THE OXFORD COMPANION TO
AMERICAN POLITICS

THE OXFORD COMPANION TO
AMERICAN POLITICS

David Coates

EDITOR IN CHIEF

VOLUME 1

Abortion–Iranian Revolution

OXFORD

UNIVERSITY PRESS

OXFORD
UNIVERSITY PRESS

Oxford University Press, Inc., publishes works that further
Oxford University's objective of excellence
in research, scholarship, and education.

Oxford New York
Auckland Cape Town Dar es Salaam Hong Kong Karachi
Kuala Lumpur Madrid Melbourne Mexico City Nairobi
New Delhi Shanghai Taipei Toronto

With offices in
Argentina Austria Brazil Chile Czech Republic France Greece
Guatemala Hungary Italy Japan Poland Portugal Singapore
South Korea Switzerland Thailand Turkey Ukraine Vietnam

Copyright © 2012 by Oxford University Press

Published by Oxford University Press, Inc.
198 Madison Avenue, New York, NY 10016
www.oup.com

Oxford is a registered trademark of Oxford University Press

The Library of Congress Cataloging-in-Publication Data

The Oxford companion to American politics / David Coates,
editor in chief.
v. cm.
Includes bibliographical references and index.
ISBN 978-0-19-976431-0
1. United States—Politics and government—Handbooks, manuals, etc.
I. Coates, David, 1946-
JK275.O94 2012
320.973—dc23   2011043405

9 8 7 6 5 4 3 2 1
Printed in the United States of America
on acid-free paper

EDITORIAL AND PRODUCTION STAFF

ACQUIRING EDITOR — Grace Labatt

DEVELOPMENT EDITORS — Stephen Wagley
Jenny Keegan

PRODUCTION EDITOR — Mark O'Malley

COPYEDITORS — Gretchen Gordon
Kristen Holt-Browning
Patricia Morris
Andrew Pachuta

PROOFREADERS — Lynda Crawford
Carol Holmes

INDEXER — June Sawyers

COMPOSITOR — Cenveo Publisher Services

MANUFACTURING CONTROLLER — Genieve Shaw

INTERIOR DESIGN — Rebecca Evans

COVER DESIGN — Brady McNamara

MANAGING EDITOR — Mary Araneo

PRODUCTION MANAGER — David Ford

EXECUTIVE EDITOR, DEVELOPMENT — Stephen Wagley

PUBLISHER — Casper Grathwohl

CONTENTS

List of Entries *ix*

Preface *xiii*

Common Abbreviations Used in This Work *xvii*

**THE OXFORD COMPANION TO
AMERICAN POLITICS**

Topical Outline of Entries, vol. 2, *449*

Directory of Contributors, vol. 2, *453*

Index, vol. 2, *465*

LIST OF ENTRIES

Abortion
Affirmative Action
Afghanistan
African Americans, History
African Americans, Contemporary
    Conditions
Africa–United States Relations
AIDS
Aid to Families with Dependent
    Children
Al-Qaeda
American Exceptionalism
American Federation of Labor and
    Congress of Industrial
    Organizations
Amnesty International
Arab-Israeli Conflict

Big Pharma
Bill of Rights
Bin Laden, Osama
Border Security
Bush, George Herbert Walker
Bush, George W.
Business-Government Relations
Business Subsidies

Cabinet Departments
Campaign Advertising
Campaign Finance and Reform
Capitalism
Capitalism, Varieties of
Capital Punishment
Carter, Jimmy

Central Asia
Charter Schools
Checks and Balances
Chicago School of Economics
Child Care
China
Christian Left
Christian Right
Church and State, Separation of
Citizenship
Civil Liberties
Civil Religion
Civil Rights
Civil Rights Act
Civil Rights Movement
Class Politics
Clean Air Act
Climate Change
Clinton, Bill
Cold War
Communism
Community Action
Community Reinvestment Act
Congress, US
Conservatism
Constitution, US
Creative Class
Crime and Punishment
Culture Wars

Darfur
Deindustrialization
Democracy
Democratic Party

Deregulation
Disability and Politics
Domestic Violence
Drugs and Politics

Economic Policy since
    World War II
Economy, American, since
    World War II
Education and Diversity
Education and Politics
Egypt
Eisenhower, Dwight D.
Elections and Electoral Behavior
Emergency Powers
Eminent Domain
Employment and Unemployment
Entitlements
Environmental Protection Agency
Equal Rights Amendment
Executive Privilege

Faith-Based Initiatives
Federal Deposit Insurance
    Corporation
Federalism
Federal Reserve Bank
Feminization of Poverty
Filibuster
Finance, International
Financial Crisis of 2008
Financial Industry
Financial Instruments, New
First Ladies

Fiscal Conservativism
Fiscal Policy
Food and Drug Administration
Ford, Gerald R.
Fordism
Free Trade and Fair Trade
Fundamentalism

Gangs
Gay Rights
Gender and Politics
Glass-Steagall Act
Global Economy and the
    United States
Global Imbalances and
    International Debt
Globalization
Government-Sponsored
    Enterprises
Gramm-Leach-Bliley Act
Grand Strategies, US
Gray Power
Great Society
Gun Control

Hate Crimes
Health Care
Health Care Reform
Hispanic Americans
Housing in the United States
Human Rights and Humanitarian
    Intervention

Immigration, Domestic
    Consequences of
Immigration, Legal and Illegal
Immigration to the United States
Impeachment
India–United States Relations
Inequalities of Wealth and Income
Insurance Companies, Health
Interest Rates
International Criminal Court
Iran
Iranian Revolution

Islam
Isolationism
Israel

Japan–United States Relations
Jihad
Johnson, Lyndon Baines
Judicial Review
Judicial Selection
Judicial System, American

Kashmir
Kennedy, John Fitzgerald
Keynesianism
King, Martin Luther, Jr.
Korea, Democratic People's
    Republic of
Korea, Republic of

Labor Force, American
Latin America Economic
    Cooperation
Latin America–United States
    Relations
Liberalism, Center-Left
Liberalism, Theory and
    History of
Libertarianism

Marriage and the Family
Marxism
McCarthyism
Media and Politics
Media Regulation
Medicare and Medicaid
Mexico
Middle Class, American
Middle East–United States
    Relations
Military-Industrial Complex
Minimum Wage
Miranda Rights
Monetarism
Monetary Policy
Mortgage-Backed Securities

NAFTA
National Security Apparatus,
    American
Native Americans
New Deal
New Left
New Media
New Right
9/11
Nixon, Richard M.
No Child Left Behind
Nongovernmental Organizations
Nonproliferation, Nuclear

Obama, Barack
Organized Crime

Pakistan–United States Relations
Patriarchy
Personal Responsibility and
    Work Opportunity
    Reconciliation Act
Philanthropy
Political Comedy
Political Consultants
Political Culture, American
Political Parties, American
Poverty, Scale and Nature of
Presidency: Governing
Presidential Nomination Process
Privacy Rights
Privatization
Progressive Movement, US
Protection
Public Opinion
Public Spending

Race, Gender, and Incarceration
Race and Racism
Reagan, Ronald
Regulation
Religion and Politics
Reproductive Politics
Republican Party
Rich, The

Roman Catholic Church
Roosevelt, Franklin Delano
Russia–United States Relations

Saudi Arabia
Savings and Loan Associations
Separation of Powers
Signing Statements
Social Mobility
Social Security
Somalia
Southeast Asia
State Politics
State Secrecy
Syria

Talk Radio
Teach for America
Tea Party

Temporary Assistance for Needy
    Families
Temporary Worker Programs
Terrorism, Domestic
Terrorism, Middle East
Think Tanks
Third Parties
Torture, Interrogation, and
    Fair-Trial Procedures
Trade Unions
Trade Unions and Democrats
Troubled Asset Relief Program
    (TARP)
Truman, Harry S.

Underclass
United Nations
Urban Sprawl
USA PATRIOT Act

Veterans Affairs, US
    Department of
Vice President, US
Vietnam War

Wal-Mart Stores
War Powers Resolution
Watergate
Welfare
Welfare State
Welfare to Work
Women and Paid Work
Women and Welfare
Work-Family Policies
World Trade Organization

Yemen

PREFACE

As this collection goes to press, the United States is in the midst of a political crisis and economic downturn of historic proportions. In the wider society beyond the Washington Beltway—as, indeed, inside it—unemployment, home foreclosures, and deepening poverty scar the land. The economy that might ease some of those burdens remains trapped in low rates of output growth and high rates of unemployment, unable to shake off the adverse impact on business confidence and consumer demand of the financial crisis that broke in September 2008. Additionally, in Washington, there is gridlock: deep partisan divides set in stone by the midterm elections of 2010—divides between those who see federal spending as the major barrier to economic recovery and those who see it as a vital defense against a return to recession. Such political divides block the emergence of clear policies and persuasive leadership. In fact, public support for Congress—as this is written, at a mere 14 percent—is the lowest it has been in modern times. The American electorate's faith in the capacity of the political system to generate solutions to the pressing social and economic issues of the day is rapidly eroding; it is eroding at the very moment, indeed, when, abroad as well as at home, the United States is facing unprecedented challenges. Militarily and in security terms, the United States remains locked in a global battle with Islamic fundamentalism. Even the 2011 capture and killing of Osama Bin Laden is proving to be simply a blip, a moment in a struggle that currently locks the United States into an open land war in Afghanistan and into covert operations in more than a hundred countries worldwide. The August 2011 downgrading of US Treasury bonds by the credit rating agency Standard and Poor's brought public criticism of US fiscal policy from none other than the Chinese government, and well it might, for in less than a decade, the United States trade deficit with China has risen more than threefold, leaving American living standards ever more dependent on the willingness of lenders in Asia (China and Japan in particular) to balance the United States' books.

In such a context of political gridlock, international tension, economic underperformance, and social division, students of American politics need to focus on more than the inner workings of their own political institutions, important as that focus is. They also need to approach their work with as wide an understanding of our contemporary international and domestic economic, social, and cultural conditions as it is possible for them to acquire quickly and easily. The two-volume *Oxford Companion to American Politics* has been designed precisely to meet the full range of those needs.

I

The content of what follows rests on a number of design principles, each of which colors all that you will find here. The first was that, in line with our publisher's requirements, we went back to the original *Oxford Companion to Politics of the World,* which Joel Krieger edited in 2001, to mine that volume for entries whose quality had enabled them to stand the test of time. We found many such entries. Some required merely updating. Some stood best unchanged, and yet others required merely supplementation with related entries drafted by new hands. The entries here on the AFL-CIO, for example, and on the Arab-Israeli conflict, on NATO, and on NAFTA, fell into the first category. Their 1990s characterization had not fundamentally changed. All they required was an update on developments since 2001. The entries on the Cold War, the Great Society, and on presidents such as Nixon and Eisenhower fell into the second. Entries on issues such as Deregulation, Deindustrialization, and Entitlements fell into the third. You will find each cross-referenced to entries that extend their insights, and the trends they have recorded, from 2001 to 2011.

The second design principle was this: recognizing that students of American politics need to know the major political actors and the institutional parameters within which they must operate, we wanted to provide as full, systemic, and rigorous descriptions of major political figures and institutions as a *Companion* of limited length could manage, without turning that *Companion* into yet another textbook on American politics. To that end, we targeted a string of discrete institutions, institutional actors, and political leaders, and we asked a relevant major scholar to synthesize existing levels of knowledge about each. In consequence, you will find entries that, to varying degrees, go back in time to set the contemporary performance of these institutions in a longer time frame, and you will find as current a characterization of those institutions and their performance as each of our contributors has been able to manage. As with the entries that we took over from the earlier *Companion,* each new entry here has a set of follow-up readings, put there specifically to enable you to go beyond the entry to explore for yourself the scholarship on which the entry is based.

When considering what overseas material to include, and in designing how to format that, a third set of design principles came into play. We split the world conceptually into two kinds of areas. In one, the United States has had long (or, even if more recent, centrally important) strategic relations; and in those areas/countries we asked our contributors to write about the US relationship and not simply the area/country itself. So, the United States' relationships with Russia, with China, with India, for example, receive individual and, indeed, lengthy entries. There are, however, places in which US strategic concerns do not currently figure large but of which any informed student of US foreign policy needs to be aware. There are so many of those, indeed, that we had to be selective; and we actually omitted some of the usual ones—Britain, for example—on the premise that much of those countries' histories and institutions are well known. Not so, of course, Sudan, or the countries of Central Asia, or Latin America taken as a whole—each of which you will find chronicled here.

The final design principle was this: it is our view that it is not possible to understand the origins, dynamics, and significance of US public policy without a full briefing on the issue/area to which that policy is addressed and without detailed knowledge of the various constituencies in play around each issue/area. Again, the scope of US public policy is so broad that we had to be selective, but at the very least, we think that scholars of modern American politics need to know significant amounts about finance and financial institutions, and about the history and contemporary character of both the US and the global economy. They need to know as much as they can about the US health care system, education system, and penal system. They need to know about the history, dominant trends, and contemporary situation of leading social categories: in demographic terms, groups differentiated by age, by gender, by wealth, and by disability; in ethnic terms, groups differentiated by their origins in Africa and Latin America, or differentiated by the longevity of their presence here and by its legality. There are in consequence many entries here that are not conventionally political. They are economic. They are social. They are cultural. They are here because modern politics cannot be understood without placing that politics in the various worlds that impinge upon it.

II

In preparing volumes of this kind, debts abound. Our main one is to Joel Krieger, Stephen Wagley, and Jenny Keegan: Joel for asking us to undertake this task, Stephen and Jenny at OUP for showing us how to do it and for guiding us (in Jenny's case) all the way to the end. The help of a number of gifted students was invaluable to us at key commissioning stages, and we would like to thank them here: Bradley Harper, Stephanie Moore, Matt Moran, Nirali Parikh, Ashley Smith, Allen Stanton, and Joe Wright. We also owe huge debts to our many contributors. Responsibility for the high quality of what follows here is ultimately theirs and theirs alone. We simply asked, and they agreed. We periodically reminded them, and they obliged. It was genuinely a pleasure to work with each of them. My final debt, as senior editor, is to my co-editors Kathy Smith and Will Walldorf.

Both are fine scholars and firm friends. This whole exercise could not have been completed without their huge and skilled input. I thank them both.

The editors collectively would like to dedicate these volumes to our colleagues in the Department of Political Science at Wake Forest University, many of whom have written entries for us here. Departments don't come academically more rigorous, or collectively more collegial, than this one. It is a very special place; and each of us has been, and remains, a great beneficiary of the professionalism we daily see around us, and of the warmth and support which in this department goes along with that professionalism. We have great colleagues, and we salute them all. We simply hope that the quality of what follows is worthy of the salute.

David Coates
Wake Forest University
March 2012

COMMON ABBREVIATIONS USED IN THIS WORK

AD	*anno Domini,* in the year of the Lord
b.	born
BCE	before the common era (= BC)
c.	*circa,* about, approximately
CE	common era (= AD)
cf.	*confer,* compare
d.	died
diss.	dissertation
ed.	editor (pl., eds.), edition
f.	and following (pl., ff.)
fl.	*floruit,* flourished
l.	line (pl., ll.)
n.	note
n.d.	no date
no.	number
n.p.	no place
n.s.	new series
p.	page (pl., pp.)
pt.	part
rev.	revised
ser.	series
supp.	supplement
USSR	Union of Soviet Socialist Republics
vol.	volume (pl., vols.)

THE OXFORD COMPANION TO
AMERICAN POLITICS

A

ABORTION

The contemporary debate over abortion pertains to clashing views about the proper powers of state and federal governments to regulate abortion practices. The issue has fostered a deep cultural and political divide among activists as well as in society more generally. Unlike most Western democracies, where this question has been resolved, the conflict ranges far and wide in the United States, maintained by two well-organized movements: pro-life and pro-choice.

The Origins of the Abortion Issue. These movements developed in response to the Supreme Court decision in *Roe v. Wade* (401 U.S. 113, 1973), which ruled that states could not prohibit doctors from performing abortions in the first and second trimesters of pregnancy. The case overturned nineteenth-century laws that had made abortion a crime except to save the life of the mother. *Roe v. Wade* was the successful outcome of the abortion reform movement that had formed in the 1960s. At first, challenges to the criminal laws came from doctors and lawyers who wanted to give doctors more leeway in offering abortion to patients who had faced special hardships. These doctors and lawyers worked with the American Law Institute (ALI) to draft a model state law allowing abortion when pregnancy threatened the physical or mental health of the mother or was the result of rape or incest. Other critics of criminal abortion laws argued that the ALI law was too

limited and did not meet the needs of women who were not mentally ill or raped, but nevertheless did not want to continue with a pregnancy. When the reform bandwagon started to gather support in the late 1960s and early 1970s, the terms of the debate changed to define abortion reform as a matter of women's rights. To feminists, the ability of women to control their bodies and fertility was essential to their overall emancipation. Along with family planning organizations, the women's movement campaigned for complete repeal of all criminal state laws and was successful in four states. Despite these victories, however, the path to abortion reform on a state-by-state basis soon suffered defeats and reversals.

As progress began to slow, the feminist litigation strategy brought two cases to the Supreme Court: one challenged the constitutionality of nineteenth-century criminal laws (as represented by Texas's law), and a second challenged the ALI conditional reform laws (in Georgia). In January 1972, the Court issued two rulings: *Roe v. Wade*, declaring the Texas law unconstitutional, and *Doe v. Bolton* (410 U.S. 179, 1973) striking down the Georgia law. The effect of these decisions was to mobilize opponents of legal abortion to action. Many were stunned when the Court declared that an unborn child was a nonperson under the Constitution and only achieved legal personhood upon birth. They saw this as an attack on what they viewed as traditional marriage, where women found fulfillment in the giving of life, not the taking of it. The Catholic Church, evangelical Protestants, and pro-family groups joined with the right wing of the Republican Party to oppose legal abortion as a threat to what they saw as fundamental values. They formed and maintained an array of organizations and tactics: marches and demonstrations; interest group lobbying; political activity related to choosing candidates; and influencing party platforms.

Advocates for legal abortion celebrated the *Roe* decision as the first step toward comprehensive reproductive rights. It took a few years for them to wake up to the threat posed by the anti-Roe forces. Between 1973 and 1980, there were intense debates in Congress over proposals to amend the Constitution to overturn legal abortion and to prevent public funds from being used for abortion services.

The movement for women's rights was growing during this period, and soon found that defending abortion rights would have to be a top priority (along with the campaign to ratify the Equal Rights Amendment). Some activists formed a central organization designed to oppose the anti-Roe actions: the National Abortion Rights Action League (NARAL).

Framing the Pro-life/Pro-choice Debate. Since the 1970s, the controversy over abortion rights has been a protracted debate between the pro-life movement and the pro-choice movement. The best way to understand this debate is to see the point of view of each side as presented here.

Pro-Life Framing. From the moment of conception when the sperm fertilizes the egg, there is a human being. Any abortion kills this innocent child; thus abortion is the same as murder. This is not a religious issue alone; advances in genetic science show that a complete genetic human being exists from the moment of conception. Current law allows abortion on demand. This means that women can kill their babies for any reason they want, no matter how irresponsible. That's not women's rights; women should protect their babies. Babies have a right to life that the state must guarantee. *Roe v. Wade* must be overturned; if the Court won't do it then we have to amend the Constitution. Until then, we must do

everything we can to protect those unborn babies and make it difficult for doctors to perform abortions or for women to get them. This legalized abortion (murder) is part of the ominous trends in our sex-saturated culture. It rewards and encourages sexual promiscuity and threatens families and social morality. It separates sex from its purpose, which is procreation, and promotes hedonism.

Pro-Choice Framing. Because pregnancy and childbirth have such a great impact on women's bodies, health, and lives, women must have the ability to choose when and if to conceive and give birth. Safe and legal abortion is an essential part of this choice, along with sex education and access to contraception. Opponents of *Roe* want to go back to a time when desperate women went to unqualified people for abortions and often lost their ability to conceive, or lost their lives, or were forced to give birth to babies they could not raise. The adverse effects on women's lives were enormous. Criminalized abortion laws won't eliminate abortion; they never have and they never will. Opponents of women's reproductive rights claim the fertilized egg is more important than the woman who will end up carrying it. We must respect women and trust them to make their own decisions about their pregnancies.

Abortion, Party Politics, and Public Opinion. An important aspect of the abortion issue in the United States is the extent to which it contributes to the ideological rift between the Republican and Democratic parties. Beginning with the 1976 convention, the Republican Party became the pro-life party. The 2008 platform continued this tradition:

> Faithful to the first guarantee of the Declaration of Independence, we assert the inherent dignity and sanctity of all human life and affirm that the unborn child has a fundamental individual right to life which cannot be infringed. We support a human life amendment to the Constitution, and we endorse legislation to make clear that the Fourteenth Amendment's protections apply to unborn children. We oppose using public revenues to promote or perform abortion and will not fund organizations which advocate it. We support the appointment of judges who respect traditional

family values and the sanctity and dignity of innocent human life.

In response, pro-choice leaders became active in the Democratic Party and to this day promote candidates and party platforms that support legal abortion and women's right to choose. From the 2008 Democratic platform:

> The Democratic Party strongly and unequivocally supports *Roe v. Wade* and a woman's right to choose a safe and legal abortion, regardless of ability to pay, and we oppose any and all efforts to weaken or undermine that right. The Democratic Party also strongly supports access to comprehensive affordable family planning services and age-appropriate sex education which empower people to make informed choices and live healthy lives. We also recognize that such health care and education help reduce the number of unintended pregnancies and thereby also reduce the need for abortions. The Democratic Party also strongly supports a woman's decision to have a child by ensuring access to and availability of programs for pre- and postnatal health care, parenting skills, income support, and caring adoption programs.

Of course, not all party members follow the official view; these platform provisions, however, continue to reflect the view of most elected party officials and those who identify with the two parties. Public opinion has remained fairly stable on the abortion issue. A minority is intensely pro-life, supporting complete criminalization of abortion, a view similar to the official Republican view. Another minority is intensely pro-choice, opposing restrictions on access to abortion. The majority is moderate, in favor of maintaining the basic provision of *Roe v. Wade* but opposing abortion on demand.

Legality of Abortion. In the context of the continuing brutal conflict between these two movements seeking to influence laws pertaining to abortion, the Supreme Court has sought to find a compromise between what many see as a collision of irreconcilable values. In *Roe v. Wade*, the justices used the trimester framework to balance the constitutional powers of states to regulate abortion practice with women's rights to privacy in matters relating to pregnancy and birth—a right established in *Griswold v. Connecticut* (281 U.S. 479, 1965) and *Eisenstadt v. Baird* (405 U.S. 438, 1972). With respect to state powers to restrict access to abortion, the court drew a line at the beginning of the third trimester, because of the severity of procedures and the likelihood that the fetus would achieve viability (ability to survive outside the uterus) during those final weeks of pregnancy: the state could prohibit abortion unless necessary to protect the life or health of the mother. Prior to the third trimester, the rights of women and doctors to make decisions in privacy prevailed and the state had no constitutional power to restrict the practice. However, in the second trimester, the state could make regulations to protect the health of the pregnant woman.

Nearly twenty years later, the Court was called upon to produce another compromise, after intense conflicts over appointments to the Supreme Court and growing demands to reverse *Roe*. This time the compromise had to consider the rights of the fetus along with women's liberty and state powers. In *Planned Parenthood of Southeastern Pennsylvania v. Casey* (505 U.S. 833, 1992), the Court eliminated the trimester framework and drew the line at viability. The justices who wrote the opinion recognized the "right of the woman to choose to have an abortion before viability and to obtain it without undue interference from the State" (846). The state's interest in protecting the fetus becomes compelling after viability. Along with the states' powers to prohibit abortion after viability, the decision recognized that they have an interest in the fetus from the beginning of pregnancy. They thus have power to erect administrative hurdles for a woman and her doctor to jump over as long as they do not constitute an "undue burden"—in other words have the "purpose or effect of placing a substantial obstacle" (877) in her path.

Since *Casey*, each side in the abortion debate has realized a victory with respect to the legal status of specific abortion procedures. In 2000, the Food and Drug Administration (FDA) approved the use of mifepristone, also known as RU486 or the "abortion pill," in the United States. Ever since it became known that medication could accomplish what had previous re-quired surgery, pro-choice activists had campaigned to make available the procedure they claimed would benefit both the health and privacy of American women. There was a strong backlash from pro-life advocates, but under the Clinton administration the pill became available.

In 2007, the pro-life movement won a victory when the Supreme Court ruled that a 2003 federal ban on so-called partial-birth abortions was constitutional. This procedure—also called dilation and evacuation—has been performed when the fetus is too large to be aborted by usual second-trimester procedures. Because it involves removing the fetus into the vagina and then killing it, the pro-life movement argued it was the same as infanticide. Doctors and pro-choice advocates countered that while serious, the procedure was sometimes necessary to protect a pregnant woman's health and fertility. The federal ban made no exception for the mother's health. In *Gonzales v. Carhart* (550 U.S. 124, 2007) the majority accepted a Congressional finding that this procedure was never necessary to protect a woman's health and thus was constitutional. Just seven years earlier the justices had ruled state laws that banned partial birth procedures would be unconstitutional unless they had a health exception. What had changed in the interim was the appointment of two justices by the Bush administration who tipped the balance away from the rights of women to liberty and health and toward the rights of the fetus.

Regulation of Access. Most of the public policy debates over abortion take place in state legislatures over proposals to restrict patient access to services. Since the 1970s, most states have enacted requirements that women under the age of eighteen either notify or get permission from parents before they can obtain an abortion. Such statutes are constitutional as long as they provide for "judicial bypass." This required exception recognizes that, sometimes, minor women face family conditions that make it impossible for them to rely on support from parents (for example, a family member may be responsible for the pregnancy). In those cases, they can seek permission from judges instead.

Pro-life activists have sought to increase the number of administrative hurdles that women must overcome to gain access to services. Most provisions have met the "undue burden" test set in *Casey*. They include the requirement of the patient's written informed consent. Some state legislators take a large view as to what "informed" might mean, requiring doctors or clinic personnel to deliver long lectures on fetuses and fetal development and abortion procedures (along with diagrams and photos). They often require extensive counseling before the patient signs the consent form. Other roadblocks include viability tests, elaborate reporting requirements, and twenty-four-hour waiting periods between initial visit/lecture/counseling and the procedure itself, requiring women to travel twice to the clinics. One requirement did not pass constitutional muster: a requirement that the patient inform her spouse and/or get his consent. The court has ruled that such a condition essentially gives veto power to the husband and is thus an undue burden on the woman's liberty.

In the 1980s and 1990s, many clinics and their patients faced high levels of determined and often violent protest from the more militant elements of the pro-life movement. Courts have ruled that such disruptions to clinic commerce are not protected speech and sustained injunctions against interfering with clinic personnel or patients. In 1994, Congress enacted the FACE (Freedom of Access to Clinic Entrances) Act, which makes it a federal crime to use force or threats of force against any organization that provides abortion services or counseling. Despite the effectiveness of these laws, violence, including murder, and threats of violence against abortion providers remain a fact of abortion politics.

Availability of Abortion Services. Although governments use their resources to keep abortion clinics open, they provide very little substantive support to women seeking abortions. The Hyde Amendment has been attached to every Congressional appropriation bill since 1978 and prohibits the use of federal Medicaid funds for abortion. Only seventeen states pay for abortions for poor women. It is constitutional for public hospitals and clinics to refuse to perform abortions, and they have been banned from military hospitals. The Affordable Care Act of 2010, which is intended to provide health insurance to all Americans, prohibits federal funds from being used to subsidize health insurance to cover abortion.

The effect of all the pro-life/pro-choice movement activism, and the partisan divide over the issue, legislation, and case law is considerable variation among the states and localities in the availability of abortion providers (hospitals, clinics, and physicians' offices). Nationally, more than 85 percent of counties accounting for 35 percent of American women have no abortion services. There are wide differences by region: 85 percent of women in the Northeastern and Western states live in counties with services, versus less than 50 percent among the Midwest and Southern states. Early medication such as mifepristone has become a regular part of the services around the country. The administrative hurdles along with location, distance to facilities, and the cost continue to present barriers, especially for poor women seeking services. Still, the Gutt-macher Institute estimates that one of five pregnancies in the United States ends in abortion, one of the highest rates in the world and signifying the high rate of unintended pregnancies among American women.

[*See also* Democratic Party; Equal Rights Amendment; Marriage and the Family; Religion and Politics; Reproductive Politics; *and* Republican Party.]

BIBLIOGRAPHY

Feldt, Gloria. *The War on Choice: The Right-Wing Attack on Women's Rights and How to Fight Back.* (New York, 2004).

Garrow, David J. *Liberty and Sexuality: The Right to Privacy and the Making of* Roe v. Wade. (New York, 1994).

Guttmacher Institute. http://www.guttmacher.org.

Hendershott, Anne. *The Politics of Abortion.* (New York, 2006).

Hull, N. E. H., and Peter Charles Hoffer. *Roe v. Wade: The Abortion Rights Controversy in American History.* 2d ed. (Lawrence, Kans., 2010).

Human Life Review. http://www.humanlifereview.com.

McBride, Dorothy E. *Abortion in the United States: A Reference Handbook.* (Santa Barbara, Calif., 2008).

Michelman, Kate. *With Liberty and Justice for All: A Life Spent Protecting the Right to Choose.* (New York, 2005).

Reagan, Leslie J. *When Abortion Was a Crime: Women, Medicine, and Law in the United States, 1867–1973.* (Berkeley, Calif., 1997).

Saletan, William. *Bearing Right: How the Conservatives Won the Abortion War.* (Berkeley, Calif., 2003).

Wagner, Teresa, ed. *Back to the Drawing Board: The Future of the Pro-Life Movement.* (South Bend, Ind., 2003).

Dorothy E. McBride

AFDC

See Aid to Families with Dependent Children.

AFFIRMATIVE ACTION

The first use of the phrase "affirmative action" is usually attributed to Executive Order 10925 issued by President John Kennedy in 1961. Two years later, when Kennedy proposed the legislation that finally became the Civil Rights Act of 1964, he and leading liberals of the 1960s assumed that by simply banning discrimination, government could create a level playing field where equal opportunity prevailed. It was an assumption that they borrowed from baseball, where Jackie Robinson and other black players had eventually thrived once racial barriers were removed, and from school desegregation cases in the South that were successful in dismantling dual educational systems.

The Civil Rights Act of 1964 prohibits any employer from discriminating because of an "individual's race, color, religion, sex, or national origin." The Act also requires that "no person in the United States shall, on the grounds of race, color, or national origin, be excluded from participation in, be denied the benefits of, or be subjected to discrimination under any program or activity receiving Federal financial assistance." This feature of the Act proved to be especially important to its implementation.

To secure passage of the Civil Rights Act of 1964 over a Southern filibuster that consumed a record eighty-three working days, it was necessary to deprive the Equal Employment Opportunity Commission (EEOC) of cease and desist authority as well as the power to sue. Accordingly, the EEOC was initially left with basically the task of being a conciliator.

To implement the Act, President Lyndon Johnson issued Executive Order 11246 to all executive departments and agencies of the federal government, which required that "each executive department and agency shall establish and maintain a positive program of equal employment opportunity." In response, the Department of Labor created an Office of Federal Compliance Program (OFCP) to implement Section VI of the Act. This left the EEOC with the core responsibility of enforcing a private right of nondiscrimination under Section VII of the Act by responding administratively to individual complaints. By 1967, the EEOC had received almost 15,000 complaints. Of these, 6,040 had been earmarked for investigation, and the tiny agency's overwhelmed investigators had completed inquiries on only 3,319. Of these, it achieved conciliation with respect to only 110 cases (involving 330 complaints). By 1968, its complaint backlog exceeded 30,000. A decade later, the EEOC's backlog had grown to 150,000 cases. In recent years, the EEOC has received about 63,000 complaints a year and is able to bring suit in no more than 500 a year. Moreover, where suit is brought, cases, as a rule, take the better part of a decade or more to reach a legal resolution.

About the same time that the EEOC was commencing its conciliatory role under the Civil Rights Act of 1964, the Department of Labor's OFCP began collecting employment records by race and using them to evaluate hiring practices. It also started a program by which contractors who had received government contracts would be required to demonstrate that they were prepared to meet affirmative action obligations. As this program was to be applied in Philadelphia (where there was only 1 percent minority membership in the craft unions), those who had received government contracts had to "provide in detail for specific steps to guaranteed equal employment opportunity keyed to the problems and needs of minority groups ... for the prompt achievement of full and equal opportunity." During Johnson's

administration, however, the Philadelphia program ran into difficulty with the General Accounting Office for introducing further requirements after contracts were awarded. There was also the worry that the affirmative action requirements of this program would run afoul of the Civil Rights Act's prohibition of quotas. However, during the Nixon administration, a revised Philadelphia program was put forward that specified its affirmative action requirements in terms of a target "range" of minorities (for 1970, it was 4–9 percent) that the contractor would try to meet and thus was able to eventually withstand a federal district court challenge that it was employing quotas. Moreover, because there were no negotiations after bids were opened in the revised Philadelphia Program, Congress determined that the plan was able to meet the objection of the Comptroller General. The success of the Philadelphia Program led the Nixon Administration to issue a new set of affirmative action guidelines that now applied to all government contractors with fifty or more employees and at least $50,000 in government business. They required contractors to take into consideration "the percentage of the minority work force as compared with the total work force in the immediate labor areas," and on the basis of that ratio design "specific goals and timetables" to correct any hiring problems.

These actions of the OFCP were clearly more effective at improving the situation of minorities than the EEOC was able to achieve through its conciliatory role. Moreover, Congress had a chance in the Civil Rights Act of 1972 to turn back the racial preference policies adopted by the OFCP (specific amendments were offered to that effect), but it refused to do so. In fact, Congress extended the requirements of the Act to state and local governments. Nevertheless, visits to government contractors in 1994–1995 to inquire about their compliance with affirmative action requirements found that 75 percent were in substantial noncompliance. In fact, since 1972 only forty-one contractors have been debarred from the list of approved federal contractors out of the thousands whose performance was judged unsatisfactory. In addition, only four of those who have been debarred were large corporations, and in these four cases, the debarment lasted less than three months. One study found that most agencies responsible for nonconstruction contractors reviewed less than 20 percent of all federal contracts. One local office had two people monitoring 29,000 contracts.

Diversity Affirmative Action. In the early twenty-first century, the most widely implemented form of affirmative action in the United States is diversity affirmative action. Its goal is not to remedy discrimination, whether present or past. Rather its goal is diversity, which in turn is justified in terms of either the educational benefits it provides or its ability to create a more effective work force in such areas as policing and community relations, or achieving equal opportunity. The legal roots of this form of affirmative action in the United States are most prominent in *Regents of the University of California v. Bakke*.

In *Bakke*, Justice Powell argued that the attainment of a diverse student body was clearly a constitutionally permissible goal for an institution of higher education. According to Powell, in an admissions program that aimed at diversity, "Race or ethnic background may be deemed a 'plus' in a particular applicant's file, yet it does not insulate the individual from comparison with all other candidates for the available seats."

For almost twenty years, Powell's opinion in *Bakke*, supported by Justices Brennan, Marshall, Blackman, and White, has been the rationale for the affirmative action used by most American colleges and universities. In 2003, the US Supreme Court again addressed the question of the use of affirmative action at the University of Michigan in *Grutter v. Bollinger* and *Gratz v. Bollinger*.

Without a doubt, the most important finding of the Court in these decisions was the constitutional permissibility to use racial preferences to achieve the educational benefits of diversity. That, of course, had been the opinion of Justice Powell in *Bakke* (1978). But there has been debate about whether Powell's opinion represents the holding of the Court in *Bakke*. In *Grutter*, Justice O'Connor, writing for the majority, cut short that discussion by adopting the

opinion of Powell in *Bakke* as the opinion of the majority in *Grutter*: "Today, we hold that the Law School has a compelling interest in attaining a diverse student body." By doing this, the Court also deferred to "the Law School's educational judgment that such diversity is essential to its educational mission." The grounds for this deference is the First Amendment to the US Constitution's protection of educational autonomy, which secures the right of a university "to select those students who will contribute to the 'robust exchange of ideas' [quoting Powell]." At the same time, the Court is moved by evidence of the educational benefits of diversity provided by the Law School and by briefs of the *amici curiae* (friends of the court): "American businesses have made clear that the skills needed in today's increasingly global marketplace can only be developed through exposure to widely diverse people, cultures, ideas, and viewpoints." What is more, high-ranking retired officers and civilian leaders of the United States military assert that a "highly qualified, racially diverse officer corps . . . is essential to the military's ability to fulfill its principle mission to provide national security."

Yet while affirming the constitutional permissibility of using racial preferences to achieve the educational benefits of diversity, the Supreme Court in *Grutter* accepted the Law School's affirmative action admissions program at the same time that the court in *Gratz* rejected the undergraduate school's program.

The difference between the two programs, according to the majority in *Grutter*, is that the undergraduate program, by automatically assigning twenty points on the basis of race or ethnicity, operated in a too-mechanical, nonindividualized manner. If race or ethnicity is to be a factor in admissions, the majority contends, there needs to be "individualized consideration of each and every applicant."

Predictably, the Supreme Court's decision in *Grutter* has met with two specific objections. Some deny that the educational benefits of diversity are an important enough state purpose to justify the use of racial preferences to achieve them. Others allow that the educational benefits of diversity are an important enough state purpose to justify the use of racial preferences; they just contend that there are other means that are preferable because they can achieve the same educational benefits of diversity in a race-neutral way.

Diversity Not Important Enough. In its brief before the Supreme Court in the Michigan cases, the Michigan Association of Scholars maintained that "even where diversity in their classrooms is a genuine merit, it is simply not the case that their work, their teaching, their research, cannot go forward successfully in its absence." When making this claim, however, opponents of affirmative action must not be thinking about what happens in classrooms when racial issues are discussed, or analogously, what happens in classrooms when gender issues are discussed. Surely, the teachers who have led discussions on racial issues in classrooms, both with and without minority students being present, know what a significant difference the presence of minorities makes in such contexts. Similarly there is a loss when gender issues are discussed in the absence of women. Thus, when opponents of affirmative action maintain that diversity is unnecessary for successful teaching, they must not be thinking about courses focused on racial (or gender) issues, but rather about courses where the subject matter is logic, math, or physics, or something similar.

Nevertheless, without denying the educational benefits of diversity, it still might be argued that achieving those benefits does not constitute an important enough state purpose to justify the use of racial preferences to secure them. This would seem to be the position of Justice Thomas in his dissent in the *Grutter* case. Thomas argues that the only kind of state purpose that would be important enough to justify the use of racial preferences in a nonremedial context is national security or, more broadly, "measures the State must take to provide a bulwark against anarchy, or to prevent violence." In the *Grutter* case, no one, except Justice Scalia, joined Thomas in defending such an extreme limitation on the use of racial preferences.

There Are Better Means. The Texas 10 Percent Plan and the Florida 20 Percent Plan are usually put forward by opponents of affirmative action as better—

that is, race-neutral—ways of securing the educational benefits of diversity.

The Texas 10 Percent Plan and the Florida 20 Percent Plan are now successfully admitting minorities into their undergraduate institutions at levels that either match, or, in Florida's case, surpass what they had accomplished with race-based affirmative action programs. This was not accomplished, however, without a substantial increase in scholarship aid for minorities, and not without, in the case of Texas, using smaller classes and a variety of remedial programs. Both plans also rely on at least de facto segregated high schools in their respective states to produce the diversity they have. If the high schools in both states were in fact more integrated, the plans would not be as effective as they are with respect to undergraduate enrollment.

Even so the plans employed still had serious drawbacks. First, they did nothing for law and medical schools, and for other graduate and professional schools ending affirmative action has been devastating. African American enrollment at the University of Texas Law School dropped from 5.8 percent (twenty-nine students) in 1996 to 0.9 percent (six students) in 1997. It rose to 1.8 percent (nine students) in 1998 and then fell to 1.7 percent (nine students) in 1999. Since then, there has been improvement in the number of African Americans enrolled at the University of Texas Law School, although the numbers have yet to approach levels when affirmative action was practiced. This holds true for most other University of Texas professional schools as well.

Second, the Texas Plan has a detrimental effect on the admission of minorities not in the top 10 percent. Minority students who are not in the top 10 percent of their high school graduating classes have little hope of admission under the Texas Plan. Third, such plans restrict universities from doing the individualized assessments that would be required to assemble a student body that is not only racially diverse, but also diverse in other ways. Fourth, an analysis of data from the Florida Plan showed that students at seventy-five of Florida's high schools could have carried a C+ average and still have ranked in the top 20 percent of their class. Fifth, such plans only work, if at all, for universities that admit primarily from a statewide population. Only 11 percent of the applicants to the University of Texas at Austin are nonresidents whereas many elite colleges and universities recruit students from a national and international pool, and thus cannot apply the percent model to their selection of student bodies.

There is yet another reason that may trump all the others as a reason for rejecting these so-called alternatives to a race-based affirmative action. It is that despite their claims to be race-neutral, these percentage-plan alternatives are really race-based themselves. They are means that are chosen explicitly because they are thought to produce a desirable degree of racial diversity. In this regard, they are no different from the poll taxes that were used in the segregated South, which were purportedly race-neutral means but were clearly designed to produce an objectionable racial result—to keep blacks from voting. Accordingly, if we are going to end up using a race-based selection procedure to get the educational benefits of diversity, it might as well be one that most effectively produces that desired result, and that is a selection procedure that explicitly employs race as a factor in admissions.

It is not surprising, therefore, that this is exactly what the University of Texas proposed to do once the Supreme Court's *Grutter* decision nullified the Fifth Circuit Court's prohibition of affirmative action. The university has also sought to limit the 10 Percent Plan to 50–60 percent of its incoming class, down from the more than 70 percent that have been admitted under the plan. Although this attempt to limit the 10 Percent Plan was rebuffed by the state legislature in 2007, the university is now using racial preference to the degree that is consistent with abiding by the Plan.

What this shows is that the practitioners of the most highly regarded alternative to affirmative action in the country, those same people who were in the best position to assess its merits and limitations, now want to use affirmative action and in other ways restrict and go beyond the 10 Percent Plan. That seems to be strong evidence against the viability of the Texas Plan and the Florida Plan as alternatives to affirmative action.

Diversity Affirmative Action to Achieve Equal Opportunity. Nevertheless, there are good reasons to expand diversity affirmative action—especially in higher education—to extend to the economically disadvantaged, not as a substitute for race-based affirmative action but rather as an addition to it with the aim of securing more equal opportunity in society.

Consider the following:

- Although the median US family income today is a little over $54,000 per year, almost 90 percent of Harvard students come from families with greater incomes, and almost 75 percent of Harvard students come from families with incomes over $100,000.
- Of the students attending the University of Notre Dame, Northwestern University, the University of Pennsylvania, Harvard University, Princeton University, the University of Virginia, and Washington University in St. Louis, less than 10 percent come from families earning less than $40,000 a year so as to qualify for Pell grants.
- At top elite colleges, only 3 percent of students come from the bottom quarter of US family incomes.

So, for the most part, elite US colleges that are supported with federal dollars and tax-exempt status are primarily attended by children from the wealthiest families.

Also consider the following:

- Most nonacademic admission preferences disproportionately benefit white, wealthy applicants.
- Although it is generally believed that athletic preferences disproportionately favor minority students, this is not the case. More than counterbalancing minority participation in basketball, football, and track is participation mainly by upper-income whites in such sports as horseback riding, skiing, sailing, fencing, golf, crew, squash, and even polo at Cornell University and the University of Virginia.
- Underrepresented minorities and athletes receive an average of 108 extra points.

- Half of Notre Dame's legacy admits each year would not have been admitted without the preference they received for being legacies.
- At Ivy League and other elite schools, legacies make up as much as 25 percent of the student body.
- Students without any nonacademic preference are vying for only 40 percent of the slots at the elite schools.

So the major beneficiaries of preferences at elite colleges in the United States turn out to be white students from wealthy or relatively wealthy families.

Putting these two "considerations" together, elite colleges in the United States are supported with federal dollars and tax-exempt status, while the students attending those colleges, almost exclusively, come from wealthy or relatively wealthy families, and a good number of them are admitted either as legacies or because they play esoteric sports that only students from wealthy or relatively wealthy families would normally have the opportunity to learn to play.

It is not surprising, therefore, that 75 percent of Americans oppose giving legacies "extra consideration for admission," according to the *Chronicle of Higher Education*. In effect, elite colleges in the United States are functioning like country clubs for students from wealthy or relatively wealthy families. Of course, there is nothing wrong in itself with the existence of institutions that are, or function like, country clubs for the rich. What is is wrong, however, is when such institutions are supported with federal dollars and tax-exempt status. The needed corrective is a significant cut in legacy preferences at elite colleges, and the replacement of legacy preferences with a corresponding number of preferences enabling more economically disadvantaged students to attend the same schools.

In the process of filling the slots at elite colleges opened up for economically disadvantaged students, it will be necessary to accept students with somewhat lower SAT scores and grade point averages (GPAs) than would otherwise have been required. Given the unequal K–12 educational system in the United States, students who come from economically disadvantaged families cannot normally be expected to secure exactly the same academic credentials as those who are admitted to these schools without any preferential treatment. They should, however, tend to match the academic credentials of those students who previously had been admitted based on legacy or athletic preferences. Under such a program, only those students would be admitted whose qualifications are such that when their selection is combined with a suitably designed educational enhancement program, they will normally turn out, within a reasonably short time, to be as qualified as, or even more qualified than, their peers.

Of course, it will be objected that elite colleges need to employ legacy and other preferences for the rich in order to maintain their endowments. As it turns out, legacy and other preferences for the rich are actually of fairly recent origin. Before World War I, although there was a tradition of alumni giving at elite US colleges and universities, the children of alumni of elite colleges and universities did not need preferences. Even Harvard and Yale were able to accept all those who passed their entrance exams and paid their tuitions. After the war, however, for a variety of reasons, the number of applications radically increased, and legacy preferences were introduced at first to help suppress Jewish enrollment.

Yet there are elite schools that manage to maintain their endowments without legacy and other preferences for the rich. The California Institute of Technology (Caltech), possibly the best or second-best engineering school in the United States, has done it, as have Oxford and Cambridge universities in the United Kingdom. The son of the former US vice president Al Gore, Albert, and the son of the former US Senate majority leader Bill Frist, Harrison, were each admitted as a legacy to their fathers' alma maters, Harvard and Princeton respectively, even though their academic credentials were considerably below the normal admission standards of those institutions. By contrast, the son of the former UK Prime Minister Tony Blair, Euan, was denied admission to Oxford, his father's alma mater, despite Euan's much better academic credentials.

In order to make the changes that are needed here, people's expectations with respect to elite colleges and universities have to change. On the one hand, if rich people expect elite colleges and universities to give preference to their children simply because they are alumni/a, then, of course, they will be disappointed if their children are not accepted by those institutions. On the other hand, if rich people expect that elite colleges and universities will maintain their educational standards and goals irrespective of alumni/a connections, then, even if their children do not gain admission, they can still respect their alma maters for not turning themselves into country clubs for the rich and for being more open to all applicants who can meet their academic criteria and goals, and they can still remain grateful to those colleges and universities for the education they themselves received. Such changes in expectations and attitudes should be able to provide an alternative basis for maintaining and growing the endowments of elite colleges and universities.

In any case, policies at elite colleges and universities cannot continue primarily favoring the wealthy and relatively wealthy with legacy and other preferences while practically excluding almost everyone else and while receiving from the government large outlays of federal dollars and tax-exempt status. To justifiably retain federal support and tax-exempt status, elite colleges and universities must transform themselves so that they are genuinely open to all qualified students. This will require putting an end to the favoritism shown to the rich and the relatively rich by instituting affirmative action programs for the economically disadvantaged that are at least as large as the race-based affirmative action programs that exist at those universities. The admissions slots needed for these new preferences for the economically disadvantaged are to be secured by a comparable cut in legacy preferences and other special preferences for the rich. As universities are able to successfully change the way they maintain and grow their endowments, it will then be possible to eliminate all legacy and other special preferences for the rich.

For some time now, there has been a vigorous debate going on in the United States over the justification of race- and sex-based affirmative action. While this debate has been raging in the halls of government, academia, and beyond, there has been the equivalent of two 500-pound gorillas sitting right in the midst of the debaters that few of the participants seems to have noticed, especially the opponents of affirmative action. The two "gorillas" are legacy and athletic preferences for white, wealthy students. Taking these preferences for the rich into account and doing an appropriate assessment of them leads to the conclusion that they should be eliminated or reduced in favor of preferences for the economically disadvantaged, the latter being a form of diversity affirmative action that seeks to secure greater equal opportunity in society.

[*See also* Civil Rights; Education and Diversity; Education and Politics; *and* Race and Racism.]

BIBLIOGRAPHY

Cohen, Carl, and James P. Sterba. *Affirmative Action and Racial Preference: A Debate.* (Oxford, 2003).

Golden, David. *The Price of Admission: How America's Ruling Class Buys Its Way into Elite Colleges—and Who Gets Left outside the Gates.* (New York, 2006).

Gratz v. Bollinger, 539 US 244 (2003).

Grutter v. Bollinger, 539 US 306 (2003).

Michaels, Walter Benn. *The Trouble with Diversity: How We Learned to Love Identity and Ignore Inequality.* (New York, 2006).

Mohrman, William F., and Eric L. Lipman. "Brief of Amicus Curiae, The Michigan Association of Scholars in Support of Petitioners." (2002), http://www.vpcomm.umich.edu/admissions/legal/gru_amicus-ussc/mas_both.pdf.

Regents of the University of California v. Bakke, 438 US 265 (1978).

Schmidt, Peter. *Color and Money: How Rich White Kids Are Winning the War over College Affirmative Action.* (New York, 2007).

Sterba, James P. *Affirmative Action for the Future.* (Ithaca, N.Y., 2009).

James P. Sterba

AFGHANISTAN

Modern-day Afghanistan, a landlocked state in Southwest Asia, has been a major preoccupation of American foreign policy for more than three decades.

It emerged in the nineteenth century as a buffer between British India and the expanding Russian empire. Given the diversity of ethnic groups within its borders (Pashtuns, Tajiks, Uzbeks, Hazaras, and many others), it has never been a "nation-state." The overwhelming majority of Afghanistan's estimated 20 million citizens are Muslims, and they are more prone to bond with those who share common ethnic or linguistic backgrounds, tribal identifications, or sectarian commitments. After nearly five decades of relative stability, Afghanistan was thrown into turmoil by a Communist coup in April 1978, followed by the Soviet invasion of Afghanistan in December 1979. Intense popular resistance within Afghanistan, supported by the Reagan Administration, was a major factor prompting the withdrawal of Soviet forces, a process completed in February 1989. In April 1992, the Communist regime collapsed. It rapidly became clear, however, that the Afghan state had collapsed as well, and thereafter the country was wracked by a struggle for control of the remaining symbols of nationwide power—notably the capital, Kabul, which suffered severe damage from rocket and artillery attacks by the Hezb-e Islami ("Party of Islam"). In 1994, the Pakistan-backed, and largely Pashtun, Taliban "student" militia appeared, and in 1996, it succeeded in taking over Kabul. The Taliban's hospitality to Osama Bin Laden and his anti-American Al-Qaeda network ensured that it would attract US attention, and following the September 11, 2001 Al-Qaeda attacks on targets in the United States, US forces were successfully deployed to oust the Taliban regime, an objective achieved by December 2001. After a lull of several years, however, the Taliban resurfaced, again with backing from Pakistan, and it continues to pose a major challenge to US strategic interests in Southwest Asia.

Until 1973, Afghanistan had a monarchical system of government; the last king, Mohammad Zahir Shah, occupied the throne from November 1933 until July 1973, when his cousin Mohammad Daoud overthrew him and established a short-lived republican regime. The monarchy presided over a ubiquitous but relatively weak array of state instrumentalities, and during Zahir Shah's rule, it took care not to challenge the key interests expressed by tribal collective leaderships. Nonetheless, the attempt from the mid-1950s to use foreign aid and asset-sales revenue to fund a centrally driven modernization process had the perverse effect of creating a new stratum of politicized Afghans whose political and social aspirations the state was unable to satisfy. It was this stratum that provided cadres for the Afghan Communist movement, which was heavily involved both in the removal of the monarchy and in the 1978 coup, but it also provided the core of the Afghan Islamist movement, which in turn formed a part of the Mujahidin resistance to Marxist rule.

The Communist regime, formally built around the bitterly factionalized "People's Democratic Party of Afghanistan," suffered problems of legitimacy from its inception and came to rely on nonlegitimate means of domination—notably coercion and the use of resources to "purchase" support—in order to survive. Following the Soviet invasion, a well-funded secret police force, KhAD (Khedamat-e Etalaat-e Dawlati, or "State Information Service") was established under the tutelage of the Soviet KGB to identify and repress opponents of the regime, especially in urban areas. Rural areas were exposed to ferocious attacks by Soviet air and ground forces, resulting in the deaths of approximately 1 million Afghans and the departure as refugees to Pakistan and Iran of a further 5–6 million. With the disintegration of the Communist regime, more than 4 million returned, but war damage, economic disruption, and fear of either persecution or antipersonnel mines blocked the return of the remainder. The subsequent rise of the Taliban—notable for their antediluvian views on gender issues and their rigidly ideological policies, which mix Islamic precepts derived from the Deobandi school with a radical and antimodernist commitment to establishing a "pure" Islamic order with no direct precedent in Afghan history—led to new refugee outflows.

Although the completion of the Soviet withdrawal from Afghanistan and the 1992 collapse of the Communist regime diminished Afghanistan's immediate significance in US eyes, that nation was not completely overlooked—although a number of commentators have observed that it received less attention than it deserved from 1992–2001. The bombing in August 1998 of US embassies in Tanzania and Kenya, for which Osama Bin Laden was blamed, saw the Clinton Administration respond with Tomahawk cruise-missile strikes against suspected Bin Laden bases in eastern Afghanistan; these strikes were followed by a US executive order in July 1999 blocking property and prohibiting transactions with the Taliban, and ultimately, in November 1999, by the imposition of sanctions against the Taliban by the UN Security Council in Resolution 1267. Nonetheless, it took the September 2001 attacks to galvanize the Bush Administration to move directly against the Taliban. On 7 October 2001, the US military launched "Operation Enduring Freedom" with a wide-ranging attack on Taliban and Al-Qaeda positions in Afghanistan, using land-based B-52 bombers and B-1 Stealth bombers (flown, respectively, from Whiteman Air Force Base near Kansas City and from the island of Diego Garcia in the Indian Ocean), together with strike aircraft (F-14 Tomcats and F-18 Hornets) from the aircraft carriers USS *Enterprise* and USS *Carl E. Vinson*. During the course of the campaign, approximately 12,000 bombs were dropped; 6700 of them were precision guided. Ordinary Afghans, witnessing this power, were quick to abandon the Taliban regime, which many in any case had hated or feared, and Kabul fell to anti-Taliban Afghan forces on November 13. The decade following the overthrow of the Taliban regime was marked by a number of achievements in Afghanistan, but more spectacularly by a severe loss of focus early in the life of its post-Taliban transition, especially following the Bush Administration's invasion of Iraq in March 2003. The course of Afghanistan's transition was set by an agreement signed in Bonn in December 2001 between non-Taliban Afghan political actors. This provided for the establishment of an interim administration for which Hamed Karzai was the consensus choice for the chairmanship, the subsequent holding of an "Emergency *Loya Jirga*" ("Great Assembly") to lift the status of the interim administration to that of a transitional administration, the holding of a Constitutional *Loya Jirga* to adopt a new constitution,

and the holding of free and fair elections for some of the key offices that the new constitution established. These benchmarks were met, but the results proved less than satisfactory.

Afghanistan's new political structures proved to be inefficient and dysfunctional. The new constitution, adopted in January 2004, established a strongly presidential system. The result, however, was that the occupant of the presidential office, Karzai, was burdened with too many responsibilities, and since Karzai had grown up politically in the state-free environment of the Pakistani city of Peshawar, where Afghan Mujahidin parties had the offices during the 1980s, he lacked the experience to drive effective policy development and implementation. Furthermore, the Bonn Agreement provided for up to twenty-nine ministries, essentially so that there would be enough rewards to satisfy the different participants from the Bonn Conference, and the result was ludicrous problems involving red tape. Not surprisingly, corruption—mainly in the form of bribe taking—emerged on a monumental scale, as cash payments were offered in the exchange for bureaucratic approvals or political patronage. Furthermore, the formal centralization of the state worked against creativity at the local level. Able young Afghan officials often found that their superiors were jealous of their talents, and keen to block their more creative endeavors.

Furthermore, the legitimacy of Afghanistan's political arrangements came increasingly to be questioned. In 2004, Karzai was comfortably elected with 55.4 percent of the vote in Afghanistan's first presidential election. He was assisted by two factors. Some 64 percent of the population, as surveyed by the Asia Foundation, felt that the country was moving in the right direction. Furthermore, he was plainly the preferred candidate of the United States, which remained the dominant external force in the country. By 2009, when the second presidential election was held, much had changed. Only 42 percent of those polled by the Asia Foundation felt that the country was moving in the right direction, and it was doubtful whether the new Obama Administration felt the same enthusiasm for Karzai that president George W. Bush had repeatedly expressed. In addition, much of the southern part of Afghanistan was deeply insecure because of the re-emergence of the Taliban. Karzai supporters responded by resorting to gargantuan fraud in order to bring about his re-election. In this they succeeded, but at the cost of putting a cloud over his political legitimacy.

Doubts also hung over whether Afghanistan could make any claim to enjoy the benefits of the rule of law. The judiciary and other potential checks on the abuse of political power were quite quickly compromised by political appointments and corruption. Powerful political figures were effectively above the law, either because of their ties to the president—on display in the 2010 Kabul Bank scandal, which saw depositors' money disappear through the making of unsecured loans to the well connected—or because they could afford to pay bribes that others could not or would not match. This permitted scandalous abuses of power that undermined the reputation of the state. These, in turn, provided opportunities that the Taliban were quick to exploit; even if the Taliban were unappetizing, many Afghans found the government not much more appealing.

Ongoing insurgency in Afghanistan contributed to poor performance by the government, which, in a vicious circle, contributed to the expansion of insurgent opportunities. The insurgency used diverse tactics, including the use of improvised explosive devices, attacks on international forces, the killing of travelers seeking to use Afghanistan's increasingly dangerous roads, and targeted assassinations of government officials at both central and local levels. President Karzai survived attempts on his life in Kandahar and Kabul, but others were not so lucky: Vice President Haji Abdul Qadir was killed in Kabul, and Karzai's half-brother Abdul Wali Karzai was killed in Kandahar. In many cases, the Taliban claimed responsibility, but it became clear that the insurgency involved more than just the "old" Taliban, linked to their leader Mullah Mohammad Omar in the so-called "*Quetta Shura*," or council (which took its name from the Pakistani city to which the Taliban had shifted when they were ejected from power in Afghanistan in 2001). A second source of difficulty

was the Hezb-e Islami, led by the veteran anti-Western politician Gulbuddin Hekmatyar. A third important strand of insurgents was the so-called "Haqqani network," associates of a former Mujahidin commander, Jalaluddin Haqqani, and his son Serajuddin. This group was responsible for some of the more dramatic insurgent attacks, including two bombings of the Indian Embassy in Kabul. All of these forces were dependent on sanctuary in Pakistan in order to be able to operate. Numerous reports attested to the connections between these groups and the Inter-Services Intelligence Directorate of Pakistan's Armed Forces, which had resented the overthrow of the Taliban and feared a growth of Indian influence in Afghan government circles. This confronted US policymakers with a considerable dilemma. On the one hand, the United States depended upon cooperation from Pakistan in order to be able to transport supplies to US forces in Afghanistan; on the other hand, Pakistan was an unreliable ally in the broader strategic environment of West Asia, since it was prepared to go to almost any lengths to exclude Indian influence from Afghanistan.

US policy toward Afghanistan after 2001 went through a number of phases and was marked by a high degree of incoherence. While the Bonn Agreement anticipated the deployment of an International Security Assistance Force (ISAF) to Afghanistan, the Bush Administration initially blocked its expansion beyond Kabul, with a view toward conserving airlift assets for use in Iraq. This led to a loss of momentum in Afghanistan's transition and signaled to regional actors that the United States' involvement in Afghanistan was mainly focused on the pursuit of al-Qaeda and that Washington had limited appetite for a wider commitment. Instead, the United States pressed its NATO and non-NATO allies to become more heavily involved in Afghanistan, notably through the development of Provincial Reconstruction Teams (PRTs) that were designed to create islands of stability for reconstruction and development. On the ground, things did not go so smoothly. The PRTs varied greatly in their resource bases, reflected diverse military cultures within the different sending states, and faced different threat levels in different parts of the country. The governments that had committed military personnel for reconstruction activities found it hard to explain mounting casualty levels to their own populations, and this put pressure on the United States to plug gaps that emerged—as occurred when the Dutch government fell in early 2010 over the issue of Afghanistan, resulting in the withdrawal of the Dutch component of the Uruzgan PRT.

A further serious problem related to the emergence of a major opium industry in Afghanistan. In the 1980s, Afghan farmers in some parts of the country had responded to the Soviet destruction of irrigation systems by planting the opium poppy, which could readily be irrigated with melting snow. In the final year before their overthrow, the Taliban had used coercive means to reduce opium cultivation, in a desperate (and failed) attempt to win some international support. With the overthrow of the Taliban, opium cultivation resurfaced. In the early phase of its re-emergence (when a policy of forced eradication might have sent a powerful message without harming too many people), US forces largely ignored what was happening, arguably because some of those involved with opium were also intelligence assets in the hunt for Al-Qaeda. By the time it was realized that opium profits were themselves filling the wallets of extremist groups, it was too late to resort to eradication, since more than a million Afghans had become involved in the industry and the income they derived as laborers made the difference between survival and destitution.

The advent to office of US President Barack Obama in January 2009 marked a new phase in the Afghanistan conflict. Where President George W. Bush had been prepared to give a largely free hand to President Karzai—especially in the period 2003–2005, when the Afghan-born Zalmay Khalilzad was US ambassador to Afghanistan—President Obama was both more distant and more critical. The consequence was a souring of President Karzai's relationship with the Obama Administration. In a leaked diplomatic cable from November 2009, US Ambassador Karl W. Eikenberry wrote that "President Karzai is not an adequate strategic partner . . . Karzai

continues to shun responsibility for any sovereign burden, whether defense, governance, or development . . . [i]t strains credulity to expect Karzai to change fundamentally this late in his life and in our relationship." Obviously aware of the way in which the Vietnam War had come to blight the presidency of Lyndon B. Johnson, President Obama initiated an elaborate review of policy toward Afghanistan. This culminated in a speech he delivered at West Point in December 2009, in which he identified three objectives for US policy: "We must deny al-Qaeda a safe haven. We must reverse the Taliban's momentum and deny it the ability to overthrow the government. And we must strengthen the capacity of Afghanistan's security forces and government so that they can take lead responsibility for Afghanistan's future." He announced a commitment of an additional thirty thousand troops to Afghanistan, but added that "After eighteen months, our troops will begin to come home." This was domestically understandable, given the reluctance of members of the Democratic Party to become involved in a burdensome overseas commitment at the expense of domestic policy initiatives, but it blunted the capacity of the troop deployment to signal an enhanced and enduring commitment to Afghanistan.

Developments on the ground in Afghanistan sent mixed signals as well. Although civilian casualties in Afghanistan were not remotely on the scale that Afghanistan had experienced through the 1980s during the Soviet occupation, they were widely publicized, and in many cases they were both heartrending and disturbing. This intensified the tensions between President Karzai and his backers. In addition, there were instabilities in the US military leadership. In May 2009, President Obama replaced General David D. McKiernan with General Stanley A. McChrystal as commander of US forces in Afghanistan. In June 2010, however, General McChrystal was removed from his position and replaced by General David H. Petraeus following the publication of a magazine story that contained indiscreet comments by McChrystal's staff about the president and his advisers. When Petraeus left Afghanistan to become head of the Central Intelligence Agency in

2011, the mood in Afghanistan was grim, and few saw on the ground the kind of breakthrough for which Petraeus had earlier received credit in Iraq.

The death of Osama Bin Laden in Pakistan in May 2011 at the hands of an elite US military team poses major questions for the future of the United States in Afghanistan. The temptation in US political circles to see this as finally accomplishing a mission that began on 12 September 2001 is obvious and understandable. It is, however, something that both Afghanistan and Pakistan have had cause to fear: Afghanistan because of the risk over time of drifting right out of Washington's field of vision and Pakistan because of the risk that improving the India-United States relationship may come to figure more prominently in the strategic calculations of the United States especially given the suspicion in some US circles that key Pakistani figures must have been aware of Bin Laden's presence on Pakistani soil. The danger for Afghanistan is that Pakistan, facing a sharp deterioration in its relations with the United States, may be tempted to interfere even more destructively in Afghanistan, if only to convey to the United States that it must be given a significant say in that country's future. How the United States responds to Pakistan's activities will be decisive in shaping the future of Afghanistan.

[*See also* Al-Qaeda; Bush, George W.; Bin Laden, Osama; Obama, Barack; Pakistan–United States Relations; *and* Terrorism, Middle East.]

BIBLIOGRAPHY

Coll, Steve. *Ghost Wars: The Secret History of the CIA, Afghanistan and Bin Laden, from the Soviet Invasion to September 10, 2001.* (London, 2005).

Maley, William. *The Afghanistan Wars.* (New York, 2009).

The 9/11 Commission Report: Final Report of the National Commission on Terrorist Attacks upon the United States. (New York, 2004.)

Rashid, Ahmed. *Descent into Chaos: The United States and the Failure of Nation Building in Pakistan, Afghanistan, and Central Asia.* (New York, 2008).

Woodward, Bob. *Obama's War.* (New York, 2010.)

William Maley

AFL-CIO

See American Federation of Labor and Congress of Industrial Organizations.

AFRICAN AMERICANS, HISTORY

More than 10 million people brought to the Americas as slaves from the sixteenth to the nineteenth centuries confronted a situation that was historically unprecedented. Never before had such a large group of people been forcibly removed from their homelands and forced to labor for the remainder of their lives in distant societies dominated by culturally and racially different people. Deprived of their freedom and torn from their cultural roots, slaves and their descendants responded to their enslavement in varied and innovative ways.

Slaves born into African societies initially relied upon their cultural traditions as they struggled against chattel slavery, but life in Africa had not prepared them to challenge European technological superiority. Some slaves saw their situation as hopeless and committed suicide rather than endure the passage to the Americas, or the harsh process of slave breaking once they arrived. Others fought their enslavers, rebelling aboard slave ships or in the Americas. Few rebellions succeeded, however, because slaves were closely supervised, unfamiliar with their new surroundings, often divided by linguistic and religious differences, and subjected to brutal punishments when disobedient. In addition, disease and malnutrition killed many slaves and weakened the ability of others to rebel. Most Africans who came to the Americas, particularly those brought to the sugar plantations of Brazil or the Caribbean islands, died without bearing children.

Those who survived found it necessary to undergo a cultural transformation. Africans from diverse cultural backgrounds became "African Americans," a group stigmatized by the color of their skin and bound together by the common experience of being subordinate to Europeans. The most basic aspect of this cultural transformation involved the adoption of European languages, which not only enabled slaves to communicate with their masters but also, in some cases, with each other. The transformation also involved the adoption of other European cultural, social, and political practices, but this did not constitute a complete abandonment of African cultural values, some of which persisted in the Americas. Nor did African slaves simply become Europeanized; rather, they simultaneously transformed European culture as they infused it with their own insights. African Americans not only endured under oppression; over time they also established families, churches, schools, self-help groups, fraternal orders, and other institutions as they sought to improve their lives collectively and individually. These institutions conformed somewhat to European American models, but they also reflected the distinctive common experiences and aspirations of slaves and their descendants.

The tendency of African Americans to utilize European cultural forms increased during the eighteenth and nineteenth centuries as a result of the religious "awakenings" and democratic revolutions that occurred in many European-dominated societies during that period of time. Emerging forms of African American Christianity combined residual elements of African religions and those aspects of Christianity that appealed to slaves and freed blacks. From the beginning of the slave era, conversion to Christianity sometimes offered a means for slaves to improve their lives, or simply to find a degree of psychological solace. Although conversion rarely led directly to emancipation for slaves—indeed, most slave masters saw Christianity as compatible with, or even mandating, slavery—in British North America democratic ideas accompanied the spread of evangelical Christianity during the eighteenth and nineteenth centuries. Methodist and Baptist religious practices in particular appealed to African Americans, because they fostered democratic ideals and encouraged individuals to assert control over their spiritual lives as well as over congregational decision-making. Prayer and prophecy became means for expressing African American aspirations. As transformed by blacks struggling to free themselves,

Christianity became a theology promoting freedom and social justice that was at least partially outside the control of whites.

The formation in 1793 of Philadelphia's Bethel African Methodist Episcopal (AME) Church was an important step in the institutionalization of African American culture and society. Bethel's minister, Richard Allen (1760–1831), initially remained within the Episcopal church hierarchy, but in 1816, when the AME Church achieved full autonomy, he became the denomination's first bishop. Other blacks would join the AME Zion denomination or one of the hundreds of Baptist and Methodist churches that gained many members as a result of the religious revivals which occurred during the decades before the Civil War. Such religious institutions provided training grounds for the development of black leadership. Moreover, Christianity was a source of insight for African Americans seeking understanding of their history and plight. They could identify their enslavement with that of the Jews, or see the Ethiopians mentioned in the Bible as their ancient ancestors.

While African Americans adapted Christianity to serve new purposes, they also transformed modern concepts of nationalism into a set of political ideas that gave them a collective identity and informed their movements for advancement. Both the American and the French revolutions of the late eighteenth century encouraged African Americans to hope that they might eventually enjoy the rights that had been won by white people. The gradual movement in Europe and the Americas toward the ideal of universal rights influenced, and was in turn influenced by, African American struggles for advancement. After the British colonies of North America gained their independence, blacks in the United States petitioned white leaders to end slavery and racial discrimination by pointing to the egalitarian sentiments expressed in revolutionary documents such as the Declaration of Independence. The French Revolution of 1789 also strengthened antislavery sentiment in the Americas and prompted a successful slave rebellion, led by Toussaint L'Ouverture (1743–1803), in the colony that became Haiti. Taken together, the American and the French revolutions provided democratic ideals for many subsequent African American political movements. The democratic idealism expressed in the American Declaration of Independence encouraged some blacks to believe the principles of equality were universal rather than limited to white men. The US Constitution of 1787 reflected the postrevolutionary decline of democratic idealism, however, by reinforcing the legal rights of slaveholders and providing African Americans with few mechanisms for effective political action against the proslavery state governments.

Whether slaves could or should seek full citizenship in white-dominated societies became central questions for nineteenth- and twentieth-century African American political movements. European Americans generally rejected the idea that African Americans should be granted equal rights. Such white resistance to racial equality led some African Americans to insist that their rights would be protected only in a black-controlled nation. In the United States, the strengthening of the slave economy after the invention of the cotton gin in 1793 lessened the possibility that slavery would be abolished peacefully. Although some emancipated blacks became politically active during the early nineteenth century, most states imposed special restrictions on their political freedom. After the exposure of major slave conspiracies in Virginia in 1800 and South Carolina in 1822, and the crushing of the Nat Turner (1800–1831) slave rebellion in Virginia in 1831, Southern whites severely restricted the ability of slaves and free blacks to assemble. In addition, the desire of African Americans to emigrate back to Africa, or at least out of the United States, grew during the antebellum years. In 1815 Paul Cuffe (1759–1817), a wealthy African American merchant mariner, brought a small group of settlers to Sierra Leone on the west coast of Africa. Most emancipated blacks found emigration to Africa impractical and undesirable, however, for they had been born in the United States and had little knowledge of life elsewhere. In 1817 a national meeting of black leaders rejected the efforts of white leaders of the American Colonization Society to encourage freed blacks to go to Africa.

The formation of the American Anti-Slavery Society in 1833 further encouraged African American antislavery agitation. Although the society's leader, William Lloyd Garrison, was a white abolitionist who believed in "moral suasion" as the best means of ending slavery, by the 1840s many black abolitionists had begun to attack slavery politically by supporting antislavery parties and candidates for political office. The most well-known black abolitionist, Frederick Douglass (1817–1895), initially allied himself with Garrison, but by the end of the 1840s he had become a proponent of political strategies. Other black leaders, such as Henry Highland Garnet and Martin Delany, urged not only political action but also slave rebellions as the best means of abolishing slavery. Garnet and Delany also became advocates of black nationalism, believing that there was little hope for black advancement in the United States. Delany's *Condition, Elevation, Emigration, and Destiny of the Colored People of the United States, Politically Considered* (1852) argued that African Americans were "a nation within a nation" and recommended emigration to Central America or Africa. Pessimism increased among African Americans about their prospects in the United States after the Supreme Court's decision in *Dred Scott v. Sandford* (1857), which concluded that blacks were not citizens but were "a subordinate and inferior class of beings."

The Civil War marked a major turning point in African American politics. Although President Abraham Lincoln initially did not see the war as a struggle against slavery, the increasing reliance of the Union army on black soldiers altered war objectives. In 1863, Lincoln's Emancipation Proclamation promised freedom to slaves in areas still held by the Confederacy. After the defeat of the Confederacy, Republican leaders recognized that citizenship rights for freed slaves were necessary for the party's success in the South during the Reconstruction period. They drafted, and obtained ratification by the states of, constitutional amendments designed to free all slaves (the Thirteenth Amendment) and to eliminate racial discrimination in laws (the Fourteenth Amendment) and voting (the Fifteenth Amendment).

During the Reconstruction period, African Americans participated in the Southern political system, but black-supported Republican state governments in the region faced strong opposition from recalcitrant white segregationists, and none survived after the last federal troops were removed in 1877.

The end of Reconstruction led to a rapid decline in black political activity, and by the early twentieth century most Southern states had enacted racially discriminatory laws that segregated blacks and prevented them from voting. Black political leaders responded to the imposition of this "Jim Crow" system in a variety of ways. Some leaders, including the AME bishop Henry McNeal Turner (1834–1915), advocated black separatism and even emigration to Africa. Others, notably Booker T. Washington (1856–1915), founder of Tuskegee Institute in Alabama, urged blacks to forgo agitation for civil rights and instead develop skills that would be attractive to white employers. Washington garnered the financial backing of white philanthropists, particularly after his conciliatory address at the Atlanta Exposition of 1895, and he dominated African American politics at the national level at the beginning of the twentieth century.

The most innovative political thinker of the period was William Edward Burghardt (W. E. B.) Du Bois (1868–1963), who combined elements of earlier nationalist thought, particularly an appreciation of the African roots of African American culture, with a strong commitment to ending racial discrimination. In 1900, Du Bois, influenced by the earlier efforts of Alexander Crummell (1819–1898) and Edward Wilmot Blyden (1832–1912), participated in the first Pan-African Conference in London, which advocated unity among all people of African ancestry. In 1905, Du Bois became a founding member of the Niagara movement, formed to promote protest activity on behalf of black civil rights, and, four years later, he joined with white reformers to establish the National Association for the Advancement of Colored People (NAACP).

Twentieth-century African American politics were greatly affected by the migration of millions of blacks from the rural South to urban areas. A massive influx of blacks to Northern cities during World War I strengthened existing African American urban religious and fraternal institutions, and led to increasing political militancy in the growing black communities. Marcus Garvey (1887–1940) organized the most substantial manifestation of the new militancy, the Universal Negro Improvement Association (UNIA), which, according to some estimates, attracted several million followers. Garvey's ultimate goal was to create a strong, independent African nation that would advance the interests of black people throughout the world. Garvey's caustic criticisms of civil rights leaders such as Du Bois made him a controversial figure among blacks and a target of government persecution. He was convicted of mail fraud in connection with his fundraising for the Black Star steamship line, and his movement declined rapidly after his deportation in 1927 to Jamaica.

Despite the persecution of Garvey, African American cultural distinctiveness continued to flourish through the movement known as the Harlem Renaissance. Poets, essayists, dramatists, novelists, and artists of the 1920s became increasingly concerned with depicting the lives of African Americans. Langston Hughes (1902–1967), the most popular and prolific of the poets of the period, summarized the sentiments of other writers when he announced in a 1926 article, titled "The Negro Artist and the Racial Mountain," published in *The Nation*: "We younger Negro artists who create now intend to express our individual dark-skinned selves without fear or shame." Other major intellectual figures of the movement included Alain Locke (1886–1954), Claude McKay (1890–1948), and Zora Neale Hurston (1901–1960). Innovative forms of African American music also appeared during the 1920s, as blues and jazz became increasingly popular in urban centers.

The worldwide economic depression of the 1930s strengthened the tendency of African Americans to seek advancement through interracial political movements and civil rights reform. A small minority of blacks, including a number of prominent artists and intellectuals, was drawn to the Communist Party, which identified itself with the ideal of universal rights and which fostered the notion that blacks could play a major role in radically transforming American society. Du Bois and Paul Robeson (1898–1976), a famed singer and actor, were prominent among blacks who remained close to the Communist Party during the 1940s and 1950s, even as other blacks, such as Hughes and the novelist Richard Wright (1908–1960), became disillusioned with the party. The dominant direction of African American political activity outside the South involved electoral participation and efforts to combat racial discrimination through litigation, lobbying efforts, and, to an increasing extent, protest activity. After 1932, black voters generally supported the Democratic Party in national elections, and most black leaders at the national level participated in interracial coalitions favoring civil rights reforms. The 1941 March on Washington movement, initiated by black union leader A. Philip Randolph, demonstrated the potential for mass protest activity as a means of bringing about civil rights reform by prodding President Franklin D. Roosevelt to establish a Fair Employment Practices Committee. Despite Randolph's success in using the threat of protest to achieve concessions, however, the strategy of nonviolent direct action had few practitioners outside of the Congress of Racial Equality (CORE), a small, interracial group formed in 1944.

The participation of black soldiers in the United States military during World War II prompted intensified demands for racial equality, but, during the decade following the war, conventional electoral politics and civil rights lobbying, rather than mass activism, characterized African American life. Both socialist and black nationalist radicalism had little impact on black politics, particularly at the national level. Instead, encouraged by the Supreme Court's *Brown v. Board of Education of Topeka* (1954) decision, civil rights organizations and their leaders sought to strengthen federal and state antidiscrimination policies. The NAACP largely shaped the national civil rights agenda, but, after the Montgomery bus boycott movement of 1955–1956, this organization faced competition from more militant local groups inspired by African independence movements, which were linked to black colleges and churches and skilled in the use of nonviolent protest tactics. The Southern Christian Leadership Conference (SCLC), formed in 1957 and led by Montgomery protest leader Martin Luther King Jr. (1929–1968), was particularly effective in organizing massive protest campaigns in Southern communities such as Birmingham in 1963 and Selma in 1965. CORE initiated a Freedom Ride campaign in 1961, pressuring the federal government to act against racial discrimination in interstate travel. The Student Nonviolent Coordinating Committee (SNCC), formed by student leaders of the sit-in movement of 1960, spearheaded the effort to achieve voting rights for blacks in Mississippi, Alabama, and southwest Georgia. The Southern protest movement prodded the federal government to enact both the Civil Rights Act of 1964, which outlawed segregation in most public facilities, and the Voting Rights Act of 1965, which abolished discriminatory practices intended to deny blacks the vote.

Even as the Southern protest movement achieved its civil rights goals, it also revived racial consciousness among African Americans. Black nationalist sentiments were evident among urban blacks during the early 1960s, but the most effective proponent of these ideas, Malcolm X (1925–1965), had little impact on national African American politics until 1964, when he broke with the religious separatist group the Nation of Islam. In the months before his assassination in 1965, Malcolm X began to establish ties with militants who had been active in the civil rights movement. By 1966, both the SNCC, under the leadership of Stokely Carmichael (1944–1998), and CORE became identified with the "Black Power" slogan, which symbolized the increasingly militant racial consciousness of many African Americans. During the decade from 1965 to 1975, many new black-controlled cultural, social, political, educational, and economic institutions came into existence. The Black Panther Party, based in Oakland, California, reflected the widespread discontent of young Northern blacks through the brash willingness of armed Panthers to confront police. For the most part, however, the majority of African American institutions of the Black Power era did not pose direct political challenges to the state, but instead emphasized African American cultural distinctiveness. During the late 1960s and early 1970s, internal ideological conflicts and external repression led to the decline of militant political groups. The National Black Political Assembly, founded at a 1972 convention in Gary, Indiana, could not reverse the disintegration of black nationalist political activity. Instead, black political activity increasingly focused on efforts to elect black politicians in predominantly black districts. In addition to the increasing number of African Americans holding elected or appointed offices, the most enduring outgrowths of the militancy of the 1960s were black studies academic programs, businesses selling products designed for blacks, and associations formed to protect the interests of black professionals.

As popular support for governmental social reforms programs declined during the 1970s and 1980s, mass protest and militancy among African Americans was increasingly supplanted by efforts to utilize conventional tactics to achieve greater control over predominantly black communities and institutions. Many studies of American racial relations during this period noted the disjunction between the economic advances of middle-class blacks and the economic stagnation of large numbers of poor or working-class blacks. Affirmative action programs came under attack not only from white conservatives but also from some blacks, who noted the adverse psychological impact of such programs on some blacks. National black leaders largely focused their efforts on the consolidation of the civil rights gains of the 1960s, but many incorporated aspects of black nationalism and Pan-Africanism into their political perspectives. Campaigns for the presidency in 1984 and 1988 by Jesse Jackson (b. 1941) demonstrated the potential strength of the black electorate. In addition, during the period after 1970, black women have increasingly won election to public office, and have assumed prominent roles in racial policy discussions.

The overriding concern of black political and intellectual life during the final decades of the twentieth century was the extent to which African Americans had become divided by class and gender identities. African American leaders were unable to formulate successful strategies to deal with the serious economic problems of blacks who did not benefit economically from civil rights legislation and affirmative action programs. The combustible elements of political stagnation, endemic poverty, and police repression contributed to major racial riots in Miami in 1980 and Los Angeles in 1991. The increasing prevalence of black households headed by single, jobless mothers; the high rates of mortality, unemployment, and incarceration among black males; and the reluctance of white Americans to support major new governmental social programs to deal with these problems led to a revival of strategies for African American self-help and cultural uplift. The most notable expression of this revival was the ascendancy of Louis Farrakhan, leader of the Nation of Islam, to national prominence as a spokesperson for discontented blacks. Farrakhan played a major role in organizing the Million Man March in Washington, D.C., in October 1995, an event that was less a protest than a collective act of atonement by black males.

The Million Man March, with its emphasis on the distinctive problems of black males within the context of broader racial solidarity, served as a counterpoint to the emergence, during the previous two decades, of a vibrant black feminist (or womanist) movement. To some degree this movement was itself a reaction against the misogyny of some black male leaders, as well as the lack of attention to black female concerns in the white feminist movement. Although black women had produced important and distinctive contributions to African American history throughout the nineteenth and twentieth centuries, a concerted effort to promote a collective consciousness among African American women was evident in numerous literary works that reached a wide readership after the mid-1970s. Seminal works in this literary and social movement were Alice Walker's *The Color Purple* (1982) and Toni Morrison's *Beloved* (1987).

Thus, at the end of the twentieth century, African Americans had succeeded in overcoming historic forms of racial discrimination, but some racial barriers remained. The economic success of some members of the group had brought about increasing diversity among African Americans, which in turn encouraged increasing variety in collective and individual advancement strategies. Increasingly likely to be involved in the mainstream of American life, African Americans continued to be concerned with distinctive and unresolved questions of group identity and destiny. The election of Barack Obama as the president of the United States in 2008 was an extraordinary event in the history and identity politics of the nation. Indeed, many have argued that it validated the successful completion of the African American struggle against the legal and social structures that have prevented them from rising to "the mountaintop" of freedom, equality, and full citizenship. However, many have also argued that such claims are outlandish and exaggerated.

[*See also* Affirmative Action; African Americans, Contemporary Conditions; Civil Rights Movement; Race and Racism; *and* Religion and Politics.]

BIBLIOGRAPHY

Aptheker, Herbert, ed. *A Documentary History of the Negro People in the United States.* (New York, 1974).

Brown v. Board of Education of Topeka, 347 US 483 (1954).

Dred Scott v. Sandford, 60 US 393 (1857).

Franklin, John Hope, and Alfred A. Moss Jr. *From Slavery to Freedom: A History of Negro Americans.* (New York, 1988).

Hine, Darlene Clark, and Kathleen Thompson. *A Shining Thread of Hope: The History of Black Women in America.* (New York, 1988).

Salzman, Jack, David Lionel Smith, and Cornel West, eds. *Encyclopedia of African American Culture and History.* (New York, 1996).

Sear, David O., Jim Sidanius, and Lawrence Bobo, eds. *Racialized Politics: The Debate about Racism in America.* (Chicago, 2000).

Wilson, William Julius. *The Bridge over the Racial Divide.* (Berkeley, Calif., 1999).

Clayborne Carson;
revised by Yomi Durotoye

AFRICAN AMERICANS, CONTEMPORARY CONDITIONS

The election of Senator Barack Obama of Illinois as the forty-fourth president of the United States of America in 2008 led many to conclude that America has now become a postracial society, a society in which no deliberate institutional, legal, or social barrier exists to deter African Americans from achieving whatever goals they set for themselves. For many others, the election of Obama to the highest office in the land was an impressive national achievement but a poor gauge of the progress African Americans have made since the legal structures of state imposed segregation, or "Jim Crow," was dismantled in the 1960s. In the wake of this argument, it is fair to ask: How much progress has been made by African Americans in their bid to achieve equity and justice, and how far do they have to go?

African American progress can be measured in relation to the corresponding existential conditions of the majority non-Hispanic, white population. Even though it is recognized that in the discussion of race relations, the majority-white/minority-black paradigm is no longer an accurate description of racial dynamics and proportionality in America, it is nevertheless sensible and methodologically appropriate to rely on such measure in this instance. A casual familiarity with American history will show that in the decades since the 1960s, African Americans have recorded relatively substantial progress in many spheres of life. Perhaps no other subject typifies the narrative of the progress that African Americans have made since the 1960s than the achievements registered in electoral politics. Thanks to the Voting Rights Act of 1965, for the first time in their history in America, all African Americans were allowed to vote in the presidential election of 1968. In less than fifty years of full participation in national politics, it is accurate to claim that African Americans have been elected into all significant political offices in the land, with the exception of the vice presidency. On the other hand, it is equally correct to argue that this claim conceals the superficiality of the progress made and the gaping racial disparities that differentiate the life circumstances of African Americans and whites. Surely, it is remarkable that the numbers of Black Elected Officials (BEOs) grew steeply from 103 in 1964 to more than 9,430 in 2002; yet, this phenomenal growth hides the fact that, at its peak, BEOs represent only about 2 percent of the elected officials nationwide.

The historic legislative victories of the civil rights struggle in the mid-1960s energized and propelled African Americans to seize the opportunity to participate in national politics with an enthusiasm that was greater than the national average. Composite figures from the Census Bureau show that, from 1964 to 2008, 64.7 percent of blacks registered to vote in presidential elections while 55.3 percent actually turned out to vote, compared to a national voter turnout average of 54.6 percent. The African American vote has consistently and overwhelmingly gone to the Democratic Party and has been crucial for the victory of the party in some elections in swing states in the Northeast and the Midwest, and has led to the extraordinary growth in the number of BEOs nationwide. Most of the BEOs come from majority-minority districts. However, in the history of statewide elections in the United States, only two African American governors and five senators have been elected. These are Governors Douglas Wilder of Virginia in 1989 and Deval Patrick of Massachusetts in 2006 and Senators Blanche Bruce and Hiram Revels from Mississippi during Reconstruction and Edward Brooke of Massachusetts, Carol Mosley Braun, and Barack Obama of Illinois in 1966, 1998, and 2004 respectively. Thus, only a handful of African Americans have won in majority-white electoral districts. The failure of African Americans to win in these elections is attributable to both the unwillingness of whites, particularly in the Southern states, to vote for African Americans and the liberal ideological platforms of African American candidates. All the same, the electoral victories of Governor Deval Patrick in Massachusetts (where African Americans constitute 16 percent of the population) and of President Barack Obama show that in order to win statewide and national elections, African Americans have to create extraordinary excitement in their candidacies,

run a racially transcendent campaign, and string together a broad coalition of minorities—Asians, Hispanics, Jews, and gays and lesbians among others—plus appeal to a substantial percentage of the white vote. Although Obama lost the white vote to McCain by 12 percentage points, he scooped up virtually all the excess votes generated by the historic increase in the voting rates for African American and Hispanic Americans and improved by one percentage point the existing record for black voter turnout for a Democratic presidential candidate.

It is anticipated that recent changes in the composition of the national population and migration patterns of African Americans may reverse the gains made in electoral politics in the past five decades. According to the 2010 census population estimates, with a population of 37.7 million, African Americans now constitute 12.3 percent of the US population, down from 14.8 percent a decade earlier. In contrast, the Hispanic population has grown to 50.5 million, making it the largest minority in the nation. Trends in population migration show that African Americans are now reconcentrating in the South. About 57 percent of African Americans lived in the South as of 2010, compared to their 53 percent share in the 1970s. Up until 1910, the South was home to roughly 90 percent of blacks in the United States. In the Great Migration between 1910 and 1970, blacks voted with their feet to escape the brutality of Jim Crow and seek employment opportunities in cities in the Midwest, Northeast, and the West. However, since 1990, many African Americans have abandoned metropolitan areas in these regions and returned to the south. Since 2000, 75 percent of African American returnees moved to Atlanta, Charlotte, Houston, Dallas, and Miami, up from 65 percent in the 1990s. The gains came at the expense of such cities as Chicago and New York. According to the 2010 census figures, of the 366 metro areas where 83.7 percent of the US population lives, Hispanics outnumber African Americans in 191 of those areas, up from 159 in 2090. It is reasonable to expect that the emergent population distribution patterns will have considerable impact on national and local politics. For one, there are greater chances that African Americans may be effectively challenged in electoral representations, as there are now fewer black-majority electoral districts than used to be the case. The redistricting that will take place in 2011 will likely see more losses of black-majority districts, given the fact that in the 2010 midterm elections the Republican Party picked up nine state houses from the Democratic Party to control twenty-nine of the fifty state houses as well as gained control of twenty-five state legislatures. In that event, politicians will probably pay more attention to Hispanics as the major minority rather than African Americans.

The gender distribution of the African American population will probably mitigate the political impact of the changes in the national population dynamics. There are more women (52.4 percent) than men (47.6 percent) among the African American population, a greater margin than in any other racial group, and they turn out to vote and vote for the Democratic Party at higher rates than their male counterparts. Effective mobilization of the African American female voters may flip the outcomes of elections in districts where African Americans recently lost their majority share. The importance of African American females is further highlighted by their roles in the black family. Nearly a third of African American families (29 percent) are headed by a single woman, the highest percentage among all racial groups. In any case, only 30.4 percent of African Americans (ages fifteen and over) are married, compared to a national figure of 50.2 percent.

The pattern of the African American family structure is partly a consequence of poverty, disproportionate high rate of unemployment, relative isolation in urban areas, and the overrepresentation of African Americans in the criminal justice system. One out of five African American families lives in poverty compared to one out of ten white families. Given the disproportional levels of poverty, African Americans are more likely to spend more than 40 percent of their income on rent, a figure that is higher than that paid by other racial groups. In addition, African Americans receive disproportionate assistance from federal programs designed to alleviate poverty. Surely, poverty increased for all racial groups during the deep recession that began in 2008, but more so for African Americans. Whereas 14.3 percent of all Americans lived in poverty in 2009, for African Americans the poverty level increased from 24.7 percent in 2008 to 25.8 percent in 2009. Similarly, the Kaiser Foundation reported that whereas in 2009 11.9 percent of nonelderly white women lived in poverty, 28.5 percent of nonelderly African American women lived in poverty, the highest among all racial groups with the exception of Native American and Native Alaskan women. In the decades since 1980, the income disparity between black and white households has consistently been around 60 percent. For instance in 2006, the median income for African American households was $32,372, the lowest of any racial group in America, compared to the white median household income of $52,375. Also, according to the Kaiser Foundation, in 2009 the median household income for women was $45,000 and while the median household income for white women was $54,536, African American women made $26,681, lowest among all racial groups except the Native Americans and Alaskans who made $24,000. Given the higher rate of women householders among the African American population, a vastly disproportionate number of their children grow up in poverty. In 2008, 35.4 percent of African American children lived in poverty, compared to 11.9 percent of non-Hispanic white children.

The high rate of unemployment among African Americans partly explains their disproportional level of poverty. Since the 1950s, the unemployment rates of African Americans were one and a half to twice those of non-Hispanic whites. In 1999, when the economy was experiencing an unprecedented boom, the overall rate of unemployment fell to 4.3 percent, which was a twenty-four-year low. Yet, while white adults' unemployment rate stood at 3.8 percent, translating into full employment for white adults according to the Humphrey-Hawkins Act, the adult unemployment rate for African Americans was 7.7 percent. At this time too, the unemployment rate for African American teenagers was 23.5 percent compared to 11.6 percent for white teenagers. Even before the deep recession that began in 2008, the unemployment rate for African Americans in December 2007 was at 9 percent, slightly more than double the white rate of 4.4 percent. Similarly, in April 2011, while the unemployment rate for whites was 8 percent, the rate of unemployment for African Americans was 16.1 percent. To make matters worse, unemployed African Americans are 25 percent less likely than unemployed whites to receive unemployment benefits due to their disproportionate representation among low-wage and part-time workers. The reasons for the disproportionately high unemployment rate among African Americans include, among others, the poor quality of education for a good majority of African Americans, the transition to a postindustrial economy, spatial mismatch, and discrimination in hiring. Even so, the earnings of African American men grew at an impressive rate between 1950 and 1990, as the wage gap between African American men and white men considerably narrowed from 74.5 percent to 55.2 percent during that period. Indeed, between 1962 and 1973, African American men's wages rose 10 percent more than the rate of increase in the wages of white men. As well, James P. Smith estimated that the number of African American males that entered the middle class or became affluent more than quadrupled between 1962 and 1997. Nevertheless, the growth in relative earnings of working poor African American men had stagnated or else declined since 1973.

Wealth inequality between African American and non-Hispanic white populations is even more pronounced than the disparities shown in wages and income. In the three decades prior to the deep recession that started in 2008, the African American median household net worth stood at 10 percent of their white counterparts. That is, African Americans own ten cents of every dollar of white disposable assets. For example, in 2007 the median net worth of non-Hispanic white households was $170,400, compared to a median net worth of $17,000 for African American families. According to a 2011 publication by the Pew Research Center, the deep recession has significantly and disproportionately worsened the racial wealth ratios. The median wealth of white households is now twenty times that of black households.

In 2009, the median net worth of the former was $113,149 compared to $5,677 of the latter. That is, African Americans now own five cents of every dollar of white disposable assets. Unquestionably, the racial disparities in income and unemployment rates partly explain the gaps in the distribution of wealth. Other significant factors that explain the persistence of the wealth disparities include portfolio composition; differences in intergenerational transfers, declining unionism, and the cumulative impacts of post–World War II federal policies on home ownership. The majority of Americans hold their wealth or disposable assets in the values of their homes. The denial of low-interest Federal Housing Administration (FHA) loans to blacks soon after World War II deprived them the opportunity to move to the emergent suburbia, while the "redlining" of communities where they lived made it difficult to buy or maintain the homes they lived in. ("Redlining" is the now illegal discriminatory practice whereby financial institutions refuse to extend mortgage and home loans to minority neighborhoods or else make it substantially more expensive when they approve such loans.) The consequent residential segregation that defines many cities across the United States results in less value and equity for black homes; poor funding for education and low-performing schools; and neighborhood decay and isolation. The wealth and potential income gaps created by the discriminatory application of these federal government policies and the selective practices of mortgage lenders have not only taken a long time to close but have actually worsened. For example, a 2007 *New York Times* analysis of loans reported under the Federal Home Mortgage Disclosure Act reveals that African Americans are 2.3 times more likely to get high-cost and high-risk loans than whites after adjusting for loan amounts and the income of borrowers.

Notwithstanding, since the 1960s, black businesses have been growing at a faster rate than all businesses. Between 2002 and 2007, the number of African American–owned businesses grew by 61 percent to 1.9 million. The receipts also rose by 55 percent to $137.5 billion, the largest of which reported a revenue of $3.2 billion. Obviously, these are all small businesses. The 2007 Census Survey reported that only 12.7 percent of African American businesses have annual revenues of more than $50,000, and 68 percent of these have four or fewer employees. However, as in the broader economy, the character of African American businesses has changed from the traditional "mom and pop" or personal-service operations to businesses in technologies, entertainment, finance, insurance, real estate, and the professions. The diversity and sophistication of these businesses, especially in the 1970s and 1980s, were made possible by the higher levels of education attained by African Americans, acquired experience and expertise, as well as affirmative action programs in education and public-sector contracting and procurement.

Education is a reliable predictor of wage and income levels. Between 1970 and 1990, African American men cut by almost half the educational deficit relative to white men from 2.02 fewer years of schooling to 1.11 years. In 2009, more than 70 percent of high school graduates enrolled in two- or four-year colleges nationwide. The African American enrollment rate was 68.7 percent, slightly lagging behind the white rate of 69.2 percent. Similarly, from 1982 to 1990, African American teenagers made significant progress in test scores, especially in math. Studies have shown that they benefited from the national effort to hold teachers and school administrators accountable, especially following the appointment of the Commission on Minority Participation in Education and American Life in 1988. The situation was also improved by other policy decisions made at the state level, such as reduced class sizes and desegregation. However, by 1990, the trends in reading and math scores declined. Some of the explanations for this decline include funding disparities, the quality of schooling, poverty, and the increasing trend toward the resegregation of schools. In 2005–2006, more than half of black students (52 percent) attended schools with less than one third (30 percent) of white students, while the average white attended schools that were 77 percent white. If the purpose of education extends beyond academics to include the preparation to function in a diverse society and a

globalized world, then the increasing isolation of students of all races is dysfunctional. For African American students, the resegregation of schools has impacted school funding. A study of nine large urban school districts in 2005 shows that African American students participate more in Title 1 supplementary services than any other racial groups, an indicator of chronic and pervasive poverty. Indeed, 63 percent of African American students attend schools where more than half of the student body is poor, compared to 21 percent of white students. Fully 13 percent of African American students attend schools where at least 91 percent of the student body is poor, compared to a mere 1 percent of whites. Where there are high levels of concentrated poverty, such schools tend to have less resources, student-discipline problems, poor parental involvement, and relatively poor-quality teachers and principals. Predictably, student performance tends to be low in such schools.

Poverty, stress, health-risk behaviors, environmental exposure, genetic factors, differential behavior of health care providers, and poor access to health care contribute to a disproportional distribution of chronic and infectious diseases, and homicide, among African Americans. A disproportionate number of African Americans suffer from hypertension, lung and heart disease, infant mortality, HIV/AIDS, and younger ages at death. In 2004, the life expectancy of whites was 78.3 compared to 73 for African Americans. High blood pressure is twice as common among them as whites. According to the Centers for Disease Control (CDC), African Americans have double the rate of "preventable hospitalization" as whites. Fully one in two cases of newly diagnosed HIV-infected persons is African American, and African Americans are less likely to report healthy diets and physical activity, especially during middle age, than non-Hispanic whites. With higher rates of poverty than whites, African Americans are more likely to rely on publicly funded services such as the State Children's Health Insurance Program (SCHIP) and Medicaid than any other racial or ethnic groups. Medicaid is the publicly funded insurance for low-income Americans, and 22 percent of those enrolled in Medicaid are black.

Few issues highlight racial disparities in the United States more than those found in the criminal justice system (CJS). African Americans are arrested and incarcerated at a higher rate than any other racial group in America. As well, other than Native Americans, African Americans are disproportionately more victimized by crimes than any other racial group, regardless of income levels. For example, the Bureau of Justice study found that between 2001 and 2005 nearly half of those murdered in the United States were African Americans. It was also found that nine out of ten African American murder victims are killed by other African Americans. Although they constitute 13 percent of the overall population, African American victims of nonfatal violent crimes account for 15 percent of such crimes. African American males are more victimized than their female counterparts, and poor African Americans in inner cities are more victimized than those of higher income or living in rural areas. Notwithstanding, violent crimes in African American communities declined as they did nationally between 1993 and 2001 and have more or less settled on a plateau thereafter.

A 2008 study by the Sentencing Project showed that 38 percent of prison and jail inmates were African Americans, compared to their 13 percent share of the national population, and while the African American youth represent 17 percent of their national cohort, they represent 46 percent of juvenile arrests and 41 percent of waivers to adult courts. There are many explanations for the racial disparity in incarceration. While Alfred Blumstein concluded in a study of 1991 national data that 76 percent of the racial disparity could be explained by the greater involvement of African Americans in criminal activities, Michael Tonry and Matthew Melewski's analysis of 2004 imprisonment data found that 61 percent of African American incarceration rate could be accounted for by disproportionate engagement in criminal activities. Other major factors that explain the disparity include drug policies, class, racial profiling, and sentencing guidelines. In the early 1980s the United States declared a "War on Drugs" that led to the incarceration of a large number of people and helped explode the prison population from

approximately 200,000 in 1972 to 1.2 million in 1997, an increase of more than 500 percent. African Americans were disproportionately the "prisoners of war" not because they committed more drug offences but for a variety of other reasons, chief among which are racial profiling in policing, racial discrimination in punishment, and poverty. According to government reports, the rates of drug offenses among all racial groups are similar, yet African Americans are more disproportionately subjected to penalties than whites. The US Department of Health and Human Services reported that, whereas in 2006 African Americans constituted 14 percent of drug users, they represented 35 percent of those arrested for a drug offense and 53 percent of drug convictions and 45 percent of drug offenders in prison in 2004. According to the Compendium of Federal Statistics, African Americans serve nearly as much time in prison for a drug offense (58.7 months) as whites do for a violent offense (61.7 months). Misapplication of sentencing guidelines is another matter. In 1986, the Congress passed a law that established a 100:1 disparity in the five-year mandatory sentencing for possession of crack cocaine compared to powder cocaine. Now, according to a 1995 US Sentencing Commission report, about two-thirds of crack cocaine users are white and Hispanic, but 88 percent of those sentenced for crack cocaine offenses are African Americans, while only 4.1 percent of those sentenced for that offense are white. After several years of resisting calls to reform this law, in August 2010, Congress passed a non-retroactive Fair Sentencing Act that reduced the disparity in the mandatory sentences for low-level crack or powder cocaine offenses from 100:1 to 28:1.

A 2008 Gallup Poll found that a majority of Americans (51 percent) believed that racism would explain the overrepresentation of blacks in the CJS compared to the 18 percent who believed that it is not a factor. Specifically, 80 percent of African Americans and a higher plurality of whites (44 percent) shared the view that racism is the major reason for the disproportional representation of African Americans in the CJS. Videotaped police brutality of African Americans only confirmed the widespread perception in the black community that the CJS is unfair to blacks. Class has also contributed to the overrepresentation of African Americans in the CJS. The majority of African American defendants are poor and are, therefore, more likely to rely on the overworked, often poorly trained, and severely under-compensated court-appointed lawyers for their defense. In 2004, the American Bar Association concluded that "too often the lawyers who provide defense services are inexperienced, fail to maintain adequate client contact, and furnish services that are simply not competent." The consequences of the overrepresentation of African Americans in the CJS are profound. For instance, nearly 1.4 million African Americans adults, that is to say 13 percent, are disenfranchised because of felony conviction state laws. In some states, for example Florida, 25 to 30 percent of all African American men are not eligible to vote. In the circumstance, because African Americans tend to vote Democratic and often impact election outcomes in swing states, the Democratic Party has probably lost some close elections in such states. Another consequence is the fragmentation of African American families and the destabilizing of African American communities, as there are more African American men of college age in prisons than are in college. Perhaps more significantly, the perception that the justice system is unfair reduces its legitimacy in the eyes of most Americans.

White supremacy and the legalized segregation and oppression of black people were officially vanquished by the heroic, often altruistic, and sometimes self-serving efforts of diverse citizens and institutions across the land in the mid-1960s. Since then, African Americans have recorded mixed results in their bid to achieve equity and justice in many areas of American life. The overall picture is that pervasive and systematic inequalities continue to exist between African Americans and non-Hispanic whites in several crucial arenas of American life such as electoral politics, income, wealth, health, welfare, education, the labor market, crime, and justice. While there are multiple causes of the observed gaping racial disparities, the conclusion that race and existential outcomes intersect cannot be ignored.

[*See also* African Americans, History; Civil Rights; Civil Rights Act; Civil Rights Movement; Crime and Punishment; Hispanic Americans; Poverty, Scale and Nature of; *and* Race, Gender, and Incarceration.]

BIBLIOGRAPHY

Brown, Michael K., et. al. *Whitewashing Race: The Myth of a Color-Blind Society.* (Berkeley, Calif., 2005).

Foreman, Christopher H., Jr., ed. *The African American Predicament.* (Washington, D.C., 1999).

Shapiro, Thomas M. *The Hidden Cost of Being African American: How Wealth Perpetuates Inequality.* (New York, 2004).

Smelser, Neil J., William Julius Wilson, and Faith Mitchell, eds. *America Becoming.* Vols. 1–2. (Washington, D.C., 2001).

Taylor, Paul, Richard Fry, and Rakesh Kochhar. "Wealth Gaps Rise to Record Highs between Whites, Blacks, and Hispanics." *Pew Social & Demographic Trends*, Pew Research Center, http://www.pewsocialtrends.org/2011/07/26/wealth-gaps-rise-to-record-highs-between-whites-blacks-hispanics/10/.

Yomi Durotoye

AFRICA–UNITED STATES RELATIONS

Although Africa's contributions to the history and culture of the United States are significant in their variety and depth, it is only in recent years that America's political relations with the states and peoples of the continent have received more than passing consideration on the part of senior officials in administrations of both parties. In fact, the recognition that the United States does have significant national interests in Africa that require it to be actively engaged there, and those interests are sufficient to sustain a long-term commitment, is one of the most dramatic policy reversals in recent American politics.

While the Moroccan Sultan Mohammed III was the first sovereign to recognize the independence of the United States in 1777, and the "Barbary Pirates" of the semiautonomous Ottoman regencies of Tripoli, Tunis, and Algiers constituted one of the early American republic's first foreign policy challenges, it was only in the nineteenth century that the

US government began developing even limited relations with the rest of Africa. In 1816, a private group founded by a group of prominent individuals, the American Colonization Society, was chartered by Congress to "repatriate" to Africa freeborn African Americans (slaves freed for the purpose), and, in cooperation with the US Navy, African slaves "recaptured" from intercepted vessels engaged in the banned transatlantic slave trade. In 1822, the Society founded the settlement of Monrovia on the West African coast, naming it after the fifth US president. Despite the role played by its citizens in the establishment of the "land of liberty," official US policy not only refused to acknowledge the de facto colony for what it was, but, after Liberia's proclamation of independence in 1847, Washington declined to recognize the new country diplomatically until 1862, due to domestic opposition from Southern politicians to accrediting envoys to and receiving representatives from a government led by persons of color.

Thus it was only in 1863, during the height of the Civil War, that President Abraham Lincoln was able to nominate Abraham Hanson as consul-general to Liberia. Hanson, who died in the post some three years later, became the first American diplomat permanently assigned to sub-Saharan Africa. Since relations with most of Africa were handled through the European capitals of the colonial powers then dividing up the continent, the minister resident in Monrovia (the office was upgraded beginning with Hanson's successor) remained the only American diplomatic chief of mission resident south of the Sahara for the rest of the century.

In 1903, Robert Peet Skinner, the US consul in Marseilles, France, was dispatched to Ethiopia with orders from President Theodore Roosevelt to secure a treaty of amity and commerce with what was, besides Liberia, the only other independent state in Africa. As a result of the pact, signed by Skinner with the Emperor Menelik II and ratified by the US Senate the following year, an American legation was opened in Addis Ababa in 1906 headed by a consul-general. However, the post, subsequently upgraded to a mission headed by a minister resident, was only intermittently filled in the period up to World War II, with American interests being otherwise entrusted to the British legation.

In 1929, the United States established its third permanent diplomatic mission in sub-Saharan Africa, when Ralph J. Totten, a career Foreign Service Officer, formerly minister at the shuttered legation in Ethiopia, was appointed minister resident and consul-general in the Union of South Africa.

Despite the eventual opening up of the Liberian interior to US economic interests—notably the Firestone Rubber and Tire Company, which acquired long-term leases to vast swathes of country in the 1920s—official US policies toward that particular West African nation and toward Africa in general continued to follow a largely "hands-off" approach well into the middle of the twentieth century, under an informal geopolitical entente which conceded Africa to the European powers while maintaining for the United States a predominant role in the Americas. Things changed just slightly with the beginning of World War II: Axis domination of the Mediterranean raised the strategic profile of the continent both as a transit point for Allied forces heading to the Middle East or South Asia and a source of natural resources, including the uranium from the Shinkolobwe mine near Lubumbashi, the capital of mineral-rich Katanga province in the Belgian Congo (present-day Democratic Republic of the Congo), used in the two atomic bombs dropped on Hiroshima and Nagasaki in 1945.

In 1942, Liberia nominally entered the war on the Allied side in exchange for American assistance with infrastructure construction. The Defense Areas Agreement of that year granted the United States the right to build, maintain, and defend military installations in Liberia. The Mutual Aid Agreement of 1943 permitted the United States to begin work on Liberia's first deep-water port. En route home from a wartime conference with British Prime Minister Winston Churchill at Casablanca, Morocco, President Franklin Delano Roosevelt stopped in Liberia on 26–27 January 1943, to call on the Liberian president Edwin Barclay, thus becoming the first American chief executive to make a state visit to an independent African nation.

After the war, however, the United States attempted to return to its secondary role in Africa, deferring once more to its European allies, although it did nudge them to allow their colonies to move toward independence. Even as the Cold War got under way, no part of the continent was even included in the American military command structure until 1952, when several North African countries were added to the "area of responsibility" of the US European Command—and then only because these territories had a historic relationship with Europe. The rest of the continent remained outside any of the Pentagon's geographic military commands—and thus were not included in the strategic planning that occurred at that level—well into the 1960s.

A break with America's longtime neglect of Africa came as the Cold War intensified, when the Soviet Union's attempts to secure a foothold in newly independent African states led the United States to respond by lavishing attention and resources on the continent, because policymakers could now understand it through the lens of the defined national interest in containing the spread of communism wherever it presented itself. A twenty-two-day tour across Africa in 1957 by Vice President Richard Nixon led to the creation of an Africa Bureau within the US Department of State, as well as the decision to establish an American embassy in every African state as each achieved its independence. Beginning in the Kennedy administration, the United States began to develop "special relationships" with geostrategically important states that were deemed to serve as bulwarks against communist expansion, including South Africa and Congo-Kinshasa (present-day Democratic Republic of the Congo).

Earlier, similar strategic ties had been cultivated with the imperial government of Haile Selassie in Ethiopia, which became a linchpin in America's containment regime along the southern tier of the Middle East. During the Second World War, the United States had begun using a communications facility outside Asmara, the capital of the Italian colony of Eritrea, then under British occupation. The facility, known as Kagnew, came to be highly valued by the US military as part of its global radio system. This

desire complemented that of the Ethiopian monarch to obtain control of Eritrea in order to gain access to the sea for his landlocked country. Consequently, after the monarch showed his support for America by sending an Ethiopian contingent to fight alongside US forces in the Korean War (the unit, dubbed the "Kagnew Battalion," was attached to the Seventh Infantry Division and fought in a number of engagements, including the famous two battles at "Pork Chop Hill"), President Dwight Eisenhower's secretary of state, John Foster Dulles, used his influence at the United Nations to arrange for Eritrea's being joined to Ethiopia in a federation in 1952. That same year, a technical program was signed between the United States and Ethiopia, followed one year later by an accord on assistance in exchange for continued American use of Kagnew and naval access to the Eritrean port of Massawa. These agreements paved the way for massive US aid, both for the emperor's military and for his broader modernization program. As the relationship acquired even greater importance following the rise of the Egyptian nationalist Gamal Abdel Nasser, Washington largely overlooked Ethiopia's steady erosion of the federal arrangements with Eritrea and effectively condoned the 1961 formal annexation of the territory into the empire.

American policy toward the former Belgian Congo was likewise emblematic of the complexities of postindependence experience of African states as well as the ambiguities faced by outsiders seeking to engage them. The fact was that the new country, covering a territory the size of the eastern United States, was woefully unprepared for the independence proclaimed on 30 June 1960. When Congo collapsed virtually immediately into violence and civil conflict (a chaos accelerated, perhaps, by ham-fisted Belgian interference, but likely to have occurred anyway) and the first United Nations peacekeeping operation floundered, the United States began assuming a progressively greater role in the country's affairs, although it never went so far as to intervene militarily—a possibility studied at one point by a NATO committee during the waning days of the Eisenhower administration. In the end,

America backed Joseph-Désiré Mobutu, a military man who seized power in 1965 with clandestine US support. While Mobutu's rule was increasingly characterized by kleptocracy and an extravagant cult of personality, Washington policymakers nonetheless counted upon him to not only keep the Soviet influence at bay in his own country, but also to aid groups fighting Marxist regimes elsewhere on the continent.

For its part, after an initial foray into West Africa, where the Marxists Ahmed Sékou Touré of Guinea and Modibo Keïta of Mali were especially receptive, the Soviet Union likewise tried to carve off spheres of influence across the African continent. Eyeing its strategic position on the Red Sea, the Soviets also concentrated their efforts on Somalia (later switching to Ethiopia after the overthrow of the Emperor Haile Selassie in 1974). They also supported Marxist-led liberation movements in Angola and Mozambique. In the latter two countries, Cuban troops were dispatched at Moscow's request to prop up the regimes that seized power following the precipitous abandonment of their colonial empire by the Portuguese in 1975. (Cuban forces also eventually fought in Ethiopia against both secessionist Eritreans and internal dissidents.) While he was initially inclined toward greater tolerance of the racist regimes of southern Africa as allies of convenience who could counter the threat posed by the military advisors the Soviet Union had introduced into the region, as well as the eleven thousand Cuban combat troops airlifted by the Soviets to assist the forces of their Angolan allies, Secretary of State Henry Kissinger eventually came around to urging a negotiated solution to head off violent conflict in the region.

During his administration, President Jimmy Carter departed from the Cold War script in attempting to help Rhodesia achieve independence under majority rule, as well as putting increasing pressure on South Africa's apartheid regime. Elsewhere, however, his administration hewed to the containment strategy, especially after the throes of Iran's Islamic Revolution and the Soviet invasion of Afghanistan in 1979 placed Moscow's forces within potential striking distance of the Persian Gulf. Access to military bases and transit authorizations were sought from Kenya, Somalia, Djibouti, Sudan, and Egypt so as to enable the newly created Rapid Deployment Force (which eventually evolved into the US Central Command) to have a staging area close to potential flashpoints in the Middle East (these countries also had the geopolitical effect of encircling Ethiopia, then Moscow's principal African ally under the brutal rule of Mengistu Haile Mariam).

With the inauguration of President Ronald Reagan in 1981, and the subsequent unveiling of the "Reagan Doctrine" of providing direct US assistance to anti-communist movements in an effort to "roll back" Soviet-backed regimes in Africa, Asia, and Latin America, prohibitions on aid to the Angolan rebel leader Jonas Savimbi's National Union for the Total Independence of Angola (UNITA) were repealed and "covert" aid from Washington of both the lethal and nonlethal varieties poured into the fight against the Soviet-backed government of the Angolan president José Eduardo dos Santos. By 1987, the United States had successfully leveraged its support of UNITA to preside over the secret negotiations in May 1988, which led to the withdrawal of both Cuban and South African troops from Angola. While the talks led by Assistant Secretary of State for African Affairs Chester Crocker left the internal struggle between the Angolan regime and UNITA unresolved, the withdrawal of foreign forces reduced the international dimension of the conflict. These moves subsequently set the stage for South Africa's agreeing to end its administration of South-West Africa the following year, and the territory's independence as Namibia.

The logic of the Cold War struggle also exercised its influence in the America-founded West African republic of Liberia, which was ruled by a quasi-literate master sergeant self-promoted to five-star general, Samuel Kanyon Doe, who killed President William Tolbert Jr. and overthrew the oligarchy descended from the "repatriated" former slaves in a 1980 coup. Despite his increasingly violent and oppressive rule, and the centralization of power in the hands of his tribal kinsmen, Doe, like his Americo-Liberian predecessors, benefited from America's Cold War willingness to turn a blind eye to the abuses of friendly despots who accommodated US interests. In Liberia, those interests included a large diplomatic and intelligence communications station comprising two 500-acre antenna fields, a 1,600-acre Voice of America broadcast relay station, a US Coast Guard maritime navigational tracking station (one of only six in the world at the time), and unlimited access for American military flights to the Robertsfield Airport—all for the extremely favorable rent of $100,000 per year. Between 1981 and 1985, US economic and military assistance to Doe amounted to over $500 million.

The end of the Cold War, however, altered America's strategic calculus: during Reagan's second term, US aid to Liberia plummeted from $53.6 million in 1986 to $19.5 million in 1989. Except for some $10 million in emergency food and other humanitarian assistance, aid to the West African country was zeroed out in the first budget submitted to Congress by the George H. W. Bush administration. The collapse of the Soviet Union and the end of the Cold War also brought about the transformation of the geopolitical world into the system characterized, however fleetingly, by America's "unipolar moment." For Africa, it largely meant that, notwithstanding the diplomatic shuttles of the Bush administration's assistant secretary of state for African affairs, Herman J. Cohen, there was even less attention to be had from an increasingly disengaged Washington, which could return to its pre–Cold War "hands-off" policy. One might even say that America shifted gears on the continent from "selective engagement" to "selective disengagement." As President Bush and his national security advisor, Brent Scowcroft, acknowledge in their joint memoirs, Liberia's civil war and other items on the African agenda were, literally, "foreign troubles" which fleetingly caught their attention between pressing concerns of greater moment.

The disastrous result of the one exception to this rule—the decision in December 1992 by the outgoing George H. W. Bush administration, expanded by the incoming Clinton administration, to send more than twenty-five thousand US troops to lead an international humanitarian effort in Somalia—served only to accelerate the pace of America's renewed disengagement from the continent. When twenty-three Pakistani soldiers who were part of the United Nations mission were ambushed in June 1993, the Security Council ordered the arrest of Mohamed Farrah Aidid, the warlord held responsible for the attack. Within two months, eight Americans had died trying unsuccessfully to achieve this objective. Then, between 3 and 4 October, in a pitched urban battle in Mogadishu seared into the popular and political consciousness by Mark Bowden's book *Black Hawk Down: A Story of Modern War* (1999) and the subsequent movie by the same title, US forces lost eighteen men and suffered eighty-four other casualties. News reports were filled with images of fallen American soldiers being dragged through the streets by frenzied mobs of 'Aideed's Hawiye clansmen.

Under intense criticism from members of Congress and facing public opposition to continued US involvement in the Horn of Africa country, President Clinton not only announced the withdrawal of US forces from Somalia just three days after the battle in Mogadishu (the United Nations followed closely behind), but also revised Presidential Decision Directive 25 to apply a litmus test of vital American interests as a prerequisite for the deployment of the nation's military forces to conflict areas abroad. While the decision to limit occasions when US personnel were put in harm's way to those involving direct threats to the country's national interests was a reasonable one, the administration also began to apply the same standard to UN missions, even those without US military involvement, especially those to places like Africa, where memories of the Somali chaos were still fresh. The retreat from Africa, however, also had an effect beyond military missions. By the end of 1994, personnel in the State Department's Bureau of African Affairs were reduced to barely 10 percent of their numbers two years earlier. The US Agency for International Development (USAID) closed nine of its missions in Africa and reduced staff in Washington by over one thousand people. The nadir was possibly hit in 1995, when the authors of the Pentagon's *US Strategy for Sub-Saharan Africa* declared that they could "see very little traditional strategic interest in Africa" and thus concluded that

"America's security interests in Africa are very limited."

Guided by this perspective, the Clinton administration largely adhered to the tendency to relegate Africa to the periphery of American strategic considerations, where it could be effectively ignored or, at best, perhaps receive occasional secondary attention. As a salve to consciences still stung by the 1994 genocide in Rwanda and a belated response to the expanding conflict around the Great Lakes region, the African Crisis Response Initiative (ACRI) was proposed as a means of establishing and training a ten-thousand-strong "All African Crisis Response Force" which would be trained by US Special Operations Forces. While several smaller countries—including Ghana, Malawi, Mali, Senegal, and Uganda—benefited from ACRI training and supplies, the skepticism of larger states like Nigeria and South Africa, as well as conditions imposed by Congress, prevented the program's full implementation.

Notwithstanding President Clinton's six-nation tour of the continent in 1998—the most comprehensive tour ever undertaken in Africa up to that time by a sitting US chief executive—as well as the president's professed wish to develop a more dynamic approach to Africa, the Clinton administration's effective disengagement from Africa was underscored by America's decision not to take a leading role in resolving the Liberian crisis, which dragged on throughout the entire eight years Clinton was in office.

It should be noted, however, that there were two exceptions to the general rule of neglect which may prove, over time, to be of far greater significance than even their architects envisioned. First, freed by the end of the Cold War from the constraints of the zero-sum competition with their Soviet competitors, American policymakers began placing a greater emphasis on democratization and good governance in their dealings with African states, which had up to then largely been characterized by various forms of authoritarian rule—it should be recalled that only two African nations, Botswana and Mauritius, had unbroken records for remaining continuously democratic since gaining their independence. By the end of the 1990s, under steady pressure from the United States and other Western nations, virtually all sub-Saharan African states—even those that had collapsed or were on the verge of collapse—opened at least partially to democratization. Second, as was the case with democratic reforms, the end of the Cold War likewise shifted leverage in economic matters to policymakers in the West, who could more freely cut off aid and other ties from states recalcitrant in accepting conditionalities. During Clinton's second term, for example, six African countries had part of their US assistance curbed for human rights abuses.

On the positive side, programs like the African Growth and Opportunity Act (AGOA), signed by President Bill Clinton in 2000 and subsequently expanded under his successor, offered tangible incentives for African countries to continue their efforts to open their economies and accelerate their integration into the global economy. AGOA provides that African countries which meet certain criteria, including improved labor rights and progress toward a market economy, could have specific goods which they enjoy a comparative advantage in producing, such as textiles and apparel, enter the American market duty-free. The legislation, which was originally set to expire in 2008, was later extended until 2015. From the American perspective, the strength of this approach was the linkage of domestic concerns (export markets for American goods and services and, hence, jobs in the United States) with foreign policy objectives (reducing foreign dependence on aid and promoting democracy), both bundles of which enjoyed broad bipartisan support in Washington.

To the surprise of many, including some of the president's own supporters, the administration of George W. Bush was extraordinarily active in Africa. Broadly conceived, there are four areas in which Africa's significance for America—or at least the public acknowledgment thereof—was amplified during the Bush years. The first was the continent's role in the "Global War on Terror" and the perceived potential of Africa's poorly governed spaces to provide facilitating environments, recruits, and eventual targets for Islamist terrorists who threaten

Western interests in general and those of the United States in particular. The second important consideration was Africa's abundant natural resources, particularly those in its burgeoning energy sector, the importance of which to the international community in general and the United States in particular has increased considerably, with the National Intelligence Council estimating that upwards of one-quarter of American oil imports will come from Africa by 2015. The third area motivating the reappraisal of Africa's strategic significance was the recognition of the role that the continent is playing in China's rapid rise to great-power status and the interest that other emerging powers, including India and Brazil, have taken in the continent. The fourth impulse was the humanitarian concern for the devastating toll which conflict, poverty, and disease, especially HIV/AIDS, continue to exact in Africa.

The Bush administration made combating HIV/AIDS on the continent a priority, with twelve of the fifteen original focus countries in the President's Emergency Plan for AIDS Relief (PEPFAR) being in Africa, including Botswana, Côte d'Ivoire, Ethiopia, Kenya, Mozambique, Namibia, Nigeria, Rwanda, South Africa, Tanzania, Uganda, and Zambia. With a $15 billion price tag during its first five years, PEPFAR, announced in 2003, has been the largest commitment ever by any nation to an international health initiative dedicated to a single disease. Through the program, which was reauthorized for another five years and expanded by Congress in 2008, more than 3.2 million people have received lifesaving antiretroviral treatment, while some 600,000 HIV-positive pregnant women have been given antiretroviral prophylaxis to prevent mother-to-child HIV transmission.

The Millennium Challenge Corporation (MCC), established in 2004, was perhaps the Bush administration's most innovative contribution with regard to foreign aid. MCC's Millennium Challenge Account provides large-scale grants to qualifying countries through multiyear "compact agreements" to fund specific host country–led programs targeted at reducing poverty by stimulating sustainable economic growth, as well as "threshold programs" to improve performance with an eye toward achieving "compact"

status. By the time Bush left office, a full half of the forty countries worldwide receiving some MCC funding, either through the "Threshold Program" or "Compact Assistance," were in Africa, including several of the largest compacts like Ghana ($547 million), Morocco ($697.5 million), Mozambique ($506.9 million), Senegal ($540 million), and Tanzania ($698 million).

The Bush administration, working with Congress, also consolidated the comprehensive trade and investment policy for Africa introduced by its predecessor in the AGOA legislation, which, for example, was credited with having increased sevenfold Africa's garment exports to America during its first decade. Furthermore, the Overseas Private Investment Corporation (OPIC), an independent US government agency, provided debt financing through its "Africa Capital Markets Fund" in an effort to mobilize $800 million in new private sector investment on the continent.

At the beginning of 2007, the administration announced the creation of a geographical command for its military organization, United States Africa Command (AFRICOM), replacing the antiquated structural framework inherited from times when the continent was barely factored into America's strategic planning, and thus military responsibility for Africa was parceled out between the European, Central, and Pacific Commands. The creation of AFRICOM was not without controversy, eliciting, in fact, a storm of protests and criticism from policymakers and commentators, not only in Africa, but also within the United States, concerned about the potential militarization of US relations with African countries. With a mission to conduct, "in concert with other US government agencies and international partners . . . sustained security engagement through military-to-military programs, military-sponsored activities, and other military operations as directed to promote a stable and secure African environment in support of US foreign policy," the new command became fully operational in October 2008. Since that time, AFRICOM has carried out training, exercises, or other collaborative programming with almost all of the continent's militaries.

The Bush administration also played a leading role in helping bring about the 2005 Comprehensive Peace Agreement (CPA) between the government of Sudan and the Sudan People's Liberation Army (SPLA), ending more than two decades of civil war that had left more than two million people dead. The accord, brokered in large part by the US presidential special envoy, former senator John Danforth, paved the way for the largely peaceful referendum on self-determination and secession of South Sudan in 2011. Tragically, just as the CPA was being negotiated, another rebellion broke out in Sudan's western Darfur region. The Sudanese regime's response led to accusations of genocide—President Omar al-Bashir was subsequently indicted by the International Criminal Court on charges of genocide as well as other war crimes—and successive US special envoys were less successful in negotiating a resolution of the crisis, although a hybrid United Nations-African Union peacekeeping force was eventually permitted to deploy to the conflicted area.

The involvement of the United States in both Sudanese crises underscored the importance of American domestic politics as a driving force in the country's relations with Africa. While the United States maintains an unmatched diplomatic network across the African continent—there are US embassies in fifty-one of Africa's fifty-four countries (relations with the Comoros, São Tomé and Príncipe, and Seychelles are handled by the embassies in Madagascar, Gabon, and Mauritius, respectively, while there has been no diplomatic presence in Somalia since the collapse of the state in 1991) as well as one accredited to African Union headquarters in Addis Ababa—US policy toward Africa in general is more likely to be influenced by various domestic groups, including those representing African Americans, evangelical Christians, and major business interests, especially the oil and other extractive industries. Within Washington, the policy process on Africa has tended to be less marked by partisan divides than it has for other issues. A not insignificant influence on policy development is still exercised by regional specialists, especially those associated with major nonpartisan foreign affairs think tanks like the Council on Foreign Relations, the Center for Strategic and International Studies, the Woodrow Wilson Center, and the Atlantic Council, all of which have Africa programs.

The inauguration of Barack Obama, the son of a Kenyan man, as the forty-fourth president of the United States of America in January 2009 raised expectations across the continent of even greater American engagement. The Obama administration's *National Security Strategy of the United States of America*, released in May 2010 after an extensive review process, shifted the emphasis of Washington's policies away from the more traditional security concerns that preoccupied the Bush administration. The focus was on broader development goals, with "priorities on strategic interventions that can promote job creation and economic growth; combat corruption while strengthening good governance and accountability; responsibly improve the capacity of African security and rule of law sectors; and work through diplomatic dialogue to mitigate local and regional tensions before they become crises." Whether or not this ambitious agenda can be achieved in a domestic political climate increasingly dominated by economic uncertainty and fiscal austerity remains to be seen, but, in any event, it seems unlikely that the now intensified relations between the United States and Africa will be diminished in the near future.

[*See also* AIDS; Clinton, Bill; Cold War; Darfur; Egypt; Somalia; *and* Yemen.]

BIBLIOGRAPHY

Buss, Terry, et al., eds. *African Security and the Africa Command: Viewpoints on the U.S. Role in Africa.* (Sterling, Va., 2011).

Cohen, Herman J. *Intervening in Africa: Superpower Peacemaking in a Troubled Continent.* (New York, 2000).

Cohen, Herman J. "A Mixed Record: 50 Years of U.S.-Africa Relations." *Foreign Service Journal* 85, no. 5 (May 2008): 17–24.

Copson, Raymond W. *The United States in Africa: Bush Policy and Beyond.* (London and New York, 2007).

Crocker, Chester A. *High Noon in Southern Africa: Making Peace in a Rough Neighborhood.* (New York, 1992).

Lyman, Princeton N., and Patricia Lee Dorff, eds. *Beyond Humanitarianism: What You Need to Know about Africa and Why It Matters.* (New York, 2007).

Mangala, Jack, ed. *Africa in the New World Era: From Humanitarianism to a Strategic View.* (New York, 2010).

Pham, J. Peter. "AFRICOM from Bush to Obama." *South African Journal of International Affairs* 18, no. 1 (April 2011): 107–124.

Rothchild, Donald S., and Edmond J. Keller, eds. *Africa-U.S. Relations: Strategic Encounters.* (Boulder, Colo., 2006).

Schraeder, Peter J. *United States Foreign Policy toward Africa: Incrementalism, Crisis, and Change.* (New York, 1994).

J. Peter Pham

AIDS

The acquired immunodeficiency syndrome (AIDS) is a relatively new disease caused by infection with the human immunodeficiency virus (HIV), which results in immune system depletion. First recognized in 1981 among white gay men in the United States, and then in Africans hospitalized in Europe, AIDS continues to spread across the globe.

HIV is transmitted from an infected person through the exchange of blood and sexual fluids, that is, through unprotected sex or through the sharing of needles and syringes used for drug injections. Pregnant and breast-feeding women, too, can transmit the virus to their fetuses or infants unless they are treated. When AIDS was first encountered it constituted a death sentence; there is still no cure and no preventive vaccine. Since 1996, however, treatment with highly active antiretroviral therapy (HAART) can reduce the level of HIV in the blood and reconstitute the immune systems of infected people.

The total number of people currently living with HIV/AIDS in the United States in 2011 was estimated at 1.1 million. By 2007, more than 576,000 had died. An estimated 56,300 people were newly infected annually from 2006. At least 200,000 people in the United States (about one-fifth of those infected) are unaware of their infection and the risk they pose to others, while an estimated 20 percent of those in need of treatment have no health insurance and no access to care through public programs due to

funding shortages. This shortfall is worrisome, since treatment of infected people is also crucial for HIV prevention. Research shows that the earlier infection is detected and treatment with antiretroviral drugs (ARVs) begun, the more likely that treatment will allow infected people to live healthily for many years without hospitalization, and the less likely they are to transmit the virus to others. Early treatment of HIV-positive pregnant women before delivery of their children virtually eliminates transmission of the virus to their infants and increases the chances of giving birth to a full-term baby with normal birth weight.

"Treat to prevent" is a cost-beneficial strategy. It not only eliminates much pain and suffering; mathematical modeling shows that the expenditures are eventually recouped by costs avoided later on. Thus, frequent health checkups and HIV testing are essential tools for prevention. Although access to care has expanded, introduction of life-extending treatment has exacerbated inequalities in HIV mortality. AIDS still results in some eighteen thousand deaths in the United States each year, especially among the poor, and proportionally, more blacks die each year than whites.

Social Epidemiology. AIDS is caused by more than a virus; it is socially produced. AIDS is not an equal-opportunity disease. "Structural violence," the powerlessness and lack of resources that result from intersecting social forces, contributes to increased levels of disease among people made vulnerable by situations they cannot change. Social epidemiology identifies the institutionalized structural factors such as poverty, racism, gender inequality and stigma that result in some people being more at risk of infection than others irrespective of personal traits. Overall, African American men, women, and children make up just 13 percent of the US population but accounted for 46 percent of new infections in 2006 and 45 percent of people living with HIV/AIDS. Corresponding rates among Latinos were 17 percent of infections and 15 percent of the population.

The majority of HIV infections, AIDS cases, and cumulative deaths from AIDS in the United States were concentrated in men (77 percent in 2007), most of whom reported having sex with men (MSM). Although others are increasingly affected, MSM still accounted for 61 percent of new infections in 2009; MSM black men were twice as likely to be infected as white men. The majority of newly infected black and Latino men were young (thirteen to twenty-nine years); white men tended to be older (thirty to thirty-nine years). The Centers for Disease Control (CDC) recognized that special efforts were needed to reach young black MSM with the knowledge and skills to prevent HIV infection. As of 2008, however, 80 percent of MSM in fifteen cities had not been reached by prevention programs.

Intravenous drug use (IDU) among people who share needles is the second-highest cause of HIV transmission among men, and among white women. Risk can be greatly reduced by programs that provide clean needles and syringes in exchange for used ones.

Early in the epidemic, AIDS in women and children was invisible, with those populations accounting for just 7 percent of infections in 1985. Females, who are more easily infected during unprotected sex than males, are increasingly affected by HIV/AIDS. Today women make up more than one-quarter (27 percent) of the total of newly infected cases, and 23 percent of those living with AIDS. With a prevalence rate of 1.49 percent, African American females made up 66 percent of the total, a rate fifteen times higher than white women.

Four-fifths of infected black women reported unprotected sex (without benefit of condom protection) with a high-risk male partner (a man who had sex with men or one who used intravenous drugs). Women were not asked specifically about partners' incarceration histories, but men who have had sex with a man in jail, whether via rape or consensual sex, often do not tell their partners. White women are more likely to have been infected through sharing needles and syringes with an infected person. In sum, among African Americans and Hispanics especially, women were at considerable risk, as were male youth, twice as many of whom became infected between nineteen and twenty-nine years of age as whites.

Women with HIV are generally poorer than men; in 1998 nearly two-thirds (64 percent) had annual incomes below $10,000, and most had small children, complicating their ability to access medical care. Despite Medicaid coverage, poor women often lack transportation, are likely to postpone care, and become too sick to go to the doctor. AIDS is the third-leading cause of death among female African Americans aged twenty-five to forty-four years.

Why Are Black MSM More Infected? To explain the "racial" (the term is placed in quotation marks because it designates a social, rather than a biological, category) disparity in rates of HIV infection observed for more than a decade, H. Fisher Raymond and Will McFarland (2009) queried gay men in San Francisco—where African American MSM were three times as likely to partner with other black men than would be expected by chance alone—about their partner preferences. Most white MSM reported that they preferred non-black partners, and that blacks were unwelcome in venues where they congregated. This leaves black men to select partners from a relatively small pool of MSM. In other words, white racism propels African American men to be more densely interconnected, with the potential for the more rapid spread of HIV even with similar numbers of partners and episodes of unprotected sex as white men. The authors conclude that "racial" disparity in HIV infection is unlikely to diminish as long as this situation continues.

This is one plausible explanation—there are additional elements to consider. Less frequently mentioned is the fact that older white men may pay poor black and Latino youth for sex; in these instances, condoms are unlikely to be used. The power differential puts the younger black and Hispanic men at risk. Additional cultural factors intervene. Sex between men is heavily stigmatized in black and Hispanic communities and some MSM do not identify themselves as gay or homosexual, particularly if they are the insertive or "top" partner in a gay relationship. They may also have relationships with women without condoms, and without telling them of their sexual relations with other men. Nearly half of all African Americans in a nationwide survey believed AIDS to be a man-made disease, created by the government as a form of genocide—a belief rooted in decades of racism in health care and in society in general. This medical mistrust is associated with lower condom use, lower testing, and lower treatment among black men than among whites.

Why Are Heterosexual African Americans More Infected? The rate of new infections among African Americans, not only MSM, but also among heterosexuals, is disproportionately higher than among whites. The first nationwide survey of HIV in heterosexual people, conducted in 2006 to 2007 by Paul H. Denning, Elizabeth A. DiNenno, and Ryan E. Wiegard (2011), provides an explanation. Researchers interviewed and tested nearly fifteen thousand people in twenty-five urban areas with high HIV prevalence across the United States. They found no statistically significant difference in prevalence either between whites and blacks, or between men and women.

What, then, explains the overall disparities in national rates that show blacks and Latinos less likely to know their HIV status, more likely to be diagnosed and treated late, and likely to die sooner than whites? The HIV-infected people in the surveyed areas were poorer; they were more likely to be unemployed, homeless, and poorly educated than those who were uninfected. In these neighborhoods of high background HIV infection, more people in these individuals' social networks are likely to be infected than among people living in areas where infection is dispersed. Of the things public health professionals generally consider to be "heterosexual risk factors" (such as crack cocaine use, exchange of sex for drugs or money, and other sexually transmitted infections, or STIs) only the STIs remained when structural factors, determined by poverty and racism, were measured. Given the generally low levels of health care available to the poor, many STIs, which greatly increase the risk of acquiring HIV infection during sex, quite likely went undetected and untreated, as did their HIV, which they then passed to partners.

Poor African Americans and Latinos suffer throughout their lives from precarious conditions of existence. They tend to live in segregated neighborhoods that are home to what Roderick Wallace calls "a synergism of plagues," with widespread and prolonged unemployment and low-wage jobs, dilapidated housing, poor schools and few recreational facilities for youth, high density of drug activity and gang violence, untreated mental illness, and sexual abuse of children and women. The number of homeless people, another risk factor for HIV, has grown with the present economic crisis. Not only has income inequality increased to the point where 1 percent of Americans hold one-third of all wealth, but the gap between whites and minorities has grown. These underlying elements of "structural violence" create disparities in virtually every measurable aspect of health and disease; nearly all have worsened in the decades leading up to the economic crisis that began in the late 2000s.

Incarceration. Incarceration, another element of the structural violence that causes AIDS to be more prevalent among African Americans and Latinos than among whites, was not studied in the CDC survey. HIV spreads through prison populations via drug use, sex (including rape), and tattooing; since clean needles are unavailable and condoms are scarce, all are risk factors for infection. Provision of condoms and clean needles would prevent the spread of HIV in prisons and in the communities to which inmates return.

Despite an overall decrease in crime rates in many cities across the nation, conservative legislators enacted stronger anticrime policies starting in the 1970s, their harshness directed principally against communities of color, albeit without reducing the availability of drugs. As a result of the "war on drugs," the United States incarcerates more people than any other nation. With just 5 percent of the world's population, it houses 25 percent of all criminals, more than 2.1 million people. Another 4 million, having completed their jail time, are on parole. More than 60 percent of people in prisons are minorities.

The "war on drugs" has targeted different users differently. Nationwide, although African Americans are just 14 percent of drug users, they are 37 percent of those arrested on charges of drug use or possession of small amounts of illegal substances. They are 56 percent of those sentenced to incarceration for drug offenses, especially for crack cocaine, even though whites are the greatest users. Middle-class whites are rarely prosecuted for possession of either expensive powder or cheaper crack cocaine, or even heroin; instead, they often escape with a warning or probation. Blacks and Hispanics, on the other hand, are more likely to use crack and to be arrested and sentenced to jail. Crack users received disproportionately higher sentences for the same amount of cocaine as did whites who received jail time for powder, although recently that disparity has been reduced.

In many cities, one-third of black men have prison records; in some cities, the lifetime rate is 50 percent. African Americans comprise 47 percent of prison inmates, nearly four times their share of the population. Since drug conviction is a federal crime, following release these men return to their communities as felons, who in many states are stripped of the right to vote. Felons, but not people convicted of violent crimes such as murder, rape, or robbery, or financial scams, are permanently barred from federal jobs and housing, from food stamps, loans for education, mortgages, and other benefits of citizenship.

Incarceration of users, rather than of "drug lords" or "kingpins," is the least cost-effective way to reduce drug use. The cost is staggering, an estimated $50 billion each year, with each prisoner absorbing $30,000 to $50,000 annually. A less costly package of services, including drug treatment, education, job training, and employment, is more likely to produce social benefits. Yet only 8 percent of drug users are in treatment and relatively few programs offer methadone, a nonaddictive substitute, to intravenous drug users.

Heterosexual Multiple Partners. The high rates of incarceration in African American communities reduce the availability of men in the age range that otherwise would support children and their mothers. This shortage leads many women to accept the multiple partnerships of their own male partners and makes them afraid to broach the issue of condom protection. In the thirtieth year of the HIV/AIDS epidemic many women still could not ask—let alone demand—that a male partner use condoms. The more expensive female condom has yet to catch on, and male partner agreement is needed in any event.

Incarceration combines with discrimination in employment to result in many children with absent fathers living in poverty. The precarious circumstances of children raised by a mother who is poorly educated, unemployed, or works at a poorly paid job create vulnerability to early sexual exploitation, STIs, early pregnancy, and HIV, perpetuating the epidemic in the next generation.

Prevention. Although there is no cure for HIV/AIDS and no vaccine, several biological measures, in addition to early treatment of those infected, contribute to lower risk of infection, and reduce the harm that infected people will do to others. Male circumcision can reduce men's risk of acquiring HIV through sexual intercourse by about 60 percent. Treatment and prevention of other STIs also reduces risk of sexual HIV infection. A vaginal microbicide gel that women can apply has been found protective but has yet to be approved for sale in the United States. Along with testing for HIV, these measure should become routine in medical practice, available free of charge to all who need them. As noted, however, many poor people do not have access to routine health care.

Injection drug users can be infected with HIV and hepatitis through sharing needles and syringes with infected people; thus free exchange of used needles and syringes for sterile ones prevents transmission. This "harm reduction" measure, demonstrated from 1996, has not been widely available. Moralist ideology triumphed over science to deny federal funds to needle-exchange programs for many years, resulting in needless loss of life.

In addition to biological measures to control the spread of HIV and social support for the affected, change in social and economic structures is required. Although the need is recognized by public health authorities, the political climate in the United States is unlikely to reduce ongoing structural violence.

Education has been called a "social vaccine." Were they widely available, creative education campaigns in mass media, schools, and communities would help to reduce risk of HIV/AIDS. While certainly not a panacea, information about how HIV infection happens and how people can take action to prevent it is nonetheless critical. To avoid message fatigue innovative communications must continually be crafted and new small-group activities initiated.

The most important nonbiological prevention of sexual transmission is the routine use of condoms. Both male and female condoms require that partners communicate with one another, not always an easy matter, especially for women who may fear violent reactions from partners, or abandonment. Communication skills can be taught and practiced in sex education classes. Comprehensive sex education, which teaches young people to delay having sex, and to protect themselves when they do, needs to begin in grades seven and eight. Since many poor children drop out in the high school years, delay leaves youth, both male and female, dangerously exposed, especially in sexual relations with older men.

Yet from the late 1990s, and especially during the administration of President George W. Bush, conservative Christian ideologues propelled federal, state, and local governments to fund ineffective abstinence-until-marriage education in school instead of comprehensive sex education, denying lifesaving knowledge to students. By 2002, hitherto declining national rates of sexually transmitted infections (STIs) and unwanted pregnancy among adolescents had reversed. HIV rates rose, especially in the southern states, where access to prevention among black adolescents was limited. In 2004, the federal General Accounting Office (GAO) evaluated the efficacy of abstinence ("just say no") programs. It not only found minimal short-term results, but noted that over the long term, most teens engaged in sexual relations despite virginity pledges taken by some. The study concluded that abstinence-only education diverted essential funds from more effective prevention. Science notwithstanding, in 2006 federal funding guidelines in the United States pushed abstinence-only prevention efforts up from the adolescent years to try to convince unmarried young adults ages twenty to twenty-nine to take a virginity pledge. In 2003, the Bush administration exported its moralist policies to Africa, requiring one-third of prevention funds to be spent on abstinence-only programs and forbidding grant recipients from providing supportive services to sex workers at very high risk for HIV/AIDS.

Policy since 2008. The economic recession of 2008–2009 saw funding cuts to many HIV/AIDS prevention and treatment services; the decline continued in 2010, and in 2011 the hoped-for recovery failed to materialize. Instead, federal and state budget cuts further reduced public sector employment at all levels and reduced provision of social services, the "safety nets" that keep the poor—more than forty-three million Americans in 2009—from utter destitution. Millions have lost their homes to predatory lenders; fewer people have insurance for health care and medications; fewer people can obtain food stamps and other public assistance. African Americans are the worst affected by the crisis, with one-fifth without any form of health insurance, twice as many unemployed, and one-quarter living in poverty, compared with 8.6 percent of non-Hispanic whites. The Health Care and Reconciliation Act should go a long way to closing the gap in health coverage. Republican lawmakers, who have dubbed the law "Obamacare," have vowed to repeal it, and several Republican governors have mounted court challenges.

In 2010 President Barack Obama's administration released the first National HIV/AIDS Strategy for fighting the epidemic. In theory, with resources allocated to "highest-risk populations," preventing new infections among African Americans should become a priority. No new funds were earmarked for its implementation, however. Instead, Congress has made deep cuts in federal funds for AIDS programs, forcing states to slash or eliminate services. Trained AIDS prevention workers have been laid off and many innovative community efforts that drove new infection rates down are ending. For example, Massachusetts, where new HIV infections fell over the past decade by more than 50 percent (from about one thousand new cases of HIV infection per year to five hundred), will lose $4.3 million, half its federal funding and one-quarter of the state budget for AIDS. Staged over the next five years, cutbacks will end free condom distribution in schools, colleges, and health centers, end needle-exchange programs and mobile vans in high risk areas, and eliminate radio, billboard, and other media ads that promote HIV testing and prevention, as well as the state's telephone information hotline. In their place, the CDC will require the state to redirect support to clinic-based HIV testing and treatment, while community agencies that assist patients in obtaining stable housing; access to medical care, food, and transportation; and ensure that they follow treatment recommendations will lose support, as will efforts to reduce stigma and discrimination that keep many from testing and treatment. Minorities will be the most severely affected. Given the social environment, treatment is not a "magic bullet."

Response to AIDS has been political from the outset of the epidemic and funding has never reached needed levels. It took many years for the role of structural violence in spreading HIV to be acknowledged in the United States and in the international arena. At the beginning of the second decade of the twenty-first century an economic crisis and cuts in social spending once again exacerbated the structural violence that creates vulnerabilities to disease and barriers to prevention, especially among the poor and disadvantaged. AIDS in black America resembles AIDS in Africa.

[*See also* African Americans, Contemporary Conditions; Drugs and Politics; Gay Rights; Health Care; Poverty, Scale and Nature of; Race, Gender, and Incarceration; *and* Race and Racism.]

BIBLIOGRAPHY

Alexander, Michelle. *The New Jim Crow: Mass Incarceration in the Age of Color Blindness.* (New York, 2011).
Bartels, Larry. *Unequal Democracy: The Political Economy of the Gilded Age.* (Princeton, N.J., 2008).
Bogart, Laura M., Frank H. Galvan, Glenn J. Wagner, et al. "Longitudinal Association of HIV Conspiracy Beliefs with Sexual Risk among Black Males Living with HIV." *AIDS and Behavior* 16, no. 6 (2010): 1180–1186.
Denning, Paul H., Elizabeth A. DiNenno, and Ryan E. Wiegard. "Characteristics Associated with HIV Infection among Heterosexuals in Urban Areas with High HIV/AIDS Prevalence—24 Cities." *CDC Morbidity and Mortality Weekly Report* 60, no. 31 (12 August 2011): 1045–1049.

Des Jarlais, Don C., Michael Marmor, Denise Paone, et al. "HIV Incidence among Injecting Drug Users in New York City Syringe-Exchange Programs." *Lancet* 348 (12 October 1996): 987–989.
Farmer, Paul. *Infections and Inequalities: The Modern Plagues.* (Berkeley, Calif., 1999).
Farmer, Paul, Margaret Connors, and Janie Simmons, eds. *Women, Poverty, and AIDS: Sex, Drugs, and Structural Violence.* 2d ed. (Monroe, Maine, 2011).
Gaiter, Juarlyn L., Roberto H. Potter, and Ann O'Leary. "Disproportionate Rates of Incarceration Contribute to Health Disparities." *American Journal of Public Health* 96, no. 7 (2006): 1148–1149.
Golembeski, Cynthia, and Robert Fullilove. "Criminal (In)justice in the City and Its Associated Health Consequences." *American Journal of Public Health* 95, no. 10 (2005): 1701–1706.
Lane, Sandra Dianne. *Why Are Our Babies Dying? Pregnancy, Birth, and Death in America.* (Boulder, Colo., 2008).
Lazar, Kay. "Mass. Services for HIV Face Cuts." *Boston Globe*, August 15, 2011.
Raymond, H. Fisher, and Will McFarland. "Racial Mixing and HIV Risk among Men Who Have Sex with Men." *AIDS and Behavior* 13, no. 4 (2009): 630–634.
Simmons, Janie. "The Interplay between Interpersonal Dynamics, Treatment Barriers, and Larger Social Forces: An Exploratory Study of Drug-Using Couples in Hartford, CT." *Substance Abuse, Treatment, Prevention, and Policy* 1 (2006): 12.
Susser, Ida B. "Sexual Negotiation in Relation to Political Mobilization: The Prevention of HIV in Comparative Context." *AIDS and Behavior* 5, no. 2 (2001): 163–172.
Swartz, Rebecca M., Denise M. Bruno, Michael A. Augenbaum, et al. "Perceived Financial Need and Sexual Risk Behavior among Urban Minority Women Following Sexually Transmitted Infection Diagnosis." *Sexually Transmitted Diseases* 38, no. 3 (2011): 230–234.
Tanne, Janice Hopkins. "Abstinence Only Programmes Do Not Change Sexual Behaviour, Texas Study Shows." *British Medical Journal* 330, no. 7487 (2005): 326.
Wakefield, Sara, and Christopher Wildeman. "Mass Imprisonment and Racial Disparities in Childhood Behavioral Problems." *Criminology and Public Policy* 10, no. 3 (2011): 791–817.
Wallace, Roderick. "A Synergism of Plagues: 'Planned Shrinkage,' Contagious Housing Destruction, and AIDS in the Bronx." *Environmental Research* 47, no. 1 (1988): 1–33.
Wilson, Phill, Kai Wright, and Michael T. Isbell. *Left Behind: Black America: A Neglected Priority in the*

Global AIDS Epidemic. (Los Angeles, 2008), http://www.blackaids.org/docs/7_08_left_behind.pdf

Wise, Tim. *Colorblind: The Rise of Post-Racial Politics and the Retreat from Racial Equality.* (Oakland, Calif., 2010).

Brooke Grundfest Schoepf, Janie Simmons, and
Diane B. Kagoyire

AID TO FAMILIES WITH DEPENDENT CHILDREN

Initially known as Aid to Dependent Children, the Aid to Families with Dependent Children (AFDC) program was established as part of the Social Security Act of 1935. Yet, even though created as part of the same legislation as the Social Security program, AFDC never enjoyed the same status or public support as that program. AFDC was commonly referred to as "welfare" and predominantly provided benefits to poor households headed by single mothers. AFDC was a social assistance rather than social insurance program, meaning that it was a noncontributory, means-tested benefit. There was considerable variation from state to state in how the program's regulations were applied, with local officials having considerable discretion in determining eligibility. Furthermore, the benefits paid out by AFDC varied significantly from state to state. Thus, despite being legislated at the federal level, the funding and regulation of AFDC was split between the federal and state governments.

When AFDC was created, eligibility for the benefit was strictly limited to those mothers deemed worthy of help. In practice, this meant widows and a few "deserted" mothers. Any claimant could find herself subject to rigorous investigation to check on her "worthiness," with these checks being particularly intrusive around issues of sexual behavior. In the 1960s the Supreme Court effectively expanded eligibility to the program by overturning state rules about residency requirements and midnight raids that found a "man in the house." Partially as a consequence of these changes the number of families receiving AFDC rose from 803,000 in 1960 to 1.9 million

in 1970. As the number of AFDC recipients continued to grow through the 1970s and 1980s, with increasing numbers of never-married mothers on the rolls, the program became increasingly controversial, and by the mid-1990s opinion polls found a high level of popular hostility to the benefit (Weaver, Shapiro, and Jacobs, 1995).

Finally, in 1996, as part of the Personal Responsibility and Work Opportunity Reconciliation Act (PRWORA), AFDC was abolished and a new benefit, Temporary Assistance for Needy Families (TANF), was introduced. When AFDC was repealed it was the first time that a major welfare entitlement had been ended. Different explanations have been advanced to explain why AFDC was so unpopular. Conservatives argued that AFDC violated widely held American values about the importance of the work ethic. In particular, critics of the program such as Charles Murray (1984) and Robert Rector (1992) maintained that what had started out as an antipoverty program had become a program that actually trapped people in poverty by promoting a culture of dependency. That is, however well-intentioned, conservatives argued that AFDC enabled people to make lifestyle choices that were self-defeating in the long run. Because of the income support provided by the government, women could choose to have children outside a stable family environment and men could abandon their responsibilities and let the government take financial care of their children. Thus, conservatives insisted, AFDC promoted reckless and irresponsible behavior.

To some liberal commentators this conservative critique of welfare harked back to the British Poor Laws of the 1830s, with the victims of economic inequalities turned into villains, and the perpetrators of their own problems (Somers and Block, 2005; Handler and Hasenfeld, 2007). In addition, liberal analysts worried that the unpopularity of AFDC was exaggerated by the racial fault line so consistently present in American public life (Gilens, 1999). Both liberals and conservatives had their views reinforced when President Ronald Reagan invoked the image of the "welfare queen." During his campaign for the Republican presidential nomination in 1976 Reagan expressed his concern that many Americans received benefits that they simply did not deserve. To illustrate his point, he talked of the "welfare queen" who was a vacationing and Cadillac-driving woman who lived heartily on AFDC benefits and food stamps. To his supporters Reagan was describing a reality whereby too many lived comfortably off the hard work, and taxes, of others. To his critics Reagan was using a shocking, and inaccurate, stereotype for political gain that exploited racial division, since by implication the "welfare queen" was an African American woman.

In the mid-1970s the conservative attack on welfare was growing but was not the dominant discourse. By the 1980s and into the 1990s these conservative ideas were gaining increasing political traction and had become the mainstream within the Republican Party. As a result bolder policy prescriptions, which advocated significant cuts to welfare benefits and the introduction of programs aimed at imposing welfare-to-work requirements on welfare recipients, came increasingly to the fore (Mead, 1992). In contrast, those few Democrats who stridently defended the program and welfare recipients themselves had little capacity for political organization.

Prior to PRWORA there had been efforts to end AFDC and replace it with other benefits. Perhaps most notably, President Richard Nixon had put forward an ambitious proposal called the Family Assistance Plan. That plan passed in the House of Representatives but died a legislative death in the Senate Finance Committee after raising the ire of an odd combination of conservatives and liberals (Waddan, 1998). President Jimmy Carter put forward proposals but did not make a serious effort to pursue legislation, while in the early days of the Reagan administration cuts were made to AFDC eligibility. In 1988 the Family Support Act made more substantive changes, but these were given little time to take effect before the welfare debate took a dramatic turn in the early 1990s. In his run for the presidency, the Democratic governor of Arkansas Bill Clinton promised to "end welfare as we know it." This phrase became central in establishing credibility for Clinton's "New Democrat" identity, as it dissociated him from the party's reputation for being too "soft" on welfare recipients. Clinton did put forward a reform plan in the summer of 1994 but this made no legislative progress. After the Republicans gained control of Congress in the midterm elections the momentum for reform increased, and the plans became more dramatic. Clinton signed PRWORA, which abolished AFDC, in August 1996. At that time over 4.4 million families received AFDC.

[*See also* Personal Responsibility and Work Opportunity Reconciliation Act; *and* Temporary Assistance for Needy Families.]

BIBLIOGRAPHY

Gilens, Martin. *Why Americans Hate Welfare: Race, Media, and the Politics of Antipoverty Policy.* (Chicago, 1999).

Handler, Joel F., and Yeheskel Hasenfeld. *Blame Welfare: Ignore Poverty and Inequality.* (New York, 2007).

Mead, Lawrence. *The New Politics of Poverty: The Nonworking Poor in America.* (New York, 1992).

Murray, Charles. *Losing Ground: American Social Policy, 1950–1980.* (New York, 1984).

Somers, Margaret, and Fred Block. "From Poverty to Perversity: Ideas, Markets, and Institutions over 200 Years of Welfare Debate." *American Sociological Review* 70, no. 2 (2005): 260–287.

Rector, Robert. "Requiem for the War on Poverty: Rethinking Welfare after the Los Angeles Riots." *Policy Review* 61 (Summer 1992): 40–46.

Waddan, Alex. "A Liberal in Wolf's Clothing: Nixon's Family Assistance Plan in the Light of 1990s Welfare Reform." *Journal of American Studies* 32, no. 2 (1998): 203–218

Weaver, Kent R., Robert Y. Shapiro, and Lawrence R. Jacobs. "The Polls–Trends: Welfare." *Public Opinion Quarterly* 59 (1995): 606–627.

Alex Waddan

AL-QAEDA

Al-Qaeda, most commonly translated into English as "The Base," is the name of a terrorist network founded by Osama Bin Laden—"terrorist" in the sense that it uses actual violence against noncombatants for political purposes, and with a view to producing psychological effects which are disproportionate to the harm actually done. Al-Qaeda was responsible for the September 11, 2001, attacks on the United States, and for many other attacks worldwide on a smaller but nonetheless significant scale.

Al-Qaeda was established in the late 1980s as the Soviet presence in Afghanistan was coming to an end. It was strongly premised on the belief that the key lesson of the Soviet-Afghan war was that Islamic faith was a force-multiplier that had proved capable of defeating even a superpower. With the rapid decline of the Soviet Union, the attention of al-Qaeda shifted elsewhere, and the deployment of US troops on Saudi territory following Iraq's invasion of Kuwait in August 1990 provided it with a new central focus, namely, anti-Americanism. This in turn set the scene for a range of attacks on US interests: on the US embassies in Kenya and Tanzania in August 1998; on the USS Cole in Aden Harbor in 2000; and finally and most dramatically, the September 11, 2001, attacks on targets in New York and Washington, D.C., which led to the ousting of the Taliban regime in Afghanistan that had been hosting Bin Laden and al-Qaeda.

These last attacks led to sudden and immediate attention being paid to the nature and organization of al-Qaeda. Its commitment to a radical, politicized form of Islamic activism had been made clear in a February 1998 *fatwa* (ruling) issued by Bin Laden and other radicals under the title of a "World Islamic Front against Jews and Crusaders," which depicted the killing of Americans as an individual duty of each and every Muslim (*fard'ayn*). Its organizational character was much less clear. Some analyses saw it as predominantly hierarchical, with Bin Laden at the apex. Others accepted Bin Laden's centrality, but saw al-Qaeda as a network rather than a hierarchy, based on cells of activists undertaking missions shaped by the distinct environments in which they worked. Carrying this further, other writers viewed al-Qaeda as a franchise, with little to unite the different components beyond a shared name and broadly shared hatreds.

The franchise model received some support from the activities of the group that came to be known as "al-Qaeda in Iraq," following the US invasion of Iraq in March 2003. The most notable figure in this group

was the Jordanian Abu Musab al-Zarqawi, whom Bin Laden recognized in December 2004 as leader of al-Qaeda in Iraq. Zarqawi was killed in a targeted strike by US jets on 7 June 2006, and was succeeded as leader by Abu Ayyub al-Masri. From that point the fortunes of the group began to wane. While it was responsible for some of the most spectacular attacks on US forces and Iraqi targets in the entire course of the conflict, the harm suffered by ordinary Iraqi civilians ultimately proved to be its downfall. Disgust at its tactics mounted, and although it bounced back with some fresh attacks in 2009, Abu Ayyub al-Masri was finally killed on 18 April 2010. Iraq no longer offers the enabling environment that it appeared to when US troops were present in large numbers

A further example of the franchise model was the formation in January 2009 of "al-Qaeda in the Arabian Peninsula," drawn from two earlier groups, al-Qaeda in Yemen and al-Qaeda in Saudi Arabia. It had been stimulated by the escape from prison in the Yemeni capital Sanaa on 3 February 2006 of twenty-three al-Qaeda figures who had been captured in earlier counterterrorism operations—an escape in which elements of the Yemeni state were most likely complicit. The group has undertaken numerous terrorist attacks in Yemen, including an assault on the US Embassy on 17 September 2008 that killed seventeen people; but it attracted the most publicity when on Christmas Day 2009, a Nigerian student, Umar Farouq Abdulmutallab, sought unsuccessfully to bring down Northwest Airlines Flight 253 from Amsterdam to Detroit by detonating explosives concealed in his underwear. Nonetheless, in the Yemeni uprising of 2011, al-Qaeda found itself marginalized as a force by both tribal actors, and civil-society protestors in the capital.

This experience, and similar experiences in Tunisia and Egypt, where radical Islamist activists proved peripheral to the revolutions of 2011, raises doubts as to how much popular support al-Qaeda can realistically claim. Here, the use of survey evidence is complicated by questions that conflate some of al-Qaeda's political causes with the instruments and tactics that it has employed to advance them. This is particularly notable in states such as Indonesia, where popular expressions of sympathy for Bin Laden have accompanied popular repudiation of suicide bombings and other terrorist tactics. Nonetheless, since only a small number of adherents are required for a group to be able to undertake destructive terrorist operations—something that al-Qaeda has clearly established—it will likely remain a major focus of international attention.

The future for al-Qaeda in the aftermath of the killing of Osama Bin Laden by US forces in Pakistan on 1 May 2011 is deeply uncertain. While it was announced that he was to be succeeded by Ayman al-Zawahiri, an Egypt-born associate whose connection with radical causes stretched back to the assassination of Anwar Sadat in Cairo in 1981, it was far from obvious that Zawahiri, who had a reputation for tetchiness and rancorous disagreement with other activists, would be able to step into Bin Laden's shoes. This could result either in the fragmentation of al-Qaeda to the point where its cells can be picked off by targeted security operations in different countries, or in the proliferation of the brand name through groups with no organizational links, but with a commitment to the values and tactics of radical Islamism.

[*See also* Afghanistan; Bin Laden, Osama; Middle East–United States Relations; Pakistan–United States Relations; Somalia; Terrorism, Middle East; *and* Yemen.]

BIBLIOGRAPHY

Burke, Jason. *Al-Qaeda: Casting a Shadow of Terror.* (London, 2003).

Gray, John. *Al Qaeda and What It Means to Be Modern* (London, 2003).

National Commission on Terrorist Attacks upon the United States. *The 9/11 Commission Report: Final Report of the National Commission on Terrorist Attacks upon the United States* (New York, 2004).

William Maley

AMERICAN EXCEPTIONALISM

American exceptionalism can be understood in at least three different but related ways. First, exceptionalism can be understood as a quasi-religious belief that the United States is a chosen and superior nation endowed by providence or the creator to be, "a city set upon a hill," (Matthew 5:14) an illustrious example and beacon for the rest of the world. Second, exceptionalism can be understood to be a claim that American society, public policy, and geography have combined to make the United States uniquely a land of economic opportunity and dynamism. Third, exceptionalism can be understood as a more neutral, social scientific claim that the United States is different from other advanced democracies in terms of its public policies, particularly those determining the extent of the roles of government or the state in the economy.

Normative and Celebratory Exceptionalism. The first two forms of exceptionalism share a belief that the United States is both different and superior. The discussion of exceptionalism here focuses more on exceptionalism as a more neutral concept, but it is important to note the first two, partly because they have significance in current politics. The belief that one's own country has a special and superior role in world history is scarcely limited to the United States, but commentators at least since Tocqueville have noted its unusual strength in that country (Tocqueville, 1961). Probably all American politicians pay tribute to the idea at some point in an election campaign. More recently, exceptionalism has been understood and promoted on the right as a justification for eschewing policies such as universal health insurance on the grounds that such policies are "European" and incompatible with American traditions. The United States in this view is a land of economic opportunity, not of mutual aid and compassion. Members of the Tea Party, a right-wing movement that attracted much attention during President Barack Obama's first term, has made much of this argument, arguing that both the Constitution and the exceptional traditions of the United States preclude anything smacking of a welfare state. For some, this is truly a religious belief and frequent use is made of the Puritan John Winthrop's famous sermon in which the "city on a hill" image is used. However, the sermon is rarely read as a whole and it is therefore less often mentioned that Winthrop was not celebrating his colony but issuing warnings of divine retribution if the colonists failed to fulfill God's expectations, which included a considerable measure of mutual care. Nonetheless, the belief voiced explicitly by a substantial minority of the American public, and felt to some degree by many more, that the United States is different and superior served to legitimate a more limited role of government in providing for social welfare than in other democracies.

More secular beliefs in the providential role of the United States are common particularly among groups whose ancestors fled persecution in Europe. Undoubtedly the United States provided a much more tolerant, safer, and freer environment for many than Tsarist or Soviet Russia, and of course, than Nazi Germany. Appropriate gratitude to the United States can result, however, in overly sharp contrasts being drawn in this respect between it and contemporary countries that have become democracies since the Second World War. Similarly, the fact that the United States never had a formalized class system complete with aristocracy, as did Europe, can lead too easily to the belief that the United States is exceptional in the opportunities it provides for social mobility. In fact, the United States is characterized by extreme inequality not only of wealth and incomes but of social class; one's parents' income is a dramatically stronger predictor of one's income in the United States than in countries such as Denmark. In the class of industrialized democracies, the ratio of the highest paid to the lowest paid is unusually large in the United States and the likelihood of upward mobility is unusually low. As in many societies, a few people rise from low income, low status backgrounds to become fabulously wealthy, but by and large Americans' position in the income hierarchy matches that of their parents. Again, however, the belief in exceptional opportunity and mobility may be more important than the facts. The belief that in the United States anyone can go from rags to riches has important cultural and political consequences.

Analytical Exceptionalism: Attitudes. Analytical exceptionalism neither approves nor celebrates patterns of public policy but merely notes that they are different. The obvious questions that arise are, different compared with what, and in which respects?

The answer to the first question is a comparison with other advanced industrialized democracies minus Japan. The sharpest contrasts are often drawn with continental Europe, but in fact contrasts with the United Kingdom, Australia, New Zealand and, as Seymour Martin Lipset emphasizes, Canada, are also at least at first glance acute (Lipset, 1990; 1996.)

One strand of analytical exceptionalism focuses on differences in attitudes between Americans and citizens of other advanced democracies. The United States is said to be exceptional by holding to a classic set of nineteenth-century liberal beliefs; individuals enjoy political rights and economic freedom. Governments govern best by governing least and allowing market forces to operate relatively unrestrained. Government should definitely not redistribute income or wealth and even its role in protecting citizens from foreseeable or likely need in old age or sickness should be very limited. This belief, combined with support for individual rights and liberty, is seen by Hartz and the other "consensus theorists" as an hegemonic, "liberal tradition" dominating American politics (Hartz, 1955).

Hartz believes that the reasons for the dominance of the liberal tradition are to be found in the exceptional character of American history. The United States has not experienced feudalism. It therefore did not have an aristocracy to support a tradition of paternalistic conservatism in which inequality and hierarchy were combined with a concern for the poorest sectors of society, linked organically to elites and leaders as the hands are to head in the human body. The rapid enfranchisement of white males meant that they were enjoying full citizenship rights well before the United States industrialized. Hartz argues that this was crucial in choking off the possibility of socialism in the United States, as for him working-class radicalism was the product of the simultaneous quest for citizenship rights and economic security. Numerous other explanations have been advanced as to why socialism was never more than a fringe movement in the United States. Lipset provides an excellent summary of explanations that have stressed the importance of a range of factors including the comparative prosperity of the American class, and the consequences of ethnic and particularly racial divisions and state-sanctioned repression in precluding the development of a socialist tradition in the United States (Lipset, 1977). Absent such a tradition, support for the growth of government in the United States was also limited. American government remained comparatively small scale because that is how Americans, their political imaginations dominated by a liberal tradition, like it.

The argument that US politics is dominated by a liberal tradition has been subjected to effective criticism. Political scientists have cast considerable doubt on whether Americans in practice are really committed to the political rights and freedoms they support if told they are part of the Constitution; over the decades, Americans have told opinion pollsters that they would deny freedom of speech and assembly to representatives of unpopular viewpoints. Indeed, contrary to the exceptionalist perspective, support for individual political rights such as freedom of speech is lower in the United States than in several other advanced democracies. Writing from a more historical perspective, Smith points out that liberalism has been far from hegemonic in US history as hierarchical, discriminatory beliefs (such as support for slavery and racism) have had considerable influence (Smith, 1993).

It might seem obvious that Americans are exceptional in their hostility to a welfare state. After all, the United States was the only advanced democracy without universal access to health care until President Obama's proposal was enacted in 2010. Republicans have continued to oppose the legislation vociferously, however, and are committed to its repeal. Perhaps surprisingly, opinion polls have shown Americans to be supportive of an extensive array of programs intended to address the problems of those in need. This includes providing access to health care, and aid to the unemployed, the sick, children, and the elderly. These findings remain strong even when respondents are reminded that these programs depend on their taxes. Skocpol and Williamson (2011) argue that even Tea Party supporters approve of programs such as Medicare and Social Security (retirement pensions) that are believed to go to deserving recipients as opposed to undeserving—in the minds of critics if not in reality—minority recipients. Important differences remain in certain crucial areas. Americans are less likely than the citizens of other advanced democracies to support government redistribution of income or wealth. Perhaps mindful of the corruption and patronage that long characterized government projects in the United States, Americans are also less likely to believe that government has the responsibility to provide jobs for the unemployed. In general, however, opinion polls show high levels of support for many government programs including some of the most expensive, such as Medicare and Social Security.

When Hartz wrote in the 1950s, it was plausible if not necessarily correct to assert that a single liberal tradition united Americans. In more recent years, the profound differences among Americans have been more apparent. While the majority of Americans may remain centrists, a significant proportion is not. The differences between American conservatives and left-of-center citizens (confusingly termed "liberals" in everyday terminology) are probably as or more profound than the differences between left and right in most democracies. On a wide range of issues such as attitudes toward gays, climate change, the desirability of universal health insurance, the permissibility of using torture to extract information from foreign detainees or even US involvement in wars such as Iraq, liberals and conservatives are deeply and passionately divided. Indeed, the citizens of a predominantly liberal state such as Massachusetts are closer to citizens of many European democracies in their political beliefs and attitudes than they are to the beliefs and attitudes of people in a state such as Mississippi (Baldwin, 2009).

Analytical Exceptionalism: Public Policy. King (1973) argues that Americans' distinctive beliefs result in distinctive policy. Much of the debate about exceptionalism has focused, however, on how different such American public policy actually is.

At the aggregate level, much depends on the measure used of the size of government. There has been an enormous contrast in the twenty-first century between the size of government in the United States as measured by expenditure, and the size of government as measured by revenues, as a percentage of gross domestic product (GDP) taken in taxes. Judged by the first measure, the United States is only modestly exceptional; judged by the second measure, it is much more so. The difference between the two figures, equivalent to about 10 percent of GDP, is the budget deficit that attracted so much discussion in the United States in 2010 and 2011. Looking at government expenditure as a proportion of GDP, government in the United States is only 8 percent smaller than the Organisation for Economic Co-operation and Development (OECD) average (42 percent in 2009 compared with the Euro area average of 50 percent.) The contrast between the size of government in the United States today and in the early twentieth century is far greater than the contrast between the size of government in the United States and the average in the OECD as a whole.

There are at least two ways—working in opposite directions in their impact on the exceptionalist argument—in which aggregate figures can be misleading. The first, reinforcing the case for exceptionalism, is that the details of policies can be importantly different from one country to another. In terms of welfare state expenditure, for example, Esping-Andersen draws a sharp distinction between the "three worlds of welfare" (Esping-Anderson, 1990). Particularly relevant in this context are his contrasts be-tween the social democratic welfare systems in which there is an entitlement to benefits for all citizens, and the insurance-based models such as the United States, in which eligibility is achieved through a history of contributions. Indeed many Americans believe—and have been encouraged to believe—that it is their own money, their accumulated contributions that they receive back in state retirement pensions (Social Security), when the reality is that the programs depend on intergenerational transfers.

The second way in which aggregate government expenditure figures can be misleading is that they ignore the impact of two policy techniques commonly used in the United States: tax expenditures and regulation. Tax expenditures (commonly referred to as "tax allowances") have been used to promote a variety of goals including reduced dependence on imported fuels, environmental goals, and home ownership. Viewed by economists as fundamentally equivalent to government expenditures, the inclusion of tax allowances would raise the size of government in the United States considerably. Similarly, regulations impose costs on businesses and other actors but generally have minimal impact on government budgets. For example, the consequences of the absence of universal health insurance in the United States have been mitigated by requirements that hospital emergency rooms provide necessary immediate treatment to those who need it, irrespective of ability to pay. While a grotesque misuse of resources (one in which facilities designed to cope with traumatic injury are used by parents without insurance to have their children's minor illnesses treated), the requirement does create a considerable extension of the social provision of health care, albeit at very little cost to the government itself. The combined consequences of the unusually heavy use of tax expenditures and regulations as policy tools in the United States reduces further the contrast between the size and scope of government in the United States and in other advanced democracies. Some of the contrasts between the United States and other advanced democracies are a result of an unusual choice of policy instrument in the United States, rather than the absence of any policy commitment.

The fierce battles over how to shrink the budget deficit of the United States during the presidency of Barack Obama do remind us, however, of the continued significance of two aspects of American exceptionalism. First, not withstanding their attachment to government programs ranging from agricultural subsidies to social security, Americans are even more reluctant than most peoples to pay higher taxes. Budget deficits can be trimmed by cutting expenditure or by raising taxes. Most countries have used a mixture of the two when facing large deficits. In the United States, however, tax increases, except for those with high incomes (defined somewhat broadly by President Obama as those making more than $250,000 a year), were ruled out. The debate focused entirely on cutting expenditures. Opponents of government domestic programs gradually realized that rather than advancing their cause by advocating the elimination of popular programs directly, it was more effective politically to "starve the beast" by arguing against the tax revenues necessary to fund them. This strategy, traceable to the Reagan years in the 1980s, contributed significantly to ballooning budget deficits both then and in the twenty-first century. Although at odds with traditional Republican commitments to balanced budgets, the strategy paid off by coupling popular concern over deficits to advocacy of budget cuts based on antipathy to certain government programs irrespective of budgetary problems.

Second, the American right has remained more profoundly opposed to government programs than its counterpart in almost any other country. Whereas British Conservatives including Margaret Thatcher promised to keep the National Health Service safe while they were in power, American conservatives have regarded it as intolerable, even immoral, for government to insure that all citizens have access to health care. Contrasts with the center right in continental countries such as Germany are even starker. With varying degrees of intensity but never abandoning the cause, American conservatives from the New Deal to the present day have remained unreconciled to the provision of a social safety net by government. Even Keynesian economics has been regarded as an alien intrusion rather than an economic policy that could be judged pragmatically. It would be a mistake to see in this opposition proof that conservatives are more attached to the liberal tradition that Hartz saw as the essence of American exceptionalism. Conservatives have been custodian to only parts of the traditions of nineteenth-century liberals, being less supportive of civil liberties and civil rights while being more willing to use state power to advance certain conceptions of sexual morality than their opponents. An explanation of the determination of the American right to oppose the expansion of the state needs therefore to account for its selective attachment to nineteenth-century liberalism. However, the deep antipathy of the American right to a wider role for the state in terms of

providing a social safety net does distinguish it from its fellow conservative groups and movements overseas. American conservatives, therefore, contribute markedly to the idea of US exceptionalism. It is tempting to see a mirror image of this on the left; American liberals are more committed to civil liberties than the Left is elsewhere. Is it, to take one example, possible to imagine an American liberal being as antipathetic to civil liberties as was the last Labour government (1997–2010) in the UK, with its support for surveillance cameras and the abolition of ancient rights such as not being tried twice for the same offense?

American exceptionalism therefore remains a fascinating but confusing topic. Viewed through the prism of the size and scope of government, it seems an unconvincing doctrine. Viewed through the prism of the willingness of Americans to pay taxes or of the attitudes of the American right toward social safety net programs, the United States does seem exceptional. The future viability of the concept depends in part on the intense struggle in American politics today between conservatives and opponents over the size and scope of government.

[*See also* Political Culture, American.]

BIBLIOGRAPHY

Baldwin, Peter. *The Narcissism of Minor Differences: How America and Europe Are Alike: An Essay In Numbers.* (Oxford and New York, 2009).

Esping-Andersen, Gosta. *The Three Worlds of Welfare Capitalism.* (Princeton, N.J., 1990).

Free, Lloyd A., and Hadley Cantril. *The Political Beliefs of Americans: A Study of Public Opinion.* (New Brunswick, N.J., 1967).

Hartz, Louis. *The Liberal Tradition in America: An Interpretation of American Political Thought Since the Revolution.* (New York, 1955).

King, Anthony. "Ideas, Institutions and the Policies of Governments: A Comparative Analysis." *British Journal of Political Science* 3 (1973): 291–313.

Lipset, Seymour Martin. *American Exceptionalism: A Double-Edged Sword.* (New York, 1996).

Lipset, Seymour Martin. *Continental Divide: The Values and Institutions of The United States and Canada.* (New York, 1990).

Lipset, Seymour Martin. "Why No Socialism in the United States?" In *Sources of Contemporary Radicalism,* edited by Seweryn Bialer and Suzanne Sluzar, pp. 115–130. (Boulder, Colo., 1977).

Skocpol, Theda, and Vanessa Williamson. *The Tea Party and the Remaking of Republican Conservatism.* (New York, 2012).

Smith, Rogers M. "Beyond Tocqueville, Myrdal and Hartz: The Multiple Traditions in America." *American Political Science Review* 87 (1993): 558–563.

Tocqueville, Alexis de. 1961 (or. 1835, 1840) *De La Democrate en Amerique.* Vol. 2. Edited by H. G. Nicholas. (London, 1961). First published in 1835, 1840.

Graham K. Wilson

AMERICAN FEDERATION OF LABOR AND CONGRESS OF INDUSTRIAL ORGANIZATIONS

The American Federation of Labor and Congress of Industrial Organizations (AFL-CIO) is the peak association representing labor in the United States. In the early twenty-first century, nearly most major unions are members; at times in the past, however, some of the very largest unions have not belonged for a variety of reasons ranging from the positions taken by the AFL-CIO on issues such as the Vietnam War, which caused the United Auto Workers to secede, to the suspension of unions for corruption, as in the case of the Teamsters in the 1960s and 1970s. More recently the AFL-CIO was weakened by the defection of a group of important unions led by the Service Employees International Union (SEIU). These unions believed the AFL-CIO was doing too little to halt union decline and after their reform movement failed, formed their own organization, Change to Win. Andy Stern, president of the SEIU and the force behind Change to Win, would be influential with the Obama administration in its early stages.

As the unwieldy title perhaps suggests, the merger of the AFL with the CIO in 1955 papered over important divisions in the ranks of American labor, rather than fully resolving them. The AFL unions were predominantly, though not exclusively, craft unions representing workers organized on the basis of a skill, such as plumbers, bricklayers, and carpenters. The CIO unions were strongly committed to organizing workers on the basis of their employment in an industry such as steel or automobile production.

Added to this difference in recruitment was a major difference in the attitudes of AFL and CIO unions toward politics.

In general, AFL unions came from the tradition associated with the founder of the AFL, Samuel Gompers, who advocated "unionism pure and simple." Gompers believed that the only way to overcome the opposition to unions in the pro-business, free market–oriented United States was to keep unions free from the taint of radicalism or socialism and to avoid antagonizing potential members by affiliating to one of the major political parties in an era in which their support was based on regional or ethnic loyalties, not class. While Gompers was successful in creating the first permanent organization of unions in the United States, his approach was seen as far too narrow by many union organizers after the First World War.

The CIO unions, which emerged in the 1930s, were aware from the first of the importance of politics. CIO unions had been able to organize in large part because of the protective legislation, passed by pro-labor legislators, known as the Wagner Act (or, more correctly, the National Labor Relations Act, passed in 1935), the beneficent attitude of some leading politicians (including President Franklin D. Roosevelt), and the support of the new government agency, the National Labor Relations Board (NLRB), which was set up to enforce new federal labor laws. The Wagner Act overcame strong, even violent, opposition by industrialists such as Henry Ford to unions by requiring that employees be able to vote in a secret ballot conducted by the NLRB on whether or not to have a union, and requiring employers to bargain in good faith with a union if it won such a ballot. Without this protection CIO unions would not have come into existence; not surprisingly, they were more actively involved in politics than AFL unions. Moreover, CIO unions tended to see themselves not merely as labor unions but as part of a social movement—the labor movement—that sought both the amelioration of the condition of workers in the broadest sense and a more just society. In this, many of the unions were closer to the social democratic traditions of Europe than the AFL unions.

The AFL and CIO were prompted to merge in spite of these differences by political setbacks in the 1940s. A resurgent Republican Party passed revisions to the NLRA over the veto of President Harry Truman. These revisions, known as the Taft-Hartley Act (1947), substantially weakened the legal position of unions and may indeed have set in place forces that would undermine the unions in the long term. While the full dangers of Taft-Hartley may not have been apparent at the time, unions were shocked that they were not able to prevent its adoption. Yet the period around the merger of the AFL and CIO was in general the high-water mark of unionism in the United States; some 35 percent of the workforce belonged to labor unions. The AFL-CIO, though not formally affiliated with the Democratic Party, played a crucial role within it, influencing the selection of presidential candidates and providing crucial support for liberal Democratic candidates through its Committee on Political Education, admired and feared as one of the best fundraising and election organizations in the country. AFL-CIO lobbyists, also respected as among the most competent in Washington, were a central element in campaigns for progressive causes, such as civil rights legislation, as well as labor legislation. Yet though the AFL-CIO was respected and feared in Washington, it was unable to change the provisions of Taft-Hartley that impeded recruiting new members for unions. The AFL-CIO's relationship with the Democratic Party was always unbalanced; the AFL-CIO supported liberal Democrats and their causes far more loyally than liberal Democrats supported the AFL-CIO on issues, such as repealing Taft-Hartley, that were important to unions. Organized labor was a constituency that many liberal Democrats felt they could take for granted while they courted new support among the white-collar, suburban, and nonunion populations. As employment drifted to regions of the United States in which unions were weak, and industries traditionally difficult to organize expanded while industries in which unions were strong (such as automobiles and steel) declined, the percentage of the unionized workforce slowly but steadily sank. An aging union leadership—epitomized by the

president of the AFL-CIO from 1955 to 1978, George Meany—proved unwilling or unable to maintain the liberal coalition of which labor had been part. The AFL-CIO took positions on many of the "new politics" issues that emerged in the 1960s and 1970s that antagonized liberal Democrats with whom it had once been allied; Meany's determined support for US involvement in the Vietnam War and refusal to endorse the liberal, antiwar Democratic candidate in the 1972 presidential election crystallized an ill-founded but widely held belief among many liberals that unions were now part of the establishment, conservative, often corrupt, and resistant to fresh ideas.

The AFL-CIO found itself without much support outside the ranks of labor when the gentle decline in labor's strength in the thirty years after the Second World War turned into a collapse in the 1980s. The reasons for the collapse of union strength in the last two decades of the twentieth century were partly economic; industries in which unions were strong declined more rapidly in part because of foreign competition. However, unions also declined in part because of political reasons. The Reagan administration signaled its tough attitude to unions by breaking the air traffic controllers' union when it called an illegal strike. Reagan also appointed people to the NLRB who took a consistently antiunion position, facilitating determined efforts by corporations to weaken unions as a prerequisite for cutting costs and remaining competitive in globalized markets in which American wages and costs were high. Meany's successor, the quiet and studious Lane Kirkland, proved incapable of crafting a strategy for recovery. However, in the 1980s and 1990s some signs of recovery emerged. Temporarily, nearly all major unions were within the AFL-CIO, as the United Auto Workers, the United Mine Workers, and the reformed Teamsters returned to the fold. Public sector unions grew strongly, and the reform movement SEIU developed within the AFL-CIO before leaving to form a separate organization.

No rejuvenation of the AFL-CIO will accomplish much, however, without major changes to labor laws facilitating recruitment and union recognition.

It was important, therefore, that relations between unions and liberals in politics were much improved. Both unions and liberals realized that their divisions had advantaged conservatives, resulting in policies during the Ronald Reagan and George H. W. Bush years which disadvantaged both of them. Unions showed greater sympathy to issues, such as women's rights, that were dear to liberals; unions and groups such as environmentalists combined to oppose further trade liberalization, most notably during a conference of the World Trade Organization in Seattle in 1999. Whereas environmental issues had divided labor from environmentalists in the 1960s and 1970s, in the 1990s both groups came to believe that they should make common cause in taking on the challenge globalization posed for workers in the United States and abroad. Liberals and unions were united in backing President Barack Obama in the election campaign in the fall of 2008. Unions played an important part in the 2008 elections; the AFL-CIO committed $200 million to it and mobilized over 200,000 volunteers. Along with the unions in Change to Win, this support was particularly important in combating head-on the working-class racism that might have cost Obama votes.

In the early twenty-first century, organized labor was in decline throughout the developed world. The situation for unions in the United States was particularly dire. Only 12 percent of the work force was unionized; in the private sector, merely 8 percent of workers belonged to unions. This would not be surprising to those who associate the United States with a strong commitment to individualism and free markets. It is important to remember, however, that in the middle of the twentieth century, deep-seated factors such as US political culture, the size and diversity of the country, and its ethnic and racial heterogeneity did not prevent American unions from being as strong in terms of the proportion of the workforce unionized as British unions were in that era, or stronger than German unions are today. Reversing union decline in the United States may be merely an extremely difficult challenge for the AFL-CIO, not an actual impossibility. However, unions have little chance of reviving unless there are fundamental changes in laws governing the right to organize, and the prospects here are not good for several reasons. First, the increased dependence of unions on the public sector creates it own political problems. Republican governors in states once associated with a union tradition, such as Wisconsin and Ohio, have been able to mobilize resentment among private-sector, nonunionized workers of the pay, pensions, and health insurance plans enjoyed by unionized public sector workers. This resentment was also evident in negative reactions to the Obama administration's rescue of General Motors and Chrysler in 2009; much of the public blamed the United Auto Workers, rather than bad management, for the companies' plight. The inherent conflict of interest between taxpayers and public-sector unions may reduce unions' appeal even further. Even before the 2010 midterm elections, Senate Republicans had been able to use that chamber's arcane procedures to block policy changes that might facilitate union growth. The majority the Republicans established in the House in those elections guaranteed that no pro-union legislation would clear Congress. In this context, the prospects for a revival of unions in general or the AFL-CIO itself were bleak.

[*See also* Labor Force, American; Trade Unions; *and* Trade Unions and Democrats.]

BIBLIOGRAPHY

Asher, Herbert B., Eric S. Heberlig, and Randall B. Ripley. *American Labor Unions in the Electoral Arena: People, Passions, and Power.* (New York, 2001).

Dark, Taylor. *The Unions and the Democrats: An Enduring Alliance.* (Ithaca, N.Y., 2001).

Goldfield, Michael. *The Decline of Organized Labor in the United States.* (Chicago, 1989).

Graham K. Wilson

AMNESTY INTERNATIONAL

Founded in 1961 by the British lawyer Peter Benenson (1921–2005), Amnesty International is a nongovernmental organization (NGO) which works primarily for the release of prisoners of conscience, fair and prompt trials for political prisoners (defined as persons in prison for their beliefs who have not practiced or advocated violence), and the abolition of the death penalty, extrajudicial killings, and all forms of torture. The organization took root quickly in Europe and the United States, but it was not until the mid-1970s that its numerical and geographical growth became remarkable. It is the largest human rights NGO in the world and sets the standards for human rights monitoring, reporting, and campaigns. It was awarded the Nobel Peace Prize in 1977.

In 1998, Amnesty claimed a membership of over 1 million active or dues-paying members in over 100 countries. Most are grouped in fifty-four national or country sections, of which thirty-three are now outside Europe and North America. The US section is headquartered in New York, as is the Secretariat's United Nations (UN) office. More than 4,200 local groups and numerous other unregistered school, university, and professional groups carry out Amnesty's projects around the world. They are served by the London Secretariat, which has a staff numbering over 300, assisted by an additional ninety-five volunteers. In 1998 the annual budget of the Secretariat was over $24 million. National sections have their own administrative structures and budgets, and they also support the budget of the Secretariat. Amnesty has strict fundraising rules. It does not accept government funds and limits the percentage of budgets at all levels that can come from a single source.

Amid the recent rapid growth in the number of human rights organizations, Amnesty International has remained unique in a number of important ways. It is a membership organization in the sense that it is supported financially and its work is carried out primarily by its worldwide membership. Policies are set every two years at International Council Meetings, where decisions are all made by representatives of the worldwide membership. Amnesty is also unique among human rights NGOs in terms of the geographic spread of its membership, emphasized by a recent decision to open outreach offices overseas, notably in Uganda in Africa.

Amnesty seeks to remain independent of external influences, particularly of governments and ideologies.

At the heart of Amnesty's commitment to independence are the standards it sets for its data collection, monitoring, and reporting. Accuracy and timeliness are major concerns of the professional staff in London, who monitor countries around the world and prepare the reports for action campaigns, both big and small. In addition to the rules about fundraising, collaboration with other NGOs is limited by specific guidelines. To assure distance from national politics, Amnesty members—with one or two exceptions such as work on the death penalty or prisons—are not allowed to work on issues within their own country. Lobbying of national legislatures is similarly limited. Amnesty, however, actively lobbies international organizations, notably the UN in New York and Geneva, the United Nations Educational, Scientific, and Cultural Organization (UNESCO), the Council of Europe and the European Community, the Inter-American Commission on Human Rights, and the Organization of African Unity.

Amnesty's advocacy methods have evolved from Benenson's original idea that exposure to public view, especially through the media, would embarrass governments into improving their practices. To achieve this goal, Amnesty has traditionally used many means: in addition to letter-writing and petitions to government officials, it sends out missions composed of experts to collect data and provide support for local human rights NGOs; it publishes reports which its members bring to the attention of officials around the world; it organizes campaigns to focus on a country or a form of violation and carries them out through national sections and members; and it runs an urgent action network which makes use of the latest technologies to alert members as to how to take immediate action on individual death penalty or prisoner of conscience cases. Increasingly Amnesty has devoted more of its budget to human-rights education and training. Promotional activities have also included consciousness-raising concert tours, scholarships for student media projects, prisoner relief, and compensation programs for the victims of human rights abuse.

Under the influence of International Council meetings, Amnesty's mandate has expanded, reflecting the breadth and interests of its members. Today the mandate includes a concern for abuses faced by refugees, women, and children. Persons in prison for homosexuality can be classified as political prisoners. The International Council meeting in Cape Town, South Africa, in December 1997 was dominated by debates on the mandate. The participants, who came from Amnesty sections from all over the world, agreed that Amnesty ought to act now, for example, to prevent abuses by non-state actors as well as by states, to work for the eradication of female genital mutilation, and to campaign against land mines and the use of children in armed conflict. The 1997 Council also agreed to launch a new four-year overall review of the mandate.

The significance of Amnesty International has been less in its individual achievements than in its success in mobilizing popular support for human rights. In this regard it has contributed more than any other single organization to the present world climate. Amnesty makes extensive use of its Web sites: that of its US office is at http://www.amnesty-usa.org, and that of its Secretariat is at http://www.amnesty.org/en/who-we-are/our-people/international-secretariat-directors. These are the easiest way to obtain recent and more detailed information on its work.

[*See also* Nongovernmental Organizations; *and* Torture, Interrogation, and Fair-Trial Procedures.]

J. Paul Martin

ARAB-ISRAELI CONFLICT

Since 1948, when Jewish inhabitants of the former British mandate of Palestine established the state of Israel, the Arab-Israeli conflict has appeared on the agenda of every session of the United Nations (UN) General Assembly. The conflict has roots which go back to the 1890s, when Jewish settlers first came from Europe and the Zionist movement began to lay the foundations for a future Jewish homeland in Palestine, with its overwhelmingly Arab population.

The clash of this Jewish state-building project with the emerging nationalist sentiment of the Palestinian Arabs aroused bitter intercommunal struggles during the mandate and led to the conflict that lay ahead. Though only a small territory was at stake—with few natural resources—the conflict was eventually magnified in international significance by the fact that the land in question is sacred to three of the world's great religions, by its intersection with politics in the world's most important oil-producing region, and by the connection of the conflict to the Cold War between the Soviet Union and the United States.

In November 1947, to the dismay of the Arabs, the UN partitioned Palestine into a Jewish and an Arab state (as well as an international enclave for Jerusalem), giving 55 percent of the territory to the Jewish state. As British forces withdrew, a civil war erupted between Jews and Arabs. When Israel declared independence in May 1948, several Arab League members sent units of their regular armies to join guerrilla forces fighting in Palestine. Israel eventually won this war, aided by weapons received from the Soviet bloc. The poorly armed Arab armies and Palestinian irregulars, badly led and unable to coordinate their operations, were no match for the Jewish forces.

After the fighting stopped in 1949, Israel gained about 5,200 square kilometers (2,000 sq. mi.) beyond the area allocated in the UN partition plan, thus occupying over 75 percent of Palestine. The UN-sponsored armistice agreements, signed between Israel and the Arab belligerents (Egypt, Jordan, Lebanon, and Syria), gave Egypt control of the Gaza Strip and Jordan some 5,200 square kilometers (2,000 sq. mi.) of eastern Palestine on the west bank of the Jordan River, including the Old City of Jerusalem. In spite of efforts by the UN Conciliation Commission for Palestine (CCP), which met separately with Arab and Israeli delegations in Lausanne, the parties made no lasting peace agreement.

Over 700,000 Palestinian Arabs fled or were driven from their homes to surrounding Arab countries, mostly to Jordan, the Gaza Strip, Lebanon, and Syria. Both the host countries and the refugees themselves insisted that those who left Palestine be permitted to return before direct negotiations with Israel. In its Resolution 194(III) of 11 December 1948 establishing the CCP, the UN General Assembly resolved "that the refugees wishing to return to their homes and live at peace with their neighbors should be permitted to do so at the earliest practicable date, and that compensation should be paid for the property of those choosing not to return." During the interim period the refugees were to be assisted by the UN Relief and Works Agency for Palestine Refugees in the Near East (UNRWA).

International efforts to resolve the conflict attempted to find a compromise between the position of Israel, which insisted on direct negotiations, and Arab demands for refugee repatriation, compensation, or both, and Israeli withdrawal from land beyond the UN partition borders. Absent a settlement, the Arab states refused to recognize Israel or to have any relations with it.

The United States offered several proposals, including plans for regional economic development that would have integrated refugees into the countries to which they had fled. All such proposals failed, however, because of political obstacles.

Political change in the Arab world sharpened the conflict between Israel and its neighbors during the 1950s. New military regimes came to power—in Syria in 1949 and in Egypt in 1952—seeking to throw off Western tutelage and to affirm Arab national identity. Gamal Abdel Nasser of Egypt in particular symbolized the new radical nationalist leadership and the growing military, economic, and political strength of the Arab world.

Israeli leaders saw Nasser as a threat. In 1954, in an effort to undermine relations between Egypt and the West, Israeli agents set off a series of bombs at US and Egyptian properties in Cairo and Alexandria. In February 1955, Israel carried out a large-scale attack on Gaza, in retaliation for infiltrators and guerrillas coming across the border. For its part, Egypt contributed to heightened tensions by continuing to refuse Israeli passage through the Suez Canal. Nasser's bellicose public rhetoric also sharpened Israeli insecurity.

In 1954, Israel began to purchase extensive military equipment from France while Nasser tried unsuccessfully to obtain arms from Western sources; Egypt finally made a deal in 1955 to buy arms from the Soviet bloc. Soviet support had shifted away from Israel and began to favor Syria and Egypt.

In July 1956, Nasser nationalized the Suez Canal, after the United States and the West rejected his requests for assistance in constructing the Aswan High Dam. Both Britain and France saw the move as a blow to their interests in the region. Soon after, at secret meetings in Europe, Israeli, French, and British leaders agreed to launch a joint military action against Egypt to regain control of the canal and overthrow the Egyptian leader. Israel began the attack in October. After its forces seized the Gaza Strip and the Sinai Peninsula, and reached the Suez Canal, British and French forces occupied the northern Canal Zone.

With uncharacteristic unity, both the United States and the Soviet Union denounced the tripartite attack and joined in a call through the UN for immediate withdrawal of the invaders. The Soviets threatened military action against Britain and France and the United States withheld vital oil supplies from both countries. These moves soon forced the invaders to withdraw.

In November the General Assembly established the UN Emergency Force (UNEF) to supervise the withdrawal and to patrol the frontiers between Egypt and Israel. Israel left Gaza in March 1957 after receiving assurances that UNEF would remain along its border with Egypt and guarantee free passage from the Gulf of Akaba through the Straits of Tiran to the Red Sea.

Following the Suez War, UNEF assured relatively stable conditions on the frontier between Egypt and Israel, although the two countries remained officially at war. More serious were Israeli border clashes with Syria and Jordan, some over the Jordan River and its sources. The Arab states opposed Israeli plans to divert Jordan River waters to the arid Negev in southern Israel, plans that would diminish their scarce water supplies. In 1960 the Arab League charged that Israel's water scheme was "an act of aggression," and in 1963 the League adopted its own diversion blueprint. Israel nevertheless went ahead with its plan.

Israel's strategic doctrine required that it develop and maintain overwhelming military superiority over all potential Arab enemies. Close relations with France enabled Israel to purchase very advanced weapons; French experts also helped Israel set up a nuclear reactor and a nuclear weapons program. Israel also developed a sophisticated weapons manufacturing capability of its own.

By 1967 tensions caused by the water dispute and by border incidents led to a number of military clashes. During May, Syria protested that Israel was massing troops on its border. Nasser threatened to prevent Israel's passage through the Straits of Tiran, demanded that UNEF forces leave Egyptian territory, and moved troops toward the Sinai border with Israel.

In early June the situation led to a political crisis in Israel, where the first national unity government was formed. On 5 June 1967, Israeli leaders decided to make a "preemptive" strike against Egypt, Syria, and Iraq. After firing on Israeli-controlled Jerusalem, Jordanian forces were also involved. The fate of the Arab armies was determined in the first few hours of war when Israeli planes destroyed most of the opposing air fleets while they were still on the ground. Within six days, Israel conquered the Sinai Peninsula from Egypt, the West Bank and East Jerusalem from Jordan, and the Golan Heights from Syria.

As a result of the Six-Day War, Israel emerged as the dominant regional power, the Arab states were thrown into disarray, and tensions deepened between the United States and the Soviet Union. After the war, the Soviet Union greatly increased support for Egypt, Syria, and Iraq, while the United States began to provide Israel with major arms and economic aid. A regional arms race began in earnest. With Israeli forces on the east bank of the Suez Canal, Egypt shut the waterway, badly damaging its own economy. Some 300,000 more Palestinians had been driven into exile as refugees, as well as nearly 100,000 Syrians who lost homes in the Golan Heights.

Differences between the Soviet Union and the United States blocked efforts to end the twenty years of conflict through the UN. Moscow supported UN resolutions condemning Israel and calling on it to return territory gained in the war, while Washington supported Israel's insistence that territory could be returned only through a final peace settlement guaranteeing Israel's security.

The stalemate was broken in November 1967 when the United States and the Soviet Union agreed to a British-sponsored compromise, Security Council Resolution 242. Its principal components included:

> the inadmissability of the acquisition of territory by war and the need to work for a just and lasting peace . . . Withdrawal of Israeli armed forces from territories of recent conflict; Termination of all claims or states of belligerency and respect for and acknowledgement of the sovereignty, territorial integrity and political independence of every State in the area . . . [and] a just settlement of the refugee problem.

Parts of the resolution were ambiguous, but it remained the basis of future negotiations. Although the United States, the Soviet Union, Israel, and most Arab states accepted the resolution, they disagreed over the phrase "withdrawal of Israeli armed forces from territories" occupied during the war. The Arab states, supported by the Soviet Union and many other UN members, insisted that withdrawal had to be complete, whereas Israel and the United States argued that partial withdrawal could satisfy the resolution.

After the war most Arab states scaled down their terms for a settlement. Few demanded that Israel retreat to the 1947 partition borders or repatriate all the refugees. They now based their demands on Resolution 242: withdrawal to the 1949 armistice frontiers and a solution of the refugee problem that could include alternatives to repatriation.

An important consequence of the 1967 war was a revival of Palestinian Arab nationalism. Palestinians now became disenchanted with leaders of the defeated Arab states and supported recently founded Palestinian groups that proposed to liberate the country by guerrilla warfare. The largest organization was Fatah; one of its leaders, Yasser Arafat, soon became leader of the new umbrella group representing Palestinian nationalism: the Palestine Liberation Organization (PLO).

The focus now shifted from conflict between Israel and Arab governments to conflict between Israel and Palestinian nationalists. The diverse Palestinian factions devised their own strategies to defeat Israel and establish an independent state. Until the 1970s, most Palestinian groups sought total victory, though they insisted that Jews in Palestine before Israel was established would be welcome in the "secular, democratic state" they sought to found. Palestinian groups tried to employ guerrillas to infiltrate Israel; they sometimes struck at targets outside of Israel; some even hijacked civilian aircraft to advance their cause. Palestinian groups and Israeli security services also waged an underground war in Europe.

The Palestinian movement won formal support and even financial backing from most Arab states, although many Arab leaders viewed the Palestinians as dangerous antagonists. By striking at states that harbored Palestinian guerrillas, Israel sought to sharpen this conflict. In 1970, Jordan was the principal Palestinian base and their armed groups became a state within a state, threatening the royal government. In September, Jordan's army attacked the Palestinians, reimposing control over the border. Because neither Syria nor Egypt permitted autonomous Palestinian presence and guerrilla bases, most Palestinian organizations withdrew to Lebanon; all but Israel's northern border were now relatively secure from guerrilla raids.

After several years Egyptian and Syrian leaders concluded they could not regain territory seized by Israel in 1967 through diplomacy alone. In 1972, Egyptian President Anwar Sadat discharged his Soviet military advisers, hoping that closer ties with the West would lead to an agreement for Israeli withdrawal. Finally disappointed, he decided to force the issue by war. After secret negotiations, Egypt and Syria opened a two-front surprise attack in October 1973. Initially they drove back the Israelis, recapturing sectors of Sinai and the Golan. Eventually, the tide of battle turned and Israel regained most territories it had occupied before.

The war, known as the October, Yom Kippur, or Ramadan War, shattered the myth of an invincible Israeli army. It nearly became a confrontation between the United States and the Soviet Union when Moscow threatened to send troops to assist Egypt; the United States then declared a high-level military alert. Both superpowers sent airborne resupplies to their allies during the heat of battle. But as the fighting ended, tensions were diffused and the two countries agreed on another Security Council Resolution—338, reaffirming Resolution 242.

An international peace conference convened in Geneva under UN auspices during December of 1973, but broke up after two days. The United States then began a "step-by-step" approach mediated by US Secretary of State Henry Kissinger, who arranged a series of disengagement agreements, two with Egypt and one with Syria, providing for gradual Israeli withdrawal from parts of Sinai and the Golan.

President Sadat of Egypt turned again to diplomacy with a surprise announcement on 9 November 1977 declaring his desire to visit Jerusalem for peace talks with Israel. The Jerusalem visit opened a new phase in Arab-Israeli relations: the first time an Arab head of state traveled to Israel for direct negotiations. When the subsequent talks faltered, US President Jimmy Carter convened the Israeli and Egyptian leaders at Camp David in September 1978. After thirteen days of acrimonious debate, Carter convinced Sadat and Israeli Prime Minister Menachem Begin to sign accords on a framework for peace.

Following further negotiations, Israel and Egypt signed a peace treaty in Washington, D.C., on 26 March 1979 providing for phased withdrawal of Israeli forces from Sinai and establishing normal ties between the two countries. Because Syrian and Palestinian territories remained occupied, Arab opinion was incensed at the Egyptian step and the country stood isolated in the region for several years.

Relations between Egypt and Israel remained strained, worsened by disputes over implementation of the Camp David Accords and by Israel's hostile relations with other Arab states, especially its attack on Lebanon in 1982. Egypt interpreted the pact to mean full Palestinian self-government; the Israeli government insisted that it was responsible only to offer "autonomy."

Between 1967 and 1987, Palestinians increasingly resisted Israeli rule in the occupied West Bank and Gaza. Israel's leaders believed that Palestinian acts of rebellion were instigated by the PLO and struck at the organization's base in Lebanon. Israel supported anti-Palestinian Maronite forces in the Lebanese Civil War, which began in 1975. It also mounted air attacks against southern Lebanese towns and villages, culminating in the 1978 invasion taking Israeli forces up to the Litani River. When its forces later withdrew, Israel maintained control over a ten-mile-deep territory north of its border assisted by antigovernment Lebanese militias.

In June 1982, Israel struck at Lebanon with a full-scale invasion by forty thousand Israeli troops, supported by massive armor and air raids. Neither the small Lebanese army, nor the Syrians (who occupied part of Lebanon), nor the Palestinian fighters were a match for this force. Israel's siege of Beirut led to international condemnation. Eventually, the United States persuaded Israel to withdraw, provided Palestinian and Syrian troops also left the city. The evacuation culminated in the Sabra and Chatila incident, in which right-wing Lebanese Christian militia forces allied with Israel massacred hundreds of Palestinian civilians in the two refugee camps.

The Sabra and Chatila incident sharpened opposition in Israel to the invasion of Lebanon, becoming a major issue in the 1982 election. After the election, Israel began a phased withdrawal, but left a fifteen-mile-wide strip in south Lebanon under its control and continued to carry out air strikes against Lebanese and Palestinian targets.

Unrest in the West Bank and Gaza erupted again in December 1987 with widespread strikes and demonstrations aimed at Israeli occupation forces. Unlike previous disturbances, the demonstrations escalated into a unified uprising called the intifada, refocusing international attention on the Palestine question. The central issue was the Palestinian demand for an independent state in the West Bank and Gaza alongside Israel.

As a result of the intifada and the confidence it inspired, the PLO recognized UN Resolutions 242 and 338 as the basis for peace discussions. It also renounced the use of terrorism and agreed to mutual recognition between the Palestinians and Israel. This led to a public dialogue between the United States and the PLO, which soon broke down. The Arabs continued to call for a return of all territories occupied in 1967, including East Jerusalem and the Golan Heights, for recognition of the PLO and creation of an independent Palestinian state. Israel refused to talk to the PLO and insisted that it would not give up any occupied territories, and built Jewish settlements in the territories instead. Migrations of hundreds of thousands of Soviet Jews to Israel, beginning in 1989, further sharpened controversy.

After the Gulf War of 1990–1991, the United States undertook yet another major effort to broker a peace agreement. In October 1991 US President George H. W. Bush renewed attempts by the United States to reach a settlement through correspondence with Mikhail Gorbachev of the Soviet Union. They agreed on an international peace conference in Madrid, Spain. Its stated objective was to achieve "a real peace . . . security, diplomatic relations, and economic relations . . . among the peoples and governments of the Middle East to shape the future." The conference framework called for bilateral and multilateral talks. Bilateral meetings were to take place between Israel and its Arab neighbors (Jordan, Syria, Lebanon, Palestine) "to resolve conflicts of the past." The multilateral tracts included five working groups focused on water, environment, arms control and regional security, refugees, and economic development. The multilateral meetings were to focus on regional problems and to serve as confidence-building measures.

Talks between Israel and the other neighbors resumed during December 1991 in Washington, D.C. They continued intermittently and were scheduled to take place in the United States, Moscow, Lisbon, Belgium, Japan, Canada, and London. In the fourth round of talks in Washington the Palestinians proposed direct elections in the West Bank. Israel rejected this proposal and the talks ended inconclusively. Some progress was reached in talks with Syria when Israel acknowledged the possibility of withdrawal from the Golan Heights conquered by Israel in the 1967 war. However, talks were discontinued when Israel indicated it would retain parts of the occupied Golan region.

In January 1993 "back-channel" talks were initiated between Israel and the PLO in Oslo, leading to open negotiations and letters of mutual recognition signed by the PLO leader Arafat and Israel's prime minister Itzchak Rabin. The Oslo talks led to recognition by Israel of Palestinian self-government in the occupied West Bank and Gaza. As a result of the PLO-Israel agreement, Israeli Prime Minister Rabin, Foreign Minister Shimon Peres, and PLO President Arafat were jointly awarded the Nobel Peace Prize in December 1994. Israel-PLO contacts were renewed after the election of the right-wing Prime Minister Benyamin Netanyahu.

In July 1994 the "Washington Declaration" ended the state of war between Israel and Jordan. During December 1994 talks between Israel and Syria were renewed in Washington between the Syrian and Israeli army chiefs of staff, but with no results.

US President George W. Bush was not optimistic about the possibility of a peace settlement between Israel and the Palestinians. But he too undertook several initiatives aimed at ending the conflict. Together with the United Nations, the European Union, and Russia, known as "the Quartet," the four parties proposed a new "Road Map for Peace" in the Palestine conflict. The plan called for a "two-state solution" (Israel and Palestine) to be achieved through several steps. Rather than imposing a timetable, the "Road Map" called on Israel and the Palestinians to reach several benchmarks or steps towards ending the conflict, beginning with a halt to violence. The proposal was aimed at ending attacks by Palestinian insurgents, especially the suicide attacks that had occurred in recent months. In return, Israel was asked to affirm its commitment to an "independent, viable sovereign Palestinian state." The "benchmarks" called for "humanitarian and economic assistance for the Palestinians." Following a transition period a permanent status agreement was to be achieved by 2005.

Although the UN Security Council endorsed the Road Map and reiterated its call for a two-state (Israel-Palestine) solution, its repeated resolutions had little if any impact on ending the Arab-Israel conflict. Nor did Israel's withdrawal of its troops or settlers from the Gaza Strip in August 2005 contribute greatly to a peace settlement. In June 2007 the Islamic fundamentalist organization Hamas took control of Gaza. During the Hamas regime Gaza became the base for terrorist attacks on southern Israel. After defeating Fatah in an open election, Hamas drove the more moderate Fatah from Gaza, permitting the region to become the base for terrorist attacks on southern Israel.

In December 2008 and January 2009 Israel responded to the continued terrorist attacks from Gaza in "Operation Cast Lead," a combination of air strikes and land strikes against Hamas in Gaza. The object of the operation was to destroy the ability of Hamas to fire rockets into southern Israel. During the operation over one thousand Palestinians, mostly civilians, were killed. A large part of Gaza's civilian infrastructure was also destroyed, resulting in major economic disruption and intensified hostility to Israel by the indigenous population. In 2009 a UN commission's report on the operation by the South African judge Richard Goldstone charged that both Israel and Hamas were guilty of war crimes during the "Cast Lead Operation." The report was rejected by both Israel and Hamas. In April 2011 Judge Goldstone modified his criticism of Israel but the UN did not repudiate the original report.

Although the fundamentalist Islamic parties—Hamas in Gaza and Hezbollah in Lebanon—remained adamant in their hostility and refusal to negotiate with Israel, mainstream Arab attitudes gradually began to accept Israel's existence. In March 2002 at an Arab summit meeting in Beirut, Crown Prince (later king) Abdullah of Saudi Arabia introduced a peace initiative. The initiative was endorsed by the Arab League and later published by the Palestinian Authority in Israeli Hebrew-language newspapers. The plan called for recognition of Israel and normalization of relations in exchange for Israel's withdrawal to the pre-1967 borders. It required Israeli acceptance and recognition of an independent Palestinian state in Israel-occupied West Bank and Gaza. The capital of the Palestinian state would be

East Jerusalem, which had been captured by Israel from Jordan in 1967. Although the plan did not call for a return to Israel of the 1948 and 1967 Palestinian refugees, it insisted on "a just solution" to the Arab refugee problem. Israel expressed interest in the plan, but objected to its implications of a mass refugee return to their original homes.

In 2007, in a final attempt to end the conflict, President Bush convened an international conference. Forty nations participated in the one-day meeting held in Annapolis at the US Naval Academy. The occasion marked the first time high-ranking Israeli and Saudi authorities met together. The one-day experience ended with a "joint understanding" between the Palestine Authority President Mahmoud Abbas and Israeli Prime Minister Ehud Olmert. They agreed to continue their meetings with the goal of reaching a peace treaty by the end of 2008. One achievement of the conference was participation by several Arab states that had not previously taken part in peace negotiations with Israel. A year later, after continued Palestine-Israel talks, President Abbas withdrew in opposition to Israel's "Cast Lead" invasion of Gaza.

In January 2009 the new US president Barack Obama indicated that he would be involved directly and actively in resolving the Arab-Israel conflict, also frequently referred to as the "Middle East problem." An initial move was to appoint former US senator George Mitchell as presidential representative in the Middle East. It was hoped that Mitchell's previous success as mediator in the Northern Ireland conflict would be repeated in the Middle East.

After a two-year hiatus in US-Syrian diplomatic relations and the absence of an American ambassador in Damascus, President Obama restored contacts by dispatching senior State Department officials to renew talks with Syrian President Assad. In June 2009, in a speech from Cairo to the Muslim world, Obama emphasized that US involvement in the region was compatible with the Muslim world's interest in settlement of the Arab-Israel conflict. Less than a year later, the president acknowledged that his Cairo speech raised Arab expectations too high, illustrating the difficulties of maintaining a

balance among the conflicting parties to the Arab-Israel conflict. Obama was rewarded for his efforts with the Nobel Peace Prize in December 2009.

As a result of the Israel Knesset (parliament) elections in February 2009, Benjamin Netanyahu, leader of the nationalist Likud Party, was reelected as prime minister. Despite meetings arranged by Obama in New York between Netanyahu and Palestinian President Abbas, little progress was achieved.

Although there was general consensus that settlement would be based on the "two-state solution," progress was blocked by differences over its parameters. A major obstacle was defining the borders between Israel and the proposed Palestinian state. Defining borders was complicated by the establishment of new Jewish settlements within the West Bank, in territory claimed by the Palestinians. Since Israel captured the West Bank in 1967, Jewish settlements there have increased several times, with the number of settlers growing from a few dozen to over 300,000. Early settlements have grown into towns, and several Jewish towns in the West Bank have become cities.

By 2010 the Jewish settlements in the occupied territories became the major obstacle to a peace accord and greatly complicated American attempts to pursue negotiations. In an attempt to lessen tensions created by the settlement issue, President Obama prevailed on Prime Minister Netanyahu to temporarily suspend construction of Jewish housing in the West Bank and East Jerusalem. However when the moratorium expired, Jewish settlement construction was renewed, leading to Palestinian suspension of further negotiations. In February 2011, the United States vetoed a UN Security Council resolution calling for a halt to Jewish housing construction in the occupied territories. In the fifteen-member UN Security Council, only the United States voted against the resolution.

In September 2010 Israeli Foreign Minister Avigdor Lieberman proposed a solution of the settlement conflict through territorial exchanges: Israel would cede parts of its territory populated by large numbers of Israeli Arab citizens in exchange for Jewish-inhabited parts of the West Bank. The guiding principle, he claimed, was "not land for peace but rather, exchange of populated territories." Instead of removing Jewish settlers from the West Bank, there would be an exchange of populated territories. This called for moving borders to reflect "existing demographic realities." Lieberman concluded that an interim agreement to implement his proposal "would take a few decades."

Leaks to the Aljazeera television network and the memoirs of former Israeli Prime Minister Ehud Olmert reveal negotiations between Olmert and Mahmoud Abbas that came close to a peace agreement. Their discussion covered the four principal issues that have blocked resolution of the conflict since 1947: boundaries of Israel and a Palestinian state, the status of Jerusalem, settlement of the 1947 Palestine refugees, and mutual security. The difference between Olmert and Abbas over the territory to be allocated to the Palestinians was less than 5 percent. The task of defining the borders between Israel and Palestine was complicated by the constantly growing number of Jewish settlements in the West Bank since 1967. Within Jerusalem—all of which was declared by Israel as its indivisible capital—over the course of more than forty years of Israeli control, the population in some Arab sectors became Jewish. This further complicated division of the city, even though in principle Olmert agreed to it.

While Abbas recognized the impossibility of "returning" 5 million Palestinian refugees (descended from 750,000 who left their homes in 1947–1948), agreement could not be reached on implementing "the right of return" or the amounts and method of compensating the refugees and their descendents. The security problem was related to defining borders, demilitarization of Palestine, and control of the border with Jordan.

These are the principal issues that have blocked attempts to resolve the conflict between Israel and the Palestinians. Failure to resolve them has also shaped relations between Israel, the Arab world and, to a large extent, relations with much of the Muslim world.

Since the 1947 UN partition the United States has often played the dominant role in the conflict. Its efforts had little success until 1979, when Israel and Egypt signed the peace treaty at Camp David under the auspices of US President Jimmy Carter. President Bill Clinton led the way to Israel's acceptance of the PLO and its leader Yasser Arafat. Although relations between Israel and Palestinians are still tenuous, the United States is still primarily responsible for maintaining continued negotiations.

[*See also* Egypt; Israel; Middle East–United States Relations; *and* Syria.]

BIBLIOGRAPHY
Caplan, Neil. *The Israel-Palestine Conflict: Contested Histories.* (Chichester, UK, 2009).
Eisenberg, Laura Zittrain, and Neil Caplan. *Negotiating Arab-Israeli Peace: Patterns, Problems, Possibilities.* 2d ed. (Bloomington, Ind., 2010).
Freeman, Charles W. *America's Misadventures in the Middle East.* (Charlottesville, Va., 2010).
Gilbert, Martin. *The Arab-Israeli Conflict: Its History in Maps.* 2d ed. (London, 1976).
Kurtzer, Daniel C., and Scott B. Lasensky. *Negotiating Arab-Israeli Peace: American Leadership in the Middle East.* (Washington, D.C., 2008).
Laqueur, Walter, and Barry M. Rubin, eds. *The Israel-Arab Reader: A Documentary History.* (New York, 1984).
Peretz, Don. *The Arab-Israel Dispute.* Library in a Book. (New York, 1996).
Peretz, Don. *Intifada: The Palestinian Uprising.* (Boulder, Colo., 1990).
Peretz, Don. *Palestinians, Refugees, and the Middle East Peace Process.* (Washington, D.C., 1993).
Peretz, Don. *The West Bank: History, Politics, Society, and Economy.* (Boulder, Colo., 1986).

Don Peretz

B

BANK FAILURES

See Federal Deposit Insurance Corporation.

BIG PHARMA

The Pharmaceutical Manufacturers Association, established in 1958, formally became known as the Pharmaceutical Research and Manufacturers Association (PhRMA) in 1994. Representing approximately fifty member companies, including names such as GlaxoSmithKline, Merck, and Pfizer, it is the trade association for the leading brand names in the pharmaceutical industry and, as such, it has developed a formidable standing as a major and effective player in the politics of Washington, D.C. This reputation has grown as PhRMA has been seen as superseding the traditional forces in health care policy and politics, such as the American Medical Association (AMA). And the evidence suggests that PhRMA's growing reputation is well deserved, as it has defeated legislative moves potentially damaging to the industry's interests. PhRMA's influence was particularly evident in the final legislative form of the Medicare Modernization Act of 2003 (MMA), which added a prescription drug benefit to the Medicare program, and was seen again in 2010 when the details of the Affordable Care Act (ACA) were finalized.

PhRMA's website (www.phrma.org) contains the following mission statement: "PhRMA's mission is to conduct effective advocacy for public policies that encourage discovery of important new medicines for patients by biopharmaceutical research companies." Critics of the pharmaceutical industry, and in particular of the power of the branded drugs sector, have a different perspective, based on how PhRMA uses its extraoridinary financial resources to bear down on groups or institutions threatening its interests (Angell, 2005). What was clear in PhRMA's response to the legislative negotiations throughout both 2003 and 2009–2010 was that it sought to minimize any government control of drug pricing through either direct intervention or through allowing government programs such as Medicare to negotiate prices downward. In addition, PhRMA was anxious to thwart efforts to allow the reimportation of drugs from abroad, ostensibly for safety reasons, but also for fear that these drugs would then be sold at prices that undercut those in the United States. Another key interest of PhRMA, putting them into conflict with other groups in the pharmaceutical sector such as the Generic Pharmaceutical Association, is to maintain the length of time that new drugs retain their patent and therefore their high value before becoming available in generic form.

One crude measure of PhRMA's presence in the political arena is its capacity to spend lavish amounts of money. During the 2009–2010 election cycle, the organization contributed over $1 million to candidates for office and individual companies also contributed heavily with, for example, Pfizer donating over $1.6 million. Other PhRMA member companies include Merck, which spent over $1 million, as did Abbott Laboratories and AstraZeneca. Interestingly, those monies were split reasonably evenly between Democratic and Republican candidates (Center for Responsive Politics, "Pharmaceuticals/Health Products"). This represented a change, first manifested in 2008, from the preceding election cycles, when the industry donated more heavily to Republican candidates. In the buildup to the 2006 elections, for example, about two-thirds of the industry's contributions went to Republican candidates. This adjustment to campaign donation strategies illustrates the instrumental nature of the industry as it adapted to the partisan balance of power in Washington. According to the then-president of PhRMA and former Republican House member from Louisiana, W. J. "Billy" Tauzin, the takeover of Congress by the Democrats in the 2006 midterm elections simply meant that "we just have more friends than we used to have," and he added, "We're trying to find more" (quoted in Birnbaum, 2008).

Yet from PhRMA's perspective, these campaign contributions were secondary when compared with the funds used to conduct lobbying endeavors. In 2003 as the MMA was under consideration, PhRMA spent over $16 million on lobbying. In 2009, as the Obama administration and congressional Democrats worked to put together comprehensive health care reform legislation, PhRMA spent over $26 million to protect what it saw as its best interests. Reflecting the importance of events that unfolded through the year, this represented nearly a 30 percent increase on lobbying expenditures in 2008. Individual companies also spent significantly. Pfizer, for example, incurred lobbying expenditures of over $25.8 million, Eli Lilly over $11.2 million, and Merck over $6.4 million in that year (Center for Responsive Politics, "Lobbying: Top Spenders 2009").

One aspect of the industry's lobbying effort is the sheer number of lobbyists involved. And, again, the industry's desire to be friends with both the main parties was witnessed in the wake of the 2006 elections when, reversing the pattern of recruiting lobbyists with Republican sympathies, many lobbyists were retained who worked for firms with ties to the Democratic Party. Part of this strategy was simply to prevent those lobbyists working for groups that were urging the Democrats to take the lead in imposing new cost controls on branded drugs. PhRMA also has an impressive record in recruiting lobbyists with ties to influential figures in Congress.

Further to this, critics have lamented the "revolving door between government regulators and industry spokespersons," as people who have written favorably of the industry get senior positions at the relevant government bodies (Olson, 2010, p. 194). For example, in the spring of 2002 when President George W. Bush was looking to appoint a new commissioner of the Food and Drug Administration, which regulates the entry of new drugs into the health care arena, one candidate was a professor of clinical pharmacology, Alastair Wood, but his name was dropped after "pharmaceutical executives complained that he would be too aggressive a regulator" (Stolberg, 2002).

In terms of public policy, PhRMA is clearly ever-vigilant in protecting its interests, but since the beginning of the twenty-first century there have been two pieces of legislation that have particularly concerned the industry. First, in 2003, was the MMA. This was a complex piece of legislation, but its headline aim was to add a prescription drug benefit to the Medicare program, because many senior citizens were struggling with the out-of-pocket expenses involved in paying for their recommended treatments. Not surprisingly, therefore, PhRMA was anxious to have its voice heard. While pleased at the prospect of selling more drugs, PhRMA was anxious that this potential new market not come with regulatory restrictions attached. One survey of congressional staff in the spring and early summer of 2003 found that they placed PhRMA as the most influential health policy interest group, ahead of traditional medical power brokers such as the AMA and the major group representing seniors, AARP (formerly the American Association of Retired Persons). It was also apparent that PhRMA was more effective when lobbying privately and alone, rather than when joining in broader coalitions of groups that worked more in the public eye (Heaney, 2006). PhRMA's tactics during the negotiations did create a sense on Capitol Hill that the organization was overly aggressive in its approach, reflected in comments that the organization "has more lobbyists than members of Congress" and "has more money than God" (Heaney, 2006, p. 922). Whatever the resentments, however, the group's interests were not only protected, as efforts to wield the size of the Medicare program as a bargaining tool to get discounts were beaten back, but were advanced, as government committed itself to helping fund a system in which seniors pay for their prescription drugs, to be administered through private delivery systems, with PhRMA playing a key role in devising the formulary lists of suitable drugs.

Unsurprisingly, PhRMA again rallied its lobbyists to influence legislators on comprehensive health care reform instigated by President Barack Obama. In this case the results were a bit more mixed for PhRMA, and there were suggestions of internal turmoil when Tauzin unexpectedly announced his resignation in February 2010. During the 2008 Democratic primary campaign, candidate Obama had run a television advertisement explicitly criticizing the manner in which the MMA had prevented Medicare from using its bargaining power to get access to cheaper prescription drugs. He also made speeches advocating the reimportation of drugs from Canada that would give Americans access to cheaper pharmaceuticals. Yet, once in the White House, Obama began to negotiate with PhRMA, and Tauzin was a regular visitor to the president. Subsequently, in July 2009 a deal was struck in which there would be no change to the rules governing prescription drug prices through Medicare, nor would reimportation be allowed. In return Tauzin agreed to new costs estimated at $80 billion over ten years, and PhRMA would throw its weight behind health reform. This support extended to providing over $100 million in pro-reform advertisements and working with Families USA, a liberal advocacy group usually on the opposing side to PhRMA in health care debates.

As the reform process unfolded this deal looked to be threatened, as the House version of reform contained clauses demanding more from pharmaceutical companies, but the Senate version stuck with the deal, which turned out to be the basis for the final legislative package.

Nevertheless, some in PhRMA still felt that Tauzin had conceded too much, and he also incurred the wrath of the United States Chamber of Commerce, which had resolutely opposed health care reform from start to finish. But PhRMA's interests had not really been impinged upon. Even the $80 billion figure in new taxes and fees looked worse than it really was, since the industry was likely to recoup funds through the expanded role of government in paying for Medicare prescription drugs that was included in the Affordable Care Act. Perhaps the more general sentiment of those who came into conflict with PhRMA was expressed by Senator Bernie Sanders of Vermont who reflected: "The drug companies form the most powerful lobby in Washington . . . They never lose" (quoted in Hamburger, 2009).

[*See also* Health Care; Health Care Reform; *and* Think Tanks.]

BIBLIOGRAPHY

Angell, Marcia. *The Truth about the Drug Companies: How They Deceive Us and What to Do about It.* (New York, 2005).

Birnbaum, Jeffrey. "Drug Firms Woo Democrats, Helping Defeat Their Bills." *Washington Post*, 12 March 2008, http://www.washingtonpost.com/wp-dyn/content/article/2008/03/11/AR2008031102620.html.

Center for Responsive Politics (Opensecrets.org). "Lobbying: Top Spenders 2009." http://www.opensecrets.org/lobby/top.php?showYear=2009&indexType=s.

Center for Responsive Politics (Opensecrets.org). "Pharmaceuticals/Health Products." http://www.opensecrets.org/industries/indus.php?ind=H04.

Hamburger, Tom. "Obama Gives Powerful Drug Lobby a Seat at Health Care Table." *Los Angeles Times*, 4 August 2009, http://www.latimes.com/features/health/la-na-healthcare-pharma4-2009aug04,0,3660985.story.

Heaney, Michael. "Brokering Health Policy: Coalitions, Parties, and Interest Group Influence." *Journal of Health Policy, Politics, and Law* 31, no. 5 (2006): 887–944.

Olson, Laura Katz. *The Politics of Medicaid.* (New York, 2010).

Pharmaceutical Research and Manufacturers of America. "About PhRMA: Who We Are." http://www.phrma. org/about/about-phrma.

Stolberg, Sheryl Gay. "After Impasse, FDA May Fill Top Job." *New York Times*, 25 September 2002, http://www. nytimes.com/2002/09/25/us/after-impasse-fda-may -fill-top-job.html?pagewanted=2&src=pm.

Alex Waddan

BILL OF RIGHTS

The Bill of Rights of the United States Constitution consists of the first ten amendments taken together, especially the first eight, which identify specific individual rights. These amendments were proposed in 1789 by Representative James Madison, who was solidly backed by President George Washington during the First Congress. Ten of the twelve congressionally approved amendments were ratified by ten states, so as to take effect on 15 December 1791. Their general tenor is to protect individual personal, political, and religious liberties against infringement by government—principally by the national government in the original conception and down to 1925, when a process of "nationalization" gradually began that has brought protection against invasion by the states of most of the rights listed and of a number only implied by (or "penumbral" to) the rights specified. The philosophical foundation of the Bill of Rights is set forth in the Declaration of Independence's first sentences, especially the announcement of "certain unalienable rights" grounded in the "laws of nature and nature's God." The effectiveness of the provisions of the Bill of Rights in protecting fundamental personal liberties through American law is uniquely dependent upon the power of judicial review as exercised by the federal judiciary, with a last resort in the Supreme Court of the United States. The judiciary determines with finality, on a case-by-case adversary basis, the meaning and force of laws under the Constitution, considered as the supreme law of the land (Article VI).

The origins of the liberties protected, as well as the general theory of rights undergirding that protection, are of great antiquity and grounded in immemorial usage (or *prescription*) and natural right, although meaning and importance were sharpened by the debate leading to American independence, and gained impetus from the eighteenth-century Enlightenment, with its emphasis upon reason and the individual. It remains generally true, however, that the rights protected substantively were part and parcel of an inherited tradition of common law liberty and rule of law that originally emerged in medieval England, and the great monument of which is the Magna Carta (1215). Decisive for the continuity of this vision of liberty through law and limited government was the education of subsequent generations of lawyers, including the American revolutionary generation and beyond, by Sir Edward Coke's *Institutes* and *Reports*. After the Glorious Revolution, the English Bill of Rights was enacted as part of the constitutional settlement (1689). Following this precedent, the bill of rights concept today may be thought of as primarily American. But the liberties protected, and institutional modes devised for their protection, are deeply moored in Anglo-American political and constitutional history, especially in the seventeenth-century resistance against absolute kingship—thereby avoided in England, unlike in most of the rest of Western Europe—with fateful consequences for free government into the present. Indeed, the securing of personal liberty and free government through rule of law is a legacy quite self-consciously reaching beyond the Magna Carta itself, back to Aristotle and Cicero in distant antiquity.

Well before 1789, when, under heavy political pressure from the Anti-Federalists and public sentiment fearful that personal liberties might be imperiled by the new Constitution, James Madison proposed his amendments, virtually *all* of the rights to be included in the federal Bill of Rights already had been set out in bills of rights ratified by eleven of the original thirteen states plus Vermont. North Carolina, for example, refused even to consider ratification until religious liberty was secured, and ratification elsewhere was conditioned on the promise of amendments to protect personal liberty and the states' integrity. Critical rights already adopted by one or another of the new American states included no establishment of religion, free exercise of religion, free speech, free press, assembly, petition, right to bear arms, searches and seizures protection, requirement of grand jury indictment and petit jury trial, protection against double jeopardy and self-incrimination, and guarantee of due process of law. The Massachusetts Declaration of Rights (1780), drafted by John Adams, even included a reserved powers clause (Article IV) analogous to the Tenth Amendment's provision. The Massachusetts document also had the merit of partly replacing the admonitory language of *ought* used by George Mason in drafting the 1776 Virginia Declaration of Rights (the model for eight other states' bills of rights), with the imperative "shall" of legal command found (along with "shall not") in Madison's Bill of Rights.

The Bill of Rights was originally applicable only to the federal government. The truly critical rights, especially those stated in the First Amendment, were considered to be the heart of "the laws of Nature and nature's God" invoked by the Declaration of Independence. These, it was thought, must at all costs be put beyond the reach of majorities, because they were antecedent to the social compact and were the essential preconditions of free government itself. They were called "rights of conscience" and thought to be emblematic of the free human being (the Magna Carta's *liber homo*). Thomas Jefferson invoked them in the powerful opening sentence of the Virginia Statute of Religious Freedom (1786): "God Almighty hath created the mind free." There was virtually no case law and judicial elaboration of the meaning of the provisions of the Bill of Rights until well after adoption of the Civil War amendments—the Thirteenth, Fourteenth, and Fifteenth Amendments. A voluminous litigable process of "absorption," "selective incorporation," and identification of liberties occupying a "preferred position" (First Amendment rights), or as being "fundamental rights," began with the Supreme Court decisions in *Gitlow v. New York* (1925) and *Near v. Minnesota* (1931) and accelerated with *Adamson v. California* (1947). This has resulted in broad application of the Bill of Rights to state governments and even to private actions,

no less than to actions of the federal government. Today the liberty protected against invasion by the states under the Due Process Clause of the Fourteenth Amendment embraces all provisions of the First Amendment and nearly all provisions of the Fourth, Fifth, Sixth, Seventh, and Eighth Amendments. The principal exceptions are the Fifth Amendment's right to a grand jury indictment in criminal cases and the Seventh Amendment's guarantee of a jury trial in civil cases. In addition, there is a substantial expanse of additional personal liberty, especially race-related civil rights, protected by the Equal Protection Clause. This expansion includes strictly extra-constitutional rights (such as privacy and the right to travel) that an activist judiciary has discovered to be long-unsuspected implications of the express rights, or has construed as being included in the Retained Rights Clause of the Ninth Amendment and, perhaps, even hidden among the "Blessings of Liberty" spoken of in the Preamble to the Constitution.

[*See also* Constitution, US; *and* State Politics.]

BIBLIOGRAPHY

Adamson v. California, 332 U.S. 46 (1947).

Gitlow v. New York, 268 U.S. 652 (1925).

Lloyd, Gordon, and Margie Lloyd, eds. *The Essential Bill of Rights: Original Arguments and Fundamental Documents.* (Lanham, Md., 1998).

Near v. Minnesota, 283 U.S. 697 (1931).

Sandoz, Ellis. *A Government of Laws: Political Theory, Religion, and the American Founding.* (Baton Rouge, La., 1990).

Schwartz, Bernard. *The Great Rights of Mankind: A History of the American Bill of Rights.* (New York, 1977).

Veit, Helen E., Kenneth R. Bowling, and Charlene Bangs Bickford, eds. *Creating the Bill of Rights: The Documentary Record of the First Federal Congress.* (Baltimore, 1991).

Ellis Sandoz

BIN LADEN, OSAMA

(b. 1957). Osama Bin Laden was the mastermind of the largest and costliest terrorist attack on the mainland territory of the United States, on September 11, 2001.

He was born on 10 March 1957 in Riyadh, Saudi Arabia. His father, Mohammad Bin Laden, was of Yemeni origin, and had grown extremely wealthy as a building entrepreneur in Saudi Arabia before his death in a plane crash. Osama studied business management at the King Abdul Aziz University in Jeddah; he obtained no formal qualifications in theology, although there was a religious studies component in his course. However, he was notably influenced by a radical Palestinian activist, Dr. Abdullah Azzam, whose writings were in turn shaped in part by the views of the Egyptian radical Sayyid Qutb. These figures broadly justified a political, as opposed to merely spiritual, understanding of the requirements of Islam.

Bin Laden's own political activity took off as a result of the Soviet invasion of Afghanistan in December 1979. He made his way to the Pakistani city of Peshawar, in the vicinity of which a number of parties in the Afghan resistance (Mujahidin) had established headquarters and training facilities, and directed his energies at supporting the struggle against the Soviet forces. The Afghan war attracted radicals from a range of Arab countries, and from 1984, he ran a guesthouse for Arab volunteers titled the Beit al-Ansar (House of Supporters). The Afghan figures to whom he was closest were Gulbuddin Hekmatyar, amir (leader) of the Hezb-e Islami (Party of Islam), and Abdul Rab al-Rasul Sayyaf, the Arabic-speaking leader of the small Ittehad-e Islami (Islamic Unity). He also sought to become involved in the Afghan war more directly, and in 1986, he established a base in the Jaji area of Paktia province. It appears to have been shortly after this that he formed al-Qaeda. His activities in Afghanistan were cut short by two events. One was the Soviet withdrawal from Afghanistan, completed in February 1989, which altered the nature of the Afghanistan conflict. The other was the assassination in Peshawar in November 1989 of his old mentor Abdullah Azzam. Bin Laden at this point returned to Saudi Arabia, but was then not allowed to leave.

By this time, Bin Laden's geopolitical interests had stretched beyond the Afghan theater of operations. As early as 1987, he voiced support for the first Palestinian intifada (uprising), and in 1988 he had reportedly described it as the duty of every Muslim to prepare to defend the holy places of Mecca and Madina from the Jews. Nonetheless, what turned him ferociously against the United States appears to have been the deployment of US forces in Saudi Arabia as part of Operations Desert Shield and Desert Storm in the aftermath of Iraq's invasion of Kuwait in August 1990. He was finally permitted to leave Saudi Arabia in April 1991. He then revisited Afghanistan and Pakistan, before making his way to Sudan, where he settled toward the end of that year. In April 1994, he was deprived of Saudi citizenship—unsurprisingly, since he had fiercely criticized the Saudi rulers for allowing US troops to enter the kingdom. In May 1996, he finally left Sudan for eastern Afghanistan—in time to aid the Taliban movement in its push to Kabul, which it overran in September 1996.

The Taliban-controlled parts of Afghanistan provided a convenient environment for Bin Laden when planning attacks on a much wider range of targets. The first major attack of this kind came with coordinated strikes against the US embassies in Kenya and Tanzania on 7 August 1998. While the vast majority of those killed were local civilians, twelve US nationals lost their lives as well. The Bill Clinton administration responded with Tomahawk cruise missile attacks on training camps in eastern Afghanistan on 20 August 1998, which killed a number of Kashmiri militants but not Bin Laden. On 7 July 1999, the administration moved against Bin Laden's Taliban hosts, freezing all Taliban assets in the United States and banning commercial and financial ties between the Taliban and the United States. The United States also moved directly against Bin Laden at the United Nations. In Resolution 1267 of 15 October 1999, the Security Council demanded that the Taliban turn over Bin Laden "to appropriate authorities in a country where he has been indicted, or to appropriate authorities in a country where he will be returned to such a country, or to appropriate authorities in a country where he will be arrested and effectively brought to justice." Neither of these measures proved effective. A further strike against the United States came on 12 October 2000, when a motorboat mounted a suicide attack on the USS *Cole* in Aden harbor in Yemen, killing seventeen sailors. Then came the September 11, 2001, attacks on the World Trade Center in New York and the Pentagon in Washington, D.C.

Operation Enduring Freedom, launched by the United States in October 2001, obliterated the Taliban regime on which Bin Laden depended for support. Bin Laden himself came close to being captured by US forces at Tora Bora in December 2001, but managed to slip across the border into Pakistan. Over the years that followed, taped material would occasionally surface that proved that he was still alive, but doubts long persisted as to his exact location. These were resolved on 1 May 2011, when US President Barack Obama announced that Bin Laden had been killed by US forces in a strike against a "safe house" in the Pakistani city of Abbottabad to which he had been traced through a laborious intelligence operation. His body was flown in a US helicopter to Afghanistan, and then buried at sea from a US vessel in the Indian Ocean to deny him a resting place that could become a destination for radical pilgrimages. Computer material in the safe house reportedly confirmed that he was still actively involved in planning attacks on US interests at the time of his death. However, it is notable that the 2011 "Arab Spring" revolutions were inspired by liberal and democratic objectives, not the establishment of an Islamic order of the kind Bin Laden had supported.

[*See also* Afghanistan; Al-Qaeda; Terrorism, Domestic; *and* Terrorism, Middle East.]

BIBLIOGRAPHY
Bergen, Peter L. *Holy War, Inc.: Inside the Secret World of Osama Bin Laden.* (New York, 2001).
Coll, Steve. *The Bin Ladens: An Arabian Family in the American Century.* (New York, 2008).
National Commission on Terrorist Attacks upon the United States. *The 9/11 Commission Report: Final Report of the National Commission on Terrorist Attacks upon the United States.* (New York, 2004).
Randal, Jonathan C. *Osama: The Making of a Terrorist.* (New York, 2004).

William Maley

BORDER SECURITY

The implications stemming from a militarized and walled US–Mexico border to economies, people, and ecosystems both north and south of the border are complex, multifaceted, and highly controversial. Although no clear definition or agreement has been established on what makes up a "secure" border by those crafting policy, enforcing its laws, or simply watching as members of the public, there are those who insist that any change to immigration policy cannot happen until the border is secured and current immigration laws enforced. Others argue that border security initiatives must work hand-in-hand with a full revamp of immigration policy. And yet other camps take a more pragmatic approach: establish legalized work programs or legal paths to citizenship that are attainable—because, they argue, only about 1 percent of the migrants who are detained at the border are dangerous and have a record of criminal offenses in their past.

A Militarized Border. The US Border Patrol was created by Congress in 1924, but the militarizing of the border only took hold in 1996, with the creation of the Illegal Immigration Reform and Immigrant Responsibility Act, which called for the construction of a triple-layered "reinforced fencing" along the shared US–Mexico border. After 9/11, immigration and security were in the spotlight again, and in 2006 President George W. Bush signed the Secure Fence Act, giving the Department of Homeland Security the green light to build "two layers of reinforced fencing," and go forward with "the installation of additional physical barriers, roads, lighting, cameras, and sensors" on 700 of the approximately 2,000-mile-long stretch that divides the US and Mexico in more ways than one.

Predator drones, high-powered night vision scopes, helicopters, Border Patrol agents, National Guard personnel, rail cargo X-ray screening machines, trucks, remote surveillance cameras, thermal imaging gadgets, partially buried alarmed sensors, and drug sniffing dogs are among the militarized assets that play a role in "securing" the US–Mexico border. Thus far approximately 650 miles of industrial-strength fencing and concrete walls have been built along that 2,000-mile border with Mexico, a terrain that can range from sand dunes and canyons to mountains, rivers, and forested regions.

In June 2011 the Associated Press (AP) reviewed congressional transcripts, White House budgets, and reports acquired through Freedom of Information Act inquiries to find out what US taxpayers are spending on the US–Mexico border. Based on their investigation and calculations, they put the price tag at $90 billion over ten years. The return on investment to the taxpayers picking up that cost, the AP contends, is a mixed bag that includes fewer undocumented immigrants, little reduction of terrorism, and no interruption to the drug supply. Ten years ago, 1.6 million undocumented migrants were caught in a year's time. In 2010, the figure had dropped to 463,000. According to the AP, that reduction was due to factors such as the recession in the United States, which meant fewer available jobs in this country. In the eyes of federal officials, the drop is also indicative that fewer migrants are trying to cross. Others suggest the drop could be influenced by the rise in border patrol corruption, for which there is recent supporting data, and both the Department of Homeland Security and the US Coast Guard indicate that, as land border security maintenance with Mexico becomes more intense through increased technology and more walls, they are seeing an increase in migrants and drug traffickers moving by ocean off of San Diego. And the number of people getting caught by Border Patrol? The lowest of these estimates claim a rate of one out of every four undocumented immigrants.

Anatomy of a Price Tag. To understand how easily $90 billion may slip through federal coffers in a decade, consider examples of the prices of some commonly used militarized assets. According to the AP, the cost to deploy 1,200 National Guard soldiers for twelve months is $110 million. A single rail cargo X-ray screening machine costs $1.75 million. The average yearly salary of a customs and border protection officer is $75,000, and the cost for the services of a drug-sniffing dog is $4,500. Depending on their design and terrain in which they are installed,

estimates for the cost of border walls range from as low as $8 million to as much as $1.7 billion per mile. According to a February 2011 General Accountability Office (GAO) report, 837 miles of the border are under "operational control" by Border Patrol, which only accounts for 44 percent of the nearly 2,000-mile southern border.

Then, of course, there's the money that has already been spent as well, as the freshly approved funding intended to help the United States keep up its border security. By the time Homeland Security Secretary Janet Napolitano decided, in January 2011, to cancel a project that was intended to develop a technology-driven "virtual fence" called SBInet (part of the Secure Border Initiative [SBI]) due to ineffectiveness and cost, the department had already spent $1 billion on it. And in August 2011, a new bill was signed into law by President Barack Obama costing $600 million, which will finance another 1,500 border agents, bringing the number of total of department agents to 21,000. The monies will also be used to acquire more unmanned surveillance drones as well as to add border patrol stations on the southwest border. Both the Senate and the House approved the bill with the kind of swiftness rarely seen in Congress lately, and to the chagrin of many grassroots groups who had hoped, and failed, to see such bipartisan support for the DREAM Act (which would have offered permanent residency to the children of illegal immigrants).

Human Impacts, Ecosystems in Peril. The reliability of border walls in addressing or deterring illegal immigration is highly contested, but their negative impacts on the safety of those trying to cross it is a different story. Thousands of migrants have died as a result of border walls. Often it is not just the solo migrant worker who attempts to cross, but whole families, including the elderly.

As walls have been erected along urban regions of the border, migrants have rerouted their courses through unpopulated areas marked by scorching deserts, rugged mountain terrains, and strong water currents. Dehydration, exposure, and drowning have claimed approximately 5,000 migrant lives as a result of this rerouting. Migrants also fall prey to unscrupulous "coyotes" who sometimes rape and beat their customers and always demand higher border crossing fees than originally agreed to. Drug cartels have also complicated the landscape. Sometimes these gangs intersect crossings and either kill migrants not willing or able to pay additional fees, or they kidnap migrants and ensnare them in human trafficking operations.

Between 1995 and 2005, the number of deaths at the border crossing doubled because of erected border walls and spikes in urban-area enforcement. Today's migrants are nearly three times more likely to perish on their trek than those who crossed the border in 2006. As of 2011, approximately 129 people die for every 100,000 apprehensions.

The property rights of US homeowners whose land is near the wall have been breached on numerous occasions. Approximately 400 individuals, farmers, families, and city governments that own land along the Rio Grande on US territory have been served with condemnation lawsuits and forced to relinquish their lands to the federal government so border walls could be built. In other instances, the placement of the wall between Nogales, Arizona, and Nogales, Mexico has caused flooding conditions on the Mexican side, when annual monsoon rains hit the area in 2008.

Public and protected lands, including wilderness areas, have been destroyed to make way for roads and walls. Erosion, water supply, ecosystem damage, habitat fragmentation and loss, and species endangerment are consequences of the frenzy to build a border wall. Nature preserves are feeling the squeeze of the walls, too, putting species such as the Mexican gray wolf, desert tortoises, ocelots, endangered jaguars, and many other mammals, reptiles, amphibians, and birds at serious risk.

Is It Worth It? Director of Policy Studies at the Institute for the Study of International Migration at Georgetown University B. Lindsay Lowell says, "The public perception is misguided. One should never expect the border to be fully effective in cutting the number of unauthorized immigrants" (Aguilera, 2011). And, "as long as the per-capita income differential between the United States (over $30,000) and

Mexico (less than $4,000) continues to be so wide, it will be difficult to stop immigrants" ("US–Mexico Border Fence/Great Wall of Mexico Secure Fence").

Indeed, the Migrant Policy Institute has found that as many as 97 percent of migrants eventually find a way to get into the United States. Ironically, the greatest number of border apprehensions in some areas of Texas, for example, has occurred in regions without walls. With human lives, property right violations, ecosystems, and species at stake on one side of the ledger and a militarized economic investment that has cost US tax payers $90 billion in ten years on the other side, it is hard to see a positive societal return on investment on this wall on either side of the border.

[*See also* Immigration, Domestic Consequences of; Immigration, Legal and Illegal; Immigration to the United States; *and* Mexico.]

BIBLIOGRAPHY
"About CBP," US Customs and Border Protection website, http://www.cbp.gov/xp/cgov/about/, accessed 8 December 2011.
Aguilera, Elizabeth. "Is US–Mexico Border Secure Enough?" *San Diego Union-Tribune*, April 2, 2011.
Archibold, Randal C. "As Mexico Border Tightens, Smugglers Take to the Sea." *New York Times*, July 18, 2009.
Beaubien, Jason. "Drug Cartels Prey on Migrants Crossing Mexico." *National Public Radio*, June 7, 2007, http://www.npr.org/2011/07/07/137626383/drug-cartels-prey-on-migrants-crossing-mexico.
"Border Security: Preliminary Observations on Border Control Measures for the Southwest Border." United States Government Accountability Office, February 15, 2011, http://www.gao.gov/products/GAO-11-374T.
Herweck, Stephanie. "Our Worst Fears About Border Wall Come True," August 15, 2011, http://notexasborderwall.blogspot.com/2011/08/our-worst-fears-about-border-wall-come.html.
McCombs, Brady. "Border Bulletin: Crossing More Dangerous Than Ever for Migrants?" *Arizona Daily Star*, August 4, 2011.
Meissner, Doris and Donald Kerwin. "DHS and Immigration: Taking Stock and Correction Course." Migration Policy Institute, February 2009, http://www.migrationpolicy.org/pubs/DHS_Feb09.pdf
Mendoza, Martha. "Border Security Comes at a Steep Cost for the US." *The Associated Press*, June 25, 2011.
Noriega, Rick. "When is the Border Secure?" *Houston Chronicle*, May 15, 2011.

O'Neil, Shannon K. "Myths and Realities of US–Mexico Border Spillover Effects." *The Atlantic*, August 2011.

Preston, Julia. "Homeland Security Cancels 'Virtual Fence' After $1 Billion is Spent." *The New York Times*, January 14, 2011.

Preston, Julia. "Obama Signs Border Bill to Increase Surveillance." *The New York Times*, August 13, 2010.

"US-Mexico Border Fence/Great Wall of Mexico Secure Fence." Global Security website, http://www.globalsecurity.org/security/systems/mexico-wall.htm, accessed 8 December 2011.

Ana Arias

BUSH, GEORGE HERBERT WALKER

(b. 1924). The forty-first president of the United States, George Herbert Walker Bush was born on 12 June 1924 into a prosperous and politically active family. (His father, a partner in a Wall Street investment firm, served as a US senator from Connecticut from 1952 until 1963.) Upon graduation from Phillips Academy, Andover, Bush entered the US Navy, where he won the Distinguished Flying Cross and three air medals during World War II. At the end of the war, Bush attended Yale University, graduating Phi Beta Kappa in 1948. Bush completed his degree in economics in just two and a half years while serving as captain of the Yale baseball team.

In 1963, having made his own fortune in the Texas oil industry, Bush entered Texas politics, winning election as a moderate candidate running against a conservative faction for the Republican Party chair of Harris County, Texas. In 1966, he was elected to represent the Seventh District of Houston, Texas, in the US Congress. In Congress, Bush was a moderate Republican, supporting such measures as a 1968 national open housing bill, despite the strong opposition of his constituents.

Bush made unsuccessful bids for a US Senate seat in Texas in 1964 and in 1970. In 1971, President Richard Nixon appointed Bush as the US ambassador to the United Nations (UN); he served in this role until 1973. In 1974 he was appointed chief of the US Liaison Office in China. Upon returning to the United States, Bush became chair of the Republican National Committee, a position which he held at the peak of the Watergate crisis. With the unpleasant task of presiding over Nixon's resignation behind him, Bush was asked by President Gerald Ford to assume the director's post at the Central Intelligence Agency in 1976. Bush lifted the morale of the CIA at a time when it was beset by a crisis of confidence brought about by congressional reforms restricting the CIA's scope and authority.

In 1980, with James Baker as his manager, Bush campaigned against Ronald Reagan for the Republican presidential nomination. Bush positioned himself as the moderate challenger to Reagan, but withdrew from the race late in the primaries after Reagan appeared to have the nomination locked up. Bush accepted Reagan's invitation to become his vice-presidential running mate on the 1980 ticket. As vice president, Bush chaired several task forces, including those on drugs and terrorism, traveled to seventy-four nations as the representative of the United States, and was designated by the president to chair the crisis management team in the White House.

After defeating Senator Bob Dole of Kansas in early contests for the Republican presidential nomination in 1988, Bush began to put some distance between himself and the Reagan administration with regard to his policy views on the environment, civil rights, and ethics in government. Bush, however, reiterated the Reagan philosophy of maintaining a strong national defense and pledged "no new taxes" during the 1988 election campaign on his way to defeating Democratic nominee Michael Dukakis in forty of fifty states.

Bush's early reputation as a moderate, pragmatic politician resurfaced in 1990 when he broke his tax pledge and supported non-income tax increases in order to curb the growing deficit. Bush's sponsorship of a comprehensive clean air program enacted by Congress also served to indicate a different policy perspective from that of his predecessor.

On the whole, however, foreign affairs dominated Bush's policy interests throughout his presidency. He met with Soviet leader Mikhail Gorbachev three times to discuss a wide array of issues, including potential agreements on the reduction of strategic and chemical weapons, and the issuance of a joint communiqué condemning Iraq for the invasion of neighboring Kuwait on 2 August 1990.

The joint communiqué on Iraq reinforced earlier US–Soviet cooperation on a UN Security Council resolution authorizing the use of military force by US-led coalition powers if economic sanctions and diplomacy failed to bring about a withdrawal of Iraqi forces from Kuwait. Bush adeptly built a coalition of twenty-eight nations, including Britain, Germany, France, Saudi Arabia, the United Arab Emirates, and Egypt. Under Bush's leadership, the coalition consisted of 440,000 combat troops, of which some 200,000 were American forces (a stark contrast to the 2003 war with Iraq, in which the United States shouldered the vast majority of the costs and provided over 80 percent of the troops). President Bush ordered a US-led attack on military targets in Iraq and Kuwait when the government of Saddam Hussein showed no intention of abiding by the UN decree to withdraw Iraqi forces by 15 January 1991. On 17 January, a forty-three-day war erupted. With a decisive victory over Saddam Hussein's army, the Bush administration adhered to the UN objectives of limiting the military campaign to removing Iraqi forces from Kuwait and crippling Iraq's capacity for future aggression against neighboring states. As a consequence of the war, Saddam Hussein's army was estimated to stand at less than 20 percent of the capacity it had possessed in 1990. President Bush, Secretary of State James Baker, National Security Advisor Brent Scowcroft, and General Colin Powell, Chairman of the Joint Chiefs of Staff, agreed that venturing into Baghdad and removing Hussein from power would not only shatter the US-led coalition, but would exact a huge cost in American lives, with no assurances that the result would produce a democratic regime in Iraq. Ironically, despite the success of the Bush administration's containment policy regarding Iraq, the President's son, George W. Bush, the forty-third president of the United States, was determined in 2003 to intervene militarily in Iraq on the basis of flawed intelligence claiming that Saddam Hussein possessed large stockpiles of weapons of mass destruction.

The 1991 war with Iraq marked the second occasion in which the administration of George H. W. Bush resorted to the use of military force after diplomacy had failed to bring about the desired resolution to an international problem. On 20 December 1989, Bush ordered 10,000 American troops into Panama to restore order after General Manuel Noriega annulled the May 1989 elections, which had been won by US.-backed opposition candidate Guillermo Endara.

Bush's leadership was characterized by most observers as collegial, broadly consultative, and flexible. Friendship and loyalty were hallmarks of Bush's personal style and were central to his conduct of foreign policy, upon which his success as president will likely be judged to a considerable degree.

Two of Bush's sons, George W. and John Ellis ("Jeb"), followed their father into Republican politics. Jeb was elected governor of Florida in 1998, and George W. was governor of Texas before winning election as president of the United States in 2000 and again in 2004.

[See also Drugs and Politics; and Presidency: Governing.]

BIBLIOGRAPHY

Barilleaux, Ryan, and Mark Rozell. *Power and Prudence: The Presidency of George H. W. Bush.* (College Station, Tex., 2004).
Campbell, Colin, and Bert Rockman, eds. *The Bush Presidency: First Appraisals.* (Chatham, N. J., 1991).

Phillip G. Henderson

BUSH, GEORGE W.

(b. 1946). George W. Bush, forty-third president of the United States, was certainly not the only controversial figure to hold the office, nor the only one to win a contested election, nor the only president to wage a war that divided the nation, nor the only president to face a severe economic crisis, nor even the only president whose father had held the same office. The distinctiveness of George W. Bush lies in the fact that *all* of these descriptions fit his presidency. During his two terms in office, there were a striking variety of comparisons to other presidents.

Born on 6 July 1946 to Barbara and George Herbert Walker Bush, who later was elected the forty-first president of the United States, George W. Bush enjoyed the advantages of a family that was both politically and financially well connected. Prescott Bush, George H. W. Bush's father, was a Wall Street banker and senator from Connecticut. Barbara Bush's father, Marvin Pierce, was a publisher. She was distantly related to the fourteenth president of the United Sates, Franklin Pierce. George W. Bush graduated from Yale University and Harvard Business School. He was the first president to receive an MBA degree. After an unsuccessful run in 1978 for the House of Representatives, in the nineteenth congressional district in Texas, George W. Bush began a career in the oil business. In 1998, partly from profits from the sale of his company, he bought a share of the Texas Rangers, a major league baseball team. George W. Bush won the governorship of Texas in 1994 and was reelected four years later. As governor, Bush enacted a tax cut and supported educational reform.

When George W. Bush was nominated by the Republican Party as its presidential candidate in 2000, commentators compared him to John Quincy Adams, the son of the second president of the United States, John Adams. Bush received a majority of the electoral college vote while losing the popular vote. The election was marred by controversy over contested ballots in Florida and was only resolved by the Supreme Court in *Bush v. Gore*. When Bush took office, he was compared frequently to Rutherford B. Hayes (who served as president from 1877 to 1881) as well as to Adams, whose elections were also contested, and both of whom had difficulty governing effectively. Bush, however, adopted a limited but successful agenda that included tax cuts and educational reform. When President Bill Clinton left office, the end of the Cold War and the economic boom of the 1990s had helped produce a $5.6 trillion surplus. The new president proposed a tax cut of $1.6 trillion as an economic stimulus. At a series of town meetings, he contended "the surplus is not the government's money. The surplus is the people's money." The Economic Growth and Tax Relief Reconciliation

Act reduced tax rates in all categories and lowered estate and capital gain taxes. Critics complained the legislation favored the wealthiest Americans, and Democrats insisted the cuts be temporary and successfully demanded an expiration date for the tax cuts (later extended in the Barack Obama administration).

The president responded to critics of his tax cut that income inequality in America was primarily the result of educational disparities. The No Child Left Behind Act, which received bipartisan support, was designed to reduce the gap between wealthy and poor student performance through the use of required standardized tests and aid to low-income school districts. Bush defended this initiative as an example of the principle of "compassionate conservatism" which he had he discussed in the 2000 presidential election: "It is compassionate to actively help our fellow citizens in need. It is conservative to insist on responsibility and on results." The program, however, has been criticized by conservatives as an unacceptable intrusion of the federal government into a domain that had always been primarily a state and local matter, while liberals questioned the effectiveness of standardized tests to measure learning and charged that the program, which began with a $42 billion appropriation, was underfunded.

The terrorist attacks on September 11, 2001, abruptly ended a brief period of relative international calm after the end of the Cold War and immediately altered the course of Bush's presidency. The swift passage of the Patriot Act and the use of military force, first in Afghanistan and then in Iraq, led commentators to compare the president to Harry S. Truman. As Truman did at the inception of the Cold War, Bush set important precedents in what he designated as the "war on terror."

In his 2002 State of the Union address, Bush expanded the scope of the war on terrorism. He identified three nations—North Korea, Iraq, and Iran—as constituting an "axis of evil" through their support of terrorists and attempts to develop a nuclear arsenal. In June, President George W. Bush expanded upon these remarks. While he acknowledged the general success of the strategy of containment during the Cold War, Bush contended that this approach must be altered in the aftermath of the 9/11 attacks, since terrorists and "rogue states" would use nuclear weapons as a first, rather than last, resort. This approach to international relations and policy would come to be known as the "Bush Doctrine." The war in Iraq was largely justified on these grounds. Iraq was invaded on 20 March 2003; Baghdad fell on 9 April.

The Bush Doctrine was not the only innovation in the use of executive power. When President Bush signed legislation limiting interrogation techniques for prisoners captured in the war on terror, he reserved the right to interpret the legislation in light of what he determined were his responsibilities as chief executive. The signing statement was one expression of the theory of the "unitary executive" advanced by administration officials who asserted that the president, in his roles as commander-in-chief and chief executive, cannot be constitutionally limited by any other branch of government.

The unitary executive claims immediately became a flashpoint for critics of the Bush administration. Opponents argued that this interpretation of presidential authority was far too broad, even threatening to place the president above the law by ignoring both the Congress and the courts. Some compared Bush's adoption of the concept to President Richard Nixon's attempt to create an "imperial presidency."

Early in 2003, the president's successes mounted. At his urging, Congress passed a third tax cut. Bush now could claim that he had reduced taxes as a percentage of national income even more than Ronald Reagan. In November, Bush signed legislation providing for prescription drug benefits to retirees. While tax cuts have long been a major focus of Republicans, this issue had been one championed by the Democratic Party. Bush could claim that his legislation was the first major expansion of Medicare since 1965 and could point to the plan as an example of the "compassionate conservatism" he had pledged to follow in the 2000 election. Some commentators detected resemblances to William McKinley after Bush's successful intervention in the 2002 midterm elections. Like McKinley, Bush seemed to be building a large, majority Republican electoral base that might last for years to come. Like McKinley, whose achievements were often credited to his advisor Mark Hanna, Bush's were attributed to his campaign consultant, Karl Rove.

As the time to begin his reelection campaign approached, however, Bush was seen to resemble yet another president, Lyndon Baines Johnson. Two months after the invasion of Iraq, the president landed in full flight gear aboard the USS Abraham Lincoln and announced the end of combat operations in Iraq. Fighting in Iraq was not over, however. Remnants of the Iraqi army, as well as forces supported by al-Qaeda, staged numerous guerilla attacks on American forces. Reports of prisoner abuse by American soldiers at the Abu Ghraib facility, and the admission that no weapons of mass destruction (WMD) had been discovered in Iraq, led to criticism of both the administration's decision to go to war and its handling of the conflict. Despite the president's declaration of "mission accomplished" in May, there were signs of the same kind of quagmire developing that Johnson had faced in Vietnam.

In the 2004 presidential election, Bush won 50.74 percent of the popular vote and 286 electoral college votes, and Senator John Kerry took 48.2 percent of the popular vote and 251 electoral college votes. Several states were almost evenly divided between the two candidates. There was also controversy about the results in Ohio, reminiscent of Florida in the 2000 election. Shortly after the election, President Bush declared he intended to spend the "political capital" earned by his victory. In his 2005 State of the Union address, he proposed restructuring Social Security by permitting those working to invest a portion of their contributions in private, personal savings accounts. Despite his reelection victory and his command of the media, the public remained skeptical and President Bush was unable to develop bipartisan support for his plan.

As Iraq appeared to be rapidly moving toward full-scale, religious-based civil war between Sunni and Shia combatants, the president faced another crisis in August 2005. Hurricane Katrina struck the Gulf Coast. Nearly two thousand people died, and damage to property was estimated at over $80 billion.

Eighty percent of New Orleans was underwater as the storm broke through the levees. The sluggish bureaucratic response; the powerful images of human suffering, particularly at the city's Superdome (which was opened as a shelter for those left homeless by the storm); the inability of the president to publicly convey authority and compassion; and the incompetence of some of his administrators combined to form a vivid image of an inept leader very different from the one who appeared with firefighters in New York after the 9/11 attacks. The president's jocular offhand statement to the Federal Emergency Management Agency director Michael Brown ("Brownie, you're doing a heck of a job") became a symbol of government failure to respond to the first major "incident of national significance" to fall under the jurisdiction of the newly created Department of Homeland Security.

As a result of these setbacks, Republicans lost thirty-one congressional seats in the 2006 midterm elections, losing control of the House after twelve years. The president, while admitting he was chastened by the results, was nevertheless unwilling to undertake any major changes in his foreign policy. Despite a bipartisan report calling for gradual withdrawal of American forces from Iraq, the president announced a "surge" of 21,500 new troops to halt the violence in that country instead. While criticism of Bush intensified, especially in the newly Democrat-controlled House, Bush's strategy did stabilize the situation in Iraq.

President Bush, however, faced one final crisis. In September 2008, several large financial firms, including the government-sponsored mortgage lenders Fannie Mae and Freddie Mac, declared bankruptcy and were near complete collapse. The stock market plunged by the greatest percentage in thirty-four years. Similar financial crises began to appear worldwide. The pattern looked eerily reminiscent of the economic collapse in 1929 that began the Great Depression. Bush was now compared to Herbert Hoover. Like Hoover, Bush's commitment to economic deregulation made him susceptible to charges that his policies were responsible for corporate mismanagement. Unlike Hoover, however, the crisis

occurred at the end of Bush's term rather than the beginning. Bush moved swiftly and boldly to deal with the crisis despite his own personal distaste for regulation and government supervision of the economy in general. The president proposed that the Department of the Treasury purchase the assets of failing financial institutions, and requested Congressional approval of over $700 billion in government funds for a "troubled asset relief program" (TARP). Congress approved his measure with major revisions and Bush signed the bill on 3 October. The legislation was the largest single economic intervention in the nation's history.

The multiple comparisons of President Bush to previous presidents may be a symptom of the rapid changes of direction characteristic of media-driven politics. Positive images of the president, such as his moment of solidarity with firefighters at Ground Zero just after the 9/11 attacks, are reinforced by supporters with comparisons to their preferred presidents, while negative ones, such as his camaraderie with FEMA director Michael Brown after Hurricane Katrina, are used by critics to connect the president to previous inept leaders. Or, these shifts may be primarily a characteristic of George W. Bush's leadership style. In the 2000 presidential election Bush portrayed himself as a "uniter," but after the attacks of 9/11, Bush for the most part abandoned that role and instead relied upon governing from his party's base. Bush's general emphasis on making decisions swiftly and resolutely often led to dramatic changes in policy.

If, despite the controversy over the decision to declare war on Iraq and the problems of the postwar occupation, Iraq establishes a stable democracy, forcing other nations in the Middle East to reform their governments, then President Bush may well be compared eventually to President Truman, whose policies were the foundation for America's ultimate success in the Cold War. If not, the president is likely to be compared to Lyndon Johnson and his failures in Vietnam. If the 2008 presidential election is followed by others that repeatedly return Republicans to office, Bush may be judged to be a twenty-first-century McKinley. If the public rejects the expansion of presidential power in Bush's administration, his concept of the unitary presidency will be compared to President Nixon's efforts to create an "imperial" presidency.

[*See also* Al-Qaeda; Bush, George Herbert Walker; Conservatism; Republican Party; Terrorism, Domestic; *and* Terrorism, Middle East.]

BIBLIOGRAPHY

Abbott, Philip, Marjorie Sarbaugh Thompson, and Lyke Thompson. "The Social Construction of a Legitimate Presidency." *Studies in American Political Development* 16 (Fall 2002): 208–230.

Bush, George W. *Decision Points*. (New York, 2010).

Caesar, James W., and Andrew Busch. *The Perfect Tie: The True Story of the 2000 Presidential Election*. (Lanham, Md., 2001).

Gregg, Gary L., and Mark J. Rozell, eds. *Considering the Bush Presidency*. (New York, 2004).

Jacobson, Gary C. *A Divider, Not a Uniter: George W. Bush and the American People*. (New York, 2007).

Schier, Steven E., ed. *High Risk and Big Ambition: The Presidency of George W. Bush*. (Pittsburgh, Pa., 2004).

Skowronek, Stephen. *Presidential Leadership in Political Time: Reprise and Reappraisal*. (Lawrence, Kans., 2008).

Philip Abbott

BUSINESS-GOVERNMENT RELATIONS

It was President Calvin Coolidge who said, "The chief business of the American people is business." This is often misquoted as "the business of America is business." Eisenhower's secretary of defense, Charles Wilson, is often misquoted as saying, "What is good for General Motors is good for the United States." (He in fact said, "What is good for the country is good for General Motors and vice versa.") The popularity of the quotations—and even more, of the misquotations—serves as a reminder that business is seen by many as having a special role in American life, a role that is reflected in the political strength of business and its influence over public policy. The famous Yale political scientist Charles E. Lindblom (1977) shocked many (as he had a somewhat conservative reputation) by arguing that American business enjoyed a "privileged position" in politics. In fact,

business-government relations are more complicated than might be supposed. American culture provides bases for criticizing business—particularly financial institutions—as "big business" run by "fat cats" indifferent to the needs of ordinary Americans, including supposedly more worthy small business people. Political scientists are far from agreed that business rules America. A number of studies have concluded that relations between business and government regulators in the United States are more adversarial and conflictual than in other democracies including Sweden and the United Kingdom (Vogel, 1986). Frank Baumgartner and colleagues (2009) claim that resources (of which business possesses plenty) are not decisive in American politics because usually there are groups with resources on both sides of an issue; the 2011 fight over the charges that banks could levy on retailers for credit or debit card transactions is a classic example, with well-financed business groups on both sides.

However, Mark A. Smith (2000) argues that when American business is cohesive and united on an issue, it is most likely to lose politically. In order to sort through these apparently contradictory perspectives, it is best to consider business-government relations under several different headings: historical perspectives, campaign contributions, and lobbying and regulation.

Historical Perspectives. In a stimulating article published in 1978, David Vogel argues that the United States had experienced a unique historical pattern of government-business relations. In most countries, state power had been established effectively before the development of the modern corporation. In the United States, in contrast, the giant corporations, particularly the railroad corporations, had been established prior to the development of the national state, with capacity to operate effectively throughout the country. The railroad corporations had a capacity to issue commands nationally that were implemented throughout the country, which the nineteenth-century American state of "courts and parties" lacked. Vogel argues that, in consequence, American business developed a culture in which government was seen as the interloper, not the large corporation. American business executives distrust and dislike government to a degree not true of their counterparts in other democracies. Indeed, in some other democracies such as France, Japan, and South Korea, government is seen as a natural partner, not an enemy.

In another of his important works, Vogel argues that the relative power of business in the United States ebbs and flows (1989). The question of how to conceptualize the political power of business is, however, difficult. There is general agreement that in the 1950s and early 1960s, American business was poorly organized politically. A major study of political activity by corporations resulted in a very negative portrayal of the size and skills of their Washington representatives (Bauer et al., 1963). On the other hand, there were remarkably few serious political challenges for business in that period.

There is general agreement that starting in the 1970s, American business began a process of political mobilization that has continued to the present day. Although the factors explaining this mobilization involve a mixture including the degree to which corporations have been made sensitive to national politics by having government as a customer, and dislike of developments in public policy, there is general agreement that the major cause of this mobilization was the rise of a public interest movement critical of business. Public opinion polls registered a sharp decline in the public's trust in major corporations, and politicians, including President Richard Nixon, responded. The creation of new federal agencies such as the Environmental Protection Agency (EPA) and the Occupational Safety and Health Administration (OSHA) in 1970, which were able to profoundly affect business life in the early 1970s, produced a backlash in corporate America. Bryce Harlow, a Proctor and Gamble executive who also worked in the Nixon administration, warned of the danger that American business might be "rolled up and put in the garbage can." The Business Roundtable was created to represent the interest of the largest corporations, while existing peak associations—such as the Chamber of Commerce, the National Association of Manufacturers (NAM), and the National Federation

of Independent Business (NFIB), which represented small businesses—were rejuvenated. Corporations moved to strengthen trade associations representing specific industries, and large corporations increasingly opened their own offices in Washington, D.C., instead of relying on peak and trade associations or Washington law firms for representation. American corporations rapidly took advantage of new opportunities to exert political influence, such as the political action committee (PAC), created by the 1974 Campaign Finance Act. Although conservative dominance in periods such as the 1980s arguably reduced the need for business mobilization, there has been little and only temporary change in the levels of business political mobilization since. Although not all large corporations have Washington offices and PACs, that is clearly now the norm.

Campaign Contributions and Lobbying. As noted above, the surge in corporate political activity in the 1970s coincided with the creation of new opportunities for political action under the Campaign Finance Act, particularly the creation of the PAC system. It is not that corporate money was absent from politics prior to the creation of PACs; one of the reasons for the creation of the PAC system was that the Watergate scandal had unearthed many illicit payments from corporations such as the global conglomerate ITT. The PAC system relied on two major safeguards; contributions were limited to $5,000 per candidate per election, and all contributions had to be publicized. Corporations can pay the operating expenses of their PACs, but the money their PACs dispense must come in contributions from executives or stockholders.

Business soon became the dominant interest in the PAC system. In fact, corporations account for about 60 percent of total PAC contributions. Nine of the largest twelve PACs are corporations or business organizations. (The Association of Credit Unions is also in the top twelve.) The pattern of their giving differs considerably from that of other interests such as labor unions. Whereas unions consistently back a single party (the Democrats), corporate PACs distribute their money more pragmatically to politicians of both parties who are in a position to help the corporation or to shape policies that most affect that particular corporation. The balance of business giving to PACs shifts over time, generally flowing to the party and candidates most likely to win.

It should also be noted that there have been constant efforts to find additional ways to funnel business money to political campaigns outside the PAC system. In the 1990s, "soft money" contributions from corporate treasuries rather than from their PACs became as large as PAC contributions. Soft money had been allowed under the Campaign Finance Act in order to strengthen party organizations, which had seemed to be withering away in favor of candidate-based campaigning. Soft money had to be given to parties rather than to candidates, although parties would then use the money to help their candidates. Moreover, donations from individual executives from a company can amount to considerably more than the contribution from its PAC. Thus in the 2008 election year, Goldman Sachs donated $2,729,709, of which only $750,000 came through its PACs; the remainder was made in individual contributions. The vast majority of the money went to Democrats. The constraints on corporate spending on campaigns were swept away in 2010 by the Supreme Court, which decided in *Citizens United v. Federal Election Commission* that the First Amendment right to freedom of speech meant that corporations had the right to spend as they wish on promoting or opposing candidates. Republicans in Congress have successfully opposed requirements that this spending be disclosed and open.

Business corporations and organizations dominate Washington lobbying, accounting for a majority of the money spent on lobbying and the number of lobbyists employed in Washington. Business organizations such as the US Chamber of Commerce and the pharmaceutical manufacturers association, and individual corporations such as General Electric, Boeing, Verizon, and General Electric, took eleven of the top twelve positions in the league table of big spenders on lobbying. Business lobbying may be conducted by a corporation's own staff, by a contract lobbyist working for the corporation, by a Washington law firm, by the trade association representing the

industry, or by a peak association such as the Chamber of Commerce. The choice of which strategy to use is based on the issues involved. Clearly if the issue is a contest between defense contractors for a Defense Department contract, the lobbying cannot be done by a trade association. Coalitions are a major part of the Washington scene; interest groups including business will often look for a variety of allies to group under a common banner with an inspiring title such as "Coalition for Growth." Such coalitions often turn to a contract lobbyist to act as leader and coordinator of the group's efforts. Finally, if business is taking what is known to be an unpopular position, corporations may prefer the relevant trade association to take the lead and any opprobrium that results, rather than chance the corporation's own reputation.

There has been an increase in not only the number but the quality of Washington lobbyists. Studies today do not echo the critical remarks about the ability of lobbyists made in some earlier studies. Lobbying today also encompasses far more than the traditional "inside the Beltway" approach. Lobbyists working on a major issue may turn to opinion researchers, media consultants, and campaign organizers to plan an integrated campaign of lobbying, advertising, and either genuine or simulated (so-called Astroturf) mobilization of support for their position. Sometimes television commercials will be shown in only a few carefully chosen locations (often including Washington, D.C., itself) to create the impression of mass political concern to key opinion makers; the famous "Harry and Louise" ads made to support for-profit hospitals as part of their campaign against universal health insurance in the early 1990s are a case in point.

While there is little controversy over the dominance of the PAC system and lobbying by business, there is considerable unresolved argument about their consequences. As noted earlier, Baumgartner and colleagues argue that resources do not determine outcomes in policy struggles because typically there are groups with resources on both sides of an issue. Innumerable studies of the impact of PAC contributions have been undertaken but there has been no success in linking them to votes in Congress.

Is it really the case that business has been wasting its money on lobbying and campaign contributions? One response would be that the "resources are not decisive" argument made by Baumgartner and colleagues is dependent on both sides using resources so that if one side left the field, the other would win. It is also likely that methodological problems complicate these questions. As congressional scholars have always emphasized, votes on the floor are only a small aspect of the work of Congress. Committee work, bargaining off the floor, and the quiet insertion of detailed amendments to legislation of great significance to the interests concerned are also important. It could also be questioned whether there really are two sides in every important decision made in Washington. For example, although dissenting voices were raised by some regulatory officials, there was no mobilization of interest groups against the successful campaign of financial institutions against regulation of complex financial instruments such as derivatives. Yet the consequences of this failure to regulate—the global financial crisis that began in 2008—were enormous. It is difficult to argue that hard-headed business executives spend money on politics needlessly.

Regulation. One of the areas in which resources count is in the drafting of regulations. Typically legislation leaves unspecified much of the detail that really matters to interest groups. For example, the Dodd-Frank Wall Street Reform and Consumer Protection Act, which constituted the American government's legislative response to the global financial crisis, will require the adoption of over 250 regulations in order to give it force. The process through which government agencies draft, amend, and finally adopt regulations is in effect an additional "legislative" process that gives interest groups the opportunity to shape and even to block policy changes that the general public assumes were settled when the legislation was passed. Draft regulations are published in the *Federal Register* and opportunities are provided for comment. Only groups such as businesses with the resources to monitor what is happening and with the technical resources to develop comments have any chance of influence.

Interest groups that dislike the way a regulatory agency is heading can mobilize pressure on it from the executive branch (including from the White House) or from Congress. Financial institutions, for example, have mobilized supporters in Congress to cut the budget of the Securities and Exchange Commission (SEC), thereby reducing its capacity to develop and defend the regulations that Dodd-Frank requires. Regulations can also be challenged in the courts, a tactic often used by both business and its opponents in the public interest groups and labor unions.

The United States has had a pattern of unstable enforcement in regulation. To a greater degree than in other countries, enforcement strategy has swung between strict enforcement and permissiveness. Much of the writing on regulation in the 1970s and 1980s sought to explain why the United States had more legalistic and adversarial relations between regulators and the regulated than was the case in other democracies. Eugene Bardach (1982), for example, argues that regulators "go by the book" in order to avoid damage to their reputations if an unlikely catastrophe does happen, and it transpired that they had shown flexibility in enforcement. However, an older tradition of scholarship on American regulation had focused on the dangers that agencies would be "captured" by the interest they regulated and therefore become too lax. More recently, there has been concern that conservative Republican administrations and congressional majorities have worked to weaken strict legislation, through cutting funding for the regulators and blocking the appointment of heads to regulatory agencies who were expected to take a tough line with they businesses they would regulate.

The Structure of Business Government, Business Organization, and Governance. Regulatory policy provides an example of a broader point: business-government relations in the United States are vigorous and active, but not necessarily conducive to good governance. To a greater degree than in most other advanced democracies, business representation is fragmented and competitive. Most political activity and lobbying is undertaken by individual corporations rather than by trade associations. Several peak associations—including the National Association of Manufacturers (NAM), the Chamber of Commerce, the Business Roundtable, and the National Federation of Independent Business (NFIB)—claim to speak on behalf of business in general or large chunks of it. This fragmentation has advantages. It allows more voices to be heard and it may help constrain the potential political power of business. However, it has two disadvantages for governance. First, business organizations do not do the work of their counterparts in countries such as Germany in aggregating sometimes conflicting or competing business interests. Second, business organizations are not able to engage in constructive problem-solving if doing so could produce a loss of membership. A classic example is health care. At the start of the Clinton administration, the Chamber of Commerce recognized that the United States had a health care problem and started to engage with the administration in finding a solution to it. However, this engagement cost it members, who defected to the more conservative NFIB. The Chamber of Commerce, also under pressure from Republicans for working with the administration, disengaged, and the health care problem was left unresolved for another fifteen years at great cost to business, the primary source of Americans' health insurance. Similarly, it is rare to find examples in the United States of industries engaging in effective self-regulation thereby avoiding the need for government action; the Chemistry Council (the trade association for chemical manufacturers) is a rare exception. In contrast, in Germany, trade associations and business organizations frequently undertake actions such as self-regulation that are effective substitutes for government action, as are the Environmental Management and Accounting System (EMAS) programs.

Conclusion. American business-government relations are like the political system as a whole: complicated, vigorous, and competitive. The large amounts that business interests spend on government relations, especially on campaign contributions and lobbying, arouse fears that business has excessive influence. No one disputes that business dominates the interest group system. Yet the fragmentation of business and the fact that individual corporation is often set against individual corporation in political argument leads some scholars to discount this as a problem. At the same time, the fragmentation of business representation, and the limited authority of trade associations and peak organizations because of this fragmentation, limits the constructive role that business can play in governance. American business is well equipped to influence, but not well organized to help solve, the problems confronting American society.

[*See also* Campaign Finance and Reform; Financial Industry; *and* Think Tanks.]

BIBLIOGRAPHY

Bardach, Eugene. *Going by the Book: The Problem of Regulatory Unreasonableness.* (Philadelphia, 1982).

Bauer, Raymond A., Ithiel de Sola Pool, and Lewis Anthony Dexter. *American Business and Public Policy: The Politics of Foreign Trade.* (New York, 1963).

Baumgartner, Frank, Jeffrey M. Berry, Marie Hojnaki, David C. Kimball, and Beth L. Leech. *Lobbying and Policy Change: Who Wins, Who Loses, and Why.* (Chicago, 2009).

Citizens United v. Federal Election Commission, 130 S.Ct. 876 (2010).

Lindblom, Charles E. *Politics and Markets: The World's Political Economic Systems.* (New York, 1977).

Smith, Mark A. *American Business and Political Power: Public Opinion, Elections, and Democracy.* (Chicago, 2000).

Vogel, David. *Fluctuating Fortunes: The Political Power of Business in America.* (New York, 1989).

Vogel, David. *National Styles of Regulation: Environmental Policy in Great Britain and the United States.* (Ithaca, N.Y., 1986).

Vogel, David. "Why Businessmen Distrust Their State: The Political Consciousness of American Corporate Executives." *British Journal of Political Science* 8 (1978): 45–78.

Graham K. Wilson

BUSINESS SUBSIDIES

Government at each level—federal, state, and local—often provides direct and indirect subsidies to private businesses. A robust definition of what a business subsidy is would take into account any spending or government program or policy that provides payments or unique benefits and advantages to specific companies or industries.

There are five main categories into which the variety of business subsidies provided by the federal government can be grouped: direct spending, tax preferences, trade barriers, government-sponsored enterprises, and loans or loan guarantees.

Direct Spending. One estimate of direct federal spending on business subsidies (estimated by this author for the Cato Institute) places the number at more than $90 billion in fiscal year 2006. (That was before the expansion of many of these expenditures and the addition of new ones enacted in the wake of the recession and the crisis in the US banking system that began in 2007.) This estimate is relatively broad and includes direct subsidies and grants to specific companies, such as cash payments to farmers and research funds to high-tech companies for "commercialization" research (as opposed to basic research), as well as indirect subsidies, such as funding for overseas promotion of specific US products and industries.

The payment of cash to farmers is a classic case of how corporate subsidy policy plays favorites. Many farmers do not receive direct subsidies from the federal government. They instead go to only about one-third of the nation's farmers and ranchers. The money goes mainly to large corporate agribusinesses and the richest farmers. The richest 10 percent of all direct subsidy recipients usually receive around 65 percent of all subsidies.

Other spending by government may benefit businesses, such as infrastructure spending and the funding of courts to enforce contracts, but these forms of expenditures also benefit the population as a whole. Expenditures that benefit all companies and citizens generally and are usually not geared to a specific activity or industry would fall outside the general understanding of what qualifies as a business subsidy.

Other examples of business subsidies are as follows:

Economic Development Administration. The Economic Development Administration (EDA) provides grants and loans to state and local governments, nonprofit organizations, and private businesses in areas with high and persistent unemployment. The EDA's activities include technical assistance grants, which provide technology transfer assistance to private firms, and development grants, which fund the construction and improvement of infrastructure for the development and expansion of private industrial parks and ports. The EDA also funds the Trade Adjustment Assistance program, which gives grants to private firms and industries that are deemed to have been adversely affected by international competition due to increased imports.

Energy Subsidies. The energy supply programs of the federal government subsidize private companies in their development and deployment of new energy technologies and the improvement of existing technologies. These activities include "applied" research and development that benefit the companies directly—quite distinct from the "basic" research that government typically funds. Research areas include solar and renewable energy, nuclear energy, and fusion energy. The fossil energy research and development (R & D) program is designed to expand the technology base for private industry engaged in developing new products and processes. These fossil fuel programs also support company-specific technology development and demonstration activities.

Foreign Military Financing Programs. Estimated to be the largest single subsidy program for the US military weapons industry, foreign military financing programs support grants to more than two dozen countries for the explicit purpose of purchasing military equipment manufactured by US firms.

Appalachian Regional Commission. The Appalachian Regional Commission (ARC) was established in the 1960s to help reduce poverty in the thirteen states of the mostly rural Appalachian region by promoting private investment and "economic development" efforts, most of which amount to subsidizing business endeavors. Today, much of the ARC's budget goes to subsidizing various private construction projects, ranging from ski resorts to football stadiums.

Trade and Development Agency. The Trade and Development Agency (TDA) provides grants to fund feasibility studies and other planning services for major economic development projects in developing countries. Those grants go largely to governments and private investors in developing countries, which then purchase goods and services from US businesses. Thus, TDA projects tend to subsidize new business opportunities for large US corporations, such as Bechtel and General Electric.

Tax Preferences. Tax preferences are described by federal law as provisions in the revenue code that award specific types of corporations or individuals "a special exclusion, exemption, or deduction from gross income or which provide a special credit, a preferential rate of tax, or a deferral of liability." Many of those provisions benefit only a small number of companies or tax filers.

Not every deduction in the tax code should be considered a form of business subsidy. Any company may avail itself of certain tax preferences, such as the tax deduction for donations to charities. It is the tax preferences that go to particular companies or particular industries that can be considered a subsidy. The best example is the tax credit that awarded $170 billion in tax liability offsets to producers of ethanol and alternative fuels. Many of those tax credits go to only a few companies. One company, Archer Daniels Midland, the multibillion-dollar agribusiness based in Decatur, Illinois, produces much of the ethanol used in the United States and receives a large share of that tax credit.

Trade Barriers. Another type of preference that the federal government provides to certain businesses and industries is the imposition of tariffs and barriers to trade with foreign countries. There are currently tariffs levied on thousands of goods, ranging from fruit juice and leather products to pressed glass and costume jewelry. Other barriers to trade include import quotas on certain farm commodities. All such barriers have the effect of protecting domestic industries from foreign competition. They also have the effect of restricting the free flow of goods in the economy, leading to decreased supply,

forgone economic production, and higher prices for consumers. The cost to consumers of the most significant trade barriers was recently estimated by the US International Trade Commission at $3.7 billion a year.

The costs of these trade barriers rarely translate into a cost associated with a line item in the federal budget. Note, however, that the federal agencies that administer trade barriers, such as the International Trade Commission, do result in a direct budgetary cost.

Government-Sponsored Enterprises. During the twentieth century, the federal government chartered corporations for certain public policy purposes. The main government-sponsored enterprises (GSEs) are the Federal Home Loan Banks (sometimes called "Flubbies"), and the Farm Credit System (which consists of the Agricultural Credit Bank, the Federal Agricultural Mortgage Corporation, and the Farm Credit Banks). Those institutions were supposed to create markets for cut-rate loans to poor families and farmers, which, it was argued, would not exist in the absence of government action.

Technically, GSEs are publicly traded corporations—they have shareholders and boards of directors. However, those companies receive many benefits that actually make them more like government-protected bureaucracies. There is also an implicit understanding that the federal government will bail out the GSEs if they are ever in threat of collapse.

The Federal National Mortgage Association (Fannie Mae) and the Federal Home Loan Mortgage Corporation (Freddie Mac) were also both prominent GSEs until September 2008, when both firms were taken into conservatorship by the federal government. The implicit assumption by the markets that these firms would be rescued by the federal government if they were close to collapse proved to be a correct assumption in this case.

Loans and Loan Guarantees. The federal government also runs programs that lend money to businesses at below-market rates, oftentimes for projects that could have gotten funding in private capital markets. In addition, they also insure (or "guarantee") certain types of loans made by private lenders. One example of this sort of program is the Overseas Private Investment Corporation (OPIC), which provides direct loans, guaranteed loans, and political risk insurance to US companies that invest in developing countries. OPIC's activities often support the foreign operations of Fortune 500 corporations, such as General Electric and Citibank.

Another example is the Export-Import Bank (Ex-Im Bank). The organization's mission statement is quite clear in stating that its main purpose is to finance the purchase of US goods in foreign markets. The loans and guarantees that Ex-Im Bank grant to US companies qualify it as the underwriter of the sales of some of the biggest Fortune 500 companies, none of which would have trouble getting funding for worthwhile overseas projects. Boeing is usually the largest corporate beneficiary of Ex-Im Bank loan activity, leading many commentators to refer to the Ex-Im Bank as "Boeing's Bank."

Supporters of the Ex-Im Bank suggest that government credit is needed to level the playing field for US companies as they compete against foreign companies that receive support from their governments. Yet the Ex-Im Bank's own internal analysis has pointed out that fewer than one-third of all its loans and guarantees go to counter subsidized foreign competition. Instead, most of the Ex-Im Bank's loan and guarantee portfolio is geared toward providing credit for overseas projects and purchases that the bank states could not receive private funding. However, almost 100 percent of capital-intensive projects in developed countries are already financed by private borrowers. Many critics point out that these statistics indicate that the bank mainly serves as a handmaiden to a small group of politically influential companies.

Arguments in Favor of and Opposition to Business Subsidies. Supporters of federal subsidies to private industry often maintain that government support of business is in the national interest. For instance, government support is said to remedy market failure by assisting disadvantaged companies that cannot receive private funding to establish new businesses. Supporters of corporate welfare programs also justify business subsidies as a way to help maintain the competitiveness of certain critical industries.

Opponents argue that those justifications do not stand up to scrutiny. They argue that government is ill-suited to successfully picking winners in an economy. The function of private capital markets is to direct investment to industries and firms that offer the highest potential rate of return. The capital markets, in effect, are in the full-time business of selecting corporate winners and losers. Yet the underlying premise of many federal business subsidies is that the government can direct the limited pool of capital funds just as effectively as, if not better than, markets can.

In addition, supporters of government programs often suggest that corporate subsidy programs are necessary to remedy some sort of "market failure." Opponents of this argument note that at least some of the proclaimed market failures simply do not exist. For instance, supporters of the Small Business Administration—a federal agency that provides subsidized loans to small businesses, among other things—allege that the agency provides credit for firms that could not get loans in the private capital markets. Others point to research on the subject that has shown that small businesses do not face insurmountable obstacles to finding willing lenders and sources of credit funding.

One thing that opponents and supporters of business subsidies tend to agree upon is the political problem that these programs create. Once these subsidies are enacted, great lobbying effort is applied to maintaining them. This creates a potentially unhealthy relationship between the private sector and the public sector which may lead to future policy decisions that continually benefit some people and organizations over others. To put it another way, once you start subsidizing businesses, it's hard to stop.

[*See also* Business-Government Relations.]

BIBLIOGRAPHY

Carney, Timothy P. *The Big Ripoff: How Big Business and Big Government Steal Your Money.* (Hoboken, N.J., 2006).

Congressional Budget Office. "Federal Financial Support of Business," (July 1995), http://www.cbo.gov/publication/10341.

Slivinski, Stephen. "The Corporate Welfare State: How the Federal Government Subsidizes US Businesses." *Cato Institute Policy Analysis,* no. 592 (14 May 2007), http://www.cato.org/pub_display.php?pub_id=8230.

"Subsidyscope." http://www.subsidyscope.org. This project of the Pew Charitable Trusts collects and updates estimates of the various sorts of federal subsidies. The data is fully downloadable.

Stephen Slivinski

C

CABINET DEPARTMENTS

Although the framers of the US Constitution anticipated the development of federal departments, the document itself contains no list of them; they are statutory creations by Congress. Nor does the word "cabinet" appear in the Constitution. At most, Article II, Section 2, vests "executive power" in the president and states that the president "may require the Opinion, in writing, of the principal Officer in each of the executive Departments, upon any Subject relating to the Duties of their respective Offices." It provides for a measure of presidential control over departments, given that the president "shall nominate, and by and with the Advice and Consent of the Senate, shall appoint . . . all other Officers of the United States, whose Appointments are not herein otherwise provided for, and which shall be established by Law." That power of nomination, however, may on occasion be statutorily limited: "the Congress may by Law vest the Appointment of such inferior Officers, as they think proper, in the President alone, in the Courts of Law, or in the Heads of Departments." In addition, the US Constitution prohibits executive officers from serving simultaneously in Congress, unlike in some parliamentary systems.

In 1789, during George Washington's first year as president, the first federal departments were created: the Department of State (briefly named the Department of Foreign Affairs), the Department of the Treasury, and the Department of War. The position of attorney general was also created that year (although the Department of Justice, over which the attorney general now presides, was not established until 1870). In 1792, the position of postmaster general was established. In 1798, the Department of the Navy was added. It would take another fifty years—with the creation of the Department of the Interior in 1849—for a new department to join the list.

One important historical development took shape early, with President Washington: the president's collective consultation with what came to be referred to as his "Cabinet." The postmaster general, however, was not included in this group, and that practice would prevail until Andrew Jackson's presidency. Another Washingtonian imprint was the issue of the president's power to remove Cabinet and other appointed officials from office; this is a question unaddressed in the Constitution. That document also does not explicitly clarify whether Senate approval is required for dismissals, given its explicit role in advising on and giving consent to initial appointments. The statutes creating the early departments contained provisions for presidential removal, and Washington exercised that power by securing a number of resignations. John Adams was the first president to fire a Cabinet member, Secretary of State Timothy Pickering, without procuring a resignation. Andrew Jackson broadly exercised his removal powers, both to punish enemies and advance his political agenda, not just to remedy wrongdoing or incompetence. Jackson's actions generated controversy with his Whig opponents which lasted beyond his presidency, but the presidential position prevailed, at least until the post–Civil War Tenure of Office Act (1867), limiting Andrew Johnson's firing powers. The Pendleton Civil Service Reform Act of 1883 removed vast numbers of positions from political patronage and established the bipartisan Civil Service Commission to regulate hiring, firing, and conditions of employment. On political appointments, the Supreme Court has occasionally weighed in. Two cases are especially important. In *Myers v. United States* (1926), the Taft court strongly ruled in favor of the president's removal powers; in *Humphrey's Executor v. US* (1935), the Court backed off a bit, exempting "quasi-legislative" and "quasi-judicial" appointees, largely in regulatory agencies, from presidential dismissal.

Over time the size of the Cabinet has expanded. As of 2011 there were fifteen Cabinet members heading federal departments. In addition, presidents have also granted other individuals "Cabinet rank." The latter is largely symbolic, and varies by presidency. President Barack Obama, for example, designated the White House chief of staff, the administrator of the Environmental Protection Agency, the director of the Office of Management and Budget, the chair of the Council of Economic Advisers, the US trade representative, and the US ambassador to the United Nations as Cabinet members. Obama discontinued, however, the Cabinet rank of the director of the Office of National Drug Control Policy.

As for the vice president's relationship to the Cabinet, John Adams attended at least one of Washington's early Cabinet meetings. However, from 1791 until Woodrow Wilson's presidency (when Vice President Thomas Marshall presided over a few meetings while Wilson was away at peace negotiations in France after World War I), vice presidents were not Cabinet members. Warren Harding invited Vice President Calvin Coolidge to meetings, but neither President Coolidge's nor President Herbert Hoover's vice presidents attended Cabinet meetings. Franklin Roosevelt (FDR), however, established the modern practice, followed by all of his successors, of including the vice president in meetings; Dwight Eisenhower instituted the practice of having the vice president preside during the president's occasional absence.

Unlike in the British and other parliamentary systems, US presidents have generally felt unconstrained by Cabinet advice. At best, it is a discretionary resource and, increasingly, largely symbolic. Presidential use of the Cabinet has varied enormously over time, and even Washington grew disappointed with its advisory role during his second term. Jackson did not even convene a meeting of his Cabinet during his first two years as president, preferring instead to rely on a more informal "kitchen cabinet" of longtime friends and associates. Abraham Lincoln appointed a strong Cabinet—a "team of rivals" that included several individuals who had run against him for the Republican presidential nomination in 1860—but while they came to respect Lincoln's leadership, they were a contentious lot with whom the president often disagreed. Hoover added an informal twist: he encouraged his Cabinet members to attend daily games of "medicine ball" on the South Lawn of the White House.

More recent presidents have taken office hoping that greater "Cabinet government" might be attainable. Richard Nixon, Jimmy Carter, and Ronald Reagan all spoke publicly about it, but each quickly became dissatisfied with the Cabinet as the chief forum for policy discussion. Perhaps the last president to use the full Cabinet as a collective body for deliberation was Eisenhower, with meetings generally scheduled on Friday and often lasting several hours. For his successors, however, meetings have been held more sporadically, and often their primary purpose is to unveil programs and policies already decided upon, particularly with the aim of garnering media and public attention. Utilization of the full Cabinet has waned not only due to its increasing size (ten departments under Eisenhower versus fifteen under Obama, plus others who are granted Cabinet rank), but also because of the increasing influence of the White House staff as a source of policy advice and development. As late as FDR's first term, the staff was small, with only a handful of aides. However, following the creation of the Executive Office of the President in 1939, the staff has grown in size (some two thousand–plus aides in a variety of policy roles) and organizational complexity. In addition, key staff members such as the chief of staff, the National Security Council (NSC) adviser, and domestic and economic aides are often the most important conduits of information and advice to the president; so too for a variety of White House policy "czars." The centrifugal pull of a Cabinet member's own department also figures in. Many cabinet members take on the particular interests, perspectives, and organizational cultures of their respective departments. The "law of bureaucratic politics" often prevails, neatly summarized in Rufus Miles's aphorism: "Where you stand, depends upon where you sit."

Individual members of the Cabinet, however, still serve as important advisers to the president, and departments continue to provide input on policy issues. Recall, for example, the central role that two treasury secretaries, Henry Paulson under President George W. Bush and Timothy Geithner under Obama, played in the financial crisis of 2008 and 2009. So, too, for prominent secretaries of state such as Henry Kissinger, George Shultz, James Baker, Madeleine Albright, Condoleezza Rice, and Hillary Clinton. (Indeed, the four members of what is termed the "inner Cabinet"—the secretaries of state, defense, and treasury, and the attorney general—are usually prominent figures and important advisers.) Still, these individual Cabinet channels face strong policy competition from the White House staff, and the latter usually serves as the powerful "gatekeeper" for what ultimately reaches the presidential level. Presidential proclivities matter too. Sometimes relationships are close and trusting, but sometimes rapport fails to develop—witness Secretary of State Colin Powell's somewhat strained dealings with George W. Bush.

Cabinet members are especially handicapped as a source of advice early in a new presidency. This is a period when a president is most strategically advantaged to advance key items on the administration's agenda. Most of the Cabinet members heading departments are confirmed by the Senate quickly (although one or two will often linger due to some controversy). However, the sub-Cabinet serving under Cabinet secretaries (and the source of inner-departmental initiative and policy input) takes longer—increasingly much longer—to nominate and confirm. According to a 2003 study undertaken by the Brookings Institution of five hundred key sub-Cabinet appointments requiring Senate confirmation, it took 2.3 months under John F. Kennedy, 3.4 months under Richard Nixon, 4.5 months under Jimmy Carter, 5.2 months under Ronald Reagan, 8.3 months under Bill Clinton, and 8.7 months under George W. Bush just to reach the halfway mark in getting the sub-Cabinet in place. (A similar study by the *Washington Post* found an eight-month halfway mark in the early Obama presidency.) Not surprisingly, the White House staff is readily at hand to fill any void.

The creation of Cabinet councils—smaller groupings of Cabinet members in functional policy areas—has seemingly offered an important avenue for ensuring Cabinet-level input, while overcoming the problem of the Cabinet's increasing size. The establishment of the NSC in 1947 provided the original model. A domestic policy council started in the Nixon presidency, and an economic council first began under Gerald Ford (the Economic Policy Board). Names and organizational boundaries have changed over time. During Reagan's first term, the number of councils grew to seven. In his second term, they were reduced to three: one on domestic matters, one on economic policy, and the NSC. Clinton made much of his early creation of the National Economic Council (NEC), although a council had existed in that area for some time. One of George W. Bush's responses to the attacks of September 11, 2001, was the creation of a new council on homeland security.

The track record of Cabinet councils has varied enormously. The NSC's has been the most enduring. Harry S. Truman met infrequently with its members at the start, although regularly once the Korean War began. Its high point occurred during the Eisenhower presidency, when regular weekly meetings were scheduled. Both John F. Kennedy and Lyndon B. Johnson disliked the NSC's size and proscribed membership, and both preferred more informal venues: Kennedy's Ex-Com and LBJ's Tuesday lunches. Kennedy, Johnson, and their successors continued to convene meetings of the NSC, but they play a lesser role than under Eisenhower or Truman. Often they have served as venues for announcing decisions determined elsewhere. The array of councils in Reagan's first term proved a mixed bag: some met regularly and productively, others infrequently and with questionable policy results. Plus, in most cases, the White House staff acts in a guiding if not determinative role: executive secretaries of councils are key White House personnel, policy staffing is White House–centered, and agendas are set by the White House.

But if their role as sources of policy advice has somewhat lessened, Cabinet members and their departments are still important forces to be reckoned with. Cabinet secretaries are presidential agents in implementing policy, and departments play a crucial role in defining the details of policy rules and regulations. Members of the Cabinet—and sometimes their subordinates—often serve as the public face of the presidency and are frequent presidential spokespersons. When new initiatives are announced and crises confronted, whether foreign or domestic, members of the Cabinet are usually front and center along with the president. Cabinet members are often called upon to float trial policy balloons; they also sometimes serve as useful presidential lightning rods.

Particularly important are the questions of what the Cabinet "looks like," what constituency interests it reflects, and what broader signals are thereby sent. Pressure is especially exerted by a variety of groups during the president-elect's transition to office. A presidential concern for diversity in the composition of the Cabinet has been present since its inception, but has also grown. In the nineteenth and early twentieth centuries, geographical and political considerations weighed heavily in making appointments. Lincoln's "team of rivals" is most notable here, reflecting his interest in building a party coalition

within the Cabinet. As for geography, the secretary of the interior usually comes from the West, the secretary of agriculture largely from the farm belt, and regional balance factors in for the rest.

Social demographics have a long history in Cabinet formation, but they have become more encompassing as well. Jackson appointed the first Roman Catholic, Attorney General Roger Taney; Theodore Roosevelt the first Jew, Oscar Straus, to what was then the Department of Commerce and Labor. In 1933, with FDR's appointment of the first woman to the cabinet—Frances Perkins as secretary of labor, a post she held until the start of the Truman administration—gender diversity began to factor in. Eisenhower appointed the next woman, Oveta Culp Hobby, at the newly created Department of Health, Education, and Welfare (HEW) in 1953. There were no female members of the Cabinet—heading departments—under Kennedy, Johnson, or Nixon; Gerald Ford's appointment of Carla Hills to Housing and Urban Development (HUD) in 1975 ended that hiatus. In total (including Obama's initial appointments), Cabinet departments have been headed by a woman twenty-eight times (fourteen appointed by Democratic presidents, fourteen by Republicans); an additional twelve have held Cabinet rank.

Lyndon Johnson appointed the first African American to the Cabinet, Robert Weaver, at the newly created HUD. As of 2010, Cabinet departments have been headed by an African American on eighteen occasions, eleven appointed by Democratic presidents, seven by Republicans (Patricia Roberts Harris is counted twice: at HUD, and then at Health, Education, and Welfare [later changed to Health and Human Services]). In 1988, Reagan appointed the first Hispanic American, Lauro Cavazos Jr., as secretary of education. Departments have been headed by Hispanics nine times, five appointed by Democrats, four by Republicans. In 2000, Norman Mineta joined the Clinton Cabinet as the first Asian American. Departments have been headed six times by Asian Americans, four appointed by Democrats and two by George W. Bush (Norman Mineta is counted twice: at Commerce under Clinton, then at Transportation under Bush).

Although their policy import has, arguably, declined, Cabinet members and their departments remain an important political feature of contemporary American government.

[*See also* Presidency: Governing.]

BIBLIOGRAPHY

Borelli, MaryAnne. *The President's Cabinet: Gender, Power, and Representation.* (Boulder, Colo., 2002).

Cohen, Jeffrey E. *The Politics of the US Cabinet: Representation in the Executive Branch, 1789–1984.* (Pittsburgh, Pa., 1988).

Fenno, Richard F., Jr. *The President's Cabinet: An Analysis in the Period from Wilson to Eisenhower.* (Cambridge, Mass., 1959).

Humphrey's Executor v. United States, 295 US 602 (1935).

Lee, Christopher. "Confirmations Fail to Reach Light's Speed." *Washington Post,* 20 June 2003.

Light, Paul Charles. *Thickening Government: Federal Hierarchy and the Diffusion of Accountability.* (Washington, D.C., 1995).

Mackenzie, G. Calvin. "The Real Invisible Hand: Presidential Appointees in the Administration of George W. Bush." *PS: Political Science and Politics* 35 (1 March 2002): 27–30.

Mackenzie, G. Calvin, ed. *The In-and-Outers: Presidential Appointees and Transient Government in Washington.* (Baltimore, 1987).

Mackenzie, G. Calvin, ed. *Innocent until Nominated: The Breakdown of the Presidential Appointments Process.* (Washington, D.C., 2001).

Myers v. United States, 272 US 52 (1926).

Reich, Robert B. *Locked in the Cabinet.* (New York, 1997).

Warshaw, Shirley Anne. *Powersharing: White House-Cabinet Relations in the Modern Presidency.* (Albany, N.Y., 1996).

John P. Burke

CAMPAIGN ADVERTISING

Perhaps few other aspects of electoral campaigns have received more attention from scholars or more ire from citizens than the televised political advertisement. The reasons for both are far from obscure. Campaign advertising is one of the primary mechanisms through which campaigns seek to communicate with voters, and thus is the single largest expenditure in most modern campaigns for federal office. Although campaigns are increasingly turning to new media venues for campaign communication, the volume of ads on TV appears to be stable or increasing, and in fact, the 2010 election featured record-breaking volume and spending on TV campaign ads, suggesting that the traditional televised spot is not going away anytime soon. In addition, there is evidence that campaign ads have become more negative and that news media have become more focused on negative campaigning associated with political spots in recent decades.

These trends fuel important normative and empirical questions about the role of advertising in American elections. To what extent does advertising (and negative advertising in particular) affect turnout and persuasion? Are campaign ads harmful to American democracy or are they in fact useful for citizen decision-making? What are the long-term consequences of negative advertising on the electorate? This article will touch briefly on what we do and do not know about political advertising in elections, with a focus on negativity.

Conventional wisdom among practitioners is that negativity works, but in order to understand the influence of advertising, we first must specify what we mean by "works." In what ways do negative ads matter? Campaign ads are, by definition, political propaganda designed to persuade citizens to support the favored candidate over the opponent. So are ads effective in influencing the votes that individuals cast? Early empirical work called into question the effectiveness and persuasive value of campaign ads, but more recent work reminds us that competing streams of information are likely to cancel each other out, and therefore, the place to be looking for evidence of persuasion is when one side has a comparative advantage in terms of the volume of messages. Studies of persuasion find that advertising does indeed lower favorability ratings of the targeted candidate, and persuasion affects even those with low political knowledge. Further, advertising advantages appear to benefit challengers more than incumbent candidates. Other studies that investigate the extent to which negativity carries a "backlash" effect—defined as a decline in support for the sponsoring candidate of an attack—largely find, however, that candidates sponsoring negativity do suffer from backlash. As Lau, Sigelman, and Rovner (2007) argue, rarely do scholars estimate the "net" effect of persuasive attacks (meaning the decline in opponent support minus backlash to the favored candidate), and therefore evidence attesting to overall (net) influence of candidate-sponsored negativity is still a bit tenuous (but see especially Brooks and Murov, forthcoming). Empirically, however, candidates air the fewest number of attack ads compared to interest groups and political parties, often preferring to leave the dirty work to others. More importantly, some research suggests that ads sponsored by interest groups may be more persuasive than ads sponsored by candidates, perhaps in part due to the fact that candidates are less likely to be punished for interest group attacks on their behalf. In a campaign finance landscape without strict disclosure laws, and thus conducive to increased interest group involvement, these findings may work to further increase the amount of negativity aired on behalf of candidates from independent groups.

Another way in which negative ads may "work" is in their ability to affect voter turnout in US elections. A wealth of academic research has focused on precisely this question, with the early experimental evidence suggesting that negativity demobilizes the American electorate (see especially Ansolabehere and Iyengar, 1995). Many have challenged this premise, arguing that advertising in fact mobilizes the electorate. Still others, including a meta-analysis assessing the state of the field, argue that negative advertising has no effect on participation. In short, although the evidence on whether advertising and negativity affect voter turnout is mixed, as Lau, Sigelman, and Rovner put it, "*The research literature provides no general support for the hypothesis that negative political campaigning depresses voter turnout.* If anything, negative campaigning more frequently appears to have a slight mobilizing effect" (2007, p. 1184, emphasis in original).

There is more scholarly consensus with regard to the effect of negativity and campaign spending on recall, knowledge, and interest. More specifically, research suggests that negative spots are more memorable than positive ones. Despite universal claims that citizens dislike negative ads, increased recall for negativity can be beneficial given negative ads contain more substantive information than positive ads and tend to stimulate higher interest in campaigns, conveying that something important is at stake. Perhaps even more importantly, scholars argue that increased campaign spending improves democratic quality by increasing citizen knowledge, and research examining advertising volume in particular suggests that the boost provided by advertising is concentrated among precisely those citizens who need it most: those with less preexisting information. As such, advertising along with increased spending and negativity can have substantial democratic benefits in the short term.

What about the potential long-term consequences of negative advertising on the electorate? Does negative advertising corrode citizen attitudes toward the political system and lower trust in government? Although perceptions of negativity have been linked to lower efficacy and lower trust in government, studies that assess the influences of negative advertising itself—though rare—tend to find little evidence suggesting that ad negativity has a harmful influence on political trust or political efficacy. Though the extent to which the actual tone of advertising is linked to perceptions of negativity has been debated, recent work suggests that the "true" tone of advertising does in fact influence citizen perceptions, but views of negativity are by no means a mirror reflection of reality. And in fact, news media speculation and focus on the campaign strategy of political ads may contribute to increased perceptions of negativity.

In summary, what we know about political advertising and negative ads in particular suggests that the short-term consequences of advertising are largely beneficial to democratic health. Advertising and negativity increase the quality of campaign discussion, raising awareness and political interest, leading to more informed citizens, especially among the citizenry that pays the least attention to politics.

Research largely suggests that advertising has the ability to persuade, but the net effect, taking into account backlash for going negative, is not fully understood. There is little evidence to suggest that negative advertising has a large depression effect on voter turnout in elections, and in fact it may occasionally boost participation. In the long run, there is weak evidence suggesting that attack ads, by increasing perceptions of negativity, may decrease political efficacy and trust in government, but it is emphatically not the case that this trend can be blamed on negative ads alone. To put it simply, then, scholarly work suggests that campaign advertising and negativity play a vital role in elections, with largely positive benefits for the democratic citizenship.

[*See also* Media and Politics; *and* Political Parties, American.]

BIBLIOGRAPHY

Ansolabehere, Stephen and Shanto Iyengar. *Going Negative: How Attack Ads Shrink and Polarize the Electorate.* (New York, 1995.)

Brooks, Deborah Jordan, and Michael Murov. "Assessing Accountability in a Post-*Citizens United* Era: The Effects of Attack Ad Sponsorship by Unknown Independent Groups." *American Politics Research*, forthcoming.

Coleman, John J., and Paul F. Manna. "Congressional Campaign Spending and the Quality of Democracy." *Journal of Politics* 62, no. 3 (2000): 757–789.

Fowler, Erika Franklin, and Travis N. Ridout. "Advertising Trends in 2010." *The Forum* 8, no. 4 (2010): http://www.bepress.com/forum/vol8/iss4/art4.

Franz, Michael, Paul Freedman, Kenneth Goldstein, and Travis Ridout. *Campaign Advertising and American Democracy.* (Philadelphia, 2008).

Freedman, Paul and Ken Goldstein. "Measuring Media Exposure and the Effects of Negative Campaign Ads." *American Journal of Political Science* 43 (1999): 1189–1208.

Freedman, Paul, Michael M. Franz, and Kenneth Goldstein. "Campaign Advertising and Democratic Citizenship." *American Journal of Political Science* 48 (2004): 723–741.

Geer, John Gray. *In Defense of Negativity: Attack Ads in Presidential Campaigns.* (Chicago, 2006).

Lau, Richard R., Lee Sigelman, and Ivy Brown Rovner. "The Effects of Negative Political Campaigns: A Meta-Analytic Reassessment." *Journal of Politics* 69, no. 4 (2007): 1176–1209.

Ridout, Travis N., and Erika Franklin Fowler. "Explaining Perceptions of Advertising Tone." *Political Research Quarterly* (December 2010): doi: 10.1177/1065912910388189. Published online before print.

Ridout, Travis N., and Michael M. Franz. *The Persuasive Power of Campaign Advertising.* (Philadelphia, 2011).

Zaller, John R. 1996. "The Myth of Massive Media Impact Revisited." In *Political Persuasion and Attitude Change,* edited by Diana C. Mutz, Paul M. Sniderman, and Richard A. Brody. (Ann Arbor, Mich., 1996).

Erika Franklin Fowler

CAMPAIGN FINANCE AND REFORM

The question of who pays for political campaigns in the United States has never been much debated. The answer is that private citizens and groups finance campaigns, not the state. However, the question of how much private citizens and groups ought to be allowed to contribute for electioneering has been at the center of a very great debate in American politics.

The American institutional features of separation of powers and federalism make campaign finance complex and at times very confusing. First, the Constitution mandates separate elections for the president (executive) and Congress (legislative). Second, the Constitution mandates fixed, staggered terms of the nationally elected bodies so that some facet of the government is conducting an election campaign during every autumn of an even-numbered year, or every two years. This means that unlike parliamentary systems, campaigns are not necessarily integrated for the executive and legislative branches. Therefore, the donors, issues, and techniques used in campaigns vary considerably. Third, federalism means that each of the individual fifty states determines its own institutional arrangements, election timetables, and campaign finance regulatory system for all offices below the federal level. Because of this last complication, the present essay will deal only with the federal campaign finance system.

Geographic dispersion, mixed electoral systems for party nominations, and a backseat on the progressive movement's agenda meant that campaign finance was lightly regulated, if at all, until the modern era. The Federal Corrupt Practices Act of 1925 did require disclosure of spending by any committee for a federal candidate, up to its $5,000 limit. However, the Act did not limit how many committees a candidate or party could have operating on his behalf and the reporting mechanism left everything to be desired, as it required reporting to officials of the House and Senate who served at the pleasure of the elected membership. Publicity surrounding large donations in the 1968 presidential race (to both major-party candidates) proved the catalyst for more comprehensive reform in the 1970s.

Campaign Finance Regulation, 1974–2002. The post-Watergate campaign finance system contained several very important provisions which changed the landscape of campaign finance entirely in the United States, even to this day. First, starting with the 1976 elections, an independent regulatory agency in the executive branch—the Federal Election Commission (FEC)—was charged with overseeing the implementation and enforcement of campaign finance laws at the federal level. This not only gave the law more credibility, it created a data repository that has been used extensively by journalists, academics, and candidates to understand and publicize the relationships at the root of the fundraising enterprise. Second, the law created two distinct campaign fi-nance regimes—one for campaigns for the presidency, the other for campaigns for Congress. The presidential system includes public money, funded through a check-off box on federal income tax returns, which subsidizes candidates for the general and primary elections, provided they abide by strict fundraising and spending limits. Public money is also given to the two major parties to defray part of the expenses of their national presidential nominating conventions. The congressional system, on the other hand, has no public money provisions whatsoever. The original legislation imposed upon congressional candidates had fundraising and spending limits similar to presidential candidates, but without the reward of obtaining a subsidy for doing so.

Buckley v. Valeo, 1976. Reformers were pleased with the outcome of the post-Watergate legislation.

However, the law came under immediate constitutional challenge because of the First Amendment to the Constitution. While reformers were concerned with the corruption, real or implied, of officeholders by wealthy donors, status quo supporters worried about Americans' free speech rights. On the one hand, it might be of concern that someone with a great deal of money—enough to finance a candidate's campaign—would have more sway over the elected official than the constituents that candidate would eventually represent. On the other hand, if a person has a significant amount of money left after having paid his or her taxes and debts, that person is theoretically free to do what he or she wishes with the remaining funds—buy a yacht, enjoy exotic vacations, or purchase political advertising in support of a favorite candidate or cause. The limitations on how individuals, candidates and interest groups use their money to purchase campaign speech communications triggered the landmark case, *Buckley v. Valeo*, which agreed with both arguments in part. The Supreme Court found that limits on how much an individual may spend on political speech per year—were inconsistent with free speech rights, and therefore unconstitutional. The court also struck down spending limits for congressional campaigns, especially in light of the lack of public funding as an incentive as in the presidential arena. However, the Court was also persuaded that the appearance of corruption from unlimited contributions to candidates was inappropriate. Hence, the Court held that while limitations on contributions to candidates, interest groups, and political parties were constitutional, as they prohibited undue influence over a particular target, the overall absolute limitations on what an individual may spend were not. The Court essentially created the category of independent expenditures, which are monies spent by individuals or interest groups without the candidate's knowledge or consent. Further, the court sanctioned the use of separate, segregated funds (via political action committees, or PACs) as a way for interest groups to spend independently but without undue influence from one employee (or owner) or direct use of union dues or corporate profits. This decision did not allow political parties to use independent expenditures (that would be reversed in *Colorado Republican Federal Campaign Committee v. Federal Election Commission*).

Enter Soft Money. While the court's "compromise" seemed to satisfy all sides for a time, those still laboring under restrictions looked for ways around the law. Political parties were frustrated with the fact that their fundraising and expenditures were limited in campaigns, putting them at a disadvantage compared to candidates and interest groups. Fortunately, some wealthy donors expressed that they would gladly give more to the party if they could. This would allow the parties to centralize their election efforts, prioritize campaigns in terms of resource need instead of visibility, and allow for efficient and effective communications between supporters and party leaders. The idea for what became known as "soft money" was that nonfederal money which was prohibited from being spent on federal election efforts could instead be spent on non-election efforts, such as party-building and issue advocacy. Nonfederal money included money from individual donors beyond the law's limits, money from union dues, and money from corporations' operating accounts. Party-building efforts included the expenses associated with running any day-to-day business of the party, even outside the traditional campaign season of the election cycle. This included office rent, office furniture and equipment, utilities, and staff salaries. If nonfederal, or soft, money could be used for these expenses, more "hard" or federally regulated money could be used for campaigning. In addition, while hard money was to be spent to advocate for candidates, soft money could be spent to advocate for issues, as long as the election or defeat of a candidate was not explicitly called for. The fine line here was the so-called "magic words" test found in a footnote in the *Buckley* decision, which distinguished the allowable uses of hard and soft money.

Issue advocacy became a dominant campaign vehicle between 1996 and 2002. Complaints about the use of this type of spending grew exponentially. The chief concern was that as the money was nonfederal, its disclosure was incomplete or nonexistent.

In other words, if individuals or groups were not expressly advocating for an election or defeat, the FEC had no authority to oversee their actions. To control this development—especially the pretense that issue ads mentioning the name of a local member of Congress and his or her views on a key issue just days before votes were to be cast was not election speech— Congress passed the Bipartisan Campaign Reform Act of 2002 (BCRA), previously known as McCain-Feingold for the two major Senate sponsors of the bill (Republican John McCain and Democrat Russ Feingold).

Bipartisan Campaign Reform Act (BCRA). BCRA was meant to level the playing field in favor of candidates and away from wealthy individuals and groups. First, BCRA indexed several of the contribution limits to inflation. This was especially important for the limits on individual contributions, whose purchasing power had eroded since 1974. While individuals could now give more money directly to candidates and political parties, the contribution limits to groups (and from groups/PACs) remained unchanged. Ultimately, inflation indexing would give donors more incentive to fund candidates and parties rather than interest groups. Increases in individual contribution limits, it was theorized, should give people less motivation to spend money for issue advocacy. Second, BCRA confronted the "sham" issue advocacy problem by changing the definition of election speech from the "magic words" test to the use of a candidate's name or likeness in broadcast communications sixty days before a general election or thirty days before a primary election. That is, any use of a candidate's name or image was considered election speech and must be paid for with limited, disclosed hard money. This was a very popular measure with many officeholders, as they felt issue advocacy allowed too much of the election dynamics to be directed by outsiders who remained anonymous. BCRA also tackled the problem of individually wealthy candidates spending personal funds on their own campaigns, to the detriment of their averagely endowed opponents. Known as the Millionaire's Amendment,. BCRA tried to equalize the playing field by allowing candidates whose opponents were self-financed wealthy individuals (millionaires) to have increased donor limits, no limits on spending by the parties in coordination with them, and stricter disclosure on the part of the wealthy candidates. Once a wealthy candidate spent $350,000 of his or her own money and the less wealthy candidate was outspent, the special provisions would kick in. In 2008, however, the Supreme Court struck down all of the provisions of the amendment in *Davis v. Federal Election Commission* in a 5–4 vote. Therefore, the amendment was only in force for the 2004 and 2006 election cycles.

Issue Advocacy vs. Election Advocacy: *Citizens United v. Federal Election Commission.* BCRA's most important provision concerning the regulation of electioneering communications was struck down in early 2010 by the Supreme Court in the *Citizens United v. Federal Election Commission* decision. BCRA insisted that any communication with the name or likeness of a candidate for federal office proximate to an election was campaign speech and should be paid for with disclosed and limited hard money contributions. Citizens United, a nonprofit corporation, held that their film about Hillary Clinton was not campaign speech, and therefore was not subjected to BCRA's limitations. The court agreed, but in a broad way that negates most of the original intent of BCRA. The majority argued that there was no way to enforce the provisions on corporate communications without having a chilling effect on free speech. Because of the ambiguities the court anticipated, they believed the FEC would have to exercise prior restraint on corporate communications, and this scenario was not acceptable to the majority. Thus, corporations would no longer be suspect in exercising speech rights, but rather treated as individuals would be. The result was that in the 2010 elections, some corporations chose to air political commercials through entities now called "Super PACs" designed to influence the outcome of the midterm congressional elections. While Super PACs have agreed to disclose their donors and spending, as designated 'independent expenditure' only committees (not contributing to or coordinating with any

candidate) but donors have no limits on their contribution amounts whatsoever.

[*See also* Elections and Electoral Behavior; *and* Political Parties, American.]

BIBLIOGRAPHY

"The Campaign Finance Institute," accessed 20 December 2011, http://www.cfinst.org/.

"The Center for Responsive Politics," accessed 20 December 2011, http://www.opensecrets.org/index.php.

Citizens United v. Federal Election Commission, 130 U.S. 876 (2010).

Colorado Republican Federal Campaign Committee v. Federal Election Commission 518 U.S. 604 (1996).

Davis v. Federal Election Commission, 554 U.S. 724 (2008).

La Raja, Raymond J. *Small Change: Money, Political Parties, and Campaign Finance Reform.* (Ann Arbor, Mich., 2008).

"The National Institute on Money in State Politics," accessed 20 December 2011, http://www.followthemoney.org/.

Steen, Jennifer A. *Self-Financed Candidates in Congressional Elections.* (Ann Arbor, Mich., 2006).

Robin Kolodny

CAPITALISM

Despite the suffix *-ism*, "capitalism" refers neither to an ideology nor a movement. It refers, if anything, to a set of economic and legal institutions, which together make the production of material objects for private profit the normal course of economic organization. In short, it is a mode of production, a way of organizing economic activity.

The word itself is of recent vintage, having been coined by William Makepeace Thackeray in the mid-nineteenth century. Capitalism may be said to have originated in Western Europe sometime in the two hundred years or so following the Black Death of 1349. Like much else about the subject, this is a controversial assertion, for exactly what constitutes capitalism—certain features of which existed in earlier periods of history and on other continents—is open to debate. Capitalism as we now know it, however, arose in Western Europe between four and six centuries ago.

Capitalism is a system marked by (1) private property in the means of production, whether land, tools, machines, or ideas; (2) a legal framework entitling the owner of those means to the profits they generate, subject only to nonarbitrary taxation; (3) a framework of contracts within which sales and purchases relevant to the production activity can be carried out, especially the right to hire and fire workers; and (4) the legal right of the owner to dispose of the profits as well as the property generating those profits in any way he or she chooses, subject to well-specified and justiciable limits.

The use of money and the existence of markets becomes ubiquitous as capitalism spreads, limited only by what individuals may hold property rights in. For its sustained growth capitalism requires investment on a continuing basis, either out of profits previously earned or from credit provided by financial intermediaries. But money, markets, and investment are necessary only inasmuch as they are instrumental to generating profits. The necessary conditions are profits in a system of private property with contractual rights.

Although money and markets have existed at least since the time of the ancient Phoenicians, and sophisticated credit markets have existed in India and China for centuries, the identification of the rise of modern capitalism with Western Europe is beyond dispute. Why capitalism should have originated there, rather than in the more prosperous and economically sophisticated (as of 1350) regions of Arabia or Asia, on the other hand, is a much-debated topic. The debate has been particularly strong among Marxists, given that the transition from feudalism to capitalism forms a major part of Marx's theory of history, as well as a rehearsal for the presumed future transition from capitalism to socialism.

The lines of debate are drawn according to whether forces internal to Western European societies, or forces external to them, are said to form the crucial element. Thus advocates of the internal explanation stress the loosening of feudal bonds on serfs via the spread of monetization and the rise of absolutist monarchies dominating the feudal baronage, along with the development of urban settlements peopled by traders and artisans. The external explanation emphasizes the shock of the encounter with Islamic civilizations during the Crusades, the search for alternate trade routes in response to the capture of overland routes by the Arabs, and the innovation of the maneuverable cannon, which fitted on to sailing ships and extended the capacity of European navies to sail farther away from their home base.

Each of these explanations is conditional upon the other, and a synthesis is needed. Any explanation must place Western Europe in a global context and must account for the force of ideas (especially religious) and technological innovations (especially military). As yet, no theory has satisfactorily explained not only why the advent of capitalism occurred in Western Europe, but also why other regions, which may have stood a better chance in terms of prior conditions, failed to develop anything similar. Explanations of the origins of capitalism have thus far taken its advent in Western Europe as a given, rather than a contingent fact to be explained.

Until the eighteenth century capitalism existed side by side with feudal structures. Especially in the realm of the technology of production, changes, if any, had been gradual over the centuries, and in some areas even ancient Roman standards had not been reattained. Money, markets, contracts, and property rights were all more or less in place by the beginning of the eighteenth century, although much more development was yet to come as well. It was the development of the steam engine during the eighteenth century that irreversibly set capitalism on its path of growth. Industrialism came to be synonymous with capitalism. The first Industrial Revolution of the 1770s in England was followed by several others over the next two hundred years, each setting off a half-century wave of expansion and contraction, only to be renewed by the next revolution. The key to capitalism seemed to lie in its releasing the potential of labor for infinite rises in productivity.

Population growth expanded in parallel with the Industrial Revolution and has been a major complementary feature wherever capitalism has developed. Factory production with large concentrations of workers in one place, the growth of rapid transport and of communications on a global scale, the growth of cities and the desertion of villages, and the breakdown of the household as a major center of production of consumables all gave capitalism a dynamism and a facility for "creative destruction" of all that was old or merely recent. Complaints of attendant social breakdown, of anomie and alienation, of the dissolution of marriage and households, of the decline of religion, were commonly—and perhaps too glibly—voiced.

It was in this combination of alienation from the rural, pre-contractual life and the concentration of large numbers in factories and towns that the first articulate opposition to capitalism arose in the form of socialism. Different schools of socialism combined the nostalgic and the futuristic elements in various ways, but as an ideology and as a movement, socialism became a powerful force of resistance to and reform in capitalism. Alongside these developments arose trade unions, a form of association hitherto unknown. While trade unions were not always socialist, their interest was in regulating the growth of capitalism in ways that would enhance workers' share in the total surplus. The collectivism of trade unions was eminently adaptable to mass politics, which increasingly became the norm in advanced capitalist countries, and these led to major qualifications to laissez-faire tendencies in capitalist countries—pensions, social security, and other social provisions associated with the welfare state. It was from these roots that, in the course of the first half of the twentieth century, the state came to play a major role in the spheres of the economy involved with the welfare of the labor force.

In the period between World War I and World War II, capitalism faced its most severe challenge. Hyperinflation following upon war, the triumph of Bolshevism in Russia, the Great Depression of the 1930s, and the rise of fascism in Germany and Italy were seen as demonstrating the weakness of individualist capitalism and the success of collectivist alternatives. The rise of welfare capitalism in the United States during the New Deal era and in Britain during World War II was a successful social innovation that revived the prospects of capitalism in the postwar period. The rise of mass consumerism with full employment was seen as a permanent solution to the problems of capitalism.

As full employment became the norm, however, the strength of the trade unions, as well as the permanence of the welfare state, threatened the sustainability of profits. By the 1970s, everywhere in advanced capitalism, the crisis of profitability led to stagflation. Reacting to these pressures, capitalism emerged in the late twentieth century renewed by new innovations in electronics and telecommunications and with a reduced commitment to the collectivist institutions of previous years. Multinational corporations, which had arisen in the early twentieth century, became the major shaping force of the newly emerging global capitalism. Capitalism seems to proceed through alternating cycles of inward-looking and outward-looking developments, and the 1980s and 1990s suggested a return to the nineteenth century, when an earlier phase of capitalism became entwined with imperialism.

In its preindustrial phase Western European capitalism had already spread its trade network to all parts of the globe, and colonial empires had been established in the Americas, Africa, and Asia. At the outset these empires were sources for plunder of gold and silver and slaves. The influx of gold from South America into the Iberian empires may even have been the cause of the first century of sustained inflation in Western Europe. But after the Industrial Revolution, the network of formal and informal empires established through trade and credit offered ready markets for the industrial products of Western European capitalism. In return, these peripheral regions became suppliers of non-slave, but still relatively unfree, labor and raw materials.

As informal trade links gave way to territorial conquest across Africa and Southeast and South Asia during the late nineteenth century, capitalism began to be widely identified with imperialism. Especially in South America, informal networks were just as influential as were formal networks. As growth spread, many former peripheral regions—North America, southern Europe, and finally during the late twentieth century East Asia—became fully capitalist and part of the advanced core.

Throughout its two-hundred-year history industrial capitalism has continued to be productive at ever-increasing levels, despite prolonged periods of depression. The capacity of the system for sustained growth is often underestimated and does not seem to have diminished. What is more difficult is to establish the reasons for this sustained growth. Some attribute it to the innovating entrepreneur, ever seeking fabulous profits and willing to take enormous risks. Others attribute it to the combination of competition in the private sphere and self-denying, laissez-faire practices on the part of the state. Others assign the state a more prominent role, especially in the earlier phases of industrial growth. Military expansionism, the Protestant ethic, gold discoveries, universalization of education and training, discoveries of science and technology—all these have been given their due prominence. The possibility of achieving large and sustained profits and the guarantee that these profits can be kept, augmented, and enjoyed would seem to be the one constant characteristic of capitalism. A variety of institutional arrangements have existed at different times within capitalism—competition and monopoly, inflation and stable prices, laissez-faire and interventionism, authoritarianism and democracy. In the end, as long as profit can be made and spent as the profit maker wishes within a nonarbitary legal framework, capitalism—no matter how unclear its workings—will flourish.

[*See also* American Exceptionalism; Deindustrialization; Finance, International; Marxism; *and* Welfare State.]

Meghnad Desai

CAPITALISM, VARIETIES OF

The "varieties of capitalism" (VOC) approach in comparative political economy focuses on the different types of capitalist organization in advanced industrialized economies. Initially, in reaction to theories in the 1990s that posited the convergence of all economies to one neoliberal model of capitalism, a large contingent of VOC scholars in the early 2000s identified two varieties of capitalism: the "liberal market economies" of Anglophone countries like the United States and the United Kingdom, and the "coordinated market economies" of Northern Europe and Japan. Their framework for analysis of VOC combined a focus on the path-dependence of institutional rules and regularities (historical institutionalism) with concern for the logistics of coordination between firms and other systemic actors (rational choice institutionalism). But since then the field has burgeoned, with scholars positing more varieties of capitalism in developed countries, focused in particular on the "state-influenced market economies" of France, Southern Europe, and Asia, adding developing countries, such as the "dependent market economies" of Central and Eastern Europe, and tracing diverging trajectories across time within as well as between clusters of countries. These approaches have also employed alternative analytic frameworks, most notably sociological institutionalism, concerned with the societal norms and cultural frames of political economic actors, and discursive institutionalism, encompassing the ideas and discourse of political economic agents that give meaning to political economic institutions and dynamics to political economic interactions. Such scholars have also become concerned with going beyond the primary preoccupation with political economic institutions to consider the impact of political institutions, policies, and politics on the varieties of capitalism.

But however one conceives of the varieties of capitalism, the treatment of the United States remains problematic. Although it has been classified within the neoliberal model, or as a "liberal market economy," it is simply too big an economy that is too geographically diverse and too politically and institutionally complex to fit the category very readily. Certain sectors and geographical areas may be seen to match the patterns of other varieties of capitalism better, while its very bigness, along with its diversity, suggests that it might be better to pair the United States with other larger and more complex political economies like the European Union or China, rather than with smaller advanced industrialized countries that are the size of US states or, at most, regions.

Neoliberal Convergence or Divergence? Capitalism has traditionally been used as a singular rather than a plural concept to describe the nature of economic organization and market relations. Since the collapse of the Soviet Union and the demise of communism as a possible alternative, however, capitalism has come to be discussed solely in terms of its varieties.

In the 1990s, scholarly debate pitted those who argued for the inevitability of convergence to a single neoliberal model, following the example of the United States, against those who instead insisted on continued divergence. While the former contended that convergence was the result of the pressures of globalization that, since the mid-1970s, had accelerated the internationalization of the financial markets and trade while pushing government programs of privatization, deregulation, and liberalization, the latter maintained that despite general economic trends and similar reform initiatives, differences among national varieties of capitalism remained (Berger and Dore, 1996). More specifically, convergence theorists pointed to market-oriented changes across countries, as firms turned to the financial markets for capital in place of the banks or the state, as multinationals became increasingly "stateless" through the internationalization of their operations, and as the state itself was in retreat, with the differences between left and right submerged (e.g., Stopford and Strange, 1991; Cerny, 1994). In contrast, the divergence theorists looked more deeply into the specific policies, practices, and ideas of different countries, challenging arguments claiming the radical decline of the nation-state and the rise of "stateless" business (Schmidt, 1995). They highlighted the continuing diversity in firms' levels of exposure to the financial markets, in the bases of firm ownership and control, in the operation of industrial sectors, in the nature of inter-firm relations, in the organization

of labor-management relations, in the patterns of production and innovation, in the rules and financing of welfare provision, and in the role of the state in the economy (e.g., Hollingsworth, Schmitter, and Streeck, 1994; Vogel, 1996; Crouch and Streeck, 1997; Scharpf and Schmidt, 2000).

The United States was very much a part of these debates in the 1990s, either as the model for neoliberal convergence—touted in particular for Wall Street's financial markets and American business' leadership in export-oriented offshoring—or as only one among many national varieties of capitalism. This was in marked contrast to the 1980s, when the United States was no model at all, having been criticized for its deindustrialization of business and its adversarial management-labor relations, and contrasted in the early 1980s with the Japanese model of just-in-time production, and in the late 1980s with the German model of export-led growth. Moving into the 2000s, however, there was to be no reversal of fortunes for the United States similar to the 1980s. Much to the contrary, the US approach to business and finance seemed increasingly to be emulated by big firms and banks across advanced industrialized countries—at least until the economic crisis that began in 2007–2008. This said, for the bulk of scholars, by the early 2000s, the United States came to be seen as encompassed by only one of two (or more) ideal-typical varieties of capitalism.

How Many Varieties of Capitalism Are There? The firm-centered approach to the varieties of capitalism pioneered by Peter A. Hall and David Soskice (2001) took comparative political economy by storm in the early 2000s. It divided capitalism into two main ideal-types: liberal market economies (LMEs) and coordinated market economies (CMEs), which are differentiated in terms of how firms coordinate with their environment. This approach, by combining historical institutionalist attention to path-dependent institutional rules and regularities and rational choice institutionalist concern with logics of coordination, produced an equilibrium model that predicted that instead of convergence to one neoliberal model, there would be constant binary divergence in two ideal-typical varieties of capitalism.

In LMEs—mainly Anglophone countries like Britain, the United States, Canada, Ireland, Australia, and New Zealand—the market coordinates interactions among socioeconomic actors. Firms depend upon the financial markets for capital, and therefore focus on short-term profits, while inter-firm relations tend to be competitive and contractual. Management-labor relations tend to be market reliant, with radically decentralized labor markets and low levels of job protections leading to bifurcated wage structures between highly paid, highly skilled workers and low-paid, low skilled workers (Hall and Soskice, 2001). The "liberal" state, if considered at all, plays at most a supportive role in creating a positive regulatory environment, acting as an agent of market preservation by locating decision-making power in companies while limiting the power of organized labor (King and Wood, 1999). The resulting system is posited as highly responsive to changing market conditions with a comparative advantage in areas where radical innovation is the key to market dominance, such as biotechnology, the new economy, and high-end financial services, and in low-end services and low-tech industries, in which workers' low wages, low skills, and minimal vocational training makes for competition on the basis of price rather than quality.

In CMEs—primarily Continental European and Scandinavian countries such as Germany, the Netherlands, and Sweden, plus Japan—socioeconomic actors engage in non-market coordination (see Hall and Soskice, 2001). Here, firms tend to be less exposed to financial market pressures, because of the more long-term investment view of providers of finance and because of the higher concentration of share-ownership through strategic investors, which also helps protect against takeover. Moreover, inter-firm relations tend to be network-based, with close, mutually reinforcing relations with suppliers, subcontractors, and customers, while labor-management relations tend to be trust-based and cooperative, ensuring that corporate governance tends to be more driven by "stakeholder" values rather than "shareholder" ones. This is reinforced by an employment system with highly skilled, highly paid labor with high levels of employment protection and long-term employment. The state, finally, plays an "enabling" role by facilitating collaborative inter-firm relations and cooperative labor management relations. The resulting system, although slower to respond to changing market conditions, has a comparative advantage in sectors such as high-precision engineering and high-value-added manufacturing, which depend upon a more stable, long-term investment environment where highly paid, technically skilled workers ensure the incremental innovation necessary to the production of high-value-added, high-quality products.

Although this binary division of capitalism has been highly seductive because of its parsimony, and has since generated a veritable cottage industry of scholarship, it has been the subject of numerous critiques. The most pervasive criticisms are that a binary division into ideal-types tends to be too reductive, overly functionalist, highly static because equilibrium-focused, too path-dependent, unable to account for institutional change—particularly in light of the very real disaggregating forces coming from globalization pressures and neoliberal policies—and unable to deal adequately with country cases that do not fit well into either ideal-type (see Crouch, 2005; Schmidt, 2002, chap. 3; and Hancké, Rhodes, and Thatcher, 2007).

Scholars have responded in various ways to these problems. Some have attempted to counter the functionalist bias of the approach by positing open rather than closed systems, with multilayered reference frames and relatively autonomous components (Becker, 2009), different patterns of interdependence in different subsystems (Deeg, 2006), or differing systemic patterns of consolidation or specialization (Fioretos, 2011). Others have sought to inject more dynamism into the explanation by positing incremental change in the institutional components of loosely connected, historically evolving varieties of capitalism (leaving open however many there might be), which change at different rates in different ways through different processes, whether through layering on of new elements, conversion through reinterpretation, drift, or even exhaustion (Streeck and Thelen, 2005), or through evolutionary trajectories of change (Steinmo, 2010). In all such approaches, the binary nature of this approach to varieties of capitalism is challenged, as open systems or incremental evolution create hybrids, or point to the disaggregation of both varieties of capitalism.

Yet other scholars have argued that the binary approach to VOC pushes to the margins a number of countries with equally distinctive patterns, but in which the state has traditionally played a larger role in the economy. This is why some scholars have argued that there are at least three varieties of capitalism (e.g., Coates, 2002; Schmidt, 2002, 2009), differentiable along lines of development from the original three postwar models (as identified by Shonfield, 1965), in which liberalism, corporatism, and statism have given way not just to "liberal market economies" and "coordinated market economies" but also to "state-influenced market economies" (Schmidt, 2009). This third variety of capitalism includes all countries in which the state plays and has played a much more active role than in the ideal-typical LME or CME—whether it was in the postwar period of "state capitalism" for France (Schmidt, 2002) or of the "developmental state" for South Korea and Taiwan or even Japan (Weiss, 1998; Woo-Cumings, 1999) or today, in what is called in France "state-enhanced capitalism" (Schmidt, 2002), or in Korea and Japan, "entrepreneurial states" (Thiberghien, 2007), or in Italy, "dysfunctional state capitalism" (Della Sala, 2004), and in Spain, "state-influenced mixed market economy" (Royo, 2008).

"State-influenced" market economies (SMEs) have a more influential state and a more state-driven or hierarchical logic of interaction between firms, labor, and the state than in the financial-market-driven, liberal market economies or the non-market managed, coordinated market economies (Schmidt, 2002, 2009). In SMEs, although the state now also seeks to create and preserve market institutions, much as in liberal market economies, this does not stop it from continuing to intervene strategically where it sees the need, mainly to protect business or labor from the worst effects of the markets—whether this means bailing out firms in difficulty, "moralizing" highly decentralized labor markets to protect

workers, as in France, or engineering corporatist agreements in wage-bargaining and pension reform, as in Italy and Spain. Firms, however, are nonetheless much more autonomous than in the past, as business has been privatized and deregulated, and as it has increasingly turned to the financial markets for capital. But this has not therefore made the financial markets the drivers of corporate strategy, since chief executive officers remain much more autonomous than in both LMEs, because their more concentrated family- or share-ownership reduces takeover risks, or in CMEs, because they are less constrained by boards of directors, networked relationships, or employees. They even remain more autonomous than CEOs in SMEs of the past, because of the retreat of the state. All of this, added to an employment system that sits somewhere between CMEs and LMEs in terms of worker pay, job protections, skills, training, and wage-bargaining systems, makes SMEs better than CMEs but behind LMEs on radical innovation, and better than LMEs but behind CMEs on incremental innovation.

Other scholars have argued for even more varieties of capitalism, once one considers additional variables and geographical regions. Thus, some have argued that there are four varieties of capitalism, with Asian countries constituting another category (Boyer, 2005; Whitley, 2005); or five, adding welfare regimes to the mix of empirical variables (Amable, 2003); or more, including regional and local varieties (Crouch et al., 2001). More recently, for Europe alone, adding to the two or three varieties of VOC has come a fourth, the dependent market economies (DMEs) of Central and Eastern Europe, defined as largely driven by outside forces, primarily capital through foreign direct investment (FDI) (Nölke and Vliegenthart, 2009), but one might also want to add the regulation coming from global as much as West European sources.

Many of these alternative analyses of the varieties of capitalism use the same historical and rational-choice, institutionalist, explanatory frameworks of the binary VOC approach, with a split between those innovating on the historical-institutionalist side through incremental (e.g., Streeck and Thelen, 2005) or evolutionary (Steinmo, 2010) approaches, and those on the rational-choice, institutionalist side through "modified historical institutionalism" (Fioretos, 2011). Increasing numbers of scholars, however, have instead moved to sociological and discursive-institutionalist frameworks. These latter add to or substitute for the rationalist logics of interests and the path-dependent logics of historical institutional rules by emphasizing sociological-institutionalist concerns with the role of cultural norms and societal mechanisms (Fligstein, 2001; Campbell, 2004), or discursive-institutionalist considerations of the role of ideas and discourse in reconceptualizing interests, reshaping institutions, and reframing culture (Blyth, 2002; Schmidt, 2002, chaps. 5 and 6, 2009; Campbell and Pederson, 2001; Hay, 2006).

The Importance of Policy, Polity, and Politics. Many scholars have also gone beyond the categorization of capitalism solely along the line of political economic institutions to show that policies, polities (i.e., political institutions), and politics matter. And when these are taken into consideration, the division of the varieties of capitalism into one, two, three, or more political economic types tends to break down.

The actual policies of countries do not always fit what the VOC literature might predict. Liberal states may be more interventionist than expected, as in the United Kingdom with its "steering state" (Moran, 2003), or Ireland with its institutionalization of social pacts in the late 1980s. Enabling states may institute policies that diminish coordinative ability, as in German capital gains tax reform in the early 2000s, which reduced structural incentives for business-bank networks. And influencing states may actually promote more non-state coordination between business and labor, as in the social pacts of Southern European countries. Moreover, although one can certainly argue that all countries have moved along a continuum from *faire* ("do") to *laissez faire* ("let do") as a result of neoliberal reforms, policy change even in the most liberal of LMEs has not produced *laissez faire* but rather a state of *faire faire* ("have do"), by having market actors perform functions that the state generally did in the past, while

even the most interventionist of SMEs has on occasion gone from *faire* ("do") not only to *faire faire* ("have do") but also to *faire avec* ("do with"), the corporatist pattern typical of CMEs (Schmidt, 2009). In a LME like the United States, for example, deregulation meant *faire faire*, as the federal government specified the guidelines that corporate actors would have to follow in carrying out their programs or the courts would have to follow in resolving disputes about those guidelines (Dobbin, 2002). In SMEs like Italy and Spain, labor market reform was successfully engaged in the 1990s through *faire avec*, via social pacts (Royo, 2008; Della Sala, 2004).

Differences in political institutions help explain why policies may differ even among countries clustered within a single variety of capitalism. This depends in large part on where countries sit on a continuum between "simple" polities, in which governing activity is channeled through a single authority (via unitary states, majoritarian representation systems, or statist policy-making processes), and compound polities, in which governing activity is dispersed through multiple authorities (via federal or regionalized states, proportional representation systems, or corporatist or pluralist policy-making; Schmidt, 2009). For example, despite both being classified as LMEs in the VOC literature, the compound United States has consistently been less able to impose radical reform than the simple United Kingdom, largely because of its institutional complexity. This was most in evidence in the 1980s, with the British prime minister Margaret Thatcher's much more radical reforms by comparison with those of the American president Ronald Reagan, despite similar electoral programs (Steinmo, 1994; King and Wood, 1999). In the 1990s, moreover, it was not only the unitary nature of the British state that enabled Prime Minister Tony Blair to impose, for example, his "New Deal" for youth employment, by contrast with President Bill Clinton's failure to negotiate more ambitious federal training and employment programs. It was also the organization of US industry, given the strength of the vehemently opposed small-business lobby, which was better organized in Washington than the pro-reform large-scale employers, which lacked a single peak association (Martin, 2000), let alone privileged access to government policy-making in coordination with unions, as in Germany. This also points to the fact that pluralist versus corporatist arrangements are as much a factor of differentiation for compound polities like the United States and Germany as federal arrangements.

Finally, politics also matters, in particular when explaining institutional change. For some VOC scholars, politics is exclusively a question of rationalist interests, and plays itself out in the interest-driven competition among political coalitions of the policy or political arena. These rationalist studies generate predictions, for example, about corporate governance policy and regulation on the basis of differing combinations of alliances among economic interest groups consisting of owners, managers, and workers (Gourevitch and Shinn, 2005), or about the distributional effects of socioeconomic policies produced by political coalitions formed under different formal electoral systems acting as incentive structures: more inegalitarian in majoritarian systems, less inegalitarian in proportional ones (Iversen and Soskice, 2006). But although this rationalist political coalition literature is a step forward by comparison with the more equilibrium-focused or path-dependent apolitical studies of earlier VOC, it still has difficulties explaining how new political coalitions are constructed and changed, let alone how the institutions in which they operate were created and reformed.

Other scholars take up the challenge of explaining institutional change by examining politics through the lens of the ideas and discourse that help alter perceptions of interests, build political coalitions, persuade policymakers of the need to construct new programs via the "coordinative discourse" of the policy arena, and convince publics of the necessity and appropriateness of such programs through the "communicative discourse" in the political arena (Schmidt, 2002, 2009; Blyth, 2002; Campbell, 2004; Hay, 2006). Such politics may explain change through the foundational economic ideas that may change at moments of "great transformation." One such moment led in the 1930s to the differentiated embedding of liberalism in countries with different national ideas about political economic organization, as in the United States and Sweden, another to its "disembedding" in the 1970s in the self-same countries (Blyth, 2002). They may explain change through the appearance of a new ideational "paradigm," as in the case of Thatcher's switch to monetarism in the United Kingdom (Hall, 1993). They may also explain change through political leaders' communicative discourse about the economic imperatives of globalization, in efforts to legitimate neoliberal reform in Europe across different varieties of capitalism (Hay and Rosamond, 2002). Or they may explain change through policymakers' coordinative discourse that, absent any overarching set of ideas, nonetheless produces an incremental layering of policy upon policy that, over time, constitutes the equivalent of a paradigm shift in welfare provision (Palier, 2005).

The focus on ideas and discourse may additionally help explain institutional continuities as well as misperceptions of reality. In the United States, for example, scholars point to how what people take for reality may really be ideology, including taking the United States for a liberal market economy when in some sectors at least it is actually a lot more coordinated and state influenced. Block (2008) makes this case with regard to the technological policy arena in the United States, which he argues is managed not by the market but by a "developmental network state," which has provided massive amounts of financing and coordination support to business technology initiatives from the 1980s forward. This reality, however, has been "hidden in plain view," because it contradicts the market fundamentalist political ideology that pervades Republican partisan politics, in which the communicative discourse presents the government as the problem, not the solution, at the same time that the discourse has served business interests by enabling them to resist being taxed on its profits.

The United States in All Its Variety as Capitalism. So where does the United States fit in all of this? Scholars who see convergence to a single neoliberal model naturally see the United States as the neoliberal political economy par excellence, while those who posit a binary division in VOC place it with other LMEs, noting the primacy of its financial markets, its profit-driven business, the radical innovation coming from its high-tech firms, the radical decentralization of its labor markets along with the bifurcation in worker skills and pay, and more. This essay has largely used these categorizations of the United States as neoliberal model and as LME when considering how the United States compares to other countries. However, although such classifications based on political economic configurations may reflect a very general sense of reality, the United States is much more complicated. Size and geography make a big difference, as do sectors, policies, political institutions, and politics of interests as well as of ideas and discourse.

There are aspects of its business-labor relationships that could make the United States look like a coordinated market economy, in particular the automotive industry in the Midwest, and especially once the state of Michigan took advantage of welfare decentralization to spend its money mostly on job training. There are elements in its business-government relationship that could make the United States appear decidedly "state-influenced," not only the hidden "developmental network state" in hi-tech, but also in the defense sector. What is more, patterns of foreign direct investment in certain parts of the country could even suggest that the United States is more of a dependent market economy—in particular in states like South Carolina and Alabama, with their massive foreign direct investment from foreign carmakers. Finally, its particular set of highly compound political institutions, its mix of *faire faire* policies, and its highly polarized ideologically charged politics make explaining the US variety of capitalism a major challenge.

All of this suggests that a truly big political economy like that of the United States does not fit categorizations made for average-sized countries' varieties of capitalism. It may very well be, therefore, that we need to develop a new way of considering capitalism, by comparing national and supranational region-sized entities rather than nation-states. This could mean contrasting the United States to the European Union, taking account of how common EU-based political economic institutions, policies, polity, and politics play themselves out in the four varieties of its member-states' capitalisms—LMEs, CMEs, SMEs, and DMEs—or to China, with the nondemocratic SME-like overall structure arguably hiding geographically located LMEs and sectorally differentiated CMEs or DMEs. But this kind of scholarship has yet to develop.

[*See also* American Exceptionalism; Business-Government Relations; *and* Financial Industry.]

BIBLIOGRAPHY

Amable, Bruno. *The Diversity of Modern Capitalism.* (Oxford, 2003).

Becker, Uwe. *Open Varieties of Capitalism: Continuity, Change, and Performance.* (Basingstoke, UK, 2009).

Berger, Suzanne, and Ronald Philip Dore, eds. *National Diversity and Global Capitalism.* (Ithaca, N.Y., 1996).

Block, Fred. "Swimming against the Current: The Rise of a Hidden Developmental State in the US." *Politics and Society* 36, no. 2 (2008): 169–206.

Blyth, Mark. *Great Transformations: Economic Ideas and Institutional Change in the Twentieth Century.* (New York, 2002).

Boyer, Robert. "How and Why Capitalisms Differ." MPIfG Discussion Paper 04/5. Max Planck Institute for the Study of Societies. (2005), http://www.mpifg.de/pu/mpifg_dp/dp05-4.pdf.

Campbell, John L. *Institutional Change and Globalization.* (Princeton, N.J., 2004).

Campbell, John L., and Ove Kaj Pedersen, eds. *The Rise of Neoliberalism and Institutional Analysis.* (Princeton, N.J., 2001).

Cerny, Philip. "The Dynamics of Financial Globalization." *Policy Sciences* 27 (1994): 319–342.

Coates, David. *Models of Capitalism: Debating Strengths and Weaknesses.* (Cheltenham, UK, 2002).

Crouch, Colin. *Capitalist Diversity and Change.* (Oxford, 2005.)

Crouch, Colin, et al. *Changing Governance of Local Economies: Responses of European Local Production Systems.* (Oxford, 2004).

Crouch, Colin, and Wolfgang Streeck, eds. *Political Economy of Modern Capitalism: Mapping Convergence and Diversity.* (London, 1997).

Deeg, Richard. "Path Dependence, Institutional Complementarity, and Change in National Business Systems." In *Changing Capitalisms? Internationalism, Institutional Change, and Systems of Economic*

Organization, edited by Glenn Morgan, Richard Whitley, and Eli Moen, pp. 21–52. (Oxford, 2006.)

Della Sala, Vincent. "The Italian Model of Capitalism: On the Road between Globalization and Europeanization." *Journal of European Public Policy* 11, no. 6 (2004): 1041–1057.

Dobbin, Frank. "Is America Becoming More Exceptional? How Public Policy Corporatized Social Citizenship." In *Restructuring the Welfare State: Political Institutions and Policy Change,* edited by Bo Rothstein and Sven Steinmo. (New York, 2002).

Fioretos, Orfeo. *Creative Reconstructions: Multilateralism and European Varieties of Capitalism after 1950.* (Ithaca, N.Y., 2011).

Fligstein, Neil. *The Architecture of Markets: An Economic Sociology of Twenty-First-Century Capitalist Societies.* (Princeton, N.J., 2001).

Gourevitch, Peter, and James Shinn. *Political Power and Corporate Control: The New Global Politics of Corporate Governance.* (Princeton, N.J., 2005).

Hall, Peter A. "Policy Paradigms, Social Learning, and the State: The Case of Economic Policy-Making in Britain." *Comparative Politics* 25 (1993): 275–296.

Hall, Peter A., and David Soskice. *Varieties of Capitalism: The Institutional Foundations of Comparative Advantage.* (Oxford, 2001).

Hancké, Bob, Martin Rhodes, and Mark Thatcher. "Introduction." In *Beyond Varieties of Capitalism: Conflict, Contradiction, and Complementarities in the European Economy.* (Oxford, 2007).

Hay, Colin. "Constructivist Institutionalism." In *The Oxford Handbook of Political Institutions,* edited by R. A. W. Rhodes, Sarah A. Binder, and Bert A. Rockman, pp. 56–74. (Oxford, 2006.)

Hay, Colin, and Ben Rosamond. "Globalisation, European Integration, and the Discursive Construction of Economic Imperatives." *Journal of European Public Policy* 9, no. 2 (2002): 147–167.

Hollingsworth, J. Rogers, Philippe C. Schmitter, and Wolfgang Streeck. *Governing Capitalist Economies: Performance and Control of Economic Sectors.* (New York, 1994.)

Iversen, Torben, and David Soskice. "Electoral Institutions and the Politics of Coalitions: Why Some Democracies Redistribute More than Others." *American Political Science Review* 100 (2006): 165–181.

King, Desmond, and Stewart Wood. "The Political Economy of Neoliberalism: Britain and the United States in the 1980s." In *Continuity and Change in Contemporary Capitalism,* edited by Herbert Kitschelt et al., pp. 371–397. (New York, 1999).

Martin, Cathie Jo. *Stuck in Neutral: Business and the Politics of Human Capital Investment Policy.* (Princeton, N.J., 2000).

Moran, Michael. *The British Regulatory State: High Modernism and Hyper-Innovation.* (Oxford, 2003).

Nölke, Andreas, and Arjan Vliegenthart. "Enlarging the Varieties of Capitalism: The Emergence of Dependent Market Economies in East Central Europe." *World Politics* 69, no. 4 (2009): 670–702.

Palier, Bruno. "Ambiguous Agreement, Cumulative Change: French Social Policy in the 1990s." In *Beyond Continuity: Institutional Change in Advanced Political Economies,* edited by Wolfgang Streeck and Kathleen Ann Thelen, pp.127–144. (Oxford, 2005).

Royo, Sebastián. *Varieties of Capitalism in Spain: Remaking the Spanish Economy for the New Century.* (Basingstoke, UK, 2008).

Scharpf, Fritz W., and Vivien A. Schmidt, eds. *Welfare and Work in the Open Economy.* 2 vols. (Oxford, 2000).

Schmidt, Vivien A. *The Futures of European Capitalism.* (Oxford, 2002).

Schmidt, Vivien A. "The New World Order, Incorporated: The Rise of Business and the Decline of the Nation-State." *Daedalus* 124, no. 2 (1995): 75–106.

Schmidt, Vivien A. "Putting the Political Back into Political Economy by Bringing the State Back Yet Again." *World Politics* 61, no. 3 (2009): 516–548.

Shonfield, Andrew. *Modern Capitalism: The Changing Balance of Public and Private Power.* (London, 1965).

Steinmo, Sven. "American Exceptionalism Reconsidered: Culture or Institutions?" In *The Dynamics of American Politics: Approaches and Interpretations,* edited by Lawrence C. Dodd and Calvin Jillson, pp. 106–131. (Boulder, Colo., 1994).

Steinmo, Sven. *The Evolution of Modern States: Sweden, Japan, and the United States.* (Cambridge, UK, 2010).

Stopford, John M., Susan Strange, and John S. Henley. *Rival States, Rival Firms: Competition for World Market Shares.* (Cambridge, UK, 1991).

Streeck, Wolfgang, and Kathleen Ann Thelen. "Introduction." In *Beyond Continuity: Institutional Change in Advanced Political Economies,* edited by Wolfgang Streeck and Kathleen Ann Thelen, pp. 1–39. (Oxford, 2005).

Thiberghien, Yves. *Entrepreneurial States: Reforming Corporate Governance in France, Japan, and Korea.* (Ithaca, N.Y., 2007).

Vogel, Steven K. *Freer Markets, More Rules: Regulatory Reform in Advanced Industrial Countries.* (Ithaca, N.Y., 1996).

Weiss, Linda. *The Myth of the Powerless State: Governing the Economy in a Global Era.* (Cambridge, UK, 1998).

Whitley, Richard. "How National Are Business Systems?" In *Changing Capitalisms? Internationalism, Institutional Change, and Systems of Economic Organization*, edited by Glenn Morgan, Richard Whitley, and Eli Moen, pp. 190–234. (Oxford, 2006.)

Woo-Cumings, Meredith, ed. *The Developmental State.* (Ithaca, N.Y., 1999).

Vivien A. Schmidt

CAPITAL PUNISHMENT

Over the great sweep of human history, capital punishment has been an important element in the judicial systems of virtually every society, and "from the very beginning, capital punishment has been an integral part of American history"(Allen and Chubb, 2008, p. 9). In past centuries, people were executed for a wide variety of crimes and were often killed in ways which amplified their pain and made their death a public spectacle. But in modern times that is no longer the case. In the early twenty-first century only a handful of major countries continue to execute people, and even fewer continue to do so in public. In 2009, just five countries accounted for 90 percent of all known executions. The top four were China, Iran, Iraq, and Saudi Arabia. Number five was the United States of America.

It was not always so. The United States has a long history of debate on the morality and effectiveness of capital punishment—a debate which even predates the break with Britain and is reflected in the presence, in the Eighth Amendment to the US Constitution, of the prohibition on "cruel and unusual punishments." For the first two centuries of the new republic, the Eighth Amendment did not block executions—there were still on average 167 each year through the 1930s, including public ones in Kentucky and Missouri—but in 1972 the Supreme Court ruled in favor of doing so. In *Furman v. Georgia* the justices decided that, because juries imposed the death penalty arbitrarily, its use did constitute cruel and unusual punishment. They accordingly voided death penalty legislation in the thirty-two states that then had such laws in place, and ordered

the 629 prisoners on death row removed. In response, many states drew up detailed guidelines for the first time, keeping the death penalty by refining it. Some made the death sentence mandatory for specific crimes. Others divided capital trials into two sections: one to determine guilt, one to determine sentencing. In 1976, *Woodson v. North Carolina* the Supreme Court struck down the first of those moves, but in *Gregg v. Georgia* it upheld the constitutionality of the second (Bakken, 2010, p. 10).

In the decades that followed this landmark judgment, the Supreme Court has ruled on a string of more specific issues related to the death penalty, including jury selection, the execution of juveniles and the mentally retarded, execution by lethal injection, and the execution of foreign nationals. Congress too has been active: in 1994 the Federal Death Penalty Act made capital punishment a possible sentence for an extended list of sixty crimes that stretched from treason and genocide to drive-by shootings and murders committed in the midst of robbery. As the bulk of the rest of the world retreated from the use of the ultimate punishment, American legislators and judges moved in the opposite direction. It is true that the Supreme Court did induce another moratorium briefly in 2007, as it pondered the constitutionality of death by lethal injection, and that at the state level, capital punishment was put on hold (in Illinois) or abandoned entirely (in New Jersey). But overall, in the United States the use of the death penalty continues, against the international trend. Since 1976 there have been 1,226 executions in the US states that allow the death penalty (now down to 35): 98 in the peak year (1999) and 46 in 2010. As of January 2010, there were 3,261 people on death row awaiting a similar fate—convicted felons who were particularly at risk in those states that regularly implement the penalty. Texas currently holds pride of place in that list, with 463 executions since 1976, 38 percent of the total (Death Penalty Information Center, 2010). The use of capital punishment remains a contested issue in contemporary American politics, with strong arguments (and even stronger convictions) held by proponents on both sides of the death penalty divide (House and

Yoder, 1991; Martinez, Richardson, and Hornsby, 2002; Lin, 2002; Bedau and Cassell, 2004).

Arguments in Favor of Capital Punishment. The arguments in favor of capital punishment turn mainly on claims about deterrence and morality.

The Deterrent Effect of So Potent a Punishment. The deterrent argument is straightforward. It is that the existence of capital punishment as a possible penalty for homicide (and in certain hands, for a wider list of other violent crimes) helps to reduce the number of such crimes committed. Advocates make their case on a priori grounds, and they make it on the grounds of available statistics.

The a priori argument has a number of dimensions. One is that executing murderers clearly prevents them from murdering again. Another is that, because the deterrent effect works to prevent acts of murder, the number of such murders deterred in this way can never be known. "There are," so the argument goes, "many, perhaps thousands, of such undocumented cases, representing many innocent lives saved by the fear of execution" but "circumstances dictate that the majority of these cases will never be documented and that the number of innocent lives saved by individual deterrence will be, and has been, much greater than we will ever be able to calculate" (Death Penalty Paper, 2009, p. 5). A third a priori argument is that among the innocent lives saved are those of prison officers and other prison inmates: if murder is punished only by life without parole, there is no disincentive on lifers not to murder again at will. Yet a fourth argument is that the deterrence effect of capital punishment is less real than symbolic, but potent still. As David Frum put it, "if societies want to wind back crime, they need to begin by sending a clear message that . . . crime won't be tolerated and will be punished to the full extent of the law. And nothing broadcasts that message like restoration of the death penalty" (2006, p. 1).

Then there are the statistics. Most everyone concedes their necessary incompleteness, seeing how difficult it is to measure deterrence when so few executions occur and so many murderers go unpunished. Many advocates of the death penalty realize well enough that great care is needed here, not least because "the test for deterrence is not whether executions produce lower murder rates, but that executions produce fewer murders than if the death penalty did not exist," and necessarily that evidence has to be "statistically elusive" (Death Penalty Paper, 2009, p. 6). Nonetheless, some statisticians and econometricians have probed for causal relationships; some have claimed to have found one, and even to have been able to put some precision on the number of lives saved. In 1975, "economist Isaac Erlich published a study arguing that each additional execution deters seven or eight murders" (Rosenzweig, 2003, p. 2). More recently, a widely cited study by three Emory University professors concluded that "each execution deters other murders to the extent of saving between eight and twenty-eight innocent lives, with the best estimate average of eighteen lives saved per execution" (Dezhbakhsh, Rubin, and Shepherd, 2001). There are at least a dozen other studies with a similar message, including studies by Paul R. Zimmerman, which argues that "a state execution deters approximately fourteen murders per year on average" (2004, p. 163), by H. Naci Mocan and R. Kay Gittings, which states that "each additional execution decreases homicides by about five" (2003, p. 5), and by Hashem Dezhbakhsh and Joanna M. Shepherd, which claims that "the results are boldly clear: executions deter murders, and murder rates increase substantially during moratoriums" (2006, p. 532). There is even evidence from Texas supporting the case: a 72 percent fall in the number of homicides in Harris County (the Houston area) since the resumption of executions there in 1982 (Death Penalty Paper, 2009, p. 10).

Taking Life to Save Lives. Ultimately the deterrence argument anchors itself in the general philosophies underpinning American jurisprudence. If deterrence is not thought credible, why have a criminal code and a prison system at all? And if deterrence in relation to homicide is not appropriate, why does the justice system work so hard to differentiate between first-degree and second-degree murder? The deterrence argument is not that capital punishment stops all homicides. It is that it deters certain kinds of homicides: those premeditated destructions of one human being by another that were rationally calculated, and the calculus of which could be altered if the certainty of execution was factored in. The moratorium that prevented executions between 1972 and 1976 did more than save the lives of those on death row. It also put at risk the lives of others—lives entirely innocent that would end in brutal slaughter because convicted murderers were themselves allowed to live.

For among those spared from execution by the moratorium were men who killed again, years later, when released. Denying the state the right to use the ultimate punishment against those willing to take the lives of others builds in an even stronger incentive for them to do just that. Kidnappers and bank robbers in the moratorium period suddenly had a greater incentive to kill witnesses than to leave them alive (Cassell, 2004), and men locked away in prison without hope of parole lack any disincentive to fatally attacking the people who must guard them or the inmates with whom they share prison space. Indeed the case can be made, and often is by advocates of capital punishment, that death is a less onerous punishment for murders than incarceration for life with no hope of parole—not that that then induces them to advocate it. On the contrary, the case is rather that capital punishment is less burdensome than permanent incarceration: less burdensome in monetary terms for the taxpayer, and less burdensome for the murderers too, on the thesis that being locked away without hope of parole for the rest of time is a worse punishment than execution—the Eighth Amendment turned upon its head.

The Moral Case for Capital Punishment. Those arguing the moral case for capital punishment normally set it alongside the deterrence argument, treating the two as a powerful package (Berns, 1991). The moral case can be made with a general or a specific focus. The general argument is that justice demands retribution (van den Haag, 2002, p. 32), and that punishment by death is a way of honoring innocent life (Fein, 2007). The specific argument is that certain crimes are so horrific that death is the only morally appropriate punishment.

Defenders of capital punishment are keen to refute the argument that by taking the life of a murderer the state itself becomes one. Killing and murder, they argue, are not the same things. States will often orchestrate killing, as in wars—indeed in wars they will often orchestrate the deaths of many innocents without the careful due process with which they execute the guilty. Murder, by contrast, is the taking of the life of one private citizen by another; and when that murder is rationally calculated and planned, it is said to enter a moral universe within which death is the only appropriate form of punishment. "It is not because retentionists disvalue life that we defend the use of the death penalty," Louis Pojman has written, "rather it is because we value human life as highly as we do that we defend the use of the death penalty" (2004, p. 73). Following Kant, he argues that "because human beings, as rational agents, have dignity, one who with malice aforethought kills a human being forfeits his right to life and deserves to die" (p. 54). Pojman at least treats this need to deploy a moral defense of the death penalty as reflective of the degree to which "we have suffered a loss of confidence in the ability of our society to carry out justice, a failure of nerve" (p. 52). Societies that have not lost their nerve understand that punishment should be proportional to the crime; and that when the crime is heinous, the punishment must match it in force to be morally sound.

If that is too general, then more specific forms of argument can be and are deployed. There are some crimes of murder, some ways of killing people—so the argument goes—that are so brutal as to require the ultimate penalty. The rape and murder of a child, the mass slaughter of a people, the random destruction of office workers by a bomb: all these kinds of crime are perpetrated by individuals whose disregard for the lives of the innocent puts them once more into that moral universe in which death is the only appropriate form of punishment. Timothy McVeigh deserved to die. Adolf Eichmann deserved to die. The four men who raped a child and killed her by stuffing clothing down her throat deserve to die. The Washington snipers deserve to die. Their callousness toward their victims requires an equal callousness on our part. To do otherwise is to disregard the suffering, and the worth, of their victims. "Killing should in aggravated cases carry consequences equal to the gravity of the harm caused" (Rosenzweig, 2003, p. 2); because, as Adam Smith had it, "mercy to the guilty is cruelty to the innocent." Executing McVeigh, Daniel Troy wrote at the time, is "perhaps paradoxically . . . the best way to affirm Americans' deeply held belief that life is a gift from God and that those who cold-bloodedly snuff it out should not continue to enjoy that gift" (2001, p. 1). We need to remember that "the recidivism rate for capital punishment is zero" (Death Penalty Paper, 2009, p. 25) and that if the data on deterrence actually holds, for certain kinds of crime capital punishment may not just be morally permissible—it may indeed be obligatory (Sunstein and Vermeule, 2006; challenged by Steiker, 2006).

Supplementary Arguments for the Death Penalty. Issues of deterrence and morality are at the core of the case here, but there are at least three supplementary arguments that are regularly deployed as well. The moral case for capital punishment is often reinforced by the citing of scripture. Not all Christians read the Bible in that fashion, but those who do insist that there are many calls by God, recorded in the Bible, for capital punishment against particularly heinous forms of criminality; go to Exodus 21:12–14 or 22–23 to find some. Go to Genesis 9:6 to find others; or go to verse 19:11 of John's Gospel, to see Christ's acceptance of the legitimacy of capital punishment even in his own case (House and Yoder, 1991, pp. 59–70). More prosaic arguments in favor of capital punishment often focus on the need to honor the victim and to ease the pain of the family of the slain. Capital punishment as closure is the key argument here. Then there is the simple matter of popular support. Advocates of the retention and use of capital punishment are able to point to significant majorities in poll after poll, majorities favoring the death penalty in specific categories of crime. When polled in 2005, three Americans in four favored the death penalty for murder convictions, and 56 percent favored the death penalty over life imprisonment without parole.

Defending Capital Punishment against Its Critics. Finally this by way of advocacy: the argument that the danger of executing the innocent is overstated. Many advocates of capital punishment concede the danger (and the reality) of mistakes in the past. They regret them, but weigh them in the balance of advantages and disadvantages taken as a whole. They insist that now, with improved DNA and forensic science, the likelihood of error is significantly diminished. And though the critics of capital punishment argue strongly that its implementation is racially biased, there are those in the pro–death penalty camp who explicitly challenge that. Kent Scheidegger is one: "debunking the racial discrimination claim" in his study of the data on capital punishment in Maryland, and advocating—if fewer white people die for killing black people than black people do for killing white ones—a process of *leveling up,* that is, eradicating any perceived bias by executing more white killers (Scheidegger, 2003, pp. 42–45). Advocates of the use of capital punishment are prepared to argue—and accept the validity of disagreement—on a whole range of key technical issues: the age at which responsibility for heinous behavior kicks in, and so the death penalty applies; the level of mental capacity necessary for responsibility; and the appropriateness or otherwise of forms of execution, from the firing squad through hanging and the electric chair to the current controversy over lethal injections. That, they say, we can talk about—but nothing else. As they see it, the general case for capital punishment is sound.

Arguments against Capital Punishment. The general response of those opposed to the use of the death penalty normally takes the following form: an argument about the flawed nature of the judicial process exercising it; about the absence of any discernible deterrence effect; about its dehumanizing impact on those administering it; and about the inappropriateness in a civilized society of capital punishment as a response even to murder (Bright, 2001; Bedau, 2004; Stark, 2006; Gerber and Johnson, 2007; Lane, 2010).

The Execution of the Innocent. Even if the deterrence and morality arguments were sound—and opponents of capital punishment insist that they are not—there is no getting away from the fact that the state has killed, and will continue to kill, innocent people; and because it has and will, the case for capital punishment as superior to life without parole becomes for many opponents of the death penalty an entirely untenable claim (Baumgartner, De Boef, and Boydstun, 2008). So long as killers are incarcerated, mistakes can be corrected. Once execution takes place, however, they cannot be. There may be no recidivism from executed killers, but there is also no way back for a state that executes in error.

Opponents point to the fact that judicial systems do execute in error. It is hard to be certain what happened in the distant past, though Amnesty International regularly cites at least twenty-three Americans wrongly executed since 1900. More telling is the number of those wrongly condemned to death in more recent times. At least "118 people have been exonerated from death row since 1972, including twenty-one from the state of Florida and eighteen from the state of Illinois" (National Coalition to Abolish the Death Penalty, 2007). The Death Penalty Information Center reported sixteen such exonerations between 1973 and 1980, rising to forty-nine between 1997 and 2004, with exonerations now averaging almost five a year and taking nine years, on average, to establish (Death Penalty Information Center, 2005). The director of the Innocence Project, while not offering DNA testing as a panacea, claimed in 2005 that post-conviction DNA testing had already exonerated 162 inmates and established the innocence of at least fourteen people sentenced to death (Jost, 2005). In the first major statistical study of modern American capital-punishment appeals (a study of 4,578 such appeals between 1973 and 1995 out of 5,670 death sentences imposed in the period), researchers at Columbia Law School found an overall pre-judicial error rate of 68 percent. "In other words, courts found serious reversible errors in nearly seven out of every ten of the thousands of capital sentences that were reviewed during the period" (Liebman et al., 2000, p. i). In fact it often took three judicial reviews to discover those errors, thus "leaving grave doubt that

we *do* catch them all" (p. i). Between 1973 and 1995, according to this report, state courts threw out 47 percent of death sentences due to errors, and federal reviews later threw out 40 percent of the rest. Eighty-two percent "of the people whose capital judgments were overturned . . . were found to deserve a sentence less than death. . . . seven percent were found to be innocent of the capital crime" (p. ii). Moreover, errors made in initial capital punishment cases were found to be neither fading nor regionally concentrated. On the contrary, the error rate exceeded 50 percent in twenty of the twenty-three study years, including seventeen of the last nineteen, and passed 50 percent in over 90 percent of all American death-sentencing states (Liebman, Fagan, and West, 2000).

Ethnic Profiling. Race is everywhere in this issue. Between 1976 and 2008, about 80 percent of those killed in cases that resulted in execution were white, even though only 50 percent of all murder victims were white. Indeed since 1977, only 14 percent of executions have been for the murder of black Americans, against 80 percent for the murder of white Americans: this in a period in which a third of all those executed were black (from a general population of which only 12 percent were African American). People of color "accounted for a disproportionate 43 percent of total executions" between 1976 and 2003, and "55 percent of those [then] awaiting execution" (American Civil Liberties Union, 2003). In those three-plus decades, 633 white men were executed, as against 383 African Americans and 79 Hispanics. In 2011, 42 percent of all those on death row were African American. Study after study has shown this ethnic imbalance (Baldus and Woodworth, 2003). The David C. Baldus study of Georgia in the 1970s found someone convicted of killing a white person to be 4.3 times more likely to be executed than was someone convicted of killing a black person (Baldus, 1983). Baldus examined Philadelphia in the 1980s, and found the odds of receiving the death penalty nearly four times (3.9) higher if the convicted prisoner was African American. (In May 2002, the governor of Maryland imposed a moratorium on executions precisely because his data showed a similar racial bias in the state's death penalty system.)

The figures for North Carolina are similar: The odds of receiving a death sentence between 1993 and 1997 increased three and a half times if the victim was white (American Civil Liberties Union, 2003; Amnesty International, 2006).

The Execution of the Poor. Opponents of the death penalty also point to issues of socioeconomic status: murders occur in all social classes in the United States, but executions do not. It is the poor who die at the hands of the state. More privileged citizens may kill, but they are rarely killed themselves. In part this is a product of access to adequate defense. Time and again, the quality of the attorneys defending the American poor against capital charges is significantly worse than is that of those defending wealthier clients. Supreme Court Justice Ruth Bader Ginsburg was very clear on that in 2001: that "people who are well represented at trial do not get the death penalty" (Death Penalty Information Center, 2007, p. 2). But good representation costs money, and "over 90 percent of defendants charged with capital crimes are indigent and cannot afford to hire an experienced criminal defense attorney to represent them" (Campaign to End the Death Penalty, 2006). Those without it are thrown back on the public defender system—or where that is missing, onto a court-appointed private lawyer—and the stories are legend of just how bad that system regularly can be. There are reports of lawyers drunk or asleep in court; of lawyers too idle, too incompetent, or simply too inexperienced to bring appropriate extenuating evidence to the attention of jurors; and of capital cases being tried and settled in less than a week—hardly time to mount an adequate defense. Inadequate counsel of this kind is not the exception; it is the rule. Indeed, as Stephen Bright has convincingly demonstrated, it is pervasive in the jurisdictions which account for most death sentences. As he notes, far too often in the contemporary United States the death penalty accrues "not for the worse crime but for the worse lawyer" (Bright, 1994). It could hardly be otherwise when "one in four condemned prisoners is represented at trial or on appeal by court-appointed attorneys who have been disciplined for misconduct at some point in their career" (Campaign to End the Death Penalty, 2006).

The Execution as a Lottery. Moreover, there are huge elements of luck and predetermination at work in the administration of justice in capital cases. Only certain states execute, and some parts of some states execute more than others. Jury selection is often a key factor, and whether capital sentences are commuted turns too often for peace of mind on the accident of who is on the bench when the sentence is appealed.

The regional variation in the use of the death penalty is particularly striking (Bakken, 2010). It is very much a matter of north against south. A northern tier of states, from Maine to Alaska, play virtually no role in the nation's execution figures. Less than 1 percent of executions occur there. A middle tier of states, from Pennsylvania to California, have the death penalty but rarely use it. The Old South, by contrast, has the penalty and does use it. Two southern states—Texas and Virginia—have nearly half the executions all to themselves. Rudolph J. Gerber and John M. Johnson call this "the 'dirty little secret' of death penalty research": that "82 percent of the 1,050 executions since 1977 have been in the Southern states" (2007, p. 59). So where you kill, as well as whom you kill, plays a defining role in whether you die for your crime or whether you do not. Even within hanging states, particular counties can often be far more death-penalty-prone than others: Chattahoochee Judicial District rather than Atlanta in Georgia, for example, or in the 1990s upstate New York rather than New York City. Currently Harris County in Texas holds the dubious distinction of being the single county in America responsible for the most death sentences and executions. Disparities between states, and within states, are currently turning capital punishment within the United States into a lethal lottery, entirely in tension with the Supreme Court's 1976 requirement that, to be constitutional, capital punishment has to be "fairly and consistently administered."

To avoid execution, would-be killers also need to pick their district attorney and their jury with care.

There is overwhelming evidence of variation here, of a situation in which "some prosecutors seek the death penalty frequently, some occasionally and some never seek it" (Bright, 1997, p. 22). Among those who do, the use of preemptive challenge against certain kinds of jurors is widespread (Dieter, 2005). District attorneys in search of a death penalty sentence do best if the jury is all white and the felon is black, or the jury pool excludes all but those predisposed to favor the death penalty for capital crimes. For this reason jury selection in capital cases can often take weeks, even months. District attorneys, state court judges, and even the occasional presidential candidate are not above gaining political capital out of the death penalty in states where public opinion heavily favors the practice. Bill Clinton did just that, denying Rickey Ray Rector clemency en route to the presidency in 1992. Supreme Court Justice Stevens has argued publicly that judicial officials elected on a "be tough on crime" or "enforce the death penalty" slate should not participate in the trials of capital crimes (Death Penalty Information Center, 1996), but they do, and on a very regular basis.

The Absence of Any Deterrence Effect. Some of these deficiencies could just be tolerated, perhaps, if they were counterbalanced by clear evidence that executing murderers deterred others from similar heinous acts. But opponents of capital punishment claim that such evidence is simply not there. It is not there when the number of murders is set against the number of executions. It is also not there when the studies claiming to find a direct effect are subject to careful scrutiny.

The chances of being executed for committing murder in the United States are minute. In the 1990s, the total number of criminal homicides each year oscillated between twenty and twenty-one thousand, of which maybe three thousand were potentially capital cases. The number of death sentences handed down was significantly lower, at about three hundred a year, and the number of executions actually carried out was lower again, averaging just fifty each year (Bae, 2007). Among those murders are

some that were rationally planned, but the vast majority were not. It is not that most would-be murderers sit around, weigh the risks against the gains, and go out and cold-bloodedly kill. Most murders are murders of the moment, and those that are not escape capital punishment in all but a miniscule number of cases. The data supporting a direct link between the death penalty and homicide rates has come under heavy question, with critics claiming that the methodology of those studies is insufficiently strong to sustain the definiteness of those numbers, given the difficulty of isolating a single causal effect in a complex social process, and the very small number of executions available to be fed into the causal equations. There are prestigious reports from such bodies as the National Academy of Science calling the findings into question (Berk, 2005); indeed, for every study that purports to show a relationship between the death penalty and homicide it is possible to find a study that reports *no* relationship at all (Bae, 2007). It is also possible to find data suggesting that capital punishment may actually *trigger* homicides rather than deter them—perhaps as many as 250 extra killings a year—and that for deterrence to work against homicides states must significantly increase the number of people they execute (Bailey, 1998). There is even one study claiming that prison conditions are a greater deterrent to criminality than execution, which plays to the "life without parole" case (Katz, Levitt, and Shustorovich, 2003). As Supreme Court Justice John Paul Stevens put it, "despite thirty years of empirical research in the area, there remains no reliable statistical evidence that capital punishment in fact deters potential offenders" (Lane, 2010, p. 74).

With the empirical research going in so many different directions, it is important to remember too that "fluctuations in execution rates during the 1970s and 1980s were *not* mirrored by substantial fluctuations in homicide rates" (Bae, 2007, p. 92), as deterrence would require. The fifteen states without a death penalty statute have, on average, *lower* homicide rates than do the thirty-five states that allow the death penalty. Opponents of the death penalty argue, therefore, that it is hard to sustain a strong case for the deterrent effect of capital punishment when, over the first twenty-four years of the reimposed death penalty, ten of the twelve states then without the death penalty actually had *below average* homicide rates, while half of the states with the death penalty had homicide rates that were well *above* the norm (Bonner and Fessenden, 2000). Michigan and Alaska apart, it would appear that in the contemporary United States homicide rates and capital punishment are prone to rise and fall together.

Killing Is No Way to Sanctify Life. The moral case for protecting life by taking it also has its detractors. There is something counterintuitive, after all, in the claim that to sanctify life the state should take the life of those who failed to sanctify it. The genuine moral conundrum represented here is often countered by those opposed to capital punishment by the deployment of a version of the "evolving standards" argument. Capital punishment stands condemned by them as a cruel and unusual punishment, inherited from a barbaric past that we have long left behind. The advocacy of "humane ways of killing" by death penalty advocates points to even their recognition of the fact that civilization requires of us different modes of behavior than those acceptable to our predecessors. Standards of decency evolve: that is the essence of civilization as a process. We do not drown witches any more; we used to, but we have long stopped doing so. And what is good for witches ought to be good enough for contemporary citizens, too. The rest of the civilized world seems to have recognized this, so why can't America? One hundred and twenty-nine countries have now abolished the death penalty in law and practice, including Canada and all twenty-seven members of the European Union. The Catholic Church is opposed to capital punishment. So too is the United Nations Human Rights Council, but the same cannot be said of popular opinion or judicial practice in the United States.

Developments in the US Debate. Broadly speaking, the dominant trends in the use of capital punishment in the United States are all downward. The forty-six executions in 2010 were less than the fifty-two executions in 2009, and well down from the eighty-five executions in the year 2000. Juries handed down death sentences 114 times in 2010 and 112 times in 2009. In 1994 that number had been 328. Majority public opinion remained in favor of the death penalty, but the margin of support was lower: 65 percent in the 2006 Gallup Poll as against 80 percent in 1994. When, in 2006, Americans were asked to express a preference for capital punishment as against the sentence of life without parole, the numbers in favor of the use of the death penalty fell below 50 percent for the first time since the 1970s, with 47 percent of those polled preferring the death penalty but 48 percent favoring life without parole.

A major driver of that downward trend in support has been the increasing awareness of error and racial bias in the application of the death penalty. The innocence of Cameron Todd Willingham—executed in 2004 for deliberately setting a fire that killed his three children—has been particularly widely discussed, with forensic evidence now making abundantly clear that the fire was not started deliberately. Certain Supreme Court justices have also added their voices to the campaign for the abolition of the death penalty. John Paul Stevens, in a widely cited article in the December 23, 2010, issue of the *New York Review of Books*, wrote that "the death penalty represents the pointless and needless extinction of life with only marginal contributions to any discernible social or public purposes." Controversy continues too regarding the efficacy of execution by lethal injection. All but 174 of the 1,063 executions carried out in the United States since 1976 have been by this method, but 2010 saw renewed evidence of the pain caused during execution by the botched use of lethal drugs, to the point at which, by early 2011, the sole manufacturer of the key ingredient—thiopental sodium—had decided permanently to halt its production. Previously manufactured in Italy, the company faced a ban on its export imposed by the Italian government because of the drug's use in the execution of condemned prisoners.

So the issue of capital punishment remains in play in contemporary American politics. Calls abound in progressive circles both for a moratorium on the practice and for extensive reforms of the judicial process surrounding the death penalty. Beyond progressive circles, the American Bar Association and the Constitution Project, housed at the University of Maryland, have added their voices to calls for changes in defense services, procedural restrictions, clemency, jury instruction, judicial independence, racial discrimination, and the sentencing of juveniles and the mentally impaired (American Bar Association, 2001; Constitution Project, 2001). The most recent in a long line of such calls can be found in Charles Lane's book *Stay of Execution*, where he argues for the restriction of the use of the death penalty to crimes of a particularly heinous nature ("the worst of the worst")) and for the elimination of the death penalty for single murders committed in the course of other common felonies such as kidnapping, robbery, and arson. As Lane puts it, "reconfiguring the death penalty as a special penalty for special crimes would restore a certain moral clarity to capital punishment" (Lane, 2010, p. 113). But even that would leave the United States as an outlier in a world in which, as Amnesty International (2009) reported, "more than two-thirds of the countries of the world have abolished the death penalty in law and in practice." In the sphere of capital punishment, as in so much else, it would appear that, for now at least, American exceptionalism continues to rule the day.

[*See also* American Exceptionalism; Crime and Punishment; Federalism; Gun Control; Hate Crimes; *and* Race, Gender, and Incarceration.]

BIBLIOGRAPHY

Allen, Howard W., and Jerome M. Chubb. *Race, Class, and the Death Penalty: Capital Punishment in American History.* (Albany, N.Y., 2008).

American Bar Association. *Death without Justice: A Guide for Examining the Administration of the Death Penalty in the United States.* (Washington, D.C., 2001).

American Civil Liberties Union. "Race and the Death Penalty." (26 February 2003), http://www.aclu.org/capital-punishment/race-and-death-penalty.

Amnesty International. "The Death Penalty in 2009." http://www.amnesty.org/en/death-penalty/death-sentences-and-executions-in-2009.

Amnesty International. "United States of America: Death by Discrimination: The Continuing Role of Race in Capital Cases." (April 2003), http://www.amnesty.org/en/library/info/AMR51/046/2003.

Bae, Sangmin. *When the State No Longer Kills: International Human Rights Norms and Abolition of Capital Punishment.* (Albany, N.Y., 2007).

Bailey, William C. "Deterrence, Brutalization, and the Death Penalty: Another Examination of Oklahoma's Return to Capital Punishment." *Criminology* 36 (1998): 711–734.

Bakken, Gordon Morris, ed. *Invitation to an Execution: A History of the Death Penalty in the United States.* (Albuquerque, N.Mex., 2010).

Baldus, David C. "Comparative Review of Death Sentences: An Empirical Study of the Georgia Experience." *Journal of Criminal Law and Criminology* 74 (Autumn 1983): 661–753.

Baldus, David C., and George Woodworth. "Race Discrimination in the Administration of the Death Penalty: An Overview of the Empirical Evidence with Special Emphasis on the Post-1990 Research." *Criminal Law Bulletin* 39 (2003): 194–226.

Baumgartner, Frank R., Suzanna L. De Boef, and Amber E. Boydstun. *The Decline of the Death Penalty and the Discovery of Innocence.* (New York, 2008).

Bedau, Hugo Adam. *Killing as Punishment: Reflections on the Death Penalty in America.* (Boston, 2004).

Bedau, Hugo Adam, and Paul G. Cassell, eds. *Debating the Death Penalty: Should America Have Capital Punishment? The Experts on Both Sides Make Their Best Case.* (Oxford, 2004).

Berk, Richard. "New Claims about Executions and the General Deterrence: Déjà Vu All Over Again." *Journal of Empirical Legal Studies* 2 (July 2005): 303–330.

Berns, Walter. *For Capital Punishment: Crime and the Morality of the Death Penalty.* (Lanham, Md., 1991).

Bonner, Raymond, and Ford Fessenden. "States with No Death Penalty Share Lower Homicide Rates." *New York Times,* 22 September 2000.

Bright, Stephen B. "Capital Punishment on the 25th Anniversary of *Furman* v. *Georgia:* A Report by the Southern Center for Human Rights." (26 June 1997), http://www.schr.org/files/resources/furman3.pdf.

Bright, Stephen B. "The Death Sentence Not for the Worst Crime but for the Worst Lawyer." *Yale Law Review* (May 1994).

Bright, Stephen B. "Will the Death Penalty Remain Alive in the Twenty-First Century? International Norms, Discrimination, Arbitrariness, and the Risk of Executing the Innocent." *Wisconsin Law Review* (2001): 1–33.

Campaign to End the Death Penalty. "Thirty Years Is Enough: End the Death Penalty National Convention 2006." http://www.nodeathpenalty.org/new_abolitionist/january-2007-issue-41/thirty-years-enough.

Cassell, Paul G. "In Defense of the Death Penalty." In *Debating the Death Penalty: Should America Have Capital Punishment? The Experts on Both Sides Make Their Best Case*, edited by Hugo Adam Bedau and Paul G. Cassell, pp. 183–217. (Oxford, 2004).

Constitution Project. "Mandatory Justice: Eighteen Reforms to the Death Penalty." Death Penalty Paper 2009, http://www.prodeathpenalty.com/DP.html.

Dezhbakhsh, Hashem, and Joanna M. Shepherd. "The Deterrent Effect of Capital Punishment: Evidence from a 'Judicial Experiment.'" *Economic Inquiry* 44 (July 2006): 512–535.

Dezhbakhsh, Hashem, Paul H. Rubin, and Joanna M. Shepherd. "Does Capital Punishment Have a Deterrent Effect? New Evidence from Postmoratorium Panel Data." *American Law and Economics Review* 5 (2003): 344–376.

Death Penalty Information Center. "Arbitrariness." http://www.deathpenaltyinfo.org/arbitrariness.

Death Penalty Information Center. "The Death Penalty in Black and White: Who Lives, Who Dies, Who Decides." (June 1998), http://www.deathpenaltyinfo.org/death-penalty-black-and-white-who-lives-who-dies-who-decides.

Death Penalty Information Center. "Facts about the Death Penalty." http://www.deathpenaltyinfo.org/FactSheet.pdf.

Death Penalty Information Center. "Innocence and Crisis in the American Death Penalty." (2005), http://www.deathpenaltyinfo.org/innocence-and-crisis-american-death-penalty.

Death Penalty Information Center. "Killing for Votes: The Dangers of Politicizing the Death Penalty Process." (October 1996), http://www.deathpenaltyinfo.org/node/379.

Dieter, Richard C. "Blind Justice: Juries Deciding Life and Death with Only Half the Truth: How Death Penalty Jurors Are Unfairly Selected, Manipulated, and Kept in the Dark." Death Penalty Information Center Report. (October 2005), http://www.deathpenaltyinfo.org/BlindJusticeReport.pdf.

Fein, Bruce. "The Death Penalty, but Sparingly." *Human Rights Magazine*, September 2001.

Frum, David. "Why Australia Needs the Death Penalty." American Enterprise Institute for Public Policy Research. (7 March 2006), http://www.aei.org/article/23966.

Gerber, Rudolph J., and John M. Johnson. *The Top Ten Death Penalty Myths: The Politics of Crime Control.* (Westport, Conn., 2007).

House, H. Wayne, and John Howard Yoder. *The Death Penalty Debate.* (Dallas, Tex., 1991).

Jost, Kenneth. "Death Penalty Controversies." *CQ Researcher.* (23 September 2005), http://www.cqpress.com/product/Researcher-Death-Penalty.html.

Katz, Lawrence, Steven D. Levitt, and Ellen Shustorovich. "Prison Conditions, Capital Punishment, and Deterrence." *American Law and Economics Review* 5 (2003): 318–343.

Lane, Charles. *Stay of Execution: Saving the Death Penalty from Itself.* (Lanham, Md., 2010).

Liebman, James S., Jeffrey Fagan, and Valerie West. *A Broken System: Error Rates in Capital Cases, 1973–1995.* (Washington, D.C., 2000).

Lin, Ann Chih, ed. *Capital Punishment (CQ's Vital Issues Series).* (Washington, D.C., 2002).

Martinez, J. Michael, William D. Richardson, and D. Brandon Hornsby, eds. *The Leviathan's Choice: Capital Punishment in the Twenty-First Century.* (Lanham, Md., 2002).

Mocan, H. Naci, and R. Kay Gittings. "Getting off Death Row: Commuted Sentences and the Deterrent Effect of Capital Punishment." *Journal of Law and Economics* 46 (October 2003): 453–478.

National Coalition to Abolish the Death Penalty. "Innocence." (2007), http://www.ncadp.org/index.cfm?content=20.

Pojman, Louis P. "Why the Death Penalty Is Morally Defensible." In *Debating the Death Penalty: Should America Have Capital Punishment? The Experts on Both Sides Make Their Best Case*, edited by Hugo Adam Bedau and Paul G. Cassell, pp. 51–75. (Oxford, 2004).

Rosenzweig, Robert. "The Death Penalty, America, and the World." Heritage Foundation. (23 October 2003), http://www.heritage.org/research/commentary/2003/10/the-death-penalty-america-and-the-world.

Scheidegger, Kent M. "Smoke and Mirrors on Race and the Death Penalty." *Engage* 4 (2003): 42–45.

Stark, Richard A. *Dead Wrong: Violence, Vengeance, and the Victims of Capital Punishment.* (Westport, Conn., 2006).

Steiker, Carol S. "No, Capital Punishment Is Not Morally Required: Deterrence, Deontology, and the Death Penalty." *Stanford Law Review* 58 (2006): 751–789.

Stevens, John Paul. "On the Death Sentence." *New York Review of Books,* 23 December 2010.

Sunstein, Cass R., and Adrian Vermeule. "Is Capital Punishment Morally Required? Acts, Omissions, and Life-Life Tradeoffs." *Stanford Law Review* 583 (2006): 703–750.

Troy, Daniel E. "Our Innate Morality Demands Execution." *Los Angeles Times*, 7 May 2001.

Van den Haag, Ernst. "Why Capital Punishment." In *The Leviathan's Choice: Capital Punishment in the Twenty-First Century*, edited by J. Michael Martinez, William D. Richardson, and D. Brandon Hornsby, pp. 29–40. (Lanham, Md., 2002).

Zimmerman, Paul R. "State Executions, Deterrence, and the Incidence of Murder." *Journal of Applied Economics* 7 (May 2004): 163–193.

David Coates

CARTER, JIMMY

(b. 1924). Jimmy Carter, the thirty-ninth president of the United States, was born in the small town of Plains, Georgia, on 21 October 1924. He was the eldest of the four children born to James Earl Carter Sr. and Lillian Gordy Carter. After graduating from Plains High School (1941), he attended Georgia Southwestern College (1941–1942), the Georgia Institute of Technology (1942–1943), and the US Naval Academy at Annapolis (1943–1946). In 1946 he married Rosalynn Smith and graduated from the Naval Academy (standing sixtieth academically in his class of 820). Between 1946 and 1953, he served, primarily, in the submarine service of the US Navy (including a stint in the nuclear submarine service headed by Admiral Hyman Rickover). He obtained the rank of lieutenant, senior grade.

Upon the death of his father in 1953, Jimmy Carter returned to Plains to manage the family farm and peanut-processing business. In 1962, he won a seat in the Georgia legislature. In 1966 he undertook an unsuccessful gubernatorial campaign. Four years later, however, he defeated the popular and moderate former governor Carl Sanders in the Democratic primaries and won the governorship. Despite a stylistically "populist" campaign that contained some covert appeals to white racist sentiment, in office Carter proved to be a racial moderate and even a progressive. He reorganized the Georgia state government, reformed the state's mental health and environmental programs, hung Martin Luther King Jr.'s portrait in the state capitol, and increased the number of black state employees.

A short-lived attempt to secure the Democratic vice-presidential nomination in 1972 was followed by a four-year campaign for the Democratic presidential nomination. Not only did Carter outflank and outmaneuver his more prominent opponents, he used symbols to great advantage. His emphasis on his religious commitments (Baptist), regional base (the South, small town), and good relations with Georgia blacks appealed to voters weary of Watergate, big government, and racial divisions. His appeals, however, were so broad that his Republican opponent in the 1976 general election, the incumbent president Gerald Ford, was able to cut into his strength with claims that he waffled on the issues. From a following of approximately 70 percent in the late summer of 1976, Carter was able to eke out only a narrow 50 to 48 percent victory over Ford.

As president, Carter showed energy and intelligence in tackling several problems of his day. In his foreign policy he secured Senate approval of the treaty returning the Panama Canal to Panama; played a key role in securing the Camp David Accords between Egypt and Israel; and curbed the export of nuclear weapons technology to countries that did not possess them. He also put human rights near the top of his foreign policy agenda and tried to adapt to revolutionary movements in the Third World (e.g., to the Sandinistas in Nicaragua).

Domestically, his presidency marked the turn of the Democratic Party toward a neoliberal program emphasizing deregulation and the conservation of energy and the environment. His programmatic successes included the deregulation of the airline industry and interstate trucking; the creation of the Departments of Energy and Education; and the passage of several conservation measures, including the Strip Mining Control and Reclamation Act of 1977 and the Alaska Land Act of 1980. After a long struggle, he also secured portions of his energy program. He also resisted AFL-CIO calls to raise the minimum wage to $3.00 per hour and deferred action for several months on the full employment provisions of the proposed Humphrey-Hawkins bill.

Several of his major policy goals, however, never were accomplished. Due to his inexperience in diplomacy, the Strategic Arms Limitation agreement was not concluded with the Soviet Union (USSR) until June 1979. Whatever chances it had for passage in the Senate were ended when the Soviets invaded Afghanistan in December 1979. He also failed in his attempts at welfare reform, as well as his endeavors to create a national no-fault insurance program and establish a federal consumer protection agency.

Despite Carter's intelligence and energy, his popular support as president was shallow. A precipitous decline in his popularity toward the end of 1979 led Senator Ted Kennedy of the Democratic Party's liberal wing to compete with him for the party's nomination in 1980. Having fended off that challenge, Carter lost the general election of 1980 to the Republican candidate, Ronald Reagan, by a vote of 41 to 51 percent (independent candidate John B. Anderson carried 7 percent of the popular vote). It was the first time since Herbert Hoover that an elected president had run for and failed to win a second term.

The reasons for Carter's lack of support in the country and in the Democratic Party have been widely debated. Some scholars argue that his problems were due to one or more of the following forces: the growing factionalism in Congress; the lack of programmatic cohesion in the Democratic Party; the difficulties the traditional Democrats have had in adapting to a more conservative political climate; and the intractable nature of the problems facing the country. Other scholars see Carter as bearing more responsibility for his political problems. They note that he lacked the kinds of political skills requisite to successful governance. He had difficulties in determining his programmatic priorities and dealing with political tradeoffs; his congressional liaison operation was amateurish at the beginning; and he often failed to consult influential individuals in the relevant policy networks as a part of the coalition-building process.

Certainly factors over which Carter had no clear control contributed to his failure to win reelection. The administration's inability to secure the release of the American hostages held in Iran caused some

voters to shift toward Reagan. But most important was the double-digit inflation of the economy. Many voters, as most of the exit polls showed, saw Carter as an ineffective president, and a plurality of the voters, for the first time since the New Deal, saw the Republican Party as the most likely to manage the economy in constructive ways.

Carter quickly assumed the role of activist former president following his presidential election defeat at the age of fifty-six. His activities focused around publications and the Carter Center. He has written twenty-eight books, with *The White House Diary* (2010) being published when he was eighty-six years old.

The Carter Center opened in 1982, with the two broad goals of improving the world by "waging peace" and "fighting disease." This nonpartisan, nonprofit, nongovernmental organization located next to the Jimmy Carter Presidential Library in Atlanta, Georgia, epitomizes the energy Carter has brought to his post-presidential activities. To help resolve international conflicts, under his leadership, eleven conflict mediations between nations have been carried out, while he has been asked by every succeeding president (except Ronald Reagan) to assist on diplomatic missions. His efforts were critical to the successful resolution of US conflicts with the Democratic People's Republic of North Korea (1994) and Haiti (1994). To promote democracy, the Carter Center led by Jimmy Carter has monitored over eighty-three elections and continues to actively pursue this function. The Center's disease prevention work is no less impressive, with the Guinea worm eradication program reducing this blinding disease by 98 percent, with the potential for total worldwide elimination.

In 1982 he became the University Distinguished Professor at Emory University in Atlanta. Accolades followed, as he was awarded the United Nations Human Rights Prize in 1998, the highest civilian medal, the Presidential Medal of Freedom, in 1999 (an honor he shared with his wife, Rosalynn), and the Nobel Peace Prize in 2002, "for his decades of untiring effort to find peaceful solutions to international conflicts, to promote democracy and human rights and to promote economic and social development."

Jimmy Carter has chosen, in his words, to use the moral authority available to former presidents to address world problems. As a former president, Carter has shaped an unusually constructive role for himself.

[*See also* Democratic Party; Presidency: Governing; *and* Reagan, Ronald.]

BIBLIOGRAPHY

Carter, Jimmy. *Keeping Faith: Memoirs of a President.* (New York, 1982).

Glad, Betty. *Jimmy Carter: In Search of the Great White House.* (New York, 1980).

Hargrove, Erwin C. *Jimmy Carter as President: Leadership and the Practice of the Public Good.* (Baton Rouge, La., 1988).

Betty Glad and Kathy Smith

CENTER-LEFT LIBERALISM

See Liberalism, Center-Left.

CENTRAL ASIA

The Central Asian republics—Kazakhstan, Kyrgyzstan, Tajikistan, Turkmenistan, and Uzbekistan—were among those least prepared for or eager for independence when the Soviet Union dissolved at the end of 1991. The United States quickly recognized their independence and immediately offered diplomatic relations to Kazakhstan and Kyrgyzstan, which were viewed as following responsible security and democratic policies. However, concern about the dangers the Central Asian states faced from Iranian-supported Islamic fundamentalism prompted the United States to ease these conditions and establish diplomatic relations with the remaining states by mid-March. Faced with calls in Congress and elsewhere that the administration devise a policy on assistance to the fragile new states of the former Soviet Union, the US president George H. W. Bush sent the Freedom Support Act to Congress, which was approved by Congress with some changes and signed into law in October 1992.

US policy in Central Asia has been tailored to the varying characteristics of these states. US interests in Kazakhstan have included securing and eliminating Soviet-era nuclear and biological weapons materials and facilities. US energy firms have invested in oil and natural gas development in Kazakhstan and Turkmenistan, and successive administrations have backed diverse export routes to the West for these resources. US policy toward Kyrgyzstan has long included support for its civil society. In Tajikistan, the United States pledged to assist in its economic reconstruction following that country's 1992–1997 civil war. US relations with Uzbekistan—the most populous state in the heart of the region—were cool after 2005, but recently have improved. Since the 2008 global economic downturn, more US humanitarian, health, and education assistance has been provided to hard-struck Kyrgyzstan and Tajikistan.

The Obama administration has listed five objectives of what it terms an enhanced US engagement policy in Central Asia:

1. to maximize the cooperation of the states of the region with coalition counterterrorism efforts in Afghanistan and Pakistan (particularly cooperation on hosting US and North Atlantic Treaty Organization (NATO) airbases, and on the transit of troops and supplies to Afghanistan along the "Northern Distribution Network"; see below);
2. to increase the development and diversification of the region's energy resources and supply routes;
3. to promote the eventual emergence of democracy and respect for human rights;
4. to foster competitive market economies; and
5. to increase the capacity of the states to govern themselves, and in particular to prevent state failure in Tajikistan and Kyrgyzstan, including by enhancing food security assistance.

Signs of this enhanced engagement by the Obama administration include the establishment of high-level Annual Bilateral Consultations (ABCs) with each of the regional states on counter-narcotics, counter-terrorism, democratic reform, rule of law, human rights, trade, investment, health, and education.

Relations after the Terrorist Attacks on the United States on September 11, 2001. Immediately after the terrorist attacks on the United States on September 11, 2001, the Central Asian governments condemned the attacks, but over the following two weeks, as US attention focused on Afghanistan, none unambiguously offered to permit overflight rights or US military airbase access. However, perhaps after receiving approval from Russia, on 23–24 September 2001, the Kazakh president Nursultan Nazarbayev pledged his country's readiness to assist an international coalition to combat the "evil" of terrorism, offering overflight rights and the use of airbases, although he averred that Kazakh forces would not fight in Afghanistan. On 24 September 2001, Turkmenistan's president at the time, Saparamurat Niyazov, gave his consent for ground transport and overflights to deliver humanitarian aid to support US antiterrorism efforts in Afghanistan. The next day, Kyrgyzstan's president Askar Akayev indicated that he had received the backing of the other regional leaders and Russia for US use of Kyrgyz airspace for antiterrorism operations in Afghanistan. Many Uzbek officials were offended by a warning from the Taliban "foreign minister" on 24 September 2001, against permitting US use of Uzbek territory to attack Afghanistan. Two days later, the Uzbek president Islam Karimov allowed US use of Uzbek airspace against Afghan-based terrorists for "humanitarian and security purposes" if Uzbekistan's security was guaranteed.

US Basing Access in Kyrgyzstan. The US military repaired and upgraded the air field at the Manas international airport near Bishkek, and it became operational in December 2001. According to the US Air Force, the Manas airbase (now termed the Manas Transit Center, see below) has served as the premier air mobility hub supporting military operations in Afghanistan. Missions have included support for personnel and cargo transiting in and out of the theater, aerial refueling, airlift and airdrop, and medical evacuation. US Secretary of State Hillary Clinton was told during her December 2010 visit to the Manas Transit Center that up to 3,500 troops every day, over 13 million pounds of cargo each month,

and 117 million gallons of fuel each year are handled by the airbase. The United States and Kazakhstan signed a memorandum of understanding on 10 July 2002, permitting US military aircraft to use Kazakhstan's airport in Almaty for emergency military landings; the accord was needed in part because military flights out of the Manas Transit Center, 120 miles away, could be disrupted by harsh weather.

On 3 February 2009, Kyrgyzstan's president Kurmanbek Bakiyev announced during a visit to Moscow that he intended to close the Manas airbase. Many observers speculated that the decision was spurred by a large loan proffered by Russia, which had become more concerned about the US military presence in Central Asia as the years had stretched on since the base was first established. After negotiations, however, the US Defense Department announced on 24 June 2009 that an agreement of "mutual benefit" had been concluded with the Kyrgyz government to keep the newly renamed "Transit Center at Manas Airport" open. A yearly rent payment for use of land and facilities at the Manas Airport would be increased from $17.4 million to $60 million per year, and the United States pledged other boosted aid. Initially after the April 2010 ouster of President Bakiyev, some officials in the interim government stated or implied that the conditions of the lease would be examined. Meeting with Secretary Clinton on 2 December 2010, the new Kyrgyz president, Roza Otunbayeva, stressed that the Manas Transit Center was a significant contributor to regional security and that Kyrgyzstan would support its operation at least through 2014, in line with US administration objectives for drawing down US forces.

US Basing Access in Uzbekistan. An agreement on US use of Uzbekistan's Khanabad airbase, near the city of Karshi, was signed on 7 October 2001, just before the commencement of coalition air attacks on Taliban forces, and a joint US-Uzbek statement on combating terrorism was broadcast on Uzbek television on 12 October. The joint statement included a vague security guarantee for Uzbekistan, in that the two sides agreed to consult in the event of a threat to Uzbekistan's security and territorial integrity.

Karimov visited the United States in March 2002, and the two sides signed a Strategic Partnership accord that reiterated the security guarantee. Uzbekistan benefited from the basing accord when US forces helped severely degrade the capabilities of the Islamic Movement of Uzbekistan (IMU), a terrorist group harbored by the Taliban, and probably killed the IMU co-leader Juma Namanganiy in November 2001. In April 2002, Karimov expressed Uzbekistan's gratitude to the United States for relieving the danger posed by the IMU to Uzbekistan.

In mid-2005, the United States criticized an Uzbek government crackdown in the southern town of Andijon, which reportedly had resulted in widespread killings of civilians. Uzbekistan responded by demanding that the United States vacate the Karshi Khanabad airbase within six months. The United States officially ceased operations at the airbase in November 2005. Many activities were shifted to the Manas airbase in Kyrgyzstan. However, appearing to signal improving US-Uzbek relations, in early 2008 Uzbekistan permitted US military personnel under NATO command, on a case-by-case basis, to transit through an airbase near the town of Termez which it has permitted Germany to operate. Further improvement in relations appeared evident in May 2009, when President Karimov announced that the United States and NATO had been permitted to use the Navoi airport (located between Samarkand and Bukhara in east-central Uzbekistan; see also below) for transporting nonlethal supplies to Afghanistan. In August 2009, Uzbekistan reportedly permitted US military air overflights of weapons to Afghanistan.

The Northern Distribution Network. Because supplies crossing Pakistan to support US and NATO military operations in Afghanistan frequently were subject to attacks, General David Petraeus, the then-commander of the US Central Command (USCENTCOM), visited Kazakhstan and Tajikistan in late January 2009 to negotiate alternative air, rail, road, and water routes. To encourage a positive response for this Northern Distribution Network (NDN), the US embassies in the region announced that the United States hoped to purchase many nonmilitary goods locally to transport to the troops in

Afghanistan. Kazakhstan and Tajikistan permitted such transit in February 2009, Uzbekistan permitted it in April 2009, and Kyrgyzstan permitted it in July 2009. According to some reports, Turkmenistan had long transported fuel and other supplies to Afghanistan.

There are broadly three land routes: one through the South Caucasus into Central Asia; one from Latvia through Russia, Kazakhstan, and Uzbekistan; and one from Latvia through Russia, Kazakhstan, Kyrgyzstan, and Tajikistan. According to the Defense Department, the amount of goods transported via the NDN has grown substantially, and in early 2011 accounted for over one-half of the nonlethal surface shipments to Afghanistan. In addition, increasing volumes of jet fuel are being purchased in Azerbaijan and Central Asia and transported to Afghanistan. Supplementing land routes, Uzbekistan's Navoi Airport reportedly is being used to transport supplies to Afghanistan. After aircraft land at Navoi, the supplies are sent by rail and truck to Afghanistan. Besides commercial shipping of nonlethal cargoes, most regional governments allegedly have quietly given US and NATO military aircraft overflight privileges for the transport of weapons and troops to Afghanistan. Some observers warn that Taliban insurgency appears to be increasing along the NDN. In September 2010, Assistant Secretary of State Robert Blake stated that the United States was assisting the countries participating in the NDN to improve border security to help them face this threat. In congressional testimony in February 2011, Director of National Intelligence James Clapper raised concerns about the stability of governments in Kyrgyzstan and Tajikistan, and their ability to surmount terrorist threats, including those emanating from Afghanistan.

Support for Operations in Iraq. Uzbekistan and Kazakhstan were the only Central Asian states that joined the "coalition of the willing" in 2003, thus signifying their endorsement of US-led coalition military operations in Iraq. Uzbekistan subsequently decided not to send troops to Iraq. In August 2003, Kazakhstan deployed some two dozen troops to Iraq, who served under Polish command and carried out water-purification, demining, and medical activities. They pulled out in late 2008.

US Foreign and Security Assistance. For much of the 1990s, and until September 11, 2001, the United States provided much more aid each year to Russia and Ukraine than to any Central Asian state. Cumulative foreign aid budgeted to Central Asia for fiscal year (FY) 1992 through FY2008 amounted to $4.7 billion—about 14 percent of the amount budgeted to all the Eurasian states, reflecting the lesser priority given to these states prior to September 11, 2001. Budgeted spending for FY2002 for Central Asia—during the launch of US operations in Afghanistan—was greatly boosted in absolute amounts ($584 million) and as a share of total aid to Eurasia (about one-quarter of such aid). The George W. Bush administration requested smaller amounts of aid in subsequent years, although it continued to stress that there were important US interests in the region. The former Bush administration highlighted the phase-out of economic aid to Kazakhstan and the Congressionally imposed restrictions on aid to Uzbekistan (see below) as among the reasons for declining aid requests. The Obama administration boosted aid to some of the Central Asian states in FY2010, but a more constrained US budgetary situation has led to some aid cuts since then.

Besides the US security interest in Central Asia's support for military operations in Afghanistan, in 1992 the US Congress passed Comprehensive Threat Reduction (CTR) legislation to provide assistance to contain proliferation threats, including those posed by loosely guarded Soviet-era nuclear, chemical, and biological weapons and materials in the region. The United States had become increasingly concerned over various incidents of attempted nuclear smuggling, and rumors that Iran had attempted to gain access to such materials. Kazakhstan was, on paper, a major nuclear weapons power after it gained its independence (in reality Russia controlled these weapons), but in May 1992, Kazakhstan signed the Lisbon Protocol to the Strategic Arms Reduction Talks Treaty (START), pledging to become a non-nuclear weapons state. In December 1993, the United States and Kazakhstan signed a CTR umbrella agreement for the "safe and secure" dismantling of 104 intercontinental ballistic missiles (SS-18s), the destruction of their silos, and related purposes. The SS-18s were eliminated by late 1994. On 21 April 1995, the last of about 1,040 nuclear warheads had been removed from SS-18 missiles and transferred to Russia, and Kazakhstan announced that it was nuclear weapons-free. Besides the Kazakh nuclear weapons, there are active research reactors, uranium mines, milling facilities, and dozens of radioactive tailing and waste dumps in Kazakhstan, Kyrgyzstan, Tajikistan, and Uzbekistan. Kazakhstan also is a major producer of low-enriched uranium. To counter the proliferation threats posed by these and other facilities and activities, US CTR assistance remains a major component of assistance to Central Asia.

US–Central Asia Trade and Energy Relations. Successive US administrations have endorsed free market reforms in Central Asia, given that these directly serve US national interests by opening new markets for US goods and services and sources of energy and minerals. US private investment committed to Central Asia has greatly exceeded that provided to Russia or most other Eurasian states, except Azerbaijan. US trade agreements have been signed and entered into force with all the Central Asian states, but bilateral investment treaties are in force only with Kazakhstan and Kyrgyzstan. In line with Kyrgyzstan's accession to the World Trade Organization, the United States established permanent normal trade relations with Kyrgyzstan by law in June 2000, so that "Jackson-Vanik" trade provisions no longer apply that call for presidential reports and waivers concerning freedom of emigration.

In June 2004, the US trade representative signed a Trade and Investment Framework Agreement (TIFA) with ambassadors of the regional states to establish a US–Central Asia Council on Trade and Investment. The Council has met yearly to address intellectual property, labor, environmental protection, and other issues that impede trade and private investment flows between the United States and Central Asia. The United States also has called for greater intraregional cooperation on trade and encouraged the development of regional trade and transport ties with Afghanistan and South Asia. The reorganization of the State Department in 2006 to create the Bureau of South and Central Asian Affairs facilitated this emphasis.

Energy Resources. Among the Central Asian states, Kazakhstan, Turkmenistan, and Uzbekistan possess substantial oil and gas resources, although at present the first two are the major regional energy exporters. The US Energy Department (DOE) reported in November 2010 that Kazakhstan possessed 30 billion barrels of proven oil reserves (comparable to Qatar). The DOE also reported estimates of 85 trillion cubic feet of proven gas reserves (comparable to the European Union countries). Kazakhstan's oil exports currently are about 1.3 million barrels per day, and it is becoming a net gas exporter. Turkmenistan's proven natural gas reserves—286.2 trillion cubic feet—are among the highest in the world, according to British Petroleum (BP) data. At present, Turkmenistan exports gas to Russia, China, Iran, and other Central Asian states, but has indicated that it wants to build pipelines to enable export to Europe and South Asia.

US policy goals regarding energy resources in the Central Asian and South Caucasian states have included supporting their sovereignty and ties to the West, supporting US private investment, promoting Western energy security through diversified suppliers, assisting ally Turkey, and opposing the building of pipelines that benefit "energy competitor" Iran or otherwise give it undue influence over the region. The encouragement of regional electricity, oil, and gas exports to South Asia and security for Caspian region pipelines and energy resources also have been recent interests.

Until recently US foreign direct investment (FDI) played a preeminent role in the development of Kazakhstani oil and gas resources, amounting to about $29 billion in Kazakhstan (over one-third of all FDI in the country) from 1993 to 2010. According to some reports, China has provided billions of dollars of loans and investment pledges to Kazakhstan's energy sector in recent years. The US Trade and Development Agency's Central Asian Infrastructure Integration Initiative (launched in 2005) and USAID's Regional Energy Market Assistance Program (launched in 2006) concentrate on encouraging energy, transportation, and communications projects, including the development of electrical power infrastructure and power sharing between Central Asia, Afghanistan, and eventually Pakistan and India. USCENTCOM also has called for developing a "silk road" trade corridor linking Central and South Asia.

US Concerns about Democratization and Human Rights. A major goal of US policy in Central Asia has been to foster the long-term development of democratic institutions and respect for human rights. Particularly since September 11, 2001, the United States has attempted to harmonize its concerns about democratization and human rights in the region with its interests in regional support for counterterrorism.

During Nazarbayev's 1994 US visit, he and the US president Bill Clinton signed a Charter on Democratic Partnership that recognized Kazakhstan's commitments to the rule of law, respect for human rights, and economic reform. During his December 2001 and September 2006 visits, Nazarbayev repeated these pledges in joint statements with the US president George W. Bush. In March 2002, a US-Uzbek Strategic Partnership Declaration was signed, pledging Uzbekistan to "intensify the democratic transformation" and improve freedom of the press. During his December 2002 US visit, Tajikistan's president Emomali Rahmon also pledged to "expand fundamental freedoms and human rights." Despite their pledges to democratize, all the leaders in Central Asia have held onto power by orchestrating extensions of their terms, holding suspect elections, eliminating possible competitors, and providing emoluments to supporters and relatives. Kyrgyzstan's October 2010 presidential election of Roza Otunbayeva was deemed to be the fairest yet held in the region.

In Congress, yearly appropriations bills since FY2003 have forbidden foreign assistance to the governments of Uzbekistan and Kazakhstan unless the secretary of state reports that the states are making progress in democratization and human rights. The secretary reported in mid-2003 that Kazakhstan and Uzbekistan were making such progress, but has reported scant progress by these states since then. However, the secretary has exercised the waiver to continue aid to Kazakhstan. In FY2008, another condition was added to block the admission of Uzbek officials to the United States if the secretary of state determines that they were involved in abuses in Andijon. Perhaps reflecting the thawing of US-Uzbek relations, appropriations in FY2010 and thereafter have permitted Uzbekistan to receive some International Military Education and Training (IMET) funds for courses in democratic civil-military relations.

[*See also* Afghanistan; 9/11; Nonproliferation, Nuclear; Pakistan–United States Relations; *and* Russia–United States Relations.]

BIBLIOGRAPHY

Blake, Robert O., Jr. "The Obama Administration's Priorities in South and Central Asia." United States Department of State. (19 January 2011), http://www.state.gov/p/sca/rls/rmks/2011/155002.htm.

Bohr, Annette. "Central Asia: Responding to the Multi-Vectoring Game." In *America and a Changed World: A Question of Leadership*, edited by Robin Niblett, pp. 109–124. (London, 2010).

International Crisis Group. "Central Asia: Decay and Decline." (3 February 2011), http://www.crisisgroup.org/en/regions/asia/central-asia/201-central-asia-decay-and-decline.aspx.

Kuchins, Andrew C. "A Truly Regional Economic Strategy for Afghanistan." *Washington Quarterly* 34, no. 2 (Spring 2011): 77–91.

"Mystery at Manas: Strategic Blind Spots in the Department of Defense's Fuel Contracts in Kyrgyzstan." Report of the Majority Staff, United States House of Representatives. (December 2010), http://merln.ndu.edu/archivepdf/centasia/Mystery_at_Manas.pdf.

Jim Nichol

CHARTER SCHOOLS

A central theme in the politics and policy of education in the United States in recent decades has been market-based reform—the idea that increasing opportunities for parents to choose their child's school will lead to general improvements in school quality, as well as decreases in the overall cost of education. While this idea can be traced at least as far back as the writings of Milton Friedman in the 1950s and 1960s, arguably the modern era of school choice began with the 1990 publication of *Politics, Markets, and America's Schools* by political scientists John Chubb and Terry Moe. This influential volume makes the case that the institutions of American democracy that govern education, such as elected school boards, actually inhibit the quality of American schools through the self-interested actions of political interest groups. Chubb and Moe make the case for a remedy based on school vouchers, with which parents can opt out of the public school system and receive a certain amount of money that can be used for private education. While such voucher regimes in various forms have captured much of the attention of education policy makers and researchers over the last twenty years, arguably a different form of school choice has been much more successful: charter schools.

Charter schools are public schools that are granted significant autonomy, relative to the traditional public school system, in exchange for increased accountability. In school year 2010–2011 there were over 5,200 charter schools (about 5.4 percent of all public schools) operating in forty states plus the District of Columbia, and educating 1.8 million students (3.7 percent of all public school students). Like any public school, charters are funded by tax dollars from local, state, and federal sources. However, unlike typical public schools, they generally operate independently of the geographical school district where they are located and are thus less constrained by many of the institutions that define the American school district, such as collective bargaining agreements and school board politics. Their operating agreement—their "charter"—generally spells out the accountability conditions that they must meet in order for their doors to remain open.

Although the fundamental definition of a charter school is common across jurisdictions, many other important aspects of these schools, such as who may charter them, how they may be governed, the contents of a school's charter, and the details of how they are funded, vary significantly across states due to differences in charter laws. However, even this variation is small in comparison to the differences among the schools themselves. One of the central theoretical justifications for charter schools is that their autonomy would yield substantial innovation in all aspects of schooling; in other words, the charters would serve as education laboratories. While the evidence of real innovation in the charters is controversial, it is clear that the schools in this sector are extremely diverse, ranging from small independent schools created by parents and teachers to large, multistate networks of schools run by "educational maintenance organizations" or EMOs.

One of the most interesting aspects of charter schools, however, is not their range of pedagogy or their diversity of organization, but the fact that they have such broad political support. Unlike school vouchers, which have generally seen their support confined to market-oriented political conservatives, charter schools have been embraced by both Democrats and Republicans, in states ranging from Arizona to Massachusetts, and charters played a central role in both President George W. Bush's signature education reforms and President Barack Obama's "Race to the Top" educational initiative.

One explanation for this bipartisan support is undoubtedly that charter schools represent a compromise between a more complete privatization model endorsed by voucher proponents and the state-centered traditional public schools. Charter schools, for some, represent the best of each—publicly funded and accountable, yet free of interest group politics and the perceived ossification of the traditional, bureaucratic school district.

Another factor explaining the political support for charter schools, however, is suggested by looking at where they are geographically. While about a quarter of American schools and just under 30 percent of students are in urban areas, over half of charter schools and students are found in America's cities. Charter schools, for pragmatic education reformers in these cities, represent just another tool to

be used to solve the herculean task of improving the nation's lowest-performing schools. The combination of well-publicized success stories like KIPP Academies and the charter schools in the Harlem Children's Zone, combined with the general frustration over the slow pace of improvement in urban schools, has led nonideological education leaders on both the left and the right to embrace charter schools as a possible policy solution.

Although questions remain about the overall educational quality of the charters relative to their traditional public counterparts and about the extent to which charter schools have really developed innovative pedagogy or programs, their bipartisan support, popularity with many parents, and growing "market share" in cities like New York, Washington, D.C., and Los Angeles suggest that they are likely to remain a significant part of American education policy in the foreseeable future. Key political debates over charter schooling in the next decades will center on issues of equitable access to the schools for difficult-to-educate populations like English language learners and students with special educational needs, as well as on the question of whether the number of charter schools in states or districts should be limited through legal "caps," or if the number of charters should be unconstrained. A key indicator of the direction that charter schools might take in the future is their role in the next reauthorization of the Elementary and Secondary Education Act, and the evolution of the interaction of school choice and standards-based accountability in federal education policy.

[*See also* Education and Politics; *and* Urban Sprawl.]

BIBLIOGRAPHY

Abernathy, Scott Franklin. *School Choice and the Future of American Democracy.* (Ann Arbor, Mich, 2005).
Buckley, Jack, and Mark Schneider. *Charter Schools: Hope or Hype?* (Princeton, N.J., 2007).
Chubb, John E., and Terry M. Moe. *Politics, Markets, and America's Schools.* (Washington, D.C., 1990).
Fuller, Bruce. *Inside Charter Schools: The Paradox of Radical Decentralization.* (Cambridge, Mass., 2000).

Henig, Jeffrey R. *Spin Cycle: How Research Is Used in Policy Debates: The Case of Charter Schools.* (New York, 2008).

Lubienski, Christopher A., and Peter C. Weitzel. *The Charter School Experiment: Expectations, Evidence, and Implications.* (Cambridge, Mass., 2010).

National Alliance for Public Charter Schools. "Schools by Geographic Locale 2009–2010 National." http://dashboard.publiccharters.org/dashboard/schools/page/locale/year/2010.

National Alliance for Public Charter Schools. "Schools Overview 2010–2011 National." http://dashboard.publiccharters.org/dashboard/schools/year/2011.

National Alliance for Public Charter Schools. "Students by Geographic Locale 2009–2010 National." http://dashboard.publiccharters.org/dashboard/students/page/locale/year/2010.

Jack Buckley

CHECKS AND BALANCES

A constitution is a framework for the exercise of political power. It establishes the institutions of decision-making and specifies their authority and methods of proceeding. In so doing, a constitution stipulates the limits of the various branches of government. Separation of powers (executive, legislative, judicial) and attendant checks and balances are the essence of this framework in American democracy.

The separationist philosophy for a constitutional order is rather simple: concentrating power in a single source cultivates bad consequences, possibly even tyranny. In the United States, the best case for this thinking was made by James Madison in the *Federalist No. 51.* Clarity was ensured because Madison explained concepts in human terms. He argued that encroachment by one department or branch on another must be controlled to prevent abuses. After all, government is "the greatest of all reflections on human nature." If "men were angels" or "angels were to govern men" checks and balances would not be necessary. Lacking angelic intercession, however, "you must first enable the government to control the governed; and in the next place oblige it to control itself." Reliance on the people in a democracy helps provide these protections. But "experience has taught mankind the necessity of auxiliary precautions." Thus separationism, with checks and balances, is justified, relying as it does on a precept of human behavior: "Ambition must be made to counteract ambition."

Madison and his colleagues at the Constitutional Convention were aware of the justification of separated powers expressed in the writings of Montesquieu and John Locke. Equally, if not more, persuasive, however, were the practical issues of governance they were seeking to resolve at hand in Philadelphia. The astute philosopher will react by warning of gridlock as a result of such inter-branch checking. For example, a government featuring counteractive legislative and executive ambitions may be stalemated, and thus fail to govern effectively. The Founders were aware of this potential. In fact, the Constitutional Convention met in large part because of the insufficiency of governance under the Articles of Confederation. Whereas protection against tyranny was fundamental, creating a workable government was equally paramount. The purpose was to separate and check, but not to the exclusion of lawmaking and its implementation. Madison, in *Federalist No. 47,* emphasizes: "The accumulation of all powers, legislative, executive, and judiciary, in the same hands . . . may justly be pronounced the very definition of tyranny." Yet he favorably cites the warning in the New Hampshire Constitution that separation be accomplished "as the nature of free government will admit or as is consistent with that chain of connection that binds the whole fabric of the constitution in one indissoluble bond of unity and amity." Separate, check, balance—but remain cognizant of the governing imperative of the chain of connection.

"Separate to unify" was therefore the bold mission to be accomplished by the Founders. Separate to prevent the certainty of tyranny with concentrated power—but do it so as to make and implement law. The result in Philadelphia was a concoction of methods of selection and bases of representation, as well as different term lengths and designated powers, for each branch of the government. Each branch was allowed to check and balance another, sometimes to perform each other's functions. The president has legislative and judicial authority (e.g., to set agendas, veto bills, nominate judges, and issue pardons), Congress can affect executive and judicial decisions (e.g., to legislate, fund the government, override vetoes, approve treaties and nominations, impeach certain officials, and establish lower courts), and the judiciary can interpret legislative and executive intent, and even measure it against a constitutional standard, following *Marbury v. Madison* (1803).

No one was certain how this fabricated government would work or how long it would last. The institutional boundaries were said to be confused and uncertain, approaching that of a *de novo* governmental experiment. An important effect of the governing system devised in Philadelphia and its uncertain institutional boundaries has been ambiguity ever since as to who can check and balance whom, when, how, and to what extent. Questions about boundaries of power and influence across the federal government are as fresh today as in 1787.

This ambiguity invites attention to shifts in the strength, perhaps even the dominance, of one branch in relation to others through history. Vagueness offers flexibility of meaning. Therefore those in each branch have identified and exercised powers from seemingly ordinary constitutional provisions quite possibly not intended for the purpose realized. Notable examples include Chief Justice John Marshall finding support for judicial review in the justices' oath of office (*Marbury v. Madison*); twentieth-century presidents spotting critical agenda-setting powers in the State of the Union and recommendation of measures provisions; and the modern Congress taking an expansive view of its power "to regulate Commerce ... among the several states." Other cases include: judicial interpretations of the First Amendment; signing statements, veto threats, war powers, and budget preparation by presidents; and detailed investigations, an expanded role in national security issues, and partisanship in approving judicial appointments on the part of Congress.

Greater world status for the United States, an enormous growth of federal government programs over time, and the attendant complexity of issues raised by these two developments explain the shifts in the relative status of the three branches. For the most part, the changes have expanded the size, reach, and responsibilities of the executive. However, Congress and the courts continue to perform significant "checking and balancing" functions.

In his book *Congressional Government: A Study in American Politics* (1885), Woodrow Wilson revealed his judgment that Congress was the dominant branch in the nineteenth century. He was critical of Congress as not sufficiently responsible to the public it was elected to represent. "Somebody must be trusted," he argued, so it will be perfectly clear who to reward or punish (pp. 283–284). Wilson did not doubt who should be so trusted: the chief executive. In fact, he participated along with Theodore Roosevelt in strengthening the president's role early in the twentieth century. Later the Great Depression and World War II contributed further to an increase in presidential power. Analysts soon wrote of an "imperial presidency," and the Twenty-Second Amendment, limiting the president to two terms of office, was ratified in 1951, following Franklin D. Roosevelt's four elections.

Checks and balances remain vital to the workings of the American government. They are dynamic features of a separated-powers system, ever adjusting to the changes in political time and ever dependent on the independence of the distinct branches. Congressional government may have given way to presidential government, but excesses by any one of the three branches are still subject to legitimate obstructions or reversals by the others. Voters too weigh in regularly to rearrange who does the checking and balancing.

[*See also* Bill of Rights; Congress, US; Federalism; Judicial System, American; Presidency: Governing; *and* Separation of Powers.]

BIBLIOGRAPHY

Bryce, James. *The American Commonwealth.* (Indianapolis, Ind., 1995). Originally published in 1893.

Casper, Gerhard. *Separating Power: Essays on the Founding Period.* (Cambridge, Mass., 1997).

Hall, Kermit L., ed. *The Oxford Guide to United States Supreme Court Decisions.* (New York, 1999).

Hamilton, Alexander, John Jay, and James Madison. *The Federalist.* (New York, 1937).

Jones, Charles O. *The Presidency in a Separated System.* 2d ed. (Washington, D.C., 2005).

Mayhew, David R. *Divided We Govern: Party Control, Lawmaking, and Investigations, 1946–2002.* 2d ed. (New Haven, Conn., 2005).

McCloskey, Robert G. *The American Supreme Court.* (Chicago, 1960).

Peterson, Mark A. *Legislating Together: The White House and Capitol Hill from Eisenhower to Reagan.* (Cambridge, Mass., 1990).

Sundquist, James L. *Constitutional Reform and Effective Government.* Rev. ed. (Washington, D.C., 1992).

Waldron, Jeremy. *Law and Disagreement.* (New York and Oxford, 1999).

Wilson, Woodrow. *Congressional Government: A Study in American Politics.* (New Brunswick, N.J., 2002). Originally published in 1885.

Charles O. Jones

CHICAGO SCHOOL OF ECONOMICS

The "Chicago School of Economics" refers to ideas emanating from the University of Chicago Department of Economics and related programs. The main figures associated with Chicago school economics are Milton Friedman (1912–2006), George J. Stigler (1911–1991), Aaron Director (1901–2004), Ronald H. Coase (b. 1910), and Gary S. Becker (b. 1930). They were influenced by earlier Chicago economists, especially Frank H. Knight (1885–1972), Jacob Viner (1892–1970), and Henry C. Simons (1899–1946). It should be noted that there is considerable diversity among the ideas of the individuals listed here, and still more diversity across the people who have taught economics at the University of Chicago. However, there are commonly held beliefs and practices that set these Chicago-based economists apart from others outside Chicago. In short, Chicago school ideas are: (1) that economic theory coupled with empirical evidence is a powerful lens through which to view society and seek solutions to social problems; (2) the centrality of political, civic, and economic liberty; (3) opposition to socialism and extensive "social engineering"; and (4) the importance

of stable monetary policy for macroeconomic stability.

Price Theory. At Chicago, economic theory is first and foremost price theory, or the theory of how resources and income are allocated in a market economy. Frank H. Knight and Jacob Viner taught price theory to doctoral students at the University of Chicago in the 1930s and 1940s, and—crucially for the formation of the Chicago school—to Milton Friedman and George J. Stigler. Knight and Viner also edited the department's in-house publication, the *Journal of Political Economy*, in which much Chicago school–focused work was published. Knight was philosophically inclined, with a keen critical eye. Viner was a virtuoso theorist, and a daunting presence in the classroom. Neither of these men, it should be noted, made heavy use of mathematics. This also is a hallmark of Chicago school economics: mathematics is the handmaiden, rather than the mistress, of economic analysis.

A related feature is that theory is developed and used within the context of "on the ground" problems. Such problems include, to draw some examples from Milton Friedman's *Price Theory: A Provisional Text* (1962), the effects of using taxes to finance medical care, the incidence of the corporate income tax, and the effects of setting a fixed limit on the number of taxicab licenses in a city. Innovations in economic theory are developed out of consideration of concrete problems such as these, rather than out of theoretical abstractions. As Milton Friedman put it in an interview about his training as a Chicago graduate student:

> The real distinction was not making price theory the focal point of the graduate curriculum. That isn't the real distinction at all. The fundamental distinction is treating economics as a serious subject versus treating it as a branch of mathematics, and treating it as a scientific subject as opposed to an aesthetic subject, if I might put it that way.... The fundamental difference between Chicago at that time and let's say Harvard, was that at Chicago, economics was a serious subject to be used in discussing real problems, and you could get some knowledge and some answers from it. (Hammond, 1992, p. 110)

Milton Friedman and George J. Stigler were the second generation of Chicago school economists. It was through their influence that the Chicago school came to be known as such. Friedman taught graduate price theory and revived interest in the quantity theory of money, at a time when it seemed to have been swept aside by the Keynesians (followers of the economist John Maynard Keynes). Stigler made extensive studies of the causes and effects of government regulation of business, showing that some regulations, thought to be important, have little actual effect, and others work to the benefit of the regulated firms. Stigler also was a pioneer in the economics of information. Gary S. Becker led a revival of economic analysis of the family and other non-market institutions. He also pioneered economic analysis of racial discrimination and of crime.

Political Ideology. Following the Russian Revolution and the Great Depression many intellectuals, including economists, saw capitalism as a failed economic system. Communism and socialism were viewed as morally superior, supposedly with more equal distributions of wealth and income, and as more productive, not subject to depressions and inflations. Both the moral and efficiency advantages of socialism were thought to be based on purposive planning, in contrast to the absence of central direction in capitalist societies. Chicago school economists stood outside the intellectual mainstream in their opposition to communism and socialism. Friedman and Stigler joined Knight and Director in 1948 as charter members of the Mont Pelerin Society, an association devoted to the defense of classical liberalism.

Countercyclical Policy. Milton Friedman and Anna J. Schwartz made a major contribution to the understanding of business cycles and policy in *A Monetary History of the United States, 1867–1960* (1963). In the late 1940s—when macroeconomics was becoming formalized mathematically—Friedman and Schwartz went against the current in embarking on a historical, relatively nonmathematical, research project on the role of money in business cycles. This study produced *A Monetary History* as well as other books and articles in which Friedman

and Schwartz took issue with presumptions widely held by economists at the time. Among these presumptions was that the Great Depression occurred despite the best efforts of the Federal Reserve to stem the tide of falling prices and output and rising unemployment. Friedman and Schwartz argued, drawing on extensive historical and empirical evidence, that the Federal Reserve actually turned a rather ordinary contraction into the Great Depression by allowing the stock of money to decline. This research led Friedman to develop his famous constant growth rate rule for the money supply. If the Federal Reserve followed this rule they would keep the money supply growing at roughly three percent per year, regardless of current or expected future economic conditions.

Chicago School Offspring. Two research programs of particular interest to political scientists that developed out of the work of the Chicago school are "law and economics," and "public choice," the latter often referred to as the "Virginia school of political economy." Henry Simons was the first economist on the University of Chicago Law School faculty; Simons was followed by Aaron Director and Director by Ronald Coase. Simons was most notable for his advocacy of policy reforms rooted in classical liberalism at a time when German National Socialism and Soviet Communism threatened to overwhelm free societies. Aaron Director is famous for bringing economic analysis into the heart of the law school curriculum, especially with regard to antitrust laws and policy. He jointly taught a course on antitrust law with Edward Levi, then later with Phil Neal, Kenneth Dam, and Richard Posner. Levi served as dean of the law school, president of the University of Chicago, and attorney general in President Gerald Ford's administration. Neal served as dean of the law school, and Dam as deputy secretary of state and of the treasury. Director's students included the future federal judges Frank Easterbrook, Robert Bork, and Posner. The *Journal of Law and Economics* was established in 1958 with Director as the first editor. Part of Director's legacy in legal thought and practice is skepticism about antitrust action, based on evidence that monopolies tend to be temporary and do little harm, unless they are sanctioned and protected by government.

Ronald Coase succeeded Director as the resident economist in the law school and as editor of the *Journal of Law and Economics* in 1964. He continued the Chicago tradition established by Director and his students of applying efficiency analysis to matters of law and regulation. Coase's scholarship had a major influence on tort law, with emphasis on the potential for property rights and markets to efficiently allocate the cost of avoiding harm.

James Buchanan (University of Chicago, PhD, 1948) was the founder of the Virginia school of political economy, so named because it was at the University of Virginia that Buchanan established this research program. Other names for the program are "public choice" and "constitutional political economy." Buchanan was influenced at Chicago by Frank Knight. Two of Buchanan's Virginia colleagues, D. Rutledge Vining and G. Warren Nutter, did their graduate work at Chicago. The key attribute of the research program was bringing insights from economic theory to public sector decision-making. In considering public policies, economists had generally treated the policy maker as being outside the economic system and presumed that he or she would make decisions in pursuit of the public good. Buchanan's innovation was to recognize that the assumption of self-interest was no less applicable to public sector than to private sector decisions. The thrust of Virginia school analysis was to ask how alternative institutional arrangements would affect the outcome of self-interested voting and self-interested decisions by public officials.

[*See also* Monetarism; *and* Monetary Policy.]

BIBLIOGRAPHY

Coase, Ronald H. *Essays on Economics and Economists.* (Chicago, 1994).

Emmett, Ross B., ed. *The Elgar Companion to the Chicago School of Economics.* (Cheltenham, UK, and Northampton, Mass., 2010).

Friedman, Milton. *Capitalism and Freedom: Fortieth Anniversary Edition.* (Chicago, 2002).

Friedman, Milton. *Price Theory: A Provisional Text.* (Chicago, 1962).

Friedman, Milton, and Anna J. Schwartz. *A Monetary History of the United States, 1867–1960.* (Princeton, N.J., 1963).

Hammond, J. Daniel. "An Interview with Milton Friedman on Methodology." *Research in the History of Economic Thought and Methodology* 10 (1992): 91–118.

Simons, Henry Calvert. *Economic Policy for a Free Society.* (Chicago, 1948).

Van Horn, Robert, Philip Mirowski, and Thomas A. Stapleford, eds. *Building Chicago Economics: New Perspectives on the History of America's Most Powerful Economics Program.* (Cambridge, UK and New York, 2011).

J. Daniel Hammond

CHILD CARE

Because the care of children is generally assigned to women, feminist analysts regard public child-care services as an essential component of women's social citizenship in modern societies. Yet the United States, unlike many advanced market democracies today, does not provide state-subsidized, universally available child care. In order to understand why this is the case, it is helpful to examine the development of US child care in comparative historical perspective.

From the early nineteenth through the early twentieth centuries, the United States witnessed the rise of "day nurseries"—local, charitable institutions intended to care for children whose mothers, unable to depend on a male breadwinner (due to absence, illness, disability, or death), were compelled to work for wages outside the home. While serving thousands of children in cities across the country, these institutions failed to establish the basis for universal public services—even after leaders in the field established a national organization, the National Federation for Day Nurseries, in 1898. Clearly intended only as emergency, stop-gap measures, nurseries offered only custodial services and served a clientele that was largely poor and working class. Their maternalist supporters had no intention of using their charities to challenge the prevailing male-breadwinner ideal by enabling women to work outside the home on a regular basis.

In many ways, the United States was little different from its modernizing counterparts in Europe; even countries that would eventually develop robust systems of universal child care, like Sweden and France, offered only custodial, class-based services for children throughout this period. These countries, however, tended to accept child care as a permanent social necessity—Sweden because of its large population of unmarried mothers who had to support themselves, France because of the many married mothers working in either factories or small businesses who were seeking ways to reconcile work and family. As these ideas about maternal employment became entrenched, they would lay the groundwork for future universal child-care provisions.

In early-twentieth-century America, however, day nurseries were becoming increasingly stigmatized, as professionalizing American social workers criticized maternal employment for undermining the mother-child bond and early childhood educators contrasted the meager services day nurseries were able to muster with the vaunted benefits of their newly founded kindergartens and nursery schools. Under the experts' influence, policy makers concerned with poor single mothers rejected child care in favor, first, of state-based mothers' or widows' pensions and later of the federal Aid to Dependent Children (ADC) program—both measures designed to keep mothers in the home. At the same time, Swedish reformers, influenced by Gunnar and Alva Myrdal's vision of an egalitarian "people's home," sought to integrate the benefits of early childhood education into existing charitable day nurseries and build public support, while in France, child care continued to expand.

World War II spiked the development of child care across Western Europe and North America, but postwar outcomes differed, depending on national contexts. In the United States, the federal government for the first time financed child care for women working in defense industries but stipulated that it was meant "for the duration only," and would thus cease with the end of the war. Never adequate to meet the needs of the thousands of mothers who poured into the labor force, public child-care centers lost their federal support immediately after the war, causing most to shut down. Maternal employment did not disappear, however; after an initial dip, it continued to rise over the ensuing decades (the baby boom notwithstanding), but neither voluntary nor commercial child care could keep pace with the need for services. Meanwhile, both Sweden and France regularized, improved, and provided public funding for a growing supply of child care. Their rationales differed somewhat: in Sweden, the goal was to expand the domestic labor force by mobilizing the nation's women rather than resorting to foreign workers, and at the same time to affirm its commitment to gender equality, while in France (where women did not even win suffrage until late 1945), policy was driven by pronatalism and continuing emphasis on work-family reconciliation.

From the 1960s on, US child-care policy was buffeted by two countervailing forces: second-wave feminism and the shift from welfare to workfare. Both called for child care as a means of promoting maternal employment, but for very different goals. Feminists sought to achieve gender equality, while conservatives were bent on stemming the tide of welfare dependency, which they believed (erroneously) was increasing disproportionately among African Americans. Feminist demands for "free, universal, twenty-four-hour child care" made no headway in Congress, but a bipartisan consensus began to form around the idea that welfare recipients should be required to work. Although lawmakers acknowledged that child care would be needed to implement such a policy, they failed to appropriate sufficient funds for it. As a result, the policy proceeded in fits and starts, never gaining enough momentum to reduce welfare rolls or enable poor and low-income women to achieve financial independence, but making it increasingly difficult for them to access needed relief.

The shift from welfare to workfare culminated in 1996 with the passage of the Personal Responsibility and Work Opportunity Reconciliation Act, which "end[ed] welfare as we have come to know it," according to President Bill Clinton, instituted harsher work requirements than ever, and brought US child policy full circle by linking it once again to the poor and impeding the development of universal provisions. Meanwhile, however, maternal employment was becoming the norm among women of all classes, increasing demands for child care that were met by an expansion of nonprofit, self-supporting services, and even more markedly, of market provisions. The high cost of formal, center-based care, coupled with erratic quality and degree of regulation, drove many parents to seek informal, family-based services for toddlers while leaving older children in "self-care." In recent years, dissatisfaction with limited hours as well as the level of quality has prompted parents with sufficient resources to hire live-in nannies— many of them low-paid female migrants from the developing world. The demand for universal child care, such as it was, has now subsided.

To a great extent, America's failure to develop universal child care may be attributed to the class- and race-based politics that has divided the constituency for services between public and private for nearly two centuries. In other words, this is a classic case of path dependency. Yet a preference for private provisions is also emerging in Sweden and France, where high-quality, state-subsidized child-care services have been the norm for decades. This has led some analysts to challenge the idea that policy feedback will normally sustain popular policies and predict that when it comes to child care (as well as other welfare policy realms, such as health care), these formerly very different welfare-state regimes may eventually converge.

[*See also* Gender and Politics; Patriarchy; Personal Responsibility and Work Opportunity Reconciliation Act; Welfare to Work; *and* Women and Paid Work.]

BIBLIOGRAPHY

Clinton, William Jefferson. "The New Covenant: Responsibility and Rebuilding the American Community: Remarks to Students at Georgetown University." (23 October 1991), http://clintonpresidentialcenter.org/georgetown/speech_newcovenant1.php

Michel, Sonya. *Children's Interests/Mothers' Rights: The Shaping of America's Child Care Policy.* (New Haven, Conn., 1999).

Michel, Sonya, and Rianne Mahon, eds. *Child Care Policy at the Crossroads: Gender and Welfare State Restructuring.* (New York, 2002).

Nyberg, Anita. "From Foster Mothers to Child Care Centers: A History of Working Mothers and Child Care in Sweden." *Feminist Economics* 6, no. 1 (2000): 5–20.

Stoltzfus, Emilie. *Citizen, Mother, Worker: Debating Public Responsibility for Child Care after the Second World War.* (Chapel Hill, N.C., 2003).

White, Linda A. "Explaining Differences in Child Care Policy Development in France and the USA: Norms, Frames, Programmatic Ideas." *International Political Science Review* 30 (2009): 385–405.

Sonya Michel

CHINA

China has achieved remarkable economic growth since Deng Xiaoping, the then-paramount leader of the Chinese Communist Party (CCP), launched the transition from a socialist command economy to a market economy in 1978. Although the process of economic transition fluctuated back and forth, due to the CCP's attempts to reconcile capitalist practices with its socialist legacy, pragmatism usually prevailed, yielding an overall forward trajectory. Even in the wake of the brutal suppression of the 1989 Tiananmen Square pro-democracy demonstration, Deng remained steadfast by declaring that "development is the only hard truth" in the early 1990s to dispel any doubt of China's quest for economic transition and growth. China continued its extraordinary growth trajectory in the 1990s and the 2000s, with an average growth of over 10 percent per year until the second half of 2008, when the world economy was hindered by the American subprime loan crisis and ensuing recession. While the US gross domestic product (GDP) fell by 5 to 6 percent during 2008 and 2009, China's economy increased 6 to 8 percent in the first half of 2009. At the World Economic Forum in Switzerland in early 2009, the Chinese premier Wen Jiabao pledged to carry on China's "opening up" policy and cooperate with the United States to avoid trade disputes, to encourage global economic stability. China continues to attract substantial investments and outsourcing contracts from many US-based companies in the manufacturing and service sectors, especially the information technology (IT) industry. This has made China a convenient target of US electoral campaigns, and of public blame for job losses in certain US industrial sectors.

As the US unemployment rate quickly rose during the economic slump, Chinese outbound foreign investment exceeded its inbound investment for the first time in 2009, even though its share, including Hong Kong and Macau's shares, of the world's stock of outward foreign direct investment remained only 6 percent, in comparison to America's 20-plus percent share. Like previous years, China's trade surplus with the United States continued to grow and left the United States with a trade deficit of $268 billion in 2008—an increase of 202 percent from $83.7 billion in 2000. Although China had adopted a "managed float" policy and appreciated the value of its currency, the *renminbi* (RMB), against the US dollar by 21 percent from June 2005 till 2008 to ease off US criticisms, the US trade deficit showed no clear signs of relief. In fact, the US trade deficit with China went up 33 percent during the same period.

The China development path has been similar to what the "developmental state" model has prescribed for latecomers to quickly catch up in economic development. With active state involvement and guidance, China adopted both fiscal and monetary policies to achieve better economic results by cultivating favorable market circumstances for its own enterprises and offering preferential treatments to selected industrial sectors for better competitive advantages in global market. The state's strenuous export-oriented strategy has made China the world's largest holder of foreign currency reserves, reaching $2.85 trillion in January 2011.

In September 2008, China surpassed Japan to become the largest foreign holder of US debt. In March 2009, Chinese financial institutions owned $1.5 trillion in US assets, implying that dollar assets account for more than 65 percent of China's total holdings of foreign assets at $2.3 trillion. Other than Chinese corporations' acquisition of US companies, China's capital accumulation through trade has made China a formidable player in the international financial market, as demonstrated in China's holding of 21 percent of US Treasury securities—valued at $906.8 billion—in October 2010. Lastly, China's sovereign wealth funds have made inroads with US financial institutions in the 2000s and have generated US financial concerns and political controversies in Washington. Such a powerful showing undoubtedly results in China's yearning for greater recognition and a stronger influence in the global economy, as well as in world politics, should the United States be incapable of dutifully performing its hegemonic role as the global "lender of the last resort," as described by Charles Kindleberger (1986).

Economic Competition and Political Impact. China's significant strides in economic growth cast doubt on the core principles of the Washington Consensus, which has been touted by the United States since the 1990s as a preferred development model for developing countries. Based on the neoclassical approach to economic development, the Washington Consensus recommends deregulation for open competition, privatization and broad tax reforms, and minimum governmental intervention in market operations. China's remarkable economic achievements have prompted the advocacy of the Beijing Consensus, vis-à-vis the Washington Consensus, as an alternative economic development model for emulation. A term coined by Joshua C. Ramo (2004), the "Beijing Consensus" highlights a state-directed, growth-driven, top-down economic development strategy and the subordination of political liberalization to economic reforms. Irrefutably, the Beijing Consensus has its strengths and weaknesses. For example, as testified by Japan's "lost decade" in the 1990s and slow recovery in the 2000s, the highly idealized interventionist, state-directed strategy might have contributed to a loss of entrepreneurship, vision, and risk-taking spirit among Japanese private enterprises due to their long-term, habitual reliance on the state for guidance and subsidies. Meanwhile, the government's political concerns over its regime stability could prevent the "brutal but fair" market from "doing the right thing" to get rid off inefficient, nonperforming, and uncompetitive enterprises.

Lastly, the either-or dichotomy between the Washington Consensus and the Beijing Consensus neglects the complementarities of both approaches in plotting a workable developmental path.

Even so, the growth trajectories of the authoritarian-statist alternative represented by China increasingly gained fair notice. The financial crisis in 2008 offered additional evidence to those skeptics of the Washington Consensus who question the United States' monopoly on influence and aspiration for other economically developing countries. China has subtly stepped up and moved beyond its usual function of a manufacturer of goods, and has begun exercising its soft power influence. When conditions have been right and opportunities have arisen, China has shown its aspiration to be a "game changer" in world politics in several areas.

First, an economic surge has augmented China's soft power for cultural influence. Launching in 2005, China's worldwide "Confucian Institute" programs have enticed numerous educational institutions throughout the world to take advantage of their basically cost-free offerings, though the program simultaneously irked some educators and politicians who questioned China's real cultural and political motives. Once denounced as a "class enemy" in countless political movements for his alleged bourgeois thinking, Confucius has regained political correctness and is now considered a "sage and great teacher." Confucian teachings of "harmony, peace, and stability" fit well with China's political needs to emphasize the necessity of social harmony and political stability to the domestic audience, and to enhance the dissemination of China's "peaceful rise" messages to the international community.

The hybrid of abundant capital resources and the enthusiastic spread of Confucianism permits China to strive to win the "hearts and minds" of other countries. It is a social constructive attempt, in Alexander Wendt's (1992) analysis, to build up a China-friendly environment. While China's successful accumulation of national wealth is, to some extent, a vindication of the intrinsic superiority of Chinese culture, the economic resources have served as a crucial force to "civilize," "socialize," or "Sinicize" other countries to appreciate and embrace China's worldview. It is a process analogous to what the United States accomplished to instill American values, beliefs, and ways of thinking through various avenues, so as to transform the world for its post–World War II hegemonic order. When the spread of Chinese cultural influence gained speed and space, it began to touch a raw nerve of uneasiness between the United States and China, because the emergence of Chinese cultural hegemony implies a possibility of excluding the *leitmotif* of American soft power influence.

Such a global cultural transition represents a change of both the framework and the rules of the game embedded in the world hegemonic structure within which state leaders deliberate and operate. As Antonio Gramsci claimed, the construction and consolidation of a cultural "hegemony" leads the subaltern to perceive the worldview of the wealthy and the powerful as a set of universal ideologies. Cultural dominance, in short, signifies the discursive power to explain how states relate to each other, what the modern world is supposed to be, and how it is likely to become.

Second, the advancement of China's economic strength and soft power has also paved the way for China to demand a bigger role in international economic institutions, such as the International Monetary Fund (IMF) and the World Bank. China's repeated demands to the IMF eventually paid off in November 2010, for example, when the IMF vaulted China's voting shares to 3.65 percent, surpassing those of Germany, France, and Britain, though behind Japan's 6.01 percent and US shares of 16.7 percent. The United States remains the sole member holding veto power, in accordance with the IMF stipulation for an 85 percent majority of the total voting power for any change in member state's quota subscription to the IMF, and accordingly, its voting shares. Nonetheless, the increase of China's IMF voting shares implied a US compromise with China's forceful request, because the timing of China's quota change decision occurred two years ahead of the IMF's regular five-year review cycle. Additionally, the 2008 global recession also offered China's central bank an opportunity to ask the world to consider a new international reserve currency, in order to avoid the perils of overdependence on the US dollar. As a move to minimize the shock of US currency value depreciation, China has signaled its plan to diversify its foreign currency holdings.

Third, huge national wealth has permitted China to provide developing countries with generous foreign aid without political strings attached—a distinctively different practice from US aid projects. In essence, China's aid program seldom places human rights and social betterment as its primary goals. Instead, its aid projects have acted as a quid pro quo for access to raw materials, energy resources, and project bidding. For example, China's trade with Africa reached $106.8 billion in 2008, with an annual growth rate of more than 33 percent in a span of eight years, 2000 to 2008. In 2010, China became Africa's largest trade partner and reduced tariffs on 95 percent of African exports to China to zero. China's charm offensive also includes $10 billion worth of preferential loans to Africa from 2010 to 2012. Economic statecraft has made China a serious competitor of the United States in influence bidding in Africa, Latin America, and other developing regions, where the United States traditionally had a powerful presence and heavy influence.

Fourth, as China's economy has grown, so have its demands for energy and natural resource supplies. Simply take oil as an example. China has surged to become the second-largest oil consumer, behind the United States, and the third-largest net oil importer, after the United States and Japan, in 2009. The US estimate is that China will import more than two-thirds of its oil by 2015 and four-fifths by 2030. China's thirst for access to energy resources has ignited frenzied competitions over energy supply among countries in regional rivalries, such as China's disputes over the Diaoyu/Senkaku Island with Japan, and the South China Sea with its Southeast Asian neighbors. China's apprehension about its energy supply sea lanes that pass through some areas under US control (for example, the Indian Ocean and the Strait of Malacca) has prompted China to obtain overland pipeline routes (for example, the Eastern Siberia–Pacific Ocean oil pipeline and two Central Asian oil pipelines) for its future energy supply.

The United States has expressed concerns over China's aggressive venture dealings for energy resources either on shaky ethical grounds or in areas where the United States has vested interests. For example, amid the horrible Darfur crisis in the mid-2000s, China's interests in securing a hefty percentage of Sudan's oil exports made it reluctant to actively support UN crisis resolution measures, and thus provoked US and international criticisms. In March 2009, China edged out the United States to become Brazil's biggest trade partner after China made lucrative business deals there, including its billions-of-dollars credit in exchange for Brazilian guaranteed shipments of oil to Chinese companies. In October 2010, China's pledge of $5 billion to Greek shipping companies to buy Chinese ships, and its announcement of intent to acquire Greek bonds, have permitted China to wield its economic clout to obtain more influence in the Euro zone, and simultaneously counter US financial power in the area.

In the East Asian region, the Association of Southeast Asian Nations (ASEAN) and other East Asian countries have desperately sought China's economic partnership beginning in the 2000s. The regional arrangements of ASEAN+1 (Chin) and aASEAN+3 (China, Japan, and South Korea) are vivid examples. A sense of optimism among regional players is best captured by a Singaporean diplomat's remark on China's regional weight: "It was China's economic power and cultural superiority that drew these countries into its orbit and was the magnet for their cultivation of relations" (Kang, 2007, p. 3). China's popularity in East Asia reflects the relative demise of the United States in this region and an alarming loss of support in the region, as the US government has had to reprioritize its global strategy, national interests, and force deployment elsewhere since September 11, 2001.

The optimistic attitude toward China in the East Asian region seems to have shifted in 2009. In an attempt to form a united front to tackle various China-related issues—including Chinese currency value and territorial disputes in the South China Sea and East China Sea—the Barack Obama administration "rediscovered" East Asia and reinforced security ties with regional actors like Japan, India, South Korea, and even Vietnam to counter a surge of Chinese triumphalism and muscle-flexing moves on regional and global matters.

Naturally, China is not problem-free on its domestic, socioeconomic front. Human rights abuses and violations, rampant corruption scandals due to ambiguous and unsecured property rights, deficiency in policy transparency and accountability, high level of nepotism, rising income inequality between the haves and have-nots, and environmental degradations all have kept Chinese leaders busy and worrying about its regime legitimacy and stability. Behind its dazzling economic growth as the world's second-largest economic entity, China's GDP per capita is far behind that of most developed countries. In 2008, more than one-tenth of China's population, approximately 150 million people, still lived on less than $1 per day. China's industrial sector continues a long and hard march in its attempt to climb up the production chain from the position of a "world factory" of labor-intensive commodities to an important provider of high-value added, sophisticated products, without having to rely heavily on foreign technology and investment for exports. Furthermore, even though the government has repeatedly prohibited data alteration, for instance in its revised 2009 Law on Statistics, frequent media reports of data falsification and inaccuracy have made China-watchers suspect the validity of official statistics and question whether the real China is accurately represented by what we read in official documents. Despite these problematic facts and figures, China seems to have gained visible economic progress, which in turn provides substantial funding to China's military modernization.

China Crosses the Great Wall. As China's economic transformation was beginning in the last decades of the twentieth century, Deng's well known quote of "*taoguang yanghui*" (literally translated as "hide brightness and nourish obscurity"), suggesting that China stay inconspicuous and remain modest in order to bide its time and build up its national strength, was the guiding principle of China's foreign and security policies. However, after many years of

patience and modesty under the US hegemonic shadow, some are now saying that it is time for China to be assertive.

By 1978, the People's Liberation Army (PLA) had relied on its revolutionary "people's war" tradition and was far behind major powers in terms of weaponry, command, control, and communication systems, even though it had an enormous military force. While China frequently lauded the PLA as a "Great Wall of Steel" (*gangtie changcheng*), in the 1980s this "Great Wall" was still characterized by outdated and inefficient communication equipment, short-range force projection capability, and slow mobility in military operation.

The 1990s saw China's renewed interest in defense technology in the wake of both its shocking realization of the significance of high-tech weapons during the first Gulf War (1990–1991) and its increasing strategic concerns over the United States and Japan's challenges to China's security interest in Taiwan, which appeared to be drifting toward independence, making war increasingly likely. Military development became crucial for China's preparation for a worst-case scenario on the Taiwan issue, if the United States were to defend Taiwan in crisis. Therefore, China began to place a higher priority on the advancement of military weapons for fighting and winning a modern high-tech war. Since 2000, China's double-digit percentage increase in defense spending every year, substantial arms transfers from abroad, and relentless indigenous research and development (R & D) efforts have together improved and upgraded China's military capabilities. Realizing its inability to modernize its defense force instantly on a complete scale, China has concentrated on selective areas, such as cyber warfare, missiles, and space technology, in order to "level the playing field" by conducting asymmetric warfare with its opponent.

Cyber warfare has been frequently discussed in Chinese military writings as "an unconventional operation other than war" to seize the initiative at the beginning stage of war to cripple an adversary's information transmission and sharing system for combat operations. Although the outside world has not acquired extensive details of the PLA's information warfare units and their operations, numerous reports of identified infiltrations and attacks from alleged China-based hackers during the period 1999–2009 in the Pentagon's reports have shown the effectiveness of China's cyber warfare capability.

In the area of missile development, China's Second Artillery has deployed more than one thousand short-range missiles on China's coast facing Taiwan, several hundreds of medium-range missiles, and more than a dozen intercontinental missiles with conventional or nuclear payloads, to gain an access denial capability to deter Taiwan from declaring independence and to make the United States think twice before launching any military operation in areas close to China. The report of China's development of "aircraft killer" missiles in 2010 also raised concerns about China's military advancement and US capability of supporting its Pacific allies in crisis.

In fact, China's endeavors in military modernization show its global ambition and preparation for a potential confrontation with the United States. Since its first manned spaceflight in 2003 and later spaceflights and successive lunar probes, China clearly has converted its space accomplishments into a source of national pride, a basis for international prestige enhancement, a show-off of national wealth, and a level of technological sophistication. With its techno-nationalistic overtones, China's space explorations carry a wide range of applications and implications for national security purposes. For instance, following the United States and Russia, China became the third country to test an anti-satellite weapon (ASAT) to successfully destroy a defunct orbiting weather satellite by using a land-based missile in January 2007, suggesting its capability of interdicting US satellite communication systems and disrupting US access to global command, control, and communication systems in an asymmetric conflict. In 2008, the United States followed suit to blow up an American malfunctioning spy satellite by using a ship-launched missile. It seems that the sky will be an area for future competition between the United States and China.

Other than missiles and space technology, there are ample strategic reasons for the United States to be alarmed by China's military development. For example, China has strengthened its submarine fleet size in the post–Cold War era to more than sixty submarines by purchasing twelve Russian Kilo-class diesel submarines in late 1990s and early 2000s and building more indigenous submarines of various classes, including diesel electric submarines (Song class), nuclear-powered attack submarines (Shang class), and nuclear-powered ballistic missile submarines (Jin class) for a regional access-denial capability. By contrast, starting from 1995, the United States has downsized its submarine fleet from one hundred to seventy-one in 2010, and further reduction is expected in the coming decade. Although qualitatively China's current submarines have not yet posed any serious threat to US submarines, the report of a Chinese Song-class submarine quietly "popping up" within its firing range of the US aircraft carrier *Kitty Hawk* during a US naval exercise in October 2006 not only dumbfounded the US Navy, but also testified to China's vigorous efforts to improve submarine stealth and long-range capability. It is no wonder that the United States has deployed thirty-one of its fifty-three attack submarines in the Pacific region in 2010.

Military analysts have also closely monitored when China will launch its first aircraft carrier for a blue-water navy since China's 1998 purchase of both a Ukrainian-built *Varyag* and its subsequent acquisition of the Soviet aircraft carrier *Minsk* as part of a military theme park in Shenzhen. In 2010, speculations among military analysts moved beyond the topic of China's aircraft carrier shipbuilding capability into debates about what type of carrier China would build, when it would be ready for deployment, and how it could be integrated into China's naval strategy to secure China's maritime power within the first island chain, an area including the East China Sea, Yellow Sea, South China Sea, and Taiwan. Once the aircraft carrier is fully deployed and successfully integrated, the Chinese navy can venture farther into the second island chain's illusionary line drawn from the Japanese archipelago to the Bonin and Marshall islands in the southern Pacific, literally swaggering in front of the US military base at Guam.

In Chinese naval advocates' minds, an overarching logic of "command of the sea" is the essence of any great power.

China's naval expansion has coincided with qualitative and quantitative improvements of its air force, such as the deployment of indigenous AWACS (airborne warning and control system) for its air defense C⁴ISR capability, the addition of long-range bombers, air transport planes, air refueling tankers, and modern fighter jets, such as the deployment of Russian SU-30, J-11 (a homemade version of Russian Su-27), indigenous J-10, the faster-than-expected progress in developing a Chinese rival (J-20) to US stealth fighter F-22 in late 2010, and the introduction of unmanned aerial vehicles for long range reconnaissance and strikes. China's air force has extended its combat radius coverage to reach the first island chain area through its aerial refueling capability. Potential competitions with and challenges to the US interests in the western Pacific are foreseeable.

Regional capability and global ambition have made China increasingly assertive in its neighboring waters. Take the example of a stern Beijing's diplomatic response to a collision incident between Japanese coast guard vessels and a Chinese trawler on 7 September 2010, in the waters off the disputed Diaoyu/Senkaku Islands. Beijing's high-profile, non-negotiable stance—comprised of suspending high-level Sino-Japanese contacts and threatening an export restriction of rare-earth metals, essential materials for high-tech products such as lasers, missiles, computers, and semiconductors, as a bargaining tool with Japan—gained worldwide attention. It was quite a stunning contrast to China's usual diplomatic, rhetorical condemnations against Japan's sovereign claim of the Diaoyu/Senkaku Islands, a position traditionally assumed to woo Japan's capital and investment in the past. Both Beijing's proclaiming the South China Sea—an area of huge energy reserves that neighbors China's military base—as one of its core national interests in August 2010, and later vehement protests of United States–South Korean joint military exercises in the Yellow Sea in response to the North-South Korean crisis in November 2010, were distinctive pronunciations of China's assertiveness. Meanwhile, the Chinese air force's unprecedented joint exercise with Turkey marked China's first crossing of Pakistan and Iran's air space for refueling, as well as a chance to participate in military exercise with a North Atlantic Treaty Organization (NATO) member and glean firsthand knowledge of NATO combat tactics and coordination. All in all, Chinese leaders and the PLA are becoming less heedful of Deng's low-key, cautious approach to global issues and more overbearing in word and deed in regard to China's far-flung security interests.

There is no doubt that China's air force and naval expansion clearly pushes its strategic vision far beyond the Taiwan issue into global reach and world influence. As long as China's robust economy continues, its military modernization will strive to fulfill the historical vision of "rich country and strong army." In 1949, Mao proudly declared that "the Chinese people have finally stood up!" to the whole country. Only this time, China intends to tell the whole world a similar message that "the Chinese are coming!" through its military modernization and spectacular economic performance.

US Policy toward China: Hedging and Engagement. Military power and economic prosperity give China an opportunity to reconstruct a Chinese self for its glorious past—a historical worldview of *tianxia*, literally meaning "all space under the heaven." This is presumably a harmonious, orderly, and stable Sino-centric order based on Confucian teachings, with China at the center. Of course, in putting forth such an identity, it may spawn an impression of threatening "others," including the United States. Stated differently, if US economic power is waning in the face of China's rapid ascent, will the economic power dynamics be sufficiently and successfully translated into world security so as to symbolize a reshuffling of power and the winding down of US preeminence in international politics? Although China has expressed its peaceful intent on numerous occasions, will China's newly gilded "great power" identity prompt it to feel strongly its hegemonic responsibility to change the existing world order? Frankly speaking, any major shift of world power structure is inevitably marked by psychological urges and social expectations of every state. Witnessing its relative slide in material strength, the incumbent power of the United States understandably desires to hold onto its hegemony and fears that the world order it built may one day be fundamentally altered by another rising power. This anxiety is not only shown among elites, but is also expressed by the public. US surveys in the 2000s tended to demonstrate the American public's concerns over China's economic rise and military expansion. On the other hand, China, "a new kid on the block," undoubtedly has an ambition to distance itself from it historical humiliation and reconstruct a new identity to proudly display its power and influence for international recognition. A glimpse at Chinese officials' speeches, media comments, and policy papers in the last decade reveals Chinese public apprehension that the United States might seek ways to slander China's ambition and block China's rise, in order to avoid the surrendering of the US hegemonic paradise.

Some scholars with inclinations to accept international liberalism tend to view the complex US-China relationship in a more positive and optimistic way. In order to avoid drastic change in the international system, in these optimists' view, the United States should interact and negotiate with China for peaceful coexistence to prevent a power duel. The further China is assimilated into the US-instituted international system, the less likely is it that China will emerge as a "revisionist" state seriously affecting US interests. As G. John Ikenberry (2008) has elaborated, the US-favored scenario is a China that would be deeply immersed, pacified, and subordinated within the US-instituted liberal order. The expectation is that the "deeply sedimented and thickened" US-instituted international rules and norms would be sticky enough to hold China to abide by the existing rules as a protector rather than a rule-breaker of the status quo. As a result, a world without a *Pax Americana*, should it occur, would remain favorable to most Western liberal states.

Furthermore, in spite of the growing US deficit, the interplay between the United States and Asian countries in trade practices and financial interactions has re-created a Bretton Woods–like system, with the United States as the center and Asia replacing Europe. Niall Ferguson and Moritz Schularick (2007), for instance, coined the term "Chimerica" to explain how Chinese and American economies work in a "division of labor" manner, with the Chinese diligently working for export earnings from the US market, and Americans cheerfully pumping out consumption demands for Chinese factories. The functional complementarities and intertwining nature between these two economies work well for each to gain what it wants. In such a framework of complex interdependence associated with sensitivity and vulnerability, Daniel W. Drezner (2009) points out that it would be an unwise move for China to use its financial power as political leverage against the United States, because any disruptive act by either side can lead to disastrous consequences to both. And Beijing's attempt to advocate the Chinese currency as one of the international currencies has surely challenged the dominance of the US dollar, but the proposal remains a remote possibility, if the long-term transition of global financial hegemony from Great Britain to the United States in the first half of the twentieth century serves as a historical precedent. With only a few endorsements from other countries, China's currency initiative was simply a symbolic gesture to placate domestic critics' charge of the Chinese government's heedless investments in the United States. Based on this trend of thought, as long as the United States continues its constructive engagement policy to deepen its relations with China and to encourage China to mesh with the liberal international system, China's discomfort with the United States should gradually evaporate, and its challenges to US hegemony should eventually diminish. Both countries will find more common ground than differences for a stable world in the years to come.

Nevertheless, Thucydides' precepts of "fear, honor, and interest" could be powerful driving forces for both China and the United States. Change breeds fears due to actors' concerns over future uncertainties, opportunities, and risks. John J. Mearsheimer

(2001) and other scholars have cautioned that power changes usually come with the reshuffling of each state's desires, interests, preferences, and proper standing in the world, how it expects to be treated by others, and how successfully others adjust their views. Hence, tension ensues with the rise of any great power. China's growth of national wealth and military strength naturally generates a sense of empowerment and national pride, as well as a desire to be recognized and accepted by the "others," including the United States. When things do not go as anticipated, public frustration and feelings of relative deprivation can run toward demands for a tougher stance abroad. Strong backing from the Chinese people may endow political leaders with a new "can-do" spirit to reshape a world in its own image for self-interests.

Even if Chinese leaders have a realistic understanding of their country's national strengths and limitations, domestic dynamics may constrain their policy choices. In the past decade, China's policy toward the United States has been complicated by its increasingly complex and fragmented decision-making process with input from the Party, government bureaucracies, think tank analysts, the media, and even groups of web bloggers and "netizens" (citizens who are active and articulate in Internet chat rooms and blogs). These individuals and organizations exert a variety of pressures, making it difficult for senior leaders to formulate a timely, coherent, and reasonable policy toward the United States.

Similarly, US policy toward China has encountered the pull and push of various interests, including the State Department's dovish inclination, the Pentagon's hawkish stand, the Central Intelligence Agency's (CIA) concern over national security, Congress's electoral concerns, business corporations' profits and market shares, labor unions' criticisms of outsourcing, ideological rivalries between Republicans and Democrats, diverse pressures from Japanese, Taiwanese, and Tibetan exiles, human rights watch groups, and the public. American willingness to see a prosperous China for mutual economic gains should not be construed as a wish to see a strong China for equivalent power-sharing in world politics.

Accordingly, the increase of federal debts and the bursting of housing bubbles in the United States, along with the frequent US pressures on China's currency undervaluation and trade imbalances, provide ample ammunition for China-bashing and demands for currency war and trade retaliation. In exchange, China's public sentiment and nationalism only fuel its combative attitude. Consequently, there has been no short supply of "China Threat" theories since the 1990s, even though China has launched numerous campaigns to mitigate the negative impact of China's increasing prominence with frequent reminders of "China's peaceful rise" and constant pledges to a "harmonious society," aimed to calm the anxiety and suspicion of outside critics.

Some pessimists, therefore, view China's rise as full of danger and instability to the world order. One can point to the long-term US frustration with China's increasingly stentorian defenses of its mercantilist trade practices and defiant stands on its currency value in the 2000s. On the other hand, Beijing perceived Washington as being deeply concerned about the inevitable decline of the United States, in contrast to China's unstoppable rise, and thus determined to block China's ascendance. To those skeptics of Chinese sincerity about its peaceful rise, the United States should adopt a policy of containment wedged deeply to preserve its hegemonic stand as much as possible.

The tug-of-war between optimists and pessimists concerning how to view and deal with China—as a friend or foe, as a benign competitor or a hostile challenger—has been a constant debate in US foreign policy. Since the historical breakthrough of President Richard Nixon's 1972 visit to China and then President Jimmy Carter's 1979 establishment of full diplomatic relations with China, American China policy has veered in extremes on the policy spectrum from engagement to containment. The tough stand against communist China was modified with President Bill Clinton's 1994 decision to delink human rights issues and the annual assessment of China's most-favored-nation trade status for the pursuit of other US core interests. Secretary of State Hillary Clinton reconfirmed a conciliatory "human rights secondary to other policy priorities" stand during her visit to China in 2009. Secretary Clinton's remark was a contrast to the tough and hostile tones against China that both she and President Obama presented during their presidential campaigns in 2008. Such a policy swing and inconsistency has been common in all US administrations since 1972, including the "human rights promoter with Chinese exception" (President Jimmy Carter in late 1970s), the "Cold War warrior" (President Ronald Reagan in the 1980s), and the "no-nonsense and China-unfriendly" leader (President George W. Bush in the 2000s).

As James Mann (1999) observed, the US policy toward China has fluctuated in a cyclical swing between attraction and friendliness on one side, and revulsion and hostility on the other side. However, in three tense standoffs—the PLA's missile tests during the Taiwan Strait crisis in 1995–1996, the accidental bombing of the Chinese embassy in Belgrade in 1999, and the US EP-3 collision with Chinese military aircraft incident in the South China Sea in 2001—both countries have demonstrated remarkable restraint to prevent military confrontation and serious rifts in their bilateral crisis interactions. Unlike the past black-and-white dichotomy in US relations with the former Soviet Union, it is difficult for the United States to categorize China clearly as either a truthful friend or a devious foe.

It is, therefore, not a surprise that the United States has adopted a dual-pronged approach, an "engaging and hedging" security strategy, toward China's hegemonic intent and security ambitions. While "engaging" promotes a "positive-sum" perspective by encouraging China to be a responsible "stakeholder and force" in the world, a precautionary realist mood of "hedging" China's potential threat settles in to protect US interests and to reassure East Asian allies. The visible presence of US forces has long been part of East Asia's "geopolitical fabric," and the US plan to fortify Guam by 2012 as a strong forward base stationing numerous advanced military jets, such as B-2 stealth bombers, B-1B, B-52, F-22 Raptors, and attack submarines, signals its strategic commitment to place East Asian allies under the US security umbrella. Other US-coordinated efforts involve the incorporation of some East Asian countries into a "hub and spoke" security arrangement, to prepare for China's security challenges.

In spite of that, hard balancing based on military strength alone may not work well in US policy toward China. While China's neighboring countries feel hemmed in by China's powerful presence in the Pacific, they are also lured by China's market and trade benefits. This puts them in a bind. Their "balancing" strategy to side with the United States to counter China's influence definitely collides with their "bandwagoning" behaviors to harvest material interests from China's economic boom. One doubts whether any of them would go all the way to cast out China as a rival in a military conflict, when their close economic ties with China call for a significant amount of goodwill. The message is that hard balancing—the policy implemented in the Cold War era—will not be a feasible option for US dealings with China.

In the end, the US "hedging and engagement" approach appears to be a reasonable and rational policy to address the concerns of both optimists and pessimists over China's rise. Great power transition is a complicated process involving multiple variables in a fast-changing environment. Since 2000, we have witnessed China begin to change the world and challenge the United States, but China has also been changing itself. It remains to be seen whether the US "hedging and engagement" strategy will accomplish its intended result of accommodating the challenge of China's rise peacefully and minimizing the negative effects of future system stability. Meanwhile, we should expect to see continuous ups and downs in US-China bilateral relations, and periodic backward and forward moves in their diplomatic tangos.

[*See also* Central Asia; Global Economy and the United States; Japan–United States Relations; Korea, Democratic People's Republic of; *and* Southeast Asia.]

BIBLIOGRAPHY

Cohen, Warren I. *America's Response to China: A History of Sino-American Relations.* 5th ed. (New York, 2010).
Deng, Yong. *China's Struggle for Status: The Realignment of International Relations.* (New York, 2008).
Drezner, Daniel W. "Bad Debts: Assessing China's Financial Influence in Great Power Politics." *International Security* 34, no. 2 (Fall 2009): 7–45.

Ferguson, Niall, and Moritz Schularick. "Chimerica and the Global Asset Market Boom." *International Finance* 10, no. 3 (2007): 215–239.

Gill, Bates. "China as an Emergent Center of Global Power." In *Great Powers and Strategic Stability in the 21st Century*, edited by Graeme P. Herd, pp. 137–153. (London, 2010).

Gilpin, Robert. *The Political Economy of International Relations.* (Princeton, N.J., 1987).

Goldstein, Avery. *Rising to the Challenge: China's Grand Strategy and International Security.* (Stanford, Calif., 2005).

Ikenberry, G. John. "The Rise of China and the Future of the West." *Foreign Affairs* 87, no. 1 (January–February 2008): 23–37.

Johnston, Alastair Iain. *Social State: China in International Institutions, 1980–2000.* (Princeton, N. J., 2008).

Kang, David C. *China Rising: Peace, Power, and Order in East Asia.* (New York, 2007).

Kindleberger, Charles P. *The World in Depression, 1929–1939.* (Berkeley, Calif., 1986).

Mann, James. *About Face: A History of America's Curious Relationship with China from Nixon to Clinton.* (New York, 1999).

Mearsheimer, John J. *The Tragedy of Great Power Politics.* (New York, 2001).

Ramo, Joshua Cooper. *The Beijing Consensus.* (London, 2004).

Shambaugh, David, ed. *Power Shift: China and Asia's New Dynamics.* (Berkeley, Calif., 2005).

Sutter, Robert G. *US-China Relations: Perilous Past, Pragmatic Present.* (Lanham, Md., 2010).

United States–China Economic and Security Review Commission (USCC). "2011 Report to Congress." http://www.uscc.gov/annual_report/2011/annual_report_full_11.pdf.

United States Office of Secretary of Defense (USDOD). "Annual Report to Congress: Military and Security Developments Involving the People's Republic of China, 2010." http://www.defense.gov/pubs/pdfs/2010_CMPR_Final.pdf.

Wendt, Alexander. "Anarchy Is What States Make of It: The Social Construction of Power Politics." *International Organization* 46 (1992): 391–425.

Wei-Chin Lee

CHRISTIAN LEFT

The tradition of left-leaning politics among Christians, primarily evangelicals, in America extends at least as far back as the decades surrounding the turn of the nineteenth century. The Second Great Awakening, a series of revivals that convulsed three regions of the new nation— New England, the Cumberland Valley of Kentucky, and upstate New York— unleashed a torrent of social reform, especially in the North, that reshaped the nation's social landscape and eventually drove an angry South to secession over demands for an end to slavery.

Theologically, the Second Great Awakening differed from the Great Awakening (which occurred in several waves, from roughly the 1730s through the 1940s) in its ascription of human ability. While Jonathan Edwards and other leaders of the First Awakening, rooted in the Calvinist tradition, believed that salvation was reserved only for the elect, and that an individual could do nothing to earn salvation, the leaders of the Second Great Awakening, notably Charles Grandison Finney, believed that individuals could indeed initiate the salvation process. Volition in personal redemption quickly translated into attitudes toward society. If it was possible for individuals to attain salvation by exercising their will, so too was it possible, with the aggregate efforts of believers, to construct a better world.

Finney himself was clear about the connections between evangelical theology and social reform. "God's rule requires universal benevolence," he wrote. "I abhor a piety which has no humanity with it and in it" (Finney, p. 348–356). An 1837 article in the *Religious Monitor & Evangelical Repository* concurred, noting that "the sentiment is rapidly gaining ground in all parts of the country, that the *church* is the divinely appointed *means* of producing moral and religious reforms."

The Second Great Awakening, then, served as a catalyst for a remarkable array of social activism, from the abolition of slavery to prison reform. Evangelicals pressed for equal rights for women, including the right to vote. Many became involved in various peace crusades. They supported public education (known as "common schools" in the nineteenth century), in an effort to provide educational opportunities for those less fortunate. "Common Schools are the glory of our land," a writer declared in the *Christian Spectator*, "where even the beggar's child is taught to read, and write, and think, for himself." Although the temperance movement came to be seen as paternalistic and overweening, it began as a sincere effort to address the debilitating effects of excessive alcohol consumption, including spousal and child abuse.

What united all of these initiatives, aside from religious motivation, was the target of their benevolence: women, slaves, prisoners, and all of those on the margins of society, those Jesus referred to as "the least of these." Elias Smith of Portsmouth, New Hampshire, was one of many evangelicals who understood the link between the teachings of Jesus and benevolent impulses directed toward those less fortunate. "Multitudes of the poor love the name and religion of Jesus Christ," Smith wrote. "There is no doubt but that God regards all his creatures; but yet from motives of mercy and compassion, there is an evident predilection for the *poor*, manifested in our Savior's preaching and ministry." Jesus Christ, Smith believed, "came to put an end to unjust inequality in the world."

Suspicion of Capitalism. For Finney and others, in fact, the focus on those less fortunate led them to denounce business and even to question the morality of capitalism itself. Finney argued that "the business aims and practices of business men are almost universally an abomination in the sight of God," and he preached explicitly against the mores of business. "The whole course of business in the world is governed and regulated by the maxims of supreme and unmixed selfishness," he said. Finney indicted capitalism itself, arguing that the "whole system recognizes only the love of self" and "the rules by which business is done in the world, are directly opposite to the gospel of Jesus Christ, and the spirit he exhibited." The man of business, by contrast, lives by the maxim: "Look out for number one."

A writer in the *New-York Evangelist* echoed Finney's sentiments, suggesting that the integrity of the church itself had been compromised by its associations with the world of business. "The prosperity of the times in the business world threatens to endanger the piety of the church," he wrote, adding that businessmen were already insinuating their principles into

the nation's pulpits. "The desire to possess, though constitutional, is one of the most dangerous affections of the human heart," he warned. "Can the heart be sanctified by constant contact with goods and merchandize, bills and invoices, notes and monies, checks and drafts?" These accouterments of business threatened the very souls of believers. "In devising as well as prosecuting their schemes of money-making, American Christians find themselves associated, if not identified with the most devoted servants of mammon, the world can afford." The author cited, in particular, the pernicious influence of "The Chambers of Commerce" and lamented that the "bias of heart toward money-making, has become an American characteristic."

In addition to their disavowal of Calvinism, antebellum evangelicals also drew on another theological strain to justify their efforts at social amelioration: postmillennialism. A reference to the millennium, the one thousand years of righteousness predicted in Revelation 20, postmillennialism holds that Jesus will return to earth *after* the millennium. The corollary to postmillennialism is that believers can bring about the millennium here on earth (and, more particularly, here in America) by reforming society according to the norms of godliness. Postmillennial optimism about the perfectibility of society, then, animated evangelical social reform in the early decades of the nineteenth century.

The carnage of the Civil War, however, began to dim hopes that a millennial kingdom was imminent. Changes in American society—urbanization, industrialization, the influx of non-Protestant immigrants who did not share evangelical scruples about temperance—prompted a reconsideration of their optimism earlier in the century. Put simply, the teeming, squalid tenements of lower Manhattan, roiling with labor unrest, hardly resembled the precincts of Zion that evangelicals had predicted.

Many evangelicals gravitated instead to a new biblical hermeneutic called dispensationalism, or dispensational premillennialism. Contrary to the optimism inherent in postmillennialism, premillennialism held that Jesus would return to earth *before* the millennium, and the corollary was that there was nothing that believers could do to make this a better world. "I look upon this world as a wrecked vessel," evangelist Dwight L. Moody famously declared, "God has given me a lifeboat and said to me, 'Moody, save all you can.'"

Social Gospel. As conservatives shifted their focus away from social reform toward individual regeneration, another group of Protestants embraced what became known as the "Social Gospel." Begun by Washington Gladden, a Congregational minister in Columbus, Ohio, and articulated most fully by Walter Rauschenbusch, pastor of New York City's Second German Baptist Church who went on to teach at Rochester Theological Seminary, the Social Gospel posited that Jesus was capable of saving not only sinful individuals, but sinful social institutions as well. Proponents of the Social Gospel worked hand in hand with the Progressive movement on behalf of the rights of workers and against corrupt political machines. In the age of the robber barons, when 10 percent of the population controlled 90 percent of the nation's wealth, Social Gospel advocates sought to mitigate the effects of unbridled capitalism.

The Social Gospel, sometimes mistaken for socialism, fell into disfavor following the Bolshevik Revolution of 1917. It was resuscitated by Howard Thurman, who in turn influenced a young African American seminary student named Martin Luther King, Jr. As the civil rights movement of the 1950s unfolded, it became clear that this iteration of the Christian Left was animated by various ideologies: the Social Gospel, the teachings on nonviolent resistance from Mohandas Gandhi, and Thurman's book *Jesus and the Disinherited* (1949), which King carried with him at crucial junctures of the civil rights movement.

Evangelicals remained, for the most part, politically quiescent during the middle decades of the twentieth century. In the late 1960s and early 1970s, however, left-leaning evangelicals began to question the morality of the Vietnam War, the growing disparity between rich and poor, the position of women as second-class citizens, and the persistence of racism. The impetus for this resurgence of the Christian Left was another seminary student, Jim Wallis of Trinity Evangelical Divinity School in Deerfield, Illinois. Wallis and some fellow students began a magazine, the *Post-American*, and lived in the Rogers Park neighborhood of Chicago before relocating to Washington, D.C., in 1975 and renaming their organization (and their publication) Sojourners.

Chicago Declaration of Evangelical Social Concern. Following the 1972 presidential campaign, when leftist evangelicals supported George McGovern's ill-fated challenge to Richard Nixon, a group of evangelicals gathered at the YMCA in Chicago to draft the Chicago Declaration of Evangelical Social Concern, calling evangelicals to repentance for their complicity in militarism, the persistence of income disparities, and racism. At the behest of Nancy Hardesty, professor of English at Trinity College, the Declaration included a statement on feminism: "We acknowledge that we have encouraged men to prideful domination and women to irresponsible passivity. So we call both men and women to mutual submission and active discipleship."

Ronald J. Sider, organizer of the gathering, went on to form Evangelicals for Social Action, and other signatories, notably Wallis, John M. Perkins of Mendenhall Ministries, and Tony Campolo, sociology professor at Eastern University, remained committed to leftist principles during the ensuing decades. Those principles also found expression in the unlikely presidential campaign of a Southern Baptist Sunday school teacher from Plains, Georgia. Jimmy Carter's concern for racial minorities and for the poor, his championing of the rights of women, his attention to human rights, and his quest for a less imperial foreign policy all mirrored the values articulated by leaders of the Christian Left.

By the time Carter ran for reelection in 1980, however, many politically conservative evangelicals had mobilized to defeat him. At the behest of Jerry Falwell and Paul Weyrich, what became the "religious right" coalesced to resist attempts on the part of the Internal Revenue Service to enforce antidiscrimination laws at Bob Jones University. By 1979 this fledgling movement added opposition to abortion into its political agenda, threw its weight behind Ronald Reagan, and denied Carter a second term.

Carter's defeat in 1980 once again signaled a decline in the fortunes of the Christian Left. For nearly three decades, during a period when the religious right exercised unparalleled, and virtually unchallenged, political influence, no national politician openly championed the values of the Christian Left. Those voices were not entirely silent, however. Wallis and Campolo, eager to demonstrate that the religious right did not speak for all evangelicals, formed Call to Renewal in 1996, which advocated environmental preservation and criticized proposals to revamp the welfare system. Ten years later, during the George W. Bush administration and once again at the behest of Wallis and Campolo, a diverse group of left-leaning evangelicals—activists, academics, and clergy—formed a loose coalition called Red Letter Christians, a reference to the words of Jesus, which are commonly printed in red ink in some editions of the Bible. The roster of Red Letter Christians included such names as Robert Franklin, Barbara Brown Taylor, Brian McLaren, Randall Balmer, Cheryl Sanders, Richard Rohr, Michael Battle, Diana Butler Bass, and Shane Claiborne. In contrast to leaders of the religious right, who continued to de-nounce abortion and same-sex marriage, Red Letter Christians discerned a much broader spectrum of moral issues: hunger, poverty, climate change, and opposition to the Bush administration's policies on torture.

Those principles resurfaced in the arena of public discourse during the presidential campaign of 2008, due in part to the perceived moral lapses of the Bush administration. The candidate who best articulated the values of the Christian Left was once again an African American, Barack Obama, someone indebted not so much to evangelicalism as to Reinhold Niebuhr, liberal Protestantism, and the Social Gospel as inflected through the black church.

[See also Christian Right; Civil Rights; Progressive Movement, US; and Religion and Politics]

BIBLIOGRAPHY

Balmer, Randall. *Thy Kingdom Come: How the Religious Right Distorts the Faith and Threatens America: An Evangelical's Lament.* (New York, 2006).

Campolo, Tony. *Red Letter Christians: A Citizen's Guide to Faith and Politics.* (Ventura, Calif., 2008).

Carter, Jimmy. *Our Endangered Values: America's Moral Crisis.* (New York, 2005).

Carwardine, Richard J. *Evangelicals and Politics in Antebellum America.* (New Haven, Conn., 1993).

Dayton, Donald W. *Discovering an Evangelical Heritage.* (New York, 1976).

Finney, Charles Grandison. *Sermons on Gospel Themes.* (New York, 1876).

Gaillard, Frye. *Prophet from Plains: Jimmy Carter and His Legacy.* (Athens, Ga., 2007).

Harvey, Paul. *Freedom's Coming: Religious Culture and the Shaping of the South from the Civil War through the Civil Rights Era.* (Chapel Hill, N.C., 2005).

Magnuson, Norris A. *Salvation in the Slums: Evangelical Social Work, 1865–1920.* (Metuchen, N.J., 1977).

Scanzoni, Letha, and Nancy Hardesty. *All We're Meant to Be: A Biblical Approach to Women's Liberation.* (Waco, Tex., 1974).

Smith, Timothy Lawrence. *Revivalism and Social Reform: American Protestantism on the Eve of the Civil War.* (New York, 1957).

Swartz, David W. "Identity Politics and the Fragmenting of the 1970s Evangelical Left." *Religion & American Culture* 21 (Winter 2011): 81–120.

Wallis, Jim. *God's Politics: Why the Right Gets It Wrong and the Left Doesn't Get It.* (San Francisco, 2005).

Young, Shawn David. "From Hippies to Jesus Freaks: Christian Radicalism in Chicago's Inner-City." *Journal of Religion and Popular Culture* 22 (Summer 2010): 1–28.

Randall Balmer

CHRISTIAN RIGHT

The Christian Right is a coalition of religious activists within the Republican Party. Evangelical Christians, who make up a majority of Christian Right activists, have always possessed a "custodial impulse." Conservative evangelicals believe God commands them to guard against amorality in the broader society. This has led them to conduct political campaigns throughout American history. The Christian Right has enjoyed increased national attention since the 1980 presidential election, in which conservative evangelical Christians helped elect President Ronald Reagan. The Christian Right's most visible institutions include national political action committees (PACs) such as the Moral Majority, the Christian Coalition, and the Family Research Council. Because these institutions emerged after 1975, most journalists and some scholars have treated the Christian Right as a relatively recent phenomenon. But an emerging scholarly consensus suggests that the Christian Right has deep roots in American history. An identifiable Christian Right has existed since the early twentieth century, and movement activists have played a role in debates over prohibition, anticommunism, civil rights, feminism, abortion, gay rights, and tax policy.

Though the Republican Party attracted former Whig Party evangelicals in the mid-nineteenth century, and has possessed a sizeable faction of religiously motivated activists since its inception, three twentieth-century developments set the stage for the rise of the Christian Right as a major player in the GOP. First, New Deal policies created an enlarged state that clashed with many evangelicals' mistrust of centralized governmental power. Although many evangelicals benefited from the New Deal—and a majority probably endorsed Franklin Delano Roosevelt's initiatives in the 1930s—evangelicals were becoming wealthier and more suburban by mid-century. This second development, which was especially pronounced in California, led suburban evangelicals to identify with the anticommunists of the radical right. Third, Southern evangelicals in the Democratic Party began shifting their allegiance to the GOP in the late 1960s. The transformation of the white South from solidly Democratic to solidly Republican meant that conservative evangelicals from Virginia to California were united within the GOP. By the time of Ronald Reagan's election to the presidency in 1980, the Christian Right had coalesced into an identifiable national movement within the Republican Party.

Anticommunism, Race, and Gender. Prior to the 1970s, anticommunism was the most visible venue of Christian Right activism. Anticommunism appealed to conservative evangelicals in part because of their theology and in part because of their understanding of America. Evangelical theology stresses the importance of individual conversion—the belief that all individuals must choose salvation for themselves by confessing their sinful nature and asking Jesus to save them. This theological emphasis, alongside classical liberalism's stress on the individual, created deep suspicion of any group that seemed to demean individual liberty. Evangelicals like the Oklahoma preacher and radio broadcaster Billy James Hargis were apt to link communism with socialism, liberalism, and religious organizations like the National Council of Churches. The thread connecting these entities in evangelical worldviews was "collectivism," or the belief that the group was more central than the individual. Many evangelicals saw collectivism as hostile to their theology and to American ideals. In fact, many evangelicals saw America as a uniquely blessed nation. They traced this blessing to their belief that America's Founders established a nation that fostered religious liberty but also depended on a "Judeo-Christian" worldview. In a Cold War context pitting "godless Communism" against "God's last best hope," conservative evangelicals believed that defending America from the Soviets was a religious duty. Hargis grew so impassioned about opposing communism (especially as he saw it influencing New Deal liberals) that he lost his Federal Communications Commission (FCC) license as a religious broadcaster for engaging in "political activities."

The racial turmoil of the 1960s played a role in the growth of the Christian Right, though historians do not entirely agree about how that turmoil factored into the Christian Right's emergence. Historians like Dan Carter (1996)) and Randall Balmer (2007), who focus on the Old South as the wellspring of the Christian Right, are more likely to see the movement as a "counterrevolution" in which white Southerners were responding directly to the civil rights revolution. In this view, Christian Right activism in the 1970s and 1980s intended to preserve white Christian mores, often at the expense of minorities. On the other hand, historians like Lisa McGirr (2001) and Darren Dochuk (2011), who center their stories on the Sunbelt, describe Christian Right activism as the outgrowth of suburbanization, anticommunism, and opposition to government activism. Though these historians describe the racial homogeneity of the Christian Right, focusing on the southwest leads them to conceive of the movement differently than do historians focused on the Old South. These Sunbelt-oriented histories describe the rhetoric of "colorblind conservatism" as the product of white suburbs that neither welcomed African Americans nor based their political agendas on opposition to civil rights. Because the Christian Right emerged in multiple locales, historians can find evidence for interpretations that stress the centrality of race in the Christian Right and for interpretations that suggest other issues stood at the center of the movement.

All historians agree that issues related to gender norms, especially feminism and abortion, acquired enormous importance to Christian Right activists in the 1970s and 1980s. The first major grassroots effort of the Christian Right involved opposition to the Equal Rights Amendment (ERA), which declared, "equality of rights under the law shall not be denied or abridged by the United States or by any state on account of sex." Congress passed the ERA in 1972. Thirty of the necessary thirty-eight states ratified the amendment within one year. Yet Christian Right activists viewed the amendment as a threat to family life, arguing that it would compel women to register for military conscription and would demean motherhood. Led by the conservative Catholic Phyllis Schlafly, conservative women across the nation joined the STOP ERA coalition and successfully defeated the ERA, which was never ratified by enough states to become part of the Constitution. Abortion also attracted significant opposition during this time period. The Supreme Court's 1973 *Roe v. Wade* decision invalidated state laws restricting abortion rights during the first two trimesters of pregnancy. Abortion rates in the United States skyrocketed, rising 700 percent nationwide between 1970 and 1977. Although the earliest abortion opponents were largely Catholic, evangelicals joined the pro-life coalition by the end of the 1970s. In 1979, the future surgeon general C. Everett Koop and the evangelical guru Francis Schaeffer cowrote a treatise against abortion called *Whatever Happened to the Human Race?* Schaeffer's son Franky turned the book into a film that aired in evangelical churches across the nation, and many evangelicals traced their opposition to abortion to viewing this film. By the time of the 1980 election, evangelicals viewed the high numbers of legalized abortions as a "holocaust"—and thus as the preeminent political issue.

The Reagan Revolution. Conservative Republicans saw evangelicals opposed to feminism and abortion as a source of grassroots activists and votes. Though many of these evangelicals had flocked to the banner of the Southern Baptist Jimmy Carter in 1976, Carter's administration endorsed feminism and abortion (though Carter said he was personally opposed to abortion). A group of evangelical leaders, including Tim LaHaye and Jerry Falwell, visited the White House in 1980 in order to ask Carter to change his stance on these two issues. When it became clear that Carter would not heed their advice, LaHaye and Falwell determined to defeat him in the election that fall. Several Republican presidential candidates courted these leaders; Ronald Reagan won their support. At a Dallas meeting in August 1980, Reagan told a throng of evangelicals, "I endorse you." Reagan's strenuous anticommunism, opposition to abortion rights, and easy command of evangelical rhetoric appealed to the Christian Right. In some ways, the love affair between Reagan and evangelicals made little sense. A divorced former actor who seldom attended church, Reagan's personal piety was suspect. But evangelicals thrilled to his endorsement and helped deliver a landslide victory to Reagan in the 1980 election.

Media reactions to the Christian Right's influence in the 1980 presidential election contained a mixture of shock, confusion, and horror. National correspondents in the northeastern corridor had paid scant attention to evangelicals for a half century; their political "awakening" took these correspondents by surprise. But networks of evangelical activists had engaged in political campaigns for decades. Ministers in southern California played key roles in the presidential campaign of the conservative Barry Goldwater in 1964 and in the gubernatorial campaign of Reagan in 1966. School board elections across the country turned on questions of morality as evangelicals questioned the introduction of sexual education and multiculturalism into school curricula. National attention to media-savvy preachers like Jerry Falwell and Pat Robertson reached new heights in 1980, but those men were simply the most visible manifestations of a pattern of evangelical activism that had existed for years.

The support for this political activism came from the strength of evangelical networks, which provided rhetoric and connections for conservative evangelicals across the nation. For instance, conservative evangelicals opened thousands of private Christian academies between 1965 and 1980. Many of these academies (especially those in the Old South) opened in response to public school desegregation. By 1980, however, they had focused their critique of public education (and, by extension, of the state itself) on schools' promotion of "secular humanism." Evangelicals said secular humanism taught students to disregard their parents' belief systems and to view themselves as autonomous agents who made moral decisions based on situational ethics. The idea that "secular humanism" dominated public schools—an idea almost nobody voiced prior to the 1970s—was pervasive among evangelicals by 1980, testifying to the power of Christian school networks. Organizations like the National Association of Christian Schools circulated periodicals that voiced a critique of secular humanism. Ministers like Tim LaHaye reinforced this critique in popular books designed to promote Christian schools. As a result, evangelicals gained both a diagnosis for the ills of public education and a desire to oust liberal school board members.

These networks also helped establish "family values" as the dominant rhetoric of the Christian Right. By the early 1980s, conservative evangelicals viewed nearly all liberal initiatives —from feminism to gay rights to higher taxes—as attacks on the family. By "family" evangelicals meant two heterosexual parents and their children, preferably with the husband as breadwinner and the wife as stay-at-home mother. They viewed the family as one of two institutions ordained by God (the other was the church), and

they opposed political initiatives that legitimized other family structures or threatened the "traditional" family. For instance, Focus on the Family, a nonprofit organization and media empire led by the child psychologist James Dobson, published critiques of the gay rights movement that identified governmental recognition of homosexuals as an attack on family values. These critiques suggested that the (heterosexual) family structure was established as normative in the Bible. Moreover, Dobson claimed that psychology had proven the deleterious effects of homosexuality on children. It followed that any society that normalized homosexuality went against both God's law and the lessons of psychology. Focus on the Family did not simply specify a normative family structure; it also endorsed a particular philosophy for parenting. Dobson argued that parents must "Dare to Discipline," bucking the trends of permissive parenting popularized in the 1960s. Dobson became emblematic of the Christian Right's rejection of 1960s liberalism and won wide popularity among evangelicals. Owing to its hugely popular radio programs and fundraising campaigns, Focus on the Family had become the most influential organization in the Christian Right by the end of the twentieth century.

Disillusionment and Retrenchment. The Christian Right's political successes during the 1980s, which included the election of Republican presidential candidates in 1980, 1984, and 1988, fell short of their ambitions. Some conservative evangelicals left the movement. They had grown disillusioned with Republican administrations that took evangelical votes for granted, and they despaired of ever overturning *Roe v. Wade*. The election of the scandal-prone Arkansas governor Bill Clinton to the presidency in 1992 seemed to them a total disaster. But evangelical conservatives in the Christian Coalition played a crucial role in the state-level success of the GOP in the 1994 midterm elections, and they won an even greater victory with the presidential election of George W. Bush in 2000. Bush memorably declared that his favorite philosopher was Jesus, and he traced his conversion to a mid-1980s conversation on the beach with the famed evangelist Billy Graham.

Furthermore, Bush staffed his campaign and administration with evangelicals and pledged to pass the agenda of the Christian Right. He won some notable victories, including the establishment of an office of Faith-Based Initiatives and the nominations of John Roberts and Samuel Alito to the Supreme Court. And yet, Christian Right leaders were once again disappointed at the end of a Republican administration in 2008, as Bush left office with historically low approval ratings and considerably less enthusiasm from his evangelical base.

This cycle of enthusiasm followed by disillusionment has characterized Christian Right activism for decades. Conservative evangelicals carry a mandate to transform society in the likeness of Christ, and their absolute-faith commitments do not admit much room for compromise. For instance, Reagan's fixation on the economy in his first term disappointed evangelicals who thought abolishing abortion rights should be the new administration's first priority. And yet, conservative evangelicals have become increasingly savvy in their political activities. Christian Right leaders have created institutions, fundraising strategies, and rhetoric that stand at the center of GOP politics. Their power encouraged the 2008 presidential nominee John McCain to nominate the Christian Right favorite Sarah Palin for the vice presidency, in spite of Palin's thin credentials. If conservative evangelicals are destined to be disappointed with political outcomes, they nonetheless show determination and maturation that will allow the Christian Right to exert significant influence in the GOP for the foreseeable future.

[*See also* Abortion; Bush, George W.; Civil Rights Movement; Cold War; Equal Rights Amendment; Faith-Based Initiatives; Gay Rights; Gender and Politics; New Deal; Reagan, Ronald; *and* Republican Party.]

BIBLIOGRAPHY

Balmer, Randall. *Thy Kingdom Come: How the Religious Right Distorts Faith and Threatens America: An Evangelical's Lament.* (New York, 2007).

Bivins, Jason. *The Fracture of Good Order: Christian Antiliberalism and the Challenge to American Politics.* (Chapel Hill, N.C., 2003).

Carter, Dan T. *From George Wallace to Newt Gingrich: Race in the Conservative Counterrevolution, 1963–1994.* (Baton Rouge, La., 1996).

Diamond, Sara. *Not by Politics Alone: The Enduring Influence of the Christian Right.* (New York, 1998).

Dochuk, Darren. *From Bible Belt to Sunbelt: Plain-Folk Religion, Grassroots Politics, and the Rise of Evangelical Conservatism.* (New York, 2011).

Lindsay, D. Michael. *Faith in the Halls of Power: How Evangelicals Joined the American Elite.* (New York, 2007).

Martin, William C. *With God on Our Side: The Rise of the Religious Right in America.* (New York, 1996).

McGirr, Lisa. *Suburban Warriors: The Origins of the New American Right.* (Princeton, N.J., 2001).

Miller, Steven P. *Billy Graham and the Rise of the Republican South.* (Philadelphia, 2009).

Williams, Daniel K. *God's Own Party: The Making of the Christian Right.* (New York, 2010).

Seth Dowland

CHURCH AND STATE, SEPARATION OF

The phrase "separation of church and state" is most commonly used to refer to the religion clauses of the First Amendment to the United States Constitution: the Establishment Clause and the Free Exercise Clause. Thomas Jefferson coined the phrase in 1802, and the US Supreme Court subsequently adopted it. The first sixteen words of the First Amendment state: "Congress shall make no law respecting an establishment of religion, or prohibiting the free exercise thereof." Put simply, the Supreme Court has said these provisions require the government to refrain from advancing or inhibiting religion and to protect the free exercise of faith by individuals and institutions.

Politicians have sometimes employed the phrase "separation of church and state" to refer to the letter and spirit of Article VI of the Constitution as well, the provision that bars the imposition of religious tests for public office. Most famously, then–presidential candidate John F. Kennedy used the phrase in this way in a speech he gave to the Greater Houston Ministerial Association in 1960. Striving to become the nation's first president who happened to be Catholic, Kennedy declared he believed in an America where church-state separation was "absolute."

Church-state separation has not always been regarded in a positive light. Some have called it a kind of code for the anti-Catholicism that was prevalent during the mid-to-late nineteenth century. In the late twentieth century, some conservatives, including then–Supreme Court Justice William Rehnquist, decried church-state separation as an extra-constitutional notion that had led the Court to overinterpret Establishment Clause commands.

Further, almost from the time Jefferson introduced the phrase, Americans have debated what church-state separation does or should mean and whether it has had a beneficial or detrimental impact on government and religion. The following sections describe the origins of the phrase and some of its uses in American public life.

Origins of the Phrase. In October 1801, the Danbury Baptist Association in the state of Connecticut wrote a letter to the newly elected president of the nation, Thomas Jefferson. They congratulated Jefferson on his election and expressed the hope that his advocacy for religious liberty would widen the freedom they enjoyed under their state's laws. At the time, Connecticut treated the Congregational Church preferentially. "We are sensible," the Danbury Baptists said, "that the President of the united States, is not the national Legislator, & also sensible that the national government cannot destroy the Laws of each State." Nevertheless, they hoped Jefferson's belief in religious freedom, "like the radiant beams of the Sun, will shine & prevail through all these States and all the world till Hierarchy and tyranny be destroyed from the Earth."

In a letter dated 1 January 1802, Jefferson thanked the Connecticut Baptists for their support. He also penned these famous words:

Believing with you that religion is a matter which lies solely between Man & his God, that he owes account to none other for his faith or his worship, that the legitimate powers of government reach actions only, & not opinions, I contemplate with sovereign reverence that act of the whole American people which

declared that their legislature should "make no law respecting an establishment of religion, or prohibiting the free exercise thereof," thus building a wall of separation between Church & State.

Jefferson may have been inspired by similar expressions of seventeenth-century thinkers such as the English philosopher John Locke and the preacher Roger Williams. In *A Letter Concerning Toleration* (1689), Locke argued that church authority must be "confined within the bounds of the church . . . because the church itself is a thing absolutely separate and distinct from the commonwealth." Williams, who was banished from Massachusetts Bay Colony in 1635 for his heretical ideas about religion and religious liberty, called for "a gap in the hedge or wall of Separation between the Garden of the Church and the Wilderness of the world" in order to keep the church pure (Gaustad 1999b). In any case, the US Supreme Court and others later adopted Jefferson's phrase.

Supreme Court Interpretation. The Supreme Court first quoted the Jefferson letter in 1878 in the case of *Reynolds v. United States*, but its most famous reference to church-state separation occurred in the 1947 case of *Everson v. Board of Education*. In *Everson*, the Court considered whether it was constitutionally permissible for the state of New Jersey to reimburse parents for the costs of transporting students to and from religious and other private schools as well as public schools. After declaring that the Establishment Clause applied to the states as well as the federal government by virtue of the Fourteenth Amendment, the Court deemed the aid to be constitutional. In an opinion written by Justice Hugo Black, however, the Court also interpreted the Establishment Clause broadly. It said:

The "establishment of religion" clause of the First Amendment means at least this: Neither a state nor the Federal Government can set up a church. Neither can pass laws which aid one religion, aid all religions, or prefer one religion over another. Neither can force nor influence a person to go to or to remain away from church against his will or force him to profess a belief or disbelief in any religion. No person can be punished for entertaining or professing religious beliefs or disbeliefs, for church attendance or non-attendance. No tax in any amount, large or small, can be levied to support any religious activities or institutions, whatever they may be called, or whatever form they may adopt to teach or practice religion. Neither a state nor the Federal Government can, openly or secretly, participate in the affairs of any religious organizations or groups and *vice versa.* In the words of Jefferson, the clause against establishment of religion by law was intended to erect "a wall of separation between church and State."

Thus, while Jefferson used this phrase to describe the combined effect of both of the First Amendment's religion clauses—the Establishment Clause and the Free Exercise Clause—the Court in *Everson* connected it only to the Establishment Clause. In subsequent cases the Court usually followed this pattern, although it sometimes noted that church-state separation protected free-exercise interests as well.

In the 1960s and 1970s, the Supreme Court struck down school-sponsored prayer and Bible readings and a variety of forms of government aid for religious elementary and secondary schools under the Establishment Clause. Broadly speaking, the Court's rationale in cases like these was that the government exceeded its jurisdiction when it sponsored religious expression or subsidized pervasively religious institutions. This overreach violated the consciences of taxpayers who properly expected the state to remain neutral in religious matters and jeopardized religion's integrity, the Court said. To a large extent, decisions like these came to define church-state separation in the mind of the American public.

In 1985, then-Justice William Rehnquist launched a broadside against the Court's references to church-state separation and its Establishment Clause doctrine more generally. In a dissenting opinion in the case of *Wallace v. Jaffree,* Rehnquist wrote: "It is impossible to build sound constitutional doctrine upon a mistaken understanding of constitutional history, but unfortunately the Establishment Clause has been expressly freighted with Jefferson's misleading metaphor for nearly forty years." The Establishment Clause was intended only to prohibit the establishment of a national religion and governmental preferences for one religion over another, Rehnquist argued; the government, therefore, was free to prefer religion over irreligion and to extend aid to religions in a nondiscriminatory manner.

Although the Court later relaxed its interpretation of the Establishment Clause as it applies to government aid and religious institutions and activities, it has not gone so far as to embrace Rehnquist's arguments on these matters. In a concurring opinion written in 1992 in the case of *Lee v. Weisman,* Justice David Souter rebutted many of Rehnquist's points.

In 2004, Supreme Court Justice Clarence Thomas argued that the First Amendment's Establishment Clause was originally intended to prevent Congress from interfering with state establishments of religion and, as such, it did not make much sense to apply that clause to the states. Thomas's argument has some popular support, but it has not drawn the vote of any other Supreme Court justice.

Prominent Uses of "Separation of Church and State" in American Politics. Beyond Thomas Jefferson, other presidents who have famously used the phrase "separation of church and state" include Ulysses S. Grant. In 1875, Grant advocated an amendment to the US Constitution that would have prohibited public funds from flowing to "sectarian" schools, and he did so in the name of separation of church and state. Grant's amendment was proposed in the midst of a raucous debate about public funds and Catholic schools at a time when anti-Catholicism was "common and loud," according to the historian Ward McAfee (2003). Catholics objected to the readings of the Protestant King James Bible that took place in the nation's public schools, and they argued that the state should fund Catholic schools as an alternative for Catholic students. Their proposal was vehemently opposed by many Americans who wanted to keep things just as they were—public funding for schools that favored Protestant practices and no public funding for Catholic schools—and a much smaller group that opposed all forms of government support for religion of any kind. In this context, President Grant gave a speech in which he said "not one dollar" that was appropriated for the public schools should flow to "sectarian schools." Grant also called for leaving "the matter of religious teaching to the family altar, the Church, and the private school, supported entirely by private contributions," and he exhorted Americans to "keep the Church and State forever separate" (Green, 2010, p. 292). Efforts to amend the federal Constitution along these lines were unsuccessful.

Almost a century later, the Catholic presidential candidate John F. Kennedy embraced church-state separation, in part to calm fears that he would take orders from the Vatican as president. In a speech to the Greater Houston Ministerial Association in 1960, Kennedy directly addressed these concerns, saying:

> I believe in an America where the separation of church and state is absolute—where no Catholic prelate would tell the President (should he be Catholic) how to act, and no Protestant minister would tell his parishioners for whom to vote—where no church or church school is granted any public funds or political preference—and where no man is denied public office merely because his religion differs from the President who might appoint him or the people who might elect him.

President Ronald Reagan had a different understanding of church-state separation. While pushing for an amendment to the Constitution that would reintroduce school-sponsored prayer, Reagan argued that preventing schools from organizing prayers actually violated the wall of church-state separation. He said: "All we asked for was to recognize that the Constitution, with that wall of separation between church and state, is interfering with the private individual's right to the practice of religion when it says you cannot pray if you want to, voluntarily, in a school. And we want that changed so that you can" (Kaylor, 2011, p. 57). This effort to amend the Constitution failed, in large part because opponents explained that Supreme Court rulings only prohibited school-sponsored prayer and religious expression, leaving students free to pray individually or in groups without state support.

A Continuing Conversation. Popular debate about church-state separation is a staple of American politics. Some have argued that it is illegitimate to use the phrase "separation of church and state" to refer to constitutional principles, because the phrase does not appear in the Constitution. Yet even though phrases and terms such as "separation of powers" and "federalism" do not appear in the Constitution, they are accepted descriptions of constitutional ideals. Also, some have said they oppose church-state separation because they believe the Supreme Court has interpreted the Establishment Clause too broadly.

On the opposite side of the spectrum, others believe the Court has interpreted the Establishment Clause too narrowly, and they have often used the phrase "separation of church and state" to agitate for constitutional doctrine that would be more to their liking. They have criticized, for example, Court decisions to uphold tax exemptions for religious entities and government-subsidized chaplains in legislatures. Some in this camp also have argued that church-state separation requires the separation of religious rhetoric from discussions about policies and politics. If the government were to impose this latter kind of separation, it would actually violate the First Amendment. Further, the wisdom and practicality of any proposed pledge along these lines is hotly disputed.

In sum, "the separation of church and state" is a well-known phrase with a rich history in American public life. Part of that history, however, has been a vigorous debate about the meaning of the phrase. In a nation with a unique framework for religious freedom and strong and varying perspectives about exactly what that framework does or should require, that debate is likely to continue.

[*See also* Civil Liberties; Constitution, US; *and* Judicial System, American.]

BIBLIOGRAPHY

Brownstein, Alan, ed. *The Establishment of Religion Clause: The First Amendment: Its Constitutional History and the Contemporary Debate.* (Amherst, N.Y., 2007).

Butler, Jon. *Awash in a Sea of Faith: Christianizing the American People.* (Cambridge, Mass., 1990).

Dreisbach, Daniel L. *Thomas Jefferson and the Wall of Separation between Church and State.* (New York, 2002).

Feldman, Noah. *Divided by God: America's Church-State Problem—and What We Should Do about It.* (New York, 2005).

Flowers, Ronald B., Melissa Rogers, and Steven K. Green. *Religious Freedom and the Supreme Court.* (Waco, Tex., 2008).

Gaustad, Edwin S. *Church and State in America.* (New York, 1999a).

Gaustad, Edwin S. *Liberty of Conscience: Roger Williams in America.* (Valley Forge, Pa., 1999b).

Green, Steven K. "Federalism and the Establishment Clause: A Reassessment." *Creighton Law Review* 38 (2005): 761–797.

Green, Steven K. *The Second Disestablishment: Church and State in Nineteenth-Century America.* (Oxford, 2010).

Greenawalt, Kent. *Religion and the Constitution: Establishment and Fairness.* (Princeton, N.J., 2008).

Greenawalt, Kent. *Religion and the Constitution: Free Exercise and Fairness.* (Princeton, N.J., 2006).

Hall, Timothy, L. *Separating Church and State: Roger Williams and Religious Liberty.* (Urbana, Ill., 1998).

Hamburger, Philip. *Separation of Church and State.* (Cambridge, Mass., 2002).

Haynes, Charles C., and Oliver S. Thomas. *Finding Common Ground: A Guide to Religious Liberty in Public Schools.* (Nashville, Tenn., 2001).

Hutson, James H., ed. *Religion and the New Republic: Faith in the Founding of America.* (Lanham, Md., 2000).

Kaylor, Brian T. *Presidential Campaign Rhetoric in an Age of Confessional Politics* (Lanham, Md., 2011).

Lash, Kurt T. "The Second Adoption of the Establishment Clause: The Rise of the Non-Establishment Principle." *Arizona State Law Journal* 27 (1995): 1085–1154.

Laycock, Douglas. "The Many Meanings of Separation." *University of Chicago Law Review* 70 (2003): 1667–1701. A critique of Philip Hamburger's book *Separation of Church and State.*

Laycock, Douglas. "'Nonpreferential'" Aid to Religion: A False Claim about Original Intent." *William and Mary Law Review* 27 (1986): 875–923.

Locke, John S. *A Letter Concerning Toleration.* (Amherst, N.Y., 1990). First published in 1689.

McAfee, Ward M. *Religion, Race, and Reconstruction: The Public School in the Politics of the 1870s.* (Albany, N.Y., 1998).

McAfee, Ward M. Remarks at an event titled *Separation of Church and States: An Examination of State Constitutional Limits on Government Funding for Religious Institutions.* Pew Forum on Religion and Public Life (28 March 2003), http://pewforum.org/Church-State-Law/Separation-of-Church-and-States-An-Examination-of-State-Constitutional-Limits-on-Government-Funding-for-Religious-Institutions.aspx.

Miller, William Lee. *The First Liberty: America's Foundation in Religious Freedom.* Expanded and updated ed. (Washington, D.C., 2003).

Walker, J. Brent. *Church-State Matters: Fighting for Religious Liberty in Our Nation's Capital.* (Macon, Ga., 2008).

Melissa Rogers

CITIES, AMERICAN

See Urban Sprawl.

CITIZENSHIP

United States citizenship is acquired either by birth within one of the fifty states, or by descent from a parent who is a US citizen, if the child is born outside of the United States, or it is conferred by Congress through a statutory process of naturalization. The naturalization process historically has included requirements such as legal entry into the United States, a residency period, intention to reside in the United States permanently, ability to speak English, and dedication to the principles of the US Constitution, determined in part through a civics test.

Early History. The United States Constitution as originally enacted mentioned the word "citizen" in only a few places (members of Congress must be citizens for a minimum number of years, and the president must be a "natural born citizen," for example), but nowhere defined the term. It did, however, confer upon Congress the authority to "establish an uniform Rule of Naturalization" in Article I, Section 8, meaning that it could choose to make US citizens of persons of other nationalities. Largely on the basis of this provision, Congress has exercised plenary power over immigration and deportation, as well as admission to citizenship for the foreign-born.

Following independence from Great Britain, Congress asserted its authority over admission to citizenship through various Naturalization Acts, permitting foreign-born white persons to apply for citizenship after residing in the United States for periods ranging from five to fourteen years, among other requirements. While Congress controlled the procedure for admission to citizenship of the foreign-born, state and federal statutes prior to the Fourteenth Amendment of the US Constitution are silent about the citizenship of native-born inhabitants. Citizenship for persons born in the United States, at least for whites, seems to have followed English common law and its adoption of the *jus soli*, a Latin term translated "law of the soil." This practice assigned citizenship on the circumstance of birth within the territorial boundaries of the nation, regardless of the parents' citizenship.

The English common law, in turn, derived the practice from *Calvin's Case*, decided in 1608, holding that all persons born within the King's territories owed allegiance to the King and hence were his "subjects." Courts in the United States early on chose "citizenship" as the relevant category to substitute for "subject" under the common-law doctrine. Numerous court cases resolved land title and inheritance disputes in cases that questioned the native-born citizenship status of one or more litigants. This background assumption of citizenship by birth within the territory seems to explain the lack of a definition of birthright citizenship in the original US Constitution.

Although the US Constitution specifies that Congress has the authority to establish the rules for admission to US citizenship for the foreign-born, some states continued to exercise a quasi-naturalization power by admitting persons to state citizenship. Indeed, until the twentieth century, state citizenship was far more important for political and civil rights. State law, for example, governed the political and civil rights of that state's inhabitants.

In *Dred Scott v. Sanford* (1857), the US Supreme Court held that people of African descent, whether slave or free, did not become United States citizens by birth on American soil—a decision that contributed to the Civil War.

The Fourteenth Amendment. Following the Civil War, the Fourteenth Amendment to the US Constitution was ratified in 1868. Section 1 of this amendment established *jus soli*—territorial birthright citizenship—as law enshrined in the Constitution. It reads, in part, "All persons born or naturalized in the United States, and subject to the jurisdiction thereof, are citizens of the United States and of the State wherein they reside." The specific intent of the Amendment's framers was to provide citizenship for the newly freed slaves and to overturn *Dred Scott*. The general intent was broader, as the US Supreme Court affirmed in the 1898 case of *United States v. Wong Kim Ark*, ruling that "all persons" was not limited to the former slaves but also included persons of Chinese descent.

An equally fundamental transformation of the Fourteenth Amendment was to protect federal citizenship rights of individuals from state interference. Persons born within the United States were specifically made citizens of the United States, as well as the state where they resided. Further, Section 1 limited state power over United States citizens: "No State shall make or enforce any law which shall abridge the privileges or immunities of citizens of the United States; nor shall any State deprive any person of life, liberty, or property, without due process of law; nor deny to any person within its jurisdiction the equal protection of the laws." The Due Process Clause and Equal Protection Clause apply to all persons present in the state, whether or not they are US citizens.

In recent years, the recognition of citizenship status for the children born in the United States to undocumented alien parents has been challenged. The US government has long assumed such children are automatically citizens of this country, while more recently some have suggested that the language of the Fourteenth Amendment does not apply to these children. The debate over birthright citizenship has two camps: those who believe Congress has the authority to limit birthright citizenship by statute, and those who insist a constitutional amendment is required. The attraction of congressional authority is obvious. It is extremely difficult to amend the Constitution, requiring two-thirds approval in both congressional houses, as well as ratification by three-fourths of the states. In the past, the Republican Party called for a constitutional amendment in its platform to change the rule of automatic citizenship at birth. The view that Congress could accomplish the same thing by legislation is of recent origin.

Most legal scholars conclude Congress has no such authority because the language of the Fourteenth Amendment is clear. Any person—regardless of their parents—acquires citizenship at birth so long as he or she is "subject to the jurisdiction" of the United States. Proponents of congressional authority reason that, because the parents are in the country illegally, they are not "subject to the jurisdiction" of the United States. But undocumented aliens clearly are subject to all manner of US law when they are here, rather than the law of their home country.

The second argument in favor of congressional authority rejects the clear language of the Fourteenth Amendment in favor of what is said to be the intention of at least some of the congressmen who voted for it in 1868. But it is clear enough from that time that the phrase "subject to the jurisdiction thereof" was intended to exclude Native Americans born on tribal land and children of diplomats, consistent with international practices. Moreover, the case of Yaser Esam Hamdi, a US citizen captured in Afghanistan and held at Guantanamo Bay as an enemy combatant, focused political debate on birthright citizenship practices. Hamdi's parents were in the United States legally at the time of his birth, but Hamdi lived in the United States for only a short time. The US Supreme Court did not address challenges to Hamdi's citizenship in its opinion (*Hamdi v. Rumsfeld*, 2004), emphasizing instead that, as an American citizen, an individual being held as an "enemy combatant" nonetheless retained the right to challenge that combatant status before a judge.

Canada and most Latin American countries also accord territorial birthright citizenship. Most of Europe, by contrast, awards citizenship based on the status of one or both parents. In recent decades, Great Britain, Ireland, and Australia have moved away from territorial birthright citizenship.

Citizenship of Persons Born in US Territories and Overseas. Persons born in United States territories and possessions, including Puerto Rico and Guam, are US citizens not by the Fourteenth Amendment but by Act of Congress. Territorial residents whose citizenship is granted by statute (including persons born on Native American tribal land within the United States) share all other rights of US citizens when present within the fifty states, including the right to vote and to enter and leave the boundaries of the United States at will. The residents of American Samoa are treated as nationals, rather than citizens, and thus may not vote in US presidential elections.

Children born overseas to at least one parent who is a United States citizen are also accorded US citizenship by Congress. Beginning in 1790, Congress provided by statute for the citizenship of persons born "beyond the seas" to citizen parents, and the statute has been amended numerous times. The statute in effect at the time of the child's birth determines the eligibility for citizenship. As of 2011, the rules varied somewhat depending upon whether both parents are US citizens, only one parent is a US citizen but is married, or the child is born out of wedlock to one US citizen parent. A record of birth abroad must be registered with a US consulate or embassy to serve as proof of citizenship, and the child may apply for a US passport or a Certificate of Citizenship. To date, persons born within one of the fifty United States must present only a birth certificate to prove citizenship.

The US Supreme Court interprets this conferral of citizenship to derive from Congress's constitutional power "to establish an uniform Rule of Naturalization" (Article 1, Section 8), so citizenship derived from one's parents is not a constitutional right but a statutory one.

Loss of Citizenship and Expatriation. Citizenship acquired through birth or naturalization may be relinquished voluntarily. In addition, naturalized US citizens may be subject to revocation of their citizenship status at any time if the naturalization has been unlawfully or fraudulently procured, but not for any acts taking place after the naturalization process is complete.

[*See also* Civil Liberties; Civil Rights; Constitution, US; *and* Immigration to the United States.]

BIBLIOGRAPHY

Motomura, Hiroshi. *Americans in Waiting: The Lost Story of Immigration and Citizenship in the United States.* (New York, 2006).

Neuman, Gerald L. *Strangers to the Constitution: Immigrants, Borders, and Fundamental Law.* (Princeton, N.J., 1996).

Price, Polly J. "Alien Land Restrictions in the American Common Law." *American Journal of Legal History* 43 (1999): 152–208.

Price, Polly J. "Natural Law and Birthright Citizenship in *Calvin's Case* (1608)." *Yale Journal of Law and the Humanities* 9 (1997): 73–145.

Schuck, Peter H., and Rogers M. Smith. *Citizenship without Consent: Illegal Aliens in the American Polity.* (New Haven, Conn., 1985).

Polly J. Price

CIVIL LIBERTIES

The United States Constitution provides for the protection of a broad set of individual liberties that the national government is prohibited from violating—prohibitions that were eventually extended to state and local governments as well. Enshrined primarily in the Bill of Rights, but contained also in the body of the Constitution, in state constitutions, and in social and historical understandings of liberty, these protections have become an essential characteristic of American political culture, reflecting the key ideals of both individualism and limited government. The history of civil liberties in the United States, however, reveals that these individual protections have always been subject to limitations imposed by majoritarian values, federalism, wartime contingencies, and the varied willingness of judges to protect individuals from the exercise of state power.

Definition and Early Understanding. At the time of the American Revolution and the drafting of the Constitution that followed, the concepts of "rights" and "liberties" tended to be used interchangeably to refer to a set of rights that citizens of a nation held in their relationship with the state. Over time, and particularly, after the Civil War (1861–1865) and during the twentieth century, the concepts of "civil rights" and "civil liberties" grew more distinct, with the notion of civil rights being about equal treatment under the law, and civil liberties being about the fundamental rights of individuals to be free from government restraint unless such restraint can be legally justified.

In the earliest understanding, the concept of civil rights and liberties was influenced by the experience of the colonists as subjects of the English throne and by the attractiveness of Enlightenment political theories that posited that certain rights were "natural" and retained by citizens even as they gave up some of their natural freedom in order to attain the safety offered by government. The English Magna Carta of 1215, and subsequent legislation by the British Parliament, laid the groundwork for the revolutionary and founding generations' understanding of their rights vis-à-vis the state. The first objections to British rule by the colonists were framed as claims to their rights as Englishmen. The Declaration of Independence, penned in 1776, relies on these rights claims to justify the breaking away of the colonies and the establishment of a new government more respectful of these rights. The "self-evident" truth is that man has "certain inalienable rights" of "life, liberty, and the pursuit of happiness" and that "whenever any government becomes destructive of these ends, it is the right of the people to alter or abolish it" in order to better secure these rights. The Declaration presents a laundry list of rights violations by the King, and it reflects two distinct, but complementary, notions about liberty. In the first place, it reflects the now common understanding of liberty as being about the absence of government restraint on individual action—but it also reflects a commitment to the human capacity for, and right to, self-government.

The first bills of rights were contained in the state constitutions adopted by the original colonies after independence. These bills varied in their levels of specificity, but had in common the idea that the state government was limited to some extent in its ability to impose on the natural rights of citizens. What exactly those rights were varied, however, depending on the political culture of the new state. For example, while there was general agreement that the "rights of conscience" were included in the notion of civil liberty, states that had established churches were slow to identify the free exercise of religious belief as being protected. Most of the states provided for some protection of freedom of speech and of the press, but as historians of the era have pointed out, there was widespread suppression of the speech and publications of those who opposed independence or who criticized state governments. In addition, the adoption of English common law rules by most states meant that libel was broadly defined, in order to justify punishment after publication of material that offended those in power.

The commitment to individualism and limited government has been widely accepted as the common understanding of the founding generation, but there is evidence that this was the understanding of only some, and not most, of those who wrote the Constitution in 1787 and the Bill of Rights in 1789. Also clearly present was an understanding of liberty as interwoven with the right of self-government. In this context, we should understand rights like freedom of speech and of the press as essential elements of democratic citizenship which allow citizens to engage with their government and hold it accountable to the people. This means that we should understand civil liberties—at least at the time of the founding—at least as much as being about freedom to engage in self-government, as about freedom from acts of government or majority suppression of minority rights. These competing understandings about rights were present during the debate over the ratification of the Constitution and the addition of the first ten amendments to that document.

Protecting Liberty with the Bill of Rights. Ratification of the Constitution, proposed by the 1787 Constitutional Convention, was not a foregone conclusion. Among the many criticisms launched by those who feared the power of the new central government was that the document contained no bill of rights that identified the liberties of the people and made clear the limits on the national government's power. In *Federalist Paper No. 84*, Alexander Hamilton responded to this criticism, arguing that a bill of rights was both unnecessary and potentially dangerous.

It was unnecessary, he claimed, because the Constitution itself was a bill of rights. Not only had it structured government in such a way (through the separation of powers and federalism) as to insure that no branch or level of government could become so powerful as to threaten liberty, but it had also included, within its original articles, the protections of liberty understood to be essential at that time: restriction on the ability to suspend habeas corpus, prohibition against the passing of bills of attainder and ex post facto laws and against the granting of titles of nobility or the use of religious tests for office; guarantee of right to a trial by jury, and a narrow definition of the crime of treason. Beyond these provisions, Hamilton noted that the history of bills of rights was one of subjects demanding these protections from the sovereign, a situation totally different from one in which the people themselves were the sovereign.

More provocative was Hamilton's argument that adding a bill of rights would be dangerous. The danger would come from the implication that government might have some regulatory power in these areas, when no such power had been granted. In addition, there was danger in creating a list that might then be interpreted as exhaustive, thus limiting liberty to those areas listed and implying government power to limit or control anything not listed. Finally, Hamilton argued that vague claims to particular freedoms—the liberty of the press, for example— had no clear meaning and thus could be subject to widely varying interpretations. In the end, the freedom of the press would depend primarily upon the people's belief in such a freedom, not on the vague words in a document.

Opponents of a Constitution without a bill of rights were not persuaded by Hamilton's argument, and ratification became contingent on an agreement that the first Congress would propose amendments to the Constitution that would add a bill of rights. Such a bill was proposed by James Madison in 1789, and the first ten amendments to the Constitution became law in 1791. These amendments included: freedom of speech, press, religion, and assembly (the First Amendment); the right to bear arms (Second); the prohibition against the forced quartering of soldiers (Third); protection from unreasonable search and seizure and the requirement for warrants (Fourth); the right to indictment by grand jury, freedom from double jeopardy and self-incrimination, the guarantee of due process, and the requirement that property not be taken without just compensation (Fifth); the right to a speedy and public trial, to confront witnesses, and to counsel (Sixth); the right to a jury trial in civil cases (Seventh); and prohibition against excessive fines and cruel and unusual punishment (Eighth). In order to address some of the concerns raised by Hamilton about interpretation, the Ninth and Tenth Amendments were added. The Ninth warned against the assumption that the list of rights was exhaustive and declared that there were other rights "retained by the people." The Tenth addressed the issue of the overall limits on the national government's power, stating that powers not delegated to the national government or prohibited of state governments were "reserved to the States respectively, or to the people." Despite these caveats, Hamilton's concerns about interpretation would prove prophetic.

Barron v. Baltimore (1833). In presenting the Bill of Rights to Congress, James Madison proposed that state governments also be constrained from interfering with these liberties, but that proposal was not accepted. In 1833, in the case of *Barron v. Baltimore,* the US Supreme Court was asked to decide whether the protections contained in the first eight amendments were also applicable to state government entities. At question was whether or not the Fifth Amendment requirement that property not be taken without just compensation applied to Baltimore. The city dredged its harbor, an action that had a negative impact on one Mr. Barron's wharf business. He claimed that the Fifth Amendment required that he be compensated for this loss, but the Court disagreed. Reviewing the ratification debate and the debate about the Bill of Rights in the first Congress, the Court concluded that the amendments applied only to the national government.

The impact of the *Barron* decision was significant. By limiting the reach of the Bill of Rights, the Court

limited the number of cases that might come before it for interpretation, since at the time most legislation and government action that could negatively affect the rights of citizens occurred at the state level, particularly in the criminal justice system. Citizens claiming rights violations were thus dependent upon their ability to affect state legislatures (in resisting or seeking repeal of problematic legislation) to amend their state constitutions, or to win in state courts on the basis of state constitutional claims. Research on state constitutionalism demonstrates that state citizens were not without success in these efforts. It bears noting, however, that these avenues for rights protection were more likely to be available to members of the majority than to minorities. The *Barron* decision also embodied a bifurcated notion of rights. One's rights as a citizen of the United States were not synonymous with one's rights as the citizen of any particular state. It required the Civil War, constitutional amendment, and years of litigation in the US Supreme Court, before *Barron* was abandoned and the liberties protected by the Bill of Rights were found to extend to the states as well as the national government.

The Fourteenth Amendment. At the close of the Civil War, it seemed clear to the Radical Republicans, who controlled Congress, that the Constitution must be amended in order to reflect the outcome of the war and to correct the Supreme Court's interpretation of the Constitution in *Barron* and in the *Dred Scott v. Sandford* (1857) case. In the latter, the Court held that the US Constitution did not recognize slaves or freed blacks as "persons" or "citizens" deserving of rights protection and, thus, that Scott had no standing to sue in federal court for his freedom. If the newly freed slaves were to become equal citizens under the law, and were to enjoy the same liberties as other citizens, these two interpretations of the Constitution would need to be undone through amendment. The Thirteenth Amendment (ratified 1865) abolished the institution of slavery. The Fourteenth Amendment (ratified 1868) dealt with various issues arising from the reintroduction of rebellious states to the Union, but most important was Section 1, which made "all persons born or naturalized in the United States . . . citizens of the United States and of the State wherein they reside." It also included particular prohibitions on the states in terms of how they could treat their citizens, including the "privileges and immunities" clause, the "due process" clause, and the "equal protection" clause. The first two of these clauses became the center of the debate among lawyers, judges, and historians about whether the Fourteenth Amendment was meant to incorporate the Bill of Rights, making its protections applicable to state governments as well as the national government, and thus eliminating the bifurcated notion of rights mentioned earlier.

Most historians of this era agree that, at a minimum, the members of Congress who wrote the Fourteenth Amendment understood it to be overturning the decisions in *Barron* (with the "privileges and immunities" clause) and *Scott* (with the "due process" and "equal protection" clauses), for they said as much on the floor of Congress. More uncertain is whether others who supported it in Congress, and those who ratified it in the states, had a similar understanding. Enterprising lawyers sought early on, but with little success, to have the US Supreme Court adopt such an understanding.

Given the goal of ensuring protection for the rights of newly freed slaves, it is ironic that in its first opportunity to interpret the Fourteenth Amendment, the Court was asked to find that the amendment prohibited the Louisiana legislature from granting a monopoly to a corporation to run slaughterhouses around New Orleans. The *Slaughterhouse Cases* (1873) provided an opportunity for the Court to interpret all three clauses in Section 1 of the amendment, and the decision had a substantial impact on the question of the extent of liberties protected from state power. Most significantly, the Court rejected the argument that the prohibition against laws "which shall abridge the privileges and immunities of citizens of the United States" meant that state governments could not infringe upon the liberty to pursue one's livelihood. Reading the clause narrowly to mean only that states may not deny certain privileges unique to US citizenship—*habeas corpus* review in federal court, for example—the Court

maintained the notion of bifurcated citizenship. It rejected a broader reading that would have overturned *Barron* by concluding that states were now under the same restrictions as the federal government in matters involving the civil liberties of their citizens—including their newest citizens, emancipated slaves—and found instead that this broader reading would be incompatible with the federal system and state sovereignty. Having made the clause largely meaningless, the decision in the *Slaughterhouse Cases* meant that those who wanted to use the Fourteenth Amendment for the protection of liberty from state action would have to look to the due process clause instead.

Liberty and the Due Process Clause. If the liberties protected in the Bill of Rights were not among the "privileges and immunities" of US citizens, might their protection be found elsewhere in the Fourteenth Amendment? The next clause in the amendment reads: "nor shall any State deprive any person of life, liberty, or property, without due process of the law." It was through interpretation of this clause, and in particular, the word "liberty," that most of the liberties identified in the Bill of Rights came to be protected from infringement by state as well as national government. The process was a gradual one, spanning more than half a century and engendering controversy within and beyond the Supreme Court. It should be understood within the larger context of post-Civil War social, political, and economic forces that were pushing the country away from its state-centered system to a far more nationalist system and a more rights-focused society. The text of the Fourteenth Amendment was clearly nationalist in intent and tone, but until the US Supreme Court was prepared to interpret it that way, it languished as a source of civil liberties for many, particularly those, like criminal defendants, who could not count on the protection of their rights through the majoritarian political processes of their states.

During the process of incorporation, there were essentially two schools of thought about how to define or interpret the word "liberty" in the due process clause. The first was an argument based on tradition. Perhaps best articulated by Justice Benjamin

Cardozo in his majority opinion in *Palko v. Connecticut* (1937), this view held that rights protected from state infringement by the Fourteenth Amendment are those that are "of the very essence of a scheme of ordered liberty" and where "neither liberty nor justice would exist if they were sacrificed." Thus, in considering whether Mr. Palko's liberty had been violated when Connecticut tried him twice for the same offense, in violation of the Fifth Amendment, Cardozo asked whether "the kind of double jeopardy to which the statute has subjected him [was] a hardship so acute and shocking that our polity will not endure it." Or, relying on an earlier decision that had refused to incorporate a different provision, he asked whether it violated "fundamental principles of liberty and justice which lie at the base of all our civil and political institutions." In Palko's case, the Court concluded that no such violation had occurred.

At the time that *Palko* was decided, the rights that were incorporated, because they met this definition, included First Amendment freedoms of speech, press, and assembly, the Fifth Amendment right to just compensation for the taking of property, and the Sixth Amendment right to counsel in capital cases. However, as the *Palko* decision demonstrated, the Court had been far more deferential to state variations when it came to the rights of criminal defendants, finding there that all that was required of the states was the ability to show that their procedures were fundamentally fair, not that they had provided all of the protections due criminal defendants in federal court.

The alternative view on incorporation was first, and best, articulated by Justice Hugo Black in his dissenting opinion in *Adamson v. California* (1947). The case raised the question of whether states were obligated to comply with the Fifth Amendment guarantee that no person be "compelled in any criminal case to be a witness against himself." California law permitted the judge and prosecutor to comment on, and the jury to consider, the failure of a defendant to explain or deny evidence against him. Adamson was convicted of murder and sentenced to death in a case where this law was applied. The

majority of the Court concluded that the California law did not interfere with the requirement of a fair trial protected by the due process clause of the Fourteenth, and thus refused to incorporate this provision of the Fifth Amendment. In his dissent, Justice Black argued for total incorporation, contending that "history conclusively demonstrates that the language of the first section of the Fourteenth Amendment, taken as a whole, was thought by those responsible for its submission to the people, and by those opposed to its submission, sufficiently explicit to guarantee that thereafter no state could deprive its citizens of the privileges and protections of the Bill of Rights." He objected to the traditional approach taken by the majority as being not only unfaithful to history, but deeply problematic in its vagueness and the degree to which it left the definition of liberty to the discretion of judges.

Justice Black's argument for total incorporation was never adopted by a majority of the Court, but over time, and in effect, it became the law. Virtually every protection outlined in the Bill of Rights, and some that were not stated explicitly, such as the right of privacy, were made applicable to the states. The greatest amount of incorporation happened during the 1960s, when all of the protections for criminal defendants contained in the Bill of Rights, except for the right to be indicted by a grand jury, were found to be essential to a concept of "ordered liberty" and thus requirements on state criminal justice systems. The last amendment to be incorporated was the Second. In 2010 the Supreme Court held in *McDonald v. Chicago* that the right to bear arms, which it had recognized the previous year as an individual right that the national government could not violate, applied to state and local governments as well.

Civil Liberties and the Clash of Values. The historical narrative as related thus far largely tells the story of the expansion of the protection of liberties in the United States, but the story is incomplete without making clearer the conflicts that this protection of civil liberties has engendered. The American constitutional commitment to individual liberty frequently has come into conflict with other important political values, most particularly, in the problems of interpretation, the desire for majorities to have their values reflected in the legislation passed by their representatives, and in the need—sometimes real, sometimes perceived—to protect the country during times of war or unrest.

Liberty beyond the Bill of Rights. Alexander Hamilton warned of the danger of writing down a list of rights that might then be interpreted as being exhaustive. The Ninth Amendment was added in order to address this concern, offering the interpretive advice that the "enumeration in the Constitution, of certain rights, shall not be construed to deny or disparage others retained by the people." But what are the "others," how are they identified, and how are they to be protected against government actions? The debate about the "right to privacy" exemplifies both this interpretive dilemma and the challenge of reconciling rights with majority values. Nowhere in the Constitution is such a right mentioned explicitly, and yet to one degree or another virtually all Americans believe they have such a right. In his dissent in the 1928 case of *Olmstead v. United States* (involving a challenge to the government use of wiretaps), Justice Louis Brandeis argued that "the most comprehensive of rights and the right most valued by civilized man" was "the right to be let alone." The challenge is in figuring out how to balance this liberty claim against the values of the majority as reflected in legislation. The lack of clear textual support makes these rights claims particularly vulnerable to challenge.

By the time that *Griswold v. Connecticut* reached the Court in 1965, it had already accepted the notion that there were protected liberties beyond those specifically enumerated in the Bill of Rights. In *Griswold*, the Court relied on the notion of a right to privacy that included the right to make one's own reproductive and childbearing decisions. Striking down a statute criminalizing the sale and use of contraceptives, the Court found the source of the right to privacy to be in the "penumbras" of the enumerated rights, in the Ninth Amendment, and in the traditions of the country. "We deal with a right of privacy older than the Bill of Rights," wrote Justice William O. Douglas in the opinion of the Court.

In 1973, in *Roe v. Wade*, the Court extended the right of privacy to include the decision to have an abortion. The decision prompted a political backlash from the Catholic Church and conservative Protestant Christians that has resonated for decades in the American political arena, reshaping the makeup of the two major political parties and influencing virtually every Supreme Court nomination battle that has followed. At the core of the legal debate about *Roe* was whether a right of privacy existed. Critics of the decision were of two minds. Some insisted that the "right to life" of the unborn must trump any vague privacy right of the mother. Others, including the dissenters on the Court, emphasized instead the nonexistence of the right in the Constitution, and thus, the right of the states to reflect the moral preferences of their citizens.

This second framing of the issue also shaped the debate on the Court and in society over homosexuality. Antisodomy statutes were defended as being reflections of majoritarian sexual morality. The question of whether such statutes violated the right of privacy came to the court in 1986 in the case of *Bowers v. Hardwick*. In a five-to-four decision, the Court concluded that there was no explicitly granted "right to engage in homosexual sodomy" and that no such right could be found by relying on the traditions of the people, as had been done in *Griswold*, since the prohibitions against sodomy were ancient. In 2003, however, the Court overturned the *Bowers* decision in *Lawrence v. Texas*, arguing instead that "liberty presumes an autonomy of self that includes freedom of thought, belief, expression, and certain intimate conduct." The decision contributed to the ongoing debate about the constitutionality of state laws that prohibit same-sex marriage. A rash of state constitutional amendments forbidding such marriages were adopted in the years following *Lawrence*, but so too have a handful of states, either through the legislature or through the state courts, concluded that marriage is an equal right of all citizens.

Liberty versus National Security. The greatest test of a nation's commitment to the protection of individual liberties comes at times when the nation feels most threatened, either at home or abroad.

Despite the First Amendment statement that "Congress shall make no law . . . abridging the freedom of speech, or of the press," and extensive requirements of due process throughout the Constitution, American history is littered with examples in which Congress, the executive, the courts, and the states did precisely that which was textually forbidden. This tendency to justify civil liberties violations in the name of national security began very shortly after the Constitution and Bill of Rights were adopted. In 1798 Congress passed the Alien and Sedition Acts, which provided for the deportation of aliens who were perceived as a threat to the government, and for the punishment of anyone who spoke out or published criticism of the government. During the Civil War, the partial suspension of habeas corpus was extended not just to those areas in open rebellion, but to other areas still within the Union but where dissent was strong.

During World War I, Congress passed the Espionage Act of 1917 and the Sedition Act of 1918. The first was used to prosecute war protesters who attempted to convince draftees to resist conscription, and the latter to prohibit criticism of the government, the military, the flag, or the Constitution. Many states adopted similar sedition acts during this time, and the Supreme Court upheld the prosecutions of war protestors under these acts. It was during this period of time that the American Civil Liberties Union (ACLU) was created for the purpose of litigating on behalf of individuals whose civil liberties were being violated by the government. Its imprint is on most of the major civil liberties cases decided by the Supreme Court since then, and it had a significant effect on creating a rights-focused legal culture in the twentieth century.

During World War II, Japanese immigrants and US citizens of Japanese descent were forced to leave the West Coast, saw most of their property confiscated and never returned, and were incarcerated in internment camps away from the coast for several years. Again, the Supreme Court approved these actions. The Cold War period that followed the Second World War saw the continued and extended suppression of domestic dissent in the name of

national security. Communist sympathizers—both avowed and alleged—were punished with prison terms, job loss, and blacklisting because of federal and state laws that prohibited forming and joining organizations that advocated the violent overthrow of the government.

The Vietnam War brought more attempts to suppress dissent, as burners of draft cards and flags were prosecuted. During this time the Court's reaction was more mixed, upholding some of these actions and rejecting others. Following the attacks on the World Trade Center and the Pentagon in 2001, and with the subsequent wars in Iraq and Afghanistan, the United States entered another period of debate about the extent to which national security concerns should trump civil liberties protections.

The clash between individual liberty and national security raises questions of the highest order for a government that embraces democratic freedoms as a fundamental value. In 1919 law professor Zachariah Chafee made the argument for liberty, arguing that free speech in wartime was essential. "Truth can be sorted out from falsehood," he wrote, "only if the government is vigorously and constantly cross-examined, so that the fundamental issues of the struggle may be clearly defined, and the war may not be diverted to improper ends" (p. 958). On the other hand, the argument for security needs trumping civil liberties has been based on a claim that the survival of the system depends on such restrictions. Defending some of his Civil War decisions, Abraham Lincoln famously argued that survival of the country had to take precedence over the survival of individual principles that would not exist if the country did not exist. Similar arguments were made during the Cold War. Finding a balance between these competing values has never been easy in the United States.

Assessment. The protection of civil liberties is a fundamental premise of the US Constitution, and claims and concerns about liberty and freedom are an ongoing part of American political culture and rhetoric. But ideals often come into conflict with political realities, and this ideal is no different. Americans have been less willing to protect the liberties of dissenters and minorities, liberty claims have often come in conflict with the desires and actions of democratic majorities, and the federal and state courts have a mixed record in protecting individuals from state power. Alexander Hamilton's claim at the time of the founding about the limits of what can be accomplished by writing down a list of rights in a constitution has been supported by the American experience. But Thomas Jefferson's counterargument, that there is an educative aspect for future generations in having these values written down, has also been proven to be true; the extension of rights protections that occurred in the twentieth century, through the process of incorporation brought about by litigation by the ACLU and other groups, seems hard to imagine without a text to guide such developments.

[*See also* Civil Rights; Constitution, US; *and* Judicial System, American.]

BIBLIOGRAPHY

Amar, Akhil Reed. *The Bill of Rights: Creation and Reconstruction.* (New Haven, Conn., 1998).

Berger, Raoul. *Government by Judiciary: The Transformation of the Fourteenth Amendment.* (Cambridge, Mass., 1977).

Bodenhamer, David J. *Fair Trial: Rights of the Accused in American History.* (New York, 1992).

Brennan, William J., Jr. "Why Have a Bill of Rights?" *Valparaiso University Law Review* 26 (1991): 1–19.

Chafee, Zechariah, Jr. "Freedom of Speech in War Time." *Harvard Law Review* 32 (1919): 932–973.

Curtis, Michael Kent. *No State Shall Abridge: The Fourteenth Amendment and the Bill of Rights.* (Durham, N.C., 1986).

Dinan, John J. *Keeping the People's Liberties: Legislators, Citizens, and Judges as Guardians of Rights.* (Lawrence, Kans., 1998).

Fisher, Louis and Harriger, Katy J. *American Constitutional Law: Constitutional Rights.* 9th ed. (Durham, N.C., 2011).

Garrow, David J. *Liberty and Sexuality: The Right to Privacy and the Making of Roe v. Wade.* (New York, 1994).

Glendon, Mary Ann. *Rights Talk: The Impoverishment of Political Discourse.* (New York, 1991).

Kurland, Philip B., and Ralph Lerner, eds. "The Founders' Constitution." http://press-pubs.uchicago.edu/founders/.

McDonald, Forrest. *Novus Ordo Seclorum: The Intellectual Origins of the Constitution.* (Lawrence, Kans., 1985).

Smith, Jeffery Alan. *War and Press Freedom: The Problem of Prerogative Power.* (New York, 1999).

Warren, Samuel D., and Louis D. Brandeis. "The Right to Privacy." *Harvard Law Review* 4 (1890): 193–220.

Wills, Garry. *Inventing America: Jefferson's Declaration of Independence.* (Garden City, N.Y., 1978).

Katy J. Harriger

CIVIL RELIGION

The concept of "civil religion," as developed in the United States, reflects the central role religion has often played, and continues to play, in the aspirations of the American people. At the nation's founding, churches in nine of the thirteen colonies ruled in conjunction with civil powers. Governments in the four remaining colonies were established as a reaction to religious pressures. The relationship between government and religion was thus rooted in the founding of the nation; Robert Bellah articulates it this way:

Although matters of personal religious belief, worship, and association are strictly private affairs, there are, at the same time, certain common elements of religious orientation that the great majority of Americans share. These have played a crucial role in the development of American institutions and still provide a religious dimension for the whole fabric of American life, including the political sphere. This public religious dimension is expressed in a set of beliefs, symbols, and rituals that I am calling the American civil religion. (1974, p. 75)

Civil religion is essentially a faith statement that describes Americans' attitudes toward America. The model for religious freedom among early American colonists was based on their interpretation of the scriptural narrative of Israel's escape from Egypt and journey to the Promised Land. This biblical analogy was frequently used by clergy such as John Winthrop, who in 1630 gave a sermon calling for the creation of a "shining City on a Hill." Similarly, Abiel Abbot's 1799 sermon asked that the colonists become a "people" united in a mission to construct an ideal society. Thomas Jefferson, Benjamin Franklin, and other members of the Constitutional Convention often asserted that the United States was founded as part of what John Adams called Providence's design "for the illumination of the ignorant and the emancipation of the slavish part of mankind over all the earth" (1765). Thus, Alexis de Tocqueville notes that for most of their history, Americans "have been repeatedly and constantly told that they are the only religious, enlightened, and free people," which results in them having "an immensely high opinion of themselves."

The Enlightenment gave rise to speculation about ideal forms of government, but the United States was deliberately designed as the manifestation of those ideals. In fact, the concept of civil religion arose as a challenge from Jean Jacques Rousseau to Plato's concept of a "civic religion." In Plato's conception, the state imposed controls and established the rituals that would develop the proper character of its people. Without a state religion, Rousseau (1762/1960) argues that civil religion emanates from the people; it is "a body of social sentiments without which no man can be neither a good citizen or a faithful subject" (p. 12). This social contract, then, is a voluntary alliance to support social order. This contract is sacralized, or "infused with religious power because it is authority derives ultimately from the Divinity" (Angrosino, 2002, p. 239). One of the main tenets of the nation, then, is that God granted equally to each man, and that government is empowered to render justice, resulting from our social contract with each other.

The sacred documents of civil religion are both religious and secular. Certainly, the Bible was one book well-educated people in the seventeenth, eighteenth, and nineteenth centuries would be expected to know, regardless of their personal religious convictions. Another sacred text of civil religion is the Declaration of Independence. In the Declaration, there are four references to the Deity that indicate the hand of Providence in the creation of the country: (1) "to assume among the powers of the earth, the separate and equal station to which the Laws of Nature and of Nature's *God* entitle them"; (2) all men are "endowed by their *Creator* with certain unalienable Rights"; (3) "appealing to the *Supreme Judge* of the world for the rectitude of our intentions"; and (4) "with a firm reliance on the protection of *Divine Providence*." Other sacred texts include the Constitution, and the *Federalist Papers*. Hundreds of speeches also reflect such views, from Abraham Lincoln's "Gettysburg Address" to Martin Luther King Jr.'s "I Have a Dream." Many of the presidential acceptance speeches at national party nominating conventions, as well as presidential inaugural speeches, espouse these same beliefs. The founding fathers were clear that the nation arose in fulfillment of God's promise, and this has been echoed in the words of its leaders ever since.

Further, the first four American universities, now secularized, were founded with evangelistic roots. Consequently, both churches and educational institutions perpetuated the notion of the centrality of religion to the life of the American nation and its people.

The symbolic practice of civil religion is important. Perhaps the prime symbol of this religion is the title of the country. Note that the name itself—the "United States of America"— implies a manifest destiny. The Americas include a far greater expanse of territory other than the United States. Yet even today, US citizens define themselves as "Americans" while designating other nationals in North, Central, and South America by their country name: for instance, Mexican, Canadian, or Brazilian. Other symbolic practices include specially consecrated days to acknowledge the nation's gratitude to the Creator. Most notably, Abraham Lincoln established Thanksgiving during the Civil War to express the nation's gratitude to God and ask for his guidance. Likewise, Memorial Day and the Fourth of July are intended to be days set aside for Americans to take time away from work in order to consider what it means to be American. Little wonder that de Tocqueville argued that "religion is therefore commingled with all the habits of the nation and all the feelings of patriotism; whence it derives a peculiar force" (1835/1945, p. 4).

Martin Marty speaks of two realms of American civil religion: the priestly and the prophetic. In times of national crisis, the role of leaders is to assume the priestly function, either to preside over religious ceremonies or to "comfort the afflicted." These include Fourth of July or Memorial Day ceremonies as well speeches and ceremonies in times of crisis, such as events marking 9/11, the *Challenger* explosion, or the assassination of an elected leader. By contrast, the prophetic role can be assumed by any of the nation's prophets whose task, according to Marty, is to "afflict the comfortable." Such prophets challenge the public to justify, change, or unify toward a course of action. For example, Lincoln in his "Meditations on Divine Will" argued that the Civil War was part of God's plan for atonement; Martin Luther King Jr., argued that the segregation culture of the 1960s did not reflect the essential character of the nation required of us by God; and in his inaugural address, President Barack Obama rallied a hopeful nation by declaring that "this is the source of our confidence—the knowledge that God calls on us to shape an uncertain destiny." Since the nation's founding, civil religion has provided the framework for unifying Americans and attempting to rally them through some rhetorically defined unifying vision, even though those defining the frameworks may espouse conflicting points of view.

The tension between religion and politics continues to provide a subtext for many political decisions. While the resonance of civil religion as a vibrant belief statement in America today is somewhat muted, the concept is useful to gaining an understanding of US culture and history, and vital to an understanding of the values that drive American life and politics.

[*See also* Religion and Politics.]

BIBLIOGRAPHY

Abbot, A. "Resemblance in the People of the United States to Ancient Israel." *South Carolina Historical Magazine* 68 (1967): 115–139.

Adams, John. "Diary of John Adams, February 21, 1765." http://www.beliefnet.com/resourcelib/docs/80/Diary_of_John_Adams_February_21_1765_1.html.

Angrosino, Michael V. "Civil Religion Redux." *Anthropological Quarterly* 75 (2002): 239–267.

Beiner, Ronald. "Machiavelli, Hobbes, and Rousseau on Civil Religion." *Review of Politics* 55 (1993): 617–638.

Bellah, Robert N. "Civil Religion in America." In *Religion American Style*, edited by Patrick H. McNamara, pp. 1–21. (New York, 1974).

Geertz, Clifford. "Religion as a Cultural System." In *The Interpretation of Culture: Selected Essays*, by Clifford Geertz, pp. 87–125. (New York, 1973).

Marty, Martin E. *Righteous Empire: The Protestant Experience in America.* (New York, 1970).

Mead, Sidney R. *The Nation with the Soul of a Church.* (New York, 1975).

Miller, Arthur H., and Martin P. Wattenberg. "Politics from the Pulpit: Religiosity and the 1980 Elections." *Public Opinion Quarterly* 48 (1984): 301–317.

Richey, Russell E., and Donald G. Jones, eds. *American Civil Religion.* (New York, 1974).

Rousseau, Jean-Jacques. "Of Civil Religion." In *Social Contract: Essays by Locke, Hume, and Rousseau*, edited by Ernest Barker, pp. 295–307. (London, 1960). First published in 1762.

Tocqueville, Alexis de. *Democracy in America.* Vol. 2. Translated by Henry Reeve. (New York, 1945). First published in 1835.

Whillock, Rita Kirk. "Dream Believers: The Unifying Visions and Competing Values of Adherents of American Civil Religion." *Presidential Studies Quarterly* 24 (1994): 375–388.

Winthrop, John. "A Model of Christian Charity." http://religiousfreedom.lib.virginia.edu/sacred/charity.html.

Rita Kirk

CIVIL RIGHTS

The terms "civil rights" and "civil liberties" often are used interchangeably in American political rhetoric about individual freedom, but they have come to have distinct meanings in the context of constitutional discourse. Civil liberties generally refer to those rights protected in the Bill of Rights and are associated with the concept of limited government. Civil rights, on the other hand, generally refer to equal treatment by the government in making and enforcing the law, and to equal participation in the democratic political process. Their constitutional protection comes largely from the Equal Protection Clause of the Fourteenth Amendment, but also from state constitutions, and from national, state, and local legislation.

Struggles for civil rights—that is, for the right of members of various groups to be treated as equal citizens under the law—have existed as long as the Constitution itself. The American experience with civil rights struggles suggests that success depends on more than winning in the courts, although victory there is important. Success also requires political action through social movements and protest activities that persuade the majority that the values embodied in the Declaration of Independence and in their constitutional texts require equal treatment of the claimant group. The most significant periods of change in the civil rights status of Americans have come in the space immediately following wars, perhaps because it is at these times that the tension between the high-minded claims about what this country stands for and the reality of discrimination against groups based on color, race, gender, or religion, is most apparent.

Equality, Rights, and the Founding Era. The Declaration of Independence, a key founding document in American politics, declared as a "self-evident" truth that "all men are created equal." This claim for equality was radical, but not for the reasons we might think of today, with a modern understanding of the concept of equality. The equality being claimed here was a direct challenge to the divine right of kings to rule, offering instead a justification for the right of individuals to govern themselves. It was not, however, a claim that "all men" could actually participate in that democratic government through equal voting rights (most states required property ownership in order to vote), or that no one should be enslaved, or that all persons, regardless of gender, would be equal citizens under the law. Thomas Jefferson, a slave owner, penned the Declaration, and many who signed it also owned slaves. On the other hand, there were many during this period who did believe that such a claim of equality required, at a minimum, the elimination of slavery, if not equal citizenship.

While these words may have had a far narrower meaning at the time they were written than their generality might imply, their existence almost immediately provided a theoretical justification for equality claims. Correspondence between Abigail and John Adams in 1776 refers to and exemplifies the way in which the concepts of liberty and equality were spreading. Abigail, noting that a "new Code of Laws" would be needed after independence was declared, asked her husband to "remember the Ladies, and be more generous and favorable to them than your ancestors." Adams's response makes clear that he did not take her seriously, but he noted that he had heard that "our Struggle has loosened the bands of Government everywhere. That Children and Apprentices were disobedient—that schools and colleges were grown turbulent—that Indians slighted their Guardians, and Negroes grew insolent to their Masters."

The revolutionary ideals spread across the new nation, leading to calls for the abolition of slavery and the extension of voting rights. Pennsylvania was the first state to abolish slavery, doing so in 1780. Advocates for abolition in the Northern states emphasized religious and natural-rights arguments and other states slowly followed Pennsylvania's lead, so that by the first part of the nineteenth century slavery was against the law throughout the North. During this period, even without laws requiring it, there were slave owners in the South who chose to free their slaves because they recognized that the practice did not comport with their revolutionary principles. During the late 1700s free blacks were permitted to vote in a number of states, subject only to the same property, taxation, or gender qualifications as whites. The Continental Congress forbade slavery in the Northwest Territory in 1787. The US Congress abolished the importation of slaves in 1808, but the practice of slavery throughout the South, and the federal constitutional protections for the institution, meant that the founding principles of rights and equality lived in uneasy tension with the reality of the acceptance of human bondage throughout a large part of the country.

Political Mobilization and Social Movements. Changes in the law, particularly when they involve expanding equality and giving up privilege, do not come easily. Legislators and judges do not suddenly change the law because they realize the gap between the law and reality. Instead, legal change requires political mobilization and the building of alliances between those lacking access to formal power and those with some power who have sympathy for the cause. It would be a mistake to imagine that courts were solely, or even primarily, responsible for the expansion of civil rights in the United States. Most important in bringing about change was the political mobilization of African Americans, women, and their white and male allies. Educating the public about the gap between ideals and reality through publications, protests, lobbying, and litigation campaigns, and taking advantage of the desire of political parties to expand their coalitions so that they might win elections, created the social change necessary to bring about legal change.

Abolitionism and the Civil Rights Movement. During the 1830s, a wave of religious fervor swept the country and included a call for the abolition of slavery. Early evangelicals contended that slavery was against God's will, since all human beings were equal in the eyes of God. The American Anti-Slavery Society was established in 1833, challenging slavery on religious grounds. Other abolitionist groups followed, and different groups represented different positions on the spectrum of abolitionism. A constitutional dispute grew out of the fact that the text of the Constitution recognized the institution of slavery in several places, including the counting of slaves as three-fifths of a person for the purposes of representation, and the fugitive slave clause in Article IV. For some abolitionists, this meant that the Constitution had to be amended in order to eliminate slavery. Other abolitionists rejected the need for amendment, arguing instead that the Constitution should be read through the lens of the natural law principles of the Declaration of Independence, which presumed the equality of humans. Others believed that the Constitution permitted the original slave states to maintain slavery, but insisted that the institution should not be permitted to spread as the country grew. Finally, there was disagreement in the antislavery forces over what the status of freed slaves should be. Many, but not all, abolitionists believed that freed slaves must be made equal citizens under the law. This position was considered to be the most radical of the abolitionist positions prior to the Civil War. By the time the war had ended, however, this view was the one that would prevail, as Congress took up the question of equality during the Reconstruction period.

After passage of the Civil War Amendments, blacks gained political power for a period of time, until the national government backed out of its Reconstruction efforts and permitted states to construct segregation regimes which disenfranchised most blacks in the South. The National Association for the Advancement of Colored People (NAACP) was established in 1909 and set as its goal the elimination of discriminatory legislation and the overturning of case law that permitted segregation. It began its efforts by publicizing the horrors of lynching and leading an effort to get federal antilynching legislation enacted. It also had some success in litigating challenges to segregated housing laws and anti-voting measures. But the organizers of the NAACP recognized that litigation alone would not be sufficient to bring about change. They encouraged the organization of chapters around the country to work locally on challenging discriminatory laws and ordinances.

The civil rights movement of the 1950s and 1960s led finally to a place where the laws of the land matched the expectations of the Fourteenth and Fifteenth Amendments. Through a campaign of civil disobedience involving protest marches, sit-ins, boycotts, and other kinds of direct but nonviolent action, African Americans pointed out the hypocrisy of a country that claimed in Cold War rhetoric to be "the land of the free," despite the existence of what was essentially institutionalized apartheid for the black population. The lives of many of these activists were lost before the laws were changed. Media coverage of the violent responses from the most entrenched Southern segregationists helped to turn the tide of public opinion in favor of reform.

The Women's Movements. The first women's movement grew out of the abolitionist movement. Women were active participants in the social reform movements of the era, but they experienced discrimination when it came to leadership and public speaking roles. There were men in the abolitionist movement who supported equality for women. They joined women abolitionists in organizing the first women's rights convention in Seneca Falls, New York in 1848. That convention produced the Declaration of Rights and Sentiments, which was modeled after the Declaration of Independence, and claimed that "all men and woman are created equal." The document was considered very radical at the time, in the same way that equal citizenship for freed slaves was seen as the most radical of the abolitionist positions.

Women's rights advocates hoped that the post–Civil War amendments guaranteeing full citizenship and voting rights for the newly freed slaves would also benefit their cause. But the reformers in Congress feared that including race and gender equality in the same package would make their proposals so controversial that they would never pass. Consequently, it took three more decades of mobilization of the women's suffrage movement, first in the states, and then nationally, for women to gain the right to vote. First introduced in 1878, the Nineteenth Amendment passed finally in 1919 and was ratified in 1920.

After women gained the right to vote, the movement divided between those who wanted to push for an Equal Rights Amendment (ERA) which would require equal treatment under the law, and those who were more concerned about the social status of women, particularly working women, and thus wanted to push for protections for women in the workforce. Despite having won the right to vote, in the decades immediately following, women voted less than men, and not that differently than men. It was the post–World War II social change in the status of women (particularly in terms of education and the labor market) that led to a new round of political mobilization among women, and renewed demands for equal rights.

Women who were part of the civil rights movement and, later, the anti–Vietnam War movement, again found that sexism within the civil rights and antiwar organizations limited their opportunities for leadership. After successfully lobbying to have sex discrimination in employment added to the 1964 Civil Rights Act, the new feminists were incensed that the Equal Employment Opportunity Commission (EEOC) refused to enforce the provision. In 1966, at a conference of state Commissions on the Status of Women, the National Organization for Women (NOW) was born, modeled after the NAACP and with a similar strategy for dismantling legislation and case law that treated women differently than men, through public education, lobbying, and litigation. They also began a process of lobbying for an Equal Rights Amendment to the Constitution, an effort that was hugely successful during the 1970s in Congress and the early ratification process, but was ultimately defeated by the countermobilization of opponents in the 1980s.

The Supreme Court and Civil Rights. The US Supreme Court has been called upon throughout American history to interpret the Constitution in disputes involving civil rights claims. Its record is a mixed one, calling into question a popular narrative that civil rights were gained primarily through litigation. For both African Americans and women, it was court decisions that drove them to mobilize in order to change those interpretations, either through constitutional amendment or legislation.

Dred Scott and the Problem of Citizenship. While abolitionists argued over whether the Constitution was inherently a proslavery document, a legal case arrived at the US Supreme Court that provided an opportunity for that court to weigh in on the issue. Dred Scott was a slave from Missouri, but argued that he had been made free by traveling with his owner in Illinois and Upper Louisiana (a free state and free territory, respectively). The question before the Court was whether or not Scott was a free US citizen, capable of bringing a case in federal court.

In *Dred Scott v. Sandford* (1857), the Court held that Scott was not a citizen with access to the federal courts. Chief Justice Roger Taney went well beyond the narrow issue of the case, ruling that Scott and all other slaves and their descendants could not be considered US citizens (even if they were citizens of individual states) under the Constitution, nor could Congress prohibit slavery in the territories. Taney argued that at the time of the founding "the legislation and histories of the times, and the language used in the Declaration of Independence, show, that neither the class of persons who had been imported as slaves, nor their descendants, whether they had become free or not, were then acknowledged as a part of the people, nor intended to be included in the general words used in that memorable instrument." If this constitutional reality is considered "unjust," wrote Taney, then the only route to change was amendment of the Constitution.

The *Dred Scott* decision clearly took a side in the constitutional debate about slavery but it certainly did not resolve the dispute. The decision made it substantially more difficult for the dispute to be worked out in the political arena, and strengthened the position of abolitionists who argued that constitutional amendment was necessary to end slavery. It was certainly one of the precipitating events for the Civil War, which was fought between 1861 and 1865.

The Promise of the Fourteenth Deferred. During the Reconstruction era following the Civil War, the Radical Republicans who controlled Congress passed, and the states ratified, the Thirteenth, Fourteenth, and Fifteenth Amendments, banning slavery, granting equal citizenship to African Americans, guaranteeing equal protection of the law, and providing voting rights for black men. Despite the lawmaking going on in Congress, however, blacks were experiencing harsh, violent, and discriminatory treatment in the states, as former slave owners resisted the new order.

The Fourteenth Amendment appeared to offer a means by which discrimination of this sort could be challenged, for the failure of state governments to protect its black citizens against violence, intimidation, and discrimination seemed to violate at least the spirit of the amendment, if not the letter. The Supreme Court decided otherwise. In the *Slaughter-House Cases* (1873), it construed the "privileges and immunities" clause so narrowly that it became almost worthless as a vehicle for protecting the rights of state citizens. It also returned to the bifurcated notion of citizenship, driven by the theory of federalism that had prevailed before the war. Despite the transformative intent of the Radical Republicans to make freedom national in scope, the Court said in this case that the amendment could not have intended to so "radically change the whole theory of the relations between the State and federal government." In 1876 it threw out the federal convictions of whites accused of violating the civil rights of blacks in Louisiana, finding that Congress did not have the authority under the Fourteenth to provide for the punishment of civil rights violations by private citizens. The Fourteenth, the Court said, required a finding of state action and allowed Congress to legislate remedies only for such action.

This limited approach was further advanced in the *Civil Rights Cases* (1883), when the Court struck down the 1875 Civil Rights Act, which prohibited discrimination in public accommodations. The Court ruled that Congress's enforcement powers under the Fourteenth did not permit the regulation of private discrimination, only of state action that discriminated.

The most infamous of interpretations by the Court came in 1896 in *Plessy v. Ferguson*, when it ruled that Louisiana's law requiring separation of the races in railroad cars did not violate the Fourteenth Amendment; the Court concluded that the Fourteenth required only legal and political equality, not social equality. As long as the state provided equal facilities, it could separate the races in order to reflect the social preferences of its citizens. The impact of this decision was significant, giving the constitutional imprimatur to discrimination by race in the law. After *Plessy*, states felt free to adopt laws requiring separation of the races, and the era of Jim Crow was officially inaugurated. For the next half of a century, the races would be legally separated throughout the South, and in some other areas of the country as well.

Early efforts by women to gain the protection of the Fourteenth were also unsuccessful. Citing the *Slaughter-House Cases*, the Court found in *Bradwell v. State* (1873) that admission to the bar was a state function not covered under the privileges and immunities clause, and thus, the state could prohibit women from practicing law if it saw fit. A concurring opinion by Justice Joseph Bradley reflected the status of women under the law at that time. Bradley wrote that "the civil law, as well as nature herself, has always recognized a wide difference in the respective spheres and destinies of man and woman. Man is, or should be, woman's protector and defender. The natural and proper timidity and delicacy which belongs to the female sex evidently unfits it for many of the occupations of civil life." Two years later the Court ruled in *Minor v. Happersett* (1875) that the Fourteenth Amendment did not cover or protect the right to vote, particularly for women.

The Rights Revolution of the Twentieth Century. President Franklin D. Roosevelt had the opportunity to fundamentally change the makeup of the Court during the New Deal period of the 1930s, and the result was important for changing the Court's interpretation of the Fourteenth Amendment. The new Court took a deferential stance vis-à-vis the national regulation of the economy, but became more aggressive in its defense of individual rights claims against state governments. In 1938, in *United States v. Carolene Products Company,* a case challenging the constitutionality of a government regulation of the milk industry, the Court upheld the regulation, stating that the government need only show a rational basis (in this case, public health) when regulating the economy. In what was to become a famous footnote, Justice Harlan Stone signaled that on matters of civil liberties and civil rights, however, the Court would impose "more exacting scrutiny." In the footnote he implied that the Court would be far less deferential where legislation had the effect of limiting access to the political process, or targeted religious or racial minorities, or was based on "prejudice against *discrete and insular minorities . . .* which tends seriously to curtail the operation of those political processes ordinarily to be relied upon to protect minorities."

The *Carolene Products* footnote proved prophetic, shaping the Court's agenda over the following

decades. What emerged finally was a three-tiered method of analysis of equal protection claims. At the lowest was the "rational basis test," which took the most deferential stance toward government action and put the burden of proof on plaintiffs claiming discrimination. This test was premised on the recognition that government creates categories in the law all the time when deciding how to allocate limited resources. It is clearly rational to have an age limit on who can drive a car, for example, or who should be eligible for retirement benefits. The government is not obligated to treat all citizens precisely equally in all circumstances. The question is whether or not categories that discriminate can be justified for reasons other than prejudice—in other words, is the discrimination rational or invidious. Mid-century the Court began to conclude with increasing frequency that laws that discriminated on the basis of race required a higher level of scrutiny than rational basis. Moving away from *Plessy's* claim that it was rational for the state to cater to the social prejudices of its time, the Court began to consider race to be a suspect classification that required a much higher burden of proof on the government.

Beginning in the 1940s with cases involving racial discrimination in higher education, the Court began to undermine the "separate but equal" doctrine by finding that separated facilities and programs were not equal. *Brown v. Board of Education* (1954) signaled the Court's full commitment to the rejection of *Plessy* and the dismantling of legal segregation. In the years that followed, the Court prohibited race discrimination in virtually all areas of public life. In order for race distinctions to be legal, they must advance a compelling state interest and be narrowly tailored to accomplish that interest.

During the 1970s, the Court was faced with litigation challenging state legislation that appeared to make arbitrary distinctions based on gender. It struggled however, to find agreement about what the appropriate standard of scrutiny should be when gender was at issue. Some justices believed that gender should be treated like race, and cases therefore required strict scrutiny. Others believed that, because there were real biological differences between men and women, it could be rational sometimes, but not always, for the state to make such distinctions. In the end, the Court adopted what has come to be called "intermediate scrutiny," which requires the state to show that there is an import state interest at stake and that the distinction is substantially related to the accomplishment of that interest. Thus, in *Craig v. Boren* (1976) the Court struck down Oklahoma's law that permitted eighteen-year-old females to buy low-alcohol-content beer, but required young males to wait until they were twenty-one. The state's interest in highway safety was certainly important, said the Court, but there was little evidence that this law actually advanced that interest.

Congress, Presidents, and Civil Rights. Political mobilization and the building of electoral coalitions has consequences for the ability to affect legal change. In the American context, the social disruption that comes with war has also been instrumental in opening the political space for legislators and presidents to support civil rights claims. In contrast, in less tense, more stable times, countermobilization and backlash have made it more difficult for legal changes to be implemented in order to significantly affect the social reality. It is impossible in this essay to give a complete accounting of how the political branches advanced or retarded civil rights but two periods stand out as exemplary: the period of Reconstruction following the Civil War, and the post–World War II adoption of the Civil Rights Act of 1964 and the Voting Rights Act of 1965.

Reconstruction and Constitutional Amendment. The period of lawmaking immediately following the Civil War transformed profoundly the understanding of citizenship and rights in the United States. One of the consequences of the Union victory in the Civil War was that the national government was seen as the protector of rights, and that all persons who had US citizenship were also automatically considered citizens of the state wherein they resided. The Radical Republicans who controlled Congress during this time sought to undo the damage of *Dred Scott* by passing laws and amending the Constitution to guarantee equal rights and citizenship

for the newly freed slaves. In doing so, they also created the legal vehicle by which other groups would claim their rights.

In 1865 Congress passed, and the states ratified, the Thirteenth Amendment, which abolished slavery and included a clause (added to the Fourteenth and Fifteenth Amendments as well) granting Congress the power to enforce the amendment "by appropriate legislation." But the experience of the newly freed slaves in this period suggested that Southern whites would not acquiesce to granting them equal rights simply because the Constitution now outlawed slavery. President Andrew Johnson, who took over when Abraham Lincoln was assassinated, was a Democrat who was sympathetic to state's rights arguments and hostile to the notion of civic equality for blacks.

Recognizing that the cause of equality could be promptly lost so soon after the war, the Radical Republicans extended the powers of the Freedman's Bureau (created after the war to help freed slaves with adjustment to their newfound freedom), and passed the Civil Rights Act of 1866, granting citizenship to all blacks and guaranteeing equality under the law. They relied on the enforcement clause of the Thirteenth Amendment to justify their action. Fearing that this legislation could be repealed when the representatives of formerly rebellious states were reseated in Congress, the Republicans decided that a constitutional amendment was necessary. The Fourteenth Amendment was designed to make these civil rights guarantees more lasting.

The Radical Republicans' goal was accomplished largely through the first section of the Fourteenth Amendment, which declared that "all persons born or naturalized in the United States" were "citizens of the United States and of the State wherein they reside." This put to rest the *Dred Scott* notion that one could be a citizen of a state, but not the United States. It went on to declare that states could not "abridge the privileges and immunities of citizens of the United States," "deprive any person of life, liberty, or property without due process of law," or "deny any person within its jurisdiction the equal protection of the laws." Because full political equality for blacks remained a controversial subject, even for Republicans, the amendment makes no mention of voting rights.

Continued resistance, often violent, to Reconstruction convinced the Republicans that full voting equality for black males was necessary. Again, acting first through legislation, Congress passed the Reconstruction Act of 1867, which provided for constitutional conventions in the rebellious states to adopt constitutions that reflected the new reality. It granted the franchise to black males, and as a consequence, coalitions of black and white Republicans gained control of state constitutional conventions and legislatures. For a period of time, this fundamentally altered politics in these states, but it also bred deep resentment among whites who had lost power. Republicans realized that without an amendment, these gains might be short-lived. The Fifteenth Amendment was thus proposed in 1869 and ratified in 1870. It seemed that full legal and political equality had been achieved, but what followed was a grim reminder that the gap—evident since the grand words of the Declaration of Independence had been adopted—between civil rights on paper and civil rights in reality was significant.

In the early 1870s violent resistance to Reconstruction laws led Congress to pass more laws authorizing federal intervention to protect the rights of citizens in the states. The last significant legislation of this sort was the Civil Rights Act of 1875, which prohibited discrimination in public accommodations, such as inns, restaurants, and public modes of transportation. Similar laws had been passed in a number of Northern states, in large part as a result of political action on the part of black citizens. With the Supreme Court decisions in the *Civil Rights Cases* and *Plessy*, and the electoral compromise of 1876 which gave the Republican Rutherford B. Hayes the White House, despite the fact that the Democrat Samuel Tilden had likely won the election, the era of Reconstruction ended. The national government withdrew from enforcing civil rights in the states and a long period of unequal rights ensued.

The Civil Rights and Voting Rights Acts. World War II, and the Cold War that followed, highlighted the gap between the rhetoric about freedom that justified the fight against Hitler, and then Communism, and the reality of the black experience in America, particularly in the South. Black soldiers who had risked their lives for their country came home to find that nothing had changed in terms of their status. Soviet propaganda emphasized the gap as well, and as each of the two great powers sought to bring newly independent states in the developing world within their sphere of influence, it became increasingly difficult for the US to defend these practices. When *Brown v. Board of Education* (1954) came before the Supreme Court, the US Justice Department filed a brief noting the embarrassment this created for the country in foreign affairs.

No great advocate of civil rights, President Dwight Eisenhower nonetheless sent federal troops into Little Rock, Arkansas, in 1958 in order to force compliance there with the *Brown* school desegregation decision. Recognizing the importance of the black vote in closely contested national elections, during the 1960 presidential election John F. Kennedy made a well-publicized call of sympathy to Coretta Scott King when her husband was imprisoned for his civil rights activism. Kennedy's claimed support for civil rights did not produce any new legislation, however, as he appeared unwilling to risk the alienation of so many southern white Democratic voters, and because southern Democrats controlled key committees in Congress through which such legislation would have to pass. He did, however, issue several executive orders that provided for fairness in federal hiring and he worked to enforce laws already on the books. Violence against civil rights activists, and the terrible images of that violence broadcast by the media, did lead to several decisions to use federal troops or agents to bring about a stop to the violence.

It would be Kennedy's vice president, Lyndon Baines Johnson, who would lead the successful effort to move meaningful civil rights legislation through Congress after Kennedy was assassinated in 1963. Johnson used his years of experience in Congress, and the country's sorrow over the loss of the president, to get the Civil Rights Act of 1964 passed by Congress. The bill prohibited discrimination in employment and in public accommodations and provided for federal remedies for civil rights violations. Following the violent response to a nonviolent voting rights march from Selma, Alabama, to the state capital, Johnson went on national television and announced the introduction of a bill that would guarantee voting rights for blacks. He noted that the march was an "effort of American Negroes to secure for themselves the full blessings of American life." The bill passed later that year and set in motion, finally, the dream of the writers of the Fifteenth Amendment a century earlier.

Power, Politics, and Civil Rights. Since its beginning, the United States has struggled with the gap between its high ideals—embodied in its founding experience and documents—and the political reality that those with power benefited from a society that was not equal. By the third century of the American experiment in democracy, substantially more people of all races, and both genders, have come under the protection of the Constitution and the laws of the states and nations, so that there is in effect universal suffrage for all adults over eighteen years of age, and there is widespread recognition and acceptance of the notion that the law should not categorize people based upon immutable characteristics like race and gender. But the story is not all one of progress and enlightenment, and many challenges to true equality remain unaddressed.

For African Americans, legal and political equality was gained a century after the Constitution was amended to guarantee equality; this required great sacrifice and considerable violence and bloodshed. They did not make these gains because those with power suddenly realized that they were not living up to the ideals they professed, but rather because activists refused to accept inequality under the law and worked relentlessly to change the status quo. Women faced a less violent reaction, but nonetheless waited more than a century for voting rights and another half century for the recognition that gender discrimination could not be reconciled with the promise of the Fourteenth Amendment. With every period of advancement came an aftermath of countermobilization and political pushback from opponents, reminding us that legal change is a dynamic process, and that victories for legal change on paper mean little if they are not followed by or supported by social change and acceptance.

Those movements, and the tactics and strategies they adopted for effecting change, have been used as models by other groups seeking equality under the law. At the start of the twenty-first century, the issue of equality for gays and lesbians has followed a track similar to earlier movements. A combination of public education, lobbying, and litigation has resulted in significant "wins" for equal rights, but corresponding backlash and setbacks in a number of states. If the history of civil rights in the United States is any guide, change will be gradual and episodic, and will require sustained political action on many fronts.

[*See also* Civil Liberties; Civil Rights Act; Civil Rights Movement; Constitution, US; Gay Rights; *and* Gender and Politics.]

BIBLIOGRAPHY

Ackerman, Bruce. *We the People: Transformations.* (Cambridge, Mass., 1998).

Andersen, Ellen Ann. *Out of the Closet and into the Courts: Legal Opportunity Structure and Gay Rights Litigation.* (Ann Arbor, Mich., 2005).

Baer, Judith. "Sexual Equality and the Burger Court." *Western Political Science Quarterly* 31 (1978): 470–491.

Dudziak, Mary L. *Cold War Civil Rights: Race and the Image of American Democracy.* (Princeton, N.J., 2000).

Fisher, Louis, and Katy J. Harriger. *American Constitutional Law: Constitutional Rights.* 9th ed. (Durham, N.C., 2011).

Foner, Eric. "The Reconstruction Amendments: Official Documents as Social History." *History Now: American History Online*, no. 2 (December 2004), http://www.gilderlehrman.org/historynow/12_2004/historian.php.

Klinkner, Philip A. With Rogers M. Smith. *The Unsteady March: The Rise and Decline of Racial Equality in America.* (Chicago, 1999).

Mansbridge, Jane J. *Why We Lost the ERA.* (Chicago, 1986).

McDonald, Forrest. *Novus Ordo Seclorum: The Intellectual Origins of the Constitution.* (Lawrence, Kans., 1985).

Morgan, Ruth P. *The President and Civil Rights: Policy-Making by Executive Order.* (New York, 1970).

Nieman, Donald G. *Promises to Keep: African-Americans and the Constitutional Order, 1776 to the Present.* (New York, 1991).

Norton, Mary Beth. *Liberty's Daughters: The Revolutionary Experience of American Women, 1750–1800.* (Boston, 1980).

Rosen, Ruth. *The World Split Open: How the Modern Women's Movement Changed America.* (New York, 2000).

Scheingold, Stuart. *The Politics of Rights: Lawyers, Public Policy, and Political Change.* (New Haven, Conn., 1974).

Tushnet, Mark V. *Making Civil Rights Law: Thurgood Marshall and the Supreme Court, 1936–1961.* (New York, 1994).

VanBurkleo, Sandra F. *"Belonging to the World": Women's Rights and American Constitutional Culture.* (New York, 2001).

Katy J. Harriger

CIVIL RIGHTS ACT

The Civil Rights Act of 1964 was "the greatest legislative achievement of the civil rights movement" (Filvaroff and Wolfinger, 2000, p. 9), the "spectacular accomplishment" of an era that was "a rare American epiphany" (Graham, 1990, pp. 152, 476). In passing it, Congress enacted the first significant federal protections for civil rights since Reconstruction and broke Southern Democrats' stranglehold on the Senate, paving the way for major subsequent legislation, including the Voting Rights Act. Still, the 1964 Act achieved far less than civil rights leaders wanted, and the compromises necessary for its passage produced a bill that was stronger in its symbolic condemnation of discrimination than in its enforcement provisions. Much subsequent political conflict over civil rights has focused on these critical questions of enforcement.

Sweeping in its coverage, the Civil Rights Act banned discrimination on the basis of race, color, religion, or national origin in such wide-ranging areas as voter registration provisions (Title I), hotels, restaurants, theaters, and other public accommodations (Title II), state and local governmental facilities (Title III), public schools (Title IV), federally funded or assisted activities (Title VI), and employment (Title VII). In the area of employment, Title VII added sex to the forms of prohibited discrimination. Additionally, Title VII created the Equal Employment Opportunity Commission (EEOC) but withheld from it key enforcement powers; Title V expanded the powers of the Civil Rights Commission; Title VIII required that commission to gather data on voter registration and voting patterns; and Title IX authorized plaintiffs to move civil rights cases from recalcitrant state courts into federal court.

Supporters of civil rights had long pressed for comprehensive civil rights legislation but Southern Democrats, using their control of key committees and the filibuster, had blocked all but 1 of 121 bills over the previous decade. Seeking to increase pressure for congressional action, in the spring of 1963 civil rights activists, led by the Reverend Martin Luther King Jr., marched in Birmingham, Alabama, home of one of the South's most repressive police forces. The police responded brutally, leading to intense domestic and international pressure on the John F. Kennedy administration to do something.

After initial hesitation, the administration responded by proposing a new civil rights bill. What civil rights leaders wanted may be illustrated by the provisions of the initial draft, written by the House Judiciary Committee under the leadership of its chair Emanuel Celler, a supporter of civil rights. It prohibited discrimination in public accommodations by every business activity licensed under state law, prohibited discrimination in federal, state, and local elections, authorized the Attorney General to sue to stop virtually any violation of civil rights (a provision aimed at addressing the persistent problem of police brutality), created the Equal Employment Opportunity Commission (EEOC), and granted the EEOC broad enforcement powers, including the authority to prosecute and to issue cease-and-desist orders. These provisions combined broad prohibitions on discrimination with powerful enforcement tools in the hands of a new agency, the EEOC, that was modeled on fair employment commissions in several states.

The administration's legislative strategists believed that neither the full House nor the Senate would accept such a broad bill and, working with key Democratic and Republican leaders in the House, they rewrote it. The revision limited the accommodations provision of Title II to businesses engaged in interstate commerce, limited the elections provision of Title I to federal elections, and eliminated the attorney general's authority to sue over police brutality. Clarence Mitchell, the lead lobbyist for the National Association for the Advancement of Colored People (NAACP), denounced the compromise as a "sell-out" (Graham, 1990, p. 133). Still, it was more than Congress had yet achieved in the area of civil rights.

Three weeks later Kennedy was assassinated, and Lyndon Johnson, upon assuming the presidency, devoted his considerable energy and political skills to pushing the bill through Congress. A broad coalition of civil rights groups, leaders of all the major religious groups, and labor unions joined in pressing Congress for passage. While this coalition was openly opposed only by conservative Southerners, business groups worked more quietly to lobby Senate Republicans for key modifications to the bill, particularly in its remaining enforcement provisions.

On the House floor, Howard Smith, Democrat of Virginia, proposed an amendment to Title VII to ban sex discrimination in employment, and it narrowly passed, significantly broadening the scope of the bill. As Smith was an ardent opponent of civil rights, some have viewed the sex discrimination amendment as a "poison pill," a provision aimed at dooming the bill to defeat in the more conservative Senate. But Smith had also been a long-standing supporter of a constitutional ban on sex discrimination, and women's rights activists had urged him to propose the amendment and then worked quietly and effectively behind the scenes to marshal votes in its favor, ultimately packing the House galleries for the final vote on the amendment (Brauer, 1983).

On 10 February 1964, the House passed the amended bill by a vote of 290 to 110, with a bipartisan Northern majority of 152 Democrats and 138 Republicans, and the action moved to the Senate. There, the Democratic majority leader Mike Mansfield of Montana diverted the bill from the Judiciary Committee, controlled by the ardent segregationist James Eastland (D-Mississippi), for immediate consideration by the full Senate. While Southern Democrats filibustered both this procedural decision and

then the bill itself, the Democrats' floor manager Hubert Humphrey (D-Minnesota) deftly used their filibuster to dramatize the evils of racial discrimination.

The minority leader Everett Dirksen, a moderate Republican from Illinois, obtained critical compromises in exchange for his assistance in marshaling Republican votes for the sixty-seven needed to end the filibuster. Adamantly opposed to creating a new enforcement agency like the National Labor Relations Board, Dirksen's amendments removed from the EEOC the powers to prosecute and to issue cease-and-desist orders in employment cases, substituting enforcement by individual plaintiffs' lawsuits. In exchange, civil rights supporters, knowing that most victims of discrimination had no capacity to bring these suits, obtained a provision authorizing judges to require employers to pay the attorneys' fees of plaintiffs who had proved at least part of their claims. Ironically, while the compromise shielded businesses from bureaucratic civil rights enforcement, its attorneys' fees provision exposed them to more employment-based civil rights litigation.

On 10 June, after a Senate debate lasting a record-breaking eighty-two working days, the Senate voted to end debate, and on 19 June passed the bill by a vote of 73 to 27. On 2 July, the House voted 298 to 126 to accept the Senate's amendments, and President Johnson signed the bill into law the same day.

The Act's impact has varied considerably since then. Its passage broke segregationists' hold on the Congress and shifted the national policy agenda in favor of civil rights. Its structure—broad prohibitions on discrimination enforced by private lawsuits funded via attorneys' fee awards—became the model for several subsequent legislative acts.

Still, the EEOC's weak enforcement powers initially led many to believe that the employment prohibition, regarded by many as the core of the Act, was empty symbolism, and much conflict and organizing focused on whether (and how) to give teeth to the employment provisions. Advocates of women's rights, frustrated with the EEOC's unwillingness to take seriously the ban on sex discrimination, formed the National Organization for Women (NOW) and pushed the agency to enforce the ban on sex discrimination. One consequence was the EEOC's endorsement of the campaign against sexual harassment and the subsequent growth of sexual harassment law. Likewise, the NAACP, collaborating with the agency, increased the requirements for compliance with Title VII, and the NAACP then enforced these with litigation. In response to these heightened compliance requirements, the human resources management profession developed employment antidiscrimination policies that, fueled by litigation pressure, have spread widely among employers in the public and private sectors. The Supreme Court, in the landmark case *Griggs v. Duke Power Company* (1971), interpreted the Act to prohibit both intentional employment discrimination and policies that, while not intentionally discriminatory, result in significant employment disparities. This crucial (and controversial) decision contributed to the development of affirmative action policies in employment. After a more conservative Supreme Court reversed *Griggs* in 1989, Congress reaffirmed the *Griggs* formula in the Civil Rights Act of 1991.

Affirmative action also grew out of the decision by federal agencies, led by the Department of Labor's Office of Federal Contract Compliance Programs (OFCCP), to interpret Title VI's prohibition on discrimination in federally assisted activities to include both a ban on job discrimination in federal contracts and a requirement for affirmative action in hiring. The Ronald Reagan administration led an effort to eradicate affirmative action, and by 2000 the Supreme Court had largely prohibited it in government policies, except to remedy a documented past history of discrimination by the employer in question.

While attention has focused especially on the protracted struggles over the Act's employment provisions, some other provisions had a more immediate, and arguably more profound, effect. Title II's ban on discrimination in public accommodations led to the almost immediate and broadscale eradication of segregation in hotels, restaurants, and the like. Title IV's prohibition on racial discrimination in public schools and Title VI's ban on federal funding for discriminatory government programs, combined with

Title III's authorization of the attorney general to file suit to eliminate patterns or practices of discrimination, provided the first powerful enforcement of the decade-old ban on racial segregation in the public schools. Within two years of the Act's adoption, most southern school districts had begun desegregating, and by the mid-1970s, they were the most racially integrated in the nation. The Reagan administration sought to free school districts from federal oversight, however, and by the 1990s the federal courts were largely agreeing to do so. Even police brutality—the only major complaint of the civil rights movement left untouched by the Act's terms—has been addressed by a broad, law-based administrative reform movement inspired by both the Act's promises and its gaps in enforcement.

While the Civil Rights Act's interpretation has varied considerably, it undoubtedly has contributed to broad and deep changes in American society. A quintessential compromise measure, its ambiguity and reliance on the ostensibly weak enforcement power of private litigation have paradoxically contributed to its influence, as fear of litigation and uncertainty about the meaning of compliance have fueled far-reaching efforts by businesses and government agencies alike to demonstrate fidelity to its lofty goals. Still, racial disparities in education, employment, health, law enforcement, and many other areas remain, provoking continuing controversy over the Act's limitations.

[*See also* Affirmative Action; African Americans, History; Civil Rights; *and* Gender and Politics.]

BIBLIOGRAPHY

Brauer, Carl M. "Women Activists, Southern Conservatives, and the Prohibition of Sex Discrimination in Title VII of the 1964 Civil Rights Act." *Journal of Southern History* 49, no 1 (1983): 37–56.

Dobbin, Frank. *Inventing Equal Opportunity*. (Princeton, N.J., 2009).

Dudziak, Mary L. *Cold War Civil Rights: Race and the Image of American Democracy*. (Princeton, N.J., 2000).

Edelman, Lauren B. "Legal Ambiguity and Symbolic Structures: Organizational Mediation of Civil Rights Law." *American Journal of Sociology* 97 (1992): 1531–1576.

Epp, Charles R. *Making Rights Real: Activists, Bureaucrats, and the Creation of the Legalistic State.* (Chicago, 2009).

Farhang, Sean. *The Litigation State: Public Regulation and Private Lawsuits in the US.* (Princeton, N.J., 2010).

Filvaroff, David B., and Raymond E. Wolfinger. "The Origin and Enactment of the Civil Rights Act of 1964." In *Legacies of the 1964 Civil Rights Act*, edited by Bernard Grofman, pp. 9–32. (Charlottsville, Va., 2000).

Graham, Hugh Davis. *The Civil Rights Era: The Origins and Development of National Policy, 1960–1972.* (New York, 1990).

Orfield, Gary. 2000. "The 1964 Civil Rights Act and American Education." In *Legacies of the 1964 Civil Rights Act*, edited by Bernard Grofman, pp. 89–128. (Charlottsville, Va., 2000).

Pedriana, Nicholas, and Robin Stryker. "The Strength of a Weak Agency: Enforcement of Title VII of the 1964 Civil Rights Act and the Expansion of State Capacity, 1965–1971." *American Journal of Sociology* 110 (2004): 709–760.

Skrentny, John David. *The Ironies of Affirmative Action: Politics, Culture, and Justice in America.* (Chicago, 1996).

Charles R. Epp

CIVIL RIGHTS MOVEMENT

The modern US Civil Rights Movement was one of the most important freedom struggles of the twentieth century. As late as the 1950s, millions of African American citizens were oppressed and disenfranchised. This reality was especially shocking because it endured in a country believed to the world's leading democracy. White leaders promoted America as the shining model to be adopted by other countries wishing to break free from their past histories of human oppression.

The historic treatment of blacks in the United States stood in sharp contrast to the American image of democracy. In fact, African Americans were forcibly transported to America as slaves. The institution of slavery lasted well over two centuries and produced the free slave labor that helped fuel the United States' enormous economic growth. Throughout the slave period, African Americans were officially defined as chattel, not human beings.

In both moral and economic terms, the US Civil War (1861–1865) was fought over the issue of slavery. With the triumph of Union forces in 1865, the formal institution of slavery was defeated. For approximately a decade following the Civil War—the Reconstruction period—blacks were granted expanded citizenship rights, such as freedom of movement, access (albeit restricted) to the franchise, and equal access to employment. If this outcome had endured it would have erased a system of white supremacy and created a society based on principles of racial equality.

By the turn of the twentieth century it had become clear that white supremacy would be reinstituted. By the early 1900s, a formal system of racial segregation known as Jim Crow was hammered into place. It required that blacks and whites be segregated on the basis of race. The two races were not allowed to attend the same movie theaters; sit on the same side of a courtroom or be sworn in using the same Bible; occupy the same place on a public bus or train; or participate equally in the political process. Although the Jim Crow system was especially entrenched in the South, it was not limited to any region, and in many respects racial segregation was national in scope. An 1896 Supreme Court ruling, *Plessy v. Ferguson*, declared that racial segregation was constitutional, enshrining the blatantly discriminatory doctrine of separate-but-equal facilities. The national scope of Jim Crow was also evident in the US military, where black soldiers served in racially segregated combat units until the post-World War II era.

By the 1950s, the overwhelming majority of Southern blacks were disenfranchised. As a result, no blacks held any significant political offices in the region. Terror and violence, including lynching, were routinely used to keep blacks subjugated. In the labor market only low-paying, undesirable jobs were usually available to African Americans. Under this arrangement white economic exploitation of blacks continued unabated. African Americans also experienced personal humiliation on a daily basis, because racial segregation set them off from the rest of humanity and labeled them as an inferior race. Human dignity was stripped from African Americans: simple titles of respect such as "Mr." or "Mrs." were withheld, and even white youngsters held authority over all blacks, however elderly or eminent.

African Americans have consistently rebelled and protested against their subordination. These protests began during the era of slavery and have endured over the succeeding generations. At times, resistance was collective and public, while at other times it remained less visible and more limited in scope. By the 1950s African Americans had a long, rich history of social protest to draw upon when confronting their oppressors. In short, the modern Civil Rights Movement was a part of the historic struggle for black liberation. The movement, which took root in the mid-1950s, was clearly one of the peaks of the historic black freedom struggle. It emerged in the Deep South, where black oppression was most intense and where the system of racial segregation was firmly entrenched.

Given the depth of oppression and the power of the white opposition, why did such a powerful civil rights movement erupt when it did? The movement took off during this period for several reasons. First, by the 1950s large numbers of African Americans had migrated to Northern cities. This urbanization of the black masses provided them with new strength derived from tightly knit communities and dense, effective communication networks. Second, by the 1950s the National Association for the Advancement of Colored People (NAACP) had won successful legal battles against the Jim Crow system, especially in the 1954 Supreme Court decision *Brown v. Board of Education*, which overturned the 1896 *Plessy v. Ferguson* decision. The *Brown* ruling concluded that separate schooling based on race was unconstitutional. This ruling served to delegitimize the entire system of racial segregation and encouraged struggles for the implementation of court orders. It also generated massive campaigns of white resistance.

Finally, the international picture was changing in the late 1950s, as African nations gained independence through anticolonial struggles. African Americans identified with those struggles, which intensified their own thirst for freedom. Moreover, the context of decolonization and Cold War rivalry made the federal government susceptible to pressure from the Civil Rights Movement, because America was determined to persuade these new African nations to model themselves after US democracy, not the Soviet alternative. Racial oppression was an obstacle that stood in the path of harmonious relations between the United States and the new African nations. Thus, the federal government came under increased and sustained international pressure to support efforts to overthrow institutionalized racial segregation.

These factors created the fertile soil in which the modern Civil Rights Movement took root. By employing the strategy of mass, nonviolent, direct action, this movement galvanized widespread social protest in the streets and within oppressive institutions. For such a strategy to succeed, white communities, businesses, and institutions had to be disrupted. To do so, the leaders and organizers of the movement persuaded tens of thousands of African Americans to challenge their oppression by becoming involved in social protest.

The Civil Rights Movement succeeded in mobilizing massive nonviolent direct action. Innovative tactics included economic boycotts (beginning with the yearlong boycott of a bus company in Montgomery, Alabama, begun in December 1955 and led by Martin Luther King, Jr.); sit-in demonstrations (started in February 1960 by black college students at a lunch counter in Greensboro, North Carolina); and mass marches (including a massive mobilization of whites and blacks in the August 1963 March on Washington, which culminated in King's "I have a dream" speech, and protest marches led by King that met with police violence in Selma, Alabama, in January 1965).

The goal of these protests was to overthrow the entire system of racial segregation and to empower African Americans by seizing the right the vote. Southern elected officials utilized their governmental power and the resistance of the larger white community in a spirited (and often brutal) effort to resist the Civil Rights Movement and to maintain legally enforced racial segregation. Participants in the movement—many of them children and college students—were often beaten and brutalized by Southern law enforcement officials, and thousands were arrested and jailed for their protest activities. Some leaders and participants were killed—such as Medgar Evers, chair of the Mississippi state chapter of the NAACP, in 1963, and three civil rights workers in Mississippi, in 1964.

Nevertheless, an endless stream of highly visible confrontations in the streets—which contrasted the brutality and the inhumanity of the white segregationists with the dignity and resolve of black protesters—made the cause of black civil rights the major issue in the United States for over a decade during the 1950s and 1960s. The nation and its leaders were forced to decide publicly whether to grant African Americans their citizenship rights, or to side with white segregationists who advocated racial superiority and the undemocratic subjugation of black people.

The movement could not be ignored. Eloquent leaders and their massive followings sustained the pressure on local elites and the federal government. Countless heroic figures inspired a massive following, among them: Rosa Parks, a dignified older woman and secretary for the local NAACP, who sparked the Montgomery bus boycott when she defied an order to move to the back of the bus in order to accommodate a white passenger; Martin Luther King, Jr., who emerged from the Montgomery bus boycott and the Southern Christian Leadership Conference (SCLC) to assume a position of preeminent moral leadership and national influence; James Forman, executive secretary of the more militant Student Nonviolent Coordinating Committee (SNCC), who was to raise questions about the SCLC's and King's strategy; the SNCC leader Stokeley Carmichael (later Kwame Toure), who introduced the slogan "Black Power"; and Fannie Lou Hamer, daughter of a sharecropper who lived on a plantation, who went to a voter registration meeting run by Forman and other SNCC members, was arrested at the courthouse in Indianola, Mississippi when she tried to register to vote, and then was beaten in prison.

These leading figures, along with thousands of movement participants, articulated black suffering and the democratic aspirations of African Americans of every generation and circumstance. In addition, thousands of whites (students, lawyers, and other civil rights workers from all walks of life) were inspired to join the movement. They participated in lunch-counter sit-ins, mass demonstrations, and campaigns such as the 1964 Mississippi Freedom Summer Project, a campaign that involved hundreds of volunteers in voter registration drives and the creation of "freedom schools." Some, like Andrew Goodman and Michael Schwerner, who were involved in the Freedom Summer campaign, and Viola Liuzzo, a Michigan homemaker shot by Klansmen after a rally in support of the march from Selma to Montgomery, lost their lives in the Civil Rights Movement and, in turn, helped inspire others.

Inevitable differences of ideology, leadership style, and approach emerged within the movement as the SCLC, SNCC, the Congress of Racial Equality (CORE), and other organizations reached different judgments about the value of nonviolent action, the role of whites in the movement, and the influence of Malcolm X. Whatever these controversies, the moral challenge and the widespread social disruption caused by the economic boycotts, the marches, the sit-ins, and other forms of nonviolent direct action, coupled with the international pressure, created an impasse in the nation that had to be resolved.

As a result, the movement achieved several important legislative victories in Congress. The landmark Civil Rights Act of 1964 outlawed discrimination in public accommodations on the basis of race, color, religion, or national origin; it granted authority to the attorney general to force the integration of schools through litigation; and it barred discrimination in employment practices on grounds of race, color, religion, national origin, or sex. The 1965 Voting Rights Act suspended the use of literacy tests, authorized the attorney general to challenge the constitutionality of poll taxes, and introduced procedures which provided for the appointment of examiners to ensure that all restrictions on black voter registration be ended. In short, it enfranchised the Southern black population.

Beyond its historic overthrow of the Jim Crow regime and specific legislative relief, the Civil Rights

Movement has affected US politics in fundamental ways. It demonstrated to the oppressed black community how such protest could be successful, and it made social protest respectable. The movement also proved that, at times, significant reform can occur through nonviolent action.

The significance of the civil rights movement extends beyond the rights and freedoms of blacks. The movement also broadened the scope of politics and inspired diverse movements for citizenship rights and social justice in the United States and abroad. Before the Civil Rights Movement, many groups in US society—women, Hispanics, Native Americans, physically disabled, and gays and lesbians, for example—were oppressed but unaware of how to resist or galvanize support. The Civil Rights Movement provided a model of successful social protest and produced a host of new tactics. Moreover, the movement had an influence on freedom struggles around the world. Participants in movements in Africa, Eastern Europe, the Middle East, Latin America, and China have made it clear that they were inspired by and learned important lessons from the US Civil Rights Movement.

For all its success and influences, however, the movement did not solve all of America's racial problems. As the twentieth century closed, African Americans and many other nonwhite groups were still at the bottom of the social and economic order. These current conditions are exacerbated by a mean-spirited political climate in which the poor and oppressed are blamed for their own suffering and oppression. Because of the success of the Civil Rights Movement, a relatively large black middle class has emerged. At the same time, over a third of the black community is trapped in poverty. Black Americans are disproportionately housed in the rapidly growing prison industry. Thus some blacks find themselves experiencing the best of times while millions of others experience the worst of times. Poverty and inequality are also widespread outside the black community. Global poverty and suffering are equally evident. It may be that protest remains the only viable means to achieve greater empowerment. If this is the case, the civil rights movement has left a rich legacy to inspire and inform future struggles.

[*See also* African Americans, History; Disability and Politics; Hispanic Americans; Inequalities of Wealth and Income; King, Martin Luther, Jr.; *and* Race and Racism.]

BIBLIOGRAPHY

Branch, Taylor. *Parting the Waters: America in the King Years, 1954–63.* (New York, 1988).
Brown v. Board of Education of Topeka, 347 U.S. 483, (1954).
Carson, Clayborne. *In Struggle: SNCC and the Black Awakening of the 1960s.* (Cambridge, Mass., 1981).
Carson, Clayborne, David J. Garrow, Gerald Gill, Vincent Harding, and Darlene Clark Hine, eds. *The Eyes on the Prize Civil Rights Reader.* (New York, 1991).
Garrow, David. *Bearing the Cross: Martin Luther King, Jr., and the Southern Christian Leadership Conference.* (New York, 1986).
Layton, Azza Salama. *International Politics and Civil Rights Policies in the United States, 1941–1960.* (Cambridge, Mass., 2000).
McAdam, Doug. *Freedom Summer.* (New York, 1988).
Morris, Aldon. *Origins of the Civil Rights Movement.* (New York, 1984).
Plessy v. Ferguson, 163 U.S. 537, (1896).

Aldon Morris

CLASS POLITICS

The concept of class has had an erratic career in the contemporary analysis of politics. There was a time, not so long ago, when class played at best a marginal role in explanations of political phenomena. In the 1950s and early 1960s, the dominant approach to politics was based on pluralism. Political outcomes in democratic societies were viewed as resulting from the interplay of many crosscutting forces interacting in an environment of bargaining, voting, coalition building, and consensus formation. While some of the organized interest groups may have been based in constituencies with a particular class character—most notably unions and business associations—nevertheless, such organizations were given no special analytical status by virtue of their class associations.

From the late 1960s through the early 1980s, with the renaissance of the Marxist tradition in the social sciences, class suddenly moved to the core of many analyses of the state and politics. Much discussion occurred over such things as the "class character" of state apparatuses, and the importance of instrumental manipulation of state institutions by powerful class-based actors. Even among scholars whose theoretical perspective was not built around class, class was taken seriously and accorded an importance in the analysis of politics rarely found in the previous period.

While class analysis never became the dominant paradigm for the analysis of politics, it was a theoretical force to be reckoned with in the 1970s. Ironically, perhaps, during the course of the 1980s, as US national politics took on a particularly blatant class character, the academic popularity of class analysis as a framework for understanding politics steadily declined. The center of gravity of critical work on the state shifted toward a variety of theoretical perspectives which explicitly distanced themselves from a preoccupation with class, in particular "state-centered" approaches to politics which emphasize the causal importance of the institutional properties of the state and the interests of state managers, and cultural theories which place discourses and symbolic systems at the center of political analysis. While the class analysis of politics has by no means retreated to the marginal status it was accorded in the 1950s, it is no longer the center of debate the way it was in the 1970s and 1980s.

This is, therefore, a good time to take stock of the theoretical accomplishments and unresolved issues of the class analysis of politics. As a prologue to the discussion, the next section briefly looks at the concept of class itself. This will be followed by an examination of three different kinds of mechanisms through which class can have an impact on politics. Using terminology adapted from the work of Robert Alford and Roger Friedland (1985), these are referred to as the situational, institutional, and systemic political effects of class. Next, this article will briefly examine the problem of variability in the patterns of class effects on politics. It concludes with a discussion of the problem of explanatory primacy of class relative to other causal processes.

The Concept of Class. The word "class" has been used to designate a variety of quite distinct theoretical concepts. In particular, it is important to distinguish between what are sometimes called gradational and relational class concepts. As has often been noted, for many, "class" is simply a way of talking about strata within the income distribution. The frequent references in contemporary US politics to "middle-class taxpayers" is equivalent to "middle-income taxpayers." Classes are simply rungs on a ladder of inequalities. For others—particularly analysts working in the Marxian and Weberian theoretical traditions—the concept of class is not meant to designate a distributional outcome as such, but rather the nature of the underlying social relations which generate such outcomes. To speak of a person's class position is thus to identify that person's relationship to specific kinds of mechanisms which generate inequalities of income and power. In a relational class concept, capitalists and workers do not simply differ in the amount of income they acquire, but in the mechanism through which they acquire that income.

It is possible to deploy both gradational and relational concepts of class in the analysis of politics. Many people, for example, use a basically gradational concept of class to examine the different political attitudes and voting behaviors of the poor, the middle class, and the rich. However, most of the systematic work on class and politics has revolved around relational class concepts. There are two basic reasons for this. First, relational concepts are generally seen as designating more fundamental aspects of social structure than gradational concepts, since the relational concepts are anchored in the causal mechanisms which generate the gradational inequalities. To analyze the determinants of political phenomena in terms of relational class concepts is therefore to dig deeper into the causal process than to simply link politics to distributionally defined class categories. Second, relational class categories have the analytical advantage of generating categories of actors who live in real interactive social relations to each other. The "rich," "middle class," and "poor" are arbitrary divisions on a continuum; the individuals defined by these categories may not systematically interact with each other in any particular way. Capitalists and workers, on the other hand, are inherently mutually interdependent. They are real categories whose respective interests are defined, at least in part, by the nature of the relations that bind them together. Building the concept of class around these relations, then, greatly facilitates the analysis of the formation of organized collectivities engaged in political conflict over material interests.

Adopting a relational perspective on class, of course, is only a point of departure. There are many ways of elaborating such a concept. In particular, much has been made of the distinction between the Marxian and Weberian traditions of class analysis. Weberians define classes primarily in terms of market relations, whereas Marxists define classes by the social relations of production. Why is this contrast of theoretical importance? After all, both Marxists and Weberians recognize capitalists and workers as the two fundamental classes of capitalist societies, and both define these classes in essentially the same way: capitalists are owners of the means of production who employ wage earners; workers are non-owners of the means of production who sell their labor power to capitalists. What difference does it make that Weberians define these classes by the exchange relation into which they enter, whereas Marxists emphasize the social relations of production?

First, the restriction of classes to market relations means, for Weberians, that classes only really exist in capitalist societies. The relationship between lords and serfs might be oppressive and the source of considerable conflict, but Weberians would not treat this as a class relation, because it is structured around relations of personal dependence and domination, not market relations. Marxists, in contrast, see conflicts over the control of productive resources in both feudalism and capitalism as instances of class struggle. This is not simply a nominal shift in labels, for it is part of the effort within Marxism to construct a general theory of historical change built around class analysis. Aphorisms such as "class

struggle is the motor of history" only make sense if the concept of "class" is built around the social relations of production, rather than restricted to market relations.

Second, the elaboration of the concept of class in terms of production relations underwrites the linkage between class and exploitation that is central to Marxist theory. In the traditional Marxist account, exploitation occurs primarily within production itself, for it is in production that labor is actually performed and embodied in the social product. Exploitation, roughly, consists in the appropriation by one class of the "surplus labor" performed by another. While the exchange relation between workers and capitalists may create the opportunity for capitalists to exploit workers, it is only when the labor of workers is actually deployed in the labor process, and the resulting products appropriated by capitalists, that exploitation actually occurs. The characteristic lack of discussion of exploitation by Weberian class analysts thus, at least in part, reflects their restriction of the concept of class to the exchange relation.

While these differences between the Marxian and Weberian concept of class are important for the broader theory of society within which these class concepts are used, in practical terms, for the analysis of capitalist society the actual descriptive class maps generated by scholars in the two traditions may not be so divergent. As already noted, both traditions see the capital-labor relation as defining the principal axis of class relations in capitalism. Furthermore, scholars in both traditions acknowledge the importance of a variety of social categories, loosely labeled the "new middle class(es)"—professionals, managers and executives, bureaucratic officials, and perhaps highly educated white-collar employees—who do not fit neatly into the polarized class relation between capitalists and workers. There is little consensus either among Weberian or among Marxist scholars on precisely how these new middle classes should be conceptualized. As a result, particularly as Marxist accounts of these "middle class" categories have become more sophisticated, the line of demarcation between these two traditions has become somewhat less sharply drawn.

While Marxist and Weberian pictures of the class structure of capitalist society may not differ dramatically, their use of the concept of class in the analysis of political phenomena is generally sharply different. Weberians typically regard class as one among a variety of salient determinants of politics. In specific problems this means that class might assume considerable importance, but there is no general presumption that class is a more pervasive or powerful determinant of political phenomena than other causal processes. Marxists, in contrast, characteristically give class a privileged status in the analysis. In the most orthodox treatments, class (and closely related concepts like "capitalism" or "mode of production") may become virtually the exclusive systematic explanatory principles, but in all Marxist accounts of politics class plays a central, if not necessarily all-encompassing, explanatory role. In the final section of this essay we will examine the problem of explanatory primacy for class. Before we engage that issue, however, we will examine the various ways in which Marxist class analysts see class as shaping politics.

How Class Shapes Politics. Robert Alford and Roger Friedland (1985), building on the analysis of Steven Lukes (1974) and others, have elaborated a tripartite typology of "levels of power" that is useful in examining the causal role of class on politics. *Situational power* refers to power relations of direct command and obedience between actors, as in Max Weber's celebrated definition of power as the ability of one actor to get another to do something even in the face of resistance. This is the characteristic form of power analyzed in various behavioral studies of power. *Institutional power* refers to the characteristics of different institutional settings which shape the decision-making agenda in ways which serve the interests of particular groups. This is also referred to as "negative power" or the "second face of power" (see Bachrach and Baratz, 1970)—power which excludes certain alternatives from a decision-making agenda without, as in situational power, actually commanding a specific behavior. *Systemic power* is perhaps the most difficult (and contentious) conceptually. It refers to the power to realize

one's interests by virtue of the overall structure of a social system, rather than by virtue of commanding the behavior of others or of controlling the agendas of specific organizations.

Alford and Friedland (1985) discuss this typology of power in an interesting way using a loose game-theory metaphor. Systemic power is power embedded in the fundamental nature of the game itself; institutional power is power embodied in the specific rules of the game; and situational power is power deployed in specific moves within a given set of rules. When actors use specific resources strategically to accomplish their goals, they are exercising situational power. The procedural rules which govern how they use those resources reflect institutional power. And the nature of the social system which determines the range of possible rules and achievable goals reflects systemic power. There is thus a kind of cybernetic relationship among these levels of power: the system level imposes limits on the institutional level which imposes limits on actors' strategies at the situational level. Conflicts at the situational level, in turn, can modify the rules at the institutional level, which cumulatively can lead to the transformation of the system itself.

The class analysis of politics is implicated in each of these domains of power and politics. Although class theorists of politics do not explicitly frame their analyses in terms of these three levels of power, nevertheless the distinctions are implicit in many discussions.

Class and Situational Power. Much of the theoretical debate over the relative explanatory importance of class has occurred at the situational level of political analysis. Marxists (and non-Marxists heavily influenced by the Marxian tradition) typically argue that actors whose interests and resources are derived from their link to the class structure generally play the decisive role in actively shaping political conflicts and state policies. Sometimes the emphasis is on the strategic action of the dominant class—that is, on the ability of capitalists to manipulate the state in their interests. Other times the emphasis is on the political effects of class struggle as such, in which case popular actions, as well as ruling class machinations, are seen as shaping state policies. In either case, class is seen as shaping politics through its effects on the behavioral interactions among political actors.

The theoretical reasoning behind such treatments of the class basis of situational power is fairly straightforward. Class structures, among other things, distribute resources which are useful in political struggles. In particular, in capitalist societies capitalists have two crucial resources available to them to be deployed politically: enormous financial resources, and personal connections to people in positions of governmental authority. Through a wide variety of concrete mechanisms—financing politicians, political parties, and policy think tanks; financially controlling the main organs of the mass media; offering lucrative jobs to high-level political officials after they leave state employment; extensive lobbying—capitalists are in a position to use their wealth to directly shape the direction of state policies. When combined with the dense pattern of personal networks which give capitalists easy access to the sites of immediate political power, such use of financial resources gives the bourgeoisie vastly disproportionate direct leverage over politics.

Few theorists deny the empirical facts of the use of politically important resources in this way by members of the capitalist class in pursuit of their interests. What is often questioned is the general efficacy and coherence of such actions in sustaining the class interests of the bourgeoisie. Because individual capitalists are frequently preoccupied by their immediate, particularistic interests (e.g., in specific markets, technologies, or regulations), when they deploy their class-derived resources politically some scholars argue that they are unlikely to do so in ways which place the class interests of the bourgeoisie as a whole above their own particularistic interests. As Fred Block (1987) among others has noted, the capitalist class is often very divided politically, lacking a coherent vision and sense of priorities. Thus, even if capitalists try to manipulate politics in various ways, such manipulations often work against each other and do not generate a consistent set of policy outcomes.

The fact that capitalists have considerable power resources by virtue of their control over capital thus does not ensure a capacity to translate those resources into a coherent class direction for politics. What is more, in terms of situational power, capitalists are not the only actors with effective political resources. In particular, as Theda Skocpol (1984, 1985), Anthony Giddens (1981), and others have stressed, state managers—the top-level politicians and officials within state apparatuses—have direct control of considerable resources to pursue political objectives. Although in many instances the interests and objectives of state managers may be congruent with the interests of the capitalist class, this is not universally the case, and when overt conflicts between state managers and the bourgeoisie occur, there is no inherent reason why capitalists will always prevail. Even more to the point, in many situations, because of the disorganization, myopia, and apathy of the capitalist class, state managers will have considerable room to initiate state policies independently of pressures from the capitalist class.

These kinds of arguments do not discredit the claim that class structures do shape both the interests of actors and the political resources they can deploy in struggles over situational power. However, the blanket claim that class-derived interests and power resources are always the most salient is called into question.

Class and Institutional Power. It was at least in part because of a recognition that, at the level of situational power, capitalists are not always present as the predominant active political actors that much class analysis of politics has centered around the problem of the institutional dimensions of power. The argument is basically this: the state should be viewed not simply as a state *in* capitalist society, but rather as a *capitalist* state. This implies that there are certain institutional properties of the very form of the state that can be treated as having a specific class character to them. The idea here is not simply that there are certain policies of the state which embody the interests of a specific class, but rather that the very structure of the apparatuses through which those policies are made embodies those class interests.

Claims about the class character of the institutional level of power involve what is sometimes called non-decision–making power or negative power. The basic argument was crisply laid out in an early essay by Claus Offe (1974). Offe argued that the class character of the state was inscribed in a series of negative filter mechanisms that imparted a systematic class bias to state actions. "Class bias," in this context, means that the property in question tends to filter out state actions that would be inimical to the interests of the dominant class. The form of the state, in effect, systematically determines what does not happen, rather than simply what does.

An example, emphasized by Claus Offe and Volker Ronge (1975) as well as by Göran Therborn (1978), would be the institutional rules by which the capitalist state acquires financial resources—namely, through taxation and borrowing from the privately produced surplus rather than through the state's direct appropriation of the surplus generated by its own productive activity. By restricting the state's access to funds in this way the state is rendered dependent upon capitalist production, and this in turn acts as a mechanism which filters out those state policies which would seriously undermine the profitability of private accumulation. Or, to take another example, given considerable emphasis by Nicos Poulantzas (1973), the electoral rules of capitalist representative democracies (in which people cast votes as individual citizens within territorial units of representation, rather than as members of functioning groups) have the effect of transforming people from members of a class into atomized individuals (the "juridical citizen"). This atomization, in turn, serves to filter out state policies that would only be viable if people were systematically organized into durable collectivities or associations. To the extent that this filter can be viewed as stabilizing capitalism, and thus serving the basic interests of the capitalist class, exclusive reliance on purely territorial, individualized voting can be viewed as having a class character.

This way of understanding the class character of an apparatus suggests a certain functionalist logic to the thesis that the state is a capitalist state; its

form is capitalist insofar as these institutional features contribute to the reproduction of the interests of the capitalist class. This functional logic has been most systematically elaborated in Göran Therborn's *What Does the Ruling Class Do When It Rules?* (1978). Therborn stresses that the real analytical bite of the thesis that the state has a distinctive class character occurs when the state is analyzed comparatively, particularly across historical epochs. The class character of the state apparatus is a variable; state apparatuses corresponding to different class structures will have distinctively different properties, which impart different class biases on state actions. If this "correspondence principle" is correct, then it should be possible to define the specific class properties of the feudal state, the capitalist state, and—perhaps—the socialist state. Take the example, already cited, of the mechanism through which the state acquires resources. In the capitalist state this occurs primarily through taxation, thus insuring the fiscal subordination of the state to private capital accumulation. In the feudal state, revenues are acquired through the direct appropriation of surplus from the personal vassals of the king. And in the socialist state, state revenues are acquired through the appropriation of the surplus product of state enterprises. In each case, the argument goes, these class forms of revenue acquisition selectively filter out political practices that might threaten the existing class structure.

Many critics of the thesis that the state has a distinctive class character have argued that this claim implies a functionalist theory of the state. This accusation is certainly appropriate in some cases. In the early work on the state by Nicos Poulantzas (1973), for example, and even more in the work of Louis Althusser (1971), there was very little room for genuinely contradictory elements in the state. The class properties of the capitalist state were explained by the functions they served for reproducing capitalism. The functional correspondence principle for identifying the class character of aspects of the state slid into a principle for explaining the properties of the state. This kind of functionalism, however, is not an inherent feature of the class analysis of the institutional level of political power. While the thesis that state apparatuses have a class character does follow a functional logic (i.e., what makes a given property have a given "class character" is its functional relation to the class structure), this does not necessarily imply a full-fledged functionalist theory of the state. To say that capitalists have situational power is to say that they command a range of resources which they can deploy to get their way. To say that they have institutional power is to argue that various institutions are designed in such a way as to selectively exclude alternatives from the political agenda which are antithetical to their interests. To say that they have systemic power is to say that the logic of the social system itself affirms their interests quite apart from their conscious strategies and the internal organization of political apparatuses.

The idea that capitalists have such systemic power has been forcefully argued by Adam Przeworski (1985), building on the work of Antonio Gramsci. Przeworski argues that so long as capitalism is intact as a social order, all actors in the system have an interest in capitalists making a profit. What this means is that, unless a group has the capacity to overthrow the system completely, then at least in terms of material interests, even groups opposed to capitalism have an interest in sustaining capitalist accumulation and profitability.

This kind of system-level power has been recognized by many scholars, not just those working firmly within the Marxist tradition. Charles Lindblom's *Politics and Markets* (1977), for example, is built around the problem of how the interests of capitalists are imposed on political institutions by the operation of markets, even without any direct, instrumental manipulation of those institutions by individual capitalists. Indeed, this essential point, wrapped in quite different rhetoric, is also at the core of neoconservative supply-side economics arguments about the need to reduce government spending in order to spur economic growth.

There are two critical differences between Marxist treatments of this systemic level of analysis and most mainstream treatments. First, Marxists characterize these system-level constraints on politics as having a distinctive *class* character. Neoconservatives do

not regard the private investment constraint on the state as an instance of "class power," because they regard markets as the "natural" form of economic interaction. The constraint comes from the universal laws of economics rooted in human nature. In contrast, the Marxist characterization of these constraints in class terms rests on the general claim that capitalism is a historically distinct form of economy.

The second important difference between Marxist and mainstream perspectives on the constraints capitalism imposes on the state is that most liberal and neoconservative analysts see this system-level logic as much less closely tied to the institutional and situational levels of analysis than do Marxists. Neoconservatives in particular grant the state considerably more autonomy to muck up the functioning of the capitalist economy than do Marxists. For neoconservatives, even though the political system is clearly dependent on the private economy for resources and growth, nevertheless politically motivated actors are quite capable of persisting in high levels of excessive state spending in spite of the economic constraints. The state, being pushed by ideological agendas of actors wielding situational power, can, through myopia, "kill the goose that lays the golden egg." Marxists tend to see state spending and state policies as less likely to deviate persistently from the functional requirements of capitalism, because they see the levels of situational and institutional power as generally congruent with the level of systemic power. The structure of state apparatuses and the strategies of capitalists, therefore, generally prevent too much deviation from occurring. Neoconservatives, on the other hand, see the three levels of politics as having much greater potential for divergence. They believe that the democratic form of institutions and the excessive mobilization of popular forces systematically generates dysfunctional levels of state spending which are not necessarily corrected by the exercise of capitalist situational power or the negative feedback.

Variability in the Effects of Class on Politics. We have reviewed three clusters of mechanisms through which class shapes politics: the class-based access to resources which can be strategically deployed for political purposes; the institutionalization of certain class biases into the design of state apparatuses; and the way in which the operation of the system as a whole universalizes certain class interests. Frequently, in the more theoretical discussions of these mechanisms, the class character of these mechanisms is treated as largely invariant within a given kind of class society. Abstract discussions of "the capitalist state," for example, emphasize what all capitalist states have in common by virtue of being capitalist states. Relatively less attention has been given to the problem of variability. In many empirical contexts, however, the central issue is precisely the ways in which class effects concretely vary across cases. Let us look briefly at such variability in class effects at the situational, institutional, and systemic levels of political analysis.

One of the central themes of much Marxist historical research is the shifting "balance of class forces" between workers and capitalists (and sometimes other classes) in various kinds of social and political conflicts. Generally, expressions like "balance of forces" refer to the relative situational power of the contending organized collectivities—i.e., their relative capacity to actively pursue their interests in various political arenas. The task of an analysis of variability in the class character of situational power is thus to explain the social determinants of these varying capacities. Generally this involves invoking mechanisms at the institutional and systemic levels of analysis. Thus, for example, the enduring weakness of the US working class within electoral politics has been explained by such institutional factors as the existence of a winner-take-all electoral system which undermines the viability of small parties, the lack of public financing of elections which enhances the political influence of financial contributors, and voter registration laws which make voter mobilization difficult, as well as such systemic factors as the location of US capitalism in the world capitalist system. Each of these factors undermines the potential situational power of the working class within electoral politics. This enduring situational weakness, in turn, blocks the capacity of the popular forces to alter the institutional properties of the state in ways which would enhance their power. While in all capitalist societies it may be the case that capitalists have disproportionate situational power, capitalist societies can vary considerably in the level of power of different subordinate groups relative to the bourgeoisie.

The same kind of variation is possible in terms of power embodied in the institutional properties of the state. In various ways, noncapitalist elements can be embodied in the institutional structure of capitalist states. Consider the example of workplace safety regulations. A variety of institutional forms can be established for implementing safety regulations. The conventional device in most capitalist states is to have a hierarchical bureaucratic agency responsible for such regulations, with actual enforcement organized through official inspections, licensing requirements, and various other aspects of bureaucratic due process. An alternative structure would be to establish workplace occupational safety committees within factories controlled by employees with powers to monitor compliance and enforce regulations. Such administration procedures, built around principles of what Joshua Cohen and Joel Rogers call "associational democracy," violate the class logic of the capitalist state by encouraging the collective organization rather than atomization of the affected people. To the extent that such noncapitalist elements can be incorporated into the institutional structure of the capitalist state, the class character of those apparatuses can vary *even within capitalism*.

Finally, some theoretical work entertains the possibilities of variation in the class character of systemic power within capitalist societies. The essential issue here is whether the overall relationship between state and economy within capitalism can significantly modify the dynamics of the system itself. Do all instances of capitalism have fundamentally the same system logic simply by virtue of the private ownership of the means of production, or can this logic be significantly modified in various ways? Most Marxists have insisted that there is relatively little variation in such system logic across capitalisms, at least as it relates to the basic class character of system-level power. The transition from competitive to "monopoly" capitalism, for example, may greatly affect the situational power of different classes and fractions of classes, and it might even be reflected in changes in the class character of the institutional form of the state (for example, petit bourgeois elements in state apparatuses might disappear as capitalism advances). But the basic system-level class logic, Marxists have traditionally argued, remains organized around the interests of capital in both cases.

There has been some challenge to this view by scholars generally sympathetic to Marxian perspectives. Gøsta Esping-Andersen (1990), for example, argues that differences in the forms of the welfare state (which he refers to as conservative, liberal, and socialist welfare state regimes) can have a basic effect on the system logic of capitalism, creating different developmental tendencies and different matrices of interests for various classes. Joel Rogers has forcefully argued a similar view with respect to the specific issue of industrial relations. He argues that there is an "inverse-J" relationship between the interests of capital and the degree of unionization of the working class. Increasing unionization hurts the interests of capitalists up to a certain point. Beyond that point, however, further increases in unionization are beneficial to capitalists, because they make possible higher levels of coordination and cooperation between labor and capital. This means that if, for example, the legal regime of industrial relations prevents unionization from passing the trough threshold in the curve (as, he argues, is the case in the United States), then unions will be constantly on the defensive as they confront the interests of capital, whereas if the legal order facilitates unionization moving beyond the trough (as in Sweden), then the system logic will sustain unionization. High unionization and low unionization capitalisms, therefore, embody qualitatively different system patterns of class power within what remains an overall capitalist framework.

Conclusion. Few scholars today would argue that class is irrelevant to the analysis of political phenomena, but there is much contention over how important class might be. The characteristic form of this debate is for the critic of class analysis to attack class reductionism—that is, the thesis that political phenomena (state policies, institutional properties, political behavior, or party strategies, for example) can be fully explained by class-based causal processes. Defenders of class analysis, on the other hand, attack their critics for claiming that political phenomena are completely autonomous from class determinants. Both of these positions, when stated in this form, have no real defenders. Even relatively orthodox Marxists introduce many nonclass factors in their explanations of any given example of state policy, and thus are not guilty of class reductionism; and even the most state-centered critic of class analysis admits that class relations play some role in shaping political outcomes.

The issue, then, is not really explanatory reductionism versus absolute political autonomy, but rather the relative salience of different causal factors and how they fit together. A good example is the discussions of the development of the welfare state sparked by the work of Theda Skocpol and others advocating a "state-centered" approach to the study of politics. In an influential paper, Ann Orloff and Skocpol (1984) argue that the specific temporal sequence of the introduction of social security laws in Britain, Canada, and the United States cannot be explained by economic or class factors. Rather, they argue, this sequence is primarily the result of causal processes located within the political realm itself, specifically the bureaucratic capacities of the state and the legacies of prior state policies.

The empirical arguments of Orloff and Skocpol are quite convincing, given the specific way they have defined their object of explanation. But suppose there was a slight shift in the question. Instead of asking, "Why was social security introduced in Britain before World War I, in Canada in the 1920s, and the United States in the 1930s?" ask, "Why did no industrialized capitalist society have social security in the 1850s while all industrialized capitalist societies had such programs by the 1950s?" The nature of class relations and class conflicts in capitalism and the transformations of the capitalist economy would surely figure more prominently in the answer to this reformulated explanatory problem.

In general, then, the issue of causal primacy is sensitive to the precise formulation of what is to be explained (explanandum). It is certainly implausible that class (or anything else) could be "the most important" cause of all political phenomena. For claims of causal primacy to have any force, therefore, it is essential that the domain of the explanations over which the claims are being made be well defined. Can we, then, specify the domain of explananda for which class is likely to be the most important causal factor? Implicit in most class analyses of politics are two very general hypotheses about the range of explanatory problems for which class analysis is likely to provide the most powerful explanations.

One hypothesis posits that the more coarse-grained and abstract the explanandum, the more likely it is that general systemic factors, such as class structure or the dynamics of capitalism, will play an important explanatory role. The more fine-grained and concrete the object of explanation, on the other hand, the more likely it is that relatively contingent causal processes—such as the specific legislative histories of different states or the detailed rules of electoral competition—will loom large in the explanation. All things being equal, therefore, the decision to examine relatively nuanced concrete variations in political outcomes across cases with broadly similar class structures is likely to reduce the salience of class relative to other causal processes.

Another hypothesis is that the more the reproduction of the class structure and the interests of dominant classes are directly implicated in the explanandum, the more likely it is that class factors—at the situational, institutional, and systemic levels—will constitute important causes in the explanation. This is not a tautology, for there is no logical reason why class mechanisms must be causally important for explaining class-relevant outcomes. Such a hypothesis also does not reject the possibility that causal processes unconnected to class might play a

decisive role in specific instances. But it does argue that one should be surprised if class-based causal processes do not play a significant role in explaining political phenomena closely connected to the reproduction of class structures and the interests of dominant classes.

Taken together, these two hypotheses help specify the applicability of class to the analysis of politics.

[*See also* Business-Government Relations; Capitalism; Inequalities of Wealth and Income; Marxism; Middle Class, American; *and* Rich, The.]

BIBLIOGRAPHY
Alford, Robert, and Roger Friedland. *The Powers of Theory.* (Cambridge, UK, 1985).
Althusser, Louis. *Lenin and Philosophy.* (New York, 1971).
Bachrach, Peter, and Morton S. Baratz. *Power and Poverty.* (New York, 1970).
Block, Fred. *Revising State Theory: Essays in Politics and Postindustrialism.* (Philadelphia, 1987).
Dahrendorf, Ralf. *Class and Class Conflict in Industrial Societies.* (Stanford, Calif., 1959).
Esping-Andersen, Gøsta. *The Three Worlds of Welfare Capitalism.* (Princeton, N.J., 1990).
Evans, Peter, Theda Skocpol, and Dieter Reuschmeyer, eds. *Bringing the State Back In.* (Cambridge, UK, 1985).
Giddens, Anthony. *A Contemporary Critique of Historical Materialism.* (Berkeley, Calif., 1981).
Lindblom, Charles. *Politics and Markets.* (New York, 1977).
Lukes, Steven. *Power: A Radical View.* (London, 1974).
Miliband, Ralph. *The State in Capitalist Society* (New York, 1969).
Offe, Claus. "Structural Problems of the Capitalist State: Class Rule and the Political System. On the Selectiveness of Political Institutions." In *German Political Studies,* vol. 1, edited by Klaus Von Beyme, pp. 31–54. (London, 1974).
Offe, Claus, and Volker Ronge. "Theses on the Theory of the State." *New German Critique* 6 (Fall 1975): 139–147.
Orloff, Ann, and Theda Skocpol. "Why Not Equal Equal Protection? Explaining the Politics of Public Social Spending in Britain, 1900–1911, and the United States, 1880s–1920." *American Sociological Review* 49, no. 6 (1984): 726–750.
Parkin, Frank. *Marxist Class Theory: A Bourgeois Critique.* (New York, 1979).
Poulantzas, Nicos. *Classes in Contemporary Capitalism.* (London, 1975).

Poulantzas, Nicos. *Political Power and Social Classes.* (London, 1973).

Przeworski, Adam. *Capitalism and Social Democracy.* (Cambridge, UK, 1985).

Roemer, John. *A General Theory of Exploitation and Class.* (Cambridge, Mass., 1982).

Therborn, Göran. *What Does the Ruling Class Do When It Rules?* (London, 1978).

Wright, Erik Olin. *Class Counts.* (Cambridge, UK, 1997).

Erik Olin Wright

CLEAN AIR ACT

The modern Clean Air Act (CAA) came into being in 1970, and although significant changes were made to it in 1977 and 1990, the basic structure of the Act has remained the same. Significant additions since 1970 include provisions addressing acid rain, chlorofluorocarbons (CFCs), indoor air, and chemical safety. In 2007, the Supreme Court confirmed the authority of the Environmental Protection Agency (EPA) to regulate greenhouse gases to mitigate climate disruption. The CAA regulates both stationary and mobile sources of pollution, taking into account the relative contributions of each to specific air pollution problems, and the relative capacity of different kinds of sources within each category to reduce their emissions. The recognition that sources using newer technology might be able to achieve greater emission reductions than older sources with older technology led to the Act's distinction, in both its stationary and mobile source provisions, between new and existing sources. Although driven by equity considerations regarding the relative financial and technical burdens of pollution reduction, this approach has unwittingly discouraged modernization or replacement of facilities and has resulted in the operation of older facilities, especially in the field of energy, beyond their expected useful life. For new sources within each industrial sector, there was recognition of the need for uniformity and also for encouraging technological innovation through the technology-forcing capability inherent in stringent standards.

The Control of Conventional and Toxic Air Pollutants. The 1970 CAA directed the EPA to set air quality criteria for pollutants that are emitted to the air "from numerous or diverse stationary or mobile sources" and "may reasonably be anticipated to endanger public health or welfare" (Section 109[a][1][A] and [B]), and to establish primary ambient air quality standards for those pollutants that protect public health with an adequate margin of safety (Section 109[b][1]). As interpreted by the courts and supported by congressional history, these standards are to be established without consideration of economic or technological feasibility. In addition, secondary ambient air quality standards are to be established to protect the public welfare within a reasonable time (Section 109[b][2]). The EPA has issued, and revised, ambient air quality standards for a relatively small number of these so-called criteria pollutants.

The CAA assigns key roles to both the federal government and the states in controlling exposure to the criteria pollutants in the ambient air. While ambient air quality (concentration) standards are established by the federal government, these ambient standards (identified below) are to be attained through (1) emission limitations placed on individual existing polluters through permits issued by state government as a part of their state implementation plans (SIPs; Section 110); (2) nationwide emission limitations for new sources, established by the EPA and known as New Source Performance Standards (Section 111); and (3) a combination of federal and state restrictions on mobile sources. Emission standards, in contrast with ambient concentration standards, are expressed as an emissions rate (milligrams emitted per 100 kg of product, per hour, per day, per week, per quarter, per year, per British thermal unit (BTU), per passenger mile, or per other unit of measurement).

The CAA does not establish ambient standards for hazardous air pollutants, but rather requires compliance with nationwide emission limitations set by the EPA (Section 112). Hazardous air pollutants are those recognized as extraordinarily toxic and eventually regarded as non- or low-threshold pollutants. Initially, these were to be regulated to protect public health with an ample margin of safety and, as with the primary ambient standards for criteria pollutants, emission standards for hazardous air pollutants were to be established without consideration of economic burden. The reliance on federal emission standards reflected congressional concern with "hot spots" of localized intense pollution, and also with intermittent versus continuous versus sudden and accidental releases of harmful substances. These pollutants, Congress determined, were sufficiently dangerous to preclude any reliance on atmospheric dispersion and mixing as a means of reducing their ambient concentrations. Moreover, ambient concentration standards were considered impractical and of little relevance for the sporadic and idiosyncratic sources of hazardous air pollutants. For all these reasons, uniform federal emission standards were considered necessary. (Note, however, that California did establish an ambient standard as a complement to the federal emission limitation on vinyl chloride.)

In the early stages of the implementation of the stationary source provisions of the Clean Air Act (approximately 1970–1975), the EPA focused on (1) the ambient air quality standards for criteria pollutants; and (2) emission standards for new sources of criteria pollutants and for all sources emitting any of seven regulated hazardous air pollutants (discussed below). Initially, prior advisory ambient standards for criteria pollutants carbon monoxide (CO), sulfur dioxide (SO2), oxides of nitrogen (NOX), large particulate matter, and photochemical oxidants were made mandatory. In 1979, the standard for photochemical oxidants was narrowed to cover only ground-level ozone and was relaxed from 0.08 parts per million (ppm) to 0.12 ppm averaged over a one-hour period. The standard for coarse particulate matter—inhalable particulates up to 10 microns in diameter (PM10)—was adopted in 1987. In 1997 and again in 2008, the ozone standard was further revised to 0.08 ppm and 0.075 ppm, respectively, but the 2008 standard has been put on hold pending further revisions. Also in 1997, the particulate standard was altered to place more stringent requirements on

smaller (less than 2.5 microns) respirable particles (PM2.5), with a twenty-four-hour limit of 65 micrograms per cubic meter of air (μg/m3). In 2006, the PM2.5 limit was further lowered to 35 μg/m3. Further revisions are under consideration. A standard for a sixth criteria pollutant, airborne lead, was promulgated in 1978, and in 2008 EPA lowered the permissible airborne concentration by one order of magnitude, from 1.5 micrograms per cubic meter of air (μg/m3) to 0.15 μg/m3. (Current primary air quality standards set under Section 109 are found in the table below.) In June 2010, EPA replaced the daily and annual sulfur dioxide standards with an hourly standard of 75 parts per billion (0.075 ppm.).

TABLE: *National Ambient Air Quality Standards*

Carbon Monoxide	*Primary* (1970) – 35 ppm averaged over 1 hr and 9.0 averaged over 8 hrs; neither to be exceeded more than once per year. *Secondary* – none.
Particulate Matter:	(PMxy below refers to particles equal or less than xy microns in diameter)
PM10	*Primary and Secondary* (1970) – 150 μg/m³ averaged over 24 hrs, with no more than one expected exceedance per calendar year; also, 50 μg/m³ or less for the expected annual arithmetic mean concentration
PM2.5	*Primary* (2006) – 35 μg/m³ averaged over 24 hrs
Ozone	*Primary* (1997) – 0.08 ppm averaged over 8 hrs
	Primary (2008) – 0.075 ppm averaged over 8 hrs (on hold)
Nitrogen Dioxide	*Primary and Secondary* (1970) – 100 μg/m³ (0.053 ppm) as an annual arithmetic mean concentration
Sulfur Oxides	*Primary* (2010) – hourly standard of 75 parts per billion; prior daily and annual standards revoked
Lead	*Primary and Secondary* (2008) – 0.15 μg/m³ arithmetic average over a calendar quarter

As noted, Congress also directed the EPA to set emission standards for "hazardous air pollutants." As originally written, Section 112 of the Act specified that all such standards should be set at a level that protects public health with an "ample margin of safety." It is likely that this phraseology reflected an early assumption that although hazardous pollutants were very dangerous, they exhibit a finite threshold (a nonzero level of exposure below which no harm would occur). As the 1970s progressed, however, there was a growing recognition that this assumption might be wrong, and that for many hazardous pollutants there was no level of exposure (at least at levels within the limits of detection) below which one could confidently predict that no harmful or irreversible effects (especially cancer or birth defects) would occur.

This presented an implementation challenge for the EPA. Arguably, given its mandate to protect public health with an ample margin of safety, the agency was required to ban the emission of several hazardous substances. This would, as a practical matter, essentially ban the use of these substances in many industries. Seeking to avoid this result, the EPA adopted a policy of setting Section 112 emission standards at the level that could be achieved by current technology. The standard-setting process was slow and had to be forced by litigation; only a few substances were regulated, and it took four to seven years to establish a final standard for each of these substances. Had the EPA continued to set standards for more substances, and had it used the technological-feasibility approach to spur the development of cleaner technology, the environmental community may well have been content to allow the implementation of Section 112 to proceed in this fashion. When the setting of new Section 112 standards all but stalled during the Ronald Reagan administration, however, the National Resources Defense Council, an environmental group, decided to press the issue in court.

National Resources Defense Council v. Environmental Protection Agency, decided by the District of Columbia Circuit Court of Appeals in 1987, complicated the EPA's approach to regulating hazardous air pollutants by ruling that the EPA must determine an acceptable (usually nonzero) risk level for a hazardous air pollutant prior to setting a Section 112 standard for that pollutant. In reaction to this case and

to revitalize the moribund standard-setting process, Congress amended Section 112 in 1990 to specify a two-tiered approach: the use of technology-based standards initially, with residual risks to be addressed (at a later date) by health-based standards. In addition, Congress listed 189 substances that must be regulated as hazardous air pollutants, and directed the EPA to add other substances to the list if they "present or may present . . . a threat of adverse human effects (including, but not limited to, substances which are known to be or may be reasonably anticipated to be, carcinogenic, mutagenic, teratogenic, neurotoxic, which cause reproductive dysfunction, or which are acutely or chronically toxic) or adverse environmental effects whether through ambient concentration, bioaccumulation, deposition or otherwise." The EPA was directed to set "maximum achievable control technology" (MACT) technology-based standards over a ten-year period for categories of major stationary sources (defined as those emitting more than ten tons per year of any single hazardous pollutant or more than twenty-five tons combined). MACT standards must require the maximum feasible degree of reduction (including a prohibition on emissions, where achievable) but must reflect the cost of achieving emissions reduction and any non-air and environmental impact and energy requirements. MACT standards for new sources must be at least as stringent as those met by the best-performing similar source, and MACT standards for existing sources must be at least as stringent as those met by the average of the best-performing 12 percent of similar sources. For categories of smaller (so-called area) stationary sources, the EPA is authorized to set standards that are less restrictive than the MACT standard, based either on "generally achievable control technology" (GACT) or on the use of specified management practices. For pollutants with an identifiable health threshold, the EPA is authorized to forgo the technology-based approach and to instead set health-based standards that ensure an ample margin of safety, essentially the original mandate of the 1970 CAA. Finally, the EPA is obligated to issue a report on the residual risk to health that remained after the adoption of the technology-based standards, which it did in 2004. If no new legislation recommended by that report is enacted by 2012, the EPA must issue such additional regulations as are necessary to "protect public health with an ample margin of safety" in general and, specifically for carcinogens, must ensure that lifetime exposure risks are less than one in one million. The EPA has made substantial progress in establishing MACT and GACT standards, but has just begun the task of developing risk- or health-based approaches. The 1990 amendments to the CAA also placed an increased emphasis on toxic air pollutants emitted by mobile sources, and in 2007 the EPA issued a Mobile Source Air Toxics rule designed to lower benzene concentrations in gasoline and restrict automotive emissions of benzene and a number of other toxic substances.

Sudden and Accidental Release of Chemicals and Chemical Accidents. Although the first congressional response to the concern generated by the deadly industrial accident in Bhopal, India, was the Emergency Planning and Community Right to Know Act of 1986, the chemical safety provisions of that law are focused almost solely on chemical accident mitigation and not on accident prevention. A much greater potential for a direct focus on accident prevention can be found in the 1990 amendments to the Clean Air Act.

As amended in 1990, Section 112 of the Clean Air Act directs the EPA to develop regulations regarding the prevention and detection of accidental chemical releases and to publish a list of at least one hundred chemical substances (with associated threshold quantities) to be covered by the regulations. The regulations must include requirements for the development of risk-management plans (RMPs) by facilities using any of the regulated substances in amounts above the relevant threshold. These RMPs must include a hazard assessment, an accident prevention program, and an emergency release program. The EPA promulgated regulations setting forth requirements for the RMPs in 1996. This RMP rule, which is estimated to affect some 66,000 facilities, requires a hazard assessment (involving an offsite consequence analysis including worst-case risk scenarios

and compilation of a five-year accident history), a prevention program to address the hazards identified, and an emergency response program.

In addition, Section 112(r) of the revised Clean Air Act imposes a general duty on all owners and operators of stationary sources, regardless of the particular identity or quantity of the chemicals used on site, to

- identify hazards that may result from [accidental chemical] releases using appropriate hazard assessment techniques,
- design and maintain a safe facility taking such steps as are necessary to prevent releases, and
- minimize the consequences of accidental releases which do occur.

Thus, firms are now under a general duty to anticipate, prevent, and mitigate accidental releases.

The amended Clean Air Act also directs each state to establish programs to provide small businesses with technical assistance in addressing chemical safety. These programs could provide information on alternative technologies, process changes, products, and methods of operation that help reduce emissions to air. However, the CAA provides no federal funding for these state programs, and they have not been uniformly implemented. Where they are established, linkage with state offices of technical assistance, especially those that provide guidance on pollution prevention, could be particularly beneficial.

Finally, the 1990 CAA amendments established an independent Chemical Safety and Hazard Investigation Board (CSHIB). The board is to investigate the causes of accidents, conduct research on prevention, and make recommendations for preventive approaches, much as the Air Transportation Safety Board does with regard to airplane safety.

Authority to Regulate Greenhouse Gases. As global climate change progresses and its detrimental impacts become clearer, it seems likely that reductions of global greenhouse gases (GHGs) will be necessary to stabilize the earth's climate system. The transportation sector remains among the largest emitters of GHGs, contributing roughly 27 percent of such emissions in the United States and 21 percent worldwide.

During the Bill Clinton administration, the EPA determined that the Clean Air Act authorizes the regulation of carbon dioxide (CO_2) emissions. In a landmark decision—*Massachusetts, et al. v. Environmental Protection Agency* (2007)—the US Supreme Court agreed. The EPA's initial regulatory response was to issue a reporting rule for GHG emissions. Acting under its information-gathering authority in Clean Air Act Sections 114 (for stationary sources) and 208 (for mobile sources), the agency has imposed reporting requirements on a variety of stationary sources (including oil and gas facilities, refineries, chemical plants, pulp and paper plants, iron and steel plants, and industrial landfills) and on car and truck manufacturers.

In 2009, the EPA made a formal finding that greenhouse gas emissions from motor vehicles pose an endangerment to public health and welfare. Thus, in 2010 the EPA and the National Highway Traffic Safety Administration issued a joint rule specifying greenhouse gas emission standards and Corporate Average Fuel Economy (CAFE)—that is, fuel efficiency—standards for new passenger cars, light-duty trucks, and medium-duty passenger vehicles for model years 2012 through 2016. Under these standards, passenger cars and light-duty trucks would be required to meet an estimated combined average emissions level of 250 grams per mile of CO_2 by the 2016 model year. The EPA's "endangerment" finding also triggered a requirement that GHG emissions from "major emitting facilities" (stationary sources) be subject to emission regulation under the CAA (Section 165[a][4]), and in 2010 the EPA promulgated the "Greenhouse Gas Tailoring Rule," which takes a phased approach and limits the types of existing and new facilities that must reduce GHG emissions.

The fate of GHG regulations under the CAA is not yet settled, however. Scores of lawsuits have been filed challenging various aspects of these regulations, the EPA has delayed implementation of many of their provisions, and Congress has threatened to amend the CAA to prevent the EPA from regulating GHGs. The ultimate resolution, then, is likely to depend as much on political considerations as on legal ones.

[*See also* Environmental Protection Agency.]

Acknowledgment
This article borrows heavily from Chapter Six, "The Clean Air Act and the Regulation of Stationary Sources," in *Environmental Law, Policy, and Economics: Reclaiming the Environmental Agenda*, by Nicholas Askounes Ashford and Charles C. Caldart, published by the MIT Press in 2008, and is reproduced here with permission.

BIBLIOGRAPHY
Ashford, Nicholas A., and Charles C. Caldart. *Environmental Law, Policy, and Economics: Reclaiming the Environmental Agenda.* (Cambridge, Mass., 2008).
Ashford, Nicholas A., and Ralph P. Hall. *Technology, Globalization, and Sustainable Development: Transforming the Industrial State* (New Haven, Conn., 2011).

Nicholas A. Ashford and Charles C. Caldart

CLIMATE CHANGE

The international community has long been concerned about the state of the global climate, and about the possibly harmful impact of human activity on the delicate balance between people and their environment. The first Earth Day celebration, which launched the environmental movement in the United States, was held in April 1970, and as early as 1972 a 113-nation conference in Sweden launched the United Nation's Environmental Program and its associated agency, the United Nations Environment Programme (UNEP). Though cooperation between nation-states is never easy to orchestrate, policy makers in the vast majority of such states have come to recognize the degree to which climate is the ultimate public good—the one dimension of the human condition in which the tragedy of the commons invites collective, rather than individual, regulation (on this, see Coates, 2011, pp. 107–108). That recognition manifested itself first in the signing, in 1988, of the Montreal Protocol on Substances That Deplete the Ozone Layer, and in the 1992 UN Earth Summit in Rio de Janeiro, at which 171 countries signed the UN Framework Convention on Climate Change. It was evident too in the negotiation of the Kyoto Protocol in 1997, which was activated in 2005 and committed industrial countries to the reduction of their level of emission of greenhouse gases (primarily carbon dioxide) to 5 percent below 1990 levels by 2012. It was evident again in the ongoing collective efforts to create a post-Kyoto international climate accord as 2012 approached: an effort initially explored at meetings in Bali in 2007, then (unsuccessfully) at Copenhagen in December 2009, and again at Cancún in December 2010. The meetings in Bali, Copenhagen, and Cancún showed just how difficult such international agreements on climate regulation are to negotiate. The meetings also demonstrated the centrality of the United States to those negotiations—and how reluctant a participant the pre-Obama White House regularly proved to be.

It is not that public policy in the United States has been long set against the regulation of the environment for the purposes of its conservation. On the contrary, the United States has an impressive record of public policy in this area, stretching back at least to the creation of a system of national parks by Theodore Roosevelt in the first decades of the twentieth century, or even back to 1872 and the creation of Yellowstone Park, and more recently involving the signing of at least 150 multilateral environmental agreements, most of them since 1970. The United States passed pathbreaking legislation on air pollution in 1970 (further amended in 1977 and 1990). It created the Environmental Protection Agency (EPA) in 1970 to police that legislation; and it passed joint legislation on air quality with Canada in 1991 and with Mexico in 1992. Indeed, the United States was the first industrialized nation to ratify the United Nations Framework Convention on Climate Change, drawn up at the 1992 Rio Earth Summit, and was an early signatory to the Montreal Protocol on ozone depletion.

Nor is it the case that the United States can safely leave global environmental protection simply to others. It cannot, in part at least, because the United States is itself a major global polluter. The US economy is no longer the main emitter of carbon dioxide (CO_2)—that dubious honor has now been transferred to the Chinese—but with just 4 percent of the world's population, the United States continues to consume 25 percent of the world's total output of oil and continues to generate 20.6 percent of all greenhouse gases, more than any other individual country or even the EU taken as a whole (China produces 14.8 percent and the EU 14 percent), and it does this as a result of lifestyle, not population size. The US per-capita emission of CO_2, at 19.8 metric tons, is double that of other leading industrial economies, including the United Kingdom, Germany, and Japan. When the World Economic Forum produced its 2008 Environmental Performance Index, ranking 149 countries on twenty-five indicators tracked across six established policy categories—environmental health, air pollution, water resources, biodiversity and habitat, productive natural resources, and climate change—it is perhaps therefore not surprising that the index placed the United States thirty-ninth in that list: down eleven places from its 2006 ranking, and well behind the majority of industrialized countries, particularly those in Western Europe, from Scandinavia to Spain.

Given that record of public policy and private practices, it might be legitimate to expect the United States to be a major driver of international agreements on climate change, regardless of the party in power in the White House. But recently that has not been the case. The main driver of such agreements of late—the pacesetter in these matters—has been the European Union. The US Congress even declined to ratify the Kyoto Protocol, the predominant view among Washington lawmakers after 1997 being that signing the protocol would seriously disadvantage American-based firms in competition with Third World producers free of Kyoto-type rules. Recent administrations—both those of George W. Bush (after 2007) and of Barack Obama—have shown more willingness to participate in any post-Kyoto settlement; but their enthusiasm for strict regulation remains restricted both by these persisting concerns about the impact on US competitiveness, and by the presence within the US Congress of a significant minority of lawmakers unconvinced of the case for climate change and its regulation. The contemporary debate within the industrialized and industrializing world is largely one of how to combat harmful climate change. The equivalent debate within the United States remains much more one of whether harmful climate change is even under way.

Debating the Science: The Science "for" Climate Change. The overwhelming consensus in the relevant academic communities would appear to be that climate change is happening, that the change which is occurring is undesirable, and that the main driver of that change is human economic activity. The reports establishing all three of those propositions are extensive and plentiful.

They include the Stern Report, prepared for the UK government by a former chief economist at the World Bank and issued in October 2006. Sir Nicholas Stern estimated that, while effective policies to curb carbon emissions would likely incur a one-off 1 percent reduction in global gross domestic product (GDP), without such policies in place it seemed wise to anticipate anything between a 5 percent and a 20 percent reduction in global GDP by 2050 because of climate-induced economic disruption. The Stern Report warned of floods from rising sea levels possibly displacing 100 million people, melting glaciers causing water shortages for one person in every six, and droughts that could create tens or even millions of "climate refugees." That "the benefits of strong early action considerably outweigh the costs," was Sir Nicholas Stern's own summation of the findings he had gathered (*Financial Times,* 2006).

Likewise, the United Kingdom's chief scientist, Sir David Anthony King, warned the UK government in May 2006 that, without action now, the world faced the possibility of a three-degree Celsius rise in average temperatures, with devastating consequences for crop production and coastal flooding: this in response to the EU decision to commit to policies designed to set a two-degree Celsius cap on global temperatures. The warning by King was based on a report from the United Kingdom's Hadley Centre, "Avoiding Dangerous Climate Change." The Hadley

scenarios were built on estimates of carbon dioxide levels of 550 parts per million (ppm) in the atmosphere. The United Kingdom's were on 450 ppm of CO_2. If Hadley is right, half the world's nature reserves and coastal wetlands face imminent destruction. Similarly stark findings are to be found in other official UK reports, including one from the chief adviser to the UK Department of Agriculture, Fisheries, and the Environment warning of a four-degree Celsius temperature rise, and from the UK government's own climate committee ("Building a Low Carbon Economy"). In May 2010 the UN added its own voice to this chorus of doom, its twentieth annual development report warning that "climate change could derail years of progress in improving the lives of the world's poor," with grain shortages alone, in a worst-case scenario, exposing a further 25 million children to the danger of starvation by 2050.

But by far the most potent of the reports warning of impending irretrievable damage has come from the Intergovernmental Panel on Climate Change (IPCC), particularly from its fourth report issued February–April 2007. Drafted by 174 lead authors and 222 contributing authors, and drawing on the work of more than 2,500 of the world's leading climate scientists, its findings were extremely stark: that, if CO_2 levels continue to rise as predicted, global temperatures would be three degrees Celsius higher by century's end—with serious food and water shortages for millions of people, lower crop yields, the spread of tropical diseases, the loss of at least one-third of animal species, extensive flooding, greater risk of wildfires, the loss of one-third of coastal wetlands, increasing storms and hurricanes, and the mass migration of people away from the worst affected regions. The IPCC report was quite clear. Without a sharp reduction in carbon dioxide emissions, climate change in the twenty-first century will spark events that have not happened in 650,000 years.

Not all such reports come from overseas agencies. US-based research often comes to similar conclusions. These, for example, were the ten key findings reported to the president in 2009 by the US Global Change Research Program:

1. Global warming is unequivocal and primarily human-induced.
2. Climate changes are underway in the United States and are projected to grow.
3. Widespread climate-related impacts are occurring now and are expected to increase.
4. Climate change will stress water resources.
5. Crop and livestock production will be increasingly challenged.
6. Coastal areas are at increasing risk from sea-level rise and storm surge.
7. Risks to human health will increase.
8. Climate change will interact with many social and environmental stresses.
9. Thresholds will be crossed, leading to large changes in climate and ecosystems.
10. Future climate change and its impacts depend on choices made today.

There is one other set of reports of relevance here: those that record the impact of human economic activity on the natural environment as a whole, that is, that attempt to measure and chart the overall human ecological footprint. Such reports generally generate two conclusions. One is that the human ecological footprint is deepening—the impact of human economic activity is becoming more threatening to ecological survival as a whole. The other is that the ecological footprint made by the United States continues to be significantly larger than that made by other major industrial economies. In 2005, a World Bank report backed by 1,360 scientists from ninety-five countries warned that as much as two-thirds of the world's resources are currently being depleted by human activity. That activity "is putting such a strain on the natural functions of the Earth," the report concluded, "that the ability of the planet's ecosystems to sustain future development can no longer be taken for granted." The study concluded with what it called a "stark warning" that basic ecosystems are being irretrievably damaged (Radford, 2005), a warning echoed in the later World Wildlife Fund (WWF) report, "The Living Planet." The WWF calculated that we are currently using 30 percent more resources each year than the Earth is capable of replenishing. Without restraint, their report concluded, at this rate we will need *two* planets by 2030.

Debating the Science: The Science "Against." Not all scientists see it that way however, particularly scientists based in the United States. That is not entirely surprising, given the areas of uncertainty remaining in climate science on such key issues as the range of likely temperature rises, the timescales involved, the differential impact of climate change on different regions of the global system, and the difficulty of predicting with any precision patterns of extreme weather or the counter-warming effects of cloud formation. It is also not entirely surprising given the number of industries that stand to lose (oil, coal, nuclear power) or gain (solar, wind, green technologies) from any public policy shift geared to the correction of humanly induced climate change. Scientists need funding, and industries need scientists. The relationship between the two is inevitably research-shaping, to some indeterminate degree.

There are politicians and scientists who remain convinced that climate change is entirely a hoax—one foisted on the American people by those keen to regulate industry for other reasons, or by scientists with a vested interest in the funding of research related to climate change. Senator James Inhofe of Oklahoma is one such politician; Richard Lindzen of the Massachusetts Institute of Technology is one such scientist. There are also scientists who remain convinced that the changes in climate are too minor to warrant the fuss; or that climate change has its own long-term natural rhythms that public policy would do well not to disturb; or that there is nothing particularly sacrosanct about existing climate patterns—that change, if and when it comes, might be all to the good. And for every one or two scientists who are convinced that human-induced climate change is under way, it is possible to find at least one scientist who is far more skeptical, and convinced that many of the major reports are overpoliticized, particularly those produced by the United Nation's Intergovernmental Panel on Climate Change. There was even a sustained controversy in 2008–2009 about the supposed fixing of results by climate change researchers at the University of East Anglia in the United Kingdom—the so-called Climategate controversy—which was only put to rest after a high-powered Select Committee of the UK House of Commons investigated the claims and found them unwarranted. That the researchers were so challenged is a mark of the intensity of disagreement between the pro- and anti-climate change camps both in the United States and in Europe (on this, see Sheppard, 2011). The fact that a Select Committee of UK members of Parliament spent time resolving the challenge is a mark of how crucial the scientific evidence is to the policy-making process in the area of climate change.

The general case against the development of public policy in this area was well put by Philip Booth in his foreword to Robert Bradley Jr.'s *Climate Alarmism Reconsidered*. Booth greeted Bradley's conclusion, that "the major threat to energy sustainability is *statism*, not depletion, pollution, reliability, or anthropogenic climate change" (Bradley, 2003, p. 15), as

a welcome reassessment of much of the accepted wisdom regarding climate change. [Bradley's] wide-ranging analysis documents a number of weaknesses in the argument that we are facing serious adverse impacts from climate change. His argument gains weight when the general context of energy sustainability is considered, where the "alarmists" on fossil-fuel reliance have been wrong time and again. There is no longer an energy depletion problem: the evidence is clear that, as long as governments do not interfere, new sources of energy can be found to meet demand at constant costs or better—not just for the next generation or two but for centuries ahead. Pollution is declining dramatically in the USA and in the EU. Energy is used with greater and greater efficiency, as the energy required per unit of output increases. And market forces have effectively addressed energy reliability/security challenges as compared with government activism. This is not to say that energy problems will not arise, but unhampered market processes inspire solutions to real problems. (Bradley, 2003, pp. 10–11)

Debating the Politics. The depth of resistance to public policy on climate change within parts of the US scientific community, and among the conservative elements now dominant within the Republican Party, helps explain the different pattern of politics associated with the issue of climate change in the United States when compared to that within the European Union.

The United Kingdom is a case in point. As late as 2005, its then–New Labour government set itself a target of reducing 1990 CO2 emission levels by 20 percent by 2010—a tougher target indeed than the 12.5 percent by 2012 initially agreed upon at Kyoto. Too tough in the event—the United Kingdom will probably miss its goal by as much as one-third—but it is still the target for which UK policy continues to strive: policy that stretches from taxation on high-emission cars through building codes for new energy-efficient buildings to the increasing use of renewable energy sources (wind, solar, biofuels, even nuclear) and the building of eco-towns. Speaking at the Delhi Sustainable Development Summit in January 2007, the then–UK energy secretary proposed a "3D" global energy revolution to which his government was committed: demand management (more efficient cars, houses, appliances), de-carbonization (using alternative fuels and capturing and storing carbon emissions), and decentralization of power sources. The United Kingdom currently possesses a cabinet-level Department for Energy and Climate Change, and a target for renewable energy use—15 percent of all energy to come from renewable sources by 2020—and such climate change targets are accepted in the United Kingdom not simply by its former center-left government but also by its current center-right government and by major business confederations based there.

The United Kingdom's climate change policies are fully in line with policies elsewhere in the European Union, where the collective response has been to establish targets for the reduction of greenhouse gas emissions over time, and to adopt policies in pursuit of those targets. The current EU target is a 20 percent reduction in 1990 levels of CO2 emissions by 2020, with the promise to increase that to 30 percent if other countries follow suit. It is a target more criticized in Europe from the Left (as too modest) than from the Right (as unnecessary); indeed, the center-right German government led by Angela Merkel was the major architect and advocate of that target when it was first formulated in 2007. Among the policies adopted in its pursuit are legally binding commitments to have 10 percent of vehicle fuel be composed of biofuels by 2020, the creation of twelve clean coal power plants by 2015 (to show the potential of carbon capture and sequestration), and new legislation on more energy-efficient consumer products, particularly cars. The European Commission in 2007 proposed Europe-wide rules requiring an 18 percent cut in CO2 emission by European car makers by 2012. It had initially wanted a 25 percent cut, and eventually settled for 2015 as its deadline. The Merkel government also pressed in 2007 for an EU commitment to another 20 percent target by 2020: this one for the percentage of European fuel use coming from renewable energy sources. The European Union remains committed from its March 2007 summit to its so-called 20/20/20 goals: a 20 percent cut in emissions and 20 percent of primary energy to be delivered by renewable fuel sources by 2020.

Moving toward Regulation: The US Case. Moves toward equivalent targets and policies were slower to begin in the United States. As late as the 2004 presidential election, the question of environmental protection surfaced only once in the three televised debates in that election cycle. By 2008 however, things had changed. They had changed partly because fuel prices had spiked—to four dollars a gallon at the height of the inflationary surge in the summer of 2007. They had changed partly because by then a series of state governors, most visibly Arnold Schwarzenegger in California, had signed groundbreaking environmental standards into state law. They had changed partly because of the global impact of former vice president Al Gore's campaign on climate change. And, they had changed partly

because, late in the day, the George W. Bush administration had taken up the cause in its own distinctive, if limited, manner. Bush insiders (including apparently the vice president's office) continued to downplay the science and the danger of climate change to the very end of the presidency, but the president at least had come around to the view (a) that the United States was dangerously overdependent on oil, and (b) that in a post-Kyoto world, the United States should be prepared to negotiate and implement limits on the emission of carbon dioxide into the atmosphere so long as other polluting nations (particularly in the developing world) were prepared to do the same. The new Bush doctrine on excessive use of fossil fuels was first delivered in the president's 2007 State of the Union Address, when he spoke of the United States as being "addicted to oil," especially foreign oil, and set new goals for fuel efficiency and the development of alternatives. The new American willingness to negotiate carbon emission standards in good faith was first delivered to an astonished world in a string of top level meetings in 2007: at the G8 meeting in Berlin in June, at the UN talks on climate change in New York in October, and at the follow-up talks in Bali in December.

Against that background, and with the Democratic Party in control of both houses of the US Congress from 2006, new climate change legislation then began to emerge, especially the December 2007 House energy bill that raised the minimum fuel efficiency standard for passenger vehicles (the first increase since 1975) and doubled the use of corn-based ethanol; also of note was the later Senate Climate Security Act (CSA), sponsored by Senators Joseph Lieberman and John Warner, which created permits ("allowances") which industries and companies contributing to pollution and global warming would be required to purchase, creating funds (as much as $800 million over ten years, it was claimed) that could be directed to the development of clean fuel technologies. The CSA proposed a cap-and-trade system to be administered by the Environmental Protection Agency, and intended a declining cap on US emissions of all types of greenhouse gas: down 4 percent by 2012 and 71 percent by 2050. Not to be left out, the US Supreme Court, in *Massachusetts v. Environmental Protection Agency*, ruled in April 2007 that the EPA must revisit its unwillingness to define carbon dioxide as an air pollutant. In addition, each leading candidate in the 2008 presidential campaign had a fully developed "green" dimension to his or her domestic policy package. Barack Obama entered the presidency supported by a "green team" of experienced environmental regulators and committed to a full set of carbon caps and targets, fuel efficiency measures, renewable electricity standards, and funding for a clean energy future. His opponent, John McCain, had been similarly innovative. In a sharp break with the previous administration, even the Republican flag-bearer in 2008 had committed any McCain-led administration to the establishment of a mandatory limit on the emission of greenhouses gases.

The Obama administration moved quickly in 2009 to reverse many of its predecessor's more intransigent rulings (including the Bush-era EPA's refusal to comply with the Supreme Court ruling in *Massachusetts v. Environmental Protection Agency*). The Obama EPA did comply, ruling in December 2009 that carbon dioxide and five other greenhouse gases were indeed a danger to public health and welfare, and thus required regulation. New rules followed that were applicable to large facilities emitting over 25,000 tons of C02 a year—some 70 percent of total US carbon dioxide emissions. From July 2011, under powers already legislated in the Clean Air Act, major emitters of greenhouse gases (coal-powered power plants particularly) need permits to operate if they release more than 100,000 tons of such gases annually, or if they increase those emissions by as much as 75,000 tons. The EPA also let it be known, in July 2010, that it would be particularly responsive, when drafting its environmental regulations and when issuing its permits, to the health concerns of low-income and minority populations. Very early in his administration, President Obama also directed the EPA to do something else that the Bush-led EPA had declined to do: reconsider granting California and other states waivers to set their own higher standards of car emissions of greenhouse gases. He

instructed the Department of Transportation to draw up new interim mileage standards to ensure that, from 2012, new vehicles reach the thirty-five-mile-per-gallon level set by Congress by 2020; those standards, when they came, required new cars and light trucks to average 35.5 miles to the gallon by 2016.

In addition, the Obama administration used its stimulus package and its first budget to give a huge boost to clean energy products and fuel efficient technologies: $59 billion of the $787 billion American Recovery and Reinvestment Act (ARRA), and $150 billion (over ten years) of the $3.35 trillion budget proposal for fiscal year 2010 were so earmarked. Both included tax credits to stimulate private sector research and development in new clean energy technologies, and funds to directly sustain clean energy research in the Energy Department's national laboratories. "By a stroke of his pen, President Obama made a federal agency the world's largest venture capitalist" and "essentially saved the renewable-energy industry in the United States" (Green, 2009, p. 84). This is how the president described his administration's early moves when addressing the UN Summit on Climate Change in September 2009:

> I am proud to say that the United States has done more to promote clean energy and reduce carbon pollution in the last eight months than at any other time in our history. We're making our government's largest ever investment in renewable energy—an investment aimed at doubling the generating capacity from wind and other renewable resources in three years. Across America, entrepreneurs are constructing wind turbines and solar panels and batteries for hybrid cars with the help of loan guarantees and tax credits—projects that are creating new jobs and new industries. We're investing billions to cut energy waste in our homes, buildings, and appliances—helping American families save money on energy bills in the process. We've proposed the very first national policy aimed at both increasing fuel economy and reducing greenhouse gas pollution for all new cars and trucks—a standard that will also save consumers money and our nation oil. We're moving forward with our nation's

first offshore wind energy projects. We're investing billions to capture carbon pollution so that we can clean up our coal plants. Just this week, we announced that for the first time ever, we'll begin tracking how much greenhouse gas pollution is being emitted throughout the country. Later this week, I will work with my colleagues at the G20 to phase out fossil fuel subsidies so that we can better address our climate challenge. And already, we know that the recent drop in overall US emissions is due in part to steps that promote greater efficiency and greater use of renewable energy.

The Pushback against Climate Change Regulation.
But then, both domestically and abroad, the push for agreed climate change policy stalled. It stalled internationally in December 2009, when the UN conference convened in Copenhagen failed to produce a post-Kyoto climate change treaty. Representatives from 193 nations had gathered in Copenhagen amid high expectations and in the full glare of world publicity; but in spite of Obama's complete reversal of the Bush administration's lack of enthusiasm for internationally negotiated targets on carbon emissions—the president actually swept in on the last day of the conference, trying (and failing) to trigger a general agreement—all that could be salvaged from two weeks of bitter wrangling was a nonbinding, three-page "accord" signed by the United States and four major developing nations (China, Brazil, India, and South Africa), who agreed to jointly monitor progress toward nationally specified emission reductions. Negotiations a year later in Cancún were equally unsuccessful, so that together in Copenhagen and Cancún—the fifteenth and sixteenth rounds of UN-sponsored global climate talks, respectively—"the failure . . . to agree on binding emission-reduction targets mark[ed] a significant scaling back from the 1997 Kyoto Protocol, the first and only international agreement to set legally binding targets" (Green-Weiskel, 2011).

The pursuit of climate change legislation stalled domestically early in 2010 when Republican Senators threatened to filibuster a renewed version of the Warner-Lieberman cap-and-trade legislation

mentioned above. The Democratically controlled House of Representatives did narrowly pass a cap-and-trade bill, the Waxman-Markey bill, in 2009, but in 2010 in the Senate, the Republican capacity to bring business there to a complete halt persuaded the Senate majority leader Harry Reid to abandon the American Power Act, sponsored by Senators John Kerry and Joseph Lieberman, even though that bill had already retreated from a general cap-and-trade stance, proposing instead a weaker set of emission standards for specific sectors of the economy. The prospect of any further progress even in the House was then derailed by the 2010 midterm capture of the House by a revitalized and ultraconservative Republican Party majority, replete with a new generation of climate-change-denying legislators. When Henry Waxman, by then simply the ranking minority member of the House Energy and Commerce Committee, introduced in April 2011 an amendment in favor of climate change regulation, not a single one of the thirty-one Republican members of the Committee was willing to vote for it. The amendment simply read: "Congress accepts the scientific findings of the Environmental Protection Agency that climate change is occurring, is caused by human activities, and poses significant risks for public health and welfare." In the light of that vote, it is hard to avoid Robert Benson's very pessimistic conclusion that "you've got to go back to the Scopes Monkey trial of 1925 for a precedent to the anti-science mania that is currently sweeping the GOP."

So while the European Union continues its drive to limit the emission of greenhouse gases (the EU climate change commissioner spent 2011 seeking renewable energy targets for 2030), the equivalent drive in the United States has, for the moment at least, stalled. This is in spite of three major developments in the field of climate change that might, in less contentious political times, have triggered major public intervention. The first was the BP oil spill into the Gulf of Mexico in 2010 (to date, America's worst man-made ecological disaster); the second was the threatened meltdown of the Fukushima Daiichi nuclear facility in Japan in the aftermath of the severe earthquake and resulting tsunami in March 2011; and the third was the clear and widely reported evidence that 2010 tied 2005 as the hottest year on record, and the 2000s are the warmest decade in modern times. But not even 660,000 barrels of oil released into the coastal waters of the United States, or the threat of a second Chernobyl, or the persistence of dramatic weather changes, could by themselves break the resistance of Republican lawmakers to the administration's attempts to create clean and safe sources of renewable energy.

Instead of new legislation or regulations to help slow down the rate of climate change, and under heavy Republican pressure that included the threat of defunding, the Obama Administration's EPA began in 2011 to retreat, delaying new intended rules on smog until July 2011 and on boiler regulation until April 2012, and putting in doubt its continued commitment to the curbing of greenhouse gas emissions. When the historians come to evaluate the Obama presidency, they will presumably note that three of his initial quartet of policy commitments—those directed to easing the recession, reforming the health care system, and tightening the regulation of Wall Street—all met some degree of success early in his term. But they will no doubt note too that the Obama presidency did not enjoy similar success in relation to its fourth commitment: to "clean energy and global warming legislation to create jobs, reduce oil use, and cut pollution" (Weiss, 2010). On that fourth commitment, the Obama record was one of small victories and large setbacks. On energy policy there was no major piece of legislation to match the ARRA, the Affordable Care Act (ACA), and the Dodd–Frank Financial Reform and Consumer Protection Act. "For a variety of reasons, large scale energy reform didn't happen. The recession, the fact that the administration's priorities put it behind a lot of other controversial items like healthcare and financial services reform" (Kirchgaessner, 2011), and the resistance of a revitalized Republican Party left the promise of 2008 still unfulfilled as America returned to the polls four years later.

[*See also* Clean Air Act; *and* Environmental Protection Agency.]

BIBLIOGRAPHY

Benson, Robert. "Three-Quarters of Senate GOP Doesn't Believe in Science—When Did the Republicans Go Completely Off the Deep End?" *Alternet.Org.* (2011), http://www.alternet.org/story/150340.

Bradley, Robert L. *Climate Alarmism Reconsidered.* (London, 2003).

Broder, John M., and Sheryl Gay Stolberg. "EPA Delays Tougher Rules on Emissions." *New York Times,* 9 December 2010.

Coates, David. *Making the Progressive Case: Towards a Stronger US Economy.* (New York, 2011).

Elliott, Larry, and Mark Tran. "UN Report Warns of Threat to Human Progress from Climate Change." *Guardian,* 4 November 2010.

Financial Times. "Editorial: Stern Review Offers Counsel of Hope," 31 October 2006.

Green, Harvey. "Better Luck This Time." *Atlantic,* July–August 2009.

Green-Weiskel, Lucia. "Climate Clash in Cancún." *Nation,* 3 January 2011.

Harvey, Fiona. "Connie Hedegaard Seeks Renewable Energy Targets for 2030." *Guardian,* 3 May 2011.

Harvey, Fiona. "Lingering Clouds." *Financial Times,* 30 August 2010.

Harvey, Fiona. "Yo, Kyoto." *Financial Times,* 2 October 2007.

Keohane, Robert O., and David G. Victor. "The Regime Complex for Climate Change." *Perspectives on Politics* 9, no. 1 (2011): 7–23.

Kirkgaessner, Stephanie. "Obama's Green Credentials Tarnished." *Financial Times,* 19 April 2011.

Layzer, Judith A. "Cold Front: How the Recession Stalled Obama's Clean Energy Policy." In *Reaching for a New Deal: Ambitious Governance, Economic Meltdown, and Polarized Politics in Obama's First Two Years,* edited by Theda Skocpol and Lawrence R. Jacobs, pp. 240–270. (Washington, D.C., 2010).

Naik, Gautum. "Last Year Tied 2005 for Hottest on Record." *Wall Street Journal,* 13 January 2011.

Radford, Tim. "Two-Thirds of the World's Resources 'Used Up.'" *Guardian,* 30 March 2005.

Revkin, Andrew, and James Kanter. "No Slowdown of Global Warming, Agency Says." *New York Times,* 9 December 2009.

Sheppard, Kate. "The Hackers and the Hockey Stick." *Mother Jones,* May–June 2011.

United States Global Change Research Program. "The National Climate Assessment." (2009), http://www.globalchange.gov/what-we-do/assessment.

Weiss, Daniel J. "Anatomy of a Senate Climate Bill Death." Center for American Progress. (2010), http://www.

americanprogress.org/issues/2010/10/senate_climate_bill.html.

David Coates

CLINTON, BILL

(b. 1946). It is probably the case that all presidents hope to "go down in history"; indeed, the goal of leaving behind a substantial "legacy" is generally regarded as an important influence on the behavior, in their last years in office, of that minority of modern presidents who have been lucky enough to serve for two full terms. William Jefferson Clinton need have no concern about whether or not his name will be recalled in the years to come. As only the second president to be impeached (although, in common with the first, Andrew Johnson, he was acquitted by the Senate), Clinton's name will often be the right answer in television quizzes and college tests. It is probable that the reasons for Clinton's impeachment will be sufficiently puzzling for future generations that—again as in the case of Andrew Johnson—a good essay question for students yet unborn will be to clarify and explain those reasons. It is reasonable to suppose that Clinton would prefer his presidency to be remembered for more positive reasons, however, than his relationship with a White House intern and the perjury he possibly committed in attempting to conceal it. What, then, was the significance of the Clinton presidency beyond trivia and scandal?

It is no disrespect to Clinton (and probably would not be seen by him as disrespectful) to say that a very important aspect of his presidency was political. Prior to Clinton's election in 1992, it had become fashionable to suggest that the Republicans had a "lock" on the presidency. The Republicans' successful use of "wedge" social issues, and the reputation that Democrats had acquired as being too far from the mainstream, suggested that the Republicans could extend their twelve-year grip on the White House. Clinton's success in defeating an incumbent president, George Bush, who had led the United States and it allies to victory in the Gulf War the year

before the election, was startling. A slight downturn in the economy helped Clinton, though ironically, the great boom of the 1990s had started before Bush left office. Yet Clinton's election strategy was regarded as "writing the playbook" on how center-left candidates could defeat their opponents, who had enjoyed success in so many democracies in the 1980s. The Clinton campaign's use of polls and focus groups, combined with adroit maneuvering on issues to steal the thunder of the Right (as in Clinton's promise to "end welfare as we know it"), provided a model that was closely observed and replicated by politicians in other countries, such as Britain's leader of the Labour Party and prime minister, Tony Blair. In the 1996 campaign, Clinton consolidated his position by developing the use of the tactic of "triangulation," positioning himself ideologically between the Republicans and the Congressional Democrats.

Even Clinton's political setbacks seemed to provide him with an opportunity to display political genius. The attempt to impeach and remove him from office, after sordid and humiliating revelations about Clinton's sex life came to light, ended up costing the Republicans politically more than it cost him. The Democrats' loss of control of Congress in the 1994 elections seemed at first a repudiation of Clinton as well as of the Democratic Party, a loss that would strip away his ability to influence events. Yet in the six years that followed, Clinton displayed consummate political skill in handling the problems presented by "divided government." Although the Republican majority had arrived in Washington armed with a long list of legislation they intended to adopt in their "Contract with America," on only one issue, welfare reform, were the Republicans able to confront Clinton with the choice between displeasing his party by signing a bill into law or displeasing majority public opinion; even on this issue, Clinton, as noted above, had signaled his willingness to change existing policies. In general, however, Clinton succeeded in blocking most of the Contract with America, and indeed often obliged the congressional Republican majorities to accept liberal, even if small-scale, incremental policy initiatives that were popular with the public, for fear that they would otherwise lose popularity and votes. Except in the year following the Republican capture of Congress, Clinton's legislative success score, as compiled by the influential *Congressional Quarterly* (the percentage of votes in Congress on which the president takes a position and wins), was unusually high. In this, Clinton was aided by rhetorical skills that allowed him to take his case to the nation ("go public") with great success.

Very few presidents have matched Clinton in his ability to enthuse voters both in person and via television. Clinton was also aided in his legislative maneuvering by continuous opinion polling and assiduous use of focus groups. Every State of the Union address, for example, was tested in advance on focus groups, like a new product being test-marketed. All presidents have been concerned about public opinion, of course. However, presidents have generally distinguished the quest for office from governing. Clinton, however, made this concern so central in policy making that his presidency has been described as a "permanent campaign."

Clinton may reasonably be regarded as a political genius. His policy legacy is more in doubt partly because divided government, which prevailed for most of his administration, always obscures who is to be blamed or praised for a policy development. Clinton's supporters gave him great credit for the economic boom that lasted throughout his presidency, in particular because of his insistence in his 1993 budget (with no Republican support) on reducing federal deficits (which disappeared completely by the end of the century), rather than increasing spending on domestic programs. Yet the boom had begun under Bush, and others (notably the chairman of the Federal Reserve Board, Alan Greenspan) were also eager to claim credit, which in any case might have been due to long-term influences such as technological change. Other significant policy initiatives such as welfare reform, ending deficits in the federal budget, and promoting economic globalization through securing Congressional approval of the North American Free Trade Agreement (NAFT) and the creation of the World Trade Organization (WTO) were the result of collaboration with

Republicans as well as Democrats. Indeed, on trade issues, Clinton received more support from Republicans than from his own party. Only a few American presidents, such as Roosevelt during the New Deal era of the 1930s or Johnson in the Great Society period of the 1960s, have had the privilege of leading a Congress controlled by their own party while making major policy changes. Clinton was not such a president. Yet those who lived through his presidency are likely to remember it as an era characterized not only by a strong economy, but also by major reductions (probably for reasons outside the president's control) in social problems, such as crime and teenage pregnancy, that had so concerned Americans for decades before Clinton entered the White House. In many respects, his presidency seemed a golden age compared with what followed; Clinton left behind budget surpluses rather than deficits, economic growth rather than recession. In foreign policy Clinton could claim that his (and Tony Blair's) 1998 bombing campaign in Iraq had ended Saddam Hussein's ability to manufacture weapons of mass destruction, without the costly war that Bush waged.

Clinton's popularity remained high at home and abroad after he left the presidency. For example, he received a rapturous reception at the annual conference of the UK Labour Party in 2006. He attempted to continue the "third way" quest for new and more effective approaches to problems such as global poverty, AIDS, and childhood obesity. Perhaps reflecting his particular popularity among African Americans, Clinton located his foundation in the Harlem neighborhood of Manhattan, long associated with African Americans.

Clinton's political impact after he left office is characteristically complicated. His time in the White House brought his wife, Hillary Rodham Clinton, into the national spotlight. A talented, impressive politician in her own right, Clinton was elected to the United States Senate, representing New York, in 2000; she was reelected with a large majority in 2006. By all accounts, she was an effective senator, taking time to learn how to operate effectively in the institution before taking on a more visible role. However, she will be remembered in large part as the first woman to be a viable candidate for the nomination of a US major political party. She lost the nomination to Barack Obama after a long and sometimes bitter struggle that divided the "Clintonistas," as the admirers of the former president were known. Bill Clinton campaigned hard, if not always effectively, for his wife, perhaps grateful to repay her to some degree for all that she had done to support him throughout his career. President Obama made Hillary Clinton his Secretary of State, a role she filled with determination, skill, and loyalty to Obama.

Although the struggle for the nomination pitted Obama against Clinton's wife, Obama's campaign can be seen as a reprise of Clinton's own strategies. Both campaigns emphasized upbeat, breezy, and rather vague themes that could appeal to unattached and younger voters. Clinton was the man from Hope (the town in Arkansas where he grew up) and the campaign played incessantly Fleetwood Mac's song "Don't Stop Thinking About Tomorrow." Obama had his theme of "Change You Can Believe In." Clinton, as noted above, had to deal with a Republican House of Representatives after 1994. Obama faced the same problem after the 2010 midterm elections. Yet it seemed unlikely that Obama would take Clinton as his model. Much of the early years of Obama's administration had been influenced, often for the worse, by a determination to do things differently to Clinton. Clinton had shown a steely willingness to call the bluff of the Congressional Republicans when they forced a shutdown of the federal government; Obama showed no such resolve in the fight with the Republicans over raising the debt ceiling in 2011. Obama derided to his staff Clinton's use of small, symbolic issues such as school uniforms, a strategy that had done much to give Clinton a bond with much of the public. Thus, while Clinton may have been something of a model for Obama in campaigning, once in office Obama was influenced more by a determination not to be like Clinton, than by a desire to emulate him. In both respects, however, Clinton cast a long shadow.

[See also NAFTA; and Presidency: Governing.]

BIBLIOGRAPHY
Campbell, Colin. The US Presidency in Crisis: A Comparative Perspective. (New York, 1998).
Campbell, Colin, and Bert A. Rockman, eds. The Clinton Legacy. (New York, 1999).
Maraniss, David. First in His Class: A Biography of Bill Clinton. (New York, 1995).
Skowronek, Stephen. The Politics Presidents Make: Leadership from John Adams to George Bush. (Cambridge, Mass., 1993).

Graham K. Wilson

COLD WAR

The term "Cold War" is used to describe the protracted conflict between the Soviet and Western worlds that, while falling short of "hot" war, nonetheless involved a comprehensive military, political, and ideological rivalry from the end of World War II through the early 1990s. The phrase entered the modern political vocabulary after World War II, as a description, popularized by the columnist Walter Lippmann, of the conflict between the Soviet and Western blocs. It was initially used to describe a historical period—the Cold War—that began with the breakdown of the wartime alliance in 1946–1947. Some writers saw an end to the Cold War in the 1950s, after the death of Stalin; others saw its demise in the 1970s with détente. The term "Second Cold War" was widely used to refer to the period after the collapse of détente in the late 1970s.

"Cold War" was, however, also used in a more analytic sense, not to refer to a particular phase of East-West rivalry, but rather to denote the very fact of the rivalry between the communist and capitalist systems itself, one that involved competition and confrontation but not all-out "hot" war. In this sense, the Cold War began not in 1945 but in 1917, with the accession of the Bolsheviks to power and their proclamation of a worldwide challenge to capitalism, and continued until the late 1980s. The communist revolutionary challenge, and the Western response to it, were checked by a variety of factors—the fragmentation of the world into separate societies and states, the power of nationalism, the fear of nuclear weapons, the limits on the power of each side—but it nevertheless endured for more than seven decades. Whatever the periodicity or meaning adopted, most writers agreed that the Cold War, in the sense of a global rivalry between two competing and roughly equal blocs, ended after Gorbachev's accession to power in 1985, with the collapse of Soviet strength and the demise of the Soviet ideological challenge to the West.

The development of East-West rivalry was marked by a set of crises, in both Europe and the Third World, and by an enduring competition in arms, especially nuclear weapons. Central as the arms race was to the Cold War, however, the latter encompassed a broader strategic and political contest. After the end of World War II, Europe was soon divided by the "Iron Curtain" of communist border controls into the Soviet and Western blocs, which led to the Berlin blockade of 1948–1949 and to the formation, in 1949 and 1955, respectively, of the North Atlantic Treaty Organization (NATO) and the Warsaw Treaty Organization. Further crises over Berlin followed in 1959 and 1961, and attempts by states under Soviet control to assert their independence were crushed by force—in the German Democratic Republic (East Germany) in 1953, Hungary in 1956, Czechoslovakia in 1968, and Poland in 1981. Yugoslavia, Albania, and Romania were able to evade Soviet domination but remained ruled by Communist parties until they, like the Soviet allies, were overwhelmed by the democratic revolutions of the late 1980s.

The rivalry of East and West was also fought out in the Third World. After the Azerbaijan crisis of March 1946 (a dispute over Soviet reluctance to pull forces out of Iran that marked the first major dispute of the Cold War), there followed the Chinese Revolution of 1949, the Korean War of 1950–1953, the Suez Crisis of 1956, the Cuban Revolution of 1959 and, in its aftermath, the missile crisis of 1962, and the US war in Vietnam of 1965–1973. In the latter part of the 1970s, the collapse of détente and the onset of the so-called Second Cold War was in part the result of US concern over the rise to power of pro-Soviet revolutionary regimes in a dozen Third World states—notably South Vietnam, Afghanistan, Ethiopia, Mozambique, Angola, and Nicaragua.

The Second Cold War came after the lessening of tensions that was evident in the 1970s with the Strategic Arms Limitation Talks (SALT I) of 1972 and the Helsinki Accords of thirty-three European nations, the United States, and Canada on European security in 1975. This amelioration had ended by the late 1970s and appeared dead when Soviet forces occupied Afghanistan in December 1979. The period after 1980 initially saw an intensification of East-West confrontation, and a concomitant increased emphasis in the West on the arms race, with the deployment of intermediate-range cruise missiles in Europe and the Strategic Defense Initiative, and an encouragement by the United States of anticommunist guerrillas in Cambodia, Afghanistan, Angola, and Nicaragua.

In the Second Cold War the Soviet leadership appeared to have retreated behind the defensive positions of the earlier Cold War, but from 1985 onward, under Gorbachev's leadership, the Soviet Union made wide-ranging concessions that brought the earlier confrontation, and the Cold War as a whole, to an end. In 1988 the Soviet Union declared an end to military support for the Eastern European communist parties that it had kept in power for forty years, and in 1989 it withdrew its forces from Afghanistan. In the same period it signed wide-ranging agreements on arms control and arms reduction with the United States and abandoned its global ideological rivalry with the capitalist West. In November 1989 the fall of the Berlin Wall signaled the end of communist power in Eastern Europe. In December 1990 the Cold War was officially declared over at the Paris Organization for Security and Cooperative in Europe (OSCE) conference. In December 1991 the Soviet Union was dissolved.

Writing on the Cold War has revolved around two broad questions. The first has been that of historical responsibility, that is, of which side caused the cold wars of the late 1940s and late 1970s. Whereas earlier writings tended to polarize around a Western view that the Soviet Union was responsible and a Soviet view that the "imperialist" countries were to blame, a later school of "revisionist" Western writing stressed forms of US responsibility. In the 1980s a "postrevisionist" school emerged, locating responsibility in both the Soviet and US blocs, while, with the advent of glasnost in the Soviet Union after 1988, Soviet writers began for the first time to concede that the policies of Stalin and Brezhnev had contributed to exacerbating East-West tensions.

The second broad set of questions concern what the Cold War was and what the sources of the conflict were. Here four broad schools of explanation have emerged. The first, a traditional application of power politics, sees it as a continuation under new ideological guises of the kind of great power rivalry for empire, influence, and domination seen in earlier epochs. A second school stresses the cognitive and subjective factors, notably the degree of misperception involved in the failure of the two sides to maintain their wartime alliance and resolve subsequent disputes, and to extricate themselves from the reinforcing anxieties of the arms race. A third school views the Cold War as only apparently a rivalry between two blocs, and a means by which the dominant states within each bloc controlled and disciplined their own populations and clients, and by which those who stood to benefit from increased arms production and political anxiety promoted a mythical rivalry. Fourth, there are those who see the Cold War not primarily as a conflict between states or as a merely military rivalry, but more as a conflict between two distinct, competing social and political systems, each committed to prevailing over the other at the global level.

Despite its rapid and, in Europe at least, relatively bloodless end, the Cold War continues to exert a hold on world affairs. In Russia there is pervasive nostalgia for world stature, exacerbated by the economic collapse that has followed the end of Soviet centralization. In China a communist party still rules, amid growing social and political pressures. Although communism as an alternative ideology is discredited, many of the tensions, both economic and social, that produced it remain acute, as the breakdown of state control in a number of areas formerly ruled by communism has produced new civil and ethnic conflicts.

[*See also* Communism; National Security Apparatus, American; *and* Russia–United States Relations.]

BIBLIOGRAPHY
Gaddis, John Lewis. *We Now Know: Rethinking Cold War History.* (Oxford, 1997).
Garthoff, Raymond. *Détente and Confrontation.* 2d ed. (Washington, D.C., 1994).
Halliday, Fred. *The Making of the Second Cold War.* 2d ed. (London, 1986).

Fred Halliday

COMMUNISM

The term "communism" originated among revolutionary societies in 1830s Paris, where it combined two meanings. The first designated a political movement, of or on behalf of the working class, dedicated to the overthrow of emerging capitalist society. The second sense referred to the kind of society that such a movement wished to inaugurate. In the first sense, communism was seen as an extreme and violent form of socialism, more fundamental in its approach to the abolition of private property than that advocated by socialists, who favored a relatively peaceful political stance and gradual social reform. This contrast finds its classic expression in the 1848 *Communist Manifesto* of Karl Marx and Friedrich Engels.

In the latter half of the nineteenth century, however, the terms "socialism" and "communism" tended to be used virtually synonymously to designate the working-class movement as a whole. Most Marxist parties, including the two largest (in Germany and Austria), used the title "Social Democratic." The Russian Revolution of 1917, the adoption by the Bolsheviks of the term "Communist" to describe their party, and, above all, the creation of the Third (Communist) International in 1921 gave the term a much more specific meaning. The aftermath of the Bolshevik revolution and the founding of the Third International involved the emergence of separate Communist parties sharply opposed to socialist or social democratic parties, and advocating policies reminiscent of early European communists. These new Communist parties were organized along Leninist "democratic centralist" lines, where power resided—formally as well as in practice—in the hands of a small Politburo. It was Lenin, too, in *The State and Revolution* (1917), who formalized the difference between communism and socialism as a project of social reorganization. Marx had already drawn a distinction between an immediately postrevolutionary society, in which reward would be granted according to merit, and a "higher stage of communist society," which would put into practice the famous slogan "from each according to his abilities, to each according to his needs." Lenin called the first of these societies "socialist" and the second "communist." The parties of the Third International, although Communist in name, were thus overseeing political systems which were, as yet, only socialist in their practices.

With the consolidation of Stalinism in the Soviet Union, a third sense of "communism" emerged, in which it was defined as a worldwide network of doctrinaire parties organized along authoritarian lines, propagating a worldview known as "dialectical materialism" and more or less completely subordinate to the political line laid down by the Communist Party of the Soviet Union (CPSU) through the operations of the Communist International. After the death of Stalin, this Communist movement entered a historical decline, the first serious symptom of which was the split between the Soviet and Chinese Communist parties in 1960, accompanied by the increasing unpopularity of and difficulties faced by the Communist regimes in Eastern and Central Europe. In Western Europe, the long postwar boom and the lack of progress made by the Communist parties there led, in the 1970s, to the emergence of a trend known as "Euro-communism." The Euro-communists, led by the Italian Communist Party, adopted a much more conciliatory attitude toward parliamentary institutions and advocated what seemed to be reforms rather than revolution—to such an extent that the post-1917 distinction between socialism and communism as opposed political tendencies seemed to be disappearing.

The 1989 revolutions in Eastern and Central Europe and the collapse of communism in the Soviet Union marked the end of this decline of European communism and its reassimilation into the general socialist movement. The anti-Stalinist communist movement represented by Leon Trotsky and his followers continues to exist, but is numerically small and politically insignificant. The vanguard parties constructed along the Leninist model still operate in such places as China, Cuba, and South Africa, but their future seems far from assured. The two central ideas of Stalinist communism—the Leninist vanguard party and an economy planned by a centralized bureaucracy—have gone into terminal decline. However, communism in the very different sense of a more principled version of socialism, an aspiration to a society in which resources are divided primarily according to human need, is likely to have a future every bit as long as its past.

[*See also* Capitalism; Class Politics; *and* Marxism.]

BIBLIOGRAPHY
McLellan, David. *Marxism after Marx.* 2d ed. (New York, 1998).
Westoby, Adam. *The Evolution of Communism.* (New York, 1990).

David McLellan

COMMUNITY ACTION

"Community action," a term that originated during the War on Poverty in the 1960s, continues to animate our understanding of interventions undertaken to tackle social ills. The historical context for what we term "community action" emerged as part of President Lyndon Johnson's Great Society, which included federal initiatives in civil rights, education, health, the environment, and poverty. Specifically, community action was associated with the Johnson Administration's Economic Opportunity Act—an initiative that was anchored in President John F. Kennedy's planned efforts to alleviate poverty. Johnson announced the War on Poverty in his first State of the Union Address in 1964. It represented a political compromise; because increasing employment through a jobs program was not politically feasible, an emphasis on services to the impoverished emerged as the key focus. The War on Poverty had two main objectives: increasing opportunity, and increasing the capacity of the poor to seize those opportunities. There were many components to the Economic Opportunity Act, including Head Start, Job Corps, the work-study program for university students, and Community Action Programs (CAP), among others.

Community Action Agencies (CAAs) were established as the local mechanisms for executing these federal goals of increasing opportunities for the poor. Federal guidelines required that 40 percent of funds to CAAs be used for services tailored to local needs (i.e., in the areas of health, education, housing, or economic development), and that 50 percent be spent on implementing national programs (i.e., Head Start, Upward Bound, legal aid, or community health centers). Within those parameters, though, the CAAs themselves had substantial influence over how funds were allocated. CAAs were conceptualized as instruments for creating institutional reform and community empowerment, in the hope that they would build reform-minded coalitions with other local organizations and institutions to improve resident well-being, and to enable community members themselves to take an active role in shaping priorities and executing plans.

The CAP initiative was the most controversial component of the War on Poverty and is often associated with its principle of "maximum feasible participation"—a concept grounded in strong democracy, and based on the idea that the poor themselves should define their priorities and participate in altering their community contexts so as to improve living conditions and resident outcomes. The idea for and implementation of CAAs, community action, and maximum feasible participation was largely patterned after the Ford Foundation's work in the 1950s and early 1960s. Maximum feasible participation was an approach that drew from two Ford Foundation demonstration projects (Mobilization for Youth and the Gray Areas program) and from the President's Council on Juvenile Delinquency (also influenced by Ford), but differed distinctly from most efforts of that era to address poverty. Departing from established norms, the War on Poverty programs,

rather than seeking experts such as economists or social workers to develop solutions via policy or programs, emphasized participation. This reflected several assumptions: understanding environment and context as causes of social problems; addressing social problems in relatively small, geographically defined units such as neighborhoods or small towns; viewing social isolation of the poor as a primary cause in perpetuating poverty; and emphasizing institutions as the locus for stimulating both individual and social change.

Another key assumption that spurred community action programs was that local governing structures—perceived as fragmented and myopic, and incapable of responding to a sprawling metropolitan urban form—were in need of reform. The War on Poverty programs, however, did not necessarily lead to coordinated neighborhood services or more streamlined bureaucracies; instead, the programs met with resistance and generated local political tensions. Initially Congress clarified that local citizen participation was a primary goal, and thus legislated that one-third of CAA board seats go to local residents, one-third to public officials, and one-third to private sector leaders. In a few short years, however, local pressure from mayors resulted in Congress reducing citizen influence by giving more control of the programs to local governments.

Although participatory approaches are connected with deeply held democratic, egalitarian values in American society, they conflict with the reality of established power at local, state, and federal levels. While participation is rhetorically appealing, in practice the principle of democracy is radical. For example, programs that encouraged participation tended to engender a heightened awareness of the ways in which the power structure was invested in deeply entrenched patterns of poverty and racism. Viewed historically, many of these tensions cannot be separated from the political activities of that era: for example, the Civil Rights Movement and its expansion from the South to Northern cities cannot be disentangled from community action efforts. As pressure for social change expanded to other constituencies, society at large was confronted with a tension between moving toward social justice and maintaining social order. Importantly, the War on Poverty programs, particularly in urban areas, excluded any examination of attendant structural causes, such as persistent racism, or job loss through deindustrialization; instead, the analysis that poverty itself was the problem assigned responsibility to the poor themselves, rather than to deeper systemic ills.

A key outcome of community action efforts from the War on Poverty was a solidifying of the concept of participation—particularly the participation of those most impacted in the definition, diagnosis, and resolution of social problems. Community action programs have been credited with the emergence of many new organizations and local initiatives such as tenant organizations, legal services, public-interest law firms, single-issue coalitions, and other rights-oriented groups; the emergence of African Americans in key bureaucratic roles in municipalities throughout the United States; and a precedent for public hearings and methods of formalizing community voice in public decision-making. Some have argued that the Great Society programs produced the most dramatic decline in poverty of the twentieth century (Califano, 1999). In contrast, critics charge that the War on Poverty was ineffective, facilitating dependency and creating a large urban underclass (Murray, 1984).

In subsequent eras, market forces have been employed as tools to reform governing structures, and privatization of service delivery has been viewed as the most efficient approach to urban problems. Nevertheless, CAPs continue to exist in many communities and provide services to those in need, although the focus of CAPs today is on individual and family service rather than collective action. The concept of community action, however, continues beyond the formal CAP structure, and is expressed through divergent approaches to addressing poverty at a community scale such as community development, comprehensive community initiatives, and community organizing. Importantly, the lasting legacy of community action is reflected in these diverse approaches, as today these and other models of community intervention all embrace participation as a central and abiding tenet.

[*See also* Great Society; Johnson, Lyndon Baines; *and* Poverty, Scale and Nature of.]

BIBLIOGRAPHY

Berry, Jeffrey M., Kent E. Portney, and Ken Thomson. *The Rebirth of Urban Democracy.* (Washington, D.C., 1993).

Califano, Joseph A. *Governing America: An Insider's Report from the White House and the Cabinet.* (New York, 1981).

Califano, Joseph A. "What Was Really Great about the Great Society." *Washington Monthly* 31 (1999): 13–20.

Daview, Gareth. *From Opportunity to Entitlement: The Transformation and Decline of Great Society Liberalism.* (Lawrence, Kans., 1996).

Halpern, Robert. *Rebuilding the Inner City: A History of Neighborhood Initiatives to Address Poverty in the United States.* (New York, 1995).

Katz, Michael B. *The Undeserving Poor: From the War on Poverty to the War on Welfare.* (New York, 1989).

Moynihan, Daniel P. *Maximum Feasible Misunderstanding: Community Action in the War on Poverty.* (New York, 1969.)

Murray, Charles A. *Losing Ground: American Social Policy, 1950–1980.* (New York, 1984).

O'Connor, Alice. "Community Action, Urban Reform, and the Fight against Poverty: The Ford Foundation's Gray Areas Program." *Journal of Urban History* 22 (1996): 586–625.

O'Connor, Alice. *Poverty Knowledge: Social Science, Social Policy, and the Poor in Twentieth-Century U.S. History.* (Princeton, N.J., 2001).

Saegert, Susan. "Building Civic Capacity in Urban Neighborhoods: An Empirically Grounded Anatomy." *Journal of Urban Affairs* 28 (2006): 275–294.

Paul W. Speer

COMMUNITY REINVESTMENT ACT

The Community Reinvestment Act (CRA) of 1977 was part of the US government's response to bank redlining, which is the identification of an area, usually a neighborhood or zip code area, where no financial services are provided; it is a form of place-based financial and social exclusion. Redlining practices were widespread during the Great Depression of the 1930s, partly because they were promoted by the Home Owners Loan Corporation (HOLC), a state agency designed to provide emergency relief to homeowners by refinancing or purchasing defaulted mortgages. The Federal Housing Administration (FHA), established in 1934 under the Franklin Delano Roosevelt administration to insure private mortgage loans, also adopted redlining policies. While FHA insurance was meant as a public backup to ensure the provision of mortgage loans, the FHA, like the HOLC, redlined areas in which private lenders were also less likely to grant mortgages, or would only grant mortgages under less advantageous conditions, such as higher down payments and higher interest rates. In the mid- and late 1960s the FHA was forced to change its policies and make mortgage insurance available in formerly redlined areas.

Origins. In the wake of the social rights movement in general and the community reinvestment movement in particular, redlining returned to the political and research agendas in the late 1960s and 1970s. Community-based organizations and others claimed that lenders were redlining large parts of inner cities. Redlining became heavily associated with racial discrimination. In 1968, discrimination in housing and mortgage lending became prohibited through the Fair Housing Act. In addition, the federal government responded by implementing the Home Mortgage Disclosure Act (HMDA) in 1975, and the CRA in 1977. The original CRA was passed by the US Congress and signed into law by President Jimmy Carter on 12 October 1977.

While the HMDA opened up mortgage data to more scrutiny, by requiring lenders to report granted loans by census tract, the CRA requires lenders to lend in all neighborhoods from which they receive deposits. The CRA thus forces banks and savings and loans institutions to meet the credit needs of the communities that they serve, including low- and moderate-income areas. The CRA, however, also emphasizes that lending activities should be undertaken in a safe and sound manner, and does not require banks to make high-risk loans at a loss. Federal regulators then examine and rate banks on their CRA performance and can impose financial

and legal sanctions to force banks to improve their lending behavior. One of the ironies of the CRA is that CRA evaluations put lenders in four different categories ranging from outstanding to substantial noncompliance in meeting community credit needs—similar to how redlining maps categorized neighborhoods in four types, ranging from hot spots in demand to places of little or no value.

The regulators can block bank mergers and acquisitions as well as branch openings and closings if a bank scores low on its CRA performance. One matter of complication is that the regulatory work is split among several entities—the Federal Reserve Board, the Office of the Comptroller of the Currency, the Federal Deposit Insurance Corporation, and the now-defunct Office of Thrift Supervision—each of which focuses on a different type of bank or savings and loans institution. The problem is that some regulating bodies are not as strict in their CRA compliance research and ratings as others, thereby providing banks with an easy way out of their community obligations. Moreover, some banks are able to switch regulators in order to be subject to an easier CRA process.

In sum: the Fair Housing Act prohibited redlining, the HMDA enabled exposure of redlining practices, and the CRA created an affirmative obligation for banks to meet community lending needs. Despite these acts and the related move of the FHA's focus to the inner city, research from the 1970s, 1980s, and early 1990s clearly shows the existence of redlining policies, mostly in inner-city areas. In many cases the research is not taken very seriously by lenders, and it is only when researchers are able to use HMDA data that redlining research is taken more seriously and is followed by lenders' financial commitments to inner-city mortgage lending. In many cases, community organizations have cooperated with academic and nonacademic researchers, and sometimes also local newspapers, to demonstrate redlining. The story of Atlanta, described superbly in an essay by Larry Keating and colleagues (1992), illustrates the potential impact that can be achieved through cooperation between community activism (the Atlanta Community Reinvestment Coalition), academic research (a 1988 MA thesis in city planning by Stan Fitterman), and media investigations and reporting (the 1988 Pulitzer Prize–winning articles by Bill Dedman). Not only in Atlanta, but across the country, HMDA and CRA helped many local community reinvestment organizations secure dozens or even hundreds of millions in community financing for home mortgage loans in non-white neighborhoods.

Changes. The Atlanta story and other experiences also led to the 1989 changes to the CRA that required regulators to publicly disclose bank performance evaluations and ratings. This, of course, increased the strength and influence of the CRA, because poor CRA ratings would now also harm the public image of the bank. In addition, it enables community organizations to request that regulators withhold approval of merges and acquisitions. More changes followed in 1995 when subjective, mostly process-oriented, factors in the bank evaluation process were replaced by more objective, performance-based, measures that also forced banks to disclose their activity in the market for small business and community development lending. The 1995 changes also allowed the regulators to make better distinctions between different types of lenders, implementing more extensive tests for large banks than for small banks.

Today, few would deny the evidence of redlining in the 1930s and 1970s–1980s, but more recent evidence of redlining is scarce. Lenders of course claim to have discontinued all redlining activities, but it could also be argued that the CRA has simply forced lenders to hide redlining better. Mortgage lenders have found ways to bypass suspicion of redlining by granting mortgage loans in the "good" part of a census tract and withholding it from the "bad" part (cherry-picking behavior). The tactics employed include: discouraging applications from certain areas; not including certain neighborhoods or parts of neighborhoods in their "catchment area" (relevant for CRA regulations); or charging higher fees in "bad" neighborhoods (known as "yellowlining" or "redlining light"). Redlining can also be "masked" by other factors, such as a requirement of private mortgage insurance for borrowers in low-income or non-white neighborhoods. Ross and Tootell (2004) have dem-

onstrated that applicants in low-income neighborhoods are more often forced to take out private mortgage insurance (PMI) in order to have a mortgage loan application approved; redlining exists when loan applicants do not apply for PMI. The PMI requirement increases the costs of a loan and works against the goals of the CRA.

Subprime Crisis. Although some changes have increased the effectiveness of the CRA, other changes have made it easier for banks to get away with lending behavior that is not CRA compliant. More importantly, the updates to the CRA were unable to keep pace with changes in the structure of the US mortgage market. In the aftermath of the subprime mortgage and foreclosure crisis that started in 2007, the CRA was heavily criticized for enabling subprime lending, and therefore playing a key role in the global financial crisis. It is argued that the CRA forced lenders to grant loans to low-income borrowers, who would not have been given a loan under "normal" conditions. However, there are at least five reasons why the CRA should not be blamed for promoting unsound lending:

1. The CRA did not call for risky loans to subprime borrowers, but rather for sound loans to minority and low-income borrowers. The CRA does not force banks to grant loans to anyone; it demands merely that access to credit is provided on equal terms.
2. The CRA only applies to the important lenders of the time the CRA was written: bank lenders and savings and loans institutions. As of 2011, more than two-thirds of all mortgage loans, and 77 to 84 percent of all subprime loans, were provided by so-called non-bank lenders, that is, lenders that fall outside the jurisdiction of the CRA and thus need not be CRA compliant.
3. Lenders did not sell risky loans because CRA forced them to do so; most subprime loans were sold to prime borrowers whose credit scores should have classified them for prime loans, implying that lenders systematically overcharged borrowers. Only 6 percent of all subprime loans were sold to low- and moderate-income borrowers by CRA-compliant lenders.

4. Most subprime loans were not used to buy a home, but were refinance loans, implying that subprime loans did not enable homeownership for minority or low-income borrowers. Most of these refinance loans were designed to appear cheaper than the original loan, but were in fact more expensive for the borrowers and more profitable for the mortgage broker and the lender.

5. Many organizations associated with the community reinvestment movement were among the first to mobilize against subprime lending. ACORN, the organization that arguably gets most of the blame, was actually one of the organizations warning against subprime loans. Moreover, organizations like ACORN actively lobbied for stringent regulation of non-bank lenders and subprime lending.

The CRA was designed to promote fair lending to all borrowers. Subprime lending, on the other hand, was designed by lenders to make money by selling risky and overpriced loans, often to people who did not need these loans or could have applied for cheaper ones. CRA loans and subprime loans are simply two different things. There are many factors that have played a significant part in unleashing the subprime mortgage crisis, but if the CRA is to be blamed for anything, it is only for not having been allowed to keep up with changes in the mortgage market.

Future Challenges. While the CRA was somewhat successful in diminishing the inequalities caused by redlining, new inequalities have emerged, characterized by less favorable loan terms and lack of adequate consumer protection from predatory practices. The rise of subprime lending has little to do with the mantra of emerging homeownership markets. With the foreclosure crisis that started in 2007, subprime lending has been decreasing fast, and non-bank lenders have been going out of business in large numbers. But not only subprime lending has decreased; it has generally become more difficult to get any type of mortgage loan. There is anecdotal evidence that some lenders have started charging higher fees for borrowers in certain zip codes—meaning, essentially, that lenders have implemented another set of yellowlining (redlining light) policies.

One of the future challenges is to adapt the CRA to cover all mortgage lenders: the rules need to be applied to both banks and non-bank lenders. Shopping around for a regulator should also be made harder, and the interpretation and implementation of CRA rules should be standardized across regulators. In addition, the CRA should also cover bank affiliates, which now, under certain conditions, can be excluded from CRA compliance. Equally important, unsound and overpriced loans—that is, the subset of subprime loans known as predatory loans, which undermine financial security—should be subject to CRA oversight and review, and result in lower CRA ratings for those approving such loans. In sum, the CRA should be updated to account for the recent structural changes in the mortgage market, and strengthened to promote sound, inclusionary lending.

[*See also* Financial Crisis of 2008; Housing in the United States; Mortgage-Backed Securities; *and* Urban Sprawl.]

BIBLIOGRAPHY

Aalbers, Manuel B. *Place, Exclusion, and Mortgage Markets.* (Oxford, 2011).

Aalbers, Manuel B. "Why the Community Reinvestment Act Cannot be Blamed for the Subprime Crisis." *City & Community* 8 (2009): 346–350.

Ashton, Philip. "CRA's 'Blind Spots': Community Reinvestment and Concentrated Subprime Lending in Detroit." *Journal of Urban Affairs* 32 (2010): 579–608.

Barr, Michael S. "Credit Where It Counts: The Community Reinvestment Act and Its Critics." *New York University Law Review* 80 (2005): 513–652.

Chakrabarti, Prabal, David Erickson, Ren S. Essen, et al., eds. *Revisiting the CRA: Perspectives on the Future of the Community Reinvestment Act.* (Boston, 2009).

Dedman, Bill. "The Color of Money." *Atlanta Journal Constitution,* 1–5 May 1988.

Hernandez, Jesus. "Redlining Revisited: Mortgage Lending Patterns in Sacramento 1930–2004." In *Subprime Cities: The Political Economy of Mortgage Markets,* edited by Manuel B. Aalbers. Oxford, 2012.

Immergluck, Dan. *Credit to the Community: Community Reinvestment and Fair Lending Policy in the United States.* (Armonk, N.Y., 2004).

Keating, Larry E., Lynn M. Brazen, and Stan F. Fitterman. "Reluctant Response to Community Pressure in Atlanta." In *From Redlining to Reinvestment: Community Response to Urban Disinvestment*, edited by Gregory D. Squires, pp. 170–193. Philadelphia, 1992.

Ross, Stephen L., and Geoffrey M. B. Tootell. "Redlining, the Community Reinvestment Act, and Private Mortgage Insurance." *Journal of Urban Economics* 55 (2004): 278–297.

Ross, Stephen L., and John Yinger. *The Color of Credit: Mortgage Discrimination, Research Methodology, and Fair-Lending Enforcement.* (Cambridge, Mass., 2002).

Squires, Gregory D., ed. *From Redlining to Reinvestment: Community Response to Urban Disinvestment.* (Philadelphia, 1992).

Squires, Gregory D., ed. *Why the Poor Pay More: How to Stop Predatory Lending.* (Westport, Conn., 2004).

Manuel B. Aalbers

CONGRESS, US

Congress is the legislative branch of the federal government of the United States. It is a bicameral legislature, consisting of a 435-member House of Representatives and a 100-member Senate. Congress acts within a federal system that also includes the executive and judicial branches. Congress makes the laws which direct the work of the agencies and departments of the executive branch. The judicial branch serves as the final arbiter of the meaning and constitutionality of the laws passed by Congress and the actions of the President and other executive branch officials.

Overview. Congress has retained its fundamental powers throughout American history. It is unlike legislatures in most countries, which play a decidedly subordinate role to the chief executive. Congress has tremendous leverage in the United States's separated system of government. To put it succinctly, it has three powers as set forth or implied in the Constitution, the nation's supreme governing document since 1788.

1. Congress *authorizes* in law what the executive branch agencies do.

2. Congress passes laws to *fund* what the executive branch does.

3. Congress, when it sees fit, *supervises* (usually referred to as *oversight*) the executive branch.

These authorities come from Article I of the US Constitution, which gives Congress the lawmaking power: "All legislative powers herein granted shall be vested in a Congress of the United States, which shall consist of a Senate and a House" (Article I, Section 1). Most of those legislative powers are specified in Section 8 of Article I. They include the powers to set and collect taxes, provide for the common defense and general welfare, borrow money, regulate commerce, raise and support armies, declare war, and many others. The so-called Necessary and Proper Clause gives Congress elastic powers to do what is needed to implement its specified authorities. Notably, the legislative power includes the power to appropriate money for federal programs, granted in Section 9 of Article I of the Constitution.

Some of the most important amendments to the Constitution, including the one that permitted a federal income tax in 1913 (Amendment XVI), and those that were meant to assure equal rights and voting rights for all Americans (Amendments XIII, XIV, XV, XIX, XXIV, and XXVI) expanded the legislative reach of the Congress, in some cases in very dramatic ways. For example, Amendment XIX giving women the vote (ratified in 1919) states: "The right of citizens of the United States to vote shall not be denied or abridged by the United States or by any State on account of sex. *Congress shall have power to enforce this article by appropriate legislation*" (emphasis added).

The supervisory, or oversight, function of the Congress has always been considered a legitimate extension of Congress's legislative powers, as Congress needs to be able to check to make sure the laws it passes are being faithfully executed by the executive branch agencies. The main ways it does this are to request or require documents and records from executive branch agencies, and to compel the testimony of executive branch officials in open hearings. In addition, Congress needs to be able to conduct oversight in order to inform its lawmaking process.

In sum, Congress has the power to set up agencies and government programs, determine the policies for those agencies, and establish the budgets for their operations.

Congress Shares Powers with the Other Branches. While the term "separated powers" is often used to describe the US system, this is not a complete or precise characterization. In fact it is a system of separate institutions (or branches) sharing powers.

The US Constitution grants each branch of government checks on the other two branches. The idea was *not* to give branches truly separate powers. If one branch of government truly did have separate, unchecked powers, the theory was that the ambitious people in that branch of government would be tempted to run wild with that power, which was just what the framers of the Constitution were trying to avoid. The framers' top priority was to prevent the central government from unnecessarily infringing upon the people's liberties. Pitting the branches against one another was thought to be the best way to accomplish this goal.

In particular, the framers were concerned with controlling the political branches, the executive and legislative. The judicial branch was thought to be the "least dangerous branch," as its pronouncements, to have any effect, would require the acquiescence of the political branches to fund (the Congress) and enforce (the president). It would have neither the "purse" nor the "sword," in the manner of speaking and writing in the late eighteenth century, so was in no position to run away with its authority. Whether the judicial branch has actually been constrained in the long course of American history is a matter of considerable debate.

As noted, in general Congress has retained its extensive, constitutionally granted powers—in fact, Congress has often interpreted its powers liberally. Of particular note, in the twentieth century Congress passed laws that expanded the reach of the federal government in the area of the regulation of commerce. In recent years a more conservative federal judiciary has circumscribed Congress's authority to regulate commerce, but only at the margins. The scope of Congress's power in this area remains controversial.

On the other hand, Congress's authority to declare war (with the president granted the commander-in-chief role) has in many ways become a dead letter—technically still law, but no longer regularly invoked. Since World War II presidents have asserted what amounts to a unilateral authority to commit the nation to war. The justification for that assertion is that the reach of modern weaponry and the complexity of the threats facing the country sometimes require an immediate response. Congressional deliberation may be too slow, and in addition, the sensitivity of some intelligence makes fully public deliberation risky.

Congress is not, however, entirely impotent in the area of war powers. Its control over military budgets and other oversight authorities gives it some ability to check the president's powers.

Congress and the Execution of the Law. The relationship between the two political branches is, however, not just a matter of one branch (the Congress) creating laws and the other branch (the executive) implementing them. There is in fact constant interaction between the branches.

Members of Congress deal with every public policy issue, including highly technical ones; as a result, it is impossible for them to be experts on everything. They are generalists, with some knowledge of a lot of issues but in-depth knowledge of very few. Laws written by the generalists in Congress are frequently, and often intentionally, broad, vague, or ambiguous. There are almost always differing opinions on how to interpret and implement these laws. Furthermore, no law can anticipate all future circumstances and will, as a result, require constant reinterpretation.

Congress recognizes these facts and often leaves a great deal of decision-making authority to the discretion of experts in executive branch agencies. In exercising their discretion, executive branch officials will not necessarily make decisions that correspond with the views of at least some current members of Congress. (This is especially common in times of divided government, when the president and congressional majorities have major ideological differences.) Confrontations between the branches and even, occasionally, major headline news may result.

The branches are, in effect, in a continuous feedback loop. The implementation of Congress's imprecise statutes by the executive branch often attracts the attention of congressional overseers (congressional aides and members), sometimes leading to various methods of persuasion and coercion (public hearings, informal communications, and other types of oversight) meant to get the agencies to reconsider their decisions. Sometimes Congress will react by introducing and passing new legislation with the hope of making its intentions clearer.

Much of this interaction between the branches revolves around funding. Executive branch agencies' funding levels are reconsidered annually, which provides Congress with a regular opportunity to poke around in executive branch business to make sure money is being spent wisely and according to its wishes.

The Nature of Congress. The Constitution gives Congress a second responsibility in addition to its legislative work.

Congress Has Two Roles. Members of Congress have a representative role. This second responsibility is essentially political. Each member of the Congress represents and is accountable to a discrete group of people that make up the member's constituency. The US Congress's essential nature is, to a large degree, determined by the tension between its legislative and representative roles.

The American Founders set up a republic. In a republic, sovereignty is vested in the voting citizenry. But since it is impractical (and, at the time of the founding, many thought unwise) for the voting citizenry literally to govern itself, the republican form of government gives power to the citizens' elected representatives. The elected representatives must face regular and frequent elections in order to retain their positions of authority.

To make the American republic operational, the Constitution set up a popularly elected House of Representatives. All of its members are up for reelection every even-numbered year. Originally members of the Senate, who were given six-year terms, were not directly elected. The Constitution stated that they would be chosen by the state legislatures. This

was changed in 1913 with Amendment XVII, which required the direct election of senators in the states. Every state now elects two senators.

The Constitution stipulates that no bill may become law without passing both the House and Senate in identical form (the so-called "Presentment Clause"), making it impossible for the government to impose anything on its citizens without their directly elected representatives' concurrence.

What was established in the Constitution was a system of accountability, which is the core principle of a republic. Citizens—the sovereign in a republic—have control over the politicians they put in power by exercising the voting franchise. It is true that politicians may do what they want while in office, but if they intend to keep their jobs they are unlikely to stray too far from voters' wishes.

Members of Congress take their representative role very seriously. All serve an ombudsman function, acting as the intermediary when constituents run into problems with government agencies. In addition to that, with respect to their consideration of legislation, most informed observers would say that members of the US Congress tend to act as delegates, doing the bidding of their constituents, rather than as trustees, exercising independent judgment. Members who do exercise independent judgment that is at odds with the views of their constituents work hard to craft an explanation so that citizens will understand why their representative took that stand. In understanding the US Congress, the bottom line is that the representative role affects nearly everything it does in the legislative arena.

A Bicameral Congress. The House of Representatives and the Senate have different types of constituencies, and thus divergent perspectives on the political world, profoundly dissimilar legislative procedures, and some distinct responsibilities. Congress's two-headed quality makes it an institution that is particularly hard—bordering on impossible at times—to coordinate. The decision to go with this kind of arrangement was a tremendously important one.

The composition of the Congress was a matter of great contention at the Constitutional Convention in 1787. Virginians put forward a plan that, among other things, proposed a single-chamber national legislature. Representation in that legislature would be based on population. Less populated states opposed the plan. Spearheaded by the New Jersey delegation, they proposed establishing a legislature that would give each state equal representation regardless of population.

Ultimately, Connecticut's Roger Sherman put forward what came to be called the Great Compromise. It proposed a bicameral arrangement, with one chamber's representation based on population and the other chamber's representation equal for every state. While there were many details that remained to be resolved, it was this plan that was adopted.

The two chambers were set up to give the Congress a wider range of representative characteristics than would have been possible had there been only one chamber. Not only were the members of the chambers answerable to different constituencies, but they would be given different time perspectives as well. The electoral cycle puts every seat of the House up for grabs every two years. The chamber as a whole was expected to be attuned and responsive to the political climate in the nation. The Senate, on the other hand, would only have one-third of its seats contested every two years. Most of the Senate, then, at any given time, did not have to be immediately concerned about the upcoming election. The thinking was that the Senate would take the long view on legislation, balancing the House's tendency to address the people's immediate concerns.

In addition, as noted earlier, originally senators were not going to be directly elected by the people. State legislatures would select them, making them more removed from the public than House members. While the Convention recognized that it was necessary to make Congress directly accountable to the people, the prevailing view was that it would be better not to have the public, which might be prone to rash and ill-considered collective judgments, directly elect the entire Congress. A directly elected House was deemed sufficient to achieve a truly accountable lawmaking body.

The Senate was also given an older age requirement: senators have to be thirty years old, while House members may be as young as twenty-five. It was presumed that with age would come wisdom. Again, the Senate was expected to be less impulsive and more statesmanlike in its decision-making, in order to check a more reactive House.

To reinforce this point, the Senate was made "more equal"; that is, it was given some weighty responsibilities that the House would not have. For a treaty to become the law of the land, the Constitution stipulated that it must meet the Senate's approval. (Two-thirds of the Senate is required to ratify a treaty.) The House was given no role in such deliberations. The Senate, as a result, would be a much bigger player in the realm of foreign affairs. The Senate's approval would also be needed for high-ranking executive branch appointments—now numbering nearly one thousand—made by the president. Again, there is no House role in this process. And nominations to the federal judiciary all the way up to the Supreme Court would also require Senate approval, with the House having no say in the matter.

On the flip side, the House was given the exclusive responsibility to originate revenue or tax bills. But this seeming advantage is really not all that significant, as the Senate must also pass tax bills for them to become law, and senators are not constrained by the Constitution from amending House-passed revenue measures in any way they see fit.

Most House members represent much smaller constituencies than senators—constituencies that are more likely to be homogeneous in terms of partisanship, ideology, economic status, ethnicity, or other factors. Most senators, representing entire states, have much more diverse constituencies in all or most of these respects. (Only seven states are so sparsely populated that they have only one House member. California is the most populated state; it has fifty-three representatives in the House.) When one considers that members of Congress seem to view themselves as delegates of their constituents, the relative homogeneity or heterogeneity of the constituencies leads to very different tendencies and approaches in the two chambers.

There are many House members who come to Washington with a strongly partisan or ideological take on their legislative work and the issues of the day because their districts are either overwhelmingly Democratic or Republican. And there are many who will focus their work primarily on a particular sector of the economy, if most of their constituents' livelihoods are dependent on it. On the other hand, most senators have to balance out the needs of a wider range of economic interests and the views of more people across the political spectrum, and consider the perspectives of people of more races and backgrounds.

Essentially, the chambers have different styles and political contexts due to their respective constituencies. As a rule, the House is a more partisan place, and a body that tends to focus more often on parochial, narrow concerns. The Senate, on the other hand, tends to be less bitterly partisan and is somewhat more apt to approach issues on a holistic basis. One can overstate these differences—for example, it is not uncommon for the Senate to have partisan struggles, and senators will certainly look out for the particular economic interests of their states. But the two chambers do have these distinct tendencies.

The Organization of Congress. The two chambers have parallel organizational units: party leadership and the committees. The party leadership in each chamber is responsible for organizing its legislative business, although the way that happens is quite different in the two bodies. The committees are specialized units meant to handle the essential legislative business of Congress: drafting and analyzing legislative proposals.

The House of Representatives. The presiding officer of the House of Representatives is the Speaker or the Speaker of the House. The Speaker is the only official position in the House listed in the Constitution. The Constitution puts the Speaker second in line for the presidency after the vice president.

The Speaker is chosen from among the majority party in the House. This is not a constitutional requirement; in fact, the Constitution does not contemplate the existence of organized political parties. But, in practice, the two parties each choose a candidate for speaker, with a roll call vote of the whole House membership determining the winner. This roll call is a formality, as the majority party candidate is always the winner.

The speaker, in a real sense, runs the House of Representatives. To aid the Speaker in developing the legislative agenda, the majority party rank and file select from their membership the House majority leader and the majority whip. The majority leader is usually put in charge of developing the party's legislative agenda, which involves constant communication with the committee chairs in the House, who work on specific bills. The majority whip's responsibility is to monitor what the rank and file is willing to support. While the leadership has ways to influence the rank and file, it is impossible to enforce strict party discipline.

The minority party has decidedly less influence in the House of Representatives. It serves essentially as the loyal opposition, typically opposing the majority's agenda but without the ability to pursue an agenda of its own.

The minority party, like the majority, elects leadership positions in a party caucus. The minority leader and the minority whip (both selected by the party's rank and file) do their best to publicize their reasons for opposing the majority on significant legislation. They also endeavor to make it difficult for the majority party to realize success by discouraging support among their rank and file for the majority's agenda.

The House currently has twenty-one committees, as listed below, most of which are authorizing committees charged with considering legislation that sets policy for the programs and agencies of the federal government. Some of the most prominent include the Energy and Commerce Committee, the Ways and Means Committee, and the Armed Services Committee. The House has one committee whose sole responsibility is to write bills to fund the functions of the government: the Appropriations Committee. All the authorizing committees as well as the Appropriations Committee conduct oversight of the executive branch agencies and programs in their jurisdiction. The Committee on Oversight and

Government Reform is notable in that it has oversight jurisdiction over the entire government. Most committees have several subcommittees that further specialize the committees' work.

Committees in the House of Representatives

- Agriculture
- Appropriations
- Armed Services
- Budget
- Education and the Workforce
- Energy and Commerce
- Ethics
- Financial Services
- Foreign Affairs
- Homeland Security
- House Administration
- Intelligence
- Judiciary
- Natural Resources
- Oversight and Government Reform
- Rules
- Science, Space, and Technology
- Small Business
- Transportation and Infrastructure
- Veterans Affairs
- Ways and Means

The majority party determines the number of members serving on each committee, as well as the ratio of party members, the accepted practice being to give each party a portion of seats roughly equal to the percentage of seats they hold in the entire House. Committee sizes range from seventy or more members (Transportation and Infrastructure) to ten (Ethics).

The one committee that always has an overwhelming majority party advantage is the Rules Committee, which for almost four decades has had a nine-to-four edge for the majority party regardless of the chamber ratio. The majority party, Republican or Democrat, has found it essential to have a clear working majority on this committee, as it has the all-important duty of structuring debate and the amendment process on legislation on the House floor. The committee's membership is handpicked by the majority party leadership.

Getting good committee assignments is crucial for members of the House. Committees are where the serious legislative work is done, establishing and funding government programs as well as writing tax law. In order to be influential in the Congress, members must be on one or more committees, giving them influence over government policy. Both parties have steering committees, composed of a geographically diverse group of mostly senior leaders, who make the assignments. It is only in extremely rare cases, usually involving criminal investigations or indictments, that members are denied committee slots.

Members of the House may obtain multiple committee assignments. Some have as many as four. But members who serve on Energy and Commerce, Appropriations, Rules, Ways and Means, or Financial Services are, by both parties' rules, usually limited to one assignment. These committees are referred to as "exclusive" committees, and have wider and more critical policy portfolios.

Most members stick with the committee assignments they have when a new Congress convenes after elections, although some may lobby for exclusive committee slots that open up due to retirement or electoral defeat. New members will always lobby for assignments that enable them to serve their constituents' interests, but they also look for assignments that are intellectually interesting to them or where their professional expertise may be particularly useful. Only in very rare cases are members stripped of committee assignments by leadership.

The position of committee chair in the House is a very important one. Committee chairs are in charge of legislation in their areas of jurisdiction. Every chair is a member of the majority party. Chairs get to hire the majority party expert or professional staff on the committee—anywhere from about twenty-five to about eighty (or even more in the case of Appropriations) people depending on the committee's importance and jurisdiction—and direct their work. The ranking member, or top person from the minority party (who would be chair were his or her party in control), gets the resources to hire about half as many professional staff. The majority needs the additional staff, as it is responsible for setting up public hearings, establishing an agenda, and moving legislation through the committee and to the House floor.

In decades past, the selection of a committee chair was automatic: the senior member in terms of service on the committee from the majority party would get the gavel. But since the 1970s both parties have embraced systems that give a wider range of membership a chance to weigh in during the selection process. Republicans have adopted a process that is heavily controlled by the leadership and the steering committee; Democrats are more likely to leave the decision to the rank and file. Republicans enforce a six-year term limit on serving as chair or ranking member; Democrats have no such limit.

Members of the House may hire staff to assist them with constituent services and legislative work in Washington and in their district offices. Members all represent approximately the same number of constituents—about 700,000—and they get roughly the same budget for setting up offices and hiring assistants. The budget, in total, is about $1.4 million. House members may hire as many as twenty-two staff members, with eighteen serving full-time, to cover Washington, D.C., and district offices.

The Senate. The presiding officer of the Senate, as stipulated in the Constitution, is the vice president of the United States. Rarely, however, does the vice president actually preside—in modern times he has usually only taken on that duty when it looks as though a vote in the Senate may end up tied and the president has an interest in the outcome. In that eventuality, the vice president may cast a vote.

The Constitution requires that the Senate select a president pro tempore, although that has become a largely ceremonial position held by the senior member of the majority party, who has no more interest than the vice president in the tedious work of presiding over endless debates and votes.

The person who really runs the Senate is the majority leader. By custom, the majority leader of the Senate has the right to be recognized first on the floor, which gives him or her the power to set the agenda in the chamber. The majority leader is assisted by the assistant majority leader, sometimes called the majority whip. Both positions are selected by the party's rank and file in the chamber.

Every member of the Senate, including those in the minority party, has a great deal of power due to standing rules, precedents, and customs. This fact enables the minority party to be a player in the establishment of the legislative agenda. (In the House, the minority is in a much weaker position.) As a result, the minority leader often must be brought into negotiations by the majority leader in the development of a legislative agenda.

The Senate currently has twenty committees, as listed below. In many respects the committee structure of the Senate resembles the House's. However, there are few exact matches. (There is no official liaison between the two chambers to enforce corresponding committee and subcommittee arrangements.) Only the Appropriations committees in the two chambers have matching jurisdictions and subcommittees.

Committees in the Senate

- Agriculture, Nutrition, and Forestry
- Appropriations
- Armed Services
- Banking, House, and Urban Affairs
- Budget
- Commerce, Science, and Transportation
- Energy and Natural Resources
- Environment and Public Works
- Finance
- Foreign Relations
- Health, Education, Labor, and Pensions
- Homeland Security and Governmental Affairs
- Indian Affairs
- Intelligence
- Judiciary
- Rules and Administration
- Select Committee on Aging
- Select Committee on Ethics
- Small Business and Entrepreneurship
- Veterans Affairs

There is one particularly notable difference that speaks to the profound variance in the operating environments of the two chambers: the Senate has no equivalent to the House Committee on Rules, which has tremendous power in structuring how legislation is handled on the House floor. In fact, no committee structures floor debate in the Senate; instead, formal and more often informal agreements are reached between the majority and minority leaders to move legislation along. (Rules and Administration handles institutional matters and has no role in structuring floor debate.)

Like the House, most Senate committees fall into the category of "authorizing committees," dealing with legislation to authorize government agencies and programs. The Senate, too, has one committee that controls funding: the Appropriations Committee. The Senate committee that focuses mostly on oversight of government programs and agencies is called the Committee on Homeland Security and Governmental Affairs.

Also like the House, most Senate committees have subcommittees to specialize the committees' work. As a general rule, House subcommittees play a larger role in the legislative process than Senate subcommittees. House members are typically on fewer committees and subcommittees than senators and are better able to turn their attention to narrower areas of policy. With only one hundred senators, most are stretched very thinly (many have multiple positions of authority in the chamber) and are unable to focus effectively at the level of subcommittee specialization.

The ratios between the parties on Senate committees always reflect very closely the ratio of the overall chamber. Senate committees range in size from about thirty (Appropriations) to six (Ethics).

Getting good committee assignments is crucial in the Senate, just as it is in the House. Senators develop expertise in their committee work, which often results in considerable standing in their areas of specialty. Of course senators try to get on committees that serve their constituents' needs and their own personal interests, as House members do, but, unlike in the House, some senators will try to get on the Armed Services Committee or the Foreign Relations Committee in order to be a more plausible presidential candidate in the future. (It is rare for House members to be considered viable presidential candidates.)

All senators serve on multiple committees, usually three or four. There simply are not enough senators to make it feasible to establish exclusive committees as the House does. Both parties guarantee all their members at least two highly influential committee assignments and at least one other assignment.

As with the House, the rank of committee chair comes with many privileges. The chair determines the agenda of the committee and gets to hire the bulk of the professional staff that works for the committee. As with the House, the minority ranking member also gets to hire staff.

Both parties in the Senate still adhere to the seniority tradition in determining committee chairs and ranking members. The seniority tradition in the Senate has come under fire in recent years, especially in the Republican Party, but it has only very rarely been violated in the selection of a chair. (As with the House, the majority party gets all the committee and subcommittee chair positions.) It is not uncommon for a particular senator to be senior in service on more than one committee. In these cases, the senator may only chair one committee.

The fact that the seniority system remains in place in the chamber gives committee chairs a measure of freedom from the dictates of the majority party leadership that their House counterparts do not always have. Another difference: Senate Democrats, upon taking power in 2007, did not put in place the six-year term limit on chairs that Republicans had enforced when they were in the majority.

Senators represent varied constituencies. Unlike the House, where the districts are all nearly the same size in terms of population, states range from Wyoming's approximately 500,000 residents to California's 36,000,000.

California senators do not quite get to hire seventy-two times as many staff as Wyoming's do, which would reflect proportionally the populations of the two states, but they do get more resources than the senators from the sparsely populated states. The big state senators usually hire from about sixty to eighty staffers to cover the Washington, D.C., and state offices, while the senators from smaller states have the resources to hire thirty to forty-five members, depending on the state.

The Importance of Party Leadership and Committees. A useful way to think about the major organizational components of the two chambers is that they are meant to aid the institution and its members in balancing legislative and representative responsibilities.

Committees, the workhorses of the institution, study, formulate, and refine legislation in all areas of federal policy. In addition, these panels conduct oversight to keep track of how the laws are being implemented and how the money they provide is being spent by the executive branch agencies. In short, congressional committees and subcommittees are the place where the serious work on national security, agriculture, taxes, and other major policy issues goes on. The authorizing and appropriations committees all have delineated policy domains and jurisdiction over specific federal agencies and departments.

But committees are hardly immune from the political pressures inherent in the representative role. Members of the House serve on anywhere from one to four committees. Senators usually serve on three or four committees. Members lobby within their parties to secure desired committee assignments. This is particularly critical for newly elected members; in order to demonstrate back home that they are relevant players in Washington, they must get on a good committee. Naturally members try to get on panels most relevant to their constituencies—perhaps the Armed Services Committee if there are naval bases in the district, or the Agriculture Committee if farming is important back home. For many reelected members, concerted efforts are made to land a desired slot on the most prestigious committees when openings occur.

The upshot is that members, as they work on policy in committee, are carefully attuned to the political ramifications back home of the bills they craft and the decisions they make. The jobs of legislator and representative cannot be neatly separated.

As the other main organizational unit in the two chambers, the party leadership decides what legislation to bring to the floor. The two parties embody distinct, if overlapping, philosophies of governance; the party that happens to be in the majority is in the advantageous position of being able to pursue its national policy goals in legislation. But in order to pursue that agenda successfully, party leaders must carefully consider their rank and file members' representative responsibilities. After all, they need to corral a sufficient number of votes to pass bills, and strict party discipline is nearly impossible to enforce in the US Congress.

The Legislative Process in the Two Chambers. The two chambers conduct legislative business very differently. The legislative agenda of the House is tightly controlled by the majority party, while in the Senate it is rarely possible for the majority to pursue an agenda without significant input from the minority party.

The House of Representatives. The legislative agenda of the House of Representatives is dictated by the majority party. Its leadership decides what bills come to the floor, how long they will be debated, and whether they will be open for amendment.

The Rules Committee in the House, whose membership is tilted heavily toward the majority, is the arm of the leadership that facilitates control over the agenda. On most major legislation it formulates a rule governing debate on the floor—the length of the debate as well as the amending procedures if any amendments are allowed. That rule must be approved by the House before the bill may come up for consideration. The majority party rarely loses a vote on the rule governing debate. In fact it is rare that the bill itself will lose, as losing a vote is considered indicative of a lack of political strength.

Normally bills are the products of the specialists (members and staff) on the committees. But if a committee product is not to the liking of the majority leadership, and no accommodation can be reached, the leadership may craft an alternative proposal and bring it to the floor. This is not the normal procedure, but it has happened more frequently in the last two decades, as party leaders have exerted control over the chamber in ways not seen since the early part of the twentieth century.

The minority party has no say in the agenda of the House except in extraordinary circumstances. Their priorities will only be addressed legislatively if they can find common ground with influential members of the majority party.

The Senate. The Senate operates very differently. While the majority leader determines what bills may be taken up for consideration, he or she has much less control over the amending process, or even whether debate will end and a vote will be taken. The US Senate, unlike almost any legislative body in the world, has no option to "move the previous question," which has the effect of bringing a bill up for a vote at once. The result is that ordinarily a bill comes up for a vote only if no member objects, which is referred to as "unanimous consent." It is in fact quite common for minor legislation to be tacitly approved by unanimous consent with no actual vote taken.

But achieving unanimity is very difficult on important legislation given the stark differences in views among the membership, which includes Republicans, many of whom are very conservative, and Democrats, who overwhelmingly are to the left of center. The majority leader often tries to negotiate with his or her minority counterpart to move forward on a bill. The majority leader normally has to agree to permit the minority to have an opportunity to change the bill in question through the amending process. This has potential pitfalls for the majority, as the minority may cleverly bring up issues in the amending process which, if adopted, may make the bill hard or impossible to pass at the end of debate. The fact that the Senate has no prohibition on non-germane amendments makes the situation trickier still for the majority.

The majority leader does have one other option. If the minority insists on offering amendments that are non-germane or otherwise noxious to the majority, the leader may attempt to invoke cloture on the floor of the Senate, which has the effect of putting an end time to debate (thirty hours hence) and gives

the leader considerable control over the amending process. Invoking cloture puts an end to dilatory tactics, which are often generically referred to as filibusters.

The problem is that cloture requires sixty votes, and it is very rare that either major party holds that many seats. The fact is that the majority leader almost always needs to negotiate with at least some of the minority party in order to get to sixty votes, thereby giving minority party members considerable influence over the chamber's agenda.

The Senate is meant to be the more deliberative body, and the sixty-vote requirement to limit debate at the very least has the effect of making it nearly impossible for the Senate to act with haste.

Congress in the Twenty-First Century. The US Congress has undergone considerable change in the last few decades, in particular the last fifteen to twenty years. Changes in the American party system have resulted in a much more partisan Congress, with important ramifications for legislative work and national policy. In addition, increasing pressures from constituents and the spiraling costs of running for office have led to a Congress focused more on its representative responsibilities than its legislative role.

Partisanship. Since the late 1970s, partisanship on roll call votes in both chambers of Congress has steadily increased. In the most recent Congresses the level of partisan voting (defined as a majority of Democrats opposing a majority of Republicans) is the highest in well over a century.

This change is due, more than anything else, to organic changes in the American political party system. While the Democratic and Republican parties have dominated politics in the country for over 150 years, their policy positions and bases of support have changed greatly since the 1960s and 1970s.

Through much of the twentieth century, both parties featured prominent factions across the ideological spectrum, from very liberal (favoring more government intervention in the economy and in other areas) to very conservative (generally opposing government intervention in the economy).

Driven by divisions on racial issues and other social questions, the parties began to sort themselves ideologically on nearly all issues of the day in the 1960s. Republicans began to be more uniformly conservative, with Democrats more uniformly liberal. There were still dozens of moderate to conservative Democrats (mainly in the Southern states) and moderate to liberal Republicans (mainly in the Northeastern states) for many years, but that changed beginning in the early 1990s, as most moderate and conservative Southern Democrats were replaced in Congress by conservative Republicans, and moderate to liberal Republicans were replaced by liberal Democrats.

In addition, the electoral environment has become much more competitive, with both parties vying every electoral cycle for control of Congress. This represents a significant change from the era of nearly unchallenged Democratic dominance in Congress from 1930 into the early 1990s.

As the parties have become more ideologically uniform and the electoral battles for power more intense, the rank-and-file membership of both parties in both chambers (although much more so in the House) have ceded considerable power and control to party leadership. Committee chairs, who once called the shots in Congress, now often play second fiddle to those in top leadership positions. Important legislation in the contemporary Congress is almost always influenced heavily by the Speaker of the House and the majority leader in the Senate, as well as influential senators of the minority party.

The Representative Role Dominates Members' Time. Throughout US history members of Congress have had to balance their national legislative responsibilities with their need to address constituents' parochial concerns. In recent decades the balance has tilted strongly toward the representative role.

As federal responsibilities increased dramatically in the middle decades of the twentieth century—a time of great expansion of programs and agencies—members' ombudsman function became much more burdensome. Most members now assign half or more of their staff to deal with constituent queries and problems they experience with executive branch agencies.

In addition, the time and resources needed for members to get reelected have greatly increased. Most spend the majority of their time back in their districts or states, and must devote a tremendous amount of time to raising money for campaigns. House members, who must run every two years, now may have to raise two or more millions of dollars, all of which must come from hundreds or even thousands of donors, given individual contribution limits. And although senators only have to face the voters every six years, the burden of raising ten million dollars, twenty million, or even more—the amount required to be viable in many states—is considerable.

Landmark Achievements, Neglect for the Essentials. The US Congress has exhibited a two-faced quality since the mid-1990s. This period has been characterized by a spate of remarkable landmark legislative achievements, but the body as a whole has been unable to keep up with its most essential and basic legislative responsibilities. This has been true under both Democratic and Republican leadership.

The radical reform of the US welfare system in 1996, achieved through negotiations between the Democratic president Bill Clinton and a Republican Congress, began a period of dramatic legislative achievement not seen since the 1960s. In the next fourteen years the Congress passed a massive spending and tax package aimed at balancing the budget (1997) and major tax legislation (2001, 2003), revamped the federal role in elementary and secondary education (2001), reorganized the vast apparatus of domestic security and intelligence gathering (2002, 2004), put in place a prescription drug plan for senior citizens (2003), and reformed the health care system and the entire financial regulatory structure (2010), to name a few major accomplishments.

But, at the same time, Congress's most important annual process—determining the budgets of all the federal agencies—has run aground, regularly leaving the agencies without the ability to move forward on new initiatives or to address new problems for months at a time. Sometimes the stasis has lasted for an entire year. In addition, regular updating of agencies' statutory authorities has often been neglected, again forcing agency officials into a difficult spot as they scramble to address pressing needs.

The Congress, then, has become a place where the two parties fight fiercely to convince the American people that they deserve to maintain or regain power. The majority in Congress, usually with the help of an ambitious president of the same party, has passed monumental legislation at a surprising clip in recent years. This has been done both to achieve policy goals and to make a case that the party deserves to stay in power. At the same time, the effort it has taken to do this, coupled with the intense pressures associated with addressing constituents' needs and running for reelection, has left little will or time for members to focus on their essential legislative duties.

[*See also* Checks and Balances; Constitution, US; Executive Privilege; Presidency: Governing; *and* State Politics.]

BIBLIOGRAPHY

Dodd, Lawrence C., and Bruce Ian Oppenheimer. *Congress Reconsidered.* 9th ed. (Washington, D.C., 2008).

Jacobson, Gary C. *The Politics of Congressional Elections.* 7th ed. (New York, 2009).

Koger, Gregory. *Filibustering: A Political History of Obstruction in the House and Senate.* (Chicago, 2010).

Mayhew, David R. *Congress: The Electoral Connection.* 2d ed. (New Haven, Conn., 2004).

Oleszek, Walter J. *Congressional Procedures and the Policy Process.* 8th ed. (Washington, D.C., 2010).

Polsby, Nelson W. *How Congress Evolves: Social Bases of Institutional Change.* (New York, 2005).

Sinclair, Barbara. *Unorthodox Lawmaking: New Legislative Processes in the US Congress.* 3d ed. (Washington, D.C., 2007).

John Haskell

CONSERVATISM

Conservatism seems to be rooted in human nature. People are often more concerned about the current possessions than future possibilities, and often attached to the old ways, just because they are the old ways. If it is conservative to heed such tendencies, conservatism is as old as politics.

As a recognized banner in party competition, however, conservatism is less than two hundred years old. There was no need for a conservative party until there came to be parties devoted to new creeds of progress or liberation. As a political designation, the term "conservative" seems to have originated in France, where it was embraced by moderate supporters of the Bourbon restoration in the 1820s. The term came into more general use a decade later, when it was taken up by the Tory Party in Britain. As a reactive doctrine, the precise policy implications of "conservatism" have varied widely from nation to nation and era to era, depending on what policies conservatives set themselves to oppose. Over the course of two centuries, "conservative" has meant as many different things as "liberal" or "progressive" or "socialist."

In some ways, American conditions might seem particularly inhospitable to "conservative" doctrines. After all, the United States began with a Declaration of Independence, grounding its claims to liberty in a universal right to revolution. Americans then established democratic constitutions which, as *The Federalist* boasted at the time, had "no model on the face of the globe." Within a decade of the founding of the nation, American politics settled into patterns of party competition which gave no assured place to men of great property or distinguished lineage. No national political party in America has embraced the word "conservative" in its official name. The successful parties have continually (and plausibly) vied with each other to establish their higher devotion to democracy, or freedom, or the well being of the common man. And almost from the beginning, Americans have led the world in technical inventions and in popular embrace of new technologies.

Yet among Western democracies, at least, America is in some ways the most conservative. It still functions under the Constitution drafted in 1787. There have been formal amendments to that Constitution, of course—most notably those adopted after the Civil War—as well as less formal changes in the understanding of what governmental powers or personal rights the Constitution confers. But arguments from the founding era remain quite relevant to contemporary constitutional debates. And political advocates of almost all stripes still invoke the authority of Thomas Jefferson, George Washington, James Madison, or even Thomas Paine to lend weight to current appeals. Surveys in the twenty-first century find that a much larger portion of Americans identify themselves as "conservative" than "progressive" or "liberal" (or even "moderate").

Yet as a political tag, "conservative"—in the United States, as in other modern democracies—means more than mere resistance to change. At least three broad themes of conservative thought continue to resonate in modern political debates. First and perhaps most important is resistance to utopian thinking. Modern technology, which has transformed so many aspects of daily life, encourages people to think that human nature itself can be transformed by social tinkering; conservatives insist on the primacy of the political models and personal virtues of the past. A second theme, which follows in a way from the first, is a respect for authority and power—combined with a wary regard for their limits and their susceptibility to abuse. Conservatives have resisted the notion that enlightenment or self-interest, solidarity or democracy will generate a spontaneous harmony among men, making recourse to force no longer necessary (or no longer recognizable as compulsion). Finally, conservatives have sought to defend particular practices and institutions—a traditional version of the family, a traditional sense of patriotic obligation, and traditional religious and moral standards. All these may be vital to a decent society, but are difficult to defend in a liberal framework that reduces all obligations to individual choice.

If these views give meaning to "conservatism," the United States remains, in important ways, more conservative than other Western democracies. It is one of the last remaining democracies that still employs capital punishment and, at the same time, acknowledges the constitutional right of citizens to keep firearms for their own self-defense. The United States has—again, almost uniquely among Western democracies—remained aloof from full participation in international human rights forums and such institutions as the International Criminal Court, largely from fear that such outside authorities might compromise America's own constitutional norms. Where almost every Western democracy has long accepted some scheme of government-provided or government-sponsored health insurance, the Obama administration encountered tremendous public resistance to its 2010 legislation requiring all citizens to purchase private health insurance under government supervision. Several courts held that the law was, in fact, unconstitutional, in suits endorsed by a majority of American state governments.

Political analysts (particularly on the left) often emphasize differences among constituencies or outlooks now commonly seen as "conservative." It is certainly true that opposition to abortion or gay marriage has no necessary connection with demands for lower taxes or less government regulation. "Social conservatives," focusing on protection of traditional "family values," might not seem natural partners with enthusiasts for free markets, as market competition often has corrosive effects on traditional ways of life. Neither might seem natural partners with advocates for stronger national security measures, which are costly and can be socially disruptive. In Western Europe and in Latin America, socially conservative Christian Democratic parties have often found it easier to cooperate with socialists than with classical liberal parties or more nationalist parties. In America's two-party system, different sorts of "conservative" claims have found shelter in each major party, making common cause with claims or constituencies that might now be seen as "progressive."

But at least in retrospect, one can discern some enduring patterns. In the 1790s, the Federalist Party denounced followers of Jefferson (party forebears of today's Democrats) for fostering the lawless and irreligious impulses of mobs in revolutionary France. The Whig Party, which succeeded the Federalists as the party of commerce and national authority, was allied with evangelical religion, championing the personal virtues necessary for success in trade. Republicans took over from the Whigs in both respects. Outside the South, for example, it was largely Republicans who supported temperance measures (culminating in the 1919 Prohibition Amendment against trade in "intoxicating liquors").

Since the 1960s, an ongoing realignment has generated more political homogeneity within the two main parties—and more polarization between them. For a century after the Civil War, blacks were denied their voting rights in the South and white voters remained wedded to the Democratic Party, providing a conservative anchor in the national councils of Democrats. The civil rights revolution of the 1960s enfranchised black voters, allowing more moderate or liberal Democrats to succeed even in the South. But in the ensuing decades, as the Democratic Party became a more reliably liberal coalition, conservative whites in the South embraced the Republican Party. Meanwhile, social upheavals in the 1960s and 1970s moved descendants of Catholic immigrants in the North, another Democratic mainstay, to embrace Republican candidates for the first time. In both regions, major constituencies that supported the regulatory and welfare policies of the New Deal in the 1930s (and for decades after) have, since the 1960s, found themselves in a new coalition with Republican opponents of such measures. The success of Ronald Reagan in the 1980s seemed to cement these new coalitions.

Is there really a common framework of ideas in this conservative coalition, or merely a set of highly contingent political alliances? In the 1950s, writers at William Buckley's *National Review* (often regarded as the premier voice of "modern conservatism") preached a "fusion" of "traditionalist" and "libertarian" strands of conservatism, thus acknowledging their differing intellectual roots and divergent policy priorities. What seems to have held this coalition together is a common distrust of centralized government programs and a common perception that the modern welfare state undermines both family and communal bonds, and the necessary disciplines

of the market. In recent decades, both "social conservatives" and "economic conservatives" have often made common cause in urging the revival of older understandings of the Constitution, as a scheme to ensure limits on government.

There is logic in such broad-ranging appeals to the "original understanding" or the traditional view of the Constitution. The American Founders were revolutionaries, but precisely because they knew themselves to be sailing in uncharted waters—pioneers, we might say, of modernity—they combined much caution with their boldness. Their constitutional system of checks and balances and decentralized power is (as progressives have complained for more than a century) an enduring brake on the visionary schemes of progressive reformers. American government is not designed to provide much central direction. American society is always changing, but incrementally, unpredictably, and not much at governmental command.

More than people in most other Western democracies, Americans have been left free—or forced by their circumstances—to rely on their own virtue, their own prudence, and their own initiative to face life's challenges. A large proportion of the American electorate remains quite suspicious of progressive nostrums, which they see as promising to relieve people of primary responsibility for directing their own lives. Conservatism will have a future in America, as long as the American past has a future.

[*See also* Christian Right; Democracy; Fiscal Conservatism; Libertarianism; New Right; Republican Party; *and* Tea Party.]

BIBLIOGRAPHY

Buckley, William F., and Charles R. Kesler. *Keeping the Tablets: Modern American Conservative Thought.* (New York, 1988).

Hayward, Steven F. *The Age of Reagan: The Fall of the Old Liberal Order, 1964–1980.* (Roseville, Calif., 2001).

Kristol, Irving. *Neo-Conservatism: Autobiography of an Idea.* (New York, 1995).

Magnet, Myron. *The Dream and the Nightmare: The Sixties' Legacy to the Underclass.* (New York, 1993).

Sowell, Thomas. *A Conflict of Visions: Ideological Origins of Political Struggles.* (New York, 2007).

Jeremy A. Rabkin

CONSTITUTION, US

The US Constitution is the world's oldest written national constitution and has been amended only twenty-seven times. As a result, many of the decisions made by delegates to the Constitutional Convention of 1787 continue to shape American politics in the early twenty-first century. Although the US Supreme Court has long played a key role in interpreting constitutional provisions—whether regarding separation of powers, federalism, or individual rights—scholars have increasingly taken note of the extent to which other public officials engage in constitutional interpretation and construction, as well as the ways that groups and movements invoke constitutional provisions in pursuit of their political goals.

Framing the Constitution. The US Constitution emerged in response to widespread dissatisfaction with the Articles of Confederation, which was drafted in 1777 and finally ratified by all thirteen states in 1781. Critics charged that the Articles of Confederation was deficient in a number of respects. Most important, the central government lacked the power to govern effectively, especially in terms of raising adequate revenue. Without an independent power to levy taxes, and on account of the states' failure to ratify amendments to the Articles that would have authorized a federal tax on imports, the central government had to requisition funds from state governments, and encountered difficulty in securing compliance with these requests. Critics also argued that the internal structure of the central government under the Articles was poorly designed, in that no provision was made for an independent executive or judiciary. Finally, and in part due to the central government's weakness, the Articles was seen as providing inadequate security for individual rights, especially in light of the passage of numerous state laws calling for printing paper money and forgiving debts, and the inability of the central government to review these measures.

After an initial meeting at Mount Vernon in 1785 between Maryland and Virginia representatives to discuss navigation of the Potomac River, and a subsequent conference in Annapolis in 1786 that attracted twelve commissioners from five states, the Annapolis Convention issued a call for a Constitutional convention to be held in Philadelphia in 1787. Fifty-five delegates from twelve states (all but Rhode Island) attended some or all of the convention, which operated according to the voting rules in place under the Articles, whereby each state cast a single vote. After much deliberation, all but three delegates in attendance at the Convention's conclusion agreed to sign the document and send it to the states for approval by popularly selected conventions, with the proviso that approval by nine states would be sufficient for the Constitution to take effect among the approving states. By July 1788, eleven states had ratified the document, and the Constitution took effect in March 1789, with North Carolina and Rhode Island eventually ratifying in November 1789 and May 1790, respectively.

In summarizing the work of the Convention in a letter to Thomas Jefferson, who was not among the fifty-five delegates, James Madison, who is considered to have been the most influential of the assembled delegates, explained that participants at the recently concluded Convention were preoccupied with four principal tasks: "1. to unite a proper energy in the Executive, and a proper stability in the Legislative departments, with the essential characters of Republican Government. 2. to draw a line of demarkation which would give to the General Government every power requisite for general purposes, and leave to the States every power which might be most beneficially administered by them. 3. to provide for the different interests of different parts of the Union. 4. to adjust the clashing pretensions of the large and small States" (Kurland and Lerner, 1987, vol. 1, p. 644).

The last of these tasks (to take them up in reverse order) generated the most controversy and came the closest to bringing the deliberations to a premature halt. Competing proposals advanced by Virginia and New Jersey delegates in the first month of the

Convention differed in many respects, but most notably in their competing means of apportioning congressional seats. Large states were generally drawn to the Virginia Plan, which called for a bicameral legislature whose members would be apportioned based on state population. Meanwhile, small states mostly supported the New Jersey Plan, which envisioned a unicameral Congress in which states enjoyed equal representation. It was only after much deliberation, and threats by some delegates to depart the proceedings if their concerns were not addressed, that the convention agreed to a bicameral Congress where states were represented equally in the Senate, and by population in the House.

The penultimate task noted by Madison—adjudicating between the different parts of the Union—centered mainly around the competing interests of Northern and Southern states and revolved to a great degree around the issue of slavery. At no time did the Convention consider authorizing the federal government to abolish slavery; such a proposal would not have been approved by Southern states. Rather, the issue surfaced in other forms, such as in how to count slaves for purposes of determining representation in the House and apportioning direct taxes (which were required to be apportioned by state population). It was to the advantage of Southern states to count slaves as equal to free citizens when apportioning House seats, but not when determining a state's tax burden. The calculus was reversed for Northern states, which were intent on preventing Southern states from enjoying undue political advantage, as would occur under any system that counted slaves in determining representation. Lacking a principled means of resolving this issue, delegates relied on a formula first proposed by the Confederation Congress for determining a state's contribution for purposes of a proposed tax amendment to the Articles. This was the origin of the clause for counting slaves as three-fifths of a person (technically the document refers to "all other persons") for purposes of representation and direct taxation.

Northern and Southern states also clashed over whether to authorize Congress to abolish the foreign slave trade (the resulting compromise allowed for congressional adoption of such a ban, but it could not take effect until 1808), and whether to allow Congress to regulate navigation by a vote of a two-thirds supermajority or a bare majority (a majority eventually carried the day, despite Southern concerns that their interests would be overridden as a result). The convention also adopted a fugitive slave clause providing that slaves who escaped into free states were not thereby freed from slavery, but rather must be returned to their owners.

Convention delegates devoted significant attention to demarcating the bounds of federal and state power. The Virginia Plan that set the Convention's early agenda would have authorized the federal government to exercise near plenary power, in that Congress would have been empowered to "legislate in all cases to which the separate States are incompetent, or in which the harmony of the United States may be interrupted by the exercise of individual Legislation" (Madison, 1966, p. 31). Moreover, Congress would have been able to "negative all laws passed by the several States" in contravention of constitutional articles and "call forth the force of the Union" against any state failing to fulfill its constitutional duties (Madison, 1966, p. 31). During the Convention, delegates modified or rejected each of these initial proposals.

Determining how best to delineate the scope and limits of federal power proved particularly challenging, with some delegates calling for the enumeration of federal powers and other delegates defending the Virginia Plan's general grant of power, on the grounds that any listing of powers would be necessarily incomplete and would hinder effective governance. The former group of delegates prevailed, in that the Constitution authorizes Congress to exercise the powers listed in Article I of the Constitution (as well as in any subsequent amendments). However, the latter group of delegates was able to secure inclusion in this list of powers—which comprises seventeen clauses, including the powers to "lay and collect Taxes . . . to pay the Debts and provide for the common Defence and general Welfare" and "regulate Commerce with foreign Nations, and among the several States"—an eighteenth and final clause permitting Congress to exercise all powers "necessary and proper to carrying into execution the foregoing powers and all other powers vested by this Constitution in the Government of the United States, or in any Department or Officer thereof."

The Convention also grappled with how best to delineate and enforce limits on state governments. Madison was a strong proponent of the provision in the Virginia Plan authorizing Congress to veto state laws that were contrary to constitutional provisions, and he returned repeatedly to this proposal throughout the Convention, only to see it defeated. Instead, the Convention opted to delineate specific limits on state authority, and then presumably rely on the Supreme Court to enforce these limits by reviewing state acts in the course of legal cases and controversies. In short, in partitioning the powers of the federal and state governments, which Madison viewed as "perhaps of all, the most nice and difficult" of the tasks before the convention (Kurland and Lerner, 1987, vol. 1, p. 645), delegates established a federal government with significantly more power than under the Articles; however, delegates also took steps to impose limits on federal power and rejected proposals seen as unduly depriving state governments of their vitality in the federal system.

Finally, delegates debated various specific questions concerning the internal structure of the federal government, with particular concern given to the establishment of an independent executive. Rejecting the notion of a plural executive that might have included representatives of various regions of the country, the convention made the key decision to vest the executive power in a single person: the president. As to the mode of selecting the president, the convention entertained various proposals and appeared at one point to have settled on Congress as the appointing body, before ultimately creating an Electoral College mechanism, which was seen as providing the president with the requisite independence from Congress and avoiding the pitfalls associated with popular election (an option given brief consideration). In addition to settling on a four-year, renewable term, the Convention provided the president with a qualified veto (capable of being overridden by a two-thirds vote of both houses of Congress) and various other powers designed to secure an "energetic Executive," in the words of Alexander Hamilton in *Federalist No. 70* (Hamilton, Madison, and Jay, 1788/1961, p. 423).

Amending the Constitution. The Constitution's amendment procedure was designed, as Madison explained in *Federalist No. 43*, to guard "equally against that extreme facility, which would render the Constitution too mutable; and that extreme difficulty, which might perpetuate its discovered faults" (Hamilton, Madison, and Jay, 1788/1961, p. 278). The procedure under the Articles was seen as overly difficult, in that changes required the unanimous approval of the states, and on several occasions a lone state prevented adoption of a proposed amendment. Meanwhile, other proposals, such as that put forth by Jefferson in an exchange of letters with Madison, were seen as permitting too-frequent change. Jefferson preferred to give an opportunity to each generation, which he calculated as lasting nineteen or twenty years, to revise the Constitution, so as to prevent one generation from binding another. In Madison's view, though, this would lead to the frequent reopening of fundamental questions and in circumstances that might not be as propitious as in the founding era, and in a way that would deprive the Constitution of the veneration necessary for governmental stability.

Article V of the Constitution establishes two means of proposing amendments and another two means of securing their ratification. Amendments may be proposed either by two-thirds of both houses of Congress, or through a convention called by Congress upon the request of two-thirds of all the state legislatures. All thirty-three amendments that have been formally proposed have followed the first path. State legislatures have on occasion tried to pursue the second path, and have come close to securing the requisite number of petitions—most recently in a push to permit a deviation from one-person, one-vote requirements for apportioning state legislatures, and also to require a balanced budget—but these efforts have never met the two-thirds majority required to call a convention.

Once proposed, amendments can be ratified either by three-fourths of state legislatures or by three-fourths of state conventions established for this purpose (Congress specifies in each instance which of these routes is to be followed). Twenty-six of the twenty-seven ratified amendments were approved by state legislatures. The one other ratified amendment, the repeal of Prohibition in 1933, was approved by state conventions, at a time when Congress was uncertain whether this amendment would be supported by state legislatures which were, at the time, dominated by rural areas seen as hostile to repeal. Another six proposed amendments failed to secure approval from the requisite number of states, including most recently an Equal Rights Amendment (ER) and a D.C. Statehood Amendment, the ratification time periods for which expired in 1982 and 1985, respectively.

Of the twenty-seven ratified amendments, the first ten, which make up the Bill of Rights, were proposed in the first Congress in 1789 and ratified by the requisite number of state legislatures by 1791. Madison, among other delegates at the Constitutional Convention, initially opposed a Bill of Rights on the grounds that it was unnecessary and potentially harmful. However, during the constitutional ratification process, Federalist supporters of the Constitution were forced to promise Anti-Federalist critics that if the document was ratified, they could propose amendments to address their concerns. Madison fulfilled this promise in the first Congress, which proceeded to approve twelve amendments for submission to the states, only ten of which were immediately ratified. Of the other two amendments, one, dealing with the apportionment of the House, was never ratified, and the other, dealing with congressional pay raise, was not ratified until 1992; it stands as the twenty-seventh and most recently approved amendment.

The Civil War Amendments—the Thirteenth Amendment (1865), the Fourteenth Amendment (1868), and the Fifteenth Amendment (1870)—are the most important amendments adopted since the first ten amendments, and none is more important than the Fourteenth Amendment, especially in view of the Supreme Court's later interpretations of its due process and equal protection clauses. The meaning and purpose of the Fourteenth Amendment have been sources of ongoing debate. Some scholars and justices have viewed the amendment as designed to achieve the important but limited goal of overturning the Supreme Court's ruling in *Dred Scott v. Sandford* (1857) to the effect that African Americans are not citizens of the United States, and then empowering the federal government to remedy state deprivations of the rights of African Americans. But others have argued that the amendment was intended to bring about a wholesale transformation in the federal system by establishing federal officials rather than state governments as the primary guarantors of individual rights across the board. After several early Supreme Court rulings took the former view, the Court from the twentieth century onward has supported the latter interpretation, most notably by determining that the due process clause incorporates nearly all provisions of the Bill of Rights (most recently the right to bear arms) and thereby renders them applicable to state governments and enforceable by Congress and federal courts.

Most of the remaining amendments throughout American history have extended the right to vote to previously disenfranchised groups, or dealt with the executive branch. The amendment process has been the vehicle for expanding the suffrage on five occasions. In addition to the Fifteenth Amendment prohibiting denial of the right to vote based on race, the Nineteenth Amendment (1920) prohibited denial of the suffrage on the basis of sex, the Twenty-Third Amendment (1961) permitted residents of the District of Columbia to participate in electing the president, the Twenty-Fourth Amendment (1964) prohibited imposition of a poll tax in federal elections, and the Twenty-Sixth Amendment (1971) established eighteen as the minimum voting age. Meanwhile, four amendments have dealt with the executive branch. The Twelfth Amendment (1804) modified the Electoral College in several respects, most notably by directing electors to cast separate votes for president and vice president. The Twentieth Amendment (1933) moved up the date of the presidential inauguration from 4 March 4 to 20 January (and also provided that congressional terms shall begin on 3 January). The Twenty-Second Amendment (1951) established a two-term presidential limit. The Twenty-Fifth Amendment (1967) established procedures for dealing with presidential disability and provided more clearly for instances of presidential and vice presidential succession.

What stands out from a review of all twenty-seven ratified amendments—which also include the Eleventh Amendment (1795) immunizing nonconsenting state governments from individual lawsuits in federal court, the Sixteenth Amendment (1913) authorizing an individual income tax, and the Seventeenth Amendment (1913) establishing direct election of senators—is the absence of the sorts of policy amendments found in American state constitutions and many other national constitutions. The only true policy amendment is the Eighteenth Amendment (1919), which banned the manufacture, sale, and transportation of intoxicating liquor and was in turn repealed by the Twenty-First Amendment (1933). To be sure, the late twentieth century saw calls for numerous policy amendments, such as in regard to authorizing prayer in public schools or banning abortion, flag desecration, and same-sex marriage; but none secured congressional approval.

Interpreting the Constitution. The Supreme Court has played a key, though far from exclusive, role in interpreting the Constitution, primarily by invalidating federal and state acts in violation of constitutional provisions. Although the Constitution does not provide explicitly for judicial review, several delegates made clear during the Convention debates that they expected the Supreme Court to exercise this power, and, employing reasoning that drew heavily on Hamilton's defense of judicial review in *Federalist No. 78*, the Supreme Court under Chief Justice John Marshall in *Marbury v. Madison* (1803) issued the first decision invalidating a congressional act. Overall, the Court has ruled unconstitutional over 160 congressional statutes and more than 950 state laws, in whole or in part.

At times, the Supreme Court has overturned congressional statutes that violate separation-of-powers provisions regarding the balance of power among the legislature, executive, and judiciary. *Marbury v. Madison* was such a ruling, in that the Court overturned a portion of the Judiciary Act of 1789 on the grounds that it improperly enlarged the Court's original jurisdiction. More often, separation-of-powers rulings have overturned efforts by Congress to assume powers properly belonging to other branches, as when Congress tried to limit the president's removal power by requiring him to obtain Senate consent before firing postmasters, or when Congress sought to rely on a legislative veto mechanism whereby one house could invalidate executive deportation orders.

On other occasions, the Supreme Court has overturned congressional statutes that violate federalism principles by exceeding congressional power as set out in the commerce and tax clauses and the Fourteenth Amendment, or by encroaching on state power protected in the Tenth and Eleventh Amendments. The Court has been particularly active in superintending the balance of state and federal power during certain eras. In the post–Civil War era, the Court overturned or limited the reach of civil rights and voting rights acts that were held to exceed congressional power under the recently adopted Civil War amendments (that is, the Thirteenth, Fourteenth, and Fifteenth Amendments). The Progressive-era Court invalidated several federal labor laws, including an employer-liability act and a child-labor act, on the grounds that they exceeded the commerce power and in some cases ran afoul of the Tenth Amendment. The New Deal–era Court was especially active, at least prior to 1937, in invoking the commerce and tax clauses to invalidate New Deal laws that regulated farming, mining, and other industries. Most recently, after a six-decade period in which only two congressional statutes were invalidated on federalism grounds, the Court under Chief Justice William Rehnquist invalidated all or part of a number of congressional statutes on federalism grounds. The Court held that the Gun-Free School Zones Act and a portion of the Violence against Women Act exceeded congressional power and that a portion of the Brady Handgun Violence Prevention

Act infringed on the Tenth Amendment. Among other federalism rulings, the Court invoked the Eleventh Amendment to prevent Congress from authorizing individual damages suits in federal court against state governments for violations of intellectual property laws, age discrimination laws, and certain aspects of the Americans with Disabilities Act.

Particularly since the mid-twentieth century, the Court's emphasis in interpreting the Constitution has been on overturning federal and state statutes that infringe on individual rights. A relatively small number of the Court's 160-plus invalidations of federal statutes have been grounded in violations of the Bill of Rights. However, a significant portion of the 950-plus state statutes that have been declared unconstitutional were struck down on grounds related to the Bill of Rights. Initially, as illustrated by the Court's ruling in *Barron v. Baltimore* (1833), the Bill of Rights was viewed as inapplicable to state governments. With the passage of the Fourteenth Amendment and its directives that no state shall "abridge the privileges or immunities of citizens of the United States" or "deprive any person of life, liberty, or property, without due process of law," or "deny to any person within its jurisdiction the equal protection of the laws," litigants began to press the Court to invalidate state acts that infringed on individual liberty. The Court, in the *Slaughter-House Cases* (1873), foreclosed the possibility that the privileges-or-immunities clause would serve any purpose broader than prohibiting state denials of the rights of African Americans. However, in an 1897 case, the Court began to interpret the due process clause as requiring that selected clauses of the bill of rights be applied to state governments, and this process of selective incorporation continued in the twentieth and twenty-first centuries, to the point that all but a few minor clauses of the Bill of Rights are now applicable to state acts. Meanwhile, the Court has interpreted the equal protection clause to prohibit state-sponsored racial segregation as well as various other forms of discriminatory treatment.

Judicial review of state legislation on due process and equal protection grounds has been responsible for a number of significant political developments in American history. *Brown v. Board of Education* (1954) relied on the equal protection clause to invalidate racially segregated public schools. *Engel v. Vitale* (1962) and various other rulings relied on the religious establishment clause, as incorporated via the due process clause, to eliminate state-sponsored prayer in public schools. *Furman v. Georgia* (1972) invoked the cruel-and-unusual punishment clause, as incorporated by the due process clause, to invalidate the death penalty as currently implemented in the states, and even after the resumption of capital punishment after a four-year moratorium, the Court has continued to impose important limitations on the states in terms of which individuals can be executed and for what offenses. Finally, *Roe v. Wade* (1973) relied on the due process clause and various Bill of Rights clauses to invalidate abortion bans in place in the vast majority of states.

Although the Supreme Court has long played an influential role in interpreting the Constitution, this task is not solely the province of the judiciary, but is also undertaken by presidents and members of Congress. In some cases, constitutional controversies never make it to the Court, and so the task of interpreting constitutional provisions falls to the president and Congress. For instance, the original Constitution was silent on whether a vacancy in the presidency should be filled by the vice president until the expiration of the original term, or whether the vice president should merely serve as acting president until a special election was called. This question surfaced in 1841, when President William Henry Harrison died soon after his inauguration and questions arose concerning Vice President John Tyler's status. Tyler interpreted the Constitution as authorizing him to assume the presidency and finish out the unexpired term, and both houses of Congress adopted resolutions endorsing his claim, without the Supreme Court becoming involved. To take another example, a leading early-nineteenth-century constitutional controversy concerned the legitimacy of federal internal improvement projects regarding roads, canals, and harbors. The Supreme Court never addressed the issue in a direct fashion, and so it was left to presidents and members of Congress to resolve the issue. In fact, at various times, Presidents Madison, James Monroe, Andrew Jackson, and Tyler vetoed internal improvement bills on the grounds that they were unconstitutional.

On other occasions, the Supreme Court has issued interpretations of constitutional provisions, but presidents have arrived at a contrary interpretation and relied on this independent interpretation in the course of exercising their duties. For instance, no issue was more heavily contested during the first half-century of American politics than the constitutionality of a national bank. After the first bank was established for twenty years and its charter allowed to expire, a second bank was established for another twenty years and subsequently challenged in the Supreme Court. Although the Court under Chief Justice Marshall upheld the constitutionality of a national bank in *McCulloch v. Maryland* (1819), when the question surfaced yet again, President Jackson in 1832 vetoed a congressional bank recharter bill and justified his veto in part on the grounds that a national bank was an unconstitutional exercise of federal power, despite the Court's ruling to the contrary.

Not only presidents have undertaken independent constitutional interpretation. Congress has occasionally declined to acquiesce in Supreme Court interpretations of constitutional provisions, and has maintained an independent interpretation of constitutional meaning despite contrary Court precedents. Thus, despite the Court's 1857 *Dred Scott* decision holding that Congress lacked the power to prohibit slavery in the territories, many members of Congress, and later, President Abraham Lincoln, refused to accept this interpretation as settling permanently the scope of federal power in this area. In 1862, Congress enacted and President Lincoln signed a law prohibiting slavery in the federal territories.

Over a century later, Congress confronted another Supreme Court ruling with which many members disagreed, and once again Congress refused to be bound by the Court's interpretation of a constitutional provision. The Court in the *Civil Rights Cases* (1883) had declared unconstitutional the Civil Rights

Act of 1875 on the grounds that, in banning racial discrimination in inns and public amusements, Congress was exceeding its power under the Fourteenth Amendment, which the Court read as applying only to state-sponsored racial discrimination. In debating the proposed Civil Rights Act of 1964, which would have banned racial discrimination in hotels and restaurants, among other places, members of Congress were forced to confront the fact that the Court's 1883 ruling had not been reversed. Undeterred, Congress approved the law, based on members' independent determination that banning racial discrimination by private actors was a legitimate exercise of federal power justifiable under the commerce clause.

On still other occasions, political groups and movements have invoked constitutional provisions in the course of rallying support for their cause. At times, groups do this as a way of building public support for their goals and persuading local, state, or federal officials to adopt or modify policies. Civil-liberties groups frequently invoke the right to free speech in political debates concerning proposed restrictions on speech; gun-rights groups rely on the Second Amendment in opposing gun-control measures; and limited-government groups have drawn on the Tenth Amendment, among other constitutional provisions, to build political support for their goals.

At times, groups and movements have also invoked constitutional provisions in the course of litigating to advance their cause, as seen recently with challenges to the Patient Protection and Affordable Care Act of 2010. In particular, individuals, groups, and state attorneys general have targeted the health care reform act's minimum coverage provision that requires nearly all individuals to carry health insurance or face a financial penalty. Federal lawsuits contend that the minimum coverage provision exceeds federal power and cannot be justified on the basis of the Constitution's commerce, tax, or necessary and proper clauses. To date, federal courts have reached mixed verdicts on these questions, with the Eleventh Circuit Court of Appeals siding with the law's challengers, but the Sixth Circuit Court of Appeals rejecting them, in a case likely to be resolved by the US Supreme Court. In this sense, the Constitution continues to figure prominently in American politics, whether on account of the actions of citizens, groups, and movements, or through decisions made by executives, legislators, and judges.

[*See also* Bill of Rights; Checks and Balances; Civil Liberties; Executive Privilege; Federalism; *and* Judicial Review.]

BIBLIOGRAPHY

Amar, Akhil Reed. *America's Constitution: A Biography.* (New York, 2005).

Beeman, Richard M. *Plain, Honest Men: The Making of the American Constitution.* (New York, 2009).

Bowen, Catherine Drinker. *Miracle at Philadelphia: The Story of the Constitutional Convention, May to September 1787.* (Boston, 1966).

Hamilton, Alexander, James Madison, and John Jay. *The Federalist Papers.* Edited by Clinton Rossiter. (New York, 1961). First published in 1788.

Kammen, Michael G. *A Machine That Would Go of Itself: The Constitution in American Culture.* (New York, 1986).

Kelly, Alfred H., Winfred A. Harbison, and Herman Belz. *The American Constitution: Its Origin and Development.* 2 vols. 7th ed. (New York, 1991).

Kurland, Philip B., and Ralph Lerner, eds. *The Founders' Constitution.* 5 vols. (Chicago, 1987).

Kyvig, David E. *Explicit and Authentic Acts: Amending the US Constitution, 1776–1995.* (Lawrence, Kans., 1996).

Madison, James.1966. *Notes of Debates in the Federal Convention of 1787.* Edited by Adrienne Koch. (Athens, Ohio, 1966).

Rakove, Jack N. *Original Meanings: Politics and Ideas in the Making of the Constitution.* (New York, 1996).

Whittington, Keith E. *Constitutional Construction: Divided Powers and Constitutional Meaning.* (Cambridge, Mass, 2001).

John Dinan

CREATIVE CLASS

"Class" is something of a dirty word in America, where values, if not practices, are overwhelmingly egalitarian. The American Dream is one of limitless economic opportunity, after all—Americans like to think that American society, economy, and politics are open to everyone and not subject to rigid class distinctions—but not so fast. To the extent that class distinctions reflect what we do and how we work, they matter profoundly—and they can help us understand how American society, economy and politics really work.

Karl Marx described an economic order that was starkly divided between labor and capital, workers and owners, the exploited and their exploiters. But where do we draw the class lines in a postindustrial economy? For decades, leading thinkers have been trying to do just that. The economist Fritz Malchup and the management guru Peter Drucker described the rise of the knowledge economy and the knowledge worker. The leading student of class, the sociologist Erik Olin Wright, charted the rise of what he called the "professional managerial class." Robert Reich identified the role of "symbolic analysts"—those members of the workforce who manipulate symbols and ideas. My concept of the creative class owes a deep debt to all of these important theories and ideas.

My theory of the creative class presumes that *the work that people do* is the most important determinant of their position in the social and economic order. The creative class includes all those who are paid for their knowledge and ideas—their creativity. Physical blue-collar work is no longer the driving force of the American economy and society—rather, it's the work we do with our minds.

Marx thought it was our capacity for physical work that bound us all together; I believe it is our capacity for creativity. The implications of my theory are no less revolutionary than Marx's. Its cornerstone is the proposition that every single human being is creative—and that our creativity will ultimately annihilate the social categories of gender, race, ethnicity, sexual orientation, and so on that we have imposed on ourselves.

The creative class numbers around 38 million American workers. Creative class occupations include: science, engineering and technology; business and management; health care, law and education; and arts, culture, design, entertainment and media. About a third of all Americans are members of the creative class, compared to about 20 percent who are blue-collar or working class. The remainder, more than 45 percent, are members of the service class, performing routine, low-paid work like food preparation and retail sales. The creative class rose from just 5 percent of all workers in 1900 to roughly 10 percent in 1950, 15 percent in 1980, and more than 30 percent by 2005. At $2.1 trillion in total earnings, they generate half of all wages and salaries in the United States (Florida, 2008, p.109).

Class is not just a function of what people do; it is also reflected in where they live. The creative class is highly concentrated in specific regions, especially Silicon Valley and the San Francisco Bay area, Washington D.C., Boston, and college towns like Boulder, Colorado and Durham, North Carolina. While older industrial cities like Detroit have experienced substantial decline, nearby Ann Arbor is a vibrant creative class center with low unemployment and high incomes.

Research has shown that regions that have high concentrations of creative workers also have certain measurable characteristics, which I have dubbed "the three Ts of economic development."

- The first "T" is technology. Research by economists like Robert Solow and Paul Romer has shown that technology is a key driver of economic growth, development, and innovation. Technology-based companies are almost always located near great universities.
- The second "T" is talent. Human capital—concentrations of skilled and highly educated people—is the key driver of economic development. Economists tend to measure human capital as the percentage of people with at least a bachelor's degree, if not a higher degree. But that leaves out great entrepreneurs like Steve Jobs and Bill Gates who never completed college—never mind the myriads of great artists and musicians who are self-schooled. The creative class includes them all, along with each and every person who uses their creativity to make their living.
- The third "T" is tolerance. Economists like to think of technology and talent as stocks that are permanently sited in certain places, like minerals in the ground. But really they are flows: technology and talented people can and do move around and seek out new locations. The key to attracting and keeping them lies in the third "T": an open-minded, diverse environment where all sorts of people can fit in.

Several studies have shown that between a third and a half of Silicon Valley high-tech startups include a foreign-born person among the members of their founding teams. When my research revealed that cities and regions with high percentages of gay people (the Gay Index) and artistic and cultural creatives (the Bohemian Index) also enjoy higher rates of innovation, higher incomes, and higher housing prices, it created no end of controversy (and even landed me on *The Colbert Report*).

My conclusion was never that gay people and bohemians drive economic growth and development directly, but rather that they are the proverbial "canaries in the coal mine" of economic growth. Places with greater concentrations of gays and bohemians are more open-minded, more open to new people and new ideas than most other places—they have ecosystems which are also attractive to innovators and entrepreneurs.

Future societies face an important challenge: how to expand the ranks of the creative class and enable more and more people to leverage their innate creativity. Tomorrow's economic winners will not only be those who can attract and retain the creative class as we know it today—the technology savants, scientists, and thinkers who are the products of top universities—but who are able to harness the creativity of their factory workers, farmers, and especially their legions of workers (60 million-plus in America today) who work in low-status, low-paid service fields.

For the first time in modern memory our economic development literally requires us to develop everyone's creative capabilities to the fullest. So maybe the rise of the creative class is the first step down the road to the classless society the United States has always aspired to be.

BIBLIOGRAPHY

Boschma, Ron A., and Michael Fritsch. "Creative Class and Regional Growth—Empirical Evidence from Seven European Countries." *Economic Geography* 85 (2009): 391–423.

Clark, Terry Nichols, Richard Lloyd, Kenneth K. Wong, and Pushpam Jain. "Amenities Drive Urban Growth." *Journal of Urban Affairs* 24, no. 5 (2002): 493–515.

Florida, Richard. *The Flight of the Creative Class: The New Global Competition for Talent.* (New York, 2005).

Florida, Richard. *The Rise of the Creative Class: And How It's Transforming Work, Leisure, Community, and Everyday Life.* (New York, 2002).

Florida, Richard. *Who's Your City? How the Creative Economy Is Making Where to Live the Most Important Decision of Your Life.* (New York, 2009).

Florida, Richard, Charlotta Mellander, and Kevin Stolarick. "Inside the Black Box of Regional Development—Human Capital, the Creative Class and Tolerance." *Journal of Economic Geography* 8 (2008): 615–649.

Florida, Richard, Charlotta Mellander, and Kevin Stolarick. "Talent, Technology and Tolerance in Canadian Regional Development." Martin Prosperity Institute Working Paper. 2009, http://www.creativeclass.com/rfcgdb/articles/Talent%20Technology.pdf.

McGranahan, David, and Timothy Wojan. "Recasting the Creative Class to Examine Growth Processes in Rural and Urban Counties." *Regional Studies* 41, no. 2 (2007): 197–216.

Mellander, Charlotta, and Richard Florida. "The Creative Class or Human Capital? Explaining Regional Development in Sweden." Working Paper Series in Economics and Institutions of Innovation, Centre of Excellence for Science and Innovation Studies, no. 79. 2007, http://papers.cesis.se/CESISWP79.pdf.

Richard Florida

CRIME AND PUNISHMENT

America's prison population has increased fivefold since the 1960s. As of 2011, there was one prisoner for every hundred adults, a rate unprecedented in American history and unmatched anywhere in the world. This article summarizes some salient aspects of America's crime and punishment field, including the country's high rates of lethal violence, the crime decline of 1990–2010, white-collar crime, women and crime, policing, prosecution, imprisonment, probation and parole, capital punishment, and miscarriages of justice.

Crime and Lethal Violence. Scholars who study crime focus on two main questions: why individuals differ in the rate at which they commit crime and why crime rates vary across societies. The answers to these questions differ markedly because the factors that put individuals at risk for committing crime overlap only a little with the forces that influence how much crime a society has. For example, young men are much more likely to commit crime than young women or older men, but most societies have roughly the same share of young men yet differ dramatically in their overall crime rates. Over the past half-century, scholars have made great gains in explaining why some people are more likely to commit crimes than other people, but they have made only modest gains in understanding what lies behind a nation's crime rate.

In comparative perspective, the United States is not an especially "high-crime" society. Indeed, for most categories of nonviolent crime—burglary, theft, and other property offenses—American crime rates are about the same as or even lower than those in other industrialized societies; and the same trend holds true for specific cities of roughly the same size, such as New York and London or Los Angeles and Sydney. In comparative perspective, what sets America apart from other developed democracies is not crime per se but rather lethal violence, especially criminal homicide. In 2009, the US homicide rate of 5.0 per 100,000 population was one-third the rate for Mexico and one-tenth the rate for Guatemala but more than double the rate for Israel, triple the rate for Canada, four times the rate for the United Kingdom, and more than ten times the rates for Japan and Singapore. In explaining America's high rates of lethal violence, it is hard to overestimate the importance of guns, which are used in about 70 percent of all homicides. Most murders in America do not originate in criminal activity such as break-ins or muggings; they stem from arguments that turn deadly because of the ready supply of lethal weapons.

Most lethal violence in the United States is concentrated in pockets of social disadvantage and committed by young men between the ages of fifteen and thirty. Criminal violence is especially concentrated among young African American males. Black males are about twice as likely as whites to become victims of property crime but five times as likely to be killed. There are also huge differences in homicide between different cities and states. In recent years, for example, the homicide rate in Flint, Michigan, has been about thirty times higher than the homicide rates in Lincoln, Nebraska, and Honolulu, Hawaii; and southern states generally have had rates of lethal violence that exceed those in other regions of the country.

Crime Decline. From the early 1990s until well into the 2000s, the rates of many crimes declined all over the United States. For most common street crimes—homicide and nonnegligent manslaughter, robbery, rape, aggravated assault, arson, burglary, motor vehicle theft, and larceny—the decline was between 35 and 40 percent. These crimes declined in cities, suburbs, towns, and rural areas; in all regions of the country; and among offenders and victims in all age groups. America's broad and sustained crime decline was not typical of other developed nations, with one striking exception—Canada. Other G-7 nations experienced crime declines in some offense categories, but only Canada reported a broad decline as deep and long as that of the United States. The parallel experience of Canada suggests that increased imprisonment, new styles of policing, and economic booms—none of which occurred in America's neighbor to the north—probably played a secondary role in the American crime decline. Canada's experience also suggests that cyclical influences not tied to economic fluctuations or criminal justice policy may have played a major role in both nations. It will not be possible to comprehend what caused crime to decline in the United States until more is known about the parallel crime decline in Canada.

The most noteworthy part of the great American crime decline concerns New York City. In the 1960s and 1970s, people of all classes in New York lived in fear that they might be mugged, assaulted, or killed; but since 1990 the city's crime rates have fallen to their lowest levels in half a century. Today, the typical New Yorker is safer than he or she has been at any time since 1960. In 2010, the homicide rate in New York City was only about 20 percent as high as it was in 1990. Similarly, New York City's rape and robbery rates were only 19 percent of what they were twenty years ago, and its burglary rate was 15 percent of what it was. Most striking of all is New York City's auto theft rate, which in 2010 was only 8 percent of what it was in 1990. A crime decline as long, wide, and deep as New York's has never been documented in a major American metropolis. New York City's crime decline suggests that cities need not be incubators of robbery, rape, and murder. Contrary to what many commentators contended in the 1970s and 1980s, high rates of serious crime are not an essential part of urban living in America. This is a fundamental surprise to many students of crime in America and one of the most hopeful insights of criminology in a century. The New York story also suggests that major changes in rates of crime can occur without major changes in society.

White-Collar Crime. To many analysts in the media and academia, crime in the suites is little more than a footnote to the "real" problem of crime in the streets. But the truth is that white-collar crime may well be the greatest crime problem in America, whether measured in terms of financial losses, deaths and injuries, or damage to the social fabric. Bernard Madoff's Ponzi scheme resulted in losses of at least $18 billion. For a run-of-the-mill robber to cause as much financial damage he or she would have to steal $50,000 from every person living in New Orleans or Honolulu. Similarly, the annual losses in the United States from antitrust violations are estimated to be ten times more than all the annual losses from all other crimes reported to the police. The asbestos industry's cover-up of the dangers of its products probably cost as many lives as all the murders in the United States for an entire decade, and another popular product, cigarettes, takes more lives than that every year. Until the Watergate scandal of the early 1970s focused attention on the issue of white-collar crime, its consequences were largely invisible. Even today, the salience of white-collar crime remains low for several reasons: because the media tend to focus on street crime, because the laws defining white-collar offenses are contested and controversial, and because the white-collar offenses that are exposed are often too complicated to fit the simple scripts that gain traction in the court of public opinion. Scholars who study white-collar crime tend to be assigned less status than their colleagues who study rape, robbery, and homicide.

Women and Crime. The subject of women and crime has been invisible for much of the history of criminology. This inattention to half the population was often justified by claims that women and girls are less involved in crime and criminal justice than men and boys are. Males in America are almost ten times more likely to commit murder than females are, and men are more likely to be victimized by most violent crimes, with the important exception of rape and the possible exception of assault (many domestic assaults go unreported). Men are also much more likely to be imprisoned—about 13 times more likely as of 2010. But crime and imprisonment rates for women and girls have grown more rapidly than those for men and boys, and there has also been a significant increase in the number of studies on gender and crime. Two central findings are that girls and women do not commit crime for the same reasons that boys and men do and that men and women have different needs and experiences in the criminal process.

Policing. In some ways policing in America has changed greatly since 1970. The most striking transformation is in the faces and backgrounds of police officers. America now has many more female and minority officers than it did in 1970, and the average level of education among police recruits is much higher. There has also been considerable experimentation in police strategy. Innovations include community policing, problem-oriented policing, broken windows policing, zero-tolerance policing, and quality-of-life policing, all of which stress (at least in principle) closer relationships between police officers and citizens, with the aim of improving public trust in the police and directly addressing disorder problems that undermine the public's sense of security.

Despite all the demographic and strategic innovation that has occurred in American policing, conventional police activities and systems still predominate in most jurisdictions. Most police personnel continue to be assigned to random patrol on the assumption that responding to citizen requests on a case-by-case basis is the best means of providing police services to the public. Most fundamentally, arrest is still widely perceived as the default response to most crime and disorder problems, for several reasons: because citizens and elected officials tend to perceive law enforcement as the central police function, because police themselves believe arrest is central to their mission, because arrest remains the most commonly rewarded form of police activity, and because police officers' discretion not to invoke the criminal process through arrest is inadequately acknowledged and structured.

Police reliance on arrest has important consequences in addition to fueling America's incarceration boom. In particular, the pressures which encourage arrest also produce searches and detentions without adequate legal justification, racially biased enforcement, the planting of false evidence, and the use of false police testimony in pretrial reports and court hearings. At the core of many persistent problems in American policing, from ineffective crime control to corruption and the excessive use of force, is misplaced faith in deterrence as the basis for how police should attempt to achieve their objectives. For deterrence to work more effectively, offenders should be given clear information about police priorities and targets; communities should be mobilized to deter specific offenders and offenses; minor sanctions should be employed more often and more quickly after an offense occurs; groups, rather than individual offenders, should be the focus of more deterrence efforts; and offenders should be engaged morally, not merely targeted with threats. By reframing the ways in which the police pursue deterrence, more crimes could be prevented.

Prosecution. Prosecutors have more control over life, liberty, and reputation than any other persons in America, largely because they possess vast discretion to decide who gets what in the criminal process.

At the core of the prosecutor's power is the process of plea bargaining, through which more than 90 percent of all criminal cases are disposed. Plea bargaining is important for two main reasons: because this is how the large majority of criminal cases are resolved and because this is what largely determines the content and quality of American criminal justice. Plea bargaining is not only the motor that makes American criminal justice run; it concentrates immense authority in the prosecutor's hands by making him or her judge and jury in his or her own case.

There are several theories of how plea bargaining achieved its dominance in American criminal justice. Some analysts argue that the burden of heavy caseloads rendered plea bargaining necessary in order to avoid collapse of the justice system. Others look beyond the criminal court community to focus on broader social forces (such as the nineteenth-century imperative of state formation) that facilitated the rise of plea bargaining. Still others contend that plea bargaining triumphed because it served the interests of powerful actors in the criminal courts. Whatever the causes of plea bargaining's historical rise and present hegemony, the likelihood of it occurring depends on a calculus which compares (1) what is offered for a guilty plea with (2) the expected sentence after trial if it should end in conviction, discounted by (3) the probability of being found guilty at trial. If the likelihood of being convicted at trial is high, then the difference between the two sentences is the chief determinate of whether a deal occurs. On the other hand, if the likelihood of acquittal at trial seems good, then the defendant will choose trial even if there is a large sentencing differential. In general, the greater the difference between the sentence offered in plea bargaining and the sentence expected after trial, the more defendants will plead guilty and waive their right to trial. In this sense, the *sentencing differential* is critically important because it determines the proportion of defendants who will go to trial. On the whole, defendants who exercise their right to a jury trial and are convicted receive much harsher sentences than they would have received if they had pled guilty and waived their right to trial. In many cases the magnitude of this trial tax is very high—two, four, or even six times higher than the expected sentence for the same offense after a guilty plea. In this respect, plea bargaining in America is coercive at its core.

The power of American prosecutors has increased with the rise in mandatory minimum sentencing laws, which shift discretion over sentencing outcomes from judges to the prosecution. America's adversarial system of criminal justice also creates incentives which encourage prosecutors to focus almost exclusively on securing convictions instead of on other objectives such as rehabilitation and reintegration. Moreover, most of the important decisions prosecutors make—especially the decisions to charge and plea bargain—are highly discretionary and almost unreviewable. Unlike judges, parole boards, and police, prosecutors in America have largely escaped the kind of scrutiny and accountability that are demanded of other legal officials. For the most part, prosecutors have been left to regulate themselves, and this self-regulation is woefully inadequate.

Imprisonment. America's incarceration rate in the early 1970s fluctuated between 100 and 150 inmates per 100,000 population. By contrast, the rate in 2008 was 750, making the United States the world incarceration leader, with a rate five times higher than that of England or Spain and eight times higher than that of France or Germany. As of 2008, more than one in every 100 adults was confined in jail or prison, saddling cash-strapped states with soaring costs while failing to have much of an effect on crime or recidivism. Nationwide, 43 percent of American convicts end up back behind bars within three years of their release, and the rates in some states exceed 50 percent. America's much increased reliance on imprisonment has had modest consequences for crime control. By most accounts, the incarceration boom that began in the 1980s accounts for less than one-fourth of the big crime decline of the 1990s and 2000s. In New York City, where the crime decline has been longer, deeper, and broader than in other American jurisdictions, the rate at which the city filled its jails and the state's prisons was well below the national incarceration pattern throughout the period while crime fell.

Mass imprisonment has not been driven by increases in crime or changes in population. It has mainly been caused by "tough on crime" policy choices that send more lawbreakers to prison for longer periods of time. In many states, the incarceration boom has also been fueled by the routine use of prison to punish persons who violate the rules of probation or parole. These policy decisions have been shaped by a variety of social and political forces, including the social organization of late modernity, the neoliberal and free-market politics that came to dominate America in the 1980s, and the benefits politicians perceive and receive from "governing through crime" (Simon 2007). For elites in many sectors of society, crime has become an important strategic issue, and leaders are seen as behaving legitimately when they act to prevent crime or other behavior that can be analogized to crime. Technologies, discourses, and metaphors of crime and punishment have also become increasingly visible features of many institutions in American society, from families and schools to workplaces and public housing.

America's incarceration boom has had serious collateral consequences. In 2007, total spending on corrections topped $49 billion, versus $12 billion in 1987. Spending on incarceration often crowds out spending on other priorities. Most notably, more money for jail and prison cells means less money for police and classrooms. Mass imprisonment also conceals poverty and inequality because the young men and women who are locked up do not get counted in official work and welfare statistics. America's penal system also deepens inequality by diminishing the life chances of the disadvantaged. One of the most pernicious consequences of America's incarceration boom concerns race. Nationwide, approximately one in three young black men are under control of the criminal justice system, and in cities such as Washington D.C. and Baltimore the proportion approaches one-half. Nearly 60 percent of black male high school dropouts born in the late 1960s were imprisoned before they turned 40. Some scholars argue that America has not really ended racial caste; it has merely redesigned it. On this view, legal segregation has been replaced by mass incarceration as a system of social control.

Probation and Parole. As of 2008, America's penal system held more than 2.3 million adults behind bars. China, with an authoritarian government and four times the population, incarcerated only about two-thirds that number. But while America relies more on imprisonment than any other nation, it uses the noncustodial punishments of probation and parole even more often than incarceration. In 2009, 5 million Americans were under supervision in the community on probation or parole—about one out of every forty-seven adults. Probationers, who are ordered to follow conditions defined by a court instead of being sent to prison, numbered 4.2 million in 2009, while parolees, who are supervised in the community after release from prison, made up the other 800,000. In 2005, only 45 percent of parolees completed their sentences successfully, while 38 percent were returned to prison and 11 percent absconded. These statistics have remained largely unchanged since 1995.

Parole has declined as imprisonment has boomed. At least sixteen states have abolished parole entirely, and four more have abolished it for certain violent offenders. During elections, politicians whose administrations parole large numbers of prisoners—or even one notorious criminal—are often attacked by their opponents for being "soft on crime." One result is an increased reluctance to grant parole even when it is available.

Prisoner reentry is a pressing problem in America. Every year, hundreds of thousands of incarcerated persons leave prison and return to society. Fewer than one in three inmates receive substance-abuse or mental health treatment while they are incarcerated, and each year fewer and fewer participate in the dwindling number of vocational or educational prerelease programs, leaving many all but unemployable. When inmates are released, many are uneducated, unskilled, and without family support. The large majority get rearrested, most within six months of release. What happens when prisoners come home is both a major public safety challenge and a revealing index of what kind of society America has become. One promising approach is to focus enforcement on certain parolees and probationers by clearly specifying the rules they must follow and then delivering the promised sanctions every time the rules are broken.

Capital Punishment. Since 1960 capital punishment has declined in many parts of the world. There remain three strongholds in the world today: Asia, the Muslim-majority nations of the Middle East, and the United States, where thirty-four states and the federal system retain the death penalty and where the vast majority of executions are concentrated in a handful of southern states. Many scholars have tried to explain why these American jurisdictions cling to capital punishment when all other developed democracies except Japan have abandoned it or stopped executing. Some argue that the main cause is a long-standing commitment to vigilante values, especially in the south. On this view, vigilante values support capital punishment by framing it as a local imperative to serve victims rather than as an issue of state power and human rights. Others stress the prominent role of degradation in American punishment. On this view, punishments in the United States are harsher than those in Europe because American traditions of egalitarianism and distrust of state power discourage the merciful and respectful treatment of offenders. Still others contend that efforts to reform capital punishment have entrenched the institution. On this view, by pruning capital punishment of some of its problems, courts and legislatures have increased the durability of what remains.

To survive in an age of abolition, American capital punishment has had to adapt. At the heart of this has been a court-centered process of reinvention which accelerated after the US Supreme Court's *Furman* decision of 1972 held that the death penalty as then practiced was unconstitutional. America's reinvented death penalty evinces three main themes. First, capital punishment must be subject to the discipline of legal rules and procedures, a mission which is grounded in the Fourteenth Amendment and which has generated many of the hallmarks of contemporary capital punishment, including infrequent executions, frequent reversals and exonerations, long delays, and high costs. Second, American capital punishment has been "civilized" and "humanized" in order to prohibit "cruel and unusual" practices that might violate the Eighth Amendment and in order to minimize the most disturbing aspects of the capital process, especially those pertaining to the moment and method of execution. Third, the death penalty in America has been democratized and localized, a purpose that is rooted in the Constitution's separation of powers and that requires returning control of capital punishment to legislators, prosecutors, jurors, and judges at the local level.

Many analysts believe America's reinvented death penalty fulfills no purposes, serves no functions, and possesses no rationale. It is used too rarely to be effective as a deterrent. It is badly infected with bias—by race, class, gender, and geography. It is administered arbitrarily and capriciously. It fails to achieve the factual and moral accuracy that theories of retribution and moral proportion require. It frustrates more victims than it serves. And it is inconsistent with the country's core values. On the whole, this scholarship concludes that American capital punishment is as incoherent a practice as leeching or rain dancing. Although these critiques are correct in so far as they go, many of them fail to consider one key question: Why does the death penalty persist in the face of so much challenge and criticism? The best answer is that capital punishment is productive and performative in a wide variety of ways, especially in the cultural realm of death penalty discourse.

Miscarriages of Justice. Decisions about who and how to punish rest on an assumption that the criminal process accurately discerns who did what to whom. Although the overall rate of error in America's criminal justice system is unknown and probably unknowable, research has revealed many wrongful convictions. For example, 138 people in twenty-six states have been released from death row since 1973 with evidence of their innocence, and more than 250 people have been exonerated by DNA testing since

1992, including seventeen who had been sentenced to death. There is also evidence that miscarriages of justice may be more common in America's adversarial system of criminal justice than in the more inquisitorial systems of northern and western Europe.

Wrongful convictions result in many serious harms. A wrongly convicted person loses his or her freedom while being forced to experience the dangers and deprivations of imprisonment. The public loses trust in the criminal process and is forced to pay for incarcerating the innocent. When the wrong person is behind bars, the real perpetrator remains free to commit other crimes. And wrongful conviction frequently remains a life-threatening trauma even after exoneration.

The main sources of wrongful conviction are eyewitness misidentification (the single greatest cause of miscarriages of justice), false confessions, perjured testimony, forensic mistakes, tunnel vision, prosecutorial misconduct, and the ineffective assistance of counsel. In addition to these primary sources (which often co-occur), racial prejudice, media pressure, and the failure of postconviction remedies contribute to many miscarriages of justice. Some reforms, such as electronically recording interrogations and conducting eyewitness lineups sequentially (one person at a time) instead of all at once, are known to reduce the likelihood of wrongful conviction; but in many American states there has been deep resistance to implementing changes that would likely make a difference for the better.

Implications. Students of crime and punishment in America can learn much from the policies and practices of other democratic nations. Many nations protect public safety better than the United States and without relying as heavily on arrest, imprisonment, and death as a criminal sanction. In America, harsh "zero-tolerance" approaches to crime may be good politics but they are bad policy because there are always more offenses than there is capacity to punish. For decades, most American jurisdictions have been trying to solve their crime problems with brute force, mainly by building more and more prisons and jails. The country's crime problem has diminished, but it remains stuck with high rates of lethal violence—and a huge incarceration problem. The first step away from brute force requires wanting to get away from it: to care more about reducing crime than about punishing offenders and to choose safety over retribution when the two are in tension.

[*See also* African Americans, Contemporary Conditions; Capital Punishment; Domestic Violence; Gun Control; Inequalities of Wealth and Income; Poverty, Scale and Nature of; Race, Gender, and Incarceration; *and* Race and Racism.]

BIBLIOGRAPHY

Alexander, Michelle. *The New Jim Crow: Mass Incarceration in the Age of Colorblindness.* (New York, 2010).
Belknap, Joanne. *The Invisible Woman: Gender, Crime, and Justice.* (Belmont, Calif, 2006).
Coleman, James W. *The Criminal Elite: Understanding White-Collar Crime.* (New York, 2006).
Davis, Angela J. *Arbitrary Justice: The Power of the American Prosecutor.* (New York, 2007).
"Death Penalty Information Center." 2011, http://www.deathpenaltyinfo.org.
Garland, David. *The Culture of Control: Crime and Social Order in Contemporary Society.* (Chicago, Ill., 2001).
Garland, David. *Peculiar Institution: America's Death Penalty in an Age of Abolition.* (Cambridge, Mass., 2010).
Gould, Jon B., and Richard A. Leo. "One Hundred Years Later: Wrongful Convictions after a Center of Research." *Journal of Criminal Law and Criminology* 100, no. 3 (2010): 825–868.
Harcourt, Bernard E. *The Illusion of Free Markets: Punishment and the Myth of Natural Order.* (Cambridge, Mass., 2011).
Huff, C. Ronald, and Martin Killias, eds. *Wrongful Conviction: International Perspectives on Miscarriages of Justice.* (Philadelphia, Pa., 2008).
Justice Policy Institute. "Finding Direction: Expanding Criminal Justice Options by Considering Policies of Other Nations." 2011, http://www.justicepolicy.org/uploads/justicepolicy/documents/finding_direction-full_report.pdf.
Kennedy, David M. *Deterrence and Crime Prevention: Reconsidering the Prospect of Sanction.* (New York, 2008)
Kleiman, Mark A. R. *When Brute Force Fails: How to Have Less Crime and Less Punishment.* (Princeton, N.J., 2009).
Langbein, John H. "Torture and Plea Bargaining." *University of Chicago Law Review* 46 (1978): 3–22.
Mauer, Marc, and Meda Chesney-Lind. *Invisible Punishment: The Collateral Consequences of Mass Imprisonment.* (New York, 2003).

Peterselia, Joan. *When Prisoners Come Home: Parole and Prisoner Reentry.* (New York, 2003).

Pew Center on the States. "One in 100: Behind Bars in America 2008." 2009, http://www.pewcenteronthestates.org/uploadedFiles/One%20in%20100.pdf.

Scott, Michael S. "Progress in American Policing? Reviewing the National Reviews." *Law & Social Inquiry* 34, no. 1 (Winter 2008): 171–185.

Simon, Jonathan. *Governing through Crime: How the War on Crime Transformed American Democracy and Created a Culture of Fear.* (New York, 2007).

Sklansky, David Alan. *Democracy and Police.* (Stanford, Calif., 2008).

Wacquant, Loic. *Punishing the Poor: The Neoliberal Government of Social Insecurity.* (Durham, N.C., 2009).

Western, Bruce. *Punishment and Inequality in America.* (New York, 2006).

Whitman, James Q. *Harsh Justice: Criminal Punishment and the Widening Divide between America and Europe.* (New York, 2003).

Wilson, James Q., and Joan Peterselia, eds. *Crime and Public Policy.* (New York, 2011).

Zimring, Franklin E. *The City That Became Safe: New York's Lessons for American Crime Control.* (New York, 2011).

Zimring, Franklin E. *The Contradictions of American Capital Punishment.* (New York, 2003).

Zimring, Franklin E. *The Great American Crime Decline.* (New York, 2008).

Zimring, Franklin E., and Gordon Hawkins. *Crime Is Not the Problem: Lethal Violence in America.* (New York, 1997).

David T. Johnson

CULTURE WARS

While the concept can be found earlier, the term "culture war" was largely popularized in the media, political discourse, and academia by James Davidson Hunter's 1991 work *Culture Wars: The Struggle to Define America.* The central assertion of the culture war thesis is that traditional cleavages, dividing Americans by class, race, region, and gender, have given way to single cleavage, dividing Americans with traditional religious and moral views from secular humanist and religious progressives. This divide between orthodox and progressive Americans is not merely the result of a variance of opinion on the issues of the day, but arises from incommensurable conceptions of the sources of moral authority, which shape those opinions. The former, orthodox group sees religion as this source, while the latter, progressive group turns to human reason and experience. In the political realm, the two sides divide over both long-standing and emerging moral and cultural issues, such as stem cell research, abortion, gay rights, gun control, the teaching of evolution, public religious displays, school prayer, and obscenity, (although the latter two have received less attention in recent years). In line with the theory, these differences extend beyond political issues to caricatured cultural differences including media preferences (Fox News and Christian talk radio versus MSNBC and National Public Radio's *Morning Edition*), entertainment preferences (NASCAR and Toby Keith versus soccer and James Taylor), shopping preferences (Walmart versus Whole Foods), and geography (rural and South or Midwest versus urban and Northeast or West), and the prioritization of values (traditional morality and religious liberty versus social justice and individual liberty).

Concomitantly, this division of values has been mirrored by the ideological division between the nation's two political parties. For most of the twentieth century Democrats and Republicans were divided primarily by economic issues. With the realignment of the parties along the moral and cultural division in the broader society, the culture war became a dominant paradigm in American politics as well as the *consensus gentium* of political and media elites. At the 1992 Republican National Convention, Patrick Buchanan famously declared that the United States was locked in a culture war for the soul of the nation. The conventional wisdom holds that as the distance between the orthodox and progressive Americans has increased, along with the number of adherents to each position, the two political parties have become increasingly polarized. Thus the culture war is played out in litigation over hot-button issues, highly contested judicial appointments, and close and contentious elections, as well as episodes such as the alleged "war on Christmas" (i.e., an intentional effort to remove sectarian references).

Since the 2000 election, the aggregate pictorial depiction of an America divided between the "red states" of the South and the heartland (i.e., those states won by George W. Bush) and the coastal "blue states" of the West and Northeast (i.e., those states won by Al Gore) seemed to vividly capture this phenomena, and the red state–blue state divide became synonymous with the culture war. Indeed, some have suggested the emergent controversy over same-sex marriage as the driving force behind the victory of George W. Bush in the 2004 presidential election.

Challenges to the Culture War Thesis. Empirical evidence has challenged some of the basic assertions of the culture war thesis. Most notably, while a new moral and cultural divide has emerged, it has not displaced the earlier economic divide. Rather, the ideological space of public opinion has become multidimensional, and while political party elites may be aligned consistently across both divides, individuals in the mass electorate are not equally "orthodox" or "progressive" across all issues. Public opinion is structured by cross-cutting divides in a multidimensional ideological space. For instance, while evangelicals are solidly in the orthodox camp on moral and cultural issues, such as abortion and same-sex marriage, their position on economic issues, such as wealth redistribution, is more variable dependent upon their socioeconomic station.

Empirical evidence also reveals public opinion has not become more polarized since the 1970s (i.e., greater numbers of people holding positions at the far ends of the political spectrum), nor have individuals become more ideologically consistent (i.e., taking the same ideological position across a range of issues). Furthermore, while the distance between public opinions on moral and cultural issues in red and blue states is statistically significant, it is substantively small, leading many scholars to describe the majority of the country as "purple," that is, neither fully red nor blue, but a blend of the two. Indeed, a single party perennially dominates major elected offices in few states. These findings mean that (1) the presence of cross-party divides makes it unlikely that two diametrically opposed camps will form; (2) the number of foot soldiers in each camp is not increasing; and (3) while geographic distinctions exist they are not substantive. These findings also appear to affirm what political science has known since the 1960s: Americans are largely ambivalent about politics and are politically unsophisticated, in that they don't organize their political behavior ideologically, so that their ideological position varies across issues and time.

Given these empirical challenges, a number of explanations have been posited to explain the perception of the presence of a culture war. One driver is a ubiquitous news media with an appetite for conflict that has embraced the rhetoric of the culture war, exaggerating the differences between Democrats and Republicans as well as misapplying real differences between political elites to the electorate as a whole. In addition, closely contested elections are not resultant from two highly committed, evenly divided camps with radically distinct ideology, but rather due to the fact that most Americans gravitate toward the center, while the candidates and political parties have become more ideologically distinct. Voters choose candidates with more extreme positions, not because they hold those positions, but because their choices are limited to the available candidates who do. Finally, the rhetoric of the culture war has been a propitious means for political elites to increase campaign contribution and mobilize voters as well as for lobbyists to rally support.

Elite Polarization. While the culture war thesis is not reflected in the quantitative distribution of the electorate, its premise does resonate with some of the contemporary realties of American politics, as political elites and activists have become more polarized, not only along moral and cultural lines, but also economic ones. The myriad causes of elite polarization include (1) the explosive growth in the size and scope of government in the second half of the twentieth century, adding an endless list of new issues to the public agenda and activists who support or stand in opposition to them; (2) democratic reforms which have weakened traditional party structures, favoring ideologues over opportunists and providing greater access for activists; and (3) the exploitation of the moral and cultural issues by strategic politicians.

This does not mean that the culture war is a myth imposed upon the electorate by political elites. Rather, strategic politicians in both parties, who saw the potential to bring new supporters into their electoral coalitions, championed distinct positions on emerging moral and cultural issues. These issues arose in part from the expanded reach of government and aligned with a genuine religious cleavage between orthodox and progressive Americans. Concomitantly, conservative and liberal political activists associated with these moral and cultural issues began to support the party of the strategic politicians whose positions aligned with their own. Both because of their advocacy within the parties and because of the potential strategic benefits they could accrue, the ideological positions of the two major parties, already divided along an economic cleavage, came to align with the latent religious cleavage. Once this shift was recognized, the mass electorate realigned itself accordingly.

Thus politicians are tapping into real differences in the electorate, and in some cases those differences are deep. American's opinion on moral and cultural issues, such as abortion and gay rights, are more likely to cluster at the extremes, in comparison to economic, educational, or environmental issues. Moreover, there is some evidence that polarization on moral and cultural issues has increased over time. These realities have led some to question whether elite attitudes can remain polarized without such polarization eventually trickling down to become reflected in the electorate. Evidence of this possibility may be seen in the increasingly negative partisan attitudes toward members of the opposition or in the increasing geographic segregation of partisans. Between 1976 and 2004, the number of voters who lived in a county where one presidential candidate captured at least 20 percent more of the vote than the opposition candidate jumped from 26 to 48 percent. Given that elite opinion drives mass opinion and elite opinion is polarized, some have cautioned that the culture war may become a self-fulfilling prophecy.

Limited Culture War. If the culture war thesis is applicable to elites, what then is the scope of the phenomena among the mass electorate? The culture war has not moved into the mass electorate largely because most Americas are politically unsophisticated, uninformed, and ambivalent. It might be surmised that if this were not the case, polarization in the electorate might mirror that among elites. Empirical evidence reveals that, while the ideological positions of most Americans have not become more polarized, they are more likely to reflect that ideology in their political behavior. As the parties have taken more distinctive positions on moral and cultural as well as economic issues, voters have been better able to sort themselves between the two parties. This is why studies measuring polarization as the increasing levels of issue-based partisan sorting find evidence for it, while those measuring it as clustering at the far ends of the political spectrum do not.

Thus, while the horizontal constraint predicted by the culture war thesis (i.e., ideological consistency across issues domains) has not increased, vertical constraint (i.e., stronger connection between certain core values and political behavior) has increased. Yet even increases in vertical constraint are not equally robust across issues domains, but have occurred primarily among moral and cultural issues. This vertical constraint does not depend only on strategic political elites adopting distinct positions on cultural and moral issues, but also on religious elites, and arguably the opinion leaders of other moral and cultural interest groups, connecting core values with issues, in turn raising their salience and driving the political behavior of their constituents. If the parties deemphasize their divergence on these moral and cultural issues—as was arguably true of the 2008 presidential race between Barack Obama and John McCain—the cleavage between orthodox and progressive Americans will have less impact on political behavior. Thus among the electorate, the culture war is limited (1) to moral and cultural issues, which can be logically connected to the underlying religious divide; and (2) to individuals who are associated with communities, typically churches, which nurture these connections, raising issue salience; and (3) to the political parties taking distinctive positions on these issues, emphasizing their divergence so that they are recognizable by voters. Given these three conditions, increasing horizontal constraint in the mass electorate, as predicted by the culture war thesis, is unlikely.

The limited scope of the culture war among the electorate is not insignificant. In the aggregate, these voters represent sizable blocs of the party coalitions, which can be mobilized by appeals to moral and cultural issues, and thus impact the vote. Accordingly these aggregate effects could expand over time, if the number of voters for whom moral and cultural issues are highly salient increases because of shifting religious demographics, or the domain of the moral and cultural issues expands to include new issues, such as the host of equal protection, employment, and family issues which could arise from the legalization of same-sex marriage. Likewise, as political allegiances based on moral and cultural divides deepen, issues which are only tangentially related to the underlying religious cleavage maybe be added. For instance, religious traditionalists overwhelmingly supported the Iraq War, while secular and religious progressives overwhelmingly opposed it. Yet, it may also be true that the political ambivalence of the electorate on most issues may lead to a backlash against the use of culture war rhetoric, which over time, if exploited by strategic politicians, could mute the impact of moral and cultural issues. Barack Obama was widely seen as employing this strategy in the 2008 election, as a candidate who ran against the culture war.

[See also Elections and Electoral Behavior.]

BIBLIOGRAPHY

Bacon, Perry, Jr., and Shailagh Murray. "Opponents Paint Obama as an Elitist: Clinton, McCain Try to Score off 'Bitter' Remark." *Washington Post*, 12 April 2008.

Baker, Wayne. *America's Crisis of Values: Reality and Perception*. (Princeton, N.J., 2005).

Bartels, Larry M. "What's the Matter with *What's the Matter with Kansas?*" *Quarterly Journal of Political Science* 1 (2006): 201–226.

Bartlett, Donald L., and James B. Steele. *America: Who Stole the Dream?* (Kansas City, Kans., 1996).

Brooks, David. "One Nation, Slightly Divisible." *Atlantic Monthly*, December 2001.

Buchanan, Patrick J. *The Death of the West: How Dying Populations and Immigrant Invasions Imperil Our Country and Civilization*. (New York, 2002).

Chapman, Roger, ed. *Culture Wars: An Encyclopedia of Issues, Viewpoints, and Voices*. Vol. 1. (Armonk, N.Y., 2010).

Davis, Nancy J., and Robert V. Robinson. "Are the Rumors of War Exaggerated? Religious Orthodoxy and Moral Progressivism in America." *American Journal of* Sociology 102 (1996): 756–787.

Davis, Nancy J., and Robert V. Robinson. "Religious Orthodoxy in Society: The Myth of a Monolithic Camp." *Journal for the Scientific Study of Religion* 35 (1996): 229–245.

DiMaggio, Paul, John Evans, and Bethany Bryson. "Have Americans' Social Attitudes Become More Polarized?" *American Journal of Sociology* 102 (1996): 690–755.

Fiorina, Morris P., Samuel J. Abrams, and Jeremy C. Pope. *Culture War? The Myth of a Polarized America*. (New York, 2005).

Frank, Thomas. *What's the Matter With Kansas? How Conservatives Won the Heart of America*. (New York, 2004).

Green, John C., James L. Guth, Corwin E. Smidt, and Lyman A. Kellstedt. *Religion and the Culture Wars: Dispatches from the Front*. (Lanham, Md., 1996).

Greenberg, Stanley. *Middle Class Dreams: The Politics and Power of the New American Majority*. (New Haven, Conn., 1996).

Hetherington, Marc J., and Jonathan Daniel Weiler. *Authoritarianism and Polarization in American Politics*. (New York, 2009).

Himmelfarb, Gertrude. *One Nation, Two Cultures: A Searching Examination of American Society in the Aftermath of Our Cultural Revolution*. (New York, 2001).

Hunter, James Davison. *Culture Wars: The Struggle to Define America*. (New York, 1991).

Layman, Geoffrey. *The Great Divide: Religious and Cultural Conflict in American Party Politics*. (New York, 2001).

Layman, Geoffrey C., and John C. Green. "Wars and Rumors of War: The Contexts of Cultural Conflict in American Political Behavior." *British Journal of Political Science* 36 (2006): 61–89.

Mouw, Ted, and Michael E. Sobel. "Culture Wars and Opinion Polarization: The Case of Abortion." *American Journal of Sociology* 106 (2001): 913–943.

Teixeira, Ruy A. *Red, Blue, & Purple America: The Future of Election Demographics*. (Washington, D.C., 2008).

Teixeira, Ruy A., and Joel Rogers. *America's Forgotten Majority: Why the White Working Class Still Matters*. (New York, 2000).

Wald, Kenneth D., and Allison Calhoun-Brown. *Religion and Politics in the United States*. 5th ed. (Lanham, Md., 2007).

Wallis, Jim. *God's Politics: Why the Right Gets It Wrong and the Left Doesn't Get It*. (San Francisco, 2005).

White, John Kenneth. *The Values Divide: American Politics and Culture in Transition*. (New York, 2003).

Williams, Rhys H., ed. *Cultural Wars in American Politics: Critical Reviews of a Popular Myth*. (New York, 1997).

Wilson, James Q. "Divided We Stand: Can a Polarized Nation Win a Protracted War?" *Wall Street Journal*, 15 February 2006.

Wolfe, Alan. *One Nation, After All: What Middle-Class Americans Really Think About: God, Country, Family, Racism, Welfare, Immigration, Homosexuality, Work, the Right, the Left, and Each Other*. (New York, 1998).

Wuthnow, Robert. *The Restructuring of American Religion: Society and Faith since World War II*. (Princeton, N.J., 1988).

Wuthnow, Robert. *The Struggle for America's Soul: Evangelicals, Liberals, and Secularism*. (Grand Rapids, Mich., 1989).

M. Joseph Burger

D

DARFUR

Darfur ("Land of the Fur") is a semiarid region in westernmost Sudan equivalent in size to Spain. A poorly developed landlocked area, Darfur lies at the heart of an important strategic junction within north-central Africa. Bordering Libya, Chad, the Central African Republic, and the Republic of South Sudan (hereafter South Sudan), Darfur has long been the focus of internal and external territorial struggles and, equally significant, has historically provided a counterweight to authority in Khartoum, Sudan's capital.

Darfur's demography is multifarious. Defining groups as simply "Arab" and "non-Arab" (or "African") obscures a complex ethnographic phenomenon and is a misleading modern-day bifurcation. Darfur's population, comprising between six and seven million people, is Muslim, indigenous, black, and African. Nevertheless, there is an abundance of subgroups within that population, each with distinct identities and fluid affiliations. Kinship is often socially and politically constructed based on nomadic or sedentary practices of agriculture and self-identity, rather than racial characteristics.

Described by the United Nations as "the world's greatest humanitarian and human rights catastrophe," Darfur became headline news in early 2003. However, Darfur's path to violence—for which the region is regrettably now renowned—is multifaceted and historic. While often cloaked in overly polemic and reductionist terms, there have long been tensions within Darfur; the outbreak of violence in 2003 represents the culmination of these hostilities.

From a Powerful Sultanate to a Marginalized Region (c. 1630–2003). For the better part of almost three centuries, Darfur prospered as an independent sultanate. It resisted destabilizing pressures to become one of the most powerful kingdoms in the area. Only in 1917, a full eighteen years after Sudan came under British administration, was Darfur officially incorporated into Sudan.

With the fall of the sultanate, the Fur—the traditional rulers of Darfur and the largest population group, comprising approximately a third of the population—saw a gradual erosion of their power. Britain left a system of economic and political imbalances across the country's governance structures, with peripheral areas like Darfur suffering overt neglect. There was little improvement in the decades following Sudan's independence, which came in 1956. Khartoum exercised significant patronage from the center, manipulated the local government apparatus, and appropriated customary mechanisms of reconciliation. This policy resulted in the elevation of some groups above others, the destabilization of the traditional land tenure system, and the polarization of large sections of Darfur's demographic. Coupled with this, "Arab" supremacy and militarization was promoted not just by Khartoum but also by Libya.

Community power struggles resulted as groups realigned themselves within a fluctuating regional governance system.

In this evolving cultural, political, and socioeconomic context, a drought, resultant famine, and desertification occurred in the early to mid-1980s. The deteriorating ecology had an asymmetric impact, leading to migration from north Darfur to south Darfur, as nomads moved to relatively plentiful areas. As northern pastoralists encroached further onto the sedentary, farming Fur population in the south, land and water became increasingly contested. Land and power have always been inextricably linked in Darfur; this tension culminated in conflict between the Fur and a coalition of nomadic "Arab" tribes from 1987 to 1989. For the first time, nearly all of Darfur's "Arabs" came together, forming a mobilized alliance armed by Khartoum, and gaining easy access to the surplus of small arms from conflicts elsewhere in the region.

A second conflict occurred from 1995 to 1999 between the Masalit (another of Darfur's "non-Arab" groups) and "Arab" groups, thus further entrenching pseudo-ethnic cleavages within the region. In segmentary opposition to the armed "Arab" alliance, a parallel "African" ideology emerged among those groups in Darfur whose livelihoods were increasingly threatened. After generations of intermarriage, Darfur's heterogeneous population coalesced over issues of identity and resource utilization, which manifested itself as a quasi-interethnic struggle. By July 2001, an expanded group of sedentary farmers, dominated by the Fur, met and vowed to thwart "Arab" activities and policies in Darfur.

A "Humanitarian and Human Rights Catastrophe" (2003–). Darfur's most recent violence stems from an insurgency waged, following the 2001 agreement, by two rebel groups: the Sudan Liberation Army (SLA) and the Justice and Equality Movement (JEM). Both accused the government of marginalization and oppression. Encouraged by the utility of violence propagated by the (southern) Sudan People's Liberation Army (SPLA)—which subsequently negotiated wealth- and power-sharing deals, and eventually independence from Khartoum—Darfur's rebels made related demands vis-à-vis the rebalance of social, political, and economic power between Khartoum and Darfur, and within Darfur itself.

The fighting, which by 2003 was widespread and systematic, initially pitted Darfur's Fur, Zaghawa, and Masalit groups against government-backed counterinsurgency proxies. In addition to military operations, the counterinsurgency paramilitaries—including many members of the armed alliance, which had mobilized in the 1980s and was supported by government forces—conducted large-scale atrocities against those civilian populations associated with the rebels. As a result of conflict, since 2003 the UN estimates that 300,000 people have died, over two million internally displaced persons (IDPs) have fled to semipermanent settlements, and a quarter of a million people have escaped to neighboring Chad. Moreover, substantial looting, bombing, and destruction of property and livelihoods have occurred, in addition to non-fatal yet exceptionally brutal violence perpetrated against noncombatants.

There has been an evolving conflict trajectory, with significant temporal and spatial variations in the nature and intensity of violence. Most of the killings and atrocities occurred in 2003 and 2004, with 90 percent of today's refugee population having fled during that period. Except for intermittent episodes, Darfur has since suffered more localized skirmishes, intra-"Arab" communal violence, abductions, and criminality. Notable exceptions include the period after the establishment of the 2006 Darfur Peace Agreement (DPA), which saw a daring, albeit unsuccessful, May 2008 JEM offensive, which was eventually repelled in the Khartoum suburb of Omdurman; and the first three months of 2011, when 70,000 individuals fled fighting in western Darfur and the government renewed its airstrikes against the rebels. At the time of South Sudan's independence in July 2011, it remained to be seen how the impact of South Sudan's independence will impact on Darfur, although the prognosis is pessimistic. Many fear that we will see a proxy war between Sudan and South Sudan in Darfur, or a renewed assault by Darfur's rebels against what they see as a now weakened central government, or Khartoum undertaking military offensives in Darfur while the international spotlight is on South Sudan, rather than Sudan's western region.

Belligerents have also diversified. There has rarely been an underlying unity among Darfur's armed factions. There has been, on occasion, a ten-fold increase in the number of rebel groups since the signing of the DPA, with frequent fragmentation, reconstitution, and coalition formation. With varying strategic and political objectives, an absence of rebel unification has been a major stumbling block to peace. Similarly, despite popular manifestations to the contrary, the counterinsurgency paramilitaries have never been a monolithic entity; rather, they include elements of disparate groups sometimes acting as government proxy forces, and often acting independently of Khartoum and each other. Moreover, much of the violence in 2010 was a consequence of intra-"Arab" disputes, rather than rebel-government fighting. A number of Darfur's "Arab" groups too have sided with rebel groups, rather than against them.

Up until a January 2010 Sudan–Chad rapprochement, violence was further complicated by the active support and safe haven granted by Chadian authorities to Darfur's rebel groups. Conversely, Khartoum allowed Chad's own rebel groups to utilize Sudanese territory, resulting in considerable conflict contagion, spillover, and proxy war between the two states.

In July 2011, the Joint African Union–United Nations Special Representative for Darfur and Joint Chief Mediator identified the principle challenges to peace as: (1) the inability to engage the larger rebel groups in the peace process; (2) the failure of the government of Sudan and rebel groups to agree on the cessation of hostilities and commit to discuss in good faith how to achieve a sustainable peace agreement; (3) the lack of an enabling environment, such as basic political and civil freedoms, to permit a credible, comprehensive, and inclusive Darfur-driven process (the so-called Darfur-based Political Process [DPP]; and (4) the inadequate grass roots ownership of a conflict resolution mechanism, which is representative of Darfur's populous and local customs.

International Efforts in Peace and Justice. The first major international protection force in Darfur

dates to 2004, when the African Union Mission in the Sudan (AMIS) arrived to monitor an April 2004 ceasefire. AMIS was supposed to showcase African solutions to African problems. However, the Mission was severely hindered by logistics, a lack of troops, an unrealistic mandate, a reliance on Khartoum to guarantee security, and operational gaps in communications, reconnaissance, and intelligence. AMIS was replaced in early 2008 by the joint AU/UN Hybrid Operation in Darfur (UNAMID). The first of its kind, at its inauguration the UN Secretary-General declared "a new and profoundly challenging chapter in the history of United Nations peacekeeping." UNAMID is the most expensive ($1.7 billion in the 2011–2012 fiscal year) and largest (approximately 23,000 authorized uniformed personnel) peacekeeping operation worldwide.

There has been a great reluctance by Khartoum to tacitly accept AMIS's failure, with the government of Sudan (however unreasonably) fearing that UNAMID is a neocolonial exercise. Ever since the idea of a transition from AMIS to UNAMID was first suggested, it has been consistently obstructed. Khartoum has hindered UNAMID's patrolling activities, confiscated funds, detained and maltreated UNAMID's national staff, issued visas at a prohibitively slow pace, grounded UNAMID helicopters, and delayed custom clearance for vital UNAMID equipment.

The internationally mediated May 2006 DPA, with its security-, power-, and wealth-sharing provisions, was a failure from the start. Under the auspices of the African Union (AU) and supported by the UN, Nigeria, Britain, and America, the government and just one rebel faction (SLM–Minni Minnawi) signed the Agreement. Two other groups present at the negotiations refused to do so (JEM and SLM–Abdel Wahid). Notwithstanding deficient leadership amongst the rebels, significant intransigence, lack of will, and distrust between the belligerents, most damning was the counterproductive strategy of deadline diplomacy pursued by the impatient international mediators in an attempt to expedite the settlement. Just five days before the external deadline imposed by the AU Peace and Security Council, the mediators presented a draft DPA to the parties allowing them insufficient ownership of the process or text.

Traditional leaders, refugees and IDPs, civil society organizations, youth groups, and academics were all conspicuously absent from the DPA process. Since 2006, there have been internationally mediated efforts toward more inclusive political and military settlements, principally by the state of Qatar, the AU High-Level Implementation Panel for Sudan (AUHIP, which is chaired by former South African President Thabo Mbeki) and the AU–UN Joint Mediation Support Team.

Deliberations in Qatar's capital, Doha, aim to include those stakeholders absent from the DPA such as the May 2011 All Darfur Stakeholders Conference which examined, *inter alia*, issues of compensation, accountability for previous human rights violations, security, and the administrative status of Darfur. Nevertheless, these more inclusive discussions have, so far, failed to end violence in Darfur. Direct talks between Khartoum and rebel movements continue to falter, with disputes over the scope and procedures of the conflict resolution process, and a number of influential groups not participating in the negotiations. Disagreements also remain between the Liberation and Justice Movement (LJM), a militarily weak rebel coalition created in early 2010 specifically as an interlocutor to the peace process, and the more established and militarily stronger rebel groups.

The most high-profile attempt to uphold principles of international justice has been the International Criminal Court's (ICC) March 2009 call for the arrest of President Omar al-Bashir, for crimes against humanity and war crimes and then, in July 2010, for genocide. The underlying rationale of the ICC decision is the conviction that justice is a critical condition for securing peace and stability in Darfur. Many have long argued, however, that the ICC decision actually undermines peace efforts in Darfur, as it entrenches positions on all sides and marginalizes Khartoum. The AU has outlined its opposition to the ICC's decision, and AU member states have shown no sign of arresting the president during his international visits. Despite UN Security Council Resolution 1593 (2005) obliging the Sudanese government to fully cooperate with the ICC, Sudan is not a signatory of the 1998 Rome Statute and thus, is not party to the ICC's jurisdiction.

The American Government's Response. The American government's response since 2003 has been dominated by strong rhetoric, significant humanitarian assistance, sanctions, and a fear of upsetting the fragile negotiations, and subsequent implementation of the January 2005 Comprehensive Peace Agreement between Khartoum and the SPLA. In mid-2004, both Houses of the US Congress declared that the events unfolding in Darfur were genocide, with then-US Secretary of State, Colin Powell, and President George W. Bush following suit later in the year.

Despite declaring that genocide was occurring in Darfur, there was no resulting military intervention. The March 2005 Darfur Genocide Accountability Act advocated the deployment of American military assets to neutralize the counterinsurgency paramilitaries targeting civilians, the implementation of a no-fly zone, and the destruction of Sudan's aerial, military and intelligence resources responsible for civilian attacks. However, the House of Representatives bill, despite significant co-sponsorship, was never passed into law. Rather, policy was driven by the much weaker Darfur Peace and Accountability Act (signed into law in October 2006) and two 2006 presidential executive orders. Influenced by ongoing Washington–Khartoum cooperation on antiterrorism, the Bush administration's non-humanitarian response favored codified bilateral sanctions against Khartoum and American citizens involved in Sudan's petrochemical industry, as well as support to AMIS.

During his 2008 presidential campaign, Barack Obama advocated a tough stance on Darfur, including the establishment of a no-fly zone. However, the Obama administration has to a large extent followed a doctrine similar to that of its predecessor. Like President Bush, Obama has continued using the term "genocide," and favors both the ICC's prosecution of al-Bashir and the use of soft power. President Obama has, however, been less isolationist toward the regime in Khartoum (albeit not toward al-Bashir himself), and in September 2010 removed some restrictions on Sudan. President Obama's former Special Envoy to Sudan, Scott Gration, was heavily criticized for being too conciliatory toward the Sudanese regime and, in March 2011, was replaced by Ambassador Princeton Lyman who, together with Ambassador Dane Smith, Senior Advisor on Darfur, coordinates the administration's Darfur policy.

President Obama has provided incentives—so far, unsuccessfully—to encourage behavioral change in Khartoum, including the normalization of diplomatic ties, support of access to bilateral and multilateral assistance, the elimination of legislative and executive sanctions, debt relief, and the removal of Sudan from the US list of state sponsors of terrorism. As part of his concurrent approach to Sudan, outlined in the administration's October 2009 Sudan Strategy, such incentives are not reliant on verifiable progress in Darfur alone, but also on relations between Khartoum and South Sudan, and Sudan's cooperation in antiterrorism efforts. Given the significance of South Sudan's independence in July 2011, many accuse the American administration of ignoring Darfur at the expense of securing final status agreements, and ensuring stability between Khartoum and the world's newest country.

Legacy of Recent Violence. There have been a range of international responses which, in turn, raise key questions as to the efficacy of conflict resolution and external involvement in conflict. The recent violence has resulted in the creation of a plethora of social advocacy movements—something unprecedented since the antiapartheid movement—such as the Save Darfur Coalition, which for better or worse have brought the conflict to the attention of large sections of the American population and have shaped its government's response. Successive American government proclamations of genocide—arguably as a direct result of campaigning by such advocacy groups—are the only instances in which any US administration has made such a declaration regarding an ongoing conflict. Despite the resulting calls for unilateral American military intervention, the response has been multilateral, first by the AU and then by the experimental AU–UN hybrid operation.

In addition to accusations of genocide, Darfur represents the first time a sitting head of state has been indicted by the ICC, which has provoked a normative discussion on justice versus peace. Equally, the humanitarian response has, at times, reignited traditional debates over the politicization of humanitarianism and impartiality, neutrality, and independence, especially following the Sudanese government's March 2009 expulsion of thirteen international aid agencies from Darfur and the closure of three domestic organizations. While the transnational link between Darfur and Chad may no longer be as relevant as it once was, the contagion between the two areas illustrates important symbiotic conflict axes, which have the potential to recur should bilateral relations deteriorate. Latent friction is not limited to within the region; the UN Security Council has itself become increasingly divided in its approach to Sudan and, by extension, Darfur.

The effects of Darfur's conflict are of course most felt by its local population. The recent violence has been devastating, and the substantial humanitarian response remains one of the largest and most complex humanitarian operations worldwide. Despite an often simplistic narrative, Darfur's violence has challenged diplomats, peacekeepers, and humanitarians alike. Given this context of deep-rooted tensions and Darfur's changing human geography, sustainable peace-building will remain challenging in the years ahead, and the legacy of violence difficult to overcome.

[*See also* Africa–United States Relations; *and* International Criminal Court.]

BIBLIOGRAPHY

Flint, Julie, and Alex de Waal. *Darfur: A New History of a Long War.* 2d ed. (London, 2008). A seminal work on Darfur by two of arguably the most respected contemporary voices on the subject.

Lanz, David. "Save Darfur: A Movement and its Discontents." *African Affairs* 108 (2009): 669–677.

Mamdani, Mahmood. *Saviors and Survivors: Darfur, Politics, and the War on Terror.* (New York, 2009).

Marchal, Roland. "Chad/Darfur: How Two Crises Merge." *Review of African Political Economy* 33, no. 109 (2006): 467–482.

Murphy, Theodore, and Jérôme Tubiana. "Civil Society in Darfur: The Missing Peace." United States Institute of Peace. (2010), http://www.usip.org/files/resources/Civil%20Society%20in%20Darfur%20-%20Sept.%202010.pdf.

Prunier, Gerald. *Darfur: A 21st Century Genocide*. 3d ed. (Ithaca, N.Y., 2008).

The Sudan Human Security Baseline Assessment (HSBA) Project, http://www.smallarmssurveysudan.org. Research and analysis on state and non-state armed groups in Sudan and South Sudan, Darfur's peace process, and the role of small arms and light weapons in Sudan and South Sudan.

Totten, Samuel. *An Oral and Documentary History of the Darfur Genocide*. (Santa Barbara, Calif., 2010).

Totten, Samuel, and Eric Markusen, eds. *Genocide in Darfur: Investigating the Atrocities in the Sudan*. (New York, 2006).

Tubiana, Jérôme. "Learning from Darfur." *Dispatches* 4 (2009): 195–218.

United Nations Sudan Information Gateway, http://www.unsudanig.org. A useful compilation of UN analysis on Darfur and Sudan.

Waal, Alex de, ed. *War in Darfur and the Search for Peace*. (Boston, 2007). A collection of essays by leading Sudanese and international specialists on Darfur, including contextualizing the conflict, the origins of Darfur's armed groups, attempts at mediation, and the role of the media.

Mark Naftalin

DEFENSE INDUSTRIES

See Military-Industrial Complex.

DEFICIT

See Public Spending.

DEINDUSTRIALIZATION

The term "deindustrialization" came into vogue in the 1980s, to describe the loss of relatively high-paying factory jobs in advanced industrial nations. From the beginning, there was confusion about what was being claimed, and about the appropriate government policies for remedying the presumed problem. While the "deindustrializers" fretted over the loss of these jobs, their critics argued that advanced nations were not really "deindustrializing" at all, since manufacturing output in the 1980s was not substantially lower, as a percentage of gross national income (GNP), than it had been in previous decades. The reason for the decline in manufacturing employment, they suggested, was that manufacturers had become so productive that they now needed fewer workers. The shift from manufacturing to more service-oriented industries within all advanced economies was an inevitable stage of development, much like the shift in the previous century from agriculture to manufacturing. The "deindustrializers" responded that, such explanations notwithstanding, well-paying manufacturing jobs were being replaced by low-paying service jobs, with the result that the United States was losing its middle class.

Most researchers have come to agree that the middle class is shrinking in the United States, although there is no consensus that "deindustrialization" is the culprit. Controlling for family size, geography, and other changes, the average income of the poorest fifth in the United States declined between 1977 and 1990 by about 9 percent, while the richest fifth became about 19 percent wealthier. That left the poorest fifth with 3.7 percent of the nation's total income in 1990, down from 5.5 percent twenty years before—the lowest portion they had received since 1954; and it left the richest fifth with a bit over half of the nation's income—the highest portion ever recorded by the top 20 percent. The top 5 percent commanded 26 percent of the nation's income, another record. Some researchers, selecting different years and using different measurements, have found the divergence to be somewhat less pronounced than this, but they note the same trend. (For post-2011 inequality data, *see* "Inequalities of Wealth and Income".)

Proposals for what to do about this widening gap are related to its presumed cause. The "deindustrializers" seek measures to preserve, protect, subsidize, or otherwise encourage the creation of well-paying manufacturing jobs that would supposedly restore middle-class incomes. Their critics—who attribute the divergence in incomes to factors such as the growth in single-parent, lower-income families, or the influx of young, unskilled, and inexperienced baby boomers and women into the work force—argue that such measures would be pointless. To the extent that the "deindustrializers" want to protect US manufacturing jobs against foreign competition, moreover, critics contend that others would bear the burden of paying substantially higher prices for the goods they purchased, and that such policies also would invite foreign nations to bar American-made goods, resulting in losses for everyone.

The argument will continue to rage, but there is mounting evidence that the widening income gap is more related to changes in the global demand for labor than to changes in US labor supply. Increases in the number of single-parent families, and in the number of baby-boomer and women job entrants, actually slowed after the late 1970s, just as the income gap in the United States began to widen precipitously. Moreover, other nations have experienced similarly diverging incomes, even without these demographic changes. This is not to suggest that the "deindustrializers" are entirely correct in attributing the widening gap to the loss of good manufacturing jobs, however. Other, broader trends are at work, involving services as well as manufacturing.

What has happened, it seems, is that national economies have become so integrated into a single global economy that labor supply and demand now operate worldwide. Highly skilled and talented workers in economically advanced nations confront an ever-larger world market for their services; thus the earnings of software engineers, lawyers, investment bankers, architects, management consultants, movie producers, and other professionals are on the rise. At the other extreme, unskilled workers—whether in traditional manufacturing industries or in services that are traded internationally, such as data processing—find themselves competing with a growing number of unskilled workers around the world, many of whom are eager to work for a fraction of the wages of unskilled workers in advanced nations.

Thus are relatively unskilled workers in advanced industrial countries pushed into local service occupations, where they must compete with labor-saving machinery, immigrants, and all the other unskilled workers who can no longer compete internationally. Their earnings are thus stagnating or declining.

The consequences for public policy are profound. The United States and other nations face three policy choices. They can attempt to preserve or protect older manufacturing jobs, or, alternatively, they can abdicate all responsibility to the magic of the global marketplace. Finally, industrialized nations may seek to enhance the capacities of their citizens to add value to the global economy, and thus command a higher standard of living from the world. Toward this end, they would increase expenditures on education, training, and infrastructure (roads, bridges, airports, and other forms of public capital), and on subsidies to global corporations that provide on-the-job training in advanced technologies.

[See also Economy, American, since World War II; Employment and Unemployment; Free Trade and Fair Trade; and Global Economy and the United States.]

BIBLIOGRAPHY

Bluestone, Barry, and Bennett Harrison. The Deindustrialization of America: Plant Closings, Community Abandonment, and the Dismantling of Basic Industry. (New York, 1982).

Lawrence, Robert Z. Can America Compete? (Washington, D.C., 1984).

Reich, Robert B. The Work of Nations: Preparing Ourselves for 21st-Century Capitalism. (New York, 1991).

Robert B. Reich

DEMOCRACY

Democracy seems to have scored a historic victory over alternative forms of governance. Nearly everyone today, whether of the left, center, or right, claims adherence to democratic principles. Political regimes of all kinds throughout the world style themselves as democracies—although there may be vast differences between statement and execution in some of these cases. Democracy seems to bestow an aura of legitimacy on modern political life: rules, laws, policies, and decisions appear justified when they are "democratic." This was not always so. The great majority of political thinkers, from ancient Greece to the present day, have been highly critical of the theory and practice of democracy. A uniform commitment to democracy is a very recent phenomenon.

The historical records contain little about democracy from ancient Greece through eighteenth-century Europe and North America. The widespread turn to democracy as a suitable form for organizing political life is less than a hundred years old. In addition, while many states today may be democratic, the history of their political institutions reveals the fragility and vulnerability of democratic arrangements. The remarkable difficulty of creating and sustaining democratic forms is illustrated by the flowering of Fascism and Nazism in twentieth-century Western Europe. Democracy has evolved in intensive social struggles, and is frequently sacrificed in such struggles. The focus here is on the idea of democracy, but in exploring the idea one cannot escape aspects of its history in theory and in practice. It will be evident that the concept of democracy and the nature of democratic arrangements are a fundamentally contested terrain.

The word "democracy" entered English in the sixteenth century from the French *démocratie*; the word is Greek in origin, having been derived from *dēmokratia*, the roots of which are *dēmos* (people) and *kratos* (rule). Democracy refers to a form of government in which, in contradistinction to monarchies and aristocracies, the people rule. It entails a state in which there is some form of political equality among the people. But to recognize this is not yet to say very much, for not only is the history of the idea of democracy marked by conflicting interpretations, but Greek, Roman, and Renaissance notions, among others, intermingle to produce ambiguous and inconsistent accounts of the key terms of democracy today: the nature of "rule," the connotation of "rule by," and the meaning of "the people."

Among the questions that require examination are: Who are "the people"? What constitutes a "people"

entitled to rule themselves? What kind of participation is envisaged for them? How broadly or narrowly is the scope of rule to be construed? Is democracy a set of political institutions or a process? How does the size of a political community affect the nature and dynamics of democracy? Must the rules of "the people" be obeyed? What is the place of obligation and dissent? Under what circumstances, if any, are democracies entitled to resort to coercion of an element of "the people," or of those outside the sphere of legitimate rule?

Within the history of the clash of interpretations about these and related questions lies a deeply rooted struggle to determine whether democracy will mean some kind of popular power (a form of life in which citizens are engaged in self-government and self-regulation), or an aid to decision-making (a means to legitimate decisions of those voted into power from time to time). This struggle has given rise to three basic variants or models of democracy. First, there is direct or participatory democracy, a system of decision-making about public affairs in which citizens are directly involved. This was the original type of democracy found in ancient Athens, among other places. Second, there is liberal or representative democracy, a system of rule embracing elected officers who undertake to represent the interests or views of citizens within the framework of the rule of law. Representative democracy means that decisions affecting a community are taken not by its members as a whole, but rather by a group of officials whom "the people" have elected for this purpose. In the arena of national politics, representative democracy takes the form of elections to congresses, parliaments, or similar national bodies and is associated with the system of government in countries as far afield as the United States, Britain, Germany, Japan, Australia, South Africa, Costa Rica, Senegal, and elsewhere. Third, there is a variant of democracy based on a one-party model (although some may doubt whether this is a form of democracy at all). Until recently, the Soviet Union, many East European societies, and some developing countries were heavily influenced by this conception. The principle underlying one-party democracy is that a single party can be the legitimate expression of the overall will of the community. Voters choose among different candidates, putatively proposing divergent policies within an overall framework, not among different parties.

In the fifth century BCE, Athens emerged as the preeminent city-state, or polis, among many rival Greek powers; the development of democracy in Athens has been taken as a fundamental source of inspiration for modern Western political thought. The political ideals of Athens—equality among citizens, liberty, respect for the law, and justice—have shaped political thinking through the ages, although there are some central ideas (for instance, the modern liberal notion that human beings are individuals with rights) that notably cannot be traced directly to ancient thought.

The Athenian city-state did not differentiate between state and society, ruled as it was by citizen-governors. In ancient Athens citizens were at one and the same time subjects of state authority, and the creators of public rules and regulations. The people (*dēmos*) engaged in legislative and judicial functions, for the Athenian concept of citizenship entailed sharing in these functions, and participating directly in the affairs of the state. Athenian democracy required a general commitment to the principle of civic virtue: dedication to the republican city-state and the subordination of private life to public affairs and the common good. The public and the private were intertwined. Citizens could only properly fulfill themselves and live honorably in and through the polis. Of course, the issue of who was to count as a citizen was a tightly restricted matter. Those who were excluded included both women, and a substantial slave population.

The Athenian city-state—eclipsed ultimately by the rise of empires, stronger states, and military regimes—shared features with republican Rome. Both were predominantly face-to-face societies, and oral cultures, and both had elements of popular participation in governmental affairs and little, if any, centralized bureaucratic control. Both sought to foster a deep sense of public duty, a tradition of civic virtue or responsibility to the republic—to the distinctive matters of the public realm. In both polities, the claims of the state were given a unique priority over those of the individual citizen. However, if Athens was a democratic republic, contemporary scholarship generally affirms that Rome was by comparison an essentially oligarchic system. Despite this, it was Rome which, from antiquity, was to prove the most durable influence on the dissemination of notions of "active citizenship."

The meaning of the concept of "active citizenship in a republic" became a leading concern in the early Renaissance, especially in the city-states of Italy. Political thinkers of this period were critical of the Athenian formulation of this idea; shaped as their views were by Aristotle—one of the leading critics of Greek democracy—and by the centuries-long impact of republican Rome, they recast the classical republican tradition. While the concept of the polis remained central to the political theory of Italian cities, most notably in Florence, it was no longer regarded as a means to self-fulfillment. Emphasis continued to be placed on the importance of civic virtue, but the latter was understood as highly fragile, subject particularly to corruption if dependent solely upon the political involvement of any one major grouping: the people, the aristocracy, or the monarchy. A constitution that could reflect and balance the interests of all leading political factions became an aspiration.

The core of the Renaissance political argument was that the freedom of a political community rested upon its accountability to no authority other than that of the community itself. Self-government is the basis of liberty, together with the right of citizens to participate—within a constitutional framework which creates distinct roles for leading social forces—in the government of their own common business. Freedom consists above all in the unhindered pursuit by citizens of their self-chosen ends. The highest political ideal is the civic freedom of an independent, self-governing republic.

In Renaissance republicanism, as well as in Greek democratic thought, a citizen was someone who participated in "giving judgment and holding office." Citizenship meant participation in public affairs.

This definition is noteworthy because it suggests that theorists within these traditions would have found it hard to locate citizens in modern democracies, except perhaps as representatives or office-holders. The limited scope in contemporary politics for the active involvement of citizens would have been regarded as most undemocratic. Yet the idea that human beings should be active citizens of a political order—citizens of their states—and not merely dutiful subjects of a ruler has had few advocates, from the earliest human associations to the early Renaissance.

The eclipse in the West of the idea of the engaged citizen—one whose very being is affirmed in and through political action—is hard to explain fully. But it is clear enough that the antithesis of *Homo politicus* is the *Homo credens* of the Christian faith: the citizen who exercised active judgment was displaced by the true believer. Although it would be quite misleading to suggest that the rise of Christianity effectively banished secular considerations from the lives of rulers and ruled, it unquestionably shifted the source of authority and wisdom from this-worldly to otherworldly representatives. The Christian worldview transferred the rationale of political action away from that of the polis or empire and toward theological framework—toward a preoccupation with how humans could live in communion with God. The Christian worldview insisted that the good lay in submission to God's will.

During the Middle Ages, the integration of Christian Europe from the Eastern Atlantic seaboard to the Balkans came to depend on two theocratic authorities above all: the Roman Catholic Church and the Holy Roman Empire. The entire fabric of medieval thought had to be challenged before the idea of democracy could reemerge. Not until the end of the sixteenth century did the nature and limits of political authority, law, rights, and obedience become a preoccupation, from Italy to England, of European political thought. The Protestant Reformation—the most significant of all the developments that triggered new ways of thinking about political authority—did more than just challenge papal jurisdiction and authority across Europe; it raised the starkest questions about political obligation and obedience. Whether allegiance was owed to the Catholic Church, a Protestant ruler, or particular religious sects was not an issue easily resolved. The bitter struggles that spread across Europe during the last half of the sixteenth century, culminating in the Thirty Years' War in Germany (1618–1648), testified to the increasing divisiveness of religious belief. Competing religions, all seeking to secure for themselves the kinds of privileges claimed by the medieval church, had engendered a political crisis, the only solution for which was to disconnect the powers of the state from the duty of rulers to uphold a particular faith.

The impetus to reexamine the nature of the relationship between society and state was given added force by a growing awareness in Europe of the variety of possible social and political arrangements that followed in the wake of the discovery of the non-European world. The relationship between Europe and the "New World," and the nature of the rights (if any) of non-Europeans, became a major focus of discussion. It sharpened the sense of a plurality of possible interpretations of political life. The direction these interpretations took was, of course, directly related to the context and traditions of particular countries: the changing nature of politics was experienced differently throughout the early modern period. But it is hard to overestimate the significance of the events and processes that ushered in a new era of political reflection, marked as it was by such dramatic occurrences as the English Revolution (1640–1688), the American Declaration of Independence (1776), and the French Revolution (1789).

Modern liberal and liberal democratic theory has constantly sought to justify the sovereign power of the state, while at the same time justifying limits on that power. The history of this attempt since Thomas Hobbes (1588–1679) is the history of arguments to balance might and right, power and law, duties and rights. On the one hand, states must have a monopoly of coercive power in order to provide a secure basis on which trade, commerce, and family life can prosper. On the other hand, by granting the state a regulatory and coercive capability, political theorists were aware that they had accepted a force that could—and frequently did—deprive citizens of political and social freedoms.

Liberal democrats provided the key institutional innovation to try to overcome this dilemma: representative democracy. The liberal concern with reason, law, and freedom of choice could be upheld properly only by recognizing the political equality of all mature individuals. Such equality would ensure not only a secure social environment in which people would be free to pursue their private activities and interests, but also that the state would do what was best in the general and public interest—for example, pursue the greatest satisfaction of the greatest number. Thus, liberal democrats argued that the democratic constitutional state, linked to other key institutional mechanisms, above all the free market, resolved the problems of ensuring both authority and liberty.

Two classical statements of the new position can be found in the philosophy of James Madison (1751–1836) and in the works of two of the key figures of nineteenth-century English liberalism: Jeremy Bentham (1748–1832) and James Mill (1773–1836). In their hands the theory of liberal democracy received a most important elaboration: the governors must be held accountable to the governed through political mechanisms (the secret ballot, regular voting, competition between potential representatives, the struggle among factions) that alone can give citizens satisfactory means to choose, authorize, and control political decisions. And by these means, it was further contended, a balance could finally be obtained between might and right, authority and liberty. But who exactly was to count as a "citizen" or an "individual," and what his or her exact role was to be, remained either unclear or unsettled. Even in the work of James Mill's radical son, John Stuart Mill (1806–1873), ambiguities remained: the idea that all citizens should have equal weight in the political system remained outside his actual doctrine.

It was left by and large to the extensive, and often violently repressed, struggles of working-class, feminist, and radical activists in the nineteenth and twentieth centuries to achieve in some countries a genuinely universal suffrage. This achievement was to remain fragile in countries such as Germany, Italy, and Spain, and was in practice denied to some groups—for instance, many African Americans in the United States, before the civil rights movement of the 1950s and 1960s. Through these struggles, the idea that citizenship rights should apply to all adults became slowly established; many of the arguments of the liberal democrats could be turned against existing institutions to reveal the extent to which the principle and aspirations of equal political participation and equal human development remained unfulfilled. It was only with the actual achievement of citizenship for all adult men and women that liberal democracy took on its distinctively contemporary form: a cluster of rules permitting the broadest participation of the majority of citizens in the selection of representatives who alone can make political decisions (i.e., decisions affecting the whole of society).

The idea of democracy remains complex and contested. The liberal democratic tradition itself comprises a heterogeneous body of thought. However, the entire liberal democratic tradition stands apart from an alternative perspective—the theory of single-party democracy. It is worth saying something more about this, because it is associated with one of the key counterpoints to liberal democracy: the Marxist tradition.

The struggle of liberalism against tyranny, and the struggle by liberal democrats for political equality, represented, according to Karl Marx (1818–1883) and Friedrich Engels (1820–1895), a major step forward in the history of human emancipation. But for them, and for the Marxist tradition more broadly, the great universal ideals of "liberty, equality, and justice" could not be realized simply by the "free" struggle for votes in the political system and by the "free" struggle for profit in the marketplace. Advocates of the democratic state and the market economy present them as the only institutions under which liberty can be sustained and inequalities minimized. However, the Marxist critique suggests that, by virtue of its internal dynamics, the capitalist economy inevitably produces systematic inequality and massive restrictions on real freedom. Although each step toward formal political equality is an advance, its liberating potential is severely curtailed by inequalities of class.

In societies marked by class, the state cannot become the vehicle for the pursuit of the common good or public interest. Far from playing the role of emancipator, protective knight, umpire, or judge in the face of disorder, the agencies of the liberal representative state are meshed in the struggles of civil society. Marxists conceive of the state as an extension of civil society, reinforcing the social order for the enhancement of particular interests—in capitalist society, the long-run interests of the capitalist class. Marx and Engels contended that political emancipation is only a step toward human emancipation, that is, the complete democratization of society as well as the state. In their view, liberal democratic society fails when judged by its own principles—and to take these principles seriously is to become a communist.

Marx himself envisaged the replacement of the "machinery" of the liberal democratic state by a "commune structure": the smallest communities, which were to administer their own affairs, would elect delegates to larger administrative units (districts, towns); these in turn would elect candidates to still-larger areas of administration (the national delegation). This arrangement is known as the "pyramid" structure of direct democracy: all delegates are revocable, bound by the instructions of their constituency, and organized into a pyramid of directly elected committees. In the Marxist-Leninist model, this system of delegation is, in principle, complemented by a separate, but somewhat similar, system at the levels of the Communist Party. In practice, however, complementarity has meant party domination. It was only during the Mikhail Gorbachev era in the Soviet Union (1988–1991) that a pyramid of councils, or *soviets*, from the central authority to those at local village and neighborhood level, were given anything more than a symbolic or ritualistic role.

What should be made of these various models of democracy today? The classical Athenian model, which developed in a tightly knit community, cannot be adapted to stretch across space and time. Its emergence in the context of city-states and under conditions of social exclusivity (no female participation, a slave economy, many other marginalized groups) was integral to its successful development. In contemporary circumstances, marked by a high degree of social, economic, and political differentiation, it is very hard to envisage how a democracy of this kind could succeed without drastic modification. The significance of these reflections is reinforced by examining the fate of the model of democracy advocated by Marx, Engels, and their followers. The suitability of their model as an institutional arrangement that allows for mediation, negotiation, and compromise among struggling factions, groups, or movements does not stand up well under scrutiny, especially in its Marxist-Leninist variant. A system of institutions to promote discussion, debate, and competition among divergent views—a system encompassing the formation of movements, pressure groups, or political parties with leaderships to help press their cases—appears both necessary and desirable. Further, the political events in Central and Eastern Europe that began in 1989 seem to have provided remarkable confirmatory evidence of this.

Inevitably, then, one must recognize the importance of a number of fundamental liberal tenets concerning the centrality, in principle, of an impersonal structure of public power; of a constitution to help guarantee and protect rights; of a diversity of power centers within and outside the state; and of mechanisms to promote competition and debate among alternative political platforms. What this amounts to, among other things, is confirmation of the fundamental liberal notion that the separation of state from civil society must be an essential feature of any democratic political order. Conceptions of democracy that depend on the assumption that the state could ever replace civil society, or vice versa, must be treated with the utmost caution.

However, to make these points is not to affirm any one liberal democratic model as it stands. It is one thing to accept the arguments concerning the necessary protective, conflict-mediating, and redistributive functions of the democratic state; it is quite another to accept these as prescribed in the model of liberal democracy from Madison or Bentham onward. Advocates of liberal democracy have tended to be concerned, above all else, with the proper principles and procedures of democratic government. By focusing on government, they have deflected attention from a thorough examination of issues such as: formal rights versus actual rights; commitments to treat citizens as free and equal versus disparities of treatment in practice; concepts of the state as, in principle, an independent authority versus involvements of the state in the reproduction of the inequalities of everyday life; and notions of political parties as appropriate structures for bridging the gap between state and society versus the array of power centers that are beyond reach of parties.

The implications of these points are profound. For democracy to flourish today it has to be reconceived as a double-sided phenomenon concerned, on the one hand, with the reform of state power and, on the other hand, with the restructuring of civil society. This entails recognizing the indispensability of a process of "double democratization": the interdependent transformation of both state and civil society. Such a process must be premised on the acceptance of the principle that the division between state and civil society must be a central feature of democratic life, and on the notion that the power to make public decisions must be free of the illegitimate constraints imposed by the private flows of capital, as Marx foresaw. But, of course, to recognize the importance of both these points is to recognize the necessity of recasting substantially their traditional connotation.

It should come as no surprise that this leaves many questions unanswered. The history of democratic theory and practice is coterminous with conflicts of interpretation and struggles for position—and this state of affairs is inevitable when politics is free of the constraints of authoritarianism in all its forms. Democratic politics is bound to the terrain of dispute and contestation. Democracy is an ingenious political arrangement for the articulation, expression, and mediation of difference. It is a testimony to the idea of democracy itself that the battle over its constitutive elements will, in all likelihood, continue.

One area where the battle will continue connects the idea of democracy to the larger framework of international affairs. The modern theory of the democratic state presupposes the idea of a "national community of fate"—a community that rightly governs itself and determines its own future. But national communities by no means exclusively program the actions, decisions, and policies of their governments, and governments by no means determine what is right or appropriate for their own citizens. For example, a decision to build a nuclear plant near the borders of a neighboring country is likely to be a decision taken without consulting those in the nearby country (or countries). Or, the decision to permit the building of a chemical factory making toxic or other noxious substances may contribute to ecological damage which does not acknowledge national boundaries or frontiers. In a world of global interconnectedness—mediated by modern communication systems and information technology—there are pressing questions about the very future and viability of national democracies. Regional and global interconnectedness contests the traditional national resolutions of the key questions of democratic theory and practice.

Therefore, one ought not to be perplexed by increasing demands for, and attempts to realize, the extension of democratic forms and processes across territorial borders. Such a policy of democratization might begin, for example, in regions such as Europe—which recognizes the need for new, transnational collaborative institutions—by creating greater transparency in the key decision-making centers of the European Union and reducing the democratic deficit across all its major political bodies. Elsewhere it would entail restructuring the United Nations (UN) Security Council to give developing countries a significant voice in decision-making; deepening the mechanisms of accountability of the leading international and transnational economic agencies; strengthening the enforcement capacity of human rights regimes (socioeconomic as well as political); and creating, in due course, a new democratic UN second chamber. Such objectives point the way toward laying the foundations for forms of accountability at regional and global levels.

A political program of this type embodies elements of what might best be understood as a cosmopolitan conception of democracy. Faced with overlapping communities of fate—with, that is, a world in which the fortunes of individual political communities are increasingly bound together—citizens in the future will need to be citizens not only of their own communities, but also of the regions in which they live, and of the wider global order. They must be able to participate in diverse political communities—from cities and subnational regions to nation-states, regions, and wider global networks. It is clear that a process of disconnecting legitimate political authority from states and fixed borders has already begun, as legitimate forms of governance are diffused "below," "above," and "alongside" the nation-state. But the cosmopolitan project is in favor of a radical extension of this process, so long as it is circumscribed by a far-reaching commitment to democratic rights and duties.

Although the history and practice of democracy has been focused up until now on the idea of a specific locality (the city-state, the community, or the nation-state, for example), it is likely that in the future it will be centered on the international or global domain as well. There are no immediate solutions to the problems posed by global interconnectedness and its complex and often profoundly uneven effects—yet an important series of questions inescapably must be addressed. Certainly, one can find many good reasons for being optimistic about finding a path forward, and many good reasons for thinking that, at this juncture, democracy will face another critical test.

[*See also* Citizenship; Civil Rights Movement; Class Politics; Human Rights and Humanitarian Intervention; Inequalities of Wealth and Income; Liberalism, Center-Left; Liberalism, Theory and History of; Marxism; Political Culture, American; Political Parties, American; *and* Roman Catholic Church.]

BIBLIOGRAPHY

Aristotle. *The Politics*. (Harmondsworth, UK, 1981).

Dahl, Robert A. *Democracy and Its Critics*. (New Haven, Conn., 1989).

Finley, Moses I. *Politics in the Ancient World*. (Cambridge, UK, 1983).

Held, David. *Democracy and the Global Order: From the Modern State to Cosmopolitan Governance*. (Cambridge, UK, 1995).

Held, David. *Models of Democracy*. 2d ed. (Cambridge, UK, 1996).

Keane, John. *Democracy and Civil Society* (London, 1988).

Marx, Karl. *The Civil War in France*. (New York, 1940).

Mill, John Stuart. *Considerations on Representative Government*. (London, 1951).

Pocock, John. *The Machiavellian Moment: Florentine Political Thought and the Atlantic Republican Tradition*. (Princeton, N.J., 1975).

Schumpeter, Joseph A. *Capitalism, Socialism, and Democracy*. (London, 1976).

Skinner, Quentin. "The State." In *Political Innovation and Conceptional Change*, edited by Terence Ball, James Farr, and Russell L. Hanson, (Cambridge, UK, 1989).

Springborg, Patricia. *Western Republicanism and the Oriental Prince*. (Cambridge, UK, 1991).

David Held

DEMOCRATIC PARTY

Political parties can be seen through a variety of lenses. Parties are structures organized by politicians and activists to meet their needs. They are coalitions formed by social and demographic groups to protect their interests. Parties are interrelationships among voters, candidates, party organization leaders, and allied interests, with each group struggling to take priority. The Democratic Party—the oldest political party in the democratic world—can profitably be analyzed from each of these perspectives.

The Party's Jeffersonian, Agrarian Roots. The Democratic Party's roots stretch back almost to the beginnings of the American republic. Although the political leaders of the time were staunchly opposed to factions, they soon formed opposing sides in reaction to the proposals of Alexander Hamilton, the first Secretary of the Treasury. Hamilton and his allies believed that a strong central, or federal, government was needed to jump-start the economic development of the new United States. They championed a series of measures, including a central bank and tariffs on imported goods, to support nascent American industries.

Thomas Jefferson and James Madison led the notables who strongly opposed Hamilton's plans. Their vision was of a largely agricultural nation, with widespread ownership of property by small landholders, in which manufacturing and merchandising would exist to benefit the planters and freeholders. A powerful federal government, they feared, would favor the development of a few big manufacturing interests. It would raise taxes and debt that would burden agriculture for the benefit of a few (Chambers, 1963, p. 173). Thus, they favored limited government and emphasized the primacy of states' rights.

Hamilton's "Federalists" dominated the early Congress. To counter the Federalists' strength in Washington, the "Jeffersonians" (also called the "Republicans" and the "Democratic-Republicans") encouraged the development of grassroots movements in the states to oppose Hamilton's proposals. This was difficult; the tremendous diversity within the states, unreliable means of communication and travel, and the general disrepute in which parties were held produced halting and uneven organizational development. Nevertheless, the Jeffersonians foreshadowed some modern political practices by appealing to a wide range of constituents and holding caucuses (meetings) to select candidates and discuss issues. Their efforts succeeded; Jefferson was elected president in 1800, and the Federalists soon declined, unable to match the Jeffersonians' mass appeal.

After an uneasy period of one-party politics in the 1810s and early 1820s, the Jeffersonians split. The party's congressional faction, eventually known as the Whigs, built on the old Federalist platform to call for internal improvements, western expansion, and high tariffs to protect industry. The presidential faction became known as the Democrats (or, later, "The Democracy"). New York party leader Martin Van Buren, a skilled tactician able to bring disparate individuals into a national alliance, revived the Democrats' organizational efforts in the late 1820s. He expanded the party by building on preexisting caucuses in several states and by extensive use of patronage. This produced a decentralized "mass party" with considerable deference to local and state political needs (Aldrich, 1995, Chapter 4).

The Solid (Democratic) South and the Northern Political Machines. For most of the 1800s, the strongest bloc of the Democratic Party, reflecting its agrarian roots, was in the South. The Southern wing of the party grew up in a region defined by the economics of slavery. As more and more white workers were drawn to the promise of cheap land and plentiful resources on the Western frontier, the Southern economy, dominated by the labor-intensive production of cotton, became even more dependent on the work of black slaves. Southern states fought the federal government in the Civil War to retain their slaves and their autonomy. After the South was defeated, the Republican-dominated federal government attempted to "reconstruct" the region by putting the former Confederate states under US Army rule, insisting on new state governments in which former Confederate officers were barred from serving, and giving land to freed slaves, as well as introducing public schools and raising taxes to support transportation improvements. Reconstruction lasted for only about a decade, but the resentment it caused among white Southerners created a Democratic "solid South" in which the only Republican enclaves were in mountainous areas that had opposed the South's secession from the Union.

After the Civil War, the growth of sizable immigrant populations in Northeastern and Midwestern cities led Democratic politicians in some of these areas to develop the form of party organization termed the "political machine." Machines created a profitable exchange by providing immigrants with needed social welfare services in return for their votes. Because the machines preferred autonomy from federal and state government interference, just as immigrants tried to protect their Catholic faith and cultural norms from assimilationist pressure, machine politicians were comfortable within the Democratic tradition of limited federal government.

So were the Southern states, which wanted freedom from national interference to maintain their racially resegregated society.

As the nation tipped from predominantly rural to increasingly urban in the early 1900s, the urban areas that favored Democrats became much more highly populated. The Democrats, who had formerly gotten most of their votes from rural areas, became increasingly an urban, Northern party, though with a powerful Southern wing. Thus, the culturally diverse Democratic Party was "a rather peculiar political alliance [in the late 1800s, early 1900s], but generally, it was an alliance that had worked" (Ware, 2006, p. 87).

This curious amalgamation is an example of the tendency of American major party coalitions to contain disparate elements. In part this reflects the exceptional diversity of a society that has incorporated immigrants from all parts of the world. It also demonstrates the fundamental pragmatism of the American parties, which have traditionally worked to build majority support by incorporating new groups into the party's coalition when the opportunity presented itself, even if the result was to muddy the party's positions on issues or to generate an uneasy alliance among groups with very different priorities.

Changing Party Philosophies in the Early 1900s and the New Deal. The immigrants pouring into Northern cities in the late 1800s not only fueled the development of the political machine, but also that of large-scale industries that drew on these immigrants as their labor pool. Powerful business monopolies grew in the absence of government regulation. Although many Democrats remained opposed to a powerful central government that would promote business, others saw that a strong federal government could also limit the excesses of these industrial monopolies. Especially in the Northeast and Midwest, some found common cause with the Progressive movement of the late 1800s and early 1900s, which championed reform, antitrust laws, and an end to political corruption. The Northern, progressive wing of the Democratic Party began to encourage a greater federal role in the economy, and especially in the regulation of business, to remedy the inequalities caused by the rapid industrial expansion.

These Yankee progressives took on increasing importance within the party, leading to the nomination of the governor of New York, Al Smith, as the Democratic presidential candidate in 1928. Smith, the first Catholic presidential nominee, was defeated by Republican Herbert Hoover, who tried to deal with the growing Great Depression through volunteer efforts, without greatly expanding the federal government's power. Because of Hoover's reluctance to respond to the economic disaster with aid to the unemployed and needy, millions of new voters entered the electorate as Democrats.

Hoover lost reelection in 1932 to another Yankee progressive, Democrat Franklin D. Roosevelt, whose activist response to the Depression set the federal government on a course of much greater intervention in the economy. Democratic strength in the South was challenged. Roosevelt tried to gain votes in Congress for his New Deal measures by supporting liberal opponents to conservative Democrats (most of them Southerners) in primary elections. But Southerners, who had also been hit hard by the Depression, remained an important element in the Democratic "New Deal" Coalition. Roosevelt's more egalitarian party program also made the Democrats more competitive in the urban East and Midwest. Other parts of this New Deal coalition included lower-income people, Catholics, Jews, labor unions, and a growing proportion of black Americans, who had previously been loyal to the antislavery Republicans, but whose economic interests now made them more amenable to supporting Democrats.

Industrialization and the Depression changed the orientation of the Republican Party as well. During the 1800s, when developing industries needed an infrastructure of roads, standardized railways, and communications, only a strong federal government could have paid the bill. Republicans, then, stood for business interests *and* a strong central government. But the needs of businesses changed in the early 1900s. Once much of the infrastructure was in place, businesses learned, especially during the New Deal, that a strong central government could also impose taxes and costly regulations and become a threat to their interests.

The New Deal Democratic coalition, large enough to win the presidency for most of the next thirty-five years, contained the seeds of its own destruction. The story is complex, involving population shifts, changes in state election law and interest group activity, and other forces. But a major chapter centers on the struggle for civil rights. As many Southern blacks migrated to the North and Northern Democratic strength grew, some Democratic activists urged their national party to stand for racial desegregation. Roosevelt sidestepped these pressures to stem the loss of white Southern support. But the next Democratic president, Harry Truman, was not as adept at holding together the diverse party coalition. By the late 1940s, objections to the national party's nod in the direction of civil rights legislation led some Southern whites to bolt to the States' Rights ("Dixiecrat") candidate for president, J. Strom Thurmond.

Civil Rights and Growing Party Polarization. A critical moment in the Democratic coalition's transformation occurred in 1964. Democratic President Lyndon Johnson pushed Congress to pass the Civil Rights Act in that year. Although previous Republican presidential nominees had favored civil rights, Johnson's opponent, Barry Goldwater, opposed the Act, claiming that it would lead to a more powerful federal government. This clearer choice prompted some white Southern Democrats to rethink their party allegiance, first voting Republican in presidential elections and then supporting Republicans at lower levels as well. The shift toward the Republicans slowed during the 1970s but regained strength with the 1980 election of Ronald Reagan.

This profound change in the parties' coalitions produced a major change in their issue positions as well. Conservative white Southerners took with them into the Republican Party not only their hostility toward racial integration but also their conservatism on abortion, same-sex marriage, and the role of religion in public life (Hershey, 2011, Chapter 7). In 1980, the Republican platform switched to a pro-life stance. Liberal activists pressed the Democrats to

adopt a pro-choice position and increasingly liberal stands on other issues, which encouraged liberal and moderate Republicans to vote Democratic. So although many analysts argued that partisanship declined from the 1960s through the late 1970s (Wattenberg, 1990), it is at least as likely that this was a time of transition, during which some people's party ties weakened and they termed themselves "independents" on their way to a new partisan home.

As Carmines and Stimson show (1989, Chapter 6), the parties' realignment on civil rights led to a polarization of members of Congress and activists. For many citizens, this elite polarization illuminated the issue differences between the parties and enabled a "partisan sorting" to take place (Levendusky, 2009): Republican identifiers became more consistently conservative and Democrats more homogeneously liberal. Whether or not citizens have become much more polarized ideologically than in the years prior to the coalitional shift, the relationship between their policy preferences and their voting choices has strengthened. In consequence, both parties have become more likely to mobilize their base voters and less likely to make cross-party appeals.

As members of Congress have polarized, they have granted more power to House and Senate party leaders, resulting in much greater congressional party cohesion in the 2000s than was the case in the 1970s (Rohde and Aldrich, 2010). In fact, in 2011, party-line voting in Congress reached levels approaching those of the legislatures in some parliamentary systems in Europe.

The party homogeneity is far from complete. Although the Democrats' large bloc of conservative Southerners is gone, there are still some moderate Democrats in the House who are more centrist in style, more inclined to oppose deficit spending, and more likely to favor budget cutting rather than tax increases. These so-called "Blue Dog Democrats" usually represent swing or marginal districts and thus are vulnerable to national political waves. When Republicans do very well nationally, these Blue Dogs, who are more "exposed" than other Democratic elected officials, tend to be swept away, as was the case in the 2010 midterm election.

Democratic President Bill Clinton, fighting to survive after the Republican midterm election victories of 1994, relied on a strategy he called "triangulation" to appeal to these centrists and to independent voters as well. Clinton sought a "third way" between liberal and conservative and found it in initiatives such as a balanced budget, deregulation of some industries, and a reform of welfare programs to reduce the incidence of long-term welfare dependency. One benefit of this strategy was that it permitted Democrats to approach big business for much-needed financial support while appealing to labor unions and liberals for aid as well. The result has been a continuing tension between the long-standing blue-collar constituency of the party and other groups, including Democrats who value a closer relationship with the business community and those who are motivated primarily by environmental, feminist, and other "postindustrial" concerns.

Expanding Organizational Capacity at the National Level. During the past five decades, the national Democratic Party organization has greatly expanded its role within the party. In the late 1960s, the national party dealt with internal conflict over civil rights and the Vietnam War by establishing the first of several reform commissions. This McGovern-Fraser Commission imposed severe limits on state party leaders' power to select national convention delegates. It also required greater representation of women, blacks, and young people in each delegation. Later reform commissions required state Democratic Parties to use proportional representation in awarding delegate seats, but also brought back the state party leaders and elected officials as "superdelegates" with guaranteed seats at the convention. Despite (or perhaps because of) all these efforts at intra-party democracy, however, the Democratic national party has remained more internally contentious than the Republican Party. William Mayer contends that this is the inevitable result of the Democratic Party's more heterogeneous coalition (Mayer, 1996).

Beginning in the mid-1990s, the national Democrats also built up their organizational capabilities with large "soft money" contributions from unions,

corporations, and individuals, used to support both federal candidates and state party organizations. The Democrats continued to adopt strategic innovations from the Republicans, including data-driven voter targeting and fundraising, so that for the first time in recent memory, the 2008 Democratic presidential candidate, Barack Obama, far outspent his Republican opponent.

Changes in the Modern Democratic Coalition. The Democratic coalition today still bears the marks of its history. Democratic voters are predominantly lower-income and disadvantaged, just as they were in the late 1800s, but the mix of disadvantaged groups has changed. Black Americans moved from increasingly to overwhelmingly Democratic, and gays, unmarried women, nonreligious people, Latino Americans, and Jews have become central to the party's support. These groups in turn have cemented more liberal stands in the party's platform. Catholics and union members, less disadvantaged than they have been in the past, have become swing voters. And as the nature of the "higher income" category changed to include more service professionals, such as trial lawyers, teachers, and mental health professionals, Democratic candidates gained a substantial share of these groups' support as well. The party's network encompasses labor unions and liberal citizen groups (environmental, women's, civil rights, and other such organizations).

Thus, the Democratic platform now favors increasing federal support for education, environmental programs, and other social services and promotes aid to cities, civil rights, and other liberal policies. Yet, also as a result of the recent coalitional changes, the Democratic platform, while viewing government as a primary means of redressing inequalities, argues for significantly *less* federal involvement in the issues of abortion and sexual orientation and in the promotion of "traditional values."

The party's electoral success has ebbed and flowed during the 2000s at a time of heightened party competitiveness. Democratic candidates built on widespread public discontent with Republican President George W. Bush to elect fifty-two new House Democrats in 2006 and 2008. And in the election of 2008,

Democrats elected the first black presidential candidate in American history, Barack Obama. He worked with a Democratic House and Senate to pass landmark legislation, including health care reform to increase individuals' access to medical care, more consistent enforcement of anti-pollution laws, greater regulation of banks and other financial services firms, and the use of tax money to stimulate the economy after the intense recession that began in 2007.

Independents reacted strongly against many of these Democratic initiatives, however, and swung toward the Republicans in the 2010 midterm elections. Republicans retook a House majority in that year and moved to repeal or blunt all of these Democratic programs. The greater polarization of the parties in the early twenty-first century meant that when party control of Congress and the presidency changes, major policy changes result.

Nonetheless, the Democrats stand a good chance of regaining majority status in the long run. Latino Americans and younger voters are the fastest growing portions of the electorate, and both groups are preponderantly Democratic. States gaining House seats after the 2010 census did so primarily because of an increase in their Latino populations, rather than in their conservative, white populations. The pro-Democratic lean of Latinos has been strengthened by many Republican officials' support for policies dealing harshly with illegal immigrants. And the youngest voters (aged 18–24) came into the electorate between 2006 and 2010 with a Democratic edge in party identification. Presuming that these partisan trends continue, Democratic strength in elections should recover and increase.

[*See also* Civil Rights; Clinton, Bill; Johnson, Lyndon Baines; Obama, Barack; Political Parties, American; Republican Party; Roosevelt, Franklin Delano; *and* Trade Unions and Democrats.]

BIBLIOGRAPHY

Aldrich, John Herbert. *Why Parties? The Origin and Transformation of Political Parties in America.* (Chicago, 1995).

Beck, Paul Allen. "A Tale of Two Electorates." In *The State of the Parties: The Changing Role of Contemporary American Parties*, edited by John Clifford Green and Rick Farmer, pp. 38–53. 4th ed. (Lanham, Md., 2003).

Brewer, Mark D., and Jeffrey M. Stonecash. *Dynamics of American Political Parties.* (Cambridge, UK, 2009).

Carmines, Edward G., and James A. Stimson. *Issue Evolution: Race and the Transformation of American Politics.* (Princeton, N.J., 1989).

Chambers, William Nisbet. *Political Parties in a New Nation: The American Experience, 1776–1809.* (New York, 1963).

Cohen, Marty, David Karol, Hans Noel, and John Zaller. *The Party Decides: Presidential Nominations Before and After Reform.* (Chicago, 2008).

Epstein, Leon D. *Political Parties in Western Democracies.* (New Brunswick, N.J., 1980).

Green, Donald, Bradley Palmquist, and Eric Schickler. *Partisan Hearts and Minds: Political Parties and the Social Identities of Voters.* (New Haven, Conn., 2002).

Hershey, Marjorie Randon. *Party Politics in America.* 14th ed. (New York, 2011).

Hofstadter, Richard. *The Idea of a Party System: The Rise of Legitimate Opposition in the United States, 1780–1840.* (Berkeley, Calif., 1969).

Levendusky, Matthew. *The Partisan Sort: How Liberals Became Democrats and Conservatives Became Republicans.* (Chicago, 2009).

Mayer, William G. *The Divided Democrats: Ideological Unity, Party Reform, and Presidential Elections.* (Boulder, Colo., 1996).

Pomper, Gerald M. *Passions and Interests: Political Party Concepts of American Democracy.* (Lawrence, Kans., 1992).

Rohde, David, and John Aldrich. "Consequences of Electoral and Institutional Change." In *New Directions in American Political Parties*, edited by Jeffrey M. Stonecash, pp. 234–250. (New York, 2010).

Ware, Alan. *The Democratic Party Heads North, 1877–1962.* (Cambridge, UK, 2006).

Wattenberg, Martin P. *The Decline of American Political Parties, 1952–1980.* (Cambridge, Mass., 1990).

Marjorie Randon Hershey

DEREGULATION

A wide-ranging deregulation of economic activity has been one of the most notable recent developments of contemporary political economy. For most of the twentieth century, the trend throughout the world had been toward more detailed and extensive regulation of business. Since the mid-1970s, however, most of the developed democracies have scaled down or abolished important regulatory programs. Many developing countries have followed suit. The privatization of municipal services and state enterprises in the Western democracies, and the liberalization of planned economies in Eastern and Central Europe, are evidence of deregulation during the last quarter of the twentieth century.

Politically, deregulation sometimes has resulted from economic or technological changes that led regulated industries to withdraw their support for regulation. For example, in the United States the introduction of new forms of personal saving forced the banking industry to support the deregulation of deposit interest.

But for the most part deregulation has reflected intellectual and political developments. Academic economists had concluded by the 1960s that regulation of pricing and entry in multifirm industries was almost always unwarranted. By the mid-1970s, certain public attitudes were adding force to the economists' critique. These included anxiety about inflation, skepticism about the efficacy of government programs, and (especially in the United States) a moralistic anger about improper collusion between government and business. In addition, the globalization of the world economy has pushed many countries toward deregulation as a means of enhancing the competitiveness of their industries.

These forces promoted deregulation primarily in one class of regulatory programs—those that controlled entry or set production quotas or minimum prices in potentially competitive industries. Major industries that experienced deregulation include transportation (including railroads, trucking, airlines, and intercity buses); financial services (such as banking, and securities brokerage); communications (including telephone equipment, long-distance service, broadcasting, and cable television); agriculture (both price supports and marketing orders); and many other industries and occupations. Although there were also efforts to reduce the cost or increase the efficiency of other regulatory programs (environmental protection, equal opportunity requirements, public utility regulation, and so on), these

programs generally did not come under severe attack.

Support for deregulation has cut across political lines. In the United States, early sponsorship was provided by both a liberal Democratic senator, Edward M. Kennedy, and a conservative Republican president, Gerald R. Ford. In Britain, deregulation was a central commitment of the conservative Margaret Thatcher government. In France, broadcast deregulation was implemented by the socialist government of François Mitterrand. The principal opposition generally came from regulated industries and their labor unions, which sought to preserve protection from competition. The ability to adopt deregulatory policy changes, therefore, typically depended on government's capacity to overcome pressure from narrow groups and act on behalf of widely shared interests. The scope and intensity of deregulation also reflected national dispositions toward market-oriented economic policies. The most wide-ranging deregulation occurred in the United States, Britain, and Australia; Canada, Italy, France, and Germany took more moderate steps toward deregulation; while Japan, Denmark, and Austria adopted very limited deregulatory measures. In the 1990s, the economic integration advanced by the European Union led to wide-ranging deregulation among all the member countries.

For the most part, deregulation has delivered on its promise of economic benefits: lower rates and more flexible service in freight transportation, accelerated technological progress in communications, expanded entertainment and information services, lower average airfares, smaller commissions for the execution of stock transactions, and higher interest rates on savings deposits, among others. In a few cases, however, there have also been adverse consequences. These have included, in the United States, fare instability in the airline industry and, most important, the collapse of the savings and loan industry in the late 1980s. But even for those industries, prior to the 2008 financial crisis, there had been little support for reregulation.

The privatization of municipal services and state enterprises in the Western democracies and the liberalization of planned economies in Eastern and Central Europe are related manifestations of a worldwide pro-market trend in recent decades.

[*See also* Regulation.]

BIBLIOGRAPHY

Button, Kenneth, and Dennis Swann, eds. *The Age of Regulatory Reform.* (Oxford, 1989).

Derthick, Martha, and Paul J. Quirk. *The Politics of Deregulation.* (Washington, D.C., 1985).

Grindle, Merilee S. *Challenging the State: Crisis and Innovation in Latin America and Africa.* (Cambridge, UK, 1996).

Paul J. Quirk

DISABILITY AND POLITICS

The late Justin Dart, the businessman-turned-disability-rights-activist, routinely urged disability rights advocates to "get into politics as if your lives depend on it—because they do." As the son of one of President Ronald Reagan's "kitchen cabinet" confidantes, Dart was steeped in politics and recognized the power of political engagement. He admonished disability advocates to enter politics—whatever one's party affiliations might be—because he knew one should not simply depend on people in power to do the right thing. Dart was a prominent contributor to campaigns and made himself visible at campaign events. He was adept at grassroots organizing and mobilizing. Dart could command a position at the forefront of the disability rights movement and gain access to high-ranking elected officials, because he knew how to get and exercise political power on behalf of people with disabilities.

Political power is the ability to influence the process of making decisions about public policies. In modern-day America, political power derives in large measure from the perceived ability to move people and money. Moving people (to vote or otherwise participate in political campaign activity) and moving money (by raising money for candidates) matters because it signals the capacity to influence elections. Perception is critical because public officials cannot precisely attribute their continued ability to

remain in office to specific individuals or groups. Persuading public officials that one has the ability to move people and money is thus every bit as important as acting on that ability.

To be sure, the perceived ability to move people and money is not the only way to influence the political process. Elected and appointed officials are motivated by various influences, including their own personal and family experiences, as well as the intrinsic appeal of certain positions rooted in our cultural heritage. Elected officials take many actions because they want to do so, not merely because they feel compelled to do so. Nonetheless, our democratic system of governance means that elected and appointed officials are ultimately subject to the will of those they believe to be responsible for their holding positions of authority—namely, the voting public.

These two broad categories of influencing the political process—one rooted in flexing political muscle and the other based on appeal to moral authority—illustrate the enigmatic status of disability in American politics. Disability rights advocates can point to a steady string of legislative and judicial victories over the past half-century. Indeed, Americans with disabilities have helped change the entire world through landmark legislative achievements such as the Americans with Disabilities Act (ADA) of 1990, which presaged similar legislation in countries around the world, and more recently the UN Convention on the Rights of Persons with Disabilities (CRPD). The ADA and CRPD proclaim that people with disabilities should be afforded certain basic rights and equality of opportunity to participate in the socioeconomic mainstream. Whatever critics may say about the relative success of the ADA, there is no question that nondiscrimination on the basis of disability has been normalized as an element of our social fabric.

It is equally clear that the ADA's limited ability to deliver on its promises is rooted, in part, in the absence of well-organized political advocacy comparable to the political mobilization achieved by other groups such as African Americans, women, Latinos, and the lesbian, gay, bisexual, and transgender (LGBT) community, as well as the recent explosion of the Tea Party movement onto the American political scene. Disability policy victories won over the last several decades owe much of their success to policy-based appeals to core values that resonate across the political spectrum, and the presence of allies already in positions of power.

People with disabilities have not needed to develop and perfect the political mobilization strategies that other groups have honed (such as grooming candidates and raising money for their campaigns) to bring attention to their issues, because they have been able to achieve so much by direct appeal to decision-makers on a bipartisan basis. However, the failure to cultivate the political power to put people in office—and to remove people from office—puts people with disabilities at risk in difficult economic times, when more powerful constituencies exert the depth of their influence. The Tea Party movement, for instance, has managed to wield significant influence in just a few years because they have proved capable of being difference-makers in elections. Irrespective of whether it is better for effective democratic governance to rely on power rooted in values more than money, the reality is that a failure to show the capacity to move people and money leaves a group vulnerable to the influence of those who do have such a capacity.

With an estimated 14.7 million people with disabilities voting in the 2010 midterm election, people with disabilities could dramatically impact elections at all levels of government. But mobilizing that potential voting bloc means undertaking a lot of organizing work and overcoming a string of longstanding challenges that have limited the ability to organize the disability community as a coherent voting bloc and political force. Prominent disability rights leaders such as Justin Dart, Tony Coelho, and Fred Fay have long recognized the need for more effective political mobilization of the disability community. But it is too soon to tell whether the disability community will take the steps necessary to realize its political potential.

Birth of a Disability Rights Movement. Analysis of "disability and politics" depends on knowing what is meant by the word "disability." Prior to the 1970s, disability was understood largely in medical terms

and focused on individual deficiency or deviance. People with impairments of various kinds—whether physical, sensory, intellectual, or psychiatric—were considered defective, sick, or impaired and, in most cases, in need of cure or rehabilitation. At its most extreme, people with disabilities were deemed worthy of outright exclusion (for instance, "ugly laws" prohibited certain people from being seen in public, many children with disabilities were barred from being educated in public schools, and immigration policies screened for various impairments) and elimination (with the US Supreme Court sanctioning forced sterilization to prevent reproduction of people it deemed "manifestly unfit" for society).

There were myriad efforts directed at improving the lives of people with disabilities, to be sure, including efforts to rehabilitate wounded veterans and injured workers, as well as charitable donation drives. However, these efforts were largely paternalistic and in many cases reinforced stigma toward people with disabilities by emphasizing the supposed tragedy of their lives, and their ability to conduct, at best, only menial tasks. People with disabilities were generally deprived the "dignity of risk," as Gerben DeJong put it in an early article that framed a new "independent living" movement in the 1970s. The dignity of risk means having the opportunity to reach one's own potential rather than have someone else decide one's fate. It means being exposed to the chance to fail as well as to succeed, and affirms the intrinsic value of self-determination over paternalism—however well intentioned.

As with other rights-based movements, the civil rights movement was a powerful catalyst for a new disability rights movement. For the past half-century, disability rights advocates have consistently linked themselves to the core principles of the civil rights movement. Although the analogy is far from perfect, people with disabilities have identified with the refusal to accept inherited stereotypes about supposedly biologically based inferiority and a particular social "place," and the need to mobilize individuals to throw off that burden. The disability rights activist Dan Wilkins captured the sentiment in a T-shirt with the slogan, "Same Struggle; Different Difference."

At its core, the disability rights movement is about rejecting inherited norms that the destinies of people with disabilities are controlled by their bodies, and affirming that each and every human being has the right to engage fully in communities of their choosing.

In a way, President Franklin Delano Roosevelt previewed the later birth of the disability rights movement. In Nazi Germany, Roosevelt would have been targeted for extermination, as unfit to make meaningful contributions to society. Fortunately, the eugenics movement did not take such insidious root in the United States. President Roosevelt's legacy as one of America's greatest presidents, like that of President Abraham Lincoln (widely believed to have had severe clinical depression), affirms that impairment need not be equated with incapacity. However, Roosevelt felt compelled to hide his polio—including by having people carry him up steps in a manner that made it look like he was walking—precisely because the stigma associated with a person who could not walk was so pervasive that his successful leadership depended on deception about his true self.

The disability rights movement embraces disability as a normal part of the human experience and offers a new framework for understanding the meaning of disability. Disability is understood more as the interaction between an individual and society rather than as an intrinsic (and detracting) trait of an individual. Individual physical or mental impairments only become "disabling" insofar as the physical and attitudinal structures of society fail to accommodate those impairments. Unfortunately, there is still no single and consistently reliable way to identify people with disabilities in the same way one can identify gender, or even race and ethnicity. Indeed, disability is defined in many different ways in different contexts. In the context of Social Security, for instance, disability is principally understood as an inability to perform "substantial gainful activity"—essentially, that is, as an inability to work.

Whether disability is defined in medical terms, in relation to employment, or based on a cultural model, there is a common thread: people with disabilities are exceedingly diverse. Unlike racial and ethnic minority status, for instance, disability does

not depend on the circumstances of one's birth. Some people are born with disabilities. But disabilities are also acquired later in life, and increase in prevalence with age. Indeed, it is often said that disability is the only minority category that one can join at any given moment. Disability advocates often refer to people without disabilities as the "temporarily able-bodied"—suggesting that if one is not disabled now one will be at some point if one lives long enough. It is also appropriately said that disability respects no boundaries. Disability is prevalent irrespective of geography, income, race, ethnicity, and political party.

Bipartisan History of Political Achievements. People with disabilities can boast an impressive string of legislative and executive achievements. Some programs critical to the lives of people with disabilities predate the Civil Rights Act of 1964. These include New Deal– and Great Society–era programs such as Social Security Disability Insurance (SSDI), Supplemental Security Income (SSI), Medicare, and Medicaid. These programs illustrate an important feature of disability politics—the way in which significant disability programs are sustained through the political strength of other powerful constituencies, particularly America's senior citizens. Although the United States's core retirement and health care programs were not created at the behest of the disability rights movement, people with disabilities benefit from being linked to the "third rail" issues of Social Security and Medicare that, for the most part, have historically enjoyed significant (if far from unanimous) support across the political spectrum.

Entitlement programs, however, can also support dependence of Americans with disabilities. Although the lives of millions of people with disabilities are supported by SSDI, SSI, Medicare, and Medicaid, many individuals can find themselves trapped by programs whose entry criteria are linked to the inability to earn more than a minimal "substantial gainful activity" level. Meeting income and asset thresholds can create incentives against working. Because working is correlated with a host of positive socioeconomic indicators, including health, income, and social participation, persistent work disincentives run the risk of harming some of the very people entitlement programs are intended to help.

A new wave of disability-related legislation took hold in the wake of the Civil Rights Act of 1964, and an ethos of integration and participation over segregation and isolation. (Indeed, there were some early attempts by disability rights advocates to amend the Civil Rights Act to encompass disability.) Beginning with the Architectural Barriers Act of 1968, which prohibited discrimination in the form of physical barriers in federal buildings, a wave of legislation aimed to give people with disabilities greater access to the workplace; places of public accommodations like movie theaters and restaurants; telecommunications, including telephones, captioned television, and the Internet; housing; transportation, including buses, trains, subways, and planes; voting; and emergency preparedness.

Important milestones include

- Architectural Barriers Act (1968)
- Rehabilitation Act of 1973
- Section 504 of the Rehabilitation Act of 1973
- Individuals with Disabilities Education Act (IDEA) (1975)
- Civil Rights of Institutionalized Persons Act (1980)
- Voting Accessibility for the Elderly and Handicapped Act (1984)
- Fair Housing Amendments Act of 1988
- Air Carriers Access Act (1986)
- Americans with Disabilities Act (1990)
- National Voter Registration Act (1993)
- Section 255 of the Telecommunications Act of 1996
- Section 508 of the Rehabilitation Act (1998)
- Ticket to Work and Work Incentives Improvement Act (1999)
- Help America Vote Act (2002)
- Post-Katrina Emergency Management Reform Act (2006)
- ADA Amendments Act (2008)
- Twenty-First Century Communications and Video Accessibility Act (2010)
- Rosa's Law (2010)

Besides the substance of these efforts aimed to improve the lives of people with disabilities, perhaps the most striking feature is the degree to which they secured broad-based bipartisan support. The ADA, for instance, was approved by huge majorities in both the House and the Senate, and by both parties. Part of the reason these bills have secured such broad-based support is that disability rights legislation has appealed to core principles on both ends of the political spectrum. The ADA, for instance, is notable because it was major nondiscrimination legislation—generally a creature of left-leaning progressive politics—that was proposed by fifteen individuals appointed by Republican President Ronald Reagan to the National Council on Disability (NCD) and signed into law by Republican President George H. W. Bush. Significant impetus for the ADA came from the Texas Republican congressman Steve Bartlett, who urged the NCD to explore ways to minimize dependence on government programs and instead promote independence. As the ADA made its way from a Reagan-appointed independent agency through a Democratic Congress to a Republican president's desk, the ADA proved capable of synthesizing a liberal commitment to disenfranchised minorities with a conservative commitment to economic self-sufficiency.

In addition to the bipartisan support for disability rights legislation, a second important feature has been that the legislative gains have come principally in the context of civil rights rather than in spending programs. Indeed, one of the anticipated hopes for the ADA was that it would *decrease* federal spending on disability, as more people were enabled to gain access to the workplace and becoming taxpaying citizens. The fact that the ADA and other laws did not center principally on appropriations of federal dollars also made it easier for people with disabilities and individual disability organizations to join forces in pushing for passage of the ADA. Indeed, there is a longstanding history of conflicts among different disability groups, because many individual disability groups depend on federal resources either as direct organization support or through reimbursement for services. When groups compete for limited resources it is harder to forge solid coalitions.

The Largest Minority Group? Disability advocates often claim that people with disabilities represent the "largest minority group," a practice now reflected in a radio show by that name. This claim is not without basis. According to a recent report issued jointly by the World Health Organization and World Bank, more than 1 billion people worldwide experience a disability, based on an estimated average prevalence rate of about 15 percent, or one in six people worldwide. However, the relative imprecision of defining disability makes it challenging to make a reliable count of the size of the population of people with disabilities. Moreover, the inherent challenge of "counting" people with disabilities has important consequences for cultivating the political power of the disability community.

Counting disability is no simple task. The estimate of more than 1 billion people worldwide is based on applying an average of individual estimated country prevalence rates to the current worldwide population of roughly 7 billion. Here in the United States, estimates of the population of people with disabilities vary significantly—both among individual states and depending on which data set is used. According to one prominent measure, the American Community Survey, in 2009 there were about 36 million, or roughly 12 percent of noninstitutionalized persons of all ages, reporting a disability. (Individual states varied in prevalence rates from 8.9 percent in Utah to 18.8 percent in West Virginia.) An oft-cited report based on the 1997 Survey of Income and Program Participation, by contrast, put the prevalence closer to 19 percent, or roughly 54 million noninstitutionalized individuals with disabilities aged five and older.

The divergent data regarding prevalence of disability is caused, in part, by (1) the inherent challenge of defining disability, (2) the dependence on self-reporting, and (3) the difficulty of identifying questions that can reliably reflect a disability definition and be likely to elicit positive self-reporting responses. A simple yes-or-no question—"Are you a person with a disability?"—would not accurately count the number of people with disabilities in the same way that someone can rely on check-boxes for "male" and "female" to estimate the numbers of men and women. Accordingly, the Census Bureau depends on a collection of questions that aim to piece together the population of people disabilities. Some questions relate to vision and hearing impairments, others to functional limitations like climbing stairs. Depending on which questions are used and how the questions are phrased, there can be significant and minor variations in the resulting numbers. Moreover, most survey data expressly omit an estimated 2 million people with disabilities who are institutionalized—completely ignoring those suffering from the most significant impact of segregation, exclusion, and loss of freedom.

Attempts to find questions that will reliably count the number of people with disabilities must be developed in the context of pervasive stigma against people with disabilities. The reason a simple yes-or-no disability question is not reliable is because many if not most people with disabilities would not answer "yes" to the question—either because they do not want to be associated with disability or genuinely do not view a particular impairment, such as difficulty in walking, reaching, bathing, concentrating, working, or leaving the home, as constituting a disability. Even where questions are particularized to avoid stigmatizing labels, many individuals may choose not to identify with any impairment.

The inherent difficulty of developing questions to count disability complicates efforts to compare disability statistics over time, or across data sets. For instance, the 1990, 2000, and 2010 census have all had questions related to disability, but the questions in each year were slightly different. Moreover, because not all data sets ask the same scope of questions besides disability-related questions, it is not possible to link a particular count of the disability population in one questionnaire to data from another questionnaire. The Social Security Administration, for instance, has a wealth of disability-related data. However, detailed Social Security data cannot be related to other demographic data documented through the Census Bureau.

Group Identity. Even assuming that the number of people with disabilities can be reliably and consistently counted through current survey methodology, there is an important difference between identifying large numbers of people with individual impairments that share in common a label of "disability" and describing those individuals as composing a "group." The challenge with claiming that people with disabilities make up a discreet minority group is that, as suggested above, people with disabilities do not necessarily identify with a label of "disability."

In political terms, the language of "group" means that there is a way to identify individuals included in the group as well as some basic shared values or issues for those in the group—even if not everyone in the group shares those attributes. Groups can be based on immutable characteristics such as race, ethnicity, or gender. Groups can also be creations of political analysts and media pundits who identify voting patterns expected to be critical in high-profile elections, such as the famous "soccer moms" and "security moms" in the 1996 and 2004 presidential elections.

One of the most important mechanisms for evaluating the extent and significance of group identity is exit polling. Exit polls and other political opinion polls enable political enthusiasts to track how identifiable groups vote, and to help identify positions and platforms that might help sway votes. Exit polling enables quick analysis of relationships between, for instance, race, sex, income, age, and a variety of other data points. Of course, counting a group is a critical prerequisite to evaluating a group's opinions and pressure points. Identification of "gay, lesbian, and bisexual" voters, for example, has been a mainstay in the national exit poll since 1990. Disability, by contrast, has not. There has been some recent interest in exit polling and disability, but so far there has been no widespread commitment to incorporate disability into the major exit polls. Not being counted means you are not visible as a voting bloc notwithstanding any claims about being "the largest minority group."

In the absence of a politically relevant mechanism such as exit polling to substantiate a disability group identity, observers are left with trying to assess the political significance of population survey data that counts tens of millions of people with disabilities.

Unfortunately, while a cadre of activists have honed extraordinary policy expertise covering the full spectrum of domestic and international disability issues, and have cultivated effective relationships with decision-makers, the disability community has not yet demonstrated an ability to harness anything close to the power of 54 million Americans with disabilities.

The Challenge of Cross-Disability Organizing. "Disability" is largely a fabricated category, in the sense that most people counted among those with disabilities do not consider themselves part of that group in the same way people identify themselves according to race, ethnicity, gender, and sexual orientation. To the extent that people identify with physical or mental impairments, they tend to do so on a disability-specific basis: as a person who is blind or visually impaired, deaf or hard-of-hearing, with spinal cord injury, or short stature, to give just a few examples.

To be sure, there is a vibrant disability rights movement that defines itself in cross-disability terms. But cultivating identity across impairment categories is an enduring challenge. The first effort to build a sustained cross-disability identity was the now-defunct organization, American Coalition of Citizens with Disabilities (ACCD). Founded in 1974 when about 150 disability rights activists convened in Washington and discussed the need for a nationwide grassroots disability movement, ACCD was initially a volunteer coalition-building organization. Its claim to fame was helping to usher in the first cross-disability nondiscrimination statute, called Section 504 of the Rehabilitation Act. However, by 1983, after less than ten years in existence, ACCD was forced to close its doors due, at least in part, to a declining stream of funding.

ACCD's early demise reflected some of the inherent tensions among disability-specific coalitions. In the early 1980s, reductions in federal grants by the Reagan Administration and other actual and proposed program cuts and eliminations forced many disability organizations to focus more narrowly on their own disability organizations. As a coalition of organizations rather than an organization of individuals, ACCD's assembly mirrored some of the very divisions within the disability community that it sought to transcend. It was easier to rally around efforts like Section 504, which broadly promised non-discrimination against all people with disabilities, than to organize amid a hostile political and economic environment and specific threats of budget cuts.

After ACCD closed its doors, the National Council on Independent Living (NCIL), formed in 1982, was quick to claim the mantle of the nation's leading cross-disability organization. With similar roots in the independent living movement, NCIL aimed to galvanize people with disabilities across the country. Ultimately, however, NCIL's focus on provision of services—particularly a perception that centers for independent living were tailored to the needs of people with physical disabilities—limited its capacity to become a genuine cross-disability organization with broad-based identification across the disability spectrum. Although NCIL had, and has, a strong grassroots connection through its network of individual centers for independent living, those connections have yet to be translated into a recognizable political force that unites people with disabilities beyond those directly connected to independent living centers.

Today, the most influential and widely recognized cross-disability organization is the American Association of People with Disabilities, or AAPD, which was founded in 1995 with a goal of uniting the diverse community of people with disabilities and their friends, families, and supporters to promote the economic, social, and political empowerment of people with disabilities. Unlike ACCD, AAPD chose to follow a model more like the AARP (formerly the American Association of Retired Persons) and be an individual-member-based organization rather than a coalition of organizations. However, in the absence of making contacts through service provision, membership in a cross-disability organization like AAPD requires a cross-disability identity. It is thus not surprising that AAPD's membership numbers sixty thousand, a fraction of the oft-quoted 54 million Americans with disabilities. AARP, by contrast, has sufficiently established itself as a powerhouse in American politics, perhaps one of the most

influential lobbying groups. But AARP's membership classification is simple: its membership is open to anyone age fifty and over, supporting AARP's ability to claim more than 40 million members.

One of the factors inhibiting the growth of organizations such as the ACCD, NCIL, and AAPD is the enduring impact of stigma. In this sense, the disability rights movement shares important similarities with the gay and lesbian rights movement. In addition to efforts to change the minds of persons of influence as well as the general public, the LGBT community's "membership" depends on self-identification. Due to powerful stigmas and overt discrimination, identifying as a person who is gay or lesbian was—and remains—a complicated and difficult personal journey. Fortunately, changing one's own attitudes as well as the general public's attitudes are mutually supportive. As more people identify themselves as gay and lesbian, their friends, families, and coworkers are challenged to put those stigmas and that discrimination in the closet. And the more public attitudes change, the easier it is for more people to take pride in the identity of being gay or lesbian.

In 2009, in the wake of the 2008 presidential election seasons, a group of disability advocates recognized the need to appeal to a broader array of people with disabilities than those directly connected with existing disability organizations, and cultivate a positive identity of "pride" in disability. A successful first-of-its-kind Disability Power and Pride Inaugural Ball led to the formation of the Committee on Disability Power and Pride. Although this new group prioritized political mobilization of the disability community rather than service delivery or policy expertise, it has encountered similar challenges as other organizations and has yet to cultivate an effective vehicle to unite the disability community in a politically recognizable way.

To the extent that disability rights advocates have succeeded in making an impact by appealing to a cross-disability identity, it has come through the efforts of a relatively small cadre of vocal and self-identified people with disabilities and policy experts. Many members of this cadre have gone through a similar process of "coming out"—of beginning to embrace a physical or mental impairment as a core part of one's identity, rather than as a mere inconvenience to surmount and hide from view as best as possible. However, the remaining more than 50 million people with disabilities are arguably people who have yet to "come out of the closet," because they continue to view disability as something negative, detracting, and stigmatizing. To claim the mantra of the nation's largest minority, disability rights advocates will need to be able to demonstrate that they can move greater numbers of their constituency group.

Disability and Political Visibility. The disability community's impressive record of political achievements, including the Americans with Disabilities Act, has paradoxically contributed to the disability community's relative lack of perceived political power when compared to other identity-based groups. For decades, African Americans, Latinos, women, and the LGBT community, for instance, have undertaken ambitious political mobilizing efforts to enhance their perceived clout. Principal among these efforts have been activities related to recruiting candidates for elected and appointed office, raising money for candidates, and rating and scoring candidates based on issues relevant to a community. Groups have made these activities a priority in large measure because they had to. In the absence of broad-based bipartisan support for their priority issues, they determined that they needed to take aggressive steps to cultivate political power.

Disability advocates and political scientists who track disability politics generally agree that following the path of other communities is essential to future success. This is particularly the case in the current budget environment. As discussed above, the disability community has been most successful in coming together when the issues do not involve money—either the direct funding of programs or indirect allocation of resources that runs along disability community fault-line issues. As pressures mount to address entitlement programs and other domestic programs that have a disproportionate impact on people with disabilities, it will likely be the case that they need to work together better to achieve their stated goals and to optimize limited resources.

The Disability Vote. Disability rights advocates and disability studies scholars have been following the disability vote for several decades. The 1988 presidential election was notable for the way in which disability was described as a potentially decisive voting bloc in turning the election in George H. W. Bush's favor. Prior survey data had indicated that the disability community leaned Democratic in its voting patterns. During the 1988 Republican convention, however, George H. W. Bush expressly advocated a civil rights law for persons with disabilities, including during his remarks at the Republican National Convention. Subsequent survey data revealed a marked shift toward Bush in the presidential election. According to one survey, the swing of the disability vote toward Bush was enough to account for the margin of victory.

According to data from the American Community Survey, there were roughly 33 million Americans with disabilities of voting age in 2009. According to studies of elections dating to the 1992 presidential election, people with disabilities vote at a rate as much as 21 percent lower than people without disabilities. In the 2008 elections, an estimated 14.7 million persons with disabilities voted, while in 2010 an estimated 11 million persons with disabilities voted. The voting turnout in 2008 and 2010 consistently amounted to between 11 and 17 percent when holding constant for age.

The estimated disability voting bloc of 14.7 million in the 2008 presidential election and 11 million in the midterm 2010 election makes the disability vote larger than the Latino vote (respectively estimated at 9.7 million and 6.6 million) and Asian American vote (an estimated 3.4 million in 2008) combined, and only slightly lower than the black vote (an estimated 16.1 million in 2008).

There is a critical difference between voter turnout and political visibility. For instance, while the numbers of whites, blacks, Asians, and Latinos, as well as men and women, in the 2008 presidential election are included in the US Census Current Population Report, the disability vote is not. Instead, in the May 2010 Current Population Report, disability is referenced only as one of the reasons for not registering or not voting. In other words, there is no disability voting bloc, according to the Census Current Population reports. The data on disability voting provided above are based on retrospective analysis of census data rather than prospective inclusion in census data linked to voter participation.

Moreover, the awareness of the rate at which, and how many, people with disabilities vote does not provide insight into *how* people vote. Census data may provide reliable estimates of aggregate numbers engaged in the voting process; but the principal mechanism for election campaigns to track voting blocs and the impact of campaign themes is through polling efforts, particularly exit polls. However, people with disabilities are generally not included in exit polls and other opinion polls. Whatever the inherent limits of polling data may be, a group needs at least to be included in the polling questions to analyze whether the polls accurately reflect voting patterns of particular voting blocs. Until people with disabilities are consistently recognized as a voting bloc that can be evaluated alongside other voting blocs in exit polls and other mainstream election analysis, the "disability vote" will remain more of an academic exercise than a political force.

Voting Accessibility. One longstanding impediment to the political participation of people with disabilities has been accessibility to voting locations. Most polling places are located in schools, libraries, and other places of public accommodation, and those facilities, as well as some voting technology, remain inaccessible to many people with disabilities. Until recently, for instance, most individuals who are blind could not vote independently but instead had to depend on others to accompany them to the voting booth and mark their preferred voting selections for them. Similarly, many individuals with mobility impairments have been blocked from accessing voting booths due to stairs or even the presence of a curb without a curb cut.

New legislation, including the Help America Vote Act of 2002, as well as advocacy efforts, including AAPD's Disability Vote Project, have helped increase the rate of polling place accessibility. According to the US Government Accountability Office, an estimated 27.3 percent of polling places in 2008 had no accessibility impediments, an improvement over 16 percent in the 2000 election. Virtually all polling places had at least one accessible voting system that enabled independent voting. However, 46 percent of voting places had systems that could pose barriers to at least some voters, such as voters using wheelchairs. The increased availability of absentee ballots has helped many people with disabilities vote. Census data indicates that 26 percent of voters with disabilities voted by mail prior to election day, compared with 15 percent of those without disabilities.

However, the impact of voting inaccessibility extends beyond the actual barriers at voting places or the availability of voting by mail. As explained above, people with disabilities vote at lower rates than persons without disabilities. However, there is only a 1 percent gap in voter registration rates. Psychological factors may play an important role, including perceptions that people with disabilities are not equally welcome to participate in the political process. While 6 percent of people with disabilities reported an actual difficulty in voting (compared with 2 percent of the nondisabled population), 33 percent of nonvoters with disabilities reported that they would expect to find difficulty at the voting place (again compared with 2 percent of the nondisabled population). This broad gap between real and perceived voting place barriers suggests that the expectation of barriers is a powerful deterrent to voting among people with disabilities.

Promoting Candidates for Elected and Appointed Office. Groups seeking to increase their political power have prioritized electing and appointing candidates from their own community. If politics is about influencing decision-making, there is arguably no more direct way to exert influence than having people in positions of power. For instance, in 1985 women's rights advocates founded a political action committee called EMILY's List with a singular objective of "electing pro-choice Democratic women to office." (The acronym stands for "Early Money Is Like Yeast.") EMILY's List now claims to have raised more than $82 million for candidates at all levels of government, and maintains a list of individual women governors, US senators, US representatives, and state and local officeholders. The efforts of EMILY's List and other women's rights organizations have successfully helped transform the demographics of the United States Congress. The first female US representative was elected in 1917. Today, a majority of the California House delegation (thirty-five of fifty-three seats) are women. The explosion of the Tea Party onto the political stage in the early twenty-first century is another example of the power of aggressive recruitment and support of candidates for elected office who share a specific political goal or objective.

Many advocacy groups have similarly made a priority of recruiting and promoting candidates for political appointments. At the presidential level, for instance, groups like the Victory Fund have developed ambitious bench-building programs to identify prospective candidates, and then work aggressively with the White House Office of Presidential Personnel to promote their appointment.

The disability community has yet to make the same inroads in elected and appointed office that other communities have made. Part of this may be attributable to the long-standing tradition of bipartisan support for disability issues, as discussed above. Moreover, because disability respects no boundaries and touches many if not most families, there have been a string of prominent elected officials who are deeply supportive of disability issues. A review of key players in Congress and in the Ronald Reagan and George H. W. Bush administrations between 1988 and 1990, during the ADA's passage, reveals extensive disability connections among those key elected officials, either through their own disability or that of their family members. Examples include Senators Bob Dole (paralyzed arm), Tom Harkin (deaf brother), Orrin Hatch (brother-in-law with polio), Ted Kennedy (son lost a leg to cancer and sister with an intellectual disability), and Lowell Weicker (son with Down syndrome); Representatives Tony Coelho (has epilepsy) and Steny Hoyer (wife with epilepsy); President George Bush (several family members with different disabilities), Attorney General Dick Thornburgh (son with intellectual disability),

and Equal Employment Opportunity Commission (EEOC) Chairman Evan Kemp (wheelchair user). These and other elected and appointed officials were passionate about the ADA in part because they lived a disability experience and wanted to better the lives of all Americans with disabilities.

There is an important difference between elected and appointed officials who happen to have disability experiences and people who are elected largely because of disability experiences. Tony Coelho is one of the most singularly influential elected officials in American disability history. However, while his disability experience motivated his decision to seek office, his rise to power did not depend on a groundswell of support from the disability community. He was not recruited to run for office by the disability community; rather, he became a champion for disability advocates because he had found his path to Congress as an effective advocate for issues related to his congressional district centered in Fresno, California.

The challenge for the disability community is that by not having an infrastructure to support continual recruitment and election of favorable candidates, the community is dependent on soliciting the support of people who have won office in large measure without support from the disability community. Of the individuals referenced above, only Tom Harkin, Orrin Hatch, and Steny Hoyer remained in office as of 2011. James Langevin, who injured his spinal cord in an accidental shooting as a seventeen-year-old police cadet and subsequently became a quadriplegic, was the most prominent person with a disability holding office in Congress in 2011. He cochaired a House Bipartisan Disabilities Caucus along with Cathy McMorris Rodgers, a Republican from Washington. The caucus was established in 2007 and launched a website around the twentieth anniversary of the ADA in July 2010; in 2011 the caucus had forty-four members. However, in contrast to other caucuses like the Congressional Black Caucus, Langevin was the only prominent member who self-identified as a person with a disability. Others, like cochair McMorris Rodgers, had family experience (in her case, as the mother of a child with

Down syndrome). It is a powerful testament to the bipartisan resonance of disability issues that so many people who are not themselves disabled want to be part of a disabilities caucus. But a disability caucus whose members are mainly people without disabilities means that people with disabilities are still not leading their own fate in the halls of Congress and remain largely dependent on the goodwill of congressional supporters.

Identifying and securing the support of candidates who happen to have or acquire disabilities while in office, or elected officials who are broadly supportive of disability policy issues, also limits the ability of people with disabilities to exert influence based on political power. Individuals like James Langevin may well continue to be elected and reelected, but so far their electoral success is due to their general appeal to broader constituencies, rather than targeted support from people with disabilities as a group.

Disability advocates who view increased political strength as important for the disability community agree that building the capacity to back qualified candidates with disabilities is critical. So far, however, there has been no concerted attempt to build an infrastructure to support candidates with disabilities. A Disability Power and Pride PAC was formed around the ADA's twentieth anniversary with a goal of supporting candidates with disabilities. However, it has yet to throw its support behind a newly recruited candidate from the disability community.

Disability advocates have generally had more success in seeing people with disabilities appointed to senior positions throughout the federal government. This is feasible because it does not rely on political electoral machinery and instead relies on more traditional largesse from both parties. After the 2008 presidential election, under the leadership of Tony Coelho and the newly formed Committee on Disability Power and Pride, disability advocates organized the most comprehensive effort to date to promote disability community candidates with the White House Office of Presidential Personnel. This effort led to new gains in seeing people with disabilities appointed across the federal government.

Approximating the success of other groups such as the LGBT community, however, will require building a sustainable bench-building effort that can survive the enthusiasm surrounding one particular election.

Fundraising. The disability community's relative political invisibility is perhaps no more clearly evident than in political fundraising—or the lack thereof. Millions of people with disabilities—and their family members and advocates—give millions of dollars to political campaigns. The problem for disability rights advocates is that those contributions are not generally identified with the disability community. Other groups have worked collaboratively with campaigns to develop tools to tag donations as being connected with a particular group. Disability rights advocates reached an important milestone in the 2008 presidential election by hosting the first-ever disability-community-sponsored presidential campaign fundraising event. By establishing a mechanism to track donations to the Barack Obama campaign, they were able to raise nearly $100,000 in less than four weeks, representing contributions from more than forty states in amounts ranging from $10 to more than $2,000. A single successful fundraising event, however, will do little to enhance the disability community's political visibility if it cannot demonstrate that fundraising can be sustained on a consistent basis.

Conclusion. Joseph Shapiro, in his pathbreaking 1994 work *No Pity: People with Disabilities Forging a New Civil Rights Movement*, about the passage of the ADA and a burgeoning disability rights movement, aptly described the disability community as a "hidden army" of people loosely linked by a shared experience of stigma and social oppression. The disability community has similarly been described in political contexts as a "sleeping giant" to signify the latent potential of disability as a significant force in American politics. For the disability community to deliver on its claims to be the largest minority and to be a potential powerful voting bloc, the so-called "hidden army" will need to become politically visible. There are signs that the community is making progress. But the potential voting bloc as yet remains largely hidden, and it is far from certain that the hidden force will have the power of an army rather than a small band of soldiers.

[*See also* Civil Rights Act; Civil Rights Movement; Community Action; Education and Diversity; Elections and Electoral Behavior; *and* Roosevelt, Franklin Delano.]

BIBLIOGRAPHY

DeJong, Gerben. "Independent Living: From Social Movement to Analytic Paradigm." *Archives of Physical Medicine and Rehabilitation* 60 (October 1979): 435–446.

National Council on Disability. *Equality of Opportunity: The Making of the Americans with Disabilities Act.* (Washington, D.C., 2010).

Rehabilitation Research and Training Center on Disability Statistics and Demographics. "Annual Disability Statistics Compendium: 2010." http://www.disabilitycompendium.org/pdf/Compendium2010.pdf.

Schur, Lisa, and Douglas Kruse. "Disability, Voter Turnout, and Polling Place Accessibility." (7 June 2011), http://www.eac.gov/assets/1/Documents/Rutger's%20-%20Disability,%20Voter%20Turnout,%20and%20Polling%20Place%20Accessibility.pdf.

Scotch, Richard. *From Good Will to Civil Rights: Transforming Federal Disability Policy.* 2d ed. (Philadelphia, 2001).

Shapiro, Joseph P. *No Pity: People with Disabilities Forging a New Civil Rights Movement.* (New York, 1994).

United States Government Accountability Office. "Voters with Disabilities: Additional Monitoring of Polling Places Could Further Improve Accessibility." (September 2009), http://www.gao.gov/new.items/d09941.pdf.

US Census Bureau. "Voting and Registration in the Election of November 2008: Population Characteristics." (May 2010), http://www.census.gov/prod/2010pubs/p20-562.pdf.

World Health Organization. "World Report on Disability." (2011), http://www.who.int/disabilities/world_report/2011/report/en/.

Jonathan Young

DOMESTIC VIOLENCE

Domestic violence—the abuse of women by their intimate partners—is the most endemic form of violence against women in the United States. It is estimated that every day in the United States, four women are killed and another fourteen thousand are battered at the hands of their partners. In contrast, males are far less likely to fall victim to domestic violence. Intimate partner violence accounts for only 3.6 percent of violent crimes committed against men, yet 21.5 percent of violent crimes against women are committed by an intimate partner. Likewise, 5.3 percent of male homicides are domestic violence-related, while 30.1 percent of female homicides are caused by domestic violence. The annual cost of domestic violence in terms of health care and lost work productivity is conservatively estimated by the Centers for Disease Control at $5.8 billion, and nationally representative random samples yield rates of domestic violence of approximately 25 percent.

Economic Factors Shaping Domestic Violence. A variety of factors play an important part in the severity of gender violence. Cultural norms and values are key, as are the particularities of the individual relationship. However, one of the most important factors is the economic power of the battered woman. Economic inequality combines with other factors such as cultural norms to deny women labor market access and jobs, which are necessary for self support. A lack of economic alternatives results in women with little power or leverage to stop the violence. A woman who is abused by her husband or partner must make a choice either to remain in this relationship or to leave. She will weigh the alternatives and choose the one that is best for herself and for her children. She has an idea what her life will be like if she stays. Her well-being if she leaves depends on her alternatives. Does she have a job? If she does, does she earn enough to support herself and her children? If she does not, can she get one? What is her educational background? Does she have any relevant professional experience? If not, can she expect welfare benefits, and how much help will these provide? Are there shelters she can escape to? Can she find job training or counseling to help with the transition? The more attractive her options outside the relationship are, the more likely it is that she will try to leave. Therefore, anything that improves her options outside the relationship increases the likelihood that she will leave.

Notably, the most important economic factor is a woman's own income, not her partner's. A woman with a wealthy husband but no personal income may be just as likely or more likely to stay in an abusive relationship than a woman from a poor household. Mounting evidence suggests that, holding other factors constant, the incidence of domestic violence falls as women's personal income increases. In contrast, many studies have found that women who are highly dependent on marriage for their economic support experience more physical abuse.

The Costs and Scope of Domestic Violence. The fact that economic independence is the key to ending domestic violence is in many ways unsurprising. Women themselves understand this and often do what they can to improve their options. Holding other factors constant, women in abusive relationships are more likely to work for pay than women who are not victims of abuse.

However, gaining economic independence and control is a difficult solution for battered women. While a woman may want to leave an abusive relationship and recognize that she needs to work and improve her economic status in order to do so, that may be easier said than done. Even while women who are victims of abuse tend to work in hopes of escaping their abusive relationship, violence lowers a woman's productivity in the workplace. Battered women often avoid going to work with visible bruises, and victims of abuse are more likely to be absent or tardy, exert less effort while working, and experience a diminished chance of advancement. Likewise, women may miss work because of serious injuries that prevent them from working or from less serious injuries that they are embarrassed about. Further, abusers often intentionally sabotage their partners' work efforts by harassing them at work or even forcing them to quit.

These negative productivity effects are extremely important and have broad implications. Not only do battered women have fewer economic alternatives and less income for themselves and their children, but the employment costs of domestic violence affect employers, coworkers, and society as whole. Employers get less productive workers and lose and

must replace already-trained workers. Coworkers may bear additional workloads due to the productivity losses and, in some cases, may be in danger when domestic violence spills over into the workplace. And the overall economy loses as valuable resources—namely, productive workers—are under- and unemployed. In the United States alone, domestic violence imposes annual costs in excess of $5.8 billion for medical care and lost productivity. Other studies have estimated losses to be as great as $10 to $67 billion annually. An estimated 2.8 million days of work are lost each year as a result of domestic violence, and the total pay lost by battered women in the United States is $96 million. Such steep costs have exposed domestic violence as a pervasive social ill.

Public Policy and Domestic Violence. Given the high costs of domestic violence, both for its immediate victims and society more broadly, policies geared at ending the abuse are important. Since victims already try to help themselves by improving their economic status, aiding in those efforts is a first step. Women who are abused are well-represented in the labor market, so the workforce is an excellent avenue for reaching out to victims of domestic abuse. Support at work including counseling, paid leaves, legal help, and advances on pay would aid a woman in building her economic power and independence enough to leave an abusive relationship. While most workplaces have ignored this important issue, corporations have supported initiatives to assist employees who are victims of domestic violence. For example, Polaroid, Liz Claiborne, Marshall's, and Verizon have a number of initiatives in place to assist employees who are victims of domestic violence, including education efforts, literature distribution, and awareness training.

In addition, services for battered women such as emergency housing, child care, counseling, and legal advocacy all play important roles in ending domestic violence. Programs that provide services to battered women may also offer alternatives to staying with abusers. Like initiatives to improve women's economic status, these services might result in more battered women being able to achieve self-sufficiency in the long run. Further, while shelters and hotlines have no significant impact on the likelihood of a woman experiencing domestic abuse, they may play important roles in mitigating the severity of abuse. The availability of legal services in the county of residence does have a significant, negative impact on the likelihood that an individual woman is battered.

However, despite the prevalence of intimate partner violence and its high social costs, insufficient services currently exist to help victims. For example, in 2003 the United States had only 1,386 shelters with a total capacity of 31,429 beds, far fewer than the approximately 1.5 million women who are abused each year in the United States. And in a given day in the United States, domestic violence programs treat seven times more individuals than emergency rooms do. Further, services are not distributed evenly across the United States, but instead tend to be most sparse in rural and poorer areas. Since local services have traditionally been provided through grassroots efforts, and grassroots efforts are more likely to flourish in well-resourced communities, these disparities make empirical sense. One explanation for the continued inadequacy of domestic violence services is the fact that low reporting levels prevent local governments from fully realizing the extent of the violence. Approximately six out of seven domestic violence assaults go unreported. Reporting levels also correlate with demographic factors like race, geographical residence, and income, potentially explaining the unequal availability of services from location to location.

Given the significant social costs that result from intimate partner violence, and the insufficient services and policies in place to prevent it, there seems to be a great need for government intervention. Although state governments have provided support to their communities to assist victims and to reduce intimate partner violence for several decades, only with the introduction of the Violence against Women Act (VAWA) in 1994 did the federal government become involved in this issue. Following the passage of the act, existing agencies expanded their offerings, but the number of overall programs only increased by 2 percent between 1994 and 2000. The Services Training Officers Prosecutors (STOP) grant program was designed as part of the VAWA and provides state-level funding for the coordination of programs or initiatives to target domestic violence. It is administered by the United States Department of Justice. While these grants have been effective in communities where they exist both in improving the overall climate for victims and bringing services to underserved groups, many counties continue to have no programs at all.

A major policy concern, therefore, should be directing VAWA funds to the neediest communities. Even with a system of awarding additional points to applications from new programs, and from programs with plans to reach underserved communities, reliance on grant proposals is likely to favor the expansion of existing programs. A more deliberate and targeted approach is required. Further, a continuation of welfare services is necessary to support battered women, as between 55 and 65 percent of women on welfare have reported being abused by an intimate partner.

Pursuing protection of battered women via criminal statutes and other legislative enactments beyond VAWA is also an important option. For example, many states have enacted laws that require police to arrest suspected abusers. However, scholars have debated the effectiveness of such statutes, and more research is needed on this topic. Laws that ensure custody rights and maintain health care benefits for women who leave abusive partners would make leaving a realistic possibility for more battered women. And perhaps most importantly, women need to be assured of their physical safety if they leave. Their economic alternatives outside the relationship are worthless if the violence continues. Women who leave are actually at a greater risk of homicide (during the first two months after separation) than women who stay in abusive relationships. And many women who leave ultimately return to their partners, only to face even greater abuse. We need better laws, enforcement, and services to ensure the safety of battered women.

[See also Marriage and the Family; and Women and Welfare.]

BIBLIOGRAPHY

Aizer, Anna. "The Gender Wage Gap and Domestic Violence." *American Economic Review* 100 (2010): 1847–1859.

Aizer, Anna. "Wages, Violence, and Health in the Household." National Bureau of Economic Research Working Paper 13494. (2007), http://www.nber.org/papers/w13494.pdf?new_window=1.

Aizer, Anna, and Pedro Dal Bó. "Love, Hate, and Murder: Commitment Devices in Violent Relationships." *Journal of Public Economics* 93 (2009): 412–428.

Bowlus, Audra J., and Shannon Seitz. "Domestic Violence, Employment, and Divorce." *International Economic Review* 47 (2006): 1113–1149.

Burt, Martha R., et al. "2001 Report: Evaluation of the STOP Formula Grants to Combat Violence against Women." Urban Institute. (2001), http://www.urban.org/url.cfm?ID=410335.

Burt, Martha R., et al. "Victim Service Programs in the STOP Formula Grants Program: Services Offered and Interactions with Other Community Agencies." Urban Institute. (2000), http://www.urban.org/url.cfm?ID=410243.

Catalano, Shannan. "Intimate Partner Violence in the United States." US Department of Justice. (2007), http://bjs.ojp.usdoj.gov/content/pub/pdf/ipvus.pdf.

Centers for Disease Control. *Costs of Intimate Partner Violence Against Women in the United States.* (Atlanta, 2003).

Department of Justice. "OVW Fiscal Year 2011 STOP Violence against Women Formula Grant Program." (2011), http://www.ovw.usdoj.gov/docs/stop-vw-program-fy2011.pdf.

DeRiviere, Linda. "Do Economists Need to Rethink Their Approaches to Modeling Intimate Partner Violence?" *Journal of Economic Issues* 42 (2008): 583–606.

Farmer, Amy, and Jill Tiefenthaler. "An Economic Analysis of Domestic Violence." *Review of Social Economy* 55 (1997): 337–358.

Farmer, Amy, and Jill Tiefenthaler. "Explaining the Recent Decline in Domestic Violence." *Contemporary Economic Policy* 21 (2003): 158–172.

Gelles, Richard J. "Abused Wives: Why Do They Stay?" *Journal of Marriage and the Family* 38 (1976): 659–668.

Iyengar, Radha, et al. "50,000 People a Day: The Use of Federally Funded Services for Intimate Partner Violence." National Bureau of Economic Research Working Paper 13785. (2008).

Kalmuss, Debra S., and Murray A. Straus. "Wife's Marital Dependency and Wife Abuse." In *Physical Violence in American Families: Risk Factors and Adaptions to Violence in 8,145 Families*, edited by Murray Arnold Straus and Richard J. Gelles, pp. 369–382. (New Brunswick, N.J., 1990).

Lloyd, Susan. "The Effects of Domestic Violence on Women's Employment." *Law and Policy* 19 (1997): 139–167.

Pagelow, Mildred Daley. *Woman-Battering: Victims and Their Experiences.* (Beverly Hills, Calif., 1981).

Pollak, Robert A. "Bargaining Power in Marriage: Earnings, Wage Rates, and Household Production." National Bureau of Economic Research Working Paper 11239. (2005).

Rennison, Callie Maries. *Rape and Sexual Assault: Reporting to the Police and Medical Attention, 1992–2000.* (Washington, D.C., 2002).

Shepard, Melanie, and Ellen Pence. "The Effect of Battering on the Employment Status of Women." *Affilia* 3 (1988): 55–61.

Solomon, C. M. "Talking Frankly about Domestic Violence." *Personnel Journal* 74 (1995).

Stanley, C. *Domestic Violence: An Occupational Impact Study.* (Tulsa, Okla., 1992).

Tauchen, Helen V., Ann Dryden Witte, and Sharon K. Long. "Domestic Violence: A Non-Random Affair." *International Economic Review* 32 (1991): 491–511.

Tjaden, Patricia, and Nancy Thoennes. "The Prevalence, Incidence and Consequences of Violence against Women: Findings from the National Violence against Women Survey." National Institute of Justice Report NCJ-172837. (1998), https://www.ncjrs.gov/pdffiles/172837.pdf.

Jill Tiefenthaler

DRUGS AND POLITICS

The regulation of the many consciousness-altering substances used by individuals recreationally has long been inextricably linked to politics, both in the United States and in other countries. In contrast to many other political issues, however, drug regulation is decidedly one-sided: apparently no one believes in or supports substance abuse. As a result, drug control has become a political symbol of larger social problems in general.

The first law banning certain psychoactive substances in the United States, the Harrison Narcotics Act, was passed in 1914; and marijuana was banned at the federal level in 1937. Since that time there have been a series of socially constructed drug "epidemics" and "drug wars" in the United States, and drug law enforcement and the related punishment of offenders has been a major component of the US criminal justice system.

The most recent drug war in the United States was initiated under the administration of President Ronald Reagan in the 1980s and continued through the 1990s and 2000s. Since 1975, there has been a tremendous increase in the number of drug arrests in the United States. Adult drug arrests increased from 322,000 in 1970 to 1,663,582 in 2009, representing 13 percent of all arrests, more than for any other offense. Despite the rhetoric on the part of some US government and law-enforcement officials that the war on drugs is focused on those who traffic in illegal substances, arrests for possession of drugs are approximately four times higher than arrests for drug trafficking. Despite the additional rhetoric that the US war on drugs is focused on "hard" drugs, in 2009 858,408 individuals were arrested for marijuana offenses, constituting 52 percent of all drug arrests in that year; 92 percent of those arrests were for simple possession of the drug. Although self-report surveys and other measures indicate that marijuana use has remained fairly constant over the last few decades, arrests for marijuana have increased substantially since the late 1980s, while arrests for cocaine and heroin have declined significantly. These data may indicate that the increased focus on marijuana has come at the expense of enforcing laws against hard drugs such as heroin, cocaine, and methamphetamine.

With respect to the sentencing of drug offenders, in 2002 (the most recent year for which data are available) drug offenders constituted 32 percent of felons convicted in state courts and, of the 240,000 felony drug offense cases in that year, 66 percent resulted in incarceration. Examined in a different way, in 2001 individuals convicted of drug offenses constituted 20.4 percent of all adults serving time in state prisons (and 55 percent of federal prison inmates). Between 1980 and 2001, the number of individuals in state and federal prisons for drug offenses increased by approximately 1,300 percent. The United States currently has more people incarcerated for drug offenses than the European Union has for all offenses combined, despite the fact that the European Union has 100 million more citizens. US drug wars have also contributed to gross racial disparities in incarceration.

These and other data leave little doubt that drugs and political issues related to drugs have been, and continue to be, an important domain in the United States. In this chapter, we trace developments in drug legislation from the early 1900s to the present. Over this period, drug legislation has been characterized by a predominantly prohibitionist, punitive approach to drug control and enforcement. Large-scale social and economic consequences have resulted from this approach, despite a lack of scientific evidence that this punitive approach has achieved success in reducing drug use and abuse. In this discussion, a number of common themes emerge: (1) the social construction of drug epidemics, (2) the association of the use of particular drugs with marginalized social groups (in particular, members of racial minority groups), (3) the influence of "moral entrepreneurs" and the government bureaucracies they are associated with in influencing drug policies, and (4) an ongoing disregard for scientific evidence in shaping drug policies. It is important to note that this chapter will not focus on drugs that are currently legal, although the distinction between legal and illegal drugs is, to at least some extent, arbitrary. In addition, space constraints do not allow for a consideration of the important role of the United States in influencing drug policies and control in other nations, especially with respect to drug-producing and transit countries.

Prohibition and Escalating Criminalization (1900–1968). In the nineteenth century, narcotic and hallucinogenic drugs were sold openly in the United States. Medicine, which lacked the scientific basis it would eventually develop in the twentieth century, relied extensively on painkillers to "treat" patients, many of which contained various derivatives of opium. In 1910, morphine was the most frequently used medical drug, while alcohol was the fifth most commonly used medical drug. The Bayer chemical company of Germany successfully synthesized heroin in 1898 and sold the drug over the counter, its advertising suggesting that heroin was a "nonaddictive" substitute for codeine and morphine. Cocaine was marketed aggressively and touted as a cure for hay fever and sinus problems, used as a food additive, and used as an ingredient in soft drinks such as Coca-Cola.

Addiction to drugs in early twentieth-century American society was fairly common—widespread drug use was facilitated by the growth of large-scale industrial organizations using mass production and advertising techniques; at the same time, many physicians and pharmacists maintained a lucrative practice by supplying opiates to drug addicts. With opiate drugs being as freely available in this period as aspirin is today, Edward Brecher (1972, p. 3) observed that "the United States of America during the 19th century could properly be described as a 'dope fiend's paradise.'" Estimates of the number of drug addicts in 1915 ranged from 200,000 to 275,000, with concentrations in the south and, importantly, among members of the middle and upper classes.

It is notable (consistent with this theme) that the first state and local government efforts to restrict the nonmedical use of drugs were aimed not at these middle- and upper-class users but instead at the immigrant Chinese population. Racial tensions, particularly in the state of California, produced a number of local ordinances and ultimately a state law prohibiting the smoking of opium in 1881. The intent of this legislation to target the Chinese was clear because opium consumption by means other than smoking in fact remained legal. Seventeen other states with some Chinese residents enacted similar laws in the late 1800s and early 1900s.

The first federal law regarding drugs in the United States—in this case related to "pharmaceutical products"—came into effect in 1848. This law banned the importation of adulterated drugs, which at the time were causing significant health problems in the United States. However, given this law's focus on drugs imported from other countries, it did not have any impact on domestically produced substances, many of which were also adulterated with drugs that are now included under federal drug-control statutes.

Approximately sixty years later, Congress passed the Pure Food and Drug Act (1906) which, among other things, prohibited interstate and foreign commerce in adulterated and misbranded food and drug products and required manufacturers to list the ingredients, including the quantity of alcohol and other drugs, in their products. Although this law did not make the use of narcotic and other drugs illegal, the accurate labeling of products served to substantially reduce their sales and, ultimately, their use. Middle-class individuals in particular, who had some awareness of the problems of addiction, tended to avoid the patent medicines that contained narcotic drugs.

Specific regulation of (in some cases, inappropriately classified) narcotics by the US federal government began with the Harrison Narcotics Act, passed in 1914. This legislation was the result of efforts by moral entrepreneurs, with some minor support from public opinion. Hamilton Wright, who served as the Department of State's opium commissioner, was one of the first to blame America's drug problems on the willingness of foreign nations to supply drugs. Seeking limitations on foreign production of drugs, the United States was instrumental in calling for the Hague Convention of 1912, with its agenda to control the international traffic in opium and cocaine.

Francis Harrison, a Democrat from New York, mediated between foreign policy advocates and domestic interest groups to shape this law. He made a series of changes in the proposed legislation to gain the support of pharmacists and physicians, who at the time were disputing the key issue of which one of their professions would control the dispensing of drugs. Interestingly, marijuana was included in the early drafts of the Harrison Act but eventually excluded in response to opposition from the pharmaceutical industry. Because the substance was used primarily in veterinary medicine and other nonintoxicating preparations, little purpose was seen in including it with the apparently more dangerous opiates and cocaine.

Race played a major role in the passage of the Harrison Act, particularly with respect to the inclusion of cocaine as one of the regulated drugs. As noted, prior to its prohibition in the United States, cocaine was a relatively popular drug—it was pure, cheap, widely distributed, and a common ingredient in various medicines, soda pop, wines, and other products. It was not the damage done to those who abused cocaine—who were primarily from the middle and upper classes—that led to demands for its prohibition. Instead, it was fear of cocaine's allegedly overstimulating powers among black users of the drug. There were numerous law-enforcement claims in circulation at the time that cocaine gave blacks superhuman strength and contributed to assaults on whites, particularly sexual assaults against white women.

The Harrison Narcotics Act thus mistakenly classified cocaine as a narcotic drug (the only true narcotic drugs are opium and its derivatives), and since 1914 the possession and sale of cocaine have been subject to the same federal penalties as those governing morphine and heroin. It has been argued that cocaine was willfully misclassified in the Harrison Act because this had certain propaganda advantages for those promoting the legislation.

The legislative intent of the Harrison Act was quite clear from the statute itself. It required that individuals and companies selling the regulated drugs register with the federal government, pay a small tax, and keep records of all their transactions. No language in the act referred to addicts or addiction, and the use of drugs for medical treatment was not prohibited. Because the Harrison Act, like the Marijuana Tax Act of 1937 that was to follow it, was framed as a revenue act, enforcement was assigned to the Treasury Department of the federal government and a narcotics division was created in the department's Bureau of Internal Revenue to administer the law.

But instead of enforcing a law that primarily involved record keeping and tax collection, the Bureau of Internal Revenue began a systematic effort to expand its powers. This effort involved first the launching of a public-relations campaign that involved using government reports and friendly newspaper reporters to portray drugs as a major threat to society. For example, the 1919 report of the bureau claimed (with no scientific evidence to support it) that there were 1 million addicts in the United States and that extensive cocaine addiction existed among children. Second, the bureau issued a series of regulations that went considerably beyond those that had been authorized under the act itself. In 1915, new regulations prohibited consumers from registering under the act, thereby requiring that addicts obtain their drugs through a physician or pharmacist. In the same year, a regulation required physicians treating addicts to systematically reduce the dosage they were providing in order to wean addicts from dependence. In essence, although the Treasury Department had no authority to regulate the practice of medicine, it had declared that drug-addict maintenance was an illegal medical practice. From a policy perspective, the Treasury Department's practices had a number of important consequences; in particular, it is notable that by 1928 almost one-third of all inmates in federal prisons were there for violations of the Harrison Act. The criminalization of drug use also created an underground "black market" for drugs, thereby generating higher drug prices and the need for at least some addicts to commit crimes to support their habits, and facilitating the involvement of organized crime in the drug trade.

There were also major scandals involving federal narcotics agents—between 1920 and 1929, a total of 752 drug-enforcement agents, representing 28 percent of all agents employed, were dismissed from their positions for actions including collusion, dereliction of duty, submitting false reports, perjury, embezzlement, and other charges. These scandals provided the impetus to reorganize the federal drug-control effort. This involved removing the Narcotics Division from the Prohibition Unit of the Treasury Department and creating the Federal Bureau of Narcotics (FBN). Harry J. Anslinger was appointed as first commissioner of the FBN, and more than any other single individual, Anslinger shaped American drug policy over the ensuing forty years. One of Anslinger's major policy accomplishments was the passage of the Marijuana Tax Act in 1937.

Recall that marijuana was not covered in the Harrison Act, although regulations in the Pure Food and Drug Act had prohibited its importation except for medicinal purposes and several states, including California, Louisiana, New York, and Texas, had passed marijuana-prohibition laws in the 1910s and 1920s. Allegations of increased marijuana use began in the South and the West, where recreational use of the substance increased with the influx of agricultural workers from Mexico.

In the early 1930s the FBN faced a very unfavorable political environment. Criticism of the agency as a result of the previously mentioned scandals was widespread, and the election of President Franklin Roosevelt, a Democrat who was committed to ending alcohol prohibition, also created problems for the bureau. In addition, the Depression had significantly reduced the FBN's budget from $1.7 million to $1.0 million.

In 1932, FBN head Anslinger apparently did not view marijuana as a serious problem but, in fact, suggested that the media were overstating use of the drug. He argued as follows: "A great deal of public interest has been aroused by newspaper articles . . . on the evils of the abuse of marijuana. . . . This publicity tends to magnify the extent of the evil and lends color to an influence that there is an alarming spread of the improper use of the drug, whereas the actual use may not have been inordinately large" (Abel, 1980, p. 112).

However, by 1935, the FBN had made a concerted effort to influence public opinion and create a moral panic over marijuana by publicizing a "marijuana menace." By using horror stories collected in bureau files, Anslinger attempted to "educate" legislators and the general public about the dangers posed by the substance. Marijuana was portrayed as a "killer weed" and the "assassin of youth," an addicting drug that led to insanity and the commission of violent and sexual crimes, often on the part of Hispanics and blacks, who were portrayed as the primary users of the drug. In an analysis of popular media (magazine) articles on marijuana, Howard Becker found that of seventeen articles published between 1937 and 1939, ten specifically acknowledged the assistance of the FBN in supplying facts and figures.

Eventually, a fairly broad consensus about marijuana emerged in the late 1930s—it was dangerous,

it caused violent crime and sexual immorality, and its use was accompanied by devastating psychological effects. This consensus was created by the moral entrepreneur Anslinger and the FBN, which dominated public discussion on the issue. As Jerome Himmelstein has noted, this happened precisely because there was no national marijuana menace, and hence, few among the general public knew anything about the drug. But through the dissemination of the bureau's information on marijuana, the public was able to place marijuana users in the preexisting category of "dope fiend"; and users of the substance became just as despicable as those who used opium, heroin, and cocaine. In addition, during the congressional hearings on the Marijuana Tax Act, Anslinger disregarded research suggesting that marijuana was a relatively benign substance that had medicinal uses and the opinion of the American Medical Association, blatantly lying to Congress in order to achieve his goal of complete marijuana prohibition.

In addition to his efforts to enact federal marijuana prohibition, Anslinger continuously pushed to strengthen other drug-related laws, to expand federal enforcement authority, and to extend his own political influence, all of which were realized in the next wave of federal drug legislation in the 1950s. He recruited other moral entrepreneurs to his cause with repeated propaganda campaigns fed to mass media sources that exaggerated the prevalence and danger of drug use, even as rates of addiction in the United States reached historic lows during the 1940s. When this rhetoric compounded with actual increases in heroin addiction following World War II and Anslinger's contention that this increase stemmed from communist attempts to brainwash Americans, public concerns and political attention to drug issues intensified. This inspired two subcommittee investigations into the "drug problem," led by Representative Hale Boggs in 1951 and Senator Pierce Daniel in 1956. The reports produced by these committees were based primarily on testimony from sympathetic experts and law-enforcement personnel, as well as Anslinger himself. They were dramatically candid about the "contagious danger" of addiction that could only be stopped by isolating addicts from society for lengthy periods and promoted the "gateway drug" theory of addiction, which asserted that, even though some might argue that drugs like marijuana are relatively benign, use of these substances inevitably led to the use of "harder" drugs such as heroin and cocaine. As a result, the Boggs Act (1951) established mandatory minimum prison sentences for all drug offenses, eliminated parole except for first offenses, and allowed capital punishment as a penalty for heroin distribution.

Shortly thereafter, the Kefauver hearings publicized the link between organized crime and drug distribution, leading to the passage of the Narcotic Control Act (also known as the Daniel Act, 1956), which quadrupled the mandatory minimum penalties prescribed by the Boggs Act and mandated increased enforcement of drug laws. In 1961, federal drug-enforcement authority further intensified, when the United States signed the Single Convention on Narcotic Drugs, which aimed to modernize and coordinate international drug-control efforts.

Brief, Limited Reorientation (1960s–1970s). Despite the harsh penalties created by the 1950s legislation, experimental drug use, in particular marijuana use, expanded considerably during the 1960s. This led to additional research, widespread experiential understanding of the effects of drug use, and the increasing normalization of marijuana use. A spirit of reform was evident, combining with other sociopolitical forces to produce a relatively brief but meaningful reorganization of federal and state drug policies. Even though federal drug policy had always officially maintained that complete prohibition of drugs was the goal, between the late 1960s and through the mid-1970s, elements of a harm-reduction approach were incorporated into US drug policy. This included the development of federal drug-treatment and -prevention agencies and programs and reduction in penalties for drug offenses at the federal level.

The 1970 Comprehensive Drug Abuse Prevention and Control Act nullified all previous drug laws and punishments, replacing them as an all-inclusive statute that reduced criminal penalties across the board; created a "scheduling" (classification) table that differentiated substances according to their alleged risk, toxicity, and medical potential; and established sanctions for different substances. The growing popularity of marijuana and mounting scientific evidence that it was a relatively benign substance led to the creation of the National Commission on Marijuana and Drug Abuse (Shafer Commission), which addressed, among other things, whether marijuana should be classified as a schedule I (highest risk) substance. The commission concluded that "neither the marijuana user nor the drug itself can be said to constitute a danger to public safety" (Shafer Commission 1972, p. 3) and recommended that marijuana be decriminalized. The Shafer report provided the foundation for President Jimmy Carter to announce (during his campaign) his intention to decriminalize marijuana if elected since "Penalties against possession of a drug should not be more damaging to an individual than the drug itself, and where they are, they should be changed" (Carter 1977). The scheduling hierarchy and the Shafer Commission report also helped to legitimize changes in drug legislation at the state level that were not aligned with federal policies. In 1973, Oregon decriminalized marijuana, as did eight other states by 1977. At the same time, drug policy in other states was going in a different direction, with a prime example being the Rockefeller laws (1973) in New York, which mandated incarceration for drug offenses and established harsh minimum sentencing guidelines.

While the 1960s and 1970s were thus a period in which the seeds of a harm-reduction approach to drugs were evident, it is also the period in which President Richard Nixon publicly declared "war" against what he referred to as "public enemy number one" (drugs). Although the term "War on Drugs" was first used by President Dwight Eisenhower in the 1950s and it could be argued that the United States has been engaged in an almost continuous war on drugs since the early 1900s, Nixon's actions elevated drug policy to national political prominence, beginning a trend that made the war on drugs one of the most salient public issues of the late twentieth century.

War on Drugs (1980–2009). During this period, increased political and media attention that focused on sensationalized, stereotypical images of drug users and the social construction of several drug "epidemics" led to a significant hardening of drug legislation. Beginning with reports about drug trafficking–related violence in Florida and Latin America in the late 1970s, media attention turned to the "crack epidemic" in the mid- to late 1980s. Reinerman and Levine (1997) note that in July of 1986 alone the three major television networks in the United States featured seventy-four evening news segments on drug-related topics, half of which were focused on crack. Between October 1988 and October 1989, the *Washington Post* presented more than fifteen hundred stories about the drug crisis. Similar to earlier themes, the media promoted the image that crack was primarily a drug used by African Americans, which served to demonize it in the eyes of many whites. While several commentators have noted that crack cocaine use never did constitute an epidemic (and that rates of use of the substance were relatively similar between whites and African Americans), the attention to this drug allowed legislators to shift the blame for many of the social problems of the 1980s (including relatively high rates of unemployment and crime) from the actions of the government to the drug-taking and trafficking of individuals.

This period also saw the passage of some of the most draconian drug (and related) laws in US history. The 1988 Anti–Drug Abuse Act reinstated mandatory minimum penalties for drug offenses, with the most important change being a distinction between crack and powder cocaine. Under this legislation, a first-time offender convicted of possession of 0.18 ounce (5.01 g) of crack cocaine was subject to a mandatory minimum penalty of five years imprisonment. For powder cocaine, however, the five-year mandatory minimum sentence did not apply until an individual possessed more than 17.64 ounces (500 g) of the substance. In passing this legislation, Congress conveniently ignored the fact that crack and powder cocaine are essentially the same drugs pharmacologically and failed to offer any rationale for the selection of the 100 to 1 ratio in amounts of powder versus crack cocaine that would trigger the mandatory minimum. Since this federal law was passed in 1986, close to 90 percent of those prosecuted under the crack cocaine provisions have been African American, despite the fact that numerically there are far more white crack users than African American crack users.

In addition to the crack cocaine legislation, other provisions of the 1988 Anti–Drug Abuse Act included enhanced mandatory penalties for individuals convicted of dealing drugs within one thousand feet of playgrounds, youth centers, swimming pools, and video arcades (several states also passed similar legislation). Studies at the state level have noted that these laws do not serve their intended purpose of protecting children and that they have disproportionately been applied against African Americans. The 1988 act also required public housing agencies to evict tenants if a tenant, a member of his or her family, or guests were involved in drug-related crime. And although these laws were not specific to drugs, the 1996 federal Welfare Reform Act stipulated that any individual convicted of a felony drug offense could be denied federal welfare benefits, including food stamps and temporary aid to needy families, for life. Similarly, under provisions of the 1998 Higher Education Act, individuals can be denied federal (student) financial aid if they have been convicted of a drug offense, including the possession of marijuana. Consistent with the severity of much drug policy in the United States, both the denial of welfare and the denial of student aid do not apply to offenders convicted of murder, rape, and other serious crimes.

While the crack cocaine "epidemic" apparently subsided in the mid-1990s, new socially constructed drug epidemics emerged in the late 1990s and early 2000s. The first of these was related to ecstasy (methylenedioxy-*n*-methylamphetamine, MDMA), with thousands of articles on this topic appearing in newspapers and magazines. These sources relied on somewhat questionable statistics on seizures of ecstasy tablets, reports of law-enforcement officials, emergency room admission data, and reports of deaths associated with use of the substance to support the claims of an epidemic. As a result of the alleged ecstasy epidemic, the RAVE (Reducing America's Vulnerability to Ecstasy) Act was passed in 2003.

This legislation targeted venues where ecstasy consumption was believed to occur and stipulated that individuals who "managed or controlled any place . . . for the purpose of unlawfully manufacturing, storing, distributing, or using a controlled substance" could be subject to twenty years imprisonment, up to $250,000 in civil penalties, and $500,000 in criminal fines. In addition to the RAVE Act, the federal government passed legislation in 2001 that increased the penalties for importing or selling ecstasy to the point where they were more severe than those associated with trafficking in powder cocaine. Under this legislation, the penalty for selling 7.05 ounces (200 g, approximately eight hundred pills) of ecstasy was increased from fifteen months to five years imprisonment.

An additional drug "epidemic" that emerged in the late 1990s was related to methamphetamine. Then drug czar General Barry McCaffrey referred to methamphetamine as "the worst drug that has ever hit America" (as quoted in Nieves 2001) and popular media sources produced literally thousands of articles documenting the scourge of methamphetamine and the bizarre acts allegedly committed by individuals under its influence. Similar to other socially constructed drug epidemics, government officials and media sources invoked somewhat questionable data to support their claims. For example, a 2005 *Newsweek* article claimed that there were 1.5 million "regular users" of meth in the United States (Jefferson 2005). However, it is important to note that this figure was based on survey respondents from the US National Household Survey on Drug Use and Health, who indicated that they had used methamphetamine at least once in the previous year—it is certainly questionable whether such use should legitimately be considered "regular."

As a result of the alleged methamphetamine epidemic, several states enacted legislation to control use of the substance, with most of these laws focusing on restricting access to products containing pseudoephedrine, which is used in manufacturing the drug and is contained in widely used cold and allergy medicines. However, it is also notable how, in comparison to the crack cocaine problem in the

mid-1980s, the federal government was relatively slow to address the methamphetamine issue. Until the summer of 2005, the Drug Enforcement Administration essentially denied that methamphetamine constituted a serious national problem, and the federal government was reluctant to consider legislation that would impose restrictions on sales of pseudoephedrine products. Some commentators have argued that this reluctance on the part of the federal government was related to the fact that users of methamphetamine were not portrayed as members of minority groups. In 2006, the federal government passed the Combat Methamphetamine Epidemic Act, which imposed controls over products containing pseudoephedrine; however, in contrast to the situation with crack cocaine, this legislation did not enhance the penalties associated with possessing or trafficking methamphetamine.

More recent socially constructed drug "epidemics" have emerged regarding the abuse of prescription drugs such as oxycontin, "K2 or Spice" (synthetic marijuana), and "bath salts," the latter of which have been referred to as "combining the worst attributes of methamphetamine, cocaine, PCP, LSD and ecstasy" (as quoted in Goodnough and Zezima 2011). As problems associated with these substances have emerged, individual states have scrambled to enact emergency legislation to ban them.

Current and Emerging Issues. While since 1980 US drug laws have been quite severe and have contributed to unprecedented levels of incarceration and gross racial disparities, there are signs that these laws may soften somewhat under the administration of President Barack Obama. Although not solely the results of Obama's efforts, a sign that the United States is moving in the direction of somewhat less stringent drug policies was the passage of the Fair Sentencing Act, which went into effect in July 2010. While still not entirely "fair" (in that it maintained a distinction between crack and powder cocaine), this legislation reduced the disparity in sentences for crack and powder cocaine offenses from 100 to 1 to 18 to 1 by raising the minimum quantity of crack cocaine necessary to trigger a five-year sentence from 0.18 ounce (5 g) to 0.99 ounce (28 g).

Some proponents of more liberal drug laws in the United States were encouraged when Obama appointed Gil Kerlikowske as his "drug czar." Kerlikowske was chief of police in Seattle, Washington, when a ballot initiative in that city required police to make marijuana possession their lowest law-enforcement priority. Kerlikowske (and the federal government, as evidenced in the 2010 National Drug Control Strategy Report) seems rhetorically committed to devoting a larger share of the federal government's drug-control budget to prevention and treatment programs as opposed to law enforcement.

At the level of state governments, however, there are indications that crime policies in general, and drug policies in particular, are becoming somewhat more lenient. As of 2011, sixteen states and the District of Columbia had passed medical marijuana legislation. And as a result primarily of fiscal constraints, states are reconsidering some of their more severe drug policies. On average, spending on corrections constitutes approximately 7 percent of state budgets, and several states are spending more on corrections than on higher education. In the past decade, a number of states have either modified or repealed mandatory minimum sentencing options for drug and other offenders, allowed earlier parole for offenders, and increased support for alternatives to incarceration such as drug courts.

For example, in 2000, California voters approved Proposition 36, the Substance Abuse and Crime Prevention Act, which mandated that first- or second-time nonviolent drug possession offenders be offered drug treatment instead of incarceration. In 2002, Washington State passed legislation to decrease the amount of time drug offenders were incarcerated and to increase substance-abuse treatment for such offenders. Similarly, in April of 2009, the state of New York, whose 1973 Rockefeller drug laws were among the most severe in the United States, changed its laws to eliminate mandatory minimum prison terms for most drug offenders, reduce sentence length, expand access to treatment, and provide for alternatives to incarceration. While these and similar developments in several other states indicate a partial softening of drug laws, it is important to stress that the changes have been primarily motivated by fiscal concerns related to the costs of incarcerating large numbers of drug offenders, as opposed to a "coddling" of such offenders.

There have also been significant developments at the international level. In addition to the fact that several other Western nations have moved in the direction of harm-reduction drug policies, in 2011 the Global Commission on Drug Policy, whose membership included the former presidents of Mexico, Colombia, and Brazil; former United Nations secretary-general Kofi Annan; and George Schultz, among others, declared that the global war on drugs was a failure. The report noted that policies have harmed low-income communities and led to overcrowding in prisons, recommended that governments "end the criminalization, marginalization, and stigmatization of people who use drugs but do no harm to others," (Global Commission on Drug Policy 2011) and encouraged governments to experiment with drug legalization.

Currently, US drug policy is at a historic crossroads, where many local, national, and international forces will be part of the political landscape in the regulation of drugs in future decades. Local and regional conflicts with federal policy will become a salient factor in determining future directions, especially with the growing number of states that have legalized medicinal marijuana and the possibility of full legalization of marijuana in a handful of states. National economic concerns will also likely factor in, with several prominent economists having publicly called for decriminalization or legalization because of billions of dollars in taxpayer savings and potential tax revenue that could be generated. Regardless of the direction that the dialogue takes, the increasingly divided political landscape and the symbolic power of the issue will ensure that drug control will remain a prominent political issue.

[See also Gangs; Gun Control; and Race, Gender, and Incarceration.]

BIBLIOGRAPHY
Abel, E. Marijuana: The First 12,000 Years. (New York, 1980).

Alexander, M. *The New Jim Crow.* (New York, 2010).

Becker, H. *Outsiders: Studies in the Sociology of Deviance.* (New York, 1963)

Brecher, E. *Licit and Illicit Drugs.* (Boston, Mass., 1972).

Carter, J. "Drug Abuse Message to Congress." (August 2, 1977), accessed 10 June 2011, http://www.presidency.ucsb.edu/ws/?pid=7908.

Global Commission on Drug Policy. "Global Commission on Drug Policy Report." 2011, http://www.globalcommissionondrugs.org/Report.

Himmelstein, J. *The Strange Case of Marijuana.* (Westport, CT, 1980)

Jefferson, D. "America's Most Dangerous Drug." *Newsweek.* (August 8, 2005), accessed 10 August 2005, http://www.thedailybeast.com/newsweek/2005/08/08/america-s-most-dangerous-drug.html.

MacCoun, R., and P. Reuter. *Drug War Heresies.* (Cambridge, UK, 2001).

Mosher, C., and S. Akins. *Drugs and Drug Policy: The Control of Consciousness Alteration.* (Thousand Oaks, Calif., 2007).

Musto, D. *The American Disease.* (New Haven, Conn., 1999).

Nieves, E. "Drug Labs in Valley Hideouts Feed Nation's Drug Habit." *New York Times.* (May 13, 2001), accessed 13 May 2001, http://www.nytimes.com/2001/05/13/us/drug-labs-in-valley-hideouts-feed-nation-s-habit.html?pagewanted=all&src=pm.

Reinerman, C., and H. Levine, eds. *Crack in America: Demon Drugs and Social Justice.* (Berkeley, Calif., 1997).

Clayton Mosher and Taj Alexander Mahon-Haft

E

ECONOMIC POLICY SINCE WORLD WAR II

Economic policy has been at the heart of American politics since World War II. The role of government in the economy has proved fundamental in shaping institutional developments, party politics, and ideological cleavages. While prosperity and growth have remained constant goals, the means of achieving them has changed over time. From 1945 to 1980, economic policy had a broadly Keynesian character that emphasized fiscal manipulation of aggregate demand to manage prosperity. Within this time frame, it underwent three distinctive phases of development: from 1945 to 1960, the Truman and Eisenhower administrations prioritized countercyclical stabilization; the new economics of the 1960s focused on maximizing jobs and productive capacity; and in the 1970s, economic management was inconsistent and incoherent in the face of stagflation. With the eclipse of Keynesianism, economic policy in the quarter-century after 1980 followed a broadly supply-side approach to enhance private-sector incentive and wealth creation through tax reduction, monetary management, and deregulation. There were three phases of development: "Reaganomics" embodied a combination of anti-statism and monetarism in the 1980s; "Clintonomics" emphasized monetary relaxation, tight budgets, and free trade in the 1990s; and a political economy of debt developed in the early twenty-first century. In 2008, however,

the worst economic crisis since the 1930s engendered a new era of governmental activism.

The Countercyclical Era. In the shadow of the Great Depression, belief in government's obligation to ensure the economy's well-being found bipartisan expression in the Employment Act of 1946. Notwithstanding its vague mandate to "promote maximum employment, production, and purchasing power," this landmark measure institutionalized federal responsibility for economic management. It also confirmed the president as chief manager of prosperity in creating the Council of Economic Advisers (CEA) to provide him with professional economic advice and by endowing him with the responsibility of preparing an annual report on the economy.

Postwar economic policy entailed a trade-off whereby most Republicans accepted that modest budget deficits (the largest was 2.6 percent gross domestic product [GDP] in fiscal year [FY] 1959) compensated for declining private demand during recession instead of being harbingers of socialism, while Democrats acknowledged that government's role was to ensure the prosperity of the private economy as the main source of jobs rather than redistribute wealth. Accordingly, Dwight Eisenhower's Republican administration operated deficits to counter recession in 1953–1954 and 1957–1958, as Harry Truman's Democratic administration had done during the 1949 downturn. Conversely, both ran surplus budgets to control inflation. In essence, each pursued a stabilizing fiscal strategy that aimed to balance the budget over the course of the business cycle.

The expansion of federal spending, particularly on Cold War–era defense, did not undermine fiscal responsibility, because the tax regime inherited from World War II generated bountiful revenues. National security funding for research and development virtually amounted to an industrial policy by government in boosting aerospace, computers, and other defense-related enterprises. The main beneficiary was California, which surpassed New York as the most populous state in 1963. Defense spending also assisted the economic renaissance of the South. Eisenhower's national security-related decision to construct the interstate highway system further promoted the development of the South and Southwest. By the end of the 1950s, therefore, federal actions had initiated a regional economic power shift from the Northeast to the Sun Belt.

Bipartisanship did not extend to every area of economic policy, however. Responding to business demands for safeguards against 1930s-style labor militancy, Republicans and conservative Democrats overrode Truman's veto to approve the Taft-Hartley Act of 1947, which reduced New Deal–created trade union rights. Conversely, Truman sustained and expanded the New Deal's industry-specific regulations over GOP objections. The slack economy of the late 1950s also occasioned partisan dispute.

The postwar economy had generated 64 million jobs by 1952, well above the full-employment target of 60 million anticipated in 1945. However, economic growth slowed as the impetus gained from World War II lost steam and federal spending diminished as a percentage of output. Annual unemployment rose to 5.1 percent in 1956–1960, compared with 3.7 percent in 1951–1955, and there were double-dip recessions in 1957–1958 and 1960. However, the principal economic policymakers remained more concerned about inflation, which was creeping toward 3 percent by the decade's end. Rejecting the Democrat-led Congress's demand for stimulus spending, Eisenhower insisted on balancing the FY1960 budget, thereby weakening recovery from recession. The Federal Reserve also focused its monetary actions on controlling inflation, thereby helping to slow the economy.

International economic concerns shaped the prioritization of inflation over jobs. Under the Bretton Woods agreement of 1944, the US dollar had fixed-rate convertibility into gold as the world's principal reserve currency. Huge dollar outflows for economic aid, military outlays, loans, and investments provided the liquidity that underwrote the postwar recovery of Western Europe and Japan, but their reconstruction was largely complete by the late 1950s. Foreign central bankers now urged the United States to operate balanced budgets as a way of forestalling a run on its gold reserves by foreign dollar-holders fearful that deficit-induced inflation would prompt devaluation. Eisenhower's parsimony preempted this danger but left unresolved the problem of the slack economy.

The New Economics. John F. Kennedy's 1960 election promise to get the country moving again led to economic growth being a key theme of his Democratic administration. To deliver this, he drew on the advice of Keynesian economists in the CEA, who recommended that fiscal policy should meet the economy's needs in a particular year rather than over the business cycle. Estimating a performance gap of 10 percent GDP between actual and potential output, the Kennedy economists advocated its closure through a demand-boosting "full employment" budget that balanced federal spending against the potential tax revenues from a full-employment economy.

This strategy provided the margin for expansionary fiscal actions within the framework of a hypothetical balanced budget. Worried about political and international reaction to real deficits, Kennedy was a hesitant convert to the "new economics." The expansionary effect of higher defense spending following the Berlin crisis of 1961 won him over. Persuaded by his advisers that tax reduction would have even greater benefits, he proposed a massive cut in personal taxes in 1963, which was enacted under Lyndon Johnson in 1964. Under its impact, economic growth exceeded 6 percent, unemployment declined to 4.1 percent, and inflation remained low in 1965.

This tax initiative marked the completion of the 1930s-initiated fiscal revolution to use the budget as the primary instrument of presidential economic management in line with the ideas of John Maynard Keynes. Breaking with balanced-budget orthodoxy, Franklin D. Roosevelt had adopted a limited Keynesianism that accepted deficits as emergency necessities but failed to provide sufficient stimulus to end the Depression. Truman and Eisenhower pursued a passive Keynesianism that used the budget for countercyclical purposes. Finally, Kennedy and Johnson engaged in active Keynesianism to maximize growth when the economy was not in recession.

Inspired by "Phillips curve" theory postulating an inverse relationship between joblessness and inflation, the CEA Keynesians were confident that manipulation of the fiscal dials would keep the economy moving ahead on a 4 percent unemployment–2 percent inflation trajectory. However, Johnson's refusal to raise taxes to pay for the Vietnam War put this goal beyond reach. His grandiose agenda of military intervention in Southeast Asia and Great Society social program expansion at home turned the budget into an engine of inflation that provided too much stimulus for an economy already operating at full employment. The deficit rose from 0.2 to 2.9 percent GDP from FY1965 to FY1968, by which point inflation was over 4 percent. This revived foreign dollar–holders' concerns that the United States would devalue its inflation-weakened currency as Britain did in 1967. To forestall a run on American gold reserves, Johnson reached an agreement with Congress for a temporary tax surcharge and social spending cutbacks, which produced a balanced budget in FY1969.

Achieving inflation-free prosperity was now the main challenge for aggregative economic policy. Keynesians remained confident of meeting it, but their intellectual ascendancy within the economics discipline was already under threat from monetarist claims that the money supply rather than fiscal policy was the real determinant of demand. Their influence would decline further in the 1970s, the most miserable economic era since the 1930s.

The Political Economy of Stagflation. The US economic experience in the 1970s was characterized by recurrent recession (1969–1970, 1974–1975, and 1980), runaway consumer-price inflation averaging above 9 percent from 1973 to 1980, the first merchandise trade deficits of the twentieth century, and energy supply problems. Fixated on resolving "stagflation" (combined stagnation and inflation), policymakers engaged in regular U-turns as measures to address one problem aggravated the other. However, the general economic malaise of the time was the result of deep-seated problems pertaining to inadequate domestic investment, excessive dependence on foreign oil, and declining productivity.

Richard Nixon's Republican administration initially aimed to control inflation and sustain growth through modest fiscal and monetary restraint. However, the Federal Reserve's excessive tightening of credit precipitated the first recession in almost a decade in late 1969. To secure his second term, Nixon manipulated the electoral-economic cycle to perfection in producing a boom for 1972. Announcing "I am now a Keynesian in economics," he increased deficit spending and benefited from a Federal Reserve change of monetary course. Meanwhile, his New Economic Policy of 1971 instituted the first peacetime wage-price controls to restrain inflation, a temporary surcharge on dutiable imports to narrow the trade gap, and suspension (made permanent in 1973) of the dollar's fixed-convertibility into gold to insulate the US from further foreign runs on its reserves.

Once reelected, Nixon reverted to tight fiscal policy in a vain effort to stifle inflation, but the removal of economic controls released a stockpile of price pressures, the devalued dollar made imports more expensive, and—most significantly—the Arab oil embargo and subsequent oil-price hike by the Organization of Petroleum Exporting Countries (OPEC) in 1973 sent energy costs skyrocketing. With inflation running at 12.2 percent in 1974, the Federal Reserve's reversion to monetary restraint set off a new recession that exerted downward pressure on prices, at the cost of the highest employment rate since 1940.

Nixon's resignation over Watergate left his successor, Gerald Ford, to sort out the economic mess.

Setting out to tackle inflation, the new Republican president had to modify course in the face of recession, but he vetoed the massive stimulus measures enacted by the Democrat-led Congress for fear of renewing price instability. This principled stand meant that unemployment was slow to fall, a major factor in Ford's narrow 1976 reelection defeat.

The inability of the new president, Jimmy Carter, to conquer stagflation undermined the Democrats' reputation as the party of prosperity that FDR had established. He began with a stimulus program to boost post-recession recovery, quickly shifted to moderate restraint, and ultimately opted for an anti-inflation austerity program that split his party and provoked Senator Edward Kennedy's unsuccessful but damaging primary challenge for the 1980 presidential nomination. Carter also had to settle for a compromise 1978 energy bill that fell far short of his ambition to halve oil imports and domestic energy consumption by 1985. Another huge OPEC oil-price hike in 1979, in the wake of the Iranian Revolution, obliterated short-term progress under this measure. Possessing the worst economic record of any president since Herbert Hoover, Carter suffered a landslide defeat in his 1980 reelection bid, in the manner of his GOP predecessor in 1932.

The last president of the Democrat-dominated New Deal order, Carter was a transitional leader in the emergence of a more conservative, market-oriented political economy. In addition to fiscal restraint, his anti-inflation initiatives included deregulation of trucking, airlines, and financial services, and oil price decontrol. Most importantly, his appointment of Paul Volcker as chair of the Federal Reserve in mid-1979 was intended to reassure inflation-sensitive financial markets. It effectively signified that monetary policy was now the essential instrument to ensure price stability, because fiscal policy had proved ineffective. This marked the emergence of the Fed chair as the chief manager of prosperity in place of the president. Volcker was a practical monetarist who shared the conservative economist Milton Friedman's conviction that inflation resulted from money supply growth exceeding overall economic growth. His draconian approach of conquering inflation through quantitative tightening of the money supply pushed up unemployment, to the detriment of Carter's reelection hopes.

"Reaganomics." America's most conservative president since Herbert Hoover, Ronald Reagan claimed a mandate to reduce government's role in the economy as the solution for stagflation. A traditional anti-statist, he advocated tax cuts, domestic expenditure reduction, and further deregulation as necessary to restore prosperity. His orthodox conservative agenda gained intellectual legitimacy from new supply-side economic ideas that enhancement of individual incentive was the real engine of growth rather than aggregate demand management.

The largest tax reduction in America's history, the Economic Recovery Tax Act of 1981 (ERTA) slashed marginal rates for the top earners from 70 to 50 percent, cut personal taxes for all other income bands by 5/10/10 percent over three years, increased depreciation allowances to boost capital equipment investment, and provided generous tax benefits to business. As amended in Congress, it also provided for indexation of all personal income tax rates to the rate of inflation from 1985, which eliminated the bracket-creep consequences of inflation-driven nominal pay increases that hit many families in the 1970s.

The president's understanding of Laffer-curve supply-side theory made him optimistic that the tax cuts would be self-funding through their revitalization of economic growth. However, White House projections of balancing the budget over four years were blown away by the worst recession of the second half of the twentieth century. In the absence of commensurate domestic retrenchment, Reagan's massive defense expansion amid conditions of a renewed Cold War also contributed to record peacetime deficits. During Reagan's presidency, fiscal imbalances averaged 4.3 percent GDP, compared with 2.2 percent in the 1970s and 1.1 percent GDP during the 1960s, and the public debt rose from 26.1 percent GDP in 1980 to 40.9 percent GDP in 1988.

The Reaganomics agenda had assumed moderate monetary restraint to control inflation while the tax cuts generated growth. Instead, the Volcker-led

Federal Reserve instituted an even stronger dose of quantitative tightening than in 1980 to throttle inflationary pressure. Its determined action achieved this end—consumer prices only rose 3.8 percent annually from 1983 to 1988—at the cost of a deep recession that lasted six quarters, until monetary policy was relaxed in late 1982. The downturn sent unemployment above 10 percent for the first time since 1940. The loss of jobs, many of which disappeared forever, was highest in the old industrial heartland, which became a declining Rust Belt in contrast to the still-booming Sun Belt.

The Reagan-era deficits exacerbated the problems of America's manufacturing sector, wherein employment declined from 21 million in 1979 to 19.3 million in 1987. These imbalances caused a collapse of national saving from 7.7 percent of national income in the 1970s to 3 percent in the late 1980s. The United States would have experienced a comparable decline in private investment had it not made up the shortfall by borrowing from abroad. America was consequently transformed from being the world's largest creditor, with net foreign assets of $141 billion in 1981, to its largest debtor, with net foreign liabilities of $111 billion in 1985. To attract the inflow of foreign capital that reached a volume of $105 billion in 1985, the Federal Reserve had to keep real interest rates (the nominal rate minus the inflation rate) some 2 percent higher than other rich nations. Having fluctuated in value since the 1973 termination of fixed-exchange rates, the dollar consequently rose by some 80 percent against a basket of eleven other major currencies between 1979 and 1985. This made foreign imports cheaper, enlarging the trade deficit from $26 billion in 1980 to a record $159 billion in 1987, to the detriment of manufacturing employment.

The 1984 presidential election became a referendum on how to deal with the troublesome deficit. Reagan had rescinded some ERTA business tax benefits to assuage the Fed's deficit concerns, but insisted on preserving the personal tax cuts to guarantee economic growth. In contrast, Democratic candidate Walter Mondale advocated deficit-reducing tax increases that would hit the middle classes as well

as the rich. Reagan's landslide victory sanctified low taxes as a dominant element of America's political culture. Capitalizing on this, he promoted the Tax Reform Act of 1986 (TRA), which simplified the personal tax code into two bands (15 percent and 28 percent) and funded this through business-tax hikes. However, he got nowhere with spending retrenchment because of the congressional Democrats' refusal to agree to domestic savings without defense cuts. Bipartisan congressional initiatives to mandate automatic installments of deficit reduction to balance the budget over time also proved ineffective.

Economic policymakers therefore had to find other ways of mitigating the deficit's effect. In 1985, Treasury Secretary James Baker and Paul Volcker negotiated the Plaza Accord with America's G-5 partners to manage dollar devaluation through enhanced foreign purchase of US Treasury securities. The most immediate effect of this was not to close the trade gap, but rather to reduce the profitability of US stocks and bonds for overseas buyers. Fears of a foreign flight from the dollar helped precipitate the worst stock market collapse since 1929 in October 1987. Prompt action by the Federal Reserve under its new chair Alan Greenspan to guarantee banks sufficient liquidity ensured that this downturn did not lead to recession. The episode also prompted political compromise over the Omnibus Trade and Competitiveness Act of 1988, the first comprehensive trade bill since the infamous Smoot-Hawley Tariff of 1930, which was widely blamed for internationalizing the Great Depression. It originally contained a Democratic provision to impose quotas on countries running large bilateral surpluses with the United States, but fears of provoking a trade war in the face of America's dependence on foreign investment led to the removal of this proposal.

Wall Street was not the only financial institution in trouble as Reagan's presidency ended. The deregulation of the ailing savings and loan (S & L) industry had not worked according to plan. Freed from longstanding government rules, S & Ls moved beyond their home mortgage domain to operate in risky financial markets. By 1989, a third were virtually bankrupt and another third were financially weak because of bad loans, risky investment, and fraudulent transactions. It would require an expensive government bailout in 1990 to rescue them.

Conservatives hailed Reagan for renewing the economy through restoration of limited government and individual liberty, but his record was not uniformly successful. Its greatest success, the conquest of inflation, was really the work of the Federal Reserve. The principal conservative achievement was reducing personal income taxes, but the consequent enlargement of the fiscal deficit distorted the operation of the economy, undermined national saving, and increased America's dependence on foreign capital.

"Clintonomics." Economic policy in the 1990s was largely centrist, pragmatic, and empirical in its domestic dimensions, but avowedly free-market abroad. "Clintonomics" (a historically useful label even if it exaggerates presidential significance) initially appeared to have resolved long-standing problems, but its success looked increasingly fragile at century's end.

The greatest fiscal success of the 1990s was the shift from a large deficit (4.7 percent GDP in FY1992) to a sizable surplus (2.4 percent GDP in FY2000). The foundations for this were laid by political compromise. In 1990, at the cost of alienating the right wing of the GOP by reneging on his "no new taxes" election pledge, President George H. W. Bush agreed to a $500 billion, five-year deficit reduction plan with the Democrat-controlled Congress. In addition to tax hikes (mainly for the wealthy), this featured spending cuts (especially defense savings as the Cold War declined) and a Budget Enforcement Act (establishing pay-as-you-go principles to prevent any new measure enlarging the deficit).

Bill Clinton won the presidency in 1992 on a New Democrat agenda promising massive new investment in education, training, and infrastructure to make America more competitive in high-tech, high-skill enterprises. After the election, he switched priorities to deficit reduction, on the advice of Alan Greenspan and fiscal hawks on his economic team, who asserted that this was essential to calm the inflationary expectations of the bond market, the

principal source of long-term investment loan funds. Otherwise, they warned, it would charge growth-throttling high interest rates as an inflation premium. In essence, Clinton shifted his supply-side focus from improving the productivity of labor to enhancing the availability of cheap capital. His 1993 omnibus measure provided for $432 billion in deficit reduction over five years, but won no Republican votes because it required significant tax increases. In 1995 the new GOP congressional majority developed a seven-year fiscal plan that entailed huge social program reduction to fund large tax cuts within a balanced budget, but presidential resistance prevented its enactment. Following Clinton's reelection, both sides agreed to a compromise proposal in 1997 that featured less painful spending cuts and some tax reduction to eliminate the deficit within five years. Revenues from accelerated economic growth unexpectedly delivered a balanced budget in FY1998, the first since FY1969.

Political progress in agreeing to deficit reduction also underwrote a relaxation of monetary policy that did much to boost revenue-enhancing economic growth. Anxious to suppress renewed inflation, Greenspan's Fed had raised interest rates in 1989–1990, thereby precipitating a brief recession, and instituted a new round of rate hikes in 1994 to temper price-rise pressures during recovery from the downturn. In 1995, however, the central bank initiated a five-year cycle of monetary relaxation as inflation subsided toward a thirty-year low later in the decade. This was partly in recognition that tight budgets no longer threatened price stability. It also reflected Greenspan's empirical analysis of economic data showing that labor productivity was rising. The annual growth rate averaged 2.7 percent from 1996 to 2000, nearly double the 1.4 percent average of the previous twenty years. While the causes of this remain under debate, Greenspan accredited the influence of new technology and globalization, inducing him to accept that improved labor productivity allowed employment to rise without fueling inflation.

If fiscal and monetary policy manifested pragmatism, trade policy was free-market in ethos. The

United States lead in high-tech enterprises—notably computers, pharmaceuticals, health care equipment, and aerospace—strengthened its export position in the 1990s. The Clinton administration vigorously supported free-trade expansion both to benefit America's commercial interests and to spread pro-market democracy. Clinton angered pro-labor Democrats, who feared blue-collar job losses, in cooperating with the Republicans to ratify the North America Free Trade Agreement (NAFTA), which had been negotiated by the Bush administration. Clinton also envisaged creation of a hemispheric Free Trade Area of the Americas and a Pacific free-trade zone under the Asia-Pacific Economic Cooperation's (APEC) aegis. The United States further promoted free trade in the Uruguay round of the General Agreement on Tariffs and Trade (GATT) in 1994, and subsequently through the World Trade Organization (WTO). However, financial crises resulting from liberalization initiatives in East Asia in 1997, Russia in 1998, and Argentina in 2001 halted the global impetus toward open markets.

The Clinton administration's enthusiasm for liberalization extended to financial market deregulation at home. Along with Alan Greenspan and many across the party divide, it supported enactment of the Financial Services Modernization Act of 1999. This effectively repealed the Glass-Steagall Act of 1933, which prevented banks, investment firms, and insurance services from entering each other's markets. To its supporters, this reform provided needed flexibility in an age of globalization, but the wisdom of Depression-era legislators would soon be confirmed.

The benefits of the short boom were neither well distributed nor sustainable. Civilian employment expanded by a remarkable 15.6 percent under Clinton, but real median family income did not exceed its 1989 level until 1998, workers with only a high school education or less experienced the least income expansion, and the 11.8 percent poverty level in 1999 was only 1 percent below the 1989 level. The doubling in value of the Dow Jones index indicated that the stock market was the main beneficiary of the boom. Receipts from capital gains and other

wealth taxes underlay the FY1998–FY2001 surplus-budget cycle, the longest since the 1920s. However, national saving still fell from 7.7 percent to 2.3 percent of disposable income from 1992 to 2000, partly because many Americans borrowed to buy shares as interest rates fell. In consequence, the United States remained dependent on foreign capital and continued to operate a trade deficit. The Federal Reserve could have pricked the speculative bubble through raising margin requirements governing how much stock could be bought with borrowed money, but desisted from fear of precipitating a financial crash. However, the collapse in early 2001 of overvalued dot-com companies sent the stock market into a tailspin and ended America's boom.

The Political Economy of Debt. The balanced budgets of FY1998 through FY2001 had fostered illusions than an age of surpluses had dawned. In the 2000 presidential election, the Democrat Al Gore and the Republican George W. Bush clashed over their differing priorities of investing the surplus in public debt elimination and trust fund replenishment (particularly Social Security and Medicare), as Gore preferred, or tax reduction, which Bush supported. However, the recession that followed the stock market collapse turned the surplus vision into a mirage. The 9/11 terrorist attacks on New York and Washington, D.C., caused further shock to the weakened economy. An increase in public and private indebtedness drove recovery, but this would again prove unsustainable.

Despite his controversial election, Bush pressed ahead to implement his tax program, claiming this was vital for recovery. However his 2001 and 2003 tax cuts, respectively the second and third largest in US history, were supply-side rather than demand-oriented measures. The bulk of the 2001 reductions benefited the top income quintile, and the phased introduction over ten years of many provisions limited their anti-recession utility. The 2003 tax cut primarily benefited the investor class and the wealthy in general. In conjunction with the post-9/11 defense expansion, revenue loss from the tax cuts and the recession sent the budget deep into the red. The swing from 2.6 percent GDP surplus in FY2000 to

3.4 percent deficit in FY2004 was a fiscal deterioration unmatched in peacetime since the Great Depression.

This development further depressed national saving, which turned negative in 2005 for the first time since 1933. The United States once again met its capital needs by importing savings from abroad and running external imbalances of historic proportions to attract foreign capital. By 2006 its current account deficit (consisting principally of the record trade deficit) ran at 6.4 percent GDP (compared to the Reagan-era peak of 3.5 percent). In contrast to the 1980s, however, the Federal Reserve could operate historically low interest rates because the savings-starved United States had entered a symbiotic relationship with the high-saving, export-oriented countries of Asia. Led first by Japan and then China, these doubled their US currency holdings from 2000 through 2004. Asian central banks then recycled the money back into America through investments and—in particular—purchase of Treasury securities to boost the dollar's value over their own currency. This secured price advantage for their countries' goods in the giant US market, further inflating the American trade deficit. It also underwrote a glut of cheap credit for America's government, business, and consumers.

Free to pursue an expansionary monetary policy, the Federal Reserve mitigated the bursting of the stock market bubble by creating another based on cheap credit. Total nongovernment debt rose from $21.7 trillion in 2000 to $40.4 trillion in 2007, with the household portion of this growing from $7 trillion to $13.8 trillion. Much of this went into real estate activity, fueling a boom that drove house price inflation to a twenty-five-year high. The combination of cheap credit, financial institution competitive pressures, and lax government regulation also generated massive issuance of so-called subprime mortgages to borrowers with low income, limited assets, and troubled credit histories, many of whom lived in economically declining inner-city neighborhoods. Of the nearly $3 trillion of home mortgage originations in 2006, a fifth fell into this category. By then, however, the Federal Reserve had started to raise interest rates to douse real estate inflation, making it increasingly difficult for subprime mortgage holders, and even middle-income homeowners who had bought at the peak of the boom, to sustain payments. By mid-2008 one in ten of all mortgage holders were either delinquent on loans or in foreclosure. This exposed many investment firms and other institutions that had taken advantage of deregulation to engage in the buying and selling of debt securities known as derivatives. The collapse of the investment bank Lehman Brothers in September 2008 set off a panic that threatened financial system meltdown that was only averted through government action.

Economic Crisis. In the space of one month, the Bush administration effectively nationalized Freddie Mac and Fannie Mae—the government-created secondary mortgage giants—took over American International Group (AIG)—the world's largest insurer—and enacted the Troubled Asset Relief Program (TARP), which permitted the Treasury to take up to $700 billion of toxic private mortgages onto its books. Entailing over $1 trillion in expansion of federal liabilities, over twice the cost of the Iraq war hitherto, these initiatives preempted systemic financial collapse.

More difficult to resolve was the deepest recessions since the 1930s, which resulted from the housing market collapse, the increasing reluctance of banks to extend credit, and the new propensity of Americans to save rather than spend amid economic insecurity. Federal Reserve quantitative easing to expand the money supply failed to generate credit-backed growth. In these circumstances, fiscal policy regained significance for economic management.

The new Democratic administration of Barack Obama enacted the American Recovery and Reinvestment Act of 2009 with a three-year cost of $787 billion distributed among spending and tax initiatives on a two-to-one ratio. Though the largest stimulus in American history, its main effect was to save rather than expand jobs. Condemning the measure as pork-barrel waste, Republicans demanded extension of the Bush tax cuts, which were set to expire at the end of 2010, as the surest economic restorative. Following GOP success in the midterm elections,

Obama agreed to carry these forward through 2012. Nevertheless, stubbornly high unemployment, low consumer confidence, and a stagnant real estate market constrained economic recovery.

The recession and the fiscal actions to counter it drove the FY2011 deficit to a peacetime high of 11 percent GDP. While economic recovery will likely improve public finances, rising Social Security and Medicare outlays as the baby-boom generation retires will exert contrary pressure. The greatest economic problem facing America in the medium-term is to avert a crisis of public debt unsustainability. The surest way of doing so is by reducing entitlement spending and raising taxes. Reaffirming the fundamental connection between politics and economics, however, the Democratic and Republican parties showed little sign at the start of the second decade of the twenty-first century of a willingness to compromise over these core issues.

From 1945 through to the early 1970s, economic policymakers looked to sustain America's position as the world's strongest economy. After the uncertainty of the stagflation-plagued 1970s, the late-twentieth-century aim was to renew American economic power through market-oriented initiatives. In the twenty-first century, the United States needs to move from its recent tendency to consume and borrow toward a new emphasis on saving and production, if it is to preserve its standard of living in a changing global economy. In addition, it faces the perennial and increasingly difficult challenge of reducing income inequalities and spreading the benefits of prosperity more widely.

[*See also* Bush, George Herbert Walker; Bush, George W.; Carter, Jimmy; Clinton, Bill; Economy, American, since World War II; Eisenhower, Dwight D.; Federal Reserve Bank; Financial Crisis of 2008; Fiscal Policy; Ford, Gerald R.; Johnson, Lyndon Baines; Kennedy, John Fitzgerald; Keynesianism; Monetarism; Monetary Policy; NAFTA; Obama, Barack; Reagan, Ronald; *and* Truman, Harry S.]

BIBLIOGRAPHY

Collins, Robert M. *More: The Politics of Economic Growth in Postwar America.* (New York, 2000).

Feldstein, Martin S., ed. *American Economic Policy in the 1980s.* (Chicago, 1994).

Frankel, Jeffrey A., and Peter R. Orszag, eds. *American Economic Policy in the 1990s.* (Cambridge, Mass., 2002).

Heller, Walter W. *New Dimensions of Political Economy.* (Cambridge, Mass., 1966).

Krugman, Paul. *Economic Sense and Nonsense in the Age of Diminished Expectations.* (New York, 1994).

Matusow, Allen J. *Nixon's Economy: Booms, Busts, Dollars, and Votes.* (Lawrence, Kans., 1998).

Morgan, Iwan. *The Age of Deficits: Presidents and Unbalanced Budgets from Jimmy Carter to George W. Bush.* (Lawrence, Kans., 2009).

Rosenberg, Samuel. *American Economic Development since 1945: Growth, Decline, and Rejuvenation.* (New York, 2003).

Sloan, John W. *Eisenhower and the Management of Prosperity.* (Lawrence, Kans., 1991).

Sloan, John W. *The Reagan Effect: Economics and Presidential Leadership.* (Lawrence, Kans., 1999).

Stein, Hebert. *The Fiscal Revolution in America: Policy in Pursuit of Reality.* 2d rev. ed. (Washington, D.C., 1996).

Stein, Hebert. *Presidential Economics: The Making of Economic Policy from Roosevelt to Clinton.* 3d rev. ed. (Washington, D.C., 1994).

Stiglitz, Joseph. *The Roaring Nineties: Seeds of Destruction.* (London, 2003).

Iwan Morgan

ECONOMY, AMERICAN, SINCE WORLD WAR II

When the delegates from the forty-four Allied nations gathered at the Mount Washington Hotel in Bretton Woods, New Hampshire, in the summer of 1944, World War II was still underway. Yet that conference laid down the principles and established the institutions that went on to govern the international economy for over three decades—and many of them are still in place over sixty-five years later. The fact that these countries gathered in the United States was no coincidence. It marked the fact that the United States was about to assume the mantle of hegemonic power in the international capitalist system. This article charts the broad contours of that hegemonic period, detailing the nature and evolution of the US economy from roughly the end of World War II up until the early years of the twenty-first century (some of the analysis and statistics on which the following discussion is based extend into the later part of the 2000s; another article deals with the 2007–2008 financial crisis and its aftermath, so that period is not the focus here).

Here, the period from 1945 to 2005 is given some analytical purchase by being organized—in the first instance at least—around the cyclical nature of economic activity. Capitalist economies—of which the United States is exemplary—tend to move in cycles of what is popularly known as "boom and bust." In a more academic parlance this is termed the "business cycle," and it has tended to take a six to ten year period to move through the stages of first an expansion of economic activity, followed by contraction. Because the US economy has been of such importance to the health of the international economy (or "global economy," as it is now characterized)—having been by far the largest single economy in the world from 1945 up through at least the mid-2000s—the business cycle as manifest in the United States has tended to have significant spillover effects into other economies. So, again as popularly presented, if the US economy "sneezed," the world economy tended to "catch a cold."

However, there is another important element to this story not quite captured by the business cycle. There is also a much longer-term and deeper aspect of economic activity which addresses structural changes. Structural changes deal with underlying features of economic activity that have a wider and more profound effect on the ability to achieve positive performance outcomes. Any trends or characteristics of these changes, however, are often difficult to identify, and they are more controversial because they appear to be beyond the possibility of being managed. But there exists, nevertheless, some longer-term structural changes onto which the shorter-term business cycles can be mapped. Sorting out, then, what is truly cyclical, and therefore what is potentially reversible as the cycle unfolds, from what is more structural, and therefore much more difficult, if not impossible, to reverse, becomes an important problem. Not all these issues can be dealt with in

a manner that would do them justice here, so this article takes a fairly straightforward approach, by dealing with the business cycle and the potential structural changes in tandem, pointing to the characteristic features of both, and trying to assess their consequences.

Cycles or Structural Changes? The way these shorter-term and longer-term considerations come into focus can be preliminarily specified by looking at growth rates. Between 1949 and 2009 there were nine business cycles of varying length, with varying average growth rates, for example: 1949–1954, 5.2 percent; 1961–1970, 4.4 percent; 1975–1980, 3.5 percent; and 1991–2001, 3.2 percent. These declining average rates over each cycle indicate a possible longer-term change. The average annual growth rate between 1949 and 1969, for instance, was just below 4 percent over those twenty years, while the latter twenty-year period, from 1969 to 2009, saw a significantly lower average growth rate of below 3 percent; toward the end of this period (2000–2009) growth rates were decidedly poor (1.8 percent).

Thus, there looks to have been a possible "structural break" emerging in the very late 1960s to early 1970s. This can be seen in respect to a number of other economic variables discussed below, though the maturing of any such shifts in these took a longer time, the entire 1970s being the appropriate period. But it is generally recognized that the "golden age" for the US economy in the postwar period was definitely between 1945 and 1970. As we will see, after that things got a lot more complicated.

The Keynesian Era. The era between the end of World War II and the mid-1970s is generally recognized as the high point of Keynesian demand management in the United States. This coincided with the very positive growth phase as just discussed. Whether this growth phase was a direct consequence of such "demand management," or whether it just happened to coincide with other positive features of economic activity, remains a disputed point. The other features that are often mentioned in this context are the rebuilding phase of economies after the widespread destruction wrought by the military conflict (this would have taken place anyway, independently of whether Keynesianism as a doctrine of economic policy existed or not); the emergence of the Cold War with the Soviet Union and Warsaw Pact countries, which stimulated an arms race and thus enormous government expenditure on military defense; and finally, the progressive internationalization of trade and investment over the recovery period, which stimulated economic activity in the United States as the major economy and creditor nation.

In part this assessment rests upon what could legitimately be considered as part of a Keynesian policy package. For some all these elements add up to a rather larger economic management regime sometimes characterized as a Keynesian *War*fare State (Clift, 1965; Chomsky, 1993), or a Keynesian *Wel*fare State (O'Connor, 1973; Gough, 1979): this would include military expenditures, domestic and international investment and trade, and an additional consideration for domestic welfare expenditures to support social policies. All these contribute to the "maintenance of aggregate demand" as a way of managing an economy. On the other hand, a somewhat narrower characterization of Keynesianism would tend to confine it to only actively managing the "boom and bust" business cycle in the interests of full employment and low inflation. These two policy goals were the core of the Keynesian project, it is suggested, along with a consideration for the balance of payments within the (semi-fixed) gold exchange standard mechanism that typified the post-Bretton Woods international monetary system until 1971–1972 (which is discussed at greater length below).

So if we were to take the narrower definition, what has been the record on employment and inflation since the later 1940s? In terms of the unemployment rate, this tended to fluctuate according to the business cycles (falling in the boom period, increasing in the subsequent downturn). From 1949 to 1970 it fluctuated between 4 and 7 percent. From 1970 it escalated to a peak in 1984 of 11 percent, and after that was on a fluctuating downward trend to about 5 percent in the early 2000s. But the unemployment rate does not record the actual number of persons available for employment at any one time. In fact,

the civilian labor force expanded enormously over these periods: from 62 million in 1949 to 147 million in 2004. Thus, one thing the United States can justly claim is its ability to prodigiously generate jobs. It has absorbed wave after wave of immigration into the labor market, for instance. But, exactly what has been happening regarding the remuneration or the quality of these jobs is a matter that will be returned to shortly.

The inflation rate was the other key variable to be targeted by policymakers. In fact, one of the great changes in policy-making that is attributed to the post-1970s period is the effective abandonment of a primary concern for unemployment among economic policymakers, as a concern for inflation rose to the top of the political and economic agenda. We return to this policy change later. But, the reasons for this change in focus may be demonstrated by the way the inflation rate escalated between 1960 and 1975 (from a modest 1 to 2 percent, to 12 percent). What is more, the seeming coexistence of relative low unemployment and relative low inflation that characterized the 1950s and 1960s—sometimes considered as an acceptable trade-off when combined with reasonable growth rates—broke down. Both unemployment and inflation rose together. When looked at alongside the growth outcomes for the business cycle over the 1970–1975 period considered above (2.8 percent), the result was deemed a period of "stagflation" (growth stagnation combined with inflation) in the 1970s. A sense of economic crisis and panic was induced by these outcomes which, to an extent at least, heralded the change in economic policy priorities discussed in a moment. Reducing inflation became the number-one priority, and it certainly fell rather significantly after 1980.

Productivity and the Labor Market. Let us now turn our attention to productivity and the labor market. Any economy needs to pay particularly close attention to its productivity record, as this represents a key determinant of economic prosperity. It is usually measured in terms of output per hour worked. This is often discussed for the non-farm business sector as a whole, and then just for the manufacturing sector.

The United States has always performed relatively well by international standards on overall business sector productivity, and very well in terms of the productivity of its manufacturing sector. And the absolute levels of productivity have been high. The "golden age" is indicated by the 1947 to 1973 period of 2.8 percent average productivity growth, a level not experienced again until the early 2000s: it plummeted between 1973 and 1979 to 1.1 percent and only slowly recovered after that. An important feature of just manufacturing productivity is the 1990s revival (1987–1990, 1.8 percent; 1990–2007, 4 percent on average), and then the decline that set in from the late 2000s (2007–2010, 1.7 percent). We will return to the characteristics and significance of these rates of productivity growth. First, let us discuss the labor market more generally.

Real wages in the United States expanded every decade between 1890 and 1970. But after that the real hourly wage rate declined (though there was a slight recovery between 2000 and 2004, which was then reversed). So real wages stagnated or declined in the United States after the mid-1970s. Thus there has been an increasing shortfall of the real wage rate relative to productivity since then. The trend after World War II was for the real wage rate to fall behind productivity in its aftermath, reaching its maximum shortfall of around 15 percent during the Korean War (1950–1953). But the gap closed during the late 1950s and 1960s until the early 1970s, when the real wage rate hit an all-time high, increasing faster than productivity by more than 5 percent in 1972.

In the aftermath of the first "oil price shock" (1973–1974), the real wage rate fell yet again behind productivity, suggesting that employees bore the brunt of the redistribution of income from the United States to the oil-producing countries. Unemployment soared from 3.5 percent in early 1970 to nearly 11 percent in the midst of the 1980–1982 recession. However, as the price of oil and unemployment fell in the 1980s the real wage rate caught up once more with productivity gains. By the spring of 1999, the gap between the real wage rate and productivity had once again been closed.

But looking only at real wages does not indicate the total factor share going to labor or the overall distribution of rewards. For this an added consideration of transfers to labor through social welfare provision is needed, which should then be compared to gross domestic product (GDP).

First, wages and salaries as a percent of GDP rose slightly from 1946 until 1970 (by 3 percent, from 50.5 percent to 53.5 percent), but then went into a slow but continuing decline, confirming the real wage decline just discussed. In fact, the share of wages and salaries fell by 9 percent, to 44.5 percent by the end of 2009. But despite these unfavorable trends in the real wage rate and wages and salaries, since the 1970s, the total compensation of employees—which includes the addition of employer contributions for Social Security and employee pension and insurance funds—shows a more complicated picture. The compensation of employees improved in the post-World War II era, increasing from 54.5 percent of GDP in 1948 to nearly 70 percent by the early 1980s. Since then it has declined, to 65.5 percent in 2008. Hence, the net loss of the compensation to employees since early 1980s is only 3.5 percent compared to 9 percent in wages and salaries and more than 10 percent shortfall in the real wage rate to productivity ratio. The smaller deterioration in the compensation of employees to wages and salaries is partly due to higher employer contributions to Social Security and employee pension and insurance funds. These contributions more than quadrupled in the post-World War II era from 2.3 percent of GDP to 10.6 percent. But the bulk of that increased employer contribution came before 1980. The share of employer contributions to GDP increased by only a tiny fraction (0.5 percent) after the early 1980s, thereby confirming the redistribution of income from employees to employers.

Debates and Explanations. What had been going on to explain all these trends and developments? A key turning point in the trajectory of the economy happened in the 1970s. First of all, in August 1971 the United States pulled out of the semi-fixed exchange rate mechanisms that had characterized the international economy since the Bretton Woods agreement. With this system the United States pegged its currency to the price of gold, and other countries could only revalue their own currencies in respect to the US dollar under extreme circumstances (hence the designation of this as a *semi-fixed* exchange rate standard). However, in the face of mounting domestic inflation, President Nixon allowed to dollar to "float," and soon other countries followed. The dollar immediately depreciated and since oil prices were (and still are) invoiced in US dollars, the real incomes of the oil-producing countries declined dramatically. Partly as a reaction to this and partly in retaliation for US support for Israel in the 1973 Yom Kippur War, the Organization of Petroleum Exporting Countries (OPEC) restricted output and instigated various embargos. The resulting price of oil quadrupled (from US$3 to US$12 a barrel), and given that the United States was heavily dependent on oil imports from OPEC, this put increased pressure on domestic prices. This oil price shock stoked the fires of domestic inflation. A recession was looming, and there was a reactive crash in the US stock market in 1973–1974. With another oil price hike in 1979 resulting from the Iranian Revolution, crude oil prices rose to an all-time high of US$39.5 per barrel. President Nixon experimented with domestic wage and price controls, but these proved unsuccessful and were short-lived.

In addition, something was happening to the international monetary system. Under the Bretton Woods gold exchange standard system, the United States was highly constrained in terms of its own domestic price and employment levels. It could not determine these independently of other nations, and it had to remain relatively passive in terms of its exchange rate, hold minimal reserves of foreign exchange, provide liquidity to the system by acting as its creditor, and anchor the world price of internationally tradable goods in terms of dollars by its own domestic monetary policy. If there was to be no international inflation, then that domestic monetary policy was constrained by the dictates of a system in which partner choices were paramount. American hegemony meant monetary independence was purely formal. But at the heart of this system lay a contradiction that proved just too difficult to surmount. The result of the long, postwar boom was an accommodating increase in the domestic money supply, but this itself proved to be potentially inflationary. In addition, by supplying liquidity to the international system—via spending abroad, for instance, to support its military and hegemonic role as the leading Western power in the Cold War era—it also fed the international economy with dollars, which to an extent was itself a stimulus to international inflationary pressures. So long as the United States remained the strongest export economy in such a system, it required a stable exchange rate and an inflation-proof regime. But that very objective was fatally undermined by the seemingly endless supply of dollars, both domestically and abroad. As this economic position began to erode, and as these contradictory pressures matured, the United States maneuvered unilaterally for some domestic economic advantage. The result was the collapse of the semi-fixed exchange rate system in 1971. But this did not staunch the global supply of money creation; indeed, to an extent, it stimulated such creation further.

As the dollar weakened between 1971 and 1980 (implying a strengthening of other currencies against the dollar), the money supplies of other countries increased. The relative passivity of the United States, by contrast, in seeking monetary autonomy to fight its own domestic inflation, meant that it did not offset this with a reduction of its own money supply, and inflation resulted. Then when the dollar unexpectedly strengthened after 1980, the adjustment took the form of severe deflations and world output contracted sharply. Thus, perhaps somewhat unexpectedly, this period saw the closer and deeper integration of the international economy, as the business cycles of all the main participants synchronized and became more pronounced. A regime designed to increase autonomy (by allowing exchange rates to float and enabling independent monetary policies) had actually led in the opposite direction.

Reactions and Changes in Policy: The Crisis of Keynesianism? The reaction to the developments in the 1970s was a profound shift in economic policy sentiment and practice. Keynesianism was accused of being mainly responsible for the predicament facing the economy because it did not pay sufficient attention to controlling inflationary pressures, and the seeming uncontrollability of the money supply was increasingly suggested as the main culprit for stimulating inflation. Monetarist theoretical sentiment gained added traction as a result, and the mood shifted from looking to manage aggregate demand as the key to economic success, to a focus on controlling the money supply, and to supply side policies of liberalization and deregulation more generally, as the means to stimulate economy activity. It was with the election of President Reagan in 1981 that this change in stance was most clearly registered. Monetarism became almost the official macroeconomic policy, while deregulation and fiscal rectitude were promoted with a vengeance (at least rhetorically). This economic change of course coincided with a sustained attack on the working conditions and wages of American labor, led by corporate interests that were determined to reverse the gains labor had made in the postwar period. The combination of all these policy changes is often summed up as a crisis for Keynesianism and the impetus to a move toward a neoliberal era.

Neoliberalism typically involves a set of ideological doctrines emphasizing the virtues of intense competition, the idea being that market solutions to problems lead to the best outcomes; it is opposed to direct state intervention in the economy, or support for socially engineered outcomes, and it stresses self-reliance. But these ideas need to be rendered into a definite project of policy formation and economic management, hence the second element. It presents a program of economic policies: the privatization of public activity; deregulation (at least in name); liberalization; reductions in taxes; the cut back on welfare expenditures; and a general retrenchment in public spending. And finally, neoliberalism is a definite political project: it presents a program for very conservative governance associated with promoting all the above features.

The Neoliberal Era: Outcomes and Consequences. Initially neoliberalism had a positive reception. It seemed to have successfully reversed the trends in inflation and unemployment, revived the cyclical growth path, and led to a sustained increase in business sector productivity growth. But was it able to tackle some of the deeper malaise affecting the economy and overcome its structural problems? If one of the objectives of neoliberalism and corporate interests was to revive business profitability, that proved less that successful. Profitability declined dramatically after World War II, and only in the early 1980s did this decline reach a plateau, to establish a steady but low rate into the 2000s.

What neoliberalism did do, however, was to change the composition of where such profitability was located, which was to have profound implications for the future of the economy overall. After 1980 there was a dramatic shift of compensation toward the financial sector and away from other sectors. This process of rewarding the financial sector at the expense of other sectors has since been designated the "financialization" of the economy, and it has taken several forms. Financial companies, in particular, saw a sharp, nearly sixfold increase in their profitability after 1982. In large part this shift was the result of financial deregulation, which began in the 1970s but was especially stimulated by the repeal of the 1933 Glass-Steagall Act in 1999, which both enabled and stimulated a vast increase in the creation of liquidity.

This liquidity was eagerly absorbed by the American household sector which—with its real incomes constrained by the trends discussed above—looked to borrowing as a way of maintaining living standards. A consumption-led "boom" followed in the 1990s, which became known as the "long moderation"—a period of seemingly effortless growth, as inflation and unemployment continued their downward trends. Household debt ratios rapidly expanded, personal savings rates plummeted, and imports were sucked in to feed the boom (so the current account balance continued to deteriorate, as will be discussed more later). What is more, this also provided the perfect conditions for financing the housing bubble in particular, but also the dot.com and other bubbles of less importance, such as commodities, shipping, and private equity. So was set a course for the American economy.

But, there are other important developments that need to be considered before we complete this picture of the overall trajectory of the post-World War II economy. Another feature of the neoliberal period was a massive redistribution of income toward the rich. While medium- and low-income households were experiencing hardships, the top earners were taking an increasing share of incomes, and taxes on their incomes were deliberately reduced. For the top 1 percent, there was an even more massive shift in their fortunes: between 1976 and 2006 they increased their share of income (including capital gains) from 7 percent of all income to 22.2 percent—a figure not equaled since 1928.

Apart from its potential adverse social impact, the problem with the successive redistribution of income to the rich is that it undercuts the possibility of easily managing aggregate demand in an economy. The rich have particular consumption patterns: they have a low overall propensity to consume but a high import-demand propensity, and they tend to save in socially non-useful ways (by investing in property and exotic financial instruments rather than in directly productive activities, for example).

The Fate of US Industry and Manufacturing. As mentioned above, to some extent US manufacturing seemed to have escaped the general problems associated with productivity decline, particularly during the 1990s and first part of the 2000s. This was, of course, the period of the "greal moderation," and was in part one of the reasons the economy seemed to be doing so well during that period. At the end of World War II, American manufacturing looked destined to rule supreme: it was, after all, the home of mass production, something at the heart of "Fordism," an industrial system that heralded efficiency and success. But even quite early on, astute commentators were pointing to the loss of dynamism among Americam manufacturing firms: management had turned its attention away from the details of production engineering, quality control, and innovation to focus instead on financial engineering, which involved mergers and aquistions, excessive attention to realizing shareholder value, and an emphasis on managerial incentives and remuneration. Thus all was not well at the heart of the manufacturing sector, even as it seemed to be at the crest of international competitiveness.

Several elements of this picture matured during the 1980s. First, as US firms expanded, they tended to do so abroad as well as at home. So was born the modern multinational firm, the development of which was led by American companies. Employment growth seemed to be slipping away as a result, taking place "off-shore" rather than in the United States itself. Secondly, competition from Japanese firms became a problem, as their products rapidly flooded traditional US domestic and international markets for consumer durables, cars, ships, electronics, and other products. This "invasion" by Japan produced a policy debate in the United States around industrial policy, and what could be done to reverse the relative decline of US manufacturing (in fact, it had been American production-quality engineers—who could find little interest in their advice from American manufacturers—who had helped the Japanese organize and secure their superior "just-in-time" Kanban manufacturing system as part of the US reconstruction package after World War II; the Kanban system eliminated the need to hold large stocks of costly inventories by organizing a system of immediate flow through from suppliers). And finally, a sense of "deindustrialization" took hold in the United States, as its traditional heavy-industry base located in the Northeast and Midwest collapsed under intense competition from overseas production.

We should not necessarily take all these negative features at face value, however; the picture is more mixed. Total industrial employment has been roughly constant at around 30 million people since the late 1970s (though there has been a steady decline since the all-time peak of 31.5 million in 2000). In addition, although total industrial employment has been relatively stable over the past forty years, the overall labor force has increased dramatically, resulting in a large reduction in the percent of the labor force engaged in industry (from over 35 percent in the late 1960s to under 20 percent in 2009). And the widespread perception of deindustrialization is largely due to shifting patterns in the geography of production (as just mentioned, away from the Northeast and Midwest and toward the South and Southwest). Then there is the increasing labor productivity, which led to higher levels of output without increases in the total number of workers. It should be remembered that US manufacturing output was still nearly 18 percent of world manufacturing output in 2008. Finally, the United States could be in the middle of a profound "technological revolution," it has been suggested, involving computers, semiconductors, and other high-technology production, based upon advances in communication and information technology. The United States leads in many areas of information processing, which is driven by the re-equipment of its domestic economy. This is having profound implications for all economic activity, it is argued. US firms accounted for over 40 percent of the world's investment in computing in the 1990s and early 2000s, spending twice as much on "infotech" as did European firms, and eight times the global average.

Clearly, productivity in manufacturing had been increasing at a much faster rate than that for the business sector as a whole, with impressive rates of growth in manufacturing in the second half of the 1990s, as pointed to above. This issue of productivity came under intense scrutiny as the US long moderation matured in the 1990s, but a detailed disaggregated breakdown showed that the bulk of the growth for the manufacturing sector's productivity could be accounted for by a relatively small industrial sector: computer manufacturing. Between 1995: fourth quarter and 1999: first quarter, output per hour productivity increased by a staggering 41.7 percent *per annum* for this industry alone. Thus, although overall manufacturing productivity growth was vigorous, it seems to have been quite "unbalanced"—confined to a single small information and communications technology sector. This itself spelled danger, and growth rates fell from the mid-2000s.

International Trends. Up until now we have been concentrating on the domestic economy, though several of its international features have been outlined in passing. But this concentration has been due to the fact that—for most of the postwar period being analyzed here—the United States *was*, for all intents and purposes, a domestic economy. This domestic orientation is illustrated by the degree of international trade integration of the US economy compared to other advanced economies. In 1970, merchandise exports and imports stood at just 7 percent of GDP (compared to the UK at 36 percent; Japan, 17 percent; Germany, 20 percent; and France, 21 percent). And even in 2008 this had only increased to 24 percent (with the UK in 2008 at 41 percent; Japan, 32 percent; Germany, 73 percent; and France, 46 percent). It was in the 1990s that there was a rather sudden increase for the United States (a jump from 11 percent in 1973 to 19 percent in 1995).

By and large, the United States remains a "continental"-sized economy compared to its immediate economic rivals: it trades a very low percentage of its production internationally, with 87 percent of its production consumed domestically in 2008. This accounts for the attitude of rather benign neglect the domestic authorities historically have taken to the US exchange rate.

But several features speak against this, particularly as the United States became more integrated into the international economy after the 1990s. First, protectionism began to raise its head politically, as domestic manufacturing jobs seemed to be slipping away and real wages fell. Was this the result of migration of unskilled workers from the South and the rather rapid increase in imports (if from a very modest base)? This question initiated a fierce debate in the 1990s. Gathered along one dimension were those who thought trade, and hence globalization, was the most important contributory factor. A key analysis employing this approach (Wood, 1995) found that a substantial proportion of the loss of market power by Northern unskilled workers was the result of the relocation of manufacturing industry and the growth of global trade: over 20 percent. This claim was challenged in another influential study by Sachs and Shatz (1994), which estimated a much smaller proportion of trade-related influences for the US economy, much nearer 6 percent. Accepting that trade influences did lie between 10 and 20 percent, estimates of the effects of migration (another "international" explanation) did not add much to this wage reduction pressure.

Other than these moderate international effects, the rest of the collapse in the demand for unskilled labor and wages can be attributable to domestic causes. Here is the second main dimension in which an explanation lies: that of skill-enhancing technical change. From this perspective, deindustrialization is, in part at least, a consequence of the impact of unequal rates of productivity growth in manufacturing and services, which has affected the United States in particular. Given the generally accepted proportions of between 10 and 20 percent attributable to trade and migration, 80 to 90 percent must still be domestic and technological in origin. So, globalization alone seems not to have had much to do with the decline in real wages of the unskilled during this period.

Finally and importantly, the United States ran a persistent current account deficit from the early 1990s, which accelerated dramatically after the late 1990s. By 2004, it exceeded US$600 billion a year. The counterpart of these deficits has been driven by the surpluses in Japan, continental Europe, and most recently by China. Thus the United States became a huge net borrower on its own capital account to finance its current account deficit.

This raised an additional question: Was this current account deficit fundamentally the result of trade imbalances, or of financial flows associated with a basic investment and savings mismatch between the United States and these other economies, itself fostered by current government fiscal deficits (which indicate a greater government expenditure than income)? The United States has run a fiscal deficit on it general government account every year since 1980 (except for a three-year period from 1999 to 2001). Thus the famous twin deficits—fiscal and balance of payments—seem to have evolved together.

Whatever one's view of the causal mechanisms operating here—and economists have been disagreeing with each other for years—the legacy remains to haunt the international financial system. The United States seems to have got itself locked into a structural imbalance, with a large and continuing financial deficit—the counterpart of which is currently the huge surplus for China—and this promises to provide the main tensions in the relationships between these two economic giants for the next decade at least.

Conclusions. We began this assessment of the American economy by focusing on short-term business cycles and the rise of American hegemony. Although such cycles look destined to continue, in the more recent period the longer term structural characteristics of the economy have come to the fore. This is associated with a widespread feeling that US economic hegemony is finally on the wane. In turn this can be couched in terms of an additional discursive cycle, which links these two aspects: a positive immediate postwar prognosis associated with a return to growth and prosperity, followed by a declinist phase during the 1970s and 1980s as these prospects faded; then a (temporary) revivalist phase over the dot.com boom and a long moderation in the 1990s and early 2000s, followed by a deeply pessimist phase associated with the 2007–2008 financial crisis and its aftermath.

[*See also* Deindustrialization; Economic Policy since World War II; Financial Crisis of 2008; Keynesianism; Labor Force, American.]

BIBLIOGRAPHY

Borjas, George J., Richard B. Freeman, Lawrence F. Katz, John DiNardo, and John M. Abowd. "How Much Do Immigration and Trade Affect Labor Market Outcomes?" *Brookings Papers on Economic Activity* 1 (1997): 1–90.

Chomsky, Noam. "The Pentagon System." *Z Magazine* (February 1993), http://www.thirdworldtraveler.com/Chomsky/PentagonSystem_Chom.html.

Clift, Tony. "Perspectives on the Permanent War Economy." *A Socialist Review* (1965): 34–40.

Deming, W. Edwards. *Out of the Crisis.* (Cambridge, Mass., 1986).

Freeman, A. (2011) "Long-term Trends in the US Economy: A Pluralist Analysis." (2011), accessed 15 June 2011, http://www.academia.edu/AlanFreeman.

Friedman, Milton. *A Program for Monetary Stability.* (New York, 1983).

Gordon, David M. *Fat and Mean: The Corporate Squeeze of American Workers and the Myth of Managerial "Downsizing."* (New York, 1996).

Gordon, Robert J. "Does the 'New Economy' Measure Up to the Great Inventions of the Past?" *Journal of Economic Perspectives* 14, no. 4 (2000): 49–74.

Gordon, Robert J. "Has the 'New Economy' Rendered the Productivity Slowdown Obsolete?" (1999), http://faculty-web.at.northwestern.edu/economics/gordon/334.pdf.

Gough, Ian. *The Political Economy of the Welfare State*. (London, 1979).

Harris, Seymour Edwin. *The New Economics: Keynes' Influence on Theory and Public Policy*. (New York, 1947).

Hirst, Paul Q., Grahame Thompson, and Simon Bromley. *Globalization in Question*. (Cambridge, UK, 2009).

Hounshell, David. *From the American System to Mass Production, 1800–1932: The Development of Manufacturing Technology in the United States*. (Baltimore, 1984).

Jorgenson, Dale W., and Kevin J. Stiroh. "Raising the Speed Limit: US Economic Growth in the Information Age." *Brookings Papers on Economic Activity* 1 (2000): 125–235.

Krugman, Paul, and Robert Lawrence. "Trade, Jobs, and Wages." *National Bureau of Economic Research*, Working Paper no. 4478. (1993).

Lawrence, Robert Z., and Matthew J. Slaughter. "International Trade and American Wages in the 1980s: Giant Sucking Sound or Small Hiccup?" *Brookings Papers on Economic Activity* 2 (1993): 161–226.

O'Connor, James. *The Fiscal Crisis of the State*. (New York, 1973).

Oliner, Stephen, Daniel E. Sichel, and Kevin J. Stiroh. "Explaining a Productive Decade." *Brookings Papers on Economic Activity* 1 (2007): 81–137.

Piketty, Thomas, and Emmanuel Saez. "The Evolution of Top Incomes: A Historical and International Perspective." *American Economic Review* 96, no. 2 (2003): 200–205.

Rothbard, Murray Newton. *Power and Market: Government and the Economy*. (Menlo Park, Calif., 1970).

Sachs, Jeffrey D., Howard J. Shatz, Alan Deardorff, and Robert E. Hall. "Trade and Jobs in US Manufacturing." *Brookings Papers on Economic Activity*, 1 (1994): 1–84.

Shewhart, Walter A. *Economic Control of Quality of Manufactured Product*. (New York, 1931).

Thompson, Grahame. "The American Industrial Policy Debate: Any Lessons for the UK?" *Economy and Society*, 16, no. 2 (1987): 1–74.

Thompson, Grahame. "The US Economy in the 1990s: The 'New Economy' Assessed." In *Where are National Capitalisms Now?* edited by Jonathan Perraton and Ben Clift, pp. 12–31. (Basingstoke, UK, 2003).

Triffin, Robert. *Gold and the Dollar Crisis: The Future of Convertibility*. (New Haven, Conn., 1961).

United States Bureau of Labor Statistics. *Charting International Labor Comparisons*. (Washington, D.C., 2010).

United States Financial Crisis Inquiry Commission. *The Financial Crisis Inquiry Report: Final Report of the National Commission on the Causes of the Financial and Economic Crisis in the United States*. (Washington, D.C., 2011).

Wood, Adrian. "How Trade Hurt Unskilled Workers." *Journal of Economic Perspectives* 9, no. 3 (1995): 57–80.

Grahame Thompson

EDUCATION AND DIVERSITY

Diversity in education encompasses a broad array of definitions, principles, and public policies that range from *promoting* differences to *protecting* the rights of individuals to participate equally in public education. Protecting the rights of individuals to equal access in public schools has been the major thrust and consequence of federal action in public education, often in the form of federal laws and legal rulings that prohibit discrimination based upon race, sex, and disability. Actions at the federal level reflect a fundamental principle of equal access to and participation in education programs that receive federal funding, from Title VI (Civil Rights Act of 1964), barring discrimination based upon race, to Title IX (Education Amendments of 1972), barring discrimination on the basis of sex. Federal action related to diversity in education has also reflected a broad set of interests and imperatives to promote educational opportunities for specific groups, notably, children in poverty, children with disabilities, and children whose native language is not English. The goals of federal legislation, most notably the Elementary and Secondary Education Act (ESEA, later known as No Child Left Behind), and the Individuals with Disabilities Education Act (IDEA) have underscored a set of public policy values: equity, access, and social justice.

The intersection of these enduring federal policies and protections gains more complexity and nuance at the state and local levels, where social, political, and economic contexts shape implementation strategies and reflect the priorities of local education leaders. These dynamics are a hallmark of American federalism as applied to education policy. Diversity issues and policies are debated (and implemented) in a decidedly local landscape and a decentralized context, with federal oversight and intervention. This relationship is underscored by a series of United States Supreme Court decisions and their aftermath, including the historic ruling on race and education in *Brown v. Board of Education of Topeka* (1954), and later, the monumental decisions that divided the Court and shifted the policy landscape on diversity: *Grutter v. Bollinger* (2003), and *Parents Involved in Community Schools v. Seattle School District No. 1* (2007). These decisions pivot across a panoply of questions related to diversity (and democracy) in education, from the constitutional basis of racial separation and integration in schools, followed by a reexamination of whether diversity is a compelling state interest, to the practical role of socioeconomic diversity as a proxy for race. Though issues related to racial diversity continue to occupy a prominent role in public discourse and policy, recent debates identify a new emphasis upon other categories of distinction and difference, including sexual orientation, family structure, and hardship. These categories of diversity require analyses and inquiry that are beyond the scope of this discussion, but are nonetheless linked to the history of racial discord (segregation) and social division (tracking) in schooling, and trigger enduring questions related to the role of public education in a civil and democratic society. In the next section, we unpack the related historical trends, policies, and empirical research in a focused review of racial and socioeconomic diversity in education; we also consider the context and concept of diverse learners. Our framework identifies these categories of distinction and difference as foundational to an improved understanding of the broader role, influence, and significance of diversity in shaping American public education.

Race. The modern definition of race began to shape perceptions about identity and societal structures during the eighteenth century. Some speculate that the concept of race was a convenient means by which to rationalize Europeans' unjust treatment of nonwhite people, as well as a preventive measure to keep the disenfranchised from banding together in rebellion across ethnic lines. Race has become

so common a construct in American society that few reflect on how or for what purposes this concept originally arose. What seems plain, however, is how this concept has continued to delineate and divide people. These divisions have permeated all institutions in society throughout the years, including that of public schooling.

Ironically, the nascence of the issue of racial diversity in schools occurred outside of the educational sphere, when Homer Plessy was arrested for attempting to travel in an all-white train car in Louisiana in 1892. Plessy maintained that segregation violated the Thirteenth and Fourteenth Amendments to the Constitution (the amendments that abolished slavery and declared citizens' equality of protection under the law, respectively). In a blow to the cause of desegregation, the Supreme Court held, in *Plessy v. Ferguson* (1896) that separate but equal facilities were legal and did not violate black Americans' rights under the Constitution. While the immediate circumstance of this landmark case pertained to transportation facilities, its application to other institutional contexts, such as schools, was inevitable. Racially segregated schools continued to exist, with reinforced support from the highest court in the land. Approximately half a century after the *Plessy* decision, the Supreme Court overturned the principle of separate but equal as far as its application to public schools in the case of *Brown v. Board of Education of Topeka* (1954). Though *Brown* refers to the surname of a black family in Topeka, Kansas, whose child was refused admittance to a white-only elementary school, the plaintiffs actually represented cases from several states, including Virginia and Delaware, which challenged the constitutionality of racially segregated public schools. The plaintiffs considered the denial of admission to white schools a violation of their Fourteenth Amendment right to equal protection under the law, since separate public educational facilities were inherently unequal. This time, the Supreme Court agreed, and asserted that educational opportunity should be made accessible to children on equal terms, regardless of race. While the principle of "separate but equal" was allowed to linger in other establishments, its application to public schools was summarily rejected. This decision laid the foundations for future progress toward racial diversity in schools.

In an interesting development, the situation that gave rise to the petitioners' case in *Brown* (i.e., the denial of school choice to promote segregation), led to students having their school choice *restricted* to promote racial integration. In *Parents Involved in Community Schools v. Seattle School District No. 1* (2007), the petitioners were parents who opposed the Seattle, Washington, and Jefferson County, Kentucky, school districts' voluntary implementation of a student assignment plan based on a binary classification of student race (e.g., white or nonwhite). The plaintiffs considered the allocation of students to public schools solely by race an abrogation of their Fourteenth Amendment right to equal protection under the law. As it had in *Brown*, the Supreme Court sided against the school boards. The Court ruled that denying or mandating admission of students to certain schools because of their race violated their constitutional rights. Furthermore, the Court opined that the school districts' student assignment plans were not narrowly tailored to meet a compelling governmental interest. In other words, the districts' aim to promote racial integration was not compelling because the government had not deemed forced integration currently necessary in their districts. Additionally, their binary racial classification system neither encompassed the breadth of racial diversity that existed in these districts, nor did it significantly change the levels of racial integration of schools.

Though the *Parents Involved in Community Schools* case pertained to issues of racial diversity at the K–12 level, the Supreme Court's decision in that case referenced judicial precedents from previous cases that addressed racial diversity concerns at the level of higher education. Three cases in particular helped to establish standards against which the Court evaluated the *Parents Involved in Community Schools* arguments. In *Regents of the University of California v. Bakke* (1978), the Supreme Court ruled that the University of California at Davis School of Medicine's admission policy of excluding applicants solely on the basis of race (i.e., nonminority students) to achieve

racial diversity was unconstitutional, although using race as one of several factors in admission was not unconstitutional. In the early 2000s, two other higher education cases solidified the need for racial diversity initiatives to be narrowly tailored to meet a compelling interest or goal. In *Grutter v. Bollinger et. al* (2003), the Supreme Court ruled that the University of Michigan Law School could indeed use race as one of many factors in its admissions policy, because of the holistic and individualized nature of the admissions process and the compelling interest of having a student body that is diverse according to more than just race. In a closely related and contemporary case, the Court judged the University of Michigan's undergraduate admissions policy as unconstitutional because it used a rigid point system in which race was a factor, and did not take a more holistic and individualized approach to ensuring a broader range of diversity in the student body.

In each of the court cases since *Brown*, the judgments have built on the idea that segregated educational facilities are inherently unequal. However, at issue has been exactly how to promote desegregation to achieve the aim of racial diversity. Time and again, the Court has supported diversity as a desirable goal, but it has exercised a critical eye as to the means by which these ends are met. The debate as to how to promote racial diversity continues today, with some observers decrying what they see as resegregation within the public school system. While it is true that black students are currently more likely to attend schools that do not have a majority of white students, this partially reflects the reality of a growing Latino population and may not signal a rollback to earlier days of segregation. Reasons for a persisting lack of racial diversity in some schools are complex, but many experts believe that persevering toward greater integration merits the effort because of its accompanying benefits to students.

Several studies suggest that racial diversity has a positive effect on academic achievement for black and Hispanic students while not having a significant effect, whether positive or negative, on white students' achievement. However, not all studies present evidence that agrees with these findings, as results depend on subject area (i.e., math or reading), how long desegregation has been implemented, and region (i.e., the northern or southern part of the United States). Some research has shown that higher achievement effects were frequently found for students who first experienced desegregation in earlier grades; initial desegregation at the point of kindergarten consistently related positively to black student achievement, while desegregation at the point of secondary school related positively to achievement in less than 50 percent of the research samples.

The effect of desegregation on nonacademic outcomes has also been examined. Some studies point out that improved interpersonal relations between white and black students may be positively associated with a school student population that is at least 20 percent black, but negatively associated with "token desegregation" (Schofield and Sagar, 1983, p. 72). The mechanism by which improved relations occur seems to be linked to actual face-to-face interaction that occurs in the classroom context. A classic study illustrates this phenomena as researchers found that, in a middle school with a student population consisting of about 48 percent black students, increased interaction over time between black students and white students occurred only for those who were in more racially balanced classrooms (Schofield and Sagar, 1977).

Research has also assessed longer-term benefits of racial diversity in schools. A report based on an analysis of national survey data states bluntly that adults who "have attended desegregated schools are more likely to have attended college, have better jobs, and live in desegregated neighborhoods" (Trent, 1997, p. 257). Exposure to desegregation early in black students' educational careers tends to be associated with future experiences in desegregated contexts at the postsecondary educational level, in the workplace, and in social settings.

Class. The earlier discussion on racial diversity cites many studies which suggest that racial integration improves black student scores. However, a different perspective proposes that simply changing the racial composition of the student body does not significantly impact black student achievement, apart

from possible educational reforms that may accompany desegregation. Perhaps a more salient factor affecting achievement differences between and within races would be family socioeconomic status, or class.

The term "class" carries with it sundry connotations, and challenges attempts at narrow definition. In a broad sense, the term refers to a combination of income, occupation, and "practices of living" including recreational reading preferences, access to health care, levels of educational attainment, and housing quality and location. Alternatively, a more easily identifiable measure of class is simply level of family income. To speak of class in the broader sense, individuals and families both live within the class structure while contributing to the development and maintenance of that structure. While class does overlap to some degree with race, class can encompass a wider range of characteristics. Similar to race, class impacts students' experience of the American educational system, and as with racial diversity, achieving class diversity has been proposed as a means to improving the achievement of less advantaged students.

Class may shape each individual family in unique ways, but a few generalities concerning how relative class levels influence students' education will help lay the foundation for arguments as to why class diversity merits attention as an educational goal. To begin, class impacts student readiness for school. Children in upper-class homes spend their early years in more print-rich environments than do children in lower-class homes. Parents who have more education tend to have more books at home, to read to their children more frequently, and to expect their children to read independently as they age. Students without these advantages may suffer in the area of print literacy as well as computer literacy, since families from lower classes are not only less likely to have print-rich environments but also less likely to own computers. Research has shown that class also influences verbal as well as literacy skills, as upper-class parents are inclined to converse with their children in ways that promote reasoning and questioning—two skills that contribute to school success.

The differences between classes persist as children enter and progress through school in part because of the disparity in activities in which children engage during their free time. For example, during their summers, middle-class children are more likely to have opportunities to develop their interests and to participate in various cultural and learning activities. This is not because lower-class parents lack the desire to provide these opportunities for their own children, but more likely because they have fewer informational, financial, and time resources to find out about programs, pay for programs, and transport children to programs. Lacking these resources, children from lower-class families have less opportunity to participate in extracurricular activities not only during the summer but also throughout the school year. Consequently, they are likely to miss out on the benefits of programs in the arts and athletics, for example, both of which can aid in building self-confidence and self-discipline.

As was mentioned earlier, class-based differences in extracurricular activities are not a result of disinterest on the part of lower-class parents, but rather a consequence of a lack of resources. Similarly, disparities in patterns of parental involvement point to gaps in social resources, as opposed to an absence of desire to promote students' school success. Upper-class parents frequently involve themselves in their children's schooling in ways that teachers find acceptable, while lower-class parents evince a greater separation between themselves and their children's schools. With increased parental involvement comes a greater likelihood that children will get all of the possible benefits available to them at school. Even if school staff make it their aim to attend to individual children for their benefit, "youngsters whose parents intervene will have an edge"; moreover, "which children get this edge is predictable by parents' social class" (Rothstein, 2004, p. 31).

Clearly, class has implications for a student's education, as evidenced by the ways it shapes children's school experiences through school preparedness, extracurricular opportunities, and parental involvement. Working-class and poorer children face greater disadvantage in the school environment as compared

to middle- and upper-class children. It follows that schools with a high concentration of lower-class children also have a high concentration of the disadvantage that too often accompanies their social stratum. Advocates of diversity in schools suggest that integration can help ameliorate this disadvantage.

Socioeconomic integration of schools could benefit lower-class students in several ways. Attending school with peers from the middle and upper classes can offer disadvantaged students opportunities to gain academic and social skills through the effects of peer influence. Lower-class students also tend to be lower achieving, but studies have shown that when they attend schools with higher-achieving students, who also tend to be middle- to upper-class, their achievement can improve. This linking of individual achievement to peer achievement reflects the ability of students to teach one another through both informal and formal means. For example, students may learn vocabulary from each other through casual conversations or through classroom tutoring.

Affective traits as well as academic traits can be shaped through peer influences. Research suggests that middle-class students have more motivation to succeed academically and may value hard work more than poorer children. Moreover, future aspirations are lower among poorer children, even when compared to wealthier children of the same achievement level. An integrated educational setting could expose lower-class students to students with higher aspirations, which could positively affect their own aspirations in turn. Integrated schools are not only more likely to have students with higher aspirations, but also are more likely to provide an environment that is safe and disciplined—two characteristics which have been associated with optimal student learning. Generally of an overall higher quality, middle- and upper-class schools benefit from parental involvement which, as was discussed above, tends to be less frequent with students from poorer families. Greater levels of parental involvement support school quality as parents volunteer in classrooms, raise funds, and give voice to concerns over learning environments that do not meet their stringent standards. Lastly, school staffs also contribute to the benefits of integrated schools, as higher-quality teachers tend to work at wealthier schools with raised expectations for student achievement and more challenging course offerings. Lower-class students who attend these schools would have access to all of these boons despite their individual families' lack of advantage.

Given that the benefits of socioeconomic integration appear manifold, promoting diversity should constitute an item on the American educational agenda. Some school boards have indeed included it on their agendas via student assignment plans that help disperse concentrations of economically disadvantaged students. Such a policy is referred to as socioeconomic integration (SEI). In North Carolina, the Wake County school system implemented a plan for SEI and capped the number of low-income students at any one school at 40 percent. The San Francisco Unified School District began using an SEI plan that considers many other student background variables and calculates a score for each student on a Diversity Index. In addition to family income, this index also evaluates the mother's educational background and academic achievement. With such efforts as these to diversify by class, racial diversity may be positively affected as a byproduct.

In addition to student assignment plans, school districts may encourage the establishment of educational choice to promote SEI. Some scholars and policymakers believe that school choice can mitigate class segregation by overcoming one of the greatest hindrances to SEI—residential segregation—while others insist that school choice will benefit wealthier families with advantaged access to information, and thereby exacerbate segregation. Two popular ways to offer school choice include voucher schools and charter schools. School tuition voucher programs can help integrate private schools by extending access to poorer families, as evidenced by income data for voucher users in cities across the nation. Larger voucher amounts and income restrictions on voucher eligibility can help to encourage lower-income families to participate in these programs. Charter schools that target lower-income families, conversely, may actually work against class (and racial) integration if their targeting efforts are very successful.

Smaller choice schools, whether charter or voucher, have the potential to promote intraschool diversity as a result of less tracking and more heterogeneous grouping within classes.

As was mentioned previously, one of the greatest hindrances to SEI is residential segregation. In addition to some school choice policies that may minimize the effects of segregated housing, policies that directly transform the physical and socioeconomic makeup of neighborhoods can potentially enhance school diversity. The federal grant program of HOPE VI encourages local housing agencies to revitalize dilapidated low-income housing by constructing "mixed-income and mixed-finance housing" (Abravanel, 2006, p. 1). A HOPE VI revitalization project in Atlanta resulted in a redeveloped neighborhood and an improved local elementary school that increased both its ranking in the district and its level of economic diversity. Predating the HOPE VI federal grant program as a lever to promote integrated housing, inclusionary zoning programs require "real estate developers to set aside a portion of the homes they build to be rented or sold at below-market prices" (Schwarts, 2010). An exemplar of educational diversity, the public school system in Montgomery County, Maryland, has benefited from an inclusionary zoning program that began in 1976. Entitled to purchase a portion of inclusionary zoned homes, the local public housing authority can offer residences to severely low-income families who consequently have access to upper-class neighborhood schools.

Class, or socioeconomic status, is most clearly marked by family income, although it encompasses much more than mere economic realities. It has far-reaching effects on how children experience school throughout their educational careers. Studies suggest SEI in schools especially benefits disadvantaged students in a number of ways. However, entrenched patterns of residential segregation impede the diversification of schools. To address this obstacle to integration, school choice policies and mixed-income housing programs have been implemented with varying degrees of success. Conveniently, many of the plans to address segregation by class also positively affect racial integration, as race and class are regularly in alignment. The next aspect of diversity to be discussed—special education—extends the integrationist perspective beyond students' race and class to students' individual abilities.

Special Education and Diverse Learners. Though race and class are complex cultural constructs that encompass many factors, they can be assessed quickly, albeit at a shallow level, with questions about ethnicity and family income. In contrast, diagnosing a disability requires explicit adherence to legal and medical definitions. As defined by the Individuals with Disabilities Education Act of 2004, students with disabilities have been rigorously evaluated according to state and federal legal requirements "as having mental retardation, a hearing impairment (including deafness), a speech or language impairment, a visual impairment (including blindness), a serious emotional disturbance ... an orthopedic impairment, autism, traumatic brain injury, an other health impairment, a specific learning disability, deaf-blindness, or multiple disabilities, and who, by reason thereof, needs special education and related services."

The American educational system has made great progress since the early twentieth century, when professionals once relegated many adults and children with disabilities to institutions or, in extreme cases, asylums. By the 1930s, urban public school systems had become more inclusive of students with special needs, through the provision of separate classes within public schools or separate public school facilities. Decades later, the very same court case that abolished the principle of "separate but equal" as a justification for racially segregated schooling (*Brown v. Board of Education*) had clear implications for integrating students with special needs. Section 504 of the Rehabilitation Act of 1973 affirmed the inherent inequality in complete segregation by prohibiting federally funded programs from excluding any qualified individual solely on the basis of disability status. Perhaps the most important piece of legislation to promote the cause of integration was passed two years later in 1975 as the Education for All Handicapped Children Act. The longevity of this legislation persists in its present form: the Individuals with Disabilities Education Act (IDEA). This act introduced the critical phrase "least restrictive" to modern special education parlance—a phrase that encapsulates the ideal of integrating students with disabilities with their nondisabled peers. In the latest version of IDEA (2004), the mandate of the "least restrictive environment" is explained in this way:

> To the maximum extent appropriate, children with disabilities, including children in public or private institutions or other care facilities, are educated with children who are not disabled, and special classes, separate schooling, or other removal of children with disabilities from the regular educational environment occurs only when the nature or severity of the disability of a child is such that education in regular classes with the use of supplementary aids and services cannot be achieved satisfactorily. (Section 1412a)

The concept of "least restrictive environment" (LRE) warrants discussion because it rests at the center of the effort to promote a diversity of abilities within public schools. LRE serves as a safeguard against removing students from their nondisabled peers when it is not absolutely necessary to do so in order to comply with the concomitant federal mandate to provide an individually appropriate education to each exceptional student. With related services ranging from speech therapy to behavioral counseling and the implementation of special education resource rooms that complement what transpires in the general education classroom, the number of reasons to remove students with disabilities from integrated settings has dwindled. Even in situations where academic services must be provided in a separate setting for exceptional students, the expectation is that nonacademic settings for physical education and art, for example, will still be integrated. Though not explicitly mandated by federal law, other considerations pertaining to the least restrictive environment include educating exceptional students with age-appropriate nondisabled peers, at the local school whenever possible, and in classrooms that are not physically segregated from the rest of the school building in which they are situated.

While there is no room to argue with the federal mandate to educate children in the LRE, educators often disagree with respect to the level of integration, or inclusion, appropriate for each student. Proponents of high levels of inclusion for exceptional students opine that labeling students has negative psychological and social effects, that being disabled is analogous to being a member of a minority group, and that ethics demands inclusion even if empirical research does not show it to be linked to higher student performance. A more moderate perspective is usually implemented in schools, however: that of a continuum of placements for students. This perspective recognizes that, while integration is valuable for all students, levels of inclusion should fit individual students' needs for the following reasons: research into labeling has been inconclusive, and labeling can actually help students receive the services they need; special educators, general educators, and parents appreciate more individualized services than inclusive settings can sometimes allow; occasionally and temporarily segregating students based on learning needs is not equivalent to segregating students based upon characteristics unrelated to learning ability (e.g., race); and, evidence does not support inclusion as being more effective than other, more individualized, learning settings.

The issue of ability diversity differs from racial and class diversity in that it may necessitate a delicate balance of integration and limited segregation. In some cases, students in special education may need intensive, individualized instruction that can only be delivered in settings apart from the general education classroom. Nevertheless, schools can promote understanding and sensitivity by including special education topics as part of their diversity programs and curriculums. By doing this, discrimination against students with disabilities—"ableism"—may be minimized. Like racism and classism, ableism defines an acceptable norm and then adopts a deficit view of anyone who does not fit that norm. Overcoming any of these pernicious "isms" that persist in our culture will require concerted efforts to understand different perspectives and experiences, promote face-to-face interactions as well as whole school integration, and value students for who they are, as opposed to devaluing them for who they are not.

[*See also* Affirmative Action; Charter Schools; Civil Liberties; Disability and Politics; Education and Politics; Federalism; No Child Left Behind; *and* Race and Racism.]

BIBLIOGRAPHY

Abravanel, Martin D., Robin E. Smith, and Elizabeth C. Cove. *Linking Public Housing Revitalization to Neighborhood School Improvement.* (Washington, D.C., 2006).

An, Brian P., and Adam Gamoran. "Trends in School Racial Composition in the Era of Unitary Status." In *From the Courtroom to the Classroom: The Shifting Landscape of School Desegregation*, edited by Claire E. Smrekar and Ellen B. Goldring, pp. 19–48. (Cambridge, Mass., 2009).

Armor, David. "Desegregation and Academic Achievement." In *School Desegregation in the 21st Century*, edited by Christine Rossell, David Armor, and Herbert Walberg, pp. 147–188. (Westport, Conn., 2002).

Braddock, Jomills Henry, II. "Looking Back: The Effects of Court-Ordered Desegregation." In *From the Courtroom to the Classroom: The Shifting Landscape of School Desegregation*, edited by Claire E. Smrekar and Ellen B. Goldring, pp. 3–18. (Cambridge, Mass., 2009).

Chin, Tiffani, and Meredith Phillips. "Social Reproduction and Child-Rearing Practices: Social Class, Children's Agency, and the Summer Activity Gap." *Sociology of Education* 77, no. 3 (2004): 185–210.

Crain, Robert L., and Rita E. Mahard. "Minority Achievement: Policy Implications of Research." In *Effective School Desegregation: Equity, Quality, and Feasability*, edited by Willis D. Hawley, pp. 55–84. (Beverly Hills, Calif., 1981).

Dawkins, Marvin P., and Jomills Henry Braddock II. "The Continuing Significance of Desegregation: School Racial Composition and African American Inclusion in American Society." *Journal of Negro Education* 63, no. 3 (1994): 394–405.

Flinspach, Susan, Karen Banks, and Ritu Khanna. "Socioeconomic Integration as a Tool for Diversifying Schools: Promise and Practice in Two Large School Systems." Color Lines Conference: The Civil Rights Project at Harvard University, Cambridge, Mass., 2003.

Gill, Brian P., Mike Timpane, Karen Ross, Dominic Brewer, and Kevin Booker. *Rhetoric versus Reality: What We Know and What We Need to Know about Vouchers And Charter Schools.* (Santa Monica, Calif., 2001).

Hallahan, Daniel P., and James M. Kauffman. *Exceptional Learners: An Introduction to Special Education.* (New York, 2006).

Hehir, Thomas. "Eliminating Ableism in Education." In *Special Education for a New Century*, edited by Lauren I. Katzman et al., pp. 11–38. (Cambridge, Mass., 2005).

Kahlenberg, Richard. *All Together Now: Creating Middle-Class Schools through Public School Choice.* (Washington, D.C., 2001).

Labaree, David. *Someone Has to Fail: The Zero-Sum Game of Public Schooling.* (Cambridge, Mass., 2010).

Lareau, Annette. "Invisible Inequality: Social Class and Childrearing in Black Families and White Families." *American Sociological Review* 67 (2002): 747–776.

Osgood, Richard. *The History of Special Education: A Struggle for Equality in American Public Schools.* (Westport, Conn., 2008).

Rothstein, Laura, and Scott F. Johnson. *Special Education Law.* (Thousand Oaks, Calif., 2010).

Rothstein, Richard. *Class and Schools: Using Social, Economic, and Educational Reform to Close the Black-White Achievement Gap.* (Washington, D.C., 2004).

Schofield, Janet Ward, and H. Andrew Sagar. "Desegregation, School Practices, and Student Race Relations." In *The Consequences of School Desegregation*, edited by Christine H. Rossell and Willis D. Hawley, pp. 58–102. (Philadelphia, 1983).

Schofield, Janet Ward, and H. Andrew Sagar. "Peer Interaction Patterns in an Integrated Middle School." *Sociometry* 40, no. 2 (1977): 130–138.

Schwartz, Heather. *Housing Policy Is School Policy: Economically Integrative Housing Promotes Academic Success in Montgomery County, Maryland.* (New York, 2010).

Smedley, Audrey. "'Race' and the Construction of Human Identity." *American Anthropologist* 100, no. 3 (1998): 690–702.

Trent, William T. "Outcomes of School Desegregation: Findings from Longitudinal Research." *Journal of Negro Education* 66, no. 3: (1997): 255–257.

Weis, Lois. "Introduction." In *The Way Class Works: Readings on School, Family, and the Economy*, edited by Lois Weis, pp. 1–9. (New York, 2008).

Claire Smrekar and Lydia Bentley

EDUCATION AND POLITICS

Education is a fascinating and complex political issue because it is intimately connected to children, jobs, taxes, religion, race, and class—in other words, to many of the most important and vexing questions confronting American government and society. Since the nation's founding, public education has been identified as the central means by which the country can promote social cohesion, civic virtue, and economic development. In the twenty-first century, social fissures, civic apathy, and the competitive pressures of the global economy have only enhanced the importance of education to the nation's well-being and its central role in political debates. Long a dominant issue in local politics, education has also become a leading issue in state and national politics as a wave of reforms—highlighted by the No Child Left Behind Act (NCLB, 2001)—has sought to address persistent racial and socioeconomic achievement gaps and the poor performance of American students on international tests.

American traditions of federalism and local control, however, have greatly complicated these reform efforts and ensured that the political debates over education occur not only within each level of government but across levels of government as well. This is what might be called the "50/14,000/130,000 problem" in American education reform—we have fifty different state education systems that collectively contain approximately 14,000 school districts and almost 130,000 schools. States have developed vastly different education systems, and tremendous variation in school funding and quality exists within and among states. Throughout American history, successive waves of concern about societal decline—whether attributed to immigration, poverty, or military or economic competition—have led citizens and politicians alike to look to the schools for solutions.

Local Control Meets the Common School, Sputnik, and Brown v. Board. The US Constitution does not mention education, and education policy-making was viewed primarily as a state and local responsibility within our federal system until the 1960s. As a result, schooling in the United States—in contrast to Europe and much of the rest of the world—has historically been a very decentralized and locally run affair. This began to change during the Progressive era of the late nineteenth century as Horace Mann initiated a movement to use state power to create "common schools" that could meet the needs of an industrializing, urbanizing, and diversifying nation.

Even as late as the first half of the twentieth century, however, the day-to-day management of schools, including such matters as personnel, curriculum, and pedagogy, remained largely in the hands of local authorities, with state and federal governments having limited influence. Prior to World War II, candidates for state and national political office generally ignored the issue of education. Education played a minor role in the political affairs of a nation where, in 1930, less than one-fifth of adults over age twenty-five had completed high school and where Progressives had fought doggedly to convince the public that schooling decisions ought to be entrusted to "nonpolitical" educational professionals. When education did emerge as a political issue, it was typically due to religious, ethnic, or racial tensions, rather than more abstract concerns about school quality.

Education gained new prominence in America after World War II, however, as high school completion became the norm and as the GI Bill spurred a dramatic increase in college enrollment. For the first time, education became part of the lexicon of the working-class American and a key to economic and social mobility. Expanding educational access also became a central objective of the civil rights movement. The Supreme Court's *Brown v. Board of Education* decision in 1954 calling for the end of segregated schools dramatically altered the politics of educational policy-making in the United States as it would engage the federal government directly and forcefully in the effort to create a more equitable system of public schooling for the first time. The publication of a large body of social science research during the 1950s and 1960s also created much greater public awareness of the economic and educational inequalities facing racial minorities and the poor in the United States. While these developments increased public support for educational equality in the abstract, federal and judicial pressure to integrate local schools would remain enormously controversial, particularly after the courts adopted a more aggressive approach (busing) and timetable for integration in the late 1960s.

America's Cold War competition with the Soviet Union also provided an impetus for greater federal involvement in education in the 1950s. The Soviet launch of Sputnik, the world's first orbiting satellite, generated fears that the United States was falling behind in the development of new technologies and underscored the importance of education to national security. These developments provided the impetus for the passage of the National Defense Education Act of 1958, which provided categorical aid to states to improve math, science, and foreign language instruction in American schools. The 1950s and early 1960s thus had a mixed legacy for the national politics of education. On the one hand, the Cold War demand for improved technical education, the greater number of Americans attending high school and college, and a growing awareness of the financial and racial inequities in the public school system combined to increase the salience of education and create significant momentum for expanded federal support for schools. Many citizens and political elites became convinced that states and localities were either unable or unwilling to address educational failures and inequities on their own. On the other hand, most Americans continued to desire that education-policy decisions should be made at the state and local levels, and the period witnessed growing and often intense opposition to federal efforts to integrate public schools.

ESEA and Interest Group Politics. President Lyndon Johnson capitalized on the growing public awareness of school inequalities and the large Democratic majority in Congress following the 1964 election to push for major federal investment in education. The Elementary and Secondary Education Act (ESEA) of 1965 enshrined an equity rationale at the heart of federal education policy—the national government would provide states with supplemental funding and programs in the hope of equalizing educational opportunity for poor and minority students. As initially designed and implemented, ESEA was enormously popular on Capitol Hill, with the education establishment, and in state capitols because it spread federal dollars around the country with few stipulations and virtually no accountability for student achievement. The politics of education at the national level between 1965 and 1994 was largely a struggle between liberal groups united by a desire to see federal spending and programs for schools expanded and conservative groups who were philosophically opposed to any federal role in education whatsoever (but practically were eager to bring home educational pork).

The most powerful interest groups in education are the two major teacher unions, the National Education Association (NEA) and the American Federation of Teachers (AFT), and the groups which represent state and local education authorities (such as the Council of Chief State School Officers and the Council of Great City Schools). Allied formally since 1969 in the Committee for Education Funding, these groups have long advocated on behalf of increased federal funding for schools and in opposition to conservative school voucher proposals. While the state education groups largely focus on policy advocacy, the teachers' unions have fashioned themselves into a major national political force by marshalling large quantities of the three most important political resources—money, votes, and campaign volunteers. Both unions are very active politically through their state affiliates and their large, well-funded national headquarters in Washington, D.C. The NEA has allied itself firmly with the Democratic Party since 1976 as a result of President Jimmy Carter's pledge to create a federal Department of Education (which opened in 1979) and congressional Democrats' steadfast support of increased federal funding for schools.

Both the NEA and the AFT consistently give over 95 percent of their campaign and soft money contributions to Democrats. The teachers' unions have been by far the Democratic Party's biggest national donor bloc, and the unions' clout is reflected during the party's presidential nominating process, where NEA and AFT members have comprised the largest block of delegates at the national convention and played an influential role on the platform committees. The unions have historically used their power within the Democratic Party—and in the political process more generally—to fight for increased federal spending for education and to oppose reforms that threaten their power over collective bargaining agreements and school policy. During the 1965–1994

period, the unions generally opposed school vouchers, choice, charter schools, rigorous standards and tests, alternative teacher licensing, merit pay, and accountability measures. For thirty years after the passage of ESEA, the unions were able to use this power to preserve the status quo in education by defeating—or effectively neutering—many of the major school reform proposals that emerged at the national level.

Republicans have also had to contend with important interest groups in their political coalition, though on the Republican side these groups have historically opposed an active federal role in education. There have been three distinct sources of opposition to federal influence in education within the Republican Party. Libertarians have opposed government activism in education generally and called for school vouchers, while states-rights groups believe that education policy is a state responsibility. Religious conservatives, such as those in the Christian Coalition, meanwhile, have fought against federal influence in education because they believe it promotes secular humanism, multiculturalism, and sex education, all of which they oppose. The influence of these conservative groups ensured that Republicans actively fought proposals to establish national education standards, tests, and accountability measures during most of the 1980s and 1990s. As late as 1996, the education plank of the Republican Party platform called for the elimination of the federal role in education and the abolition of the US Department of Education. One significant consequence of this dynamic was that conservative educational interest groups and think tanks did not develop comprehensive alternative education reform plans until the late 1990s.

Despite their political and philosophical differences then, during the 1965–1994 period interest groups on both the Left and Right had a stake in preserving the old education policy regime and in opposing expanded federal efforts to promote school reform. Liberals sought to keep the federal focus on disadvantaged students and increasing funding, and education groups wanted to minimize new federal requirements that threatened their members.

Conservatives sought to minimize federal influence in education and to promote local control. This unusual alliance was politically powerful and largely successful in limiting efforts to transform and expand the federal role in schools until the 1990s. The result was that federal education spending, programs, and regulation expanded incrementally in the thirty years after ESEA was created but did so largely within the context of the program's original equity framework.

Shattering the Old Consensus: The New Politics of Education. The early consensus around federal education policy began to unravel in the 1980s and 1990s. The seeds of change were sown with the publication of the high-profile *A Nation at Risk* report in 1983, which challenged the legitimacy of the old equity approach to school improvement. The report highlighted increasing concern across the country about student achievement and its impact on economic development and global competition among state leaders, business and trade groups, and voters generally. Since Republicans (first Ronald Reagan and then George H. W. Bush) who opposed an active federal role in schools occupied the White House for nine years following the report, there was little movement toward a new policy regime at the national level. President George H. W. Bush convened an important educational conference with governors in Charlottesville, Virginia, in 1989 and advanced a proposal for voluntary national academic standards with his America 2000 plan; but in the end no major changes to federal policy were made, and these efforts proved largely symbolic. As a result, the initial policy response to *A Nation at Risk* during the 1980s was largely confined to the state level.

The legacy of *A Nation at Risk* was significant, however, as it served as a crucial focusing event that heightened media—and ultimately citizen—attention to education reform to an unprecedented degree. Since 1980 education has risen rapidly on the national political agenda and the state and federal roles in schools have undergone a remarkable expansion and transformation. In 1976, voters did not even rank education as one of the country's top twenty concerns; but the issue began a steady climb in the

1980s, and by 2000 many polls showed it to be the number one issue on the public agenda. This political shift has accorded debates over school reform a prominent place in state and national elections in the contemporary era as well as in broader partisan and ideological struggles over the proper size and scope of the national government.

A number of developments came together in the 1990s to fundamentally challenge the old politics of education and transform the national education policy arena. Several important groups became disenchanted with the slow pace of state education reforms and began to doubt whether states would be able to generate meaningful change in the absence of federal pressure. As Paul Manna (2006) has noted, reform-minded governors sought to "borrow strength" by leveraging federal authority to advance their own school reform agendas. They were joined in this effort by business groups, which were increasingly concerned about the training and productivity of American workers and civil rights groups, which hoped to use such reforms to document and close racial achievement gaps. This alliance of governors, business leaders, and civil rights groups blurred the long-standing ideological divisions over school reform and represented a potent outside political force for change in state capitals and Washington, D.C.

A second set of developments inside Washington ensured that the reform alliance would find a more receptive audience of policymakers at the federal level. The election of New Democrat Bill Clinton, a reform-minded education governor, as president in 1992 pushed Democrats to embrace a more centrist position on education and led to the passage of two major school reform bills in 1994—Goals 2000 and the Improving America's Schools Act. Many of the reform ideas that would later form the core of NCLB—such as standards, assessments, adequate yearly progress, school report cards, and corrective action—found their first expression in the 1994 ESEA reauthorization. Though the new laws did not include many mandates for states, they signified a sea change in federal education policy and codified the shift from the historical focus on ensuring resource equity for disadvantaged students to a new commitment to improve the academic performance of all students.

These reforms, however, were initially greeted with considerable hostility by many members of both parties in Congress. Liberal Democrats (and their allies in the teachers' unions) feared that the reforms would shift attention away from resource issues, and conservative Republicans lamented the expansion of federal influence into areas of school governance, which had historically been the prerogative of the states. Together they effectively pressured the Clinton administration to weaken the enforcement of the reforms in the field, particularly after the switch of party control in Congress to the Republicans in 1995. The Improving America's Schools Act ostensibly required states to adopt standards, assessment, and accountability policies; but it was weakly enforced, and by 2002 only sixteen states had fully met its requirements.

Under the leadership of Speaker of the House Newt Gingrich, Republicans in the mid-1990s once again tried to reduce federal involvement in education by cutting federal spending, by converting it into block grants or vouchers, and by eliminating the Department of Education entirely. These conservative positions on education, while popular with the party's base, proved extremely unpopular with the general public and particularly with moderate swing voters. The extent of public displeasure with the conservative agenda on education was revealed forcefully in the 1996 presidential election, when voters favored Clinton over Dole on the issue by more than a two-to-one margin. More broadly, between 1984 and 1996, polls showed that Democrats maintained a double-digit advantage over Republicans in the percentage of the public who felt the party best addressed education.

The partisan education gap became increasingly costly for the Republicans because by the end of the 1990s education had risen to the top of the public agenda and become a decisive national electoral issue. In addition, the failure of most states to comply with the 1994 federal mandates or to make significant progress in closing achievement gaps despite greatly increased federal and state education spending put pressure on national policymakers to undertake more substantive education reform. The unpopularity of the earlier Republican focus on deregulation and privatization and the discrediting of the Democratic focus on resources and process regulation led to a new bipartisan consensus around standards, testing, and accountability. In the 2000 election, voters ranked education as the single most important issue of the election, and presidential candidates George W. Bush and Al Gore proposed remarkably similar plans for an expanded federal role in schools that became the basis for NCLB.

NCLB and an Expanded Federal Role. If congressional Republicans and Democrats had softened their opposition to a new reform-oriented federal role in education by the late 1990s, it would take the election of a former Republican governor, George W. Bush, as president to cement the foundation of a new policy regime. Where earlier Republican presidential candidates had either ignored the issue of education or run in opposition to a federal role, Bush made education the number one issue of his campaign and a crucial part of his compassionate conservative philosophy. In an effort to close the gap on education and appeal to swing voters such as women and Latinos, for whom education was a top issue, Bush adopted a pragmatic and centrist education agenda that called for an active but reformed federal role in promoting school improvement. Bush entered office declaring that education reform would be his first priority and used his success on the issue in the election to forge a bipartisan coalition behind NCLB. The final vote on the conference report of NCLB was overwhelming and bipartisan in both the House (381–41) and Senate (87–10) and President Bush signed NCLB into law on 8 January 2002.

NCLB requires states to create academic standards, annually test children in reading and math in grades three through eight (and once in high school), and hold them accountable for the results. States must determine which students are proficient, identify schools where an insufficient number of students are proficient, ensure that specified measures are taken with regard to schools that fail to make "adequate yearly progress," and set targets that ensure

100 percent of children are proficient in reading and math by 2014. One of the most important mandates in the law is that school report cards must disaggregate student test score data for subgroups based on race or ethnicity, economically disadvantaged status, limited proficiency in English, and classification as in need of special education. Crucially and controversially, a school which does not meet the proficiency target for *any one of these groups* is placed in "in need of improvement status," and states are required to take an escalating series of steps to intervention (including the offering of public school choice, tutoring, technical assistance, and restructuring) with schools and districts that persistently fail to meet achievement targets.

The scope, specificity, and ambition of the law's mandates signaled something akin to a revolution in federal education policy. With NCLB the federal government for the first time pressured states in a sustained way to undertake systemic change in their education systems and held them accountable for the academic performance of their students. NCLB's requirement that states conduct annual testing and report student scores has forced them to build new data-gathering and dissemination systems and produced a greater degree of transparency in public education than ever before. Parents, advocacy groups, the media, and policymakers have access to a wealth of disaggregated student performance data, which they have used to shine a bright light on previously dark corners of neglect in the educational system. School report cards, demands that schools make escalating progress toward closing achievement gaps, and a corrective action and restructuring process that specifies steps that persistently underperforming schools must take to improve have all directed an unprecedented amount of attention and resources at turning around failing schools. By holding states clearly accountable for the performance of their public schools, NCLB has also prodded state departments of education to expand their capacity to monitor local districts, provide technical assistance, and intervene where necessary.

A variety of concerns have been raised about the design and implementation of the test-based accountability at the heart of NCLB and the ways in which it has fallen short of its goals and produced unintended negative consequences in American classrooms. States have bristled at the coerciveness and prescriptiveness of the law's mandates and have struggled mightily to implement them on the ground. As David Cohen and Susan Moffit (2009) have observed, the federal government's ambitious goals in education have not been matched by sufficient attention to how teachers and administrators can realize these goals; there has been a large disconnect between policy and practice. As a result, each year more and more schools have failed to meet their state proficiency targets, thus triggering escalating corrective actions. Critics of test-based accountability believe that the tests in use are an invalid measure of student learning and that they have pushed schools to teach to the test and narrow the curriculum. And there is considerable evidence that states have used their broad discretion to set their own standards, tests, and proficiency levels to game the system by lowering their expectations for student achievement.

Obama, Race to the Top, and Competing Narratives of Education Reform. The election of Barack Obama as president in 2008—combined with Democratic control of Congress—gave the Democratic Party an opportunity to assert a new vision of education reform. Many observers initially assumed that this would lead to a move away from school accountability and a reassertion of a traditional liberal focus on school resources, integration, and social welfare programs. But Obama called for the continuation of annual testing in ESEA, expanded federal efforts to restructure the worst performing schools, and a new focus on innovation, charter schools, and teacher accountability. The centerpiece of the Obama education agenda has been the $4.35 billion Race to the Top (RTT) and $650 million Investing in Innovation (I3) funds. Unlike traditional categorical grant programs, which allocated money to districts on the basis of need-based formulas, the RTT and I3 funds were distributed through a competitive grant process in which states and districts were rewarded for developing effective school reforms that are aligned with the federal emphasis on innovation and accountability. In particular, state applications were graded according to the rigor of the reforms proposed and their compatibility with five administration priorities: the development of common standards and assessments; improving teacher training, evaluation, and retention policies; developing better data systems; the adoption of preferred school turnaround strategies; and building stakeholder support for reform.

The department also established a number of criteria that states had to meet to even be eligible to apply for the RTT funds, and these requirements have had a major effect on state school reform efforts, independent of the specific grant proposals which the states have submitted. Among the fourteen criteria for RTT eligibility is that a state does not have a cap on the number of charter schools that are permitted to operate and that it does not have a firewall preventing the linking of student achievement data with individual teacher information. This served to stir the pot politically in states over school reform as never before by forcing different interest groups to publicly stake out their positions on the various reform components of RTT in the debate over whether to apply and under what conditions. The competition also attracted a tremendous amount of media attention to the issue of school reform, shone a bright light on dysfunctional state policies, and helped create new political coalitions at the local and state levels to drive reform. There is evidence, for example, that RTT's emphasis on expanding charter schools and revamping teacher evaluations has helped to change the political climate around these controversial issues, thus paving the way for the passage of reform legislation in many states. The Obama administration has announced a second RTT competition as well as its desire to distribute more federal education funding though competitive grant programs in the future.

The new focus on teacher quality and accountability (in tandem with the major postrecession fiscal crisis in states) has also led to a nationwide debate over the proper scope of teacher compensation, benefits, and collective bargaining rights, which

has prompted a vigorous pushback by the teachers' unions and a growing split within the Democratic Party. Recent developments have also highlighted the emergence of two competing narratives of school reform that have come to dominate the political discourse around education. These different narratives are largely captured in the platforms of the Broader, Bolder Approach to Education (BBA) and the Education Equality Project (EEP). While advocates of the BBA and EEP share similar goals in terms of advancing educational equity, they have different visions of the obstacles that stand in the way and the policies that states and the federal government should adopt to pursue it. The BBA narrative attributes racial and socioeconomic achievement gaps primarily to the effects of poverty and segregation. Since schools cannot be expected to remedy educational deficits which have social or economic roots, in this view NCLB and the standardized testing and accountability movement, more generally, are at best a waste of time and at worst dangerously counterproductive. American neighborhoods and schools remain strikingly segregated by race and class, and concentrated poverty produces concentrated educational disadvantage that is impossible to rectify absent a major effort to expand home and school resources that can enhance the "opportunity to learn."

The EEP narrative of school reform, meanwhile, sees centralized testing and accountability policies as essential to changing the political dynamics around education reform—to breaking a status quo that has prevented schools from taking action to close racial and socioeconomic achievement gaps despite a large increase in federal and state education spending since 1970. The political power of teachers' unions and upper- and middle-class families prevents states and localities from adopting policies on behalf of poor children, and ossified bureaucratic school systems are unable or unwilling to address their own problems. The public school system is seen as broken in many ways, particularly in urban areas; and the purpose of state and federal reforms should be to foster/require policy change and innovation and to ensure that school leaders and teachers have meaningful consequences attached to their efforts to close achievement gaps. While historically much of the debate about education has been partisan in nature, this is much less true today, with adherence to these different narratives—and support for the BBA and EEP—crossing party lines.

The Future of Education Politics. Since 1980 the country has witnessed a dramatic shift in politics and policy-making in education. That the problems identified by *A Nation at Risk*—large socioeconomic and racial achievement gaps and concerns that even America's "good schools" are not good enough—persist is not the subject of much dispute. The particular source of the country's educational maladies and the best prescription to remedy them, however, continue to engender enormous disagreement among educators, researchers, citizens, and politicians. The new federal focus on academic performance and the extension of federal policy to cover every student and every school mark a major shift in the governance of elementary and secondary education in the United States. As states have struggled to meet NCLB's ambitious goals and chafed at the reforms rewarded by RTT, some of the initial philosophical reservations within both parties about the new federal emphasis on accountability have come storming back to the surface. Many Republicans resent the coerciveness of the new federal role, while many Democrats are concerned about the impact of standardized testing on instruction and the focus on schools over broader economic and social change.

But the contemporary debate over NCLB and RTT has also revealed that the politics of education have changed significantly in the first decade of the twenty-first century in ways that are likely to have lasting influence on efforts to bring about educational improvement and equity. Ongoing debates about how to improve teacher quality and accountability, develop common standards and assessments, restructure failing schools, expand school choice, and refine the federal role in school reform will ensure that the education issue will remain highly salient and contentious in local, state, and national politics for the foreseeable future.

[*See also* Charter Schools; Education and Diversity; *and* No Child Left Behind.]

BIBLIOGRAPHY

Berkman, Michael, and Eric Plutzer. *Ten Thousand Democracies: Politics and Public Opinion in America's School Districts*. (Washington, D.C., 2005).

Cohen, David, and Susan Moffitt. *The Ordeal of Equality: Did Federal Regulation Fix the Schools?* (Cambridge, Mass., 2009).

Cooper, Bruce, James Cibulka, and Lance Fusarelli, eds. *Handbook of Education Politics and Policy.* (New York, 2008).

Davies, Gareth. *See Government Grow: Education Politics from Johnson to Reagan.* (Lawrence Kans., 2007).

DeBray, Elizabeth. *Politics, Ideology, and Education: Federal Policy during the Clinton and Bush Administrations.* (New York, 2006).

DeBray, Elizabeth, and Patrick McGuinn. "The New Politics of Education: Analyzing the Federal Education Policy Landscape in the Post-NCLB Era." *Educational Policy* 23 (2009): 15–42.

Hochschild, Jennifer, and Nathan Scovronick. *The American Dream and the Public Schools.* (Oxford, UK, 2003).

Kirst, Michael, and Frederick Wirt. *The Political Dynamics of American Education*, 4th ed. (Richmond, Calif., 2009).

Manna, Paul. *School's In: Federalism and the National Education Agenda.* (Washington, D.C., 2006).

McDermott, Kathryn. *Controlling Public Education: Localism vs. Equity.* (Lawrence, Kans., 1999).

McGuinn, Patrick. "Creating Cover and Constructing Capacity: Assessing the Origins, Evolution, and Impact of Race to the Top." American Enterprise Institute, December 2010, http://www.aei.org/paper/100165.

McGuinn, Patrick. *No Child Left Behind and the Transformation of Federal Education Policy, 1965–2005.* (Lawrence, Kans., 2006).

Mitchell, Douglass, Robert Crowson, and Dorothy Shipps, eds. *Shaping Education Policy: Power and Process.* (New York, 2011).

Moe, Terry. *Special Interest: Teachers Unions and America's Public Schools.* (Washington, D.C., 2011).

National Commission on Excellence in Education. *A Nation at Risk: The Imperative for Educational Reform.* (Washington, DC, 1983).

Spring, Joel. *The Politics of American Education.* (New York, 2011).

Stone, Clarence, Jeffrey Henig, Bryan Jones, and Carol Pierannunzi. *Building Civic Capacity: The Politics of Reforming Urban Schools.* (Lawrence, Kans., 2001).

Patrick McGuinn

EGYPT

Egypt was formed as a centralized state from a province of the Ottoman Empire in the early nineteenth century. The new state promoted agriculture and modern industry, and expanded its empire abroad from the Sudan to Syria. In 1839, however, European states intervened to reestablish nominal Ottoman authority, forcing Egypt to disarm itself and remove restrictions on the penetration of European commerce and capital.

The building of the Suez Canal and a modern transport and irrigation network during the 1850s and 1860s accelerated Egypt's incorporation into the European world economy, principally as a producer of raw cotton. The American Civil War ended the US domination of the global cotton trade, encouraging a boom in Egyptian production. Export agriculture concentrated landownership in the hands of a Turkish-speaking elite and produced a new stratum of European and Levantine financiers and merchants tied to powerful European banks. The resumption of US exports after the Civil War, followed by the worldwide economic crisis of 1873–1879, ended the Egyptian boom and bankrupted the state, allowing foreign banks to establish direct supervision of state revenues. In 1881 a reformist movement attempted to replace absolutist rule subservient to European creditors with representative government, but within a year British troops invaded Egypt and reestablished a client regime.

A second nationalist revolt broke out in 1919, demanding an end to the British occupation. The nationalist leaders appealed to US President Woodrow Wilson for support, invoking his adoption of the principle of self-determination, but the United States supported Britain's continued control. Unable to defeat the nationalist movement, in 1922 Britain agreed to recognize Egypt as a sovereign state under a constitutional monarchy. However, the British retained their military presence, control of Egyptian foreign policy, and considerable influence over domestic affairs. In 1936 Britain withdrew its troops to the Suez Canal zone. The economic hardships of World War II, and Egypt's defeat in the Palestine War

of 1948–1949, led to violent popular protest against the British presence and the incompetence of the monarchy. In 1952, army officers led by Gamal Abdel Nasser seized power, abolished the monarchy, and negotiated Britain's withdrawal from Suez. The United States initially supported the new regime, as a military-run alternative to more populist forces and as a means of strengthening Washington's position in its regional rivalry with Britain. In the later 1950s and 1960s, however, Egypt's support for anti-imperialist movements in Africa and the Arab world discouraged the United States from developing closer ties, allowing the Soviet Union to become a rival source of economic and political support.

Under the military government, Egypt adopted a one-party system. The regime suppressed existing parties and replaced them with the Liberation Rally, which was renamed the Arab Socialist Union (ASU) in 1962 and organized in communities and workplaces as an agency of popular political mobilization. The ASU leadership weakened after the death of President Nasser in 1970, and after conservative forces reasserted themselves under his successor, Anwar Sadat. In 1976 Sadat permitted rival political organizations to form, first as platforms within the ASU and then, from 1978, as separate parties.

The ASU itself became the National Democratic Party, and the ruling political party (it would ultimately remain so until 2011). Closely linked to the government and the state-controlled media and security forces, it was assured of large electoral majorities. Left-leaning intellectuals and Nasserists organized the National Progressive Unionist Party; its support was strong among industrial workers, and its criticisms prompted the regime to establish the religious-nationalist Socialist Labor Party as a more loyal opposition. The center-right New Wafd, successor to the popular pre-1952 nationalist party, emerged as the most influential opposition party.

Communist, Nasserist, and Islamic political parties continued to be banned. Labor unions, an important force before 1952, were under the control of a government federation, whose monopoly over labor organizing was confirmed by law in 1976. The Muslim Brotherhood, a mass political movement formed in 1929 and suppressed after 1954, was allowed to reorganize semilegally in the 1970s, as an alternative to the Left and the labor movement. After the assassination of President Sadat in 1981 by members of a militant Islamic cell, the Brotherhood was also seen as an alternative to religious extremism. Its program of social and cultural conservatism was supported by powerful elements in the state, including parts of the judiciary, and by the religious establishment. Its members won People's Assembly seats under the name of other parties and dominated elections to many professional organizations. Under Sadat's successor, Hosni Mubarak, opposition newspapers were allowed more freedom. Since the state banned the holding of public meetings, the press provided the only public forum for criticism of government policy. But its efforts in the late 1990s to expose financial corruption, especially in the presidential family, led to new restrictions that reestablished the limits to political dissent.

Under the 1971 constitution, Egypt was ruled by a president nominated to a six-year renewable term of office by the People's Assembly and approved by the electorate. The president appointed the prime minister and other members of the government, issued decrees with the force of law, declared states of emergency and war, and was the supreme head of the armed forces and the police. The judiciary was protected by the constitution from political interference and in practice maintained significant independence—to the extent that the regime was forced to evade its powers by the almost continuous use of martial law and military courts.

With public protest forbidden, popular discontent with the regime was increasingly channeled via the moral and organizational resources of Islamic associations. In the 1980s, radical elements among these groups were recruited into the US-supported forces fighting in Afghanistan. Returning home a decade later, the jihadists attempted to destabilize the regime through violence. In 1992 the Islamic Group (al-gama' a al-islamiyya) launched a terror campaign in Cairo and the south, targeting foreign tourism as a mainstay of the economy and a symbol of Egypt's corruption by the West. The state suppressed the group at the cost of many hundreds of lives. Anxious for the support of less subversive Islamic activists, however, the regime was unwilling to halt a persistent, occasionally violent, campaign against prominent Egyptian secularists, and used the threat of destabilization to refuse the demand of opposition parties and human rights groups for effective democratic rights.

After 2000, secular opposition developed outside the formal political system, through a growing number of human rights organizations, an increase in labor organizing among industrial and government-sector workers, and a rise in protest groups supporting Palestinian rights and opposing the 2003 US invasion of Iraq. The Egyptian Movement for Change, also known as Kefaya ("enough"), was formed in 2004 to bring opposition forces together under a campaign for constitutional reforms that would allow an effective electoral challenge to Mubarak and the NDP, where the president's son, Gamal Mubarak, was building a campaign to succeed his father. Opposition groups made increasing use of the Internet and social media to mobilize support and to expose the brutality of the security forces.

In response to the pressure for reform, including mild criticism from the United States, the regime amended the constitution in 2007 to allow multicandidate elections to the presidency, but under conditions that prevented an effective challenge to the ruling party's candidate. The amendments also restricted judicial independence, including the role of judges in monitoring elections, and turned emergency powers of the state into normal legal prerogatives. The tightening of control enabled the NDP to dominate the parliamentary elections of 2010, effectively eliminating opposition parties from the People's Assembly.

In 2011 a popular uprising brought down the Mubarak regime. Its overthrow was a key moment in the wave of revolutionary uprisings across the Middle East known as the "Arab Spring" and a turning point in Egypt's modern history. Encouraged by protests in Tunisia that removed the president from power, the uprising began on 25 January with a carefully planned popular demonstration that seized control of central Cairo. A violent crackdown by security forces failed to suppress the protests, which spread to other cities and were supported by strikes that paralyzed the government and economy. On 11 February the armed forces stepped in to remove Mubarak and his government from power. The United States, which had been calling for Mubarak to reform the government but not for his removal, supported the transfer of power.

The Supreme Council of the Armed Forces assumed control, suspended the constitution, appointed an interim government, and issued a provisional constitution to govern the election of a new president and legislative assembly, which was to draft a permanent constitution. The reform restored judicial supervision of elections, limited the president to two terms in office, and provided for multiparty elections. Popular protests and strikes continued throughout 2011. The opposition groups fought to prevent the military from entrenching itself in power in collaboration with the Muslim Brotherhood and members of the dissolved NDP. A resurgent labor movement fought for a wider transformation to address the country's enormous economic and social inequality. Wider social change was resisted by supporters of the old order, still powerful in the upper ranks of the bureaucracy and the armed forces; among a small class of entrepreneurs and property speculators, some controlling large, family-based conglomerates; and among large landowners. These groups benefited from the previous regime's policies of economic deregulation and military growth and had depended on the state for protected markets, contracts, and commissions.

Over 40 percent of the country's population is now urban, concentrated in the two major cities of Cairo and Alexandria. Although the industrial workforce is more than a million strong, most of the urban population is employed in the service sector. The rural population remains predominantly agricultural, but despite reform measures, land is still concentrated in a few hands. In 1987, 48 percent of farmland was held in farms of more than five acres (the maximum size of a family farm) by the top 10 percent of landholders. This stratum continues to holds political power in the countryside, but has been challenged by the emergence of a movement of small farmers during the 2011 revolution.

Egypt's population is largely Muslim, with Christians estimated at 10 percent. During the colonial period, parts of the Christian community prospered as intermediaries for European capital and political power, but since the 1950s their position of relative privilege has declined. This has contributed to Christian-Muslim animosity and sometimes violence, especially in areas where the Islamic movement is strong.

Women in Egypt benefited from the emergence of a feminist movement early in the twentieth century, in the context of the nationalist struggle. After 1952 they gained the right to vote and to stand for election, as well as wider access to education and employment. As education moved them into the workplace, many women adopted a modern form of veiling, with motives ranging from piety and political activism to dealing with the discomforts of a male-dominated public space. At the same time, the wider growth of the Islamic movement carried with it a reassertion of the male prerogatives weakened by these economic and social changes. Women activists played a leading role in many of the groups that launched the uprising of 2011.

The Nasser regime undertook a program of state-controlled economic development labeled "Arab socialism." The 1952 agrarian reforms dispossessed the small, landed aristocracy and guaranteed the security of tenant farmers. The regime initially sought international investment, but when the United States refused to finance the keystone of its development program, the Aswan High Dam, the state was forced into a more active economic role. The Suez Canal was nationalized, and after the abortive Suez invasion by Britain, France, and Israel in 1956, the regime Egyptianized European banks and enterprises. Egyptian business elites and landowners prospered, but were unwilling to invest in rapid industrialization to promote wider prosperity and reduce pressure from the Left, which was subject to growing repression.

In the 1960s the military regime moved against the power of private Egyptian capital, nationalizing banks, major companies, and industries, and passed laws giving workers shares of profits, a minimum wage, and free health care and education. Five-year planning focused on a program of import-substitution industrialization in iron and steel, aluminum, chemicals, and other heavy industry, and efforts were made to extend the land reform. Egypt's defeat in the June 1967 Arab-Israeli War (the Six-Day War) weakened the regime, however, and enabled the emergent bureaucratic and military elite, together with large landowners and the urban bourgeoisie, to resist further reform.

The Sadat and Mubarak regimes reflected these interests. The 1974 economic *infitah* ("opening") encouraged foreign investment in collaboration with local capital, but the boom occurred in construction, property speculation, consumer imports, tourism, and other services, rather than renewed industrial growth. By the mid-1990s, services accounted for 60 percent of the country's gross domestic product (GDP), while industry and agriculture contributed only 20 percent each. Oil and gas exports, Suez Canal tolls, tourism, and the remittances of millions of men who went to work in the Gulf became the major sources of foreign income—all of them highly volatile.

Unable to promote self-sustaining growth or further redistribution, the regime preserved social order through the 1980s and 1990s by subsidizing the cost of food and other necessities. This was financed by borrowing from abroad, including subsidized US loans and grain sales on a scale that exceeded US aid to all the rest of Africa combined. Together with extensive purchases of US arms, these loans drew the government heavily into debt. Although part of the debt was later forgiven, the collapse of oil prices after 1985 forced the government to seek aid from the International Monetary Fund (IMF) to refinance its obligations. In exchange, in 1991 and 1996 Egypt accepted IMF economic programs that cut social spending and price controls, began the privatization or liquidation of state enterprises, and opened the country more fully to private foreign investment and trade. By the late 1990s the reforms had stabilized inflation, the currency, and

the fiscal balance, but deregulated prices had caused havoc in agriculture and in textiles (Egypt's major industry), and export growth was lagging behind the surge in imports. There was a speculation boom in property and in the revived Cairo stock exchange, but the level of long-term investment and job creation remained low. The state abandoned its lingering commitment to redistribution of wealth and revoked many of the economic rights won in the Nasser period, in particular rent controls and the security of tenant farmers against eviction.

In 2004, as opposition to the regime began to intensify, Mubarak appointed a government led by market-oriented economic reformers, who reduced social spending, increased the military and security budget, and accelerated the privatization of state-owned industry. The loss of jobs and employment rights that followed triggered the largest wave of labor unrest since before the 1952 coup, preparing the way for the revolutionary events of 2011.

Egyptians live with high unemployment and declining access to adequate housing, nutrition, health care, and education. The population doubled from 40 million in 1980 to over 80 million in 2010, although family planning programs have now slowed the annual growth rate to under 2 percent, well below the median rate for Africa and the Arab world. Almost one-third of the population in 2010 was under the age of fifteen.

Egypt's economic and military dependence on the United States since the mid-1970s has reduced its international role. Until oil wealth financed the growth of Saudi Arabia and Iraq, Egypt was the predominant Arab power and a leader in wider coalitions such as the Non-aligned Movement and the Organization of African Unity. Israel's unsuccessful 1956 Suez invasion affirmed Nasser's leadership of a populist Arab nationalism, and was followed in 1958 by political union with Syria to form the short-lived United Arab Republic. The United States opposed Arab nationalism, which threatened its more oligarchic Arab allies, forcing Egypt and other populist states to depend increasingly on the Soviet Union. In 1967 Israel again invaded Egypt, this time with US support, after Israeli-Syrian clashes had led Egypt to reimpose its pre-1956 blockade of Israeli shipping in the Gulf of Aqaba. In response to a humiliating defeat, Egypt began realigning itself to gain US support. The October 1973 war forced Israel into military disengagement talks. Sadat's November 1977 trip to Jerusalem led to the 1979 Camp David peace accords, under which Israel withdrew in stages from Egyptian territory and promised some form of autonomy to the Palestinians in the West Bank and the Gaza Strip.

The other Arab states opposed a peace treaty that left Israel holding the West Bank and Gaza under military occupation, and broke diplomatic relations with Cairo. Egypt's formal isolation lasted a decade, interrupting aid from the Gulf states and increasing Cairo's dependence on Washington. The Iran-Iraq War (1980–1988), however, drew Egypt closer to Saudi Arabia and Jordan in joint support of Iraq, and after the war ties with Syria and Libya were strengthened. Egypt's participation in the Gulf War (1991) strengthened the regime's position both at home and in Washington. After the 1993 Oslo Agreement giving the Palestinians in Israeli-occupied territories limited self-rule, Egypt was unable to push Israel or the United States to support full Palestinian statehood. The Palestinian uprising of 2000–2001, which Israel put down by force, and the US invasion of Iraq in 2003, placed increasing domestic pressure on an Egyptian regime allied with Washington and dependent on American military and financial support. The United States continued to support the Egyptian state as a mainstay of the wider regional system of oligarchy and inequality, through which it believed its interests were protected. The Egyptian revolution of 2011 challenged the political oppression that had maintained this unequal and autocratic order. It challenged, in turn, America's longstanding reliance on militarism and regional security arrangements as a means of defending its weakening influence in Egypt and the Arab world.

[*See also* Arab-Israeli Conflict; *and* Middle East–United States Relations.]

BIBLIOGRAPHY

El Mahdi, Rabab, and Philip Marfleet, eds. *Egypt: The Moment of Change*. (New York, 2009).

Goldschmidt, Arthur. *Modern Egypt: The Formation of a Nation State*. (Boulder, Colo., 2004).

MacLeod, Arlene. *Accommodating Protest: Working Women, the New Veiling, and Change in Cairo*. (New Haven, Conn., 1991).

Malek, Anouar Abdel. *Egypt: Military Society*. (New York, 1968).

Springborg, Robert. *Mubarak's Egypt*. (Boulder, Colo., 1989).

Timothy Mitchell

EISENHOWER, DWIGHT D.

(1890–1969). Born in Denison, Texas, on 14 October 1890, Dwight D. Eisenhower was the son of a railroad section hand. The family moved to Abilene, Kansas, in 1891; he grew up there and graduated from high school in 1911. He won an appointment to the US Military Academy at West Point, from which he graduated, and received a commission as a second lieutenant in the US Army. His army career was marked by slow, gradual promotion and high praise from his superiors, one of whom was General Douglas MacArthur.

In December 1941, Chief of Staff George C. Marshall brought Lieutenant Colonel Eisenhower to Washington, gave him a temporary promotion to major general, and put him in charge of the Operations Division of the War Department. In June 1942, Marshall sent Eisenhower to England to take command of the European Anglo-American invasion of North Africa. In May 1943, he forced the surrender of the German-Italian military units in Africa; in July, he commanded the Anglo-American invasion of Sicily; in September, forces under his command invaded Italy at Salerno. In December 1943, President Franklin Roosevelt selected him to command Operation Overlord, the invasion of German-occupied France at Normandy.

In June 1944, Eisenhower launched the assault. By late August, his troops had liberated France from the Germans. In December, his forces met and hurled back the last great German offensive of the war, in Belgium, known as the Battle of the Bulge. In March 1945, British, US, and Canadian troops crossed the Rhine River and overran Germany. On 7 May 1945, at his headquarters in Reims, France, Eisenhower presided over the unconditional surrender of Germany.

Eisenhower emerged from World War II as the most successful and famous general in the world. He was also immensely popular personally. A political career seemed natural and inevitable. In 1948, Democrats and Republicans alike wanted to nominate him for the presidency, but he declared that a professional soldier ought not get involved in partisan politics. He retired as chief of staff and took the position of president of Columbia University.

In 1951, at President Harry Truman's request, he left Columbia to become the first Supreme Allied Commander, Europe, a position that made him the head of the military arm of the North Atlantic Treaty Organization (NATO). The Republicans, desperate after losing five presidential elections in a row, were eager to nominate him in 1952. Party leaders convinced him that if he did not run, Senator Robert Taft would be the Republican nominee; Taft was an isolationist who had voted against NATO, and would pull the United States out of NATO if he became president. If the Democrats won, the leaders predicted it would be the end of the two-party system and the beginning of socialism in the United States. To avert such perceived potential calamities, Eisenhower reluctantly agreed to accept the nomination.

Eisenhower won a landslide victory over Democratic nominee Adlai Stevenson in 1952, and did so again when he ran for reelection in 1956. As president, he was extremely popular. Partly this was a result of his sunny disposition, his big grin, his "there's nothing to worry about" manner, and his ability to project himself as "just plain folks." Mainly, however, his popularity was a product of his policies. Eisenhower was a political conservative who always sought the middle of the road. His philosophy was that the extremes on any political debate were always wrong. He wanted a balanced budget, but not at the expense of the social programs created by the New Deal Democrats in the 1930s. He was a moderate on civil rights, willing to enforce the law as laid down by the Supreme Court in *Brown v. Board of*

Education of Topeka (1954), but unwilling to move aggressively to integrate the schools. He wanted to eliminate communist influence in the schools and in government, but was opposed to the methods used by Senator Joseph McCarthy.

Eisenhower greatly expanded the nation's infrastructure. More schools were built during his administration than any other (they were, admittedly, necessary because of the baby boom). The St. Lawrence Seaway was one of his achievements. His proudest boast was that he initiated and carried through the Interstate Highway System, the greatest public works project in history.

Eisenhower was a general who hated war. He ended the Korean War with an armistice six months after taking office, and entered no others, in a decade in which the Cold War was especially tense and dangerous. Nearly all his advisers wanted him to save the French position in Vietnam in 1954, but he refused to commit US troops to that conflict. War with China seemed all but certain on three occasions during his presidency, but he always managed to find a peaceful solution.

In 1955, he went to Geneva for a summit with Nikita Khrushchev—the first time a US president had met with a Soviet leader since the end of World War II—to establish a system of peaceful coexistence. Eisenhower held down the costs and dangers of the arms race through the 1950s in a particularly skilled and effective way. Both political parties demanded more defense spending—especially after the Soviets launched the first satellite, Sputnik, in 1957—but Eisenhower consistently held that building more weapons would not create more security, and that a balanced budget was more important than defense spending. Eisenhower was no reformer. Except for his appointment of Earl Warren as chief justice, black Americans had little to thank him for; neither did women, nor the poor. He opposed McCarthy's witch-hunting methods, but did almost nothing personally to stop the senator. Nor was he a risk-taker. The counterpoint to his success in achieving and maintaining peace was his failure to "roll back" communism in Central and Eastern Europe (as he had promised to do in the 1952 campaign), or to stop the spread of communism to Vietnam and Cuba. To his critics, he appeared to be a do-nothing president, content to "stand pat" and preside over a rich, happy, self-satisfied nation. He left his party vulnerable to Senator John F. Kennedy's 1960 presidential campaign charges that he had allowed the nation to "fall behind" the Soviets. Eisenhower gave the nation eight years of peace and prosperity, a claim no other president in the twentieth century could make. In 1961, he retired to his farm in Gettysburg, Pennsylvania. He died on 28 March 1969. He was survived by his wife Mamie and his son John.

[*See also* Cold War; Communism; Kennedy, John Fitzgerald; New Deal; Roosevelt, Franklin Delano; *and* Truman, Harry S.]

BIBLIOGRAPHY

Ambrose, Stephen E. *Eisenhower: Soldier and President.* (New York, 1990).
Eisenhower, Dwight D. *Crusade in Europe.* (Garden City, N.Y., 1948).
Eisenhower, Dwight D. *The White House Years.* 2 vols. (Garden City, N.Y., 1962–1963).

Stephen E. Ambrose

ELDERLY

See Gray Power.

ELECTIONS AND ELECTORAL BEHAVIOR

American presidential elections at the end of the twentieth century and the beginning of the twenty-first century produced some of the most unique races in US history. The 1990s saw the third-party candidate Ross Perot participating in debates, running a significant advertising campaign, and gathering millions of supporters to his cause on Election Day. The following decade also witnessed consequential third-party candidates—most notably Ralph Nader's run as a Green Party candidate in 2000—but the elections were more notable for their competitiveness. The Democrat Al Gore won more ballots

than the Republican George W. Bush in 2000, but he lost the Electoral College vote and therefore the presidency. The 2004 election was almost as competitive; President Bush won both the Electoral College and the nationwide popular vote, but by narrow margins. Even in the 2008 election, which seemed to be a "regular" election in that there were only two major candidates and no dispute over the winner, Americans took the historic step of electing the nation's first racial minority president.

Though these decades gave us truly unique elections, they also reveal persistent features of the American political system. For example, they show the centrality of the two major political parties in American elections. This is not to say that third parties have no impact, but they fall well short of winning elections and taking over the policy-making apparatus. Recent history also shows that the major political parties are not fixed points; in other words, they are capable of changing their positions over time. This is how George W. Bush can run as a "compassionate conservative" and add a massive prescription drug benefit plan to Medicare, while Barack Obama can take the position that the nation's largest financial institutions are too big to fail and spend billions ensuring their financial health.

How do we make sense of these competing forces of stasis and change? Why do some parts of American politics seem to be a permanent fixture in presidential campaigns while others not? This article touches on this question by examining several topics related to American presidential campaigns and elections. While the United States has a plethora of elected political offices at the national, state, and local levels, this article concentrates on the central components surrounding modern presidential elections. Important characteristics of the electoral system, research on voting behavior, and campaign dynamics are addressed in some detail.

Specifically, some thoughts on the institutional parameters surrounding American elections are provided. Next, some historical context is introduced to illustrate how elections are constitutionally established, and the evolutionary process that developed its procedures. Then, the current understanding of political behavior as it relates to voter turnout and voter choice is reviewed. Political scientists have spent a great deal of time analyzing the decision to go to the polls and the decision of whom to vote for. Both can be predicted, in part, based on an individual's social and demographic characteristic. The complex notion of modern campaigning is tackled. With the expenditures of the 2008 presidential contest totaling over a billion dollars, campaigns have a variety of options in how to allocate their resources and maximize their electoral chances of winning.

Institutional Environment. Americans have a penchant for representative democracy that permeates every level of government. In addition to the choice of president, Americans use elections to select Senators, members of the House of Representatives, an array of statewide officeholders, state legislators, and numerous local officials ranging from city council members and mayors to more specific functionaries such as school board members. With elections embedded at virtually every level of American social and political life, the basic ground rules for running elections play an important role in organizing these choices and avoiding the potential chaos so many decisions could create. It would be an overstatement to say that electoral rules have never changed in American history, but the principles underlying them have changed very little.

The most important institutions for understanding elections are the rules determining who can vote, and how ballots translate into who wins the office. In the original constitutional framework, voters only directly cast ballots for their member of Congress; other federal offices were determined through processes of indirect election. In the case of senators, these positions were originally filled by state legislatures, a practice that ended with passage of the Seventeenth Amendment in 1913. Presidential elections use the last remaining process of indirect election, the Electoral College, a system of choice whereby the president is selected by the states. Each state gets a number of votes equal to its representation in Congress (two senators plus the size of the congressional delegation, itself is determined by the population of the state). The candidates then compete for these state-level votes, with 270 out of 538 needed to win. Because all but two of the states distribute all of their Electoral College votes to the statewide winner, the popular vote victor can lose the Electoral College.

Also of note are the rules for determining winners of legislative elections. The United States has winner-take-all single-member districts in legislative elections, meaning only one candidate can win per legislative district or state. As first discussed by Maurice Duverger, these rules are key for explaining the structure of competition in elections. In the United States, unlike in a proportional representation system, the only parties that get any representation are those that win a plurality of the vote. Consequently, groups that might form electoral parties in democracies like France or Germany tend to support one of the two major parties rather than establishing their own. Though such rules do not prevent the evolution of multiple national parties with localized two-party competition, this is suppressed in the United States by its presidential system of government and nomination process.

Of interest is the fact that these elections are governed by national *and* state laws, even though they are all federal elections. Each state has its own procedures determining how candidates get on the primary and general election ballots. And though suffrage is protected by constitutional amendments (the Fifteenth, Nineteenth, Twenty-Fourth, and Twenty-Sixth) and Supreme Court cases (e.g., *Louisiana v. United States*, 1965; *South Carolina v. Katzenbach*, 1966) which ensure that most citizens aged eighteen and over are eligible to vote, there remain substantial differences between the states in how they register voters and count ballots. Candidate behavior during campaigns is governed by federal law, most notably campaign finance laws, though the restrictions do not stretch past national positions, leaving the majority of subnational elections covered by state laws.

A final note should be added here on what kind of participation is legitimate in America, and on what grounds. Two basic principles govern US elections: equality in voting and freedom of expression. Though it took the nation nearly two hundred years to remove most formal and informal barriers to voting rights, the guiding goal has always been the pursuit of equality, embodied by the principal of "one man, one vote." Inequities in voter registration still exist, but the general trend has been to reduce these barriers. Ironically, as much as equality has been the focus when it comes to voting, participatory inequality is protected elsewhere. As long as there have been elections, there have been concerns about unfair election practices (e.g., bribing voters) and the sale of political influence (e.g., bribing candidates). Even though national, state, and local laws try to limit such situations, some Americans wield substantially more influence than their fellow citizens on the basis of differences in wealth. Such differences inevitably crop up in campaigns, which are for the most part privately financed and frequently expensive. This means that a multimillionaire who is willing to give money to candidates for office can potentially have more influence over policymakers than regular voters. Such behavior is legal, and yet can potentially limit electoral competition, contribute to low electoral turnover, and affect the attention given to particular issues. The underlying justification for these actions is that spending money in politics is a form of free speech and thus an allowable form of inequality.

Voting Behavior: Turnout. Other developed democracies like Italy, Sweden, and Germany frequently experience voter turnout levels of over 70 percent, but this has not occurred in the United States since 1900. During the 1990s, US turnout levels during presidential elections were around 50 to 55 percent, although this moved closer to 60 percent in 2004 and 2008. Much of this difference can be attributed to the fact that voting is a two-step process in the United States. Potential voters must first register to vote—usually in a specific place and in advance of elections—and only then are they eligible to exercise their right to vote. The process of registering can be seen as a barrier to voting, but also seen as necessary for preventing electoral fraud. According to the US Census Bureau, registered voters turned out at a rate close to 90 percent in 2008, but registering to

vote remains a "hurdle" that many citizens see as more effort than the act of voting itself.

America's comparatively low voter turnout is an issue that has been tackled by both public officials in Washington and legislative bodies in individual states. The Constitution outlined major expansions on who may vote when it allowed African American men to vote with the passage of the Fifteenth Amendment in 1870, and then women, with the passage of the Nineteenth Amendment in 1920. Further protections to minorities were instilled with the Civil Rights Act of 1964 and the Voting Rights Act of 1965. More recently, the federal government has taken steps to increase voter turnout by easing the voter registration process, such as by allowing citizens to register when they renew their driver's license. It remains unclear, however, whether such efforts actually increase turnout levels.

Beyond federal government activity, some specific policy proposals adopted in states demonstrate noteworthy effects on voter turnout. First, states that allow same-day registration are also states that rank at the top in voter turnout levels. Same-day registration laws allow citizens to register to vote at the polling facility the day of the election. States will require different forms of identification, such as proof of address, and some states require voters to register with a political party. Voter turnout averages from the 1996 to 2008 presidential elections see a turnout increase of 9 to 11 percent in those states with same-day registration. Minnesota, one such state with same-day registration, typically ranks as having the highest turnout rates in the nation, with over 70 percent of the voting-age population showing up at the polls in many of the recent presidential elections.

The second advantageous policy is early voting. Early voting can take several forms, such as voting early via mail (as opposed to absentee ballots, which are submitted by voters who are unable to make it to the polling place on Election Day). In other states, voters can simply visit their county clerk's office and vote weeks before Election Day. Excuses such as work commitments or traveling are occasionally required for such actions, but states are increasingly moving to "no excuse" early voting. Political scientists are still debating the effects of early voting, but in recent presidential elections a marginal increase in voter turnout can be seen in early voting states.

While there is a trend toward making voting easier, some state policies to prevent voter fraud may deter voters from the polls. Specifically, some states are adopting laws requiring government-issued photo identification cards to vote. In South Carolina, one of the states with such a law, the *Sun-News* reported that around 178,000 registered voters did not have a government-issued photo identification card at the time of the law's passage. This equates to over 6 percent of the state's electorate and is expected to disenfranchise older and poorer voters.

The decision to vote versus the decision to "stay home" is usually described in academia as a form of rational behavior. Voting can be seen as irrational behavior because the only "benefit" to voting is that you may change the outcome of the election. This probability is so near zero that it is never taken as a serious explanation for why someone votes. That means the "costs" of voting outweighs the "benefits" of voting. The costs of voting are typically identified as (1) registering to vote, (2) learning who to vote for, and (3) physically appearing at the polling facility on Election Day. The fact that many Americans do vote, and it is perceived to be irrational, produced a paradox for rational choice theorists, who now argue that participation stems from a sense of a civic duty.

Another point on voter turnout should be made in association with presidential campaigns and mobilization efforts. Political pundits emphasize a political party's "enthusiasm gap" during electoral seasons. However, the reason why voters of one party are more "enthused" about their candidates over the voters of another party is a discussion that political pundits fail to fully address. Perhaps such enthusiasm is exogenous to the candidates and the party organization. Indeed, electoral scholars hypothesize that (1) salient issues of the day activate certain blocs of voters, and (2) the political party out of power gets an enthusiasm boost from the public

because of their desire to alter Washington's political makeup. On the other hand, greater enthusiasm for a candidate may be the result of mobilization efforts conducted by the parties and the campaigns to maximize turnout by their strongest supporters. Campaign advertisements, candidate events, and other forms of increased campaign intensity are perceptually believed to have persuasive effects while mobilization is more often ignored, but likely holds greater campaign effects.

As the United States becomes more diverse, and minority populations steadily rise, election observers become increasingly more interested in who votes in American elections. The importance of who votes is quite simple to grasp: if political representation from government officials is beholden to voters and elections, then equal representation of society and its political values is most likely to occur when all sects of voters are participating. If, however, certain sects of voters—such as poor people, Hispanics, Native Americans, or young people—are not participating in the electoral process, then their political interests are less likely to be tended to from the government's elected leaders. While ideally the United States would have experienced voter turnout levels equally distributed across race, religion, gender, age, education, and income, this has not been the case. Hispanics, the fastest growing minority group in the United States, had 47 percent turnout in 2004 and 50 percent turnout in 2008. By comparison, the US Census Bureau measures voting-age whites and African Americans as generally going to the polls at over 60 percent in recent presidential election years. Education levels, another powerful predictor of turnout, consistently show college graduates voting at ten to twenty points higher than those with only a high school diploma or less.

Voting Behavior: Choice. By far the most important factor in understanding voter choices is partisan identification. As originally conceptualized, this refers to how closely an individual identifies with the two major political parties. The typical seven-point measure used by academics includes the *direction* of identification (Democratic, Republican, or Independent) as well as the *strength* of that identification (strong identifier, weak identifier, or an Independent who leans toward a party). These identities tend to be very stable within a person's lifetime and are strongly embedded in a person's race, class, gender, region, family, and other sociodemographic traits.

The strength of this partisan stability is clearly illustrated by data from the American National Election Studies (ANES), a nationally representative sample survey of Americans that has been administrated since 1948. Beginning in 1952, when the survey first asked about partisan identification, the percentage of Americans harboring at least some partisan leanings has been remarkably steady. Since that time, the percentage of voters claiming to be Democrats has been over 60 percent once and under 50 percent four times in all the congressional and presidential elections surveyed since 1952. Likewise, the percentage of Republican identifiers has never been lower than 30 percent and has only been over 40 percent four times. Another display of stability in party coalitions can be seen when partisan identification is broken down by an individual's social and demographic characteristics. Over 80 percent of Africans Americans consistently vote for Democratic presidential candidates, and since 2000, white men have been voting for Republican presidential candidates at around 60 percent. Income is another reliable predictor of presidential candidate preference, in that the wealthier one is, the more likely one is to vote Republican. For instance, only 28 percent of those wealthiest Americans (within the 96th percentile of family income) voted for Barack Obama in 2008. Even though these are some of the most dynamic elections in American history, there was a remarkable amount of partisan stability.

How we can have electoral change in a system with such stability in underlying predispositions? One possibility is that partisanship may not predict voting behavior. Unlike the strong parties seen in other developed democracies, American parties do not have membership requirements, dues, or responsibilities that tie citizens to them very closely. However, a closer look at the evidence provided by the ANES shows American partisans remain loyal at the ballot box. In the last three decades, Democratic

identifiers have voted for their presidential candidate no less than 72 percent of the time (1984) and frequently at a rate as high as 91 percent (1992, 2004, 2008). Republican identifiers during that same period have supported their candidate no less than 84 percent of the time (1996) and as high as 95 percent (1984).

Nevertheless, evidence shows that parties must increasingly work harder for this support. First, there has been a rise in split-ticket voting, where voters cast their presidential ballot for one party and their legislative ballot for another. Some debate exists about whether this reflects the lack of competition in many legislative races or a citizen preference for divided government, but what is important is that voters show a willingness to support candidates from other parties even when they have partisan loyalties. Second, there has been a decline in the strength of partisan loyalties. While the number of hardcore partisans has not changed much, there has been an increase in the number of people who only weakly identify with or lean toward a party. These voters may still be fairly partisan in many ways, but there remains evidence that their votes can be clearly affected by the issues of the specific election.

As important as party identification is in understanding American elections, it cannot provide a complete explanation for how voters make choices. Most remaining research on this subject focuses on the role of political issues. In contrast to the concept of party identification, the idea of issue voting is not supposed to be reflexive. Here the classic work is Anthony Downs's book *An Economic Theory of Democracy* (1957), where he argues that (among other things) voting behavior can be best understood as a function of benefits and votes. The principal benefit of voting in Downs's treatment derived from the issue positions of candidates/parties and voters. He started with the assumption that each voter, V, had an "ideal" policy that would maximize their personal utility. Candidates would then offer voters a choice of policies represented by their own ideal points, Ci and Cj. The voter would then compare these positions, $|V\text{-}Ci|$ and $|V\text{-}Cj|$, to his or her own to determine which one was closer, such that if $|V\text{-}Ci|>|V\text{-}Cj|$

then V chooses Ci and, if $|V\text{-}Ci|<|V\text{-}Cj|$ then V chooses Cj.

In addition to benefits, however, Downs explicitly acknowledged the importance of costs in his model. These are incorporated through the idea of information, which he argued was scarce in politics precisely because people had little incentive to gather it. These information costs create uncertainty for voters in a variety of ways, such as the actual policies of candidates and which ones will benefit the voters.

In this Downsian world, the lack of certainty among voters trying to maximize their own interests has a number of theoretical consequences. First, parties and candidates should build an ideological brand that will help simplify vote choices. It is rational, in this view, for individuals to base their votes not on specific positions but on the basis of reputations. Second, voters should be *retrospective* rather than *prospective*, meaning voters should not believe promises, but rather evaluate past performance, because it provides more reliable information to voters. Finally, Downs's model expects voters to be generally uninformed about politics, particularly when it comes to specific facts about policy. Such predictions are supported in the empirical literature. Although there is ideological heterogeneity *within* the parties, there are clear and persistent ideological differences *between* the parties. Importantly, voters clearly respond to those ideologies, even when the voters themselves do not exhibit the traits of ideological thinking themselves. Voters often have backward-looking criteria for evaluating candidates, with voters punishing unpopular incumbents and voting for change when the economy is unfavorable. And, by nearly any standard, the average voter is uninformed about basic political facts and salient political affairs.

Despite such limitations, other evidence shows that issues still play a key role in the choices made by voters. Though voters are not political experts, they have adapted in ways that allow them to make reasonable decisions in the face of complicated information flows. Citizens can use some mix of personal and social political conditions to make voting decisions, such as punishing incumbent parties when the economy is not sound. They can evaluate whether a presidential candidate is on the "right side" of an issue rather than the more complicated judgment of which candidate is "closest" to being right. And, of course, voters belong to different social groupings based on gender, race, age, and other social categories that can help them prioritize particular issues and connect them with candidates.

The contrast between reflexive, partisan voters and rational, issue-driven voters raises a host of new questions about voting behavior in US presidential elections. It remains clear that American voters are not rational thinkers in elections, but nor are they unthinking automatons. A more realistic view is that they are reasoning voters, who think about their choices when necessary, are uncertain about politics, and use a variety of psychological shortcuts for "filling in the blanks." This has led to a great deal of interest in how voters use information. One conclusion is that American voters are less like filing clerks, who keep information stored away for later reference, than they are online thinkers who have emotional, continuously changing impressions of candidates. Another conclusion is that voters can use heuristics (think of them as information shortcuts) as substitutes for the "hard information" that they lack. Research shows that voters use candidate traits such as likability, partisanship, and social characteristics to make educated guesses as to which candidate might be best for them.

Presidential Campaigns. Where do campaigns fit in? Conventional wisdom holds that campaigns ought to be persuasive, using any means necessary to convince voters that Candidate A is better than Candidate B. Take campaign commercials, for example; cable and network television is now so overloaded with them during a presidential election year that public exhaustion and overload is a very real possibility. Television ads are not cheap and perhaps the money could be better spent elsewhere. Do campaigns really think that voters will suddenly change their minds and vote for the other candidate based on seeing a television advertisement? No, but they do hope it will affect a small subset of independent-minded voters and impassion their party base.

Electoral studies since the 1960s have been dominated by the minimal effects hypothesis, which suggests that campaigns generally do little more than activate political predilections. This does not mean that campaigns are inconsequential. Even if only a small slice of voters are persuadable, that is still enough to change election outcomes. Thus, these persuadable voters are vital to campaigns because electoral outcomes are often determined by just a few percentage points. Those campaign events that consistently appear to have an effect on candidate support include party conventions, debate victories, and campaign appearances. Of course, scandals and blunders, both big and small, have a negative effect on candidate support.

Take the 2004 presidential election as an example of how campaigns can influence the electorate. Campaign poll numbers from the National Annenberg Election Survey during the weeks of July and early August had the Democratic challenger John Kerry leading the race, reaching a high point of 53 percent just days after the Democratic National Convention ended on 29 July. In late July electoral support for George W. Bush was at its lowest; less than 40 percent of the poll's sampled population stated they would vote for him. To little surprise, Bush also received a bump in the polls after the Republican National Convention ended on 2 September. Indeed, the GOP convention was the campaign spark Bush needed to surpass Kerry's poll numbers, and he held onto the slightest of leads (1.5 to 6 percent) through Election Day. This lead remained steady even after the public and pundits alike agreed that Kerry outperformed Bush in the debates in late September and mid-October.

It would be remiss to not recognize the important role that media communications now play in presidential campaigns. All together, the Federal Election Commission (FEC) calculates that media-related costs for the 2008 presidential election topped out at over $711 million. This total not only includes television advertising, but other forms of advertising (e.g., online, print, radio, etc.), production costs, and contracts with corporate consultants. Campaigns view media communications as critical to their success

because, in part, the media allows a candidate's campaign messages to be conveyed to voters. Modern presidential campaigns target swing states, allocating millions of dollars to certain geographic markets for media buys in order to maximize electoral payoffs. Campaigns must strategically use their funds, targeting ads in those "battleground" states, while ignoring those states where poll numbers show they are either strongly ahead or far behind.

Overall, each presidential campaign must establish a core set of issues to run on, and the political environment may call for different emphases regarding this messaging. After all, a poor economy may call for presidential candidates to concentrate on job creation and other recession-busting ideas, while major military conflicts abroad may call for candidates to concentrate on defense-related issues. Campaign messages vary from election to election. For instance, it should be of no surprise that Jimmy Carter won the 1976 election based on his Washington outsider persona, just a few short years after Richard Nixon's resignation. Those who followed the 1988 election closely recognized that George H. W. Bush was able, early on in the race, to frame the relatively unknown Michael Dukakis as soft on crime and defense. Four years later Bill Clinton was out in front of the economic issues of the day, and made sure voters knew that. George W. Bush ran his 2004 reelection campaign on national security concerns, and a conservative interest group ran the infamous "Swift Boat Veterans for Truth" ads against John Kerry to discredit his military background and leadership potential. These examples exemplify that presidential candidates want to (a) create a positive issue content area for themselves, and (b) create a negative content area for their opponents. Both must resonant with voters. While the party base is generally not persuaded by such campaign tactics, those certain few persuadable voters are listening.

Conclusion. Underlying this overview of presidential elections in the United States are decades of research attempting to understand the role campaigns play in connecting political candidates to citizens. Though there are broad areas of agreement, there are also significant differences on important issues. One approach to understanding today's electoral environment focuses on the nature of political conflict that underlies the US political system, particularly as it relates to voters and candidates. A lasting impact of the last few presidential elections, as well as the intervening midterm elections and legislative sessions, has been the highlighting of what seems to be a new era of hyper-partisanship among the elites and its roots in the electoral system. Another area of particular importance is whether rising levels of economic inequality pose a threat to the political system. As noted earlier, unequal participation with money is tolerated. But new questions are being raised about the political sources of economic inequality and its potential for disempowering voters in the United States. Finally, there are serious questions being raised about the nature of communications in campaigns. These concerns revolve around the potential lack of deliberation, the implications of new and nontraditional media for engaging or disengaging voters, and the seeming pervasiveness of information in some venues that is entirely absent elsewhere.

[*See also* Political Parties, American.]

BIBLIOGRAPHY

Bartels, Larry M. *Unequal Democracy: The Political Economy of the New Gilded Age.* (Princeton, N.J., 2010).

Downs, Anthony. *An Economic Theory of Democracy.* (New York, 1957).

Duverger, Maurice. *Political Parties: Their Organization and Activity in the Modern State.* (Paris, 1954.)

Louisiana v. United States, 380 US 145 (1965).

Masket, Seth E. *No Middle Ground: How Informal Party Organizations Control Nominations and Polarize Legislatures.* (Ann Arbor, Mich., 2009).

Patterson, Thomas E. *The Vanishing Voter: Public Involvement in an Age of Uncertainty.* (New York, 2003).

Shaw, Daron R. *The Race to 270: The Electoral College and the Campaign Strategies of 2000 and 2004.* (Chicago, 2006).

Solt, Fredrick. "Does Economic Inequality Depress Electoral Participation? Testing the Schattschneider Hypothesis." *Political Behavior* 32, no. 2 (2010): 285–301.

South Carolina v. Katzenbach, 383 US 301 (1966).

Scott D. McClurg and Matthew L. Bergbower

EMERGENCY POWERS

At some point, every country will face a crisis or threat that calls upon the government to exercise extraordinary powers. These "emergency powers," or governmental powers exercised outside the normal channels and means of government, are the subject of substantial controversy. The question that always must be asked is, "Does the Constitution have the tools within to save itself?" That is, does the exercise of emergency powers represent the exercise of a constitutional authority, or will the exercise of emergency powers sometimes require the government to go outside the Constitution? Furthermore, what are the limits of these extraordinary powers, even in the most extraordinary times?

Over the last 250 years, the courts have established a relatively coherent view of the exercise of emergency powers. The general principle that the courts seem to follow is that in an emergency, the government can do whatever is necessary to protect itself and the nation, as long as the regular processes of government are not available and those emergency actions are subject to review. Thus, in an emergency, the government can engage in activities that range anywhere from the seizure of property, to indefinite terms of detention, to trial for capital offenses by military tribunal.

While there were several minor controversies in the earliest days of the nation in regards to the exercise of emergency powers, the most important and pivotal expansion of such powers occurred in the first few months of the Civil War. When the Confederates fired on Fort Sumter, Congress was out of session. President Abraham Lincoln, on his own authority, ordered the blockade of southern ports, the purchase of armaments, the seizure of property, interception of the mails, and the indefinite detention of suspected spies.

Lincoln's authority was challenged in the courts with the most important decision made in the *Prize Cases* (1862), when the owners of a number of vessels seized by the US Navy sued in court for the return of their property. The plaintiffs argued that their ships were seized illegally inasmuch as there had been no formal declaration of war, and therefore the president had exceeded his powers as commander in chief. But the Supreme Court declared that at the time of the seizures a state of insurrection did exist. Consequently, the president acted properly in suppressing the revolt, whether or not Congress had approved the action. Furthermore, since Congress did endorse Lincoln's actions after the fact, post hoc approval by Congress conferred retroactive legal authority for the president to act.

The Civil War created a number of controversies concerning the civil liberties of civilians and combatants. One of the most important cases in that regard involved a Confederate spy arrested in Indiana. The defendant had been tried before a special military tribunal and sentenced to death. On appeal, the Supreme Court ruled that because Indiana was not a war zone and the defendant not a combatant, the federal government had no right to try a civilian in a military court; the operative principle here being that if the civilian courts were available they should be utilized (*Ex parte Milligan*, 1866).

World War II again occasioned extensive exercise of emergency powers, and the courts were often asked to rule on the legality of such actions. Particularly notable were a series of decisions that validated the activities of the government in sanctioning everything from special military tribunals for captured spies (*Ex parte Quirin*, 1942) to the wholesale transport of a group of people, many of whom were American citizens, to internment camps (*Korematsu v. United States*, 1944). What is telling is the Court's relatively consistent reliance on exigency as a justification for extraordinary measures. Perhaps one of the most clear-cut examples of this type of logic was outlined by the Court when, in 1946, landlords sued to lift wartime rent controls. In *Woods v. Cloyd W. Miller Co.* (1948), the Court ruled that because economic conditions occasioned by the war still existed, even though the fighting was over, the government still had the power to impose wartime regulations.

In 1952, at the beginning of the Korean War, President Truman ordered the government seizure of several American steel mills to avert a steelworkers'

strike. The owners sued and the Supreme Court ordered the steel mills returned; Truman complied. Many analysts cite *Youngstown Sheet & Tube Co. v. Sawyer* (1952) as a rare example of the Court imposing limits on the president's emergency powers. But it can also be argued that this decision is consistent with precedent. As it turns out, when the president seized the mills, he sided with the steelworkers in their dispute against the owners. Because the only legal authority he had at his disposal at the time to intervene in a labor dispute was the Taft-Hartley Act—a law passed over his veto a few months before, a law that did not allow him to intervene on the side of the workers—Truman may have simply been using the war as an excuse to intervene on behalf of the unions in a labor dispute. The Court certainly saw it that way. Thus, *Youngstown* is consistent with the principle that emergency powers are only justified when no other action can be taken.

Indeed, during the Civil War and World War II, arguably the most serious crises in American history, national elections were held in 1864 and 1944 (even while elections were suspended in Britain for the duration of World War II). Only when the government could prove otherwise, was the regular exercise of authority circumvented. In retrospect, then, even the Court's decision in *Korematsu,* while an embarrassment, was understandable given the possibility of imminent attack.

More recently, in the aftermath of the terrorist attack on the World Trade Center in 2001, the administration of President George W. Bush tried several times to exercise extraordinary powers. However, while slow to act, the signal expression of the Court's rejection of the Bush administration's claim to expansive powers came in the *Hamdan v. Rumsfeld* (2006) decision. In that case the Court ruled that the military commissions authorized by Congress and operated by the Bush Administration to try Guantanamo detainees were illegal under the Geneva Convention. Furthermore, in dismissing the administration's pleadings, the Court granted itself jurisdiction in the case. The "War on Terror," it seemed, was not enough of a crisis to prevent the regular administration of justice.

Emergency powers, then, are those powers exercised by the government when there is no alternative. What makes them constitutional is a demonstrable claim that the emergency is genuine and that the regular channels of government are not available. The government's actions in such an instance are not wrong until judged so by a court of law. However, once ordered to comply, suspend, or compensate, the government must obey a Court's decision. Furthermore, any of the other regular processes of government, such as elections, must continue unobstructed unless the government can provide a verifiable excuse for suspension.

BIBLIOGRAPHY

Corwin, Edward Samuel. *Total War and the Constitution: Five Lectures Delivered at the University of Michigan, March 1946*. (New York, 1947).

Ex parte Milligan, 71 US 2 (1866).

Ex parte Quirin, 317 US 1 (1942).

Fisher, Louis. *Presidential War Power*. 2d rev. ed. (Lawrence, Kans., 2004).

Franklin, Daniel P. *Extraordinary Measures: The Exercise of Prerogative Powers in the United States*. (Pittsburgh, Pa., 1991).

Genovese, Michael A. "Democratic Theory and the Emergency Powers of the President." *Presidential Studies Quarterly* 9 (Summer 1979): 283–289.

Hamdan v. Rumsfeld, 548 US 557 (2006).

Henkin, Louis. *Constitutionalism, Democracy, and Foreign Affairs*. (New York, 1990).

Koenig, Louis William. *The Presidency and the Crisis: Powers of the Office from the Invasion of Poland to Pearl Harbor*. (New York, 1944).

Korematsu v. United States, 323 US 214 (1944).

Prize Cases, 67 US 635 (1863).

Rossiter, Clinton Lawrence. *Constitutional Dictatorship*. (New York, 1963).

Smith, Jean Edward. *The Constitution and American Foreign Policy*. (St. Paul, Minn., 1989).

Woods v. Cloyd W. Miller Co., 333 US 138 (1948).

Youngstown Sheet & Tube Co. v. Sawyer, 343 US 579 (1952).

Daniel P. Franklin

EMINENT DOMAIN

"Eminent domain" refers to a government's power to take possession of private property for public use. In the United States, the Just Compensation Clause (also known as the Takings Clause) of the Fifth Amendment, and equivalent provisions in state constitutions, require that governments must pay the fair market value of private property taken through eminent domain proceedings. Considered an inherent power of government, the right to take property for public use is not specified in the federal or most state constitutions. However, the principle that governments have the power to take private property but must pay "just compensation" has long been a part of the common law. In *Calder v. Bull* (1798), Justice Samuel Chase stated that "the very nature of our free Republican governments" placed limits on government authority, such as the basic proposition that "a law that takes property from A and gives it to B" is void.

"Condemnation" is the usual term for the process by which a government institutes the exercise of eminent domain. The measure of "just compensation" is the fair market value of the property, a value which property owners can challenge in judicial proceedings. Once the fair market value has been finally determined and paid, the government assumes complete domain over the property, including the ability to evict homeowners from their residence.

Two issues are of central concern in modern debates about eminent domain: first, whether government actions that lessen the fair market value of property without any physical appropriation should be compensated as a "taking" (the so-called regulatory takings issue); and second, whether the "public use" limitation means that governments may not take private property for assignment to developers for other private uses.

Regulatory Takings. The "police power" refers to a state government's authority to protect the health, welfare, and safety of its citizens through legislation designed to restrict certain conduct. Most state and local laws regulating use of property, including zoning ordinances, are justified as an exercise of this power. The extent to which an exercise of the police power unconstitutionally deprives an owner of a property right is a central debate in modern takings law.

Government regulation of private property that deprives an owner of substantial value of the property may rise to the level of a "regulatory taking," requiring compensation under the Takings Clause even though no physical invasion or transfer of property to the government has occurred. The regulatory takings doctrine generally balances the public interest in, and need for, the regulation against the decline or impairment of value to an individual's property. Regulatory takings are determined on an ad hoc, case-by-case basis, with two exceptions: If the regulation results in a permanent physical invasion of one's land, or if the regulation deprives a land owner of "all economically viable use" of the land, a court will likely find that a taking has occurred without the need to balance the government's asserted need for the regulation. The regulatory takings doctrine is based on the view that the Takings Clause requires courts to consider whether the public at large, rather than a single owner, must bear the burden of an exercise of state power in the public interest.

"Inverse condemnation" is the technical term for a claim that a government's property use restriction is a "regulatory taking." The phrase "inverse condemnation" generally describes a cause of action against a defendant in which a land owner may recover just compensation for a "taking" of his property under the Fifth Amendment, even though the formal condemnation proceedings in exercise of the sovereign's power of eminent domain have not been instituted by the government entity.

In *Penn Central Transportation Co. v. City of New York* (1978), the US Supreme Court held that a city ordinance that prevented modification of a designated historic structure did not constitute a taking of private property. Although the Court upheld the city's historic preservation law as applied in this instance, the Court indicated that a regulation designed to preserve historic structures could result in a compensable taking in other situations. The Court identified three factors for determining whether a taking has occurred: the nature of the governmental action; the regulation's economic impact on the property owner; and the extent to which the regulation interfered with "distinct, investment-backed expectations." These three factors continue to form the standard inquiry in most regulatory takings claims.

Public Use. In *Hawaii Housing Authority v. Midkiff* (1984), the Court held that the requirement of a "public use" in eminent domain cases is quite broad, stating that if the state's use of its eminent domain power is "rationally related to a legitimate state purpose," the public use requirement is satisfied. Historical circumstances in the state of Hawaii had led to a concentration of private property in the hands of a small number of landowners. In an attempt to lessen the disparity, the state used its eminent domain power to purchase land from large landowners and sell the lots to the tenants living on them. Upholding the plan, the Court pointed to the fact that the state's strategy was a rational attempt to remedy a social and economic ill.

The "public use" requirement received prominent attention in the United States as a result of the Supreme Court's decision in *Kelo v. City of New London* (2005). The city of New London, Connecticut, instituted eminent domain proceedings in a residential area in favor of a comprehensive economic development plan it hoped would create a substantial number of jobs and increase tax revenue. The development corporation was a private entity. In a 5–4 decision, the Supreme Court upheld the city's actions, stating that the "public purpose" of economic development, even in private hands, could satisfy the "public use" restriction in the US Constitution.

Although the decision was consistent with prior Supreme Court cases, it was widely criticized on the ground that local governments may be subject to political "capture" in favor of private developers. As one justice noted in dissent, "Any property may now be taken for the benefit of another private party, but the fallout from this decision will not be random. The beneficiaries are likely to be those citizens with disproportionate influence and power in the political process, including large corporations and development firms."

After the *Kelo* decision, forty-two states enacted legislation limiting local government exercise of eminent domain for economic development, severely limiting potential transfers of private property to other private entities.

[*See also* Deregulation; *and* Regulation.]

BIBLIOGRAPHY

Calder v. Bull, 3 US 386 (1798).

Ely, James W. *The Guardian of Every Other Right: A Constitutional History of Property Rights.* 3d. ed. (New York, 2008).

Epstein, Richard Allen. *Supreme Neglect: How to Revive Constitutional Protection for Private Property.* (New York, 2008).

Hawaii Housing Authority v. Midkiff, 467 US 229 (1984).

Kelo v. City of New London, 545 US 469 (2005)

Paul, Ellen Frankel. *Property Rights and Eminent Domain.* (New Brunswick, N.J., 2008).

Penn Central Transportation Co. v. City of New York, 438 US 104 (1978).

Price, Polly J. *Property Rights: Rights and Liberties under the Law.* (Santa Barbara, Calif., 2003).

Polly J. Price

EMPLOYMENT AND UNEMPLOYMENT

After a slow start, the US economic recovery from the recession of the early 1990s generated job growth so strong that unemployment fell to its lowest rate in thirty years, and economic observers began referring to the "great American jobs machine." Other advanced countries were urged to emulate what many claimed was the root of this American success in job creation: more competitive labor (and to a lesser degree, product) markets.

This success in generating overall employment growth in the late 1990s also drowned out criticisms from those worried about the rising US trade deficit and its mirror image, a rise in financial savings leaving the poorer developing world and being sent to the richer United States (a direction of savings flows that is directly opposite of what textbook macroeconomics would predict, as capital is assumed to be scarce and its return large in poorer countries). These rising trade deficits displaced jobs from American tradable goods sectors (mostly manufacturing), but the inward flow of global savings lowered interest rates, and hence boosted jobs in interest-sensitive industries (mostly construction of residential housing). But because economy-wide job growth remained strong, the sectoral problems of

manufacturing were often characterized as irrelevant to the overall health of the economy.

While many pointed to investments in information technology or policies that reduced the federal budget deficit as primary reasons for the strong job growth of the 1990s, a simpler explanation for extraordinarily fast economic and job growth—which explains both overall employment strength as well as large trade deficits—was the stock market bubble which boosted consumer spending to post–World War II highs (supporting jobs) while also leading to falling personal savings rates that more than offset the swing toward federal budget surpluses (which led to trade deficits, as reduced domestic saving necessitated borrowing from abroad). In short, a rise in aggregate demand that was not preemptively choked off by the Federal Reserve, and not market flexibility, could account for the rapid job growth during the late 1990s.

This explanation was bolstered as the business cycle spanning 2001 to 2007 (which followed the bursting of the stock market bubble) saw the "great American jobs machine" begin sputtering badly. Even with another asset market bubble (housing, this time), which boosted consumption and lowered savings rates, the decline in demand spurred by rising trade deficits and falling business investment did not allow job growth at anywhere near the pace that characterized the 1990s. Employment growth from the 2001 peak of economic activity to the 2007 peak was the worst since World War II: payroll employment rose just 0.6 percent per year during this cycle, only one-third as fast as the rate that characterized the previous business cycle.

Then, 8.7 million jobs—over 6 percent of the entire workforce—were lost between December 2007 and February 2010. Unemployment averaged 4.5 percent for the first half of 2007, and by December of that year (the last month before the start of the recession) stood at 5 percent. By October 2009 it had more than doubled, reaching 10.1 percent. And even two full years after the official start of the recovery from the Great Recession (dated June 2009), there remained 6.9 million fewer jobs in the US economy than existed before the recession began, and the unemployment rate stood at 9.2 percent. This is a scale and length of job loss that dwarfs any that had occurred since the Great Depression.

Most economic forecasters, both public and private, did not expect the year-round unemployment rate to return to its prerecession levels until 2016. Notably, these forecasts were made before a sharp deceleration in economic growth in the first quarter of 2011. Further, these forecasts were also made before it became likely that short-term cuts to government spending were going to be made as concessions to increase the debt ceiling of the United States in the summer of 2011. Such cuts will place a drag on growth going forward and could delay (perhaps substantially) the eventual return to prerecession unemployment rates.

The eventual trajectory of overall economic growth and, by extension, unemployment, has far-reaching political consequences as well. It is widely thought among political scientists that one of the most powerful predictors of electoral success for incumbents is the recent (i.e., one year) *change* in economic conditions prior to the election. Perhaps surprisingly, these same researchers argue that the simple *level* of the unemployment rate in the period of time right before the election is largely incidental to its outcome (once the change is accounted for). That said, it was quite likely that most of the presidential election season of 2012 would take place against the backdrop of an unemployment rate over 8 percent. No president since Franklin Delano Roosevelt has been elected with an unemployment rate over 7.4 percent in the quarter prior to Election Day.

The political salience of the unemployment rate means that many ideas have been put forward to explain its movement, and numerous policy proposals offered to reduce it more quickly. In the aftermath of the Great Recession, two perennially competing explanations for stubbornly high unemployment— structural (or Classical) versus cyclical (or Keynesian)— have again been jostling for primacy. During the 1990s, structural explanations for American success in generating jobs generally held sway. In a sense, the structural versus cyclical argument about the

aftermath of the Great Recession is a continuation of a debate that has been ongoing for decades.

The structural argument for stubbornly high unemployment in the aftermath of the Great Recession is that jobs lost due to the bursting housing bubble (which are generally characterized as construction jobs) required a different set of skills than those required in the post-bubble economy. This "skills mismatch" was what was keeping unemployed workers from finding jobs. The primary piece of evidence cited in favor of the structural argument is an outward shift in the "Beveridge curve," which is a relation charting the unemployment rate versus the job-vacancy rate. An outward shift in this curve means that there are more unemployed workers for every level of vacancies, which could suggest a less efficient movement of people out of unemployment and into open positions.

The cyclical argument is simply that overall employment and unemployment over short time periods is driven by the level of aggregate demand for new spending in the economy. The bursting of the housing bubble of the early years of the twenty-first century led to sharp reductions in this aggregate demand, as households and businesses found themselves much less wealthy and with fewer customers, leading to less spending and investment. This reduction in spending led to layoffs and rising unemployment. A primary piece of evidence cited in favor of this explanation was simply the ratio of job seekers to job openings. In 2007 there were 1.6 unemployed workers for each job vacancy. At the peak of the recession this ratio was 6.9 to 1, while even two years into the official economic recovery in June 2011 it remained at 4.6 to 1. Both arguments as to the sources of rising unemployment have corollaries as to what can reverse this rise. The trajectory of employment and unemployment in coming years will be determined in large part by whether or not the right cause and remedy of unemployment is identified and enacted by policymakers.

The remedy for structural unemployment concerns policies that make it easier to move the jobless into vacancies. These policies can include retraining to match the skills of jobless workers and vacancies more easily. They can even include cutting the duration or generosity of unemployment insurance, as unemployment benefits may be keeping jobless workers from accepting new employment in the vacant positions available in the economy.

The remedy for cyclical unemployment instead focuses on increasing aggregate demand, that is, boosting the spending of households, businesses, and governments. These policies include interventions by the Federal Reserve to encourage spending by attempting to lower economy-wide interest rates, as well as fiscal policies that either increase government spending directly or transfer money to households or businesses in an attempt to boost their spending. And in the case of unemployment benefits, the cyclical diagnosis would argue that extending the duration of unemployment benefits, or increasing the amount of those benefits, would, by supporting spending by private households, improve the unemployment situation, not worsen it.

As of spring 2011, any consensus as to the causes and preferred remedies for high US unemployment across political parties had broken down, and coming years looked to be plagued by this relative indecision. Republicans were nearly unanimous in rejecting the diagnosis that insufficient aggregate demand is the root cause of today's high unemployment, which made continuing an aggressive Keynesian policy response after the American Recovery and Reinvestment Act of 2009 particularly difficult. While the Obama administration secured more fiscal support in December 2010 by agreeing to an extension of the Bush-era tax cuts for richer households, it also agreed to significant spending cuts in order to pass the 2011 budget and will likely agree to more cuts to secure the legislated raising of the statutory debt ceiling.

It is worth noting that policy disagreements about the causes of and remedies for economic stagnation that consign advanced economies to decades of slow job growth and high unemployment are far from rare. The 1990s in Japan are often referred to as the "lost decade" because growth was so far below potential: the Japanese economy did not see a robust recovery from the bursting of asset market bubbles in the early 1990s until 2002.

Further, many researchers have begun reassessing the relatively high unemployment rates in Europe in the 1990s. These high rates were often attributed to labor market rigidities that resulted in high levels of structural unemployment. This diagnosis led the policy discussion in Western Europe to focus on labor market "liberalization," that is, reducing the power of unions and other labor market institutions, reducing the generosity of social insurance programs, and reducing legislated employment protections. However, relatively new research has suggested that much of this excess unemployment may have been driven significantly by the failure of policy to ensure that aggregate demand grew sufficiently fast to keep pace with supply—indeed, researchers at the German Bundesbank have estimated, using some measures of the output gap, that the German economy was performing below potential for twenty-seven of the past thirty-two years.

In short, the stakes involved in correctly diagnosing and remedying the causes of labor market stagnation could not be higher—literally decades of less-than-potential growth could be the outcome of incorrectly reacting to this challenge. Further, the weak growth of typical (median) families' incomes, and the sputtering job market of the 2000s, have already resulted in essentially a lost decade: between 2000 and 2007 median family income was essentially flat, rising only 0.4 percent over the entire seven-year period. By 2009, median family incomes had fallen to their lowest levels since 1997. Given the very strong relationship between elevated unemployment and poor income growth for median families, it seems quite likely that 2007 income levels will not be reached again for another decade, unless policymakers move correctly and aggressively to reduce joblessness.

Lastly, it should be noted that while failure to remedy high rates of unemployment in the United States inflicts widespread damage to the economy, the damage is predictably greater for more vulnerable members of the workforce. The unemployment rate among blacks, for example, tends to be double the rate for whites at each point in the business cycle. The Hispanic unemployment rate tends to be

1.5 times as high as the white rate. The unemployment rate for those workers without a four-year college degree tends to be twice as high as the rate for workers with such a degree. And poverty rates for black families tend to be much more sensitive to changes in the unemployment rate than those for nonblack families.

The US economy entered the second decade of the twenty-first century with its once-secure reputation as a great "job-creating machine" rightfully damaged. It is hard to imagine a more important goal of public policy than to restore this reputation to reality, but doing so requires a serious analytical look as to why the US economy had such success in generating jobs during the 1990s while many of its advanced-country peers did not. Much evidence suggests that this success has deeper roots in macroeconomic developments (as opposed to the structure of labor and product markets) than conventional wisdom has generally recognized. Hopefully this evidence will inform policymakers' attempts to deal with joblessness going forward.

[*See also* Economy, American, since World War II; Labor Force, American; *and* Poverty, Scale and Nature of.]

BIBLIOGRAPHY

Altig, David. "A Curious Unemployment Picture Gets More Curious." Federal Reserve Bank of Atlanta's MacroBlog. (2010), http://macroblog.typepad.com/macroblog/2010/07/a-curious-unemployment-picture-gets-more-curious.html.

Baker, Dean, et al. "Labor Market Institutions and Unemployment: A Critical Assessment of the Cross-Country Evidence." In *Fighting Unemployment: The Limits of Free Market Orthodoxy*, edited by David Howell, pp. 72–118. (Oxford, 2004).

Bartels, Larry M. "Econometrics and Presidential Elections." *Journal of Economic Perspectives* 11, no. 3 (Summer 1997): 195–196.

Bivens, Josh, and John Irons. "A Feeble Recovery: The Fundamental Weakness of the 2001–2007 Expansion." Economic Policy Institute, Briefing Paper 214. (2008), http://epi.3cdn.net/ff1869e11dfc0ef295_xxm6b9cj9.pdf.

Congressional Budget Office. "The Budget and Economic Outlook: Fiscal Years 2011 to 2021." (2011), http://www.cbo.gov/ftpdocs/120xx/doc12039/01-26_fy2011outlook.pdf.

Kocherlakota, Narayana. "Inside the FOMC." (2010), http://www.minneapolisfed.org/news_events/pres/speech_display.cfm?id=4525.

Mishel, Lawrence. "Debunking the Case for Structural Unemployment." (2011). Economic Policy Institute, http://www.epi.org/publication/debunking_the_theory_of_structural_unemployment/.

Organization for Economic Cooperation and Development. *The OECD Jobs Study, Evidence and Explanations, Part 1: Labor Market Trends and Underlying Forces of Change.* (Paris, 1994).

Posen, Adam S. "The Realities and Relevance of Japan's Great Recession: Neither *Ran* nor *Rashomon.*" Peterson Institute for International Economics Working Paper No. 10–7. (2010), http://papers.ssrn.com/sol3/papers.cfm?abstract_id=1623828.

Schettkat, Ronald, and Rongrong Sun. "Monetary Policy and European Unemployment." *Oxford Review of Economic Policy* 25, no. 1 (2009): 94–108.

Josh Bivens

ENTITLEMENTS

Social protections and benefits owed by a state to its citizens are known as entitlements. In the most general sense, entitlements are akin to social rights, in which a government promises to ensure its citizens access to various goods and services, such as minimum income, housing, health care, or employment. The notion of entitlements became particularly important in the welfare states created by advanced industrial societies after World War II.

The use of the term "entitlement" varies across nations. In most Western European nations, entitlement expresses a general political commitment by the state to provide social benefits. In the United States, entitlement has taken on a more specific meaning. Reflecting the importance of legal mechanisms in US policy-making and the absence of a tradition of social rights, entitlements have been enumerated in detail and defined as legal claims in the United States. This way of defining entitlements grew out of the legal movements of the 1960s, which sought to define social policy benefits as a form of property. Although the Supreme Court has declined to endorse formally this view of policy, in practice courts have struck down numerous administrative barriers that reduced access to social benefits, and have guaranteed clients the right to appeal decisions altering these benefits.

This legal defense of access to social policy benefits has been accompanied by an increasingly detailed description of the components of an entitlement in the United States. The value of itemizing entitlements in this way is debated among theorists of the welfare state. American liberals, who tend to favor this approach, argue that it ensures access to social benefits. Critics, such as the British social theorist Richard Titmuss, charge that the "fragmentation of entitlement" removes needed discretion and deprives beneficiaries of choice. At the same time, critics fear that itemizing entitlements creates a ceiling defining the maximum level of benefits.

Entitlements have been the subject of considerable contention in US budgetary politics since the 1970s. Because the benefits of entitlement programs must be made available to all who are eligible for them, the costs of these policies are difficult to control. As administrative barriers fell and new programs were established, expenditures for entitlement programs expanded rapidly from 1965 to 1974. When the American economy stagnated in the 1970s and deficits soared in the 1980s, government officials expressed strong concern about the uncontrolled nature of spending for entitlement programs, which accounted for nearly half of the national budget by the 1990s. But entitlement programs, which include Social Security and Medicare, remained politically popular because the broad majority of American families relied on them. This popularity made politicians reluctant to cut these programs.

During the early years of the Clinton administration, the Bipartisan Commission on Entitlement and Tax Reform was created to consider how the costs of entitlements could be contained. Although the commission drew substantial attention to the growth of entitlement programs, political divisions blocked any action, and a declining budget deficit eventually reduced the salience of the issue. The single most significant change in entitlements occurred in 1996, when Congress voted to abolish Aid to Families with Dependent Children (AFDC), the entitlement program serving poor families. In its place, Congress created a new program, Temporary Assistance for Needy Families, in which benefits are subject to time limits and to various conditions set by the state and federal governments, as a part of Clinton's major welfare restructuring legislation, the Personal Responsibility and Work Opportunity Reconciliation Act. The abolition of AFDC, however, reflected the political weakness of programs that provide assistance to the nonworking poor in the United States, rather than a substantial challenge to the concept of entitlements. Entitlements remain popular as the key social programs that serve the American middle class.

[*See also* Medicare and Medicaid; Social Security; Temporary Assistance for Needy Families; Welfare State; Welfare to Work; *and* Women and Welfare.]

BIBLIOGRAPHY

Abel-Smith, Brian, and Kay Titmuss, eds. *The Philosophy of Welfare: Selected Writings of Richard M. Titmuss* (London, 1987).

Weaver, R. Kent. "Controlling Entitlements." In *The New Direction in American Politics,* edited by John E. Chubb and Paul E. Peterson, pp. 307–341. (Washington, D.C., 1985).

Margaret Weir

ENVIRONMENTAL POLITICS

See Climate Change.

ENVIRONMENTAL PROTECTION AGENCY

Like most government organizations, the Environmental Protection Agency (EPA) was not created from whole cloth, but resulted from the amalgamation of other organizations, most of which existed in the Departments of the Interior, Agriculture, and Health, Education, and Welfare (today called Health and Human Services). Unlike many agencies, however, the EPA was created not by Congress but rather by executive order—in this case, one signed by President Richard Nixon in 1970.

In the EPA's early years, government officials made key decisions regarding how to structure the agency and how to pursue national policies when dealing with geographically variable concerns. The EPA has also come to embody tensions which have made it a lightning rod for attention and controversy. Even so, the agency has significant accomplishments to its credit, even as it continues to face an array of new and continuing challenges.

When he signed the executive order creating the EPA, President Nixon suggested that the concept behind his reorganization of government functions was to provide a comprehensive approach to improving the quality of the environment in the United States. He wanted a coordinated approach to environmental issues and "functional management," rather than an approach directed toward specific "media" such as air and water.

Congress showed little interest in this style of organizing. It continued to pass legislation, and to structure funding, along the lines of specific environmental needs. In addition to the responsibilities transferred to the EPA from other agencies, Congress added new authorities for waste and toxic substance management in the 1970s, and these new responsibilities led to the creation of new "media-based" organizational capacities within the EPA. These decision-making processes were driven not by President Nixon's interest in integrated public management, but by legislative processes that facilitated congressional oversight and accountability, both of which are of continuing concern to Congress.

In its early years, the EPA also made arrangements to enable organizational flexibility in order to deal effectively with geographic variations in environmental problems. Ten regional offices were created within the agency, with responsibility for managing national environmental programs within the states in their specific region. The EPA regional offices were given considerable autonomy. Each regional administrator, for example, is politically appointed and reports to the EPA administrator, rather than to the national

program managers, who are appointed to manage the agency's media-based program offices in Washington, D.C.

Congress also enabled states to manage a number of the EPA's environmental programs through "delegations" of authority (or "primacy" arrangements), allowing states to administer EPA programs relating to air, water quality, drinking water, and waste within their jurisdictions. In these cases, the EPA provided oversight and assistance, rather than implementing federal programs. Most states have now been delegated authority to manage numerous federal programs within their jurisdictions.

When the EPA was originally established, it had about five thousand employees and a budget of approximately $1 billion. During the following decade, the agency's workforce grew steadily as Congress passed new regulatory laws for it to implement: the Clean Air Act of 1970, the Clean Water Act of 1972, the Safe Drinking Water Act of 1974, the Resource Conservation and Recovery Act of 1976, and the Toxic Substances Control Act of 1976, to name just a few. By 1980, the EPA had a workforce of about thirteen thousand and a budget of between $4 and $5 billion. The election of Ronald Reagan to the presidency in 1980 produced controversy for the EPA, however. President Reagan believed that the EPA's regulatory programs inhibited economic growth and proposed cutting the agency's budget, and a number of these cuts were implemented. By 1983, the agency's workforce had dropped below eleven thousand and its budget had been reduced to $3.7 billion.

These events highlighted one tension inherent in the EPA's environmental policies: the need to protect the environment and public health without hindering economic growth. When Anne Gorsuch Burford resigned as EPA administrator in 1983, President Reagan reappointed the EPA's first administrator, William Ruckelshaus, to help the agency address this challenge. Ruckelshaus sought to reorient the EPA's activities toward targeted risk reduction, which he hoped would be more efficient and effective than the "command and control" regulatory strategies that dominated the 1970s. Building on this conceptual foundation and on new laws passed by Congress, the agency expanded in the late 1980s and 1990s to a workforce of about seventeen thousand and a budget of $7 billion. Later in the 1990s, this risk reduction orientation was supplemented by sustainable development strategies; both approaches sought to align environmental protection goals more closely with economic development.

Another tension within the EPA has been the conflict among professionals of different backgrounds within the organization. Many EPA employees are hired for their scientific expertise, and some of them have had conflicts with the agency's political leadership. This kind of conflict has been most pronounced under Republican presidents but has not been absent under Democratic chief executives. It is highlighted when EPA scientists and others accuse political officials of selective perception in evaluating scientific evidence, an accusation that appears to be more common in recent years.

The viewpoints of scientists also differ from other employees. Years ago, engineers were at the center of environmental protection efforts as command and control regulatory requirements used technology-based solutions. More recently, the EPA has increased its reliance on biologists, toxicologists, and behavioral scientists to help address a changing mix of environmental problems, such as greenhouse gas emissions, nonpoint source water pollution, and diffuse exposures to lead, mercury, and other toxic contaminants. With these changes in the relevant science and scientific training have come differences of opinion on how best to deal with changing environmental problems.

There have also been conflicts among legal, economic, and environmentalist conceptions of EPA policy. For example, economists have tended to emphasize market- and, to a lesser extent, information-based regulatory tools that are considered cost-effective, while environmentalists tend to be more concerned with simply abating pollution, regardless of the economic implications. Likewise, EPA lawyers deal with complex legal issues surrounding the implementation of environmental laws, and may not support either the economists or the environmentalists.

Another tension that has become central to the EPA's work is a mismatch between the aggressiveness of the agency's legal mandates and the resources available from Congress to implement these mandates. A key objective of the federal Clean Water Act, for example, is to eliminate discharges of pollutants into the nation's waterways. However, the resources available to the EPA to accomplish ambitious goals such as this have not increased with the demands made on the agency. Indeed, the number of EPA employees has hovered around seventeen thousand to eighteen thousand since the early 2000s, and the overall budget for the agency has hovered between $7 and $8 billion since the 1990s (with the notable exception of a significant yet temporary increase to about $10 billion in 2010, when President Barack Obama and Congress increased funding throughout the government to stimulate the national economy).

In spite of these ongoing challenges, the EPA has achieved measureable results in addressing a number of important environmental problems. Emissions of criteria pollutants such as sulfur dioxide, carbon monoxide, and lead, regulated by the Clean Air Act, have been reduced. Through implementation of the Clean Water Act, the number of households discharging raw sewage to American waterways is now significantly reduced. These are just two examples of problems which the EPA has addressed with notable levels of success.

Even so, major environmental challenges remain, as diffuse and global environmental problems increasingly supplement the local and regional problems that dominated debate in the 1970s. The agency also continues efforts to reconcile the tensions and conflicts mentioned above. Over the long term, the EPA's success will depend on its ability to build capacities to address new and more complex environmental problems in a coordinated and cost-effective fashion.

[*See also* Clean Air Act; *and* Climate Change.]

BIBLIOGRAPHY

Association of State and Interstate Water Pollution Control Administrators. *Clean Water Act Thirty-Year*

Retrospective: History and Documents Related to the Federal Statute. (Washington D.C., 2004).

Collin, Robert W. *The Environmental Protection Agency: Cleaning up America's Act.* (Westport, Conn., 2006).

Hoornbeek, John. "Information and Environmental Policy: A Tale of Two Agencies." *Journal of Comparative Policy Analysis: Research and Practice* 2, no. 2 (2000): 145–187.

Landy, Marc K., Marc J. Roberts, and Stephen R. Thomas. *The Environmental Protection Agency: Asking the Wrong Questions: From Nixon to Clinton.* (New York, 1994).

National Academy of Public Administration. *Setting Priorities, Getting Results: A New Direction for EPA.* (Washington, D.C., 1995).

U.S. Environmental Protection Agency. "EPA's Budget and Workforce, 1970–2003." (2006).

World Resources Institute. *The 1992 Information Please Environmental Almanac.* (Boston, 1992).

B. Guy Peters and John Hoornbeek

EQUAL RIGHTS AMENDMENT

In 1923, three years after women won the suffrage in the United States, the first Equal Rights Amendment (ERA) to the Constitution of the United States was introduced in the US Congress. Its primary proponents were the professional and upper-middle-class suffragist militants of the National Women's Party. The amendment was opposed by "social feminists," Progressives, and union leaders, who, in the absence of a strong labor movement in the United States, were trying to institute protections for at least women workers—special protections that would have had to be dropped, or else extended to men by an ERA's requirement of formal equality.

By the 1960s, a number of professional associations and both political parties supported the ERA; however, Democratic President John Kennedy's Commission on the Status of Women concluded that such a "constitutional amendment need not now be sought." One year later, opponents of the Civil Rights Act added "sex" as a protected category to the proposed act, hoping to induce some representatives to vote against it. but the Act passed as amended. By 1970, the federal Equal Employment Opportunity Commission (EEOC) had interpreted the 1964 Act

to forbid precisely those special protections for women (in most cases extending the protections to men) that had made the unions oppose the ERA.

In 1970, therefore, the Pittsburgh chapter of the newly formed National Organization for Women (NOW) took direct action to promote the ERA, which NOW had given first place on its Bill of Rights for Women. After two years of controversy, the ERA passed in the House of Representatives with a vote of 354 to 23, and it passed in the Senate with a vote of 84 to 8. The amendment's substantive clause read: "Equality of rights under the law shall not be denied or abridged by the United States or by any State on account of sex."

The ERA then went immediately to the states, with Hawaii ratifying it on 22 March 1972, the very day the Senate passed the amendment. Twenty-nine more states ratified in 1972 and early 1973, the earliest with unanimous or nearly unanimous votes. By 1973, however, the opposition had begun to organize, led by Phyllis Schlafly, a maverick from the right wing of the Republican Party. A skilled political entrepreneur, Schlafly tied the ERA to fears of the cultural upheaval entailed by the growing number of women in the paid labor force, the increasing rate of divorce, and other larger social changes that had emerged along with the growing women's liberation movement in the United States. She tied the ERA as well to conservative and mainstream legislators' anger at the Supreme Court's liberal decisions, and to state legislators' fears of losing control over most issues regarding women, which the US federal system allocates primarily to the states. Nevertheless, five more states ratified in 1974, 1975, and 1977. However, none ratified after 1977, despite the triumph of ERA proponents in 1978 in getting Congress to extend the original 1979 deadline to 1982. On 30 June, the final deadline for ratifying the ERA passed, with only thirty-five of the required thirty-eight states having ratified.

In public opinion polls, a majority of the US public (57 percent in the "average" survey) always supported the ERA. Men were as likely to support it as women, the working class as likely as the middle class, blacks somewhat more than whites, and Catholics somewhat more than Protestants. Fundamentalist and evangelical Christians, frequent churchgoers, parents with large families, older people, and rural residents tended to oppose the amendment. The amendment lost because it came to be linked with abortion (the Supreme Court decision in *Roe v. Wade* had legalized abortion in 1973), and could be portrayed as dividing women (homemakers versus women in the paid labor force). Its proponents failed to overcome objections that the amendment would force changes that most Americans disapproved (e.g., drafting women for combat in the armed forces). It stopped being a nonpartisan issue (the right wing came to power in the Republican Party with the candidacy of Ronald Reagan and withdrew the ERA from its platform), and it had to be ratified by states with fewer than 15 percent women legislators (in the states that did not ratify, 79 percent of the women legislators, but only 39 percent of the men legislators, favored the amendment).

Although feminists criticized it for detracting from other causes, in the long run the struggle for the ERA helped build the prestige and budget of NOW (its budget rose from $700,000 in 1977 to $8.5 million in 1982), making the organization the strongest independent feminist organization in the world, and putting it in a position to demand successfully that the Democratic Party run a woman for vice president of the United States in the 1986 election. The ERA struggle also helped build the feminist movement in the United States, to the point at which, by 1989, one out of three women in the United States was reporting to poll takers that she considered herself a "feminist"—about the same percentage as considered themselves Democrats or Republicans.

Argentina (1853) and Iran (1907) were the first countries to guarantee in their constitutions equality for "all inhabitants," including women. After 1945, when the United Nations (UN) Charter affirmed the "equal rights of men and women," many of the world's nations adopted similar clauses in their constitutions. In 1982, the Charter of Rights in Canada's new constitution guaranteed "the right to the equal protection and equal benefit of the law without discrimination and, in particular, without discrimination

based on . . . sex," generating litigation under that clause that has greatly extended women's rights. The impact of each of these constitutional clauses, including the "equal protection" clause of the US constitution, which now governs legislation affecting women in the absence of an ERA, must be judged by the policy decisions reached under it.

[*See also* Congress, US; Federalism; Feminization of Poverty; Gender and Politics; *and* Kennedy, John Fitzgerald.]

BIBLIOGRAPHY

Berry, Mary Frances. *Why ERA Failed: Politics, Women's Rights, and the Amending Process of the Constitution.* (Bloomington, Ind., 1986).

Boles, Janet K. *The Politics of the Equal Rights Amendment: Conflict and the Decision Process.* (New York, 1979).

Mansbridge, Jane. "Whatever Happened to the ERA?" In *Women and the US Constitution: History, Interpretation, and Practice*, edited by Sibyl Schwarzenbach, pp. 365–378. (New York, 2004).

Mansbridge, Jane. *Why We Lost the ERA.* (Chicago, 1986).

Siegel, Reva B. "Constitutional Culture, Social Movement Conflict and Constitutional Change: The Case of the *de facto* ERA." *California Law Review* 94 (2006): 1323–1419.

Soule, Sarah A., and Brayden G. King. "The Stages of the Policy Process and the Equal Rights Amendment, 1972–1982." *American Journal of Sociology* 111 (2006): 1871–1909.

Jane J. Mansbridge

EXECUTIVE PRIVILEGE

The subject of executive privilege is a convoluted one. The complications begin with the term itself. Although it is generally accepted that "executive privilege" refers to the president's right to withhold official information, there has long been a degree of uncertainty about *what* categories of information can be withheld under this heading, and from *whom*. When the term first entered into circulation in the early 1950s, it referred to the president's right to withhold, from both of the other branches of the federal government, information relating both to national security as well as the internal deliberations of the executive branch. Since that time, however, the president's right to withhold classified information from the courts has come to be discussed under a different heading, namely, the "state secrets privilege." In addition, even though a number of presidents have invoked executive privilege to withhold information about internal deliberations and operations—most notably in the context of Senator Joseph McCarthy's hearings in 1954 and the Supreme Court's demand for White House tape recordings in *United States v. Nixon* (1974)—the president's right to withhold this category of information has begun to be discussed under a new heading, namely, the "deliberative process privilege."

Although these terminological developments complicate discussions of executive privilege, they are welcome for two reasons. First, using the term "executive privilege" to refer to the president's right to withhold both classified and nonclassified but confidential information invites analytical confusion, since the justification offered on behalf of the former differs from that offered on behalf of the latter. Indeed, it is not uncommon to encounter arguments that claim to vindicate "executive privilege," but that in fact defend the president's right to withhold only one of these categories of information. Second, the right to withhold information relating to internal deliberations, which is justified by concerns for the candor and privacy of officials, is not claimed by the executive branch alone; it is also claimed by a variety of other institutions including central banks, courts, and legislatures. Therefore, it is not clear why this right should be discussed under the heading of "executive" privilege. By contrast, the right to withhold classified information on grounds of national security is claimed by the executive branch alone. Hence, it seems more fitting to use the term "executive privilege" to refer to this right alone.

The complications surrounding executive privilege are not only terminological, but also substantive. In particular, there are deep disagreements over whether the president really has the right to withhold classified information from Congress. Broadly, three defenses have been offered. The first, put forward by successive attorneys general, and championed by Abraham Soafer and Mark Rozell, rests on precedent.

The emphasis here is on identifying instances, stretching back to the early Republic, where presidents have successfully withheld information from Congress. However, the utility of this evidence has been called into question by Bernard Schwartz and Saikrishna Prakash, both of whom have persuasively argued that Congress's failure to challenge the president cannot be interpreted as establishing the constitutionality of the practice. A second defense of executive privilege rests on claims about the intellectual and political context in which the Constitution was framed. The argument here, developed by Rozell again, is that the political turmoil associated with the post-Revolutionary period convinced the Framers of the Constitution of the importance of secrecy in government. Unfortunately, the contextual evidence in favor of this claim is thin. For instance, there is no discussion of the privilege in the debates of the Constitutional Convention. Furthermore, the diverse and often contradictory intellectual and political movements that characterized the late eighteenth century make it difficult to discern exactly how context affected the Framers. Thus, Raoul Berger has drawn on historical materials to argue that the Framers actually intended for Congress to exercise penetrating oversight. A third defense of executive privilege rests on the doctrine of implied powers. The claim here, put forward by David Crockett and Gary Schmitt, is that even though the Constitution does not explicitly authorize an executive privilege, this privilege can nevertheless be derived from the president's responsibilities as commander in chief and chief executive. However, this claim too has encountered stiff resistance. For instance, Louis Fisher has argued that Congress has an independent right to national security information because the Constitution vests it with its own national security powers and responsibilities.

There is little prospect of the debate over the constitutionality of executive privilege being resolved any time soon. The relevant materials—precedents, intentions, and historical texts—are simply not amenable to conclusive interpretation. To make matters worse, the courts have shied away from the issue, citing in *United States v. AT&T* (1977) the need to "avoid a resolution that might disturb the balance of power between the two branches and inaccurately reflect their true needs." Given the circumstances, scholars have begun to focus less on questions about strict constitutionality and more on the general arguments for and against allowing the president to control the flow of national security information to Congress. Perhaps the most promising such argument in favor of executive privilege points to structural differences between the executive branch and Congress that make the former less susceptible to making damaging, unauthorized disclosures of classified information. This argument, made by George Calhoun and Stephen Knott, draws attention to the manner in which the hierarchical structure and more ideologically cohesive membership of the presidency make it less vulnerable to indiscipline (a point brought home by President Dwight Eisenhower's oft-cited warning to his Cabinet that any official who violated the confidentiality he wanted to protect "won't be working for me that night." This argument has been countered by the claim, made recently by Heidi Kitrosser, that executive privilege threatens the separation of powers. The idea behind the separation of powers is that governmental authority should be allocated to the political branch in a way that makes the exercise of power dependent on the mutual consent of the other branches. The point of arranging things this way is to prevent any branch from exercising unchecked power. It is not difficult to see that executive privilege threatens this arrangement because it complicates Congress's ability to mount an informed challenge to the president's policies.

Unfortunately, arguments about the broader merits of executive privilege have failed to provide a conclusive answer either. In the interim, a number of scholars, most notably Neal Devins and Peter Raven-Hansen, have drawn attention to the means by which Congress can obtain access to information regardless of whether the privilege is ultimately determined to be constitutional or not. These means include withholding appropriations, refusing to confirm nominees, and using Congress's subpoena power. In practice, though, there has been little need for such measures, because unauthorized disclosures from the executive branch have routinely brought wrongdoing to the attention of Congress, for instance

recently in the case of flawed intelligence on Iraq's purported weapons of mass destruction program. In other words, informal transfers of information have thus far precluded the president and Congress from demanding a formal answer to the question of whether executive privilege is constitutional or not. Whether scholars, lawyers, and judges will be forced to provide such an answer remains to be seen: it depends on whether the president and Congress can make their peace with the current arrangement, or if they decide to press for a resolution of the matter.

[*See also* State Secrecy.]

BIBLIOGRAPHY

Banks, William C., and Peter Raven-Hansen. *National Security Law and the Power of the Purse*. (New York, 1994).

Berger, Raoul. *Executive Privilege: A Constitutional Myth*. (Cambridge, Mass., 1974).

Calhoun, George W. "Confidentiality and Executive Privilege." In *The Tethered Presidency: Congressional Restraints on Executive Power*, edited by Thomas Franck, pp. 172–195. (New York, 1981).

Crockett, David. "Executive Privilege." In *The Constitutional Presidency*, edited by Joseph Bessette and Jeffrey K. Tulis, pp. 203–228. (Baltimore, 2009).

Devins, Neal. "Congressional-Executive Information Access Disputes: A Modest Proposal—Do Nothing." *Administrative Law Review* 48 (1996): 109–137.

Fisher, Louis. *The Politics of Executive Privilege*. (Durham, N.C., 2004).

Kitrosser, Heidi. "Secrecy and Separated Powers: Executive Privilege Revisited." *Iowa Law Review* 92 (2007): 489.

Knott, Stephen F. *Secret and Sanctioned: Covert Operations and the American Presidency*. (New York, 1996).

Prakash, Saikrishna B. "A Critical Comment on the Constitutionality of the Executive Privilege." *Minnesota Law Review* 83 (1999): 1143.

Rozell, Mark J. *Executive Privilege: Presidential Power, Secrecy, and Accountability*. (Lawrence, Kans., 2002).

Schmitt, Gary J. "Executive Privilege: Presidential Power to Withhold Information from Congress." In *The Presidency in the Constitutional Order: An Historical Examination*, edited by Joseph M. Bessette and Jeffrey Tulis, pp. 154–194. (Baton Rouge, La., 1981).

Soafer, Abraham D. *War, Foreign Affairs, and Constitutional Power: The Origins*. (Cambridge, Mass., 1976).

United States v. A.T&T, 567 F.2d 121 (D.C. Cir. 1977).

Rahul Sagar

F

Faith-Based Initiatives

Implementation of the faith-based initiative program began at both the state and federal levels in 1996. The original implementation of the faith-based initiative, then known as Charitable Choice, passed as a component of the 1996 Personal Responsibility and Work Opportunity Reconciliation Act. There were two underlying goals of the Charitable Choice legislation. The first was to increase the amount of cooperation between religious groups and government agencies, eliminating perceived barriers to funding for those religious groups. The second goal was to increase the amount of funding going to faith-based organizations that provided necessary social services. Combined, the ultimate goal was to "unleash the armies of compassion" and create a broad base of government-funded, religion-based social services. The passage of Charitable Choice, and the subsequent faith-based initiative policies that followed in 2001, were the result of many years of lobbying from elite evangelical activists, who used their power within the Republican Party to push forward on these measures and create a new and sustained faith-based bureaucracy at both the state and federal levels.

Like many social movements, the faith-based movement is made up of a broad coalition of supporters that include conservative evangelical activists, the African American religious population, and some members of the Catholic Church. Together these actors formed a loose coalition that often did not agree on which goal was the most important to meeting the end result of increasing the role of religious groups in social services. Elite-level evangelicals, like former attorney general John Ashcroft, largely focused on eliminating barriers to faith-based groups, working to ensure them access to public funds on what some considered an unequal playing field. However others, including the former White House staffer David Kuo, Catholic supporters, and African American activists favored greater fiscal support in conjunction with eliminating barriers. While each of these groups offered important political support, none was as influential as the resurgent conservative evangelical movement, without which early victories for the faith-based initiative, at both the federal and state level, would not have been achieved. Unprecedented access was first gained in Texas under then-governor George W. Bush. In 1996, Bush created the first state-level, faith-based liaisons, and worked with state legislators to significantly alter state law regarding religion in the social service sector. After Texas's original implementation of a variety of laws, including the creation of multiple state faith-based liaisons, elimination of licensing requirements for faith-based social services, and support for funding for evangelical prison ministries, other states followed suit with similar laws, including South Carolina, Oklahoma, and New Jersey.

After President Bush assumed office in 2001 he made clear, through his formation of the White House Office of Faith-Based and Community Initiatives, that expansion and support of faith-based initiatives would be his top domestic priority. Bush also created the Compassion Capital Fund (CCF) to aid faith-based and community-based organizations. The CCF remains the only federal government effort to provide funding to faith-based organizations, delivering over $140 million to numerous faith-based groups throughout the country for a variety of programs, including assistance in grant writing and direct funding to some services. However, very little of the originally promised $8 billion in funding actually materialized, leading some supporters to feel betrayed.

After 2001 many states saw the president's focus as a new mandate, and began to find various ways to implement faith-based policies and practices with little input from the federal government. States were left on their own to interpret what the faith-based initiative was, and how to get religious groups more involved in providing social services. In 1996 in Texas and again in 2001 in Washington, D.C., George W. Bush signaled both directly and indirectly to states that the best way for them to enact faith-based policies was to create faith-based offices modeled after the ones in Texas and the White House. In 2001, letters were sent from his White House Office of Faith-Based and Community Initiatives to state governors asking them to implement state-level Offices of Faith-Based and Community Initiatives. Some movement actors confidently assumed that the creation of these offices would help states win federal funding and political support.

Since 1996, twenty-four states have created both a faith-based office and a related liaison position; an additional thirteen states have created only a liaison position. In general these offices have offered minimal assistance and outreach to faith-based groups, as well as some help in connecting them with state organizations and navigating the federal government grants system. Consequently, these efforts did little to add to appropriations or funding of faith-based organizations. Rather, these offices worked with faith-based organizations, using the few resources available, to help them attempt to get funds that were already in the system. This led some academics and some movement insiders to characterize these accomplishments (that is, the creation of faith-based liaisons and offices) as largely symbolic administrative gestures. In addition to creating faith-based offices, states have begun to put various faith-based practices into law, creating over 270 pieces of legislation between 1996 and 2009. These laws include limiting regulations on faith-based day cares, establishing faith-based advisory boards, and regulating faith-based prison wings.

After President Bush left office, the faith-based initiative remained part of the White House landscape, but under a different name and with a somewhat different direction. President Barack Obama renamed the office the White House Office of Faith-Based and Neighborhood Partnerships, hoping to refocus the initiative on the "community" segment many felt had been ignored under President Bush. Since then supporters have felt the office has remained rather quiet, especially in comparison to its predecessor, and has not done as much as needed to help bring religious groups into the social services fold. Others, such as Barry Lynn, director of Americans United for the Separation of Church and State, have noted that Obama also failed to make good on a campaign promise to reverse one of the most controversial parts of the initiative, which allows religious groups that receive federal funds to hire on the basis of religion. Even though the federal government has remained somewhat quiet on these issues and has stayed out of any public controversy, and although the faith-based initiative has long slipped off the front page, it has become well established on the legal and political landscape and will likely remain so for some time.

[*See also* Bush, George W.; Christian Right; Civil Religion; *and* Religion and Politics.]

BIBLIOGRAPHY

Bartkowski, John, and Helen Regis. *Charitable Choices: Religion, Race, and Poverty in the Post-Welfare Era.* (New York, 2003).

Chaves, Mark. "Going on Faith: Six Myths about Faith-Based Initiatives." *Christian Century,* 12–19 September 2001.

Chaves, Mark. "Religious Congregations and Welfare Reform: Who Will Take Advantage of the Faith-Based Initiatives?" *American Sociological Review* 64 (1999): 836–846.

Formicola, Jo Renee, Mary C. Segers, and Paul Weber, eds. *Faith-Based Initiatives and the Bush Administration: The Good, the Bad, and the Ugly.* (Lanham, Md., 2003).

Kuo, David. *Tempting Faith: An Inside Story of Political Seduction.* (New York, 2006).

Loconte, Joseph. "Keeping the Faith." *First Things* 123 (May 2002): 14–16.

Lynn, Barry. "It's Time for Obama to Fix the Faith-Based Initiative." *HuffingtonPost.com* (29 March 2010), http://www.huffingtonpost.com/barry-w-lynn/its-time-for-obama-to-fix_b_517249.html.

Sager, Rebecca. *Faith, Politics, and Power: The Politics of Faith-Based Initiatives.* (New York, 2010).

Wineburg, Robert J. *Faith-Based Inefficiency: The Follies of Bush's Initiatives.* (Westport, Conn., 2007).

Wineburg, Robert J. *A Limited Partnership: The Politics of Religion, Welfare, and Social Science.* (New York, 2001).

Rebecca Sager

FEDERAL DEPOSIT INSURANCE CORPORATION

The Federal Deposit Insurance Corporation (FDIC) is a federally chartered, independent agency that insures retail bank deposits. It was created in 1933 to prevent increasingly frequent bank runs then affecting the Depression-bound American economy. National and state banks regulated by the Federal Reserve System are required to join the FDIC, which examines their books, takes them into receivership if they fail, and pays customer deposits if the worst should happen (a similar institution insures nonprofit credit unions). The principle of deposit insurance has not been politically controversial, although the banking industry has periodically sought—and won—congressional intervention to reduce the FDIC's regulatory and financial costs. During the financial crisis of 2008, the FDIC earned a reputation as an aggressive defender of savers, borrowers, taxpayers, and smaller banks, as opposed to bond-holders and Wall Street more generally.

Bank collapses were a regular feature of the late nineteenth century, with hundreds of America's tiny local banks failing each year during the vicious downturns of the post–Civil War decades. Failures spiked in the years after 1929, with 1,352 banks closing in 1930, 2,294 in 1931, 1,456 in 1932, and more than 4,000 in 1933. State-imposed bank "holidays" became a regular occurrence in the winter of 1932–1933. Immediately following his inauguration, President Franklin Delano Roosevelt worked with the Democratic Congress to pass the Banking (Glass-Steagall) Act of 1933, which split investment and retail banking and, among other things, created the FDIC. At the urging of his advisers, the new president overcame personal reservations that deposit insurance would increase the prevalence of moral hazard in banking. At first, individual accounts were guaranteed up to $5,000; this figure had outpaced inflation to reach $100,000 by the first decade of the twenty-first century. Once in place, the new regulatory regime had the desired effect, and until financial deregulation began in the 1980s, bank failures were extremely rare.

Banks that fail are taken over by the FDIC, which makes depositors whole from its reserve fund and then liquidates the bank, selling the bank's assets to recover the insured loss. Generally failures are rare and isolated, but during periods of financial crisis, and especially when very large banks fail, the strains on deposit insurance grow.

The FDIC reserve fund is maintained through bank premiums, and has fluctuated between approximately 1.1 percent and 1.5 percent of total insured deposits. The FDIC also has borrowing authority in case the fund is depleted, as it was during the 1980s and again in the wake of the costly 2008 crisis. On the other hand, Congress has repeatedly ensured that reserve fund arrangements favored the banking industry, which naturally wanted lower premiums. For example, the FDIC was required to rebate contributions to member banks if its fund exceeded 1.5 percent of deposits, and was barred from collecting additional premiums from most banks if its fund stood at 1.25 percent or more—ostensibly because these banks were well capitalized and therefore at low risk of failure.

For libertarian economists, deposit insurance and its regulatory corollaries create unacceptable moral hazard, since savers need no longer monitor the banks they patronize. Mainstream economists and lawmakers, by contrast, observed that average depositors had rarely exercised such due diligence, having neither the resources nor the inclination to do so. As a result, throughout the late nineteenth and early twentieth centuries, savers periodically lost everything and, more seriously, the broader public suffered the externalities of bank panic contagion. For five decades after the 1930s, the FDIC was an elegant solution. It spread the insurance risk nationally and solved the regulatory collective action problem. On the other hand, in a context of deregulated finance, the moral hazard of deposit insurance accumulated in banks' executive suites and boardrooms. In 1999, two decades of financial deregulation culminated in the Gramm-Leach-Bliley Act, which repealed Glass-Steagall's separation of investment and commercial banking. As a result, federally insured bank deposits could no longer be isolated from a bank's securities trading operations. Arguably, systemically important banks that traded on their own account took on higher risks and generated higher returns than they would otherwise have been able to, safe in the knowledge that their primary obligations were taxpayer-insured at effectively subsidized rates.

This high-level moral hazard was compounded by other trends in the industry—eroding internal controls and risk management, for example—and by weak corporate governance more generally. There was little incentive for anyone to question the arrangement as long as financial corporations were generating large and growing returns for future retirees, their institutional fund managers, and for individual investors. The fact that the banks grew larger and larger, and more and more interconnected with broader financial markets and the "shadow" banking system of nonbank financial institutions, meant that the systemic threats of single-bank failures grew well beyond those anticipated or funded by the FDIC. This is true not merely because of the number of failures itself, but because multiple failures lead to asset price devaluation and so lower effective recoveries in individual liquidations. Hence, there is a long-neglected systemic component to deposit insurance.

The FDIC played a significant role before and during the financial crisis of 2008. In 2000, Chairwoman Donna Tanoue proposed guidance on how banks might avoid purchasing securitized predatory subprime loans, and urged higher capital standards for subprime loans. She was opposed by members of Congress from both parties and by the bankers themselves. Again ignoring bankers' wishes, the FDIC opposed implementation of the Basel II reserve requirements, which were less onerous than existing American standards. Partly as a result, when the crisis hit, US banks were better capitalized than their European counterparts. Sheila Bair, whom President George W. Bush appointed to chair the agency in 2006, was widely viewed as a more assertive regulator than her colleagues in Washington and New York. In 2007 she warned about poor mortgage lending standards and took a notably more aggressive and even populist tone than her Treasury or Federal Reserve counterparts as the crisis developed.

One problem for reformers like Tanoue and Bair is that the FDIC is but one part of the complex patchwork of federal and state financial regulation. It shares authority with the Federal Reserve System, the Office of the Comptroller of the Currency, and other agencies. Historically, this complexity has permitted regulatory competition that may favor industry interests, and the agencies ultimately answer to a heavily lobbied Congress. Moreover, whatever the policy views of its leadership, each body has a strong self-interest in preserving (or expanding) its remit. During passage of financial reform following the crisis, for example, the FDIC joined other incumbent regulators in opposing any loss of authority to the anticipated Consumer Financial Protection Agency.

While not at the center of decision-making in either the George W. Bush or Barack Obama administration's crisis management, the FDIC joined efforts to ensure continued liquidity. The insured deposit ceiling was raised to $250,000 to ensure that systemic liquidity problems did not provoke panic.

At the urging of the Treasury and the Federal Reserve, the FDIC extended guarantees to as much as $1.5 trillion of new bank holding company debt, and was involved in several bank restructurings. After the crisis, Bair attempted to make clear that large banks would not be bailed out in the future, but instead would be wound down. She even went so far as to warn the rating agency Standard & Poor's that it should not include any assumed FDIC bailout in assessing financial institutions. Before leaving her post in 2011, Bair argued that banks should no longer be allowed to grow "too big to fail," and that systemically important institutions must be very closely watched by regulators who could then more aggressively manage the "resolution" (winding down) of failing firms in the interest of taxpayers.

[*See also* Financial Industry; Glass-Steagall Act; Gramm-Leach-Bliley Act; *and* Regulation.]

BIBLIOGRAPHY

Bair, Sheila. "We Must Resolve to End Too Big to Fail." *FDIC Quarterly* 5, no. 2 (2011): 25–29.

Johnson, Simon, and James Kwak. *13 Bankers: The Wall Street Takeover and the Next Financial Meltdown.* (New York, 2010).

McClean, Bethany, and Joe Nocera. *All the Devils Are Here: The Hidden History of the Financial Crisis.* (New York, 2010).

Alistair Howard

FEDERALISM

Modern federalism, according to the British political scientist K. C. Wheare (1964), was invented in Philadelphia two hundred years ago by the authors of the US Constitution. Until then, a federal country had been seen as a league or club of member states. Under the US Constitution, however, each citizen is a citizen of two governments: the national government and the state government.

There is general agreement among experts that a functioning federal system, composed of a number of regional governments, must have a democratic and pluralist political system that provides opportunities for access and participation by citizens at both the national and state levels. Otherwise, the idea of self-expression by the regional component governments would not be meaningful. (The term "state" is used to refer to various regional entities—states, provinces, republics, cantons, *Länder*—in this article.) Most experts also agree that an effective federal form needs to operate under a written constitution that stipulates the responsibilities of the central and state governments, the role of the states in the amendatory process, and the rights of citizenship.

Advocates of federalism see it as a way to protect against central tyranny, increase citizen participation, encourage innovation (seeing the states as "laboratories" for new policies and approaches), and strengthen community identity and values. Opponents of the federal form criticize its slowness to respond to new challenges, its perceived inability to take advantage of technological advances, and the allegedly cumbersome nature of its governmental decision-making and implementation processes.

The basic objective of federalism is to reconcile unity and diversity. In particular, federalism has been adopted in various forms by many nations as a way to balance the interests of different ethnic and language groups—although this was not the purpose of the founders of US federalism—in some cases where former colonies covering a large territory with a vast unsettled frontier were joined together. The Swiss federation, founded in 1848, has twenty-three cantons (the equivalent of states in the United States). For over one hundred years, it has balanced the interests of three major ethnic and language groups (German, French, and Italian). Federalism in India and Canada likewise seeks to reconcile the interests of different ethnic and language groups, although the tensions in these countries have, at various times, caused serious problems for the federalism bargain.

Among political scientists, there are debates about the nature of federalism. One school stresses the amorphous nature of federalism and its operational complexity. The US political scientist Morton Grodzins, a leading exponent of this position, likened modern federalism to a marble cake (rather than a layer cake) characterized by constantly shifting, swirling patterns of functions, finances, and administrative arrangements. Some members of the Grodzins school describe federalism as inevitably progressing toward a centralized governmental system. According to this view, federalism is, in effect, a way station on the path toward unitary government.

A second school highlights the distinctive role of regional governments in federal systems, however designated: states, provinces, republics, cantons, *Länder*. Some members of this second school view federalism as cyclical in nature, noting that the role of states tends to increase in some periods and contract in others. Generally speaking, the role of the central government tends to expand in liberal periods (that is, periods in which progovernmental views are strong) and to contract in conservative periods (in which, in turn, the role of the states expands).

Many nations have attempted to institute a federal form, sometimes copying the actual wording of the US Constitution. Often, however, they either have not carried out the intent or have tried to do so but were unable to establish or maintain a federal form. The Caribbean Federation and the East African Federation are examples of failed federations. The Soviet Union was federal in its formal constitution but not in actual behavior; it has now been replaced by a far looser association that includes the Russian federation, which consists of twelve republics. The emergence of a unified market among the member nations of the European Union (EU) raises the interesting prospect of a movement toward a federal system in Europe.

A useful way to view the federal bargain is to focus on major aspects of the role of state governments including, for example: (1) the political and constitutional aspect of the federal relationship, referring to the powers of the states to determine, organize, and control their own legal and electoral systems; (2) their fiscal role, referring to the way in which, and the degree to which, the states can set and levy their own taxes; (3) the programmatic dimension of federalism, referring to the functional areas of governmental activity over which the states have sole or predominant responsibility; (4) the role of state governments in the policy-setting process of the central government (for example, in the upper house of the legislature); and (5) the role of the states in determining the form, functions, and finances of local units of government.

Countries currently and frequently classified as federal are Australia, Canada, Brazil, the Federal Republic of Germany, India, Malaysia, Nigeria, Russia, Switzerland, and the United States.

[*See also* Citizenship; *and* Constitution, US.]

BIBLIOGRAPHY

Anton, Thomas Julius. *American Federalism and Public Policy: How the System Works.* (New York, 1989).

Nathan, Richard P., and Margaret M. Balmaceda. "Comparing Federal Systems of Government." In *Decentralization, Local Governments, and Markets: Towards a Post-Welfare Agenda*, edited by Robert J. Bennett. (Oxford, 1990).

Wheare, K. C. *Federal Government.* 4th ed. (New York, 1964).

Richard P. Nathan

FEDERAL RESERVE BANK

The Federal Reserve System ("the Fed") is America's independent central bank, wielding monetary policy to influence the macro-economy. Shrouded in technocratic mystique, the Fed is generally admired by economists and neglected by political scientists. This is unfortunate, given its considerable ability to act decisively, its distributive significance, and the periodic outbursts of populist hostility it attracts.

Most prominently, the Fed is expected to slow or halt macroeconomic downturns by influencing the amount of credit made available to banks, and thereby to businesses and consumers. In the past it has also assiduously worked against the inflationary pressures of overly rapid growth. Indeed, one chairman described his role as "to take away the punchbowl just when the party gets going." Today, some fault Alan Greenspan's Fed for not restraining housing and credit bubbles prior to the financial crisis of

2008, thereby making the inevitable collapse all the worse. Whatever its culpability, under its new chairman, Ben Bernanke, the Fed took unprecedented measures once the bubble burst.

The Fed also has less visible functions. It is lender of last resort and supervisor of member banks; it is the settler of inter-bank transactions; and it is the banker to the federal government. It pays Treasury obligations, holds its deposits, and creates the currency. Ultimately, as well, it could "monetize" the national debt by reducing the dollar's value, so joining a time-honored tradition of currency debasement. Going into the second decade of the 2000s, this is the great fear of the populist Tea Party movement and its doyen, Congressman Ron Paul.

Operation and Functioning. Formally, a board of governors and twelve reserve banks make up the Federal Reserve system. Reflecting early fears of a central bank, the Fed is decentralized, with regional banks handling financial and regulatory functions for member commercial banks. At the national level, macroeconomic policy decisions are made at regular meetings of the Federal Open Market Committee (FOMC), with target interest rates reflecting competing views on relative inflation and deflation risks.

Policy is implemented through three monetary policy tools, each of which influences the level of bank reserves, and so also the money supply: they are open market operations, the discount rate at which the Fed lends to member banks, and bank reserve requirements. Open market operations are most important, and involve buying and selling securities to large banks, which effectively increases or decreases those banks' reserves.

The Fed ensures financial stability by acting as lender of last resort. Indeed, it was created in 1913 not for macroeconomic purposes but to prevent bank failures. Early fractional reserve banking was prone to liquidity problems, as when customers demanded more cash than the bank had at hand. America's many thousands of local banks regularly lost customer's confidence, suffered "runs," and were forced to deny savers their money. Even when unfounded, these episodes were self-fulfilling and

extremely contagious. Too often fellow banks were unable or unwilling to lend support. Today the Fed provides short-term liquidity to some fifteen hundred of the nation's leading commercial (retail) banks, and in return shares supervisory responsibility for them.

By 2007, however, decades of deregulation meant that systemic liquidity risks were no longer confined to member banks. The rise of market-based finance and a shadow banking system caused a mismatch between the Fed's banking focus and new sources of risk. During the financial crisis the Fed went well beyond its conventional remit, extending liquidity to markets and even nonfinancial corporations.

Independence and Mandate. Neoliberal economists prefer independent central banks with narrow mandates. The Fed is a model in the first respect but not in the second. It is insulated from political influence in several ways. It is not formally part of the executive branch and is not funded through congressional appropriations. Legislative oversight is achieved largely through regular reporting and congressional hearings, and narrowly defined audit. Although the president appoints the seven board governors (with Senate consent), they serve staggered fourteen-year terms. The president's greatest occasional power is to appoint the board's chair for renewable four-year terms. Over the decades, several strong chairmen governed the Fed, setting the direction of policy and leaving a prominent macroeconomic legacy.

The Fed's legislative mandate is broad. While the European Central Bank and Bank of England privilege monetary stability, American law sets "maximum employment, stable prices, and moderate long-term interest rates" as goals. Beyond that it has considerable discretion, and while it does not explicitly target inflation rates, it has historically prioritized monetary stability.

Historical Controversies. Because of the varied distributive effects of fighting inflation and deflation, the Fed's macroeconomic role attracts the greatest political attention. Constraining credit to prevent inflation slows investment, growth, and employment over the short term. There remains an inherent division between inflation's losers (savers, those on fixed incomes, bond markets) and those with less to lose (debtors and workers who can extract nominal pay increases). Insulated from elections, central bankers often fear inflation more than unemployment, and argue that only stable money promotes sustainable employment. Yet following the 2008 financial crisis, a Japan-style decade of deflation loomed, despite signs of commodity inflation, and the FOMC responded accordingly.

By contrast, during the early 1920s, the 1930s, and the early 1980s, critics attacked the Fed for prioritizing inflation over unemployment. It induced severe contractions (1920–1921 and 1981–1982) and then kept money tight in the face of sluggish employment growth. It arguably also allowed sector-specific deflation, as during the mid-to-late 1980s in the case of manufacturing and agriculture. Chairman Paul Volcker's famous and successful battle against 13.5 percent inflation in 1980 resulted in a contraction of 3 percent in 1981–1982, and the unemployment rate hovered near 10 percent. Inflation was conquered and aggregate headline unemployment did eventually fall.

The significance of the "Volcker shock" went beyond its proximate goal of killing inflation. It signaled the triumph of neoliberalism and, less comprehensively, of monetarism. It demonstrated that the Fed's chief constituents were bond markets rather than the broader political-economic groupings of labor, agriculture, and industry. The practical and intellectual significance of markets continued to grow throughout subsequent decades.

Ronald Reagan appointed Alan Greenspan to succeed Volcker, and he served for seventeen years, during what was known as the "Great Moderation"— a period of relative macroeconomic stability and low inflation. Greenspan's command of the Fed was widely celebrated and the *Financial Times* described him, in the end, as "the most powerful man in the world."

Greenspan believed as a matter of principle that government was in no position to second-guess markets, or to determine whether they were overvalued. The dominant working assumption was that deregulated financial markets, because of their very complexity, priced assets properly. On the one hand, individual investors were sophisticated and presumably best able to bet their money (or their client's money) appropriately. On the other, the efficient markets hypothesis guaranteed that, like the wise crowd of popular legend, the collective outcome was proper, at least in the long run. One consequence was that the Fed found itself mopping up after asset bubbles burst, rather than deflating them as they inflated.

With the bursting of the Internet bubble in 2000, the 9/11 attacks, and long-term structural erosion of wages, Greenspan's Fed cut rates between 2001–2003, and with support from Ben Bernanke as a Fed governor, allowed ever greater private debt to accumulate. Surplus-trading countries that recycled dollar earnings into American assets further inflated the bubble. But at the Fed the practice of "leaning against" the prevailing winds of the business cycle was ignored, at least on the upside.

The Financial Crisis. With signs of trouble in the securitized mortgage market spreading throughout the American financial system, liquidity dried up in the late summer of 2007. As banks' and nonbank financial institutions' assets lost value rapidly, contagion threatened general financial stability in the banking system; through no fault of their own, companies large and small found it hard to access the day-to-day financing needed to operate in a complex economy. The Fed pushed interest rates down from 5.25 percent to 0.25 percent in just sixteen months. At the same time, it began supplying the market with more funds than needed to achieve those rates (it was engaged in quantitative easing) and interest rates fell even further.

Using its emergency powers for the first time since the 1930s, the Fed became the lender of last resort well beyond the banking system. During 2008–2009, the Fed more than doubled reserve bank credit, injecting $1.5 trillion into America's $14 trillion economy. It lent not only to its member institutions but also to nonmember financial institutions deemed systemically important, like Bear Stearns and American International Group (AIG). It purchased troubled assets from Citigroup and Bank of America. Its Term Securities Lending Facility and Primary Dealer Credit Facility enabled the Fed to further support its "primary dealers"—the largest Wall Street and international financial institutions with which it conducts open market operations. It assisted the largest domestic and foreign institutions by taking on their illiquid assets as collateral in return for loans of US Treasuries, and by loaning cash directly. It entered commercial paper markets, lending directly to nonfinancial companies. Ultimately it also supported the two "government-sponsored entities" in the American housing market—Fannie Mae and Freddie Mac—after they had been taken into receivership by the government. All of this amounted to a fantastic transfer of risk from the private to the public sector—something neither expected in Congress nor sanctioned in legislation. It also prevented wholesale financial collapse at a time when the executive and legislative branches of the government seemed incapable of decisive action.

Fighting Stagnation. Even as the Fed keeps interest rates near zero for long periods, banks may refuse to lend. Interest rate policy thus "loses traction." One option is to influence longer-term rates by "qualitative easing," or purchasing Treasury bonds with longer maturities. A more dramatic initiative is "quantitative easing," in which the Fed "expands its balance sheet" by exchanging money for assets it will hold. This directly increases the money supply further. The Fed did this twice with the onset of the 2008 crisis-induced recession. With unemployment high and inflation below 2 percent, the Fed launched another round of quantitative easing in November 2010. There were loud complaints from some quarters. The politician David Stockman called it an injection of "high-grade monetary heroin" that would kill the patient. Others saw it as an effort to monetize the debt, and likely to create inflation. Foreign governments, including those of China and Germany, complained that it further reduced the strength of the dollar. Yet quantitative easing need not be permanent: in an upturn the Fed can raise reserve requirements and sell its bonds, thereby soaking up liquidity and guarding against inflation.

Criticisms and Populist Fears. For all its alacrity, the Fed is again enduring a period of unpopularity, both with Tea Party populists and mainstream conservatives. The latter argue the Fed should be relieved of its employment mandate and focus solely on monetary stability, perhaps through inflation targeting. This would require less monetary stimulus and reduce the likelihood of any monetization of the debt. Periodically, too, Congress highlights more commonplace administrative controversies, including the Fed's famed secrecy, insufficient internal controls, and undue political influence on legislation. The Fed's extraordinary initiatives after 2007 brought these issues to the fore, and added several more. In particular, critics objected to the Fed's loans to nonmember firms, to nonfinancial corporations, to foreign banks, and even to foreign central banks.

The latter was especially outraging to the Tea Party movement. Small groups of left- and right-wing populists have long portrayed the Fed as an unconstitutional source of profits for its member "stockholders" (in fact, it pays its surpluses into the Treasury) and as an unreliable bastion of the fiat currency. More reasonably, perhaps, they are uncomfortable with the quasi-public–semi-private nature of the Fed in an administrative state marked by well-defined, formal boundaries between public and private. Longstanding efforts in the House of Representatives to audit the Fed—to discover exactly what it does, and for whom—were reinvigorated by the 2010 midterm Republican victory, not least because its perennial critic Ron Paul rose to chair the key oversight committee.

A final source of anger is concern that the Fed is monetizing the federal debt, or at least that it facilitates deficit spending. Rick Perry, the Texas governor and a candidate for the 2012 Republican presidential nomination, made early headlines in mid-2011 by charging that Chairman Bernanke's quantitative easing was tantamount to treason.

Given the remarkable autonomy and economic power of the Federal Reserve, and its insulation from legislative influence and party control, it will likely continue to attract such hostility. And perhaps for the same reasons, economists and policy analysts will continue to admire it.

[*See also* Financial Crisis of 2008; Financial Industry; *and* Monetary Policy.]

BIBLIOGRAPHY

Greider, William. *Secrets of the Temple: How the Federal Reserve Runs the Country.* (New York, 1987).

Livingston, James. *Origins of the Federal Reserve System.* (Ithaca, N.Y., 1986).

Thomas, Lloyd Brewster. *The Financial Crisis and Federal Reserve Policy.* (New York, 2011).

Alistair Howard

FEMINIZATION OF POVERTY

The phrase "feminization of poverty" came into use in the late 1970s as an expression encapsulating the phenomenon of women's increasing presence among the ranks of the poor. The US sociologist Diana Pearce coined the phrase in 1978, and the popular media began to use it by the early 1980s. In 1981, the President's National Advisory Council on Economic Opportunity made the prediction that "all other things being equal, if the proportion of the poor in female headed families were to continue to increase at the same rate as it did from 1967 to 1978, the poverty population would be composed solely of women and their children by the year 2000." This prognosis was widely mentioned in discussions of domestic policy during the 1984 presidential election. By 1990, the feminization of poverty was commonly cited whenever poverty and gender were discussed together.

Although there are analytic problems with the term, its popularity served the important purpose of bringing the particularities of women's poverty to political attention. There are two major reasons why women in most societies have been historically and are currently vulnerable to poverty. First, women's access to breadwinner's wages, and the social benefits accruing to them, have been limited by cultural expectations, discrimination, and employment and educational segregation. Second, most cultures have assigned women the bulk of society's unpaid caregiving work: child care, care for elderly and infirm family members, and general family maintenance duties.

Such nurturing obligations compete for women's time and attention when they enter the wage labor market, and yield the label "dependence" when they are supported economically by the paid employment of husbands, by government transfer payments, or by private charity.

Several social changes which began to take root in the late twentieth century have caused women's long-standing poverty to represent an increasing proportion of the entire poverty population, increasing from 50 percent of all poor adults in the United States in 1960 to 62 percent by 1995. Most important has been that the growing acceptability of women's participation in the labor market has contributed to a dramatic rise in the numbers of two-parent families with both adults employed outside the home. Consequently, more two-parent families have been able to escape poverty status—even as the related overall lessening of the "family wage" has left families or households with only one wage earner more vulnerable to poverty. At the same time, a complex set of social forces—including the increased cultural tolerance for divorce and the expansion of social welfare benefits—has led to a dramatic increase in the number of divorced and never-married mothers: in the United States, families headed by women have doubled in proportion to all families since the late twentieth century. In addition, gender differences in longevity within the expanding elderly segment of the population mean that more older women live longer as singles, and are therefore more likely to live in poverty at some point during their lives.

Taken together, these trends yield a poverty population in most Western industrial nations that is increasingly composed of single women and their children. Policy advocates, politicians, and feminists have viewed this situation with alarm and have called for a wide array of responses aimed at both changing the nature of the problem, and responding directly to the needs of poor women and their families. The most widespread political responses have been two-pronged. On the one hand, there has been a call among mainstream politicians and policy advocates for more public support for "family-friendly" policies, to promote greater self-sufficiency for women who face problems finding jobs with adequate wages in the labor market (e.g., child care subsidies, child support assurance, earned income tax credits, paid family leave). On the other hand, the more significant policy response has been to overhaul the income maintenance supports that have historically been targeted toward single mothers. Especially in English-speaking nations, and most profoundly in the United States, "welfare reform" has been proposed as the solution to women's pauperization, at least, if not to the problem of women's poverty itself.

In the United States, since the 1980s, wide political support grew for the idea that women's poverty was sustained, if not caused, by the existence of a welfare system that offered an entitlement to income without a mandate that all adults (single-parent mothers as well as all fathers and most married mothers) must rely on private employment, and not government subsidies, as their primary source of income. In 1988, the Family Support Act altered the national welfare system that had been established as part of the Social Security Act of 1935, so that the basic federal family income subsidy (Aid to Families with Dependent Children, or AFDC) was linked much more closely to employment. This was accomplished primarily through inclusion of mandated work requirements, as well as permission for a host of state options mandating that women participate in work, training, or community service activities in exchange for support. From 1989 until 1996, heated policy debates occurred in Congress, and in state legislatures, over the future direction of "welfare reform."

As the research and debates continued, the policy focus shifted away from creating an overt response to the feminization of poverty, or even to the existence of poverty itself. Instead the goal for many became, in President Bill Clinton's 1992 campaign phrase, to "end welfare as we know it." The passage, after rancorous debate, but finally with significant bipartisan support, of the Personal Responsibility and Work Opportunity Reconciliation Act (PRWORA) in August 1996 was the culmination of this debate. Among other things, this important piece of legislation

"devolved" responsibility for income maintenance to the states—replacing AFDC as a federal entitlement with the Temporary Assistance to Needy Families (TANF) program, available through a federal block grant structure. PRWORA mandated a five-year time limit for receipt of federal income subsidies to families headed by able-bodied adults, and linked provision of federal funding to work participation among increasing numbers of recipients. There was a de-emphasis on education and training, and an explicit approach of "work first," whereby welfare recipients should be helped—even pushed—into employment as a condition for receipt of child care, training, and other subsidies. There were provisions aimed at reducing teen pregnancy and "illegitimacy" rates as well.

From 1995 through 1998, welfare rolls in the United States began a dramatic decline, of over 30 percent in many states. Many, including former President Clinton, have seen this drop as an indication that state and federal welfare reform is working. Others have pointed out that, despite low unemployment rates, family poverty is not decreasing, but rather is increasing or holding steady, and that a decline in welfare participation may increase children's poverty. For a range of reasons, women's poverty, as such, commands little public attention except in terms of providing the transitional child care, transportation, employment, and health care subsidies that are required to move people from "welfare to work."

Other countries, especially English-speaking nations, have begun to consider proposals for reforming their income maintenance programs along the US model—again with the stated goal of reducing "welfare dependence," not necessarily women's poverty. Indeed, by the early twenty-first century, the "feminization of poverty" may well have become a historical term useful for crystallizing the debates of the 1980s, and still descriptive of the problems facing single mothers, but anachronistic in relation to ongoing policy debates in the United States and other industrial nations.

[*See also* Aid to Families with Dependent Children; Gender and Politics; Personal Responsibility and

Work Opportunity Reconciliation Act; Temporary Assistance for Needy Families; *and* Welfare State.]

BIBLIOGRAPHY

Albelda, Randy, and Chris Tilly. *Glass Ceilings and Bottomless Pits: Women's Work, Women's Poverty.* (Boston, 1997).

Dujon, Diane, and Ann Withorn, eds. *For Crying Out Loud: Women's Poverty in the United States.* (Boston, 1996).

Edin, Katherine, and Laura Lein. *Making Ends Meet: How Single Mothers Survive Welfare and Low Wage Work.* (New York, 1997).

Ann Withorn

FILIBUSTER

The "filibuster" is an informal term describing a technique of extended debate in the US Senate. On most legislation, the Senate's rules do not limit debate. As long as a senator seeks recognition to speak, or a senator continues to speak, debate cannot be limited. By filibustering, senators attempt to prevent a vote on a measure or amendment.

The term "filibuster" was adopted to describe such extended debate in the mid-nineteenth century. The term was imported from the then-popular Spanish word *filibustero*, which used to describe pirates and marauders who plundered the Spanish West Indies and other parts of the Americas. The term came to be used to describe a rebellious technique for disrupting Senate action.

Between 1806 and 1917, the Senate had no rule that allowed a motion to limit debate and cause a vote. In 1917, the Senate adopted Rule 22, which allowed two-thirds of senators present and voting to invoke cloture. In 1949, the rule was amended to raise the threshold to two-thirds of all elected senators and to allow cloture on procedural motions, except motions to consider changes in Senate rules. In 1959, the rule was amended again to reduce the threshold to two-thirds of senators present and voting, and to allow cloture on measures related to Senate rules. In 1975, the threshold was reduced to three-fifths of all elected senators, except for measures related to Senate rules, which continued to be subject to the two-thirds present and voting threshold.

In the late twentieth and early twenty-first century, filibusters and threatened filibusters have become more common. They are used by members of the minority party to block legislation and to gain bargaining leverage with the majority party.

[*See also* Congress, US.]

BIBLIOGRAPHY

Binder, Sarah A., and Steven S. Smith. *Politics or Principle? Filibustering in the United States Senate.* (Washington, D.C., 1997).

Burdette, Franklin L. *Filibustering in the Senate.* (Princeton, N.J., 1940).

Steven S. Smith

FINANCE, INTERNATIONAL

International finance refers to monetary transactions across political borders, usually involving the exchange of currencies. Because different economies use different currencies, basic transactions such as trade, loans, and asset sales are more risky and complicated when conducted internationally.

Arrangements for setting exchange rates are the core of the international monetary system. At one extreme, nations can fix (or "peg") the price of their currency relative to others. In the late nineteenth century, for example, most currencies were convertible into gold, effectively fixing their exchange rates. The result was a predictable environment for international transactions, with a strong anti-inflationary bias. But it was also an environment that gave national monetary authorities little autonomy or discretion. At the other extreme, currency rates can be determined on a daily basis in the marketplace. They fluctuate (or "float") as supply and demand varies among currency traders, importers, and exporters. Monetary authorities may still intervene, either to dampen short-term volatility or to influence the long-term direction of rates (so-called "managed floating"), but they are not committed to either fixed rates or to specified target zones. Such floating rates pose uncertainties for traders and investors, but they give monetary authorities wide scope to determine national policies.

All these varied monetary arrangements have been tried since World War II. As the war drew to a close, the United States and Great Britain organized a multilateral conference to reconstruct the world financial system. Meeting at Bretton Woods, New Hampshire, in 1944, they devised a new system of fixed exchange rates. Though nominally based on gold, the Bretton Woods system was actually based on the one currency that was widely accepted for exchange and reserve purposes: the US dollar. Reconstruction proved slower than anticipated, and most European currencies did not become fully convertible until the late 1950s. But once established, the Bretton Woods system of pegged rates lasted for more than a decade, providing a stable framework for trade and investment among the world's major economies.

The central principle of this system was its stable exchange rates; rates varied only within narrow bands, and larger changes were permitted only to cope with fundamental balance-of-payments problems. The International Monetary Fund (IMF), which was established at Bretton Woods, monitored the system and provided short-term resources to help states hold their currencies within these bands. A crucial element of the arrangements was the informal US pledge to redeem dollars for gold at $35 per ounce. Foreign central banks relied on that pledge, and held dollars as well as gold to settle their balance-of-payment shortfalls. This "dollar-exchange" system of pegged rates permitted world trade to grow steadily on a base of expanding dollar reserves.

There were, however, fundamental difficulties in implementing the system. One overriding worry was the problem of earning enough hard currency to overcome the "dollar shortage" of the 1940s and 1950s. Economist Robert Triffin (1960) looked further ahead and saw that the real crisis would not be too few dollars, but rather too many. As dollars slowly accumulated in foreign central banks, they would eventually exceed US gold holdings. When that happened, the US pledge to redeem dollars for gold would become untenable, and the system itself unstable.

Triffin's point and its implications were soon acknowledged by experts, but the structural problems were never solved.

The Bretton Woods arrangements suffered another fundamental problem that festered throughout the 1960s: its uneven impact on balance-of-payment adjustment. While deficit countries faced clear pressures to deflate in order to maintain exchange rates, surplus countries such as Germany did not face similar constraints and were not forced to revalue. The dollar—the linchpin of the system—also faced mounting difficulties. Although the United States had unique advantages as the creator of dollar reserves, it had no effective way to depreciate a currency that was becoming increasingly overvalued.

The strong dollar profoundly affected America's role in the world economy. It stimulated vast increases in US foreign investment, which became a contentious issue in Western Europe, especially in France. At home, it damaged exports and encouraged imports, hurting all traded-good industries. America's international deficits were growing, and the Bretton Woods system offered no clear avenue to limit them. Unlike other deficit countries, the United States could simply fund its shortfall by printing the world's reserve currency, and it did so. Private speculators added to the pressures to realign exchange rates. With capital markets now closely linked, they could move large sums into stronger currencies, such as the deutsche mark, instantly and at low risk.

The Bretton Woods system finally collapsed in August 1971, when France and the Federal Republic of Germany (West Germany) began converting their burgeoning dollar reserves into gold, forcing the United States to abandon its convertibility pledge. Efforts to restore a fixed-rate system using new parities (the 1971 Smithsonian Agreement) ultimately failed. By default, the world's major currencies began floating. (Less developed economies continued to peg their exchange rates to one or two large trading partners.) This unplanned system has persisted ever since, combining floating rates and ad hoc intervention by monetary authorities. The major economic powers have sometimes intervened jointly, as they did after the 1985 Plaza Agreement and the 1987

Louvre Accord. The aim of this informal (and often short-lived) cooperation is to manage the crucial nexus of the dollar, yen, and deutsche mark.

Since the breakdown of Bretton Woods, the only sustained institutional effort to control exchange rates has been a regional one in Europe. Beginning in 1972, the European Community (EC), which was known as the European Economic Community until 1993, led by France and Germany, sought to facilitate trade and investment by narrowing their regional currency movements. Their cooperation was formalized in 1979 against the backdrop of continued dollar instability. The stated goal was to create "a zone of monetary stability in Europe." Not only has the European Monetary System succeeded; its leading members actually managed to create a usable common currency (the euro) and an independent monetary authority (the European Central Bank), all complementing the larger process of European integration.

Outside of Western Europe, central banks have found it extremely difficult to manage exchange rates. Private financial markets now determine currency rates on a day-to-day basis. To affect these rates directly, central banks buy and sell foreign exchange in the markets, in the hope of shifting private agents' expectations, and thus the composition of their currency portfolios. It is a difficult task and often an unsuccessful one, made more difficult by traders' ability to move vast sums of short-term capital electronically across borders. These private markets dwarf the scale of intervention by monetary authorities, even joint intervention, and proved to be a major source of instability during the Asian financial crisis of the late 1990s.

Ironically, private currency markets are so large partly because floating rates are so volatile. To control their exposure to currency movements, multinational corporations hedge with foreign-exchange contracts and use international capital markets to match longer-term assets and liabilities in multiple currencies. The result is a vast international market for short-term capital—a market that dwarfs the underlying transactions of importers, exporters, and long-term investors. The growth of these interdependent

markets for capital and foreign exchange represents an important shift in international financial structure. The world's largest capital market, the London-based Euromarket, is now an essentially unregulated one. Along with other "offshore" banking centers, it eliminates many of the costs and constraints of domestic banking.

The offshore markets began in the early 1960s, fostered by US restrictions on interest rates and a tax on foreign borrowing. Major US banks responded by allowing their London subsidiaries to accept deposits and grant loans denominated in dollars. The Euromarkets grew rapidly because of their cost advantages for large-scale depositors and borrowers. They benefited from low regulatory overhead and intense competition among international banks. These offshore markets—from London to Hong Kong—became centers of global finance, increasing the pressures to deregulate national financial markets in Western Europe, Japan, and North America.

The Euromarket's largest participants are multinational firms, but the most controversial members are Third World states. Their borrowing started in the early 1970s, aimed at sustaining rapid growth without dependence on direct foreign investment. Debts grew dramatically after the oil shock of 1973–1974, funded, ironically, by bank deposits from oil-producing states ("petrodollar recycling"). Lending standards seemed relaxed, at least in retrospect, but commercial credits were still limited to larger economies in Latin America and Asia, plus a few states with rich natural resources. Weaker economies, such as those of sub-Saharan Africa, had to rely on aid donors.

Banking syndicates made their loans on standard commercial terms, usually five to ten years, with principal due at the conclusion of the agreement. Interest rates were recalculated periodically to reflect the banks' cost of funds. Profits came from initial fees and negotiated "spreads" above the interest costs. These arrangements marked a substantial change from foreign lending practices over the past 150 years. Earlier loans were mostly bonds, sold by banking houses to individual investors. Defaults were not uncommon, but they generally harmed bondholders and not the banking system. The quality of Euromarket loans, on the other hand, directly affects the solvency of large banks. National monetary authorities are thus drawn into foreign loan problems and their renegotiation.

After a second oil shock in the early 1980s, these loan problems proliferated. The world economy contracted and commodity prices fell sharply. Real interest rates soared and remained high. As a result, debt burdens rose while debt-servicing capacity plummeted. In August 1982, Mexico announced its inability to meet current debts. It was soon followed by most other major debtors among the developing countries, including Brazil, Argentina, and Venezuela. The debt crisis was initially understood as a short-term emergency, requiring an infusion of liquidity and a sharp contraction of imports. The banks moved to reschedule immediate obligations, but offered no debt forgiveness. Before any rescheduling, they insisted that debtors agree to austerity programs supervised by the International Monetary Fund.

Perceptions of the debt crisis gradually changed as it persisted through the 1980s and early 1990s. Debtors paid a high price in political instability, forgone income, and lower future productivity, but without returning to creditworthiness. Commercial banks, export-credit agencies, and aid donors finally began to set aside major loan-loss reserves and to write down their impaired credits. Official US policies were also changing. The initial focus had been almost exclusively on the banking system's stability, and that remains important. But beginning in 1985, the United States also began to promote structural adjustment and economic growth as longer-term solutions. The Baker Plan, developed under Treasury Secretary James Baker, was underfunded and unsuccessful, but it did signal a policy shift. The 1989 Brady Plan, also from the Treasury, went further and encouraged commercial debt relief. Even so, the largest debtors continue to face heavy payments and find it difficult to attract voluntary lending. With credit markets so tight, a number of less developed countries have changed their approach to international finance, reversing their long-standing opposition to

multinational firms and inviting new equity investments. Some poorer states in Africa and Asia, however, have been unable to attract either new loans or significant foreign investment. Unable to meet their current interest payments, they have been forced to reschedule debts and seek large-scale relief from private creditors and aid donors.

BIBLIOGRAPHY

Eichengreen, Barry. *Globalizing Capital: A History of the International Monetary System.* (Princeton, N.J., 1996).

Kahler, Miles, ed. *The Politics of International Debt.* (Ithaca, N.Y., 1986).

Lipson, Charles. *Standing Guard: Protecting Foreign Capital in the Nineteenth and Twentieth Centuries.* (Berkeley, Calif., 1985).

Sachs, Jeffrey D. *Developing Country Debt and Economic Performance.* (Chicago, 1989).

Triffin, Robert. *Gold and the Dollar Crisis.* (New Haven, Conn., 1960).

Charles Lipson

FINANCIAL CRISIS OF 2008

Both the severity and the length of the "great recession" that unfolded in the wake of the 2008 financial crisis were unprecedented in the postwar era. Other periods of downturn, such as those associated with the "stagflation" of the 1970s or that resulting from the bursting of the dot.com bubble at the end of the 1990s, were of significantly lesser magnitude. If the nine preceding recessions that the National Bureau of Economic Research (NBER) has charted are considered, the US economy had, seven quarters after the beginning of the recession, grown by an average of 4 percent when compared to its prerecession peak. In the "great recession," the economy was, at a comparable point, still 3.2 percent smaller than it had been at the prerecession peak. (It should be noted, however, that although the 2007–2009 recession was longer, the unemployment rate during the recession at the beginning of the 1980s was higher. At the end of 1982 it reached 10.8 percent.) In all, there was a six-quarter or eighteen-month contraction from peak to trough beginning in December 2007, constituting the longest period of downswing and recession since March 1933.

Even after the NBER pronounced that the recession had come to a close, recovery was slow and hesitant. Indeed, at times, the shallow character of the upswing triggered fears of a "double-dip" recession. Despite a 5 percent annualized growth rate in the last quarter of 2009, growth in the eighteen months following the end of the recession averaged less than 3 percent. This should be set against estimates suggesting that the US economy requires 2.5 percent growth just to keep pace with increases in the size of the working-age population.

The anemic character of recovery that followed the recession was reflected in the unemployment figures. The jobless rate reached 10.2 percent in October 2009. This, however, provides only part of the economic picture. Alongside the headline unemployment rate, the Bureau of Labor Statistics also releases broader figures based upon the U6 measure of unemployment. This also includes the underemployed and those who have withdrawn from the labor market. The U6 figure for the same month was 17.5 percent (Leonhardt, 2009).

Other economic and social indicators also provided testimony to the severity and depth of the crisis. The numbers in poverty reached their highest level, at 43.6 million, in fifty-one years. Although senior citizens increased their income levels between 2007 and 2009, all other age cohorts lost ground. Those aged fifteen to twenty-four saw their income fall by 6.5 percent (Cauchon and Wolf, 2010). At the same time, and despite measures intended to assist those who faced losing their homes, foreclosures reached 2.8 million in 2009, a 21 percent increase when compared to 2008 and a 120 percent rise compared with 2007 (*International Business Times*, 2010).

Household wealth had begun to fall at an early stage. Although there were widespread variations, house prices dropped by 32 percent between 2006 and early 2009 (Financial Crisis Inquiry Commission, 2011: pp. 391–92). Indeed, they were still falling during 2011. There was a 3 percent drop in the first quarter of 2011 when compared with the preceding quarter, the largest fall since the first three months

of 2008 (Timiraos and Wotapka, 2011). During 2010 there were more than a million foreclosures, generally triggered by unemployment and negative equity (Herron, 2011). Stock values slid downward amid economic anxieties and as institutional stockholders sought safety in Treasury securities. As a corollary, local and state governments, many of which were bound by balanced budget statutes or constitutional requirements, faced falling revenue and growing demands upon the forms of provision that they offered.

The crisis extended well beyond American shores. As Joseph Stiglitz (2010, p. 21) has noted, "The world is too interlinked; a downturn in the United States could not but lead to a global slowdown." However, as in the Great Depression, although no country escaped its impact, the character of that impact was neither even nor uniform. Although Brazil, Russia, India, and China together with the "Next 11" (which includes nations such as Bangladesh, Egypt, and Indonesia) were hit by the loss of export markets, the contraction of world trade, and the losses incurred through the holding of American securities, growth for the most part continued, thereby accelerating the process of "catch-up" with the more advanced economies. Against this background, earlier descriptions of US decline and its weakening as a hegemon gained renewed impetus.

The European economies suffered more seriously. In some, there had been property bubbles and their banking industries were dangerously exposed. In a number of the smaller economies, this was then compounded by sovereign debt crises because of financial guarantees given at an early stage, large-scale structural deficits, or excessive borrowing. At the G-20 summit held in Washington, D.C., there was a joint commitment to strengthen financial markets and regulatory regimes and, at the same time, to ensure "closer macroeconomic cooperation." It was agreed that participating nations would "use fiscal measures to stimulate domestic demand to rapid effect, as appropriate, while maintaining a policy framework conducive to fiscal sustainability" (Council on Foreign Relations, 2008). Nonetheless, despite these affirmations, talk of "Bretton Woods II," and a commitment to hold interest rates at a minimal level by both the Federal Reserve and the European Central Bank, fiscal policy responses were very largely determined at a national level. Whereas some countries introduced large fiscal packages consisting of tax concessions, financial assistance for subnational governments, and expenditure projects, others (such as the United Kingdom) adopted more modest measures. Furthermore, by the end of 2009, some nations were already seeking an "exit route" and looking instead toward fiscal retrenchment and paying down of government debt.

Within the United States, there appeared, for a period at least, to be more political space for significant structural reform than in many of the countries of Europe. This had opened up at the end of 2008 and, following Barack Obama's inauguration, during the early months of 2009. Nonetheless, although political space allowed for the passage of the American Recovery and Reinvestment Act (a $787 billion fiscal stimulus package) in February 2009, it quickly closed off. Instead, in an even more pronounced way than in many other countries, the locus of political discourse quickly shifted to deficit reduction and to concerns about the overall size of government. This was reflected in the president's falling approval ratings; the defection of many independent voters away from the Democrats; the revitalization of the Republicans, who had initially been dispirited by President George W. Bush's last years in office and the outcome of the 2008 presidential election; and, most visibly, the rise of the Tea Party movement. By the beginning of 2011, the Obama administration had begun to place greater emphasis on the federal deficit. In contrast, therefore, with the economic crises of the 1930s and 1970s, there have been few signs that the "great recession" will give rise to a paradigmatic shift so far as public policy is concerned or a process of electoral realignment.

Proximate Causes. The proximate causes of the crisis and the recession have been well-charted. Accounts invariably point to the housing bubble earlier in the decade. Although there were significant variations between states and regions, house prices often rose dramatically. In California, a house

purchased for $200,000 in 1995 could have been sold, just nine years later, for $454,428 (Financial Crisis Inquiry Commission, 2011: p. 85). This gave individuals the confidence to buy larger or second properties and take on bigger mortgages. People also increasingly borrowed on the basis of the equity that they held in their properties. Against this background, housing market activity took an increasingly speculative form. "Flippers" secured easy profits by buying and quickly selling properties (particularly in the condominium and vacation-home markets). Others bought so as to rent. Some commentators were later to recall and apply Federal Reserve chair Alan Greenspan's earlier comment about the "irrational exuberance" of markets, although it raises some questions about the extent to which the actions of individuals and firms can be considered irrational. It might be argued that they were pursuing a course based upon perceptions of rational self-interest.

Through the wealth effect, rising property prices and growing home ownership contributed much to sustain overall US economic expansion during the years that followed the end of the dot.com boom at the beginning of the new century. Every $1,000 increase in housing wealth has been estimated to add to consumer spending by $50 a year (Financial Crisis Inquiry Commission, 2011: p. 86). There was, furthermore, a direct boost to the construction industry and demand for consumer durables. In turn, both the housing bubble and consumer spending (which also owed much to the increased availability of credit card loans as well as the use of housing equity) were facilitated by the Federal Reserve's commitment to low interest rates. From May 2000 onward, the federal funds rate was progressively reduced to just 1 percent in June 2003. It remained below 4 percent until late 2005.

The bubble set the stage for the expansion of home ownership to "subprime" borrowers (those who had low or irregular sources of income, had poor credit records, or had yet to establish credit histories), who had traditionally been excluded from the mortgage market. The process was further facilitated by securitization as well as new technology, which reduced transaction costs and simplified the calculation of risk. Although the subprime share of the market had grown from the beginning of the decade, efforts to extend the market still further by developing more creative forms of lending intensified as the overall mortgage market started to cool. The volume of mortgage originations fell by 27 percent between 2003 and 2004 (Calabria, 2011: p. 2). Lenders were increasingly squeezed as interest rates began to edge upward, transaction fee income fell (as the volume of mortgage originations declined), and their arbitrage profits fell as the yield curve for different forms of debt narrowed.

Against this background, the proportion of mortgage originations that were defined as subprime rose, reaching 23.5 percent in 2006 (Financial Crisis Inquiry Commission, 2011: p. 70). Such borrowers were offered enticements. Smaller down payments were required. Many of the loans were adjustable-rate mortgages that permitted low monthly payments (or "teaser rates") during an initial period. There was, reportedly, less concern about the integrity of the claims that mortgage applicants made in their applications; and the term "liar loan" was increasingly heard within the industry. Instead of the insurance cover customarily required for larger loans, borrowers were encouraged to take out second mortgages. Borrowing levels were often close to 100 percent of a property's market value.

These developments were tied to, and in some ways facilitated by, *securitization*. In a process sometimes dubbed "originate-to-distribute" (which superceded "originate-to-hold"), individual mortgages were bundled together so as to create securities that could in turn be traded. Then, from about 2000 onward, those tranches of mortgage-backed securities that were seen as being at higher risk of default were repackaged into collateralized debt obligations (CDOs). As risk was seemingly distributed (thereby, it was believed, reducing the possibility of a generalized crisis), about 80 percent of these would be rated by the credit agencies, such as Moody's, as AAA (the highest rating). As the Financial Crisis Inquiry Commission (2011, p. 127) noted, "it was not obvious that a pool of mortgage-backed securities rated BBB could be transformed into a new security that is

mostly rated triple-A. But math made it so." Further derivatives, including "CDOs-squared" (which were backed by CDOs rather than other forms of security) and credit-default swaps, were constructed on the basis of this edifice.

The property boom was unsustainable. Although there were regional variations, house prices started to fall in 2006 and the drop had become pronounced by early 2007. The bubble had burst, and there were reports that growing numbers of householders faced the prospect of negative equity. At about the same time, the number of mortgage delinquencies increased dramatically, particularly among those holding adjustable-rate subprime mortgages and in California, Arizona, Nevada, and Florida.

Although it appeared for almost eighteen months that these difficulties could be contained, the consequences of market collapse for the financial structures built on the basis of mortgages quickly became evident as the realizable value of assets fell or uncertainty arose about their value. There was growing talk of "toxic assets." The process of bundling so as to create securities had initially seemed to minimize risk. Now, the uncertainties that arose from bundling increasingly magnified risk.

As early as March 2007, Moody's announced that CDOs incorporating large numbers of mortgage-backed securities would probably be subject to "severe" downgrades. By late 2007, firms such as Citigroup and Merrill Lynch were reporting significant losses because of their CDO holdings. Although J.P. Morgan's federally assisted rescue of Bear Stearns in March 2008 seemed to stave off a more generalized crisis, the respite was only temporary. In September 2008, in developments that dramatically intensified the sense of panic and fears of a systemic collapse, the Federal National Mortgage Association (Fannie Mae) and the Federal Home Loan Mortgage Company (Freddie Mac), the government-sponsored enterprises that had underpinned much of the housing market through mortgage securitization, were abruptly taken into conservatorship by the Federal Housing Finance Agency. Just days later, Lehman Brothers, the investment bank, which was particularly dependent upon short-term funding and the "repo" market (within which securities are quickly repurchased at a higher price), filed for bankruptcy. Despite earlier claims from some that the larger financial institutions were "too big to fail," fears of creating a moral hazard ensured that there was no government bailout. Credit ratings for the American International Group, then the largest insurance company in the world and the holder of large numbers of credit default swaps, were downgraded. It was only saved through the provision of a credit facility by the Federal Reserve. Against this background, a political crisis broke, shaking up the course of the presidential election campaign. There were fears for the future of the entire financial sector, and in a memorable phrase, President George W. Bush warned congressional leaders that "this sucker could go down" (quoted in Reich, 2011, p. 38).

Nonetheless, financial institutions survived. Their survival owed much to the federal government's efforts, particularly the eventual passage of the Emergency Economic Stabilization Act of 2008 and the creation of the Troubled Asset Relief Program. Nonetheless, despite this, the damage to the "real economy" caused by the bursting of the housing bubble and the financial meltdown quickly became evident. As asset values fell, credit lines to both individuals and firms were tightened (a "credit crunch"), and personal debt reduction became paramount, consumer expenditure was cut and investment plans were curbed. The recession, which had begun in late 2007, seemed likely to become a prolonged depression. Comparisons with the 1930s abounded.

Narratives and Theories. Nonetheless, although the events and developments that defined the unfolding of the financial crisis can easily be charted, there were different accounts of its less proximate origins and competing narratives of its underlying causes.

Regulatory Failure. The most widely accepted narrative of the crisis (which informed the 2010 Dodd-Frank Wall Street Reform and Consumer Protection Act) rests upon claims that it arose from the underregulation of the financial sector and the ways in which this permitted excessive risk taking, excessive executive compensation, institutional as well as individual greed, and the creation of perverse incentives. Barack Obama spoke in these terms while he was on the campaign trail in 2008. The National Commission on the Causes of the Financial and Economic Crisis, which was established by Congress and President Obama in May 2009, similarly concluded that

> financial institutions made, bought, and sold mortgage securities they never examined, did not care to examine, or knew to be defective; firms depended on tens of billions of dollars of borrowing that had to be renewed each and every night, secured by subprime mortgage securities; and major firms and investors blindly relied on credit rating agencies as their arbiters of risk. What else could one expect on a highway where there were neither speed limits nor neatly painted lines? (Financial Crisis Inquiry Commission, 2011, p. xvii)

Some commentators point to particular examples of deregulation. The Securities and Exchange Commission's decision in 2004 to permit investment banks to double their leverage has been cited. Others, such as Paul Krugman (2009), point to deregulatory processes during the Reagan era, such as the 1982 Garn-St. Germain Depository Institutions Act. They ended the requirement that mortgage borrowers make substantial initial down payments and thereby increased their exposure and risk. More commonly, commentators such as Robert Kuttner (2007), in his testimony to the House Committee on Financial Services, stress the part played by the Financial Services Modernization Act of 1999 (more commonly known as the Gramm-Leach-Bliley Act), which repealed the 1933 Glass-Steagall Act and removed the already much eroded barriers between banks, securities firms, mortgage lenders, and insurance companies and suggest that this contributed to structural conflicts of interest that added to financial risk.

Others emphasize the ways in which regulatory systems failed to keep pace with the growth and changing character of the financial sector. They point, in particular, to the increasing weight of the "shadow" banking system, which, they argued, bypassed the regulatory structures that were established in earlier decades. Savings that had traditionally been placed in regulated banks had been transferred to structured investment vehicles, which were subject to markedly less regulation, and used to purchase CDOs: "those who worried about the fact that this brave new world of finance lacked a safety net were dismissed as hopelessly old-fashioned" (Krugman, 2009).

Fred Block (2008) links together deregulatory processes of the Reagan era with the tax cuts enacted during the same period. Much of the additional income secured by those in the wealthiest cohorts was, he argues, placed in hedge funds. These were subject to few controls, accepted significant levels of risk, secured high rates of return, and paved the way for other financial institutions to develop innovatory products and move into ever-riskier forms of activity.

Underregulation, it was said, permitted the growth of the subprime market and securitization. The dangers posed by these were compounded by related but distinct and separate forms of risk. There was predatory lending to those who had little hope of making repayment. The system by which individual bonuses were paid at the highest level within the financial sector encouraged irrationality. The ratings agencies, which assigned AAA status to CDOs that would, with the onset of the crisis, lose much of their earlier value, were not, it has subsequently been said, subject to effective scrutiny. The models they employed assigned insufficient weight to the possibilities of generalized market failure. They were, furthermore, funded by the sellers of securities, who had a direct interest in securing the highest possible ratings.

What explains the absence of regulation? Some point to bureaucratic inertia. The Securities and Exchange Commission was, it has been suggested, focused on the dangers posed by insider trading. There were intragovernmental tensions. Fannie Mae and Freddie Mac may have been caught between the US Treasury and Housing and Urban Development and thereby escaped oversight. Many, however, have placed particular emphasis on the political weight of the financial sector. Before his election as US president, and although his own campaign was a beneficiary, Barack Obama was among those pointing to the resources devoted by the industry to the lobbying process and the scale of its campaign contributions. This, it has been argued, led the Bush administration to cap the level of lending that Fannie Mae and Freddie Mac could undertake, a move that allowed private lenders to secure a greater market share.

Polling data suggest that, at least during the most severe period of crisis, majorities embraced a form of narrative structured around the relative absence of regulation. A March 2009 ABC News/*Washington Post* poll found that 56 percent of respondents felt that banks and other financial institutions deserved "a great deal" of blame "for taking unnecessary risks." Just 4 percent said that they deserved none or "hardly any" (PollingReport.com, 2011).

Nonetheless, the claims around which the narrative is structured are open to question. President George W. Bush increased the budget for the Securities and Exchange Commission, which had regulatory responsibility for much of the financial sector, by 76 percent in real terms. There was a corresponding increase (26 percent) in the commission's staff numbers (Calabria, 2009: p. 5). Furthermore, although the executive-compensation thesis suggests that financial institutions were guilty of excessive risk taking, 81 percent of the mortgage-backed tranches that they purchased were rated AAA. Although seemingly safer, they delivered lower returns than tranches rated AA or below: "Bankers who were indifferent to risk because they were seeking higher return, hence higher bonuses, should have bought the lower-rated tranches universally, but they did so only 19 percent of the time" (Friedman, 2009). There is also little evidence that the repeal of the Glass-Steagall Act had a direct impact on the course of events. Relatively few financial holding companies brought their investment and commercial banking activities together. The two best-known firms, Bear Stearns and Lehman Brothers, were not tied to depository institutions.

A Systemic Crisis. In place of the errors committed by policymakers, some stress the systemic character of the crisis. As the financier George Soros asserted, "the salient feature of the current financial crisis is that it was not caused by some external shock like OPEC. . . . The crisis was generated by the system itself" (quoted in Skidelsky, 2009, p. 168). Having said this, the character of the "system" to which systemic accounts refer is not always evident. In some narratives, it is the financial sector and the logic of speculative activity to which the sector is tied. This has been tied to a revival of interest in the work of Hyman Minsky (1919–1996) and the financial instability hypothesis that he put forward. Minsky saw financialization as an endogenous process within the business cycle. Periods of boom permit and encourage speculation and borrowing. Over time, that activity progresses from hedging (whereby borrowers can pay off both the interest and the principal from current earnings) to speculation (the borrower can only make interest payments) and then to Ponzi borrowing, whereby debts are serviced through the appreciation of the price of the asset. This eventually triggers a crisis, bringing forth greater government regulation of the financial sector. For some, there is a direct correspondence between the expansion of the subprime mortgage market and Minsky's schema. Indeed, there have been references to the "Minsky moment."

Other accounts, particularly those drawing upon the Marxian tradition, go beyond the financialization process (which might be open to containment through reform and regulation) and point more broadly to the laws and dynamics of capitalism. Although there are sometimes claims that such accounts have difficulty reconciling the laws of motion that, they suggest, govern the development of capitalism, and the specificities of the 2008 financial crisis, John Bellamy Foster and Fred Magdoff (2009) bring them together by focusing on the inherent tendency within capitalism toward economic stagnation (which is defined as the chronic underuse of productive capacity) as investment outlets and the opportunities to absorb the surplus generated by mature capitalism dry up. Financialization and debt grew because, together with government spending, they constituted countertendencies by

offering a temporary stimulus, thereby delaying capitalist stagnation. The bursting of the bubble brought that stimulus to an end: "Since financialization can be viewed as the response of capital to the stagnation tendency in the real economy, a crisis of financialization inevitably means a resurfacing of the underlying stagnation endemic to the advanced capitalist economy" (Foster and Magdoff, 2009, p. 133).

Inequality and Stagnation. A third narrative or explanatory framework edges toward a systemic critique but for the most part holds back from this and is instead structured around the defining characteristics of the processes that took place during the decade or so that preceded the crisis. In particular, there is an emphasis on the growth in income inequality, the relative lack of economic mobility, and the long-term failure of real wages to rise significantly. Indeed, there has been real wage stagnation. Between 2000 and 2007, typical family incomes grew by less than half a percent. Growing inequality has been compounded by a decline in economic mobility rates from about 1980 onward.

This has economic consequences. Robert Reich (2011), labor secretary during the early years of the Clinton administration, argues that the growing concentration of income among the highest earners has reduced effective demand levels because those in the higher-income cohorts have a lower marginal propensity to consume. Even more significantly, real wage stagnation created the basis for the crisis. Widespread borrowing using the equity offered rising house prices, which Josh Bivens (2011, p. 14) suggests was equivalent to almost 8 percent of disposable personal income, was an attempt to compensate for this: "In short, Americans were using the housing bubble to give themselves the 8% raise that the job market, hampered by anemic growth, was not generating for them."

Ideational Variables. A fourth account draws upon ideational variables and stresses the hegemony of discourses structured around the self-correcting character of free markets, the ability of markets to calculate risk, and, as a subsidiary claim, the seeming efficacy of the policy tools developed in preceding decades. From this perspective, the crisis owed much to the hubris of elites in the years that preceded it.

In its popular form, the narrative saw the resilience of the US economy and its ability to avoid recession after 1991 as testimony to "Reaganomics" and the implementation of supply-side policies. Many within the economics profession drew upon the efficient-markets hypothesis and the rational-expectations hypothesis. These provided a generalized affirmation of faith in market principles and the deregulation of capital markets and at the same time legitimized risk models by bolstering the belief that market-clearing processes could not permit the systematic mispricing of financial assets such as CDOs.

A subsidiary claim rests upon the proposition that the Federal Reserve could use interest rates and other forms of monetary policy in far more advanced ways than in the past. In his 2003 presidential address to the American Economic Association, Professor Robert Lucas of the University of Chicago used words that would later be cited as an example of hubris in critiques of the part played by mainstream economics in the crisis: "macroeconomics . . . has succeeded: Its central problem of depression-prevention has been solved, for all practical purposes, and has in fact been solved for many decades" (Lucas, 2003, p. 1). In particular, it has been said, Alan Greenspan, chair of the Federal Reserve between 1987 and 2006, through the judicious and pragmatic anticipation of both external shocks and the course of cyclical processes had successfully curbed the excesses of the business cycle. Indeed, he was dubbed "the maestro" by *Washington Post* writer Bob Woodward. At the end of the 1990s, Greenspan was, according to *Time* magazine (together with Lawrence Summers and Robert Rubin, who at that point headed the US Treasury), part of the "committee to save the world." Federal Reserve policy had, it was said, contained the economic fallout from the 1987 stock market crash, the 1997–1998 Asian financial crisis, the collapse of Long-Term Capital Management, and the bursting of the dot.com bubble two years later. It had, furthermore, contributed much to the strength and resilience of the "new economy" during the latter half of the 1990s.

Having said this, it should be noted that there were always doubters who challenged Greenspan's credentials. Indeed, it is fair to talk of counterhegemonic discourses. Some commentators argued that monetary tightening by the Federal Reserve had contributed to, or perhaps caused, the recession at the beginning of the 1990s. Others noted that he did not accept that the role of the Federal Reserve was to prick asset bubbles. Instead, he felt, it should restrict its activities to their consequences for the "real economy." (Zandi, 2009, p. 68). He, more than anyone else, has faced assertions that he was guilty of uncritical faith in market processes. In testimony before the House Committee on Oversight and Government Reform, Greenspan himself later acknowledged that he should have supported a greater measure of regulation: "Those of us who have looked to the self-interest of lending institutions to protect shareholder's equity—myself especially—are in a state of shocked disbelief. . . . I have found a flaw. I don't know how significant or permanent it is. But I have been very distressed by that fact" (Andrews, 2008).

Government Failure. A fifth explanatory framework, largely associated with the conservative and libertarian movement, takes issue with claims that the crisis arose from the inherent irrationality of market forces or the suboptimal outcomes that they delivered and instead argues that the crisis was caused by the distortion, or corruption, of those forces by political diktat. In other words, from this perspective, the crisis was rooted in governmental actions rather than the market: "The current financial crisis is not—as many have said—a crisis of capitalism. It is in fact the opposite: a demonstration that well-intentioned government intervention in the private economy can have devastating consequences" (Wallison, 2011, p. 172).

Successive administrations and congressional majorities, of whichever partisan hue, promoted the principle of home ownership. In many eyes, widespread home ownership not only had positive spillover effects for society but was the embodiment of the American dream.

Many small-scale incremental legislative and regulatory changes increased the demand for home ownership and made mortgages more attractive in relative terms. For example, the Tax Reform Act of 1986 ended income tax relief on the interest paid for other forms of debt but allowed unlimited deductions for mortgages on both first and second homes. At the end of 2003, President George W. Bush reaffirmed his faith in home ownership and signed the American Dream Down Payment Assistance Act, which enabled local governments to help first-time home buyers.

There are, furthermore, suggestions that the rights-based forms of discourse that emerged in the latter half of the twentieth century added weight to charges that racial and ethnic minorities seeking mortgages faced institutionalized discrimination by lenders. Minorities were, it was said, underrepresented in the home-owning sector because of racism. Political pressures were placed on the financial sector to compel them to lower the barriers that had customarily faced potential borrowers. The 1977 Community Reinvestment Act required that federally insured banks served the entire "community." Against this background, they extended loans to those who quickly encountered financial difficulties. At the same time, the lowering of underwriting standards created a moral hazard that laid a basis for irresponsibility. Borrowers who were asked to make only a small down payment or none at all had no stake in the property. They might gain if house prices rose but could, if problems arose, walk away. In most states, "without-recourse" laws or the burdens involved of enforcing mortgage obligations removed penalties from those who did this.

From this perspective, government actions contributed to the crisis in other ways. From about 2001 onward, the Federal Reserve lowered interest rates below a point that historical experience would suggest was prudent. Seemingly driven by deflationary fears, monetary policy was "loose fitting." Not only were interest rates excessively low for a prolonged period but the Federal Reserve also signaled that they would not be raised for "a considerable period" and would then rise only at a "measured pace" (Taylor, 2008, pp. 2–3). Furthermore, whereas fiscal and monetary policy had often served to check and

counteract each other, as in the 1990s when fiscal restraint went together with a relatively loose monetary policy, the picture from 2001 onward was significantly different. Alongside the reduction in interest rates, the Bush administration and Congress added to federal government spending levels. As Austrian-school adherents argue, artificial economic stimuli such as these lead to capital malinvestment, resource misallocation, and the emergence of asset bubbles.

Conservative theorists also charge that the demand for CDOs (rather than, for example, Treasury bills) was fueled by government regulation and its unintended consequences. The Recourse Rule, a 2001 amendment to the Basel I Accord, gave bonds such as mortgage-backed securities a 20 percent risk weight, compared to a zero risk weight for cash and a 50 percent risk weight for an individual mortgage. As a consequence, commercial banks could resell mortgages, regardless of their individual soundness, to investment banks and then buy them back through mortgages-backed securities, thereby freeing up additional capital for lending.

The conservative narrative also stresses the part played in the housing market by Fannie Mae and Freddie Mac. Although publicly traded, both are government-sponsored enterprises, created in 1938 and 1970, respectively. They buy mortgages on the secondary market, package them together, and resell them as mortgage-backed securities. The public interest rationale was that this added to the supply of funds available for mortgage lending and thereby extended home ownership. The "implicit guarantee" that they enjoyed as government-sponsored enterprises reduced borrowing costs and provided them with a competitive advantage over others in the housing market.

Both Fannie Mae and Freddie Mac were, it has been argued, in the forefront of the efforts to increase the number of subprime borrowers. In part, they sought to meet the housing goals, particularly those for low- to moderate-income borrowers, initially set by Congress and periodically revised upward by the secretary of Housing and Urban Development. However, they were also attempting "to maintain the outsized profits and revenue growth experienced from 2000 to 2003" (Calabria, 2011, p. 3). Using their implicit guarantee of federal government backing should difficulties arise, they built upon the "substantial lead" that they had already secured.

Having said this, there are counterclaims. Although depicted as market leaders by the Right, they were, others suggest, only followers of market trends. They had "largely faded from the scene during the height of the housing bubble" (Krugman, 2008). Indeed, Fannie Mae and Freddie Mac were subject to extended forms of regulation that inevitably curtailed the part that they could play. In particular, they were legally prevented from taking on subprime loans: "So whatever bad incentives the implicit federal guarantee creates have been offset by the fact that Fannie and Freddie were and are tightly regulated with regard to the risks they can take. You could say that the Fannie–Freddie experience shows that regulation works" (Krugman, 2008).

Global Imbalances. A final narrative is structured around the global context within which both the housing boom and the crisis took place. Developments within the United States are attributed to transnational relationships and trends. In 2005, a year before he was appointed as chair of the Federal Reserve, Ben Bernanke referred to a "global savings glut." It is a contentious claim. John B. Taylor (2008), who served in the George W. Bush administration, has argued that there is no evidence that there was such a glut. Indeed, he notes that there was, when comparisons are drawn with earlier periods, a savings shortage. As a proportion of global gross domestic product, the savings rate was significantly lower than in the 1970s and 1980s.

Nonetheless, although the term "glut" is open to argument, there were imbalances. High savings rates within the rising economic powers, most notably China, provided a basis for large-scale lending to Western governments and banks. The globalization process and the growing mobility of capital allowed both the US federal government and the consumer to take advantage of Chinese frugality as well as the worldwide hunger for dollars. The inflow of funds allowed continuing borrowing, permitted a current

account deficit, curbed upward pressures on interest rates, and prevented a "crowding-out" effect on private-sector investment.

Conclusion. Some of these narratives are counterposed. Whereas many of those on the left have pointed to market failure, emphasized the weakness of regulatory structures, and pointed to the close political associations between the financial sector and those serving in successive administrations and Congress, the conservative right has offered a profoundly different narrative, resting upon the claim that government intervention and the pursuit of political interests undermined market-clearing processes.

Other narratives overlap and are interlinked. Indeed, there were institutional complementarities (many of which arose unintentionally) within and beyond the mortgage lending industry. Although such complementarities may take different forms, many of these reinforced each other so as to fuel the taking of risk and the institutionalization of it. US borrowing levels and the underregulation of the financial sector were tied to the long-term stagnation of real incomes and the global imbalances between nations. If this is accepted, it follows that, despite the hopes of policymakers, financial reform and debt repayment may not be sufficient to address the underlying causes of the crisis.

[*See also* Economy, American, since World War II; Federal Deposit Insurance Corporation; Federal Reserve Bank; Finance, International; Financial Industry; Financial Instruments, New; Glass-Steagall Act; Global Imbalances and International Debt; Gramm-Leach-Bliley Act; Housing in the United States; Mortgage-Backed Securities *and* Regulation.]

BIBLIOGRAPHY

Andrews, Edmund L. "Greenspan Concedes Error on Regulation." *New York Times*, October 23, 2008, http://www.nytimes.com/2008/10/24/business/economy/24panel.html.

Associated Press. "Record Number of Foreclosures in 2009." *International Business Times*, January 14, 2010, http://www.ibtimes.com/contents/20100114/record-number-foreclosures.htm.

Bivens, Josh. *Failure by Design: The Story behind America's Broken Economy.* (Ithaca, N.Y., 2011).

Bivens, Josh. "Worst Economic Crisis Since the Great Depression? By a Long Shot." Economic Policy Institute, January 27, 2010, http://www.epi.org/economic_snapshots/entry/snapshot_20100127/.

Block, Fred. "Mortgage Meltdown for Dummies: Defining the Changes We Need." *Dissent*, April 8, 2008, http://www.dissentmagazine.org/online.php?id=64.

Bureau of Economic Analysis. "National Economic Accounts." 2011, http://www.bea.gov/national/index.htm#gdp.

Bureau of Labor Statistics. "Labor Force Statistics from the Current Population Survey." 2011, http://data.bls.gov/cgi-bin/surveymost.

Calabria, Mark A. "Did Deregulation Cause the Financial Crisis?" *Cato Policy Report*, 31, no. 4 (July/August 2009): 5–8, http://www.cato.org/pubs/policy_report/v31n4/cpr31n4-1.pdf.

Calabria, Mark A. "Fannie, Freddie, and the Subprime Mortgage Market." Cato Institute Briefing Papers 120. (Washington, D.C., 2011).

Campbell, John L. "The US Financial Crisis: Lessons for Theories of Institutional Complementarity." *Socio-Economic Review* 9 (2011): 211–234.

Cauchon, Dennis, and Richard Wolf. "Number of People in Poverty Reaches Highest Level in 51 Years." *USA Today*, September 17, 2010, http://www.usatoday.com/news/nation/census/2010-09-16-poverty-rate-income-numbers_N.htm.

Council on Foreign Relations. "Statement from G-20 Summit, November 2008." November 15, 2008, http://www.cfr.org/financial-crises/statement-g-20-summit-november-2008/p17778.

Federal Reserve Board. "Remarks by Governor Ben S. Bernanke: The Global Saving Glut and the U.S. Current Account Deficit." March 10, 2005, http://www.federalreserve.gov/boarddocs/speeches/2005/200503102/.

Financial Crisis Inquiry Commission. *The Financial Crisis Inquiry Report.* (New York, 2011).

Foster, John Bellamy, and Fred Magdoff. *The Great Financial Crisis: Causes and Consequences.* (New York, 2009).

Friedman, Jeffrey. "Three Myths about the Crisis: Bonuses, Irrationality, and Capitalism." September 14, 2009. http://causesofthecrisis.blogspot.com/2009/09/three-myths-about-crisis-bonuses.html.

Gamble, Andrew. *The Spectre at the Feast: Capitalist Crisis and the Politics of Recession.* (Houndmills, UK, 2009).

Herron, Janna. "Banks Repossessed 1 Million Homes Last Year—and 2011 Will Be Worse." MSNBC.com, January 13, 2011, http://www.msnbc.msn.com/id/41051419/ns/business-eye_on_the_economy/.

Krugman, Paul. "Fannie, Freddie and You." *New York Times*, July 14, 2008, http://www.nytimes.com/2008/07/14/opinion/14krugman.html.

Krugman, Paul. "Reagan Did It." *New York Times*, May 31, 2009, http://www.nytimes.com/2009/06/01/opinion/01krugman.html.

Kuttner, Robert. "Testimony of Robert Kuttner before the Committee on Financial Services, U.S. House of Representatives," Washington, D.C., October 2, 2007, http://archives.financialservices.house.gov/hearing110/testimony_-_kuttner.pdf

Leonhardt, David. "Broader Measure of U.S. Unemployment Stands at 17.5%." *New York Times*, November 6, 2009, http://www.nytimes.com/2009/11/07/business/economy/07econ.html?em.

Lucas, Robert E. Jr. "Macroeconomic Priorities." AEA 2003 Presidential Address. January 10, 2003, http://home.uchicago.edu/%7Esogrodow/homepage/paddress03.pdf.

Mishel, Lawrence, Jared Bernstein, and Heidi Shierholz. *The State of Working America 2008–2009.* (Ithaca, N.Y., 2009).

National Bureau of Economic Research. "US Business Cycle Expansions and Contractions." 2011, http://www.nber.org/cycles/.

Obama'08. "Barack Obama's Plan to Restore Confidence in the Markets, Tackle the Housing Crisis and Help Protect Families from the Economic Slowdown." 2008, http://obama.3cdn.net/f9836ef496f75a9be0_39gimvt5b.pdf.

PollingReport.com. "Business Issues in the News." 2011, http://www.pollingreport.com/business2.htm.

Reich, Robert B. *Aftershock: The Next Economy and America's Future.* (New York, 2011).

Skidelsky, Robert. *Keynes: The Return of the Master.* (New York, 2009).

Stiglitz, Joseph E. *Freefall: America, Free Markets, and the Sinking of the World Economy.* (New York, 2010).

Taylor, John B. "The Financial Crisis and the Policy Responses: An Empirical Analysis of What Went Wrong." November 2008, http://www.stanford.edu/~johntayl/FCPR.pdf.

Timiraos, Nick, and Dawn Wotapka. "Home Market Takes a Tumble." *Wall Street Journal*, May 9, 2011, http://online.wsj.com/article/SB10001424052748704810504576309532810406782.html.

Wallison, Peter J. "Housing Initiatives and Other Policy Factors." In *What Caused the Financial Crisis*, edited by Jeffrey Friedman, pp. 172–182. (Philadelphia, Pa., 2011).

Zandi, Mark. *Financial Shock: Global Panic and Government Bailouts—How We Got Here and What Must Be Done to Fix It.* (Upper Saddle River, N.J., 2009).

Edward Ashbee

FINANCIAL INDUSTRY

In a modern capitalist economy, the financial system serves two main functions: (1) facilitating financial transactions and (2) intermediating flows of capital from *savers* (people with more cash than productive investment opportunities) to *borrowers* (people with more productive investment opportunities than cash). The financial sector also insures households and organizations against different types of risk. For these reasons, a stable, efficient financial industry is an important component of a healthy economy.

Industry Structure. Financial transactions are executed by the payments system, composed largely of traditional banks and a central bank that regulates the money supply. Financial intermediation takes two broad forms: banking and capital markets. In traditional banking, households and organizations deposit excess cash in a bank in exchange for a low interest rate. The bank then lends out that money, at a higher rate, to households or organizations with investment opportunities. In the capital markets, by contrast, borrowers transact directly with lenders. For example, investors pay cash to companies and governments in exchange for *bonds* (promises to repay the cash over time, with interest). While financial institutions often broker such transactions, once the transaction is completed, the resulting obligations flow directly between the investor in the bond and the issuer of the bond. Finally, households and companies protect themselves from risk by paying an annual premium to an insurance company in exchange for an insurance policy, which is a promise to pay the insured in the event of specific types of loss.

In the United States, the financial industry is made up overwhelmingly of private-sector entities, although they are subject to significant government oversight. The Federal Reserve System, the country's central bank, includes twelve private banks, overseen by a board of governors appointed by the president. From the 1930s until the late 1990s, the law effected a relatively clear separation between traditional banking, the capital markets, and insurance. The Banking Act of 1933 (commonly known as the Glass-Steagall Act), enacted in response to the crash of 1929 and the Great Depression, required a strict separation between commercial banks, which take deposits from customers, and investment banks, which underwrite and trade securities. Even before 1933, banks were historically prohibited from underwriting insurance by the terms of their charters. These barriers were dismantled in the 1980s and 1990s, culminating in the Financial Services Modernization Act of 1999 (Gramm-Leach-Bliley Act), which allowed financial holding companies, through their subsidiaries, to engage in traditional banking, investment banking, and insurance. Because of historical factors, however, most of the financial industry, as well as its regulatory agencies, remains broadly divided along traditional lines.

The US banking industry has the curious distinction of being both highly fragmented and highly concentrated. In 2010, there were approximately sixteen thousand commercial banks, savings institutions, and credit unions in the United States. Together with their holding companies, they held $16.7 trillion in assets, or about 114 percent of US annual gross domestic product, according to the Flow of Funds report from the Federal Reserve. At the same time, however, the four largest bank holding companies held $7.7 trillion in assets, or 52 percent of gross domestic product. This concentration was the product of a merger wave that began in the early 1990s and accelerated after restrictions on interstate banking were relaxed in 1994, resulting in the assembly of coast-to-coast banking networks by Bank of America, J.P. Morgan Chase, Citigroup, and Wells Fargo. As of 2009, those four banks together had an over 50 percent share in major consumer markets such as mortgage issuance and credit cards. By number, however, the vast majority of banks remain community banks with less than $1 billion in assets.

Investment banking has become similarly concentrated as securities firms have combined with each other and have been acquired by traditional commercial banks. Of the five largest investment banks at the end of 2008, three were divisions of J.P. Morgan Chase, Citigroup, and Bank of America, which were historically commercial banks. In the first half of 2009, three banks—J.P. Morgan Chase, Goldman Sachs, and Morgan Stanley—accounted for 42 percent of the market for initial public offerings. Derivatives trading was even more concentrated, with the top five banks capturing 95 percent of all trades by US institutions.

The growth of the capital markets has seen, in addition, the growth of "buy-side" firms that invest in securities (as opposed to "sell-side" investment banks, which underwrite and sell securities). These asset-management firms include mutual fund companies that manage over $10 trillion in assets, largely gathered from individual investors, and thousands of hedge funds, that together manage over $2 trillion on behalf of pension funds, municipalities, and rich individuals. In both cases, investors, instead of buying assets directly, entrust their money to an investment fund, which then invests in assets (or in other funds); in exchange for this investment service, the fund manager earns a fee, typically a percentage of the assets being managed.

Increasing capital markets intermediation has also led to the creation of specialized firms that perform some, but not all, banking functions. For example, while mortgages were traditionally originated, financed, and held by banks and savings institutions, those functions have become separated. During the recent credit bubble, mortgages were often originated by mortgage brokers; financed by mortgage lenders, who raised money through lines of credit from investment banks; sold by the mortgage lenders to investment banks; and then sold by the investment banks to stand-alone entities, which raised money by issuing mortgage-backed securities. As of 2008, $9 trillion of outstanding securities

had been manufactured from what were once traditional loans, mainly by investment banks or by government-sponsored enterprises created for this purpose, such as Fannie Mae and Freddie Mac.

Despite the Gramm-Leach-Bliley Act, the insurance industry has remained largely separate from the banking system and the capital markets, except as major investors. (Because insurance companies collect premiums in advance of paying claims, they usually have large amounts of money to invest, mostly in securities.) As of 2010, property-casualty and life insurance companies held $6.5 trillion of financial assets. The insurance industry is similar to the banking industry in that there are several thousand insurance companies, most of them very small, as well as a handful of large companies with nationwide operations.

Regulatory System until 2010. Regulation of the US financial industry has been highly fragmented. In addition to the division between state and federal regulation, different regulators are responsible for different types of financial institutions. While this makes sense in principle, it has become increasingly problematic as individual firms engage in more and more types of activity and has resulted in competition between regulators for the "business" of financial institutions. The regulatory structure has also not kept pace with recent developments in financial markets.

A banking institution's primary federal regulator may be the Federal Reserve, the Office of the Comptroller of the Currency (OCC), the Office of Thrift Supervision (OTS; until its dissolution, mandated in 2010), the Federal Deposit Insurance Corporation (FDIC), or the National Credit Union Administration (NCUA), depending on whether it is a commercial bank, a savings institution, or a credit union (all of which provide similar services) and whether it is chartered by a state or the federal government; if it is state-chartered, it will also be regulated by the appropriate state agency. Bank holding companies are regulated by the Federal Reserve. Virtually all depository institutions are insured either by the FDIC (banks and savings institutions) or the NCUA (credit unions). These deposit insurance funds have been largely successful in ensuring depositor confidence and preventing bank runs similar to those seen in the early 1930s. In exchange for these stabilizing benefits, banks are subject to additional regulation to ensure that they are not likely to become insolvent and require a government takeover. Bank regulation has primarily been concerned with ensuring bank solvency, but banks are at least nominally subject to various consumer-protection laws such as the Truth in Lending Act, which mandates certain disclosures to customers entering into credit agreements. Before 2010, the Federal Reserve had responsibility for enforcing consumer-protection laws, although it did not appear to give them a high priority.

This fragmented system meant that a complex financial institution could have multiple regulators and could effectively choose its primary regulator. This, combined with the fact that several agencies are dependent for funding on fees paid by the institutions they regulate, created the opportunity for regulatory arbitrage: firms could select the regulator they wanted, and regulators could compete for business (and fees) by offering lax regulation. It is widely believed that this was one reason that major institutions including Countrywide and American International Group (the largest insurance company in the country) selected the OTS as their primary regulator, even though it lacked the skills and experience necessary to oversee such large and complicated organizations.

In addition, because this regulatory scheme is based on how institutions are chartered rather than what they do, it created blind spots that could be exploited by new types of firms. For example, as mortgage financing shifted from banks to the capital markets, mortgages could be originated by mortgage lenders, who financed themselves in the capital markets rather than by raising deposits. Because they were not depository institutions, these "nonbanks" largely escaped traditional banking regulation and often led the way in developing and marketing the subprime loan products that helped create the credit bubble of the 2000s.

The grand bargain of the Glass-Steagall Act was that investment banks would not have a government safety net and in return would face relatively light regulation. The Securities Act of 1933 and the Securities and Exchange Act of 1934 established a disclosure-based regulatory regime that, very roughly speaking, requires companies that issue securities to provide specific information to investors, prohibits fraud, and otherwise largely leaves the markets to themselves. Primary regulation of securities firms was entrusted to self-regulatory organizations, at first the National Association of Securities Dealers and then the Financial Industry Regulatory Authority (FINRA), which are not government agencies; FINRA, however, is itself overseen by the Securities and Exchange Commission (SEC). In 2004, several of the largest investment banks subjected themselves to direct SEC oversight under the Consolidated Supervised Entities program. However, this program was dissolved in September 2008 after the financial crisis made it clear that it had completely failed.

The asset-management industry is largely governed by the Investment Company Act of 1940 and the Investment Advisers Act of 1940. These acts, which are also enforced by the SEC, regulate the behavior of mutual funds, mutual fund companies (which create mutual funds and manage their money), and investment advisers, primarily through disclosure requirements, antifraud rules, and limits on self-dealing. Before 2010, they did not apply to most hedge funds, which escaped regulation by raising money only from a relatively small number of institutions and rich individuals.

This regulatory system did not adequately adapt to changes in the financial industry itself. During the past twenty years, derivatives have become an increasingly important market, particularly for major investment banks. For historical reasons, jurisdiction over many derivatives is vested not in the SEC but in the Commodity Futures Trading Commission (CFTC). The first widely used derivatives were agricultural futures contracts that farmers, for example, would use to lock in sale prices for their crops. However, many derivatives came to be based on securities that are overseen by the SEC and some on both commodities and securities, leading to confusion concerning jurisdiction over new products. Merging the SEC and CFTC is periodically proposed but generally considered politically impossible since each agency is overseen by a different Senate committee.

In contrast to the rest of the financial industry, insurance companies are primarily regulated by state law and state insurance commissioners. From 1868 to 1944, insurers were protected from federal regulation by a Supreme Court ruling that insurance was not "commerce" and, hence, not subject to congressional action. The Supreme Court reversed itself in 1944, but the industry successfully pressured Congress into passing the McCarran-Ferguson Act of 1945, which endorsed the existing system of state regulation. Most insurance companies are thought to prefer state regulation because of their presumably stronger ties to state legislators. The National Association of Insurance Commissioners, by coordinating activities among state regulators, has helped to reduce some of the potential problems of regulatory fragmentation.

Political Influence and Deregulation. Since 1980, the financial sector has been a powerful force in American politics and has benefited from a succession of industry-friendly policies in Washington.

Channels of Influence. The financial/insurance/real estate sector has been the top financial contributor to electoral campaigns in every election cycle for which the Center for Responsive Politics has collected data from 1990 through late 2010. In each electoral cycle, the broad financial sector has contributed more than twice as much as any other distinct sector (not counting sectors such as "miscellaneous business" and "lawyers and lobbyists"), reaching $478 million in 2008, split almost evenly between Democrats and Republicans. Over the same period, as the cost of the average seat in the House of Representatives tripled, contributions from the securities industry grew fivefold from $12 million to $66 million, making it the top industry (not counting "retired" and "lawyers/law firms"). From 1998 to late 2010, the financial sector spent over $4.2 trillion on lobbying, more than any other sector.

The Wall Street investment banks in particular have been able to place some of their strongest advocates in powerful positions in Washington, in both Democratic and Republican administrations. Presidents Ronald Reagan, George H. W. Bush, Bill Clinton, and George W. Bush all selected treasury secretaries who had previously headed Wall Street banks: Donald Regan (Merrill Lynch), Nicholas Brady (Dillon Read), Robert Rubin (Goldman Sachs), and Henry Paulson (Goldman Sachs). Goldman Sachs alone supplied treasury undersecretaries and chairs of the National Economic Council to both the Clinton and George W. Bush administrations, a chair and a president of the Federal Reserve Bank of New York, and a chief of staff to George W. Bush. Perhaps even more important was the appointment of Alan Greenspan, self-styled libertarian and fervent defender of unregulated markets, as chair of the Federal Reserve from 1987 to 2006. At lower levels, the revolving door between finance and government has been turning rapidly. For example, Frank Newman was chief financial officer of Bank of America, then deputy Treasury secretary, and then chief executive officer of Bankers Trust; John Dugan, conversely, was a Treasury official who advocated financial deregulation, then a lawyer who advised the American Bankers Association, and later head of the OCC in the years leading to the financial crisis.

Deregulation and Nonregulation. Since 1980, the federal government oversaw the near-complete deregulation of the financial system. Restrictions on interest rates and on the activities of savings institutions were relaxed in 1980 and 1982—leading in part to the savings and loan crisis of the late 1980s and early 1990s, in which more than two thousand banks collapsed. Limits on interstate banking were eliminated by the Riegle-Neal Act of 1994. The separation between commercial and investment banking was broken down by a series of Federal Reserve decisions in the 1980s and 1990s and finally collapsed by the Gramm-Leach-Bliley Act of 1999.

Government policies also fostered the growth of new markets that were major sources of profits for financial institutions. One of these markets was private label securitization, in which banks bundled together assets (such as mortgages) in new entities that issued bonds backed by those assets. Securitization was made possible by laws passed in 1984 and 1986 that eliminated regulatory and tax issues that threatened this new market. These decades also saw the growth of the market for customized, "over-the-counter" (OTC) derivatives from essentially nothing to over $35 trillion in gross market value by the end of 2008. In 1994, the banking industry (with the help of the Clinton Treasury Department) defeated proposed regulation in Congress; in 1998, the industry again enlisted the Clinton administration, the Federal Reserve, and the SEC to fight off an attempt at regulation by the CFTC; and finally, in 2000, the Commodity Futures Modernization Act effectively prevented any federal regulation of OTC derivatives. Securitization and derivatives together provided the building blocks for structured finance, in which banks engineered exotic new financial products by combining existing assets with derivative contracts.

Federal policy contributed to the credit bubble of the 2000s in other ways. As subprime loans became more exotic and more widespread and the Federal Reserve declined to intervene despite growing complaints from consumer groups, several states passed anti-predatory-lending laws. In response, the banks successfully lobbied both the OTS and the OCC to overrule state law in favor of more lax federal regulation. In an attempt to increase home ownership, both the Clinton and George W. Bush administrations pressured Fannie Mae and Freddie Mac to increase lending to lower-income households. Fannie and Freddie responded in part by buying more securities backed by subprime mortgages. In addition, the Federal Reserve kept interest rates low for several years following the 2001 recession, increasing demand for housing.

Regulators also allowed financial institutions to take on more risk during the credit bubble. In 2001, the federal agencies published a rule allowing banks to rely on credit ratings when determining capital requirements for securitizations where they retained some of the risk. This meant that banks could take on large amounts of risk as long as they could obtain favorable ratings from the rating agencies. In 2004, the SEC allowed the five largest investment banks to use their own internal models in determining their net capital requirements, effectively (and consciously) allowing them to increase their leverage.

The net effect of government policy in this period was to give free rein to the financial sector. On issues ranging from interstate banking to mortgage origination to capital requirements, the federal government adopted policies favored by the financial industry. One possible explanation is that government officials were consciously doing the bidding of industry, perhaps because they were attracted by the vastly larger sums of money available on Wall Street than in Washington. However, it is also possible that regulators and administration officials simply agreed with the positions of the financial sector. Many of the people charged with overseeing financial institutions were themselves veterans of those institutions. The technical complexity of many issues meant that the primary source of expert opinion was the banks themselves and their law firms and lobbyists. Finally, this was a period when academic opinion—at least the flavor disseminated outside the academy itself—favored free financial markets and opposed financial regulation. In any case, the financial sector was largely able to obtain the policies it wanted from the American political system.

Financial Crisis and Aftermath. Those policies were significant contributing factors to the financial crisis that began in 2007 and triggered the most severe recession since the Great Depression. The crisis created considerable political momentum for reform and provoked widespread debates about the financial system and the need for regulation. Those debates demonstrated the continued political power of the industry but also culminated in wide-ranging reform legislation that will likely govern the relationship between finance and government for decades to come.

The Politics of Reform. At the peak of the crisis in late 2008, many observers expected fundamental changes in the financial sector, particularly in investment banking. The crisis itself triggered a historic shift in industry structure: of the five major stand-alone investment banks, one went bankrupt, two were acquired by major commercial banks, and the last two transformed themselves into bank holding companies in order to qualify for additional assistance from the Federal Reserve.

As the major financial institutions began to recover in 2009, however, they began a determined fight against additional regulation. The financial sector as a whole spent $468 million on lobbying in 2009 and over $340 million more by late 2010. The complexity of many legislative provisions, such as new derivatives regulations, played into the hands of the financial institutions and their lobbyists, who could use their technical expertise to influence the drafting process. In addition to direct lobbying, the industry enlisted support from other groups within the business community. The US Chamber of Commerce lobbied and advertised heavily against several legislative proposals, including a new consumer financial protection agency, claiming that it constituted unnecessary regulation that would stifle business. Executives from major nonfinancial corporations also lobbied against new derivatives regulations, arguing that they would be harmed by excessive regulation.

At the same time, the financial crisis and widespread public anger toward "Wall Street"—widely seen as both the cause of the crisis and the chief beneficiary of the bailouts that followed it—created a new coalition backing substantive financial reform. This loose coalition included organized labor, consumer groups, and other progressive activist organizations. During the 1990s and 2000s, financial deregulation had been a bipartisan affair with no major opposition, taking place outside of public view. In 2009 and 2010, by contrast, financial reform was fought out in public, and the popular pressure for real change pushed a significant portion of the Democratic Party into positions that at least seemed to be "tough on finance."

In this political context, the Obama administration took a centrist position, advocating a significant overhaul of the regulatory regime that fell short of structural change in the financial sector itself. The administration's proposals included new powers for regulators to monitor and take action against systemic risk, higher capital requirements, restrictions on proprietary trading, new regulations governing OTC derivatives, and a new consumer financial protection agency. At the same time, the administration either opposed or helped weaken more aggressive proposals, including those to place strict size or leverage limits on banks. In general, the administration's position reflected the view that the problems of the existing financial system could be remedied by granting additional authority to regulatory agencies.

In the end, the Obama administration's strategy was largely successful. The Dodd-Frank Wall Street Reform and Consumer Protection Act, signed into law in July 2010, generally conformed to the administration's blueprint. The financial sector was able to defeat or water down some of the most threatening legislative proposals, including a strict size limit that would have required a breakup of the largest banks, a provision allowing the consumer-protection agency to mandate "plain vanilla" versions of basic financial products, and a tax on large banks to provide funding for potential future rescues. Even before the major reform bill, the banks defeated an Obama administration proposal to allow bankruptcy judges to reduce the principal balance on home mortgages (prompting Senator Dick Durbin to say, of Capitol Hill, "the banks . . . own the place"). Perhaps more importantly, the financial sector and its political allies were able to defer much of the substance of financial reform to the regulatory rulemaking phase that followed official enactment of the Dodd-Frank Act. That is, the true extent of financial reform will depend heavily on decisions made by regulators over how to interpret and implement the act, giving the financial sector a further opportunity to influence the law.

The Future. Although it did not reach as far as some reform advocates wanted and its eventual impact is yet to be determined, the Dodd-Frank Act was the most comprehensive overhaul of financial regulation since the 1930s. It significantly expanded the mandate of federal regulators, brought new segments of the industry under regulation, and placed new restrictions on the activities of financial institutions.

One failing of the previous regime was that it was largely based on prudential regulation—ensuring that a given bank did not become insolvent—with insufficient attention to the problem of systemic risk. In response, the Dodd-Frank Act established the Financial Services Oversight Council (a committee of regulators) with the power to identify systemically important institutions. Those institutions will be subject to more stringent capital, liquidity, and risk-management regulations and to more rigorous oversight. Because of the widespread perception that certain financial institutions were "too big to fail"—and therefore had to be bailed out during the recent crisis—the act gave regulators new powers to deal with the potential failure of these firms. Most importantly, a new Orderly Liquidation Authority regime allows regulators to take over and break up or liquidate a financial institution whose failure would endanger the financial system, without requiring it to go through bankruptcy. (Previously, the FDIC had the ability to take over insured depository institutions such as banks but not bank holding companies or other financial institutions—including Lehman Brothers, whose bankruptcy in September 2008 triggered the most extreme phase of the crisis.) There is debate about whether Orderly Liquidation Authority would be invoked in a future crisis and whether it would be sufficient to deal with a crisis, but the threat of using it may in itself change financial institutions' behavior.

Another major failure that contributed to the financial crisis was the nonregulation of OTC derivatives, particularly the credit default swaps that caused the collapse of American International Group. The Dodd-Frank Act explicitly subjects OTC derivatives to regulation. While OTC derivatives had previously been traded in private, confidential transactions, the act in principle requires that they be traded on exchanges, cleared through central clearinghouses (where the clearinghouse bears the risk that one of the parties to the trade may default), and disclosed to regulators. Again in principle, these requirements should increase price transparency, lowering prices for customers, and should give regulators more visibility into outstanding derivatives positions, reducing systemic risk.

A third major achievement of the Dodd-Frank Act was the creation of a Consumer Financial Protection Bureau (CFPB), with the power to write rules implementing consumer-protection statutes as well as to examine large financial institutions and enforce those rules as necessary. The CFPB is a division of the Federal Reserve, but it is largely independent, with a director nominated by the president. After a credit bubble during which banking regulators often seemed to put the interests of "their" banks ahead of the interests of the banks' customers, the CFPB was envisioned as an agency that would put the interests of consumers first. If successful, the CFPB could restrain the ability of the financial sector to take advantage of less sophisticated consumers, which could in turn limit some of the excesses that helped to produce the financial crisis.

These are only a few of the major components of the Dodd-Frank Act. Other notable provisions include a version of the "Volcker Rule," limiting the ability of insured banks to participate in proprietary trading, hedge funds, and private equity; expanded registration requirements for hedge funds; new rules governing credit rating agencies; and the dissolution of the now discredited OTS, with the transfer of its functions to other agencies. (The breadth of the act also makes its failure to do anything about Fannie Mae and Freddie Mac—the mortgage market giants whose collapse led to their emergency takeover by the government in September 2008—particularly notable.)

The Dodd-Frank Act, however, remains very much a work in progress whose effectiveness could be severely limited by several factors. It grants a large amount of discretion to the regulatory agencies, both to write implementing rules and to enforce those rules in the future. The law firm Davis Polk counted 243 rulemakings (which it considered a significant underestimate) and sixty-seven one-time reports or studies specified by the legislation. The act's sponsors considered this broad grant of authority to be necessary given the highly technical nature of financial regulation. However, it means that much of the substance of financial reform will be written in the comparative quiet of the rulemaking process, giving financial institutions and their lobbyists another chance to shape the new regulatory regime out of public view. The act also continues the tradition of delegating quasi-regulatory functions to nongovernmental ("self-regulatory") organizations; for example, the initial determination of what derivatives will be centrally cleared will be made by the clearinghouses, which are themselves influenced by the major derivatives dealers. In addition, many of the new regulatory powers are themselves discretionary, such as the power to impose constraints on firms that pose risks to the financial system. Given the apparent confluence of opinion between the financial sector and its regulators, some people are skeptical that those powers will be used appropriately during the next financial boom.

The act is also riddled with exceptions, the contours of which will be determined in that rulemaking process. For example, the derivatives regulations contain a general exemption for nonfinancial entities using derivatives for hedging purposes, and the restrictions on proprietary trading do not apply to transactions conducted "on behalf of customers." How these provisions are implemented could determine if they become exceptions that swallow their surrounding rules. The CFPB's authority to regulate financial products has exceptions not only for insurance (which remains under the jurisdiction of state insurance commissioners) and for investment activities regulated by the SEC or the CFTC but also for auto dealers, despite the important role of financing in auto sales.

Another potential weakness is the reliance of the new regulatory system on international coordination. During the debates over financial reform, the administration resisted attempts to write specific capital requirements into the statute, preferring to leave those decisions to international negotiations. The resulting Basel III Accord, announced in 2010, did increase capital requirements for financial institutions but did not fix several problems with the previous Basel II Accord, such as the usage of banks' internal risk-management models for determining capital requirements.

The global financial crisis that began in 2007 provided both intellectual justification and political pressure for a comprehensive reform of the financial system. However, resistance from the financial sector and its political allies succeeded in blocking the most aggressive reform proposals, resulting in a bill that attempts to overhaul the regulatory regime more than the financial system itself. The technical nature of financial regulation and the wide latitude granted to regulatory agencies give industry participants further opportunities to weaken reforms or turn them to their advantage. Whether financial reform is ultimately successful, of course, will not be known for decades, if ever.

[*See also* Deregulation; Federal Deposit Insurance Corporation; Federal Reserve Bank; Financial Crisis of 2008; Financial Instruments, New; Glass-Steagall Act; *and* Gramm-Leach-Bliley Act.]

BIBLIOGRAPHY

Bebchuk, Lucian, and Holger Spamann. "Regulating Bankers' Pay." *Georgetown Law Journal* 98 (2010): 247–287.

Carnell, Richard Scott, Jonathan R. Macey, and Geoffrey P. Miller. *The Law of Banking and Financial Institutions.* 4th ed. (Austin, Tex., 2009).

Carpenter, Daniel. "The Contest of Lobbies and Disciplines: Financial Politics and Regulatory Reform." Chapter 4 in Theda Skocpol and Lawrence R. Jacobs, eds., *Reaching for a New Deal: Ambitious Governance, Economic Meltdown, and Polarized Politics in Obama's First Two Years* (New York, 2011).

Hacker, Jacob S., and Paul Pierson. *Winner-Take-All Politics: How Washington Made the Rich Richer—And Turned Its Back on the Middle Class.* (New York, 2010).

Igan, Deniz, Prachi Mishra, and Thierry Tressel. "A Fistful of Dollars: Lobbying and the Financial Crisis." In Daron Acemoglu and Michael Woodford, eds., *NBER Macroeconomics Annual 2011*, vol. 26.

Johnson, Simon, and James Kwak. *13 Bankers: The Wall Street Takeover and the Next Financial Meltdown.* (New York, 2010).

Macey, Jonathan R. "The Distorting Incentives Facing the U.S. Securities and Exchange Commission."

Harvard Journal of Law and Public Policy 33 (2010): 639–670.

Moss, David A. "An Ounce of Prevention: Financial Regulation, Moral Hazard, and the End of 'Too Big to Fail.'" *Harvard Magazine* (September–October 2009): 24–29.

Warren, Elizabeth. "Unsafe at Any Rate." *Democracy: A Journal of Ideas* (Summer 2007): 8–19.

James Kwak

FINANCIAL INSTRUMENTS, NEW

Finance is a dynamic and innovative industry, and new financial instruments have proliferated over recent decades. As elaborated by Raghuram Rajan (2005), financial innovation is driven by a combination of *technological changes*, reducing the cost and increasing the speed of both communication and computation; *deregulation*, breaking down barriers to market entry and encouraging competition; and *institutional changes* that have produced new financial entities, such as hedge funds. Some financial innovation is demand driven, developed to satisfy needs currently unfulfilled by the market. Other innovations are supply driven, supported by the fact that financial products are not conducive to patent protection. Firms have little ability to reap the "monopoly rents" of innovation, even for the short term, so they must constantly develop new, unique products to gain market share. The existence of standardized financial instruments is hardly new; a rice futures exchange started in Japan in the late 1600s, and stocks and bonds were well embedded in European economies in the nineteenth century. The focus here is on more recent developments, with an emphasis on those instruments and institutions (the two are sometimes indistinguishable, as with hedge funds) seen as playing a role in the 2008 financial crisis. Even limited as such, space prohibits a comprehensive review. All financial instruments, however, be they novel or well established, can serve multiple functions: to facilitate payments, mobilize savings, channel productive investment, or effectively allocate risk to those willing and able to bear it. The important question is whether they fulfill these roles in ways that are, in the net, economically beneficial or damaging.

Financial innovation is often seen as the preserve of Wall Street, yet many of the most noteworthy developments relate to personal finance. Networked automated teller machines (ATMs) and online banking now allow for twenty-four-hour access to personal accounts. Credit cards and debit cards offer both convenient payment and ready access to credit. Credit scoring has "democratized credit," allowing lenders to more easily determine creditworthiness and expand consumer credit. Adjustable rate mortgages (ARMs) perform a similar function in the housing market, while home equity lines of credit allow individuals to tap into the value of their homes. While all are relatively recent, by now they have become so pervasive that we hardly think of them as new.

Gaining more attention are those instruments prevalent in the financial sector proper. Various investment funds serve in mobilizing savings, channeling resources toward lucrative investments. Money market funds are specialized mutual funds that invest in relatively secure assets, allowing consumers to earn more interest than a standard deposit account while maintaining liquidity. Alternative mutual funds climb the ladder of risk and reward. Indexed mutual funds are tied to stock market indices or baskets of equities and securities. Exchange trade funds (ETF) are similarly structured but, as the name implies, are traded in the same manner as stocks and bonds. Introduced in 1993, the value of ETFs in the United States has risen from $66 billion in 2000 to just under $1 trillion in 2010. At the top of the risk-reward ladder are the largely unregulated hedge funds. Rather than hedging against market risks, hedge funds serve as vehicles for sophisticated investors to leverage capital into investments offering superior potential returns adjusted for the risk. Perhaps the most notorious hedge fund was Long-Term Capital Management (LTCM), which found itself excessively overleveraged in 1998, resulting in a private bailout organized by the Federal Reserve and the eventual dismantling of the hedge fund. Finally, sovereign wealth funds are similar to other investment funds, except that they invest the surpluses of governments, especially from countries flush with oil wealth.

Another method for maximizing returns is through the process of securitization: taking illiquid assets (e.g., mortgages), bundling them together, and selling them as securities that provide a payment stream for investors. In spreading the risk of default, the intention is to increase the supply of funds available. Securitization has produced a veritable alphabet soup of new financial instruments. All are variations on the same theme, the difference lying in the connection between investors and the underlying asset. The first mortgage-backed securities (MBSs) were sold by the Government National Mortgage Association (Ginnie Mae) in 1970. These were "plain vanilla" securities in which the principle and interest payments of the collective mortgage holders would flow through to investors. Asset-backed securities (ABSs) offer the same idea, but are built on alternative assets, such as credit card accounts or student loans. The complexity in securitization comes in with collateralized mortgage obligations (CMOs) or collateralized debt obligations (CDOs). Confusingly, these terms are frequently used interchangeably. The fundamental difference between the two is that a CMO is built on mortgages while a CDO proper can include mortgages and other assets. The key trait of CMOs and CDOs is that the securities are divided into portions (or "tranches," the French word for "slice"), with different levels of risk and return. The upper tranches are first in line for payment in exchange for a lower return; after that, the "waterfall" of payments cascades down to the mezzanine tranches, and then the junior or "equity" tranches. In principle this structure effectively matches investors to their risk preferences. However, investment banks could only buy these securities if they were highly rated. The major ratings agencies, using probability models, determined that the likelihood of the senior tranches not getting paid was very low, even if the bond was based entirely on subprime mortgages. Those tranches were thus sold with high AAA ratings, leading in turn to a proliferation of even more subprime mortgages: 7.4 percent of mortgage originations in 2002, up to 23.5 percent in 2006.

This fed a bubble in CMOs and CDOs, which went from just $5 billion issued in 1996 to $520 billion in 2006. These instruments were frequently bought and sold, moreover, through structured investment vehicles (SIVs), also known as the "shadow banking system." First introduced by Citigroup in 1988, SIVs were formally separate from banks, but generally connected to them through lines of credit. By funneling investments through SIVs, they remained off the bank's balance sheets and thus did not apply toward their capital requirements. This allowed banks to reduce capital minima, increase leverage, and increase profits. In concept, securitization would diversify risk and enhance credit. In practice, it concentrated and accentuated risk.

One means of hedging against such uncertainty is through purchasing derivatives. These are financial contracts, and their final price is determined (or "derived") by the value of underlying asset or outcome. Used as well for speculation, some derivatives have a long genealogy, notably futures (a contract to pay in advance for the future delivery of some item, typically a commodity) and options (a contract giving the holder the right to purchase a financial instrument at a future date for a predetermined price). These types of derivatives are sold through organized and regulated exchanges, such as the Chicago Board of Trade. Over the counter (OTC) derivatives are traded by large investment firms. Treated as one-off contracts between buyers and sellers, these exchanges are neither centralized nor regulated. Credit default swaps (CDSs) were a key OTC derivative during the financial crisis. On one level, CDSs are insurance policies taken out against a debt, such as an MBS. Unlike a normal insurance policy, however, one need not be the holder of the underlying asset in order to insure against its default. One could simply bet on default as a form of speculation. Equally, traditional insurance companies are required to hold reserves in case of loss. Those selling CDSs, most notably American International Group (AIG), faced no such requirement in the unregulated derivative market.

In explaining the 2008 financial crisis, many analysts have pointed accusatory fingers at the new financial instruments. The key point is that it is generally not the instruments themselves that are inherently problematic, rather, it is how they are used or misused. Mortgage securitization can in fact distribute risk and increase the volume of mortgage funds available to homeowners. The system falls apart, however, when subprime mortgages are packaged as AAA bonds. The problem was not that AIG sold credit default swaps per se; it was that they kept selling them without building up any capital to back up the potential claims. That is not to say all new financial instruments are unproblematic. The Brookings Institution scholar Robert E. Litan, in his sweeping review of financial innovation, concludes that the majority of innovations have had a positive impact on the financial sector and the overall economy. However, he specifically singles out SIVs and the particularly complex and opaque CDOs developed in the last decade for condemnation. Despite the scars of 2008, the factors that drove the development of new financial instruments in the three decades preceding the crisis are still prevalent and will continue to nurture financial innovations in the near term.

[*See also* Financial Crisis of 2008; *and* Financial Industry.]

BIBLIOGRAPHY

Litan, Robert E. "In Defense of Much, But Not All, Financial Innovation." Brookings Institution. (2010), http://www.brookings.edu/~/media/Files/rc/opinions/2010/0217_financial_innovation_litan/0217_financial_innovation_litan.pdf.

Rajan, Raghuram G. "Has Financial Development Made the World Riskier?" *The Greenspan Era: Lessons for the Future*, Federal Reserve Bank of Kansas City Symposium, Jackson Hole, Wyo., August 25–27, 2005.

United States Financial Crisis Inquiry Commission. (2011) *The Financial Crisis Inquiry Report: Final Report of the National Commission on the Causes of the Financial and Economic Crisis in the United States.* (Washington, D.C., 2001).

Terrence Casey

FIRST LADIES

The United States presidency has received extensive scholarly attention, but the position of first lady has often received only superficial coverage. The position, and even the title, can evoke contradictory expectations. George Washington's wife, Martha, was greeted in 1789 as "Lady Washington." This evocation of an aristocratic title did not please many citizens of the newly independent nation, however, and was discontinued. While Dolley Madison (the wife of President James Madison) was addressed as "Her Majesty" and "Lady Presidentress," later wives were called simply "Mrs. President." Not until 1870 did the journalist Emily Briggs, under the pseudonym "Olivia," use the title "First Lady" to discuss Martha Washington and Julia Grant (the wife of President Ulysses S. Grant). Only with the inauguration of President Rutherford B. Hayes in 1877 was the term "First Lady" repeatedly used by correspondents to describe his wife, Lucy Hayes. But the use of the title "First Lady" highlights the domestic and social side of the position and deemphasizes the potential for active and significant political involvement.

The popular expectation for a woman's public role and individual voice has fundamentally altered in America since the nation's founding, but the first lady is often still held to an antiquated model. In 2011, there is less media coverage of First Lady Michelle Obama's public antiobesity campaign for children or her activities for increased support for armed service spouses than of her clothes, her hair, and her sense of style. Jackie Kennedy (the wife of John F. Kennedy) in the 1960s or Abigail Adams (the wife of John Adams) in the eighteenth century would have both been the subjects of similar focus. But this social dimension is only one facet of this potentially powerful position.

American history is replete with examples of presidential spouses fulfilling openly political functions, including roles as: presidential representative, campaigner, public liaison, lobbyist, presidential adviser, and individual policy actor. Although the first lady is unelected, not mentioned in the Constitution, and unimpeachable, she is rarely criticized, and often praised, for acting as a presidential representative at ceremonial functions such as weddings, funerals, and coronations. But in 1977, when President Jimmy Carter asked his wife, Rosalynn Carter, to represent him and explain American foreign policy to heads of state in seven Latin American countries early in his administration, the media coverage was extensive but not universally positive. Her role as a legitimate spokesperson for the president was challenged, although she was briefed by the president daily and was following his request. Interestingly, President Carter sent the first lady only on more traditional trips for the remainder of his administration.

An active role during the presidential campaign has become an expected duty of the potential first lady, with Lou Hoover (the wife of President Herbert Hoover) being the first potential first lady in the twentieth century to give formal campaign addresses and speak over the radio. Individual spouses have varied in their enthusiasm for campaigning, with Mamie Eisenhower accompanying her husband, Dwight Eisenhower, at public events but never speaking, and Jackie Kennedy withdrawing from campaigning in 1960 because of her pregnancy but still writing a weekly newsletter for the Democratic Party workers called "Campaign Wife." The advantages, however, of an active campaigner are numerous. They include extending the candidate's symbolic presence into two places simultaneously; balancing the ticket by increasing the traits in the presidential team; allowing the voters to get to know a person who may well become a close presidential adviser; attracting additional media coverage; and possibly receiving a more courteous reception from a hostile audience. When Lady Bird Johnson, the wife of President Lyndon B. Johnson, traveled through the Deep South from 6–9 October 1964, covering 1,682 miles by train on the "Lady Bird Special," her Southern accent and wide web of Southern family and friends assured her favorable receptions, even as her husband struggled for Southern support in the wake of his backing for the civil rights movement. More recent first ladies, such as Laura Bush, the wife of President George W. Bush, have not all enjoyed campaigning, but they have all become actively involved in the campaigns nonetheless. Many, including Rosalynn Carter, Hillary Clinton (the wife of President Bill Clinton), and Michelle Obama were known as key campaign strategists. The media and the public have

come to expect an active campaigner in the candidate's spouse.

A first lady can humanize a presidential administration and act as a liaison to the public. The Office of the First Lady, located in the East Wing of the White House, has a staff to deal with the voluminous quantity of mail arriving daily from the citizenry. Some letters want assistance, some give advice, some criticize, and some commiserate, but they all are reaching out to the first lady on a personal level. Laura Bush was praised by media correspondents in May 2005 when she did a stand-up comedy routine before three thousand reporters at the White House Correspondents' Association dinner, delivering wisecracking one-liners about her husband during a rough time in his presidency. She helped reveal the personal and universally human side of the president. First ladies have also corresponded publicly through their writings. For example, Eleanor Roosevelt wrote a daily syndicated column called "My Day," and Hillary Clinton wrote a weekly newspaper column called "Talking It Over" and published a book, *It Takes a Village and Other Lessons Children Teach Us*. With her candid discussion of her own breast cancer, Gerald Ford's wife, Betty Ford, highlighted a significant health concern shared by many women, and prompted an increase in individual cancer screenings among American women.

At times first ladies have taken active roles as lobbyists. This is a potentially controversial path, since public issues generally have both supporters and opponents. Betty Ford continued to advocate for the passage of the Equal Rights Amendment (ERA), which was not supported by the Republican establishment, including her husband. Less controversially, Rosalynn Carter had a long-term interest in mental health policy. In 1979, when President Carter submitted to Congress the Mental Health Systems Act, she actively lobbied for the bill's passage by giving a wide range of speeches on mental health and specifically entertaining members of the congressional committee considering the bill at the White House. Additionally, for the first time since 1945, when Eleanor Roosevelt testified before Congress, Rosalynn Carter testified before the Subcommittee on Health and Scientific Research of the Senate Human Resources Committee. Other examples of advocacy include Laura Bush's speeches advocating the passage of the No Child Left Behind Act and Hillary Clinton's chairing of the Task Force on National Health Care Reform. The criticism directed at Clinton for her role is a good indicator of the limits still placed on the proper role of the first lady by some Americans.

First ladies have advised their presidential spouses nearly from the founding of the nation. Abigail Adams wrote over two thousand letters to her often absent husband John Adams, which included advice and overtly political observations. What makes a first lady a powerful presidential adviser is not the institutional position, but the highly personal respect and trust achieved in a good marriage partnership. From a conservative Nancy Reagan or Barbara Bush to a liberal Hillary Clinton or Michelle Obama, the similarities tying their strong advising roles together is certainly not ideology but rather their relationship with the president. Some, like Rosalynn Carter, took a public advising role by attending cabinet meetings, while more commonly, the wife's advice comes privately but constantly throughout the president's term. Strong challenges to the propriety of this role came from the actions of Edith Wilson following President Woodrow Wilson's stroke in 1919, when she blocked all visitors but the doctors from her husband's chambers, yet emerged with presidential signed documents. This was an extreme circumstance, but today the assumption is that the first lady will have an important role, as the president hashes out decisions and evaluates strategies. From Ford onward through Obama, all presidents have publicly acknowledged the significance of their wives' advice in their own decision-making processes.

Finally, first ladies have also used their very public podium to influence the agenda-setting function of the media, so as to direct the American people's attention toward a favorite cause. The following examples are not comprehensive but only illustrative of the variety of projects. Jackie Kennedy focused on historic restoration and the White House renovation. Lady Bird Johnson became associated with natural beautification efforts and promoted the planting of wildflowers along interstate highways. Betty Ford focused on alcohol and drug addiction, as did Nancy Reagan with the "Just Say No" campaign against drug use. Laura Bush was active in the "Ready to Read, Ready to Learn" early childhood literacy program. Hillary Clinton promoted children's welfare, and Michelle Obama promotes healthy food and exercise for children. Many of these projects fall within the traditional women's areas of health, children, and beautification.

First ladies play an important role in the operation of the American presidency. The power of this position lies with the president's attitude toward it, the personality of the first lady herself, and the cultural expectations of the American people. The changing role of women in society allowed First Lady Clinton to run for and win the position of US Senator from New York in 2000, and after leaving the White House, continue her career as US secretary of state under President Barack Obama. The term "first lady" may be an archaic one, but the position continues to evolve with the times.

BIBLIOGRAPHY

Boller, Paul F. *Presidential Wives: An Anecdotal History.* (New York, 1988).

Caroli, Betty Boyd. *First Ladies.* (New York, 1987).

Gould, Lewis L., ed. *American First Ladies: Their Lives and Their Legacy.* (New York, 1996).

Gutin, Myra G. *The President's Partner: The First Lady in the Twentieth Century.* (New York, 1989).

Watson, Robert P. *The Presidents' Wives: Reassessing the Office of First Lady.* (Boulder, Colo., 2000).

Wertheimer, Molly Meijer, ed. *Leading Ladies of the White House: Communication Strategies of Notable Twentieth-Century First Ladies.* (Lanham, Md., 2005).

Kathy Smith

FISCAL CONSERVATISM

Fiscal conservatism is a political philosophy that focuses on low taxes, reduced government spending, and minimal government debt. Most fiscal conservatives also support less government regulation and little oversight of business and free trade. In general fiscal conservatives are skeptical of government's ability to stimulate the economy or create jobs, and support only a minimal role for the government in redistributing resources. While fiscal conservatives often are aligned with corporate interests on issues such as lower taxes and less regulation, they frequently break with businesses on issues such as subsidies or government "investment" in the economy.

In many ways, fiscal conservatism stems from a classical liberal tradition that is suspicious of government authority and supportive of individual choice. This preference for individual as opposed to government action leads toward a laissez-faire approach to economic issues. Fiscal conservatives stand in contrast to contemporary liberals, who argue that the state should use tax money to regulate the economy and provide social services.

Fiscal conservatives form one of the traditional three legs of the conservative movement, along with social conservatism and national-defense conservatism. While the categories are not mutually exclusive, a significant subgroup of fiscal conservatives might be broadly described as libertarian, meaning they hold more liberal views on social issues and tend to support a noninterventionist foreign policy, along with their support for lower taxes and less government spending.

Historically, fiscally conservatives have tended to vote for Republicans. However, during the George W. Bush administration, Republican big spending alienated many fiscally conservative voters, and during the 2006 and 2008 congressional elections, these voters deserted Republicans in droves, leading to a Democratic takeover of Congress. However, most fiscally conservative voters were deeply unhappy with the growth in government spending during the first years of the Barack Obama administration, and in the 2010 midterm elections swung back to the Republican Party, helping to return control of the House of Representatives to the GOP.

The recent growth in the size of government, in particular the rising level of government debt, has been an important factor in the rise of the "Tea Party" movement, which is focused on the need to reduce government spending, the deficit, and the national debt. Among the politicians most closely identified with fiscal conservatism today are New Jersey Governor Chris Christie, Senators Tom Coburn (Rep.–Okla.) and Rand Paul (Rep.–Ky.), and Representative Paul Ryan (Rep.–Wis.).

While fiscal conservatives generally agree on the goal of a smaller, less expensive government, there are significant disagreements over priorities. One subgroup of fiscal conservatives could be categorized as "deficit hawks." Their emphasis is on balancing government budgets and reducing the size of government debt. They see government debt as both economically damaging and morally dubious, since it passes obligations on to future generations who have played no part in present-day tax and spending decisions. Therefore, they are willing to consider tax increases if the additional revenue will be used to reduce debt rather than to increase spending.

A second group puts their primary emphasis on tax cuts rather than spending cuts or debt reduction. Many embrace "supply-side economics," arguing that because high taxes discourage economic activity and investment, tax cuts would result in increased economic growth, leading in turn to higher government revenues. The additional revenues would, in the long term, reduce government debt. Therefore, this group would argue for reducing taxes even if it were to lead to short-term increases in the deficit. Some supply-siders have even argued that the increased revenues make drastic expenditure cuts unnecessary. This would mean that conservatives could avoid messy debates about the proper size and role of government. As former Representative Jack Kemp, a leading cheerleader for supply-side economics, put it, they could govern "with no political pain, i.e., having to convince the voters to accept any real absolute cuts in government spending."

A third faction makes little distinction between debt and taxes. They agree with the Nobel Prize–winning economist Milton Friedman that the true "cost" of government is the level of spending, not how that spending is financed. Every dollar that government spends is a dollar that is siphoned from American workers, regardless of whether it is raised through debt or taxes. Taxes simply redistribute purchasing power, and do so in a particularly inefficient manner, reducing the incentives to produce or hire. Borrowing simply forces businesses and investors to anticipate higher taxes down the road. Therefore, this group emphasizes reductions in spending rather than tax policy.

Economic conservatives argue their position on both practical and moral grounds. Practically, most fiscal conservatives concede that a certain amount of government spending is necessary. Governments must provide certain basic services, such as dispute adjudication, police and defense functions, and the infrastructure maintenance necessary for a functioning economy. Thus, under a scenario with zero government spending there would be little if any economic growth. But beyond a certain level, fiscal conservatives argue that the costs of government exceed the benefits it provides, leading to lower economic growth. For example, if government consumed 100 percent of gross domestic product (GDP), there would be little or no economic growth. In between is a curve, with rising initial growth accompanying increased government spending, followed by declining growth once government gets too large.

Fiscal conservatives also argue that many government programs do not work or are counterproductive. They point out, for example, that despite massive increases in education spending, student test scores have not improved. Or they suggest that government welfare payments contribute to a variety of social ills and encourage dependency. From a moral perspective, fiscal conservatives point out that government spending fundamentally reduces human liberty. Since government has no money of its own, all government revenue must ultimately be extracted from others. Every dollar consumed by the government, therefore, is one less dollar that individuals can spend in the way they choose.

[See also Conservatism; Fiscal Policy; Liberalism, Theory and History of; Public Spending; and Republican Party.]

BIBLIOGRAPHY

Edwards, Chris. *Downsizing the Federal Government.* (Washington, D.C., 2006).

Friedman, Milton. *Capitalism and Freedom.* (Chicago, 1962).

Hazlett, Henry. *Economics in One Lesson: The Shortest and Surest Way to Understand Basic Economics.* (New York, 1979).

Smith, Adam. *The Wealth of Nations.* (London, 1991). First published in 1776.

von Hayek, Friedrich A. *The Fatal Conceit: The Errors of Socialism.* (Chicago, 1988).

Michael Tanner

FISCAL POLICY

In the 1960s, a scholar looking for an authoritative reference on fiscal policy in the United States would have been told to read Musgrave. The reference is to *The Theory of Public Finance* by Richard Musgrave (1959). Musgrave set out what he called "A Multiple Theory of the Public Household." His theory encompassed the determination of government budget policies to achieve allocation, distribution, and stabilization goals. He thus integrated previous theories of government spending and taxation with the relatively new Keynesian idea of fiscal policy as a macroeconomic stabilization tool. He did this at the dawn of the "New Frontier" of the John F. Kennedy administration, which employed fiscal stabilization policy along Keynesian lines.

At the beginning of the twenty-first century, Musgrave is still a good starting point to describe the course of US fiscal policy. This article begins with a brief summary of Musgrave's framework and then considers how it has been challenged, modified, and found useful or not over the years. Some major applications of fiscal policy over the past half-century will be described as well.

Musgrave's Public Household. Musgrave conceived of fiscal policy decisions being made by three branches of an imaginary "Fiscal Department," each linked to one set of policy objectives. Each branch would pursue its objective, assuming that the other two branches performed their functions properly. The allocation branch would determine the level of spending on public goods relative to private. The distribution branch would set a structure of tax and transfer rates to achieve the proper distribution of income. The stabilization branch would see to it that high employment and price stability were achieved without interfering with the goals of the other branches; this would be done by taxes and transfers.

All this seems like a tall order and, well, imaginary. Musgrave was reacting to what he saw as a situation in which budget policies had been assessed as practical matters of legislation and administration. His aim was to apply the general body of economic theory to public finance.

For the problems of optimal allocation of resources between public and private uses and the best possible distribution of income, Musgrave drew upon a large body of previous work going back to David Ricardo, Knut Wicksell, and John Stuart Mill, and extending to A. C. Pigou, Erik Lindahl, and Paul Samuelson, among others. Onto this literature he grafted the Keynesian analysis of compensatory finance—the goal of ensuring the full employment of factors of production.

Musgrave's analysis of stabilization policy was conducted within the Keynesian model of the time. This was basically John R. Hicks's Investment Saving/Liquidity Preference Money Supply (IS/LM) model, along with a labor market that exhibited downward rigidity of the money wage and money illusion on the part of labor suppliers. There were thus real effects from fiscal policy-induced changes in aggregate demand, and consequently a substantive role for discretionary stabilization and for automatic fiscal stabilizers. The conduct of fiscal policy as set out by Musgrave and other prominent Keynesians of the day was not the simplistic caricature found in some contemporary textbooks and retrospectives on the period. It was not composed of "fine-tuning" and "social menu curves." There was recognition of disincentive effects on labor supply and the saving-investment choice that came from taxation. The short-run nature of the output-inflation trade-off was recognized. Policies such as investment tax credits were proposed to foster investment and capital formation. But at heart Musgrave's compensatory finance was an application of what Franco Modigliani (1977) called the fundamental practical

message of John Maynard Keynes's *The General Theory of Employment, Interest, and Money* (1936): "that a private enterprise economy using an intangible money *needs* to be stabilized, *can* be stabilized, and, therefore *should* be stabilized by appropriate monetary and fiscal policies" (p. 1).

Public Choice Theory. When President Kennedy asked the Yale economist James Tobin to join his Council of Economic Advisors (CEA), Tobin demurred, saying that he was an "ivory tower" economist. Kennedy responded that he intended to be an ivory tower president. Tobin, along with other prominent Keynesian economists including Walter Heller, Arthur Okun, Gardner Ackley, Kermit Gordon, Charles Schultze, Otto Eckstein, and Warren Smith, served in the Kennedy and Lyndon Johnson administrations. They went on to guide the conduct of Musgrave's public household. In addition to serving on the CEA, Keynesian economists provided all four directors of the Bureau of the Budget and two undersecretaries of the Treasury during the Kennedy and Johnson years.

James Buchanan and Richard Wagner, in *Democracy in Deficit* (1977), viewed these economists as having "the Presumptions of Harvey Road" (Harvey Road being the street where the Keynes family lived in Cambridge). The presumptions were that fiscal policy would be carried out as prescribed by an ideal framework such as Musgrave's. Buchanan and Wagner maintained that we must instead look at the application of "Keynesian economics in a political setting where . . . policy decisions are made by professional politicians who respond to demands both of the public and the bureaucracy itself" (p. 35).

In the setting of the United States economy Buchanan and Wagner, as well as others who take the public-choice approach, see the results of the application of Keynesian economics as far from the ideal. They see politicians vying for votes via public spending projects and tax cuts while avoiding unpopular tax increases, with a resulting deficit bias in fiscal policy. This bias is strengthened in the view of some public-choice writers by the belief that output growth is at most times a more pressing concern to voters than is inflation. William Nordhaus

(1975) and others also saw discretionary fiscal policies resulting in a political business cycle, as the economy was "pumped up" prior to elections followed by postelection austerity. Fiscal policy was a cause rather than a remedy with respect to the business cycle.

The remedy in Buchanan and Wagner's view was a return to the pre-Keynesian norm of a balanced budget. Other public-choice theorists favor alternative rules such as ones to restrain the growth in government spending. Rather than having enlightened economists directing the branches of Musgrave's public household, we would be better served with, as Nordhaus put it, "the lame leading the sometimes wicked."

A Fractured Consensus. When Musgrave's book appeared in 1959, the theory of macroeconomic policy was guided by the Keynesian-neoclassical consensus. This dominant view held that while prices and wages would adjust to achieve high employment in the long run, demand management via monetary and fiscal policy was required for economic stability in the short to medium run. There was a monetarist minority position which held, in Milton Friedman's words, that "the state of the budget by itself has no significant effect on the course of nominal income, on deflation, or cyclical fluctuations" (1969, p. 51). The monetarist-fiscalist debate was, however, a sideshow. The challenges to the Keynesian view of the role of stabilization in the 1970s and 1980s from the new classical and real business cycle theories were fundamental.

New classical models developed by Robert Lucas (1972, 1981) and others held the position that systematic aggregate demand management policies, monetary or fiscal, would not affect the distribution of real variables, including output and employment. Real-business-cycle models such as those in Robert J. Barro (1989) go further in arguing that the business cycle as an equilibrium phenomenon is not suboptimal. The practical message of Keynes's *General Theory*, the underlying premise of Musgrave's analysis, was seen as false; the real economy neither could, nor perhaps even should, be stabilized by monetary or fiscal policy. What was left was stabilization of

inflation best accomplished by monetary policy rules; Musgrave's stabilization branch, the thinking went, should be shuttered.

The late 1970s and early 1980s also witnessed the rise of supply-side economics. While not an essentially new theory, supply-side economics focused on the incentive effects of marginal tax rates, the wedge that tax rates formed affecting labor-leisure and saving-investment choices. These aspects of fiscal policy were emphasized, rather than stabilization of aggregate demand. The separation of allocation, distribution, and stabilization goals was blurred relative to Musgrave's approach.

In the presence of diverse and conflicting theoretical perspectives, debates over fiscal policy became much more contentious. In particular, fiscal stabilization initiatives along Keynesian lines no longer commanded clear majority support. As concerns about growing budget deficits and public debt increased in the 1980s and 1990s, measures for fiscal stimulus were greeted with increased suspicion. Thus even when the New Keynesians resuscitated welfare-based stabilization policy analysis in the 1990s, they concentrated on monetary policy. Only under the pressure of events described below did New Keynesian economists revisit subjects such as the "Simple Analytics of the Government Expenditure Multiplier" (Woodford, 2011).

Interplay with Events. The changes in economic theory and policy analysis so far discussed took place in the context of events in the United States and other developed economies over the past half century. The high point of Keynesian policy influence probably came with the tax cut of 1964. The public-choice and political-business-cycle views were fueled by failures of fiscal policy during the Vietnam War years, as described by Okun (1970), and the stop-go fiscal and incomes policies preceding the 1972 presidential election. The dissatisfaction with Keynesian economics in general grew during the stagflation of the 1970s. Growing deficits and debt in the United States after 1980 led to a reliance on monetary policy both to restrain inflation and stabilize output. During the post-1980 period, expansionary fiscal policies resulted only when stabilization goals of

Keynesians coincided with the desire of supply-side economists for lower tax rates (1980–1982, 2001–2003). Tax increases were enacted only when aimed at deficit reduction (1990–1993 and 1996–1998).

The financial crisis and severe recession in 2008 revived interest in Keynesian fiscal stabilization policies, as major world economies tried stimulus programs to stave off depression and spur recovery. By 2009 monetary policy in the United States was faced with the zero-bound problem, as the federal funds rate was reduced to virtually zero. Many nontraditional monetary policy measures were tried, but policymakers became convinced that tax cuts and spending increases were required to restart the economy. There was a Keynesian revival. Then an anti-Keynesian reaction set in as recovery took hold, and the politicians and the public turned their concern again to deficits and debt.

Where We Are Now. It is too early to assess the success of the fiscal stimulus program undertaken in the United States in the wake of the 2008 financial crisis. Even if in the future it is viewed as at least somewhat successful, fiscal stabilization will still be viewed as a tool of last resort. The theoretical consensus remains shattered, and conflicts over fiscal policy goals are still evident. A common view during 2009 was that, just as there are no atheists in foxholes, during financial crises we are all Keynesians. But crises end and economists return to their previous faiths. As the economy recovers and interest rates return to more normal levels, alleviating the zero-bound problem, monetary policy will likely regain primacy in stabilization policy.

Fiscal policy will for several years be constrained by long-term deficit and debt problems, due mostly to rising health care costs. So far these problems have resulted in squabbles over continuing resolutions, possible government shutdowns, and debt-limit increases. The current budget fights fit a description Alexis de Tocqueville gave to an after-shock of the French revolution: "a bad tragedy performed by actors from the provinces." In the spring of 2011, for example, Congress and the Obama administration sparred over $30 billion in spending cuts barely three months after approving more than

ten times that amount in deficit-increasing tax cuts. Budget identities are, however, stubborn things, and US Congresses and presidents will have to reach compromises on spending and revenues that result in sustainable levels of debt and deficits.

[*See also* Financial Crisis of 2008; Keynesianism; Monetarism; *and* Monetary Policy.]

BIBLIOGRAPHY

Barro, Robert J. *Modern Business Cycle Theory.* (Cambridge, Mass., 1989).

Buchanan, James M., and Richard E. Wagner. *Democracy in Deficit: The Political Legacy of Lord Keynes.* (New York, 1977).

Friedman, Milton, and Walter Heller. *Monetary vs. Fiscal Policy.* (New York, 1969).

Froyen, Richard T., and Alfred V. Guender. *Optimal Monetary Policy under Uncertainty.* (Cheltenham, UK, 2007).

Galí, Jordi. *Monetary Policy, Inflation and the Business Cycle: An Introduction to the New Keynesian Framework.* (Princeton, N.J., 2008).

Keynes, John Maynard. *The General Theory of Employment, Interest, and Money.* (New York, 1936).

Lucas, Robert E. "Expectations and the Neutrality of Money." *Journal of Economic Theory* 4 (April 1972): 103–124.

Lucas, Robert E. *Studies in Business-Cycle Theory.* (Cambridge, Mass., 1981).

Modigliani, Franco. "The Monetarist Controversy or Should We Forsake Stabilization Policies?" *American Economic Review* 67 (March 1977): 171–186.

Musgrave, Richard. *The Theory of Public Finance.* (New York, 1959).

Nordhaus, William. "The Political Business Cycle." *Review of Economic Studies* 42 (1975): 169–190.

Okun, Arthur M. *The Political Economy of Prosperity.* (Washington, D.C., 1970).

Tufte, Edward R. *Political Control of the Economy.* (Princeton, N.J., 1978).

Woodford, Michael. "Simple Analytics of the Government Expenditure Multiplier." *American Economic Review: Macroeconomics* 3 (January 2011): 1–35.

Richard T. Froyen

FOOD AND DRUG ADMINISTRATION

Like all democratic republics, the United States government engages in regulation of its national economy, and much of this regulation is carried out by administrative agencies endowed with powers by statute, by tradition, and by popular legitimacy. American politics knows no more powerful regulatory agency than the US Food and Drug Administration (FDA), the scope and powers of which are telling, because they gesture toward often unrecognized powers of administrative and regulatory agencies in American politics.

The FDA is an executive branch agency resting in a Cabinet-level executive department, the Department of Health and Human Services. It grew from a set of networks, organizations, and powers in the US Department of Agriculture (USDA), and many observers date its founding to the 1906 Pure Food and Drug Act, which empowered the USDA's Bureau of Chemistry to regulate food and drugs in interstate commerce.

The FDA's power is most stark, and most distinct from that of other regulatory agencies in American government, in its gatekeeping power over health products. No drug or medical device can be marketed in interstate commerce without prior authorization as "safe and effective" by the FDA. Gatekeeping power is an important form of "approval regulation" (Carpenter, 2004), whereby an agency need not act affirmatively in order to regulate, but can fail to act (that is, decline to approve a new product or delay in doing so), and thereby cause companies to adjust their operations and behavior toward its preferences. Gatekeeping power dates from the 1938 Federal Food, Drug, and Cosmetic Act (FFDCA), which required FDA determinations of product safety in order for new drugs to be marketed in the United States, and which stands as one of the most important pieces of regulatory legislation in American history. In the area of drugs and medical devices, the FFDCA was strengthened by a set of developments in the 1940s and 1950s that created protocols (phased testing) and standards (efficacy, or how well a drug works, as opposed to the toxicity standards inherent in safety standards) for drug review. Following the thalidomide crisis of 1960 and 1961, efficacy standards were formally added to those of safety as necessary demonstrations for marketing approval in the Drug Amendments of 1962, and similar standards were applied to medical devices in the Medical Device Amendments Act of 1976.

The FDA is critical to American politics because it is one of the most recognized agencies in American government. Several surveys taken in the past decade suggest that it may have the highest public recognition among all federal agencies. American citizens have repeatedly demonstrated great concern for the safety of their foods and health products, and the FDA has become, deservedly or not, the source and object of trust (and sometimes, distrust) when it comes to the safety of basic household items. Underlying much of this trust is a widely shared but little recognized cultural assumption. Americans often believe that a food or drug product has been tested first before it gets to their table or medicine cabinets—they believe, in other words, that some form of approval regulation is protecting them.

Gatekeeping power in regulation exists among other forms of power, both "directive power" (the ability of an agency to command and control private subjects) and "conceptual power" (the ability of regulators to shape vocabularies and structures of thought). Of these, the FDA's conceptual power is especially significant. The agency's procedures and institutions for regulating drugs have been copied by many agencies around the world, not least those organizations (such as China's State Food and Drug Administration, or equivalent "FDAs" in South Korea and Saudi Arabia) that have copied the agency's name. But there are more profound dependencies of global regulation on the FDA, including the worldwide adoption of the three-phase system of medical experiments for drugs, the regulatory definition of efficacy, the idea of an administrative "new drug application," or the definition of "bioequivalence" by which generic drugs can substitute for pioneer molecules.

The FDA's important role in politics and society stems in part from its critical role in the economy. It is commonly estimated that one-quarter to three-tenths of US gross domestic product (GDP) is regulated by the FDA. Whenever there is an outbreak of food-borne illness in the United States, or when safety problems are discovered with a drug, cosmetic, or device, the FDA takes center stage in national and global news. The agency's ubiquity in economic matters and in the media points to a "politics of reputation," a primary force strengthening and constraining the agency. Reputation is a political force that buffets numerous administrative agencies in US government, yet its importance for the FDA is paramount because the agency has long possessed a reputation for consumer protection and scientific vigor—essentially, for getting matters and decisions "right" in critical situations such as the thalidomide tragedy—that gives it partial immunity from the anti-government strain of American political culture. In the twentieth century especially, few government agencies carried such historical legitimacy with them, and the FDA's broad and robust reputation was a primary source of its legal, political, cultural, and economic strength.

Reputational politics have strongly shaped the recent history of the FDA. When the worldwide health crisis of AIDS surfaced in the 1980s, activists from the gay health movements and from libertarian causes combined to agitate for quickened access to new drugs and reduced barriers to experimentation. In ways that echoed the pressure of cancer organizations, these activists and their allies induced the FDA to reshape some of its institutions. They did so primarily by challenging the flexibility and moral reputation of the agency, asking how a compassionate program of regulation could keep potentially lifesaving treatments from those who had no other therapeutic options. Among the important changes were the accelerated approval paradigm, and the Prescription Drug User Fee Act (PDUFA), first passed in 1992 and renewed every five years since. Under PDUFA, drug and device companies are charged a per-application tax, the revenues of which are dedicated to hiring more review staff and, especially since 2007, other drug regulation functions. The user-fee act also imposes review deadlines upon the FDA, such that most new drug applications must be reviewed within six to ten months; some political science and medical studies (e.g., Carpenter, Zucker, and Avorn, 2008) suggest that these deadlines are

associated with safety problems in the drugs approved right at the deadline times. Others argue that the user-fee act has compromised the independence of the FDA (see Avorn, 2004).

One important social and cultural commodity that long resisted the FDA's governance—tobacco products, especially cigarettes, which constitute one of the defining commodities and experiences of twentieth-century America—has recently come under the FDA's purview. Under the Family Smoking Prevention and Tobacco Control Act (FSPTCA) of 2009, the FDA can broadly regulate the design, manufacture, and marketing of cigarettes and all new tobacco products, including those that claim to offer reduced risk to consumers.

The FDA's gatekeeping power and other regulatory authorities render it an object of furious and intense political and economic pressure. The agency receives criticism from numerous organizations, and food, cosmetic, pharmaceutical, and medical device companies in the global realm are especially keen to attempt to persuade its decision-makers. The global pharmaceutical industry is one of the most powerful players in Washington and in European and Asian capitals, and has deployed intense lobbying efforts to influence legislation governing the FDA, and indeed the very culture of the FDA. The agency has also witnessed the rise of particular libertarian attacks in the past thirty years, as many libertarians see approval regulation as antithetical to free market operations in the field of health products. Yet with popular support and broad legitimacy among medical specialists, health professions, and the scientific community, approval regulation for health products and other regulations at the FDA continue apace.

[See also AIDS; Deregulation; Drugs and Politics; Environmental Protection Agency; Health Care; and Regulation].

BIBLIOGRAPHY
Avorn, Jerry. Powerful Medicines: The Benefits, Risks, and Costs of Prescription Drugs. (New York, 2004).
Brandt, Allan M. The Cigarette Century: The Rise, Fall, and Deadly Persistence of the Product That Defined America. (New York, 2007).

Carpenter, Daniel. "Protection without Capture: Product Approval by a Politically Responsive, Learning Regulator." *American Political Science Review* 98, no. 4 (November 2004): 613–631.

Carpenter, Daniel. *Reputation and Power: Organizational Image and Pharmaceutical Regulation at the FDA.* (Princeton, N.J., 2010).

Carpenter, Daniel, and Gisela Sin. 2007. "Policy Tragedy and the Emergence of Economic Regulation: The Food, Drug, and Cosmetic Act of 1938." *Studies in American Political Development* 21, no. 2 (Fall 2007): 149–180.

Carpenter, Daniel, Evan James Zucker, and Jerry Avorn. "Drug Review Deadlines and Safety Problems," *New England Journal of Medicine* 358 (2008): 1354–1361.

Daemmrich, Arthur. *Pharmacopolitics: Drug Regulation in the United States and Germany.* (Chapel Hill, N.C., 2003).

Hilts, Philip. *Protecting America's Health: The FDA, Business, and One Hundred Years of Regulation.* (New York, 2003).

Daniel Carpenter

FORD, GERALD R.

(1913–2006) Gerald R. Ford became the thirty-eighth president of the United States upon Richard Nixon's resignation. The only president never elected by voters beyond his congressional district, he spent thirty months working to restore the credibility of the presidency, combating both inflation and recession, and reestablishing America's international leadership after Vietnam. He defeated Ronald Reagan for the 1976 Republican nomination before losing the presidential election to Jimmy Carter.

Pre-Presidential Years. Leslie Lynch King Jr. was born 14 July 1913 in Omaha, Nebraska, and moved to Grand Rapids, Michigan, when his parents' marriage ended in 1915. There his mother married Gerald R. Ford, who adopted "Junior." Efforts to curb Junior's ambidexterity contributed to a stuttering problem. The Fords left the Dutch Calvinist church (which emphasized the Ten Commandments and punishment) for Grace Episcopal Church (emphasizing mercy, repentance, and forgiveness of sins). In short, young Ford had two fathers, two names, two hometowns, two churches, was ambidextrous, and

false-started his words. At the University of Michigan, Ford became an All-American football center by hiking the ball to the stars of the team and blocking for them, as the coach tried to force opposition mistakes. Ford's personal philosophy therefore valued family, love, discipline, and community; winning through teamwork by accentuating the best in his teammates and capitalizing on his adversaries' mistakes; and forgiving rather than punishing. He explained: "Everyone, I decided, had more good qualities than bad. If I understood and tried to accentuate those good qualities in others, I could get along much better. Hating or even disliking people because of their bad qualities, it seemed to me, was a waste of time."

Ford attended Yale Law School and coached football. He began a Grand Rapids law firm but served in the navy during World War II. He led an effort that defeated the Grand Rapids Republican boss Frank McKay in 1946, and in 1948 challenged Congressman "Barney" Jonkman. With the incumbent trapped in Washington by President Harry S. Truman's challenge for the Republican "do nothing" Congress to enact their platform, Ford campaigned alone in the district. He forced Jonkman into mistakes on which he capitalized to win the primary by a margin of two to one, and then the Fifth District seat with 61 percent of the vote.

Gerald Ford wanted to be Speaker of the House and so became a coalition builder. He was an idealist with a pragmatic and moderate legislative style, who quickly earned the respect of his colleagues. His memoirs criticize three men who tried to steer Republicans toward rigid conservatism: Joseph McCarthy, Barry Goldwater, and Spiro Agnew. In 1964 Republicans chose Ford to replace Charlie Halleck (a smoke-filled-room leader operating in the television age) as minority leader. Being one step away from Speaker, Ford declined Nixon's invitation to run as vice president in 1968 because he expected Republicans to take the House. But with the Democrat Hubert Humphrey closing the presidential gap and George C. Wallace winning the Deep South, Republicans fell thirty-six seats short and Ford remained minority leader. When Nixon's personal landslide gained only thirteen seats in 1972, Ford was again denied his goal, and he decided to return to private life in 1977.

But Ford underestimated the toll of the Watergate scandal. With the White House under siege, Spiro Agnew resigned the vice presidency, charged with accepting bribes as governor of Maryland. President Nixon asked Ford to be vice president and he was easily confirmed despite the climate of fear, anger, and suspicion. When Nixon resigned on 8 August 1974, lest he be impeached, Gerald R. Ford became president.

Ford's Presidential Years. Gerald Ford's presidency followed "Junior's" early life with two "inaugurals," two pardons, and vetoes that punted bills back to Congress, and he nurtured teamwork to heal the nation. Ford's inaugural remarks—"a little straight talk among friends"—began by highlighting division with fourteen references to others ("those," "them,") and none to "America" or "togetherness," then pivoted on "We must go forward together" to emphasize commonality ("our" rather than "your" and "God," "America," and "together" rather than "Congress," "them," and individuals). He proclaimed that, "our long national nightmare is over" but pledged himself to the country with thirteen self-references that minimized his accountability to anyone but himself.

Three days later Ford reminded Congress that "I told you I was a Ford, not a Lincoln," but added, "I am not a Model T." He also said "my motto toward the Congress is communication, conciliation, compromise, and cooperation." But this address also overindulged in self-references—"*I do not want* a honeymoon, *I want* a good marriage. *I want* progress, and *I want* problem solving . . . *I believe* in the very decency and fairness of America. *I believe* in the integrity and patriotism of the Congress" (emphases added)—such that President Ford introduced himself as a man standing alone with his principles.

Gallup's first poll reported 71 percent presidential approval and only 3 percent disapproval. But the unelected president had won that approval by cultivating personal legitimacy to compensate for his tenuous claim to the structural legitimacy of the

presidency. He needed to keep the Nixon loyalists on board, strengthen his relationship with Congress, maintain favorable press relations, bolster Republican morale during the ninety-day congressional campaign, and translate his public approval into support for his policy leadership.

Although 80 percent of the public regarded inflation as the most pressing problem facing the nation, they were deeply divided over Vietnam and Watergate. Ford moved swiftly to end those nightmares, using his constitutional authority to pardon Nixon and draft evaders, but justified both pardons with his personal morals.

A Veterans of Foreign Wars (VFW) member, Ford addressed the VFW in Chicago on 19 August. He was warmly received, especially when vowing to "humanize the VA." Then Ford surprised everyone by justifying selective pardons for draft evaders. The Pentagon had differentiated "amnesty" and "pardons" (both presume misconduct and guilt and remove punishment, but amnesty forgives the offense, whereas a pardon affirms the guilt even as it removes the punishment). But unlike the Pentagon, Ford differentiated between "*blanket* amnesty" and "pardons *in individual cases*," reaffirming his moral opposition to blanket amnesty. He invoked "the urgent problem of how to bind up the Nation's wounds" and ordered the departments of Defense and Justice to consolidate "the known facts and legal precedents" so that he could decide "how best to deal with the different kinds of cases." Thus Ford's characteristic willingness to pardon became part of the effort to end the war, inviting veterans to consider the offenders as fellow casualties of war. By "throwing the weight of my Presidency into the scales of justice on the side of leniency," he used his religious training to address the problem. At his first press conference nine days later, there were no questions about the pardon.

Instead, questions convinced Ford to face the Nixon issue. President Ford unexpectedly announced "a full, free and absolute pardon unto Richard Nixon for all offenses against the United States which he, Richard Nixon, has committed or may have committed or taken part in during the period [of his Presidency]" on the morning of Sunday, 8 September.

The proclamation explained that a trial would not begin for a year, during which "the tranquility to which this nation has been restored . . . could be irreparably lost" in the controversy over "bringing to trial a former President" and "thereby exposing to further punishment and degradation a man who has already paid the unprecedented penalty of relinquishing the highest elective office of the United States." But Ford's remarks included additional justifications, including the absence of precedent, and the possibility that Nixon "would be cruelly and excessively penalized" with regard to the presumption of innocence and "speedy determination of his guilt." Should the courts find due process had been denied, the verdict of history would be "even more inconclusive." Ford concluded that, "My conscience tells me it is my duty, not merely to proclaim domestic tranquility but to use every means that I have to insure it."

Nixon accepted the pardon but the House held hearings, and although the holdovers from the previous administration did not defect, Ford's press secretary resigned, and the press and public were displeased. Ford's memoirs describe the 1915 precedent in which "justices found that a pardon 'carries an imputation of guilt, acceptance, a confession to it.'" Had Ford mollified Nixon's critics by saying this, he would have tipped his hand to Nixon, divided Republicans, and alienated the Nixon holdovers keeping his administration afloat.

Ford's pardon remarks used sixty-four first-person-singular references to explain his personal decision-making. His remarks enabled Ford to sell the pardon to Nixon, but unnecessarily and unwisely invested his personal credibility in the Nixon pardon. When he lost the 1976 election voters cited the Nixon pardon more frequently than any other reason for preferring Jimmy Carter to Ford.

After using the pardons to end the Vietnam and Watergate nightmares President Ford attacked his own policy agenda by convening a Conference on Inflation on 5 September 1974. He declared war on inflation in October with his "Whip Inflation Now" (WIN) campaign. But by 15 January he had to say that the primary economic difficulty was not inflation but jobs. The situation had so changed that his temporary $5 billion tax increase became a $12 million tax rebate to stimulate the economy.

The 1976 Election. Ford planned to retire from public life in 1977 but realized that he needed to run in 1976 for his leadership to be taken seriously. Ronald Reagan used the proposed "giveaway" of the Panama Canal to win the North Carolina primary, but Ford won the nomination nevertheless. His acceptance address claimed that "Americans have made an incredible comeback since August 1974. Nobody can honestly say otherwise. And the plain truth is that the great progress we have made at home and abroad was in spite of the majority who run the Congress of the United States." Although this was his best speech, he already trailed Carter by 33 percent.

Thus Ford became the first incumbent president to debate his challenger. The only memorable moment occurred during the second debate, when Ford said that Eastern Europe was not under Soviet domination. Within twenty-four hours, 62 percent gave the debate to Carter, who ultimately turned a 1.7 percent popular vote edge into a 297–240 electoral vote victory.

Conclusions. Gerald Ford never aspired to the presidency, but was swept into it through unique circumstances. He brought to the job an orientation toward teamwork, forgiveness, cautious conservatism, and a tendency to capitalize on others' mistakes. But the modern presidency presumes that presidents play offense. Many scholars compare presidents to Franklin D. Roosevelt, who thought of himself as a quarterback balling plays, evaluating their success, then calling another. But Ford had always hiked the ball to quarterbacks, and his inexperience at calling plays became a liability. Because he justified his play-calling with references to his personal judgment, the man rather than the office took the blame. Nevertheless, only eighteen thousand more votes in Ohio and Mississippi could have given Ford the presidency.

[*See also* Carter, Jimmy; Nixon, Richard M.; *and* Reagan, Ronald.]

BIBLIOGRAPHY

Berquist, Goodwin. "The 1976 Carter-Ford Presidential Debates." In *Rhetorical Studies of National Political Debates*, 2d ed., edited by Robert V. Friedenberg, pp. 29–44. (Westport, Conn., 1994).

Brock, Bernard L. "Gerald R. Ford Encounters Richard Nixon's Legacy: On Amnesty and the Pardon." In *Oratorical Encounters: Selected Studies and Sources of Twentieth-Century Political Accusations and Apologies*, edited by Halford Ross Ryan, pp. 227–240. (Westport, Conn., 1988).

Ford, Gerald R. *A Time To Heal: The Autobiography of Gerald R. Ford*. (New York, 1979).

"Gerald R. Ford Library." University of Michigan, http://www.fordlibrarymuseum.gov/library/aboutlib.asp.

Hartmann, Robert. T. *Palace Politics: An Inside Account of the Ford Years*. (New York, 1980).

Klumpp, James F., and Jeffrey K. Lukehart. "The Pardoning of Richard Nixon: A Failure in Motivational Strategy." *Western Journal of Speech Communication* 41 (1978): 116–123.

"The Public Papers of the President: Gerald R. Ford," http://www.presidency.ucsb.edu/gerald_ford.php.

Smith, Craig Allen, and Kathy B. Smith. *The White House Speaks: Presidential Leadership as Persuasion*. (Westport, Conn., 1994).

Stelzner, Hermann G. "Ford's War on Inflation: A Metaphor That Did Not Cross." *Communication Monographs* 44 (November 1977): 284–297.

Craig Allen Smith

FORDISM

A remarkable fusion of incremental technological change and radical social innovation, Fordism was first achieved in the Ford Company's Highland Park, Michigan plant immediately prior to World War I; it was soon recognized as a world-historical force, with the stunning immediacy of a natural upheaval. The chasm that separated traditional craft methods of automobile manufacture from the new Fordist mass production system appeared almost without warning, although the fault lines which coalesced to produce it often traced their origins well into the past. Improvements to established practice in component manufacturability, product design, equipment specialization, materials flow, work coordination, and business organization had already expanded

the annual output of Ford's Model T automobile more than thirty-fold in the five years before the moving assembly line was introduced in 1912–1913. With even more fundamental changes in the social organization of production accompanying the imposition of line-paced continuous manufacture, labor time for constructing each automobile was further reduced from twelve and a half hours only a few months earlier, to just ninety minutes.

Ford's system not only revolutionized automobile production (within a few years, Ford had captured 55 percent of the US auto market), but, in successfully applying mass production methods to so complex a product, it established a universal logic of industrial production, portending fundamental transformation in many areas of manufacturing, and the potential historical regression of societies unable to deploy the new techniques effectively. Its economic and cultural implications were so vast that, even at its inception, contemporaries recognized that Fordism laid claim to defining the epoch.

Thus freighted with historical significance, it was inevitable that Fordism should become interpretively overburdened. In stark contrast with its most famous product—a single model of car appealing to a range of desires (and memorably described as "available in any color a customer wants so long as it is black")—"Fordism" is, in fact, a broad term masquerading as a singular concept. Some equate it with the scientific fragmentation of tasks and the specialized division of labor. For others, Fordism is synonymous with the assembly line. Somewhat more inclusively, Fordism is identified with mass production, or, the use of specialized machinery and semiskilled labor to manufacture standardized products in large quantities.

Fordism has also been conceptualized as an "accumulation regime," or a growth path governed by positive feedback loops connecting mass production and mass consumption. At the other end of the spectrum, Fordism achieves a meaning as nebulous as it is all-encompassing when it is understood as definitive of American culture or, still more broadly, as the essence of a particular stage in the development of industrial civilization. The contemporary catchphrase intended to suggest its eclipse—"post-Fordism"—suffers from a similar problem of diverse and often vague applications.

Fordism proper involved a refinement and synthesis of disparate, if intersecting, trends within the realm of production method and industrial organization—that is, something rather more than a single element of the production process, and rather less than a totalistic cultural form. The essential precondition for the possibility of Fordist mass production was the practical manufacture of precisely interchangeable parts, which was first accomplished in small arms production under the auspices of the US Ordnance Department, and eventually was applied to the fabrication of sewing machines, agricultural equipment, bicycles, and then automobiles. The very idea of exactly duplicated components eliminated the craft worker's raison d'être: the ability to create a wide variety of different products or models and to provide experience-based solutions to fabrication problems. Ford pushed this idea to its limit: "There cannot be much hand work or fitting if you are going to accomplish great things."

With parts interchangeability, tasks and processes can be disconnected from each other (and from the same worker) and, thus separated out, they can be reordered in new configurations. As a consequence, substantial experimentation in task rationalization had already occurred in Ford's plants independently of F. W. Taylor's application of the "armory system's" norms of precise measurement and exact replication to the practice of human labor itself. The central tenets of Taylorism—the analytical separation and standardization of movements and tasks to their smallest efficient scope; functional specialization or the assignment of discrete tasks to distinct workers; scientific selection of the work force; a clear division of labor between the tasks of conception and execution—were all manifest in Fordist production. Yet Fordism and Taylorism were quite divergent, in that Taylor's system focused on individual conformity to objective task requirements, whereas Ford was far more concerned with the coordination of tasks or posts and the flow of work between them.

The constant refinement of parts interchangeability, machine specialization, and work standardization compelled an engineering focus on the systemic integration of machine operations, materials circulation, the distribution of labor, and work organization. Constant, if pragmatic, exploration of integrative techniques and practices culminated in the moving assembly line and the concomitant organization of large-scale manufacture as an integrated, continuous flow—a genuine social innovation.

This same preoccupation led Ford also to build on tendencies toward vertical integration already advanced in other industrial sectors. The "visible hand" of industrial organization was pushed to its logical conclusion at Ford's gigantic River Rouge complex, which constituted a virtually self-contained manufacturing system—from the production of raw materials to shipping of the finished product—at a single location. The final step in this extensive nesting process—the integration of discrete work stages into a coherent manufacturing process, and of the manufacturing process into a sequentially coordinated production system—was to link the production system directly with the economy as a whole. This connection was established through Ford's distinctive concern with reducing the final product price, as opposed to sustaining high-price monopolistic market control—a strategy that presupposed a combination of mass production and mass consumption.

Despite its extraordinary achievements, the inherent rigidity of the supply-driven Fordist system rendered it rapidly obsolete: in less than two decades, Ford's market share declined from three-fifths to less than one-fifth, as the company was bested by more flexible rivals. Ford's commitment to specialization was so rigorous, and its production system so tightly interdependent, that significant engineering improvements (battery-powered ignition, electric starters, shock absorbers) could not be accommodated. Model redesigns were resisted as long as possible, and the coordination of sales levels and output became increasingly difficult. When substantive model overhauls occurred (as with the replacement of the fifteen-year-old Model T with the Model A), they required long-term plant closures and equipment scrapping and retooling on a massive scale. High levels of vertical integration proved counterproductive when declines in demand increased unit costs more rapidly for Ford than for its competitors. Henry Ford's propensity for maintaining personal leadership of the firm further reduced organizational responsiveness and innovative capabilities. The impact of employment security and high wages on workers was undermined by the constant acceleration of the assembly line—the only possible Fordist response to deteriorating competitiveness.

Far from monolithically defining industrial society in general, or even particular national economies, Fordism remained one logic of production among others: indeed, imperial conceptualizations of Fordism have left largely unexplored its relationship to, and integral dependence on, non-Fordist sectors of the economy. Insofar as Fordism diffused beyond the United States, it was modified substantially by existing institutional structures and industrial cultures. It is not clear that skill-based manufacturing in Germany or Japanese forms of collaborative manufacturing owe much to Fordism at all. The growth of mass consumption certainly preceded the advent of Fordism, and rapid advances in national income levels, such as those occurring in postwar Europe, owe as much to factors like urbanization and the conversion of traditional sectors to capitalist techniques as to national adaptations of Fordist practice.

In this context, the question of "post-Fordism" also seems quite misplaced. To the extent that mass production was not defined by Fordism alone, the reality of post-Fordism long preceded its conceptual formulation. On the other hand, to the degree that post-Fordism denotes the end of mass production, it neglects the continuing salience of Fordist principles in the movement toward more flexible forms of manufacturing. These include large-scale organization and economies of scale, the capital cost constraints inherent in flexible automation, and the ability of mass production firms to achieve greater flexibility, as in contemporary forms of modular production (the achievement of high levels of product customization on the basis of extensive component

and subassembly standardization), through simultaneous refinement and transcendence of Fordist techniques.

[*See also* Deindustrialization.]

BIBLIOGRAPHY
Arnold, Horace Lucian, and Fay Leone Faurote. *Ford Methods and the Ford Shops.* (New York, 1915).
Hounshell, David A. *From the American System to Mass Production, 1800–1932: The Development of Manufacturing Technology in the United States.* (Baltimore, 1984).
Jessop, Bob. "Fordism and Post-Fordism: A Critical Reformulation." In *Pathways to Industrialization and Regional Development*, edited by Michael Storper and Allen John Scott, pp. 42–62. (Boston, 1992).
Maier, Charles S. *In Search of Stability: Explorations in Historical Political Economy.* (Cambridge, UK, 1987).

Richard Gordon

FREE TRADE AND FAIR TRADE

The unalloyed advantages of free trade are among the most unquestioned premises of the current age. On both sides of the political divide in the United States, all but a few isolated voices subscribe to the view that free trade is necessarily good for all the parties associated with it: good for companies and workers in advanced industrial economies; good for companies and workers in the developing world; and good for the consolidation of peaceful relationships between competing nations. In arguments that parallel those for the deregulation of internal markets—about which there is greater political controversy—the conventional wisdom in Washington, D.C., and indeed in the finance and trade ministries of most industrialized economies, is that the lowering of trade barriers, and the concentration by each economy on the production of goods and services in which it enjoys a comparative advantage, can only add to the prosperity and growth of the entire global economic system. Lowering trade barriers and exposing domestic producers to global competition lowers prices, enhances quality, and widens variety and choice, and so boosts the living standards of consumers in both the global "north" and the global "south." It squeezes out inefficient producers, so enhancing the general productivity of both the manufacturing and service sector. It encourages the adoption, by all producers, of the latest technology and the cheapest raw materials. It encourages innovation, and it avoids the corrupt "crony capitalism" that came with import substitution industrialization (ISI). ISI was the development strategy widely canvassed, particularly in post–World War II Latin America, as a better route to economic growth and rising living standards than that guaranteed by opening domestic markets to the full force of global competition, and ISI failed.

In the view of most advocates of free trade policies, as the world's leading economy the United States is especially well placed to benefit from the lowering of tariff walls; and indeed the United States has pressed for such lowering in each global trade round since 1945. The 2007 Economic Report of the President even put a figure on that benefit: post-1945 free trade "has contributed an additional $10,000 to the typical American household of four" (Terry, 2007). The Petersen Institute had a grander figure still: gains from trade liberalization since 1947 of $1.4 trillion were claimed, equivalent by 2003 to roughly 10 percent of total US gross domestic product (GDP) (Bradford, Grieco, and Hufbauer, 2006). In a world that is unavoidably "flat" (Friedman, 2005)— and amid the greater globalization of the US economy as "driven by three fundamental changes: growth of the global economy, reduced government barriers to international trade and investment, and the spread of new technologies" (Griswold, 2009, p. 5)— protectionism in any form can only buy temporary advantage at the cost of long-term decline. By contrast, once an economy equips its labor force with the skills to compete, then increased trade across open borders can only generate a cumulative race to the top, raising living standards north and south by creating ever-wider global markets into which US corporations will be able to sell with greater and greater ease. Daniel T. Griswold (2009) put the general case this way:

I hope that readers open to persuasion will see that we should really be "mad about trade"—mad as in crazy in love with the opportunities that our new and

more open world is creating before our eyes, not only for ourselves but, more importantly, for our children. We should have the same positive feelings towards free trade and globalization as we do towards digital cameras, iPods, email, online shopping, a well-fed child going off to school, and peace on earth. (p. 10)

The counterargument for managed trade is that "the benefits of free trade and globalization are overrated and the costs thereof underestimated" (Dunkley, 2004, p. xv). The counterargument is that, given the uneven development of a global economy inherited from an age of colonialism and capitalist-communist competition, lowering tariff barriers and inviting in cheaply produced goods from previously Second World and Third World economies can only produce a generalized "race to the bottom" that will ultimately destabilize both the global system as a whole and its leading high-wage economies. As US corporations struggle to compete with foreign-based producers enjoying access to the latest technology and to large pools of skilled but low-paid labor, the outsourcing of core manufacturing employment becomes endemic. Recent data on this is clear. American multinational corporations employing a fifth of all American workers "cut their workforces in the United States by 2.9 million during the 2000s while increasing overseas employment by 2.4 million . . . a big switch from the 1990s when they added jobs everywhere: 4.4 million in the United States and 2.7 million abroad" (Wessel, 2011, p. 1). The result, in the United States, is a self-sustaining downward spiral often labeled "the Wal-Mart effect" (Coates, 2011, pp. 70–72). In that spiral, pressure on suppliers to hold down prices triggers the redeployment of production to cheap labor sites in Asia and South America, eroding internal US employment and wages as it does so, and leaving more and more American consumers so income-depleted that their lifestyle depends on the availability of low-cost products in big-box stores like Wal-Mart—stores that themselves survive only by intensifying the pressure on suppliers to hold down costs still further.

Critics of free trade find no comfort, as many free trade advocates do, in the notion that only low-skilled jobs are outsourced. They see low-cost foreign producers steadily moving up the value chain, with US-based corporations responding by outsourcing employment among skilled workers and even professionals. They see the new jobs created in the wake of deindustrialization paying less than did the jobs that were lost. They see the resulting trade imbalance—between low-cost producers (particularly China) and previously high-wage economies now sustaining their consumption by a mixture of lower wages and increased personal debt (particularly the United States)—as inevitably leaving Americans ever more dependent for their living standards on foreign creditors, and leaving the global system as a whole ever more vulnerable to credit crises triggered by that indebtedness. As Jeff Faux (2011) put it:

> For three decades, both Democratic and Republican administrations have been making trade deals with elites of other countries that favor the interests of multinational investors over the interests of American producers and workers. US-based banks and corporations get access to cheap labor and to the financial systems of other nations. In return, US workers are exposed to competition from countries where wages are suppressed (Mexico) or where governments run effective industrial policies (Germany) or both (China). As a result, a chronic trade deficit has made us the world's largest debtor, undercut the bargaining power of the working middle class, and hollowed out US manufacturing. Because our labor markets are integrated, the damage has spread to virtually every industry, occupation, and region. Real wages and benefits have stagnated even as the value of what Americans produce keeps rising." (2011, p. 2)

Those more sanguine about the limits of free trade tend toward the view that "the impacts of international trade can be beneficial or they can be adverse, depending on how it is managed" (George, 2010, p. x). Advocates of "fair trade" emphasize the right of developing economies to protect their local producers from full exposure to competition from heavily capitalized industrial economies, and urge consumers in those more advanced economies to pay heed, as they purchase, to the working conditions surrounding the commodities they buy. Advocates of managed trade in the north argue for free trade between economies of roughly equivalent levels of development and wages, and managed trade between unevenly developed economies—managed in ways that pull wages in the south up to those of the north, and protect in the north hard-won welfare rights now threatened by the spread of unregulated global competition.

The political battle between these fiercely held and competing views of the contemporary fit between US national interests and the lowering of tariff barriers remains hugely lopsided. The interests of large US corporations in ever bigger global markets, and the immediate interests of US consumers in lower prices, normally combine to keep Washington a free-trade town. The Barack Obama administration, like the George W. Bush administration before it, regularly pushes for trade agreements with targeted economies. The Bush administration signed seven such trade agreements, and the Obama administration has recently signed new ones with South Korea, Panama, and Colombia.

[*See also* Business-Government Relations; Deindustrialization; Deregulation; Global Economy and the United States; Protection; Regulation; *and* World Trade Organization.]

BIBLIOGRAPHY

Baucus, Max, and John Kerry. "The Colombia Trade Deal: A Different Kind of Jobs Bill." *Wall Street Journal*, 14 April 2011.

Bivens, Josh. *Everyone Wins, Except for Most of Us: What Economics Teaches about Globalization.* (Washington, D.C., 2008).

Bradford, Scott, Paul Grieco, and Gary Hufbauer. "The Payoff to America from Globalisation." *World Economy* 29, no. 7 (July 2006): 893–916.

Coates, David. *Making the Progressive Case: Towards a Stronger U.S. Economy.* (New York, 2011).

Dunkley, Graham. *Free Trade: Myth, Reality, and Alternatives.* (London, 2004).

Faux, Jeff. "America's Trade Policy of the Absurd." *American Prospect*, 7 February 2011.

Friedman, Thomas L. *The World Is Flat: A Brief History of the Twenty-First Century.* (New York, 2005).

George, Clive. *The Truth about Trade: The Real Impact of Liberalization.* (London, 2010).

Griswold, Daniel T. *Mad about Trade: Why Main Street America Should Embrace Globalization.* (Washington, D.C., 2009).

Miller, Terry. *Free Trade: Media Should Include Facts with Opinion Polls.* Heritage Foundation WebMemo No. 1670, 18 October 2007, http://www.heritage.org/research/reports/2007/10/free-trade-media-should-include-facts-with-opinion-polls.

Tonnelson, Alan. *The Race to the Bottom: Why a Worldwide Worker Surplus and Uncontrolled Free Trade Are Sinking American Living Standards.* (Boulder, Colo., 2000).

Wessel, David. "Big U.S. Firms Shift Hiring Abroad." *Wall Street Journal*, 19 April 2011.

Wilkinson, Daniel. "The Killers of Colombia." *New York Review of Books*, 23 June 2011.

Williamson, Elizabeth. "Trade Pacts Tied to Aid for Workers." *Wall Street Journal*, 17 May 2011.

David Coates

FUNDAMENTALISM

Fundamentalism is a deep and total commitment to a particular religious creed, involving a return to supposed fundamentals, away from doctrinal compromises with modern social and political life. The term is used to describe a wide range of political and religious phenomena, including Protestant denominations, Jewish groups, Buddhist movements, Hindu political parties, and Islamic governments.

The term has its origins in US religious history. In the early twentieth century, fundamentalism arose as a US Protestant movement, guided by the doctrine of complete faith in the five fundamentals: the absolute truth of the Bible, the virgin birth of Jesus, the supernatural atonement, the physical resurrection of Jesus, and the authenticity of the Gospel miracles. A variety of Protestant groups have been described as fundamentalist because of their adherence to these (or similar) fundamental principles. Fundamentalism has been a significant political force in the United States since the 1920s.

In recent decades, fundamentalism has come to have a broader meaning and it has been increasingly seen as a global phenomenon, as movements analogous to those in the United States have appeared in many countries and regions. Though the concept is somewhat problematic outside the context of US Christianity, the term is now very widely used, both in the popular news media and in scholarly literature. It denotes a variety of movements worldwide, both religious and religio-political.

The historical process of secularization provides a background for all discussions of fundamentalism. Societies and individuals have moved away from the dominance of religious institutions and ideas. Religion and state have been separated, and religious-based laws and prohibitions have been abolished. Fundamentalism, however, rejects this secularization process and seeks to reverse it.

Fundamentalism takes so many forms, in so many different religious and cultural traditions, that generalizations can be only approximate. Fundamentalist ideology typically centers on the following four beliefs: (1) there is one set of religious teachings that contains the fundamental, basic, and essential truth about humanity and the deities; (2) this truth is opposed by forces of evil, which must be vigorously fought; (3) this truth must be followed according to unchangeable traditions; and (4) those who espouse this ideology have a special relationship with the deities.

Fundamentalists are commonly individuals who feel threatened by urbanization, industrialization, and modern secular values. Their ideology may have little substantial social or political consequences as long as it remains within the religious realm and is limited to a relatively small group. Typically, fundamentalist beliefs are tied to political conservatism, authoritarianism, and prejudice. Fundamentalist ideology thus reflects a hostile confrontation with modern society. The fundamentalist strategy not only rejects any accommodation to modern, secular society, but also contains a utopian vision for reconstructing that same society.

The messianic or apocalyptic dreams of many religious groups include the idea of their own political domination of a state (or even the world). Believers may take such dreams seriously, and the fantasy of future greatness and domination can compensate for their current deprivation. In some cases, adherents translate messianic dreams into plans for political action. The ideology of fundamentalism then becomes a political ideology embodied in a substantial political movement, which may gain mass support, or even political power.

By contrast to secularization, which calls for the separation of religion and politics, fundamentalism looks to the resacralization of politics and the politicization of religion. Fundamentalism rejects modernity, though it does not necessarily reject modern technology. It opposes the modern ideals of individualism, voluntarism, pluralism, free speech, and the equality of women. Fundamentalist movements often present a telling critique of late capitalist society, which they portray as being composed of alienated, atomistic, selfish individuals, engaged in the obsessive pursuit of pleasure without heed for its consequences for others (or even for themselves). Fundamentalist ideologies share a critique of modernity and its costs—materialism, selfishness, tolerance for uncontrolled sexualities, decline of family ties, and urban crime.

This cultural aspect accounts for some of the breadth of the fundamentalist appeal. The deprivations and stresses of modernity—be they economic, psychological, or cultural—feed fundamentalist movements, as the crisis of global capitalism is felt in both central and peripheral nation-states. As a solution to alienation and dislocation, fundamentalism prescribes a commitment to gender role, family, and community. A rhetoric of "family values" and patriarchal authority can be heard in fundamentalist doctrine from Oklahoma to Tehran. The fundamentalist ideology everywhere appears as collectivist and communalist—individual rights are seen as secondary to the interests of the community. Fundamentalists call for reversing the historical course of secularization and modernity, and recreating a premodern (or precolonial), idealized past.

Fundamentalism thrives in conditions of economic and social crisis. In countries on the periphery in particular, fundamentalism has often arisen where secular, authoritarian governments have held power and failed. In these circumstances, fundamentalism arises as an alternative project, and its antimodern ideology assumes wide appeal because of its similarity to the ideology of anti-imperialism and the hostility to Western domination. In some cases, ironically, fundamentalism has been supported and manipulated by foreign countries in their efforts to influence local or regional politics. This was very clear in Afghanistan, where the Islamic guerrilla movements resisting the Soviet occupation in the 1980s were funded and trained by the United States, with support from Pakistan and Saudi Arabia. Conservative governments have also promoted fundamentalist political groups as a counterweight to left oppositions, as was the case in Egypt under Sadat in the 1970s.

Fundamentalist ideology has much to say about the lives of women and reproductive rights. Fundamentalist movements are usually opposed to contraception, and favor modest dress and the overall subordination of women to men. Fundamentalist regimes have often issued dress codes and laws about the segregation of the sexes in public. They also typically limit women's involvement in public life, their freedom of movement, and their legal rights. Male superiority and privilege is formally embodied in the law. Yet fundamentalist movements have attracted much support from women, whose domestic role is especially threatened by market relations and extreme individualism.

Political fundamentalism rejects liberal democracy and proposes an elite ruling class, made up of religious leaders or leaders sanctioned by the religious authority. Fundamentalist regimes are authoritarian because a religious state must follow the religious authority invested in the clergy, who alone can interpret the scriptures. Some may describe this as totalitarian, because religious law is applied to all aspects of life.

Fundamentalism is inclined to suppress the rights of other religious or secular forces in society, and even to organize violence against them. In India, Hindu fundamentalist movements have attacked Muslims and burned mosques. In Israel, Jewish fundamentalists have demanded religious-based laws and practices (closing down all public transportation on the Sabbath, for example) and some have violently attacked Palestinians. In the United States, fundamentalists have demanded that Christian prayer be practiced in public schools, and some Christian fundamentalists have been involved in the murder of doctors practicing abortions.

Fundamentalism as a religio-political ideology can be found all over the world. As a significant political movement aspiring to create a religious state it can be found in about thirty nations, but as a dominant power it exists in very few countries. We find the label applied to Christian groups with political influence in Southern Africa and Latin America, to Mormons in the United States, and to Buddhists in South Asia. Sinhala-Buddhist fundamentalism in Sri Lanka, inspired by a vision of the Sinhala as the curators of Buddhism, is a factor in the protracted and bloody conflict between Sinhalese and Tamils. Another example of Buddhist fundamentalism, the Dalai Lama, represents a vision of a feudal Tibetan state ruled by the clergy.

Many important fundamentalist movements, and even several fundamentalist regimes, are to be found in the Islamic world, a vast region from Indonesia and Malaysia at one end, to Algeria and Morocco at the other, and from the so-called Islamic republics of the former Soviet Union to West Africa, especially Nigeria. In some of these countries, fundamentalists' attempts to make their version of Islam binding on the whole population have led to serious conflicts. Afghanistan, Algeria, and Egypt are three cases where fundamentalists gained wide followings and their bids for power led to extreme violence. Each one of these countries suffered from deep economic and social crises and from failed authoritarian secular regimes.

Have fundamentalist movements and regimes, which seek to reverse secularization and to create a theologically based political system, succeeded in their goal? In a few cases, and in the short term, the answer may be yes. But over the longer term, most evidence suggests they have not succeeded. Even where fundamentalism appears to have triumphed, as in Iran, its success has been transitory and based on a population still deeply religious and not yet secularized. As the Iran case shows, even when a fundamentalist clergy control political power for twenty years (1980–2000), they cannot hold back secularizing trends. Eventually the Iranian population opted for a more open and tolerant kind of politics, pushing religion back toward a more restricted or private sphere.

Fundamentalism may not be as potent a force as some thought in the 1980s, but it remains an important religious, social, and political phenomenon. In a world of wrenching change and uncertainty, millions of people will continue to turn to fundamentalist movements in their search for a more secure and morally grounded social order.

[*See also* Conservatism; Gender and Politics; *and* Religion and Politics.]

BIBLIOGRAPHY

Beit-Hallahmi, Benjamin, and Michael Argyle. *The Psychology of Religious Behaviour, Belief, and Experience.* (London, 1997).

Davidson, Lawrence. *Islamic Fundamentalism.* (Westport, Conn., 1998).

Marty, Martin E., ed. *The Fundamentalisms Project.* 5 vols. (Chicago, 1991–1995).

Benjamin Beit-Hallahmi

G

GANGS

Gangs have been documented in the United States since the mid-1800s. In the early 1900s, the journalist Herbert Asbury described conflicts among the immigrant gangs of New York, and Frederic Thrasher, who is considered to be the nation's first gang researcher, studied the gangs of Chicago. In Thrasher's 1927 book *The Gang: A Study of 1313 Gangs in Chicago*, he explained that gangs originate as "play groups" of boys, which eventually morph into a gang through conflict with other groups. This early explanation of how and why groups evolve into gangs continues to receive support from contemporary gang researchers. Research suggests that most gangs are neighborhood-based, with origins as small, informal groups, and that their violence is generally directed at other such groups located in the same geographic area.

Defining a gang and differentiating it from other types of groups remains a troubling issue for researchers and law enforcement. Statutory definitions vary by state, but typically consider a gang to be a group of two or more (or three or more) individuals engaged in a collective pattern of delinquency or crime. There are other common characteristics of gangs, which are sometimes incorporated into definitions, including the use of colors, symbols, signs, tattoos, or graffiti designating the group or its territory. However, there is no standard nationwide definition for how to define a gang, a gang member,

or gang crime, and therefore the statistics on any of those issues are subject to jurisdictional variations. The statutory and practical distinctions between "street gangs" and other types of groups involved in criminal behavior, such as drug gangs and organized crime groups, can create further difficulties for researchers and practitioners attempting to understand and address these problems. What is defined as a gang one year, in one jurisdiction, could possibly be defined as a drug-dealing organization or organized crime group in another year, or in the same jurisdiction at a different time period, depending on how the statutory definitions are interpreted, and by whom and for what purpose.

Given the varying definitions for gangs, gang membership, and gang crime, the aggregate statistics on the prevalence of gangs and gang crime must be interpreted with caution. According to the National Longitudinal Survey of Youth, about 8 percent of youth (from a nationwide representative sample) admitted to having belonged to a gang at some point between the ages of twelve and seventeen. Other survey research in cities with known gang problems has revealed higher membership rates; for example, 32 percent of the youth sampled in a Rochester, New York, study claimed to have been gang-affiliated at some point during adolescence.

The National Youth Gang Survey annually asks law enforcement departments throughout the country to estimate the number of gangs, gang members, and gang-related crimes in their jurisdiction. The vast majority of large cities in the US report a significant gang problem and the number of jurisdictions noting gang activity has grown; for example, in the 1970s only nineteen states reported gang problems, but by 2000, all states reported gang activity. The National Youth Gang Survey data reveal that of all gang members nationwide, about 50 percent are Latino, 32 percent are African American, and 11 percent are Caucasian. However, it is important to note that police estimates of racial minority involvement in gangs are generally higher than the proportion of minority involvement revealed via other research. For example, in some city-based self-report surveys, in which youth were asked to report whether they are gang-involved, the rate of white membership was comparable to that of other racial groups. Racial representation in gangs obviously varies by community, but both law enforcement data and research studies suggest that all racial and ethnic groups in the United States are involved in gangs; in recent years gang problems have escalated on Native American reservations.

Although law enforcement statistics and most survey research reveal that males make up the vast majority of gang members, there has been increasing concern about female gang membership in recent years. It is impossible to say whether female gang involvement has actually increased (due to a lack of previous data for comparison purposes), but there is some anecdotal evidence and research to suggest this may be the case. Girls have always played a role in gangs, typically in one of the following ways: auxiliary or affiliate groups that are governed by or in some way attached to male gangs; coed groups, in which girls and boys share membership and responsibilities; or independent or autonomous groups, which are completely separate from males. These three types of groups remain the primary ways in which girls are involved in gangs, but studies also reveal that girls may have strong connections to male gang members (e.g., a boyfriend) without actually being officially gang involved themselves. Research has found that girls' gang membership bears both similarities and differences to boys'

and warrants separate analysis and prevention and intervention strategies.

Research consistently reveals that when asked why they have joined a gang, the primary reasons given by both male and female members is that they were seeking a sense of family, belonging, or love; the protection and safety they believed the gang could offer; and the status or respect that membership could convey. Communities with concentrated poverty, joblessness, and poor schools generally have a stronger gang presence than those exhibiting greater economic and social stability. Youth with family members, neighbors, and friends involved in a gang are at greater risk for joining a gang themselves, and research indicates that youth who have risk factors across multiple domains (e.g., family, community, school, individual, and peer group) are more likely to join a gang than youth with fewer risk factors (see Vigil, 2002, for a discussion of "multiple marginality"). But contrary to the common perception that gang members are committed to their group for life, longitudinal research reveals that most individuals do not remain in youth gangs very long; the average length of time in a gang is about two years. Studies suggest that once in a gang, individuals may stay involved because they are making money (e.g., through drug sales) and are economically reliant on the group. Research on why and how gang members leave their groups indicates that experiencing or witnessing a traumatic violent incident (e.g., the death of a loved one through gang violence) is often an impetus for departure.

Although not all gangs or gang members are violent, longitudinal research on juvenile delinquency, drug use, and gangs reveals that individuals who are involved in gangs are more likely to be involved in crime than those who are not. Most gang violence appears to be retaliatory in nature and directed at other gangs. Research also suggests that gang-related crime is of the "cafeteria-style" variety, meaning that the majority of gangs do not specialize in one particular type of offense, but are opportunistic and partake in what is available (Klein, 1995).

A wide variety of gang suppression, prevention, and intervention strategies and programs have been implemented to combat gangs and gang violence. Most large, urban police departments have a designated gang suppression unit. Such units investigate gang crimes and maintain a database of individuals identified as gang members. Specialized gang units within prosecutors', probation, and parole offices are now common as well. A variety of police suppression tactics have been used to address gangs and gang violence, including deterrence-based sweeps, but to date there has been minimal evidence supporting suppression as an effective stand-alone strategy. Most gang experts (and indeed even law enforcement officers) acknowledge that police suppression efforts (with the goal of arresting and incarcerating gang members) may take some dangerous gang members off the street, but cannot address the underlying social conditions, which make gangs an attractive option for some youth. Given that gangs are most entrenched in poor, marginalized communities wherein hopelessness pervades, strengthening those communities, families, and schools, and developing better economic opportunities (e.g., jobs) for youth living there, is essential to combating gang problems.

Although no one suppression, intervention, or prevention program has greatly reduced or eliminated gangs, several cities have experienced some success with multiagency, collaborative approaches that coordinate and integrate all three types of strategies. The "Ceasefire" model was first used effectively in Boston in the mid-1990s and various versions of it have been implemented nationwide. In the original Boston Ceasefire, law enforcement targeted violent gang members through investigation and arrest, while street outreach workers, clergy, and social service agencies attempted to get kids out of gangs (intervention) or keep them from joining (prevention) by providing greater employment, recreation, and education opportunities. This strategy was credited for the city's significant decrease in gang-related youth homicide and violence. More recently, an evaluation of Chicago's Ceasefire gang-violence program, which is based on a public-health model of violence, also suggests that some success can be achieved with a multipronged, coordinated response.

The Office of Juvenile Justice and Delinquency Prevention (OJJDP) provides a Comprehensive Gang Strategy, with detailed guidance for communities that are attempting to address their gang problems.

[*See also* Organized Crime; Race, Gender, and Incarceration; *and* Underclass.]

BIBLIOGRAPHY
Asbury, Herbert. *The Gangs of New York.* (New York, 1927).
Decker, Scott, and Barrik Van Winkle. *Life in the Gang: Family, Friends, and Violence.* (New York, 1996).
Egley, Arlen Jr., James C. Howell, and John P. Moore. *Highlights of the 2008 National Youth Gang Survey.* U.S. Department of Justice, Office of Justice Programs, Office of Juvenile Justice and Delinquency Prevention, https://www.ncjrs.gov/pdffiles1/ojjdp/229249.pdf.
Esbensen, Finn-Aage, Dana Peterson, Terrance Taylor, and Adrienne Freng. *Youth Violence: Sex and Race Differences in Offending, Victimization, and Gang Membership.* (Philadelphia, 2011).
Kennedy, David M., et al. *Reducing Gun Violence: The Boston Gun Project's Operation Ceasefire.* (Washington, D.C., 2001).
Klein, Malcolm. *The American Street Gang.* (New York, 1995).
Miller, Jody A. *One of the Guys: Girls, Gangs, and Gender.* (New York, 2001).
Moore, Joan W. *Going Down to the Barrio: Homeboys and Homegirls in Change.* (Philadelphia, 1991).
Office of Juvenile Justice and Delinquency Prevention. *Best Practices to Address Community Gang Problems: OJJDP's Comprehensive Gang Model.* U.S. Department of Justice, Office of Justice Programs, Office of Juvenile Justice and Delinquency Prevention, https://www.ncjrs.gov/pdffiles1/ojjdp/222799.pdf.
Skogan, Wesley G., et al. 2008. *Evaluation of Cease Fire-Chicago.* Report. Washington, D.C.: US Department of Justice, Office of Justice Programs, Office of Juvenile Justice and Delinquency Prevention, https://www.ncjrs.gov/pdffiles1/nij/grants/227181.pdf.
Thornberry, Terence P., et al. *Gangs and Delinquency in Developmental Perspective.* (New York, 2003).
Thornberry, Terence P., and Marvin D. Krohn, eds. *Taking Stock of Delinquency: An Overview of Findings from Contemporary Longitudinal Studies.* (New York, 2003).
Thrasher, Frederic. *The Gang: A Study of 1,313 Gangs in Chicago.* (Chicago, 1927).
Vigil, James Diego. *A Rainbow of Gangs: Street Cultures in the Mega City.* (Austin, Tex., 2002).

Dana Nurge

GAY RIGHTS

The politics of gay rights is as notable for the rapidity of its success in the courts as it is for the empowerment and enrichment of conservative organizations that have fought these rights and constricted their meanings. As a consequence, gay rights have challenged the way many think about what rights do, and the political and social costs that are associated with legal victories in a post–civil rights era.

Post–World War II political action to expand the meaning and purview of the collective rights won by many white workers in the 1930s—actions made possible by increased access to courts and active government assistance—remade the idea of civil rights and liberties into a broad antidiscrimination regime extended to socially marginal and politically oppressed identities of race, gender, and sexual choice and self-presentation; status issues of age and national origin; physical ability; and respect for treaty rights of indigenous peoples. While this growing culture of liberal legalism, buoyed by the imagined successes of the civil rights movement in the 1960s, promised expansive forms of recognition along with access to justice, there was early evidence of countervailing arguments about the limited elasticity of civil rights. Judicial unwillingness to expand "strict scrutiny" of newly "protected classes" as well as acceptance of "reverse discrimination" claims, and political resistance to integration, abortion, affirmative action, and comparable worth, suggest that the more recent opposition to gay rights is not unique. However, the use of popular plebiscites and other mobilizing efforts to roll back antidiscrimination protection and constitutionalize restrictions on same-sex marriage in a majority of states since 1998, and the partial federalization of marriage law through the Defense of Marriage Act (1996), do suggest that gay rights have been at least as significant to liberal and labor rights activists as they have been to conservative social movements.

Gay rights in the United States have come to represent a wide range of issues, including the decriminalization of homosexual relations (achieved in 2003); establishment of antidiscrimination statutes protecting employment, housing, and people with AIDs; access to adoption by same-sex couples; immigration sponsorship for gay spouses and lovers; the ability to serve openly in the armed forces; and the ability to marry or contract a civil union with the person of one's choice. In addition, many of the privacy and antidiscrimination protections of gay rights implicitly or by statutory language have been extended to include other sexual minorities, such as transsexual and transgender people and those identifying or identified as bisexuals—the broader LGBT coalition.

The possibility of a rights regime governing sexual minorities has always been dependent upon restricting alternative forms of governance, many of which continue to this day. Oppression of sexual minorities in the twentieth century was justified by medical discourses that equated homosexuality with mental illness and disease, as well as national and economic security concerns due to the ease of blackmailing gay officials; such policies drove many gays and lesbians underground (and continued to do so as well under military policy until very recently). The 1969 uprising at the Stonewall Inn, a bar in New York City, in which patrons and neighbors fought back against a police vice raid, brought a more public face to antidiscrimination demands and a movement for "gay liberation." Although it echoed many slogans of the civil rights and women's movements of the 1960s and early 1970s, gay liberation was about many things beyond rights: it stood for a more visible cultural politics that could lessen shame and instill pride in order to challenge sexual roles and the cultural place and dominant form of the family, the norm of monogamy, and the political restrictions against passion, and it served as a counterpoint to more assimilationist tactics advanced by earlier homophile groups. It also had an economic dimension, as its demands for rethinking the family took place at the very time that middle-class family relations were changing under the demise of Fordism and the family wage.

The Stonewall uprising symbolically centered the question of how best to restrain state power and use the state to disrupt economic forms of discrimination.

Some activists turned to a politics of rights along the model of the NAACP Legal Defense Fund. Lambda Legal Education and Defense Fund, founded in 1973, was one such organization that promoted legal rights as a form of cultural change, later developing into one of the leading firms fighting for equal marriage rights. Others, who were more committed to developing a gay culture in its many social and cultural dimensions, rejected the cultural expectation for normality and civility attendant on those who demanded human and civil rights. This internal tension persists today among those pursuing a civil rights agenda symbolized by the fight for marriage rights and equal military service (though more broadly committed to antidiscrimination and privacy issues), and those who have chosen to develop a queer community antagonistic to the politics of normalization.

Since the late 1970s, conservatives have used this internal tension to help mobilize their opposition to gay rights, and in the process build their own political movements and activist legal firms. In one of the earliest public efforts to eliminate rights, Anita Bryant, a former Miss America, successfully organized conservative Christians under the banner "Save Our Children, Inc." to defeat an antidiscrimination ordinance. Her political strategy was to revive older fears of sexual predation of children and the fear of radical cultural upheaval with images emerging from the radical wing of the gay movement, in an effort to reverse the political gains of a more liberal and conformist rights-oriented agenda. Bryant's campaign inspired successful repeal efforts of antidiscrimination ordinances in four urban areas by 1980 and fueled many more anti-antidiscrimination contests in years afterward. It also framed the tactics of numerous efforts to place state constitutional barriers to same-sex marriage since 1998. Whether won or lost, these anti-rights efforts strengthened local and national conservative groups—organizations that played a significant role in the administration of President George W. Bush.

The conservative effort to roll back legal gains had consequences for gay rights activists, forcing them to reframe rights claims in less expansive ways. It also encouraged the cultural development of rights-alternatives such as officially unrecognized marriages, and inspired workers in labor unions to demand same-sex spousal benefits and other protections from their employers. Opposition to gay rights also encouraged the growth of "homonormative" activism preaching the achievement of cultural equality as a prelude to state protection, through efforts at assimilation and outright rejection of more liberationist cultural objectives. For some observers, this has led to a pernicious form of cultural governance, in which lesbians and gays are tolerated only to the extent they conform to culturally dominant values.

These conservative influences have also crept into doctrinal interpretations of gay rights. The constitutional elimination of antisodomy statutes (already repealed in thirty-six states and the District of Columbia by the time of *Lawrence v. Texas* in 2003) that had kept alive the symbolic if not actual threat of criminal law as a tool of governance, doctrinally established what the scholar Katherine Franke (2004) has called a scheme of "domesticated liberty." In this scheme, sexual freedom was protected only in private spaces under the rubric of due process, and equal protection rights were denied (thereby eliminating doctrinal arguments for same-sex marriage and military service). Similarly, the decision in *Romer v. Evans* (1996), which ruled unconstitutional statewide efforts to prevent antidiscrimination legislation, never affirmatively granted constitutional protection to lesbians and gays, enabling what the political scientist Evan Gerstmann (1999) calls a "constitutional underclass." These and other critical readings of legal doctrine acknowledge the political and cultural forces that have limited what gay rights have achieved.

The hard-fought issue of same-sex marriage raises important questions about whether these limits will endure. Long a contentious issue within the LGBT community, marriage equality was seen by some as a plastic contribution to citizenship rights generally, and by others as a move toward conformity. Since San Francisco and Massachusetts began allowing same-sex marriages in 2004, five additional states now marry same-sex couples, and six others and Washington, D.C. contract civil unions. This has made marriage a real option for some, and has increased its appeal for many others, in part because of the public acknowledgement of equal rights that marriage bestows. Conservatives who mobilized against same-sex marriage have led a long effort to challenge the meaning of this equality, suggesting that equal rights diminish the status of heterosexual marriages, and hide more radical aims that will indelibly alter American cultural values. President Barack Obama's recent refusal to litigate to uphold the Defense of Marriage Act, and support for same-sex marriage by the prominent conservative lawyer and former solicitor general Theodore Olson, who has joined the high-profile challenge to Proposition 8 that has limited judicially declared equal rights to marriage in California, suggest a possible political convergence that may make gay rights less contentious. Whether these rights still hold the potential to be culturally transformative, as many LGBT activists have hoped and many conservatives have feared, or whether the mainstreaming of gay rights has only been won through the domestication of gay demands for equality, will be soon seen.

[*See also* AIDS; Christian Right; Civil Liberties; *and* Marriage and the Family.]

BIBLIOGRAPHY

Dudziak, Mary L. *Cold War Civil Rights: Race and the Image of American Democracy*. (Princeton, N.J., 2000).

Duggan, Lisa. "The New Homonormativity: The Sexual Politics of Neoliberalism." In *Materializing Democracy: Toward a Revitalized Cultural Politics*, edited by Dana D. Nelson, pp. 175–194. (Durham, N.C., 2002).

Epp, Charles R. *The Rights Revolution: Lawyers, Activists, and Supreme Courts in Comparative Perspective*. (Chicago, 1998).

Eskridge, William, and Nan Hunter. *Sexuality, Gender, and the Law*. (Westbury, N.Y., 1997).

Fetner, Tina. "Working Anita Bryant: The Impact of Christian Anti-Gay Activism on Lesbian and Gay Movement Claims." *Social Problems* 48, no. 3 (2001): 411–428.

Fortin, A. J. "AIDS, Surveillance, and Public Policy." *Research in Law and Policy Studies* 4 (1995): 173.

Franke, Katherine M. "The Domesticated Liberty of *Lawrence v. Texas*." *Columbia Law Review* 104 (2004): 1399–1426.

Gerstmann, Evan. *The Constitutional Underclass: Gays, Lesbians, and the Failure of Class-Based Equal Protection*. (Chicago, 1999).

Goldberg-Hiller, Jonathan. "Do Civil Rights Have a Face? Reading the Iconography of Civil Rights." In *Queer Mobilizations: LGBT Activists Confront the Law*, edited by Scott Barclay, Mary Bernstein, and Anna-Maria Marshall, pp. 231–256. (New York, 2009).

Goldberg-Hiller, Jonathan. *The Limits to Union: Same-Sex Marriage and the Politics of Civil Rights*. (Ann Arbor, Mich., 2004).

Goldberg-Hiller, Jonathan, and Neal Milner. "Rights as Excess: Understanding the Politics of Special Rights." *Law and Social Inquiry* 28 (2003): 1075–1118.

Hilbink, Thomas. 2009. "The Right's Revolution? Conservatism and the Meaning of Rights in Modern America." *Studies in Law, Politics, and Society* 48 (2009): 43–67.

Hull, Kathleen E. *Same-Sex Marriage: The Cultural Politics of Love and Law*. (Cambridge, UK, 2006).

Hunt, Gerald. *Laboring for Rights: Unions and Sexual Diversity across Nations*. (Philadelphia, 1999).

Johnson, David K. *The Lavender Scare: The Cold War Persecution of Gays and Lesbians in the Federal Government*. (Chicago, 2003).

Muñoz, José Esteban. *Cruising Utopia: The Then and There of Queer Futurity*. (New York, 2009).

Patton, Cindy. "Refiguring Social Space." In *Social Postmodernism: Beyond Identity Politics*, edited by Linda Nicholson and Steven Seidman, pp. 216–249. (Cambridge, UK, 1995).

Rollins, Joe Neil. *AIDS and the Sexuality of Law: Ironic Jurisprudence*. (Houndmills, Basingstoke, UK, 2004).

Stoddard, Thomas. "Bleeding Heart: Reflections on Using the Law to Make Social Change." *New York University Law Review* 72 (1997): 967.

Sullivan, Andrew. *Virtually Normal: An Argument about Homosexuality*. (New York, 1996).

Teles, Steven Michael. *The Rise of the Conservative Legal Movement: The Battle for Control of the Law*. (Princeton, N.J., 2008).

Vaid, Urvashi. *Virtual Equality: The Mainstreaming of Gay and Lesbian Liberation*. (New York, 1995).

Warner, Michael. *The Trouble with Normal: Sex, Politics, and the Ethics of Queer Life*. (New York, 1999).

Yoshino, Kenji. *Covering: The Hidden Assault on Our Civil Rights*. (New York, 2006).

Jonathan Goldberg-Hiller

GENDER AND POLITICS

In a 1776 letter to her husband John, who was attending the Second Continental Congress in Philadelphia, Abigail Adams famously declared:

> I long to hear that you have declared an independency. And, by the way, in the new code of laws which I suppose it will be necessary for you to make, I desire you would remember the ladies and be more generous and favorable to them than your ancestors.
>
> Do not put such unlimited power into the hands of the husbands.
>
> Remember, all men would be tyrants if they could. If particular care and attention is not paid to the ladies, we are determined to foment a rebellion, and will not hold ourselves bound by any laws in which we have no voice or representation.

Of course, John Adams and the other delegates to the Continental Congress, as well as their later peers at the Constitutional Convention, crafted no such code of laws. The status of women was never mentioned in the new system of government, and women's political and civil rights in the new nation were more reflective of English common law than a great revolution in political thought and practical politics. Any and all laws affecting women in the early republic, thus, came from the state governments.

But, as Abigail Adams cautioned, this negligence on the part of the national government eventually led to rebellion. Over time, women began to tire of their unequal political status and nonexistent representation, particularly in a land that made lofty pronouncements about liberty, equality, and individual freedom. Slowly, a woman's movement began to foment. The power of this political movement has ebbed and flowed over time, but, taken as a whole, it has effected significant change in American politics.

This article explores the forces that have led to the transformation of the American woman. It begins with the history of women's movements in the United States from 1848 to the present and evaluates how these movements have altered the status of women today. Then, it considers how this progress has informed a growing body of scholarship on gender and American politics. Finally, it concludes with a note on future goals and directions for women in practical politics.

Gendering Politics. Here, the terms "women and politics" and "gender and politics" will be used somewhat interchangeably. In practice, however, "women and politics" and "gender and politics" refer to very different constructs. The former refers only to sex, a simple biological difference between man and woman that is dictated largely by physical features. In contrast, the latter is a much more complicated socially constructed concept. Gender considers any features that distinguish between male and female. This may include a variety of factors, such as the norms, roles, and stereotypes implied by ideas of male and female.

Popular use of the phrase "gender and politics" is a relatively new phenomenon; into the twenty-first century, the top journal in the political science subfield was still titled *Women and Politics*. In more recent years, however, gender has become the preferred terminology, because it implies a much deeper understanding of the forces that drive political behavior. (The journal, too, has been renamed *Politics and Gender*.) Thus, the act of "gendering" politics refers to the considering of how political life is and has been affected by the inherent differences between male and female.

Women in the United States. The journey of women into the world of politics, specifically in the United States, has been a difficult one. Theoretical and historical barriers have restricted access, and, until recently, social, legal, political, and economic limits have bounded feminist activism. The few early women who did dare to enter the political world were regarded as heathens, lesbians, or morally questionable characters. Their successors, in some cases, were met with little more favor. Only at the end of the twentieth century did social movements begin to secure legal change. At the same time, visible numbers of women began to win election to political office.

Women in the Early Republic. The roots of our understanding of gender and politics lie in the theoretical conceptions of power that informed even the earliest societies. In these early societies, separate spheres developed for men and women. The public sphere became "masculine." Men were expected to play an active role in society, and held most, if not all, of the political power. Women, on the other hand, were encouraged be the center of home and family, to be helpmeets to their husbands, and to raise good children (particularly sons, who would be faced with handling the public affairs of the next generation). As a result, the private sphere came to be viewed as "feminine."

In the colonies and early American republic, women enjoyed a status somewhat outside these norms. Women were valued, first, for their role in the creation and protection of the nuclear family. But, they (and the children they produced) also provided much-needed labor. They worked alongside and in place of their husbands in family farms and businesses. Though they did not engage actively in the political world and retained only limited civil rights under the law, American women were probably as well off as any women in the world at the time.

But, as the Industrial Revolution led to the development of the modern American family in the 1830s, American women saw their status in society begin to change. Cities developed and factory labor and new technology became more common, and new divisions in society began to emerge. These splits cut across not only gender, but also race and class. Poor and immigrant women, for example, were sent to work in the growing factories in mill towns such as Lowell, Massachusetts. Here, women as young as ten years old worked long hours in unsafe working conditions. They were compensated little, and most of those earnings were not used for their own pleasure, but for expenses of other family members, including the education of male siblings.

Lives changed for African American women and families during this time, as well. The development of the cotton gin, which made harvesting and processing cotton more efficient, did not slow the growth of slavery. Instead, perhaps counterintuitively, the cotton gin increased the need for slaves on many Southern plantations, as owners began to expand their operations. Many families were broken apart as slaves were sold and relocated from one plantation to another.

Social divisions between men and women also began to grow in upper- and middle-class white homes. As subsistence gave way to commerce, nineteenth-century gentlemen increasingly began to work outside the home for wages. Of course, their work also led to social exploits and celebrations that rarely included their wives, but often included alcohol, tobacco, and prostitutes. With the exception of attending church on Sundays, women retreated within the household. (Though, given the poor sanitation and safety standards of many nineteenth-century cities, this may have been little sacrifice.) Cooking, cleaning, and childrearing soon became the republican duty of the nineteenth-century woman. Clear gendered distinctions between public and private took root in the United States, with many men publicly suggesting that their wives lacked the brainpower or fundamental social skills necessary to succeed outside the home.

Soon, some women—largely, though not exclusively, upper-middle-class whites—became restless. Though they had resisted the inevitable "rebellion" cautioned by Abigail Adams for much of the first fifty years of the nation's existence, American women were not wholly content in their status. A growing number desired social and political rights, such as property ownership, and access to education, divorce, and credit, to say nothing of the more controversial right to vote.

Abolition and Suffrage. The earliest serious efforts to organize a woman's movement in the United States have their roots in the abolition movement. In 1840, two American women, Elizabeth Cady Stanton and Lucretia Mott, accompanied their husbands on a transatlantic journey to the meeting of the World Anti-Slavery Society in London. Upon their arrival in Great Britain, the women were informed that they could not participate in the convention; they were relegated to the balcony to observe the activities of the meeting. Here, the women reflected on their status compared to that of the slaves they sought to free. They reached the conclusion that they, too, lacked fundamental human rights. Stanton and Mott resolved that, upon their arrival home in the United States, they would hold a meeting to discuss the political and legal status of women.

Eight years later, in 1848, the first convention for the civil and political rights of women was held in Seneca Falls, New York. Here, the delegates drafted and approved the Declaration of Sentiments, a list of grievances written to mirror the Declaration of Independence that, in turn, has become a model for more recent reports on women's social and legal status itself. Among the women's objections were limitations on the right to own property, pursue an education, and seek employment. The women also expressed their frustration with a lack of political representation, as well as the loss of all social and political rights after marriage. All of the sentiments expressed in the document received the unanimous approval of the attendees except one: the right to vote. Some attendees, including Mott, feared that adding this provision would render the others ridiculous in the eyes of the public.

Following Seneca Falls, the women's movement continued to operate alongside the abolition movement. These women believed strongly in linked fate—African Americans and women would defeat white patriarchy together. Thus, when it became clear at the conclusion of the Civil War in 1865 that the national government was going to extend citizenship and suffrage to African Americans, women believed they would also be included in the new constitutional protections. However, the Reconstruction Congresses had no interest in this objective. The women's once-loyal allies in the abolition movement were also unwilling to sacrifice their gains for the goals of the woman's movement; Stanton and her sisters were told that now was "the Negro's hour." To add insult to injury, the Fourteenth Amendment, which granted African Americans the rights of citizens, specifically added the word "male" to the Constitution for the first time.

Votes for Women. The ratification of the Civil War Amendments divided suffragists. Some women, such as Stanton and Susan B. Anthony, felt betrayed by this action, and broke ties with those who supported the Civil War Amendments. Other women, such as Lucy Stone, were willing to support the amendments and saw their ratification as a logical step toward rights for women.

By 1869, this division led to the creation of two separate groups dedicated to the continued battle for woman suffrage. The more radical Stanton and Anthony founded the National Woman Suffrage Association, which lobbied the national government for policy change, both in suffrage and other areas of the law. Stone and her more conservative allies, on the other hand, formed the American Woman Suffrage Association, which concentrated its efforts on lobbying for suffrage in the states.

For almost twenty years, the two groups simultaneously pursued their similar goals. In 1890, however, the groups agreed to a merger and became the National American Woman Suffrage Association (NAWSA). Unity was clearly necessary to the achievement of the ultimate goal, and the progress toward winning votes for women in the states accelerated after the merger. But, NAWSA also had a problem. By the turn of the century, many of its leaders were quite old, and the organization was literally dying off. The group's efforts to reach out to younger women were met with mixed results; though many young women began their activism in the group, they eventually looked to express their more radical ideals elsewhere, such as in the National Woman's Party (NWP).

Key to the ultimate achievement of the ratification of the Nineteenth Amendment was the support of President Woodrow Wilson. After years of lobbying by women's organizations, as well as marches, protests, rallies, and even picketing outside the White House, Wilson finally endorsed the suffrage movement wholeheartedly in 1918. How much of this endorsement was due to interest groups' efforts and how much of it was the result of Wilson's need for women's support for World War I will never be known. Nevertheless, with Wilson's endorsement, the House and Senate passed the suffrage amendment, which had been proposed in every Congress since 1872, and sent it to the states for ratification in 1919. One year later, the new Nineteenth Amendment was officially added to the Constitution: women had won the much-sought-after right to vote. NAWSA soon morphed into the bipartisan League of Women Voters, and most of the women who had joined the suffrage movement went back to lobbying for other goals, such as better libraries and safer streets.

The dissolution of the 1920s women's movement was compounded by the Great Depression, which slowed progress for many women in the 1930s, stretching their already thin economic prospects even thinner. Narrow gains, however, were made through New Deal programs that provided benefits to families, including rural electrification projects. Some women, including First Lady Eleanor Roosevelt, also began to gain political voice during this time, working for expanded civil and political rights for all people. Eleanor Roosevelt also encouraged and helped her husband, President Franklin D. Roosevelt, to develop a network of prominent female political advisers, including Secretary of Labor Frances Perkins and Florence Allen, who was the first woman to serve on a federal court of appeals.

Women's role in American society was once again reexamined in the 1940s, with the beginning of World War II. With men, who made up the majority of the American workforce, headed off to war, companies, particularly those manufacturing supplies necessary for war, were forced to rely on women to fill positions on assembly lines. Though some (especially married) women were reluctant at first, the propaganda machine—most notably embodied by "Rosie the Riveter"—actively encouraged women to join the workforce, suggesting that the very lives of American soldiers, and indeed, peace and security themselves, hinged on women's efforts. By the end of World War II, women made up more than a third of the workforce.

The contributions of women to the war effort did not end in the factories. Women were expected to hold families together while fathers served abroad, to ration certain foods, to raise Victory Gardens, and attend knitting bees. With the exception of the seventy thousand women who served in the army and navy nurse corps, men were most of the soldiers on the front lines. But women were the lynchpin of the behind-the-scenes effort.

A New Movement for Women's Rights. The 1950s housewife was a vision in pearls and heels, with a vacuum cleaner in one hand and a television dinner in the other. She was, more often than not, married by twenty and had three children by her thirtieth birthday. She was the consummate June Cleaver; she was perfection in every way. And, as Betty Friedan expressed in her 1963 book *The Feminine Mystique*, she was exhausted, unfulfilled, and questioning if there was more to life. The 1963 report of the President's Commission on the Status of Women underscored those feelings; "American Woman" documented the extensive discrimination against women in all areas of life, from education to religion to politics.

These sentiments, coupled with weak enforcement of the 1964 Civil Rights Act, fueled a new wave of the American women's movement in the 1960s. Perhaps the most well-known of the early events of this movement came in 1966, when a group of political activists came together to form the National Organization for Women (NOW). NOW and other traditional interest groups, such as the National Women's Political Caucus, were dedicated to fighting for the equality of all women through litigation, lobbying, and grassroots campaigns.

But, not all women interested in greater rights in the late 1960s supported the avenues taken by NOW. Younger women, especially those who had worked as organizers in the civil rights and antiwar movements, saw NOW and its lobbying tactics as pale, old, and stale. In the younger women's view, NOW was an interest group for their mothers. Thus, these younger women helped to organize a radical wing of the women's movement dedicated to raising consciousness of gender issues through less traditional avenues. Women in this more radical branch of the movement, for example, symbolically shed symbols of male oppression by removing their bras in public. They also started domestic violence shelters and worked with police for better treatment of rape victims.

The two branches of the 1960s women's movement—the more conservative women in NOW and other interest groups and the more radical women associated with the New Left—had very different tactics. NOW worked within the existing political system, however patriarchal it may have been, while the radical women fundamentally rejected that system and attempted to build a new politics. But, both NOW and the New Left desired the same end: an elevation of the status of women in American society. The substantial gains achieved in the 1960s and early 1970s in the areas of equal pay, pregnancy discrimination, credit, child care, and education, to name a few, could not have been achieved without their combined efforts.

Backlash. Not all women rallied around the causes of the women's movement in the 1960s and 1970s. Conservative women, perhaps most visibly represented by the Republican activist Phyllis Schlafly, resisted what they saw as the radical goals of the movement, arguing that it was destroying the American family and ruining women's lives. Two political events in the 1970s—the Supreme Court's decision legalizing abortion in *Roe v. Wade* (1973) and the struggle to ratify the proposed Equal Rights Amendment (ERA)—gave these women an opportunity to mobilize political support.

Abortion. English common law, which formed the foundation for many of the earliest codes of laws in the United States, allowed abortion until the time of "quickening," or the first movement of the fetus. This was the custom for much of the early republic. By 1900, however, most American states had passed laws declaring abortion illegal. Though these laws criminalized the activity, they did not stop the action entirely. Perhaps their only effect was to make abortion less safe than it might otherwise have been, as organizations and individuals provided women with abortion services in "back alleys" and other secret places.

A series of events in the early 1960s put the abortion issue on the agenda of American governments, both state and national. First, a scare involving birth defects as a result of the drug thalidomide, which had never been sold in the United States, but had been available in Europe, raised concerns about women's access to safe, legal abortions in medically necessary situations. In addition, the Supreme Court's 1965 decision in *Griswold v. Connecticut*, which used a judicially created right to privacy to legally protect a married woman's access to contraception, increased the salience of issues surrounding family planning. As a result, some states, notably Hawaii and New York, began to liberalize their abortion laws.

The most significant change in abortion law in the United States would come as a result of the Supreme Court's decision in *Roe v. Wade* (1973). In this case, the Supreme Court declared that the right to privacy, as construed in *Griswold*, extended to a woman's right to obtain an abortion, although this right was not absolute. Justice Harry Blackmun, writing for the Court, tied a woman's right to access an abortion to the trimester of her pregnancy. In reaching this conclusion, the Court overturned the laws of forty-seven states and the District of Columbia.

Pro-choice groups, who were well-organized at the time of the Court's decision, were elated; victory on the abortion issue had come much more quickly than they had expected. Pro-life activists, on the other hand, were outraged by the Court's decision. Aided heavily by the Roman Catholic Church, they wasted little time organizing and building interest group infrastructure in the American states. This provided opportunities for conservative political activism and began to give voice to a segment of American women that did not feel represented by the 1960s women's movement.

The Equal Rights Amendment. Perhaps nothing, however, better gave voice to conservative women than the battle over the proposed Equal Rights Amendment (ERA). Liberal women viewed the amendment as a simple modification to the Constitution—a few words to correct an oversight and grant women constitutional protection for their civil and political rights. It stated only: "Equality of rights under the law shall not be denied or abridged by the United States or by any State on account of sex."

Women's rights activists had been fighting to add the ERA to the Constitution since soon after receiving the right to vote in the 1920s. In 1972, Congress finally adopted the amendment and sent it to the states for ratification. Thirty states assented to the

ERA's provisions in the first two years. But, securing the support of the remaining eight states to add the amendment to the Constitution proved to be a much more difficult struggle. On one hand, activists found it difficult to convince some people that the amendment was truly necessary—the gains of the 1960s women's movement had already made illegal many of the most glaring forms of discrimination against women. Though there is a legal difference between constitutional and statutory protection for civil rights, and while many sex discrimination statutes were not being uniformly enforced, the necessity of the amendment proved complicated and difficult to explain to the general public.

Moreover, many people wondered just how far this Equal Rights Amendment would go. Courts declared that women would have to register for the military draft. Would it also result in women being allowed to play on men's sports teams? Would it lead to single-sex restrooms? Would married men still be required to support their wives? Though these questions seemed, to some degree, frivolous and silly, they raised fear in the hearts and minds of many Americans. State legislatures became increasingly reluctant to ratify the amendment, and some even rescinded their initial ratifications.

By the time the Republican president Ronald Reagan was elected in 1980, the number of states that had approved the amendment still stood at only thirty-five. No additional states would ratify the amendment by its 30 June 1982 expiration date. The remaining years of the Reagan and George H. W. Bush administrations would prove to be a difficult time for women, as activists attempted to dismantle the Supreme Court's decision in *Roe* and a struggling economy limited opportunities for women's advancement.

The Year of the Woman. In 1991, President George H. W. Bush nominated Judge Clarence Thomas to fill a vacant seat on the US Supreme Court. Commentators almost immediately questioned Thomas's qualifications for the position. He had little previous judicial experience, and received a rare low rating on his qualifications from the American Bar Association. But, perhaps no incident surrounding Judge Thomas's nomination received greater attention than the testimony of law professor Anita Hill before the Senate Judiciary Committee.

Hill had worked for Thomas at the Department of Education and the Equal Employment Opportunity Commission. During her time at these agencies, she charged, Thomas made improper sexual advances and took actions that created a hostile and uncomfortable work environment. Though Hill did not report Thomas's actions at the time, her allegations were made public during his confirmation hearings and she was called to appear before the Judiciary Committee to address potential questions about Thomas's character.

Hill's testimony was initially received with a great deal of skepticism; in the days following the hearings, most Americans did not believe Anita Hill. But, opinion began to change as more women, including a group of navy and marine corps officers, came forward with their stories of workplace discrimination. Questions also began to arise about the fairness of forcing Hill, a black woman, to testify before an all-white, all-male Senate Judiciary Committee.

The Hill hearing ultimately contributed to a year of unprecedented electoral success for female candidates in 1992. The gains of women candidates in this year were also aided by a number of other factors, including redistricting and scandals that created a near record number of open seat opportunities for women to run for office. In addition, women candidates, many of them Democrats, enjoyed a weak economy with an incumbent Republican president. Women's gains were so significant that 1992 became known as "The Year of the Woman." Twenty-one women won election to statewide office, and record numbers won legislative seats in the states and in Washington, D.C. The numbers of women in both the House and Senate, for example, nearly doubled. In 1993, when the new Congress was sworn in, fifty-four women were serving in the institution: seven in the Senate and forty-eight in the House.

Studying the Political Woman. As the women's movement took root in 1970s America, opportunities arose for women in a wide variety of fields once reserved largely for men. Among these was academia; by the late 1970s and early 1980s, a cohort of young female scholars interested in exploring the women and the movement that had given them such great opportunities began to emerge. These scholars helped to develop the body of political science scholarship that we today call gender (or women) and politics. This research has explored women in all aspects of political life. The important contributions of scholars on the gender gap, political ambition, and women in government are highlighted in the following sections.

The Gender Gap. At their most basic level, gender gaps are the result of differences between men's and women's attitudes, actions, beliefs, or behaviors. Scholars have observed these gaps in issue salience, political participation, electoral behavior, and partisanship. Perhaps the most famous application of the idea of a gender gap is to the observable gaps in men's and women's voting behavior. Though these gaps have existed since at least 1952, scholars and practitioners of politics first paid significant attention to them following the election of President Ronald Reagan in 1980. In this year, scholars noted, there was an 8 percent gap in women's support for the Democratic candidate, President Jimmy Carter, when compared to Reagan.

Political science research probing the causes of the gender gap followed soon after. The earliest scholars evaluating this gap hypothesized that feminist women, who appeared to be shifting away from the Republican Party to support the Democratic Party, caused the gap. These ideas were rooted in the history of the 1960s women's movement and the subsequent backlash against it. Traditional wisdom dictated that during this time period, the once pro-woman Republican Party was transformed, as activists in the women's movement visibly and vocally began to increasingly identify with the Democratic Party. Scholars found empirical support for this hypothesis; feminist women were indeed more likely to identify as and vote Democratic than their non-feminist counterparts.

The next generation of scholars advanced this line of thinking to consider not only feminist women, but also feminist men. In effect, these researchers broadened the definition of a feminist identity to include anyone who valued equality between men and women, acknowledging that gender consciousness may not be a fundamentally gendered construct. Using data on both foreign and domestic policy issues, they showed that feminist women and feminist men had very similar attitudes. This data demonstrated that the women's movement and a subsequent awakening in women could not be the sole source of the gender gap in voting behavior and party identification.

More recently, scholars have uncovered evidence that has completely debunked the idea that the gender gap is caused by changes in women's attitudes. Instead, this scholarship suggests that it is *men* whose party identification has shifted since 1952. As the Republican Party took on less of a social welfare agenda and began to oppose government involvement in the private sphere, men increasingly came to identify with that party's agenda. Women, on the other hand, have identified with the Democratic Party at remarkably stable levels since 1952. This scholarship suggests that understanding the dynamics of gender and politics does not always come back to the political behavior of women. Instead, the beliefs, attitudes, and actions of men may be equally important to understanding gender divides in political behavior.

Political Ambition. Studies of women as political candidates find that when women run for political office, they win at rates similar to those of their male counterparts. However, women are far less likely than similarly situated men to express a desire to run for political office. They are, additionally, more reluctant to explore policies regarding how to declare candidacy and raise funds to run for office. And, when women do run for office, they typically eschew national offices such as Congress, preferring instead to run for more local, lower visibility offices, such as school boards or judgeships.

This gender gap in political ambition has been the subject of much consternation for scholars in recent years. Three main gendered explanations have been offered for the sources of this divide: family roles, self-perceptions, and patterns of recruitment. First, women, as the traditional center of the home and family, may be more reluctant to leave their children and their community to run for political office. As a result, if women run at all, they are more likely to delay running for office until they—and their children—are older. Second, women appear to have a crisis of confidence; they are less likely to see themselves as qualified for political office than their similarly situated male counterparts. They often doubt the relevance of their own abilities and experiences in the political world, even when they have worked in fields such as law and business that are popular training grounds for political leaders. Finally, traditional hierarchies of power in American party organizations may leave women sitting on the sidelines. Even politically active women report that they are less likely to be asked by their parties to run for office than their male counterparts. This recruitment problem may be particularly significant in the Republican Party, which has historically had a more top-down organizational structure emphasizing hierarchy and compliance.

Women in Government. As the numbers of women serving in government have increased, scholars have begun to ask whether the descriptive representation of women increases the substantive representation of women. These explorations of whether the presence of women in politics translates into more woman-friendly policies have found somewhat mixed results. The strength of the linkage between the two constructs varies widely on the type of behavior, the political institution, the political climate, and the personal and political characteristics of actors involved.

In state legislatures and in Congress, for example, scholars have found that, in general, women act, vote, and lead differently from their male counterparts at all stages of the legislative process. From committee membership to committee chair to the floor of the legislature, women are more likely to embody an inclusive style of leadership, support women's issue bills in speeches and comments, and cast votes in support of that legislation. However, the magnitude of these effects varies significantly with the member's party affiliation, with Democratic women being more likely to engage in these types of behaviors than their Republican counterparts.

Studies of judicial decision-making, on the other hand, have revealed that women judges at all levels of the judicial system behave similarly to their male colleagues in most types of cases. However, significant differences appear in some issue areas. Most notably, women judges are much more likely to support sex discrimination claimants than their male counterparts. What is more, the presence of women judges on judicial panels appears to also influence their male colleagues' support for sex discrimination claimants.

Fewer women have served in high-visibility positions in the executive branch, both in state capitals and in Washington, D.C., making systematic analysis challenging. The research that does exist demonstrates that women Cabinet ministers tend to follow somewhat different career paths than their male counterparts, coming to office with less education, at a younger age, and less likely to be married or have children. Once in office, women in the executive branch tend to emphasize collaborative leadership. They are also more likely to prioritize so-called women's issues and to provide opportunities for other women to advance within the bureaucracy.

Is There a Glass Ceiling? The 2008 presidential election provided a platform for women that had not been seen before in American politics. Hillary Clinton contended for the Democratic Party's nomination, ultimately losing in a long and hard-fought contest to now-President Barack Obama. The Republican Party, too, placed a memorable woman in a visible role, nominating Alaska Governor Sarah Palin as Senator John McCain's vice presidential running mate.

Yet, neither of these women was ultimately successful. And two years later, in 2010, women candidates for the House, Senate, and state legislatures suffered losses not seen since before the Year of the Woman. Though Republican women, particularly gubernatorial candidates, fared better than their Democratic counterparts, commentators still expressed concern at what appeared to be a new glass ceiling for the progress of women in politics.

The United States, after all, still ranks behind most industrialized democracies in women's representation in government. It also ranks behind some emerging nations, such as China, which have quotas reserving seats for women in government. Nations such as Canada, India, and Great Britain have already elected female chief executives.

What it will take to elevate the United States to this level is not immediately clear. On one hand, it clearly takes a candidate willing to face the media onslaught and demands of running for office. But, on the other, it also takes voters who are willing to support that candidate, both as they enter the political pipeline and as they aspire to and run for higher offices. This requires infrastructure, support, and unity among those most dedicated to the cause, and may suggest the need for a new and very different type of twenty-first-century women's movement.

A number of factors could potentially mobilize such a movement. The publication of the 2011 White House report "Women in America," which chronicles the continued pervasive discrimination against women in all walks of life, may provide some inspiration. The potential for a series of conservative Supreme Court decisions that may dismantle legal protections for sex discrimination and abortion—rights most young women take for granted—may also act as a catalyst in the coming years.

[*See also* Child Care; Civil Rights; Domestic Violence; Elections and Electoral Behavior; First Ladies; Women and Paid Work; *and* Women and Welfare.]

BIBLIOGRAPHY
Baker, Jean. *Sisters: The Lives of America's Suffragists.* (New York, 2005).
Collins, Gail. *When Everything Changed: The Amazing Journey of American Women from 1960 to the Present.* (New York, 2009).
Conover, Pamela Johnston. "Feminists and the Gender Gap." *Journal of Politics* 50 (1988): 985–1010.
Cook, Elizabeth Adell, and Clyde Wilcox. "Feminism and the Gender Gap: A Second Look." *Journal of Politics* 53 (1991): 1111–1122.
Cushman, Clare. *Supreme Court Decisions and Women's Rights.* (Washington, D.C., 2000).
Dolan, Julie, Melissa M. Deckman, and Michele L. Swers. *Women and Politics: Paths to Power and Political Influence.* 2d ed. (New York, 2010).
Faludi, Susan. *Backlash: The Undeclared War against American Women.* 2d ed. (New York, 1992).
Ford, Lynne E. *Women and Politics: The Pursuit of Equality.* 3d ed. (Boston, 2011).
Friedan, Betty. *The Feminine Mystique.* (New York, 1963).
Kaufmann, Karen M., and John R. Petrocik. "The Changing Politics of American Men: Understanding the Sources of the Gender Gap." *American Journal of Political Science* 43 (1999): 864–887.
Krook, Mona Lena, and Sarah Childs, eds. *Women, Gender, and Politics: A Reader.* (New York, 2010).
Langbein, Laura, and Kimberly Cowell-Meyers. "Linking Women's Descriptive and Substantive Representation in the United States." *Politics and Gender* 5 (December 2009): 491–518.
Lawless, Jennifer L., and Richard L. Fox. *It Still Takes a Candidate: Why Women Don't Run for Office.* Rev. ed. (New York, 2010).
McGlen, Nancy E., et al. *Women, Politics, and American Society.* 5th ed. (New York, 2010).
O'Connor, Karen, ed. *Gender and Women's Leadership: A Reference Handbook.* (Thousand Oaks, Calif., 2010).
O'Connor, Karen, Sarah E. Brewer, and Michael Philip Fisher, eds. *Gendering American Politics: Perspectives from the Literature.* (New York, 2005).
Palmer, Barbara, and Dennis Simon. *Breaking the Political Glass Ceiling: Women and Congressional Elections.* 2d ed. (New York, 2008).
Rosen, Ruth. *The World Split Open: How the Modern Women's Movement Changed America.* (New York, 2006).
Sanchez, Leslie. *You've Come a Long Way, Maybe: Sarah, Michelle, Hillary, and the Shaping of the New American Woman.* (New York, 2009).
Swers, Michele L. *The Difference Women Make: The Policy Impact of Women in Congress.* (Chicago, 2002).
United States Department of Commerce, Economics and Statistics Administration. "Women in America: Indicators of Social and Economic Well-Being." (March 2011), http://www.whitehouse.gov/sites/default/files/rss_viewer/Women_in_America.pdf.
Whitaker, Lois Duke, ed. *Women in Politics: Outsiders or Insiders?* 5th ed. (New York, 2010).

Karen O'Connor and Alixandra B. Yanus

GLASS-STEAGALL ACT

The Glass-Steagall bill, commonly referred to by the names of its congressional authors, was formally titled the Banking Act of 1933; Franklin Delano Roosevelt signed it into law on Friday, 16 June 1933.

Carter Glass, a Democratic senator from Virginia, was the central figure in the bill's history. Henry B. Steagall, a Democrat and the House representative from Alabama, was the less willing partner. The Republican Party was largely absent from the legislative debate, having been resoundingly defeated in the 1932 elections, partly due to public perception of its responsibility for the Great Depression.

The bill circumscribed the activities of commercial banks. The term "commercial bank" is critical to understanding Glass-Steagall, because the legislation segregates commercial banking from investment banking. Commercial banks were defined by membership in the national Federal Reserve System, created in 1913 to fulfill the functions of a central bank, including serving as a lender of last resort to banks. At the time, banks could seek charters from state governments or the national government. Banks with national charters were required to join the Federal Reserve system, meaning they held stock in one of the regional Federal Reserve Banks and deposited non-interest-bearing reserves with the Federal Reserve. After 1980, legislation required all deposit-taking banks in the United States, including state-chartered banks, savings banks, savings and loan institutions, and credit unions, to hold reserves at the Fed.

Glass-Steagall prohibited commercial banks from having investment-banking affiliates or sharing members of their boards of directors with investment-banking affiliates. Any organization earning more than 10 percent of its income from issuing, underwriting, or distributing securities or trading them for the organization's own account was an investment bank. The law exempted from this definition one form of security: US government bonds. Banks were given one year from the bill's signing to choose between implementing a commercial or investment bank business strategy. The main argument for separation was the conflict of interest arising when banks both underwrite and trade stocks and encourage their depositors to purchase those securities.

While the separation of commercial and investment banking is the most prominent element of the Glass-Steagall Act, it also introduced Federal Deposit Insurance for deposit-taking banks and moved conduct of open-market operations from the New York branch of the Federal Reserve to the Board of the Federal Reserve system, based in Washington, D.C. As with most legislation, some of the stipulations resulted from the process of building legislative support for the final bill.

By the time it came up for vote, the bill enjoyed such strong support that it was vetted through voice vote rather than a legislator-by-legislator roll call. The politics behind the development of the bill operated at two levels: public debate centered around the Pecora hearings in the Senate (described later), while more private networking went on within and between financiers and regulators.

The public politics of Glass-Steagall revolved around Senate hearings and their press coverage. The Republican-controlled Senate launched investigation into the bank failures following the stock market crash in 1929 (around 20 percent of all US banks failed during that crash). The investigation was troubled; two successive lawyers hired to run the investigation were fired and a third resigned because he could not secure subpoena authority. This added credibility to those who viewed the investigation as a whitewash intended to mollify public critics of Wall Street. In January 1933 Ferdinand Pecora, the assistant district attorney for New York County, took on oversight of the investigation and, as chief counsel to the Senate Banking and Currency Committee, soon won permission to convene Senate hearings. Pecora called many prominent investment bankers to testify and exposed unethical, if not criminal, activity related to both corporate and individual conduct. (The public was incensed to learn that many partners in J.P. Morgan and Company, for example, paid very little or no income taxes.) These hearings galvanized public opinion against the investment banks.

At the center of the behind-the-scenes politics of the Glass-Steagall Act was Senator Carter Glass himself, who wrote and negotiated many specific aspects of the bill. He had been a vocal critic of speculative stock trading, arguing long before 1933 that stocks should be purchased as investments, but that if a stock was bought "with a view of selling it even before delivery physically could be made, the next hour, or with a view of anticipating the future of tomorrow or the next day, that was . . . pure gambling—just as much gambling as if Senators were to sit at a roulette table and bet on the outcome of the game." Stock market speculators, he went on, "sell things they do not possess," and "buy things they never expect to get, and thereby disturb the whole commercial fabric of this country, and it ought to be stopped." Glass also felt that the New York Federal Reserve Bank had contributed to the speculative bubble by pursuing expansionary monetary policy.

Glass walked a fine line between serving the public interest and, perhaps unwittingly, serving the interests of one segment of the financial industry over another. Increasingly after 1865, the larger US banks shifted toward a universal banking model of combining loan and investment activity in one business. The genesis was competitive pressure. As trust companies, predominantly in the investment business, moved into the lending business, commercial banks sought the power to engage in investment activities by requesting charter revisions. For instance, fueled by the lucrative business of gaining critical ownership stakes in industrial firms such as US Steel and General Electric, by the 1920s, J.P. Morgan, an investment bank that had evolved from the trust company of Drexel, Morgan and Co., controlled the commercial bank First National Bank of New York. Large financial institutions, such as the Rockefeller-affiliated Chase National Bank, which began this shift later, had less to lose from the separation of investment and commercial banking activities. They moved preemptively to spin off investment banking activity and support the bill Carter Glass was writing. Piling on to support a regulatory move that would most severely penalize Morgan interests and limit the power of the New York Federal Reserve were large Chicago banks and the California banking ancestor of today's Bank of America. For support from the House of Representatives, Glass won over Henry Steagall with the inclusion of the provision for Federal Deposit Insurance.

Over the course of the twentieth century the Glass-Steagall separation of commercial and investment banking gradually eroded. Building competitive pressure in the 1980s and 1990s spurred industry lobbying for outright repeal. Political momentum gained further traction in Congress after the resounding defeat of Democratic candidates in the 1994 midterm elections. In 1999, with support of President Bill Clinton's Treasury Department, Congress passed the Gramm-Leach-Bliley Act, which effectively ended the Glass-Steagall prohibitions.

[*See also* Financial Crisis of 2008; Gramm-Leach-Bliley Act; *and* Regulation.]

BIBLIOGRAPHY

Benston, George J. *The Separation of Commercial and Investment Banking: The Glass-Steagall Act Revisited and Reconsidered.* (New York, 1990).

Calomiris, Charles W. *US Banking Deregulation in Historical Perspective.* (New York, 2006).

Chernow, Ron. *The House of Morgan: An American Banking Dynasty and the Rise of Modern Finance.* (New York, 1990).

Geisst, Charles R. *Wall Street: A History from Its Beginnings to the Fall of Enron.* (New York, 2004).

Spong, Kenneth. "Banking Regulation: Its Purposes, Implementation, and Effects." 5th ed. (2000), http://www.kansascityfed.org/publicat/bankingregulation/RegsBook2000.pdf.

Tabarrok, Alexander. "The Separation of Commercial and Investment Banking: Morgans vs. Rockefellers." *Quarterly Journal of Austrian Economics* 1, no. 1 (1998): 1–18.

Sylvia Maxfield

GLOBAL ECONOMY AND THE UNITED STATES

In 1944, as World War II entered its final phase, the United States found itself in the unexpected position of single most powerful country in the world. Amounting to 40 percent of the world's total gross domestic product (GDP) and producing about 50 percent of the world's industrial output, the United States also dominated the global economy. The magnitude of America's economic primacy was unprecedented in the modern age: by comparison, the British economy—at its relative peak in 1899—had constituted just 9 percent of the world economy.

Given this unique concentration of economic power, the United States would press ahead with its vision of an open and liberal world economy and try to reverse the process of international economic disintegration that had started with the outbreak of World War I in 1914, and had led to a breakdown of the liberal order with the rise of fascism in the 1930s. However, as soon as the geopolitical rivalry of the Cold War got under way in the late 1940s, the world was ideologically divided between East and West— a division that would last until 1989. In the East, the Soviet Union under Joseph Stalin, its satellite states in Central and Eastern Europe, as well as China under Mao Tse-tung, along with other parts of East and Southeast Asia—together adding up to one-third of the total world population—would organize their economies based on communist-socialist principles and the teachings of Karl Marx and Friedrich Engels. The United States and the West organized the rest of the world economy following the logic of open markets, free trade, and private property rights, as originally outlined by Adam Smith, David Ricardo, and John Locke.

In the mid-1940s, the Democratic presidents Franklin D. Roosevelt and Harry S. Truman led America and the West (including Japan, South Korea, and Taiwan) in building an international economic system which would internalize the lessons of the Great Depression of the 1930s. What came to be known as the "Bretton Woods" system—based on relatively free trade and a fixed exchange rate system, with managed international capital flows centered on the US dollar—defined international economic relations from 1944 to 1971 in the West. New international organizations such as the United Nations (UN), the International Monetary Fund (IMF), the World Bank (WB), and the General Agreement on Tariffs and Trade (GATT) all combined liberal and realist principles of international relations, and US leadership was indispensable in their foundation during the 1940s.

The Harvard scholar John Gerard Ruggie (1982) refers to this early postwar period as the era of

"embedded liberalism," since policymakers combined the principles of a relatively open world economy with the domestic constraints and demands of modern democracies, that is, the need to maintain a high level of growth and employment along with stable prices. Interestingly enough, the eventual collapse of the dollar-centric Bretton Woods system in 1971 did not lead to an existential crisis among liberal economic ideas and institutions. And with the opening up of China under Deng Xiaoping starting in the late 1970s, the fall of the Berlin Wall in 1989, and the breakup of the Soviet Union in 1991, the liberal ideas and institutions the United States put in place after World War II not only seem to have survived, but the East eventually embraced Western economic ideas and applied to join its international economic institutions, in a seeming ideological triumph of the West in the early 1990s.

However, America's relative economic power started to decline quite rapidly from 1945 onward due to the rise of the rest ("catch-up and convergence"). And given the increasing frequency and magnitude of financial crises and their contagious impact on the rest of the world economy, as well as the "state capitalist" alternatives currently on offer in places like China and Russia, it is far from evident that the world economy will remain organized based on the US liberal economic paradigm.

Charles Kindleberger's Hegemonic Stability Theory (HST), one of the most influential international political economy (IPE) theories to date, explains the resilience and relative stability of the open world economic system since World War II. Kindleberger (1981) argues that the necessary, though not sufficient, condition for stability is the existence of "one hegemon." According to HST, Great Britain played the role of hegemon between 1815 and 1914, and managed the relative stability of that period, making the first age of globalization possible. After World War I, crippled by the war effort and financially weakened, Britain was no longer able to play that role. The United States, though able, was initially reluctant in 1919 to take over from Britain, and only embraced its hegemonic task from the Bretton Woods conference onward. Kindleberger maintains that the lack of a hegemon in the 1920s and the 1930s led to a reversal of globalization and explains the length and depth of the Great Depression, or what E. H. Carr (1939) referred to as the "twenty years' crisis" in international relations.

Given the absence of a major systemic conflict since 1945, Robert Keohane (1984) has argued that once international regimes have been established with the vital backing of a hegemonic power, they tend to live a life of their own and can survive as long as a critical coalition of states supports the existing regime. It remains to be seen whether an increasingly pluralistic world—with economic and political power distributed much more evenly among states—will be able to maintain and strengthen the liberal institutions that were created by the United States after World War II.

Generally, four broad themes have informed the thinking of academics and policymakers in their analysis of the United States' relationship with the global economy. The first theme is that of relative economic decline and renewal. The United States has strived to maintain its international competitiveness in the face of the "rise of the rest," while its own internal economic structure has been in turn affected by globalization and technological change, leading to alternating periods of declinist fears and renewed optimism in the country's capacity to rebound. The second theme is the exponential growth of international financial markets and the role of the dollar in the international monetary system. With the movement toward an increasingly plural monetary system by the beginning of the twenty-first century, with rivaling currencies like the euro and the potential future role of the Chinese renminbi as a global reserve currency, the "exorbitant privilege" the dollar has enjoyed since 1944 is being called into question. The third theme is the constant tension between multilateralism and regionalism in international trade relations and negotiations, with the establishment of the World Trade Organization (WTO) in 1994 as the main multilateral triumph, but the mushrooming of preferential trade agreements from the late 1980s onward as a clear sign of intensifying regional integration, which could be a considerable stumbling block toward global free trade. The fourth and final theme is the political and security dimension of America's international economic relations, with high defense spending and chronic budget deficits linked to persistent current account deficits, a weakening external position (with the United States switching from a "creditor nation" to a "debtor nation" in 1985), and the inevitable economic costs of what Paul Kennedy (1987) called "imperial overstretch."

These four broad themes inform the evolution of the place of the United States in the world economy in the period since World War II. For analytical purposes, this description is divided into three subperiods. The first subperiod runs from 1944 to 1971, dubbed the "thirty glorious years," when the United States was the undisputed center of a fast-growing world economy. The second subperiod begins in 1971, with the breakdown of the Bretton Woods system of fixed exchange rates. The final subperiod starts in 1991, with the end of the Cold War and a relatively short world recession at the end of the first Gulf War.

The "Thirty Glorious Years" and the Rise and Fall of Bretton Woods, 1944–1971. The first subperiod was characterized by US activism and a clear vision for US leadership in the world economy. Once it dawned on Washington's policy elites soon after the war, when the ideological battle over the world economy with the Soviet Union got under way, that Europe and Japan were experiencing a serious dollar shortage and were unable to pay back their war debts without direct American support, the Americans decided to step in with the Marshall Plan for Europe and the Dodge Plan for Japan. Both programs were acts of genuine American generosity (the Marshall Plan adding up to 10 percent of the federal budget in its first year of operation) sold to Congress as a necessary tool to stave off communism in those strategically important parts of the world, and both helped Europe and Japan rebuild their economies by importing the capital goods needed to build up their infrastructure and to develop their export industries. The plans laid the foundation for miracles of economic growth in both regions during the subsequent thirty years.

With much faster growth rates in Continental Europe and Japan, it would not be long before those countries started to catch up and converge with the living standards of the American economy, giving way to fears of relative economic decline in Washington. There was also a significant security dimension to these declinist frustrations. Since the United States was providing security to both Europe (through NATO) and Japan (through the US-Japan Alliance) at a considerable cost to its purse (at some point during the 1950s, NATO usurped close to half of America's total defense budget), the Americans found it increasingly difficult to balance their modern democracy's need for both "guns and butter." Since Europe and Japan (and soon South Korea after the 1950–1953 Korean War) could shelter under the American security umbrella, they did not have to worry about guns and were able to create their universal welfare states, with generous social safety nets, and health and pensions systems—something the United States was unable to do to the same extent, given its global military commitments. More often than not, this apparent "free-riding" behavior led to tensions between the United States and its European and Asian allies, especially over international trade and monetary negotiations. American presidents Eisenhower, Kennedy, and Johnson, in the 1950s and 1960s, found themselves caught in a constant balancing act between the need for more burden-sharing from its allies to make its containment strategy a success, and the relative weakness of those allies adding to the fear of further communist aggression from Moscow and Beijing, especially during and after the wars in Korea and Vietnam.

In the summer of 1944, over seven hundred government representatives and delegates from forty-four allied countries gathered at the Mount Washington Hotel in Bretton Woods, New Hampshire, to discuss how to rebuild the international monetary and financial system after the Great Depression. The two main protagonists of the conference were the British economist John Maynard Keynes and the American treasury department official Harry Dexter White. The compromise they reached was an attempt at reconciling a commitment to an open multilateral

world economy, with new domestically oriented priorities of addressing unemployment and social welfare. Key elements of the agreement included the institution of a "gold exchange" standard, with currencies pegged in relation to the gold content of the US dollar, currency convertibility for current account transactions, capital controls designed to manage speculative and "disequilibrating" private financial flows, as well as the establishment of two new international economic organizations: the International Monetary Fund (IMF) and the World Bank (WB). The IMF was founded to provide short-term loans to help countries finance temporary balance of payments deficits and to manage international economic imbalances through oversight of the adjustable peg system, leverage use of its lending capacity, and the use of its "scarce currency" clause. The WB was founded to provide long-term loans for reconstruction and development after the war. Until about 1958, the Bretton Woods system was in virtual "cold storage": the currencies of European countries were not convertible, and the US government and regional institutions were playing the roles the IMF and WB should have. However, from 1958 to 1971, the IMF and the WB became more active lenders.

An agreement to establish an International Trade Organization (ITO), intended to complement the World Bank and the IMF, was concluded in 1948 in Havana. Since the US Congress failed to ratify the agreement, the international community had to fall back on the General Agreement on Tariffs and Trade (GATT), a multilateral contract embodying trade rules negotiated by the United States in 1947. The GATT, never intended to function as an international organization, provided a structure for the regulation of the international trade system, and was partly a mechanism to ensure that countries did not reintroduce protectionism once tariffs were lowered. The main principle of the GATT and the cornerstone of the international trade system was the idea of "non-discrimination," with article I (most favored nation principle) and article III (national treatment) addressing issues of external and internal discrimination. The GATT sponsored various rounds of multilateral negotiations to liberalize trade, with the first four rounds in the late 1940s and 1950s addressing institutional matters but failing to make significant progress in liberalizing world trade. In those rounds, negotiations took place bilaterally and were then made multilateral through the "most favored nation" principle. The first significant round was the Kennedy round of 1963–1967, which led to an average tariff reduction of about 35 percent, introduced an anti-dumping code, and saw the European Community participating as a single unit for the first time.

The 1960s—by all measures a very successful decade for the United States and the global economy overall—saw the deep flaws of the dollar-centered Bretton Woods system come to the fore. Furthermore, the relatively fast growth and technological innovations of the Soviet Union under Nikita Khrushchev, together with the protracted military conflict in Vietnam, only underscored the latent fears of US relative decline in Washington. The inherent instability and eventual collapse of the Bretton Woods system had been predicted as early as 1960 by the Yale economist Robert Triffin. He had argued that, in a system where the dollar was the sole reserve asset, the only way to expand international liquidity was for the United States to run a persistent balance of payments deficits to provide the world with more dollars; but the more and the longer it did so, the more this very process would also undermine the credibility of the US commitment to convert dollars into gold at the fixed rate of $35 per ounce. The "Triffin Dilemma" was to choose between a liquidity crisis (the world being starved of dollars, leading to deflation), or a credibility crisis (with all countries simultaneously wanting to convert their dollars into gold).

Given the ongoing process of globalization in the 1960s, with the gradual liberalization of capital flows and the increasing importance of international trade, a very large "Eurodollar" market developed in London, and the pressure on the Bretton Woods system threatened to spiral out of control. As US currency abroad grew considerably larger than the amount of gold that the US government held to back it up, the writing was already on the wall. Initially, however, the dollar-credibility issue was averted

when both West Germany and Japan agreed not to convert their dollar reserves into gold. However, other allies, such as Charles de Gaulle's France, who were more skeptical of America's intentions, and saw that nation as abusing its "exorbitant privilege" to export inflation to the rest of the world, refused to do so. When speculative pressures against the dollar reached a peak in 1971, President Richard Nixon was forced to close the gold window in August of that year, formally ending dollar convertibility into gold. Nixon also imposed a surcharge of 10 percent on imports and a 90-day freeze of wages, prices, and dividends under the cloak of a "New Economic Policy" for the United States. A new period of uncertainty in the global economy followed, with floating exchange rates and accelerating inflation, which would end the so-called thirty glorious years.

The "Great Inflation," Reagan's Recovery, and the End of the Cold War, 1971–1991. The 1970s and 1980s were two difficult decades for the United States and the world economy, with increased uncertainty in the geopolitical, monetary, and trade realms, as well as a fundamental shift in the governing economic paradigm from the "embedded liberal" ideas of John Maynard Keynes to the free market ideas of Friedrich Hayek and Milton Friedman. The 1970s started out quite promisingly, with an economic boom after Nixon's embrace of Keynesian demand stimulus and his reelection in 1972. However, this proved to be short-lived; inflation, already creeping up because of increased spending on Great Society programs at home and Vietnam abroad, spiraled out of control after the first of two oil shocks in 1973–1974 (following the Yom Kippur War). A deep stagflationary recession followed during the short-lived Ford Administration of 1974–1975.

When the Democrat Jimmy Carter was elected US president in 1976, he tried to revive the US economy's flagging fortunes through traditional Keynesian means, but was also forced to make a policy U-turn after the second oil shock in 1979 was triggered by the Iranian revolution and the fall of the shah in Tehran. Unable to recognize the sea change in economic ideas under way in the West during the 1970s, Carter publicly spoke of a "malaise" in the American economy, and his presidency too was short-lived, after unemployment started to rise when the newly appointed Fed chairman Paul Volcker embraced monetarism to fight inflation. Ronald Reagan swept to power in 1981, promising to revive America's economic prowess through a supply-side program of deregulation, privatization, and liberalization, combined with large tax cuts to stimulate investment and big increases in defense spending to win the Cold War. Reagan hoped to unleash the creative forces of the free market, but with ballooning budget and trade deficits at the end of the 1980s (the "twin deficits"), together with the economic challenges to US competitiveness from a fast-growing Japan and the four original Asian "mini-dragons" (South Korea, Taiwan, Hong Kong, and Singapore), fears of US "declinism" were back in vogue.

After the collapse of the Bretton Woods system, the United States tried to mend international monetary relations with the Smithsonian Agreement, which heralded a very short return to fixed exchange rates allowing wider fluctuation bands. However, the oil shock of 1973 put an end to that agreement, and the United States started to embrace a new financial liberalism, including the phasing out of capital controls and the full acceptance of a floating dollar, often referred to as a US dollar policy of "benign neglect." It was clear that the growing size of speculative international financial flows had complicated governments' efforts to peg currencies, forcing policymakers to reevaluate the merits of floating rates. In 1978, this new policy turn was reflected in an amendment of the IMF's Articles of Agreement, which legalized floating exchange rates, thus formally ending the adjustable peg system. In the 1980s, spurred by Volcker's high-interest-rate policy and a more open US capital market, the US economy attracted vast capital inflows which quickly led to an overvalued dollar, hurting US competitiveness while financing growing budget and current-account deficits. Those longer-term misalignments led to more coordinated depreciation of the US dollar and more managed exchange rates among the "Group of 5" (G5) nations of the United States, Japan, the United Kingdom, West Germany, and France,

resulting in the Plaza Agreement in 1985 and the Louvre Accord of 1987. This also increased monetary tensions between the United States, Europe, and Japan, with West Germany and Japan arguing that the United States was shifting the cost of adjustment squarely onto them.

The United States pushed for further trade liberalization in the GATT during the Tokyo Round (1973–1979) and the Uruguay Round, which started in 1987 but was only completed in 1994. The successful tariff reductions of the Kennedy Round in the 1960s were repeated in the Tokyo Round, with average reductions of about 35 percent of industrial nations' tariffs, but the focus of the Tokyo Round was on non-tariff barriers (NTBs) to trade. In contrast to previous GATT negotiations, the Tokyo Round was a rule-making exercise of major proportions, resulting in six legal codes covering customs procedures, import licensing, product standards, subsidies and countervailing duties, government procurement, and anti-dumping. The decision to launch a new trade round in the 1980s came after the United States argued that it was necessary to expand the GATT regime to keep it relevant in a changing world economy. The Reagan administration demanded the inclusion of new issues, such as services, investment, and intellectual property rights. Disagreement between developing and developed economies led to long negotiations, which were only completed well into the 1990s.

The 1980s also saw a new interest in the United States in regional trade agreements, given the apparent integration success of the European Community after the signing of the Single European Act in 1986, and selective government intervention to boost international competitiveness, which a growing body of research argued had played a crucial role in the Asian economic miracle. Reagan's free-market policies, after a rocky start during his first two years in office with another deep recession, seemed to have been successful, at first glance, by the middle of the 1980s. Inflation was down by the mid-1980s and the US economy grew quickly during the rest of the decade. But with exploding deficits and a growing debt burden due to beefed-up military budgets and multiple rounds of tax cuts, a persistent current account deficit with emerging Asia and Europe, a very brief episode of declinist fear returned. But that episode was soon put to rest by the fall of the Berlin Wall in 1989 and the final collapse of the Soviet Union in 1991. In the battle for the world economy, the United States, it seemed, had triumphed. The end of the Cold War meant that the ideological battle over how to run a modern economy was over, and a new "neoliberal" consensus on how to reap the full benefits of economic globalization gained widespread acceptance, and would soon come to be universally known as the "Washington Consensus."

Globalization, the New Economy, Blowing Bubbles, and the "Great Recession," 1991–2011. The end of the Cold War had profound consequences for the relationship between the United States and the world economy. From the early 1990s until 2001, the US economy was on a seemingly unstoppable path of high productivity growth, low inflation, and low unemployment, thanks to the swift application of information and communications technology, and America was easily outpacing its direct competitors in Europe and East Asia. Also, after the all-but-painless military victories in the 1990s over Saddam Hussein's Iraq in Kuwait, and over Slobodan Milosevic's Serbia in Bosnia and Kosovo, the US military had an air of invincibility about it, and the "peace dividend" that had come with the end of the Cold War allowed presidents George H. W. Bush and Bill Clinton to drastically cut back on military spending and put the country's fiscal house back in order. This resulted in a series of large federal budget surpluses by the end of the decade. In that "unipolar moment," American elites were enamored with the idea of a "new economy" and the end of the business cycle, convinced that America was the "indispensable nation" that could lead the world economy well into the future. All over the world, Clinton administration officials were touting the benefits of free trade, economic liberalization, and deregulation, convincing the formerly communist states to join the American-led international economic organizations such as the IMF, the World Bank, and the WTO.

The flip side of the two consecutive US booms was that the two decades following the end of the Cold War saw an unprecedented series of financial crises, including currency, banking, and financial crises (or combinations of all three) in places including Mexico, East Asia, Russia, Brazil, Turkey and Argentina. The Mexican peso crisis in 1994 forced the United States to intervene directly and put together a package of loans and guarantees totaling close to $50 billion, in concert with the IMF and the Bank for International Settlements (BIS). The Asian financial crisis in 1997 raised fears of a worldwide economic meltdown due to financial contagion, and also saw the IMF step in and put together "structural adjustment programs" for all affected Asian nations. In the meanwhile, with the advent of Europe's single currency, or euro, in 1999, the dollar was no longer the sole international reserve currency of choice. For the first time since the interwar period, international investors had an alternative to the greenback as reserve currency.

The bursting of the dot.com bubble at the end of 2000 and the terrorist attacks of September 11, 2001, would forever shake the country's sense of invulnerability. The economic downturn was quickly countered with aggressive monetary easing by Alan Greenspan's Federal Reserve and two consecutive rounds of fiscal expansion during the presidency of George W. Bush, combining large tax cuts for the relatively well-off with increases in defense spending to fight the "War on Terror," with initial quick successes in Afghanistan and Iraq. Winning the war, however, would prove easier than winning the peace. The Bush stimulus soon led to another boom, now in housing markets and financial products, made possible by the continuing policies of deregulation and fueled by cheap credit at home and large financial inflows from abroad, mainly China and Japan. The boom of the 2000s did not result in fiscal surpluses as they had in the 1990s, and the US current account went deeper into deficit every year. Eventually, the financial crisis of 2008—largely blamed on cheap credit and the reckless lending practices by Wall Street's major banks, which were made possible by the deregulatory ideas of the

Washington Consensus—plunged the United States and the world economy into its deepest recession since the Great Depression of the 1930s.

The "great crash of 2008" put into question, for the first time since 1945, whether the United States was fit to lead the world economy and whether it was in the rest of the world's interest to emulate Western economic ideas. In addition, the 2008 crisis saw renewed currency rivalries between emerging markets and developed economies, with the undervalued Chinese *Renminbi* a thorn in the side of the United States, given America's record bilateral trade deficit with China, largely blamed by the Americans on Chinese currency manipulation.

For international trade, the 1990s were a decade full of multilateral and regional trade activism. The United States joined Canada and Mexico in a regional trading bloc called the "North American Free Trade Agreement" (NAFTA), which went into effect in 1994. In Marrakesh, the Uruguay Round of the GATT was finalized in April 1994, after the United States and the European Union (EU) settled their differences on agricultural subsidies in a deal informally known as the "Blair House Accord." The various agreements reached at the Uruguay Round expanded the rules of the international trade system by including services, as well as trade-related investment measures (TRIMs) and intellectual property rights (TRIPs). The most obvious outcome of the Uruguay Round was the creation of the World Trade Organization (WTO), with a permanent secretariat in Geneva and the establishment of a formally integrated dispute settlement mechanism (DSM). The WTO was a victory for the rules-based, as opposed to power-based, approach to trade relations, with the United States giving up part of its sovereignty to a supranational organization. Both the establishment of the WTO and the creation of NAFTA were not without controversy, given the opposition of American labor and environmental groups fearing a global race toward the bottom. The Uruguay Round also was seen as detrimental to developing countries. To remedy that perception, the United States and the European Union decided to launch the Doha Round in 2001, calling it the "development round" of international trade. By 2011, the Doha Round still had not been concluded, because of differences between developed economies and emerging economies over the size of agricultural subsidies and market access for manufactures.

The War on Terror, apart from being a significant drain on the US federal budget, also left the United States engaged in two costly ground wars, in Afghanistan (since 2001) and Iraq (2003–2011). Given the fact that both wars were sold to the American public as relatively easy-to-win and necessary wars, the slow progress in both conflicts by 2011 laid bare the state-building weaknesses of America's military forces. While the Barack Obama administration tried to disengage from both conflicts, the United States also tried to lead the reform of the world's financial architecture under the auspices of the Group of 20 (G20), and to get the WTO to successfully complete negotiations over the Doha Round. Given the large budget deficits, growing since 2008, the Doha Round's deadlock, and the relatively modest Dodd-Frank financial reforms at home, the United States seems to prefer only moderate reform to the global financial architecture and bilateral trade deals.

Questions about the Future: The United States as a Frugal Superpower in a Multipolar World. The long-term federal budget question, given the future demands of an aging population, together with the need for fiscal austerity at home, has made the United States gradually turn more inward. The era of the "frugal superpower" has begun, and the ghost of decline has returned in the face of much faster growth in the emerging markets, especially in the two Asian giants, China and India, but also in Latin America and Southeast Asia. Previous certainties about America's role in the world economy have been called into question, such as the central role of the dollar, its quasi-veto power in international economic organizations, future US competitiveness in the face of rising economic powers in the East, and whether America can lead the next wave of technology in an age of austerity.

America still has many advantages over its direct competitors: its unique geography; a young and dynamic population; a relatively open policy toward immigration; the best universities in the world; flexible labor markets; continuing consumer strength thanks to its large domestic market; a positive attitude toward risk taking; and its resilience in the face of economic shocks. Despite the financial crisis, Wall Street still dominates the financial world, free market ideas are still in vogue in most parts of the world, and the country will be able to continue to borrow cheaply in world markets.

There are also disadvantages and future concerns, such as military overstretch; the limitations of democracy in making tough but necessary decisions; a huge debt overhang; largely structural current account deficits; energy dependence; unskilled-male unemployment; lagging competitiveness in industry and manufacturing; and to some extent, a lack of new ideas to replace the Washington Consensus.

America's future economic strength and competitiveness in the world economy will depend on how well the US economy will be able to deal with its own problems and reform its economic system from within. But, the main dilemma of the twenty-first century remains how America can manage to combine liberal institutions with a more traditional realpolitik-based system of power balancing.

[*See also* Economic Policy since World War II; Economy, American, since World War II; *and* Financial Crisis of 2008.]

BIBLIOGRAPHY

Bhagwati, Jagdish. "Regionalism and Multilateralism: An Overview." In *New Dimensions in Regional Integration*, edited by Jaime de Melo and Arvind Panagariya, pp. 22–51. (New York, 1993).

Calleo, David. *The Bankrupting of America: How the Federal Budget Is Impoverishing the Nation.* (New York, 1992).

Calleo, David. *Beyond American Hegemony: The Future of the Western Alliance.* (New York, 1987).

Calleo, David. *Follies of Power: America's Unipolar Fantasy.* (New York, 2009).

Calleo, David. *The Imperious Economy.* (Cambridge, Mass., 1982).

Carr, E. H. *The Twenty Years' Crisis, 1919–1939: An Introduction to the Study of International Relations.* (New York, 1939).

Chase-Dunn, Christopher, et al. "A Trajectory of the United States in the World-System: A Quantitative Reflection." *Sociological Perspectives* 48, no. 2 (2005) 233–254.

Eichengreen, Barry. *Exorbitant Privilege: The Rise and Fall of the Dollar and the Future of the International Monetary System.* (Oxford, 2011).

Fukuyama, Francis. *The End of History and the Last Man.* (New York, 1992).

Gilpin, Robert, and Jean M. Gilpin. *Global Political Economy: Understanding the Economic World Order.* (Princeton, N.J., 2011).

Gray, John. *False Dawn: The Delusions of Global Capitalism.* 2d rev. ed. (London, 2009).

Helleiner, Eric. "The Evolution of the International Monetary and Financial System." In *Global Political Economy*, 3d ed., edited by John Ravenhill, pp. 215–243. (Oxford, 2011).

Helleiner, Eric. *States and the Reemergence of Global Finance: From Bretton Woods to the 1990s.* (Ithaca, N.Y., 1994).

Kagan, Robert. *The Return of History and the End of Dreams.* (New York, 2008).

Kennedy, Paul. *The Rise and Fall of the Great Powers: Economic Change and Military Conflict from 1500 to 2000.* (New York, 1987).

Keohane, Robert O. *After Hegemony: Cooperation and Discord in the World Political Economy.* (Princeton, N.J., 1984).

Keynes, John Maynard. *The General Theory of Employment, Interest, and Money.* (London, 1936).

Kindleberger, Charles P. "Dominance and Leadership in the International Economy: Exploitation, Public Goods, and Free Rides." *International Studies Quarterly* 25, no. 2 (June 1981): 242–254.

Mandelbaum, Michael. (2010), *The Frugal Superpower: America's Global Leadership in a Cash-Strapped Era.* (New York, 2010).

Mandelbaum, Michael. *The Ideas That Conquered the World: Peace, Democracy, and Free Markets in the Twenty-First Century.* (New York, 2004).

Matthijs, Matthias. *Ideas and Economic Crises in Britain from Attlee to Blair (1945–2005).* (London, 2010).

Pauly, Louis. "The Political Economy of Global Financial Crises." In *Global Political Economy*, 3d ed., edited by John Ravenhill, pp. 244–272. (Oxford, 2011).

Reinhart, Carmen M., and Kenneth S. Rogoff. *This Time Is Different: Eight Centuries of Financial Folly.* (Princeton, N.J., 2009).

Ruggie, John Gerard. "International Regimes, Transactions, and Change: Embedded Liberalism in the Postwar Economic Order." *International Organization* 36, no. 2 (Spring 1982): 379–415.

Williamson, John. "What Washington Means by Policy Reform." In *Latin American Adjustment: How Much Has Happened?* edited by John Williamson, pp. 41–53. (Washington, D.C., 1990).

Winham, Gilbert. "The Evolution of the Global Trade Regime." In *Global Political Economy*, 3d ed., edited by John Ravenhill, pp. 137–172. (Oxford, 2011).

Matthias M. Matthijs

GLOBAL IMBALANCES AND INTERNATIONAL DEBT

International lending is a subset of international investment, and has long been a prominent feature of world economic and political affairs. Cross-border debts have been important to economic activity in many nations and have frequently given rise to domestic and international political conflict.

The economic principles of international lending are relatively straightforward. Loans across national borders normally respond to differences in rates of return: capital flows from where it is plentiful (and interest rates are low) to where it is scarce (and interest rates are high). From the standpoint of the investor, this difference in rates of return makes foreign lending attractive. However, these higher rates also reflect the generally greater risk of foreign, as compared to domestic, borrowers. If the foreign debtor refuses to service its debt, the creditor has fewer collection options than he does domestically—especially if the foreign debtor is a national government, because creditors cannot foreclose on a sovereign state. In return for accepting a higher degree of risk, foreign lenders demand a higher interest rate (that is, a higher risk premium).

From the standpoint of borrowing nations, such as the United States in the nineteenth century or most developing countries in the twentieth century, foreign loans have several interrelated effects. First, they increase the local supply of capital, allowing national investment to exceed savings. Second, they increase the supply of foreign currency, allowing national imports to exceed exports. Third, inasmuch as they are extended to governments, they increase

the financial resources of the public sector, allowing the government to spend more than it takes in.

Foreign loans generally make economic sense to the borrower if they serve, whether directly or indirectly, to increase national output and ability to export (or to produce previously imported goods). To repay foreign lenders eventually, the country must use loans to contribute to economic growth and the country's earnings of foreign currencies. This process can be indirect, but sooner or later loans must increase growth if they are to justify themselves. For example, borrowing might allow a government to increase spending on transportation infrastructure that is not directly productive, and does not directly increase exports, but that allows private economic agents to increase output and exports (perhaps by opening up access to new agricultural or mining regions).

In addition to the underlying economic relationship, international debt has important institutional features. Typically, a large proportion of international loans is made to governments: from the standpoint of a foreign lender, national governments are generally better credit risks than are national firms, which are themselves in any event subordinate to government control. Before 1965, most long-term loans were made in the form of bond flotations; since then, bank lending has also been important. In either instance the number of creditor financial institutions (investment banks or commercial banks) is generally small. International loan markets are often characterized by credit rationing, in which some countries are unable to borrow at any interest rate. This is due, among other things, to the fact that the ability of creditors to enforce contractual compliance on foreign governments is very limited in the absence of a binding judicial system, such as undergirds domestic financial relations. And, for reasons that are controversial, international lending tends to cycle through waves of boom and bust: generally, a ten- or twenty-year period of easy money is followed by an equivalent period of little lending.

The political implications of international debt are generally clearest when debt must be serviced (i.e., interest payments must be made, and principal must be repaid). At this point the favorable economic effects of capital inflow are reversed. The country must save more than it invests in order to send capital abroad; it must export more than it imports in order to send foreign currencies abroad; and its government must bring in more than it spends. These three adjustments can be painful, especially if they have to be undertaken rapidly.

The two most prominent modern experiences with international lending were in the interwar period, and since 1970. In the 1920s, US and British capital markets lent heavily to semi-industrial countries in central, eastern, and southern Europe and in Latin America. When the Great Depression of the 1930s hit and the prices of these countries' exports plunged, most of them defaulted on their debts amid great domestic and international political turmoil. Since 1970, international banks and investors have lent hundreds of billions of dollars to developing countries. Such countries as Brazil, Mexico, and the Republic of Korea (South Korea) grew very rapidly at least in part because of the availability of ample foreign finance.

This lending was interrupted in the early 1980s, when interest rates rose dramatically amid a generalized recession. As a result, many debtors did not make payments, once more against the backdrop of domestic and international political turmoil. Indeed, most of Latin America spent the 1980s mired in recession, inflation, and political conflict, as the debt burden exacted an enormous socioeconomic and political toll. The resumption of lending in the 1990s was also punctuated by crises in Mexico and East Asia.

The global politics of international debt are dominated by the complexity of enforcing property rights, such as the creditor's contractual right to debt service payments, across national borders and against sovereign governments. Creditors have tried to induce compliance by debtors through a number of methods. One is military force: in the pre–World War II era, military intervention by home governments of creditors—up to and including direct colonialism—sometimes served to enforce contracts (although whether debt problems were important causes of such intervention is controversial). China, Egypt, and the Caribbean are among the regions in which foreign military interference was associated with foreign lending. Another is the formation of clubs or committees by a country's creditors, which can collaborate to use such economic threats as a cutoff of future loans or trade credits to bring pressure to bear. A third option, common over the last few decades, is to rely on an international organization such as the International Monetary Fund (IMF) to monitor and attempt to enforce loan contracts.

In the final analysis, however, the absence of an international bankruptcy court means that resolution of debt problems depends on the interaction of the two sides involved. When debt comes due, debtors wish to pay as little as possible, while creditors want to receive as much as possible. Debtors threaten to reduce or halt debt service payments. Creditors threaten to seize assets the debtor may have overseas (the national airline's airplanes, bank deposits), or to exclude the debtor from future borrowing, or to retaliate by other means; sometimes they offer new loans or other side payments as an incentive to encourage the debtor to honor past obligations.

Careful studies have found that over the very long run (decades or more) and on average, debt problems are bargained out to where the final rate of return on the loan, taking into account unpaid interest and principal, ends up being roughly equivalent to the return on domestic financial assets. This is evidence that, in the final analysis, international loan markets are relatively efficient, in that risk premiums charged to borrowers that may default tend, on average, to reflect the actual probability of default.

Hostilities between debtors and creditors can affect broader political relations among nations, and are sometimes blamed for wars both small and large-scale. In the 1930s, the heavy economic burden of foreign debts contributed to the rise of highly nationalistic, often fascistic, movements in central, eastern, and southern Europe, and to the resentment of these countries and their populations toward the creditor nations of western Europe and North America. The debt crisis of the 1980s exacerbated North-South political tensions, as many in the developing world felt that they were suffering solely to line the coffers of international banks.

In addition to international conflict over the distribution of costs and benefits involved in international lending, there are many analogous domestic disputes. There is no guarantee that those within a borrowing nation who benefit from foreign loans are the ones who will be asked to sacrifice to repay them. Foreign finance can go toward reducing borrowing costs for industry, for example, while the resources to service this debt can be extracted from agriculture. Such domestic distributional patterns are sure to give rise to political struggles.

Just as foreign borrowing tends to increase the domestic supply of capital and foreign exchange, making loans and imports cheaper, the need to service debt reduces this supply, making loans and imports more expensive. By the same token, inasmuch as foreign borrowing by the government allows it to provide more services with lower taxes, servicing debt requires a curtailment of public services and increased taxes. Those who had, during borrowing, come to rely on inexpensive loans and imports, and on government services, can be expected to protest the reversal, as can those required to pay higher taxes.

The requirements of foreign debt service can impose severe burdens on debtor societies. The need to raise funds for service of the foreign debt is often associated with domestic depressions, severe unemployment, and spiraling inflation. Debt problems were factors in the dismal economic performance of Latin America in the 1980s and Southeast Asia in the 1990s. Issues related to the foreign debt have been central to political turmoil, the collapse of authoritarian regimes, and pressures to undertake politically difficult economic reforms.

The domestic and international politics of foreign debt interact. In a country burdened with costly debt service payments, those economic interest groups hardest hit by the impact of these payments clamor for the government to take a tougher stance against its creditors—to shift some of the burden onto foreigners. Such demands are countered by other domestic economic interest groups, who may rely on their ties with overseas markets or who are concerned about the precedent set by government disregard for private property rights. At the same time, creditors press the debtor government for prompt and full debt service payments with whatever means they have at their disposal.

In the midst of a full-fledged debt crisis, such as those involving many semi-industrial countries in the 1930s and the 1980s, a swirling spiral of domestic and international political conflict can cause great political and economic instability. International debt issues exacerbated domestic and international conflict during the Great Depression, while the debt crisis of the 1980s also saw major changes in domestic politics and foreign policies throughout the developing world.

For most of modern economic history, the principal international borrowers have been relatively poor countries in the process of rapid economic development, and the principal lenders have been relatively rich countries. But since about 1980, many rich nations have become major foreign debtors, and they have borrowed from both rich and poor countries alike. The most prominent example of this is the experience of the United States.

After 1980, in the aftermath of substantial tax cuts, the US government began running large budget deficits. Much of this deficit spending was financed by borrowing from abroad. Deficits continued, and the federal government's debt grew continually, for over ten years. In the middle and late 1990s, a combination of spending cuts and tax increases succeeded in balancing the budget and even created a large surplus by the year 2000. But in 2001 a new round of tax cuts plunged the federal budget into deficit again, and began another substantial increase in foreign borrowing. It was not just the federal government that borrowed overseas: foreigners lent substantially to American corporations during the 1996–2000 boom in information technologies, and to American banks and households during the 2002–2007 housing finance boom. As is typically the case, this foreign borrowing was uncontroversial so long as the national economy was growing.

In 2007, as the American housing boom collapsed, the issue of the country's foreign debt came to the fore. One issue was the longer-term implications of a multi-trillion-dollar debt owed to foreigners and foreign institutions. This was of special concern because many believed that the borrowed funds had not been used particularly wisely, that is, in ways that contributed to the nation's productive capacity. Another issue was the fact that much of the debt was owed to the Chinese government. This last issue raised fears on two counts. First, there was some fear that this might give an authoritarian government undue leverage over the United States. Second, there was a widespread view that China's lending was in large part due to its manipulation of its currency to give its exports an advantage in American markets. Both the economic and the national-security implications of America's debt to China—and more broadly to foreigners in general—contributed to the kinds of political conflicts over foreign debt that had previously been more characteristic of developing countries.

Foreign loans can be important contributors to economic development, and international financial flows are an important component part of an integrated international economy more generally. However, international debt is inherently political, and frequently conflictual. Economic and political factors interact to determine whether foreign debt will be an unproblematic contribution to national development and international economic growth, or the cause of major domestic and international political strife.

[*See also* Finance, International; *and* Financial Crisis of 2008.]

BIBLIOGRAPHY

Chinn, Menzie David, and Jeffry A. Frieden. *Lost Decades: The Making of America's Debt Crisis and the Long Recovery.* (New York, 2011).

Cline, William R. *International Debt Reexamined.* (Washington, D.C., 1995).

Sachs, Jeffrey, ed. *Developing Country Debt and Economic Performance.* (Chicago, 1989).

Stallings, Barbara, and Robert Kaufman, eds. *Debt and Democracy in Latin America.* (Boulder, Colo., 1989).

Jeffry A. Frieden

GLOBALIZATION

Globalization can be conceived as a process (or set of processes) that embodies a transformation in the spatial organization of social relations and transactions, expressed in transcontinental or interregional flows and networks of activity, interaction, and power. It is characterized by four types of changes. First, it involves a *stretching* of social, political, and economic activities across frontiers, regions, and continents. Second, it is marked by the *intensification*, or the growing magnitude, of interconnectedness and flows of trade, investment, finance, migration, and culture. Third, it can be linked to a *speeding up* of global interactions and processes, as the development of worldwide systems of transport and communication increases the *velocity* of the diffusion of ideas, goods, information, capital, and people. And, fourth, the growing *extensity, intensity*, and *velocity* of global interactions can be associated with their deepening *impact,* such that the effects of distant events can be highly significant across the world, and specific local developments can come to have considerable global consequences. In this sense, the boundaries between domestic matters and global affairs become increasingly fluid. Globalization, in short, can be thought of as the widening, intensifying, speeding up, and growing impact of worldwide interconnectedness.

Three broad accounts of the nature and meaning of globalization can be identified, referred to here as the hyperglobalist view, the skeptical view, and the transformationalist view. These define the conceptual space of the current intensive debate about globalization.

The Hyperglobalists. What distinguishes the present era from the past, argue the hyperglobalists, is the existence of a single global economy transcending and integrating the world's major economic regions. In variously referring to "manic capitalism," "turbo-capitalism," or "supraterritorial capitalism," these globalists seek to capture the qualitative shift occurring in the spatial organization and dynamics of a new global, capitalist formation. Inscribed in the dynamics of this new global capitalism is, they argue, an irresistible imperative toward the denationalization of strategic economic activities. Today it is global finance and corporate capital, rather than individual states, that exercise decisive influence over the organization, location, and distribution of economic power and wealth.

Since the authority of states is territorially bound, global markets can escape effective political regulation. In this borderless economy, states have no option other than to accommodate global market forces. Moreover, the existing multilateral institutions of global economic surveillance—especially the Group of 7 (G-7), the International Monetary Fund (IMF), the World Bank (WB), and the World Trade Organization (WTO)—largely function to nurture this nascent "global market civilization."

In this "runaway world," nation states are becoming "transitional modes of economic organization and regulation," since they can no longer effectively manage or regulate their own national economies. Economic globalization spells the end of the welfare state and social democracy. In effect, the hyperglobalists hold, the autonomy and sovereignty of nation-states have been eclipsed by contemporary processes of economic globalization.

The Skeptics. By comparison, the skeptical position is much more cautious about the revolutionary character of globalization. While generally recognizing that recent decades have witnessed a considerable intensification of international interdependence, the skeptical interpretation disputes its novelty. By comparison with the belle epoque of 1890–1914, the intensity of contemporary global interdependence is considerably exaggerated. Moreover, the spatially concentrated nature of actual patterns of economic interdependence suggest that globalization is primarily a phenomenon largely confined to the major Organisation for Economic Co-Operation and Development (OECD) member-states. Further, these states have been the very

architects of a more open liberal international economy. Dismissing the idea of a unified global economy, the skeptical position concludes that the world is breaking up into several major economic and political blocs, within which very different forms of capitalism continue to flourish. The emphasis upon footloose capital and a new global capitalist order is overstated, as is the decline of the welfare state. Rather than a new world order, the post–Cold War global system has witnessed a return to old-style geopolitics and neo-imperialism, through which the most powerful states and social forces have consolidated their global dominance. In presuming the novelty of the present, so the skeptical position suggests, the hyperglobalists ignore the continued primacy of national power and sovereignty.

What is to be made of these accounts? Are we on the edge of a fundamental global shift in the world order? Or is the narrative of globalization simply mere rhetoric? Is a productive synthesis between these two positions possible?

An Intermediate Way: The Transformationalist Analysis. To begin with, it is crucial to acknowledge that globalization does not simply denote a shift in the extensity or scale of social relations and activity. Much more significantly, argue the transformationalists, it also involves the spatial reorganization and rearticulation of economic, political, military, and cultural power. The current debate about globalization ought primarily to be about the question of power: its modalities, instrumentalities, organization, and distribution. Globalization can thus be understood as involving a shift or transformation in the scale of human social organization that extends the reach of power relations across the world's major regions and continents. It implies a world in which developments in one region can come to shape the lives of communities in distant parts of the globe. Highly uneven in its embrace and impact, it divides as it integrates. Globalization may mean a shrinking world for some, but for the majority it creates a distancing, or profound disembedding, of power relations. As the East Asian crisis of 1997–1998 demonstrated, key sites of global power can be quite literally oceans apart from the subjects and communities whose future they determine.

Globalization too has to be understood as a multidimensional process which is not reducible to an economic logic, and which has differential impacts across the world's regions and upon individual states. It is not a novel process, but rather has a long history—from the age of premodern empire building to the contemporary era of corporate empires. Of course, its contemporary articulation has many unique and distinctive attributes—not least among them near real time communication.

Historically, globalization has always been, and remains, a vigorously contested process—from the struggles against slavery and the movements for national independence to the more recent global protest against the WTO's millennium trade round. Indeed, it can be argued that across many domains—from the cultural to the technological—globalization has contributed to a remarkable politicization of social life, while also creating new modalities and institutional arenas through which its imperatives are contested. Such developments are most in evidence with respect to economic and political globalization.

Economic Globalization. Contemporary patterns of economic globalization have been strongly associated with a reframing of the relationship between states and markets. Although the global economy as a single entity is by no means as highly integrated as the most robust national economies, the trends point unambiguously toward intensifying integration within and across regions. Patterns of contemporary economic globalization have woven strong and enduring webs across the world's major regions, such that their economic fate is intimately connected. Levels of interregional trade are largely unprecedented, while the forms that such trade takes have changed considerably. Despite the fact that there is a tendency to exaggerate the power of global financial markets, ignoring the centrality of states to sustaining their effective operation, especially in times of crisis, there is much compelling evidence to suggest that contemporary financial globalization is a market-driven, rather than a state-driven, phenomenon. Reinforced by financial liberalization, the accompanying shift toward markets and private financial institutions as the "authoritative actors" in the global financial system poses serious questions about the nature of state power and economic sovereignty.

Alongside financial integration, the operations of multinational corporations integrate national and local economies into global and regional production networks. Under these conditions, national economies no longer function as autonomous systems of wealth creation, because national borders are no longer significant barriers to the conduct and organization of economic activity. The distinction between domestic economic activity and worldwide economic activity (as the range of products in any superstore will confirm) is becoming increasingly difficult to sustain.

Central to the organization of this new global capitalist order is the multinational corporation. In 1999, there were over 60,000 multinational corporations worldwide with 500,000 foreign subsidiaries, selling $9.5 trillion of goods and services across the globe. Today, transnational production considerably exceeds the level of global exports, and has become the primary means for selling goods and services abroad. Multinational corporations now account, according to some estimates, for at least 20 percent of world production and 70 percent of world trade. It is global corporate capital, rather than the state, which exercises decisive influence over the organization, location, and distribution of economic power and resources in the contemporary global economy.

Contemporary patterns of economic globalization have been accompanied by a new global division of labor brought about, in part, by the activities of multinationals themselves. Developing countries are being reordered into clear winners and losers, as the experience of the East Asian Tiger economies shows. Such restructuring is, moreover, replicated within countries, both North and South, as communities and particular locales closely integrated into global production networks reap significant rewards, while the rest struggle at the margins. Economic globalization has brought with it an increasingly unified world for elites—national, regional, and global—but divided nations and communities as the global workforce is segmented, within rich and poor countries alike, into winners and losers.

Furthermore, the globalization of economic activity exceeds the regulatory reach of national governments while, at the same time, existing multilateral institutions of global economic governance have limited authority because states, still jealously guarding their national sovereignty, refuse to cede these institutions substantial power. Under such conditions, global markets may effectively escape political regulation. For the most part, the governance structures of the global economy operate principally to nurture and reproduce the forces of economic globalization, while also serving to discipline and streamline this nascent "global market civilization." Yet, in some contexts, these governance structures may carve out considerable autonomy from the dictates of global capital or the G-7 states. Hence, multilateral institutions have become increasingly important sites through which economic globalization is contested, both by weaker states and by the agencies of transnational civil society. The G-7 states and representatives of global capital have found themselves on many occasions at odds with collective decisions or rule making. Moreover, the political dynamics of multilateral institutions tend to mediate great power control—for instance through consensual modes of decision-making—such that they are never merely tools of dominant states and particular social groupings.

Alongside these global institutions, there also exists a parallel set of regional bodies, from Asia-Pacific Economic Cooperation (APEC) to the European Union (EU), which represent an additional attempt to shift the terms of engagement with global market forces. Within the interstices of this system operate the social groups of an emerging transnational civil society, from the International Chamber of Commerce to the Jubilee 2000 campaign, seeking to promote, or to contest and bring to account, the agencies of economic globalization. Economic globalization has been accompanied by a significant internationalization of political authority associated with a corresponding globalization of political activity.

Political Globalization. Two fundamental transformations have shaped the constitution of contemporary political life. The first of these involved the development of territorially based political communities—that is, modern nation-states. The second, more recent transformation has by no means replaced the first in all respects, but it has led to a break in the exclusive link between geography and political power. It can be illustrated by a number of developments.

In the first instance, there has been an institutionalization of a fragile system of multilayered global and regional governance. At the beginning of the twentieth century there were thirty-seven intergovernmental organizations (IGOs). By the close of the century, nearly three hundred were delivering important global or regional collective goods. This multilateral system institutionalizes a process of political coordination among governments, and intergovernmental and transnational agencies—both public and private—designed to realize common purposes or collective goods through making or implementing global or transnational rules, and managing transborder problems (e.g., the WTO). Of course, it is scarred by enormous inequalities of power, and remains a product of the interstate system. But it has, nevertheless, created the infrastructure of a global polity and new arenas through which globalization itself is promoted, contested, or regulated. It has also instigated new forms of multilateral, regional, and transnational politics.

A remarkable transnationalization of political activity has been associated with this internationalization of the state. In 1909 there were 371 officially recognized, international, nongovernmental organizations (INGOs); by 2000 there were approximately 25,000 (including the International Chamber of Commerce, the International Confederation of Free Trade Unions, and Greenpeace International). These include a proliferation of associations, social movements, advocacy networks—from the women's movement to Nazis on the Internet—and citizens groups mobilizing, organizing, and exercising people power across national boundaries. This explosion of "citizen diplomacy" creates the basis of communities of interest or association that span national borders, with the purpose of advancing mutual goals or bringing governments and the formal institutions of global governance to account for their activities. Whether it constitutes the infrastructure of a translational civil society remains open to debate.

There has, moreover, been an important change in the scope and content of international law. Twentieth-century forms of international law—from the law governing war to those concerning crimes against humanity, environmental issues, and human rights—have created the basis of an emerging framework of "cosmopolitan law," that is, law that circumscribes and delimits the political power of individual states. In principle, states are no longer able to treat their citizens as they think fit. Although, in practice, many states still violate these standards, nearly all now accept general duties of protection and provision, as well as of restraint, in their own practices and procedures. This internalization or nationalization of international law has been evident in other areas too. There has, for instance, been an explosive growth of private international and commercial law. These developments have encouraged what some legal scholars refer to as a shift from a monistic conception to a polycentric conception of legal sovereignty.

As governments and their citizens have become embedded in more expansive networks and layers of regional and global governance, they have become subject to new loci of authority above, below, and alongside the state. Indeed, the form and intensity of contemporary political globalization poses a profound challenge to the Westphalian "states as containers" view of political life. In particular, political space and political community are no longer coterminous with national territory, and national governments can no longer be regarded as the sole masters of their own or their citizens' fate. But this does not mean that national governments or national sovereignty have been eclipsed by the forces of political globalization; the state is not in decline, as many hyperglobalists suggest.

Globalization and the Transformation of Political Community. Contemporary globalization is associated with a transformation of state power, as the roles and functions of states are rearticulated, reconstituted, and re-embedded at the intersection of globalizing and regionalizing networks and systems. The metaphors of the loss, diminution, or erosion of state power can misrepresent this reconfiguration. For while globalization is engendering, for instance, a reconfiguration of state–market relations in the economic domain, states and international public authorities are deeply implicated in this very process. Economic globalization by no means necessarily translates into a diminution of state power; rather, it is transforming the conditions under which state power is exercised. Moreover, in other domains, such as the environmental, states have adopted a more activist posture, while in the political domain they have been central to the explosive growth and institutionalization of regional and global governance. These are not developments which can be explained convincingly through the language of the decline, erosion, or loss of state power, because such metaphors (mistakenly) presume that state power was much greater in previous epochs. On almost every conceivable measure, states, especially in the developed world, are far more powerful than their antecedents. So too are the demands placed upon them. The apparent simultaneous weakening and expansion in the power of states under conditions of contemporary globalization is symptomatic of an underlying structural transformation. This is nowhere so evident as in state sovereignty and autonomy, which constitute the very ideological foundations of the modern state.

There are many good reasons for doubting the theoretical and empirical basis of claims that states are being eclipsed by contemporary patterns of globalization. It should be emphasized that, while regional and global interaction networks are strengthening, they have multiple and variable impacts across diverse locales.

Neither the sovereignty nor the autonomy of states are simply diminished by such processes. Indeed, any assessment of the cumulative impacts of globalization must acknowledge their highly differentiated characters, because they are not experienced uniformly by all states. Globalization is by no means a homogenizing force. The impact of globalization is mediated significantly by a state's position in global political, military, and economic hierarchies; its domestic economic and political structures; the institutional pattern of domestic politics; and specific government as well as societal strategies for contesting, managing, or ameliorating globalizing imperatives. The ongoing transformation of the Westphalian regime of sovereignty and autonomy has differential consequences for different states.

While, for many hyperglobalizers, contemporary globalization is associated with new limits to politics and the erosion of state power, the transformationalist argument developed here is critical of such political fatalism. For contemporary globalization has not only triggered and encouraged a significant politicization of a growing array of issue-areas, but has also been accompanied by an extraordinary growth of institutionalized arenas and networks of political mobilization, surveillance, decision-making, and regulatory activity which transcend national political jurisdictions. This has expanded enormously the capacity for, and scope of, political activity and the exercise of political authority. Neither the hyperglobalists nor the skeptics provide the proper conceptual resources to grasp this. Globalization does not prefigure the "end of politics," nor the simple persistence of old state ways; instead, it signals the continuation of politics by new means. Yet, this is not to overlook the profound intellectual, institutional, and normative challenges which it presents to the organization of modern political communities.

Political communities are in the process of being transformed. At the heart of this lies a growth in transborder political issues and problems which erode clear-cut distinctions between domestic and foreign affairs, internal political issues and external questions, the sovereign concerns of the nation-state, and international considerations. In nearly all major areas of public policy, the enmeshment of national political communities in regional and global processes involves them in intensive issues of transboundary coordination and regulation. Political space for the development and pursuit of effective government and the accountability of political power is no longer coterminous with a delimited national territory. The growth of transboundary problems creates "overlapping communities of fate"—that is, a state of affairs in which the fortune and prospects of individual political communities are increasingly bound together. Political communities are locked into a diversity of processes and structures which range in and through them, linking and fragmenting them into complex constellations. National governments by no means simply determine what is right or appropriate exclusively for their own citizens.

This condition is most apparent in Europe, where the development of the European Union has created intensive discussion about the future of national sovereignty and autonomy. But the issues are important not just for Europe and the West, but for countries in other parts of the world, for example, Japan and the Republic of Korea (South Korea). These countries must recognize new emerging problems, for instance, problems concerning AIDS, migration, and new challenges to peace, security, and economic prosperity, which spill over the boundaries of nation-states. There are emerging overlapping communities of fate generating common problems within and across the East Asian region.

Political communities today are no longer discrete worlds. Growing enmeshment in regional and global orders, and the proliferation of transborder problems, has created a plurality of diverse and overlapping collectives which span borders, binding together directly and indirectly the fates of communities in different locations and regions of the globe. In this context the articulation of the public good is pried away from its embeddedness in the bounded political community: it is being reconfigured in the context of global, regional, and transnational orders. The contemporary world is no longer "a world of closed communities with mutually impenetrable ways of thought, self-sufficient economies and ideally sovereign states" (O'Neill, 1991, p. 282). This is not to assert that territorial political communities are becoming obsolete but, rather, to recognize that they are nested within global, regional, and transnational communities of fate, identity, association, and solidarity. Political community today is being transformed to accord with a world of "ruptured boundaries."

[*See also* Capitalism; Finance, International; Non-governmental Organizations; *and* World Trade Organization.]

BIBLIOGRAPHY

Held, David, et al. *Global Transformations: Politics, Economics and Culture.* (Cambridge, UK, 1991).

Hirst, Paul Q., and Grahame Thompson. *Globalization in Question.* 2d ed. (Cambridge, UK, 1999).

Ōmae, Ken'ichi. *The Borderless World: Power and Strategy in the Interlinked Economy.* (New York, 1990).

O'Neill, O. "Transnational Justice." In *Political Theory Today*, edited by David Held. (Cambridge, UK, 1991).

David Held and Anthony McGrew

GOVERNMENT-SPONSORED ENTERPRISES

The government-sponsored enterprise (GSE) is an enterprise that is neither purely private nor purely public. Examples of GSEs include Fannie Mae, Freddie Mac, Sallie Mae, Amtrak, and the US Postal Service. The United States has a long history of hybrid institutions. For example, while railroads were built by private companies in the nineteenth century, they were financed in part by land grants from the United States government and in part by bonds backed by the United States government.

The most well-known government-sponsored enterprises, Fannie Mae and Freddie Mac, had their roots in the Great Depression. The financial crash led the US government to invent at least five housing-related financial institutions: the Federal Home Loan Bank system, the Home Owners Loan Corporation, the Federal Housing Administration, the Federal National Mortgage Association, and the Federal Deposit Insurance Corporation. These institutions were developed to stabilize a banking system that was on the verge of moving from a horrible condition to a catastrophic condition. One might argue that these were policy responses to a legitimate problem and therefore were not "political." But both the Herbert Hoover administration—which brought about the Federal Home Loan Banks—and

the Franklin D. Roosevelt administration felt hamstrung by the demands of banks. Lenders rarely modified loans in a meaningful way during the 1930s. Just as is the case today, from the perspective of individual lenders, it might have made sense for banks not to provide debtor relief, but from the standpoint of the market as a whole, debtor relief was crucial to restarting the market.

The fact that the Federal Home Loan Banks were a creature of the Hoover administration suggests how desperate public officials were in the 1930s. Hoover and his treasury secretary, Andrew Mellon, are often viewed as paragons of laissez-faire policy. Yet the Federal Home Loan Bank system represented an enormous government intervention into private markets.

The Federal Home Loan Bank system was set up as a cooperative of member institutions, all of whom owned equity in the system, which was largely funded by government-backed debt. Members could draw advances from the system to finance mortgages when other sources of such funds were not available. It was similar to the Reconstruction Finance Corporation, which provided similar arrangements for the funding of infrastructure.

The most remarkable institution of the time, from a public-choice standpoint, was the Home Owners Loan Corporation (HOLC). This entity could raise money with government backing through capital markets. It used the capital it raised to buy nonperforming mortgages from troubled lenders. While this helped inject capital into lender balance sheets, it also required lenders to realize losses, as the HOLC purchased loans at a discount. Many of the loans had what are known as "maturity defaults": borrowers had kept current on their payments, but when their loan balances came due, they were unable to obtain funds to pay them off. The HOLC reinstated the loans and allowed them to amortize over fifteen years, which at the time was a long period. The HOLC conducted this business for two years, and then stopped; it ran off its portfolio of loans as they got paid off over the next fifteen years, and then put itself out of business in 1951. On net, it returned more money to taxpayers than it cost them.

The Federal National Mortgage Association (FNMA), the predecessor to Fannie Mae, was in many respects the successor to HOLC. Founded in 1938, the FNMA was created to raise capital for mortgages that were insured by another government-sponsored enterprise, the Federal Housing Administration, or FHA (this would be expanded in 1949 to both FHA and Veterans Administration loans). The Federal Housing Administration insured loans against default. Borrowers paid a premium that went into a fund that would hold lenders harmless against losses arising from loans that did not fully pay off.

The FNMA was actually a government agency until 1954, at which point it became a "public-private" entity, where lenders drawing on funds from the FNMA were required to be common shareholders in the organization. Nevertheless, Fannie Mae was quite small until 1966, when a liquidity crisis in mortgages led lenders to turn to the FNMA for funding. The reason lenders needed to turn to the FNMA is that depositors were fleeing banks and savings and loans, the principal sources of mortgage finance. The exodus arose because deposit ceilings prevented depositories from paying competitive interest rates in a market where short-term rates rose above 4 percent for the first time after the Great Depression. The FNMA could pay its bonds holders a market rate of interest, and so could raise the funds necessary to finance mortgages. An alternative policy available to Congress would have been to eliminate ceilings on deposits, but that would not happen until 1980, with the passage of the Depository Institutions Deregulation and Monetary Control Act.

Even if depositories were allowed to pay market interest rates, however, the mortgage business would have faced difficulty in 1966, as the rates they would have needed to pay on deposits would have sharply reduced the profitability of the long-term mortgages they already held. By this time, Americans were used to obtaining long-term, fixed-rate housing finance, something that made America quite unusual. Among the few other countries that offered long-term, fixed-rate mortgages were Germany and Denmark—countries that, not coincidentally, relied on capital markets rather than depositories for mortgages.

The larger role played by the FNMA in mortgage markets led Congress and the Lyndon Johnson administration to amend its charter. The FNMA was split into two parts: public-sector Ginnie Mae (for Government National Mortgage Association) and private-sector Fannie Mae. Ginnie Mae's role would be a continuation of Fannie Mae's old role—it would purchase FHA and VA loans, and have the full backing of the United States government. The privatized Fannie Mae would now be responsible for raising money in private markets to fund private loans that it would hold in its own portfolio. Some have argued that President Johnson was concerned that Fannie Mae's growth was weakening the national balance sheet, and so he wanted Fannie Mae's debt to be private. That said, Fannie Mae's history created ambiguity in the minds of investors about whether it was truly private or whether it was backed by the government. W. Scott Frame and Lawrence White (2005) suggest that Fannie and Freddie took advantage of this ambiguity, telling Congress that they were really private but winking to investors that they in fact had the backing of the US government, and that capital markets believed that they had the backing of the US government. In any event, they ultimately became so large that, like Bank of America and Citibank, they were considered "too big to fail" when the financial crisis of 2008 hit the United States.

The fact that Fannie Mae was joined by a competitor, Freddie Mac, is also an artifact of politics. While some sources maintain that Freddie Mac was invented to "compete" with Fannie Mae, it was at the beginning a somewhat different institution than Fannie. Fannie Mae was always a portfolio lender—it would buy and hold loans. At its beginning, Freddie Mac essentially filled a brokerage function, allowing savings and loans to trade money for loans. The privatization of Fannie Mae, a national lender, led savings and loans, who were local lenders, to worry that they could not compete. Savings and loans associations implored Congress to set up an institution that would allow savings and loans with excess deposits to purchase mortgages from savings and loans with insufficient deposits. Freddie Mac was set up for just this purpose.

In 1971, Freddie Mac revolutionized the mortgage business by offering the first conventional (i.e. non-government-backed) mortgage security, the Mortgage Participation Certificate (PC). Freddie bundled together mortgages it purchased from savings and loans and stitched them together into a security that investors could purchase. This accomplished two things. First, it brought diversification benefits to investors: owning one-thirtieth of thirty mortgages is less risky than owning a single mortgage. Second, it brought liquidity to the mortgage market. At the time, Freddie imposed strict underwriting standards on the loans it would purchase, and as such, the loans it purchased were homogenous. This made mortgage securities commodities, and led them to be liquid. Fannie Mae then followed suit with a guaranteed mortgage-backed security of its own.

Freddie and Fannie were not well-known institutions until Fannie Mae ran into financial trouble in the early 1980s. Fannie alone became troubled because it was a portfolio lender, and was as such subject to interest rate risk. For the period 1979 to 1981, the Treasury yield curve was strongly inverted: short-term interest rates were considerably higher than long-term interest rates. This meant that any institutions that used short-term funding for long-term assets would become troubled. Savings and loans essentially became insolvent, as did Fannie Mae. Congress made a deliberate decision to engage in forbearance. With savings and loans, Congress did not just forbear—it doubled down, so to speak, allowing savings and loans to move into risky businesses that they had previously been forbidden from entering. In the case of Fannie Mae, Congress simply hoped that short-term interest rates would fall, the yield curve would become more normal, and Fannie would return to solvency. The treatment of the savings and loans turned failure into worse failure, as executives who could privatize gains and socialize losses did so. In the case of Fannie Mae, however, patience proved a virtue; when the yield curve returned to normal, Fannie returned to solvency.

From the mid-1980s through the late 1990s, Fannie Mae and Freddie Mac were celebrated, if not beloved, for connecting capital markets with individual borrowers. The institutions had allies. Depositories liked Fannie and Freddie, because the GSEs allowed them to move loans off their balance sheets. Private mortgage insurance companies liked them, because all Fannie and Freddie loans that had loan-to-value ratios in excess of 80 percent were required to carry private mortgage insurance.

It is difficult to pinpoint the precise moment when Fannie and Freddie's downfall began, but it was likely around the time of the long-term capital management crisis of 1998. During this period, spreads on all types of lending widened dramatically, with one exception: home mortgage lending. Both Fannie Mae and Freddie Mac saw even small changes in spreads as profit opportunities. Because investors perceived that Fannie and Freddie had government backing, the GSEs could raise money in capital markets at low cost. They began purchasing and retaining mortgages in large numbers: the size of Fannie Mae's portfolio increased from a little under $100 billion in 1986 to $1 trillion in 2003; Freddie's increased thirty-five times, from $23 billion to $803 billion, over the same period. The business proved highly profitable, as both institutions had very low capital requirements. While banks needed overall capital of 8 percent to be adequately capitalized, Fannie and Freddie needed to hold capital of only 2.5 percent against their portfolios. Both companies had teams of lobbyists to assure that they would retain their favorable capital position. Freddie Mac's management promised shareholders double-digit earnings growth: portfolio growth along with leverage allowed management to deliver.

Yet the GSEs also overreached. For example, they attempted to persuade Congress that private mortgage insurance companies did not need to insure high loan-to-value ratio loans. This, along with the GSEs' use of their "implicit guarantee," began to produce a lobbying backlash. A number of large banks set up an organization called FM Watch, whose purpose was to underscore the systemic risk the GSEs were creating by virtue of their increasing size. Ironically, FM Watch emphasized the danger endemic in interest rate risk; in the end, it would be credit risk that would lead to the companies' fall.

In any event, the GSE's profitability may have led to hubristic decisions on the part of both companies to fudge their earning numbers in their reports to shareholders. This led to accounting scandals and the eventual ouster of both companies' senior management, as well as higher capital requirements. The higher capital standards led to some retrenchment, which may have produced the vacuum into which private label securities—the purely private counterpart to Fannie and Freddie mortgage-backed securities—leapt.

Between 2001 and 2004, the market share of Fannie Mae and Freddie Mac mortgage-backed securities dropped substantially. In 2001, outstanding mortgage debt in the United States grew by $707 billion; Fannie and Freddie mortgage-backed securities grew by $339 billion. In 2004, however, Fannie and Freddie mortgage-backed securities contributed only $40.8 billion of the $1.3 trillion in net new mortgages. The new senior management of the companies, seeing their market share deteriorate, began purchasing private label securities, which undermined the credit quality of their portfolios. When the US housing market collapsed in 2007 and 2008, so did the financial position of the GSEs, which led to a government conservatorship beginning on 6 September 2008.

In the end, the government committed to backing Fannie Mae and Freddie Mac debt, at least in part because many central banks around the world had purchased their debt and mortgage-backed securities.

[*See also* Housing in the United States; *and* Mortgage-Backed Securities.]

BIBLIOGRAPHY

Federal Housing Finance Agency. "Annual Report to Congress." (2011).

Frame, W. Scott, and Lawrence White. "Fussing and Fuming over Fannie and Freddie: How Much Smoke, How Much Fire." *Journal of Economic Perspectives* 19, no. 2 (2005): 159–184.

Harriss, C. Lowell. *History and Policies of the Home Owners' Loan Corporation.* (New York, 1951).

Rose, Jonathan D. "The Incredible HOLC? Mortgage Relief during the Great Depression." *Journal of Money, Credit, and Banking* 42 (September 2011): 1073–1107.

Van Order, Robert A. "A Microeconomic Analysis of Fannie Mae and Freddie Mac." *Regulation* 23, no. 2 (2001): 27–33.

White, Richard. *Railroaded: The Transcontinentals and the Making of America.* (New York, 2011).

Richard K. Green

GRAMM-LEACH-BLILEY ACT

The Financial Services Modernization Act of 1999 (more commonly known as the Gramm-Leach-Bliley Act, or GLBA) repealed the decades-old prohibition against financial firms offering both commercial and investment banking. The Gramm-Leach-Bliley Act repealed sections 20 and 32 of the Glass-Steagall Act, which Congress had passed in the aftermath of the US financial collapse of 1929. The rationale for separating commercial and investment banking was to protect individual bank depositors from bank insolvency or conflicts of interest due to activities such as banks investing their own assets in securities (stocks and bonds), making unsound loans to shore up the prices of securities the banks owned, or pressuring banking customers to buy securities that the bank owned in order to boost security prices.

In the 1950s, when financial firms began circumventing the separation of investment and commercial banking by forming bank holding companies that owned subsidiary enterprises specializing in different financial services, Congress reinforced the Glass-Steagall prohibition through the Bank Holding Company Act of 1956. The Bank Holding Company Act illustrates a key point pertinent to the history of the GLBA. In the financial services sector of the economy, technology and other factors contribute to a cycle of regulated entities devising ways to circumvent regulations, thus in turn creating a need for regulation to evolve with the industry or become less and less effective. At the time Congress voted the GLBA into law, the separation of commercial and investment banking had been eroding for a long time.

Many activities contributed to the erosion of the separation of commercial and investment banking prior to the first vote on the Financial Services

Modernization Act in 1998. Commercial banks began to offer securities investment services to household customers, and to offer corporate finance services such as advice on mergers and acquisitions. Investment banks began to engage in activities that encroached on commercial bank business. Instead of seeking loans from commercial banks to finance their businesses, they issued bonds. Spurred by the creation of the Government National Mortgage Association, more colloquially known as Ginnie Mae, mortgages were financed through securities markets rather than with the deposits commercial banks gathered from retail and business customers. Created in 1972, money market mutual funds offered an attractive savings alternative for household savers challenging the more heavily regulated commercial, savings, and thrift banks.

The changes in activities of commercial and investment banks accompanied a gradual erosion of tight financial regulation. Deregulation of stockbroker commission rates in the 1970s opened the door to discount brokerages, which attracted savings deposits away from deposit-oriented banks. In 1987, the Federal Reserve allowed commercial banks to engage in some limited securities underwriting, and continued in the 1990s to loosen restrictions on securities business conducted by commercial banks. In 1996 a Federal Reserve decision allowed commercial banks to derive up to 25 percent of their business from nontraditional activities. A Supreme Court decision that same year gave commercial banks limited permission to sell insurance. By facilitating the expansion of commercial banks into new lines of business, these measures spurred a wave of both offensive and defensive consolidation in the US financial sector, which ultimately created tremendous pressure to repeal Glass-Steagall once and for all.

The 1996 Federal Reserve decision freed US commercial banks to compete more effectively with European commercial banks, unhindered by Glass-Steagall separations, by buying US investment and brokerage firms. Investment banks also became bidders for these firms in order to defend themselves from the encroachment of commercial banks.

Insurance companies sought to create commercial banking subsidiaries and commercial banks sought to merge with insurance companies. Insurance giant Travelers, which had recently acquired an investment bank, merged with Citibank in 1997. In this merger, industry lobbyists for financial modernization, most of them previously from the investment banking side, gained a large new commercial bank ally, because under Glass-Steagall provisions regulators would have had to force the breakup of Citicorp within five years of the merger.

Also paving the way for passage of the GLBA were changes in the partisan balance in the US Congress and the structure of congressional committees with jurisdiction over financial matters. The Democratic Party suffered an epic electoral defeat in the midterm elections of 1994, second only to the 2010 elections in history in the number of seats lost. They lost fifty-four seats in the House and Jim Leach (Rep.–Iowa) replaced Henry Gonzalez (Dem.–Tex.) as chair of the House Committee on Banking, Finance, and Urban Affairs. After that election, party leaders agreed to strip the House Energy and Commerce Committee of most of its jurisdiction over financial markets, simplifying the internal congressional politics of developing and shepherding financial modernization legislation through the House of Representatives.

Senator Phil Gramm (Rep.–Tex.) first introduced the Financial Services Modernization Act in 1998, but it failed to win sufficient support to pass into law. Two aspects of the legislation shaped the politics of the bill's evolution: the extension of the Community Reinvestment Act (CRA) as the financial sector evolved due to financial modernization; and the balance of regulatory authority between the Federal Reserve Board (FRB) and the Treasury Department. Gramm's bill increased the regulatory authority of the Fed at the expense of the Treasury Department, angering then-President Clinton's Treasury Secretary Robert Rubin. Once rewritten to expand the scope of the CRA and reinforce the regulatory authority of the Treasury Department, the bill passed in 1999 with broad support. The Senate bill passed in a party-line vote, but it received bipartisan support in the House of Representatives with seventy-four Democrats, who voted against the 1998 version, switching to a "yes" vote. Among these Democrats was Nancy Pelosi, who, as Speaker of the House, brokered the huge congressional bailout of the US financial system in 2008.

The Gramm-Leach-Bliley Act paved the way for continued consolidation of the US financial services sector, spurring creation of entities that were "too big to fail" and at the same time creating a regulatory vacuum in the financial securitization and security derivatives arena. The GLBA accorded macro-prudential supervision of financial holding companies (those combining deposit-taking and securities businesses) to the FRB but did not explicitly assign micro-level oversight pertinent to these business lines to any particular public sector entity. As the "umbrella supervisor" under the GLBA, the FRB was to rely on other regulatory entities such as the Federal Deposit Insurance Corporation (FDIC), the Securities and Exchange Commission (SEC), or state insurance regulators for information and to examine entities itself only if it believed that their activities created risk for the deposit-taking bank that was affiliated under the financial holding company. In other words, under the GLBA, only if the FRB believed that Lehman Brothers put a large deposit-taking bank at risk did the FRB have authority to pressure the Securities and Exchange Commission to report results of the micro-prudential supervision of Lehman Brothers's capital adequacy.

[*See also* Financial Industry; Financial Instruments, New; Glass-Steagall Act; *and* Regulation.]

BIBLIOGRAPHY

Barth, James R., R. Dan Brumbaugh Jr., and James A. Wilcox. "Policy Watch: The Repeal of Glass-Steagall and the Advent of Broad Banking." *Journal of Economic Perspectives* 14, no. 2 (2000): 191–205.

Goldberg, Lawrence G., and Lawrence J. White. *The Deregulation of the Banking and Securities Industries.* (Washington, D.C., 2003).

Kolodny, Robin, and Sandra Suarez. "Paving the Road to 'Too Big to Fail': Business Interests and the Politics of Financial Deregulation in the US." *Politics and Society* 39, no. 4 (2011): 74–102.

Macey, Jonathan R. "The Business of Banking: Before and After Gramm-Leach-Bliley." Yale Law School Faculty Scholarship Series, Paper 1412. (2000), http://digitalcommons.law.yale.edu/fss_papers/1412.

Wang, Charles C. Y., and Yi David Wang. "Explaining the Glass-Steagall Act's Long Life, and Rapid Eventual Demise." (2010), http://papers.ssrn.com/sol3/papers.cfm?abstract_id=1722373.

Sylvia Maxfield

GRAND STRATEGIES, US

US grand strategies have been shaped by both events and intellectual ideas. This essay examines five US grand strategies: isolationist (neo-isolationist), nationalist, realist, liberal internationalist, and conservative internationalist. Each strategy identifies with a particular historical period and reflects a coherent logic about the way the world works. They constitute America's grand strategy traditions.

The isolationist tradition derives from George Washington's famous farewell address and influenced the new republic's early relationships with Europe. The nationalist tradition emerged with Andrew Jackson and the relentless expansion of the new republic across the continent. The realist grand strategy picks up with Theodore Roosevelt and the eruption of the United States on the world stage as a global power. The liberal internationalist tradition associates with Woodrow Wilson and Franklin Roosevelt and America's leadership in spreading democracy through the development of universal international institutions. More recently, a conservative internationalist grand strategy identifies with Ronald Reagan, and perhaps earlier with Harry Truman (at least in contrast to Franklin Roosevelt), and involves the quest to defend and spread democracy through a more forceful diplomacy that relies less on universal institutions than military strength, alliances, and coalitions of the willing.

US grand strategy traditions differ intellectually as well as historically. As I argue elsewhere, these traditions place different relative emphasis on three factors that shape foreign policy and international outcomes: ideas, institutions, and power. Isolationists, who emphasize American "exceptionalism," place heavy emphasis on ideas and example and relatively less on activist diplomacy and the balance of power. Nationalists, who see America as "unique" or different but not exceptional, place less emphasis on ideas and more on power and assume that all nations defend themselves, precluding the need for an activist US foreign policy beyond the Western Hemisphere. Realists see America as "ordinary" rather than unique and stress the need to manage the balance of power in other hemispheres (Europe and Asia) to preserve global peace and stability. Liberal internationalists consider America "exceptional," like isolationists, but place less emphasis on power and more on universal international institutions, particularly those that practice collective security, pool authority, and eventually substitute for the balance of power by settling disputes peacefully through "domestic-like" means of compromise and the rule of law. Conservative internationalists also consider America exceptional but place more emphasis on the use of force to defend and spread democracy around the world rather than cooperation with tyrants in international institutions.

Isolationism (Neo-isolationism). Isolationism, some may argue, is no longer a relevant grand strategy tradition. Given America's preeminent power in the world today, the United States is unlikely to withdraw into isolationism. But isolationism was a factor as late as the middle of the twentieth century, and neo-isolationism, as Eric Nordlinger incisively argues, remains relevant and is evident in the growing unhappiness with America's wars in Afghanistan and Iraq and declining economic prospects. This foreign policy tradition could easily reassert itself.

Isolationists focus overridingly on America's domestic political experiment. Liberal isolationists stress American ideals: liberty, and equality; conservative isolationists stress American folk culture, robustness, and self-reliance. Foreign involvement threatens this domestic experiment either by fostering a large military and industrial establishment (garrison state) or by contaminating American culture.

For liberal isolationists, an active US foreign policy directly undermines a "republican" domestic policy.

It encourages large military forces and powerful multinational corporations, both of which militate against decentralized government and individual liberty. Moreover, foreign involvement is unnecessary. The Old World is largely benign and nonthreatening, populated by diverse cultures that have a right to coexist and may even offer some desirable features that America could use. (Radical interpretations of American foreign policy, such as the writings of Noam Chomsky, often embody this view.) To engage this world is imperialistic because every country has something to contribute. Liberal isolationists are often pacifists, not out of a fear of war but out of a conviction of peace.

Conversely, conservative neo-isolationists see the Old World as alien and threatening, populated by despots that disdain the New World of liberty. (Some libertarian analysts, such as Ted Carpenter, take this view.) To engage actively in this Old World only risks making America more like the despots. It also opens up America to excessive immigration and baleful foreign cultural influences.

Thus, for isolationists on the right and left, the world remains either hostile or benign and there is little that America can or should do abroad that can make the world a better place. The best course is to stay home and nurture America's uniqueness, as conservatives emphasize, and respect other nations, as liberals advocate.

Hence, war and foreign entanglements are to be avoided at all costs. America inhabits a "delightful spot" and, as George Washington intoned, "why forego the advantages of so peculiar a situation? Why quit our own to stand upon foreign ground?" (Gilbert, 1961, 145). The United States enjoys "strategic immunity." It is the only major power in history that is separated by two large oceans from other regions and does not confront a great power rival in the western hemisphere, as other great powers do in Europe and Asia.

Hence, America defends itself best by simply reassuring other nations that it will not threaten them unless they threaten America's core interests. For isolationists, core interests constitute at a minimum the defense of American borders and at a maximum the defense of territorial seas and the Caribbean in the Western Hemisphere. Beyond this strictly "homeland" security policy, the United States has no stake in world affairs. Private groups can engage in low-risk, limited interventions on behalf of democracy and free trade; but the government has no strategic interests in these activities.

Isolationism developed its roots in the early American republic. Foreign policy was mostly about domestic policy. Should the government be centralized or decentralized, authoritarian or democratic? America's first political parties formed around these issues. Alexander Hamilton, Treasury secretary under the new constitution, and the Federalist Party he nurtured favored a strong central government that not only assumed debts of the states under the Articles of Confederation but also exercised executive authorities similar in some ways to the emerging constitutional monarchy in England. Thomas Jefferson, first secretary of state and third president under the new republic, and the Republican Party he nurtured feared an American-style monarchy and supported the new populist democracy that emerged in the early days of the French Revolution.

These domestic preferences dictated foreign policy views. Hamilton championed the Jay Treaty, which aligned the United States with Great Britain, while Jefferson supported the old Revolutionary War alliance with France. George Washington's famous warning in his farewell address "to steer clear of foreign alliances" was a message to both emerging parties not to let foreign interests intrude in the creation of the new American identity. It was a warning less against American involvement in the world than against foreign involvement in the United States. After all, the United States gained its independence through a crucial alliance with France. And the United States expanded into "foreign" territory through the Louisiana Purchase. Rather, Washington counseled that Americans should not give foreigners the opportunity to meddle in the great domestic experiment of American liberty. John Adams, second president of the United States, referred to foreign influences as "one of the most baneful foes of Republican government" (Padover, 1955, p. 321). For

isolationists then, as for neo-isolationists today, American foreign policy is all about domestic politics and American exceptionalism can only be corrupted by foreign policy.

Nationalism. By contrast, nationalists are less impressed by American exceptionalism and more focused on national defense and power. They believe that the world is unlikely to be influenced significantly by the American domestic experiment, through either example or coercion. America is neither "good, bad nor ugly." (McDougall, 1977:1) If it is exceptional, its exceptionalism is unique and not particularly relevant in foreign affairs. "Self-government," which applies to all nations, trumps liberty, which may be unique to a few. But the United States is vulnerable, like all other nations. The overriding imperative of foreign policy for all nations therefore is defense. The United States must spare no effort to defend its independence. Other countries will do the same. And because they defend themselves no less vigorously than the United States, there is little need for the United States to help them by entering into alliances or foreign adventures with them. Nationalists, on the whole, are fiercely independent and favor unilateralism whenever possible. Alliances are acceptable only if they do not infringe on the sovereignty of an independent nation.

For nationalists, the world is anarchic and dangerous but foreign conflicts are self-balancing. All countries put defense first and confront threats to their independence with vigor and tenacity. Thus, threats to the United States are unlikely to emerge in other parts of the world because nations historically divided in those regions will balance off one another and fight to defeat threats to independence long before they reach America's shores. Look at how the former Soviet Union almost singlehandedly defeated Nazi Germany in World War II. As the nationalist strategist Pat Buchanan argues, the United States benefited by delaying the establishment of a second front in World War II and would have benefited even more if it had stayed out of the war altogether. So, unlike realists, nationalists see no need to balance power actively around the world in order to defend the United States at home.

On the other hand, if America is attacked, nationalists are fierce to strike back and destroy the enemy. They carry the revolutionary banner "Don't Tread on Me." In war, national honor, not just national interest, is at stake. And there is only one possible outcome in foreign affairs, victory. George W. Bush reflected this sentiment after the 9/11 attacks. Originally seeking a more humble (that is, nationalist) American foreign policy, he reacted strongly to attacks on the American homeland. "The people who knocked these buildings down," he told the first responders gathered on the rubble of the twin towers; "will be hearing all of us soon." (Bones555a, 2007). Later, he taunted the enemy, "Bring them on" (Frazza, 2003), and displayed the "Mission Accomplished" banner on the aircraft carrier USS *Abraham Lincoln* touting victory, the only outcome of war nationalists accept. Once the enemy is defeated, however, nationalists are eager to return home. There is nothing more to do. Nation building is not for Americans or any nation, except at home. Bush lost his nationalist following quickly once he waded into the weeds of nation building and democracy promotion in Iraq and the Middle East.

Nationalists also reject engagement to secure economic benefits. Conservative nationalists see trade as potentially entangling or directly detrimental to national welfare. Protectionism is preferable. American jobs are not for export. More liberal nationalists embrace free trade but see no need to defend it by protecting sea lanes or allies. Countries trade because they benefit from it. They will continue to do so as long as the benefits outweigh the costs. When they stop and decide to block free trade, they hurt themselves as much as others. No American foreign policy should try to rescue them from their own folly.

Alliances are admissible to defend the country. But they should not be considered permanent. And they remain acceptable only as long as the United States needs or dominates these institutions to advance its independent national interests.

The nationalist grand strategy emerged in the course of the nineteenth century. The Monroe Doctrine in 1823 elevated the idea of being wary of foreign intervention in American affairs (but not necessarily America's intervention in world affairs—matching the intent of Washington's warning) to a grand strategy embracing the entire hemisphere. The United States would accept no interference by European or Asian powers in the Western Hemisphere. It rejected any new colonies, transfer of colonies, or reversion of independent states back to colonial status in the region. Foreign powers were put on notice that the United States would defend the status quo in the rest of the hemisphere.

At the same time, the United States was free to alter that status quo unilaterally and expand the American republic across the continent from sea to shining sea. The Monroe Doctrine proscribed foreign, but not US, expansion in the hemisphere. And it embraced US expansion with no explicit commitments to alliances or the spread of democracy. To be sure, the United States benefited from implicit protection by British naval power. But, before issuing the Monroe Doctrine, the United States rejected a British offer to act jointly. Unlike the realist tradition, the nationalist grand strategy shuns alliances unless they are absolutely necessary for survival. Nationalist logic also eschews any special obligations of American foreign policy to export liberty. Unlike the liberal and conservative internationalist strategies, nationalists expand to defend security and promote development (the justification for seizing Indian lands) but never to spread democracy. Liberty may be desirable, but culture is more determining. Nationalists are champions of assimilation and at times are charged with racism and xenophobia.

Andrew Jackson and disciples such as James K. Polk epitomized the nationalist tradition. They championed the union but not necessarily freedom (they supported slavery) and used force to expand a country increasingly divided by slavery. (Jackson's famous quip at the Jefferson Day dinner in 1830 made it clear that union mattered more than liberty or slavery: "Our Federal Union; it *must* be preserved" (Brands, 2005, p. 446). The United States seized Indian lands, annexed the Texas and Mexican territories, and negotiated the acquisition of the Oregon territories. And it did all of this without alliances; indeed, it expanded precisely to preempt the need for alliances which might have followed if European powers had colonized parts of the continent. For nationalists, foreign policy is not dangerous or irrelevant, as it is for isolationists; rather, it is essential to unite and preserve the nation. But it entails no obligation to help other nations. It is intended to prevent foreign interference at home, not to abet American intervention abroad. Nationalists extol the exploitation of new frontiers, such as space and missile defense; but they aim only to fulfill national needs, not to gain international advantage.

Lincoln and the Civil War resolved the division in America's domestic politics that made the initial republic so vulnerable and foreign intervention so dangerous. Freedom eclipsed slavery, and the country's domestic experiment became an increasing influence in American foreign policy. The "new birth of freedom" both ignited a massive economic boom and hoisted the specter of America's commitment to support freedom abroad. The next three grand strategy traditions bring these elements to the fore. Realism trumpets American power in world affairs, and liberal and conservative internationalism showcase American ideals.

Realism. Realists, like nationalists, consider American ideas to be no better or worse than those of other nations but have less confidence than nationalists that the balance of power will automatically defend national interests. Global alliances are necessary to head off power imbalances; and international diplomacy, including some international institutions such as concerts of great powers, may be needed to ensure stability and peace. Realists differ on the configuration of power that best ensures peace. Offensive realists, such as John Mearsheimer, believe that hegemony stabilizes and that America, which is a regional hegemon in the western hemisphere, should strive to maintain that status. Defensive realists, such as Henry Kissinger, believe that equilibrium stabilizes and they would urge the United States to anticipate and accommodate counterbalancing challenges, whether from democracies (e.g., Europe) or nondemocracies (China, Russia, Venezuela, Iran, etc.).

Realists are very skeptical about the role of values in international affairs. Classical realists, such as George Kennan, champion free societies; but they do not advocate the export of freedom, except by example and emulation. Even then, this outcome is not an explicit objective of grand strategy. Kennan foresaw already in 1948 that America's best defense against the Soviet Union was to strengthen its own free society. But he advocated military containment (balancing) to deter the Soviet Union and never expected that freedom would or should spread to the Soviet Union. He predicted instead that the Soviet Union would return to its Russian roots and authoritarian nationalist traditions. And he opposed the injection of ideology in foreign policy, rejecting every extension of containment against the Soviet Union (Korea, Vietnam, etc.) that went beyond the principal defense perimeter of central Europe. He anticipated the end of the Cold War, which other realists like Henry Kissinger, who were more skeptical of domestic institutions, did not. But neither Kennan nor Kissinger expected a Boris Yeltsin to emerge and seek to liberalize communism in the 1990s, albeit with limited success.

Realists support free trade and institutional cooperation among allies but not with adversaries. Trade brings mutual benefits, as liberal nationalists believe; but it also distributes those benefits unequally. While it makes sense to strengthen allies under certain circumstances, it makes no sense to strengthen adversaries. And while some cooperation is possible among great powers, relying too heavily on universal institutions undercuts American foreign policy. The United Nations Security Council gives a veto to Russia and China. These countries are not current adversaries, but they may become such; and no American grand strategy can commit itself to work primarily through international institutions that formally depend upon the goodwill of other powerful states.

Realism became a grand strategy choice once America became powerful. And America became powerful in the generation after the Civil War. American wealth and power expanded explosively, similar to that of Germany around the same time and China in the twenty-first century. The presence of the United States was felt on the scales of world power, and President Theodore Roosevelt adopted a realist grand strategy to deploy that power.

Roosevelt celebrated the virtues of American power and energy. A Rough Rider in Cuba during the Spanish–American War, he savored the sacrifice as well as glory of the warrior. He understood that the United States was a rising power and deserved a place at the table of world powers. His intervention in the Russo–Japanese War established America's credentials. He saw the crucial importance of the American navy and engineered the acquisition of the Panama Canal. Altogether, he thrust the new power onto the world stage of great power diplomacy.

The United States did not form any alliances immediately and resisted standing alliances until after World War II. Yet, informally, it forged a closer and closer association with the world power it was replacing, Great Britain. This alignment proved critical to the allied victory in World War I. And after the war, Roosevelt and other realists, such as Henry Cabot Lodge, favored codifying this alliance to defend Europe against a resurgent Germany. However, as Colin Dueck points out, the realists strongly opposed the League of Nations as a substitute for more concrete alliance commitments and the balance of power.

Realism does not exclude values—and neither did Roosevelt and early proponents of realism. Roosevelt promoted the values of Western civilization and embraced America's role as a colonial power and standard-bearer for civilization in the Philippines. But values for realists are parochial and relative, not universal and absolute. If anything, they are superior or subordinate, not relative or universal; and Roosevelt, a classical realist, left no doubt that he believed Western cultural values were superior.

Liberal Internationalism. Unlike nationalists and realists, liberal internationalists give priority to ideas and institutions over power. They see international institutions playing a key role to "domesticate" international politics and eventually shift the international system from military balances to domestic-like police actions. They envision the day when the liberal experiment prevails across the globe, but they believe the world gets to that point best, not by relying on example or the balance of power but by including all nations whether democratic or not in universal international institutions that regularize procedures and the rule of law for resolving international disputes peacefully without the use of force.

Treating countries equally, whether free or not, through a process of open diplomacy and trade is the best way to encourage them over the long term to become free and democratic. Liberal internationalists do not exclude the use of force. They use it vigorously to defend America. Nevertheless, they insist that force can be used beyond America's borders legitimately only with the approval of universal institutions. In contrast to realists, they see force not as a normal instrument of global diplomacy but as an instrument of "last" resort after diplomacy has failed. In the long run, they hope that the use of force becomes a "past" resort as international politics is "domesticated" and transformed from military balances to police enforcement.

Woodrow Wilson is the author and lodestar of the liberal internationalist grand strategy. He designed the first permanent universal institution to manage the affairs of war and peace. The League of Nations constituted a new approach to international security, one that relied on collective security and the common pooling of force rather than national security and the balance of power. Wilson was quite self-conscious about what he was doing. He was committing the United States to the security of the world, not just to the security of the United States.

The logic of the League of Nations was clear. All nations would consider threats anywhere to be threats everywhere. Peace was indivisible. And all nations would act to deter such threats, first by automatic and collective economic sanctions and then, if necessary, by the combined military forces of the world. Peace was universal. Because the world's combined military forces would overwhelm any recalcitrant country, it was unlikely these forces would have to be deployed. In fact, the world could promote disarmament and still marshal sufficient military forces to prevail against offending states.

The league promised to do for international politics what national governments had done for domestic politics—reduce matters of war and peace to police actions.

As John Ikenberry argues, the liberal internationalist grand strategy relies on the exercise of cooperation to instill the habit of cooperation. Nations working together daily in international institutions will get used to one another and increasingly empathize, maybe even identify, with one another. Agreement among them will become easier and easier. An unspoken expectation is that such cooperation will engender values of pluralism, tolerance, and eventually democracy. These values are not prerequisites of cooperation but consequences over time. The best way to spread democracy is to treat all states equally and cooperatively, whether they are initially democratic or not. Thus, except in dire emergencies, such as direct attack, liberal internationalists are not only comfortable but eager to work with nondemocracies. Cooperation is sticky, and as long as the glue is democratic (a big article of faith), cooperation builds a world community of free and peaceful states. The democratic peace, in which power remains decentralized but democratic states do not go to war with one another, is the eventual outcome.

The League of Nations went too far for American nationalists and realists. A combination of them, led by William Borah and Henry Cabot Lodge, defeated it. But the league idea did not fade away, even in the wake of its abject failure in the interwar period. It was resurrected after the war in the United Nations (UN). This time, however, Franklin Roosevelt gave it a realist twist. The Security Council required unanimity only among the great powers, not among all nations great and small. A major concession to realism, this feature improved the odds that the great powers would join the UN and, if they agreed, ensure its success. That hope was quickly eclipsed by the Cold War. But briefly, when the Cold War ended in 1990–1991, the UN functioned as it was envisioned by liberal internationalists. The world went to war to expel Iraq from its conquest of Kuwait. With sovereignty restored, Kuwait rejoined the community of nations. But Saddam Hussein's regime in Iraq

remained sovereign as well. The UN did not sanction regime change in Baghdad. Eventually, disagreement over how to deal with Iraq almost destroyed the UN. Since 1991 it has never functioned again as a collective security institution.

Conservative Internationalism. Since World War II, US foreign policy has cycled between realist and liberal internationalist grand strategies. Presidents Eisenhower, Nixon, and Ford were considered to be realists; Presidents Truman, Kennedy, Johnson, and Carter were considered to be liberal internationalists. The cycle broke down with Ronald Reagan however. As the writings of John Lewis Gaddis and Martin and Annelise Anderson document, he opposed both the realist containment strategy of Richard Nixon and the liberal internationalist human-rights campaign of Jimmy Carter. He adopted a strategy that used force or the threat of force assertively, as realists recommended, but aimed at the demise of communism and the spread of democracy, as liberal internationalists advocated. Reagan pursued the aims of liberal internationalism with the means of realism. He succeeded brilliantly. The Cold War ended, the Soviet Union disappeared, and the United States emerged as the first preeminent "global" power in the history of the world. Even former critics such as Henry Kissinger now concede that Reagan was on to something.

So what tradition did Reagan represent? He was internationalist but not liberal. And he was realist but not cynical or pessimistic. He did not base his grand strategy on the stickiness of international institutions, but he did believe that democracy mattered and could be spread. In a sense, as Louis Hartz argued, Reagan and all Americans are liberals. They reject traditional authoritarianism and believe in liberal democracy. But some are classical liberals, while others are social liberals. Reagan and many Republicans are classical liberals; they give priority to freedom over equality. They hesitate to accept nondemocracies as equals in international institutions until the nondemocracies respect freedom and give their citizens political rights. Carter and many liberal Democrats are social liberals; they give priority to equality over freedom. They favor the use of government and international institutions to engage nondemocracies and encourage liberty by granting them social equality.

Reagan and classical liberals represent a different foreign policy tradition of conservative internationalism. Like realists, conservative internationalists focus on threats, peace through strength, and the balance of power. But unlike realists, they do not seek just global stability and mutual coexistence or the balance of power. Instead, like liberal internationalists, they promote democracy, yet they do so more through unilateral or competitive, especially market, mechanisms than through government institutions, which liberal internationalists favor. If they work with the balance of power, they nevertheless seek to tilt it toward freedom, believing that the struggle against despotism requires more than multilateral diplomacy in which despots participate and obstruct.

Defined in this way, conservative internationalism also has historical precedents. As I have demonstrated elsewhere, four presidents stand out for aggressively expanding freedom through assertive military and diplomatic action. Thomas Jefferson is claimed by isolationists and liberal internationalists, but he was neither. He doubled the size of American territory, and although this expansion took place on the North American continent when America was militarily weak, Jefferson's policies can hardly be called isolationist or pacifist. In fact, he used all the military, especially naval, power that the United States had at the time and combined threats and diplomacy deftly to grab Louisiana when the opportunity arose. The Louisiana Purchase may have fallen into his lap, as some historians argue; but he had to place his lap in the right position to catch it.

James Polk too is claimed by other traditions. Nationalists extol his military aggressiveness toward Mexico, realists his preemption of European alliances on the continent, and liberal internationalists his deft diplomacy to annex the Oregon territory. But unlike nationalists or realists, including his alter ego Andrew Jackson, Polk did more than preserve the union. He expanded American territory by another

60 percent. And, while criticized by liberal internationalists as racist, he expanded American freedom as well, however tarnished that expansion was by black slavery (which Mexico had abolished in 1829). In 1848 the United States was the most advanced republic on earth. It gave the vote to more white male citizens than any other country. It was also the country that was on a trajectory of future emancipation which, with all its blemishes, would lead the world toward liberty for all minorities and women. Polk was one of the most ambitious and successful American presidents, and while his star, like that of Jefferson and Jackson, has been diminished by rearview-mirror charges of racism and imperialism, he was, again like Jefferson and Jackson, a pioneer of his day not only in expanding liberty but also in understanding the close and reciprocal interaction between force and diplomacy, a particular emphasis of conservative internationalist thinking.

Harry Truman expanded the cause of freedom for the first time beyond the confines of the Western Hemisphere. He inspired the Cold War policy of militarized containment that incubated democracy in Japan, Germany, and throughout Western Europe. Had Truman not inserted American forces on European soil to stop a potential Soviet advance from Berlin to the English Channel, liberty might well have been lost in the very countries where it originated. As Wilson Miscamble points out, Truman made the UN work–for example in Korea–but without the Soviet Union and hence not as the universal institution envisioned by Roosevelt.

Finally, Ronald Reagan transformed Truman's containment policy from a defensive, status quo posture into a competitive strategy to defeat, not just coexist with, the Soviet Union. He saw the opportunity to end Soviet oppression in Eastern Europe, which none of his predecessors saw, and ultimately opened the doors of freedom for communist Europe and a good part of the rest of the world.

Conclusion. All of America's grand strategy traditions remain in play. Neo-isolationists on both the left and right vigorously oppose America's wars in Iraq and Afghanistan. Especially in times of economic crisis, such wars, they believe, are unaffordable and destructive of domestic freedom and harmony. Nationalists bristle at the breach of American borders by terrorists and illegal immigrants and at America's vulnerability to the nuclear aspirations of rogue states. They call for bringing American troops home from Europe and Asia, erecting border guards and fences, and fully deploying national missile defenses. Realists see the need to balance power in the Middle East and South Asia but prefer to do it by an offshore, counterterrorism strategy that deters adversaries by naval forces and long-distance missile strikes to destroy terrorist camps when they emerge. They propose greater burden sharing by allies and oppose misguided efforts to spread democracy in cultures that are not Western or Christian.

Conservative internationalists advocate a more aggressive strategy to counter terrorism. They support a counterinsurgency approach that deploys boots on the ground to root out terrorists in Iraq and Afghanistan and supports vigorous nation-building efforts to train local forces and governments to assume a larger role under stronger democratic constraints and transparency. Conservative internationalists are skeptical that socially liberal allies in Europe care as much about freedom in the world as Americans do and opt to work with coalitions of the willing when allies demur to fight. Liberal internationalists decry the unilateralism and militarism of conservative internationalists and work to restore American standing and leadership in international institutions. They prioritize international collaboration to curb nuclear proliferation, fight global warming, convert to green energy sources, and tame failed capitalist financial markets.

US grand strategy traditions and the debates among them are unlikely to disappear soon. They are solidly rooted in both the history and logic of the country's circumstances and creed. In many ways, as Walter Russell Mead argues, all are indispensable. Through an ongoing competition and debate, US grand strategies ensure that America considers all of the elements of a changing world and brings different perspectives to bear to meet the challenges of specific times.

[*See also* Afghanistan; American Exceptionalism; Military–Industrial Complex; Native Americans; Protection; Reagan, Ronald; Roosevelt, Franklin Delano; Truman, Harry S.; *and* United Nations.]

BIBLIOGRAPHY

Anderson, Martin, and Annelise Anderson. *Reagan's Secret War: The Untold Story of His Fight to Save the World from Nuclear Weapons.* (New York, 2009).

Brands, H. W. *Andrew Jackson: His Life and Times.* (New York, 2005).

Buchanan, Patrick J. *Churchill, Hitler, and the Unnecessary War.* (New York, 2008).

Carpenter, Ted Galen. *Smart Power: Toward a Prudent American Foreign Policy.* (Washington, D.C., 2008).

Chomsky, Noam. *Hegemony or Survival: America's Quest for Global Dominance.* (New York, 2003).

Dueck, Colin. *Hard Line: The Republican Party and US Foreign Policy since World War II.* (Princeton, N.J., 2010).

Frazza, Luke. "Bush: 'Bring on' attackers of U.S. troops," *USA Today*, July 2, 2003, http://www.usatoday.com/news/world/iraq/2003-07-02-bush-iraq-troops_x.htm.

Gaddis, John Lewis. *Strategies of Containment: A Critical Appraisal of American National Security Policy during the Cold War.* (New York, 2005).

Gilbert, Felix. *To the Farewell Address.* (Princeton, N.J., 1961).

Hartz, Louis. *The Liberal Tradition in America.* (New York, 1955).

Ikenberry, G. John. *Liberal Leviathan: The Origins, Crisis, and Transformation of the American System.* (Princeton, 2011).

Kennan, George F. *Around the Cragged Hill: A Personal and Political Philosophy.* (New York, 1993).

Kissinger, Henry. *Diplomacy.* (New York, 1994).

McDougall, Walter A. *Promised Land, Crusader State: The American Encounter with the World since 1776.* (Boston, Mass., 1997).

Mead, Walter Russell. *Special Providence: American Foreign Policy and How It Changed the World.* (New York, 2002).

Mearsheimer, John J. *The Tragedy of Great Power Politics.* (New York, 2001).

Miscamble, Wilson D. *From Roosevelt to Truman: Potsdam, Hiroshima, and the Cold War.* (Cambridge, 2007).

Nau, Henry R. *At Home Abroad: Identity and Power in American Foreign Policy.* (Ithaca, N.Y., 2002).

Nau, Henry R. "Conservative Internationalism: Jefferson to Polk to Truman to Reagan." *Policy Review* 150 (August–September 2008): 3–45.

Nau, Henry R. *Perspectives on International Relations: Power, Institutions and Ideas.* (Washington, D.C., 3rd Edition, 2011).

"9/11: George Bush Jr at the Trade Center, 9/14/2001," YouTube video. 2:46, posted by "bones555a," August 14, 2007, http://www.youtube.com/watch?v=MkiHW jX1yX0.

Nordlinger, Eric A. *Isolationism Reconfigured: American Foreign Policy for a New Century.* (Princeton, N.J., 1995).

Padover, Saul K. *The Washington Papers.* (New York, 1955).

Henry R. Nau

GRAY POWER

"Gray power" refers to the real or alleged phenomenon that growing numbers of older people in the United States (and other industrial nations) are exercising a vast and, in some estimations, an excessive degree of political influence. Books by prominent authors, with titles such as *Gray Dawn: How the Coming Age-Wave Will Transform America—and the World* and *The Coming Generational Storm: What You Need to Know About America's Economic Future*, have received wide exposure. Evidence marshaled on behalf of an imposing degree of gray power includes the large and growing proportion of older voters in the American electorate, the presumed political self-identity of those voters, the size and influence of aging-oriented interest groups, and the size of major public policies devoted exclusively or largely to older Americans. There are widely varying opinions as to whether this large number of individuals, groups, programs, and dollars constitutes genuine "gray power," or whether there are perhaps a variety of mitigating factors which make this major presence less imposing than it might seem at first glance.

The Mass Political Presence of Seniors. Until recently, the growth of the older population has been quite steady and gradual, with persons aged sixty-five and older constituting roughly 12 percent of the population in 2005. Generating much additional interest is the impending entry into old age of the Baby Boom generation, which will elevate seniors' presence in the population by 76 million people by 2030; at that point, the elderly will constitute 20 percent of the population. Boomers are often seen as having had profound effects on social institutions in the realms of education, employment, and consumption, and many believe that they will transform the shape and meaning of retirement and public policy in their old age.

In the world of politics, the presence of older people can already be shown to exceed that suggested by raw population figures alone, a standing seen most directly from voting data. Two trends in that data are particularly notable. First, older people now vote at a higher rate than any other age group, whereas in 1968 they voted less than all but those aged eighteen to twenty-four. Second, older persons' voting participation has increased over the forty-year period, while the participation of all other groups has decreased. In midterm elections, the age-based differentials are yet more pronounced, with turnout for seniors reaching 73 percent in 1998, and that for the youngest voters having fallen to 30 percent. In short, seniors' electoral presence has increased in both absolute and relative terms since the 1960s. Older people's growing political involvement is seen as well in their now being as active as the middle-aged in expressed political interest and in contacting public officials. Perhaps most remarkably, older people now contribute financially to political campaigns more than any other age group.

Despite these impressive numbers, there exists considerable controversy around how much power or influence older voters actually exercise. On the one hand, there is no doubt that they are disproportionately represented in the electorate and that political parties actively solicit their support. Yet, despite their growing numbers, voters sixty-five and older constituted no more than 16 percent of the electorate in 2008. Moreover, there have been only minor variations in the partisan voting patterns of older and younger voters over the years—a convergence that tends to negate the influence that seniors' higher rates of participation might otherwise have. The 2008 election appeared as something of an exception to this pattern, with younger voters disproportionately supporting Barack Obama and older ones supporting John McCain. But that difference appears to have been much more about broad political ideology (and the candidates' ages) than any kind of reflection of "senior interests" manifesting themselves.

The Lobbying Presence of Senior Organizations. This same time period has seen a remarkable growth in advocacy representation on behalf of older Americans in Washington. In addition to three mass membership organizations—AARP (formerly the Association for the Advancement of Retired Persons), with some 46 million members, being by far the most well known—there are numerous national organizations, both advocating for seniors and delivering publicly funded services to them. Sixty-six of these organizations now constitute their own entity, the Leadership Council of Aging Organizations (LCAO), which is "dedicated to preserving and strengthening the well-being of America's older population."

How singularly influential these organizations have been in furthering senior interests remains open to question. There is scant evidence that any of the major aging-oriented social programs—Social Security, Medicare, Medicaid, the Older Americans Act—came into existence largely because of pressure from these groups. In fact, most of the groups came into existence in the wake of these policy enactments, not prior to them. Yet, the groups now being very much in existence, there is little question that they constitute a substantial firewall against initiatives they oppose (notably, President Bush's 2005 attempt to partially privatize Social Security) and lend critical support to programs that they favor (AARP's support of the Medicare Part D prescription drug program). While it is not clear that these groups, including AARP, can "deliver the elderly," there is little willingness among political officials to upset or oppose these groups if it can be avoided.

Power and Public Policy. The most compelling case to be made in favor of senior power is found in the concentration of American social policy expenditures directed toward them. Whatever shortcomings public policies for seniors may have in the United States—and there are many—older Americans benefit from a range of policies far beyond those directed toward any other social policy constituency. In 2004, social policy expenditures for the aged totaled $767 billion, or 57 percent of the nation's total health and human services spending. Observers critical of this high level of federal spending for the elderly ($21,144 per capita) compare it to that made on behalf of children ($2,895 per capita). Without question, old-age expenditures are a core component of the debate swirling around Washington about the federal deficit, despite counterarguments to the effect that Social Security does not contribute to the deficit, or that rising Medicare expenditures are much more closely tied to spiraling health care costs overall than to older people's entitlement to acute health care services.

Contemporary scholarship demonstrating the independent role of public policy in shaping political events (Skocpol, 1985; Pierson, 1993: Mettler, 2005) is of great relevance to understanding the present standing of both senior policies and senior power. In short, it appears in a majority of cases that policies on behalf of older Americans were largely responsible for heightened political activity of the old and of the rise of the LCAO groups, rather than such activity being responsible for enactment and initial expansion of the policies. Campbell's (2003) study of how Social Security generated much of the political activity mentioned above is the most central contribution. In addition, Walker (1983) found that over half of the senior groups came into existence after enactment of the major policies of the 1960s: Medicare, Medicaid, the Older Americans Act, and the Age Discrimination in Employment Act. Acknowledging the policies' independent role, there also develops a critical symbiotic relationship between the policy and subsequent political activity. Whereas the policies may have generated political interest and support, older people and aging-based organizations, once galvanized, come to serve as critical bulwarks in the defense of those very policies. It is in this sense that Teles (2005) refers to Social Security as the cornerstone of what he labels "welfare state conservatism."

Does Senior Presence Demonstrate "Gray Power"?
The intriguing question left unanswered is the degree to which the unquestioned political and policy standing of older Americans is about power or, perhaps, about something else. Historically, it was almost certainly not about power. Older people were singularly poor, frail, and isolated. Old-age interest groups did not even exist. AARP did not come into being until 1958 and, as recently as 1973, opposed as inflationary a Democratic proposal to raise Social Security benefits by 20 percent. If not power, what then accounts for the pathbreaking age-related policy enactments of the 1930s and 1960s? The answer appears to lie in a combination of political legitimacy (widespread public opinion then and now believes older people *should* receive these benefits) and political utility (reformers invoked the needs of the aged to further initiatives which they hoped would come to include additional populations). With the partial exception of Medicare, every major enactment on behalf of older people prior to the mid-1980s was based more on these considerations than on any exercise of raw political power.

More recently, however, such power has been manifest in the social policy arena. Repeal of the Medicare Catastrophic Care Act, Bill Clinton's ability to forestall massive cuts in Medicare and Medicaid in the mid-1990s, the passage of the Part D prescription drug legislation, and the derailing of George W. Bush's Social Security privatization proposal each very much owe their outcomes to a senior electorate selectively mobilized around such issues and an advocacy infrastructure in place to channel those energies.

Presently, a political cold front is clearly building around age-based policies. In Schattschneider's (1975) famous words, "the scope of conflict has expanded." As a result, the social construction of the aged as target population appears now to have shifted twice over the course of seventy-five years, from "deserving" to "advantaged" during the late 1970s, and to "contenders" within the last five or ten years. In short, the aged today have indisputably attained a powerful and institutionalized political standing. Whether that standing will be sufficient to overcome the enormous pressures now building against welfare state spending—spending that is heavily concentrated on seniors—is one of the most pressing public policy questions facing the United States in the years ahead.

[*See also* Medicare and Medicaid; Social Security; *and* Welfare State.]

BIBLIOGRAPHY

Campbell, Andrea. *How Policies Make Citizens: Senior Political Activism and the American Welfare State.* (Princeton, N.J., 2003).

Campbell, Andrea, and Robert H. Binstock. "Politics and Aging in the United States." In *Handbook of Aging and the Social Sciences*, 7th ed., edited by Robert H. Binstock and Linda K. George, pp. 265–279. (London, 2010).

Hudson, Robert B. "Conflict in Today's Aging Politics: New Population Encounters Old Ideology." *Social Service Review* 73 (1999): 356–377.

Hudson, Robert B. "The 'Graying' of the Federal Budget and Its Consequences for Old-Age Policy." *Gerontologist* 18 (1978): 428–440.

Iglehart, John K. "Medicare Prescription-Drug Benefit—Pure Power Play." *New England Journal of Medicine* 350 (2004): 826–833.

Isaacs, Julia B. "Spending on Children and the Elderly." Brookings Institution. (2009), http://www.brookings.edu/reports/2009/1105_spending_children_isaacs.aspx.

Kotlikoff, Laurence J., and Scott Burns. *The Coming Generational Storm: What You Need to Know About America's Economic Future.* (Cambridge, Mass., 2004).

Leadership Council of Aging Organizations, http://www.lcao.org.

Lew, Jacob. "Social Security Is Not the Problem." *USA Today*, February 21, 2011.

Marmor, Theodore, and Jerry Mashaw. "A Thinly Disguised Assault on Medicare." *Philadelphia Inquirer*, April 19, 2011.

Mettler, Suzanne. *From Soldiers to Citizens: The G.I. Bill and the Making of the Greatest Generation.* (New York, 2005).

Pear, Robert. "In Ads, AARP Criticizes Plan on Privatizing." *New York Times*, December 30, 2004.

Peterson, Peter G. *Gray Dawn: How the Coming Age-Wave Will Transform America—and the World.* (New York, 1999).

Pierson, Paul. "When Effect Becomes Cause: Policy Feedback and Political Change." *World Politics* 45 (1993): 595–628.

Pratt, Henry. *The Gray Lobby.* (Chicago, 1976).

Schattschneider, E.E. *The Semi-Sovereign People: A Realist's View of Democracy in America.* (New York, 1975).

Schneider, Anne, and Helen Ingram. "The Social Construction of Target Populations." *American Political Science Review* 87 (1993): 332–347.

Skocpol, Theda. "Bringing the State Back In." In *Bringing the State Back In,* edited by Peter Evans, Dietrich Rueschemeyer, and Theda Skocpol, pp. 3–37. (New York, 1985).

Teles, Stephen. "Social Security and the Paradoxes of Welfare State Conservatism." In *The New Politics of Old Age Policy,* edited by Robert B. Hudson, pp. 90–107. (Baltimore, 2005).

U.S. Bureau of the Census. "Voting and Registration," http://www.census.gov/hhes/www/socdemo/voting/publications/historical/index.html.

Walker, Jack L. "The Origins and Maintenance of Interest Groups in America." *American Political Science Review* 77(1983): 390–406.

Robert B. Hudson

GREAT SOCIETY

The "Great Society" is the name that President Lyndon Baines Johnson gave to the outpouring of social and economic policies enacted in the United States during the 1960s. New initiatives increased the federal government's role in the domains of health care for the poor and elderly, education, and low-income housing. These policies were complemented by Keynesian macroeconomic management to promote full employment; civil rights measures to ensure equal opportunity for African Americans; and a highly visible "War on Poverty," which sought to end poverty in the United States.

The Great Society represented a completion of many initiatives which had been first contemplated in the 1930s during the New Deal. With it, the US federal government assumed a role in promoting the social welfare of its citizens akin to that assumed by many European nations immediately after World War II. However, the Great Society featured distinctly American approaches to social policy and remained less far-reaching than most European welfare state programs. The programs inaugurated during the Great Society sought to promote equal opportunity, rather than to redistribute income or to guarantee social rights.

A variety of economic, political, and social factors created a favorable environment for social reform in the 1960s. Postwar growth had boosted the US economy, but "pockets of poverty" continued to exist in areas left behind by industrial transformation. Some groups were more economically vulnerable than others: the elderly and African Americans suffered from particularly high rates of poverty as the United States entered the 1960s. Although the decade began with a sluggish economy, by the mid-1960s, unprecedented prosperity allowed the federal government to increase spending on social programs without raising taxes.

As Patterson (1981) has noted, this secure economic climate took the sting out of increased public spending; social reform could be accomplished without redistributing wealth.

Politics, too, moved in directions favorable to social reform in the 1960s. Since the 1950s, congressional Democrats had been pressing for action on a range of social policy issues including education, health care, and unemployment. And, after a decade of struggle, the southern civil rights movement succeeded in drawing national attention to the exclusion of African Americans from the economic prosperity and political rights enjoyed by the majority of whites.

The shock of President John F. Kennedy's assassination in 1963 finally jolted Congress into action. The unfulfilled promise of the Kennedy administration, which had vowed to get the country "moving again," provided renewed impetus for reformers. When combined with President Johnson's considerable legislative skill, these circumstances made Congress more amenable to social legislation than it had been for several decades. This predilection to increase the federal role in ensuring social welfare was strongly reinforced in 1964, when Americans elected the most liberal Congress since 1936.

Many of the Great Society programs had been on the nation's agenda for decades. The Medicaid and Medicare programs, which established health insurance for the poor and the elderly, respectively, represented a compromise that established a federal role in ensuring the nation's health, but fell short of the national health insurance proposed since the 1930s. The panoply of low-income housing programs enacted in the late 1960s, and the establishment of a Department of Housing and Urban Development in 1965, extended federal activity in the field of housing beyond the small public housing programs authorized in the 1930s. The Keynesian tax cut enacted in 1964, which aimed to stimulate the economy and reduce unemployment, represented the triumph of an economic strategy first tried in 1938.

Other initiatives reflected concerns that had grown during the 1950s. Support for federal aid to education—traditionally the province of states and localities—mounted, as localities struggled to accommodate the explosive demands on public education created by the postwar baby boom, and as concern about the different capacities of local governments grew. Although federal aid to education actually increased very little during the 1960s, the acknowledgment of a federal role in funding public education represented a new development in American political culture. A second new area of federal activism was civil rights. In 1964, the Civil Rights Act outlawed discrimination in public facilities, ending more than fifty years of legally sanctioned racial segregation in the South. The Voting Rights Act, passed a year later, sought to ensure black political rights, and laid the foundation for the conquest of political power by a generation of black politicians in the following decade.

The newest and most visible element of the Great Society was the War on Poverty. Although many of the components of the attack on poverty were not new, the effort to package them into a concerted effort to end poverty was novel. The charter legislation for the War on Poverty, the Economic Opportunity Act of 1964, created programs for youth job training, public service employment for youth, a volunteer national services corps, and a new Office of Equal Opportunity, operating out of the Executive Office of the President. The most innovative aspect of the War on Poverty was the community action agency; these agencies were established in localities across the country to administer the new programs with the "maximum feasible participation" of the poor. In creating these agencies, the federal government bypassed state and city government to establish the first direct relationship between community groups and the federal government.

Despite its flamboyant rhetoric, the War on Poverty did not commit the federal government to major spending to reduce poverty; its greatest gains were in promoting black political empowerment. Although the War on Poverty was officially race-neutral, in practice it focused on urban minorities. Black communities seized on community action programs to challenge the exclusionary practices of local governments and service bureaucracies. As race riots spread across urban America in the 1960s, the federal government used community action agencies to funnel resources into these troubled communities.

The social reform launched by the Great Society lost its momentum in the late 1960s, as spending on the Vietnam War limited funds for domestic social purposes. Equally important was dwindling support for the War on Poverty in the wake of urban rioting. Although federal social spending would rise under the Nixon administration, the emphasis on federal activity and the focus on the poor that characterized the War on Poverty diminished in the 1970s. And, as inflation and unemployment grew in the 1970s, confidence that government could solve economic and social problems declined.

The Great Society left an uneven institutional legacy. Some of the policy innovations of the 1960s have survived: the federal government continues to help finance health care for the poor and elderly and provides modest aid to education. Many of the neighborhood community organizations created by the community action programs still deliver social services to poor neighborhoods. Some of the programs pioneered in the War on Poverty, including early childhood education such as that provided by Head Start, have survived attempts to eliminate them. But the programs that have survived, particularly those aimed at the poor, are poorly funded and struggle for resources. Other policy innovations, including most of the job training and employment efforts of the Great Society, have been abandoned altogether.

The intellectual and policy legacy of the Great Society remains hotly contested. Liberal supporters point to successes in reducing poverty levels and call for extensions of many programs including health care, job training, and education. Critics from the left blame the limited focus of the Great Society for its failure to sustain political support, and call for broader policies that can appeal to both the middle class and the poor. Conservatives, by contrast, argue that the social policies of the 1960s distorted the work incentives of the poor, and are consequently responsible for the growth of an urban underclass dependent on government subsidies.

The central vision of the Great Society—that federal government should provide equal opportunity for all citizens—unraveled as funds grew tight and new policies proved unable to sustain public support. But, because of its bold ambitions, the Great Society will continue to provide the touchstone for future debates about social policy in the United States.

[*See also* African Americans, History; Civil Rights Movement; Johnson, Lyndon Baines; Kennedy, John Fitzgerald; New Deal; Underclass; *and* Welfare State.]

BIBLIOGRAPHY

Aaron, Henry J. *Politics and the Professors: The Great Society in Perspective*. (Washington, D.C., 1978).

Matusow, Allen J. *The Unraveling of America: A History of Liberalism in the 1960s*. (New York, 1984).

Patterson, James T. *America's Struggle against Poverty, 1900–1980*. (Cambridge, Mass., 1981).

Margaret Weir

GUN CONTROL

Gun ownership per capita is far higher in the United States than in any other modern industrial democracy, with the possible exception of Israel and Switzerland. There are currently some 200–250 million privately owned guns in the United States, one-third of which are said to be handguns. There is much controversy about the actual numbers of guns in circulation, if not about their overall scale; but we do know for certain that about 2 million new handguns are bought by private citizens in the United States each year, that currently around 40 percent of all American homes contain at least one gun, and that gun ownership is heavily concentrated in the hands of just one-quarter of the entire population. We also know that around thirty thousand Americans lose their lives to guns each year—in 2004 over eleven thousand as victims of homicide and sixteen thousand through suicide—and that the revenues of the firms making and selling those guns is huge: currently $2+ billion a year. (An estimated fifty thousand persons die annually in the United States from violence-related injuries. Homicide is the second leading cause of death for persons aged fifteen to twenty-four years, the third leading cause for persons aged ten to fourteen and twenty-five to thirty-four years, and the fourth leading cause for persons aged one to nine years. Suicide is the second leading cause of death for persons aged twenty-five to thirty-four years, the third leading cause for persons aged fifteen to twenty-four years, and the fourth leading cause for persons aged ten to fourteen and thirty-five to forty-four years.) Guns are as ubiquitous in American life as are cars and fast food; and like those two defining features of modern America, they are also big business.

At the federal level, the purchase and use of guns in the United States are regulated by three major statutes and by a string of minor ones. The big three are the 1938 Federal Firearms Act, which established the system of licensed dealers; the 1968 Gun Control Act, which established categories of prohibited gun purchasers and banned the importation of non-sporting guns; and the 1994 Brady Law, which set up the system of background checks on would-be gun owners. (The system of background checks was strengthened by legislation passed in 2007 in the wake of the shootings at Virginia Tech. A fourth piece of federal legislation, the Violent Crime Control and Law Enforcement Act of 1994, banned for 10 years the possession and sale of nineteen types of assault weapon.

The ban expired in 2004.) Most gun-control legislation, however, is state, rather than federal, in origin. There may be as many as three hundred different state statutes regulating gun use in the United States. Currently, most states have statutory waiting periods before handguns can be purchased, though forty of them also have "right-to-carry" laws on the books—laws allowing adults to carry concealed handguns once they have passed a background check and paid a fee. (Some of these states require gun training before the gun can be carried. Others do not.) It was not always so. As recently as 1985, only eight states had such laws. Nor is it universal. As late as 2003, Missouri voted down a "right-to-carry" law and Washington, D.C., maintained for thirty-one years a complete ban on the possession of handguns even in private homes. It was that 1976 ban, the most restrictive in the country, that opponents of gun control challenged regularly, and eventually successfully, in federal court. The 2008 Supreme Court ruling in *District of Columbia v. Heller* found the ban to be in violation of the Second Amendment and, as such, unconstitutional; and a follow-up ruling in 2010 (similarly a 5–4 vote by the Supreme Court justices) extended that decision to equivalent handgun bans in Chicago and Oak Park, Illinois. A flood of litigation is now expected, challenging handgun and other gun restrictions in states and cities across the Union.

The fact that the Washington, D.C., ban was in place to be challenged tells us that there are powerful advocates of tighter gun control currently operating in the United States. There are most notably Americans for Gun Safety, the Brady Campaign to Prevent Gun Violence (which includes chapters of The Million Mom March), and the Coalition to Stop Gun Violence. The fact that the ban was challenged successfully attests to the fact that there are also in play equally well-organized opponents of stricter regulation. The 3+-million-strong National Rifle Association (NRA) is the most visible; but there are others, including the Gun Owners of America, the Second Amendment Foundation, Jews for the Preservation of Firearms Ownership (who define themselves as "America's most aggressive defender of firearms ownership"), and the 650,000+-strong Citizen's Committee for the Right to Keep and Bear Arms. There is a broadly partisan dimension to this pattern of support and opposition to stricter gun control. Gun control is, in the main, a liberal issue— a cause long advocated by the Democratic, rather than the Republican, wing of the American political class and by many activists at the base of the Democratic Party. But gun control is not exclusively a liberal concern. There is support for tighter gun-control legislation in certain Republican quarters. James Brady was, after all, Ronald Reagan's press secretary, not Jimmy Carter's. There are also strong Democratic Party opponents of gun control, not least because the tight regulation of firearms does not play well among potential Democratic voters in America's rural areas and small towns, especially the male voters. The 2004 presidential campaign by John Kerry was derailed by the Republican Party's effective deployment of the "3G's" against him: "gays" and "God" were two of the three electorally sensitive issues on which Kerry and the Democrats were held to be vulnerable, but "guns" was the other.

Arguments against Gun Control. Those opposing the further regulation and restriction on gun ownership and use in the contemporary United States tend to use some or all of the following arguments in support of their case.

The Constitutional Right to Bear Arms. The Second Amendment to the Constitution is invariably the starting point of the gun-control debate, insisting as it does that "a well regulated militia, being necessary to the security of a free state, the right of the people to keep and bear arms shall not be infringed." Opponents of gun control put the weight of their interpretation of that amendment on the second part. Within the gun lobby as a whole, attitudes still vary significantly on the degree of gun regulation, if any, that is compatible with Second Amendment rights. The NRA regularly supports a degree of gun regulation. More libertarian voices within the gun lobby, by contrast, do not. Contrary to popular claims, very few progun activists are in favor of the deregulation of semimilitarized weapons. Indeed, they would prefer the regulatory activities of state and federal officials to be focused there. Most (though not all) law-abiding gun owners also see the virtue of background checks and brief moratoriums before guns can be purchased. But they are adamant that guns bought for sporting purposes and handguns bought for individual self-defense are not part of any gun problem. Tighter gun control, particularly gun control designed and implemented by federal authorities, is said by its opponents to strike at the very core of American freedom. Tighter federal gun control strikes at the freedom of states to self-regulate; and it strikes at the right of private citizens to live free of interference from the government, no matter what its level. States' rights and antigovernment sentiments are key themes in the thinking of many gun advocates: states' rights for traditionally conservative ones and a general antistatism for their more libertarian colleagues. In this debate at least, more than the Second Amendment to the American Constitution is at stake. So, too, according to many gun advocates, is the Tenth.

Guns as Self-Protection. One reason given for a generous interpretation of the Second Amendment by opponents of tighter gun control is the ability of gun owners to use those guns to protect themselves and their families against attack. On the relationship between guns and crime, the central assertion of the gun lobby is that guns help to prevent, rather than augment, crime and that handguns in particular provide an essential element of self-protection to law-abiding citizens in a society in which criminal elements are already armed and beyond the reach of the very gun control that liberals advocate. When states introduce "right-to-carry" laws, so the argument goes, the number of multiple public-victim shootings and attempted murders (including attempts on still-armed police officers) falls, rather than rises—and falls by large percentages. In the states that adopted a right-to-carry law between 1977 and 1999, the number of attacks is said to have fallen by 60 percent and the number of deaths and injuries from multiple shootings by 78 percent. In states where people can legally carry concealed weapons for the purposes of self-defense, that self-defense is said to be highly effective. It is effective in

general, and it is effective specifically for groups of citizens especially vulnerable to armed crime—the young, the elderly, women, and racial minorities (particularly black males). The number of incidents of effective self-defense is difficult to tabulate but is claimed to be substantial: perhaps as many as 2.5 million cases in the United States each year, the vast majority of which go entirely unrecorded.

Persistent Mythologies. The gun controversy refuses to go away, many gun advocates insist, not because guns are a problem but because antigun activists continue to maintain a series of assertions that are entirely untrue. *Myth 1*: Guns in the home do not make homes safe. Yes, they do. It is a little reported fact that fewer toddlers die from gun accidents in American homes each year than die from drowning in bathtubs and plastic water buckets. *Myth 2*: Gun control reduces crime. No, it does not. What it actually does is disarm the victims of crime. *Myth 3*: The gun lobby opposes reasonable regulations. No, it does not, as any careful examination of the NRA record will clearly demonstrate. *Myth 4*: Countries with tougher gun laws have less crime. They do not. *Myth 5*: Firearm offenses in the United States are soaring. No, they are not. If anything has soared, it is the number of guns privately owned in the United States—up 70 million since 1991; violent crimes are actually down, some 38 percent over the same period. *Myth 6*: Guns in this country are under-regulated. No, they are not. There are at least three hundred—some claim as many as twenty thousand—statutes already on the books at the state and federal levels. And *Myth 7*: Tighter gun regulation can end these episodic mass slaughters in US public places. No, sadly, according to most gun advocates, it cannot.

There is a *Myth 8* too, according to the opponents of further regulation. It is that blame for gun violence ultimately rests on those who make and sell weapons. It does not. Gun makers are no more liable for the misuse of their product than automakers are for the misuse of the car; and cars, of course, kill far more Americans each year than guns do. In truth, guns do not kill. Nor do cars. People are killed not by machines but by people. It is with the dangerous drivers and the misguided shooters that the moral buck needs to stop.

Ineffective Legislation. Tightening gun controls is also said to be neither necessary nor productive. It is not necessary: we have gun regulations enough—regulations which need better enforcement, not supplementation. It is not productive because the very people the regulations seek to control—the lone madman, the suicide killer, and the professional criminal—are precisely the people who will not be influenced by these regulations. On the contrary, the evidence would suggest that loosening gun regulation is the better way forward. The ten-year ban on assault weapons expired in 2004, yet violent crime using the previously banned weaponry did not rise as the ban's supporters anticipated that it would. The only piece of gun legislation that does correlate systematically with falling rates of violent crime is legislation that allows law-abiding citizens greater freedom to keep and bear arms, legislation giving citizens the right to carry handguns. "Overall, the states in the United States with the fastest growth rates in gun ownership during the 1990s" were also the states that "experienced the biggest drops in violent crime" (Lott, 2005a, p. 1). The United States has no monopoly on the horror of school shootings: gun-control advocates reputedly "conveniently ignore that the nations with the highest homicide rates have gun bans" (Lott, 2005b, p. 2).

Complex Causes. Gun-control advocates are also said to ignore the fact that, even with guns set aside, America is still a more violent society than many others. The United Kingdom is often singled out as a key comparator here, the US non-gun-based homicide rate being at least three times as high as the British rate. It is not the gun culture that is the core problem, according to some. It is the wider culture of which the guns are but a part.

It is extremely difficult to establish causal relationships even in strong cases of correlation, of course, because so many other variables are in play; but that complexity, gun advocates claim, can only strengthen their case. Violent crime has many causes, including the spread and depth of poverty, the spread of drugs, entrenched racism, the orchestration of

cultures of masculinity by an uncontrolled entertainment industry, and inadequate levels of law enforcement. Guns play a part. That is conceded. Easy access to guns does make deadly violence more common in drug deals, gang fights, and street corner brawls, as even the most ardent gun advocates recognize. But take the guns out of the equation, and the impulse to violence will still be there; and in fact, you cannot take guns out of the equation because so many are already in circulation. If quickening the rate of fall of violent crime is the target, public policy needs therefore to be directed at its social and economic causes and not at the weaponry used. "The real tragedy," Robert Levy (2000, p. 1) has written, "is not the availability of guns but illegitimacy, unemployment, dysfunctional schools and drug and alcohol abuse." So why focus on the guns rather than "the social pathology of the underclass"? Because, so the argument goes, "it's easier to blame an inanimate object than to come to grips with troublesome inner-city afflictions."

Arguments for Gun Control. The counterarguments in this ongoing debate tend to be deployed as follows.

The Problem of Gun-Related Deaths. The figures on guns and death in the United States are striking and disturbing. More than a million Americans have died in firearm homicides, suicide and unintentional killings since 1962—more slaughtered Americans in fact between 1979 and 1997 than in all wars since 1775. In 2001 alone, 29,573 people were killed by guns in the United States. That was approximately eighty fatalities a day and one in five of all American injury-induced deaths that year. (An estimated additional 58,841 people were treated for nonfatal firearm-related injuries in 2001—about 160 a day.) It is figures like these that have left the United States with the highest gun mortality rate among the top thirty-six high-income and middle-income countries in the United Nations and given it first place in "the industrialized world in firearm violence of all types—homicides, suicides, and unintentional deaths" (Violence Policy Center, 2000, p. 1). Currently, the rate of gun mortality in the United States is running "8 times higher than in other high income countries"

(Johns Hopkins Center for Gun Policy and Research, 2004, p. 1). This largesse in death and injury has occurred in spite of the falling number of American households possessing firearms and the spiraling cost of the consequences of their misuse. Between 1972 and 2006 the percentage of US households reporting gun ownership fell significantly: from a peak of 54 percent in 1977 to only 34.5 percent in 2006. The Johns Hopkins Center on Gun Policy and Research estimated the lifetime medical costs of gun-induced injuries and deaths at $2.3 billion and the wider economic and social costs at an estimated $100 billion per year.

Far from Making Americans Safe, Guns Put Americans at Risk. Because of the widespread availability of guns, there is an increased risk of death from homicide in the United States, there is the distinct possibility of accidental gun injury and death, and there is a greater ease of suicide, with all of these highly undesirable outcomes impacting both the general population and specific highly vulnerable groups—children, women, and members of ethnic minorities. There is definitely an enhanced vulnerability to homicide in a land full of guns, one that is not reduced by the possession of a gun as a form of self-defense. Firearms are currently "used to kill two out of every three homicide victims in America" and homicide rates are actually "higher in states where more households have guns" than in those where gun ownership is less (Harvard School of Public Health, 2007, p. 1). Keeping a gun at home for self-defense actually increases the probability of accidental injury or death. "Simply put, guns put in the home for self-protection are more often used to kill someone you know than to kill in self-defense: 22 times more likely according to a 1998 study in the *Journal of Trauma*" (Brady Center, 2002, p. 1). And in 2004, 16,750 Americans took their own lives by using firearms on themselves. No one is arguing that taking the guns out of the equation will end suicides. There are many ways to achieve that end for those who are so determined, but "the presence of a gun in the home increases the risk of suicide fivefold" (Brady Center, 2002, pp. 1–2). Unlike many other forms of suicide, sadly the use of a gun is nearly always successful.

Certain groups of American are thereby put especially at risk, particularly women, children, and African Americans. Women are especially at risk from the general availability of handguns. In 1998, for example, "for every time a woman used a handgun to kill an intimate acquaintance in self-defense, 83 women were murdered by an intimate acquaintance with a handgun" (Violence Policy Center, 2001a, p. 3). "In 2007, there were more than 18,000 homicides in the U.S. While men are more likely to be homicide victims, women are over 3 and a half times more likely to be killed by an intimate partner compared to men" (Johns Hopkins Center for Gun Policy and Research, 2003, p. 2). Children and teens are vulnerable too. More are killed each year with handguns than with any other weapon: on average, twenty-seven deaths annually throughout the 1990s. Most youth handgun deaths are in fact "homicides—with children and teens involved as both victims and offenders"(Violence Policy Center, 2001b, p. 1) and involved at an internationally excessive rate. In 1997 the firearms homicide rate for children under age fourteen in the United States was sixteen times higher than the rate in all the other twenty-five major industrial nations combined. Young black males are particularly vulnerable here: 51 percent of all deaths among African American teens between 1999 and 2004 were gun-related. For Caucasian teens, the equivalent figure was 18 percent.

Gun Regulators Are Not Opposed to Sports Guns; They Are, However, After Uzis . . . Very few people in the gun-regulation lobby object to the availability and use of guns for sporting purposes. There are some, appalled by the notion that killing animals for sport (as distinct from killing them for food) is legitimate in a civilized society; but in general, gun-regulation advocates have recognized the pleasure that gun sport gives to many Americans and have no desire to end it. Semimilitarized weapons, however, are quite a different matter. Many sensitive people have difficulty applying the "sporting justification" to weapons that shoot a string of bullets automatically or semiautomatically or which discharge bullets large enough to deconstruct animal (and human) flesh rather than simply penetrate it. The case against them all is that they are way too powerful for legitimate sporting purposes, that their presence in the gun market opens the way to their use by criminals, and that accordingly two key categories of American citizen are put especially at risk: the victims of violent crime and the police officers charged to prevent it.

... and Concealed Handguns. There is one additional set of smaller weaponry to whose general distribution and use the gun-control lobby is systematically opposed: handguns carried in a concealed manner and used for individual self-protection. As was noted earlier, the claims for the benefits of concealed weapons are substantial: that concealed weapons significantly reduce the scale of, and threat posed by, crimes of theft and assault and that the evidence demonstrating the positive effect of concealed weapons is clear and unambiguous. The counterargument is that neither of those claims is true. The evidence used to sustain them is misleading, and the effects are not positive for either crime or safety. Two-thirds of all Americans killed in gun-related incidents since 1962 were killed by a handgun, in an era in which handguns have been systematically refined to carry more and bigger bullets while being ever easier to conceal. Yet in that same era, when handguns accounted for 80+ percent of all killings, woundings, and gun crimes, the number of handguns in circulation remained only half that of rifles and shotguns. Violent gun crime is now a major problem in the United States. "From 1996 through 2005, there were almost 5 million violent crimes committed with firearms in this country." (Brady Center, 2006a, p. 1) There were 477,000 victims of violent gun crime in 2005 alone—146,000 more than were reported in 2004. So far from easing legal limits on the carrying and use of handguns, there is a strong case to be made for banning them outright, a case predicated on the huge loss of human life associated with what the Violence Policy Center calls "the explosive growth of the handgun population over the past generation" (2000, p. 1) and on the ever more lethal nature of the handguns now on sale.

Second Amendment Rights. Finally, the regulation of gun ownership and use is not the same as the banning of guns per se. The Second Amendment gives American citizens the right to keep and bear arms—that is not in dispute. But what is also not in dispute is that that amendment has never prevented the judicial branch of government from upholding the right of the legislature to set limits on how Americans can bear arms and on which arms they can bear. When the Bill of Rights was passed, no one could have foreseen the dramatic increase in the potency of the weaponry available to be carried. Nor could they have anticipated the scale and character of the criminality that is currently strengthened by easy and unregulated access to guns. The Second Amendment's linkage of the bearing of arms to the existence of a militia points to the governing concern in 1791 that the United States be able to defend itself. That defense is now properly located in the hands of a standing army and in the existence of civilian law enforcement. No one is proposing to disarm either the military or the police. The case for the regulation of private access to (and use of) guns is rather that in modern times we should grant a *monopoly of the legitimate use of force* to just those entities. The Second Amendment was never designed to be a vigilantes' charter, and the existence now of professional law enforcement and defense points to a more limited area in which private gun use and ownership remains legitimate. Guns for sport, yes; guns for self-defense, no: that should be the progressive position on the Second Amendment. The alternative is the persistence of periodic carnages in our workplaces and schools. After all, victims have rights too; and the Second Amendment is of no use to them if they are dead.

Gun-Control Issues and the Obama Administration. Gun-control issues did not figure largely in US politics in the first two years of the Obama administration, but the fear of gun control did. Obama the candidate had supported the restoration of the Brady ban on the sale of assault weapons, and that was enough to bring the NRA heavily into play, stoking fears of fresh controls from the incoming administration. Those fears proved misplaced however. The White House remained largely silent on even the restoration of the Brady ban, as did the Democratic

Party leadership in the House, conscious as that leadership was of the lack of support for further gun controls among many Democratic lawmakers elected from districts with significant numbers of gun owners. Democratic Party restraint did not, however, prevent a postelection surge in gun sales by buyers fearful of restrictions to come.

Though the administration was largely inert on this issue—to the point, indeed, in 2009 of signing into law permission for visitors to national parks to carry loaded and concealed weapons—the NRA and the wider gun lobby were not. The NRA continued actively to block moves to bar people on the Federal Bureau of Investigation's (FBI's) terrorist watch list from buying guns and explosives. The NRA continued to oppose the computerization of gun-ownership records at the National Tracing Center or any significant increase in the number of Bureau of Alcohol, Tobacco, Firearms, and Explosives (ATFE) agents supervising the retail gun industry. (The agency currently has the same number of agents as it did forty years ago, to police the nation's sixty thousand gun dealerships.) But even this careful and sustained lobbying was not enough for the more radically libertarian wing of the gun lobby, who pressed the NRA and legislators in 2010 for the right to openly carry pistols in public places and to more easily purchase semiautomatic rifles. Indeed, in the hot summer of 2010, as the Tea Party rank and file mobilized angrily against health-care reform, right-wing vigilante groups made an issue of the right to bear arms at political rallies—and, indeed, demonstrated that right in a major protest rally at Mount Vernon in Virginia. There was counterpressure in the opening years of the Obama administration. Mayors against Illegal Guns (a bipartisan coalition of 450 mayors) issued their own report in October 2009, urging tighter supervision of gun shows and the creation of an interstate firearms tracking unit; and the well-known Republican pollster Frank Luntz found, in a survey commissioned by the mayors, that NRA members in general were more open to sensible gun-control measures than the NRA leadership liked to claim. (For example, 69 percent of those polled supported closing the gun-show loophole, and 82 percent favored banning gun sales to suspected terrorists on

the FBI list.) Overall, however, the balance of pressure on the administration was definitely heavier and more effective from the gun lobby than from its opponents throughout 2009 and 2010.

That was not entirely surprising, given the history and organizational potency of the NRA. By 2010 the NRA had a long and consistent track record of opposition to new gun regulation and of initiatives designed to weaken existing gun controls. From its 1986 proposal, the Firearms Owners' Protection Act, designed to weaken large sections of the 1968 Gun Control Act, through to its steadfast opposition to the passing of the Brady Act and its support for the right to carry concealed weapons, the NRA has consistently attempted to keep restrictions on gun use to the minimum and advocated positions favoring the gun industry and individual gun owners. Of late, the NRA has been particularly active in designing and lobbying for legislation to give the gun industry legal immunity from prosecution of the kind so successfully used against the tobacco industry. It has also continued its prolonged battle to restrict the powers and limit the resources of the one federal agency that is charged with oversight of the manufacture and use of guns: formerly the ATF, now the ATFE. The NRA is a large and well-financed organization. Its membership is close to 3 million. Even a decade ago, its annual revenues exceeded $100 million and its lobbying arm had a $30 million budget and a staff of more than fifty; and as early as 1992 its political spending put it in the big league—ninth that year among all political action committees in congressional spending.

The NRA is politically active, but it is not politically even-handed. The continual reassurance given by leading Democrats that hunting and sporting guns are safe in their party's hands is regularly discounted by NRA leaders, who help to sustain the belief that the Democratic Party is out to deny law-abiding Americans their Second Amendment rights. By 2000, the NRA board of directors contained two Republican congressmen, the head of the right-wing Americans for Tax Reform, and the chair of the Conservative Political Activist Conference. With board members like Congressman Bob Barr, Senator Larry Craig, lobbyist Grover Norquist, and Conservative

Political Action Conference chair Larry Keene, the NRA's campaign contributions in the tightly contested 2000 presidential election went overwhelmingly to the Republican cause: over $1 million to the Republican National Committee compared to $111,000 to the Democrats. And not just to the Republican mainstream: the NRA lines up more easily with the Republican right. Before his death, Charlton Heston regularly linked NRA concerns about Second Amendment rights to the wider fight against terrorism abroad and gay rights at home; and other NRA leaders are also on record as on occasion mixing their gun lobbying with a strong dose of sexism, racism, and homophobia. Whatever else the NRA is or has become, politically it is not liberal. On the contrary, it is now firmly embedded on the right flank of the Republican Party and is a key element in the Republicans' persistent campaign to win over white working-class voters, particularly white working-class men.

It is not simply the lobbying of the NRA that so infuriates gun-control advocates. It is also the state of the gun industry itself. There is particular irritation in many gun-control quarters at the behavior of the retail side of the gun industry. "Tupper parties for criminals" is how the Violence Prevention Center has characterized gun shows, arguing that access to lethal weaponry by criminal and terrorist elements is far too easy at many of them. It is noticeable that "cities in states with strong gun laws tend to be flooded with guns sold at dealerships in states with weaker gun laws" (Brady Center, 2007b, p. 9), many of them acquired at gun shows because at most gun shows unlicensed gun dealers are allowed to sell guns without any obligation to carry out background checks on would-be purchasers. The legal fiction here is that the unlicensed dealers are only selling from their personal collections. Yet it was from just such a "personal collection" that several of the guns used in the Columbine High School shooting were easily obtained and that, in the run up to 9/11, Hezbollah supporters in the United States were found to be arming themselves. Rogue arms dealers then compound the problem, particularly rogue dealers operating at legal gun shows. Federal crime gun data show more than "that gun shows provide a

forum for illegal firearms sales and trafficking." They also show that "most crime guns originate with a relatively small number of dealers . . . that about one percent of the Nation's gun dealers account for almost 60 percent of guns recovered in crime" (Brady Center, 2007b, p. 9). The complicity of these dealers with criminals, gang members, and juveniles is clear. The Brady Center holds them responsible for a string of preventable "shady dealings" that include large-scale sales of handguns to single individuals, repeat customers buying guns over and over again, or a single purchaser buying multiple numbers of the same weapon. According to the Brady Center, slowing down the flow of new guns to criminals is particularly vital because it is new guns that the criminal fraternity prefers. New guns cannot be traced back to old crimes. They are more reliable than old guns, and they are steadily more potent. They are steadily more potent because competition between gun manufacturers has long built a deadly logic into the heart of this industry, persistently driving up the potency of both weapons and ammunition and creating demands and markets that were hitherto more modest in their scale and requirements. New markets are targeted purely for reasons of profitability—women have been a particular focus of much recent gun advertising. New weapons are regularly developed, particularly of late ever smaller handguns attractive to those keen on the carrying of concealed weapons. The gun industry stands accused too of a persistent "institutional blindness" to the small number of dealers whose names regularly appear in the ATFE's trace data as the source of guns used in crime. "The gun industry knows who the high-trace dealers are," the Brady Center (2006a, p. iv) has argued, but it has consistently "refused to stop selling those guns or force them to reform." Instead, the industry continues to work assiduously to discredit and silence ATFE trace data—seeking, through the so-called Tiahrt amendment, to block publication of those data. It also continues to seek unprecedented protection from any liability for the misuse of its products through legislation at the state and federal levels.

Finally, two issues of public concern are pulling the debate away from NRA concerns and back toward greater gun control. One is the growing evidence of the contribution of inadequately regulated US gun retailers to the growing gun violence in Mexico and to the strengthening (within the United States and south of its border) of drug gangs equipped to kill more effectively than the state forces organized to defeat them. The other is the safety of legislators themselves. That lack of safety was graphically underlined in January 2011 by the attempted assassination of Representative Gabrielle Giffords, an attempt that cost the lives of six bystanders. The would-be assassin was armed with a semiautomatic handgun whose magazine released thirty-one bullets into the crowd that was meeting and greeting the congresswoman. In the wake of that shooting, Senator Frank Lautenberg and Representative Caroline McCarthy introduced legislation to ban high-capacity ammunition clips. It was a particularly appropriate response by Caroline McCarthy, whose own husband had been killed in 1993, and her son critically injured, when a mentally disturbed gunman opened fire in a Long Island railway carriage—appropriate but not immediately effective: at the time of going to press, any new legislation remains stuck in committee.

BIBLIOGRAPHY

Brady Center. *Firearm Facts*. (Washington, D.C., April 2007a).

Brady Center. *Guns in the Home*. (Washington, D.C., April 2002).

Brady Center. *Shady Dealing*. (Washington, D.C., January 2007b).

Brady Center. *Trivial Violations?* (Washington, D.C., September 2006a).

Brady Center. *Without a Trace*. (Washington, D.C., April 2006b).

District of Columbia v. Heller, 554 U.S. 570 (2008).

Doherty, Brian. *Gun Control on Trial*. (Washington, D.C., 2008).

CDC. *Morbidity and Mortality Weekly Report*, 59, no. SS-4 (May 14, 2010).

Fallis, David S. "450 Mayors Petition Obama to Adopt Broad Gun Reform." *Washington Post*, October 3, 2009.

Grimaldi, James V., and Sari Horowitz. "As Mexico Drug Violence Runs Rampant, U.S. Guns Tied to Crime South of the Border." *Washington Post*, December 13, 2010.

Harvard School of Public Health. "States with Higher Levels of Gun Ownership Have Higher Homicide Rates," press release, January 11, 2007, http://www.hsph.harvard.edu/news/press-releases/2007-releases/press01112007.html.

Johns Hopkins Center for Gun Policy and Research. *Firearm Injury and Death in the United States*. (Baltimore, Md., 2004).

Johns Hopkins Center for Gun Policy and Research. *Fact Sheet: Intimate Partner Violence and Firearms*. (Baltimore, Md., 2003).

Levy, Robert A. "On the March: Clinton, Gore and a Million Moms." Cato Institute. May 11, 2000, http://www.cato.org/pub_display.php?pub_id=4708.

Lott, Jr., John R. "Disarming Facts." American Enterprise Institute. March 23, 2005a, http://www.aei.org/article/22168.

Lott Jr., John R. "Don't Blame American Guns." American Enterprise Institute. October 28, 2005b, http://www.aei.org/article/23387.

Lott Jr., John R. *Why People Fear Guns*. American Enterprise Institute. January 3, 2004, http://www.aei.org/article/19691.

Moorhouse, John C., and Brent Wanner. "Does Gun Control Reduce Crime or Does Crime Increase Gun Control?" *Cato Journal* 26, no. 1 (Winter 2006): 103–124.

National Rifle Association, Institute for Legislative Action. NRA-ILA Fact Sheets. "Right-to-Carry 2010," http://www.nraila.org/news-issues/fact-sheets/2010/right-to-carry-2010.aspx?s=right%20to%20carry%202010&st=&ps=.

Poe, Richard. *The Seven Myths of Gun Control*. (New York, 2003).

Spitzer, Robert J. *The Politics of Gun Control*. (Washington, D.C., 2008).

Squires, Peter. *Gun Culture or Gun Control?* (New York, 2000).

US Department of Justice. *Guns in America*. (Washington, D.C., 2007).

Violence Policy Center. "A Deadly Myth: Women, Handguns and Self-Defense." 2001a, http://www.vpc.org/studies/myth.htm.

Violence Policy Center. "Gun Shows in America: Tupperware Parties for Criminals." 1998, http://www.vpc.org/studies/tupstudy.htm.

Violence Policy Center. "Kids in the Line of Fire." 2001b, http://www.vpc.org/studies/firecont.htm.

Violence Policy Center. 'Unsafe in Any Hands," 2000, http://www.vpc.org/studies/unsafe.htm.

David Coates

H

Hate Crimes

A hate crime is a criminal act motivated at least in part by the victim's perceived group identity. Typical hate crimes would include such acts as assaulting a person because the attacker believes the victim is gay, vandalizing a synagogue, or burning a cross in front of an African American family's home. Hate crimes are sometimes also known as "bias crimes" or "crimes of ethnic intimidation."

Although crimes based on prejudice are hardly new, most hate crime laws are fairly recent. After lobbying by advocacy groups, states began passing special hate crime legislation in the early 1980s; by 2011, every state except Wyoming had enacted some form of hate crime law. In addition, a federal hate crime law was enacted in 2009. These laws vary considerably, but many of them work by enhancing the penalties for criminal acts motivated by the victims' perceived identity group. The specific protected groups also vary. All hate crime laws encompass crimes committed because of the victims' race, ethnicity, national origin, or religion; many include sexual orientation or gender; and some include gender identity, disability, age, or political affiliation. Canada, Australia, and many European countries have also adopted laws aimed at bias-motivated crime, but these laws tend to differ considerably from US laws in function and scope.

Hate crime laws have engendered a number of vigorous legal and policy debates. Among these have been arguments concerning the laws' constitutionality. Some have asserted that because the laws provide enhanced punishment for specific motives—a characteristic that is nearly unique among US laws—they are essentially punishing offenders' thoughts, which would be a clear violation of the First Amendment. Other people have countered that it is not the thoughts themselves that are being punished, but rather the actions based on those thoughts. Furthermore, it has been argued that hate crimes are qualitatively different from other offenses, in that they are more harmful to victims and communities. Empirical evidence for this assertion is weak, but when the US Supreme Court addressed the constitutionality of hate crime laws in *Wisconsin v. Mitchell* (1993), the Court held that these laws are permissible. However, the Court has distinguished hate *crime* laws from hate *speech* laws. Hate speech laws attempt to prohibit harmful or offensive expressions without requiring some underlying criminal act. Examples of hate speech might include calling someone a racial epithet, distributing leaflets or creating a web page with content that is defamatory to a particular group, or displaying images such as swastikas. In general, hate speech is protected by the First Amendment and courts have usually struck down laws that attempt to prohibit such speech.

Although many of the constitutional issues related to hate crimes have been settled by the courts, other debates remain. One of the more lively of these debates concerns which groups to protect; most of the controversy around this issue has centered over whether to include within hate crime laws crimes committed because of the victims' sexual orientation. The US federal hate crime law, eventually titled the Matthew Shepard and James Byrd Jr. Hate Crimes Prevention Act, was debated in Congress for well over a decade before being signed into law in 2009. The primary obstacle to its passage was the fact that crimes on the basis of sexual orientation were included within the law's scope; some conservative and religious organizations and individuals strongly opposed this language. As of 2011, the hate crime laws in twenty-nine states and the District of Columbia included sexual orientation as a protected class, while the remainder of the states' laws did not.

For over two decades, attempts have been made to measure the number of hate crimes that are committed in the United States, and to determine who is victimized. Initially, much of this work was done by private advocacy organizations such as the Anti-Defamation League, but in 1990 Congress passed the Hate Crime Statistics Act, which requires the Department of Justice to collect hate crime data from law enforcement agencies. These data are now included within the annual Uniform Crime Reports.

In 2009, the FBI reported nearly eight thousand hate crimes in the United States. This number was a small decrease over the previous year; in general, the FBI reports between eight and ten thousand hate crimes each year. However, these numbers likely represent only a small portion of the offenses that actually occur. There are a large number of problems associated with the collection of hate crime data. Among these are the relatively low rates of reporting by victims to the police, difficulties in the way police departments collect and categorize offenses, and the often ambiguous nature of the offenses themselves. Hate crime reporting rates are likely especially low among certain victims such as those who are in the country illegally, those who live in communities with poor relationships with law enforcement, and those who are reluctant to be identified as victims.

Despite the problems with the official data, some victimization patterns for hate crimes seem clear. In most jurisdictions, the most common motivation for hate crimes is racial or ethnic bias, and the most common victims of these crimes are African Americans. The second most common motivation varies depending on the jurisdiction. In some places it is religious bias (with Jews being the most frequent targets), and in some places it is sexual orientation bias (with gay men being most often victimized). These patterns can sometimes vary, however. For example, shortly after the events of September 11, 2001, there was a sharp increase in crimes against those who were perceived to be Muslim or Middle Eastern.

While thousands of hate crimes are reported to the police each year, actual convictions are rare. For example, in 2009 in California, 1,100 hate crimes were reported to the police, 283 of these were actually prosecuted as hate crimes, but there were only 131 hate crime convictions. One of the primary reasons for the low conviction rates is that it is often very difficult to determine a person's motive for committing a crime, and even more difficult to prove that motive beyond a reasonable doubt. Even some acts that might seem fairly unambiguous, such as a swastika spray-painted on a synagogue, might be committed more out of youthful indiscretion than true animosity toward a specific group. In fact, research on hate crime offenders suggests that very few of them belong to organized hate groups and many of them have other motives as well, such as impressing their friends, demonstrating their own masculinity, or alleviating boredom. Of course, this does not mean that prejudice plays no part in their behavior, but at least some states require that it be the primary or a primary motive, and proving that can be very challenging.

Although the body of research remains small, some studies have been conducted to obtain better estimates of the extent and effects of hate crime victimization. For example, studies by Gregory

Herek (2009) suggested that over one-third of gay men in the United States have had a hate crime committed against them or their property. While being a victim of a crime can certainly be physically and psychologically harmful, it remains unclear whether this harm is quantitatively or qualitatively different from that suffered by victims of other crimes.

Research has also been conducted to investigate hate crime offenders. As mentioned above, few offenders—perhaps only 5 percent—belong to organized hate groups. Most seem to be young men acting in small, informal groups. It is unclear the extent to which these offenders are influenced by hate group propaganda or, in fact, by biased messages received from the media and society in general. The extent of recidivism among hate crime offenders is also unknown, nor have many studies been conducted on the most effective methods of treating or rehabilitating offenders. However, some small studies have suggested that restorative justice approaches such as victim-offender mediation may be useful, at least in some cases.

One of the main reasons that supporters have given for favoring hate crime laws is that the laws will deter bias motivated crimes. It is unlikely, however, that many people are really deterred by these laws. Even if potential offenders are aware that the laws exist, and even if they engage in some type of risk-benefit analysis in which the enhanced punishments carry a weight that ordinary punishments do not, most people probably conclude—correctly—that the chances of receiving sanctions for their actions are slim. However, that does not mean that hate crime laws are without value; it has been argued that the laws themselves serve a symbolic purpose, conveying the message that such behaviors are not acceptable within a community. On the other hand, some scholars have argued that the laws can also be harmful, in that they encourage resentment of minorities, whom some might mistakenly see as getting "special treatment," or that they increase intergroup antagonism. The laws may also inspire complacency among policy makers, who will be deterred from pursuing more meaningful ways of reducing bias.

[*See also* Civil Liberties; Crime and Punishment; Gay Rights; *and* Gender and Politics.]

BIBLIOGRAPHY

Federal Bureau of Investigation. "Latest Hate Crimes Statistics." http://www.fbi.gov/news/stories/2010/november/hate_112210/hate_112210.

Gerstenfeld, Phyllis B. *Hate Crimes: Causes, Controls, and Controversies.* 2d ed. (Thousand Oaks, Calif., 2011).

Harris, Camala D., and California Department of Justice. "Hate Crime in California 2010." http://ag.ca.gov/cjsc/publications/hatecrimes/hc10/preface10.pdf.

Herek, Gregory M. "Hate Crimes and Stigma-Related Experiences among Sexual Minority Adults in the United States: Prevalence Estimates from a National Probability Sample." *Journal of Interpersonal Violence* 24 (2009): 54–77.

Jacobs, James B., and Kimberly Potter. *Hate Crimes: Criminal Law and Identity Politics.* (New York, 2000).

Jenness, Valerie, and Ryken Grattet. *Making Hate a Crime: From Social Movement to Law Enforcement.* (New York, 2004).

Perry, Barbara, ed. *Hate Crimes.* 5 vols. (Santa Barbara, Calif., 2009).

Phyllis B. Gerstenfeld

HEALTH CARE

Among the health systems of developed countries, America's is unique. Only the United States built its health insurance system by linking access to insurance with employment. Though the 2010 Patient Protection and Affordable Care Act may change this substantially, this reliance on job-based health insurance accounts for the very high number of Americans without coverage: more than 50 million people, or 16 percent of the population.

US medical costs are the highest in the world by a significant margin. This is a consequence of higher prices for services, the rapid adoption and heavy use of new medical technologies, the absence of curbs by payers on their use, and the widespread use of fee-for-service reimbursement, which encourages providers to deliver a high volume of services. Neither the government nor private payers exerts much control over the price or volume of medical services. Physicians, hospitals, and other providers are politically powerful. Almost half of all US health spending is public, but most of the administration of insurance coverage remains firmly in private hands.

Despite its high spending, the United States ranks at the middle or bottom of most comparative measures of health outcomes, such as mortality and morbidity, among industrialized nations. This reflects, in large part, the relative lack of resources devoted to public health and the lack of coordination between the acute health care system, which treats short-term injuries and episodes of illness, and public health systems, which attempt to create and maintain the conditions necessary for the health of the US population as a whole.

The uniqueness of the US health system has led, in turn, to distinctive ways of debating health care issues in American politics. Through the 1970s, debates revolved around physician demands for autonomy, and physician hostility toward any measures that would thwart this independence, including oversight by managed care plans or government programs such as Medicare. Since the 1970s, the debate has turned more to the issue of rising health costs, which contribute to federal deficits and state budget gaps and cause competitive difficulties for American manufacturers in global trade. And studies that have called the quality of overall US health care into question have brought demands for redesigning the way care is delivered, with the aim of getting better value for medical spending.

Beginnings Count: How a Private System Evolved.
Before the late nineteenth century, medicine was a true cottage industry, in which doctors in the United States operated as small business owners not very differently from cobblers or barrel makers. In the words of the historian Roy Porter (1997), medicine was "small-scale, disaggregated, restricted, and piecemeal in its operations" (p. 628). In many ways it remained so until the 1960s and 1970s. Though mutual aid societies flourished in some quarters, and in particular in New York and Philadelphia, doctors tended to practice alone and patients paid them directly for services.

The evolution of medicine as a profession, in the United States and in other countries, began in the late nineteenth century. It paralleled and drew upon the rise in scientific knowledge and the growth of institutions that applied science to everyday life. Advances in biomedical research and revolutions in surgical procedures and pharmacy practices went hand in hand with the growth of philanthropies that could support them, not to mention large fortunes. A growing middle class, at the same time, became able to avail itself of new medical discoveries and began to expect them to roll out with regularity.

American physicians and religious and ethnic groups built hospitals, embraced new technologies, and aggressively marketed their products. Before the late nineteenth century, hospitals had been closer to "alms houses" which housed the chronically ill or victims of plagues or emergencies. By the early twentieth century, they became places where middle-class Americans routinely went when they became ill. Hospital admissions in the United States rose from an estimated 146,500 annually just after the Civil War to more than 29 million in the late 1960s and over 37 million today.

This growth and expansion of hospitals, however, took place on terms that preserved physician autonomy and cemented the power of doctors, who stood at the top of a medical hierarchy. Doctors were granted admitting privileges at multiple hospitals but remained in independent practice. Bans on the "corporate practice of medicine" prevented hospitals from employing physicians directly or investors from owning hospitals. New licensure regulations distinguished medically schooled physicians from homeopaths and osteopaths.

Except in emergencies and for basic regulation and licensure, the government was only intermittently involved in health care. Public health became a separate profession in the early twentieth century and especially during World War I. It principally took the form of responding to epidemics and crafting public service announcements on behalf of the government, employers, and good government associations. From the outset, public health agencies were never institutionally linked in the United States with hospitals and clinics in ways that were commonplace in other countries.

The origins of the current health insurance system help explain its fee-for-service orientation and its links to employment. Until the Great Depression, most patients paid their doctors directly for medical services rendered. As incomes declined and more prospective patients were either unemployed or financially strapped, hospital admissions and revenues declined during this period. Hospitals turned to the idea of insurance as a way to keep beds full and maintain a steady base of patients. In 1929, Baylor University Hospital in Dallas offered to provide up to twenty-one days of hospital care each year to a group of schoolteachers for the sum of six dollars each. Such prepaid hospital payment plans, supported by the American Hospital Association, quickly spread to California and New Jersey and then throughout the country. Since doctors were paid on a fee-for-service basis, which the American Medical Association (AMA) and its affiliates preferred, such arrangements gained favor from the medical profession as well. In 1939, Blue Shield plans offering comparable coverage for physician bills began, though because these costs were less steep than hospital payments, these plans spread more slowly.

During World War II, the federal government imposed a freeze on wages and prices to counter the threat of rising inflation in a wartime economy. However, in 1942, the federal War Labor Board, which administered the freeze, ruled fringe benefits exempt from limits on wages. This meant that employers competing for scarce labor could offer health insurance to attract workers. Largely as a result, the number of Americans covered by Blue Cross plans increased almost fourfold during the war, from 7 million to 26 million.

The link between employment and access to insurance coverage tightened further after the war. In 1954, Congress affirmed an Internal Revenue Service (IRS) decision that health benefits offered through employment were not wages and therefore not taxable. This treatment of benefits created a large tax exclusion (now amounting to around $200 billion annually) and increased the attractiveness of coverage through employment. Commercial insurers entered the market alongside the not-for-profit

Blue Cross and Blue Shield plans and competed for customers.

This creation of a private marketplace for health insurance moved the United States in a different direction from many other countries, which at mid-century were consolidating national, government-run, universal insurance programs. It meant that insurers focused on employed Americans, who tended to be healthier and better-off, and overlooked older Americans, or those with low incomes who could not afford insurance premiums without subsidies. And, it shaped the subsequent structure and politics of US health care through path dependency, that is, the tendency for institutions to move in a direction consistent with earlier decisions. In the United States, with its relatively weak executive department, and political powers dispersed between multiple branches of government and the states, this tendency is especially pronounced.

Medicare and Medicaid: Cornerstones of the Current System. For many years before the creation of Medicare in 1965, the plight of older Americans was clear. Older Americans went to the hospital more often, had higher medical costs, and lacked insurance at a much higher rate than younger Americans. Just over half of seniors had insurance coverage and only one-third of those who were out of the workforce were covered. Since most seniors were presumably in need of financial assistance, it was politically attractive to cover all of them. Many believed that starting with such a sympathetic group would open the path to universal insurance coverage for all.

Lyndon B. Johnson's landslide presidential victory in 1964 and strong Democratic hold on both houses of Congress facilitated the passage of Medicare. Thanks to an aggressive implementation strategy and a rapid embrace of the program by seniors, most older Americans were covered for hospital insurance by 1966, one year after the program was launched, and 17.6 million seniors, out of roughly 19 million eligible, signed up for the voluntary Part B of Medicare, which covered physician services. Moreover, the desegregation of Southern hospitals was accomplished swiftly through the insistence of federal officials that no hospital that discriminated on the basis of race would receive federal funding.

While the passage of Medicare addressed a vital need, it also reinforced the essentially private structure of the US medical system and helped contribute to the inflationary spiral of US health spending. Medicare's distinction between "Part A" for hospital care (mandatory, paid for through a payroll tax) and "Part B" for physician services (voluntary, paid for through premiums and general government revenues) followed customary practices among "the Blues" (that is, the insurance programs of Blue Cross and Blue Shield). Blue Cross and Blue Shield were responsible for the day-to-day administration of Medicare claims. To help blunt opposition from the powerful AMA and from physicians, the statute promised that Medicare would pay doctors' "customary and reasonable costs" and would not "interfere with the practice of medicine."

Acquiescence on rates and control meant generous and rising payments to physicians, many of whom set prices based on what they expected Medicare to be able to bear rather than on the basis of previous practice. Private insurers followed Medicare's lead on physician reimbursement, and Medicare rates tended to become a floor rather than a ceiling. As costs predictably went up, Congress responded first by freezing the Medicare benefit package in place, rather than allowing the program to evolve in ways that kept pace with how patients with private coverage were generally treated. As a result, Medicare did not cover any preventive services until 1980, and did not cover outpatient prescription drugs until 2004.

Medicare's rising costs and projections about the exhaustion of the "Part A Trust Fund" for hospital care made it a perennial part of budget politics from the early 1980s to the present day. Congress played catch-up by establishing a Prospective Payment System (PPS) for Medicare in 1984, which set a fixed rate for hospitalization fees paid based on a patient's diagnosis. While Medicare's costs over time grew roughly at the same pace as those in the private sector, its rate of growth has been the subject of perennial debates and blue-ribbon commissions.

Moreover, Medicare's considerable spending (almost four percent of the gross domestic product [GDP]) means that the program always occupies a central role during debates over the federal budget. For example, cuts in Medicare provider rates accounted for the bulk of the short-lived federal budget surplus of 1999–2000, while the current Affordable Care Act expects $130 billion in savings to come from reduced payments to private plans which serve Medicare beneficiaries. Many have recommended that Medicare be put on a private footing. This has resulted in the considerable expansion of private managed care plans in Medicare, and perennial calls for a fixed budget contribution ("premium support") for older Americans.

To the surprise of most contemporary observers, the 1965 legislation also created Medicaid, which expanded federal health care spending to states. Federal and state spending jointly funded Medicaid, but Washington offered a higher "match rate" for money spent on Medicaid by less wealthy states. Republicans in Congress had wanted to build on existing (but sparsely used) programs to help states pay for the health care of their aged and indigent populations, instead of creating a universal program of entitlements and contributions. Led by Wilbur Mills, chairman of the House Ways and Means Committee, the Democratic leadership used this opening to seek new funding for the health care of low-income Americans.

From the outset, distinctions between Medicare and Medicaid were sharp. Medicare was a universal federal program funded principally through the payroll tax, for which almost all seniors qualified. Its benefit package was largely standardized on a national basis. Medicaid, on the other hand, was a joint federal-state commitment paid for by general revenues, with strict means-testing and eligibility requirements that excluded most poor adult men and others, and with a benefit package left largely to the discretion of the states. Medicaid has expanded greatly over the past thirty years, however, with the result that it is now larger than Medicare on the basis of enrollment and a near equal in spending. The Affordable Care Act, for the first time, will cover through Medicaid all Americans making less than or close to the federal poverty line, meaning that it comes close to being a universal coverage program for low-income Americans.

The "three-layer cake" of Medicare Part A, Medicare Part B, and Medicaid dramatically reduced the financial burden of care for seniors, though that burden has crept up over time through the effect of cost-sharing for expensive procedures. For Medicare, the adequacy of the benefit package over time has been its Achilles heel. For Medicaid, which pays much lower rates to providers, keeping an adequate network of providers and avoiding state budget cuts during economic downturns have been its traditional challenges. By accommodating the private medical industry, Medicare and Medicaid mustered the political capital necessary to succeed. Along with several other government-funded health programs such as the Veterans Administration, the Public Health Service, the Indian Health Service, and Tricare (military health care), they normalized the idea of the federal government as a major payer for health care. At the same time, Medicare's policy of not interfering with the "usual and customary practice of medicine" and paying "customary and reasonable costs" helped set off a long period of medical inflation and contributed to the rapid growth of a vast medical industry.

Health Costs Take Center Stage. If one distinguishing feature of US health care is its historic link between insurance and employment, another is its unusually high rate of spending relative to other countries. As early as the 1930s distinguished commissions such as the Committee on the Costs of Medical Care issued warnings about the potential for runaway medical spending, but these concerns took a backseat to encouraging access to newer technologies and financing wider access to insurance coverage. As Roy Porter (1997) puts it, "From the 1930s the United States has invested in more, more elaborate, and more expensive health care for the well-off" (p. 658). Especially by the late 1970s and early 1980s, corporate managers and government officials were becoming increasingly troubled by the costs of medical care. A top General Motors

executive, for instance, observed that Blue Cross and Blue Shield had become a bigger supplier to GM than US Steel.

Between 1950 and 1970, US health spending rose from $12.7 to $71.6 billion, or from 4.5 to 7.3 percent of the gross national product. (The health workforce grew from 1.2 to 3.9 million Americans over the same period.) By 1980, medical expenditures had reached $230 billion, or almost ten percent of GNP. The figures are $2.6 trillion and 17 percent of the economy today, or from one-third more to more than twice what other countries spend on a per capita basis.

Why did the United States come to lead the world in medical spending? Partly this growth reflected deliberate expansions of capacity coming to maturity. The federal government invested heavily both in applied science and in hospital construction after World War II. Prewar investment in science had been almost entirely private, but government spending, which grew rapidly during the war years and after, rose from $81 million to $400 million between 1955 and 1960. Under the Hill-Burton Act, the federal government spent $3.7 billion between 1947 and 1971 to construct hospitals in what were deemed underserved areas. This funding contributed to 30 percent of all community hospital-building projects, and accounted for roughly 10 percent of the total construction cost of all hospitals. The rapid expansion of medical schools, again with considerable government support, tended to produce a rising number of specialists who could charge more for their services.

Moreover, Americans spent more on health care because medicine was often successful. Physicians increasingly found treatments and interventions for conditions that they previously had been able, at best, to diagnose. What one scholar calls the "resurrectionist" capacity of technology holds a special appeal for middle-class Americans, as indicated by their fascination with innovations such as the iron lung and penicillin. This has made Americans more willing to spend federal dollars to promote new medical technologies, and also more fiercely resistant to policies, such as single-payer health reform or deliberate curbs on new hospital construction, which might, even if only in theory, crimp innovation and its diffusion.

Medical innovation has paid dividends even as it has driven up costs. One researcher, for instance, has argued that improvements in the care of heart disease alone, on the basis of years of life added, could justify the entire increased spending on US health care since the mid-twentieth century (Cutler 2005). The sharp growth in Medicare expenditures when the program began to cover dialysis treatment for end-stage kidney failure demonstrated vividly how the widespread expansion of new technologies could extend lives, even as its high costs helped block further expansion of the program's benefits.

Certain mutually reinforcing features of the US health system meant that health care spending grew much more rapidly than it did in other countries. Until the 1970s, the key premise was that more medical care was better, and that private voluntary institutions—doctors, medical schools, and hospitals—were best suited to decide how these systems should be organized. These groups strongly opposed any forms of payment other than fee-for-service, which encouraged more procedures to be performed. Suppliers of care—from doctors to drug manufacturers to device makers—tended to be highly organized and politically savvy, while payers were diffuse and disorganized. No entity had the power to say "no" to rising prices and higher insurance premiums, and by the time government, employers, and unions joined the fray, the power of the medical industry was entrenched. Employers were responsible for tens of thousands of slightly different benefit packages and their employees were insulated from the full cost of care, thanks to the exclusion of health benefits from taxation.

In short, this fragmentation of payers and weak government powers created a permissive environment in which health costs rose rapidly, as both supply and demand increased. New technologies were swiftly embraced as reimbursement was quickly approved. In the absence of a single strong payer, hospitals, doctors, and others associated with medicine achieved higher prices for all services and products, often by two or three times per unit of service,

than anywhere else in the world. The personal debt that physicians regularly incurred in their training, which in other countries is publicly subsidized, also played a significant role in driving up rates. The swift demise of President Carter's proposal to cap hospital rates and President Clinton's proposal to cap insurance premiums demonstrated this power to resist regulation of prices.

While medical spending grows in tandem with the wealth of nations, according to a 2009 McKinsey estimate, the United States spends $650 billion more on health care than would be expected, even when adjusting for its wealth relative to other countries. The main reasons are high prices (in particular for pharmaceuticals), high administrative costs (two-thirds of these in the private sector), and the high costs of outpatient care. Population aging, malpractice, and other possible explanations play a relatively minor role. Though high inpatient hospital costs clearly played a major earlier role in medical inflation, hospitals have shifted their work toward same-day elective care and high-margin procedures. Hospitals and physician groups have also established specialty hospitals and institutes that solely perform procedures with high reimbursement rates, such as cardiac care. Sixty-five percent of hospital treatments are now delivered in these and other outpatient settings, up from 43 percent in 1980. While the number of visits by Americans to doctors has remained relatively flat, more is done, at higher prices, to Americans during each encounter. And the United States lags in the adoption of cost-saving methods, such as electronic health records (EHRs), which might counter the inflationary effects of administrative and payer fragmentation. While more than three-quarters of doctors in most European countries use EHRs for instance, fewer than one in five American doctors does the same.

Rising US health costs had three main political consequences: they made health care-related politics more salient; they made the solving of the problem of the uninsured both more urgent and more difficult; and they made the pursuit of reform more complicated, since the expansion of the medical industry widened the scope, size, and power of its interests. In the 1970s, only a few score health lobbyists walked the halls of Congress. Current estimates put their number at over 3300, or over six lobbyists per lawmaker.

The Rise of "Managed Care" and the Clinton Plan. The most prominent early strategy for rolling back the growth of spending—itself an approach which relied heavily on private institutions—was managed care. The idea behind managed care was to assign to a group or organization the responsibility for providing necessary care to a group of patients at a fixed cost. The concept itself was not new; it harked back to prepayment arrangements in mining and lumber camps in the Pacific Northwest at the turn of the twentieth century, and it was enshrined in a large prepaid group practice, the Kaiser Foundation and the Permanente Medical Group, which gained a strong foothold in California beginning in World War II.

The idea received new life thanks to the HMO Act of 1973, which required large employers to include at least one health maintenance organization (HMO) among the choices of insurance coverage for employees. These insurance products featured tightly controlled networks of providers who were paid a flat fee per person per month, a system known as "capitation." The incentives of working within a fixed budget, managed care proponents argued, would encourage doctors to minimize unneeded care and to emphasize prevention and primary care. The hope, as well, was that insurance products could be tailored more directly to the needs of particular patients at an affordable price. As one expert put it, "The health insurance firms of the future will offer multiple provider networks, rather than remain wedded to a single design, in order to accommodate the heterogeneity among consumers in what they are willing to buy and among physicians in what they are willing to sell" (Robinson 1999, p. 64).

HMOs became the cornerstone of a universal coverage strategy backed by President Nixon and Republicans, who were responding to proposals by Senator Edward Kennedy and others for a single, universal, federal health insurance system operating under a national budget. No fewer than six major

initiatives for universal coverage were launched during the 1970s and 1980s, and all failed to clear the launch pad. The hurdles to achieving comprehensive reform mounted as the years passed and the system organized around employer coverage and fee-for-service reimbursement. As the health industry expanded, its stakeholders gained power both in Washington and in each congressional district. Providers chafed at, and beat back, government efforts to restrict supply, such as plans to limit new hospital construction and prevent the unchecked spread of new technologies such as magnetic resonance imaging machines (MRIs).

Growing deficits and suspicion of government, federal bureaucracies, and taxation that might redistribute wealth made many Americans wary of coverage expansion. Because most Americans were satisfied with their own physician even if they expressed discontent with the system as a whole, they mistrusted any policy proposals that they felt might affect that doctor-patient relationship. And the question of which health reforms to pursue typically fell prey to a growing ideological cleavage in American politics between liberal and conservative views. Liberals (who tended to view health care as a collective good) argued for a government single-payer approach consistent with that of other countries; conservatives (who tended to see health care as a matter of personal responsibility and a private good best distributed by the market) backed ideas such as health savings accounts and higher cost-sharing for patients.

For a time, President Bill Clinton's health proposal, which he had championed on the campaign trail, looked like it might be the exception to this trend of failed reforms. Instead, it became its capstone. The plan was distinguished by its ambition both to achieve universal access and to control costs. It tried to do so in a way that appealed both to believers in government and in markets alike. Featuring "managed competition" within a budget, it envisioned cost-conscious payers choosing between tightly organized and efficient managed care systems. Employers were mandated to cover their employees or to pay a substantial fee ("pay-or-play") which would have financed much of the coverage for the uninsured, mostly through regional health alliances that would have paid insurers based on the relative health of their enrollees.

This hybrid public and private approach tended to unite health policy analysts and attracted support among some business interests, who favored its approach to cost containment. Unfortunately, Clinton and his team spent little time consulting with industry stakeholders, who disliked both the employer mandate and the scope of the regional alliances, and perhaps even less time with the key members of the Congressional committees who were vital to passing the bill both in whole or in part. The Health Insurance Association of America spent $12 million dollars on a single ad campaign attacking the proposal, featuring an older homespun couple referred to colloquially as "Harry and Louise." Policy entrepreneurship was one thing, but passage another, and the Clinton plan failed even to come to a vote before the full Congress, despite almost a year of preparation.

As an alternative to the president's proposal, employers looked to one of its elements: managed care. For several years in the early 1990s, the expanded use of managed care plans played a major role, according to most analysts, in keeping the growth of health costs flat. Over time, however, under pressure from both doctors and patients, it evolved in the direction of less restrictive products such as preferred provider organizations (PPOs), which failed to keep a lid on costs. Popular culture, and especially Hollywood films, gave the impression that managed care inevitably meant the denial of needed care. While many hospitals and doctors encouraged the pushback against managed care despite limited evidence, the industry did itself few favors by trying to insure only the healthiest patients rather than attempting to keep a cross-section of beneficiaries well. Almost all the original HMOs were not-for-profit, but the growing prominence of for-profit HMOs accelerated this self-destructive trend.

In the absence of a global budget for health care and general price reductions, there are few ways to control costs other than through the kinds of tools—selective contracting, capitation, network management, and so on—that managed care pioneered. While managed care continues to operate on a modest scope, a version of the practice may make a comeback under the umbrella of physician-led accountable care organizations (ACOs), which have been tested in several pilot programs. These entities are tasked with coordinating an individual's care over a number of separate providers in return for sharing any savings with the payer.

Quality and Evidence-Based Medicine. Some physicians and researchers have been concerned about the quality of American medical care and the challenges of linking medical interventions with outcomes since the beginning of organized medicine, although their influence until recently has been slight. Congress held hearings on the subject of medical quality in the early 1980s. The Agency for Health Research and Quality published landmark findings in the 1980s and 1990s before its funding was slashed (it questioned the value of certain kinds of back surgery, and spine surgeons mounted a successful political counterattack.) But the widespread idea that medical care was falling short came to public consciousness after the publication of two reports issued by the prestigious Institute of Medicine (IOM) in 1998 and 2001: "To Err is Human" and "Crossing the Quality Chasm." These reports revealed that as many as 98,000 Americans died each year from medical error; that 85 percent of all everyday medical treatments have never been scientifically validated; and that it takes, on average, seventeen years for clinical research findings to make their way into everyday practice. In the words of David Eddy, a pioneer in quality measurement: "The perception we all want to have is that medicine is firmly based on reality and [that] information is transmitted speedily to [doctors], who apply it unerringly. Unfortunately, the truth is that the practice of medicine is not based firmly on reality ... [t]he transmission of research information into practice is precarious and the results are used selectively by practitioners" (Eddy, 2009).

The release of these IOM reports and similar findings began to expose the shaky foundations of the quality of medical care to policy makers and gradually to the broader public. The growing focus on quality has begun to affect the medical profession and has started to alter the politics surrounding US health care. Until the early 1990s, the dominant narrative pitted access versus cost. The salient question was assumed to be how to extend the fruits of what was assumed to be the best medical system in the world to everyone, not just the well insured. In the wake of these reports, and also because of several heavily publicized deaths of prominent individuals at prestigious teaching hospitals, the redesign of care delivery has become a major part of the health care debate.

While delivery redesign has been led by particular hospital systems such as Mayo, Geisinger, Intermountain Health, Virginia Mason, and others, it has been heavily supported by employers and government payers as well. It has received new impetus from the growing scrutiny of costs. It uses a variety of approaches: redesigning professional education, improving peer review of physician practice, reengineering systems of care; increasing competition between provider organizations; reporting of public data; paying for performance; and continuously managing quality.

While each of these strategies has had mixed success and has tended to result in pockets of excellence rather than reliable systems, they together represent a departure from the piecemeal, uncoordinated, and procedure-oriented past of American medicine. They include numerous small-scale examples of primary care physicians taking charge of the total care of patients, often in teams, and the hospital procedures revamped using an approach pioneered in Japanese companies aimed at creating streamlined industrial efficiency. For example, the reduction of bloodstream infections, caused by improper placement of central line catheters, declined by 63 percent from 2001 to 2009 nationwide, largely due to a program begun by Peter Pronovost in Michigan that has now spread to forty-five states. Good progress, as well, has been made on other hospital-acquired infections and on unnecessary hospital readmissions.

Closely related to the quality improvement and care redesign movement is the pioneering research on practice variation conducted by Dartmouth's John Wennberg and his team. Wennberg has found unwarranted variation in delivery practices nationwide that "cannot be explained on the basis of illness, medical evidence, or patient preference." Nor can these differences be justified by better health outcomes in regions that spend more. State-by-state variations in per-person Medicare spending can differ by more than 100 percent without comparable (or any measurable) returns to health. More expensive areas appear to have a higher concentration of specialists and teaching hospitals, suggesting that a greater supply of physicians tends to lead to overutilization and higher costs.

Wennberg's thesis has been challenged on various grounds, especially on the point that these differences may reflect only the experience of Medicare beneficiaries and not under-sixty-five Americans covered by commercial insurers. At the very least, however, it offers an opportunity to distinguish between the rational use of limited resources and more arbitrary rationing of care.

The quality movement has strong political salience. It has contributed to the gradual realization that physicians and hospitals cannot be the only stewards of the medical system and that they cannot have *carte blanche* in organizing their practices if cost and health outcomes are the vital measure of success. Or, if they are to maintain this leadership role, they need to do so on a much more accountable and transparent basis.

The Affordable Care Act and New Directions in Health Reform. In the early years of the twenty-first century, the longstanding model of doctors as independent practitioners started to wane. The history of the US health system in the twentieth century in many ways revolves around the erosion of the professional authority and independence of physicians even as greater specialization, the superior effectiveness of treatments, and the emergence of multiple payers has made them financially better off. Doctors are moving rapidly into closer association with hospitals, largely seeking higher reimbursement or better hours, a trend which is likely to affect both the practice and the politics of health care. Hospital purchases of medical groups have gone up 40 percent since the year 2000, and far more doctors are seeking direct salaried employment in hospitals. The advent of ACOs is likely only to accelerate this trend.

What is unclear is whether this trend toward the "corporate practice of medicine" will result in more specialized groups of physicians who work in high-reimbursement areas such as cardiac care, orthopedics, and dermatology; or a greater emphasis on primary care and care-coordination teams with an eye toward lowering costs; or both. An influential article published in *The New Yorker* in 2009 by surgeon and author Atul Gawande on the small city of McAllen, Texas, which has some of the highest per person Medicare costs in the country, strongly contrasts the business-oriented and reimbursement-focused approach, as practiced in McAllen and many other cities, with an approach that tries to integrate specialists and primary care through focusing on redesigning the way care is delivered, working in teams, and paying salaries to physicians to discourage unnecessary care.

Chronically ill patients are poorly served by a procedure-dominated, acute-care model, in particular if good health outcomes at the lowest costs are the goal. Americans with chronic illnesses like congestive heart failure, diabetes, and asthma account for more than 70 percent of health care expenditures. Even major killers such as heart attacks and cancer are increasingly coming to resemble chronic illness in the ways they are treated and the survival rates of patients. The need for both early diagnosis and coordinated team-based treatment is essential both for preventing the onset of chronic illnesses and for managing their symptoms.

The landmark Patient Protection and Affordable Care Act (PPACA), which passed Congress in March 2010, tries to build upon the sea changes that are underway both in the structure of the medical profession and in treating illness. Hundreds of provisions in the Act, such as provisions that encourage the growth of ACOs and payment reforms, as well as new organizations that will examine the relative effectiveness of different treatments, speak directly to the coordination of care and quality issues that have come to the fore since the demise of the Clinton plan. The Act tries to encourage coordinated, team-based care across settings and wants hospitals and physicians to take the lead by responding to the modest economic incentives included in reform.

The Affordable Care Act represents in some ways a new direction in US health reform and in others a relatively cautious departure from the past. The Act intends to cover 32 million uninsured Americans by 2019, principally by expanding Medicaid and by subsidizing the individual purchase of insurance on state-based health exchanges. Its goal is to extend to all Americans the security of coverage offered through employers without disrupting the base of existing employer coverage. While a substantial number of Americans preferred a single-payer approach and favored a "public option" or government-run insurance plan available on the exchanges, this preference wasn't strongly considered either by the president or by Congress. The political success of the bill stemmed largely from its proponents' skillful reassurance that existing coverage would not be altered and that what was contemplated was reform of the widely unpopular insurance industry, not the health system as a whole. Indeed, the (un)timely announcement, on the eve of final debate on the bill, that Anthem/Blue Cross of California had raised premiums by 39 percent in the individual market is credited by most observers with making the final difference between passage and failure.

The Affordable Care Act, like the universal coverage bill passed four years earlier in Massachusetts, accommodates health interests by expanding access first and promising to tackle costs later. The lack of concerted opposition by these interests goes a long way to explain why the Act was successful where the Clinton plan failed. Nevertheless, the timing of the Act was somewhat surprising. While individuals worried about personal health costs, and polls showed that these fears affected those higher on the income ladder, such concerns were lower in 2009 than in the early 1990s. Reforming health care had not been the principal campaign pledge of incoming

President Obama nor in fact had he espoused this particular model of reform on the campaign trail. Despite the propitious political circumstances, members who voted for the bill paid a steep political price in the midterm elections, although the lagging economy and not health care was the single most important factor behind Republican gains in Congress.

In short, passage of the Affordable Care Act, despite its lack of overt bipartisanship, represented something of an elite consensus that unchecked health costs, if not reined in, could sink the overall economy. The Congressional Budget Office's argument about declining US competitiveness carried substantial weight. Stakeholders felt that unless some action was taken, business as usual in the health industry might not continue. That the bill was in fact a moderate, middle-of-the-road bill, which resembled, in fact, the GOP alternatives proposed to the Clinton plan in the 1990s, helped politically. By the same token, it was bound to dissatisfy both those who preferred a single-payer system of financing or thought more pressure should be put on individuals to seek lower-priced insurance plans. That the overall goal had been a central plank in Democratic platforms for several generations, and had been blessed by Edward Kennedy (who passed away during the debate over the bill), also helped cement the deal politically. While its central provisions—notably the individual mandate to require the purchase of private insurance coverage—remain under challenge in the courts and its fate is too soon to judge, its passage has once again put health care in the center of US politics.

[*See also* Health Care Reform; Insurance Companies, Health; *and* Medicare and Medicaid.]

BIBLIOGRAPHY

Anderson, Gerard F., Uwe E. Reinhardt, Peter S. Hussey, and Varduhi Petrosyan. "It's The Prices, Stupid: Why the United States is So Different From Other Countries." *Health Affairs* 22, no. 3 May–June 2003): 89–105.

Barr, Donald. *Introduction to US Health Policy: The Organization, Financing, and Delivery of Health Care in the United States.* (San Francisco, 2002).

Bodenheimer, Thomas S., and Kevin Grumbach. *Understanding Health Policy: A Clinical Approach.* (New York, 2002).

Brownlee, Shannon. *Overtreated: Why Too Much Medicine Is Making Us Sicker and Poorer.* (New York, 2007).

Cutler, David. *Your Money or Your Life: Strong Medicine for America's Health System.* (New York and Oxford, 2005).

Docteur, Elizabeth, et al. "The US Health System: An Assessment and Prospective Directions for Reform." *Organisation for Economic Co-operation and Development* (OECD). Economics Department Working Papers, No. 350 (February 27, 2003).

Emanuel, Ezekiel. *Healthcare, Guaranteed: A Simple, Secure Solution for America.* (New York, 2008).

Enthoven, Alain, and Laura A. Tillen, eds. *Toward a 21st Century Health System: The Contributions and Promise of Prepaid Group Practice.* (San Francisco, 2004.)

Field, Robert. *Health Care Regulation in America: Complexity, Confrontation, and Compromise.* (New York, 2007).

Gawande, Atul. *Complications: A Surgeon's Notes on an Imperfect Science.* (New York, 2002).

Gawande, Atul. "The Cost Conundrum." *The New Yorker,* June 1, 2009.

Hacker, Jacob S. *The Road to Nowhere: The Genesis of President Clinton's Plan for Health Security.* (Princeton, N.J., 1997).

Halvorson, George. *Health Care Reform Now: A Prescription for Change.* (San Francisco, 2007).

Herzlinger, Regina. *Who Killed Health Care?* (New York, 2007).

Johnson, Haynes, and David Broder. *The System: The American Way of Politics at the Breaking Point.* (Boston, 1996).

Lantos, John D. *Do We Still Need Doctors?* (New York, 1997).

Kenney, Charles. *The Best Practice: How the New Quality Movement is Transforming Medicine.* (New York, 2008).

Kenney, Charles. *Transforming Health Care: Virginia Mason's Pursuit of the Perfect Patient Experience.* (New York, 2011).

Marmor, Theodore R. *The Politics of Medicare.* 2d ed. (New York, 2000).

Millenson, Michael L. *Demanding Medical Excellence: Doctors and Accountability in the Information Age.* (Chicago, 1997).

Moon, Marilyn. *Medicare Now and in the Future.* 2d ed. (Washington, 1996).

Porter, Roy. *The Greatest Benefit to Mankind: A Medical History of Humanity.* (London, 1997).

Quadagno, Jill. *One Nation Uninsured: Why the US Has No National Health Insurance.* (New York, 2005).

Rettenmaier, Andrew, and Thomas Saving, eds. *Medicare Reform: Issues and Answers.* (Chicago, 1999).

Robinson, James C. *The Corporate Practice of Medicine: Competition and Innovation in Health Care.* (Berkeley, Calif., 1999).

Smith, David G. *Paying for Medicare: The Politics of Reform.* (New York, 1992).

Starr, Paul. *The Logic of Health Care Reform: Why and How the President's Plan Will Work.* (New York, 1994).

Weissert, Carol S., and William G. Weissert. *Governing Health: The Politics of Health Policy.* (Baltimore, 1996).

Wennberg, John E. *Tracking Medicine: A Researcher's Quest to Understand Health Care.* (New York, 2010).

Leif Wellington Haase

HEALTH CARE REFORM

Health care reform in the United States tends to occur in twenty-year cycles, with each cycle culminating in a political response to the problems emerging as a result of the settlement made two or more decades before. The United States witnessed major moves to reform health care provision in the immediate postwar years, when the Truman push for universal health care failed, but free health care for veterans was put in place, and employer-funded health care increasingly became the norm. Major developments occurred again in the 1960s with the creation of Medicare and Medicaid, and again in the 1990s with the failure of the Clinton initiative and the creation of the State Children's Health Insurance Program (SCHIP), a system of free health care for uninsured children whose parents' income, while not high, is too high to qualify them for Medicaid. This incremental extension of coverage necessarily created boundary problems, with some categories of Americans just barely missing out on coverage. It also created a patchwork of public programs built around, and acting as supplements to, the core of the health care system: private insurance-funded health care coverage, provided by fee-taking general practitioners, medical specialists, and private hospitals. Much of that private health insurance was linked to employment contracts, such that those with generous benefits received health care free (except for limited co-payments) so long as they maintained their employment, with their contribution to the insurance premium treated as pre-tax income. By 2007, the old had Medicare. Children of the poor (though very few of the poor without children) had Medicaid. Children of the near-poor had SCHIP. Veterans could go to VA hospitals run by the US Department of Veterans Affairs; 59 percent of those employed had employer-provided health insurance; and everyone else either bought their own insurance (without the tax relief) or went without insurance coverage of any kind. (The uninsured remained able to use the emergency facilities of local hospitals free of charge, and did so in increasing numbers). Insurance companies had by then created a huge white-collar labor force who processed claims and passed them on to other providers; and over time more and more employers, particularly small employees, found themselves unable to offer their employees either any health coverage at all, or health coverage that was in any way comprehensive in its scope. The share of American firms offering health benefits fell from 66 percent to 60 percent between 1999 and 2007.

Such a patchwork settlement ultimately satisfied no one, leaving in place, as it did, a series of problems unique to the American health care system. There was a problem of excessive cost. There was a problem of access. There was a problem of quality control. There was a problem of overutilization by the insured. And, there was a problem of variation of standards by region, class, and ethnicity. By 2006 the United States was spending 16 percent of its gross domestic product (GDP) on health care, up from 8.5 percent in 1975 and more than twice the proportion common in health care systems in other fully industrialized countries. Health cost costs were rising at twice the rate of inflation—in 2000, "the average family premium was $6,800. By 2007, it had risen to $12,700" (Furnas, 2009)—in the process placing competitive burdens on US companies operating in foreign markets, and triggering at home a steady increase in levels of co-pay and a steady decrease in both the number of employees covered and in the scope of that coverage. Soaring health care costs were the major driver of federal expenditure before the 2008 financial meltdown, absorbing between a quarter and a fifth of the entire federal budget. Yet for all the expenditure, the United States remained the one major industrialized economy unable to guarantee even basic health coverage to all its citizens. In January 2009, more than 51 million Americans under 65 lacked health insurance; and in 2007–2008, "approximately 87 million Americans under 65—nearly one in three—went without health insurance for some period" (Furnas, 2009). On a series of international health indicators, the United States continued to lag behind the best of the rest. That lag was regularly demonstrated in a series of international comparative reports, including one by the Commonwealth Fund in 2007. The Fund reported that "among the six nations studied—Australia, Canada, Germany, New Zealand, the United Kingdom, and the United States . . . the US ranks last, as it did in the 2006 and 2004 editions . . . on dimensions of access, patient safety, efficiency, and equity" (Commonwealth Fund, 2007, p. 2. Little wonder then that, during the George W. Bush presidency and the Obama one, the fundamental reform of the US health care system again came at times to dominate federal politics.

The broad answer from the right of the political spectrum to the unique problems of American health care was to focus on costs as a barrier to access, and to urge competition among providers as a spur to cost reduction. Conscious that the existing system mixed private-market provision with state-funded programs, and aware too that employer-provided health care insurance protected the users of health care from any direct exposure to the actual costs of the health care they used, conservative reformers sought ways to give consumers accurate information on costs and the ability to choose medical services in the light of those costs. For conservatives, more public expenditure was not the answer. That route could only lead to "increased demand, overconsumption, higher prices, and enormous waste" (Cannon, 2004, p. 86). The way forward was to get government out of the health care system: out as a source of funding, out as a regulator, out as a

disturber of the free play of market forces. Quite how to achieve that end varied, depending on the conservative: at its most modest, the proposal—from President George W. Bush in his 2007 State of the Union Address—was simply to level the playing field between those receiving tax relief on their employer-provided health care insurance and those obliged to buy their cover in the open market. At the most extreme, in the Ryan budget proposed by Representative Paul Ryan (R-WI) and passed in the House of Representatives in early 2011, the proposal was the replacement of Medicare and Medicaid for those born after 1955 by vouchers (and individual health saving accounts)—personal funds with which a new generation of seniors, now individual health care consumers, could pick their way through the myriad of health care products available to them.

The broad answer on the left was entirely otherwise. For progressives, cost control had to take second place to solving the issue of access, ideally through reforms that could also, over time, lower the rate of increase in health care charges. Some liberal reformers advocated a universal health care system along Canadian lines—Medicare for all—with private suppliers of health care paid by the state and with private insurance companies no longer part of the picture. Others advocated a deepening of the private insurance model, with employers obliged either to "pay or play": free, that is, to go on providing health care insurance if they wanted to, or to pay into a general fund to finance health care indirectly—the idea being that such a fund, with so many participants, would significantly reduce the cost per patient. And yet others advocated the subsidized purchase of at least basic health care plans by those unable to pay for the purchase unaided, with a requirement that all adults make such a purchase—a system based, that is, on an individual mandate to participate in health care insurance when healthy, the better to have properly funded health care services when sick.

In the clash between those competing visions in 2010, the Obama administration eventually passed the Patient Protection and Affordable Care Act. The incoming president's preference had been for a universal health care system, but he lacked the majorities necessary (particularly in the Senate) for anything so drastic. He was not even able to call into existence a nationwide public option, a government-provided insurance package to compete with packages offered by private insurers (his Republican opponents' commitment to the cost-cutting propensities of competition did not stretch that far). Instead, the Affordable Care Act required insurers (from 2014) to offer policies at the same premium to all potential customers regardless of age, gender, location, and preexisting conditions (other than tobacco use). It also immediately created a temporary high-risk insurance pool for people currently uninsured and afflicted by a preexisting health condition, and allowed dependent children to remain on their parents' health insurance plan until age twenty-six. The Act proposed the phasing in of Medicaid eligibility to all families with incomes less than 133 percent of the poverty level, and the provision of federal subsidies on a sliding scale for health insurance purchase by families with income placing them above Medicaid eligibility, but that is still less than 400 percent of the poverty level. Alongside these access provisions—estimated by the Congressional Budget Office (CBO) to bring health care coverage of at least a basic kind to some 32 million additional Americans—the Act required the creation of health insurance exchanges in each state, and (from 2018) the taxation of employer-provided health plans of the "Cadillac" variety—that is, those plans with an actuarial value of $10,200 for an individual or of $27,500 for families. The Act also established what became known as "the individual mandate:" the requirement that all adults under age sixty-five purchase and comply with an approved insurance policy or pay a penalty. Employers not providing health insurance directly to their employees (if the number of employees exceeded fifty) would also be required to pay into a general fund if the federal government was subsidizing the purchase of health insurance by those the firm employed.

The Act's critics on the left condemned the settlement as simply channeling taxpayer dollars into private health insurance companies without adequate public regulation. Their commitment to the creation of a Medicare-for-all system remains intact, if not widely discussed in political circles in the years immediately following passage of the Act. That silence was and remains a product of, and a reaction to, the ferocity of the condemnation of the Affordable Care Act from the Right. The Act is condemned for embedding the very system of subsidized health care that, in the view of the Right, encouraged over-usage and rising prices in the first place. It is condemned for being so generous with the new subsidies as to encourage many employers to stop offering insurance altogether, thus pushing their employees into the new health care exchanges and burdening the taxpayer even further. And the Act is condemned for infringing on individual liberties—in mandating private citizens to buy a particular product from a set of private companies for the first time in US history—and, it is argued, making an unconstitutional use of the Commerce Clause in the US Constitution.

The constitutionality of the individual mandate remained in question in 2011. So too does funding for Medicare and Medicaid, as Congress continues its drawn-out battle over deficit reduction. If the Act is eventually struck down, in whole or in part, no doubt the political conversation on health care reform will return to the fundamental divide noted above. If it is not struck down, however, the United States faces a decade of readjustment to a health care system that covers more Americans, but which remains far more costly to deliver than its equivalents elsewhere in the advanced industrial world. In either case, this round of health care reform seems far from over.

[*See also* Health Care; *and* Medicare and Medicaid.]

BIBLIOGRAPHY

Cannon, Michael. "Medicare and Medicaid." In *The Cato Handbook on Policy,* pp. 85-86. (Washington, D.C., 2004).

Coates, David. *Answering Back: Liberal Responses to Conservative Arguments.* (New York, 2010).

Commonwealth Fund. *Mirror, Mirror on the Wall: An International Update on the Comparative Performance of American Health Care.* (New York, 2007).

Douthat, Ross. "Reforming the Reform." *The New York Times*, January 23, 2011.

Furnas, Ben. "American Health Care Since 1994: The Unacceptable Status Quo." Center for American Progress. (2009), http://www.americanprogress.org/issues/2009/01/health_since_1994.html.

Healthreform.gov. "Hidden Costs of Health Care: Why Americans are Paying MORE but Getting LESS." (2009), http://www.healthreform.gov/reports/hiddencosts/index.html

Jacobs, Lawrence R., and Theda Skocpol. *Health Care Reform and American Politics: What Everyone Needs to Know.* (New York, 2010).

Kaiser Foundation. "The Uninsured: A Primer: Key Facts About Americans Without Health Insurance." (2010), http://www.kff.org/uninsured/upload/7451-06.pdf.

Kaiser Foundation. "Summary of New Health Reform Law." (2010), http://www.kff.org/healthreform/upload/8061.pdf.

Reich, Robert. "Why the New Healthcare Law Should Have Been Based on Medicare (And What Democrats Should Have Learned By Now." (2011), http://www.opednews.com/articles/Why-the-New-Healthcare-Law-by-Robert-Reich-110816-923.html.

Tanner, Michael. *Bad Medicine: A Guide to the Real Costs and Consequences of the New Health Care Law.* (Washington, D.C., 2011).

David Coates

HISPANIC AMERICANS

US cities have witnessed major demographic changes since the 1960s, although the national African American population has remained relatively stable since the 1960s, near 12 percent. In the 1970s, Latinos made up a smaller share of the population (approximately 5 percent), yet the Latino population has been growing significantly since the middle of the twentieth century. By the year 2000, Latinos reached parity with African Americans, and are now the largest immigrant and minority group, making up 16.3 percent of the US population. From 2000 to 2010, Latinos accounted for more than 50 percent of the nation's growth in population. The Pew Research Center projects that the Latino population will continue to grow, and by the year 2050, Latinos will make up approximately 30 percent of the US population.

Hence, the significant growth of the Latino population triggers the following question: What is the role of Latinos in the political landscape in the United States? Some may argue that the theories of political behavior and identity of African Americans, a minority group which has experienced similar social, political, and economic struggles as Latinos, would automatically extend to Latinos. Others would argue that Latinos' proximity to the immigrant experience and the fact that not all are citizens would lead them to be specifically concerned about legislation regarding legal and illegal immigration, language policy, assimilation, and naturalization—topics not commonly associated with African Americans. Therefore, in order to examine Latinos' role in the US political landscape comprehensively, we must examine Latinos' demographic profile, political identity and behavior, the importance that Latinos place on immigration, recent immigration legislation, and the implications that Latino attitudes have for the Latino vote in the 2012 presidential election.

A Demographic Portrait of Latinos in the United States. There are noteworthy demographic characteristics of the Latino population that distinguishes its members from each other as well as from other racial groups. First, national origin greatly distinguishes Latinos. The top four national origin groups among Latinos in the United States are Mexican (65.5 percent of Latinos), Puerto Rican (9.1 percent), Salvadoran (3.6 percent), and Cuban (3.5 percent). Some come to the United States as political refugees, others as migrants, and many come as immigrants (with the intention to remain for an unlimited amount of time) seeking improved job opportunities and education opportunities for their children.

Latinos also differ by place of birth, and their nativity, coupled with citizenship rates and age, have strong implications for their political behavior. Native-born Latinos account for 9.9 percent of the total US population, and foreign-born Latinos account for 5.9 percent. Among the 37.4 percent of Latinos who are foreign-born, some are citizens (11 percent), yet the majority are noncitizens (26.5 percent). Since the Latino population has contributed to an extensive rise in the total US population in the last decade, it should not be surprising that Latinos are overall younger in age than whites and African Americans today. The median age for Latinos is twenty-seven years, but the median age for whites is forty-one years, for African Americans is thirty-two years, and for Asians is thirty-five years. Since a substantial number of Latinos are not of voting age, combined with 27 percent of Latinos identifying as noncitizens, the eligible voter population among Latinos is much smaller than among whites and African Americans, resulting in Latinos' likely unstable or minimal political power at the voting booth.

Furthermore, it is important to note that not all Latinos identify by the same race. Since Hispanic/Latino origin is considered an ethnicity, the US Census provides Latinos the opportunity to identify by race. The majority identifies as white (63 percent); some classify themselves as some other race (29 percent); and very few (1.9 percent) Latinos identify as black. The fact that a substantial portion of Latinos identify as some other race provides support for the fact that some Latinos may perceive "being Latino" as a race and not an ethnicity. Moreover, Latinos' strong racial identification with whites and not with African Americans may shed light on the likelihood that Latinos perceive that they are closer to whites than African Americans, and thus are more likely to form political coalitions with whites instead of African Americans.

Latinos' presence in distinct geographic locations also has implications for their political behavior in the United States. Since 2000, Latinos have remained heavily concentrated in traditionally Latino areas, yet a substantial number have relocated to non-traditionally Latino areas, such as rural areas in the South. In California and Texas, Latinos make up approximately 37 percent of each state's population. Latinos also consist of a significant portion of the populations in Nevada (26.5 percent) and Arizona (30.8 percent). In New Mexico, Latinos make up a striking 45.6 percent of the state population. Nonetheless, from 2000 to 2009, several nontraditional Latino states in the South have seen a striking percentage change in the Latino population.

For instance, South Carolina (115.5 percent increase), West Virginia (112.8 percent), Arkansas (101.3 percent), Kentucky (98.5 percent), and North Carolina (90.2 percent) have seen extraordinary increases in their Latino populations. States' distinct histories of Latino presence as well as their political, social, and economic climates influence the formation of congressional districts as well as the policies that they establish in response to the changes that Latinos import.

Although Latinos have made headway in population growth throughout the United States, their education level in comparison to whites, African Americans, and Asians are not as encouraging. For instance, compared to whites, African Americans, and Asians, Latinos have the smallest high school graduation rate (26 percent). The Latino high school dropout rate in 2009 was approximately 9.2 percent, more than twice the number for non-Hispanic whites (3.9 percent), and substantially larger than the rate for African Americans (6.6 percent) and Asians (2.0 percent). Fortunately, the high school dropout rate has decreased for all groups since the beginning of the twenty-first century, and for Latinos the rate has almost been cut in half. Similar to the high school graduation rates, Latinos' college graduation rates rank the lowest (12.7 percent) compared to African Americans (17.7 percent), Asians (9.9 percent), and whites (31.1 percent) today and at the turn of the century.

Nonetheless, it is important to recognize that a college education is not as accessible to all Latinos as it is to other racial groups. For example, only eleven states (California, Texas, Illinois, Kansas, Nebraska, New Mexico, New York, Oklahoma, Utah, Washington, and Wisconsin) allow undocumented immigrants to receive in-state tuition rates, and three states (Arizona, Colorado, and Georgia) bar illegal immigrants from paying in-state tuition rates completely. South Carolina goes as far as excluding undocumented immigrants' entry into state colleges. The implications of these policies are significant, given that states that allow in-state tuition rates for illegal immigrants are slightly stronger financially than other states, attract a greater number of undocumented immigrants to attend college, and have a 14 percent decrease in high school dropout rates among undocumented Latino students.

It is not surprising, given Latinos' generally low education levels, that Latinos concentrate in low-income brackets and earn less than African Americans, whites, and Asians. More than African Americans and whites, 46.2 percent of Latinos have an individual income of less than $20,000. Furthermore, only 14.2 percent of Latinos earn more than $50,000 in comparison to African Americans (18.4 percent), whites (30.7 percent), and Asians (36.9 percent).

Partisan Identification. Current and previous research asserts that given Latinos' low socioeconomic status overall, most Latinos are stronger supporters of the Democratic Party than the Republican Party. However, among Latinos, Cubans are more likely to identify as Republican, primarily due to the fact that individuals who immigrate from communist or postcommunist regimes are more predisposed to adopting capitalist values and identifying with the Republican Party. Length of time in the United States and gender frequently surface as determinants of Latino party identification. The longer Latinos are in the United States, the more likely that they identify as Democrats. Furthermore, similar to whites, Latinas adopt greater support for the Democratic Party than Latinos. Latinas' stronger identification with the Democratic Party was recently illustrated in a Latino Decisions poll leading up to the 2010 midterm elections.

Although Latinos have commonly identified as Democrats, it is not always clear whether they will vote for Democratic candidates all the time. A recent Latino Decisions national poll indicates that only 43 percent of registered Latinos intend to vote for President Barack Obama in 2012. Furthermore, a majority of Latinos surveyed perceive that the Democratic Party has not conducted sufficient outreach among the Latino population, yet a very small percentage of Latinos perceive that Republicans are reaching out appropriately. One way or another, outreach is critical to Latinos' vote choice, since it significantly affects whether Latinos vote for a Republican or Democratic candidate.

Voter Turnout. The extensive growth in Latino population has not been matched by growth in Latino power at the voting booth. Latinos may be the largest minority group in the United States, yet they vote at lower rates than similarly situated whites and African Americans in non-presidential elections. An obvious reason for this is that not all Latinos are US citizens. The process to obtain US citizenship is painstakingly long, and some immigrants deliberately delay naturalization, perceiving it as a betrayal to their homeland. Nevertheless, newly naturalized Latinos have a greater predisposition to turn out at the voting booths than native-born Latinos. Another fundamental reason why Latinos are not eligible to vote is that they are considerably younger than whites, African Americans, and Asian Americans.

Several other key determinants of Latino voter turnout behavior have been cited in the literature. Similar to the factors that influence Anglo voting, socioeconomic status influences Latino turnout; Latinos with higher income and education levels have greater participation rates. In comparison to African Americans and whites, Latinos' lack of political socialization (particularly little contact with electoral institutions and government) depresses their turnout rate. However, mobilization, particularly get-out-the-vote initiatives, increase Latino turnout. Latinos who participate in campaign activity have higher turnout rates than others, yet for several decades, political parties did not dedicate as much time or resources to engage Latinos in campaign activity as compared to other racial groups. Nonetheless, political parties today are slowly realizing the Latino voting population's potential power and influence on electoral politics. With Latinos' concentration in certain areas of the country comes the creation of majority-minority districts. These districts increase Latino descriptive representation and are so influential on Latino behavior that Latinos who live in these districts have greater turnout rates than other Latinos.

Besides the differing effects that majority-minority districts have on African American and Latino turnout, Latinos distinguish themselves from African

Americans in the way that they perceive voting. While African Americans perceive voting as an instrument for change and providing a sense of group purpose, Latinos, like Asian Americans, view electoral participation as a duty, which in turn increases their turnout rate. On the other hand, perceptions of discrimination against their group increases Mexican Americans' participation at the voting booth.

A notable difference between Latinos and African Americans is the latter's strong sense of group-based solidarity. Latinos strongly identify with their national origin group and are less likely to adopt a pan-ethnic identity and identify themselves primarily as "Latino" or "Hispanic." The implications of this are profound, given that group identification increases participation in campaign contributions, contact with the media, and participation in groups to solve social problems. Latinos' national-origin identification is due in part to their concentration in particular regions and by national origin. However, with the recent increase in dispersion of Latinos across several areas in the country, Latinos' strong national-origin identification may decrease, paving the way for many to adopt a pan-ethnic identity and, also, increase the likelihood of adopting comparable interests and increasing political power. Consequently, differences between African Americans and Latinos may be significant, yet Latinos' movement to non-traditional Latino areas combined with their increasing pan-ethnic identification may increase the parallels between the political identities and behaviors of these two groups.

At the start of the twenty-first century a large gap in registration rates remained between Latinos and African Americans and Latinos and whites: only 60 percent of Latino citizen adults were registered to vote in comparison to African Americans at 70 percent and whites at 74 percent. Nevertheless, given Latinos' vast growth in population in the first decade of the century and the fact that they are positioned to influence presidential votes considerably in several traditional and emerging Latino states, Latinos' strength at the polls can potentially be greater than ever.

Latinos and Immigration. Immigration has considerable political effects on the political attitudes, behavior, and policy challenges of Latinos and Asian Americans, but not so much for African Americans—at least not until very recently. The issue of immigration frames the entire political environment of Latinos in the United States and, thus, it is not surprising that immigration is a top issue among Latinos. A recent Latino Decisions poll indicates that Latinos think it is the most important issue that Congress and President Obama should address, taking precedence over the economy, job growth, and education. Latinos place such an importance on immigration that if Congress does not pass immigration reform, most Latinos want the president to take action. Approximately 66 percent of Latinos favor an executive order that would halt the deportation of undocumented, immigrant, college-age youth who have not committed any crimes. This feeling is shared by Democrats as well as Republicans.

A significant portion of Latino Democrats, independents, and Republicans support comprehensive immigration reform, and Congress has made several attempts in the last decade to pass such legislation, yet has not been successful, largely due to partisan differences. In 2010 the DREAM (Development, Relief, and Education for Alien Minors) Act was proposed, providing illegal immigrants, particularly those who attend college or participate in the military, a path to citizenship. This act was voted on in the Senate but did not pass. While on the campaign trail in 2008 as well as throughout his presidency, President Obama has expressed a significant interest in addressing numerous social, economic, and political issues associated with immigration yet he has not been successful in pushing for immigration legislation at the national level. Actually, since President Obama has taken office, the number of deportations has increased and in 2010 alone slightly less than 400,000 individuals were deported, with the majority not listed as convicted criminals.

Since the beginning of the twenty-first century, several states have taken immigration issues into their own hands. The most controversial state law,

SB 1070, was passed in Arizona in 2010. It restricted immigration in a variety of ways. Some of the law's key provisions include (1) allowing local police departments and federal immigration enforcement officers to coordinate immigrant deportations; (2) permitting law enforcement officers to arrest an individual without a warrant if the officer has probable cause that the individual has performed a public offense resulting in deportation; (3) prohibiting illegal immigrants from searching for employment or working; (4) prohibiting individuals from transporting, concealing, or shielding undocumented immigrants; and (5) requiring employers to participate in the federal government's E-verify program. After a legal battle, the first two aforementioned provisions were no longer enforced. Georgia, a state with a booming Latino population, has passed a new immigration law requiring all businesses that hire more than ten employees to adopt the federal E-Verify system to determine individuals' eligibility to work. Moreover, Alabama has recently passed immigration legislation that some consider the most restrictive law against illegal immigration in the United States. Some of the main provisions include permitting police officers to detain individuals suspected of having an illegal status; prohibiting undocumented immigrants from attending public postsecondary institutions; and prohibiting individuals from hiring, transporting, providing shelter, or renting property to undocumented immigrants. These recent state laws, led by Republican legislators, create an unwelcoming environment for immigrants, increasing Latinos' skepticism in government and decreasing their perception that they have a say in what government does.

Therefore, it is not surprising that Latinos' attitudes toward immigration also influence their evaluation of political parties and President Obama. The political scientist Sylvia Manzano (2011) emphasizes the importance that Latinos place on immigration and states that the "GOP has lost traction among Latinos because of immigration politics and diminished Latino enthusiasm for Democrats is also attributable to the issue" (p. 2). Furthermore, it is worth noting that 33 percent of Latinos think that Obama did not push for comprehensive immigration reform strongly enough, and 48 percent do not think that during his first term he handled immigration issues well.

Conclusion. Scholarship on Latinos' role in the US political landscape has provided significant insights into how comparable and different Latinos are from each other and from whites, African Americans, and Asian Americans. Some theories that explain white, African American, and Asian American political behavior and identity apply to Latinos, and others do not. Latinos' association with immigration, as immigrants or descendants of immigrants, and the importance that they place on comprehensive immigration reform, distinguish them greatly from several racial groups, including African Americans.

Moreover, unlike many other minority groups, Latinos today are being courted by political parties to obtain their support. However, the way that political parties address immigration may ultimately decide Latinos' solid support for a particular party. Latinos' significant growth in population and wavering political party support provides the ideal moment for them to capitalize on their potential political power. Nevertheless, this can only be accomplished if they begin to identify pan-ethnically and register to vote at mass levels. Now, more than ever, Latinos can and must flex their political muscle to establish a stable and vast presence in a country that values as well as questions their presence.

[*See also* African Americans, History; African Americans, Contemporary Conditions; Immigration to the United States; *and* Latin America–United States Relations.]

BIBLIOGRAPHY

Barreto, Matt. "Perceptions of Party Outreach to Latinos Key to 2012 Vote." Latino Decisions. (2011), http://latinodecisions.wordpress.com/2011/04/12/perceptions-of-party-outreach-to-latinos-key-to-2012-vote/.

Barreto, Matt. "Where Latinos Will Matter in 2012." Latino Decisions. (2011), http://latinodecisions.wordpress.com/2011/03/31/where-latino-votes-will-matter-in-2012/.

Barreto, Matt, Gary Segura, and Nathan Woods. "The Mobilizing Effect of Majority Minority Districts on

Latino Turnout." *American Political Science Review* 98 (2004): 65–75.

Cain, Bruce, D. Roderick Kiewiet, and Carole Uhlaner. "The Acquisition of Partisanship by Latinos and Asian-Americans." *American Journal of Political Science* 35 (1991): 390–422.

Cassel, Carol. "Hispanic Turnout: Estimates from Validated Voting Data." *Political Research Quarterly* 55 (2002): 391–408.

Dawson, Michael. *Behind the Mule: Race and Class in African-American Politics.* (Princeton, N.J., 1994).

Foner, Nancy, and George M. Fredrickson. *Not Just Black and White: Historical and Contemporary Perspectives on Immigration, Race, and Ethnicity in the United States.* (New York, 2004).

Gay, Claudine. "The Effect of Black Congressional Representation on Political Participation." *American Political Science Review* 95 (2001): 589–602.

Greenblatt, Alan. "Arizona Immigration Law is a Challenge for Police." *National Public Radio*, 28 July 2010, http://www.npr.org/templates/story/story.php?storyId=128820774.

Jervis, Rick and Alan Gomez. "Tough Immigration Law Raises Fear in Alabama." *USA Today*, 18 October 2011, http://www.usatoday.com/NEWS/usaedition/2011-10-19-1AAlabama-CV_CV_U.htm.

Jones-Correa, Michael. *Between Two Nations: The Political Predicament of Latinos in New York City.* (Ithaca, N.Y., 1998).

Jones-Correa, Michael, and David Leal. "Becoming 'Hispanic': Secondary Pan-Ethnic Identification among Latin American–Origin Populations in the United States." *Hispanic Journal of Behavior Sciences* 18 (1996): 214–254.

Lien, Pei-te. "Ethnicity and Political Participation: A Comparison between Asian and Mexican Americans." *Political Behavior* 16 (1994): 237–264.

Lohr, Kathy. "Georgia Farmers Brace for New Immigration Law." *National Public Radio*, 2011, http://www.npr.org/blogs/thetwo-way/2011/06/10/137107117/friends-and-foes-call-alabamas-immigration-law-the-nations-toughest.

Mangan, Catherine. "In-State Tuition for Illegal Immigrants Can Be a Plus for Both States and Students." *Chronicle of Higher Education*, 18 May 2011, http://chronicle.com/article/In-State-Tuition-for-Illegal/127581/.

Manzano, Sylvia. "One Year after SB1070: Why Immigration Will Not Go Away." *Latino Decisions*, http://latinodecisions.wordpress.com/2011/05/09/one-year-after-sb1070-why-immigration-will-not-go-away/.

Marrero, Pilar. "Immigration Is a Critical Issue for Latinos." *Latino Decisions.* (2011), http://latinodecisions.wordpress.com/2011/06/10/june-tracking-poll-immigration-is-a-critical-issue-for-voters/.

Marrero, Pilar. "Latinos Divided on Obama and Immigration." *Latino Decisions.* (2011), http://latinodecisions.wordpress.com/2011/06/13/latinos-divided-on-obama-and-immigration/.

Mascaro, Lisa, and Michael Muskal. 2010. "Dream Act Fails to Advance in Senate." *Los Angeles Times*, 18 December 2010.

Pantoja, Adrian, Ricardo Ramirez, and Gary Segura. "Citizens by Choice, Voters by Necessity: Patterns in Political Mobilization by Naturalized Latinos." *Political Research Quarterly* 54 (2001): 729–750.

Passel, Jeffrey S., and D'Vera Cohn. "Mexican Immigrants: How Many Come? How Many Leave?" Pew Hispanic Center. (2009), http://pewhispanic.org/reports/report.php?ReportID=112.

Passel, Jeffrey S., and D'Vera Cohn. "US Population Projections: 2005–2050." Pew Hispanic Center. (2008), http://pewhispanic.org/reports/report.php?ReportID=85.

Passel, Jeffrey S., D'Vera Cohn, and Mark Hugo Lopez. "Hispanics Account for More than Half of Nation's Growth in the United States." Pew Hispanic Center Publications. (2011), http://pewhispanic.org/reports/report.php?ReportID=140.

Pedraza, Francisco. "Why State Immigration Policies Turn Off Latino Voters." *Latino Decisions.* (2010), http://latinodecisions.wordpress.com/2010/10/13/why-state-immigration-policies-turn-off-latino-voters/.

Peralta, Eyder. "Friends and Foes Call Alabama's Immigration Law the Nation's Toughest." *National Public Radio*, 10 June 2011, http://www.npr.org/blogs/the-two-way/2011/06/10/137107117/friends-and-foes-call-alabamas-immigration-law-the-nations-toughest.

Pew Hispanic Center. "A Statistical Portrait of Hispanics in the US, 2009." (2011), http://pewhispanic.org/factsheets/factsheet.php?FactsheetID=70.

Project Vote Smart. "Alabama Key Vote: Immigration Enforcement." (2010), http://votesmart.org/issue_keyvote_detail.php?cs_id=35346.

Project Vote Smart. "Arizona Key Vote: Expanding Undocumented Immigration Enforcement." (2010), http://www.votesmart.org/bill/10810/28910/expanding-undocumented-immigration-enforcement.

Segura, Gary M., and Helena Alves Rodrigues. "Comparative Ethnic Politics in the United States: Beyond Black and White." *Annual Review of Political Science* 9 (2006): 375–395.

Shaw, Daron, Rodolfo de la Garza, and Jongho Lee. "Examining Latino Turnout in 1996: A Three-State, Validated Survey Approach." *American Journal of Political Science* 44 (2000): 332–340.

Smith, Dylan. "Appeals Court Rules against SB 1070." *Tucson Sentinel,* 11 April 2011, http://www.tucsonsen tinel.com/local/report/041111_sb1070_appeals/ appeals-court-rules-against-sb-1070/.

Soto, Victoria DeFrancesco. "Latinos Are from Mars, Latinas Are from Venus—in Politics Too!" *Latino Decisions.* (2010), http://latinodecisions.wordpress. com/2010/09/29/latinos-are-from-mars-2010/.

Welch, Susan, and Lee Sigelman. "A Gender Gap among Hispanics? A Comparison with Blacks and Anglos." *Western Political Quarterly* 45 (1992): 181–199.

Wilkinson, Betina Cutaia. "Commonality, Competition, and Stereotypes: Can Whites, Blacks, and Latinos Play Politics Together in the US?" PhD dissertation, Louisiana State University, 2010.

Betina Cutaia Wilkinson

HIV/AIDS

See AIDS.

HOUSING IN THE UNITED STATES

This article briefly summarizes the evolution of institutional mortgage markets in the United States from the early twentieth century to the advent of the subprime crisis in the late 2000s. It begins by detailing how federal involvement enabled the development of a stable and generally sound housing finance system—albeit one that suffered from significant problems of racial and social inequities. It then describes how active and passive deregulation and the rise of highly structured finance undermined this system, leading eventually to the subprime crisis.

The Development of Institutional Mortgage Markets in the United States. The rise of stable mortgage markets in the broad middle part of the twentieth century—epitomized by the dominance of the thirty-year, fixed-rate mortgage—was dependent on a persistent role for the federal government. These markets were not without serious and pervasive problems, including discrimination and redlining.

However, their basic structure constituted a strong base upon which to build a sound and fair housing finance system, and in the late 1960s and the 1970s, a number of federal statutes—the Fair Housing Act, the Home Mortgage Disclosure Act, the Equal Credit Opportunity Act, and the Community Reinvestment Act—helped move markets toward greater social equity. While implementation and enforcement of these laws were frequently lackluster, there were periods of time when significant progress towards fair, affordable, and sustainable home finance was made.

The timeline of US mortgage market development and change is not one of bright lines and and clear boundaries, although there were periods during which change occurred quite rapidly. Rather, different outside forces—including those based in technology, policy, and demography—interacted with each other to produce a variety of new financial products, changes in market structures, and opportunities and vulnerabilities among households and neighborhoods.

Since at least the early 1920s, the federal government had been a supporting, and sometimes catalyzing, actor in the promotion of homeownership in the United States. However, it was not until the 1930s that Congress and the executive branch became key participants in the development and expansion of homeownership and mortgage finance. Before the 1930s, many Americans, even many with decent incomes, found it very hard to borrow sufficient funds to purchase a home. The homeownership rate at the turn of the century was just above 46 percent and, despite the very large economic expansion of the 1920s, it had climbed to only just under 48 percent by 1930. The structure and availability of homeownership finance certainly played a key role in the relatively limited extent of homeownership prior to the 1930s.

The Local Building and Loan. From the early twentieth century through at least the 1970s, no single type of lender was more important to the development of risk-limiting mortgage markets than the building and loan (B and L), later called the savings and loan (S and L). Early B and Ls were primarily local institutions, with many member-depositors knowing each other or having some common association. Social and geographic cohesiveness gave B and Ls an informational advantage that kept underwriting costs and defaults low. The fate of B and Ls rested closely with the success of borrowers. Besides B and Ls, life insurance and mortgage companies were important providers of mortgages in the late nineteenth and early twentieth centuries. Mortgage companies made loans, and then sold either individual loans or bonds backed by the loans to investors.

Local B and Ls grew significantly in the early twentieth century. After the Panic of 1907 and through the boom period of the early 1920s, the number of local B and Ls grew, buttressed by the social and cultural mores that favored homeownership and by the general growth in real estate and the economy. With the real estate collapse of the late 1920s and the advent of the Great Depression, the number of B and Ls declined, but at the beginning of the Great Depression, savings and loans still held about one-third of the outstanding home mortgages in the United States.

There were significant differences in the structure and nature of credit provided by different types of lenders. B and Ls provided longer-term loans with higher loan-to-value ratios (but still rarely ever exceeding 80 percent) than banks or insurance companies. In the 1920s, the average term of mortgages was eleven years for those written by B and Ls, versus six to eight for those from insurance companies and two to three for those from commercial banks. Average loan-to-value ratios were 60 percent for B and Ls and 50 percent for other lenders. Borrowers with the shorter-term loans had to take out new loans much more frequently, and so incurred the upfront borrowing costs more often. Loans with lower loan-to-value ratios typically required the involvement of a substantial second mortgage, which came with very high fees and interest rates.

The 1930s: Federal Leadership in Home Finance. Federal involvement in the mortgage market began with the Federal Home Loan Bank Act of 1932, which President Hoover proposed and signed. This bill created the Home Loan Bank system to provide liquidity to B and Ls and to increase their role in the mortgage market. The Home Loan Bank system effectively endorsed the B and L-type loan and was the first direct government vehicle for dealing with the long-term/short-term liquidity mismatch that faced B and Ls with short-term deposits.

The Roosevelt administration pushed for more aggressive interventions in the housing market. The Home Loan Banks did little in the near term for homeowners who were losing their homes to foreclosure during the Great Depression. Roosevelt and Congress passed the Home Owners' Loan Act (HOLA) of 1933, which created the Home Owners' Loan Corporation (HOLC). The HOLC purchased mortgages in default from lenders. It also made refinance loans directly to homeowners, with the intent of providing a more manageable loan. The HOLC was capitalized and owned by the federal government and governed by the Federal Home Loan Bank Board. The HOLC has generally been perceived as successful. It made loans from 1933 to 1936 and did not incur substantial net losses over the long term. The HOLC served approximately 20 percent of homeowners with existing mortgages. It has been accused of institutionalizing redlining practices through the use of its risk rating maps; however, recent research suggests that the agency did not disseminate their risk rating maps, did not cooperate with the Federal Housing Administration (FHA) in its aggressive redlining practices, and actually made many loans in areas that it rated as high-risk. The HOLA also created the federal savings and loan (S and L) charter. The federal S and L increased the standardization and professionalization and helped turn a "movement" into an "industry."

The next major development in federal mortgage policy was the National Housing Act of 1934, which created the Federal Housing Administration (FHA). The FHA was created in large part to stimulate job creation, but also was responsible for introducing a key credit enhancement—FHA mortgage insurance—which had a strong direct effect on credit availability and served as a model for modern private mortgage insurance.

In addition to offering mortgage insurance, the FHA established the twenty-year, and later thirty-year, fully amortizing, fixed-rate mortgage with an 80 percent loan-to-value ratio as the dominant mortgage format for the remainder of the twentieth century. FHA loans also increased the standardization of mortgages generally, setting the stage for the eventual expansion of secondary market activity and securitization that dominated the last quarter of the twentieth century.

The FHA increased the supply of mortgage credit and allowed for predictable, low-risk financing. From the 1930s to the 1940s, the average term for mortgages made by S and Ls increased from eleven years to fifteen years. For insurance companies, who were larger FHA users, the average term increased from six to eight years to twenty years. Overall, the average loan-to-value for mortgages increased from less than 60 percent to 75 percent, and the bulk of loans became fully amortizing, helping homeowners to build equity over time.

The FHA had a large impact on the overall housing market. By the early 1940s, the FHA accounted for 45 percent of single-family loan originations. The end of World War II saw the advent of the Veterans Administration (VA) program. From 1945 to 1956, during the peak of the postwar suburbanization boom, VA loans accounted for 35 percent of net new mortgage flows, with the FHA accounting for another 14 percent. The FHA program gradually declined in significance until the late 1960s, when Congress authorized a substantial expansion of FHA activity, including a major subsidized loan component.

In 1938, the federal government created the Federal National Mortgage Association (now known as Fannie Mae) to create a secondary market in FHA-insured loans. In 1968, Fannie Mae became a "government-sponsored enterprise" (GSE), a for-profit, privately owned corporation subject to some, albeit limited, federal oversight. Its mission also soon had changed, to a focus on providing liquidity to the non-GSE, or conventional, mortgage market.

Thus, the two major "circuits" for housing finance developed in the United States both relied heavily on federal support over the course of their development.

The S and L circuit was supported by deposit insurance and the Home Loan Banks, while also drawing some support from FHA and VA programs. In the meantime, mortgage companies, commercial banks, and insurance companies made loans supported by FHA and VA programs and by Fannie Mae. Prior to the 1960s, the FHA/VA circuit was particularly important. Beginning in the late 1960s, as VA and FHA programs declined in their overall share of mortgages, the S and L circuit grew more dominant. This persisted until the 1980s and the explosion of the GSE secondary markets and securitization, which essentially superseded the old FHA/VA circuit.

The Growth of Plain-Vanilla Securitization. Mortgage securitization is a process in which funding of, or investment in, mortgage loans is separated from the origination (and originator) of the loans. The loans stand, in pools with many other loans, "on their own" and are not tied to the fate of the originating lender. In general, the alternative is either for the loans to be sold as individual "whole loans" to buyers who assume these loans as individual loans that they (or their agent) then service, or for the loan to remain on the balance sheet of the lender. Securitization led directly to the widespread "vertical disintegration" of the lending process (Jacobides, 2005). It enabled the origination process to be separated from the process of the funding and servicing of the loan. Vertical disintegration meant that more contractual relationships were now required among originators, issuers of the securities, investors that purchased the securities, credit rating agencies, servicers, and other mortgage market participants.

Securitization has often been portrayed as a private-sector financial innovation. Yet, it was the Government National Mortgage Association (Ginnie Mae), the federal agency that purchased FHA loans after Fannie Mae became a private firm, that issued the first residential mortgage-backed securities (RMBS) in 1970. RMBS increased the number and types of investors in the mortgage market, as well as the number of new lenders in the market. Also in 1970, the Emergency Home Finance Act created the Federal Home Loan Mortgage Corporation, now Freddie Mac, to provide secondary market capacity for the Home Loan Bank system members and allowed Fannie Mae and Freddie Mac to perform secondary market operations for conventional mortgages.

The first generation of residential mortgage-backed securities was the "pass-through" certificate, in which loans are purchased and assembled into pools. The securitizer then issues certificates, in which the cash flow generated by the loans in the pool is passed through to the investors in a pro-rata fashion. This sort of relatively simple security does not involve any complex hierarchical structuring into different layers of risk.

This plain vanilla securitization via the GSEs provided greater diversification in risks in the value of a lender's assets, yielded more liquidity to lenders because these diversified assets are more marketable than whole loans, and redistributed credit supply across regions, so that regions with few local sources of credit suffered from fewer constraints on credit flows. One consequence of the growth of securitization and the GSEs was that mortgage companies gained access to inexpensive funds and were able to offer long-term, fixed-rate mortgages at competitive interest rates. The national scope of mortgage companies and their lack of branches allowed them to benefit from lower costs and economies of scale. S and Ls were still both savings and lending institutions that had relied upon their local knowledge for competitive advantage. In the age of securitization, such advantages became less relevant.

In its early forms at least, securitization promoted the standardization of mortgage terms and underwriting requirements. This standardization reduced the benefit of local information, and the scale and inherent subsidies of the secondary markets meant that they offered lenders lower-cost capital for making mortgages. These changes resulted in growing economies of scale for most of the stages of the lending process, including funding and servicing. At the same time, large national lenders—mostly mortgage companies or bank-owned mortgage companies—developed more "wholesale" lending channels, in which they originated loans through large networks of localized mortgage brokers.

The Rise of Structured, Risk-Inducing Securitization. Pass-through residential mortgage-backed securities, though helping to geographically diversify the underlying default risk that investors faced, did little to deal with another sort of risk: prepayment risk. When interest rates decline, borrowers prepay their loans by refinancing. This can hurt investors who want a predictable income stream from residential mortgage-backed securities, and with lower interest rates, it is difficult to find investment opportunities that will generate the similar returns at similar levels of risk as the original investment in the security.

Partly to deal with this problem, Freddie Mac issued the first collateralized mortgage obligation (CMO) in 1983. A CMO is a more complicated form of the residential mortgage-backed security because it allocates prepayment risk across different investors by structuring the securitization into different segments that pay back over varying schedules. In addition, CMOs can provide a vertical hierarchy of default risk by allowing more risk-tolerant bondholders to bear losses associated with defaults of the underlying loans before the holders of less risky senior bonds. These different segments of risk are called "tranches" (French for "slices") and are generally classified according to the rating they receive from the credit rating agencies, such as AAA, AA, A, BBB, BB, or B.

CMOs had a large impact because they peeled apart various types and degrees of risk and allocated these to different investors depending on their appetite for risk. Investors who would not invest in a pass-through security backed by loans exhibiting anything but the lowest default risks could invest in a bond that was designed to be highly secure. These AAA, senior tranche bonds would provide modest interest rates to investors, with riskier tranches earning somewhat higher rates. CMOs appealed to a broader segment of investors and drew more capital into mortgage markets. They also enabled the capital markets to provide credit to a wider spectrum of credit risk at the point of loan origination.

Therefore, securitization encouraged risk-based pricing rather than credit rationing, where essentially no institutional lender would lend to borrowers below certain risk thresholds. The more mortgage cash flows were repackaged, the more risk could be tolerated in the home financing transaction. As the risk at the origination level increased, however, defaults and foreclosures increased, which produced substantial negative spillovers into communities.

The issuance of residential mortgage-backed securities in the subprime market increased from $87 billion in 2001 to almost $450 billion by 2006. In the Alt-A market—which includes many stated-income mortgages, mostly to borrowers with strong credit scores—issuance of residential mortgage-backed securities increased from approximately $11 billion in 2001 to more than $365 billion by 2006. The securitization of subprime and Alt-A loans together almost equaled total GSE issuance by 2006 ($814 billion versus $905 billion).

The simple growth of CMOs does not completely explain why so much capital flowed into high-risk mortgage markets starting in 2002 and 2003. There were fundamental shifts in the financial engineering of mortgage securities. A new form of highly complex security was used heavily to the subprime and Alt-A mortgage markets: the collateralized debt obligation, or CDO. The CDO involved the additional layering between the institutional investor and the borrowers. In CDOs, RMBS bonds—particularly those with less than AAA ratings—are themselves pooled with RMBS bonds derived from other loan pools, which may be of varying quality or ratings. The cash flows from these bonds are then pooled and a new set of CDO bonds are produced, with senior and subordinate tranches. By this tranching of the cash flow coming from a pool of residential mortgage-backed securities (and potentially other CDO bonds), the "sow's ear" of lower-grade bonds produced what were thought to be "silk purses," in the form of higher-rated CDO bonds. The CDO is generated from a spectrum of residential mortgage-backed securities and sometimes other kinds of bonds, some of which may be other CDO bonds. The CDO increased the demand for and value of higher-risk, lower-rated CMO bonds, thus increasing the market's overall appetite for higher risk lending.

Another innovation employed in the second high-risk lending boom was the credit default swap (CDS), which is effectively a private, unregulated, insurance agreement that allows investors in mortgage-backed and other securities to hedge their investments. What came to be known as "structured finance"—the engineering of CMOs, CDOs, CDSs and other complex mortgage-related investment vehicles—turned out to suffer from a broad array of perverse incentives and transactional failures. Without sufficient regulatory oversight or interventions, these vehicles helped produce large amounts of default risk in the origination of home loans.

Federal Policy in the Late Twentieth Century: Support for Securitization, the Decline of Originate-to-Hold Lending, and Active and Passive Deregulation. Although Fannie Mae was created in 1938 and Ginnie Mae and Freddie Mac introduced residential mortgage-backed securities in 1970 and 1971, the eventual dominance of securitization in mortgage markets by the late twentieth century is perhaps best attributed to federal financial deregulation of the early 1980s, followed by some specific industry-supported legislation later in that decade. By explicitly favoring the securitization circuit over the traditionally dominant S and L circuit, federal policy makers helped shift the structure of the mortgage industry in at least three ways: 1) from a predominantly local to a predominantly national system; 2) from an originate-to-hold model to an originate-to-distribute model; and 3) from one in which most loans were made by relatively more regulated lenders (e.g., S and Ls) to one in which predominantly unregulated mortgage companies and a growing set of essentially unregulated mortgage brokers dominated. Combined with the failure of policy makers and regulatory agencies to increase regulatory supervision of these emerging lenders—a form of "passive" deregulation—and the federal preemption of state regulations, these moves meant that the path toward greater overall deregulation of the mortgage marketplace was well paved by the middle to late 1980s. Moreover, legislators and regulators constructed policy that allowed for better-regulated depository institutions, especially commercial banks, to acquire or affiliate with less regulated entities so that the new financial conglomerates could conduct most of their mortgage lending through lightly regulated subsidiaries and affiliates.

A critical ingredient to the growth of securitization was the Depository Institutions Deregulation and Monetary Control Act (DIDMCA) of 1980, which phased in the general abolition of state usury limits on first mortgages by 1986. DIDMCA also extended the ability of national banks to be governed only by the usury limits of their home state; this ability, labeled "interest rate exportation," allowed depositories to override state usury limits.

With the adoption of the Alternative Mortgage Transaction Parity Act (AMTPA) in 1982, federal policy makers overrode state laws that regulated various terms of "alternative" loans, including those with features such as adjustable interest rates and balloon payments. The law also allowed mortgage companies, which are primarily state-regulated, to opt for regulations issued by the federal S and L regulator (now the Office of Thrift Supervision) rather than comply with the lending regulations of the state in which they were operating. Thus, AMTPA provided significant federal preemption to nondepository lenders, and these nondepositories were precisely the sort who relied especially on securitization as a means of funding their loans.

In 1982, the President's Commission on Housing argued that all sorts of lenders and borrowers should have "unrestricted access" to the money and capital markets. Moreover, the Commission advocated that mortgage-market participants (and by this it appears they were thinking more of investors and originators than of borrowers) should have "reliable ways of managing interest-rate risk" (Colton, 2002, p.11). The Commission went on to recommend a variety of proposals to more closely link broader capital markets to the "underlying demand" for housing credit.

At least two statutes followed directly from the recommendations of the President's Commission. First, the 1984 Secondary Mortgage Market Enhancement Act (SMMEA) facilitated non-GSE or "private-label" securitization in various ways, including exempting residential mortgage-backed securities from state-level registration, and expanding the ability of banks and thrifts to hold residential mortgage-backed securities as assets on their balance sheets. The CMO was also directly supported by the 1986 Tax Reform Act, which created the Real Estate Mortgage Investment Conduit (REMIC), a legal structure for trusts that are used in structured residential mortgage-backed securities, especially CMOs. The REMIC eliminated any problems with potential "double" taxation of cash flows, as they flow through the CMO.

By the 1990s, Fannie Mae's and Freddie Mac's loan purchases accounted for more than one-half of new mortgage originations. The preemption of state consumer protections increased the market for residential mortgage-backed securities by increasing the returns to investors (by increasing fees and rates paid by borrowers). By stoking the creation and growth of a new set of lenders, by removing deposit rate regulations favoring S and Ls, and by fostering the development of the mortgage brokerage industry, federal policy essentially constituted the death knell for S and Ls, and installed a regime of both government-sponsored and private-label securitization as the dominant sources of mortgage capital.

The decline of the S and L circuit began in the mid-1970s, as the issuance of residential mortgage-backed securities began. When S and L market share began dropping in the 1980s, it was essentially absorbed by GSE residential mortgage-backed securities. Private-label residential mortgage-backed securities began slowly in the middle 1980s but began to grow at a faster pace in the early 1990s, as the early subprime mortgage market developed. By 1995, the GSEs and GSE-mortgage residential mortgage-backed securities accounted for 51 percent of outstanding mortgage credit. Banks had reached a share of 19 percent, with thrifts down to 14 percent. Thrifts were down from a high of 58 percent in 1973 and 26 percent in 1989, the year of the savings and loan crisis bill, the Financial Institutions Reform, Recovery, and Enforcement Act (FIRREA). Private-label residential mortgage-backed securities were just beginning to get started, rising from 2 percent of outstanding mortgages in 1990 to 6 percent in 1995.

Policy Debates over Regulating High-Risk Mortgage Lending, 1995–2008. The now well-known boom in high-risk mortgages from 2002 to 2007 followed a major, albeit smaller, increase in subprime lending in the late 1990s. Although some minor changes in federal regulation of subprime lending occurred in 2001 following this first subprime boom, the financial services industry successfully fought off most calls for increased regulation, and even received assistance from some federal regulators in overriding state attempts to regulate lending more strongly.

As problems of predatory lending and higher foreclosure rates among subprime loans came to light in the late 1990s, consumer groups around the country became increasingly focused on the issue. In 1994, the Home Ownership and Equity Protection Act (HOEPA) was adopted. However, HOEPA focused only on increasing regulation of the very highest-cost home equity and refinancing loans, leaving the bulk of the subprime market not covered by the law.

Advocates for stronger mortgage regulation found some initial success at the state level. In the summer of 1999, the North Carolina legislature passed the first comprehensive anti-predatory lending legislation in the country. Following North Carolina, advocates in other states pushed for anti-predatory lending regulations. By 2003, the National Conference of State Legislatures listed more than thirty states as having passed anti-predatory lending statutes. However, many state statutes were not very comprehensive or very strong. Some essentially just recreated the federal HOEPA protections in state law. Many so-called "anti-predatory lending" laws at the state level had been heavily influenced by state banking lobbyists.

When consumer advocates attempted to strengthen state lending regulations, they were often thwarted by industry advocates and lobbyists. Banking and financial services lobbyists have traditionally had a great deal of influence on state legislatures. Key actors in state-level policy debates included the GSEs, Fannie Mae and Freddie Mac, and the three primary credit rating agencies, Standard & Poor's, Moody's, and Fitch. These firms had significant leverage over state policy makers. The GSEs could refuse to purchase certain types of loans in a state. The rating agencies could refuse to rate mortgage-backed securities containing loans covered by certain state laws, severely limiting regular liquidity and marketability of such loans, at least in the near term.

In Georgia in early 2003, for example, the credit rating agencies became actively involved in influencing state legislation by proclaiming that they would not rate securities containing any loans covered by the state's new anti-predatory lending law. Soon after the law went into effect, Standard & Poor's issued a press release saying that it would not rate securities backed by Georgia mortgages for fear that some of the underlying loans might violate the Georgia Fair Lending Act (GFLA). This press release, which was later followed by similar actions by Moody's and Fitch, was the critical factor in enabling opponents of GFLA to weaken the law after it was initially passed.

Federal Regulators Study Abusive Lending and Warn of Subprime Risks to Banks. In 1999, the US Department of Housing and Urban Development (HUD) and the US Treasury Department created a task sorce to develop federal policy recommendations to address predatory lending. The HUD-Treasury Task Force held hearings in five large cities in the spring of 2000 and issued a report containing a number of federal policy recommendations, including calling on the Federal Reserve Board to use more of its authority under HOEPA to outlaw predatory practices.

In the late 1990s and early 2000s, opposing bills were introduced in Congress backed by consumer and industry interest groups, but neither side made substantial headway. State and local policy developments, the HUD-Treasury report, and public and congressional concern led the Federal Reserve Board to hold public hearings in 2000 on potential revisions to HOEPA regulations. At the end of 2000, the Board proposed some modest changes to the HOEPA rules. However, the Board failed to use its broader powers under the Act to substantially expand the coverage or impact of the law.

Federal Regulators Act to Preempt State Regulation of High-Risk Lending. As more states began to adopt predatory lending regulations in 2001 and 2002, lenders began to turn to Washington to override state laws. The lending industry pursued a mixed strategy of seeking a federal statute aimed at preempting state laws and, at the same time, trying to get federal bank regulators to preempt state laws. The first approach would remain difficult as long as Senator Paul Sarbanes, a supporter of increased regulation, retained the ranking Democratic seat on the Senate Banking committee.

Therefore, lenders also appealed to their federal regulators to preempt state regulations. Federal regulators have a vested interest in preempting state consumer protection laws, because the ability to preempt state law is perhaps the greatest source of value in the federal thrift and national bank charters. Regulators can gain political power based on the number and size of the banks that fall under their regulatory supervision. In the some cases, a regulator's operations are funded by levying fees on the institutions they regulate. If a regulator does not use its ability to allow banks under its supervision to preempt state consumer protection regulations, the bank may change its charter so that it is regulated by a more lender-friendly agency.

The Office of Thrift Supervision (OTS) moved first to override state mortgage regulations by preempting key provisions of Georgia's predatory lending law in January of 2003, so that federal thrifts were exempted from the law. The Office of the Comptroller of the Currency (OCC) had issued a letter to national banks in November of 2002, asserting its jurisdiction over state regulators and asking banks to inform it if a state regulator may have asserted authority over a national bank. It was not long before National City Bank of Cleveland requested that the OCC preempt the Georgia law, and the OCC obliged.

In the early to middle 2000s, consumer advocates called on federal regulators to do more to regulate the affiliates of banks that were increasingly dominating the subprime market. In early 2004, the US General Accounting Office (GAO) issued a report calling for stronger regulatory supervision in the subprime market, and specifically called for giving the Federal Reserve explicit power to conduct regular examinations of bank affiliates. Earlier, in 2000, Edward Gramlich, a Federal Reserve Board Governor, had urged Alan Greenspan, Chairman of the Board, to direct examiners to inspect the lending of bank affiliates on a pilot basis. The suggestion was rebuffed by Chairman Greenspan.

More generally, even though federal regulators had issued cautions to banks holding subprime loans on their balance sheets, they generally supported the growth of the subprime market. Regulators issued statements and studies arguing that subprime lending provided increased homeownership opportunities, which in turn gave support to industry lobbyists working against efforts to increase regulation.

In 2006 and early 2007, as problems in the subprime market became much clearer and began to cause significant disruptions to broader financial markets, regulators responded with additional proposals and hearings. The Federal Reserve Board held hearings related to subprime and predatory lending in both 2006 and 2007 and, in early 2007, issued a draft proposal for increased regulation of the subprime market. After the 2007 hearings, the Board issued a more complete set of regulatory proposals, with particular attention to using HOEPA to regulate a substantially broader portion of the subprime market, rather than just the very highest-cost segment.

After the 2006 election, when Democrats gained control of the House of Representatives, there was also some movement in the legislative arena. Barney Frank (D-MA), the powerful chair of the House Financial Services Committee, sponsored a bill that contained many substantive regulations which consumer advocates had been proposing for over a decade. However, the bill that eventually passed the House in 2007 was once again weakened by industry lobbyists in some critical ways.

Of course, by 2007, a good deal of the damage had already been done and the subprime market had substantially shut down. Over 2009 and 2010, congressional debate would continue and culminate in the Dodd-Frank Act, which created a new Consumer Financial Protection Bureau in the Federal Reserve

System with broad rule-making authority, and authorized a number of stronger initiatives to regulate high-risk lending. The regulatory process now largely shifts to the rule-making process, where debates over appropriate levels of regulation will take place. Many of these debates are likely to resemble, both politically and substantively, the debates that took place over the last twenty years. The outcomes of these rule-making processes will be critical determinants of whether, and to what degree, the nation is likely to see a reprise of the US mortgage crisis.

[*See also* Deregulation; Regulation; *and* Savings and Loan Associations.]

BIBLIOGRAPHY

Ashcraft, Adam B., and Til Schuermann. "Understanding the Securitization of Subprime Mortgage Credit." Federal Reserve Bank of New York, Staff Report no. 318. (2008), http://www.newyorkfed.org/research/staff_reports/sr318.pdf.

Colton, Kent W. "Housing Finance in the United States: The Transformation of the US Housing Finance System." Joint Center for Housing Studies, Harvard University, Working Paper W02-5. (2002), http://www.jchs.harvard.edu/research/publications/housing-finance-united-states-transformation-us-housing-finance-system.

Crossney, K., and D. Bartelt, D. "The Legacy of the Homeowners Loan Corporation." *Housing Policy Debate* 16 (2005): 547–572.

Green, Richard K., and Susan M. Wachter. "The Housing Finance Revolution." Prepared for the Thirty-first Economic Policy Symposium: Housing, Housing Finance and Monetary Policy. Kansas City: Federal Reserve Bank of Kansas City. (2007), http://www.kansascityfed.org/publicat/sympos/2007/PDF/2007.08.21.WachterandGreen.pdf.

Gries, John, and James Ford. *Home Finance and Taxation: Reports of the Committees on Finance and Taxation.* (Washington, D.C., 1932).

Hoffman, Susan. *Politics and Banking: Ideas, Public Policy, and the Creation of Financial Institutions.* (Baltimore, 2001).

Hutchinson, Janet. "Shaping Housing and Enhancing Consumption: Hoover's Interwar Housing Policy." In *From Tenements to the Taylor Homes: In Search of Urban Housing Policy in Twentieth Century America,* edited by John F. Bauman, Roger Biles, and Kristin M. Szylvian, pp. 81–101. (University Park, Penn., 2000).

Immergluck, Dan. "Community Responses to the Foreclosure Crisis: Thoughts on Local Interventions." Federal Reserve Bank of Atlanta Discussion Paper. Atlanta: Federal Reserve Bank of Atlanta. (2008).

Immergluck, Dan. *Credit to the Community: Community Reinvestment and Fair Lending Policy in the United States.* (Armonk, N.Y., 2004).

Immergluck, Dan. *Foreclosed: High-Risk Lending, Deregulation and the Undermining of the American Mortgage Market.* (Ithaca, N.Y., 2009).

Jacobides, Michael G. "Industry Change Through Vertical Disintegration: How And Why Markets Emerged In Mortgage Banking." *Academy of Management Journal* 48 (2005): 465–498.

Klaman, Saul B. *The Postwar Residential Mortgage Market.* (Princeton, N.J., 1961).

Lea, Michael. "Innovation and the Cost of Mortgage Credit: A Historical Perspective." *Housing Policy Debate* 7 (1996): 147–174.

Mason, David Lawrence. *From Buildings and Loans to Bail-Outs: A History of the American Savings and Loan Industry, 1831–1995.* (Cambridge, UK, 2004).

McCoy, Patricia A., and Elizabeth Renuart, E. "The Legal Infrastructure of Subprime and Nontraditional Home Mortgages." Joint Center for Housing Studies, Harvard University. (2008), http://www.jchs.harvard.edu/research/publications/legal-infrastructure-subprime-and-nontraditional-home-mortgages.

National Conference of State Legislatures. "Banking and Financial Services: Subprime and Predatory Mortgage Lending." (2003), http://www.ncsl.org/default.aspx?tabid=12511.

United States General Accounting Office. "Consumer Protection: Federal and State Agencies Face Challenges in Combating Predatory Lending." (2004). http://www.gao.gov/new.items/d04280.pdf.

Vale, Lawrence J. "The Ideological Origins of Affordable Homeownership Efforts." In *Chasing the American Dream: New Perspectives on Affordable Homeownership,* edited by William M. Rohe and Harry L. Watson, pp. 15–40. (Ithaca, N.Y., 2007).

Vandell, Kerry D. "FHA Restructuring Proposals: Alternatives and Implications." *Housing Policy Debate* 6, no. 2 (1995): 299–383.

Dan Immergluck

HUMAN RIGHTS AND HUMANITARIAN INTERVENTION

The linkage between American politics and human rights is replete with paradoxes, if not outright contradictions. The American Revolution, and the subsequent founding of various levels of government, were made in the name of human rights—even as severe discrimination continued against Native Americans, African Americans, women, and others. Many saw the country as professing a special global mission to lift up others toward more personal freedom and democracy, even as the federal government sometimes aligned itself with various repressive circles abroad, and engaged in harsh interventions and occupations. Over time, official American rhetoric pledging commitment to human rights at home and abroad did not wane, but this did not prevent the United States from turning a blind eye to major violations of human rights in both domestic and foreign policy. In the final analysis, the abstract idea of human rights remains a mainstay of American political culture, but two overlapping central tensions endure in a globalized world: how to link the dominant American version with the international law of human rights, and how to advance human rights in the face of competing views regarding national security and economic competition.

History. Most educated Americans know that the country was founded on the ideas of Lockean liberalism and Jeffersonian justification of rebellion: governments were instituted to protect not just national security but also the "rights of man," and when governments transgressed these fundamental human rights, individuals were justified in rebelling in order to form more legitimate institutions. The notion of universal human rights had been invented by European Enlightenment philosophers like the Englishman John Locke in the seventeenth and eighteenth centuries, however much such ideas were informed by various philosophical and religious traditions from around the world—(for example, the biblical injunction to "do unto others as you would have them do unto you"). These notions of universal personal rights were first applied on a national, political basis in the American Revolution (1776) and the French Revolution (1789–1799); during this era, leading rights advocates like Thomas Jefferson and Thomas Paine were influential on both sides of the Atlantic.

In the case of the United States in the eighteenth century, the idea of universal human rights was interlinked with notions of providential nationalism. The Puritans in New England in particular, having given up on Europe, saw the Americans as the new chosen people of God and the United States as the new Jerusalem, or a new "city on a hill," a beacon and model to others. In this view, articulated especially by Massachusetts governor and Puritan preacher John Winthrop, from the beginning the United States was not an ordinary nation, but rather a unique country blessed by Providence to show the world the way to greater religious and political freedoms. The idea of providential nationalism linked to personal freedoms proved enduring—so much so that Winthrop's sermons were resurrected by the not-especially-religious Ronald Reagan in the 1980s, to great popular acclaim. American political debates in 2010 still featured much attention to "American exceptionalism," that is, a special role for the divinely blessed United States. Notions of personal freedom and human rights loomed large in this discourse. It has been said that Americans worship at the altar of freedom, although the abstract conception of "freedom" entails many meanings.

It made little difference to many Americans that other nations also manifested their version of providential nationalism. That is to say, the British, French, Russians, Germans, Dutch, and others also claimed Providence's blessing as they exported their political experience abroad. For example, under the religious tzars, Russian expansion into central Asia as part of "the Great Game" against British power and control in the nineteenth century invoked the deity's blessing. Likewise, British, French, and Dutch colonialisms were all accompanied by the rhetoric of bringing progressive advance to inferior peoples as part of God's plan. British rhetoric about the "white man's burden," or French claims about a *mission civilitrice*, were derived from a religious foundation. The fact that American exceptionalism was not so exceptional did not diminish its appeal over time within America—a nation notoriously weak in maintaining comparative historical perspectives.

When Jefferson and the other founding fathers referred to the "God-given rights of man," this universalist rhetoric was accompanied by the assumed, if often unstated, restrictions of that time. It was understood to exclude women, Native Americans, and racial minorities. In fact, despite the rights rhetoric, the gentry class that led the American Revolution emphasized the special leadership privilege of propertied white males. But over time, a more egalitarian and democratic ethic took hold, at least for white males. And once articulated, the principle of personal rights for all, without negative distinctions, made it difficult to sustain discrimination based on gender or national origin. As is evident, in the United States discrimination against women, African Americans, and others did not dissipate quickly or easily. Women did not gain political rights until the 1920s, and African Americans did not benefit from vigorous enforcement of federal civil rights laws until the 1960s and after. All vestiges of gender, racial, and religious biases have yet to be erased. Yet the notion of personal equality and personal rights played its role in the evolution of the conception of rights, accentuating the contradiction between the foundational principles based on universal human rights and the reality lived by many Americans on a daily basis. As is normal, abstract values, norms, and laws do not implement themselves; rather, they are implemented through the struggle of interested and committed persons.

Both in France and the United States, from about 1770 to 1790, the universalist rhetoric about human rights was applied in strictly national ways. As the antimonarchical revolution faltered in France, the semidemocratic United States adopted a foreign policy of selective engagement with the world, which at times manifested elements of nonalignment and isolationism. An exiting President George Washington counseled against permanent and entangling alliances. Jefferson worried about how an activist foreign policy tended to undermine democracy at home, leading as it often did to an "imperial presidency." And John Adams admonished the country not to go abroad in search of monsters to destroy. His version of American exceptionalism would perfect American society at home, thus allowing the young nation to serve as a mostly passive beacon to others. The United States not only did not

recognize the independence of black-led Haiti in 1804, because that might encourage African American unrest in the American South, but also did not actively support European democratic revolts in 1848. Early US use of force abroad tended to be employed in pursuit of strictly expedient goals, such as the elimination of piracy from North Africa, which interfered with American commerce. There was not—and in fact never has been—a moralistic crusade for human rights in American foreign policy that ignored expedient concerns. Despite the early universalist rhetoric of human rights in France and the United States, and later elsewhere as well, human rights obligations were not written into general international law until 1945.

The United States and the Establishment of International Human Rights Norms. It was only with the ratification of the United Nations (UN) Charter after World War II that attention to human rights was made a general obligation of all states in public international law. The United States led the way in this important change. Before then, as indicated above, while there existed a moral and political rhetoric of universal human rights, institutional developments in this domain, whether positive or negative, tended to be strictly national. National legal and political developments might or might not emphasize human rights, while human rights tended to be generally downplayed in much national foreign policy.

The record of President Woodrow Wilson, and US decisions after World War I, did not make a large dent in the existing pattern. Wilson had supposedly entered World War I primarily to make the world safe for democracy and to vindicate international law, the latter arguably prohibiting German unrestricted submarine warfare. Wilson and the British entered the Versailles Peace Conference in 1919 planning to write the norm of religious freedom into the League of Nations Covenant. But when the Japanese responded by pushing for acknowledgment of the norm of racial equality, the arch-segregationist Wilson abandoned any mention of any form of human rights in the Covenant. Moreover, Wilson resisted pressures for the United States to assume a humanitarian protectorate over Christian Armenians in the collapsing Ottoman Empire, even though they had been subjected to genocidal policies by their Turkish masters. While the League did take up various matters such as slavery in Liberia or certain refugee situations (mainly in Europe), among other subjects, it did not officially do so as a matter of human rights, but rather as a matter of social welfare. And the United States chose to participate or not in League activities according to strictly national decisions, not being legally bound by the Covenant. As is well known, the US Senate failed to give its advice and consent to the Versailles Treaty with the Covenant of the League of Nations attached. Human rights were not internationally institutionalized during the period from 1919 to 1945. American racial discrimination was one factor accounting for this fact. (At home, Wilson insisted that the federal work force be segregated.)

By comparison, even before World War II ended, US officials began planning for the United Nations, the postwar international organization, essentially a reformed League of Nations, which would have primary responsibility for international peace and security, as guided by five so-called great powers, or permanent members of the UN Security Council. The UN Charter, unlike the League Covenant, contained references to human rights from early drafts. In part this was because President Franklin D. Roosevelt was convinced that the origins of World War II lay in the violations of human rights by the Nazi, fascist, and militarist powers that had engaged in persecution at home and aggression abroad. Harry S. Truman, who became president upon Roosevelt's death in the spring of 1945, agreed, and continued the push for human rights language at the San Francisco conference in August 1945 that created the United Nations. Thus the White House supported the general idea that protection of individual human rights was linked to peace. In this view, brutal, authoritarian regimes committed aggression, while rights-protective democracies did not. While various other parties, both public and private, also pushed for human rights language in the Charter, it was the US government, under Roosevelt and Truman, that first drafted key provisions, and then insisted that the language remain general rather than specific, and detailed enough to be enforced by courts.

Both Roosevelt and Truman, and their advisers, wanted to ensure Senate acceptance of the UN Charter. They believed persistent US engagement with the world was necessary for the national interest, lest the country repeat what they saw as its misguided policies of limited engagement during the interwar years. They also recalled Wilson's failure to attain advice and consent for the Versailles Treaty and the League Covenant. In this regard, both presidents understood all too well the power of senators from the American South, where discrimination and even lynchings against African Americans were still prevalent. Just as FDR had prioritized his economic "New Deal" at the expense of vigorous action for civil rights, so he planned to keep the human rights language in the UN Charter vague in order not to generate opposition in the Senate. Truman, who was to racially integrate the US military, saw the logic of this thinking and likewise did not push the human rights language beyond what the political traffic would bear. In the final analysis, the Charter's Article 55 did obligate all member states to take unspecified action to advance human rights and fundamental freedoms, and the United States did ratify the Charter and become a UN member. From the US perspective, weak institutionalization of human rights at the UN was the product of careful political calculation about congressional opinion. (While the Senate alone voted on treaties like the UN Charter, both houses voted on implementing legislation). Paradoxically, US foreign policy led on human rights in 1945, but in the context of continuing racial discrimination at home.

The same process more or less prevailed regarding the 1948 Universal Declaration of Human Rights. The UN Charter required support for internationally recognized human rights, but international law at that time did not define any such rights. Thus the new UN Human Rights Commission—a body of state representatives reporting to the UN Economic and Social Council—set about identifying thirty general human rights principles. They pertained to civil, political, economic, social, and cultural rights, thus going beyond the US Constitution, which addresses only civil and political rights. The commission was headed by Eleanor Roosevelt, who facilitated international agreement in several ways, even if she did not often enter into the substance of detailed negotiations. As the vote on the Universal Declaration approached in the UN General Assembly, set for 10 December 1948, Eleanor Roosevelt made clear the view that the document was not immediately legally binding, but rather a statement of aspirations. On this understanding, Truman supported the Declaration and US diplomacy "twisted arms" to secure a positive vote. It passed without negative vote (but with eight abstentions). Once again the United States had been active on universal human rights standards, but in a way that did not require immediate change in American society. US leaders wanted the image of standing for individual freedoms around the world, but in a way that did not accentuate human rights violations in the United States.

After 1948, state representatives at the UN turned to the negotiation of binding human rights treaties that would specify, in enforceable ways, the general language of the Declaration. This process led to two core Covenants on civil-political and economic-social-cultural rights. This was followed by a raft of treaties on genocide, torture, racial discrimination, religious freedom, rights of women, refugees, rights of the child, and many other subjects. The United States participated actively in these negotiations. It ratified some of these treaties (e.g., civil-political rights, genocide, religious freedom, refugees) while declining to ratify others (e.g., economic-social-cultural rights, women's rights, rights of the child, etc.) Often US ratification was accompanied by reservations, understandings, and declarations (RUDs) that either made some provisions, or the entire treaty, unenforceable within US jurisdiction. In most cases of ratification, the United States wanted to be seen as supportive of internationally recognized human rights, but without agreeing to make major changes in American society or to give international courts,

such as the International Court of Justice (ICJ), the authority to make a binding interpretation of what the treaty required (as seen in the US reservation to the Genocide Treaty).

In the meantime, the United States played a leadership role in the development of International Humanitarian Law (IHL), also called the laws of war or the law of armed conflict, or even the law for human rights in armed conflict. In 1949 Washington supported the International Committee of the Red Cross (the private guardian of IHL), and the host Swiss government in a diplomatic conference that produced the four Geneva Conventions of that year. A principle goal of these four interlocking treaties was to reduce the human distress of war by providing humanitarian protections for prisoners of war and civilians affected by war or occupation. Washington ratified all four in 1955 and later passed implementing legislation (the War Crimes Act). From 1974 to 1977 it was a major player in the negotiation of two additional Protocols to the 1949 law, although as events played out the United States ratified neither. It did strongly support a third Protocol in 2005 that added a red crystal to the red cross and red crescent as neutral emblems in war. This Protocol worked to the advantage of Israel and its official aid agency, Magen David Adom (MDA), since use of the newly approved red crystal in international operations obviated the need for MDA to use the red cross or red crescent, which it had refused to do. MDA was therefore allowed to join the family of "Red Cross" actors, which was seen by some as an extension of Israeli legitimacy in world affairs. Such was the interplay of "humanitarian" and "political" factors in contemporary international relations, with the powerful United States at the center of all developments.

Beyond Establishing Standards: US Protection of Human Rights. It is one thing to agree that there is an international law of human rights and humanitarian affairs, or even to ratify some of the treaties that make up this part of international law (along with the complex subject of customary international law, not discussed here). It is another thing to take the law seriously and ensure that international law affects public policy at home and abroad. It has often been remarked that while there is much human rights law for peace and war, there remains a great gap between the law on the books and the law in action. Or, as one commentator remarked, the twentieth century had the best norms and the worst realities of any century on record. What is the US record on implementation of human rights norms?

Human Rights at Home. First, in general, internationally recognized human rights have not had a great influence on American society, at least not directly in terms of legal process. The dominant view in the United States is that human rights are an American export, not an international import. Human rights are thus seen as a matter of civil and political freedoms that the United States teaches to others. This is consistent with American providential nationalism, and the view that the United States is a beacon to others. When the United States ratifies a human rights treaty, most of the time it has to defend its subsequent record of implementation before a UN committee of experts, a so-called monitoring mechanism. But the comments and questions of these experts are not legally binding in the short run, and there is not much evidence that this review process, or other relevant UN proceedings, are given great weight by Washington policy makers. Human rights advocacy groups like Amnesty International have documented many violations of internationally recognized human rights in the United States, such as the treatment of prisoners. But this private criticism, fashioned against the background of international standards, likewise does not seem to have had much impact on American society.

Furthermore, as noted above, most of the time when the United States has ratified a human rights treaty it has attached reservations by whatever name to ensure that would-be plaintiffs cannot use that law to determine cases in US courts. Thus the International Covenant on Civil and Political Rights cannot be the basis for judicial resolution of disputes in the United States. This is in addition to the fact that Washington has never ratified the

International Covenant of Economic, Social, and Cultural Rights. The United States does not accept what is widely accepted in the rest of the world, including in all industrialized democratic counties—namely, that citizens have a human right to adequate food, clothing, shelter, and health care. In this sense the United States preaches universal human rights, but practices cultural relativism or national particularity. When the international law of human rights fits with traditional American values, officials say that the law is binding on all. When the international version of human rights does not fit with the traditional American approach, as on socioeconomic rights, most officials hold to the traditional national view. In general, Americans revere the US Constitution and the US court system, not wanting either to be trumped by international law and international agencies. (The situation is otherwise in democratic Europe, where the European Court of Human Rights makes the controlling interpretation of what is required under the European Convention on Human Rights and Fundamental Freedoms.) When Americans engaged in health care reform in 2009–2010, the notion of a human right to health and health care was almost totally absent from official proceedings.

There are three major exceptions to this first generalization that the international law of human rights has not manifested much impact on American society. The first two exceptions pertain to formal legal process. The 1951 Convention on Refugees (as affected by its 1967 Protocol) has been held to be a self-executing treaty. US courts will adjudicate claims under this treaty, and have required changes in US decision-making pertaining to asylum seekers and refugees, although not consistently so. Also, if IHL is included as part of international human rights law, it is clear that US courts will sometimes require a change in US policy with regard to various detainees linked to the so-called War on Terror. In light of the George W. Bush administration's claim to have been engaged in armed conflict against various state and non-state actors after the attacks of September 11, 2001, the US Supreme Court has held, among other judgments, that parts of the 1949 Geneva

Conventions pertain to all detainees held at the Guantanamo Bay naval base, geographically located on the island of Cuba (but under US de facto sovereignty, in the view of the Court). In other ways, too, it is now very clear that IHL has affected US public policy, either in the decisions of various courts, or in legal interpretations made by various parts of the executive branch—namely, legal interpretations made by government lawyers in the Justice Department, Pentagon, State Department, White House, etc. So the existence of the Geneva Conventions, which overlaps in coverage with the UN Convention against Torture and Other Cruel, Inhuman, and Degrading Treatment, has indeed affected US public policy.

The American federal structure can complicate the role of international human rights law in the United States. For example, the federal government has accepted a part of international law that requires aliens charged with capital crimes to have access to consular representation, in order to ensure adequate defense counsel. But most charges entailing a possible death penalty occur in state courts. The US Supreme Court has held that the federal government has no constitutional authority to control state courts. Thus a bipartisan effort in Washington to comply with US international obligations about due process in judicial proceedings has run into a roadblock, stemming from the federal nature of US domestic law. Some states (e.g., California) have changed state law to comply with US treaty provisions. Other states (e.g., Texas) have not.

As for the third exception, politically rather than legally speaking, the presence after 1945 of an international law of human rights caused those sensitive to US foreign policy needs to seek some changes in American society. Given the tendency, especially of the Soviet Union and its satellite communist states to highlight "the race question" in the United States, several US presidents were historically sensitive to the damage done to US foreign policy by the continuation of human rights violations at home. In the 1950s and 1960s, several presidential administrations were aware that it was hard to win the hearts and minds of developing and other non-aligned

states in Cold War competition with communism when African Americans and others were clearly the victims of discrimination and persecution. These administrations were sensitive to the needs of US soft power—that is, the reputation the United States needed to maintain in order to assume the high moral ground in political struggles. President John F. Kennedy, for example, came around to paying more attention to civil rights changes at home, in part because of the glaring contrast between US official support for civil and political rights in international affairs and the continuing violation of the civil and political rights of blacks in the American South.

Human Rights Abroad. However, it cannot be denied that during the Cold War the United States often aligned itself with various repressive governments because of the immediate needs of national security, as perceived by Washington. This was not a new development, as the United States had supported the brutally and sometimes irrationally murderous Stalin in order to maximize the effort against Hitler. The list of major autocrats supported by the United States in the name of freedom, in the face of Soviet-led communism, is a long one: Tito in Yugoslavia, Ceausescu in Romania, Pinochet in Chile, the military junta in Argentina, Mobutu in Zaire, the Somoza dynasty in Nicaragua, and others. The United States came late to the struggle against white minority rule in southern Africa. And from 1971 it aligned with Mao's China in order to complicate the life of the Soviet Union. Mao was one of the major mass murders of the twentieth century—but then, so was Stalin. So while many US foreign policy officials wanted to improve the US domestic record on human rights, at the same time they found it expedient to align with foreign governments engaging in serious violations of human rights.

The pattern continued after the Cold War, and especially after the al Qaeda attacks of 9/11. To offset the actions of militant Islamists, the United States found it expedient to continue to align with repressive governments in places including Egypt, Saudi Arabia, and Uzbekistan. Priority was given to immediate security threats. The George W. Bush

510 HUMAN RIGHTS AND HUMANITARIAN INTERVENTION

administration argued that, through its invasion of Iraq in 2003, it hoped to stimulate democracy via a falling-dominoes effect in the Middle East, which would enhance overall US security. But the reality was that the Bush administration—and the following Barack Obama administration—continued to support pro-American autocrats in countries like Egypt and Jordan, and to court and cooperate with other repressive regimes, like Syria. Because of US security policies, Iraq and Afghanistan were somewhat more democratic than they previously had been (which inherently means they gave more attention to civil and political rights), but this relative advance was purchased at the price of great violence in those two countries, and reinforced repression in neighboring states.

Either because of the economic dimension to national security, or because of the search for advantage by American corporations, a similar logic played out on the economic chessboard of international relations. Countries like Saudi Arabia and China were seen as so important to the American economy, which after all is part of the foundation for US national security, that it was rare for US officials to publicly criticize, much less apply sanctions against, their human rights violations. Moreover, if the United States did impose economic sanctions on countries like Sudan or Burma/Myanmar, other corporations from other states simply moved in and reaped whatever profits were to be made. It was relatively easy for Washington to vote in favor of sanctions on the Mugabe government of Zimbabwe because of human rights violations, that country being of little strategic or economic value to the United States. But the situation was otherwise for major trading partners and especially for those with valuable natural resources, either from a national security or for-profit view.

Trying to protect the human rights of others in a system of international relations that still featured the norms of state sovereignty and national self-determination was not an easy task. US security and economic well-being were not assured in a world of competing states, some of whom aligned with various armed, non-state parties. Important political figures in America did not believe that, in a dangerous world, one should give high priority to internationally recognized human rights. Thus after 9/11, Vice President Dick Cheney openly stated that US security needs would compel Washington to go "to the dark side" in dealing with Islamic Jihadists. As a result, the country had to defend itself against charges of torture and other cruel, inhuman, and degrading treatments, as meted out to security detainees in secret prisons run by the Central Intelligence Agency (CIA) and in military prisons run by the Pentagon. So, exactly how the quest for national security and economic well-being was supposed to be pursued, while maintaining a proper commitment to human rights in peace and war, was a subject of great debate.

The Subject of Humanitarian Intervention. The UN Charter can be read as continuing a long effort to restrict the first use of military force to strictly defensive measures, unless the UN Security Council authorizes other uses of force. Thus states have an inherent right of individual and collective self-defense, but other uses of force constitute illegal aggression or breach of the peace—unless the Security Council decides otherwise. This means that, presumably, state use of force to protect individuals from human rights violations within the jurisdiction of foreign states is illegal, unless approved by the Council.

After the Cold War, with Soviet power no longer an effective check on the United States and its North Atlantic Treaty Organization (NATO) allies, certain developments resurrected a debate about humanitarian intervention. In 1991, Saddam Hussein's persecution of Iraqi Kurds in the north of that country produced a refugee flow that upset both Turkey and Iran. The Security Council labeled the situation a threat to international peace and security, and a group of Western nations, led by the United States, employed military force to restrict Saddam Hussein's control to the south of Iraq. Then in 1999, the Bill Clinton administration led NATO in a bombing campaign against Serbia, ostensibly in response to Serbian ethnic cleansing of Albanian Kosovars (Kosovo was then a part of Serbia), despite the fact that NATO neither claimed self-defense nor secured the prior approval of the Security Council. Much argument in the West contended that whereas the bombing campaign might have been illegal, it was morally justified. In 2003, the George W. Bush administration, having invaded Iraq on charges that it had weapons of mass destruction—weapons that were never found—then claimed that its invasion was justified on grounds of removal of a brutal dictator and the construction of a democratic state.

By 2005 the international community replaced much contentious debate about humanitarian intervention by shifting to the notion of R2P, the responsibility to protect. This formula was endorsed at a UN summit meeting in that year. Thus it was agreed, in the abstract, that the sovereign territorial state had the primary responsibility to implement the international law of human rights and humanitarian affairs. But if the state proved unable or unwilling to do so, outside parties had a responsibility to deal with the situation. To the authors of R2P, the role of the international community was not simply to threaten or use military force at a crisis stage, but rather to help prevent the crisis by timely diplomacy, perhaps to use force as a last resort, and then to engage in postconflict reconstruction in a rights supportive manner. It remained unclear what the role of individual states might be when the Security Council or other international organization did not authorize outside involvement.

As with most general agreements, the key question than became one of whether the political will existed for outside parties to act when a state was unwilling or unable to prevent gross violations of human rights like genocide, crimes against humanity, or major war crimes. In the long-running atrocities in places like Sudan (e.g., Darfur) and Democratic Republic of Congo (e.g., Ituri province) it was clear that the necessary political will to terminate the atrocities was absent. The new norm of R2P worked somewhat better as Kenya slid toward becoming a failed state through emerging ethnic violence.

Various outside parties acted in a timely way to help stabilize that situation. However, it was reasonably clear that taking casualties to protect the rights of others was not popular in democratic states. The United States withdrew from coercive state building in Somalia in 1993 after the deaths there of eighteen US military personnel. It then failed to intervene in Rwanda in 1994 to stop genocide against the Tutsi group. Similar withdrawals after casualties occurred were carried out by the Belgians in Rwanda and the Dutch in the Bosnian massacre at Srebrenica in 1995.

The emergence of the norm of R2P had, in effect, tried to redefine the notion of state sovereignty from a right to reject outside interference in domestic affairs, to a responsibility to protect human rights—with a failure to do so perhaps leading to permissible outside involvement. The continuation of gross violations of human rights in even small and weak states like Burma/Myanmar and Zimbabwe, inter alia, called into question how much practical progress had been made in countering the negative aspects of state sovereignty. If use of force abroad could not be easily linked to national self-interest, it proved difficult to sustain costly ventures on purely human rights and humanitarian grounds. American and congressional opinion was not supportive of US soldiers being killed to advance rights-protective governance in Somalia. President Clinton's avoidance of intervention in Rwanda was met by quiet approval at home, despite ample knowledge of the genocide via the American media. Such was the role of narrow nationalism, leading to weak transnational solidarity. The evenhanded protection of universal human rights proved an admirable but difficult goal in a world fractured by nationalism and narrow views of national interest. Brutal terrorism operating out of failed and weak states only intensified the problems—with the United States, as usual, deeply involved in one way or another in most developments.

BIBLIOGRAPHY
Evans, Gareth. *The Responsibility to Protect: Ending Mass Atrocity Crimes Once and for All.* (Washington, D.C., 2008).

Hunt, Michael H. *Ideology and US Foreign Policy.* (New Haven, Conn., 1987).

Ignatief, Michael, ed. *American Exceptionalism and Human Rights.* (Princeton, N.J., 2005).

Schulz, William F., ed. *The Future of Human Rights: US Policy for a New Era.* (Philadelphia, 2008).

Vogelgesang, Sandy. *American Dream, Global Nightmare: The Dilemma of US Human Rights Policy.* (New York, 1980).

Wood, Gordon S. *The Radicalism of the American Revolution.* (New York, 1992).

David P. Forsythe

I

Immigration, Domestic Consequences of

While many view the question of immigration to the United States as an only recently controversial issue, domestic political conflict regarding immigration has been an enduring reality of US politics since the country's founding. The first immigrants did not settle with the permission of the Native Americans, and the United States is a country that has experienced wave after wave of immigration since its earliest days (forced in the case of Africans, and voluntary in the case of Europeans and Asians). It has long been recognized that immigrants have acted as an engine of economic growth for the country, supplying cheap and willing labor and later setting the foundation for the American middle class. However, immigration has also consistently generated economic, social, and cultural tensions. These tensions have transformed immigration into a contentious political issue under three principal conditions: (1) when immigration has been limited or heavily regulated (making illegal the natural immigration flows that stem from larger world economic forces); (2) in times of economic privation, when new immigrants increase competition for jobs, housing, and social services (when historically such social services have existed); and (3) where massive immigration has originated in one or a few countries and is interpreted as a threat to the dominant culture and national identity.

The current wave of Latino (and mostly Mexican) immigration to the United States has recently met all three of these criteria. Opponents of immigration contend that immigrants take jobs away from native citizens, force downward pressure on wages, increase crime rates, burden the country's social services, and threaten the basic tenets of American culture, including the country's much-vaunted entrepreneurial spirit.

How valid are these points? What do hard facts and data say about the domestic impact of Latino immigration to the United States? Do Latino immigrants provide a net gain or a net loss for the US economy? How do they affect wages and working conditions in the United States? What impact do immigrants have on US culture? The answers to these questions are complex and controversial. Statistics are often carelessly wielded by one side of the immigration debate or the other in order to make a political point. Fundamentally, the answers depend on how costs and benefits are calculated. Those who contend that undocumented workers exact a cost on the US economy and labor market tend to only consider the potential for downward pressure on wages, and the costs associated with providing schooling and health and social welfare benefits for the undocumented. They often fail to take into account the overall contribution of immigrants to the broader economy with respect to cheap food, housing, and services. Nor do they take into account the multiplier effect of immigrants putting more money into the economy which, in turn, potentially supports further economic growth and employment. On the other side of the equation, proponents of more liberalized immigration reform often overlook how immigrants' reliance on public services and education, concentrated in particular areas of the United States, can exact an unfair burden on certain populations, given the maldistribution of the costs and benefits of illegal immigration.

In order to understand the impact of illegal immigration on the jobs picture in the United States, it is important to understand the demographics of new and illegal immigrants to the United States. Most who arrive are more educated than the Mexican population in general, though less educated than native-born US workers. In terms of socioeconomic status, while most depictions of illegal immigrants paint them as the poorest of the poor, immigrants tend to be slightly better off than the lowest economic quintile in Mexico. It takes some resources and a certain level of education and cultural adeptness to successfully make the journey north. Nonetheless, illegal immigrants do tend to be less educated than their documented compatriots in the United States. Also significant with respect to competition over jobs, the smallest educational gap between major racial groups within the United States is between new Latino immigrants and African Americans.

This educational and, in turn, skills gap has a substantial impact on how Mexicans fit into the US labor force, and the nature of competition over jobs. Overwhelmingly, undocumented workers are concentrated in a few key areas of the US economy. These workers make up large percentages of the labor force in the farming, construction, cleaning, food preparation, and landscaping industries. In terms of competition for employment, many studies find an overwhelming skills gap developing in the US employment market. That is to say, at the bottom of the jobs ladder there are fewer native-born US citizens willing to do the jobs that undocumented workers are doing. At the same time, the supply of low-skill jobs is growing faster than high-skill jobs,

meaning that immigrant labor may actually be instrumental in propping up the US economy. Immigrant employment in the United States has historically followed a pattern in which the most recent arrivals perform the lowest-status and lowest-paying jobs until they are able to move up the employment ladder. In this sense, anecdotal evidence which shows that the native-born population is unwilling to perform certain jobs at the same pay level as immigrants fits into the United States's historic employment patterns for immigrants.

In terms of wages, the claim that illegal immigration depresses wages generally is not supported by most studies. This is a counterintuitive finding. The simple law of supply and demand would suggest that when immigrants are willing to do work for a lower price than the native-born population, there should be a downward pressure on wages. The wage story is much more complex. In effect, one can speak of two different labor markets with two different skill sets. It is clear that among the highly skilled (which new immigrants tend not to be), the influx of labor at the higher end of the wage scale has little effect. Immigrants are simply unable to compete at this level. As one moves down the wage scale, however, this dynamic changes, and it is well documented that wages are depressed for workers with very few skills. Wage losses and downward pressure on wages is likely to be felt by the least advantaged in the labor force and, in particular, other recent immigrants and unskilled African American males.

The impact of immigrants on the education, health, and social welfare systems of the United States is perhaps the most visible and controversial aspect of the country's current immigration debate. It is also easy to exaggerate the impact. Claims are often made that illegal immigrants exact a disproportionate cost on the penal and judicial systems, ignoring the fact that the rate of incarceration is lower for illegal immigrants than the general population. Proponents of harsher immigration policy argue that immigrants rely excessively on "welfare" without specifying particular costs or to which programs they are referring. In addition, it is important to differentiate between legal and illegal immigrants.

Undocumented immigrants are legally banned from taking advantage of most social welfare programs related to food aid and income assistance. Legal immigrants, on the other hand, do disproportionally take advantage of these programs. However, even legal immigrants face a five-year waiting period before they are allowed to take advantage of food stamps and Social Security insurance. Further, as recent arrivals, these legal immigrants also simply happen to have lower incomes, making them just as likely as the native-born population with similar incomes to qualify and take advantage of these programs. This new-immigrant poverty usually fades with the passage of the generations, and the entrance of new immigrants' children and grandchildren into higher status and higher-paying jobs. In addition, it is important to note that Social Security, Medicare, and other social programs are facing shortfalls fundamentally because of demographics. A large influx of young and healthy workers provides a potential solution to the impending demographic imbalance that threatens these programs.

One area where undocumented residents do exact an undeniable cost is public education. Immigrants are more likely to be younger and to have young families. Almost one-fifth of school-age children in the United States in 2005 were Latino, though the percentage of these that is undocumented is uncertain. These students put a particularly heavy burden on states where most illegal immigration is concentrated, including New York, California, and Florida. In these states, and many others, public education systems are overburdened at a time when education budgets are also drying up. As class sizes swell and budgets are cut, more and more school systems—and in turn, politicians—point to the children of undocumented workers as one of the principal problems in meeting strained educational budgets.

Nonetheless, when weighing costs and benefits of immigration, an important and overlooked reality is that, contrary to common assertions, immigrants do pay taxes. Undocumented workers pay sales tax, and indirectly pay property tax through their rents. About one-half of undocumented workers have false papers, and so they often also pay Medicare taxes, income taxes, and Social Security. The use of false (or other peoples') Social Security numbers means that undocumented workers are paying into accounts on which they will never be able to draw. The tax money paid into the system by illegal immigrants is often not included in the calculations of the net costs of illegal immigration.

The controversy surrounding immigration is not just economic. The effect of such large-scale immigration from a single region on US culture and national identity is another area of intense debate. Fear and mistrust have always greeted immigrants, given the tensions that often arise when cultures collide. Many object to such large-scale immigration, claiming that a large influx of Spanish-speaking and Catholic people with "Hispanic values" threatens the Anglo-Saxon, Protestant values of the United States, and potentially the entrepreneurial spirit that has underwritten the country's economic success. Leaving aside the issue of whether this depiction of the United States as an "Anglo-Saxon culture" is accurate, does the sheer size and homogenous origins of this newest wave of immigrants undermine American culture and national identity? With respect to assimilation, decades of research has shown that the children of immigrants quickly acquire the language and culture markers of social assimilation characteristic of the dominant culture. What is more, it is questionable whether the sociocultural characteristics of Latinos are all that different from those of dominant US culture. In essence, study after study has shown that Latinos tend to be highly religious, individualistic, family-oriented, risk-takers who value hard work and the virtues of laboring to move ahead and raise children that are more successful than they are. These are values that are often held up as quintessentially American.

Any effort to determine the overall impact of immigration, both legal and illegal, must take into account the overall growth in US gross domestic product (GDP), increases in competiveness and productivity, and the positive impact on prices that unskilled immigrant labor provides. Fundamentally, the jury is still out on whether immigrant labor provides a net gain or a net loss for the US economy, though most mainstream economists do note that illegal immigration likely provides a modest net positive gain. What is certain, however, is that the costs and benefits of immigration are unevenly distributed, and this has deeply affected the debate on immigration within the United States. While it is difficult to clearly tie an increase of a few percentages in the total GDP to immigrant labor, it is easy to see the costs associated with immigration with respect to social services, when the costs for providing them are concentrated in particular communities. One key to successful immigration reform is a better balance of the distribution of these costs and benefits, to ease the burden on communities that foot the bill for immigration, in order to finance the likely net gain it provides the United States as a whole. More equitable distribution of costs and benefits will likely also lead to fewer tensions related to culture and national identity.

[*See also* Hispanic Americans; Immigration, Legal and Illegal; *and* Immigration to the United States.]

BIBLIOGRAPHY

Coates, David. "The Economic Impact of Immigration." In *Getting Immigration Right: What Every American Needs to Know*, edited by David Coates and Peter Siavelis, pp. 83–96. (Washington, D.C., 2009).

Fraga, Luis, and Gary Segura (2009). "The Immigration Aftermath: Latinos, Latino Immigrants, and American National Identity." In *Getting Immigration Right: What Every American Needs to Know*, edited by David Coates and Peter Siavelis, pp. 63–79. (Washington, D.C., 2009).

Huntington, Samuel. *Who Are We? The Challenges to America's National Identity.* (New York, 2005).

Massey, Douglas, Jorge Durand, and Nolan J. Malone. (2002). *Beyond Smoke and Mirrors: Mexican Immigration in an Era of Economic Integration.* (New York, 2002).

Ottaviano, Gianmarco, and Giovanni Peri. *Rethinking the Effects of Immigration on Wages.* (Cambridge, Mass., 2006).

Passel, Jeffrey. "Background Briefing Paper Prepared for Task Force on Immigration and America's Future." Pew Hispanic Center. (2005), http://pewhispanic.org/files/reports/46.pdf.

Passel, Jeffrey. "The Size and Characteristics of the Unauthorized Migrant Population in the US." Pew Hispanic Center. (2006), http://pewhispanic.org/files/reports/61.pdf.

Rumbaut, Rubén, and Walter Ewing. *The Myth of Immigrant Criminality and the Paradox of Assimilation: Incarceration Rates among Native and Foreign-Born Men.* (Washington, D.C., 2007).

Peter M. Siavelis

IMMIGRATION, LEGAL AND ILLEGAL

There are few issues as complex as that of transnational migrants and their families who lack the legal status to reside or be employed in the United States. These immigrants, also referred to as "undocumented workers" or, more pejoratively, as "illegal aliens," are a critical component of the labor force in a number of employment sectors, and yet at the same time are the recipients of some of the most vitriolic and hostile rhetoric, action, and legislation at present in the United States. It is also the case that they drive much of the current debate regarding comprehensive immigration reform.

The Pew Hispanic Center estimates that as of March 2010, there were an estimated 11.2 million unauthorized immigrants in the United States, representing 3.7 percent of the nation's population and 28 percent of the foreign-born population. In 2000 it was estimated that there were 8.4 million residents and workers of unauthorized status, and this number steadily increased to a high of 12.0 million in 2007, declined to 11.6 million in 2008, and further declined to 11.1 million in 2009. The stability in the estimates of the illegal population in 2009 and 2010 suggests that the influx of new unauthorized immigrants to the United States has declined substantially. The country from which the largest group of these immigrants originate is Mexico, which accounts for 58 percent of all illegal immigrants. Other countries in Latin America account for 23 percent of the unauthorized; 11 percent are from Asia; 4 percent are from Europe and Canada; and 3 percent are from Africa.

It is also estimated that in 2010, the overwhelming majority of these immigrants—8 million or 71.4

percent—were workers active in the labor force. These workers represented approximately 5.2 percent of all workers in the United States. Moreover, adult unauthorized immigrants were parents to 8 percent of all children born in the United States from March 2009 to March 2010. Of these children, approximately 70 percent have at least one parent from Mexico; 17 percent from other countries in Latin America; 7 percent from countries in Asia; 2 percent from Europe; and Canada; and 3 percent from Asia.

The primary reasons for the influx of these immigrants are often organized into two clusters: push factors and pull factors. Among the primary push factors are limited opportunities for long-term employment that pays sustainable wages in home countries; the modernization and international integration of home-country economies driven by the globalization of capital; and political unrest. The reason so many unauthorized immigrants come to the United States to work is that they cannot find sufficient employment in their home countries. One major segment of these migrants has limited job skills and generally takes low-wage jobs in the United States. What is less well understood, however, is that this is often driven by shifts in sectors of national economies that are the result of the increased integration of the United States and other national economies within international markets, which then results in international competition. For example, corn farmers in Mexico have been devastated by competition with US farmers made possible by the North American Free Trade Agreement (NAFTA). Farmers who previously could survive on subsistence farming can no longer do so. Immigration to the United States becomes a reasonable alternative for many such individuals. One can think of these individuals as economic refugees who see themselves as forced to leave their home countries in search of employment to feed their families and relatives both in the United States or back in the home country. Other illegal immigrants come to the United States because of political unrest, and at times persecution, in their countries of origin.

Immigrants came from a number of places in Central America during the 1970s and 1980s, when civil wars ravaged those nations. Immigrants from some countries in Africa have come due to unrest in their home states.

Equally and perhaps even more important, are pull factors that provide incentives for individuals to come to the United States to work. Although finding work has become more difficult for everyone since the downturn of the US economy in 2008, employment is still likely in the United States for those who are unauthorized. Components of the agricultural sector in the United States have come to rely heavily on workers who are undocumented—"out of status"—to labor in their fields, and especially to pick grapes, strawberries, apples, peaches, and many other crops during harvest time. Farmers have been known to complain that they cannot find enough American-born individuals to do this work at the wages they generally pay. Until 2008, it was also common for undocumented immigrants to come to the United States to work in construction, child care, senior care, and low-skill service jobs such as in restaurants and hotels. Oftentimes this work is hard and the pay is not lucrative. However, compared to the opportunities in sending countries, the employment opportunities are still very desirable.

The politics related to undocumented immigrants includes some of the most heated and divisive rhetoric and argument present in US politics today. Public opinion polls reveal that a majority of Americans—depending on the poll, from 51 to 72 percent—support a path to citizenship for those who currently live in the United States out of status, as long as they pass a criminal background check, pay a fine, pay back taxes, and learn English. However, a majority of Americans—between 65 and 78 percent—*also* favors increased border security to reduce the number of undocumented immigrants. Support for increased border enforcement increased immediately after the 9/11 terrorist attack in the United States.

In general, only the latter call, for border security, has been answered by elected officials in Washington.

For example, in 2006, the Secure Fence Act allotted at least $1.2 billion to the construction of seven hundred miles of reinforced fence and a comprehensive surveillance system. Proposals have been made for comprehensive immigration reform that included a path to legalization for undocumented individuals, the cleaning up of immigration application backlogs, a revised and regularized system of visa allocation for different types of workers, and increased border enforcement. Such legislation was considered in 2006, the Comprehensive Immigration Reform Act, but it did not receive majority support in either chamber of Congress. In 2011, Senator Charles Schumer (Dem.–N.Y.) and Senator Lindsey Graham (Rep.–S.C.) were reportedly eager to initiate yet another effort to establish a set of principles that could guide discussion of comprehensive immigration reform. As of early 2012, this discussion had not led to any formal proposal.

A relatively small (estimated at about 20 to 25 percent) but extremely well-organized group of advocates consistently call for a border-security-only immigration policy, to stop any and all illegal immigrants from entering the United States; some of these border-security advocates also call for the immediate deportation of all those who are not authorized to be in the United States. They consistently flood the phone lines of senators, members of the House, and the White House when immigration-related legislation is being considered. An increasing number of candidates and other leaders, particularly in the Republican Party, have openly supported this position. Advocates on behalf of immigrants have been less successful in their efforts to influence political leaders to enact comprehensive immigration reform, despite public support from the Barack Obama administration. Interestingly, the Obama administration has been responsible for the deportation of undocumented immigrants in numbers greater than any previous administration. It has justified this as a consequence of new efforts to focus on those who have committed serious crimes. In 2011 the Obama administration issued what it hoped were clarifying regulations to limit the number of those deported to only those who committed serious crimes. It is estimated that two-thirds of those deported during each year of the Obama administration did *not* commit serious felonies. It is apparent that the disjunction between a desire for legalization of illegal immigrants and increased border enforcement has yet to be reconciled in the nation's legislative politics.

The problem of illegal immigration to the United States has only existed since 1929. Previously, when the United States experienced massive immigration from the mid-nineteenth to the early twentieth century, there was no legal category of "illegal alien" that would allow for deportation. It was during a period of severe economic downturn that would ultimately result in the stock market crash of 1929 and the Great Depression of the 1930s that legislation was enacted to create this new legal category. Nonetheless, the United States effectively addressed the issue of undocumented immigrants most recently in 1986 through the Immigration Reform and Control Act, which was signed by President Ronald Reagan and supported by a bipartisan coalition. Integrating those out of status into American society is possible. Such legislation today could be based on six principles:

- Provide a clear and earned path to citizenship for immigrants who are undocumented;
- Clear immigration backlogs, so that millions who have filed legal applications can be considered;
- Ensure appropriate ways for workers to come with proper status, full worker rights, and labor protections;
- Ensure due process and fundamental rights for all;
- Promote immigrant integration into US civil society though language classes and civics training; and
- Enhance the country's continuing needs for security and safety through a fair and responsible enforcement policy.

Comprehensive immigration reform in the United States has only occurred through bipartisan coalition-building based on compromise and effective leadership from the White House. Despite its pronouncements, the Obama administration has not been able to overcome the partisan divisiveness, and the disagreements within its own party, on how the issue of undocumented immigrants should be addressed. This seemed even more unlikely during the 2012 presidential campaign. The result of this lack of action will be a country that will continue to have strong and differing opinions as to what to do, and workers whose status will make them permanently vulnerable to being fired, underpaid, or deported, depending on changes in enforcement efforts.

[*See also* Border Security; Immigration to the United States; *and* Mexico.]

BIBLIOGRAPHY

Passel, Jeffrey S., and D'Vera Cohn. "Unauthorized Immigrant Population: National and State Trends, 2010." Pew Hispanic Center. (2011), http://pewhispanic.org/reports/report.php?ReportID=133.

Luis Ricardo Fraga

IMMIGRATION TO THE UNITED STATES

Americans have been ambivalent about the effects of international migration since the inception of the American republic. The impasse over the need for, and content of, comprehensive immigration reform that began during the Nixon administration endured to the Obama administration with no end in sight despite the widespread view that US immigration policy was "broken." Yet, the United States scarcely stood alone as a state mired in controversies and rancor over international migration. Nor was it the only state in which immigration policies produced a pattern of untoward or unanticipated outcomes. Since roughly 1970, the growing saliency of international migration-related concerns in domestic politics, bilateral and regional relationships, and at the global level, as witnessed by the convocation of high-level meetings about migration and development at the United Nations in 2007, became a defining feature of the "age of migration."

Virtually all states around the world confront important issues pertaining to international migration. The specificity of the United States in this respect is best grasped through cross-national and chronological (diachronic) comparisons.

The Legacy of the Colonial Era. The founding of the American republic came nearly three centuries after the European discovery of the New World. The areas that would become the thirteen British colonies in North America were settled in diverse ways and at different times. The New England colonies varied sharply from Pennsylvania and New York, for instance, in that the European-background population of the latter was much more diverse, due in part to the fact that Pennsylvania and New York encompassed parts of the former New Netherland that England conquered in 1664. It is further important to recall that, of the European powers competing for domination of the New World, only Great Britain welcomed large-scale settlement of foreigners, like Germans, in its colonies. The aforementioned colonies in turn differed sharply from the Virginia and Carolina colonies in that African slave labor was more extensive in colonies with large-scale plantation agriculture. Transatlantic arrivals of African slaves far exceeded arrivals of Europeans until the 1830s.

What transpired in the colonial era still resonates in differing views Americans hold about their identity. One tradition anchors American identity in English and Protestant forbearers. Alexis de Tocqueville's highly influential *Democracy in America* reflected this understanding. Later, such views would be propagated by influential professors such as Louis Hartz and Samuel Huntington. However, the historical accuracy of the viewpoint is contested. The non-English population may have constituted up to half of the population of the early American republic. To some Americans, immigration has long threatened their core culture and identity. To others, the diversity of American society has constituted a great strength, especially in that it beckons newcomers and facilitates their integration. Fault lines of this nature have stoked American debates over immigration.

Another durable legacy of the colonial era dates from the English conquest of New Netherland in 1664 and its conquest of New France in 1763. In the first instance, a number of conciliatory concessions were granted the mainly Dutch-speaking inhabitants of New Netherland; but no commitment was made to maintain the Dutch language and culture, although Dutch cultural specificity would endure, especially in New York City. This established a colonial-era precedent for a later monocultural American republic.

In contrast, the treaty ending what in America is called the French and Indian War in 1763 established bicultural governance in the newly acquired British dominions that formerly constituted New France. Eventually, Canada would embrace multiculturalism and Canadian governments would perceive an obligation to maintain cultural diversity in sharp contrast to the evolution of its neighbor to the south, where English has always been the unquestioned language of government and where the federal government has never endeavored to maintain cultural diversity except where obligated by treaties. Nevertheless, this state of affairs frequently is misunderstood as witnessed by widespread public support for the English-only movement that took shape in the 1980s and pressed many of the fifty constituent states to adopt legislation barring use of languages other than English in governmental endeavors.

Another legacy of the colonial era involved the centrality of race. Even though Europeans had long viewed themselves as backward and inferior to empires and civilizations to the east, European settlers of the New World of whatever provenance tended to view themselves as superior to the indigenous populations they encountered and to the African slaves, who for centuries outnumbered Europeans in the Americas. The Christianity embraced by most European settlers strongly influenced their views.

European- and African-borne diseases decimated Native American populations. And while the various European powers competing to dominate the New World frequently sought out allies among indigenous peoples, a strategy paramount to the Spanish conquistadores' ability to defeat the Incas and the Aztecs, the British colonists of the Atlantic seaboard proved particularly aggressive. Indeed, a perception of inherent superiority held by British colonists facilitated a pattern of encroachment upon Indian lands that lay in the background to the French and Indian War and became a central concern in the North American British colonies' relations with the British Crown in the years between 1763 and 1776.

The grievances held by many, but by no means all, British subjects in the area soon to become the thirteen colonies, after Delaware separated from Pennsylvania, were numerous. The French and Indian War brought a major British expeditionary force to North America for the first time, and the British government expected the colonies to foot the bill. Moreover, the British sought to dissuade the colonists from pushing westward into Indian lands, but the colonists continued to do so. Many of the colonists also opposed British governmental efforts to prevent emigration of British subjects to the Atlantic seaboard colonies. Such grievances precipitated the American Revolution.

From the Early Republic to the First World War. The first decades of the new and quite precarious American Republic witnessed relatively little international migration. Nevertheless, the population of the United States grew rapidly due to a high birth rate. The paucity of immigration facilitated a palpable homogenization of the quite heterogeneous areas that comprised the newfound republic between 1790 and 1830. Speaking of non-English languages declined in many areas, and many churches with non-English language services Americanized. Several broke affiliations with kindred faithful in Europe, most American Anglicans became Episcopalians, as did Swedish Lutherans in New Jersey.

An early immigration-related disagreement arose between the supporters of Thomas Jefferson and Alexander Hamilton, the latter of whom favored enactment of a law that would empower the government to expel radical immigrants. The pro-Hamiltonians also sought to increase dramatically the number of years of residency required for aliens to become eligible for naturalization. They feared that newly arriving immigrants, especially from Ireland and France, might bring with them radical political ideas and, worse yet, vote for Jefferson and his allies. Hence, the Alien and Sedition Acts were promulgated and the years required to become eligible for naturalization were briefly extended. But these measures came too late to forestall new immigrants from contributing to electoral victories by Jefferson and his allies.

This marked an early episode of the "feedback loop," a reference to the propensity of recent immigrants to vote in favor of political parties, especially for what became the Democratic Party, which pursue policies favorable to newcomers. Relatively easy access for immigrants to political enfranchisement, a matter controlled by the constituent federal states, and to acquisition of citizenship became hallmarks that long helped ensure that the American Republic would remain open to European immigrants.

By the 1820s, many of the federal states had granted additional rights, which were coupled with obligations like military service in time of war, that enabled male European immigrants to become electors in state and federal elections, among other rights. After two years of residency, a male immigrant could declare his intent to become a US citizen and thereby acquire such additional rights and obligations as determined by the federal states. Many of the states competed to attract immigrants.

The first major wave of immigrants arrived in the 1830s and 1840s from Ireland, which in 1801 had become part of the United Kingdom but had experienced an enormous population explosion that led large numbers of mainly Roman Catholic, and often poor, people to emigrate to England and other areas of the United Kingdom. What was generally viewed as an untoward development began to erode the British government's adherence to the long prevailing antiemigration norm embedded in mercantilism. British authorities soon began to pay for the voyage across the Atlantic as this was less expensive than providing for the indigents in the United Kingdom. Declines in the cost of transatlantic passage eventually made the New World accessible to the European masses. Between 1820 and 1920, nearly 60 million Europeans would emigrate, mainly to the United States.

The waves of Irish immigrants precipitated an anti-immigrant reaction. Many Atlantic seaboard states witnessed anti-Irish violence and the adoption of state- and local-level measures to restrict further arrivals of Irish. These measures were struck down in the landmark Supreme Court ruling on the Passenger Cases in 1849, which held that the federal government possessed plenary power over immigration law and policy.

The nativist or anti-immigrant political reaction crested in the 1850s with substantial support for the Know-Nothing movement. But the issue of slavery eclipsed all other concerns as civil war loomed and the Know-Nothings merged into the new Republican Party.

Before and after the Civil War, the feedback loop would help to ensure that the United States remained open to massive emigration from Europe. For instance, in the new state of Wisconsin, which achieved statehood in 1848, enfranchisement of noncitizens greatly enlarged the electorate and favored the electoral prospects for the Democratic Party, which received overwhelming support from German immigrants in elections of the 1850s. Later, however, the German vote would bifurcate as German Protestants came to support the new Republican Party, whereas most voters of German Roman Catholic background stuck with the Democratic Party. German Protestants had begun to perceive the Democratic Party as a Catholic party. Noncitizen and immigrant-background ethnic voters did not vote monolithically but often gave substantial majorities to one of the two major parties. This pattern has endured into the twenty-first century, as witnessed, for instance, by Hispanic voting trends in favor of the Democratic Party.

The sheer magnitude of the European arrivals differentiated the United States from other areas of the New World, such as Australia, New Zealand, and Canada, but also areas of South America, especially the Southern Cone. The influx of immigrant labor enabled the expansion of the American economy and society such that, by the turn of the century, the United States had been transformed into a world power.

This transformation did not proceed without resistance. Opposition to an influx of Chinese immigrants led to the Chinese Exclusion Act of 1882, which proved a harbinger of more extensive restrictions to come. The changing composition of European immigration, as more and more immigrants from southern and eastern Europe arrived, also caused alarm. As in Germany, France, and the United Kingdom, the influx of east European Jews to the United States played an important role in growing opposition to immigration.

Such concerns led to the creation of the first federal commission to study the effects of immigration upon the United States. What became known as the Dillingham Commission engaged in the first significant social science inquiry into immigration. This reflected the influence of the Progressive movement, which had emerged as a political force in the upper Midwest and which held that public policies should be informed by the best possible social science understanding. The gist of the commission's recommendations favored curtailment of immigration.

Subsequent congressional efforts to restrict immigration were blocked by repeated presidential vetoes, testifying to the significance of the United States' unusual institutional arrangements for understanding the evolution of US immigration policies. The division of power between the three branches of the federal government makes it difficult to change an immigration status quo once it is in place.

By the turn of the century, many of the distinctive effects of mass immigration upon American society and politics had become discernible. One of the most important of these concerned political parties. Unlike what transpired in most European societies, the American socialist movement did not become a major force, except in certain areas. Many factors contributed to this outcome, including electoral laws favoring two-party competition; early enfranchisement of males, including many immigrants; and specific features of the trade union movement. Due to the absence of a feudal heritage, class consciousness did not develop. Instead, ethnic, racial, religious, and regional allegiances prevailed.

The Democratic Party, in particular, long cultivated electoral support from immigrants by favoring proimmigration and proimmigrant policies. The feedback loop enabled by easy enfranchisement and naturalization empowered immigrants. This figured importantly in the series of presidential vetoes of restrictive immigration legislation prior to 1914.

From World War I to the 1965 Amendments. American entry into World War I profoundly affected immigration and immigration policy. Immigration from Europe declined precipitously, never to recover to pre-1914 levels, although as late as 1965 major changes to immigration law would be effected to increase immigration from Europe. The declaration of war precipitated a patriotic (which is to say nationalistic) outburst similar to the one experienced after the 9/11 terrorist attacks. Nationalism often entails xenophobia, which was much in evidence in the United States during and after World War I. The altered political landscape enabled adoption of restrictive immigration legislation in 1917, which would be supplemented by even more restrictive legislation in 1921 and 1924 that would greatly curtail immigration from Europe and enshrine a discriminatory national origins visa distribution system that endured until 1965. Immigration statistics testify to the magnitude of the change wrought. In 1921, after transatlantic civilian shipping had been restored, 652,364 Europeans were admitted. This amounted to more than half of the record number of arrivals recorded in 1907. But by 1929 only 158,598 European immigrants were recorded.

Significantly, the military mobilization in 1917 led to the perception of labor shortages, especially in the Southwest where labor migration from Mexico had grown after 1900. The secretary of labor granted a waiver to the 1885 law barring contract labor, thereby enabling American employers to hire Mexican temporary workers legally. Of the estimated five hundred thousand Mexican workers who came to the United States over the duration of the first *bracero* program, which ended in 1921, roughly half took up employment legally.

It is important to note that US immigration history entails repeated recourse to temporary foreign worker admissions in addition to the prevalent pattern of immigrants arriving and naturalizing. Of course, an important fraction of European-origin migrants elected to return home. Thus, one should not overdraw differences among states in the transatlantic area. American *bracero* policies can be usefully compared to guest worker and seasonal foreign worker policies implemented on the other side of the Atlantic.

The restrictive pattern led to the discontinuation of noncitizen voting in local and federal elections in the 1920s, thereby decreasing the significance of recent immigrants to electoral outcomes. In many states, Americanization efforts began to ensure that recent immigrants became loyal US citizens.

The onset of the Depression led to state and local efforts to repatriate Mexicans, somewhat similar to French measures to repatriate Polish workers at roughly the same juncture. President Franklin D. Roosevelt would convene the Evian Conference in 1938 to respond to the Jewish refugee crisis in Europe, but there was no chance that many Jewish refugees would find a haven in the United States. The United States did not have a refugee policy, and the employment situation precluded other than minor US measures to alleviate the plight of European Jewry.

American entry into World War II prompted a second *bracero* program with Mexico. Reflecting the evolution of international norms during the interwar period, the recruitment was authorized by a bilateral treaty intended to protect the interests of all parties. Between 1942 and 1964, 5 million Mexican workers were admitted.

The history of the second *bracero* period figured importantly in the political stalemate over comprehensive immigration reform that began circa 1970. Opponents of wider recourse to temporary foreign worker admissions often cite a path dependency of temporary foreign worker policies not working as planned and resulting in exploitation of migrant workers as good reason to oppose such policies. Their opponents often view the same history in a different light. Disagreements of this nature are not unique to the United States as decisions to admit

foreign workers are never based on incontrovertible evidence of labor shortages and always reflect political outcomes. After World War II, the United States did admit large numbers of displaced persons from Europe, most of whom were not Jewish.

In 1952, a new immigration law was promulgated over a presidential veto, reflecting growing opposition to the national origins system for visa distribution. Significantly, the legislation did not impose legal sanctions against employers who hired aliens ineligible to work. Such measures had been included in the bills adopted by both houses of Congress but were altered during the conference committee to produce instead the Texas Proviso, which exempted employers of unauthorized aliens from punishment. Into the first decade of the twenty-first century, thus, the United States would not have a credible employer-sanctions regime, although a 1986 law would enact legal sanctions that were weakly enforced. Nor did the 1952 law scrap the national origins system for visa distribution, which had prompted President Harry Truman's veto.

By 1965, political support for reform of immigration policy had grown. The ethos of the civil rights era diminished support for retention of the national origins system. And growing concern over the plight of migrant workers and displacement of Mexican American farm workers enabled unilateral discontinuation of *bracero* recruitment by the US government in 1963. The Mexican government pointedly expressed its disagreement with the change in policy.

The 1965 amendments to the 1952 law finally ended the national origins system and replaced it with a nondiscriminatory system of visa distribution on a first come, first served basis within quantitative and qualitative limitations. Somewhat surprisingly, the new visa system was intended to reinvigorate immigration from Europe. No one of significance to the debates appears to have noticed that most west European countries had since become immigration lands in their own right. This historic transformation of first western and later eastern Europe would significantly narrow transatlantic differences in the realm of immigration law and policy. But, in 1965, the eventuality of a European analogue to the "feedback loop" remained beyond comprehension, for both Americans and Europeans.

The Transatlantic Immigration Policy Stalemate. By the 1970s, a new legal immigration system had taken shape. A much larger number of visas, almost three hundred thousand, became available for distribution on an annual basis to applicants from around the world, not only from Europe. Immediate family members of US citizens were not subject to quantitative restrictions. The quantitative and qualitative delimitations also applied to those from the Western Hemisphere, and legal immigration from any given country was capped at twenty thousand per year. Imposition of the cap reflected fears of the implications of the population explosion in Latin America. The 1965 amendments, like most past and future reforms of US immigration law and policy, combined liberalizing and restrictive measures. The single most important outcome of the amendments was entirely unforeseen, namely, the changed composition of post-1965 immigrants. Instead of Europeans, the vast majority of immigrants since the late 1960s have been non-European in origin, thereby creating even greater diversity in American society.

The unilateral termination of *bracero* admissions did not result in an end to Mexican labor migration. By the early 1970s, alarm grew over mounting illegal Mexican migration to the United States even though there were only 750,000 legally resident Mexican citizens in the United States. President Richard Nixon ordered federal agencies to prepare a federal response to mounting illegal migration. This would eventually lead to the creation of a second federal commission to study the effects of legal and illegal immigration, during the Carter administration of the late 1970s. The Select Commission on Immigration and Refugee Policy would recommend to Congress and a new president, Ronald Reagan, that illegally resident aliens be enabled to legalize, that employers of unauthorized foreign workers be punished, that a counterfeit resistant employment eligibility document be implemented, and that there be no return to large-scale temporary foreign worker recruitment.

The commission's recommendations were supposed to reflect a bipartisan consensus but encountered intense opposition by various politically powerful interest groups. The result was legislative stalemate until late 1986 when a compromise enabled passage of new legislation during a lame-duck session of Congress. Significantly, the compromise gutted the counterfeit resistant employment eligibility document and added a legalization opportunity for farm workers with different rules from the principal legalization program.

Nearly 3 million, mainly Mexican, migrants would gain legal status as a result. For the first time, it became illegal for employers to hire unauthorized aliens; but it quickly became apparent that the lack of a counterfeit resistant employment eligibility document would foster massive circumvention of the new law. Moreover, very few resources were allocated to enforcement of the employer-sanctions provision.

Meanwhile, yet another federal commission was authorized to study alternative approaches to prevention of illegal migration. This would eventually lead to the creation of the North American Free Trade Agreement (NAFTA) between the United States, Canada, and Mexico, which entered into effect on 1 January 1994. NAFTA was supposed to decrease illegal migration by liberalizing trade, which would create a better environment for job-producing investment in Mexico. Instead, NAFTA ravaged the *ejido* sector of the Mexican economy, thereby uprooting millions of Mexican workers and their families, many of whom joined the northward exodus. Unlike regional integration in Europe, NAFTA included only minor measures involving immigration admission between the partner states.

Nevertheless, with the election of Mexican president Vicente Fox in 2000 and of US president George W. Bush the following year, it seemed that the decades-long stalemate over immigration reform would be resolved. But this did not happen in part because of miscalculations but also changed circumstances. The terrorist attacks of September 2001 unleashed forces that mitigated against comprehensive immigration reform.

The impasse over US immigration policy is part of a global pattern. Uneven socioeconomic development as in the past continues to spur international migration, generally from lesser developed, manpower-surplus areas to more developed, relative manpower-scarce zones. One result has been a kind of convergence between the member states of the Organization for Economic Cooperation and Development on migration-related policy concerns. Features once distinctive to traditional immigration lands like the United States have become features of politics and society in new environments. Now the vote of naturalized Turks in Germany increasingly matters. Immigration is reforging states and societies but not only in an American mold.

The United States in the Age of Migration. Very slowly, and still incompletely, the American populace and its political leadership have begun to understand that international migration has long constituted a global phenomenon that centrally shapes states and societies. Recent inquiry into the history of Europe in the first millennium CE points to the centrality of migration processes in key transformations such as the collapse of the western Roman Empire and the emergence of a new political order in which Mediterranean-based politics no longer dominated Europe as had Greece and Rome prior to roughly the fifth century CE.

Not unsurprisingly, the central processes driving mass and elite migration into the late western Roman Empire involved dynamics similar to those affecting global migration in the twenty-first century. Human mobility across interstate boundaries fundamentally reflects dynamics of socioeconomic development, especially movement from less developed to more developed areas, and the role of state policies. International migration, hence, is inherently political in nature; and in the long run, political outcomes shaped by international migration often outweigh the significance of the socioeconomic effects of international migration.

By the 1970s, the growing pace of globalization began to foster understanding that states and societies formerly viewed as highly disparate in fact shared commonalities that rendered them less distinctive. For instance, Western Europe and the United States differed enormously in how the significance of their respective immigration histories was viewed. Nevertheless, both Western Europe and the United States increasingly encountered similar problems and issues in their attempts to prevent illegal migration.

By the twenty-first century, the relationship between the European Union and its southern periphery, most notably North Africa, had come to closely resemble the impasse witnessed in North America, although there remain important dissimilarities between the two contexts. This was emblematic of the age of migration.

More broadly, the transatlantic migratory flows so central to the shaping of Western history since roughly 1500 have found an echo in all other regions of the world. W. R. Boehning, the long-serving head of the Migrants Branch at the International Labor Organization, was not far off the mark when he famously wrote "that the history of mankind is the history of migration" (Heather, 2009, p. 2). To the extent this is true, the United States is less exceptional than often supposed.

[*See also* Border Security; Bush, George W.; Democratic Party; Hispanic Americans; Immigration, Domestic Consequences of; Immigration, Legal and Illegal; Labor Force, American; NAFTA; *and* Reagan, Ronald.]

BIBLIOGRAPHY

Archdeacon, Thomas. *Becoming American*. (New York, 1983).

Castles, Stephen. "The Factors that Make and Unmake Migration Policy." *International Migration Review* 38, no. 3 (2004): 852–884.

Castles, Stephen, and Mark J. Miller. *The Age of Migration*. 4th ed. (New York, 2009).

Curtin, Philip. "Africa and Global Patterns of Migration." In *Global History and Migrations*, edited by Wang Gungwu, pp. 63–94. (Boulder, Colo., 1997).

Daniels, Roger. *Guarding the Golden Door*. (New York, 2004).

Fowler, Robert Booth. *Wisconsin Votes: An Electoral History*. (Madison, Wisc., 2008).

Gungwu, Wang. *Global History and Migrations*. (Boulder, Colo., 1997).

Hatton, Timothy J., and Jeffrey G. Williamson. *Global Migration and the World Economy*. (Cambridge, Mass., 2008).

Heather, Peter. *Empires and Barbarians*. (Oxford, UK, 2009).

Huntington, Samuel P. *Who Are We?* (New York, 2004).

Kagan, Robert. *Dangerous Nation*. (New York, 2006).

Kiser, George C., and Martha Woody Kiser. *Mexican Workers in the United States*. (Albuquerque, N.Mex., 1979).

Lipset, Seymour M., and Gary Marks. *It Didn't Happen Here*. (New York, 2000).

Martin, Philip L., and Martin Ruhs. "Labor Shortages and US Immigration Reform: Promises and Perils of an Independent Commission." *International Migration Review* 45, no. 1 (2011): 174–187.

Motomura, Hiroshi. *Americans in Waiting: The Lost Story of Immigration and Citizenship in the United States*. (New York, 2006).

O'Brien, Peter. *European Perceptions of Islam and America from Saladin to George W. Bush*. (New York, 2009).

Select Commission on Immigration and Refugee Policy. *U.S. Immigration Policy and the National Interest: The Final Report and Recommendations of the Select Commission on Immigration and Refugee Policy with Supplemental Views by Commissioners, March 1, 1981*. (Washington, D.C., 1981).

Shorto, R. *The Island at the Center of the World*. (New York, 2004).

Siavelis, Peter. "Beyond Push and Pull: Neoliberalism, NAFTA, Immigration Policy and the Structural Incentives for Mexican Immigration." In *Getting Immigration Right*, edited by David Coates and Peter Siavelis. (Dulles, Va., 2009).

Silver, Peter. *Our Savage Neighbors*. (New York, 2008).

Taylor, Alan. *American Colonies*. (New York, 2001).

Tichenor, Daniel. *Dividing Lines*. (Princeton, N.J., 2002).

Zeidel, Robert F. *Immigrants, Progressives, and Exclusion Politics: The Dillingham Commission, 1900–1907*. (DeKalb, Ill., 2004).

Zolberg, Aristide. "The Exit Revolution." In *Citizenship and Those Who Leave*, edited by Nancy L. Green and François Weil. (Urbana, Ill., 2007).

Zolberg, Aristide. *How Many Exceptionalisms? Exploration in Comparative Macroanalysis*. (Philadelphia, Pa., 2008b).

Zolberg, Aristide. "International Migration in Political Perspective." In *The Migration Reader: Exploring Politics and Policies*, edited by A. Messina and G. Lahav. (Boulder, Colo., 2006).

Zolberg, Aristide. *A Nation by Design: Immigration Policy in the Fashioning of America*. (Cambridge, Mass., 2008a).

Mark J. Miller

IMPEACHMENT

"Impeachment," in Anglo-American jurisprudence, is the authority of a legislative body to legally accuse a public official of a crime and remove that person from office. Impeachment originated in England as one of the few instruments of power that could be used by Parliament to rein in an abusive monarch; it gave Parliament the ability to remove royal ministers from office (and sometimes execute them as well).

From the first impeachment in 1376 through 1397, the House of Commons impeached eighteen officers of the king, and all were convicted by the House of Lords. During the Tudor period, although accepted in principle, impeachment fell into disuse; however, it was revived again in the seventeenth century to counter the absolutist pretentions of the Stuarts.

The framers of the US Constitution were steeped in British history, and adopted impeachment as a check on the executive branch, as had most of the newly created states after the Revolution. Alexander Hamilton, in *The Federalist no. 65*, called the British process of indictment by the House of Commons and conviction (or acquittal) by the House of Lords the "model" for US constitutional procedures. The original Virginia Plan gave control of impeachments to the national judiciary. But the Constitution vests "the sole Power of Impeachment" in the House of Representatives and gives the Senate the "sole Power to try all Impeachments."

Although "all civil Officers of the United States" are subject to impeachment, the Framers saw impeachment primarily as a safety valve to check a perfidious president. James Madison argued that "some provision be made for defending the Community against the incapacity, negligence or perfidy of the chief Magistrate" (Farrand, vol. 2, 1911, p. 65).

An early draft of the Constitution provided for impeachment for treason (narrowly defined) and bribery. George Mason, however, argued that "Attempts to subvert the Constitution" might not be covered by the terms "treason" or "bribery" and suggested that "maladministration" be added to the offenses to be remedied. Madison objected that the term was too vague, and so Mason substituted "other high crimes & misdemeanors" against the United States. The term "high crimes and misdemeanors" was a legal term of art used in British impeachments and was used to denote crimes against the state, rather than merely private or petty crimes. The word "other" in the above constitutional phrase implies that impeachable offences would be comparable to treason and bribery.

The political nature of impeachment was emphasized by Hamilton in *The Federalist no. 65*, in which he noted that impeachment was a "method of NATIONAL INQUEST into the conduct of public men." Its purpose was to be a "bridle in the hands of the legislative body upon the executive servants of the government." According to Hamilton, "offenses which proceed from the misconduct of public men, or, in other words, from the abuse or violation of some public trust. They are of a nature which may with peculiar propriety be denominated POLITICAL, as they relate chiefly to injuries done immediately to the society itself."

The political nature of impeachment is further indicated by the constitutional provision that punishment of the official "shall not extend further than to removal from Office, and disqualification to hold and enjoy any Office of honor, Trust or Profit under the United States." Nevertheless, the former official is still subject to "Indictment, Trial, Judgment and Punishment, according to Law" (Article I, Section 3). In the words of Joseph Story, the great American jurist, in his *Commentaries on the Constitution of the United States*, impeachment is "a proceeding purely of a political nature. It is not so much designed to punish an offender as to secure the state against gross official misdemeanors. It touches neither his person nor his property, but simply divests him of his political capacity" (Berger, 1973, p. 79).

Throughout US history, impeachments at the federal level have been rare, with fewer than twenty officials having been impeached, and all of those convicted have been federal judges. Two presidents (Andrew Johnson and William Clinton) were impeached, and one (Richard Nixon) resigned before probable impeachment by the House and conviction in the Senate. Both impeached presidents were acquitted by the Senate.

President Andrew Johnson was impeached by the Republicans in 1867 for violating the Tenure of Office Act, which had just been passed. The real reason for impeaching him, however, was that the House felt that Johnson was undermining harsh Reconstruction policies in the South after the Civil War. The Senate refused to convict Johnson by a margin of one vote.

The Judiciary Committee of the House of Representatives adopted three articles of impeachment against President Nixon in 1974. The articles charged that he had obstructed the Watergate criminal investigation, that he had abused his power by using the Internal Revenue Service (IRS) and Federal Bureau of Investigation (FBI) to violate the constitutional rights of citizens, and that he did not comply with congressional subpoenas of his White House tapes. Before the full House took up the issues, Nixon resigned on 9 August 1974, making the case moot.

President Clinton's impeachment was a result of his having had a sexual affair with a young White House intern. Clinton denied that he had had the affair before a grand jury in a civil case brought against him (which was later thrown out of court). His false testimony, however, was the focus of one article of impeachment. The second article accused him of obstruction of justice, because it was alleged that he encouraged his secretary to lie about evidence relating to the affair. The Republican leaders thwarted attempts by Democrats to censure Clinton rather than impeach him, and in December 1998 the House passed the two articles of impeachment.

Impeachments of presidents are politically disruptive and usually reserved for severe crimes against the state. As James Bryce observed in the late nineteenth century:

> Impeachment . . . is the heaviest piece of artillery in the congressional arsenal, but because it is so heavy it is unfit for ordinary use. It is like a hundred-ton gun which needs complex machinery to bring it into position, and an enormous charge of powder to fire it, and a large mark to aim at. (Bryce, 1891, p. 208)

So far in US history the Senate has not deemed any presidential impeachment sufficient to meet that test.

[*See also* Presidency: Governing.]

BIBLIOGRAPHY

Berger, Raoul. *Impeachment: The Constitutional Problems.* (Cambridge, Mass., 1973).

Black, Charles L., Jr. *Impeachment: A Handbook.* (New Haven, Conn., 1974).

Bryce, James. *The American Commonwealth.* (London, 1891).

Farrand, Max. *The Records of the Federal Convention of 1787.* Vols. 1–4. (New Haven, Conn., 1911).

Labovitz, John R. *Presidential Impeachment.* (New Haven, Conn., 1979).

James P. Pfiffner

INDIA–UNITED STATES RELATIONS

Despite Americans at the time being mainly indifferent toward and ignorant of South Asia, the United States under President Franklin D. Roosevelt strongly supported India's independence from British rule (much to Winston Churchill's chagrin). When this finally happened in August 1947, and Indian leaders immediately began putting together a democratic constitution, it would have been assumed that the world's oldest democracy and the world's largest democracy were bound to enjoy friendly relations. What transpired instead was a mostly prickly relationship, whereby the two countries were neither close friends nor foes, but rather coexisted warily as "estranged democracies" (Kux, 1993). This continued until the end of the Cold War, when the new, unipolar, international system headed by the United States combined with India's failed socialist economy to usher in a strategic partnership that stands to significantly impact international relations during the twenty-first century.

The Cold War Years. America's preeminent goal during the Cold War era was to contain the spread of communism. This consideration conditioned its relations with other states, and South Asian countries were no exception.

Independent India's elites, knowing full well how British colonialism had denuded the subcontinent's resources and humiliated Indians, were staunchly anti-imperialist. Jawaharlal Nehru and other prominent Indian elites also associated imperialism with capitalism, even as they admired how Soviet leaders had, within a generation, transformed a country with a mainly peasant economy into a global power. Newly independent India thus embraced a socialist economy, which was hardly controversial, given that many European countries that were part of the Western alliance against the Soviets had also embraced various socialist practices. What became controversial and caused tension with the United States was the way India positioned itself within the Non-Aligned Movement (NAM).

Nehru strongly believed that there was no reason for countries like India to become entangled in the Cold War by having to choose between the United States and the Soviet Union; on the contrary, he felt that India and other influential Third World states could adopt a neutral position, thereby acting as a bridge between the superpowers, and in doing so also advance the interests of many countries in the international system. Thus NAM came into being in the mid-1950s, and the Eisenhower administration initially sympathized with India's desire for geopolitical neutrality, given that the United States too had embraced a similar position for 150 years following its independence. But Indian bias toward the Soviet Union—amply manifested when it severely criticized the United Kingdom, France, and Israel over the Suez Crisis in October 1956, but a month later abstained from voting for a United Nations resolution that condemned the Soviet invasion of Hungary, and likewise refused to condemn the

Soviet-led invasion of Czechoslovakia in August 1968 and the Soviet invasion of Afghanistan in December 1979—exasperated American policymakers. This Indian bias was partly influenced by the view that the Soviets lacked a colonial history and were not a colonial power, whereas the United States was a more materialistic substitute for Britain. US Secretary of State John Foster Dulles especially frowned on India's claims regarding nonalignment, and argued that countries that were not aligned with the United States should be considered as standing against it. Such reasoning, combined with Pakistan leveraging its strategic location vis-à-vis the Soviet Union and the Middle East, led the United States to sign a Mutual Defense Assistance Agreement with that country in 1954.

India considered itself Britain's successor in ensuring stability in South Asia and the Indian Ocean, but the US-Pakistan alliance undermined this claim to being a regional hegemon. The claim was further vitiated when the United States resorted to a policy of parity when dealing with India and Pakistan, thereby disregarding the asymmetrical nature of the two countries. Such "coupling" of the two states emboldened Pakistan's military leaders to act adventurously over the disputed region of Kashmir and also to interfere in Pakistan's domestic politics, even as it made India insecure and slowly drove the country into cultivating closer ties with the Soviet Union. Furthermore, American diplomats in the United Nations, lacking expertise on South Asia and hence taking their cue from their British counterparts, initially adopted a pro-Pakistan stance when seeking to resolve the Kashmir imbroglio (after India referred the dispute to the United Nations). They did reverse themselves and propound a more impartial position, but all of this led to strong anti-American currents throughout the Indian body politic—so much so that even American aid to India was viewed suspiciously.

The high points for bilateral relations during the Cold War years would include Jacqueline Kennedy's visit to India in March 1962, US arms shipments to India following the Sino-Indian war in October and November the same year (albeit not to the levels we now know Nehru requested), and Prime Minister Rajiv Gandhi's visit to the United States in June 1985, which generated serious interest among American businesses about investing in India, and also led to certain US technologies that were hitherto barred now being transferred to India. A low point was when the Lyndon B. Johnson administration, overlooking the effects of a major famine in India, suspended food assistance to the country in July 1965. The administration's supposed goal was to induce agricultural reforms in India, but irate Indian leaders felt their country's sovereignty was being violated and that they were being punished for opposing the escalating war in Vietnam.

The lowest point in the relationship most certainly came during the 1971 India-Pakistan war that led to the creation of Bangladesh. On that occasion President Richard Nixon's animus toward Prime Minister Indira Gandhi and US partiality toward Pakistan (at a time when Pakistan was conniving with the United States to further US-China relations) caused the administration to vilify India and its prime minister (with Nixon and his national security advisor Henry Kissinger referring to Indira Gandhi as a "witch" and a "bitch"), and to deploy the USS *Enterprise* aircraft carrier to the Bay of Bengal as a show of support for Pakistan. Both Nixon and Kissinger knew little about and cared even less for South Asia, and their dealings with the region were based on Cold War calculations. Indians, however, to this day bristle when reminded about the so-called *Enterprise* incident, which merely confirmed Indian perceptions of American arrogance.

Notwithstanding United States policymakers, especially those associated with Republican administrations, who considered nonalignment in the face of Soviet designs to be immoral, and American diplomats who sometimes resented having to deal with assertive Indian counterparts wont to pontificating about their country's splendid ancient history and supposedly dispassionate foreign policies, successive American administrations admired India's democratic credentials and appreciated the fact that the country hardly challenged US security interests. Consequently, US-India relations during the Cold

War years were, in the main, conducted amid friendly nonchalance.

The Bill Clinton Era. The end of the Cold War and the 1991 economic reforms India was forced to enact suggested that the United States and India were likely to enjoy better ties going forward. This appeared to be confirmed when India allowed US aircraft to refuel on Indian soil during the Persian Gulf War in 1990–1991. The strong US commitment to nonproliferation, however, saw the Clinton administration pressuring India to sign the Non-Proliferation Treaty (NPT), when it was extended indefinitely in 1995, and the Comprehensive Test Ban Treaty (CTBT), when the UN General Assembly adopted it in 1996. Indian policymakers adamantly refused to do so because they sincerely believed that the treaties discriminated against states without nuclear capability, even while ignoring nuclear proliferation among the nuclear powers. They also resented the United States making nonproliferation the major basis for dealing with India while overlooking the illegal nuclear collaboration between Pakistan and China (the two states with the worst record of nuclear proliferation in the last quarter century). These policymakers thus criticized the United States for embracing a colonial mindset and even accused it and the West of practicing "nuclear apartheid" (Singh, 1998). This impasse ensured that relations during the first Clinton term took place in an erratic manner.

India conducted its first nuclear test in May 1974, making it the first country besides the five permanent members of the UN Security Council to do so. This capability conditioned US-India relations for the next quarter century. India conducted five more tests in May 1998, embarrassing the United States intelligence community, which had failed to discover the preparations leading up to them. The tests also infuriated the Clinton administration, which felt the Indian action undermined the NPT and CTBT regimes. The tests led to automatic US sanctions against India (and Pakistan, for reciprocating with six tests of its own).

The Clinton administration was sensitive to India's claim about needing a nuclear deterrent to counter the Chinese nuclear threat amid that country's increasingly assertive stance vis-à-vis the unsettled India-China border and growing involvement in South Asia, but it made clear that the United States would not recognize India (and Pakistan) as nuclear weapons states within the NPT, which meant that India was to be denied benefits (primarily concerning nuclear energy to generate electricity) that came to those states that had joined the NPT regime. President Clinton preferred to see India roll back its nuclear weapons program but knew this was not an option, and so he sought to get the country to sign the NPT and CTBT. This was the basis for the fourteen rounds of talks and semiofficial meetings that took place between Bill Clinton's representative Strobe Talbot and the Indian external affairs minister Jaswant Singh during June 1998 and July 2000. While ultimately producing no agreement promoting nonproliferation, the talks enabled an ongoing dialogue and an opportunity for both to share and appreciate their countries' concerns, and were a turning point in US-India relations.

The 1999 Kargil War between India and Pakistan especially bolstered US-India ties, by strengthening Indian confidence in American diplomacy. The Kargil conflict ensued after the Pakistani military deployed soldiers and militants to a strategic mountainous location in Kashmir which Indian forces had temporarily vacated during the winter, and India tried to wrest the territory back. With both India and Pakistan having proven their nuclear capability, the United States sought to ensure the crisis did not escalate. When Pakistan sought to use the crisis to force India to agree to a deal on Kashmir, the Clinton administration refused to go along and instead demanded that Pakistan withdraw its forces from the Kargil sector. This was the first time that the United States openly and assertively jilted Pakistan in favor of India, and it helped build India's trust in the superpower.

Bill Clinton, aware that India felt it was insufficiently respected, had called the country "the Rodney Dangerfield of great nations" (Talbott, 2004, p. 78). Yet by the time President Clinton went to India the following year—becoming the first US president to visit the country in twenty-two years—India's self-confidence and appreciation for the United States and its president had soared, and Clinton was given a rapturous welcome. During this March 2000 trip to the subcontinent, Clinton spent five days in India and only five hours in Pakistan, where he gave a short speech in which he warned the Pakistanis (with reference to Kashmir) that the contemporary era did not reward those who tried to alter their borders with blood. Clinton thus reiterated the current US preference for the Line of Control separating India and Pakistan in Kashmir to be recognized as the international border. As noted above, India's policymakers had long resented the United States equating and coupling India with Pakistan. President Clinton's stance on Kargil, together with his trip to South Asia, initiated the decoupling process; building on Clinton's progress, under the George W. Bush administration a "dehyphenation" policy would be instituted effectively (Tellis, 2008).

The George W. Bush Era. President Clinton's visit to India heralded an improved phase in US-India relations, but none could have predicted how far the George W. Bush administration would go to lay the groundwork for a strategic partnership between the two countries.

President Bush projected a predilection for countries that were democracies, and nothing compared with India's vibrant and noisy democracy. The neoconservatives in the administration were also concerned about China's rapid rise, and recognized a potential ally in India to balance against it. Additionally, the Bush administration apparently adopted a RAND report's recommendation that partly said India was an emerging "great power," Pakistan was "unsettled and troublesome on multiple counts," and the United States should decouple relations with the two states (Carlucci, Hunter, and Khalilzad, 2000, p. 45). The administration evidently agreed that, even though both India and Pakistan were important to US interests, "their respective geopolitical weights were radically divergent, their prospects for success as pivotal states in the international system were remarkably dissimilar, and their significance to US grand strategic interests in various geographic and functional arenas were so

unalike that they could not be discussed in the same breath" (Tellis, 2008, p. 23). Thus the Bush administration quickly made it clear that it would pursue closer ties with India. India's strong support for President Bush's plans for a missile defense shield, notwithstanding Russia's disapproval, only further endeared the country to the new administration. That some in the right-wing government in India at the time also seriously considered participating in the Iraq War was also much appreciated.

The geostrategic considerations aside, there were two other developments that promoted stronger US-India ties. Trade between them had grown dramatically after India introduced economic reforms in 1991, and the US business community clamored for stronger relations. The 1990s also saw the Indian population in the United States grow by nearly a million thanks to Indian students (who by the late 1990s were among the largest foreign contingents) staying on to pursue careers in the United States, and American companies hiring Indians to work in great numbers, especially in the information technology sector. This was exemplified by the so-called Y2K (or year 2000) problem, which saw Indian information technology specialists ensuring that US computer software and operating systems were compliant with the onset of the new millennium. The already established Indian diaspora (representing mainly physicians, engineers, and business people) had helped create the Congressional Caucus on India and Indian Americans in 1993, and the new arrivals gradually joined them to lobby American legislators ever more effectively.

A major reason the United States and India had endured an estranged relationship during the Cold War was because the United States was not consistently involved in South Asia's political, economic, and military affairs except when crises propelled it to engage Pakistan (which in turn upset India). Lyndon B. Johnson had disengaged the United States from the subcontinent following the 1965 Indo-Pakistan war, and the country did not get seriously involved in the region again until the Soviet Union invaded Afghanistan in December 1979. Thus during the 1980s, America worked through Pakistan's

Inter-Services Intelligence (ISI) to funnel weapons to the Mujahedeen (Soldiers of God), who assembled from all over the world to fight the Soviets, even as it overlooked Pakistan's nuclear weapons program. No sooner had the Mujahedeen triumphed over the Soviets than the United States extricated itself from the region and imposed sanctions on Pakistan for pursuing nuclear weapons. While the United States did engage India and Pakistan during various crises, both countries were, in the main, dissatisfied with it: Pakistan justifiably felt it had been used and abused, while India felt America's hidebound position on nonproliferation failed to consider its own responsible track record (which contrasted favorably with that of other nuclear states). Following the withdrawal of the Soviets from Afghanistan, Pakistan's ISI began using the Mujahedeen and various other extremist forces to stoke separatism in India-administered Kashmir, destabilize other parts of India, and also control events in Afghanistan. India therefore also resented what it perceived as US soft-pedaling of the ISI's terror-sponsoring activities, even as it vigorously opposed any outside involvement regarding Kashmir.

Al-Qaeda's September 11, 2001, terrorist attacks on America prompted India to share its intelligence on terror groups in South Asia with the United States. Indeed, India became the first country to support the Bush administration's "War on Terror." The terrorist strikes also forced Pakistan's President Pervez Musharraf to claim his country was fore-swearing its ties to the Taliban, which Pakistan had sponsored, and throwing its support behind the United States. With al-Qaeda and the Taliban having joined forces and operating out of Afghanistan and Pakistan's tribal regions, Pakistani support became indispensible for waging the War on Terror. One would have, especially in light of the administration's newfound mission, expected relations with Pakistan to be revived at India's expense. But the Bush administration instead effectively decoupled relations, dealing with Pakistan principally with regard to the war against the Taliban and al-Qaeda while strengthening economic, security, and foreign policy ties to India, with an eye toward China.

India's standard line vis-à-vis China was and is that the two countries will resolve their border dispute and differences over the Dalai Lama and Tibetan activists in India peacefully. But Indians have not forgotten the humiliating defeat China inflicted on their country in 1962 and are troubled by their economically and militarily superior neighbor's increased involvement in Pakistan (including Pakistan-controlled Kashmir), its expanding entanglements in the rest of South Asia, and the periodic strident rhetoric in government-sanctioned Chinese media. Indian policymakers in general are averse to any alliance that pits India against China—and this is a mindset influenced by India's previous non-aligned posture—but many hawks within India's security establishment see their country as having little choice but to position itself against a future Chinese superpower. This, together with fears over the spread of radical Islam in the subcontinent, coincided with the worldview of Washington's neoconservatives (especially in think tanks like the American Enterprise Institute) who supported the landmark nuclear agreement between the countries.

In July 2005 the United States and India signed a Civilian Nuclear Agreement in Washington, D.C. In doing so, the Bush administration recognized India as a de facto nuclear state and created a framework for India to benefit from civilian nuclear cooperation without signing on to the NPT. The agreement allowed India to use its existing fuel to develop nuclear weapons while using the purchased fuel for power generation purposes; the nonproliferation lobby strongly opposed the deal by arguing that it undermined the NPT. But the president and his supporters justified their decision by playing up the responsible way in which India had conducted itself with its nuclear know-how. In doing so, the administration apparently vitiated the hitherto emphasized distinction between NPT signatories and nonsignatories and promoted instead a new standard of gauging states based on their "responsible" and "non-responsible" nuclear records (Sharma, 2008, p. 65).

In September 2008 the Nuclear Suppliers Group (NSG), a voluntary body comprising forty-five countries with the wherewithal to produce nuclear weapons, finally caved in to US lobbying and lifted the ban that had hitherto prevented India from engaging in nuclear commerce. The irony was that the NSG was formed in reaction to India's first nuclear test in 1974, to prevent nuclear proliferation by putting in place rules that controlled the transfer of enrichment and reprocessing equipment and technology. Once the NSG ban was lifted, American business interests that stood to benefit from nuclear commerce with India and the increasingly influential Indian-American community began lobbying wavering members of Congress to ensure that the US House of Representatives and Senate passed the US-India Agreement for Civil Nuclear Cooperation, which President Bush signed into law in October 2008.

As part of the agreement, India promised to not conduct additional nuclear tests, to separate its civilian plants from its military nuclear plants, and to permit the International Atomic Energy Agency to inspect fourteen of its twenty-two nuclear power reactors. In return, India was allowed to purchase nuclear fuel from countries within the NSG, negotiate to buy dual-use technologies, continue its nuclear weapons program, and eventually sell its own nuclear fuel through the NSG. For all practical purposes, the nuclear deal the United States pushed through ensured that India was now recognized as the world's sixth nuclear power. By refusing to pursue a similar agreement with Pakistan, the Bush administration also unequivocally signaled that "dehyphenation" or "decoupling" was now very much a part of US policy when dealing with India and Pakistan.

Ultimately, George W. Bush "did more for India than he did for any NATO ally, including the United Kingdom, notwithstanding Tony Blair's lonely reputation-destroying support for the war in Iraq" (Perkovich, 2010, p. 8). Critics of the US-India nuclear agreement argue that Bush cultivated close ties with India without receiving much in return, neglecting multilateral institutions and weakening the NPT in the process. It is with good reason that President Bush left office being more popular in India than almost anywhere else in the world, despite Indians

strongly opposing the War on Terror and the US invasion of Iraq.

The Barack Obama Presidency. Given the upsurge in US-India relations during especially the Bush administration's second term, Indian policymakers and supporters found Barack Obama's first year as president to be anticlimactic. America's fiscal woes and attendant weakened position on the global stage saw President Obama engage China as an equal partner. Besides dealing with the wars in Iraq and Afghanistan, Obama began pushing for a peace deal between Israelis and Palestinians and recalibrating relations with Russia. India seemed to be left behind. To make matters worse, candidate Obama had discussed how a solution to the Kashmir dispute was imperative if the United States were to defeat the Taliban and al-Qaeda and extricate its forces from Afghanistan, implying that India was indirectly responsible for exacerbating America's position in Afghanistan. Within two days of his inauguration Obama made clear where he intended to focus in South Asia when he (after considering Bill Clinton) designated Richard Holbrooke to be the special envoy for Afghanistan and Pakistan (Af-Pak). India considers Kashmir an integral part of the country and lobbied hard to ensure it was not included in Holbrooke's brief. Indeed, Holbooke and his team were dissuaded from visiting New Delhi whenever India felt Kashmir might crop up. Notwithstanding India's initial discomfiture on Af-Pak, US focus on the two countries, especially following the decoupling of the India-Pakistan equation, highlighted where the region's real problems lay.

Yet another perceived impropriety took place when President Obama visited China in November 2009 and released a joint statement that partly said the countries will "work together to promote peace, stability and development" in South Asia. This and talk of how the United States and China were now in a "G2" relationship grated Indian officialdom, given China's burgeoning involvement in the subcontinent through which it has encircled India. India even objects to the US proclivity to couple it with China, as in China-India, especially when the formulation pits India as the junior partner. Overall, Obama's policies toward South Asia during the initial months of his presidency deeply troubled New Delhi.

China's vociferous claims over the South China Sea, its expanding maritime and satellite capabilities targeting the Pacific, and its intentions to curtail US influence in East Asia led the Obama administration to also cultivate closer relations with India. It reassured India by hosting Prime Minister Manmohan Singh to its first state dinner in November 2009. A year later President Obama made a hugely successful visit to India, accompanied by around two hundred American chief executives, that led to business deals worth $10 billion. During the trip Obama encouraged India to not merely look toward East Asia but to engage it, a comment likely made to compensate for the faux pas committed in the US-China joint statement noted above. When addressing the Indian Parliament, Obama said that "India has emerged," and for the first time promised United States support for India's bid to become a permanent member of the UN Security Council (which France, the United Kingdom, and Russia also support but China apparently does not). The president also promised to promote India's candidacy in four nonproliferation clubs (including the NSG) and announced that two major state-owned research and military establishments—the Defense Research and Development Organization (DRDO) and the Indian Space and Research Organization (ISRO)—would be taken off the Entities List, which determines high-technology export-control restrictions.

The United States would like India to open up its banking, insurance, pharmaceutical, defense, and retail sectors and also provide its seed technology companies greater access to India's vast agricultural sector. India, among other things, would like the United States to treat it as no second to America's European allies when dealing with dual-use technologies. The Obama administration, in accordance with the president's promise, has now dropped from the Entities List certain subsidiaries associated with the DRDO and ISRO. Many in the US nonproliferation lobby, however, worry that India may utilize the dual-use technology it can now access to develop more precise and potent nuclear weapons. Evidence

supporting such use or further Indian testing of a nuclear weapon could set back the progress made in US-India relations in the first decade of the twenty-first century.

India opposes the rise in H1B and L1 (intracompany transfer) visa fees that the Obama administration introduced, as they disproportionately affect Indian high-tech personnel. Indian politicians and especially businesspersons (and their American business colleagues) have also opposed the related anti-outsourcing policies that were implemented following the US economic downturn, even as they consider the occasional bashing of Bangalore, India's foremost high-tech hub, to be counterproductive, given the robust pro-American sentiment among that city's computer fraternity.

In 2011, the United States and India found themselves on opposite sides on global warming, as India placed the onus for climate change on the advanced industrialized countries. The two countries also disagreed within the World Trade Organization, with India among the leaders of the developing countries opposing the US stance on agricultural subsidies, even as it protected its predominantly poor formers via import controls and high tariffs. India has spurned US entreaties to recognize Kosovo as an independent country, as it fears doing so may legitimize the claims of separatists in Kashmir and elsewhere in India. It has also refused to take a hard line against the military junta in Myanmar and the regime in Sudan, as it would like to access these states' oil and gas exports.

The US-India nuclear agreement was a major boon for India with the United States receiving hardly anything in return. The real payback was supposed to follow when India began spending over $100 billion in the next two decades to develop nuclear energy. Thus passage in September 2010 of the nuclear liability law, which imposes stiff penalties on suppliers and operators for any accidents in civilian plants, has upset American government officials and suppliers like General Electric and Westinghouse.

In 2011 the NSG voted to ban the sale of enrichment and reprocessing technology and equipment to countries outside the NPT, thereby questioning the NSG waver granted to India in September 2008. Indian leaders, however, appear confident that the bilateral agreements they have negotiated with nine states (including France, Russia, Canada, Argentina, South Korea, and the United States) would continue notwithstanding the ban. How the United States responds to this NSG rule and to what extent India tweaks its nuclear liability law will determine how much nuclear trade takes place between the two states.

In addition to the nuclear sector, United States companies and officials have lobbied furiously to benefit from India's military modernization. For instance, both during and after his visit to India, President Obama too lobbied hard for Boeing and Lockheed Martin to be provided the contract for fighter jets worth $11 billion. However, in April 2011 India announced that the contract would go to a European company. While India continues to purchase other American military aircraft, the United States on this occasion refused to sell its most advanced fighter jets because India refused to sign the requisite monitoring and verification agreements, which further highlights India's aversion to being superintended or treated as a junior partner. But the decision to grant the contract to a European company, which infuriated some American officials, may have also been political given the fear among senior defense officials, like the Indian defense minister A. K. Anthony, that such military deals and their potential for interoperability are drawing India into an undesirable alliance with the United States. That the aircraft on offer were similar to those the United States has sold Pakistan may have also influenced the Indian decision. Closer India–United States defense ties are bound to come at the expense of Russia, which began collaborating with India militarily in the late 1960s. Some suspect that continuing ties between officials in the Research and Analysis Wing, which is India's external intelligence agency, and their Russian counterparts who were part of the former Soviet KGB may also be preventing greater military cooperation between India and the United States.

During Barack Obama's first year in office it was common to hear Indian officials rue the end of the George W. Bush administration. Given America's current fiscal problems and Obama's commitment to nonproliferation, it is hard to see India continue to benefit disproportionately as it did under the Bush administration. President Obama, however, has done well to put US-India relations on a more balanced trajectory even while furthering the relationship.

The Future of US-India Relations. The US-India relationship is not an alliance. It is currently a qualitatively improved, more trusting, and mature partnership that is based mainly on trading and strategic considerations. While bilateral relations continue to improve, India's position on various global issues coincides more with the so-called BRICS (Brazil, Russia, India, China, and South Africa) than with the United States. Its stance in multilateral forums would need to converge with the United States position, and the country would need to feel sufficiently threatened, before there would likely be any alliance between them.

The United States appreciates India's measured response to terrorist attacks against its citizens, despite clear evidence that many such attacks were orchestrated by elements operating freely in Pakistan. The United States also considers India's consistent support for UN peacekeeping operations and its attempts at deterring piracy off the Horn of Africa to be invaluable. The Obama administration has, consequently, encouraged India to develop interoperable capabilities in peacekeeping and piracy so as to promote the country as an alternate Asian power. Indian officials clamor for great power status, but they do not want to come across as subservient to the United States, and also worry that China would construe such interoperability as an attempt to balance against it.

Such concerns have not prevented military-to-military ties from soaring. The countries have held over sixty joint military exercises since 1992, and this despite US concerns over the general readiness, corruption, and extrajudicial activities of India's security forces. Indeed, the two countries today conduct more military exercises with each other than with any other country. Their security personnel collaborate on cyber-security and counterterrorism; and the focus on Indian homeland security following the Mumbai terror attacks has seen a demand among private companies for surveillance and detecting equipment, which stands to benefit American businesses. While US businesspeople (and officials) are often exasperated by India's hard bargaining, widespread red tape, and protected sectors of the economy, they also realize that there is no alternative but to engage the world's second fastest growing economy. Bilateral trade reached $50 billion in 2010 (with India enjoying around $10 billion surplus), and will only grow as trading links are inevitably strengthened.

India began serving a two-year term as a rotating member of the UN Security Council in January 2011 and how it votes on resolutions will also affect bilateral ties. For instance, India abstained from voting for the military operation against Libya in March 2011. It enjoys relatively good relations with Iran and it would likely not support sanctions or military action against that nation, if it came to that. India did vote in September 2005 to have the International Atomic Energy Agency refer Iran's nuclear program to the UN Security Council, but this was after the Bush administration linked the vote to congressional support for the US-India nuclear agreement. The fact remains that India tries not to offend the sensibilities of the NAM consensus within the various UN bodies, which explains why it has only voted around 20 percent of the time with the United States within the UN General Assembly.

Many among India's political class and literati tend to be leftist in their outlook, and they especially remain suspicious about closer links with the United States. Some among the Indian establishment also resent the United States for supporting every single military dictator who usurped power in Pakistan and continuing to arm that country, which uses the same hardware to target India. This noted, it is hard to locate an upper-middle-class family in India today without a relative who has studied, worked, or lived in the United States. These links, combined with

burgeoning business interactions and the strong pro-India lobby in the United States (exemplified by the US-India Business Council and the United States India Political Action Committee), have caused an ideological shift so that Indians today view America more positively than ever before.

Indian Americans are the fastest growing population among Asian Americans and currently number approximately 3 million. They assimilate exceedingly well and Indian American students are generally recognized for their stellar educational achievements. Indian Americans are also playing an increasingly prominent role in US politics, with Governors Bobby Jindal of Louisiana and Nikki Haley of South Carolina topping the list . Such involvement will only accelerate as the next generation of Indian Americans comes of age, and it will only contribute toward closer ties between the two countries.

What currently matters most to the United States is the war in Afghanistan and how India may help stabilize that country and the region. India has carried out significant nation-building activity in Afghanistan and enjoys good relations with the present Afghan government and most of its population. The United States has lauded Indian involvement in Afghanistan and would like to collaborate on projects there. It would, ideally, also like to see India and Pakistan reach an understanding on Afghanistan and avoid competing for a foothold there. Pakistan, however, believes India uses Afghanistan to curtail its influence beyond its western border and to aid separatists in the Pakistan province of Baluchistan. Pakistan has therefore sought to distinguish between "good" and "bad" Taliban: the former promotes its influence in Afghanistan, while the latter are those who seek to brutally replace the Pakistani state with a caliphate. India in turn fears that a complete American withdrawal from Afghanistan would strengthen Pakistan-sponsored anti-India factions and further radicalize Pakistan itself.

A US withdrawal from Afghanistan could lead American policymakers to rethink relations with Pakistan, especially given its links to terrorism and rabid anti-Americanism. That would force Pakistan to become ever more dependent on China. In 2011

Pakistan and China were in the process of consolidating further their relationship, with the countries even set to agree to a civil nuclear deal similar to the US-India agreement. The irony for the United States is that China-Pakistan ties have long remained stronger than US-Pakistan ties, notwithstanding the $20 billion in aid the United States has poured into the country during the past decade. Pakistan refers to China as an "all-weather friend" and its ambassador to Beijing recently claimed that their countries' friendship "is higher than the mountains, deeper than the oceans, stronger than steel, dearer than eyesight, [and] sweeter than honey" (*Economist*, 2011). The ramifications of all this may prove India's anti-China hawks right and force the country closer to the United States.

From an American standpoint Pakistan scares, China challenges, and India frustrates. Yet the upsurge in US-India relations across three administrations amid various disagreements shows that the two countries can now differ without acrimony, which is a welcome change from the past. The disagreements notwithstanding, the United States has indicated that it supports a strategic partnership that secures both countries' interest in Asia and the Pacific. The extent to which India agrees to engage the United States bilaterally and multilaterally will determine how much more robust US-India relations become.

[*See also* Kashmir; *and* Pakistan–United States Relations.]

BIBLIOGRAPHY

Carlucci, Frank, Robert E. Hunter, and Zalmay Khalilzad, eds. *Taking Charge: A Bipartisan Report to the President-Elect on Foreign Policy and National Security.* (Santa Monica, Calif., 2000).

Cohen, Stephen Philip. *India: Emerging Power.* (Washington, D.C., 2001).

DeVotta, Neil. "International Relations." In *Understanding Contemporary India.* 2d ed., edited by Neil DeVotta, pp. 95–122. (Boulder, Colo., 2010).

Kapur, S. Paul. "India and the United States from World War II to the Present: A Relationship Transformed." In *India's Foreign Policy: Retrospect and Prospect*, edited by Sumit Ganguly, pp. 251–274. (New Delhi, India, 2010).

Kirk, Jason A. "India's Season of Discontent: U.S-India Relations through the Prism of Obama's 'Af-Pak' Policy, Year One." *Asian Affairs: An American Review* 37 (2010): 147–166.

Kux, Dennis. *Estranged Democracies: India and the United States, 1941–1991.* (New Delhi, India, 1993).

Perkovich, George. *Toward Realistic US-India Relations.* (Washington, D.C., 2010).

Schaffer, Teresita C. "The United States, India, and Global Governance: Can They Work Together?" *Washington Quarterly* 32, no. 3 (July 2009): 71–87.

Sharma, Shalendra D. "The Making of the US-India Nuclear Accord." *Global Asia* 3, no. 4 (Winter 2008): 64–70.

Singh, Jaswant. "Against Nuclear Apartheid." *Foreign Affairs* 77, no. 5 (September–October 1998): 41–52.

"Sweet As Can Be." *Economist*, 14 May 2011.

Talbott, Strobe. *Engaging India: Diplomacy, Democracy, and the Bomb.* (Washington, D.C., 2004).

Tellis, Ashley J. "The Merits of Dehyphenation: Explaining US Success in Engaging India and Pakistan." *Washington Quarterly* 31, no. 4 (Autumn 2008): 21–42.

Neil DeVotta

INEQUALITIES OF WEALTH AND INCOME

Wealth represents a stock of accumulated assets; income represents a flow of current output. Families not only receive income over the course of a year, but also save part of their income. Such accumulated savings are referred to as "wealth." The first part of this article develops the concept of household income and wealth. The second presents time trends in the inequality of income and wealth in the United States. The third part examines some of the causes of rising income and wealth inequality, while the fourth explores some of the consequences. The last part comments on some of the policy implications of these trends.

What Is Household Income and Wealth? The most important component of personal income is labor earnings, which accounted for 60 percent of total personal income in 2009. This is the sum of wages and salaries received by employees. A related component is called proprietors' earnings, which accounted for 10 percent of total income in 2009. There are many businesses that are operated by single individuals (or partnerships) and are unincorporated. Income received by such self-employed individuals is considered personal income.

A third component is the rental income received by individuals from the real estate that they own. The fourth is dividends paid to owners of corporate stock. The fifth component is interest income, which individuals receive on savings accounts, bonds, and other financial instruments. These three components, collectively called property income, made up 15 percent of total income in 2009. The last component is government transfer payments. The most common of these are Social Security benefits, unemployment benefits, and welfare. This group made up another 15 percent of income in 2009.

The conventional definition of household wealth includes assets and liabilities that are directly or indirectly marketable. Marketable wealth (or net worth) is defined as the current value of all marketable assets less the current value of debts. In 2007, homes were the most important household asset, accounting for 33 percent of total assets. Land, rental property, and other real estate made up another 11 percent of assets. Unincorporated business equity, which refers to small businesses owned directly by individuals, composed another 20 percent. Liquid assets (like bank deposits and money market funds) composed 7 percent of total assets. Pension accounts, such as individual retirement accounts and 401(k)s, made up another 12 percent. Financial securities amounted to only 1.5 percent of total assets, whereas corporate stock and mutual funds amounted to almost 12 percent.

On the liability side, the major form of household debt is the home mortgage. In 2007, mortgage debt accounted for 75 percent of total household debt. The remaining 25 percent consisted of such items as automobile and consumer loans and credit card debt. Total household debt amounted to 15 percent of the value of household assets.

Wealth and Income Inequality Trends in the United States. Wealth inequality, after rising steeply between 1983 and 1989, showed an ambiguous trend from 1989 to 2007. The share of wealth held by the top 5 percent of earners rose by 2.8 percentage points from 1983 to 1989, that of the top quintile by 2.2 percentage points, and the Gini coefficient (an index that ranges from zero to one, where a higher number indicates greater inequality) increased from 0.80 to 0.83. Between 1989 and 2007, the share of the top 5 percent increased by 2.9 percentage points, and that of the top quintile rose by 1.5 percentage points, but the Gini coefficient remained virtually unchanged.

The top 5 percent of families (as ranked by income) earned 37 percent of total household income in 2007, and the top 20 percent accounted for 61 percent of income—large figures, to be sure, but lower than the corresponding wealth shares. Income inequality, in contrast to wealth inequality, showed a sharp rise from 1983 to 1989, and an equally large increase from 1989 to 2007. Between 1983 and 1989, the Gini coefficient rose from 0.48 to 0.52, and the share of the top 5 percent rose from 26 percent to 30 percent. There was then a further increase of the Gini index by 0.043 points from 1989 to 2007, and of the shares of the top 5 percent and 20 percent (see Wolff, March 2010, for further details).

Causes of Rising Inequality. With regard to income inequality, it is important to distinguish between the top 10 percent and the bottom 90 percent of the distribution. With regard to the latter, changes in the inequality of labor income dominate movements of overall income inequality, because the vast majority of the income of this group derives from labor earnings. Indeed, the United States witnessed a steep rise in inequality among this group from about 1980 through 2010. The most popular hypothesis explaining this rise in inequality is skilled biased technical change (SBTC). The argument advanced is that technological change since the early 1970s has favored highly educated and skilled workers over less educated and less skilled workers. This view is connected with the so-called information technology revolution dating from the early 1970s. One result of this technological revolution is a transformation of the skills required in the labor market, favoring more educated and skilled workers. One important piece of evidence in support of this view is the steep rise in the returns to education, particularly to a college degree, that has occurred in the United States since 1975.

Increasing trade liberalization, beginning in 1973 with the end of the Bretton Woods Agreement and continuing through the 1980s and 1990s, is, perhaps, the second leading contender to explain rising inequality. Imports into the US economy grew from 5.4 percent of gross domestic product (GDP) in 1970 to 14 percent in 2003. Many of these new imports were from low-wage, less developed countries. The argument here is that the rising share of imports into the United States effectively increased the supply of low-wage labor, thereby lowering the relative wages earned by low-skilled laborers in the United States. A related argument is that rising immigration since the early 1980s may have also increased the relative pool of low-skill workers, likewise putting downward pressure on their relative wages.

A third leading argument involves institutional changes, notably declining unionization and a declining minimum wage in real terms. The proportion of the workforce represented by unions peaked in 1954, at 25.4 percent. After 1954, the trend was downward, and by 2003 only 12.9 of the total workforce were union members. It is suggested that the decline in unions has led to widening differentials in the overall wage structure. The second factor is the declining minimum wage in real terms. The federal minimum wage fell by 34 percent in real terms between its peak in 1968, and 2003. This has put downward pressure on the wages of unskilled workers and may account, in part, for the growing wage disparities between unskilled and skilled workers.

Factors regarding the top of the income distribution—which here refers to approximately the top 10 percent of earners, and most notably the top 1 percent—are different than those for the bottom part. For this group, so-called winner-take-all and tournament effects, whereby the rewards of competition become more and more concentrated at the top, may be a primary factor. Another explanation is that the expansion of information technology and associated markets, particularly for media, led to rising revenue to firms in the sports and entertainment industry and consequent increases in the earnings of top athletes and stars. Another source is the astronomical rise in compensation for CEOs and other top business executives, which can be traced to huge expansion in firm size. Lawyers and other professionals have also witnessed huge increases in earnings, as the value of "deals" has risen and the winner-take-all effect has come into play. The importance of political economy factors like lobbying, campaign contributions, the formation of social networks, and the provision of jobs to politicians when they leave office have also been emphasized. The rising importance of these factors has led to a government much more sympathetic to the rich, and to expanding concrete measures that benefit the rich.

With regard to rising wealth inequality, the main factor is rising income inequality, according to an analysis performed by Wolff (2002). A secondary factor is the rise in the ratio of stock prices to housing prices, since stocks are heavily concentrated among the rich and homes are the principal asset of the middle class.

Consequences of Rising Inequality. Perhaps the main consequence of rising inequality is the stagnation of wages and middle-class income. According to authorial computations, 44 percent of the total gain in household income between 1983 and 2007 accrued to the top 1 percent, and 87 percent of the gain went to the top 20 percent (the comparable figures for household wealth are 35 percent and 89 percent, respectively.) As a consequence, economic growth since roughly the late 1970s has left significantly less income and wealth for the rest of the population. The result is that real wages actually declined between 1973 and 2007 in the United States, while median family income rose by only 24 percent over these years, compared to a doubling between 1947 and 1973.

Another, perhaps even more troubling implication of rising inequality in the United States is that democracy, in the classic sense of equal political power for each individual, is now fraying. With the rising concentration of income and wealth, the rich have come to exert a disproportionate control over the political process.

Policy Relevance. Inasmuch as the top 20 percent, and particularly the top 1 percent, have enjoyed spectacular gains and have garnered the vast majority of economic growth, tax rates for the rich have fallen significantly more than for other groups. Indeed, the top marginal tax rate in the United States fell from 70 percent in 1980 to 35 percent in 2011—much more, in percentage terms, than for the middle class or poor. Another important tax benefit for the rich is the preferential treatment of capital gains and dividends, which is a major source of income for the rich, with a maximum tax rate of 15 percent, compared to 35 percent for ordinary income today. The increasing political power of the rich has manifested itself in favorable tax treatment, among other benefits provided by the government.

[*See also* Class Politics; Minimum Wage; Poverty, Scale and Nature of; *and* Trade Unions.]

BIBLIOGRAPHY

Atkinson, Anthony B., Thomas Piketty, and Emmanuel Saez. "Top Incomes in the Long Run of History." *Journal of Economic Literature* 49 (2011): 3–71.

Bartels, Larry M. *Unequal Democracy: The Political Economy of the New Gilded Age.* (Princeton, N.J., 2010).

Frank, Robert H., and Philip J. Cook. *The Winner-Take-All Society: Why the Few at the Top Get So Much More Than the Rest of Us.* (New York, 1995).

Gordon, Robert J. "Misperceptions about the Magnitude and Timing of Changes in American Income Inequality." National Bureau of Economic Research, Working Paper No. 15351. (September 2009), http://www.nber.org/papers/w15351.

Gordon, Robert J., and Ian Dew-Becker. "Controversies about the Rise of American Inequality: A Survey." National Bureau of Economic Research, Working Paper No. 13982. (May 2008), http://www.nber.org/papers/w13982.

Piketty, Thomas, and Emmanuel Saez. "Income Inequality in the United States, 1913–1998." *Quarterly Journal of Economics* 118 (2003): 1–39.

Rosen, Sherwin. "The Economics of Superstars." *American Economic Review* 71, no. 5 (December 1981): 845–858.

Wolff, Edward N. *Poverty and Income Distribution.* 2d ed. (New York, 2009).

Wolff, Edward N. "Recent Trends in Household Wealth in the United States: Rising Debt and the Middle-Class Squeeze—An Update to 2007." Levy Economics Institute, Working Paper No. 589 (March 2010), http://www.levyinstitute.org/pubs/wp_589.pdf.

Wolff, Edward N. "Rising Profitability and the Middle Class Squeeze." *Science and Society* 74, no. 3 (July 2010): 429–449.

Wolff, Edward N. *Top Heavy: A Study of Increasing Inequality of Wealth in America.* (New York, 2002).

Edward N. Wolff

INSURANCE COMPANIES, HEALTH

The modern health insurance industry began in Dallas, Texas, in 1929, when Baylor University Hospital developed the nation's first public, prepaid hospitalization plan, sparking similar nonprofit insurance plans across the nation, known as "Blue Cross" plans. The political influence of these early health insurance plans was dwarfed by that of organized medicine, which opposed all reform proposals as "socialism" that would undermine American freedoms. The groups' interests aligned in 1949 after President Harry Truman—appalled that millions of men were deemed unfit for military service during World War II, as they had to that point lacked access to proper medical care—won the presidential election by promising to provide public health care. The physicians, however, blocked Truman with an unprecedented lobbying campaign that urged Americans to buy private, voluntary insurance. Major employers began paying for workers' health insurance in 1950, and insurers, including a few for-profit companies, were basing premiums on the claims history of a company's workers. By 1963, nearly 80 percent of Americans were employer-insured. (By 2007 that figure was down, to 59 percent.) The health insurance industry in 2010 consisted of roughly two hundred nonprofit and for-profit companies that covered 195 million people through more than one thousand subsidiaries. The industry also manages benefits for more than 97 million people enrolled in public health programs (Medicare for the elderly and disabled and Medicaid for low-income and disabled people).

For years, Blue Cross plans enjoyed tax breaks as "insurers of last resort." But the establishment of

Medicare and Medicaid meant "the Blues" no longer had to cover millions of elderly, disabled, and poor Americans. While this freed them to focus on for-profit activities and a healthier segment of the population, it did not restrain medical costs, and left tens of millions uninsured. In 1993, President Bill Clinton proposed fixing the problem by creating mandatory, state-based, health-insurance-purchasing cooperatives. Insurers, threatened by the proposal, crafted a $300 million public relations campaign to delegitimize the plan. When the smoke cleared, insurers were left unscathed and allied with the party controlling the legislative agenda, the Republicans. The Blue Cross and Blue Shield Association, a nonprofit stronghold, promptly permitted its franchisees across the nation to convert to public-stock companies, refocusing them away from local service and nonprofit status and toward national entities that could overwhelm competitors. By 2005, Blue Cross plans in fourteen state markets had converted into for-profits and become subsidiaries of WellPoint Inc. One-third of the nearly 100 million Blue Cross subscribers are in WellPoint plans. Other for-profit companies have pursued similar growth strategies with non–Blue Cross insurance companies. Health insurers were in more than four hundred corporate mergers, including deals worth more than $62 billion from 2004 to 2009. The industry has evolved into a powerful for-profit cartel dominated by WellPoint, UnitedHealth Group Inc., Cigna Corp., Aetna Inc., and Humana Inc. Health-insurance market concentration has reached unprecedented levels, limiting price competition. Among 313 metropolitan markets, 99 percent were highly concentrated in 2009, up from 94 percent the year before.

Insurers, including nonprofits and investor-owned local and national companies, determine which consumers may access nonemergency care. They accomplish this by setting premium and benefit levels and by adjudicating claims. As health costs have risen, insurers have raised premiums faster than medical or overall inflation, and have tightened consumer access to coverage and to expensive treatments, with little interference from regulators. There has been minimal transparency about claims

denials, underwriting rules, payments to providers, death rates, and racial or ethnic health disparities among subscribers. Although this data would be valuable to public health planning, it is considered proprietary. These marketplace advantages enabled the largest for-profit insurers in 2009 to breeze through the worst economic downturn since the Great Depression and report record profits, even as they shed 2.7 million enrollees from commercial plans. The share of premiums spent on actual medical care also declined.

The industry considers its net income—more than $25 billion a year—to be reasonable. The earnings have enriched its executives and motivated them to preserve the status quo. Including exercised stock options and pensions, CEOs of the ten largest for-profit health insurers collected nearly $1 billion in compensation from 2000 to 2009. The companies regularly use premium cash to boost returns for shareholders by repurchasing company stock. The five largest health insurance companies spent $64 billion on such maneuvers from 2003 to 2010. The $800-billion-a-year private health insurance industry wields significant political influence in Washington and state capitals, and is a significant obstacle to the correction of structural defects in the American health care system. The health insurance companies' ability to exclude individuals based on medical history, discriminate against population subgroups, and raise premiums with impunity left 51 million Americans without insurance in 2009. Experts estimate another 25 million have inadequate coverage, leaving them at risk of financial ruin should they suffer a serious illness.

The industry was prepared for battle after President Barack Obama was elected in 2008 on a promise to reform health care. As the Patient Protection and Affordable Care Act was being crafted, the industry spent substantial sums to shape it. Among the weapons wielded by the industry were a phalanx of lobbyists on Capitol Hill, a sophisticated public relations campaign to engender mistrust of the law, funding for front groups and think tanks that sustain political opposition, support for groups pursuing constitutional challenges to the law, extensive political campaign advertising, and campaign contributions to political allies who advocate repeal of the law. A landmark 2010 Supreme Court ruling that freed corporations and unions to spend without limit to influence the outcome of elections further enhanced their power. Partly as a result of the industry's clout, the law

- included no government-run health plan to compete with private insurers
- requires uninsured people who can afford to purchase private coverage to do so or pay a fine
- provides subsidies to lower-income people to buy insurance
- provides tax credits to small businesses that cover their workers

Main provisions of the law take effect in 2014, when state-based health-insurance exchanges open to sell coverage to individuals and small employers. But in the interim, health insurance companies pushed to modify or kill provisions they oppose. The industry supported the subsidies but wanted higher penalties for going without coverage; objected to barriers designed to resist insurers' double-digit premium rate hikes; and opposed rules requiring minimum portions of customer premiums to be spent on actual health care rather than administration, profit, and executive pay.

The passage of the Affordable Care Act presented the health insurance industry with a historic opportunity to add 32 million Americans to its rolls. In the aftermath of the politically divisive legislative process, the industry in 2011 was focused on limiting the federal government's regulatory authority over the industry's offerings and preserving its influence at the state and national levels. The industry is certain to continue wielding its political power and vast financial resources to fend off initiatives that limit its profits or introduce a government-run health plan to compete with it.

[*See also* Health Care; *and* Health Care Reform.]

BIBLIOGRAPHY

American Medical Association. "AMA Study Shows Competition Disappearing in the Health Insurance Industry." (23 February 2010), http://www.ama-assn.org/ama/pub/news/news/health-insurance-competition.page.

Balto, David. "Testimony before the House Judiciary Committee, Subcommittee on Courts and Competition Policy, on HR 3596, the 'Health Insurance Industry Antitrust Enforcement Act of 2009.'" http://judiciary.house.gov/hearings/pdf/Balto091008.pdf.

Health Care for America Now. "Breaking the Bank: CEOs from Ten Health Insurers Took Nearly $1 Billion in Compensation, Stock from 2000 to 2009." (2010), http://healthcareforamericanow.org/wp-content/uploads/2012/02/BREAKING-THE-BANK-CEOs-From-10-Health-Insurers-Took-Nearly-1-Billion-in-Compensation-Stock-From-2000-to-2009.pdf.

Health Care for America Now. "Health Insurance Industry Profits Surge Again." (2010), http://hcfan.3cdn.net/d605c2281191ac1f04_kam6bn3ga.pdf.

Health Care for America Now. "Medical Benefit Ratios of Private Insurers, Public Medicare Plan, 1993 to 2007." (2010), http://hcfan.3cdn.net/15b2e716998ad2bdd0_ktm6bz8u0.pdf.

Potter, Wendell. *Deadly Spin: An Insurance Company Insider Speaks Out on How Corporate PR Is Killing Health Care and Deceiving Americans.* (New York, 2010).

Quadagno, Jill. *One Nation, Uninsured: Why the US Has No National Health Insurance.* (New York, 2005).

Skocpol, Theda. "The Rise and Resounding Demise of the Clinton Plan." *Health Affairs* 14, no. 1 (Spring 1995):66.

Starr, Paul. *The Social Transformation of American Medicine.* (New York, 1982).

Wynn, Paul. "What the For-Profit Trend in Health Care Really Means." *Managed Care*, June 1996, http://www.managedcaremag.com/archives/9606/9606.profit.html.

Avram Goldstein

INTEREST RATES

Interest rates are among the most important prices in an economic system, but also among the most difficult to understand. This essay will explain what interest rates are and their economic significance, and discuss policies to influence and make use of interest rates.

Interest Rates Are Prices. An interest rate is a price, just like the price of a loaf of bread. Prices are ratios expressing the rate at which goods and services are exchanged for one another. If the price of bread is $4.00 per loaf this means that four US dollars trade for one loaf of bread, and also that one-quarter of a loaf of bread trades for one US. dollar. This price is referred to as a "nominal price," because one of the items being traded is money. If at the same time that the price of bread is $4.00 per loaf the price of milk is $2.00 per quart, then one loaf of bread trades for two quarts of milk. Thus the real, or "relative" price of bread is two quarts of milk per loaf.

Interest rates are prices just as these bread and milk prices are—except that interest rates are different. First, and most important, interest rates are "intertemporal" prices, expressing the rate at which, for instance, one dollar today exchanges for dollars one year from today. If the price of $1.00 today is $1.04 one year from today, then the price of $1.00 one year from today is $.96 today. Second, while the price of bread is expressed in units (dollars or quarts of milk for instance), interest rates are unit-free numbers. This is because both the numerator and denominator of the price ratio are the same item—the dollar, in our example. Third, interest rates are expressed as percentages. In our example the interest rate is 4 percent. Fourth, even in a nonmonetary economy there would be interest rates. For example, if the price of 100 ounces of milk today is 104 ounces a year from today, the interest rate is 4 percent.

The Economic Role of Interest Rates. Because intertemporal trade is ubiquitous, as intertemporal prices, interest rates have an especially important role. They provide signals and incentives for decisions people make about saving and drawing down past savings to spend, lending and borrowing, investing and disinvesting . These pairs of activities are interrelated, for saving may be the source of funds that are lent, and these funds may finance investment (i.e, production of new capital goods). Accumulation of capital is a source of economic growth.

If interest rates rise people are more likely to save, to lend, and to disinvest. When interest rates fall people tend to spend, borrow, and invest. The key role of interest rates is to coordinate the separate decisions people make about these activities so that,

for instance, the volume of planned borrowing is matched by the volume of planned lending. This is the key role of any price, to provide for market "clearing." In the context of borrowing and lending, the interest rate is the price of loanable funds. If we think of borrowing as the source of funds to purchase new capital goods, then the interest rate can be seen as the cost of capital.

In Keynesian theory of "speculative" demand for money, the interest rate has a central role as the price of money balances. The basic idea is that money balances earn either no interest, or low rates of interest. Higher interest rates are available on bonds. Keynes regarded people as having an idea of a "normal" rate of interest on bonds. When interest rates on bonds rise relative to this normal rate, people expect capital gains on bonds and thus shift their savings portfolio from money to bonds. If bond interest rates fall below the normal rate, they expect capital losses and move funds from bonds to money balances. The speculative demand for money is one piece of the IS-LM (investment saving–liquidity preference money supply) macroeconomic model. The upshot of the model is that an increase in the supply of money leads to lower interest rates and higher real income.

Consideration of money, bonds, and interest rates leads to the role of interest rates in the capitalization of streams of income received, or payments made, over time. In this context the interest rate is often called the "discount rate." The simplest example is one that we have already considered, the promise of $1.00 one year from today. If the interest rate is 4 percent, the present value of this future payment is $.96. In May 2011, one-year US Treasury bills were selling for $9,983 per $10,000 face value. This implies an interest rate of .17 percent, extremely low by historical standards. Through the 1990s the average rate on one-year Treasury bills was 5.36 percent. This implies that a $10,000 Treasury bill would have sold for $9,491.

Interest Rate Policy. The Federal Reserve Board is the locus of interest rate policy in the United States. Interest rates serve as both targets and indicators of monetary policy. A rationale for interest rate targets is found in the aforementioned IS-LM model. If the Federal Reserve pushes interest rates down, this stimulates aggregate demand for goods and services, as would be appropriate when a business cycle recession is looming. Pushing interest rates up restrains aggregate demand, appropriate when inflation is the problem. The federal funds rate, which is the rate on interbank loans of cash reserves, is the particular rate that the Federal Reserve uses as its target.

The second monetary policy function of interest rates, as an indicator, arises because monetary policy actions have their effects on income and prices only after a considerable lag. Interest rate movements provide an indication of what the effect is likely to be. A problem arises with interest rate indicators, however, when there is inflation. This is because rising interest rates indicate tight monetary policy, while expansionary monetary policy causes inflation, which in turn causes interest rates to rise. So if the Federal Reserve is pursuing what is in fact inflationary policy, rising interest rates from the inflation will indicate tight policy. If the Federal Reserve then loosens policy to avoid recession, this makes inflation all the worse. Thus interest rate indicators can lead to a vicious cycle of inflationary policy. The situation is as if the level of mercury in a thermometer was affected by air pressure as well as temperature.

In September 2007, the Federal Reserve began an expansionary policy with a series of reductions in the target federal funds rate to offset the then-looming financial crisis. The federal funds rate target began at 5.25 percent. By December 2008 the target was between zero and .25 percent. With interest rates close to zero conventional policy strategy was in a bind, for negative interest rates do not make economic sense so long as people prefer more to less. This led to the Federal Reserve shifting attention away from interest rates and toward the size and composition of the asset side of its balance sheet. In a policy referred to as "quantitative easing," the Fed embarked on a massive increase in holdings of US Treasury debt and of other public and private debt obligations.

This policy is unprecedented, and therefore difficult to evaluate as to its likely effects. The first novelty is the sheer size of the expansion: roughly a threefold increase in the size of the Fed's balance sheet since 2007. This implies a huge increase in available liquidity, which was intended to provide relief for troubled businesses and households—but carries the risk of igniting inflation. Second, while the Fed in the past purchased US Treasury securities in the open market to influence interest rates and liquidity, since the financial crisis it has purchased mortgage-backed securities and long-term debt of government-sponsored enterprises (e.g., Fannie Mae and Freddie Mac), and made loans to private financial firms. This has put the Fed more directly in the business of allocating capital rather than just providing liquidity to the market. Third, with interest rates near zero, the Fed is exposed to the risk of large losses on its portfolio should interest rates rise (and the price of securities it holds fall). At near zero there is effectively only one direction for interest rates to move, and that is up. Since most of the Fed's profits are remitted to the US Treasury, the prospect of losses is not without consequence for Congress and fiscal policy.

So, over the past several years the Federal Reserve has sailed into uncharted waters. Traditional interest rate policy of using open market purchases and sales of US Treasury securities to influence the money supply has apparently been deemed inadequate in the face of the 2008 financial crisis and ensuing recession. It remains to be seen whether the new policies will lead the economy into safe port or new storms.

[*See also* Federal Reserve Bank; Financial Crisis of 2008; Keynesianism; *and* Monetary Policy.]

BIBLIOGRAPHY

Alchian, Armen A., and William R. Allen. "Capital Values, Interest Rates, and Wealth." In *University Economics: Elements of Inquiry*, 3d ed., by Armen A. Alchian and William R. Allen, pp. 174–196. (Belmont, Calif., 1972).

Wood, John H. *A History of Central Banking in Great Britain and the United States*. (New York, 2009).

J. Daniel Hammond

INTERNATIONAL CRIMINAL COURT

The International Criminal Court (ICC), located in The Hague, Netherlands, in operation since 1 July 2002, is the first and only standing international court intended to prosecute individuals for atrocity crimes: genocide, crimes against humanity, and war crimes. Although the United States played a major role in the international negotiations that produced the court's Statute, it opposed the final text. US opposition to the court at first increased during President George W. Bush's administration, but then declined as the costs of its stance became clear. Under the succeeding Obama administration, relations improved. Conservative politicians' continuing mistrust of multilateral organizations generally, and the ICC in particular, prevents US ratification of the Statute; cooperation with the court, however, will likely continue.

The idea behind the ICC is old, dating back to at least the mid-nineteenth century. The successful initiative to bring it into being, however, is recent, dating from the end of the Cold War. In late 1989, the United States and the Soviet Union supported proposals in the United Nations General Assembly (UNGA) for reinvigorating long-stalled discussions in the International Law Commission (ILC) over a statute for an international criminal court with jurisdiction over perpetrators of international crimes, including international drug trafficking. Similarly, in October 1990, the US Congress recommended that the president "explore the creation of an international criminal court in hopes of more effectively combating egregious transnational crimes." While the immediate impetus for the UNGA and US congressional action was international drug trafficking, the ILC developed a draft statute for a court with potentially much broader jurisdiction, presenting it to the General Assembly in 1994.

Meanwhile, in response to atrocity crimes that began to take place in 1990 as disintegrating Yugoslavia descended into war, and erupted in Rwanda during the 1994 genocide, the United States supported the United Nations Security Council's (UNSC) creation of the International Criminal Tribunals for Yugoslavia (ICTY, 1993) and for Rwanda (ICTR,1994). US State Department legal experts were largely responsible for drafting the tribunals' statutes. They also vigorously participated in ongoing negotiations that led to the Rome Conference on the Statute of the ICC that took place in June and July, 1998. The ICC proposed by the ILC in 1994 and championed by the United States would, like the tribunals, have been subordinated to the UNSC; however, by the time the Rome Statute was complete, the UNSC could only refer conflict situations to the court for investigation and could suspend court proceedings (for twelve months, renewable) in situations under the purview of the Council pursuant to UN Charter Chapter VII (International Peace and Security). Otherwise, the court was independent.

During the Rome negotiations, the United States sought to protect state sovereignty and limit the court's purview by permitting states that joined the Statute to opt out of the court's jurisdiction, by restricting that jurisdiction to individuals whose countries of citizenship had joined the Statute, by permitting states to attach reservations to their ratifications of the Statute, and by opposing the addition of the crime of aggression to genocide, crimes against humanity, and war crimes under ICC jurisdiction. The United States lost on all these points, although compromises went part way toward its positions on the opt out and on aggression. On the opt out, a French initiative for a one-time, seven-year opt out (for crimes against humanity and war crimes) was adopted. On aggression, the Statute granted ICC jurisdiction but postponed *exercise* of jurisdiction until the crime could be defined and modes of implementation devised in amendments to be considered not earlier than the first Statute review in 2010.

US opponents of the emerging ICC sought to insulate US citizens from the court's jurisdiction, charging that it was part of international efforts to promote global institutions that undermine sovereignty generally and especially the US's ability to carry out its worldwide security responsibilities. ICC proponents argued that the Statute negotiators, largely in response to US pressure, protected states' sovereign prerogatives. Under the court's so-called "doctrine of complementarity," cases are admissible only when states with the responsibility to do so are genuinely unable or unwilling to investigate and prosecute Statute crimes, so states have primary jurisdiction (unlike the ICTY and ICTR, whose jurisdiction could supersede domestic courts). Moreover, before the ICC prosecutor can proceed to investigate a situation under his or her own authority (*proprio motu*) or pursuant to a state referral, his or her action must be approved by a Pre-trial Chamber of three judges. Although states that are party to the Statute are obligated to make cooperation with the Court possible by aligning their domestic laws with the Statute (enabling, for example, the arrest of an individual accused of the crimes over which the Court has jurisdiction) and by responding to requests for assistance and information, the Court has no way autonomously to compel cooperation or to enforce its warrants.

At the end of the Rome Conference the United States was one of only seven states that sought procedurally to prevent approval of the Statute, which then took place by acclamation. As President Bill Clinton's administration continued, US negotiators still participated in activities preparatory to the Statute coming into force and played major roles in developing crucial court documents, including the ICC's Rules of Procedure and Evidence and its Elements of Crimes. On 31 December 2000, in the last days of the Clinton administration, the United States signed the Statute in order to "be in a position to influence the evolution of the court," although recommending that the Treaty not be submitted to the Senate for ratification "until our fundamental concerns are satisfied."

Clinton's successor, George W. Bush, and his administration, particularly in the person of Undersecretary of State for Arms Control and International Security John Bolton, vigorously opposed the court. The new administration terminated US participation in ICC preparatory meetings and on 6 May 2002, in what Bolton called his "happiest moment" at State, informed UN Secretary-General Kofi Annan that the United States did not intend to submit the Statute for Senate ratification (the so-called "unsigning"), and therefore did not consider itself bound by any of the Statute's provisions.

The Bush administration supported Congressional legislation forbidding US cooperation with the Court (the American Service members' Protection Act, or ASPA), and pursued so-called bilateral immunity agreements (BIAs) with other states guaranteeing that they would not transfer US citizens to the Court. Under the ASPA, countries declining to accede to the BIAs would lose International Military Education and Training (IMET) support and Foreign Military Funds (FMF). The administration also supported annual (for 2005, 2006, and 2008) amendments to the Defense Appropriations Act that cut off Economic Support Fund (ESF) aid to such countries. The United States sought and gained from the UNSC an exemption from ICC jurisdiction of US personnel involved in UN peacekeeping activities as a condition for the 2002 reauthorization of UN forces in Bosnia-Herzegovina. (This turned out to be a one-time event. After the American invasion of Iraq in 2003, there was no support in the UNSC for continuing such an exception.)

The first George W. Bush term proved the high point of US opposition to the Court. US diplomats in The Hague were forbidden to interact with Court officials and the United States gained BIAs with more than 100 countries and threatened others with aid cutoffs. As a consequence of these actions, foreign policy problems rapidly surfaced. European Union members castigated the United States for its opposition to the Court. Latin American states resented US pressure to sign BIAs, and some major allies refused. Moreover, American desire to act against atrocity crimes in the Sudan was impeded by the Bush administration's opposition to the Court.

A special commission supported by the United States reported to the UNSC in late 2004 that acts of genocide, war crimes, and crimes against humanity appeared to be taking place in Darfur in the Sudan. While the commission recommended that the UNSC refer the Darfur situation to the ICC, the United States sought an alternative venue. It found no international support for the idea. With Condoleezza Rice as the new Secretary of State, and the departure of John Bolton as UN ambassador, US opposition to the court softened and the United States abstained on the Darfur vote. The UNSC referred Darfur to the ICC.

The BIAs turned out to be costly. The Pentagon's Quadrennial Defense Review noted that the cutoff of assistance to Latin American countries that refused to sign BIAs was damaging US relations in the region. As a consequence, in October 2006, the ASPA was amended to eliminate the IMET restriction, and in 2008 FMF restrictions were ended. The ESF proscription lapsed in 2009.

Once President Barack Obama entered office, the United States resumed participation—as an observer only—in ICC Assembly of States Parties meetings. At the June 2010 Kampala Review Conference of the Parties to the Rome Statute, Ambassador-At-Large for War Crimes Issues Stephen Rapp and Department of State Legal Adviser Harold Koh led a large US delegation closely engaged in the most controversial matter at the conference: whether and how the court could exercise jurisdiction over the crime of aggression. A compromise was developed—with major US participation—defining the crime and specifying joint ICC-UNSC triggers, establishing that states would have the right individually to opt in or opt out of ICC jurisdiction over aggression, and postponing implementation pending further discussions and a vote that could not take place prior to 2017. Both advocates and opponents of extending ICC jurisdiction over aggression claimed success. As Ambassador Rapp and Legal Adviser Koh asserted, the United States had promoted its interests much more by engaging at Kampala than it could have by boycotting.

Congressional attitudes toward the ICC, much like those toward other international organizations, remain divided. Significant numbers of politicians regard these organizations as threats to US sovereignty. No overwhelming constituency exists to propel ratification of US signature of the Statute; however, the idea of joining international efforts to counter impunity for perpetrators of atrocity crimes remains attractive. The United States will likely stay engaged with the Court but remain outside of the Statute.

[*See also* Darfur.]

BIBLIOGRAPHY
American Non-Governmental Organizations Coalition for the International Criminal Court, http://www.amicc.org/.
American Society of International Law. "The US and the International Criminal Court: Report from the Kampala Review Conference." (June 16, 2010), http://www.asil.org/files/Transcript_ICC_Koh_Rapp_Bellinger.pdf.
Feinstein, Lee, and Todd Lindberg. *Means to an End: US Interest in the International Criminal Court.* (Washington, D.C., 2009).
McGodlrick, Dominic, Peter Rowe, and Eric Donnelly, eds. *The Permanent International Criminal Court: Legal and Policy Issues.* (Portland, Or., 2004).
Paris, Erna. *The Sun Climbs Slow: The International Criminal Court and The Struggle for Justice.* (New York, 2009).
Schabas, William. *An Introduction to the International Criminal Court.* 2d ed. (Cambridge, UK, 2010).
Schiff, Benjamin N. *Building the International Criminal Court.* (Cambridge, UK, 2008).

Benjamin N. Schiff

IRAN

A relatively large country (636,000 square miles; 1,648,000 square kilometers) in Southwest Asia, Iran's twentieth-century political history was strongly affected by international rivalry for influence over its oil resources. Prior to World War I, the principal foreign threat came from neighboring Tsarist Russia and the British Empire, each interfering in Iran's domestic politics to promote friendly governments. Foreign intervention dramatically declined between 1921 and 1939, when Moscow was preoccupied with creating the Soviet Union and London perceived few threats to its expanding oil interests in southwestern Iran. Although Iran acted more independently in this period, its economy became more integrated into the international market system. The outbreak of World War II revived foreign interest in the country's policies and resources, culminating in a joint Anglo-Soviet invasion in August 1941.

These persistent foreign interventions prompted intense debates within Iran over the most effective means of securing the country's independence and led to the emergence of two major political currents: secular and religious nationalism. Secular nationalists—mostly political activists educated in Europe,

North America, or, after 1940, Iran's public education system—generally believed their country could prevent foreign interference by adopting Western-style political institutions, economic programs, and social policies. In contrast, the religious nationalists believed such imitation reinforced the country's dependence on the West, and so they advocated a return to traditional cultural values, especially those of Shia Islam, the religion of 90 percent of the population. Despite their different perspectives, both secular and religious nationalists viewed the country's shahs (kings) as compromising with foreign powers in order to maintain royal autocracy. Consequently, secular and religious groups sometimes cooperated to restrict the shah's powers, most notably in the 1905–1907 Constitutional Revolution and the 1978–1979 Revolution. More typically, shahs exploited conflicts among secular and religious nationalists to enhance royal prerogatives.

The Pahlavi dynasty (ruled 1926–1979) generally tried to co-opt the secular nationalists by promoting many economic and social reform policies they advocated. These programs initiated the industrialization and urbanization processes that significantly transformed Iranian society, especially after rising oil prices, beginning in the late 1950s, dramatically increased state revenues. The government's diverse development projects supported a large bureaucracy, a national army, and internal security forces—institutions that greatly strengthened the central government. The secular nationalists favorably referred to all reforms as "modernization." Nevertheless, because the first Pahlavi shah (ruled 1926–1941) effectively ruled as a dictator, he failed to develop a political support base among secular nationalists. His social policies generally antagonized the religious nationalists and cost him support among the clergy as well.

Following World War II, Iran became one of the earliest scenes of the emerging Cold War struggle between the West and the Soviet bloc, as each sought to incorporate the country within its own alliance system. Iran's efforts to pursue a neutral foreign policy ended in August 1953, when an American- and British-supported military coup d'état overthrew

Prime Minister Mohammad Mosaddeq, who had forced the shah, Mohammad Reza (ruled 1941–1979), to reign as a constitutional monarch. Subsequently, the shah consolidated a royal dictatorship while cultivating close ties with the United States. The shah's policies alienated both secular and religious nationalists, who in 1978 formed a broad-based coalition under the charismatic leadership of the exiled clergyman Ayatollah Ruhollah Khomeini. This coalition mobilized Iranians in cities and towns throughout the country to participate in mass anti-shah demonstrations and strikes that paralyzed the economy by the end of 1978. The spreading but nonviolent popular revolutionary movement demoralized the extensive security forces, and in February 1979 the army declared its neutrality in the political struggle, effectively enabling the movement under Khomeini's leadership to overthrow the monarchy and establish a republic. The new provisional government terminated Iran's longstanding alliance with the United States and began to chart a neutral course vis-à-vis the superpowers.

The secular-religious coalition began to dissolve soon after the initial success of the revolution. The various secular parties faced a serious disadvantage in the post-revolutionary political contest, because they appealed primarily to the small urban elite of college students and professionals in a society where 80 percent of adults had not completed high school. The religious parties appealed more broadly to shopkeepers and artisans in the urban bazaars, lower-ranking civil servants, industrial workers, and peasants. In general, the religious nationalists successfully portrayed the secularists as Westernized "liberals" who had lost touch with their Islamic cultural roots and wished to create a "democratic" republic that would be un-Islamic and ultimately as dependent upon the West as the shah's regime had been. Through their control of revolutionary organizations that assumed judicial and security functions, the religious nationalists effectively intimidated their secular rivals. Significantly, those religious groups affiliated with Khomeini capitalized on his nationwide popularity to draft a constitution, approved in a December 1979 referendum, that vested ultimate political authority in a senior Shiite theologian, or *faqih*, with broad powers to appoint the chief military and judicial authorities. The constitution designated Khomeini the first *faqih* and provided that his successors be chosen by a special assembly of high-ranking clergy.

The constitution also provided for an elected president as the head of government; the president serves a four-year term and may be reelected once. Although the president appoints the cabinet, each minister must be approved by the legislature, or Majlis, which first was created in 1906, but in its new form as the Islamic Consultative Assembly is a single-chamber body of 290 members elected every four years. The Majlis is independent of the executive, which has no power to dissolve it. A unique institution, known as the Council of Guardians, reviews all Majlis legislation and is empowered to veto any laws it deems as violating Shia Islamic principles or the constitution. The judiciary is independent of both the executive and the Majlis. The chief judicial authorities must be clergy with advanced training in the codices of Shia Islamic law.

Despite the personal popularity of Khomeini, there was significant opposition to the notion of the Shiite clergy having any special authority to rule in an Islamic government. The Mujahidin-e Khalq, a prerevolutionary clandestine organization that developed into a mass political movement after 1979, was one of the main groups contesting Khomeini's conception of an Islamic Republic. In June 1981, it launched a nationwide, armed uprising against the government, with support from smaller Marxist and ethnic opposition groups. Iran was involved in a war with Iraq, which had been initiated by an Iraqi invasion of southwestern Iran in September 1980, and the patriotic fervor that emerged in response to that conflict was a factor that helped the regime to contain and eventually crush the internal rebellion; over an eighteen-month period, at least 13,000 Iranians were killed in the suppression of the revolt, an estimated 90 percent of whom were between the ages of eighteen and thirty. Since 1983, the leadership of the Mujahidin and also of various secular opposition parties has been based outside of the country.

The Islamic Republic inherited an economically and socially diverse society. Although the government did not alter the primarily capitalist nature of the economic system, one of its aims was to distribute wealth from oil revenues more equitably. The country's 70,000 villages, where 32 percent of the total 71 million population resided in 2006, were the beneficiaries of major development programs that provided them with roads, electricity, piped water, primary and secondary schools, and health clinics. Price-support policies for agricultural commodities and interest-free credit to finance crop production helped transfer more money to rural areas. The regime's policies were less successful in ameliorating living conditions for the urban poor, however. City population increased an average of 4 percent annually between 1979 and 1996, because of high migration from the villages. Tehran—the capital and one of Asia's largest and most congested cities—has failed to resolve problems associated with its pollution, inadequate water and sewerage systems, and inefficient and poorly maintained public transportation services. Five other cities with populations over one million face similar problems: Mashhad in the northeast; Isfahan on the central plateau, Tabriz in the northwest; Karaj, to the west of Tehran; and Shiraz in the south.

Disagreement over economic and social policies opened ideological rifts among Iran's postrevolutionary political elite. During the first decade of the Islamic Republic, preoccupation with foreign policy goals, especially the eight-year war with Iraq, as well as the authority of Khomeini, helped to maintain de facto political unity. The end of the war in August 1988 and the death of Khomeini one year later paved the way for a formal political split among those exercising power. More pragmatic political leaders, self-identifying themselves as Reformists, argued that the government's failure to promote economic growth threatened the revolution's future. They used both the Majlis and the press as forums to present their essentially neoliberal economic ideas, arguing that past policies stressing economic self-sufficiency had contributed to economic recession, and Iran must abandon its isolationism and cooperate with

Western countries to obtain resources for creating a just, Islamic society at home. Such views alarmed the Conservatives, who argued that extensive diplomatic ties and commercial relations, especially foreign loans and investments, would make Iran dependent upon Western states, compromise the aims of the revolution, and ultimately undermine the very legitimacy of the Islamic Republic.

Nevertheless, the Reformists' emphasis on programs designed to alleviate immediate economic difficulties had broad appeal between 1989 and the early 2000s. During the presidential administration of Ali Akbar Hashemi Rafsanjani (1989–1997), two social movements emerged: Islamist intellectuals, most prominently Abdolkarim Soroush, began reinterpreting Islamic texts in ways that harmonized them with international conceptions of democracy and human rights; and women self-identifying themselves as Islamic feminists began reinterpreting the same religious texts to support gender equality. Shirin Ebadi, a woman lawyer active in the efforts to expand the legal rights of women and minorities, was awarded the 2003 Nobel Prize for Peace, the first Iranian and also first Muslim woman ever to earn this honor. By 2000, over half of all undergraduate college students in Iran were women, and educated women were active as educators, engineers, entrepreneurs, filmmakers, health care professionals, managers, publishers, scientists, and writers. Both the democratization and women's movements were important in the election of Reformist Mohammad Khatami as president in 1997. During his eight-year tenure, Khatami stressed creating a domestic "civil society" in which individual rights are protected by transparent laws, and pursuing a foreign policy based on a "dialogue of civilizations."

Conservatives opposed Khatami's efforts to democratize Iran, arguing that average citizens are not qualified to make morally correct political decisions, but rather must be guided by clergy with specialized knowledge of religious texts that reveal God's plan for an Islamic society. Conservatives, who had occupied powerful positions in the judiciary and security services since the early 1990s, won control of the legislature in 2004, and of the presidency in 2005.

They have used their positions in state institutions to marginalize the Reformists and to weaken or cancel many of the latter's pre-2005 political reforms. The 2009 presidential election escalated tensions between the factions, as the Reformists accused the Conservatives of manipulating the counting of ballots to ensure the reelection of President Mahmoud Ahmadinejad.

[*See also* Iranian Revolution; Islam; *and* Religion and Politics.]

BIBLIOGRAPHY

Abrahamian, Ervand. *A History of Modern Iran.* (Cambridge, UK, 2008). The author generally is considered the principal historian of twentieth century, and this book provides a useful overview of change and continuity in the Iranian state and society from the late nineteenth century up to the early 2000s.

Bahramitash, Roksana, and Eric Hooglund, eds. *Gender in Contemporary Iran: Pushing the Boundaries.* (London, 2011). A unique collection of essays by prominent scholars of Iranian society examining the role of women in education, employment, the media, and sports, as well as their efforts in the legal, political, and religious spheres to obtain gender equality.

Ghamari-Tabrizi, Behrouz. *Islam and Dissent in Postrevolutionary Iran; Abdolkarim Soroush, Religious Politics, and Democratic Reform.* (London, 2008). Analysis of the discourse pertaining to the legitimacy and permissible extent of political dissent in a government constitutionally defined as an Islamic Republic in accordance with the theory of *velayat-e faqih* (guardianship of the religious jurist).

Hooglund, Eric, ed. *Twenty Years of Islamic Revolution: Political and Social Transition in Iran since 1979.* (Syracuse, N.Y., 2002). Analyses of various cultural, economic, and social changes during the first twenty years of the Islamic Republic.

Katouzian, Homa, and Hossein Shahidi, eds. *Iran in the 21st Century: Politics, Economics, and Conflict.* (New York, 2008). Academic experts on Iran analyze aspects of the country's economic policies, political contestation, and foreign relations during the presidential administration of Mohammad Khatami (1997–2005).

Middle East Report, The Islamic Revolution at 30 (special issue) 250 (Spring 2009). Reflective and research-based essays by such leading scholars of Iran as E. Abrahamian, K. Ehsani, H. Hoodfar, E. Hooglund, A. Keshavarzian, and F. Sadeghi.

Moslem, Mehdi. *Factional Politics in Post-Khomeini Iran.* (Syracuse, N.Y., 2002). This comprehensive analysis of the ideological positions that underlay the contestation over economic and political issues during the 1990s provides essential background for understanding the subsequently intense factionalism that emerged among the postrevolutionary political elite after 2000.

Eric Hooglund

IRANIAN REVOLUTION

The Iranian Revolution of 1978–1979 was one of the most momentous and unique events of the postwar epoch: it challenged the established distribution of power in much of the Middle East and the Islamic world, and paved the way to major international conflicts with the United States and Iran's neighbor, Iraq. The revolution itself began in 1978, at a time when the shah, or Persian king, had been in apparent control for twenty-five years, and had used the substantial oil revenues that Iran had been earning in the 1970s to build up his country's economy and international importance. By September 1978, the shah's government was confronted with widespread protests, involving millions of people, in the major cities of Iran. Although the first protests had been led by secular opponents of the regime, leadership had quickly passed to the Islamic clergy under the leadership of Ayatollah Khomeini, in exile since 1964.

By January 1979 the shah was forced to flee. Khomeini returned to Iran on 1 February of that year, and after a brief armed uprising against the remnants of the shah's army on 11–12 February, he took power. Within weeks he had proclaimed the establishment of the Islamic Republic of Iran, and proceeded to transform the political, social, educational, and cultural life of the country to meet what he regarded as Islamic principles.

Power lay in the hands of the leading clergy and the networks of Islamic committees set up throughout the country. The ministries of state and the armed forces were subjected to clerical control. Opposition to Khomeini's regime continued for several years and led to armed clashes with opponents of the clergy, both left-wing guerrillas in the cities and Kurdish insurgents in the western mountains.

Khomeini proclaimed a policy of militant neutrality, under the slogan "Neither East nor West," and appealed to the Islamic and other oppressed peoples of the world to rise up against their rulers. In many parts of the Islamic world, in particular, underground and opposition groups looked to Iran for support and example against governments seen as secular or tied to the West. Iranian influence was especially strong among Shia in Lebanon.

Two conflicts in particular came to dominate Iranian foreign policy. The first was with the United States and began on 5 November 1979, when a group of Islamic militants, proclaiming themselves to be students following the Imam's line, seized the staff and buildings of the US embassy in Tehran. The Iranian government stood behind these militants and made a series of demands, including the handing over of the shah, then in the United States, and the return of his wealth to Iran. The United States froze all Iranian assets and, unsuccessfully, attempted military action to free the hostages. In January 1981, the hostages were released in return for a financial settlement of US-Iranian claims and counterclaims.

The second major conflict came in September 1980 when Iraq, angered by Iranian calls for the overthrow of the Ba'thist regime in Baghdad, invaded Iran in the hope of toppling the Khomeini government. In the ensuing war, in which over a million people are said to have died, neither side was able to prevail or to overthrow the other's government. In 1987 the US Navy and other Western navies, anxious about Iranian influence, entered the war on Iraq's side, and in August 1988 Iran finally accepted a UN Security Council resolution on a cease-fire.

The Iranian Revolution was the first successful upheaval of modern times to justify itself in religious terms and to be led by clergy. More than any other revolution, it rejected modern ideas of progress, democracy, and material well-being. At the same time, it was distinct from most Third World revolutions in taking place in cities and in involving relatively little armed conflict. Some analyses stress the particular power of radical Islamic ideology, others the appeals of ideological returns to the past, and others the particular conflict between the shah's state, sustained by oil-based modernization, and society.

[*See also* Iran; Islam; *and* Religion and Politics.]

BIBLIOGRAPHY

Abrahamian, Ervand. *Iran Between Two Revolutions.* (Princeton, N.J., 1982).

Bakhash, Shaul. *The Reign of the Ayatollahs.* (London, 1985).

Keddie, Nikki. *Roots of Revolution: An Interpretive History of Modern Iran.* (New Haven, Conn., 1981).

Sick, Gary. *All Fall Down: America's Tragic Encounter with Iran.* (New York, 1985).

Fred Halliday